Formula 1 The Knowledge

records and trivia since 1950

by David Hayhoe Foreword by Ben Edwards

The right of David Hayhoe to be identified as the Author of this work has been asserted in accordance with the Copyright, Design & Patents Act 1988.

First edition published in 2016 by
David Hayhoe Publications
6 Meadow Way
Seaford
East Sussex
BN25 4QT
England

Front cover photographs:
Juan Manuel Fangio leading Stirling Moss at the 1955 Dutch Grand Prix, each in a Mercedes-Benz W196 (LAT Photographic).
Lewis Hamilton (Mercedes-Benz F1 W06) at the 2015 British Grand Prix (Jakob Ebrey Photography).

Back cover photographs:
Juan Manuel Fangio in 1954 (The GP Library).
Lewis Hamilton in 2015 (Jakob Ebrey Photography).

Publisher: David Hayhoe Publications
e-mail: djhayhoe@gmail.com

Designed by David Hayhoe

Creative design, artwork and pre-print production by Bamb

Printed and bound by The Printing House

A catalogue record of this book is available from the British Library.

ISBN: 978-0-9935329-0-0

Contents

Foreword by Ben Edwards

As a commentator on motorsport, I sometimes feel that every two weeks I am being thrown back into the exam room at school to ransack the extremities of my brain for interesting or obscure facts. Recalling medieval battles and politicians of the 18th century used to leave me cold, but set me to work on the history of a particular Grand Prix, and I can lose several hours happily scanning old race reports, checking results and rediscovering drivers and incidents that created the complex backdrop to the current day.

David Hayhoe's previous tome was the *Grand Prix Data Book* and for many years that served as my key reference in terms of checking results and pulling together statistics. It was produced before the internet became our one click stop for checking information, whether it be the winner of the 1968 Monaco Grand Prix or the recipe for banana cake. Nowadays we have access to so much material that it can be daunting to know where to start, and indeed which sources to trust. Having first met David when I was commentating for Eurosport in the mid 1990s, I can attest to his dedication and relentless pursuit of accuracy, but also to his keen eye for the obscure, the strange coincidence and bizarre happenstance that all the F1 races since 1950 have managed to create. Hence in *The Knowledge* he has assembled a mind-blowing series of related facts and figures that are fascinating, sometimes surprising and always entertaining.

I have some particular favourites; the random elements that make Lewis Hamilton's choice of race number at 44 so perfect, the fact that six grands prix have been run on a Monday, the gem of a story about the only time one driver drove two different makes of car in one grand prix, and the fact that Kevin Magnussen tops a fairly significant statistic which will be hard to beat. The sheer scope of the book is breathtaking; I can't imagine many people in the world who would have had the patience to compile it, but I do know several who will devour it for their festive period or grand prix barbecue quiz, and as a resource for commentators, journalists and all round motorsport anoraks, it is gold dust.

Introduction

A radio programme about the 1980 Grand Prix season first sparked my interest in Formula 1. After that, television coverage, *Autosport* and other periodicals helped develop my knowledge and before long I was keeping notes on cars, drivers and general race statistics.

By 1982 I had started delving into the history of Formula 1, but without computers, I had to compile manuscript records. This was also the season I attended my first F1 race, the British Grand Prix at Brands Hatch.

My record-keeping grew into what would become *Grand Prix Data Book*, first published in 1989 by Haynes. This led, two years later to Richard Poulter at Hazleton Publishing inviting me to take on the role of statistician for *Autocourse*, the leading Grand Prix annual. It's a position I proudly hold to this day. There have been various other publications that I have contributed to as statistician, reporter or photographer.

Alongside my business career in the Civil Service and aviation security, I further developed my Formula 1 database in order to produce a more comprehensive second edition of *Grand Prix Data Book*. This was published in 1995 and two further editions followed. A highly popular chapter in those books was *Records and Trivia*, and it is this that forms the basis for this, my latest project.

I am grateful to motorsport commentator, Ben Edwards for sparing the time to write the foreword. Also, during the process of compiling the book, a select group of Formula 1 enthusiasts and record-keepers have been of great assistance. First and in tribute, the late Ben Horne, formerly of McLaren, who was enormously helpful at the outset. And secondly, with my sincere thanks to Clifford Birch, João Paulo Cunha, Jacques Deschenaux, Peter Dick, Steve Hirst, Richard Jenkins, Aleks Kruz, Aleš Norsky, Doug Nye (The GP Library), Travis Posthumus, Steve Small, David Smith and Roger Smith, who coined the title: *Formula 1 **The Knowledge***.

David Hayhoe
Seaford
East Sussex

The Formula 1 World Championship

Total seasons = 66
> (to the end of 2015)

Total races = 935
> (inc. 11 at Indianapolis 500, 1950 - 60)

Total circuit venues = 70

Total countries to host a race = 31

Total laps in the world championship = 61,297
> (inc. 2,138 at Indianapolis 500)

Total distance = 302.699 km/ 188,089 miles
> (inc. 8,602 km/ 5,345 miles at Indianapolis 500)

Total drivers entrants in the world championship = 904
> (inc. 178 only at Indianapolis 500)

Total starting drivers = 760
> (inc. 103 only at Indianapolis 500)
> (4 drivers started in Formula 1 grands prix and the Indianapolis 500)

Total non-starting drivers (attempted to qualify) = 144
> (inc. 75 only at Indianapolis 500)

Total practice only drivers = 36

Total cars starting in the world championship = 21,103
> (inc. 363 at Indianapolis 500)

For eleven years from 1950 until 1960, the Indianapolis 500 race was included in the Formula 1 world championship, to boost the number of races. Indianapolis 500 data is separated in this book, given that only four drivers who started there, participated in grands prix. Throughout the book, where drivers' achievements in consecutive races are referred to, the Indianapolis 500 has been excluded from the sequence.

Information within this book is taken to the end of the 2015 season.

Chapter 1: Coincidences

1. The two American world champions

There have been two American world champions (Phil Hill, 1961 and Mario Andretti, 1978). In BOTH cases they clinched their titles in the Italian Grand Prix at Monza, in BOTH cases on Sunday, September 10th, in BOTH cases they entered that race with only their team-mate still in contention for the title, and in BOTH cases their team-mate was killed in the race, sealing the title for the American.

2. Jackie Stewart and number 11

Jackie Stewart has an interesting relationship with the number "11". He was born on the 11th of the month, 11 years before the Formula 1 World Championship began, he became the 11th different or new World Drivers' Champion, and clinched that on the day he achieved his 11th grand prix win (Monza 1969).

3. Jackie Stewart's 392 day championship reigns

Jackie Stewart's three reigns as world champion each lasted exactly 392 days.

4. François Cevert and the psychic

François Cevert had been told by a psychic that while he would achieve great fame in his chosen field, he would not live to see his 30th birthday. The race meeting at which he was killed was the last race he was due to drive before turning 30.

5. First French champion: Prost instead of Cevert

Few doubt that François Cevert, if not killed so young, would have been France's first World Drivers' Champion. Cevert died on October 6th. Twelve years later, France finally did crown their first Formula 1 World Champion. The date Alain Prost clinched that first French title - October 6th - almost like history righting a wrong.

6. Cevert and Peterson in common

For François Cevert, Watkins Glen, the circuit where he won his one and only grand prix, was also the circuit where he died. Similarly Ronnie Peterson had the most success of any circuits in his career at Monza, where he won three times. It was also the circuit at which he died.

7. August 1st in Germany

August 1st was a dangerous day to be racing in Germany - it was the date of Jean Behra's fatal accident at AVUS (1959), Niki Lauda's near-fatal Nürburgring crash (1976), and Patrick Depailler's fatal testing crash at Hockenheim (1980).

8. Lorenzo Bandini's chicane

Lorenzo Bandini was the driver-consultant that helped advise John Frankenheimer on staging a realistic Formula 1 crash at the chicane at Monaco (1966) for his classic film "Grand Prix". The following year he died in an accident at the very chicane.

9. The Hill connection
Graham Hill and son Damon Hill have a strange point of connection...both were team-mate to the greatest driver of their era - Graham to Jim Clark at Lotus, and Damon to Ayrton Senna at Williams, when that great driver was killed. In each case, following the shocking death of the leading F1 driver (1968, 1994) the devastated team had to rely on "their" Hill to assume team leadership. In both cases, shortly thereafter, the team was delivered their first post-Clark/post-Senna win by Hill. In both cases that win came in Spain, and in both cases, the driver, to the surprise of many, surpassed expectations and led the team to either a championship title winning, or a very near championship title winning season (respectively).

10. Alboreto and Berger at Ferrari
For three consecutive seasons, Ferrari had team-mates Michele Alboreto and Gerhard Berger, and during those seasons they wore the numbers 27 and 28 respectively. As it happens, Alboreto was the 27th different driver to win a grand prix for Ferrari since the championship began, and Berger was Ferrari's 28th winner.

11. Prost at Monza
Alain Prost won the Italian Grand Prix at Monza every four years - 1981, 1985, 1989, and in his final appearance there, four years later in 1993, was leading when his engine blew. Based on the 'pattern', he should have won that.

12. Crashed into the Monte-Carlo harbour
Two drivers have crashed into the harbour at Monte-Carlo: Alberto Ascari in 1955 and Paul Hawkins in 1965. Neither were fatal, although Ascari died four days later at Monza on 26 May, and Hawkins died four years after his Monaco accident, at Oulton Park in England, coincidentally also on 26 May.

13. Unlucky 13 and Jochen Rindt
The only season to produce a posthumous champion (1970, Jochen Rindt) was also the only season in Formula 1 history to have 13 races!

14. A year to forget for Ferrari
1982 was a bad year for Ferrari - strangely, Gilles Villeneuve's fatal accident in practice at Zolder, and Didier Pironi's career-ending crash in practice at Hockenheim, were 13 weeks apart, to the day!

15. World champions in common
What do Fangio, Moss, Ickx, and Stewart all have in common? All had their last Formula 1 win at the Nürburgring.

16. English & Scottish world champions
Britain has produced more different world champions than any other country, and has had more years producing champions than any other country. All the champions have either been English or Scottish. For the first 59 years of the championship, prior to Jenson Button in 2009 (he broke the pattern!), ALL English world titles occurred in even-numbered years, while ALL Scottish world titles occurred in odd-numbered years. In 2009 Button became the first English driver to win an F1 title in an odd-numbered year, breaking the pattern that had existed for almost 60 years!

17. Four Taylors in the 1959 British Grand Prix
The most drivers with the same surname to enter a grand prix, was four in Britain 1959: Dennis, Henry, Mike & Trevor Taylor, none of whom were related to each other. They all made their debut at that race.

18. Justice at Monza in 2012
Coincidentally, the three drivers who were taken out in the accident caused by Romain Grosjean at the start of the 2012 Belgian Grand Prix, filled the podium a week later at Monza. The three were Lewis Hamilton, 1st in Italy, Sergio Pérez, 2nd and Fernando Alonso, 3rd.

19. Birthday winners
Only two drivers have won a grand prix on their birthday: James Hunt on his 29th birthday at Netherlands in 1976 (his fifth win) and Jean Alesi on his 31st at Canada in 1995 (his only win).

20. 1, 2 and 3-time champions in 1st, 2nd and 3rd
Australia 2013 was the first time that the 1st, 2nd and 3rd placed drivers have respectively had 1, 2 and 3 championship titles to their credit (Kimi Räikkönen, Fernando Alonso and Sebastian Vettel).

21. Lewis Hamilton's "tell-tale" event for the title
Lewis Hamilton has won the British Grand Prix three times in his nine seasons of Formula 1...all (2008, 14 and 15) being in the year that he won the championship. So, the British GP has acted as a "tell-tale" event for Lewis...he wins the championship during (and only in) seasons in which he wins the British Grand Prix!

22. 44 an obvious number for Lewis Hamilton
Some interesting stats around Lewis Hamilton's choosing no. 44 as his permanent race number. Lewis has said it is because it was the number he mostly used in his karting days, and has always seemed like a good-luck number for him. But there are four very strong coincidences also attached to him adopting the number 44:
1) It is exactly double the number he wore on his car when he won his first world title;
2) It is the country code for England when you call it from around the world;
3) Barack Obama is the 44th United States president - they are linked by the fact that Hamilton became the first ever black F1 world champion and Obama became the first ever black U.S. president within two days of each other in 2008. They are also both sons of mixed marriages with a black father and white mother;
4) If you add up the car numbers that Lewis carried in F1 during the first 7 years of his F1 career (2007 - 2013 prior to adopting a permanent number), they add up to - 44! (2+22+1+2+3+4+10=44).
Clearly that number is the obvious choice for Lewis!

Chapter 2: **Car Numbers**

From the Belgian Grand Prix of 1973, the same car number would generally be allocated to a driver for the whole season, with the reigning world champion taking number 1 and his team-mate, number 2. The main exceptions to this rule were the occasions of the reigning champion not being active in the following season: in 1993 and 94 the reigning world champions (Nigel Mansell, 1992 and Alain Prost, 1993) were not present, so the team for which they achieved the championship title (Williams) was allocated numbers 0 and 2. Williams had famously been associated with numbers 5 and 6 and Ferrari with 27 and 28. However from 1996, numbers were applied to teams based on their finishing position in the previous season. For 2014, drivers were asked to pick their preferred number to use for the rest of their careers. Number 1 would continue to be reserved for the reigning world champion each season, should he wish to use it.

Section

23   Wins
24   Pole positions
25   Races started with the same car number
26   Car number coincidences and records

23. Wins *(Most)*

No. 1	181 **	No. 8	47 *
No. 5	133 *	No.12	37
No. 2	83	No. 4	37 *
No. 6	65 *	No.11	36
No. 3	58	No. 7	27

* Includes 1 Indianapolis 500 race, ** Includes 2 Indianapolis 500 races

24. Pole positions *(Most)*

No. 1	166	No. 3	44 *
No. 5	125	No. 4	39
No. 2	99 *	No. 8	31 *
No. 6	81 *	No. 7	26
No.12	60 *	No.16	25

* Includes 1 Indianapolis 500 race

25. Races started with the same car number

	car no.	races			
Jacques Laffite	26	132	Brazil 1976	- Britain 1986	(Ligier inc. Talbot-Ligier)
Michael Schumacher	1	119	Brazil 1995	- China 2005	(Benetton, Ferrari)
Gerhard Berger	28	112	Brazil 1987	- Australia 1995	(Ferrari, McLaren)
Riccardo Patrese	6	111	Brazil 1983	- Australia 1993	(Brabham, Williams, Benetton)
Nigel Mansell	5	91	Brazil 1985	- Australia 1992	(Williams)
John Watson	7	89	Argentina 1977	- South Africa 1983	(Brabham, McLaren)
Rubens Barrichello	2	85	Australia 2001	- China 2005	(Ferrari)
Michele Alboreto	27	80	Brazil 1984	- Australia 1988	(Ferrari)
Pierluigi Martini	23	79	Detroit 1988	- Germany 1995	(Minardi)
Andrea De Cesaris	22	78	Canada 1980	- Australia 1990	(Alfa Romeo, Rial, Dallara)
Patrick Depailler	4	78	Argentina 1974	- Canada 1978	(Tyrrell)

26. Car number coincidences and records

1-2-3-4 classified in numerical order

The only race in which cars 1, 2, 3 and 4 have finished in that order was in Spain 1999, Mika Häkkinen, David Coulthard, Michael Schumacher and Eddie Irvine.

1-2-3 classified in numerical order

Apart from the race above, the only time that cars 1, 2 and 3 finished in that order was Brazil 2013, Sebastian Vettel, Mark Webber and Fernando Alonso.

top cars on the grid in numerical order
At Australia 2000, the top seven on the starting grid were numbered 1 to 7 in order, whilst at Japan 2002 the top six were numbered in order 1 to 6. At the following races, cars 1, 2, 3 and 4 lined up on the grid in that order: San Marino 1999, Brazil 2000 and Bahrain 2004. Cars numbered 1, 2 and 3 lined up 1, 2 and 3 in: Germany 1956, Australia 1999, Australia 2001, United States 2002, Australia 2003, Australia 2004, Canada 2006 and Europe 2011.

number 13
From 2014, with drivers choosing their own permanent race number, Pastor Maldonado selected number 13. Prior to 2014, the only time that car number 13 had started a grand prix, was in Mexico 1963, driven by Moisés Solana (BRM). Divina Galica (Surtees) did not qualify in car 13 in Britain 1976.

number 0
Car number 0 has only been used by two drivers: Jody Scheckter (McLaren) in Canada and United States 1973, and by Damon Hill (Williams) throughout 1993 and 94.

highest number to enter an event
The highest car number was 208, sponsored by Radio Luxembourg (208 being the radio frequency). It was a Brabham driven by Lella Lombardi in Britain 1974 (non-qualified).

numbers higher than 99
Germany 1952 was the only race to feature numbers higher than 99 (car numbers ranged from 101 to 136).

highest number to start a race
The highest car number to start was 136, a BMW driven by Rudolf Krause in Germany 1952.

highest number to win
The highest car number to win was 101 in Germany 1952, driven by Alberto Ascari (Ferrari).

lowest number never used
The lowest number never to be used in the world championship (including Indianapolis 500) is 63. The lowest number never to be used in grands prix is 47.

lowest number never to win
Apart from 13 (which has rarely been used, although it was Pastor Maldonado's number in 2014 and 15), the lowest number never to win is 29.

Chapter 3: When & Where

27. Circuits used

		races	seasons
Monza	Italy	65	1950 - 2015
Monte-Carlo	Monaco	62	1950 - 2015
Silverstone	Great Britain	49	1950 - 2015
Spa-Francorchamps	Belgium	48	1950 - 2015
Nürburgring	Germany	40	1951 - 2013
Montréal	Canada	36	1978 - 2015
Hockenheim	Germany	34	1970 - 2014
Interlagos	Brazil	33	1973 - 2015
Hungaroring	Hungary	30	1986 - 2015
Zandvoort	Netherlands	30	1952 - 85
Imola	Italy	27	1980 - 2006
Spielberg (a)	Austria	27	1970 - 2015
Suzuka	Japan	27	1987 - 2015
Catalunya	Spain	25	1991 - 2015
Buenos Aires	Argentina	20	1953 - 98
Kyalami	South Africa	20	1967 - 93

		races	seasons
Melbourne	Australia	20	1996 - 2015
Watkins Glen	United States	20	1961 - 80
Indianapolis (b)	United States	19	1950 - 2007
Magny-Cours	France	18	1991 - 2008
Sepang	Malaysia	17	1999 - 2015
Mexico City	Mexico	16	1963 - 2015
Brands Hatch	Great Britain	14	1964 - 86
Paul Ricard	France	14	1971 - 90
Estoril	Portugal	13	1984 - 96
Shanghai	China	12	2004 - 15
Adelaide	Australia	11	1985 - 95
Reims/ Reims-Gueux	France	11	1950 - 66
Sakhir	Bahrain	11	2004 - 15
Jacarepaguá	Brazil	10	1978 - 89
Zolder	Belgium	10	1973 - 84
Jarama	Spain	9	1968 - 81
Long Beach	United States	8	1976 - 83
Marina Bay	Singapore	8	2008 - 15
Mosport Park	Canada	8	1967 - 77
Detroit	United States	7	1982 - 88
Istanbul	Turkey	7	2005 - 11
Jerez de la Frontera	Spain	7	1986 - 97
Yas Marina	Abu Dhabi, UAE	7	2009 - 15
Anderstorp	Sweden	6	1973 - 78
Dijon-Prenois	France	6	1974 - 84
Aintree	Great Britain	5	1955 - 62
Bremgarten	Switzerland	5	1950 - 54
Rouen-les-Essarts	France	5	1952 - 68
Valencia	Spain	5	2008 - 12
Austin	United States	4	2012 - 15
Clermont-Ferrand	France	4	1965 - 72
Fuji	Japan	4	1976 - 2008
Montjuïc	Spain	4	1969 - 75
Yeongam	South Korea	4	2010 - 13
Buddh	India	3	2011 - 13
East London	South Africa	3	1962 - 65
Phoenix	United States	3	1989 - 91
Aida	Japan	2	1994 - 95
Las Vegas	United States	2	1981 - 82
Mont-Tremblant	Canada	2	1968 - 70
Nivelles-Baulers	Belgium	2	1972 - 74
Pedralbes	Spain	2	1951 - 54
Porto	Portugal	2	1958 - 60
Sochi	Russia	2	2014 - 15
Âin-Diab	Morocco	1	1958
AVUS	Germany	1	1959
Bugatti au Mans	France	1	1967
Dallas	United States	1	1984
Donington Park	Great Britain	1	1993
Monsanto Park	Portugal	1	1959
Pescara	Italy	1	1957
Riverside	United States	1	1960
Sebring	United States	1	1959
Zeltweg	Austria	1	1964

(a) Formerly known as A1-Ring/ Österreichring.
(b) Includes 11 Indianapolis 500 races.
Monza has been present on the calendar every year except 1980, when the Italian Grand Prix was held at Imola.
Germany was officially West Germany until re-unification on 3 October 1990. UAE - United Arab Emirates.

28. Countries hosting races

	races	seasons		races	seasons
Italy	93	1950 - 2015 (a)	Argentina	20	1953 - 98
Germany	75	1951 - 2014 (b)	Malaysia	17	1999 - 2015
Great Britain	69	1950 - 2015 (c)	Mexico	16	1963 - 2015
United States	66	1950 - 2015 (d)	Portugal	16	1958 - 96
Monaco	62	1950 - 2015	China	12	2004 - 15
Belgium	60	1950 - 2015	Bahrain	11	2004 - 15
France	59	1950 - 2008 (e)	Singapore	8	2008 - 15
Spain	52	1951 - 2015 (f)	Turkey	7	2005 - 11
Canada	46	1967 - 2015	United Arab Emirates	7	2009 - 15 (h)
Brazil	43	1973 - 2015	Sweden	6	1973 - 78
Japan	33	1976 - 2015 (g)	Switzerland	5	1950 - 54
Australia	31	1985 - 2015	South Korea	4	2010 - 13 (i)
Hungary	30	1986 - 2015	India	3	2011 - 13
Netherlands	30	1952 - 85	Russia	2	2014 - 15
Austria	28	1964 - 2015	Morocco	1	1958
South Africa	23	1962 - 93			

(a) Includes 1 Pescara Grand Prix & 26 San Marino Grands Prix (Imola). (b) Includes 12 European & 2 Luxembourg Grands Prix (Nürburgring). (c) Includes 3 European Grands Prix (2 at Brands Hatch & 1 at Donington Park). (d) Includes 11 Indianapolis 500 races and 2 Caesars Palace (Las Vegas), 1 Dallas, 7 Detroit & 8 United States West Grands Prix (Long Beach). (e) Includes 1 Swiss Grands Prix (Dijon-Prenois). (f) Includes 7 European Grands Prix (2 at Jerez de la Frontera & 5 at Valencia). (g) Includes 2 Pacific Grands Prix (Aida). (h) Abu Dhabi Grand Prix. (i) Korean Grand Prix.

29. Races held every season
The British and Italian Grands Prix are the only two to be held every year since 1950.

30. Season length

Longest

	months, days
1968	10m, 2d
1965	9m, 23d
1967	9m, 20d
1977	9m, 14d
1960	9m, 13d

Shortest

	months, days
1952	3m, 20d
1950	3m, 21d
1961	4m, 25d
1951	5m, 1d
1966	5m, 1d

31. Interval between seasons

Longest

	months, days
1950 - 51	8m, 24d
1961 - 62	7m, 12d
1965 - 66	6m, 29d
1958 - 59	6m, 22d
1951 - 52	6m, 21d

Shortest

	months, days
1959 - 60	1m, 26d
1964 - 65	2m, 7d
1966 - 67	2m, 10d
1967 - 68	2m, 10d
1976 - 77	2m, 16d

32. First race in the season

Earliest

1 January	1965	South Africa
1 January	1968	South Africa
2 January	1967	South Africa
9 January	1977	Argentina
12 January	1975	Argentina
13 January	1957	Argentina
13 January	1974	Argentina
13 January	1980	Argentina
15 January	1978	Argentina
16 January	1955	Argentina

Latest

27 May	1951	Switzerland
26 May	1963	Monaco
22 May	1966	Monaco
20 May	1962	Netherlands
18 May	1952	Switzerland
14 May	1961	Monaco
13 May	1950	Britain
10 May	1959	Monaco
10 May	1964	Monaco
12 April	1987	Brazil

33. Last race in the season

Earliest

2 September	1956	Italy
3 September	1950	Italy
7 September	1952	Italy
8 September	1957	Italy
11 September	1955	Italy
13 September	1953	Italy
25 September	1982	Caesars Palace
3 October	1972	United States
5 October	1975	United States
5 October	1980	United States

Latest

29 December	1962	South Africa
28 December	1963	South Africa
12 December	1959	United States
29 November	2015	Abu Dhabi
27 November	2011	Brazil
25 November	2012	Brazil
24 November	2013	Brazil
23 November	2014	Abu Dhabi
20 November	1960	United States
15 November	1987	Australia

34. Interval between races in a season *(Longest)*

			months, days
1965: Round 1 to Round 2:	1 Jan (South Africa)	30 May (Monaco)	4m, 29d
1954: Round 1 to Round 2:	17 Jan (Argentina)	31 May (Indianapolis)	4m, 14d
1953: Round 1 to Round 2:	18 Jan (Argentina)	30 May (Indianapolis)	4m, 12d
1968: Round 1 to Round 2:	1 Jan (South Africa)	12 May (Spain)	4m, 11d
1955: Round 1 to Round 2:	16 Jan (Argentina)	22 May (Monaco)	4m, 6d
1957: Round 1 to Round 2:	3 Jan (Argentina)	19 May (Monaco)	4m, 6d
1967: Round 1 to Round 2:	2 Jan (South Africa)	7 May (Monaco)	4m, 5d
1956: Round 1 to Round 2:	22 Jan (Argentina)	13 May (Monaco)	3m, 22d
1960: Round 1 to Round 2:	7 Feb (Argentina)	29 May (Monaco)	3m, 22d
1958: Round 1 to Round 2:	19 Jan (Argentina)	18 May (Monaco)	3m, 30d

35. Races not held on a Saturday or Sunday

Netherlands 1958	Monday, 26 May
Netherlands 1960	Monday, 6 June
Netherlands 1961	Monday, 22 May
South Africa 1965	Friday, 1 January
South Africa 1967	Monday, 2 January
South Africa 1968	Monday, 1 January
Spain 1972	Monday, 1 May

Indianapolis 500	
1950	Tuesday, 30 May
1951	Wednesday, 30 May
1952	Friday, 30 May
1954	Monday, 31 May (a)
1955	Monday, 30 May
1956	Wednesday, 30 May
1957	Thursday, 30 May
1958	Friday, 30 May
1960	Monday, 30 May

(a) Fell out of the sequence of being held on 30 May, as racing was not permitted there on a Sunday.

36. The last occasion of a grand prix on Saturday

This was 3 November 1985 at Kyalami, in South Africa.

37. Night races

Singapore hosted the first night race on 28 September 2008 (starting time: 20:00) with all the subsequent races at the circuit being held at night. The Bahrain Grand Prix became a night race with effect from 2014 (starting time: 18:00). The Abu Dhabi Grand Prix has been the only day-to-night race, with the first being held in 2009 (starting time: 17:00).

Summary of night/ day-to-night races

Singapore	8	2008 - 15 (night)
Abu Dhabi	7	2009 - 15 (day-to-night)

Bahrain	2	2014 - 15 (night)

38. Countries producing a winner, but never hosted a race
The only countries to produce a race winning driver and yet never host a grand prix are Colombia, Finland, New Zealand and Venezuela.

39. Countries staging another country's race

France (Dijon-Prenois)	Switzerland 1982	(1 race)
Italy (Imola)	San Marino 1981 - 2006	(26 races)
Germany (Nürburgring)	Luxembourg 1997 - 98	(2 races)

40. Countries staging more than one race during a season

3 races

	number of seasons		
United States	1	1982	United States West (Long Beach), Detroit & Caesars Palace (Las Vegas)

2 races

France	1	1982	France (Paul Ricard) & Switzerland (Dijon-Prenois)
Germany	13	1984, 95, 96, 99 - 2006	Germany (Hockenheim) & Europe (Nürburgring)
		1997, 98	Germany (Hockenheim) & Luxembourg (Nürburgring)
Great Britain	3	1983, 85	Britain (Silverstone) & Europe (Brands Hatch)
		1993	Britain (Silverstone) & Europe (Donington)
Italy	27	1957	Pescara & Italy (Monza)
		1981 - 2006	San Marino (Imola) & Italy (Monza)
Japan	2	1994, 95	Pacific (Aida) & Japan (Suzuka)
Spain	7	1994, 97	Spain (Catalunya) & Europe (Jerez de la Frontera)
		2008 - 12	Spain (Catalunya) & Europe (Valencia)
United States	10	1959	United States (Sebring) & Indianapolis 500
		1960	United States (Riverside) & Indianapolis 500
		1976 - 80	United States West (Long Beach) & United States (Watkins Glen)
		1981	United States West (Long Beach) & Caesars Palace (Las Vegas)
		1983	United States West (Long Beach) & Detroit
		1984	Detroit & Dallas

41. Countries with the most grand prix venues

United States	10	Austin, Dallas, Detroit, Indianapolis, Las Vegas, Long Beach, Phoenix, Riverside, Sebring, Watkins Glen
France	7	Bugatti au Mans, Clermont-Ferrand, Dijon-Prenois, Magny-Cours, Paul Ricard, Reims/ Reims-Gueux, Rouen-les-Essarts
Spain	6	Catalunya, Jarama, Jerez de la Frontera, Montjuïc, Pedralbes, Valencia
Great Britain	4	Aintree, Brands Hatch, Donington Park, Silverstone
Belgium	3	Nivelles-Baulers, Spa-Francorchamps, Zolder
Canada	3	Mont-Tremblant, Montréal, Mosport Park
Germany	3	AVUS, Hockenheim, Nürburgring
Italy	3	Imola, Monza, Pescara
Japan	3	Aida, Fuji, Suzuka
Portugal	3	Estoril, Monsanto Park, Porto

42. Opening venue *(Most seasons)*

Melbourne, Australia	18	1996 - 2015
Buenos Aires, Argentina	15	1953 - 80
Kyalami, South Africa	8	1967 - 93
Jacarepaguá, Brazil	7	1983 - 89
Monte-Carlo, Monaco	5	1959 - 66
Interlagos, Brazil	3	1976 - 95

43. Closing venue *(Most seasons)*

Adelaide, Australia	11	1985 - 95
Watkins Glen, United States	8	1961 - 80
Interlagos, Brazil	7	2004 - 13
Mexico City, Mexico	7	1964 - 70
Monza, Italy	6	1950 - 57
Suzuka, Japan	6	1996 - 2003

44. Races in a season

Most

20	2012
19	2005, 10, 11, 13, 14, 15
18	2004, 06, 08
17	1977, 95, 97, 2000, 01, 02, 07, 09

Fewest

6	1950 *, 55 *
7	1951 *, 52 *, 56 *, 57 *
8	1953 *, 54 *, 59 *, 61

* Excludes Indianapolis 500.

Total for each season

1950 - 6, 1951 - 7, 1952 - 7, 1953 - 8, 1954 - 8, 1955 - 6, 1956 - 7, 1957 - 7, 1958 - 10, 1959 - 8, 1960 - 9, 1961 - 8, 1962 - 9, 1963 - 10, 1964 - 10, 1965 - 10, 1966 - 9, 1967 - 11, 1968 - 12, 1969 - 11, 1970 - 13, 1971 - 11, 1972 - 12, 1973 - 15, 1974 - 15, 1975 - 14, 1976 - 16, 1977 - 17, 1978 - 16, 1979 - 15, 1980 - 14, 1981 - 15, 1982 - 16, 1983 - 15, 1984 - 16, 1985 - 16, 1986 - 16, 1987 - 16, 1988 - 16, 1989 - 16, 1990 - 16, 1991 - 16, 1992 - 16, 1993 - 16, 1994 - 16, 1995 - 17, 1996 - 16, 1997 - 17, 1998 - 16, 1999 - 16, 2000 - 17, 2001 - 17, 2002 - 17, 2003 - 16, 2004 - 18, 2005 - 19, 2006 - 18, 2007 - 17, 2008 - 18, 2009 - 17, 2010 - 19, 2011, 19, 2012 - 20, 2013 - 19, 2014 - 19, 2015 - 19

Excludes Indianapolis 500 with 1 race each year from 1950 until 1960.

45. Race length (time)

Longest

	hours, mins, secs
Canada 2011	4h, 04m, 39.537s (a)
Germany 1954	3h, 45m, 45.800s
Germany 1956	3h, 38m, 43.700s
Germany 1957	3h, 30m, 38.300s
Germany 1951	3h, 23m, 03.300s
France 1951	3h, 22m, 11.000s
Spain 1954	3h, 13m, 52.100s
Monaco 1950	3h, 13m, 18.700s
Monaco 1957	3h, 10m, 12.800s
France 1957	3h, 07m, 46.400s

Indianapolis 500	
1951	3h, 57m, 38.050s
1955	3h, 53m, 59.530s
1956	3h, 53m, 28.840s
1953	3h, 53m, 01.690s
1952	3h, 52m, 41.880s
1954	3h, 49m, 17.270s
1958	3h, 44m, 13.800s
1957	3h, 41m, 14.250s
1959	3h, 40m, 49.200s
1960	3h, 36m, 11.360s

(a) Race was stopped for over two hours with the clock left running (see section 55).

Shortest

Australia 1991	24m, 34.899s	(Heavy rain. Result declared after 14 of the scheduled 81 laps) (b)
Spain 1975	42m, 53.700s	(Rolf Stommelen's accident which killed five spectators. Result declared after 29 of 75 laps) (b)
Malaysia 2009	55m, 30.622s	(Heavy rain. Result declared after 31 of 56 laps) (b)
Austria 1975	57m, 56.690s	(Heavy rain. Result declared after 29 of 54 laps) (b)
Monaco 1984	1h, 01m, 07.740s	(Heavy rain. Result declared after 31 of 77 laps) (b)
Italy 1978	1h, 07m, 04.540s	(Restarted after a long delay, following the first lap accident and terminated after 40 of the 52 laps due to darkness)
Belgium 2001	1h, 08m, 05.002s	(Reduced length due to delays. The start had been aborted and the race was later stopped after Luciano Burti's accident. Eventually restarted for 36 of the scheduled 44 laps)
Italy 2003	1h, 14m, 19.838s	(c)
Italy 2005	1h, 14m, 28.659s	(c)
Italy 1987	1h, 14m, 47.707s	(c)

All were shortened races except (c) which were full distance. (b) Half points awarded..

See Appendix 2 for regulations on race length and distance through the years

46. Race length (distance)

Longest

	km	miles
France 1951	601.808	373.947
Belgium 1951 - 56	508.320	315.855
Belgium 1960	507.600	315.408
France 1954 - 56	506.406	314.667
Spain 1954	505.280	313.966
Italy 1950 - 54	504.000	313.171
France 1957	503.734	313.006
Germany 1954 - 57	501.820	311.816
France 1953	500.838	311.206
Italy 1957	500.250	310.841
Indianapolis 500		
1951 - 60	804.672	500.000
1950	555.224	345.000

Shortest

	km	miles
Australia 1991	52.920	32.883
Monaco 1984	102.672	63.797
Spain 1975	109.929	68.306
Austria 1975	171.419	106.515
Malaysia 2009	171.833	106.772
Monaco 1997	208.692	129.675
Belgium 1981	230.148	143.007
Italy 1978	232.000	144.158
Brazil 2003	232.656	144.566
Canada 1997	238.734	148.342

47. Circuit length

Longest

	km	miles
Pescara 1957	25.579	15.894
Nürburgring 1967 - 76	22.835	14.189
Nürburgring 1951 - 66	22.810	14.173
Spa-Francorchamps 1950 - 56	14.120	8.774
Spa-Francorchamps 1958 - 70	14.100	8.761
Monza 1955 - 56, 60 - 61	10.000	6.214
Sebring 1959	8.369	5.200
Reims 1953	8.3473	5.1868
Reims 1954 - 66	8.30175	5.15850
AVUS 1959	8.300	5.157

Shortest

	km	miles
Monte-Carlo 1955 - 72	3.145	1.954
Monte-Carlo 1950	3.180	1.976
Zeltweg 1964	3.200	1.988
Long Beach 1976 - 81	3.251	2.020
Long Beach 1983	3.275	2.035
Monte-Carlo 1973 - 75	3.278	2.037
Dijon-Prenois 1974	3.289	2.044
Jarama 1981	3.312	2.058
Monte-Carlo 1976 - 85	3.312	2.058
Monte-Carlo 1986 - 96	3.328	2.068

48. Laps in a race

Most

United States 1963 - 65	110
United States 1966 - 70	108
Austria 1964	105
Monaco 1957	105
Britain 1956	101
Argentina 1957	100
Monaco 1950 - 56, 58 - 67	100
Netherlands 1955	100
United States 1961 - 62	100
Argentina 1956	98

Additionally, the Indianapolis 500 ran a full distance of 200 laps from 1951 to 1960 and 138 laps in 1950.

Fewest

Germany 1971	12
Australia 1991	14 (a)
Germany 1968 - 69, 72 -76	14
Germany 1958, 61 - 67	15
Germany 1952 - 53	18
Pescara 1957	18
Germany 1951	20
Germany 1954 - 57	22
Belgium 1958	24
Belgium 1966 - 70	28

(a) Race was stopped early due to heavy rain.
Apart from (a), these races had few laps due to being run on long circuits.

49. Laps raced in a season

Most

2012	1,192
2005	1,180
2015	1,149
2006	1,137
2014	1,134
2011	1,133
1977	1,132
2013	1,131
2010	1,129
1995	1,124

Fewest

1950	391 *
1951	415 *
1952	447 *
1956	468 *
1955	472 *
1961	490
1957	499 *
1954	522 *
1953	536 *
1959	536 *

* Excludes Indianapolis 500.

50. Distance raced in a season

Longest

	km	miles
2012	6,084.9	3,781.0
2011	5,794.4	3,600.5
2010	5,793.4	3,599.9
2013	5,792.3	3,599.3
2005	5,779.0	3,590.9
2015	5,778.2	3,590.5
2014	5,717.4	3,552.7
2008	5,480.9	3,405.6
2006	5,478.8	3,404.4
2004	5,472.4	3,400.4

Shortest

	km	miles
1950	2,447.6	1,520.9 *
1955	2,552.2	1,585.9 *
1961	2,988.1	1,856.7
1959	3,006.9	1,868.4 *
1952	3,039.6	1,888.7 *
1957	3,122.2	1,940.1 *
1956	3,190.2	1,982.3 *
1951	3,236.7	2,011.2 *
1971	3,276.9	2,036.2
1966	3,284.3	2,040.7

* Excludes Indianapolis 500.

51. Fastest and slowest circuits

(based on fastest speeds recorded in all qualifying and official practice sessions and the race at each circuit venue, regardless of track changes)

Fastest

	km/h	mph		session	
Monza	262.242	162.950	Juan Pablo Montoya (Williams FW26 - BMW)	2004	1st qualifying practice
Silverstone	258.983	160.925	Keke Rosberg (Williams FW10 - Honda)	1985	2nd (final) timed practice
Österreichring (a)	256.621	159.457	Nelson Piquet (Williams FW11B - Honda)	1987	1st timed practice
Hockenheim	252.219	156.722	Nigel Mansell (Williams FW14 - Renault)	1991	2nd (final) qualifying practice
Spa-Francorchamps	244.744	152.077	Chris Amon (March 701 - Ford Cosworth)	1970	race
AVUS	240.000	149.129	Tony Brooks (Ferrari Dino 246)	1959	race
Kyalami	236.898	147.202	Nigel Mansell (Williams FW10 - Honda)	1985	2nd (final) timed practice
Suzuka	235.011	146.029	Michael Schumacher (Ferrari 248 F1)	2006	qualifying practice Q2
Reims	233.852	145.309	Lorenzo Bandini (Ferrari 312)	1966	3rd (final) practice
Melbourne	228.552	142.016	Sebastian Vettel (Red Bull RB7 - Renault)	2011	qualifying practice Q3
Indianapolis 500					
Indianapolis	240.759	149.601	Jim Hurtubise (Christensen - Offenheiser)	1960	qualifying

(a) Now known as Spielberg.

Slowest

	km/h	mph		session	
Dallas	144.720	89.925	Nigel Mansell (Lotus 95T - Renault)	1984	1st timed practice
Detroit	147.344	91.556	Ayrton Senna (Lotus 98T - Renault)	1986	2nd (final) timed practice
Long Beach	150.631	93.598	Nelson Piquet (Brabham BT49 - Ford Cosworth)	1980	2nd (final) timed practice
Aintree	153.001	95.070	Jim Clark (Lotus 25 - Climax)	1962	4th (final) practice
Pescara	157.517	97.876	Juan Manuel Fangio (Maserati 250F)	1957	2nd (final) practice
	157.517	97.876	Stirling Moss (Vanwall VW5/57)	1957	race
Monsanto Park	159.362	99.023	Stirling Moss (Cooper T51 - Climax)	1959	practice
East London	161.850	100.569	Jim Clark (Lotus 33 - Climax)	1965	2nd practice
Monte-Carlo	163.520	101.707	Kimi Räikkönen (McLaren MP4-21 - Mercedes)	2006	qualifying practice Q2
Phoenix	164.488	102.208	Ayrton Senna (McLaren MP4/6 - Honda)	1991	2nd (final) qualifying practice
Jarama	164.503	102.217	Jacques Laffite (Ligier JS11 - Ford Cosworth)	1979	2nd (final) timed practice

52. The safety car

The safety car is deployed as soon as Race Control considers that is unsafe for cars to continue racing due to an accident, incident or adverse weather conditions. The safety car remains on the track with the cars running in formation behind, no overtaking being permitted. When it is considered safe for the racing to resume, the safety car will return to the pit lane.

The first appearance of a safety car was on 23 September 1973, at Mosport in the Canadian Grand Prix, a Porsche 914 driven by Eppie Wietzes (a Formula 1 driver who raced at two Canadian Grands Prix). It was from the start of the 1993 season that the safety car was officially introduced for action when required at every grand prix. From Brazil that year, it was a FIAT Tempra. Cars have been from a variety of manufacturers, but from 1996, Mercedes-Benz has had the contract to provide a safety car at each grand prix.

The current safety car is the Mercedes-Benz SLS AMG GT S with a twin-turbocharged 4-litre, V8 engine and a power output of 510 bhp. It has a top speed of 193 mph and covers 0 to 100 km/h (62 mph) in just 3.8 seconds.

races starting behind the safety car due to wet conditions

Belgium 1997, Belgium 2000, Brazil 2003, Japan 2007, Italy 2008, China 2009, Korea 2010, Canada 2011, Japan 2014

races finishing behind the safety car

Canada 1999	Heinz-Harald Frentzen's accident.
Australia 2009	Debris from accident involving Sebastian Vettel and Robert Kubica.
Italy 2009	Lewis Hamilton's accident.
Monaco 2010	Accident involving Jarno Trulli and Karun Chandhok.
Brazil 2012	Paul Di Resta's accident.
Canada 2014	Final lap accident involving Felipe Massa and Sergio Pérez.
Japan 2014	Jules Bianchi's accident in heavy rain.

most deployments of the safety car in a race

Six in Canada 2011.

53. Races in two parts, with times aggregated

Germany 1959	Intentionally a two-part race.
Austria 1978	Stopped after 7 laps, due to heavy rain and accidents involving Mario Andretti, Jody Scheckter, Carlos Reutemann and Jean-Pierre Jabouille. Restarted for the remaining 47 laps.
South Africa 1979	Stopped after 2 laps, due to heavy rain. Restarted for the remaining 76.
France 1981	Stopped after 58 laps, due to Jacques Laffite's accident. Restarted for the remaining 22 laps.
Detroit 1982	Stopped after 6 laps, due to accident involving Riccardo Patrese and Roberto Guerrero. Restarted for the remaining laps, but the race had to be stopped after a further 56 (at the 2-hour maximum limit), thereby leaving the race eight laps short of the originally scheduled distance.
Britain 1984	Stopped after 11 laps, due to Jonathan Palmer's accident. Restarted for the remaining 60 laps.
Mexico 1987 (a)	Stopped after 30 laps, due to Derek Warwick's accident. Restarted for the remaining 33 laps. Nelson Piquet crossed the finishing line first, but on aggregated time, Nigel Mansell was the overall winner. The race had been scheduled for 68 laps.
San Marino 1989	Stopped after 3 laps, due to Gerhard Berger's accident. Restarted for a further 55 laps, three less than scheduled.
France 1992	Stopped after 18 laps, due to heavy rain. Restarted for a further 51 laps, three less than scheduled.
San Marino 1994	Stopped after Ayrton Senna's fatal accident. Run over 5 and 53 laps, three less than scheduled.
Japan 1994	Stopped due to heavy rain and Martin Brundle's accident. Run over 13 and 37 laps, three less than scheduled.

(a) The only race where the driver leading at the chequered flag was not the winner on aggregate times.

54. Other races stopped and restarted for a reduced number of laps

Italy 1978	Stopped on lap 1, due to an accident. Restarted for 40 of the scheduled 52 laps.
Belgium 2001	Stopped after 5 laps, due to accidents. Restarted for a new race of 36 of the scheduled 44 laps.

On numerous other occasions, races were aborted due to accidents at the start, cars stalling or being out of position on the grid. These races were consequently run for a reduced number of laps to accommodate the extra parade lap(s).

55. Races stopped and restarted after an interval with the clock left running

	stoppage time	
Europe 2007	24m 20s	Stopped after 4 laps, due to heavy rain and accidents, notably that of Vitantonio Liuzzi. Restarted for the remaining 56 laps.
Korea 2010	48m 08s	Stopped after 3 laps, due to very wet track condition. Restarted for the remaining 52 laps.
Monaco 2011	20m 43s	Stopped after 71 laps, after accidents involving Adrian Sutil, Lewis Hamilton, Jaime Alguersuari and Vitaly Petrov. Restarted for the remaining 7 laps.
Canada 2011	2h 04m 03s	Stopped after 24 laps, due to heavy rain. Restarted for the remaining 46 laps.
Malaysia 2012	51m 01s	Stopped after 8 laps, due to heavy rain. Restarted for the remaining 48 laps.
Monaco 2013	24m 24s	Stopped after 45 laps, following the accident involving Pastor Maldonado & Max Chilton accident. Restarted for the remaining 33 laps.
Britain 2014	59m 22s	Stopped after 1 lap, due to the Kimi Räikkönen & Felipe Massa accident. Restarted for the remaining 51 laps.
Japan 2014	19m 55s	Stopped after 2 laps, due to very wet conditions. Restarted for the remaining 42 laps.

All of the above races were restarted behind the safety car.

56. Races stopped early and not restarted

Indianapolis 1950	Result declared over 138 of the scheduled 200 laps (heavy rain).
Canada 1971	Result declared over 64 of the scheduled 80 laps (fog).
Brazil 1974	Result declared over 32 of the scheduled 40 laps (heavy rain).
Spain 1975	Result declared over 29 of the scheduled 75 laps (Rolf Stommelen's car crashed into a public area, killing five spectators).
Britain 1975	Result declared over 56 of the scheduled 67 laps (heavy hail storm).
Austria 1975	Result declared over 29 of the scheduled 54 laps (heavy rain).
Argentina 1978	Chequered flag waved in error, after 52 of the scheduled 53 laps.
Belgium 1981	Result declared over 54 of the scheduled 70 laps (heavy rain).
Monaco 1984	Result declared over 31 of the scheduled 77 laps (heavy rain).
Britain 1985	Chequered flag waved in error, after 65 of the scheduled 66 laps.
Portugal 1990	Result declared over 61 of the scheduled 71 laps (accident involving Aguri Suzuki and Alex Caffi).
Australia 1991	Result declared over 14 of the scheduled 81 laps (heavy rain).
Canada 1995	Result declared over 68 of the scheduled 69 laps (crowd invasion of the track).
Canada 1997	Result declared over 54 of the scheduled 69 laps (Olivier Panis' accident).
Brazil 2003	Result declared over 54 of the scheduled 71 laps (Mark Webber and Fernando Alonso accidents).
Malaysia 2009	Result declared over 31 of the scheduled 56 laps (heavy rain and accidents).
China 2014	Chequered flag waved in error, after 54 of the scheduled 56 laps.
Japan 2014	Result declared over 44 of the scheduled 53 laps (Jules Bianchi's accident).

57. Races stopped due to running out of time

(2-hour limit)

1974	Spain		1989	United States, Australia
1975	Monaco		1991	United States
1981	Brazil, Canada		1996	Monaco
1982	Detroit		1997	Monaco
1984	Dallas		2008	Monaco
1985	Portugal		2012	Singapore
1986	Hungary		2014	Singapore

The 2-hour maximum race limit came into being from the 1973 season. See Appendix 2 for regulations on race length and distance through the years.

58. Cars on the starting grid

Most

Germany 1953	34
Italy 1961	32
Britain 1952	31
United States 1972	31
Belgium 1974	31
Germany 1952	30
Italy 1953	30
Britain 1954	30
Britain 1961	30
United States 1971	29

Excludes Indianapolis 500 races which had 33 cars on each grid.

Fewest

United States 2005	6 (a)
Argentina 1958	10
Belgium 1951	13
Belgium 1955	13
Argentina 1956	13
Spain 1968	13
France 1969	13
San Marino 1982	13 (b)(c)
Belgium 1950	14
Belgium 1954	14
Monaco 1956	14
Argentina 1957	14
Spain 1969	14

(a) An additional 14 Michelin runners were withdrawn on the parade lap, due to tyre safety concerns.
(b) Excludes Derek Warwick (Toleman - Hart) who retired on the parade lap.
(c) The field for this race was depleted as a result of a dispute involving ten teams which refused to participate. Teams aligned to the Formula One Constructors' Association were boycotting the race. They were protesting about the decision to disqualify the top two cars in the Brazilian Grand Prix which were found to be under the minimum permitted weight. The teams had argued that they had inserted a water tank which gradually emptied during the race, not to run the cars under weight, but to cool the brakes.

59. Starting grid formats

From Germany 1973, every starting grid has been in a two by two format. Before that, grids could contain as many as four cars on a row, as was the case at the nunerous races until 1967. The most rows on a starting grid was 16 at the Italian Grand Prix in 1961 and Belgian Grand Prix in 1974.

Front row format summary:
2 cars in 759 races (Italy 1961 - Abu Dhabi 2015)
3 cars in 125 races (Monaco 1950 - Netherlands 1973)
4 cars in 40 races (Britain 1950 - Germany 1967): at AVUS, Buenos Aires, Monza, Nürburgring, Pedralbes, Silverstone and Zeltweg
Additionally, all 11 Indianapolis 500 races had 3-car front rows.

60. Cars running at the race finish

Most

Europe 2011	24	(Narain Karthikeyan, HRT F111 - Cosworth, has been the only Formula 1 driver in history to be classified 24th in a grand prix).
Brazil 2010	23 (a)	
China 2011	23	
Japan 2011	23	
China 2012	23	
Germany 2012	23	
Britain 1952	22	
Turkey 2011	22	
United States 2012	22	

Excludes Indianapolis 500.

Fewest

Monaco 1996	4 (b)
Monaco 1962	5
Spain 1968	5
Monaco 1968	5
Spain 1969	5
Spain 1970	5
Monaco 1982	5
South Africa 1993	5

(a) Includes 1 not classified (ie did not complete 90% of race distance).
(b) Includes 1 car in the pits at the end of the race.

61. Cars on leading lap at the race finish *(Most)*

Most

Japan 2011	19	Germany 2008	16
Britain 2013	18	Europe 2010	16
Germany 2009	17	Abu Dhabi 2010	16
China 2012	17	Singapore 2012	16
Abu Dhabi 2012	17	United States 2013	16
Korea 2013	17	Singapore 2014	16

Excludes Indianapolis 500.

Winning speed *(Fastest/ Slowest)*. See section 253
Winning margin *(Largest/ Smallest)*. See section 254

62. Margin of victory of less than one second

1950: Switzerland, 1954: France, 1955: Netherlands, Britain, Italy, 1956: France, 1959: United States, 1961: Netherlands, Belgium, France, 1967: Italy, 1969: Italy, 1970: Germany, Austria, 1971: Italy, 1973: Italy, United States, 1974: Belgium, Sweden, Italy, 1976: Netherlands, 1977: United States West, Monaco, 1978: South Africa, Netherlands, 1979: Monaco, Italy, 1980: Austria, 1981: Spain, 1982: San Marino, Austria, 1985: Netherlands, 1986: Spain, 1988: Hungary, Italy, 1990: Hungary, 1991: Japan, 1992: Monaco, Australia, 1993: France, Portugal, 1994: Portugal, 1996: Europe, Hungary, 1997: Argentina, 1998: Australia, Germany, Belgium, 1999: Canada, Austria, 2000: Canada, Malaysia, 2001: Monaco, 2002: Brazil, Austria, Europe, Hungary, Italy, United States, Japan, 2003: Brazil, Monaco, Canada, 2004: Monaco, 2005: San Marino, 2006: Germany, 2007: Hungary, 2009: Australia, Belgium, 2010: Monaco, Singapore, Japan, 2011: Spain, 2012: Monaco, Abu Dhabi, United States, 2013: Britain, 2014: Spain, 2015: China

For the smallest winning margins, see section 254.

63. Closest top threes

	seconds	
Italy 1971	0.090	1: Peter Gethin (BRM), 2: Ronnie Peterson (March - Ford Cosworth), 3: François Cevert (Tyrrell - Ford Cosworth)
Italy 1969	0.170	1: Jackie Stewart (Matra - Ford Cosworth), 2: Jochen Rindt (Lotus - Ford Cosworth), 3: Jean-Pierre Beltoise (Matra - Ford Cosworth)
Spain 1981	0.580	1: Gilles Villeneuve (Ferrari), 2: Jacques Laffite (Talbot-Ligier - Matra), 3: John Watson (McLaren - Ford Cosworth)
Monaco 2012	0.947	1: Mark Webber (Red Bull - Renault), 2: Nico Rosberg (Mercedes-Benz), 3: Fernando Alonso (Ferrari)
Canada 2003	1.355	1: Michael Schumacher (Ferrari), 2: Ralf Schumacher (Williams - BMW), 3: Juan Pablo Montoya (Williams - BMW)
France 1953	1.400	1: Mike Hawthorn (Ferrari), 2: Juan Manuel Fangio (Maserati), 3: José Froilán González (Maserati)
China 2004	1.469	1: Rubens Barrichello (Ferrari), 2: Jenson Button (BAR - Honda), 3: Kimi Räikkönen (McLaren - Mercedes)
Australia 2009 (a)	1.604	1: Jenson Button (Brawn - Mercedes), 2: Rubens Barrichello (Brawn - Mercedes), 3: Jarno Trulli (Toyota)
Monaco 2010 (a)	1.675	1: Mark Webber (Red Bull - Renault), 2: Sebastian Vettel (Red Bull - Renault), 3: Robert Kubica (Renault)
Monaco 2003	1.720	1: Juan Pablo Montoya (Williams - BMW), 2: Kimi Räikkönen (McLaren - Mercedes), 3: Michael Schumacher (Ferrari)

(a) Race finished behind the safety car.

64. Within one minute of the winner *(Most cars)*

16	Europe 2010, China 2012, Britain 2013
15	Japan 2009, Britain 2012, Abu Dhabi 2012, Italy 2013
14	Singapore 2008, Abu Dhabi 2010, Monaco 2013, Monaco 2015, Mexico 2015
13	Germany 2008, Belgium 2009, Abu Dhabi 2009, Britain 2010, Belgium 2010, Canada 2012, Germany 2013, Korea 2013, Bahrain 2014
12	Britain 2004, Canada 2007, France 2008, Monaco 2010, Australia 2012, Europe 2012, Italy 2012

65. Cars retiring in a race

Most

South Africa 1993	21
Italy 1961	20
Britain 1975	20
San Marino 1986	20
Italy 1950	19
Austria 1982	19
Detroit 1984	19
Belgium 1987	19
Germany 1987	19
Australia 1988	19
United States 1989	19
Monaco 1990	19
Indianapolis 500	
1951	25
1953	21
1955	19
1958	19

(a) Not only were there were no retirements at Netherlands 1961, there is no record of any pit stops either.

Fewest

Netherlands 1961	0 (a)
United States 2005	0
Italy 2005	0
Europe 2011	0
Argentina 1958	1
Britain 2005	1
France 2008	1
Italy 2008	1
Bahrain 2009	1
Brazil 2010	1
China 2011	1
Turkey 2011	1
Japan 2011	1
China 2012	1
Germany 2012	1
Bahrain 2013	1
Abu Dhabi 2013	1
United States 2013	1
Japan 2015	1
Brazil 2015	1
Abu Dhabi 2015	1

66. Cars retiring before end of first lap *(Most)*

Germany 1994	11	Italy 1978	5
Monaco 1950	10	Argentina 1979	5
Britain 1973	10	Europe 1984	5
Germany 1976	9	Italy 1993	5
Belgium 1966	8	Monaco 1996	5
Australia 2002	8	Canada 1998	5
Belgium 1998	7	Belgium 2001	5
United States 2006	7	Australia 2008	5
Italy 2000	6	**Indianapolis 500**	
Monaco 1974	5	1958	7

67. Laps completed before first retirement *(Most)*

Hungary 2012	58	Turkey 2011	44
Germany 2012	56	Canada 2015	44
Brazil 2010	49	Canada 2013	43
Japan 2015	49	Portugal 1996	41
Bahrain 2009	48	Hungary 2015	41
Monaco 2006	46		

There were four races with no retirements (see section 65).

68. Drivers leading in a race *(Most)*

Italy 1971	8	France 1990	6
Canada 1973	7	Italy 1995	6
Britain 1975	7	United States 2003	6
Canada 2008	7	Belgium 2004	6
Australia 2013	7	Japan 2005	6
France 1961	6	Japan 2008	6
Italy 1966	6	China 2011	6
Italy 1967	6	China 2013	6
Italy 1970	6		
Spain 1975	6		

Based on drivers leading at the end of each lap, across the finishing line.

69. Pole to podium conversion
(illustrates the number of cars on pole position which reached the podium)

	races	pole to podium		pole to 1st		pole to 2nd		pole to 3rd	
		no.	(%)	no.	(%)	no.	(%)	no.	(%)
all circuits	935	566	(60.5)	383	(41.0)	122	(13.0)	61	(6.5)
Istanbul	7	7	(100.0)	5	(71.4)	-	-	2	(28.6)
Austin	4	4	(100.0)	1	(25.0)	3	(75.0)	-	-
Buddh	3	3	(100.0)	3	(100.0)	-	-	-	-
Âin-Diab	1	1	(100.0)	-	-	1	(100.0)	-	-
AVUS	1	1	(100.0)	1	(100.0)	-	-	-	-
Donington Park	1	1	(100.0)	-	-	-	-	1	(100.0)
Monsanto Park	1	1	(100.0)	1	(100.0)	-	-	-	-
Pescara	1	1	(100.0)	-	-	1	(100.0)	-	-
Riverside	1	1	(100.0)	1	(100.0)	-	-	-	-
Sepang	17	15	(88.2)	9	(52.9)	3	(17.6)	3	(17.6)
Indianapolis (a)	8	7	(87.5)	3	(37.5)	4	(50.0)	-	-
Shanghai	12	10	(83.3)	7	(58.3)	2	(16.7)	1	(8.3)
Dijon-Prenois	6	5	(83.3)	2	(33.3)	3	(50.0)	-	-
Sakhir	11	9	(81.8)	5	(45.5)	2	(18.2)	2	(18.2)
Mexico City	16	13	(81.3)	8	(50.0)	2	(12.5)	3	(18.8)
Catalunya	25	20	(80.0)	19	(76.0)	1	(4.0)	-	-
Aintree	5	4	(80.0)	3	(60.0)	1	(20.0)	-	-
Valencia	5	4	(80.0)	3	(60.0)	1	(20.0)	-	-
Magny-Cours	18	14	(77.8)	5	(27.8)	7	(38.9)	2	(11.1)
Marina Bay	8	6	(75.0)	6	(75.0)	-	-	-	-
Clermont-Ferrand	4	3	(75.0)	2	(50.0)	-	-	1	(25.0)
Yeongam	4	3	(75.0)	1	(25.0)	2	(50.0)	-	-
Suzuka	27	20	(74.1)	12	(44.4)	7	(25.9)	1	(3.7)
Hockenheim	34	25	(73.5)	18	(52.9)	3	(8.8)	4	(11.8)
Paul Ricard	14	10	(71.4)	8	(57.1)	1	(7.1)	1	(7.1)
Zolder	10	7	(70.0)	5	(50.0)	2	(20.0)	-	-
Estoril	13	9	(69.2)	6	(46.2)	2	(15.4)	1	(7.7)
Jarama	9	6	(66.7)	4	(44.4)	2	(22.2)	-	-
East London	3	2	(66.7)	2	(66.7)	-	-	-	-
Nürburgring	40	26	(65.0)	15	(37.5)	4	(10.0)	7	(17.5)
Long Beach	8	5	(62.5)	4	(50.0)	1	(12.5)	-	-
Mosport Park	8	5	(62.5)	4	(50.0)	1	(12.5)	-	-
Interlagos	33	20	(60.6)	13	(39.4)	4	(12.1)	3	(9.1)
Hungaroring	30	18	(60.0)	13	(43.3)	4	(13.3)	1	(3.3)
Melbourne	20	12	(60.0)	9	(45.0)	1	(5.0)	2	(10.0)
Spa-Francorchamps	48	28	(58.3)	16	(33.3)	8	(16.7)	4	(8.3)
Montréal	36	21	(58.3)	16	(44.4)	4	(11.1)	1	(2.8)
Jerez de la Frontera	7	4	(57.1)	3	(42.9)	-	-	1	(14.3)
Monte-Carlo	62	35	(56.5)	28	(45.2)	2	(3.2)	5	(8.1)
Imola	27	15	(55.6)	9	(33.3)	5	(18.5)	1	(3.7)
Spielberg (b)	27	15	(55.6)	7	(25.9)	7	(25.9)	1	(3.7)
Silverstone	49	27	(55.1)	17	(34.7)	7	(14.3)	3	(6.1)
Watkins Glen	20	11	(55.0)	10	(50.0)	1	(5.0)	-	-
Adelaide	11	6	(54.5)	5	(45.5)	1	(9.1)	-	-
Reims/ Reims-Gueux	11	6	(54.5)	6	(54.5)	-	-	-	-
Monza	65	33	(50.8)	23	(35.4)	5	(7.7)	5	(7.7)
Zandvoort	30	15	(50.0)	12	(40.0)	3	(10.0)	-	-
Anderstorp	6	3	(50.0)	1	(16.7)	2	(33.3)	-	-
Fuji	4	2	(50.0)	2	(50.0)	-	-	-	-
Aida	2	1	(50.0)	-	-	1	(50.0)	-	-
Nivelles-Baulers	2	1	(50.0)	1	(50.0)	-	-	-	-
Porto	2	1	(50.0)	1	(50.0)	-	-	-	-
Sochi	2	1	(50.0)	1	(50.0)				
Buenos Aires	20	9	(45.0)	7	(35.0)	2	(10.0)	-	-
Brands Hatch	14	6	(42.9)	4	(28.6)	2	(14.3)	-	-
Detroit	7	3	(42.9)	3	(42.9)	-	-	-	-
Yas Marina	7	3	(42.9)	2	(28.6)	1	(14.3)	-	-
Kyalami	20	8	(40.0)	4	(20.0)	2	(10.0)	2	(10.0)
Jacarepaguá	10	4	(40.0)	1	(10.0)	2	(20.0)	1	(10.0)
Bremgarten	5	2	(40.0)	1	(20.0)	1	(20.0)	-	-

	races	pole to podium		pole to 1st		pole to 2nd		pole to 3rd	
		no.	(%)	no.	(%)	no.	(%)	no.	(%)
Rouen-les-Essarts	5	2	(40.0)	2	(40.0)	-	-	-	-
Phoenix	3	1	(33.3)	1	(33.3)	-	-	-	-
Montjuïc	4	1	(25.0)	-	-	1	(25.0)	-	-
Bugatti au Mans	1	-	-	-	-	-	-	-	-
Dallas	1	-	-	-	-	-	-	-	-
Sebring	1	-	-	-	-	-	-	-	-
Zeltweg	1	-	-	-	-	-	-	-	-
Las Vegas	2	-	-	-	-	-	-	-	-
Mont-Tremblant	2	-	-	-	-	-	-	-	-
Pedralbes	2	-	-	-	-	-	-	-	-
Indianapolis 500									
Indianapolis	11	4	(36.4)	2	(18.2)	-	-	2	(18.2)

(a) Excludes Indianapolis 500.
(b) Formerly known as Österreichring & A1-Ring.

70. Interval between races

	no. of years				no. of years	
Portugal	24	1960 - 84		Argentina	12	1960 - 72
Mexico	23	1992 - 2015		Austria	10	1987 - 97
Mexico	16	1970 - 86		Japan	10	1977 - 87
Argentina	14	1981 - 95		Austria	9	2003 - 14
Spain	14	1954 - 68		United States	9	1991 - 2000

71. Cancelled races

1951: Netherlands (Zandvoort), 22 July.

1952: Spain (Pedralbes), 26 October (financial); Brazil (La Gavea, Rio de Janeiro), 14 December.

1953: Spain (Pedralbes), 25 October (financial).

1954: Netherlands (Zandvoort), 7 June (financial).

1955: France (Reims), 3 July (rumours suggested a re-scheduling for 9 October, but that was also cancelled); Germany (Nürburgring), 31 July; Switzerland (Bremgarten), 21 August; Spain (Pedralbes), 23 October (all due to the fatal accident at Le Mans 24 hours race on 11 June, which killed 83 spectators in addition to Pierre Levegh driving a Mercedes-Benz 300 SLR).

1956: Netherlands (Zandvoort), 17 June (financial); Switzerland (Bremgarten), 19 August (racing now banned in Switzerland); Spain (Pedralbes), 28 October.

1957: Belgium (Spa-Francorchamps), 2 June (financial); Netherlands (Zandvoort), 16 June (financial); Spain (Pedralbes), 20 October (financial - cancelled pre-season).

1959: Argentina (Buenos Aires No.2), 25 January; Belgium (Spa-Francorchamps), 14 June (financial); Morocco (Âin-Diab), 11 October.

1960: Germany (AVUS); Morocco (Âin-Diab), 1 October.

1961: Morocco (Âin-Diab), 29 October.

1964: South Africa (East London), 26 December (held a week later as the first race of 1965).

1965: Austria (Zeltweg), 22 August (circuit safety concerns).

1969: Belgium (Spa-Francorchamps), 8 June (the circuit decided not to invest in safety improvements resulting in British and Italian teams withdrawing from the event - cancelled in early April).

1970: Australia (Warwick Farm), 22 November (run as a non-F1 grand prix).

1971: Belgium (Spa-Francorchamps), 6 June (safety upgrades not carried out); Mexico (Mexico City), 24 October (circuit crowd safety concerns - cancelled pre-season).

1972: United States West (Ontario), 9 April (financial); Netherlands (Zandvoort), 18 June (circuit safety concerns); Mexico (Mexico City), 22 October (lack of interest following Pedro Rodríguez's death - replaced by Canada on 24 September).

1975: Canada (Mosport Park), 21 September (financial).

1976: Argentina (Buenos Aires No.15), 11 January (economic and political problems).

1978: Japan (Fuji), 16 April (cancelled pre-season).

1979: Sweden (Anderstorp), 16 June (due to Swedish driver, Ronnie Peterson being killed at the 1978 Italian Grand Prix - there was never to be another Swedish Grand Prix).

1980: Mexico (Mexico City), 13 April (cancelled pre-season); Sweden (Anderstorp), 14 June (cancelled pre-season); Caesars Palace (Las Vegas), 12 October (moved to 2 November, but also cancelled).

1981: United States (Watkins Glen), 4 October (cancelled in May due to bankruptcy - replaced by Caesars Palace on 17 October).

1982: Argentina (Buenos Aires No.15), 7 March (concerns over the country's political situation); Spain (Jarama), 27 June (cancelled pre-season).

1983: Argentina (Buenos Aires No.15), 30 January (cancelled pre-season); Switzerland (Dijon-Prenois, France), 10 July (Swiss TV refused to televise the race outside their own country and French RTF refused cover more than one race per year); Russia (Moscow), 21 August (bureaucratic barriers - cancelled pre-season); United States (Flushing Meadows, New York), 25 September (cancelled in June as insufficient time to complete environmental review - replaced by European Grand Prix at Brands Hatch); Caesars Palace (Las Vegas), 9 October (failed to attract TV coverage).

1984: United States (Flushing Meadows, New York), 23 September (cancelled pre-season); Spain (Fuengirola), 21 October (scheduled as a race on public roads - replaced by Portuguese Grand Prix).

1985: Dallas, 9 June (financial/safety concerns - cancelled pre-season); United States (Flushing Meadows, New York), 29 September; Europe (Rome) (circuit not ready and moved to 13 October, but cancelled and replaced by the European Grand Prix at Brands Hatch on 6 October).

1986: Argentina (Buenos Aires No.15), 9 March (political); South Africa (Kyalami), 26 October (apartheid policies). Both cancelled pre-season.

1987: Canada (Montréal), 14 June (legal battle following the promoter signing a sponsorship deal with Molson when rival company Labatt claimed to have first-refusal rights - cancelled pre-season).

1988: Austria (Österreichring), 14 August (essential widening and resurfacing work not completed - cancelled pre-season).

1993: Asia (Autopolis, Japan), 11 April (financial - cancelled pre-season and replaced by European Grand Prix at Donington Park); Mexico (Mexico City) (circuit safety concerns - cancelled pre-season).

1994: South Africa (Kyalami), March (financial - cancelled pre-season); Argentina (Buenos Aires No.6), 16 October (circuit safety concerns and replaced by European Grand Prix at Jerez).

1996: Pacific (Aida), 6 October (decided that location too remote - cancelled pre-season).

1997: Portugal (Estoril), 26 October (cancelled in early summer due to safety concerns and replaced by the European Grand Prix at Jerez).

1998: Portugal (Estoril), 11 October (safety upgrades demanded - cancelled pre-season).

1999: Argentina (Buenos Aires No.6), 28 March (no financial agreement). China (Zhuhai), October (failed to meet international standards). Both cancelled pre-season.

2003: Belgium (Spa-Francorchamps), 31 August (tobacco sponsorship ban - cancelled pre-season).

2006: Belgium (Spa-Francorchamps), 17 September (withdrew pre-season due to lack of time to complete circuit improvements).

2009: Canada (Montréal), 7 June (withdrawn pre-season and replaced by Turkey on that date); France (Magny-Cours), 28 June (withdrawn previous October when French federation withdrew finance).

2011: Bahrain (Sakhir), 13 March (civil unrest and the consequent security and safety concerns - in February it was postponed to 30 October, but that was cancelled due to international disapproval).

2013: America (Port Imperial, New Jersey), 16 June (financial difficulties and contractual dispute - cancelled pre-season).

2014: Korea (Yeongam), 27 April (financial), America (Port Imperial, New Jersey), 1 June (circuit not ready); Mexico (Mexico City), 9 November (circuit upgrades delayed). All were cancelled pre-season.

2015: Korea (Yeongam), 3 May (financial - added to calendar in December 2014, cancelled in January); Germany (Nürburgring), 12 July (financial, as well as a change of circuit ownership - cancelled soon after the season began).

Additionally, these were scheduled, but later declared non-championship races:

1980: Spain (Jarama), 1 June [FISA, the governing body of Formula 1 declared the race illegal, but the race was sanctioned by FOCA and proceeded without Ferrari, Alfa Romeo and Renault. At a meeting the day after the race, it was decided that it would not be part of the world championship, no points being awarded. The result was: 1: Alan Jones (Williams - Ford Cosworth); 2: Jochen Mass (Arrows - Ford Cosworth); 3: Elio De Angelis (Lotus - Ford Cosworth). Pole position: Jacques Laffite (Ligier - Ford Cosworth). Fastest lap: Alan Jones].

1981: South Africa (Kyalami), 7 February [Scheduled as the first race of 1981, but because of a dispute between the Formula One Constructors' Association and FISA, a revised date was requested, but rejected by the race organisers. The race went ahead as originally scheduled, but only teams with an allegiance to FOCA raced. The race was downgraded to Formule Libre instead of Formula 1 with no points being awarded. The result was 1: Carlos Reutemann (Williams - Ford Cosworth); 2: Nelson Piquet (Brabham - Ford Cosworth); 3: Elio De Angelis (Lotus - Ford Cosworth). Pole position: Piquet. Fastest lap: Reutemann].

72. Postponed races

1985: Belgium (Spa-Francorchamps), 2 June (track surface was disintegrating - the first qualifying session took place before the event was abandoned - re-scheduled for 15 September with the original qualifying times being declared void).

1995: Pacific (Aida, Japan), 16 April (due to the Great Hanshin earthquake - the race was held on 22 October).

73. Milestones: races

	(including Indianapolis 500, 1950 - 60)		(excluding Indianapolis 500, 1950 - 60)
1st	Britain 1950 (Silverstone)	1st	Britain 1950 (Silverstone)
100th	Germany 1961 (Nürburgring)	100th	South Africa 1962 (East London)
200th	Monaco 1971 (Monte-Carlo)	200th	Spain 1972 (Jarama)
250th	United States 1974 (Watkins Glen)	250th	Germany 1975 (Nürburgring)
300th	South Africa 1978 (Kyalami)	300th	Italy 1978 (Monza)
400th	Austria 1984 (Österreichring)	400th	France 1985 (Paul Ricard)
500th	Australia 1990 (Adelaide)	500th	Belgium 1991 (Spa-Francorchamps)
600th	Argentina 1997 (Buenos Aires No.6)	600th	Austria 1997 (A1-Ring)
700th	Brazil 2003 (Interlagos)	700th	Italy 2003 (Monza)
750th	China 2005 (Shanghai)	750th	France 2006 (Magny-Cours)
800th	Singapore 2008 (Marina Bay)	800th	Britain 2009 (Silverstone)
900th	Bahrain 2004 (Sakhir)	900th	Singapore 2014 (Marina Bay)
900th	Bahrain 2004 (Sakhir)	900th	Singapore 2014 (Marina Bay)

Chapter 4: World Champion Drivers

74. World champions

year	driver	nat	car-engine	decided	2nd	3rd
1950	Giuseppe Farina	I	Alfa Romeo	Italy, 3 Sep (a)	Juan Manuel Fangio	Luigi Fagioli
1951	Juan Manuel Fangio	RA	Alfa Romeo	Spain, 28 Oct (a)	Alberto Ascari	José Froilán González
1952	Alberto Ascari	I	Ferrari	Germany, 3 Aug	Giuseppe Farina	Piero Taruffi
1953	Alberto Ascari	I	Ferrari	Switzerland, 23 Aug (b)	Juan Manuel Fangio	Giuseppe Farina
1954	Juan Manuel Fangio	RA	Maserati & Mercedes-Benz	Switzerland, 22 Aug	José Froilán González	Mike Hawthorn
1955	Juan Manuel Fangio	RA	Mercedes-Benz	Italy, 11 Sep (a)(c)	Stirling Moss	Eugenio Castellotti
1956	Juan Manuel Fangio	RA	Lancia-Ferrari	Italy, 2 Sep (a)	Stirling Moss	Peter Collins
1957	Juan Manuel Fangio	RA	Maserati	Germany, 4 Aug	Stirling Moss	Luigi Musso
1958	Mike Hawthorn	GB	Ferrari	Morocco, 19 Oct (a)	Stirling Moss	Tony Brooks
1959	Jack Brabham	AUS	Cooper - Climax	United States, 12 Dec (a)	Tony Brooks	Stirling Moss
1960	Jack Brabham	AUS	Cooper - Climax	Portugal, 14 Aug (d)	Bruce McLaren	Stirling Moss
1961	Phil Hill	USA	Ferrari	Italy, 10 Sep	Wolfgang von Trips	Stirling Moss

year	driver	nat	car-engine	decided	2nd	3rd
1962	Graham Hill	GB	BRM	South Africa, 29 Dec (a)	Jim Clark	Bruce McLaren
1963	Jim Clark	GB	Lotus - Climax	Italy, 8 Sep	Graham Hill	Richie Ginther
1964	John Surtees	GB	Ferrari	Mexico, 25 Oct (a)	Graham Hill	Jim Clark
1965	Jim Clark	GB	Lotus - Climax	Germany, 1 Aug	Graham Hill	Jackie Stewart
1966	Jack Brabham	AUS	Brabham - Repco	Italy, 4 Sep	John Surtees	Jochen Rindt
1967	Denny Hulme	NZ	Brabham - Repco	Mexico, 22 Oct (a)	Jack Brabham	Jim Clark
1968	Graham Hill	GB	Lotus - Ford Cosworth	Mexico, 3 Nov (a)	Jackie Stewart	Denny Hulme
1969	Jackie Stewart	GB	Matra - Ford Cosworth	Italy, 7 Sep	Jacky Ickx	Bruce McLaren
1970	Jochen Rindt	A	Lotus - Ford Cosworth	United States, 4 Oct	Jacky Ickx	Clay Regazzoni
1971	Jackie Stewart	GB	Tyrrell - Ford Cosworth	Austria, 15 Aug	Ronnie Peterson	François Cevert
1972	Emerson Fittipaldi	BR	JPS Lotus - Ford Cosworth	Italy, 10 Sep	Jackie Stewart	Denny Hulme
1973	Jackie Stewart	GB	Tyrrell - Ford Cosworth	Italy, 9 Sep	Emerson Fittipaldi	Ronnie Peterson
1974	Emerson Fittipaldi	BR	McLaren - Ford Cosworth	United States, 6 Oct (a)	Clay Regazzoni	Jody Scheckter
1975	Niki Lauda	A	Ferrari	Italy, 7 Sep	Emerson Fittipaldi	Carlos Reutemann
1976	James Hunt	GB	McLaren - Ford Cosworth	Japan, 24 Oct (a)	Niki Lauda	Jody Scheckter
1977	Niki Lauda	A	Ferrari	United States, 2 Oct	Jody Scheckter	Mario Andretti
1978	Mario Andretti	USA	JPS Lotus - Ford Cosworth	Italy, 10 Sep	Ronnie Peterson	Carlos Reutemann
1979	Jody Scheckter	ZA	Ferrari	Italy, 9 Sep	Gilles Villeneuve	Alan Jones
1980	Alan Jones	AUS	Williams - Ford Cosworth	Canada, 28 Sep	Nelson Piquet	Carlos Reutemann
1981	Nelson Piquet	BR	Brabham - Ford Cosworth	Caesars Palace, 17 Oct (a)	Carlos Reutemann	Alan Jones
1982	Keke Rosberg	FIN	Williams - Ford Cosworth	Caesars Palace, 25 Sep (a)	Didier Pironi	John Watson
1983	Nelson Piquet	BR	Brabham - BMW	South Africa, 15 Oct (a)	Alain Prost	René Arnoux
1984	Niki Lauda	A	McLaren - TAG Porsche	Portugal, 21 Oct (a)	Alain Prost	Elio De Angelis
1985	Alain Prost	F	McLaren - TAG Porsche	Europe, 6 Oct	Michele Alboreto	Keke Rosberg
1986	Alain Prost	F	McLaren - TAG Porsche	Australia, 26 Oct (a)	Nigel Mansell	Nelson Piquet
1987	Nelson Piquet	BR	Williams - Honda	Japan, 31 Oct (e)	Nigel Mansell	Ayrton Senna
1988	Ayrton Senna	BR	McLaren - Honda	Japan, 30 Oct	Alain Prost	Gerhard Berger
1989	Alain Prost	F	McLaren - Honda	Japan, 22 Oct (f)	Ayrton Senna	Riccardo Patrese
1990	Ayrton Senna	BR	McLaren - Honda	Japan, 21 Oct	Alain Prost	Nelson Piquet
1991	Ayrton Senna	BR	McLaren - Honda	Japan, 20 Oct	Nigel Mansell	Riccardo Patrese
1992	Nigel Mansell	GB	Williams - Renault	Hungary, 16 Aug	Riccardo Patrese	Michael Schumacher
1993	Alain Prost	F	Williams - Renault	Portugal, 26 Sep	Ayrton Senna	Damon Hill
1994	Michael Schumacher	D	Benetton - Ford Cosworth	Australia, 13 Nov (a)	Damon Hill	Gerhard Berger
1995	Michael Schumacher	D	Benetton - Renault	Pacific, 22 Oct	Damon Hill	David Coulthard
1996	Damon Hill	GB	Williams - Renault	Japan, 13 Oct (a)	Jacques Villeneuve	Michael Schumacher
1997	Jacques Villeneuve	CDN	Williams - Renault	Europe, 26 Oct (a)	Heinz-Harald Frentzen (g)	David Coulthard
1998	Mika Häkkinen	FIN	McLaren - Mercedes	Japan, 1 Nov (a)	Michael Schumacher	David Coulthard
1999	Mika Häkkinen	FIN	McLaren - Mercedes	Japan, 31 Oct (a)(h)	Eddie Irvine	Heinz-Harald Frentzen
2000	Michael Schumacher	D	Ferrari	Japan, 8 Oct	Mika Häkkinen	David Coulthard
2001	Michael Schumacher	D	Ferrari	Hungary, 19 Aug	David Coulthard	Rubens Barrichello
2002	Michael Schumacher	D	Ferrari	France, 21 Jul	Rubens Barrichello	Juan Pablo Montoya
2003	Michael Schumacher	D	Ferrari	Japan, 12 Oct (a)	Kimi Räikkönen	Juan Pablo Montoya
2004	Michael Schumacher	D	Ferrari	Belgium, 29 Aug	Rubens Barrichello	Jenson Button
2005	Fernando Alonso	E	Renault	Brazil, 25 Sep	Kimi Räikkönen	Michael Schumacher
2006	Fernando Alonso	E	Renault	Brazil, 22 Oct (a)	Michael Schumacher	Felipe Massa
2007	Kimi Räikkönen	FIN	Ferrari	Brazil, 21 Oct (a)	Lewis Hamilton	Fernando Alonso
2008	Lewis Hamilton	GB	McLaren - Mercedes	Brazil, 2 Nov (a)	Felipe Massa	Kimi Räikkönen
2009	Jenson Button	GB	Brawn - Mercedes	Brazil, 18 Oct	Sebastian Vettel	Rubens Barrichello
2010	Sebastian Vettel	D	Red Bull - Renault	Abu Dhabi, 14 Nov (a)	Fernando Alonso	Mark Webber
2011	Sebastian Vettel	D	Red Bull - Renault	Japan, 9 Oct	Jenson Button	Mark Webber
2012	Sebastian Vettel	D	Red Bull - Renault	Brazil, 25 Nov (a)	Fernando Alonso	Kimi Räikkönen
2013	Sebastian Vettel	D	Red Bull - Renault	India, 27 Oct	Fernando Alonso	Mark Webber
2014	Lewis Hamilton	GB	Mercedes-Benz	Abu Dhabi, 23 Nov (a)	Nico Rosberg	Daniel Ricciardo
2015	Lewis Hamilton	GB	Mercedes-Benz	United States, 25 Oct	Nico Rosberg	Sebastian Vettel

For key to nationalities, see foot of section 125.
(a) Final race of the season.
(b) Some sources regard the German Grand Prix as the decider, but at that time, it was expected that the Spanish race would be run in October and that three more races would allow Fangio or Farina to overtake Ascari for the title.
(c) It would seem that the British Grand Prix was the decider, but by the Italian race, it was still expected that an extra race in France would be run in October (so the championship wasn't decided until Italy).
(d) Some sources give Italy as the decider, but it was known that Bruce McLaren had withdrawn from that race, so only had one race in which to beat Brabham's total points (the Italian Grand Prix could not have provided enough points for him to become champion).
(e) The day before the Japanese Grand Prix when Nigel Mansell flew home after his qualifying accident, becoming out of contention for the title.
(f) Confirmed on the day of McLaren's appeal hearing (31 October) when Senna's disqualification from the race was upheld.
(g) Michael Schumacher would have been runner-up, but was disqualified from the championship for causing an accident with Villeneuve at the European Grand Prix.
(h) Häkkinen had been world champion temporarily after Schumacher's disqualification from the Malaysian Grand Prix, but after Ferrari's successful appeal, later that week, it meant he didn't become champion until the final race, in Japan.

75. Posthumous world champion
Jochen Rindt was the only posthumous world champion. By the time he was killed during qualifying for the 1970 Italian Grand Prix at Monza, his closest rival, Jack Brabham was 20 points behind. Rindt's points tally of 45 was not beaten by the end of season and he won the title by 5 points from Jacky Ickx.

76. World champions who never started a race as a world champion
Apart from Jochen Rindt, the only driver to never start as a world champion was Mike Hawthorn, who clinched the title in the final race of 1958 (Morocco) and retired from the sport at that race.

77. World championship titles

Michael Schumacher	7	1994, 95, 2000, 01, 02, 03, 04	Mario Andretti	1	1978
Juan Manuel Fangio	5	1951, 54, 55, 56, 57	Jenson Button	1	2009
Alain Prost	4	1985, 86, 89, 93	Giuseppe Farina	1	1950
Sebastian Vettel	4	2010, 11, 12, 13	Mike Hawthorn	1	1958
Jack Brabham	3	1959, 60, 66	Damon Hill	1	1996
Lewis Hamilton	3	2008, 14, 15	Phil Hill	1	1961
Niki Lauda	3	1975, 77, 84	Denny Hulme	1	1967
Nelson Piquet	3	1981, 83, 87	James Hunt	1	1976
Ayrton Senna	3	1988, 90, 91	Alan Jones	1	1980
Jackie Stewart	3	1969, 71, 73	Nigel Mansell	1	1992
Fernando Alonso	2	2005, 06	Kimi Räikkönen	1	2007
Alberto Ascari	2	1952, 53	Jochen Rindt	1	1970
Jim Clark	2	1963, 65	Keke Rosberg	1	1982
Emerson Fittipaldi	2	1972, 74	Jody Scheckter	1	1979
Mika Häkkinen	2	1998, 99	John Surtees	1	1964
Graham Hill	2	1962, 68	Jacques Villeneuve	1	1997

78. World champions by nationality
Argentina:	Juan Manuel Fangio, 5
Australia:	Jack Brabham, 3; Alan Jones, 1
Austria:	Niki Lauda, 3; Jochen Rindt, 1
Brazil:	Nelson Piquet, 3; Ayrton Senna, 3; Emerson Fittipaldi, 2
Canada:	Jacques Villeneuve, 1
Finland:	Mika Häkkinen, 2; Kimi Räikkönen, 1; Keke Rosberg, 1
France:	Alain Prost, 4
Germany:	Michael Schumacher, 7; Sebastian Vettel, 4
Great Britain:	Lewis Hamilton, 3; Jackie Stewart, 3; Jim Clark, 2; Graham Hill, 2; Jenson Button, 1; Mike Hawthorn, 1; Damon Hill, 1; James Hunt, 1; Nigel Mansell, 1; John Surtees, 1
Italy:	Alberto Ascari, 2; Giuseppe Farina, 1
New Zealand:	Denny Hulme, 1
South Africa:	Jody Scheckter, 1
Spain:	Fernando Alonso, 2
United States:	Mario Andretti, 1; Phil Hill, 1

Summary

	world titles	drivers		
Great Britain	16	10	1958 (Mike Hawthorn)	- 2015 (Lewis Hamilton)
Germany	11	2	1994 (Michael Schumacher)	- 2013 (Sebastian Vettel)
Brazil	8	3	1972 (Emerson Fittipaldi)	- 1991 (Ayrton Senna)
Argentina	5	1	1951 (Juan Manuel Fangio)	- 1957 (Juan Manuel Fangio)
Australia	4	2	1959 (Jack Brabham)	- 1980 (Alan Jones)
Austria	4	2	1970 (Jochen Rindt)	- 1984 (Niki Lauda)
Finland	4	3	1982 (Keke Rosberg)	- 2007 (Kimi Räikkönen)
France	4	1	1985 (Alain Prost)	- 1993 (Alain Prost)
Italy	3	2	1950 (Giuseppe Farina)	- 1953 (Alberto Ascari)
Spain	2	1	2005 (Fernando Alonso)	- 2006 (Fernando Alonso)
United States	2	2	1961 (Phil Hill)	- 1978 (Mario Andretti)
Canada	1	1	1997 (Jacques Villeneuve)	
New Zealand	1	1	1967 (Denny Hulme)	
South Africa	1	1	1979 (Jody Scheckter)	

79. Drivers of the same nationality in the final top championship positions

Great Britain	5	1958	1: Mike Hawthorn, 2: Stirling Moss, 3: Tony Brooks, 4: Roy Salvadori, 5 Peter Collins
Italy	3	1952	1: Alberto Ascari, 2: Giuseppe Farina, 3: Piero Taruffi
Great Britain	3	1964	1: John Surtees, 2: Graham Hill, 3: Jim Clark
Great Britain	3	1965	1: Jim Clark, 2: Graham Hill, 3: Jackie Stewart
Argentina	2	1954	1: Juan Manuel Fangio, 2: José Froilán González
Great Britain	2	1962	1: Graham Hill, 2: Jim Clark
Great Britain	2	1963	1: Jim Clark, 2: Graham Hill

80. World champion age
(on the day that the title was decided)

Youngest

	years, days	
Sebastian Vettel	23y, 134d	2010
Lewis Hamilton	23y, 300d	2008
Fernando Alonso	24y, 58d	2005
Emerson Fittipaldi	25y, 273d	1972
Michael Schumacher	25y, 314d	1994
Niki Lauda	26y, 197d	1975
Jacques Villeneuve	26y, 200d	1997
Jim Clark	27y, 188d	1963
Kimi Räikkönen	28y, 4d	2007
Jochen Rindt	28y, 169d	1970 (a)

(a) Would have been that age, but deceased by that time.

Oldest

	years, days	
Juan Manuel Fangio	46y, 41d	1957
Giuseppe Farina	43y, 308d	1950
Jack Brabham	40y, 155d	1966
Graham Hill	39y, 262d	1968
Nigel Mansell	39y, 8d	1992
Alain Prost	38y, 214d	1993
Mario Andretti	38y, 194d	1978
Damon Hill	36y, 26d	1996
Niki Lauda	35y, 242d	1984
Michael Schumacher	35y, 239d	2004

81. Back-to-back championship titles

Michael Schumacher	5	2000 - 04
Juan Manuel Fangio	4	1954 - 57
Sebastian Vettel	4	2010 - 13
Fernando Alonso	2	2005 - 06
Alberto Ascari	2	1952 - 53
Jack Brabham	2	1959 - 60
Mika Häkkinen	2	1998 - 99
Lewis Hamilton	2	2014 - 15
Alain Prost	2	1985 - 86
Michael Schumacher	2	1994 - 95
Ayrton Senna	2	1990 - 91

82. Back-to-back champion age

	years, days	
Sebastian Vettel	24y, 98d	2011
Fernando Alonso	25y, 85d	2006
Michael Schumacher	26y, 292d	1995
Lewis Hamilton	30y, 291d	2015
Mika Häkkinen	31y, 33d	1999
Ayrton Senna	31y, 213d	1991
Alain Prost	31y, 244d	1986
Jack Brabham	34y, 134d	1960
Alberto Ascari	35y, 41d	1953
Juan Manuel Fangio	44y, 79d	1955

83. Three consecutive championships age

	years, days	
Sebastian Vettel	25y, 145d	2012
Michael Schumacher	33y, 199d	2002
Juan Manuel Fangio	45y, 70d	1956

84. Four consecutive championships age

	years, days	
Sebastian Vettel	26y, 116d	2013
Michael Schumacher	34y, 282d	2003
Juan Manuel Fangio	46y, 41d	1957

85. Two-time champion age

	years, days	
Sebastian Vettel	24y, 98d	2011
Fernando Alonso	25y, 85d	2006
Michael Schumacher	26y, 292d	1995
Emerson Fittipaldi	27y, 298d	1974
Niki Lauda	28y, 222d	1977
Jim Clark	29y, 150d	1965
Lewis Hamilton	29y, 320d	2014
Ayrton Senna	30y, 214d	1990

Mika Häkkinen	31y, 33d	1999
Nelson Piquet	31y, 59d	1983
Alain Prost	31y, 244d	1986
Jackie Stewart	32y, 65d	1971
Jack Brabham	34y, 134d	1960
Alberto Ascari	35y, 41d	1953
Graham Hill	39y, 262d	1968
Juan Manuel Fangio	43y, 59d	1954

86. Three-time champion age

	years, days	
Sebastian Vettel	25y, 145d	2012
Lewis Hamilton	30y, 291d	2015
Ayrton Senna	31y, 213d	1991
Michael Schumacher	31y, 279d	2000
Jackie Stewart	34y, 90d	1973

Alain Prost	34y, 240d	1989
Nelson Piquet	35y, 75d	1987
Niki Lauda	35y, 242d	1984
Jack Brabham	40y, 155d	1966
Juan Manuel Fangio	44y, 79d	1955

87. Four-time champion age

	years, days	
Sebastian Vettel	26y, 116d	2013
Michael Schumacher	32y, 228d	2001

Alain Prost	38y, 214d	1993
Juan Manuel Fangio	45y, 70d	1956

88. Date crowned champion

Earliest

21 Jul 2002	Michael Schumacher
1 Aug 1965	Jim Clark
3 Aug 1952	Alberto Ascari
4 Aug 1957	Juan Manuel Fangio
14 Aug 1960	Jack Brabham
15 Aug 1971	Jackie Stewart
16 Aug 1992	Nigel Mansell
19 Aug 2001	Michael Schumacher
22 Aug 1954	Juan Manuel Fangio
23 Aug 1953	Alberto Ascari

Latest

29 Dec 1962	Graham Hill
12 Dec 1959	Jack Brabham
25 Nov 2012	Sebastian Vettel
23 Nov 2014	Lewis Hamilton
14 Nov 2010	Sebastian Vettel
13 Nov 1994	Michael Schumacher
3 Nov 1968	Graham Hill
2 Nov 2008	Lewis Hamilton
1 Nov 1998	Mika Häkkinen
31 Oct 1987	Nelson Piquet
31 Oct 1999	Mika Häkkinen

89. Clinched the title on home soil

Giuseppe Farina is the only driver to do this, at Monza in the 1950 Italian Grand Prix.

90. Countries where the championship was decided

Japan	13 (a)	Australia	2	Belgium	1		
Italy	12	Hungary	2	Britain	1 (d)		
United States	7	South Africa	2	Canada	1		
Brazil	6	Spain	2 (b)	France	1		
Germany	3	Switzerland	2	India	1		
Mexico	3	United Arab Emirates	2 (c)	Morocco	1		
Portugal	3	Austria	1				

(a) Includes Pacific Grand Prix 1995 (Aida).
(b) Includes European Grand Prix 1997 (Jerez de la Frontera).
(c) Abu Dhabi Grand Prix.
(d) European Grand Prix 1985 (Brands Hatch).

91. Championship decided in final race of the season

		in contention for the title
1950	Italy	Juan Manuel Fangio, Luigi Fagioli, Giuseppe Farina (wc)
1951	Spain	Juan Manuel Fangio (wc), Alberto Ascari, José Froilán González
1955	Italy	Juan Manuel Fangio (wc), Stirling Moss
1956	Italy	Juan Manuel Fangio (wc), Peter Collins
1958	Morocco	Mike Hawthorn (wc), Stirling Moss
1959	United States	Jack Brabham (wc), Stirling Moss, Tony Brooks
1962	South Africa	Graham Hill (wc), Jim Clark
1964	Mexico	Graham Hill, John Surtees (wc), Jim Clark
1967	Mexico	Denny Hulme (wc), Jack Brabham
1968	Mexico	Graham Hill (wc), Jackie Stewart, Denny Hulme
1974	United States	Emerson Fittipaldi (wc), Clay Regazzoni, Jody Scheckter

	in contention for the title	
1976	Japan	Niki Lauda, James Hunt (wc)
1981	Caesars Palace	Carlos Reutemann, Nelson Piquet (wc), Jacques Laffite
1982	Caesars Palace	Keke Rosberg (wc), John Watson
1983	South Africa	Alain Prost, Nelson Piquet (wc), René Arnoux
1984	Portugal	Niki Lauda (wc), Alain Prost
1986	Australia	Nigel Mansell, Alain Prost (wc), Nelson Piquet
1994	Australia	Michael Schumacher (wc), Damon Hill
1996	Japan	Damon Hill (wc), Jacques Villeneuve
1997	Europe	Michael Schumacher, Jacques Villeneuve (wc)
1998	Japan	Mika Häkkinen (wc), Michael Schumacher
1999	Japan	Eddie Irvine, Mika Häkkinen (wc)
2003	Japan	Michael Schumacher (wc), Kimi Räikkönen
2006	Brazil	Fernando Alonso (wc), Michael Schumacher
2007	Brazil	Lewis Hamilton, Fernando Alonso, Kimi Räikkönen (wc)
2008	Brazil	Lewis Hamilton (wc), Felipe Massa
2010	Abu Dhabi	Fernando Alonso, Mark Webber, Sebastian Vettel (wc), Lewis Hamilton
2012	Brazil	Sebastian Vettel (wc), Fernando Alonso
2014	Abu Dhabi	Lewis Hamilton (wc), Nico Rosberg

(wc) World champion that season.

Summary (by country)

Japan	5	Suzuka, 4; Fuji, 1
United States	4	Las Vegas, 2 (a); Sebring, 1; Watkins Glen, 1
Brazil	4	Interlagos
Italy	3	Monza
Mexico	3	Mexico City
Australia	2	Adelaide
South Africa	2	East London, 1; Kyalami, 1
Spain	2	Jerez de la Frontera, 1 (b); Pedralbes, 1
United Arab Emirates	2	Yas Marina (c)
Morocco	1	Âin-Diab
Portugal	1	Estoril

(a) Caesars Palace Grand Prix. (b) European Grand Prix. (c) Abu Dhabi Grand Prix.

92. Eventual champion not leading the championship going into final race of the season

Giuseppe Farina	1950	(3rd at the start of the final race, behind Juan Manuel Fangio & Luigi Fagioli)
John Surtees	1964	(2nd behind Graham Hill)
James Hunt	1976	(2nd behind Niki Lauda)
Nelson Piquet	1981	(2nd behind Carlos Reutemann)
Nelson Piquet	1983	(2nd behind Alain Prost)
Alain Prost	1986	(2nd behind Nigel Mansell)
Jacques Villeneuve	1997	(2nd behind Michael Schumacher)
Mika Häkkinen	1999	(2nd behind Eddie Irvine)
Kimi Räikkönen	2007	(3rd behind Lewis Hamilton & Fernando Alonso)
Sebastian Vettel	2010	(3rd behind Fernando Alonso & Mark Webber)

93. Races remaining after the championship was decided *(Most)*

		(world champion)			(world champion)
2002	6	(Michael Schumacher)	1963	3	(Jim Clark)
1992	5	(Nigel Mansell)	1965	3	(Jim Clark)
2001	4	(Michael Schumacher)	1969	3	(Jackie Stewart)
2004	4	(Michael Schumacher)	1971	3	(Jackie Stewart)
2011	4	(Sebastian Vettel)	2013	3	(Sebastian Vettel)
2015	3	(Lewis Hamilton)			

94. Seasons where the points leader after two races was not the champion

		eventual position				
1950	Juan Manuel Fangio (a)	2nd		1976	Niki Lauda	2nd
1951	Giuseppe Farina	4th		1977	Carlos Reutemann	4th
1952	Piero Taruffi (a)	3rd		1979	Jacques Laffite	4th
1955	Maurice Trintignant	4th		1981	Carlos Reutemann (a)	2nd
1956	Jean Behra	4th			Alan Jones (a)	3rd
1958	Luigi Musso	8th		1982	Alain Prost	4th
1960	Bruce McLaren	2nd		1983	Niki Lauda	10th
1961	Wolfgang von Trips (a)	2nd		1984	Alain Prost	2nd
	Stirling Moss (a)	3rd		1985	Michele Alboreto	2nd
1963	Bruce McLaren	6th		1986	Ayrton Senna	4th
1964	Jim Clark (a)	3rd		1987	Nigel Mansell	2nd
	Graham Hill (a)	2nd		1988	Alain Prost	2nd
1965	Graham Hill	2nd		1993	Ayrton Senna	2nd
1966	Lorenzo Bandini	9th		1997	David Coulthard (a)	3rd
1970	Jackie Stewart	joint 5th		1999	Eddie Irvine	2nd
1972	Denny Hulme	3rd		2003	Kimi Räikkönen	2nd
1973	Emerson Fittipaldi	2nd		2007	Fernando Alonso	3rd
1974	Clay Regazzoni	2nd		2010	Fernando Alonso	2nd
1975	Emerson Fittipaldi	2nd		2012	Fernando Alonso	2nd
				2014	Nico Rosberg	2nd

(a) Joint leader on points in the title race.

95. Race starts taken to achieve their first championship title
(Relates to the title deciding race. In brackets, race starts before first title winning season)

Giuseppe Farina	7	(0)		James Hunt	52	(36)
Juan Manuel Fangio	13	(6)		Michael Schumacher	52	(38)
Alberto Ascari	15	(11)		Niki Lauda	55	(42)
Jack Brabham	24	(16)		Jochen Rindt	60	(51)
Emerson Fittipaldi	25	(15)		Sebastian Vettel	62	(43)
Denny Hulme	26	(15)		Fernando Alonso	67	(51)
Phil Hill	27	(20)		Damon Hill	67	(51)
Jim Clark	30	(23)		Ayrton Senna	77	(62)
Jacques Villeneuve	33	(16)		Mario Andretti	79	(65)
Lewis Hamilton	35	(17)		Alan Jones	80	(67)
Graham Hill	41	(32)		Alain Prost	87	(73)
John Surtees	41	(31)		Jody Scheckter	97	(84)
Mike Hawthorn	45	(35)		Mika Häkkinen	112	(96)
Jackie Stewart	47	(39)		Kimi Räikkönen	121	(104)
Nelson Piquet	49	(34)		Jenson Button	169	(153)
Keke Rosberg	51	(36)		Nigel Mansell	176	(165)

96. World championship runner-up

Stirling Moss *	4	1955, 56, 57, 58		Ayrton Senna	2	1989, 93
Alain Prost	4	1983, 84, 88, 90		Jackie Stewart	2	1968, 72
Fernando Alonso	3	2010, 12, 13		Michele Alboreto *	1	1985
Graham Hill	3	1963, 64, 65		Alberto Ascari	1	1951
Nigel Mansell	3	1986, 87, 91		Jack Brabham	1	1967
Rubens Barrichello *	2	2002, 04		Tony Brooks *	1	1959
Juan Manuel Fangio	2	1950, 53		Jenson Button	1	2011
Emerson Fittipaldi	2	1973, 75		Jim Clark	1	1962
Damon Hill	2	1994, 95		David Coulthard *	1	2001
Jacky Ickx *	2	1969, 70		Giuseppe Farina	1	1952
Ronnie Peterson *	2	1971, 78 (a)		Heinz-Harald Frentzen *	1	1997
Kimi Räikkönen	2	2003, 05		José Froilán González *	1	1954
Nico Rosberg *	2	2014, 15		Mika Häkkinen	1	2000
Michael Schumacher	2	1998, 2006 (b)		Lewis Hamilton	1	2007

Eddie Irvine *	1	1999
Niki Lauda	1	1976
Felipe Massa *	1	2008
Bruce McLaren *	1	1960
Riccardo Patrese *	1	1992
Nelson Piquet	1	1980
Didier Pironi *	1	1982
Clay Regazzoni *	1	1974

Carlos Reutemann *	1	1981
Jody Scheckter	1	1977
John Surtees	1	1966
Sebastian Vettel	1	2009
Gilles Villeneuve *	1	1979
Jacques Villeneuve	1	1996
Wolfgang von Trips *	1	1961 (c)

Never a world champion.
(a) Fatal accident at the Italian Grand Prix - was runner-up in the championship at his death.
(b) In 1997, he would have been runner-up, instead of Frentzen, but was disqualified from the championship for causing an accident with Jacques Villeneueve at the European Grand Prix.
(c) Fatal accident at the Italian Grand Prix - was leading the championship at his death.

97. Reigning champions who won the opening race of the following season

	title winning season
Alberto Ascari	1952
Juan Manuel Fangio	1954
Juan Manuel Fangio	1955
Juan Manuel Fangio	1956
Graham Hill	1962
Jackie Stewart	1971
Emerson Fittipaldi	1972
Emerson Fittipaldi	1974
Lewis Hamilton	2014
Niki Lauda	1975

Alan Jones	1980
Alain Prost	1986
Ayrton Senna	1990
Michael Schumacher	1994
Michael Schumacher	2000
Michael Schumacher	2001
Michael Schumacher	2003
Fernando Alonso	2005
Sebastian Vettel	2010

98. Reigning champions who fared worst in the opening race of the following season

	title winning season	following season opening race result
Damon Hill	1996	did not start: retired on the parade lap (throttle sensor)
Keke Rosberg	*1982*	*disqualified from 2nd (push-start in the pits)*
Nelson Piquet	1981	retired after 3 laps (accident)
Sebastian Vettel	2013	retired after 3 laps (engine)
Alain Prost	1989	retired after 21 laps (oil leak)
Niki Lauda	1984	retired after 27 laps (fuel metering unit)
Alain Prost	1985	retired after 30 laps (engine)
James Hunt	1976	retired after 31 laps (rear suspension)
Nelson Piquet	1983	retired after 32 laps (turbo)
Michael Schumacher	1995	retired after 32 laps (brake fluid loss)
Jack Brabham	1960	retired after 38 laps (ignition/ misfire)
Jack Brabham	1959	retired after 43 laps (gearbox)
Jody Scheckter	1979	retired after 45 laps (engine)
Jim Clark	1965	retired after 60 laps (rear suspension)
Ayrton Senna	1988	finished 11th
Jack Brabham	1966	finished 6th

99. No wins in the season before winning the title

Mike Hawthorn	1957	(Lancia-Ferrari 801) - only podiums 1 x 2nd & 1 x 3rd
	1958	champion (Ferrari Dino 246)
Jack Brabham	1958	(Cooper T45 - Climax) - best result 1 x 4th
	1959	champion (Cooper T51 - Climax)
Graham Hill	1961	(BRM P48/57 - Climax) - best result 1 x 5th
	1962	champion (BRM P57)
Jack Brabham	1965	(Brabham BT11 - Climax) - only podium 1 x 3rd
	1966	champion (Brabham BT19, BT20 - Repco)
Denny Hulme	1966	(Brabham BT20 - Repco, BT22 - Climax) - only podiums 1 x 2nd & 3 x 3rd
	1967	champion (Brabham BT19, BT20, BT24 - Repco)
Graham Hill	1967	(Lotus 43, 33, 49 - BRM, Ford Cosworth) - only podiums 2 x 2nd
	1968	champion (Lotus 49, 49B - Ford Cosworth)
Emerson Fittipaldi	1971	(Lotus 72C, 72D - Ford Cosworth, 56B - Pratt & Whitney) - only podiums 1 x 2nd & 2 x 3rd
	1972	champion (JPS Lotus 72D - Ford Cosworth)
Jody Scheckter	1978	(Wolf WR1, 3, 4, 5, 6 - Ford Cosworth) - only podiums 2 x 2nd & 2 x 3rd
	1979	champion (Ferrari 312T3, 312T4)

Keke Rosberg	1981	(Fittipaldi F8C - Ford Cosworth) - no points, 9th his best placing
	1982	champion (Williams FW07C, FW08 - Ford Cosworth)
Niki Lauda	1983	(McLaren MP4/1C - Ford Cosworth), MP4/1E - TAG Porsche) - only podiums 1 x 2nd & 1 x 3rd
	1984	champion (McLaren MP4/2 - TAG Porsche)
Fernando Alonso	2004	(Renault R24) - only podiums 1 x 2nd & 3 x 3rd
	2005	champion (Renault R25)
Kimi Räikkönen	2006	(McLaren MP4-21 - Mercedes) - only podiums 2 x 2nd & 4 x 3rd
	2007	champion (Ferrari F2007)
Jenson Button	2008	(Honda RA108) - only points finish 1 x 6th
	2009	champion (Brawn BGP 001 - Mercedes)

1993 world champion, Alain Prost was not active in 1992, taking a sabbatical after being fired by Ferrari for being critical of the team.

100. No wins in the season after winning the title
(of those who were active)

Alberto Ascari	1953	champion (Ferrari 500)
	1954	(Maserati 250F, Ferrari 625, Lancia D50) - retired in each of the four races started
Juan Manuel Fangio	1957	champion (Maserati 250F)
	1958	(Maserati 250F) - only entered two races, finishing 4th in both
Jack Brabham	1960	champion (Cooper T51, T53 - Climax)
	1961	(Cooper T55, T58 - Climax) - 1 x 4th, 1 x 6th place & six retirements
Phil Hill	1961	champion (Ferrari 156)
	1962	(Ferrari 156) - only podiums 1 x 2nd & 2 x 3rd
John Surtees	1964	champion (Ferrari 158)
	1965	(Ferrari 158, 1512) - only podiums 1 x 2nd & 2 x 3rd
Mario Andretti	1978	champion (JPS Lotus 78, 79 - Ford Cosworth)
	1979	(Lotus 79, 80 - Ford Cosworth) - best results 1 x 3rd & 2 x 4th
Jody Scheckter	1979	champion (Ferrari 312T3, 312T4)
	1980	(Ferrari 312T5) - best result 1 x 5th
Nelson Piquet	1987	champion (Williams FW11B - Honda)
	1988	(Lotus 100T - Honda) - only podiums 3 x 3rd
Damon Hill	1996	champion (Williams FW18 - Renault)
	1997	(Arrows A18 - Yamaha) - only podium 1 x 2nd
Jacques Villeneuve	1997	champion (Williams FW19 - Renault)
	1998	(Williams FW20 - Mecachrome) - only podiums 2 x 3rd
Sebastian Vettel	2013	champion (Red Bull RB9 - Renault)
	2014	(Red Bull RB10 - Renault) - only podiums 1 x 2nd & 3 x 3rd

101. Did not participate in the season following winning the title
(of those who were active)

Juan Manuel Fangio	1951	(broke his neck in a non-F1 championship race at Monza, pre-season)
Mike Hawthorn	1958	(retired from F1, then killed in a road accident in January 1959)
Jochen Rindt	1970	(fatal accident in 1970 Italian Grand Prix qualifying)
Jackie Stewart	1973	(retired from F1)
Nigel Mansell	1992	(moved to IndyCar World Series, returning to F1 in 1994)
Alain Prost	1993	(retired from F1)

102. Failed to qualify for one of the races in the season after winning the title
The only occasion was for 1981 World Champion, Nelson Piquet. Qualifying for Detroit 1982 in the Brabham BT50 - BMW turbo, he encountered engine problems and was 28th on the time sheet.

103. Switched teams at the end of their championship title winning season

	title winning season	following season
Alberto Ascari	1953, Ferrari	1954, Maserati
Juan Manuel Fangio	1955, Mercedes-Benz	1956, Ferrari
Juan Manuel Fangio	1956, Ferrari	1957, Maserati
Denny Hulme	1967, Brabham	1968, McLaren
Jackie Stewart	1969, Matra	1970, March (a)
Niki Lauda	1977, Ferrari	1978, Brabham
Nelson Piquet	1987, Williams	1988, Lotus
Alain Prost	1989, McLaren	1990, Ferrari
Michael Schumacher	1995, Benetton	1996, Ferrari
Damon Hill	1996, Williams	1997, Arrows
Fernando Alonso	2006, Renault	2007, McLaren
Jenson Button	2009, Brawn	2010, McLaren

(a) With Tyrrell Racing Organisation.

104. Total period as a champion

Longest

	days	title winning seasons
Michael Schumacher	2,513	1994, 95, 2000, 01, 02, 03, 04
Juan Manuel Fangio	1,799	1951, 54, 55, 56, 57
Alain Prost	1,532	1985, 86, 89, 93
Sebastian Vettel	1,470	2010, 11, 12, 13
Jackie Stewart	1,176	1969, 71, 73
Niki Lauda	1,106	1975, 77, 84
Nelson Piquet	1,080	1981, 83, 87
Jack Brabham	1,051	1959, 60, 66
Ayrton Senna	1,022	1988, 90, 91
Jim Clark	812	1963, 65

Lewis Hamilton will enter this list during 2016.
(a) Killed before becoming world champion.

Shortest

	days	title winning seasons
John Surtees	280	1964
Jochen Rindt	315	1970 (a)
James Hunt	343	1976
Mario Andretti	364	1978
Jacques Villeneuve	371	1997
Damon Hill	378	1996
Denny Hulme	378	1967
Kimi Räikkönen	378	2007
Alan Jones	384	1980
Keke Rosberg	385	1982
Jody Scheckter	385	1979

105. Continuous period as a champion

Longest

	years, days	title winning seasons
Michael Schumacher	4y, 352d	2000 - 01 - 02 - 03 - 04
Juan Manuel Fangio	4y, 58d	1954 - 55 - 56 - 57
Sebastian Vettel	4y, 9d	2010 - 11 - 12 - 13
Fernando Alonso	2y, 26d	2005 - 06
Alain Prost	2y, 25d	1985 - 86
Alberto Ascari	2y, 19d	1952 - 53
Mika Häkkinen	1y, 342d	1998 - 99
Michael Schumacher	1y, 335d	1994 - 95
Ayrton Senna	1y, 300d	1990 - 91
Jack Brabham	1y, 272d	1959 - 60

Shortest

	days	title winning seasons
Graham Hill	253d	1962
Juan Manuel Fangio	280d	1951
John Surtees	280d	1964
Graham Hill	308d	1968
Jochen Rindt	315d	1970
Emerson Fittipaldi	336d	1974
James Hunt	343d	1976
Niki Lauda	343d	1977
Nelson Piquet	343d	1981
Lewis Hamilton	350d	2008
Niki Lauda	350d	1984

106. Championship title winning margin

Narrowest (net points)

	points	world champion	runner-up
1984	0.5	Niki Lauda	Alain Prost
1958	1	Mike Hawthorn	Stirling Moss
1961	1	Phil Hill	Wolfgang von Trips
1964	1	John Surtees	Graham Hill
1976	1	James Hunt	Niki Lauda
1981	1	Nelson Piquet	Carlos Reutemann
1994	1	Michael Schumacher	Damon Hill
2007	1	Kimi Räikkönen	Lewis Hamilton
2008	1	Lewis Hamilton	Felipe Massa
1983	2	Nelson Piquet	Alain Prost

	points	world champion	runner-up
1986	2	Alain Prost	Nigel Mansell
1999	2	Mika Häkkinen	Eddie Irvine
2003	2	Michael Schumacher	Kimi Räikkönen

Widest (net points)

from 2010 with new points system			
2013	155	Sebastian Vettel	Fernando Alonso
2011	122	Sebastian Vettel	Jenson Button
2014	67	Lewis Hamilton	Nico Rosberg
2015	59	Lewis Hamilton	Nico Rosberg
before 2010			
2002	67	Michael Schumacher	Rubens Barrichello
2001	58	Michael Schumacher	David Coulthard
1992	52	Nigel Mansell	Riccardo Patrese
1997	39	Jacques Villeneuve	Heinz-Harald Frentzen (a)
2004	34	Michael Schumacher	Rubens Barrichello
1995	33	Michael Schumacher	Damon Hill
1971	29	Jackie Stewart	Ronnie Peterson
1969	26	Jackie Stewart	Jacky Ickx
1993	26	Alain Prost	Ayrton Senna
1963	25	Jim Clark	Graham Hill

(a) Michael Schumacher would have been runner-up, just four points behind Villeneuve, but was removed from the championship table for causing an accident with him in the European Grand Prix.

107. Seasons where the champion was beaten in terms of total wins

	champion	beaten by
1958	Mike Hawthorn, 1	Tony Brooks, 3; Stirling Moss, 4
1964	John Surtees, 2	Jim Clark, 3
1967	Denny Hulme, 2	Jim Clark, 4
1977	Niki Lauda, 3	Mario Andretti, 4
1979	Jody Scheckter, 3	Alan Jones, 4
1982	Keke Rosberg, 1	René Arnoux, 2; Niki Lauda, 2; Didier Pironi, 2; Alain Prost, 2; John Watson, 2
1983	Nelson Piquet, 3	Alain Prost, 4
1984	Niki Lauda, 5	Alain Prost, 7
1986	Alain Prost, 4	Nigel Mansell, 5
1987	Nelson Piquet, 3	Nigel Mansell, 6
1989	Alain Prost, 4	Ayrton Senna, 6
2008	Lewis Hamilton, 5	Felipe Massa, 6

Scored more points in a season than the champion. See section 464

108. Fewest wins in their championship title winning season

Mike Hawthorn	1	1958
Keke Rosberg	1	1982
Jack Brabham	2	1959
Phil Hill	2	1961
Denny Hulme	2	1967
John Surtees	2	1964

109. Fewest poles in their championship title winning season

Denny Hulme	0	1967
Niki Lauda	0	1984
Jack Brabham	1	1959
Graham Hill	1	1962
Nelson Piquet	1	1983
Alain Prost	1	1986
Keke Rosberg	1	1982
Jody Scheckter	1	1979

110. Champions with fewest wins in their career

Mike Hawthorn	3		Denny Hulme	8		Alberto Ascari	13
Phil Hill	3		James Hunt	10		Graham Hill	14
Giuseppe Farina	5		Jody Scheckter	10		Emerson Fittipaldi	14
Keke Rosberg	5		Jacques Villeneuve	11		Jack Brabham	14
Jochen Rindt	6		Alan Jones	12		Jenson Button	15
John Surtees	6		Mario Andretti	12			

All of the above won fewer races in their career than Stirling Moss who was never world champion.

111. Wins before their first championship title winning season

Nigel Mansell	21	Jacques Villeneuve	4	Mika Häkkinen	1
Alain Prost	16	Jim Clark	3	Phil Hill	1
Damon Hill	13	Juan Manuel Fangio	3	James Hunt	1
Kimi Räikkönen	9	Nelson Piquet	3	Jochen Rindt	1
Jody Scheckter	7	Alberto Ascari	2	John Surtees	1
Mario Andretti	6	Mike Hawthorn	2	Jack Brabham	0
Ayrton Senna	6	Niki Lauda	2	Giuseppe Farina	0
Alan Jones	5	Michael Schumacher	2	Graham Hill	0
Jackie Stewart	5	Fernando Alonso	1	Denny Hulme	0
Sebastian Vettel	5	Jenson Button	1	Keke Rosberg	0
Lewis Hamilton	4	Emerson Fittipaldi	1		

112. Championship titles with more than one constructor

driver	constructors, no. of seasons
Juan Manuel Fangio	Alfa Romeo, 1; Maserati, 2 (a); Mercedes-Benz, 2 (a); Ferrari, 1
Jack Brabham	Cooper, 2; Brabham, 1
Emerson Fittipaldi	Lotus, 1; McLaren, 1
Lewis Hamilton	Mercedes-Benz, 2; McLaren, 1
Graham Hill	BRM, 1; Lotus, 1
Niki Lauda	Ferrari, 2; McLaren, 1
Nelson Piquet	Brabham, 2; Williams, 1
Alain Prost	McLaren, 3; Williams, 1
Michael Schumacher	Ferrari, 5; Benetton, 2
Jackie Stewart	Tyrrell, 2; Matra, 1

(a) In 1954, Fangio drove Maserati and Mercedes-Benz cars to his championship title.

113. Won the drivers' championship in their first ever season with the constructor

Jenson Button	2009	Brawn	Alain Prost	1993	Williams
Giuseppe Farina	1950	Alfa Romeo	Kimi Räikkönen	2007	Ferrari
Emerson Fittipaldi	1974	McLaren	Keke Rosberg	1982	Williams
James Hunt	1976	McLaren	Jody Scheckter	1979	Ferrari
Juan Manuel Fangio	1954	Mercedes-Benz (a)	Ayrton Senna	1988	McLaren
Juan Manuel Fangio	1956	Ferrari			

(a) Incomplete season with Mercedes-Benz. Drove the early races of 1954 with Maserati.

114. Champion in own car
The only driver to become world champion in his own car was Jack Brabham in 1966 driving a Brabham BT19 and BT20.

115. Won championship titles driving four different makes of car
Juan Manuel Fangio is the only driver to do so, with Alfa Romeo, Ferrari, Maserati and Mercedes-Benz.

116. Races without a champion on the starting grid

1950	Britain - Italy (all season)
1958	Monaco - Belgium (3 races), Britain - Morocco (5 races)
1959	Monaco - United States (8 races, ie all season)
1960	Italy (Jack Brabham did not enter)
1975	Spain (Emerson Fittipaldi did not start)
1982	San Marino (Piquet and Lauda did not enter)
1994	Monaco - Canada (3 races), Britain - Portugal (6 races without Mansell)

All of these races were run with drivers who would later become world champion.
Excludes Indianapolis 500.

117. Champions on the starting grid *(Most)*

the most world champions to be active throughout a season is 6:

2012 (20 races): Fernando Alonso, Jenson Button, Lewis Hamilton, Kimi Räikkönen, Michael Schumacher, Sebastian Vettel

5 champions were active throughout these seasons:

2011 (19 races): Fernando Alonso, Jenson Button, Lewis Hamilton, Michael Schumacher, Sebastian Vettel
2013 (19 races) and 2014 (19 races): Fernando Alonso, Jenson Button, Lewis Hamilton, Kimi Räikkönen, Sebastian Vettel

5 were also active during these seasons:

1968 (1 race: South Africa): Jack Brabham, Jim Clark, Graham Hill, Denny Hulme, John Surtees
1969 (2 races: Canada - United States): Jack Brabham, Graham Hill, Denny Hulme, Jackie Stewart, John Surtees *(once Stewart had clinched the title at Monza)*
1970 (8 races: South Africa - Monaco, Britain - Germany, Canada - Mexico): Jack Brabham, Denny Hulme, Jackie Stewart, Graham Hill, John Surtees
1985 (1 race: Australia): Alan Jones, Niki Lauda, Nelson Piquet, Alain Prost, Keke Rosberg *(once Prost had clinched the title at Brands Hatch and Jones was back on the grid)*
2015 (17 races): Fernando Alonso, Jenson Button, Lewis Hamilton, Kimi Räikkönen, Sebastian Vettel *(although a 19 race season, Alonso did not start in Australia and Button did not start in Bahrain)*

118. Champions in the top placings in a race

Top 5	
Italy 2011	1: Sebastian Vettel, 2: Jenson Button, 3: Fernando Alonso, 4: Lewis Hamilton, 5: Michael Schumacher
China 2013	1: Fernando Alonso, 2: Kimi Räikkönen, 3: Lewis Hamilton, 4: Sebastian Vettel, 5: Jenson Button
Top 4	
Hungary 2011	1: Jenson Button, 2: Sebastian Vettel, 3: Fernando Alonso, 4: Lewis Hamilton
Abu Dhabi 2012	1: Kimi Räikkönen, 2: Fernando Alonso, 3: Sebastian Vettel, 4: Jenson Button
Top 3	
Britain 1953	1: Alberto Ascari, 2: Juan Manuel Fangio, 3: Giuseppe Farina
South Africa 1965	1: Jim Clark, 2: John Surtees, 3: Graham Hill
Britain 1965	1: Jim Clark, 2: Graham Hill, 3: John Surtees
Netherlands 1966	1: Jack Brabham, 2: Graham Hill, 3: Jim Clark
Italy 1967	1: John Surtees, 2: Jack Brabham, 3: Jim Clark
South Africa 1970	1: Jack Brabham, 2: Denny Hulme, 3: Jackie Stewart
Brazil 1973	1: Emerson Fittipaldi, 2: Jackie Stewart, 3: Denny Hulme
Australia 1988	1: Alain Prost, 2: Ayrton Senna, 3: Nelson Piquet
United States 1991	1: Ayrton Senna, 2: Alain Prost, 3: Nelson Piquet
Canada 2010	1: Lewis Hamilton, 2: Jenson Button, 3: Fernando Alonso
Spain 2011	1: Sebastian Vettel, 2: Lewis Hamilton, 3: Jenson Button
Monaco 2011	1: Sebastian Vettel, 2: Fernando Alonso, 3: Jenson Button
Japan 2011	1: Jenson Button, 2: Fernando Alonso, 3: Sebastian Vettel
India 2011	1: Sebastian Vettel, 2: Jenson Button, 3: Fernando Alonso
Abu Dhabi 2011	1: Lewis Hamilton, 2: Fernando Alonso, 3: Jenson Button
Australia 2012	1: Jenson Button, 2: Sebastian Vettel, 3: Lewis Hamilton
Europe 2012	1: Fernando Alonso, 2: Kimi Räikkönen, 3: Michael Schumacher
Germany 2012	1: Fernando Alonso, 2: Jenson Button, 3: Kimi Räikkönen
Belgium 2012	1: Jenson Button, 2: Sebastian Vettel, 3: Kimi Räikkönen
Singapore 2012	1: Sebastian Vettel, 2: Jenson Button, 3: Fernando Alonso
United States 2012	1: Lewis Hamilton, 2: Sebastian Vettel, 3: Fernando Alonso
Australia 2013	1: Kimi Räikkönen, 2: Fernando Alonso, 3: Sebastian Vettel
Canada 2013	1: Sebastian Vettel, 2: Fernando Alonso, 3: Lewis Hamilton
Hungary 2013	1: Lewis Hamilton, 2: Kimi Räikkönen, 3: Sebastian Vettel
Belgium 2013	1: Sebastian Vettel, 2: Fernando Alonso, 3: Lewis Hamilton
Singapore 2013	1: Sebastian Vettel, 2: Fernando Alonso, 3: Kimi Räikkönen

119. Champions as team-mates

Alberto Ascari & Giuseppe Farina (Ferrari)	Netherlands 1952	- Italy 1953 (10 races, 8 wins)
Jim Clark & Graham Hill (Lotus)	South Africa 1967	- South Africa 1968 (12 races, 5 wins)
Emerson Fittipaldi & Denny Hulme (McLaren)	Argentina 1974	- United States 1974 (15 races, 4 wins)
Niki Lauda & Alain Prost (McLaren)	South Africa 1985	- Australia 1985 (2 races, 1 podium)
Alain Prost & Keke Rosberg (McLaren)	Brazil 1986	- Australia 1986 (16 races, 4 wins)
Alain Prost & Ayrton Senna (McLaren)	Australia 1988	- Australia 1989 (17 races, 11 wins)
Jenson Button & Lewis Hamilton (McLaren)	Bahrain 2010	- Brazil 2012 (58 races, 18 wins)
Fernando Alonso & Kimi Räikkönen (Ferrari)	Australia 2014	- Abu Dhabi 2014 (19 races, 2 podiums)
Kimi Räikkönen & Sebastian Vettel (Ferrari)	Australia 2015	- Abu Dhabi 2015 (19 races, 3 wins)
Fernando Alonso & Jenson Button (McLaren)	Malaysia 2015	- Abu Dhabi 2015 (17 races, 0 podiums)

Other cases where two world champions drove the same make of car in a race, but were not team-mates:

Denny Hulme & John Surtees (McLaren)   South Africa 1970   - Monaco 1970 (3 races, 1 podium)

Hulme drove for Bruce McLaren Motor Racing whilst Surtees was with Team Surtees.

120. Champions with worst performing main team-mate

	world champion	main team-mate	final championship position of team-mate
1972	Emerson Fittipaldi	Dave Walker	- (0 points), John Player Lotus (10 of 12 races)
1970	Jochen Rindt	John Miles	19th, Gold Leaf Team Lotus (9 of 13 races) (a)
1963	Jim Clark	Trevor Taylor	15th, Team Lotus
1968	Graham Hill	Jackie Oliver	15th, Gold Leaf Team Lotus (10 of 12 races)
1982	Keke Rosberg	Derek Daly	13th, TAG Williams Team
1981	Nelson Piquet	Hector Rebaque	10th, Parmalat Racing Team (Brabham)
1985	Alain Prost	Niki Lauda	10th, Marlboro McLaren International
1994	Michael Schumacher	Jos Verstappen	10th, Mild Seven Benetton Ford (10 of 16 races)
1976	James Hunt	Jochen Mass	9th, Marlboro Team McLaren
1983	Nelson Piquet	Riccardo Patrese	9th, Fila Sport (Brabham)
1962	Graham Hill	Richie Ginther	8th, Owen Racing Organisation (Lotus)
1965	Jim Clark	Mike Spence	8th, Team Lotus
1974	Emerson Fittipaldi	Denny Hulme	7th, Marlboro Team Texaco (McLaren)
2008	Lewis Hamilton	Heikki Kovalainen	7th, Vodafone McLaren Mercedes
1956	Juan Manuel Fangio	Eugenio Castellotti	6th, Scuderia Ferrari
1959	Jack Brabham	Bruce McLaren	6th, Cooper Car Co. (7 of 9 races)
1986	Alain Prost	Keke Rosberg	6th, Marlboro McLaren International
2012	Sebastian Vettel	Mark Webber	6th, Red Bull Racing

(a) Withdrew from what would have been his 10th race, following Rindt's fatal accident.

121. Interval between championship titles *(Longest)*

Niki Lauda	7 years	1977 - 84 (a)
Jack Brabham	6 years	1960 - 66
Lewis Hamilton	6 years	2007 - 14
Graham Hill	6 years	1962 - 68

Michael Schumacher	5 years	1995 - 2000
Nelson Piquet	4 years	1983 - 87
Alain Prost	4 years	1989 - 93 (b)

(a) Not active in 1980 - 81.
(b) Not active in 1992.

122. Interval between first & last championship titles *(Longest)*

Michael Schumacher	10 years	1994 - 2004
Niki Lauda	9 years	1975 - 84 (a)
Alain Prost	8 years	1985 - 93 (b)
Jack Brabham	7 years	1959 - 66
Lewis Hamilton	7 years	2008 - 15

Juan Manuel Fangio	6 years	1951 - 57 (c)
Graham Hill	6 years	1962 - 68
Nelson Piquet	6 years	1981 - 87
Jackie Stewart	4 years	1969 - 73

(a) Not active in 1980 - 81. (b) Not active in 1992. (c) Not active in 1952.

123. Led the championship, but has not become a champion

Michele Alboreto (1985), René Arnoux (1980), Lorenzo Bandini (1966), Jean Behra (1956), Peter Collins (1956), David Coulthard (1997, 2003), Elio De Angelis (1985), Patrick Depailler (1978), Giancarlo Fisichella (2005), Eddie Irvine (1999), Robert Kubica (2008), Jacques Laffite (1979), Felipe Massa (2008,10), Bruce McLaren (1960, 63), Stirling Moss (1958, 61), Luigi Musso (1958), Didier Pironi (1982), Clay Regazzoni (1974), Carlos Reutemann (1977, 78, 81), Pedro Rodríguez (1967), Nico Rosberg (2014, 15), Piero Taruffi (1952), Maurice Trintignant (1955), Gilles Villenuve (1979), Wolfgang von Trips (1961), John Watson (1982), Mark Webber (2010)

124. Milestones: world champions
(eg Lewis Hamilton was the 30th driver to become world champion)

1st	Giuseppe Farina	1950
10th	Denny Hulme	1967

20th	Keke Rosberg	1982
30th	Lewis Hamilton	2008

Chapter 5: Race Starting Drivers

	Nat	St	W	Pod	PP	FR	FL	Pts	Date of birth	Date of death	First start	Last start
George ABECASSIS	GB	2	-	-	-	-	-	-	21 Mar 1913	18 Dec 1991	CH 1951	CH 1952
Kenny ACHESON	GB	3	-	-	-	-	-	-	27 Nov 1957		ZA 1983	I 1985
Philippe ADAMS	B	2	-	-	-	-	-	-	19 Nov 1969		B 1994	P 1994
Kurt ADOLFF	D	1	-	-	-	-	-	-	5 Nov 1921	24 Jan 2012	D 1953	D 1953
Kurt AHRENS	D	4	-	-	-	-	-	-	19 Apr 1940		D 1966	D 1969
Christijan ALBERS	NL	46	-	-	-	-	-	4	16 Apr 1979		AUS 2005	GB 2007
Michele ALBORETO	I	194	5	23	2	4	5	186.5	23 Dec 1956	25 Apr 2001	RSM 1981	AUS 1994
Jean ALESI	F	201	1	32	2	10	4	241	11 Jun 1964		F 1989	J 2001
Jaime ALGUERSUARI	E	46	-	-	-	-	-	31	23 Mar 1990		H 2009	BR 2011
Philippe ALLIOT	F	109	-	-	-	-	-	7	27 Jul 1954		BR 1984	B 1994
Cliff ALLISON	GB	16	-	1	-	-	-	11	8 Feb 1932	7 Apr 2005	MC 1958	MC 1961
Fernando ALONSO	E	253	32	97	22	37	21	1,778	29 Jul 1981		AUS 2001	ABU 2015
Chris AMON	NZ	96	-	11	5	19	3	83	20 Jul 1943		B 1963	D 1976
Bob ANDERSON	GB	25	-	1	-	-	-	8	19 May 1931	14 Aug 1967	GB 1963	GB 1967
Conny ANDERSSON	S	1	-	-	-	-	-	-	28 Dec 1939		NL 1976	NL 1976
Mario ANDRETTI	USA	128	12	19	18	24	10	180	28 Feb 1940		USA 1968	LV 1982
Michael ANDRETTI	USA	13	-	1	-	-	-	7	5 Oct 1962		ZA 1993	I 1993
Marco APICELLA	I	1	-	-	-	-	-	-	7 Oct 1965		I 1993	I 1993
René ARNOUX	F	149	7	22	18	34	12	181	4 Jul 1948		B 1978	AUS 1989
Peter ARUNDELL	GB	11	-	2	-	-	-	12	8 Nov 1933	16 Jun 2009	MC 1964	MEX 1966
Alberto ASCARI (a)	I	31	13	17	14	25	12	140.14	13 Jul 1918	26 May 1955	MC 1950	MC 1955
Peter ASHDOWN	GB	1	-	-	-	-	-	-	16 Oct 1934		GB 1959	GB 1959
Ian ASHLEY	GB	4	-	-	-	-	-	-	26 Oct 1947		D 1974	USA 1977
Gerry ASHMORE	GB	3	-	-	-	-	-	-	25 Jul 1936		GB 1961	I 1961
Bill ASTON	GB	1	-	-	-	-	-	-	29 Mar 1900	4 Mar 1974	D 1952	D 1952
Richard ATTWOOD	GB	17	-	1	-	-	1	11	4 Apr 1940		MC 1965	D 1969
Luca BADOER	I	51	-	-	-	-	-	-	25 Jan 1971		ZA 1993	B 2009
Giancarlo BAGHETTI	I	21	1	1	-	-	1	14	25 Dec 1934	27 Nov 1995	F 1961	I 1967
Julian BAILEY	GB	7	-	-	-	-	-	1	9 Oct 1961		RSM 1988	RSM 1991
Mauro BALDI	I	36	-	-	-	-	-	5	31 Jan 1954		BR 1982	RSM 1985
Marcel BALSA	F	1	-	-	-	-	-	-	1 Jan 1909	11 Aug 1984	D 1952	D 1952
Lorenzo BANDINI	I	42	1	8	1	5	2	58	21 Dec 1935	10 May 1967	B 1961	MC 1967
Fabrizio BARBAZZA	I	8	-	-	-	-	-	2	2 Apr 1963		ZA 1993	F 1993
John BARBER	GB	1	-	-	-	-	-	-	22 Jul 1929		RA 1953	RA 1953
Skip BARBER	USA	5	-	-	-	-	-	-	16 Nov 1936		NL 1971	USA 1972
Paolo BARILLA	I	9	-	-	-	-	-	-	20 Apr 1961		J 1989	B 1990
Rubens BARRICHELLO	BR	323	11	68	14	34	17	658	23 May 1972		ZA 1993	BR 2011
Edgar BARTH	DDR/D	5	-	-	-	-	-	-	26 Jan 1917	20 May 1965	D 1953	D 1964
Giorgio BASSI	I	1	-	-	-	-	-	-	20 Jan 1934		I 1965	I 1965
Erwin BAUER	D	1	-	-	-	-	-	-	17 Jul 1912	3 Jun 1958	D 1953	D 1953
Zsolt BAUMGARTNER	H	20	-	-	-	-	-	1	1 Jan 1981		H 2003	BR 2004
Elie BAYOL	F	7	-	-	-	-	-	2	28 Feb 1914	25 May 1995	I 1952	MC 1956
Don BEAUMAN	GB	1	-	-	-	-	-	-	26 Jul 1928	9 Jul 1955	GB 1954	GB 1954
Günther BECHEM (b)	DDR/D	2	-	-	-	-	-	-	21 Dec 1921	3 May 2011	D 1952	D 1953
Jean BEHRA (c)	F	53	-	9	-	10	1	51.14	16 Feb 1921	1 Aug 1959	I 1951	F 1959
Derek BELL	GB	9	-	-	-	-	-	1	31 Oct 1941		I 1968	D 1974
Stefan BELLOF	D	20	-	-	-	-	-	4	20 Nov 1957	1 Sep 1985	BR 1984	NL 1985
Paul BELMONDO	F	7	-	-	-	-	-	-	23 Apr 1963		E 1992	E 1994
Tom BELSØ	DK	2	-	-	-	-	-	-	27 Aug 1942		ZA 1974	S 1974
Jean-Pierre BELTOISE	F	86	1	8	-	2	4	77	26 Apr 1937	5 Jan 2015	D 1966	CDN 1974
Olivier BERETTA	MC	9	-	-	-	-	-	-	23 Nov 1969		BR 1994	H 1994
Allen BERG	CDN	9	-	-	-	-	-	-	1 Aug 1961		DET 1986	AUS 1986
Georges BERGER	B	2	-	-	-	-	-	-	14 Sep 1918	23 Aug 1967	B 1953	F 1954
Gerhard BERGER	A	210	10	48	12	32	21	385	27 Aug 1959		A 1984	EUR 1997
Eric BERNARD	F	45	-	1	-	-	-	10	24 Aug 1964		F 1989	EUR 1994
Enrique BERNOLDI	BR	28	-	-	-	-	-	-	19 Oct 1978		AUS 2001	D 2002
Mike BEUTTLER	GB	28	-	-	-	-	-	-	13 Apr 1940	29 Dec 1988	GB 1971	USA 1973

	Nat	St	W	Pod	PP	FR	FL	Pts	Date of birth	Date of death	First start	Last start
Jules BIANCHI	F	34	-	-	-	-	-	2	3 Aug 1989	17 Jul 2015	AUS 2013	J 2014
Lucien BIANCHI	B	17	-	1	-	-	-	6	10 Nov 1934	30 Mar 1969	B 1960	MEX 1968
Gino BIANCO	BR	4	-	-	-	-	-	-	22 Jul 1916	8 May 1984	GB 1952	I 1952
Hans BINDER	A	13	-	-	-	-	-	-	12 Jun 1948		A 1976	J 1977
Clemente BIONDETTI	I	1	-	-	-	-	-	-	18 Oct 1898	24 Feb 1955	I 1950	I 1950
'B' BIRA	T	19	-	-	-	-	-	8	15 Jul 1914	23 Dec 1985	GB 1950	E 1954
Pablo BIRGER	RA	2	-	-	-	-	-	-	6 Jan 1924	9 Mar 1966	RA 1953	RA 1955
Harry BLANCHARD	USA	1	-	-	-	-	-	-	30 Jun 1929	31 Jan 1960	USA 1959	USA 1959
Michael BLEEKEMOLEN	NL	1	-	-	-	-	-	-	2 Oct 1949		USA 1978	USA 1978
Trevor BLOKDYK	ZA	1	-	-	-	-	-	-	30 Nov 1935	19 Mar 1995	ZA 1963	ZA 1963
Mark BLUNDELL	GB	61	-	3	-	-	-	32	8 Apr 1966		USA 1991	AUS 1995
Raul BOESEL	BR	23	-	-	-	-	-	-	4 Dec 1957		ZA 1982	ZA 1983
Bob BONDURANT	USA	9	-	-	-	-	-	3	27 Apr 1933		USA 1965	MEX 1966
Felice BONETTO	I	15	-	2	-	1	-	17.5	9 Jun 1903	21 Nov 1953	CH 1950	I 1953
Jo BONNIER	S	104	1	1	1	5	-	39	31 Jan 1930	11 Jun 1972	I 1956	USA 1971
Roberto BONOMI	RA	1	-	-	-	-	-	-	30 Sep 1919	10 Jan 1992	RA 1960	RA 1960
Slim BORGUDD	S	10	-	-	-	-	-	1	25 Nov 1946		RSM 1981	USAW 1982
Luki BOTHA	ZA	1	-	-	-	-	-	-	16 Jan 1930	1 Oct 2006	ZA 1967	ZA 1967
Valtteri BOTTAS	FIN	56	-	8	-	2	1	326	28 Aug 1989		AUS 2013	ABU 2015
Jean-Christophe BOULLION	F	11	-	-	-	-	-	3	27 Dec 1969		MC 1995	PAC 1995
Sébastien BOURDAIS	F	27	-	-	-	-	-	6	28 Feb 1979		AUS 2008	D 2009
Thierry BOUTSEN	B	163	3	15	1	1	1	132	13 Jul 1957		B 1983	B 1993
David BRABHAM	AUS	24	-	-	-	-	-	-	5 Sep 1965		MC 1990	AUS 1994
Jack BRABHAM	AUS	126	14	31	13	38	12	261	2 Apr 1926	19 May 2014	GB 1955	MEX 1970
Bill BRACK	CDN	3	-	-	-	-	-	-	26 Dec 1935		CDN 1968	CDN 1972
Vittorio BRAMBILLA	I	74	1	1	1	1	1	15.5	11 Nov 1937	26 May 2001	ZA 1974	I 1980
Toni BRANCA	CH	3	-	-	-	-	-	-	15 Sep 1916	10 May 1985	CH 1950	D 1951
Eric BRANDON	GB	5	-	-	-	-	-	-	18 Jul 1920	8 Aug 1982	CH 1952	GB 1954
Tom BRIDGER	GB	1	-	-	-	-	-	-	24 Jun 1934	30 Jul 1991	MA 1958	MA 1958
Tony BRISE	GB	10	-	-	-	-	-	1	28 Mar 1952	29 Nov 1975	E 1975	USA 1975
Chris BRISTOW	GB	4	-	-	-	-	-	-	2 Dec 1937	19 Jun 1960	GB 1959	B 1960
Peter BROEKER	CDN	1	-	-	-	-	-	-	15 May 1929	4 Nov 1980	USA 1963	USA 1963
Tony BROOKS	GB	38	6	10	3	11	3	75	25 Feb 1932		GB 1956	USA 1961
Alan BROWN	GB	8	-	-	-	-	-	2	20 Nov 1919	20 Jan 2004	CH 1952	I 1953
Warwick BROWN	AUS	1	-	-	-	-	-	-	24 Dec 1949		USA 1976	USA 1976
Adolf BRUDES	D	1	-	-	-	-	-	-	15 Oct 1899	5 Nov 1986	D 1952	D 1952
Martin BRUNDLE	GB	158	-	9	-	-	-	98	1 Jun 1959		BR 1984	J 1996
Gianmaria BRUNI	I	18	-	-	-	-	-	-	30 May 1981		AUS 2004	BR 2004
Clemar BUCCI	RA	5	-	-	-	-	-	-	4 Sep 1920	12 Jan 2011	GB 1954	RA 1955
Ronnie BUCKNUM	USA	11	-	-	-	-	-	2	5 Apr 1936	23 Apr 1992	D 1964	MEX 1966
Ivor BUEB	GB	5	-	-	-	-	-	-	6 Jun 1923	1 Aug 1959	MC 1957	GB 1959
Sébastien BUEMI	CH	55	-	-	-	-	-	29	31 Oct 1988		AUS 2009	BR 2011
Luiz BUENO	BR	1	-	-	-	-	-	-	16 Jan 1937	8 Feb 2011	BR 1973	BR 1973
Ian BURGESS	GB	16	-	-	-	-	-	-	6 Jul 1930	19 May 2012	GB 1958	D 1963
Luciano BURTI	BR	15	-	-	-	-	-	-	5 Mar 1975		A 2000	B 2001
Roberto BUSSINELLO	I	2	-	-	-	-	-	-	4 Oct 1927	24 Aug 1999	I 1961	I 1965
Jenson BUTTON	GB	284	15	50	8	24	8	1,214	19 Jan 1980		AUS 2000	ABU 2015
Tommy BYRNE	IRL	2	-	-	-	-	-	-	6 May 1958		A 1982	LV 1982
Giulio CABIANCA	I	3	-	-	-	-	-	3	19 Feb 1923	15 Jun 1961	I 1958	I 1960
Mário CABRAL	P	4	-	-	-	-	-	-	15 Jan 1934		P 1959	I 1964
Alex CAFFI	I	56	-	-	-	-	-	6	18 Mar 1964		I 1986	AUS 1991
John CAMPBELL-JONES	GB	2	-	-	-	-	-	-	21 Jan 1930		B 1962	GB 1963
Adrián CAMPOS	E	17	-	-	-	-	-	-	17 Jun 1960		BR 1987	RSM 1988
John CANNON	CDN	1	-	-	-	-	-	-	21 Jun 1933	18 Oct 1999	USA 1971	USA 1971
Eitel CANTONI	ROU	3	-	-	-	-	-	-	4 Oct 1906	6 Jun 1997	GB 1952	I 1952
Ivan CAPELLI	I	93	-	3	-	-	-	31	24 May 1963		EUR 1985	ZA 1993
Piero CARINI	I	3	-	-	-	-	-	-	6 Mar 1921	30 May 1957	F 1952	I 1953
Eugenio CASTELLOTTI	I	14	-	3	1	7	-	19.5	10 Oct 1930	14 Mar 1957	RA 1955	RA 1957
Johnny CECOTTO	YV	18	-	-	-	-	-	1	25 Jan 1956		BR 1983	DAL 1984

	Nat	St	W	Pod	PP	FR	FL	Pts	Date of birth	Date of death	First start	Last start
François CEVERT	F	47	1	13	-	3	2	89	25 Feb 1944	6 Oct 1973	D 1969	CDN 1973
Eugène CHABOUD	F	3	-	-	-	-	-	1	12 Apr 1907	28 Dec 1983	B 1950	F 1951
Jay CHAMBERLAIN	USA	1	-	-	-	-	-	-	29 Dec 1925	1 Aug 2001	GB 1962	GB 1962
Karun CHANDHOK	IND	11	-	-	-	-	-	-	19 Jan 1984		BRN 2010	D 2011
Dave CHARLTON	ZA	11	-	-	-	-	-	-	27 Oct 1936	23 Feb 2013	ZA 1967	ZA 1975
Eddie CHEEVER	USA	132	-	9	-	1	-	70	10 Jan 1958		ZA 1978	AUS 1989
Andrea CHIESA	CH	3	-	-	-	-	-	-	6 May 1964		MEX 1992	F 1992
Max CHILTON	GB	35	-	-	-	-	-	-	21 Apr 1991		AUS 2013	RUS 2014
Ettore CHIMERI	I/YV	1	-	-	-	-	-	-	4 Jun 1921	27 Feb 1960	RA 1960	RA 1960
Louis CHIRON	MC	15	-	1	-	-	-	4	3 Aug 1899	22 Jun 1979	GB 1950	MC 1955
Johnny CLAES	B	23	-	-	-	-	-	-	11 Aug 1916	3 Feb 1956	GB 1950	NL 1955
Jim CLARK	GB	72	25	32	33	48	28	274	4 Mar 1936	7 Apr 1968	NL 1960	ZA 1968
Peter COLLINS	GB	32	3	9	-	8	-	47	6 Nov 1931	3 Aug 1958	CH 1952	D 1958
Bernard COLLOMB	F	4	-	-	-	-	-	-	7 Oct 1930	19 Sep 2011	F 1961	D 1963
Erik COMAS	F	59	-	-	-	-	-	7	28 Sep 1963		BR 1991	J 1994
Franco COMOTTI	I	2	-	-	-	-	-	-	24 Jul 1906	10 May 1963	I 1950	F 1952
George CONSTANTINE	USA	1	-	-	-	-	-	-	22 Feb 1918	7 Jan 1968	USA 1959	USA 1959
John CORDTS	CDN	1	-	-	-	-	-	-	23 Jul 1935		CDN 1969	CDN 1969
David COULTHARD	GB	246	13	62	12	37	18	535	27 Mar 1971		E 1994	BR 2008
Piers COURAGE	GB	28	-	2	-	-	-	20	27 May 1942	21 Jun 1970	D 1966	NL 1970
Chris CRAFT	GB	1	-	-	-	-	-	-	17 Nov 1939		USA 1971	USA 1971
Jim CRAWFORD	GB	2	-	-	-	-	-	-	13 Feb 1948	6 Aug 2002	GB 1975	I 1975
Antonio CREUS	E	1	-	-	-	-	-	-	28 Oct 1924	19 Feb 1996	RA 1960	RA 1960
Tony CROOK	GB	2	-	-	-	-	-	-	16 Feb 1920	21 Jan 2014	GB 1952	GB 1953
Geoffrey CROSSLEY	GB	2	-	-	-	-	-	-	11 May 1921	7 Jan 2002	GB 1950	B 1950
Jérôme d'AMBROSIO	B	20	-	-	-	-	-	-	27 Dec 1985		AUS 2011	I 2012
Fritz d'OREY	BR	3	-	-	-	-	-	-	25 Mar 1938		F 1959	USA 1959
Cristiano da MATTA	BR	28	-	-	-	-	-	13	19 Sep 1973		AUS 2003	D 2004
Nano da SILVA RAMOS	F/BR	7	-	-	-	-	-	2	7 Dec 1925		NL 1955	I 1956
Chuck DAIGH	USA	3	-	-	-	-	-	-	29 Nov 1923	29 Apr 2008	B 1960	USA 1960
Yannick DALMAS	F	23	-	-	-	-	-	-	28 Jul 1961		MEX 1987	P 1994
Derek DALY	IRL	49	-	-	-	-	-	15	11 Mar 1953		GB 1978	LV 1982
Christian DANNER	D	36	-	-	-	-	-	4	4 Apr 1958		B 1985	CDN 1989
Jorge DAPONTE	RA	2	-	-	-	-	-	-	5 Jun 1923	9 Mar 1963	RA 1954	I 1954
Anthony DAVIDSON	GB	24	-	-	-	-	-	-	18 Apr 1979		H 2002	E 2008
Colin DAVIS	GB	2	-	-	-	-	-	-	29 Jul 1933	19 Dec 2012	F 1959	I 1959
Andrea De ADAMICH	I	30	-	-	-	-	-	6	3 Oct 1941		ZA 1968	GB 1973
Elio De ANGELIS	I	108	2	9	3	6	-	122	26 Mar 1958	15 May 1986	RA 1979	MC 1986
Andrea De CESARIS	I	208	-	5	1	2	1	59	31 May 1959	5 Oct 2014	CDN 1980	EUR 1994
Maria Teresa De FILIPPIS	I	3	-	-	-	-	-	-	11 Nov 1926	9 Jan 2016	B 1958	I 1958
Emmanuel de GRAFFENRIED	CH	22	-	-	-	-	-	9	18 May 1914	22 Jan 2007	GB 1950	I 1956
Peter De KLERK	ZA	4	-	-	-	-	-	-	16 Mar 1935	11 Jul 2015	ZA 1963	ZA 1970
Pedro de la ROSA	E	105	-	1	-	-	1	35	24 Feb 1971		AUS 1999	BR 2012
Alfonso de PORTAGO	E	5	-	1	-	-	-	4	11 Oct 1928	12 May 1957	F 1956	RA 1957
Max De TERRA	CH	2	-	-	-	-	-	-	6 Oct 1918	29 Dec 1982	CH 1952	CH 1953
Alejandro de TOMASO	RA	2	-	-	-	-	-	-	10 Jul 1928	21 May 2003	RA 1957	USA 1959
Charles de TORNACO	B	2	-	-	-	-	-	-	7 Jun 1927	18 Sep 1953	B 1952	NL 1952
Emilio de VILLOTA	E	2	-	-	-	-	-	-	26 Jul 1946		E 1977	A 1977
Jean-Denis DELÉTRAZ	CH	3	-	-	-	-	-	-	1 Oct 1963		AUS 1994	EUR 1995
Patrick DEPAILLER	F	95	2	19	1	7	4	141	9 Aug 1944	1 Aug 1980	F 1972	GB 1980
Lucas Di GRASSI	BR	18	-	-	-	-	-	-	11 Aug 1984		BRN 2010	ABU 2010
Paul Di RESTA	GB	58	-	-	-	-	-	121	16 Apr 1986		AUS 2011	BR 2013
Pedro DINIZ	BR	98	-	-	-	-	-	10	22 May 1970		BR 1995	MAL 2000
José DOLHEM	F	1	-	-	-	-	-	-	26 Apr 1944	16 Apr 1988	USA 1974	USA 1974
Martin DONNELLY	GB	13	-	-	-	-	-	-	26 Mar 1964		F 1989	P 1990
Mark DONOHUE	USA	14	-	1	-	-	-	8	18 Mar 1937	19 Aug 1975	CDN 1971	D 1975
Robert DOORNBOS	NL	11	-	-	-	-	-	-	23 Sep 1981		D 2005	BR 2006
Ken DOWNING	GB	2	-	-	-	-	-	-	5 Dec 1917	3 May 2004	GB 1952	NL 1952

	Nat	St	W	Pod	PP	FR	FL	Pts	Date of birth	Date of death	First start	Last start
Bob DRAKE	USA	1	-	-	-	-	-	-	14 Dec 1919	18 Apr 1990	USA 1960	USA 1960
Paddy DRIVER	ZA	1	-	-	-	-	-	-	13 May 1934		ZA 1974	ZA 1974
Piero DROGO	I	1	-	-	-	-	-	-	8 Aug 1926	28 Apr 1973	I 1960	I 1960
Johnny DUMFRIES	GB	15	-	-	-	-	-	3	26 Apr 1958		BR 1986	AUS 1986
George EATON	CDN	11	-	-	-	-	-	-	12 Nov 1945		USA 1969	CDN 1971
Guy EDWARDS	GB	11	-	-	-	-	-	-	30 Dec 1942		RA 1974	CDN 1976
Vic ELFORD	GB	13	-	-	-	-	-	8	10 Jun 1935		F 1968	D 1971
Paul EMERY	GB	1	-	-	-	-	-	-	12 Nov 1916	3 Feb 1993	GB 1956	GB 1956
Tomáš ENGE	CZ	3	-	-	-	-	-	-	11 Sep 1976		I 2001	J 2001
Paul ENGLAND	AUS	1	-	-	-	-	-	-	28 Mar 1929	17 Jun 2014	D 1957	D 1957
Marcus ERICSSON	S	35	-	-	-	-	-	9	2 Sep 1990		AUS 2014	ABU 2015
Harald ERTL	A	19	-	-	-	-	-	-	31 Aug 1948	7 Apr 1982	D 1975	A 1978
Nasif ESTÉFANO	RA	1	-	-	-	-	-	-	18 Nov 1932	21 Oct 1973	RA 1960	RA 1960
Philippe ETANÇELIN	F	12	-	-	-	-	-	3	28 Dec 1896	13 Oct 1981	GB 1950	F 1952
Bob EVANS	GB	10	-	-	-	-	-	-	11 Jun 1947		ZA 1975	GB 1976
Corrado FABI	I	12	-	-	-	-	-	-	12 Apr 1961		BR 1983	DAL 1984
Teo FABI	I	64	-	2	3	3	2	23	9 Mar 1955		RSM 1982	AUS 1987
Pascal FABRE	F	11	-	-	-	-	-	-	9 Jan 1960		BR 1987	E 1987
Luigi FAGIOLI	I	7	1	6	-	4	-	32	9 Jun 1898	20 Jun 1952	GB 1950	F 1951
Jack FAIRMAN	GB	12	-	-	-	-	-	5	15 Mar 1913	7 Feb 2002	GB 1953	I 1961
Juan Manuel FANGIO	RA	51	24	35	29	48	23	277.64	24 Jun 1911	17 Jul 1995	GB 1950	F 1958
Giuseppe FARINA	I	33	5	19	5	27	5	127.33	30 Oct 1906	30 Jun 1966	GB 1950	B 1955
Ralph FIRMAN	GB/IRL	14	-	-	-	-	-	1	20 May 1975		AUS 2003	J 2003
Rudi FISCHER	CH	7	-	2	-	-	-	10	19 Apr 1912	30 Dec 1976	CH 1951	I 1952
Mike FISHER	USA	1	-	-	-	-	-	-	13 Mar 1943		CDN 1967	CDN 1967
Giancarlo FISICHELLA	I	229	3	19	4	11	2	275	14 Jan 1973		AUS 1996	ABU 2009
John FITCH	USA	2	-	-	-	-	-	-	4 Aug 1917	31 Oct 2012	I 1953	I 1955
Christian FITTIPALDI	BR	40	-	-	-	-	-	12	18 Jan 1971		ZA 1992	AUS 1994
Emerson FITTIPALDI	BR	144	14	35	6	16	6	281	12 Dec 1946		GB 1970	USA 1980
Wilson FITTIPALDI	BR	36	-	-	-	-	-	3	25 Dec 1943		E 1972	USA 1975
Theo FITZAU	DDR/D	1	-	-	-	-	-	-	10 Feb 1923	18 Mar 1982	D 1953	D 1953
Jan FLINTERMAN	NL	1	-	-	-	-	-	-	2 Oct 1919	26 Dec 1992	NL 1952	NL 1952
Ron FLOCKHART	GB	13	-	1	-	-	-	5	16 Jun 1923	12 Apr 1962	GB 1954	USA 1960
Gregor FOITEK	CH	7	-	-	-	-	-	-	27 Mar 1965		USA 1990	D 1990
George FOLLMER	USA	12	-	1	-	-	-	5	27 Jan 1934		ZA 1973	USA 1973
Norberto FONTANA	RA	4	-	-	-	-	-	-	20 Jan 1975		F 1997	EUR 1997
Franco FORINI	CH	2	-	-	-	-	-	-	22 Sep 1958		I 1987	P 1987
Philip FOTHERINGHAM-PARKER	GB	1	-	-	-	-	-	-	22 Sep 1907	15 Oct 1981	GB 1951	GB 1951
Heinz-Harald FRENTZEN	D	157	3	18	2	12	6	174	18 May 1967		BR 1994	J 2003
Paul FRÈRE	B	11	-	1	-	-	-	11	30 Jan 1917	23 Feb 2008	B 1952	B 1956
Patrick FRIESACHER	A	11	-	-	-	-	-	3	26 Sep 1980		AUS 2005	GB 2005
Joe FRY	GB	1	-	-	-	-	-	-	26 Oct 1915	29 Jul 1950	GB 1950	GB 1950
Beppe GABBIANI	I	3	-	-	-	-	-	-	2 Jan 1957		USAW 1981	B 1981
Bertrand GACHOT	F	47	-	-	-	-	1	5	23 Dec 1962		F 1989	AUS 1995
Patrick GAILLARD	F	2	-	-	-	-	-	-	12 Feb 1952		GB 1979	A 1979
Nanni GALLI	I	17	-	-	-	-	-	-	2 Oct 1940		NL 1971	MC 1973
Oscar GÁLVEZ	RA	1	-	-	-	-	-	2	17 Aug 1913	16 Dec 1989	RA 1953	RA 1953
Fred GAMBLE	USA	1	-	-	-	-	-	-	17 Mar 1932		I 1960	I 1960
Howden GANLEY	NZ	35	-	-	-	-	-	10	24 Dec 1941		ZA 1971	BR 1974
Frank GARDNER	AUS	8	-	-	-	-	-	-	1 Oct 1930	29 Aug 2009	GB 1964	I 1965
Jo GARTNER	A	8	-	-	-	-	-	-	24 Jan 1954	1 Jun 1986	RSM 1984	P 1984
Tony GAZE	AUS	3	-	-	-	-	-	-	3 Feb 1920	29 Jul 2013	B 1952	D 1952
"GEKI"	I	2	-	-	-	-	-	-	23 Oct 1937	18 Jun 1967	I 1965	I 1966
Olivier GENDEBIEN	B	14	-	2	-	1	-	18	12 Jan 1924	2 Oct 1998	RA 1956	USA 1961
Marc GENÉ	E	36	-	-	-	-	-	5	29 Mar 1974		AUS 1999	GB 2004
Bob GERARD	GB	8	-	-	-	-	-	-	19 Jan 1914	26 Jan 1990	GB 1950	GB 1957
Gerino GERINI	I	6	-	-	-	-	-	1.5	10 Aug 1928	17 Apr 2013	RA 1956	MA 1958
Peter GETHIN	GB	30	1	1	-	-	-	11	21 Feb 1940	5 Dec 2011	NL 1970	GB 1974
Piercarlo GHINZANI	I	76	-	-	-	-	-	2	16 Jan 1952		B 1981	AUS 1989

	Nat	St	W	Pod	PP	FR	FL	Pts	Date of birth	Date of death	First start	Last start
Bruno GIACOMELLI	I	69	-	1	1	1	-	14	10 Sep 1952		I 1977	ZA 1983
Dick GIBSON	GB	2	-	-	-	-	-	-	16 Apr 1918	17 Dec 2010	D 1957	D 1958
Richie GINTHER	USA	52	1	14	-	8	3	107	5 Aug 1930	20 Sep 1989	MC 1960	MEX 1966
Yves GIRAUD-CABANTOUS	F	13	-	-	-	-	-	5	8 Oct 1904	30 Mar 1973	GB 1950	I 1953
Ignazio GIUNTI	I	4	-	-	-	-	-	3	30 Aug 1941	10 Jan 1971	B 1970	I 1970
Timo GLOCK	D	91	-	3	-	1	1	51	18 Mar 1982		CDN 2004	BR 2012
Chico GODIA	E	13	-	-	-	-	-	6	21 Mar 1921	28 Nov 1990	E 1951	F 1958
Carel GODIN de BEAUFORT	NL	28	-	-	-	-	-	4	10 Apr 1934	2 Aug 1964	D 1957	NL 1964
Christian GOETHALS	B	1	-	-	-	-	-	-	4 Aug 1928	26 Feb 2003	D 1958	D 1958
José Froilán GONZÁLEZ	RA	26	2	15	3	12	6	77.64	5 Oct 1922	15 Jun 2013	MC 1950	RA 1960
Óscar GONZÁLEZ	ROU	1	-	-	-	-	-	-	10 Nov 1923	5 Nov 2006	RA 1956	RA 1956
Aldo GORDINI	F	1	-	-	-	-	-	-	20 May 1921	28 Jan 1995	F 1951	F 1951
Horace GOULD	GB	14	-	-	-	-	-	2	20 Sep 1921	4 Nov 1968	GB 1954	RA 1958
Jean-Marc GOUNON	F	9	-	-	-	-	-	-	1 Jan 1963		J 1993	P 1994
Keith GREENE	GB	3	-	-	-	-	-	-	5 Jan 1938		GB 1960	D 1962
Masten GREGORY	USA	38	-	3	-	1	-	21	29 Feb 1932	8 Nov 1985	MC 1957	I 1965
Georges GRIGNARD	F	1	-	-	-	-	-	-	25 Jul 1905	7 Dec 1977	E 1951	E 1951
Romain GROSJEAN	CH/F	83	-	10	-	1	1	287	17 Apr 1986		EUR 2009	ABU 2015
Olivier GROUILLARD	F	41	-	-	-	-	-	1	2 Sep 1958		BR 1989	AUS 1992
André GUELFI	MA/F	1	-	-	-	-	-	-	6 May 1919		MA 1958	MA 1958
Miguel Angel GUERRA	RA	1	-	-	-	-	-	-	31 Aug 1953		RSM 1981	RSM 1981
Roberto GUERRERO	CO	21	-	-	-	-	-	-	16 Nov 1958		USAW 1982	EUR 1983
Maurício GUGELMIN	BR	74	-	1	-	-	1	10	20 Apr 1963		BR 1988	AUS 1992
Dan GURNEY	USA	86	4	19	3	22	6	133	13 Apr 1931		F 1959	GB 1970
Esteban GUTIÉRREZ	MEX	38	-	-	-	-	1	6	5 Aug 1991		AUS 2013	ABU 2014
Hubert HAHNE	D	3	-	-	-	-	-	-	28 Mar 1935		D 1966	D 1968
Mike HAILWOOD	GB	50	-	2	-	-	1	29	2 Apr 1940	23 Mar 1981	GB 1963	D 1974
Mika HÄKKINEN	FIN	161	20	51	26	39	25	420	28 Sep 1968		USA 1991	J 2001
Bruce HALFORD	GB	8	-	-	-	-	-	-	18 May 1931	2 Dec 2001	GB 1956	F 1960
Jim HALL	USA	11	-	-	-	-	-	3	23 Jul 1935		USA 1960	MEX 1963
Duncan HAMILTON	GB	5	-	-	-	-	-	-	30 Apr 1920	13 May 1994	GB 1951	GB 1953
Lewis HAMILTON	GB	167	43	87	49	90	28	1,867	7 Jan 1985		AUS 2007	ABU 2015
David HAMPSHIRE	GB	2	-	-	-	-	-	-	29 Dec 1917	25 Aug 1990	GB 1950	F 1950
Walt HANSGEN	USA	2	-	-	-	-	-	2	28 Oct 1919	7 Apr 1966	USA 1961	USA 1964
Mike HARRIS	RSR	1	-	-	-	-	-	-	25 May 1939		ZA 1962	ZA 1962
Cuth HARRISON	GB	3	-	-	-	-	-	-	6 Jul 1906	21 Jan 1981	GB 1950	I 1950
Brian HART	GB	1	-	-	-	-	-	-	7 Sep 1936	5 Jan 2014	D 1967	D 1967
Masahiro HASEMI	J	1	-	-	-	-	-	-	13 Nov 1945		J 1976	J 1976
Paul HAWKINS	AUS	3	-	-	-	-	-	-	12 Oct 1937	26 May 1969	ZA 1965	D 1965
Mike HAWTHORN	GB	45	3	18	4	17	6	127.64	10 Apr 1929	22 Jan 1959	B 1952	MA 1958
Boy HAYJE	NL	3	-	-	-	-	-	-	3 May 1949		NL 1976	B 1977
Willi HEEKS	D	2	-	-	-	-	-	-	13 Feb 1922	13 Aug 1996	D 1952	D 1953
Nick HEIDFELD	D	183	-	13	1	2	2	259	10 May 1977		AUS 2000	H 2011
Theo HELFRICH	D	3	-	-	-	-	-	-	13 May 1913	28 Apr 1978	D 1952	D 1954
Brian HENTON	GB	19	-	-	-	-	1	-	19 Sep 1946		GB 1975	LV 1982
Johnny HERBERT	GB	161	3	7	-	-	-	98	25 Jun 1964		BR 1989	MAL 2000
Hans HERRMANN	D	18	-	1	-	-	1	10	23 Feb 1928		D 1953	D 1966
François HESNAULT	F	19	-	-	-	-	-	-	30 Dec 1956		BR 1984	D 1985
Hans HEYER	D	1	-	-	-	-	-	-	16 Mar 1943		D 1977	D 1977
Damon HILL	GB	115	22	42	20	47	19	360	17 Sep 1960		GB 1992	J 1999
Graham HILL	GB	176	14	36	13	42	10	289	15 Feb 1929	29 Nov 1975	MC 1958	BR 1975
Phil HILL	USA	48	3	16	6	9	6	98	20 Apr 1927	28 Aug 2008	F 1958	MEX 1964
Peter HIRT	CH	5	-	-	-	-	-	-	30 Mar 1910	28 Jun 1992	CH 1951	CH 1953
David HOBBS	GB	7	-	-	-	-	-	-	9 Jun 1939		GB 1967	I 1974
Ingo HOFFMANN	BR	3	-	-	-	-	-	-	28 Feb 1953		BR 1976	BR 1977
Kazuyoshi HOSHINO	J	2	-	-	-	-	-	-	1 Jul 1947		J 1976	J 1977
Nico HÜLKENBERG	D	94	-	-	1	1	1	290	19 Aug 1987		BRN 2010	ABU 2015
Denny HULME	NZ	112	8	33	1	23	9	248	18 Jun 1936	4 Oct 1992	MC 1965	USA 1974
James HUNT	GB	92	10	23	14	24	8	179	29 Aug 1947	15 Jun 1993	MC 1973	MC 1979

	Nat	St	W	Pod	PP	FR	FL	Pts	Date of birth	Date of death	First start	Last start
Gus HUTCHISON	USA	1	-	-	-	-	-	-	26 Apr 1937		USA 1970	USA 1970
Jacky ICKX	B	116	8	25	13	25	13	181	1 Jan 1945		D 1966	USA 1979
Yuji IDE	J	4	-	-	-	-	-	-	21 Jan 1975		BRN 2006	RSM 2006
Jesús IGLESIAS	RA	1	-	-	-	-	-	-	22 Feb 1922	11 Jul 2005	RA 1955	RA 1955
Taki INOUE	J	18	-	-	-	-	-	-	5 Sep 1963		J 1994	AUS 1995
Innes IRELAND	GB	50	1	4	-	3	1	47	12 Jun 1930	23 Oct 1993	NL 1959	MEX 1966
Eddie IRVINE	GB	146	4	26	-	4	1	191	10 Nov 1965		J 1993	J 2002
Chris IRWIN	GB	10	-	-	-	-	-	2	27 Jun 1942		GB 1966	MEX 1967
Jean-Pierre JABOUILLE	F	49	2	2	6	11	-	21	1 Oct 1942		F 1975	E 1981
John JAMES	GB	1	-	-	-	-	-	-	10 May 1914	27 Jan 2002	GB 1951	GB 1951
Jean-Pierre JARIER	F	134	-	3	3	3	3	31.5	10 Jul 1946		I 1971	ZA 1983
Max JEAN	F	1	-	-	-	-	-	-	27 Jul 1943		F 1971	F 1971
Stefan JOHANSSON	S	79	-	12	-	1	-	88	8 Sep 1956		GB 1983	CDN 1991
Leslie JOHNSON	GB	1	-	-	-	-	-	-	22 Mar 1912	8 Jun 1959	GB 1950	GB 1950
Bruce JOHNSTONE	ZA	1	-	-	-	-	-	-	30 Jan 1937		ZA 1962	ZA 1962
Alan JONES	AUS	116	12	24	6	13	13	206	2 Nov 1946		E 1975	AUS 1986
Oswald KARCH	D	1	-	-	-	-	-	-	6 Mar 1917	28 Jan 2009	D 1953	D 1953
Narain KARTHIKEYAN	IND	46	-	-	-	-	-	5	14 Jan 1977		AUS 2005	BR 2012
Ukyo KATAYAMA	J	95	-	-	-	-	-	5	29 May 1963		ZA 1992	EUR 1997
Rupert KEEGAN	GB	25	-	-	-	-	-	-	26 Feb 1955		E 1977	LV 1982
Eddie KEIZAN	ZA	3	-	-	-	-	-	-	12 Sep 1944		ZA 1973	ZA 1975
Joe KELLY	IRL	2	-	-	-	-	-	-	13 Mar 1913	28 Nov 1993	GB 1950	GB 1951
Loris KESSEL	CH	3	-	-	-	-	-	-	1 Apr 1950	15 May 2010	B 1976	A 1976
Nicolas KIESA	DK	5	-	-	-	-	-	-	3 Mar 1978		D 2003	J 2003
Leo KINNUNEN	FIN	1	-	-	-	-	-	-	5 Aug 1943		S 1974	S 1974
Hans KLENK	D	1	-	-	-	-	-	-	28 Oct 1919	24 Mar 2009	D 1952	D 1952
Christian KLIEN	A	49	-	-	-	-	-	14	7 Feb 1983		AUS 2004	ABU 2010
Karl KLING	D	11	-	2	-	3	1	17	16 Sep 1910	18 Mar 2003	F 1954	I 1955
Ernst KLODWIG	DDR/D	2	-	-	-	-	-	-	23 May 1903	15 Apr 1973	D 1952	D 1953
Kamui KOBAYASHI	J	75	-	1	-	1	1	125	13 Sep 1986		BR 2009	ABU 2014
Helmut KOINIGG	A	2	-	-	-	-	-	-	3 Nov 1948	6 Oct 1974	CDN 1974	USA 1974
Heikki KOVALAINEN	FIN	111	1	4	1	5	2	105	19 Oct 1981		AUS 2007	BR 2013
Rudolf KRAUSE	DDR	2	-	-	-	-	-	-	30 Mar 1907	11 Apr 1987	D 1952	D 1953
Robert KUBICA	PL	76	1	12	1	4	1	273	7 Dec 1984		H 2006	ABU 2010
Daniil KVYAT	RUS	37	-	1	-	-	-	103	26 Apr 1994		AUS 2014	ABU 2015
Robert La CAZE	MA	1	-	-	-	-	-	-	26 Feb 1917	1 Jul 2015	MA 1958	MA 1958
Jacques LAFFITE	F	176	6	32	7	11	7	228	21 Nov 1943		D 1974	GB 1986
Franck LAGORCE	F	2	-	-	-	-	-	-	1 Sep 1968		J 1994	AUS 1994
Jan LAMMERS	NL	23	-	-	-	-	-	-	2 Jun 1956		RA 1979	AUS 1992
Pedro LAMY	P	32	-	-	-	-	-	1	20 Mar 1972		I 1993	J 1996
Chico LANDI	BR	6	-	-	-	-	-	1.5	14 Jul 1907	7 Jun 1989	I 1951	RA 1956
Hermann LANG	D	2	-	-	-	-	-	2	6 Apr 1909	19 Oct 1987	CH 1953	D 1954
Nicola LARINI	I	49	-	1	-	-	-	7	19 Mar 1964		E 1987	MC 1997
Oscar LARRAURI	RA	7	-	-	-	-	-	-	19 Aug 1954		MC 1988	AUS 1988
Gérard LARROUSSE	F	1	-	-	-	-	-	-	23 May 1940		B 1974	B 1974
Niki LAUDA	A	171	25	54	24	31	24	420.5	22 Feb 1949		A 1971	AUS 1985
Roger LAURENT	B	2	-	-	-	-	-	-	21 Feb 1913	6 Feb 1997	B 1952	D 1952
Giovanni LAVAGGI	I	7	-	-	-	-	-	-	18 Feb 1958		D 1995	P 1996
Chris LAWRENCE	GB	2	-	-	-	-	-	-	27 Jul 1933	13 Aug 2011	GB 1966	D 1966
Michel LECLÈRE	F	7	-	-	-	-	-	-	18 Mar 1946		USA 1975	F 1976
Neville LEDERLE	ZA	1	-	-	-	-	-	1	25 Sep 1938		ZA 1962	ZA 1962
Geoff LEES	GB	5	-	-	-	-	-	-	1 May 1951		D 1979	F 1982
Arthur LEGAT	B	2	-	-	-	-	-	-	1 Nov 1898	23 Feb 1960	B 1952	B 1953
J J LEHTO	FIN	62	-	1	-	-	-	10	31 Jan 1966		E 1989	AUS 1994
Lamberto LEONI	I	1	-	-	-	-	-	-	24 May 1953		RA 1978	RA 1978
Les LESTON	GB	2	-	-	-	-	-	-	16 Dec 1920	13 May 2012	I 1956	GB 1957
Pierre LEVEGH	F	6	-	-	-	-	-	-	22 Dec 1905	11 Jun 1955	B 1950	I 1951
Jack LEWIS	GB	9	-	-	-	-	-	3	1 Nov 1936		B 1961	D 1962
Stuart LEWIS-EVANS	GB	14	-	2	2	5	-	16	20 Apr 1930	25 Oct 1958	MC 1957	MA 1958

	Nat	St	W	Pod	PP	FR	FL	Pts	Date of birth	Date of death	First start	Last start
Guy LIGIER	F	12	-	-	-	-	-	1	12 Jul 1930	23 Aug 2015	MC 1966	MEX 1967
Roberto LIPPI	I	1	-	-	-	-	-	-	17 Oct 1926	31 Oct 2011	I 1961	I 1961
Vitantonio LIUZZI	I	80	-	-	-	-	-	26	6 Aug 1980		RSM 2005	BR 2011
Lella LOMBARDI	I	12	-	-	-	-	-	0.5	26 Mar 1941	3 Mar 1992	ZA 1975	A 1976
Ernst LOOF	D	1	-	-	-	-	-	-	4 Jul 1907	3 Mar 1956	D 1953	D 1953
André LOTTERER	D	1	-	-	-	-	-	-	19 Nov 1981		B 2014	B 2014
Henri LOUVEAU	F	2	-	-	-	-	-	-	25 Jan 1910	7 Jan 1991	I 1950	CH 1951
John LOVE	RSR	9	-	1	-	-	-	6	7 Dec 1924	25 Apr 2005	ZA 1962	ZA 1972
Pete LOVELY	USA	7	-	-	-	-	-	-	11 Apr 1926	15 May 2011	USA 1960	USA 1971
Roger LOYER	F	1	-	-	-	-	-	-	5 Aug 1907	24 Mar 1988	RA 1954	RA 1954
Jean LUCAS	F	1	-	-	-	-	-	-	25 Apr 1917	27 Sep 2003	I 1955	I 1955
Brett LUNGER	USA	34	-	-	-	-	-	-	14 Nov 1945		A 1975	USA 1978
Mike MacDOWEL	GB	1	-	-	-	-	-	-	13 Sep 1932	18 Jan 2016	F 1957	F 1957
Herbert MacKAY-FRASER	USA	1	-	-	-	-	-	-	23 Jun 1922	14 Jul 1957	F 1957	F 1957
Lance MACKLIN	GB	13	-	-	-	-	-	-	2 Sep 1919	29 Aug 2002	CH 1952	GB 1955
Damien MAGEE	GB	1	-	-	-	-	-	-	17 Nov 1945		S 1975	S 1975
Tony MAGGS	ZA	25	-	3	-	-	-	26	9 Feb 1937	2 Jun 2009	GB 1961	ZA 1965
Umberto MAGLIOLI	I	10	-	2	-	-	-	3.33	5 Jun 1928	7 Feb 1999	I 1953	D 1957
Jan MAGNUSSEN	DK	25	-	-	-	-	-	1	4 Jul 1973		PAC 1995	CDN 1998
Kevin MAGNUSSEN	DK	19	-	1	-	-	-	55	5 Oct 1992		AUS 2014	ABU 2014
Guy MAIRESSE	F	3	-	-	-	-	-	-	10 Aug 1910	24 Apr 1954	I 1950	F 1951
Willy MAIRESSE	B	12	-	1	-	2	-	7	1 Oct 1928	2 Sep 1969	B 1960	D 1963
Pastor MALDONADO	YV	95	1	1	1	2	-	76	9 Mar 1985		AUS 2011	ABU 2015
Nigel MANSELL	GB	187	31	59	32	56	30	482	8 Aug 1953		A 1980	E 1995
Sergio MANTOVANI	I	7	-	-	-	-	-	4	22 May 1929	23 Feb 2001	I 1953	RA 1955
Robert MANZON	F	28	-	2	-	3	-	16	12 Apr 1917	19 Jan 2015	MC 1950	I 1956
Onofré MARIMÓN	RA	11	-	2	-	-	1	8.14	19 Dec 1923	31 Jul 1954	F 1951	GB 1954
Helmut MARKO	A	9	-	-	-	-	-	-	27 Apr 1943		A 1971	F 1972
Tarso MARQUES	BR	24	-	-	-	-	-	-	19 Jan 1976		BR 1996	B 2001
Leslie MARR	GB	2	-	-	-	-	-	-	14 Aug 1922		GB 1954	GB 1955
Tony MARSH	GB	4	-	-	-	-	-	-	20 Jul 1931	7 May 2009	D 1957	D 1961
Eugène MARTIN	F	2	-	-	-	-	-	-	24 Mar 1915	12 Oct 2006	GB 1950	CH 1950
Pierluigi MARTINI	I	118	-	-	-	1	-	18	23 Apr 1961		BR 1985	D 1995
Jochen MASS	D	105	1	8	-	-	2	71	30 Sep 1946		GB 1973	F 1982
Felipe MASSA	BR	229	11	41	16	27	15	1,071	25 Apr 1981		AUS 2002	ABU 2015
Michael MAY	CH	2	-	-	-	-	-	-	18 Aug 1934		MC 1961	F 1961
Tim MAYER	USA	1	-	-	-	-	-	-	22 Feb 1938	28 Feb 1964	USA 1962	USA 1962
François MAZET	F	1	-	-	-	-	-	-	26 Feb 1943		F 1971	F 1971
Gastón MAZZACANE	RA	21	-	-	-	-	-	-	8 May 1975		AUS 2000	RSM 2001
Kenneth McALPINE	GB	7	-	-	-	-	-	-	21 Sep 1920		GB 1952	GB 1955
Bruce McLAREN	NZ	100	4	27	-	7	3	196.5	30 Aug 1937	2 Jun 1970	D 1958	MC 1970
Allan McNISH	GB	16	-	-	-	-	-	-	29 Dec 1969		AUS 2002	USA 2002
Graham McRAE	NZ	1	-	-	-	-	-	-	5 Mar 1940		GB 1973	GB 1973
Carlos MENDITÉGUY	RA	10	-	1	-	-	-	9	10 Aug 1915	27 Apr 1973	RA 1953	RA 1960
Roberto MERHI	E	13	-	-	-	-	-	-	22 Mar 1991		MAL 2015	ABU 2015
Arturo MERZARIO	I	57	-	-	-	-	-	11	11 Mar 1943		GB 1972	USAW 1979
Roberto MIÈRES	RA	17	-	-	-	-	1	13	3 Dec 1924	26 Jan 2012	NL 1953	I 1955
François MIGAULT	F	13	-	-	-	-	-	-	4 Dec 1944	29 Jan 2012	A 1972	B 1975
John MILES	GB	12	-	-	-	-	-	2	14 Jun 1943		F 1969	A 1970
André MILHOUX	B	1	-	-	-	-	-	-	9 Dec 1928		D 1956	D 1956
Gerhard MITTER	D	5	-	-	-	-	-	3	30 Aug 1935	1 Aug 1969	NL 1963	D 1967
Stefano MODENA	I	70	-	2	-	1	-	17	12 May 1963		AUS 1987	AUS 1992
Franck MONTAGNY	F	7	-	-	-	-	-	-	5 Jan 1978		EUR 2006	F 2006
Tiago MONTEIRO	P	37	-	1	-	-	-	7	24 Jul 1976		AUS 2005	BR 2006
Andrea MONTERMINI	I	20	-	-	-	-	-	-	30 May 1964		BR 1995	F 1996
Robin MONTGOMERIE-CHARRINGTON	GB	1	-	-	-	-	-	-	23 Jun 1915	3 Apr 2007	B 1952	B 1952
Juan Pablo MONTOYA	CO	94	7	30	13	26	12	307	20 Sep 1975		AUS 2001	USA 2006
Gianni MORBIDELLI	I	67	-	1	-	-	-	8.5	13 Jan 1968		BR 1990	L 1997
Roberto MORENO	BR	42	-	1	-	-	1	15	11 Feb 1959		J 1987	AUS 1995

	Nat	St	W	Pod	PP	FR	FL	Pts	Date of birth	Date of death	First start	Last start
Dave MORGAN	GB	1	-	-	-	-	-	-	7 Aug 1944		GB 1975	GB 1975
Silvio MOSER	CH	12	-	-	-	-	-	3	24 Apr 1941	26 May 1974	GB 1967	I 1971
Stirling MOSS	GB	66	16	24	16	37	19	186.64	17 Sep 1929		CH 1951	USA 1961
Gino MUNARON	I	4	-	-	-	-	-	-	2 Apr 1928	22 Nov 2009	RA 1960	I 1960
David MURRAY	GB	4	-	-	-	-	-	-	28 Dec 1909	5 Apr 1973	GB 1950	GB 1952
Luigi MUSSO	I	24	1	7	-	6	1	44	28 Jul 1924	6 Jul 1958	I 1953	F 1958
Bernd NACKE. Pseudonym for Günther BECHEM.												
Kazuki NAKAJIMA	J	36	-	-	-	-	-	9	11 Jan 1985		BR 2007	ABU 2009
Satoru NAKAJIMA	J	74	-	-	-	-	1	16	23 Feb 1953		BR 1987	AUS 1991
Shinji NAKANO	J	33	-	-	-	-	-	2	1 Apr 1971		AUS 1997	J 1998
Alessandro NANNINI	I	76	1	9	-	-	2	65	7 Jul 1959		BR 1986	E 1990
Emanuele NASPETTI	I	6	-	-	-	-	-	-	24 Feb 1968		B 1992	P 1993
Felipe NASR	BR	18	-	-	-	-	-	27	21 Aug 1992		AUS 2015	ABU 2015
Massimo NATILI	I	1	-	-	-	-	-	-	28 Jul 1935		GB 1961	GB 1961
Brian NAYLOR	GB	7	-	-	-	-	-	-	24 Mar 1923	8 Aug 1989	D 1957	I 1961
Tiff NEEDELL	GB	1	-	-	-	-	-	-	29 Oct 1951		B 1980	B 1980
Patrick NÈVE	B	10	-	-	-	-	-	-	13 Oct 1949		B 1976	CDN 1977
John NICHOLSON	NZ	1	-	-	-	-	-	-	6 Oct 1941		GB 1975	GB 1975
Helmut NIEDERMAYR	D	1	-	-	-	-	-	-	29 Nov 1915	3 Apr 1985	D 1952	D 1952
Brausch NIEMANN	ZA	1	-	-	-	-	-	-	7 Jan 1939		ZA 1963	ZA 1963
Gunnar NILSSON	S	31	1	4	-	-	1	31	20 Nov 1948	20 Oct 1978	ZA 1976	J 1977
Hideki NODA	J	3	-	-	-	-	-	-	7 Mar 1969		EUR 1994	AUS 1994
Rodney NUCKEY	GB	1	-	-	-	-	-	-	26 Jun 1929	29 Jun 2000	D 1953	D 1953
Robert O'BRIEN	USA	1	-	-	-	-	-	-	11 Apr 1908	10 Feb 1987	B 1952	B 1952
Jackie OLIVER	GB	50	-	2	-	1	-	13	14 Aug 1942		D 1967	S 1977
Danny ONGAIS	USA	4	-	-	-	-	-	-	21 May 1942		USA 1977	BR 1978
Arthur OWEN	GB	1	-	-	-	-	-	-	23 Mar 1915	27 Apr 2002	I 1960	I 1960
Carlos PACE	BR	72	1	6	1	7	5	58	6 Oct 1944	18 Mar 1977	ZA 1972	ZA 1977
Nello PAGANI	I	1	-	-	-	-	-	-	11 Oct 1911	19 Oct 2003	CH 1950	CH 1950
Riccardo PALETTI	I	2	-	-	-	-	-	-	15 Jun 1958	13 Jun 1982	RSM 1982	CDN 1982
Torsten PALM	S	1	-	-	-	-	-	-	23 Jul 1947		S 1975	S 1975
Jonathan PALMER	GB	83	-	-	-	-	1	14	7 Nov 1956		EUR 1983	J 1989
Olivier PANIS	F	158	1	5	-	-	-	76	2 Sep 1966		BR 1994	J 2004
Giorgio PANTANO	I	14	-	-	-	-	-	-	4 Feb 1979		AUS 2004	I 2004
Max PAPIS	I	7	-	-	-	-	-	-	3 Oct 1969		GB 1995	EUR 1995
Mike PARKES	GB	6	-	2	1	2	-	14	24 Sep 1931	28 Aug 1977	F 1966	B 1967
Reg PARNELL	GB	6	-	1	-	1	-	9	2 Jul 1911	7 Jan 1964	GB 1950	GB 1954
Tim PARNELL	GB	2	-	-	-	-	-	-	25 Jun 1932		GB 1961	I 1961
Riccardo PATRESE	I	256	6	37	8	28	13	281	17 Apr 1954		MC 1977	AUS 1993
Al PEASE	CDN	2	-	-	-	-	-	-	15 Oct 1921	4 May 2014	CDN 1967	CDN 1969
Roger PENSKE	USA	2	-	-	-	-	-	-	20 Feb 1937		USA 1961	USA 1962
Cesare PERDISA	I	7	-	2	-	-	-	5	21 Oct 1932	10 May 1998	MC 1955	RA 1957
Sergio PÉREZ	MEX	93	-	5	-	-	3	266	26 Jan 1990		AUS 2011	ABU 2015
Larry PERKINS	AUS	11	-	-	-	-	-	-	18 Mar 1950		E 1976	B 1977
Xavier PERROT	CH	1	-	-	-	-	-	-	1 Feb 1932	8 Dec 2008	D 1969	D 1969
Henri PESCAROLO	F	57	-	1	-	-	1	12	25 Sep 1942		CDN 1968	USA 1976
Sandro PESENTI-ROSSI	I	3	-	-	-	-	-	-	31 Aug 1942		D 1976	I 1976
Josef PETERS	D	1	-	-	-	-	-	-	16 Sep 1914	24 Apr 2001	D 1952	D 1952
Ronnie PETERSON	S	123	10	26	14	25	9	206	14 Feb 1944	11 Sep 1978	MC 1970	I 1978
Vitaly PETROV	RUS	57	-	1	-	-	1	64	8 Sep 1984		BRN 2010	BR 2012
Charles PIC	F	39	-	-	-	-	-	-	15 Feb 1990		AUS 2012	BR 2013
François PICARD	F	1	-	-	-	-	-	-	26 Apr 1921	29 Apr 1996	MA 1958	MA 1958
Ernie PIETERSE	ZA	2	-	-	-	-	-	-	4 Jul 1938		ZA 1962	ZA 1963
Paul PIETSCH	D	3	-	-	-	-	-	-	20 Jun 1911	31 May 2012	I 1950	D 1952
André PILETTE	B	9	-	-	-	-	-	2	6 Oct 1918	27 Dec 1993	B 1951	B 1964
Teddy PILETTE	B	1	-	-	-	-	-	-	26 Jul 1942		B 1974	B 1974
Luigi PIOTTI	I	5	-	-	-	-	-	-	27 Oct 1913	19 Apr 1971	RA 1956	I 1957
David PIPER	GB	2	-	-	-	-	-	-	2 Dec 1930		GB 1959	GB 1960
Nelsinho PIQUET	BR	28	-	1	-	-	-	19	25 Jul 1985		AUS 2008	H 2009

	Nat	St	W	Pod	PP	FR	FL	Pts	Date of birth	Date of death	First start	Last start
Nelson PIQUET	BR	204	23	60	24	44	23	485.5	17 Aug 1952		D 1978	AUS 1991
Renato PIROCCHI	I	1	-	-	-	-	-	-	23 Jun 1933	29 Jul 2002	I 1961	I 1961
Didier PIRONI	F	70	3	13	4	6	5	101	26 Mar 1952	23 Aug 1987	RA 1978	F 1982
Emanuele PIRRO	I	37	-	-	-	-	-	3	12 Jan 1962		F 1989	AUS 1991
Antônio PIZZONIA	BR	20	-	-	-	-	-	8	11 Sep 1980		AUS 2003	CHN 2005
Jacques POLLET	F	5	-	-	-	-	-	-	28 Jul 1922	16 Aug 1997	F 1954	I 1955
Ben PON	NL	1	-	-	-	-	-	-	9 Dec 1936		NL 1962	NL 1962
Dennis POORE	GB	2	-	-	-	-	-	3	19 Aug 1916	12 Feb 1987	GB 1952	I 1952
Sam POSEY	USA	2	-	-	-	-	-	-	26 May 1944		USA 1971	USA 1972
Charles POZZI	F	1	-	-	-	-	-	-	27 Aug 1909	28 Feb 2001	F 1950	F 1950
Jackie PRETORIUS	ZA	3	-	-	-	-	-	-	22 Nov 1934	30 Mar 2009	ZA 1968	ZA 1973
David PROPHET	GB	2	-	-	-	-	-	-	9 Oct 1937	29 Mar 1981	ZA 1963	ZA 1965
Alain PROST	F	199	51	106	33	86	41	798.5	24 Feb 1955		RA 1980	AUS 1993
Tom PRYCE	GB	42	-	2	1	2	-	19	11 Jun 1949	5 Mar 1977	B 1974	ZA 1977
David PURLEY	GB	7	-	-	-	-	-	-	26 Jan 1945	2 Jul 1985	MC 1973	F 1977
Dieter QUESTER	A	1	-	-	-	-	-	-	30 May 1939		A 1974	A 1974
Ian RABY	GB	3	-	-	-	-	-	-	22 Sep 1921	7 Nov 1967	GB 1963	GB 1965
Bobby RAHAL	USA	2	-	-	-	-	-	-	10 Jan 1953		USA 1978	CDN 1978
Kimi RÄIKKÖNEN	FIN	231	20	80	16	34	42	1,174	17 Oct 1979		AUS 2001	ABU 2015
Pierre-Henri RAPHANEL	F	1	-	-	-	-	-	-	27 May 1961		MC 1989	MC 1989
Roland RATZENBERGER	A	1	-	-	-	-	-	-	4 Jul 1960	30 Apr 1994	PAC 1994	PAC 1994
Hector REBAQUE	MEX	41	-	-	-	-	-	13	5 Feb 1956		D 1977	LV 1981
Brian REDMAN	GB	12	-	1	-	-	-	8	9 Mar 1937		ZA 1968	MC 1974
Alan REES	GB	3	-	-	-	-	-	-	12 Jan 1938		D 1966	D 1967
Clay REGAZZONI	CH	132	5	28	5	21	15	212	5 Sep 1939	15 Dec 2006	NL 1970	USAW 1980
Carlos REUTEMANN	RA	146	12	45	6	22	6	310	12 Apr 1942		RA 1972	BR 1982
Lance REVENTLOW	USA	1	-	-	-	-	-	-	24 Feb 1936	24 Jul 1972	B 1960	B 1960
Peter REVSON	USA	30	2	8	1	5	-	61	27 Feb 1939	22 Mar 1974	B 1964	BR 1974
John RHODES	GB	1	-	-	-	-	-	-	18 Aug 1927		GB 1965	GB 1965
Alex Dias RIBEIRO	BR	10	-	-	-	-	-	-	7 Nov 1948		USA 1976	J 1977
Daniel RICCIARDO	AUS	88	3	10	-	3	4	360	1 Jul 1989		GB 2011	ABU 2015
Fritz RIESS	D	1	-	-	-	-	-	-	11 Jul 1922	15 May 1991	D 1952	D 1952
Jochen RINDT	A	60	6	13	10	18	3	109	18 Apr 1942	5 Sep 1970	A 1964	A 1970
John RISELEY-PRICHARD	GB	1	-	-	-	-	-	-	17 Jan 1924	8 Jul 1993	GB 1954	GB 1954
Richard ROBARTS	GB	3	-	-	-	-	-	-	22 Sep 1944		RA 1974	ZA 1974
Pedro RODRÍGUEZ	MEX	55	2	7	-	3	1	71	18 Jan 1940	11 Jul 1971	USA 1963	F 1971
Ricardo RODRÍGUEZ	MEX	5	-	-	-	1	-	4	14 Feb 1942	1 Nov 1962	I 1961	I 1962
Alberto RODRÍGUEZ LARRETA	RA	1	-	-	-	-	-	-	14 Jan 1934	11 Mar 1977	RA 1960	RA 1960
Franco ROL	I	5	-	-	-	-	-	-	5 Jun 1908	18 Jun 1977	MC 1950	I 1952
Tony ROLT	GB	3	-	-	-	-	-	-	16 Oct 1918	6 Feb 2008	GB 1950	GB 1955
Bertil ROOS	S	1	-	-	-	-	-	-	12 Oct 1943		S 1974	S 1974
Keke ROSBERG	FIN	114	5	17	5	10	3	159.5	6 Dec 1948		ZA 1978	AUS 1986
Nico ROSBERG	D	185	14	41	22	40	14	1,209.5	27 Jun 1985		BRN 2006	ABU 2015
Louis ROSIER	F	38	-	2	-	-	-	18	5 Nov 1905	29 Oct 1956	GB 1950	D 1956
Ricardo ROSSET	BR	27	-	-	-	-	-	-	27 Jul 1968		AUS 1996	L 1998
Alexander ROSSI	USA	5	-	-	-	-	-	-	25 Sep 1991		SIN 2015	BR 2015
Huub ROTHENGATTER	NL	25	-	-	-	-	-	-	8 Oct 1954		CDN 1984	AUS 1986
Lloyd RUBY (a)	USA	1	-	-	-	-	-	-	12 Jan 1928	23 Mar 2009	USA 1961	USA 1961
Giacomo RUSSO. See "GEKI".												
Troy RUTTMAN (a)	USA	1	-	-	-	-	-	-	11 Mar 1930	19 May 1997	F 1958	F 1958
Peter RYAN	CDN	1	-	-	-	-	-	-	10 Jun 1940	2 Jul 1962	USA 1961	USA 1961
Bob SAID	USA	1	-	-	-	-	-	-	5 May 1932	24 Mar 2002	USA 1959	USA 1959
Carlos SAINZ	E	19	-	-	-	-	-	18	1 Sep 1994		AUS 2015	ABU 2015
Luis SALA	E	26	-	-	-	-	-	1	15 May 1959		BR 1988	J 1989
Eliseo SALAZAR	RCH	24	-	-	-	-	-	3	14 Nov 1954		RSM 1981	USAW 1983
Mika SALO	FIN	110	-	2	-	-	-	33	30 Nov 1966		J 1994	J 2002
Roy SALVADORI	GB	47	-	2	-	2	-	19	12 May 1922	3 Jun 2012	GB 1952	ZA 1962
Consalvo SANESI	I	5	-	-	-	1	-	3	28 Mar 1911	28 Jul 1998	I 1950	GB 1951
Stéphane SARRAZIN	F	1	-	-	-	-	-	-	2 Nov 1974		BR 1999	BR 1999

	Nat	St	W	Pod	PP	FR	FL	Pts	Date of birth	Date of death	First start	Last start
Takuma SATO	J	90	-	1	-	1	-	44	28 Jan 1977		AUS 2002	E 2008
Ludovico SCARFIOTTI	I	10	1	1	-	2	1	17	18 Oct 1933	8 Jun 1968	NL 1963	MC 1968
Giorgio SCARLATTI	I	12	-	-	-	-	-	1	2 Oct 1921	26 Jul 1990	D 1956	F 1961
Ian SCHECKTER	ZA	18	-	-	-	-	-	-	22 Aug 1947		ZA 1974	CDN 1977
Jody SCHECKTER	ZA	112	10	33	3	13	5	255	29 Jan 1950		USA 1972	USA 1980
Harry SCHELL	USA	56	-	2	-	5	-	32	29 Jun 1921	13 May 1960	MC 1950	RA 1960
Tim SCHENKEN	AUS	34	-	1	-	-	-	7	26 Sep 1943		A 1970	USA 1974
Albert SCHERRER	CH	1	-	-	-	-	-	-	28 Feb 1908	5 Jul 1986	CH 1953	CH 1953
Mimmo SCHIATTARELLA	I	7	-	-	-	-	-	-	17 Nov 1967		EUR 1994	MC 1995
Heinz SCHILLER	CH	1	-	-	-	-	-	-	25 Jan 1930	26 Mar 2007	D 1962	D 1962
Jean-Louis SCHLESSER	F	1	-	-	-	-	-	-	12 Sep 1948		I 1988	I 1988
Jo SCHLESSER	F	3	-	-	-	-	-	-	18 May 1928	7 Jul 1968	D 1966	F 1968
Bernd SCHNEIDER	D	9	-	-	-	-	-	-	20 Jul 1964		MEX 1988	USA 1990
Rudolf SCHOELLER	CH	1	-	-	-	-	-	-	27 Apr 1902	7 Mar 1978	D 1952	D 1952
Rob SCHROEDER	USA	1	-	-	-	-	-	-	11 May 1926	3 Dec 2011	USA 1962	USA 1962
Michael SCHUMACHER	D	307	91	155	68	116	77	1,566	3 Jan 1969		B 1991	BR 2012
Ralf SCHUMACHER	D	180	6	27	6	19	8	329	30 Jun 1975		AUS 1997	BR 2007
Vern SCHUPPAN	AUS	9	-	-	-	-	-	-	19 Mar 1943		B 1974	A 1977
Adolfo SCHWELM CRUZ	RA	1	-	-	-	-	-	-	28 Jun 1923	10 Feb 2012	RA 1953	RA 1953
Archie SCOTT BROWN	GB	1	-	-	-	-	-	-	13 May 1927	19 May 1958	GB 1956	GB 1956
Piero SCOTTI	I	1	-	-	-	-	-	-	11 Nov 1909	14 Feb 1976	B 1956	B 1956
Wolfgang SEIDEL	D	10	-	-	-	-	-	-	4 Jul 1926	1 Mar 1987	D 1953	GB 1962
Ayrton SENNA	BR	161	41	80	65	87	19	614	21 Mar 1960	1 May 1994	BR 1984	RSM 1994
Bruno SENNA	BR	46	-	-	-	-	1	33	15 Oct 1983		BRN 2010	BR 2012
Dorino SERAFINI	I	1	-	1	-	-	-	3	22 Jul 1909	5 Jul 2000	I 1950	I 1950
Chico SERRA	BR	18	-	-	-	-	-	1	3 Feb 1957		USAW 1981	MC 1983
Doug SERRURIER	ZA	2	-	-	-	-	-	-	9 Dec 1920	4 Jun 2006	ZA 1962	ZA 1963
Johnny SERVOZ-GAVIN	F	12	-	1	-	1	-	9	18 Jan 1942	29 May 2006	MC 1967	E 1970
Tony SETTEMBER	USA	6	-	-	-	-	-	-	10 Jul 1926	4 May 2014	GB 1962	D 1963
Hap SHARP	USA	6	-	-	-	-	-	-	1 Jan 1928	7 May 1993	USA 1961	MEX 1964
Brian SHAWE-TAYLOR	GB	2	-	-	-	-	-	-	29 Jan 1915	1 May 1999	GB 1950	GB 1951
Carroll SHELBY	USA	8	-	-	-	-	-	-	11 Jan 1923	10 May 2012	F 1958	I 1959
Tony SHELLY	NZ	1	-	-	-	-	-	-	2 Feb 1937	4 Oct 1998	GB 1962	GB 1962
Jo SIFFERT	CH	96	2	6	2	5	4	68	7 Jul 1936	24 Oct 1971	B 1962	USA 1971
André SIMON	F	11	-	-	-	-	-	-	5 Jan 1920	11 Jul 2012	F 1951	I 1957
Moisés SOLANA	MEX	8	-	-	-	-	-	-	26 Dec 1935	27 Jul 1969	MEX 1963	MEX 1968
Alex SOLER-ROIG	E	6	-	-	-	-	-	-	29 Oct 1932		ZA 1971	E 1972
Raymond SOMMER	F	5	-	-	-	-	-	3	31 Aug 1906	10 Sep 1950	MC 1950	I 1950
Mike SPARKEN	F	1	-	-	-	-	-	-	16 Jun 1930	21 Sep 2012	GB 1955	GB 1955
Scott SPEED	USA	28	-	-	-	-	-	-	24 Jan 1983		BRN 2006	EUR 2007
Mike SPENCE	GB	36	-	1	-	-	-	27	30 Dec 1936	7 May 1968	I 1963	ZA 1968
Alan STACEY	GB	7	-	-	-	-	-	-	29 Aug 1933	19 Jun 1960	GB 1958	B 1960
Gaetano STARRABBA	I	1	-	-	-	-	-	-	3 Dec 1932		I 1961	I 1961
Will STEVENS	GB	18	-	-	-	-	-	-	28 Jun 1991		ABU 2014	ABU 2015
Ian STEWART	GB	1	-	-	-	-	-	-	15 Jul 1929		GB 1953	GB 1953
Jackie STEWART	GB	99	27	43	17	42	15	360	11 Jun 1939		ZA 1965	CDN 1973
Jimmy STEWART	GB	1	-	-	-	-	-	-	6 Mar 1931	3 Jan 2008	GB 1953	GB 1953
Siegfried STOHR	I	9	-	-	-	-	-	-	10 Oct 1952		BR 1981	NL 1981
Rolf STOMMELEN	D	54	-	1	-	-	-	14	11 Jul 1943	24 Apr 1983	D 1969	USA 1978
Philippe STREIFF	F	53	-	1	-	-	-	11	26 Jun 1955		P 1984	AUS 1988
Hans STUCK	D/A	3	-	-	-	-	-	29	27 Dec 1900	8 Feb 1978	CH 1952	I 1953
Hans-Joachim STUCK	D	74	-	2	-	1	-	-	1 Jan 1951		RA 1974	USA 1979
Danny SULLIVAN	USA	15	-	-	-	-	-	2	9 Mar 1950		BR 1983	ZA 1983
Marc SURER	CH	82	-	-	-	-	1	17	18 Sep 1951		USA 1979	B 1986
John SURTEES	GB	111	6	24	8	21	10	180	11 Feb 1934		MC 1960	I 1972
Adrian SUTIL	D	128	-	-	-	1	1	124	11 Jan 1983		AUS 2007	ABU 2014
Aguri SUZUKI	J	64	-	1	-	-	-	8	8 Sep 1960		J 1988	PAC 1995
Toshio SUZUKI	J	2	-	-	-	-	-	-	10 Mar 1955		J 1993	AUS 1993
Jacques SWATERS	B	7	-	-	-	-	-	-	30 Oct 1926	10 Dec 2010	D 1951	E 1954

	Nat	St	W	Pod	PP	FR	FL	Pts	Date of birth	Date of death	First start	Last start
Tora TAKAGI	J	32	-	-	-	-	-	-	12 Feb 1974		AUS 1998	J 1999
Noritake TAKAHARA	J	2	-	-	-	-	-	-	6 Jun 1951		J 1976	J 1977
Kunimitsu TAKAHASHI	J	1	-	-	-	-	-	-	29 Jan 1940		J 1977	J 1977
Patrick TAMBAY	F	114	2	11	5	9	2	103	25 Jun 1949		GB 1977	AUS 1986
Gabriele TARQUINI	I	38	-	-	-	-	-	1	2 Mar 1962		RSM 1987	EUR 1995
Piero TARUFFI	I	18	1	5	-	4	1	41	12 Oct 1906	12 Jan 1988	I 1950	I 1956
Henry TAYLOR	GB	8	-	-	-	-	-	3	16 Dec 1932	24 Oct 2013	GB 1959	I 1961
John TAYLOR	GB	5	-	-	-	-	-	1	23 Mar 1933	8 Sep 1966	GB 1964	D 1966
Mike TAYLOR	GB	1	-	-	-	-	-	-	24 Apr 1934		GB 1959	GB 1959
Trevor TAYLOR	GB	27	-	1	-	1	-	8	26 Dec 1936	27 Sep 2010	NL 1961	GB 1966
Mike THACKWELL	NZ	2	-	-	-	-	-	-	30 Mar 1961		CDN 1984	CDN 1984
Alfonso THIELE	I/USA	1	-	-	-	-	-	-	5 Apr 1920	15 Jul 1986	I 1960	I 1960
Eric THOMPSON	GB	1	-	-	-	-	-	2	4 Nov 1919	22 Aug 2015	GB 1952	GB 1952
Leslie THORNE	GB	1	-	-	-	-	-	-	23 Jun 1916	13 Jul 1993	GB 1954	GB 1954
Sam TINGLE	RSR	5	-	-	-	-	-	-	24 Aug 1921	19 Dec 2008	ZA 1963	ZA 1969
Desmond TITTERINGTON	GB	1	-	-	-	-	-	72.33	1 May 1928	13 Apr 2002	GB 1956	GB 1956
Maurice TRINTIGNANT (c)	F	81	2	9	-	2	1	-	30 Oct 1917	13 Feb 2005	MC 1950	I 1964
Jarno TRULLI	I	252	1	11	4	15	1	246.5	13 Jul 1974		AUS 1997	BR 2011
Esteban TUERO	RA	16	-	-	-	-	-	-	22 Apr 1978		AUS 1998	J 1998
Guy TUNMER	ZA	1	-	-	-	-	-	-	1 Dec 1948	22 Jun 1999	ZA 1975	ZA 1975
Toni ULMEN	D	2	-	-	-	-	-	-	25 Jan 1906	4 Nov 1976	CH 1952	D 1952
Bobby UNSER	USA	1	-	-	-	-	-	-	20 Feb 1934		USA 1968	USA 1968
Alberto URÍA	ROU	2	-	-	-	-	-	-	11 Jul 1924	4 Dec 1988	RA 1955	RA 1956
Nino VACCARELLA	I	4	-	-	-	-	-	-	4 Mar 1933		I 1961	I 1965
Eric van de POELE	B	5	-	-	-	-	-	-	30 Sep 1961		RSM 1991	I 1992
Giedo van der GARDE	NL	19	-	-	-	-	-	-	25 Apr 1985		AUS 2013	BR 2013
Dries van der LOF	NL	1	-	-	-	-	-	-	23 Aug 1919	24 May 1990	NL 1952	NL 1952
Gijs van LENNEP	NL	8	-	-	-	-	-	2	16 Mar 1942		NL 1971	D 1975
Basil van ROOYEN	ZA	2	-	-	-	-	-	-	19 Apr 1939		ZA 1968	ZA 1969
Jean-Eric VERGNE	F	58	-	-	-	-	-	51	25 Apr 1990		AUS 2012	ABU 2014
Jos VERSTAPPEN	NL	107	-	2	-	-	-	17	4 Mar 1972		BR 1994	J 2003
Max VERSTAPPEN	NL	19	-	-	-	-	-	49	30 Sep 1997		AUS 2015	ABU 2015
Sebastian VETTEL	D	158	42	79	46	70	25	1,896	3 Jul 1987		USA 2007	ABU 2015
Gilles VILLENEUVE	CDN	67	6	13	2	8	8	107	18 Jan 1950	8 May 1982	GB 1977	RSM 1982
Jacques VILLENEUVE	CDN	163	11	23	13	23	9	235	9 Apr 1971		AUS 1996	D 2006
Luigi VILLORESI	I	31	-	8	-	5	1	49	16 May 1909	24 Aug 1997	MC 1950	I 1956
Ottorino VOLONTERIO	CH	3	-	-	-	-	-	-	7 Dec 1917	10 Mar 2003	E 1954	I 1957
Rikky von OPEL	FL	10	-	-	-	-	-	-	14 Oct 1947		F 1973	NL 1974
Wolfgang von TRIPS	D	27	2	6	1	4	-	56	4 May 1928	10 Sep 1961	RA 1957	I 1961
Jo VONLANTHEN	CH	1	-	-	-	-	-	-	31 May 1942		A 1975	A 1975
Fred WACKER	USA	3	-	-	-	-	-	-	10 Jul 1918	16 Jun 1998	B 1953	I 1954
Dave WALKER	AUS	11	-	-	-	-	-	-	10 Jun 1941		NL 1971	USA 1972
Peter WALKER	GB	4	-	-	-	-	-	-	7 Oct 1912	1 Mar 1984	GB 1950	GB 1955
Heini WALTER	CH	1	-	-	-	-	-	-	28 Jul 1927	12 May 2009	D 1962	D 1962
Rodger WARD (a)	USA	2	-	-	-	-	-	-	10 Jan 1921	5 Jul 2004	USA 1959	USA 1963
Derek WARWICK	GB	146	-	4	-	-	2	71	27 Aug 1954		LV 1981	AUS 1993
John WATSON	GB	152	5	20	2	11	5	169	4 May 1946		GB 1973	EUR 1985
Mark WEBBER	AUS	215	9	42	13	37	19	1,047.5	27 Aug 1976		AUS 2002	BR 2013
Karl WENDLINGER	A	41	-	-	-	-	-	14	20 Dec 1968		J 1991	AUS 1995
Peter WESTBURY	GB	1	-	-	-	-	-	-	26 May 1938	7 Dec 2015	D 1969	D 1969
Ken WHARTON	GB	15	-	-	-	-	-	3	21 Mar 1916	12 Jan 1957	CH 1952	I 1955
Graham WHITEHEAD	GB	1	-	-	-	-	-	-	15 Apr 1922	15 Jan 1981	GB 1952	GB 1952
Peter WHITEHEAD	GB	10	-	1	-	-	-	4	12 Nov 1914	20 Sep 1958	F 1950	GB 1954
Bill WHITEHOUSE	GB	1	-	-	-	-	-	-	1 Apr 1909	14 Jul 1957	GB 1954	GB 1954
Robin WIDDOWS	GB	1	-	-	-	-	-	-	27 May 1942		GB 1968	GB 1968
Eppie WIETZES	CDN	2	-	-	-	-	-	-	28 May 1938		CDN 1967	CDN 1974
Mike WILDS	GB	3	-	-	-	-	-	-	7 Jan 1946		USA 1974	BR 1975
Jonathan WILLIAMS	GB	1	-	-	-	-	-	-	26 Oct 1942	31 Aug 2014	MEX 1967	MEX 1967
Roger WILLIAMSON	GB	2	-	-	-	-	-	-	4 Feb 1949	29 Jul 1973	GB 1973	NL 1973

	Nat	St	W	Pod	PP	FR	FL	Pts	Date of birth	Date of death	First start	Last start
Justin WILSON	GB	16	-	-	-	-	-	1	31 Jul 1978	24 Aug 2015	AUS 2003	J 2003
Vic WILSON	GB	1	-	-	-	-	-	-	14 Apr 1931	14 Jan 2001	I 1960	I 1960
Manfred WINKELHOCK	D	47	-	-	-	-	-	2	6 Oct 1951	12 Aug 1985	ZA 1982	D 1985
Markus WINKELHOCK	D	1	-	-	-	-	-	-	13 Jun 1980		EUR 2007	EUR 2007
Reine WISELL	S	22	-	1	-	-	-	13	30 Sep 1941		USA 1970	S 1974
Roelof WUNDERINK	NL	3	-	-	-	-	-	-	12 Dec 1948		E 1975	USA 1975
Alexander WURZ	A	69	-	3	-	-	1	45	15 Feb 1974		CDN 1997	CHN 2007
Sakon YAMAMOTO	J	21	-	-	-	-	-	-	9 Jul 1982		D 2006	ROK 2010
Alex YOONG	MAL	14	-	-	-	-	-	-	20 Jul 1976		I 2001	J 2002
Alessandro ZANARDI	I	41	-	-	-	-	-	1	23 Oct 1966		E 1991	J 1999
Ricardo ZONTA	BR	36	-	-	-	-	-	3	23 Mar 1976		AUS 1999	BR 2004
Renzo ZORZI	I	7	-	-	-	-	-	1	12 Dec 1946	15 May 2015	I 1975	E 1977
Ricardo ZUNINO	RA	10	-	-	-	-	-	-	13 Apr 1949		CDN 1979	RA 1981

(a) One of four who also started Indianapolis 500 race(s) in the world championship, so also has an entry in section 126.
(b) Bechem started the first of his races (Germany 1952) under the pseudonym of Bernd Nacke to keep his racing a secret from his family who were unhappy about the activity.
(c) At Italy 1951, it appears likely that Jean Behra took over Maurice Trintignant's car, so Behra has been credited here with the race start. The situation was disguised with Behra wearing Trintignant's helmet (see section 558).

As is now common practice, drivers retiring on the formation lap are not counted as having started.
Where races have been subject to a restart, those retiring during an initial race are included as having started.
For non-starters see section 559 and for drivers who only ever entered practice, see section 561.

Key to column headings:

Nat	- Nationality
St	- Starts
W	- Wins
Pod	- Podium positions
PP	- Pole positions
FR	- Front row positions
FL	- Fastest laps
Pts	- Points

Key to nationalities and races:

A	- Austria	IRL	- Ireland
ABU	- Abu Dhabi	J	- Japan
AUS	- Australia	L	- Luxembourg
B	- Belgium	LV	- Caesars Palace, Las Vegas
BR	- Brazil	MA	- Morocco
BRN	- Bahrain	MAL	- Malaysia
CDN	- Canada	MC	- Monaco
CH	- Switzerland	MEX	- Mexico
CHN	- China	NL	- Netherlands
CO	- Colombia	NZ	- New Zealand
CZ	- Czech Republic	P	- Portugal
D	- Germany	PAC	- Pacific
DAL	- Dallas	PL	- Poland
DDR	- East Germany	RA	- Argentina
DET	- Detroit	RCH	- Chile
DK	- Denmark	ROK	- Korea (South)
E	- Spain	ROU	- Uruguay
EUR	- Europe	RSM	- San Marino
F	- France	RSR	- Southern Rhodesia (now Zimbabwe)
FIN	- Finland	RUS	- Russia
FL	- Liechtenstein	S	- Sweden
GB	- Great Britain	SIN	- Singapore
H	- Hungary	T	- Thailand
HK	- Hong Kong	USA	- United States
I	- Italy	USAW	- United States West
IL	- Israel	YV	- Venezuela
IND	- India	ZA	- South Africa

	Nat	St	W	Pod	PP	FR	FL	Pts	Date of birth	Date of death	First - last start
Walt ADER	USA	1	-	-	-	-	-	-	15 Dec 1913	25 Nov 1982	1950
Freddie AGABASHIAN	USA	8	-	-	1	3	-	1.5	21 Aug 1913	13 Oct 1989	1950 - 57
George AMICK	USA	1	-	1	-	-	-	6	24 Oct 1924	4 Apr 1959	1958
Red AMICK	USA	2	-	-	-	-	-	-	19 Jan 1929	16 May 1995	1959 - 60
Keith ANDREWS	USA	2	-	-	-	-	-	-	15 Jun 1920	15 May 1957	1955 - 56
Frank ARMI	USA	1	-	-	-	-	-	-	12 Oct 1918	28 Nov 1992	1954
Chuck ARNOLD	USA	1	-	-	-	-	-	-	30 May 1926	4 Sep 1997	1959
Alberto ASCARI	I	1	-	-	-	-	-	-	13 Jul 1918	26 May 1955	1952
Manny AYULO	USA	4	-	1	-	-	-	2	20 Oct 1921	16 May 1955	1951 - 54
Bobby BALL	USA	2	-	-	-	-	-	2	26 Aug 1925	27 Feb 1954	1951 - 52
Henry BANKS	USA	3	-	-	-	-	-	-	14 Jun 1913	18 Dec 1994	1950 - 52
Tony BETTENHAUSEN	USA	11	-	1	-	1	1	11	12 Sep 1916	12 May 1961	1950 - 60
Art BISCH	USA	1	-	-	-	-	-	-	10 Nov 1926	4 Jul 1958	1958
Johnny BOYD	USA	6	-	1	-	-	-	4	19 Aug 1926	27 Oct 2003	1955 - 60
Don BRANSON	USA	2	-	-	-	-	-	3	2 Jun 1920	12 Nov 1966	1959 - 60
Walt BROWN	USA	2	-	-	-	-	-	-	30 Dec 1911	29 Jul 1951	1950 - 51
Jimmy BRYAN	USA	9	1	3	-	1	-	18	28 Jan 1926	19 Jun 1960	1952 - 60
Bill CANTRELL	USA	1	-	-	-	-	-	-	31 Jan 1908	22 Jan 1996	1950
Duane CARTER	USA	8	-	1	-	-	-	6.5	5 May 1913	8 Mar 1993	1950 - 60
Bill CHEESBOURG	USA	3	-	-	-	-	-	-	12 Jun 1927	6 Nov 1995	1957 - 59
Joie CHITWOOD	USA	1	-	-	-	-	-	1	14 Apr 1912	3 Jan 1988	1950
Bob CHRISTIE	USA	5	-	-	-	-	-	-	4 Apr 1924	1 Jun 2009	1956 - 60
George CONNOR	USA	3	-	-	-	-	-	-	16 Aug 1908	29 Mar 2001	1950 - 52
Ray CRAWFORD	USA	3	-	-	-	-	-	-	26 Oct 1915	1 Feb 1996	1955 - 59
Larry CROCKETT	USA	1	-	-	-	-	-	-	23 Oct 1926	20 Mar 1955	1954
Art CROSS	USA	4	-	1	-	-	-	8	24 Jan 1918	15 Apr 2005	1952 - 55
Jimmy DAVIES	USA	5	-	1	-	-	-	4	18 Aug 1929	11 Jun 1966	1950 - 55
Jimmy DAYWALT	USA	6	-	-	-	1	-	-	28 Aug 1924	4 Apr 1966	1953 - 59
Duke DINSMORE	USA	4	-	-	-	-	-	-	10 Apr 1913	12 Oct 1985	1950 - 56
Len DUNCAN	USA	1	-	-	-	-	-	-	25 Jul 1911	1 Aug 1998	1954
Don EDMUNDS	USA	1	-	-	-	-	-	-	23 Sep 1930		1957
Ed ELISIAN	USA	5	-	-	-	1	-	-	9 Dec 1926	30 Aug 1959	1954 - 58
Walt FAULKNER	USA	5	-	-	1	1	-	1	16 Feb 1920	22 Apr 1956	1950 - 55
Pat FLAHERTY	USA	6	1	1	1	1	-	8	6 Jan 1926	9 Apr 2002	1950 - 59
Myron FOHR	USA	1	-	-	-	-	-	-	17 Jun 1912	14 Jan 1994	1950
George FONDER	USA	2	-	-	-	-	-	-	22 Jun 1917	14 Jun 1958	1952 - 54
Carl FORBERG	USA	1	-	-	-	-	-	-	4 Mar 1911	17 Jan 2000	1951
Gene FORCE	USA	2	-	-	-	-	-	-	15 Jun 1916	21 Aug 1983	1951 - 60
A J FOYT	USA	3	-	-	-	-	-	-	16 Jan 1935		1958 - 60
Don FREELAND	USA	8	-	1	-	-	-	4	25 Mar 1925	2 Nov 2007	1953 - 60
Billy GARRETT	USA	2	-	-	-	-	-	-	24 Apr 1933	15 Feb 1999	1956 - 58
Elmer GEORGE	USA	1	-	-	-	-	-	-	5 Jul 1928	30 May 1976	1957
Paul GOLDSMITH	USA	3	-	1	-	-	-	6	2 Oct 1925		1958 - 60
Cecil GREEN	USA	2	-	-	-	-	-	3	30 Sep 1919	29 Jul 1951	1950 - 51
Cliff GRIFFITH	USA	3	-	-	-	-	-	-	6 Feb 1916	23 Jan 1996	1951 - 56
Bobby GRIM	USA	2	-	-	-	-	-	-	4 Sep 1924	14 Jun 1995	1959 - 60
Sam HANKS	USA	8	1	4	-	-	-	20	13 Jul 1914	27 Jun 1994	1950 - 57
Gene HARTLEY	USA	8	-	-	-	-	-	-	28 Jan 1926	13 Mar 1994	1950 - 60
Mack HELLINGS	USA	2	-	-	-	-	-	-	14 Sep 1915	11 Nov 1951	1950 - 51
Al HERMAN	USA	5	-	-	-	-	-	-	15 Mar 1927	18 Jun 1960	1955 - 60
Bill HOLLAND	USA	2	-	1	-	-	-	6	18 Dec 1907	20 May 1984	1950 - 53
Jackie HOLMES	USA	2	-	-	-	-	-	-	4 Sep 1920	1 Mar 1995	1950 - 53
Bill HOMEIER	USA	3	-	-	-	-	-	1	31 Aug 1918	2 May 2001	1954 - 60
Jerry HOYT	USA	4	-	-	1	1	-	-	29 Jan 1929	10 Jul 1955	1950 - 55
Jim HURTUBISE	USA	1	-	-	-	-	-	-	5 Dec 1932	6 Jan 1989	1960
Jimmy JACKSON	USA	2	-	-	-	-	-	-	25 Jul 1910	25 Nov 1984	1950 - 54
Joe JAMES	USA	2	-	-	-	-	-	-	23 May 1925	5 Nov 1952	1951 - 52

	Nat	St	W	Pod	PP	FR	FL	Pts	Date of birth	Date of death	First - last start
Eddie JOHNSON	USA	9	-	-	-	-	-	1	10 Feb 1919	30 Jun 1974	1952 - 60
Al KELLER	USA	5	-	-	-	-	-	-	11 Apr 1920	19 Nov 1961	1955 - 60
Danny KLADIS	USA	1	-	-	-	-	-	-	10 Feb 1917	26 Apr 2009	1954
Jud LARSON	USA	2	-	-	-	-	-	-	21 Jan 1923	11 Jun 1966	1958 - 59
Bayliss LEVRETT	USA	1	-	-	-	-	-	-	14 Feb 1913	13 Mar 2002	1950
Andy LINDEN	USA	7	-	-	-	1	-	5	5 Apr 1922	10 Feb 1987	1951 - 57
Bill MACKEY	USA	1	-	-	-	-	-	-	15 Dec 1927	29 Jul 1951	1951
Mike MAGILL	USA	3	-	-	-	-	-	-	8 Feb 1920	31 Aug 2006	1957 - 59
Johnny MANTZ	USA	1	-	-	-	-	-	-	18 Sep 1918	25 Oct 1972	1953
Ernie McCOY	USA	2	-	-	-	-	-	-	19 Feb 1921	4 Feb 2001	1953 - 54
Johnny McDOWELL	USA	3	-	-	-	-	-	-	29 Jan 1915	8 Jun 1952	1950 - 52
Jack McGRATH	USA	6	-	2	1	5	1	9	8 Oct 1919	6 Nov 1955	1950 - 55
Jim McWITHEY	USA	2	-	-	-	-	-	-	4 Jul 1927	1 Feb 2009	1959 - 60
Chet MILLER	USA	2	-	-	-	-	-	-	19 Jul 1902	15 May 1953	1951 - 52
Duke NALON	USA	3	-	-	1	1	-	-	2 Mar 1913	26 Feb 2001	1951 - 53
Mike NAZARUK	USA	3	-	1	-	-	-	8	2 Oct 1921	1 May 1955	1951 - 54
Cal NIDAY	USA	3	-	-	-	-	-	-	29 Apr 1916	14 Feb 1988	1953 - 55
Pat O'CONNOR	USA	5	-	-	1	2	-	-	9 Oct 1928	30 May 1958	1954 - 58
Johnnie PARSONS	USA	9	1	1	-	-	1	12	4 Jul 1918	8 Sep 1984	1950 - 58
Dick RATHMANN	USA	5	-	-	1	1	-	2	6 Jan 1926	1 Feb 2000	1950 - 60
Jim RATHMANN	USA	10	1	4	-	3	2	29	16 Jul 1928	23 Nov 2011	1950 - 60
Jimmy REECE	USA	6	-	-	-	1	-	-	17 Nov 1929	22 Sep 1958	1952 - 58
Jim RIGSBY	USA	1	-	-	-	-	-	-	6 Jun 1923	31 Aug 1952	1952
Mauri ROSE	USA	2	-	1	-	1	-	4	26 May 1906	1 Jan 1981	1950 - 51
Lloyd RUBY	USA	1	-	-	-	-	-	-	12 Jan 1928	23 Mar 2009	1960
Eddie RUSSO	USA	4	-	-	-	-	-	-	19 Nov 1925	14 Oct 2012	1955 - 60
Paul RUSSO	USA	8	-	1	-	-	1	8.5	10 Apr 1914	13 Feb 1976	1950 - 59
Troy RUTTMAN	USA	7	1	1	-	1	-	9.5	11 Mar 1930	19 May 1997	1950 - 60
Eddie SACHS	USA	4	-	-	1	3	-	-	28 May 1927	30 May 1964	1957 - 60
Carl SCARBOROUGH	USA	2	-	-	-	-	-	-	3 Jul 1914	30 May 1953	1951 - 53
Bill SCHINDLER	USA	3	-	-	-	-	-	-	6 Mar 1909	20 Sep 1952	1950 - 52
Bob SCOTT	USA	3	-	-	-	-	-	-	4 Oct 1928	5 Jul 1954	1952 - 54
Chuck STEVENSON	USA	5	-	-	-	-	-	-	15 Oct 1919	21 Aug 1995	1951 - 60
Len SUTTON	USA	3	-	-	-	-	-	-	9 Aug 1925	4 Dec 2006	1958 - 60
Bob SWEIKERT	USA	5	1	1	-	-	-	8	20 May 1926	17 Jun 1956	1952 - 56
Marshall TEAGUE	USA	3	-	-	-	-	-	-	22 May 1921	11 Feb 1959	1953 - 57
Shorty TEMPLEMAN	USA	3	-	-	-	-	-	-	12 Aug 1919	24 Aug 1962	1955 - 60
Johnny THOMSON	USA	8	-	1	1	1	1	10	9 Apr 1922	24 Sep 1960	1953 - 60
Bud TINGELSTAD	USA	1	-	-	-	-	-	-	4 Apr 1928	30 Jul 1981	1960
Johnnie TOLAN	USA	3	-	-	-	-	-	-	22 Oct 1918	2 Jun 1986	1956 - 58
Jack TURNER	USA	4	-	-	-	-	-	-	12 Feb 1920	12 Sep 2004	1956 - 59
Jerry UNSER	USA	1	-	-	-	-	-	-	15 Nov 1932	17 May 1959	1958
Bob VEITH	USA	5	-	-	-	-	-	-	1 Nov 1924	29 Mar 2006	1956 - 60
Bill VUKOVICH	USA	5	2	2	1	1	3	19	13 Dec 1918	30 May 1955	1951 - 55
Lee WALLARD	USA	2	1	1	-	1	1	9	8 Sep 1911	28 Nov 1963	1950 - 51
Rodger WARD	USA	10	1	2	-	1	-	14	10 Jan 1921	5 Jul 2004	1951 - 60
Spider WEBB	USA	4	-	-	-	-	-	-	8 Oct 1910	29 Jan 1990	1950 - 54
Wayne WEILER	USA	1	-	-	-	-	-	-	9 Dec 1934	13 Oct 2005	1960
Chuck WEYANT	USA	4	-	-	-	-	-	-	3 Apr 1923		1955 - 57
Dempsey WILSON	USA	2	-	-	-	-	-	-	11 Mar 1927	23 Apr 1971	1958 - 60

Fastest lap at the Indianapolis 500 relates to the fastest leading lap of the race.

127. Races started *(Most)*

Rubens Barrichello	323	Jacques Laffite	176	Adrian Sutil	128
Michael Schumacher	307	Niki Lauda	171	Jack Brabham	126
Jenson Button	284	Lewis Hamilton	167	Ronnie Peterson	123
Riccardo Patrese	256	Thierry Boutsen	163	Pierluigi Martini	118
Fernando Alonso	253	Jacques Villeneuve	163	Jacky Ickx	116
Jarno Trulli	252	Mika Häkkinen	161	Alan Jones	116
David Coulthard	246	Johnny Herbert	161	Damon Hill	115
Kimi Räikkönen	231	Ayrton Senna	161	Keke Rosberg	114
Giancarlo Fisichella	229	Martin Brundle	158	Patrick Tambay	114
Felipe Massa	229	Olivier Panis	158	Denny Hulme	112
Mark Webber	215	Sebastian Vettel	158	Jody Scheckter	112
Gerhard Berger	210	Heinz-Harald Frentzen	157	Heikki Kovalainen	111
Andrea De Cesaris	208	John Watson	152	John Surtees	111
Nelson Piquet	204	René Arnoux	149	Mika Salo	110
Jean Alesi	201	Eddie Irvine	146	Philippe Alliot	109
Alain Prost	199	Carlos Reutemann	146	Elio De Angelis	108
Michele Alboreto	194	Derek Warwick	146	Jos Verstappen	107
Nigel Mansell	187	Emerson Fittipaldi	144	Pedro de la Rosa	105
Nico Rosberg	185	Jean-Pierre Jarier	134	Jochen Mass	105
Nick Heidfeld	183	Eddie Cheever	132	Jo Bonnier	104
Ralf Schumacher	180	Clay Regazzoni	132	Bruce McLaren	100
Graham Hill	176	Mario Andretti	128		

128. Laps completed

Most

	km	miles			km	miles
Michael Schumacher	16,825	81,188	50,878	Mark Webber	10,976	54,493	33,860
Rubens Barrichello	16,631	80,585	50,073	Alain Prost	10,540	48,978	30,434
Jenson Button	15,182	75,513	46,922	Nico Rosberg	9,957	49,982	31,057
Fernando Alonso	13,838	68,967	42,854	Nelson Piquet	9,871	45,566	28,313
Felipe Massa	12,672	63,150	39,240	Gerhard Berger	9,793	45,647	28,364
David Coulthard	12,394	59,727	37,113	Nick Heidfeld	9,701	47,146	29,295
Jarno Trulli	12,368	60,383	37,520	Jean Alesi	9,645	45,295	28,145
Kimi Räikkönen	12,106	59,711	37,103	Lewis Hamilton	9,318	46,802	29,081
Giancarlo Fisichella	11,509	55,678	34,597	Ralf Schumacher	9,166	44,279	27,514
Riccardo Patrese	11,346	52,129	32,391	Graham Hill	8,791	44,232	27,484

Fewest

0 laps

Marco Apicella (Jordan)	Italy 1993
Miguel Angel Guerra (Osella)	San Marino 1981
Ernst Loof (Veritas)	Germany 1953
Graham McRae (Iso-Marlboro)	Britain 1973
Massimo Natili (Cooper)	Britain 1961
Arthur Owen (Cooper)	Italy 1960

1 laps

Erwin Bauer (Veritas)	Germany 1953
Leslie Johnson (ERA)	Britain 1950
Roberto Lippi (de Tomaso)	Italy 1961
André Lotterer (Caterham)	Belgium 2014
Josef Peters (Veritas)	Germany 1952
Lance Reventlow (Scarab)	Belgium 1960
Bob Said (Connaught)	United States 1959

2 laps

Bill Aston (Aston-Butterworth)	Germany 1952
Ben Pon (Porsche)	Netherlands 1962
Bertil Roos (Shadow)	Sweden 1974
André Lotterer (Caterham)	Belgium 2014
Josef Peters (Veritas)	Germany 1952
Lance Reventlow (Scarab)	Belgium 1960
Bob Said (Connaught)	United States 1959

Günther Bechem (AFM), whilst he only completed 2 laps in his career (in Germany 1953) with that name, using his pseudonym Bernd Nacke, he completed a further 5 laps in Germany 1952 (BMW).

3 laps

Kurt Adolff (Ferrari)	Germany 1953
Theo Fitzau (AFM)	Germany 1953
Rudolf Schoeller (Ferrari)	Germany 1952

Excludes Indianapolis 500.

129. Laps completed in a season *(Most)*

Kimi Räikkönen	1,191	2012
Felipe Massa	1,178	2012
Daniel Ricciardo	1,175	2012
Sebastian Vettel	1,162	2012
Heikki Kovalainen	1,153	2012
Paul Di Resta	1,137	2012
Mark Webber	1,131	2012
Sebastian Vettel	1,127	2015
Jenson Button	1,126	2013
Tiago Monteiro	1,125	2005
Sergio Pérez	1,123	2015
Rubens Barrichello	1,122	2005
Fernando Alonso	1,120	2010
Lewis Hamilton	1,120	2015
Sebastian Vettel	1,120	2013
Jenson Button	1,120	2014
Sergio Pérez	1,116	2013
Nick Heidfeld	1,112	2008
Kevin Magnussen	1,111	2014
Valtteri Bottas	1,110	2014

130. Distance completed in a season *(Most)*

	km	miles	
Kimi Räikkönen	6,081	3,779	2012
Daniel Ricciardo	6,023	3,743	2012
Felipe Massa	6,011	3,735	2012
Sebastian Vettel	5,920	3,679	2012
Heikki Kovalainen	5,881	3,654	2012
Paul Di Resta	5,767	3,583	2012
Jenson Button	5,766	3,583	2013
Mark Webber	5,748	3,572	2012
Fernando Alonso	5,733	3,562	2010
Sebastian Vettel	5,727	3,559	2013
Sergio Pérez	5,722	3,555	2013
Sebastian Vettel	5,681	3,530	2015
Sergio Pérez	5,657	3,515	2015
Paul Di Resta	5,654	3,513	2011
Jenson Button	5,647	3,509	2014
Max Chilton	5,647	3,509	2013
Fernando Alonso	5,641	3,505	2011
Valtteri Bottas	5,636	3,502	2014
Lewis Hamilton	5,631	3,499	2015
Jenson Button	5,613	3,488	2012

131. Consecutive races started *(Most)*
(ie started every race in the period)

Riccardo Patrese	187	Belgium 1982	- Australia 1993	
Nico Rosberg	185	Bahrain 2006	- Abu Dhabi 2015	
Fernando Alonso	176	France 2005	- Abu Dhabi 2014	
Jenson Button	179	France 2005	- China 2015	
David Coulthard	175	Brazil 1995	- Canada 2005	
Rubens Barrichello	167	Germany 2002	- Brazil 2011	
Lewis Hamilton	167	Australia 2007	- Abu Dhabi 2015	
Alain Prost	160	United States West 1981	- Brazil 1991	
Sebastian Vettel	157	Hungary 2007	- Abu Dhabi 2015	
Mark Webber	157	France 2005	- Brazil 2013	
Ayrton Senna	149	Europe 1984	- San Marino 1994	
Thierry Boutsen	138	Canada 1984	- Australia 1992	
Rubens Barrichello	133	Monaco 1994	- San Marino 2002	
Gerhard Berger	132	Mexico 1989	- Spain 1997	
Jean Alesi	129	Monaco 1994	- Japan 2001	
Michael Schumacher	124	Malaysia 1999	- Brazil 2006	
Heinz-Harald Frentzen	118	Spain 1994	- Monaco 2001	
Michele Alboreto	117	Austria 1981	- Brazil 1989	
Jacques Villeneuve	117	Australia 1996	- Australia 2003	
Johnny Herbert	116	Japan 1991	- Japan 1998	

132. Seasons of starting races *(Most)*

Rubens Barrichello	19	1993 - 2011
Michael Schumacher	19	1991 - 2012
Graham Hill	18	1958 - 75
Riccardo Patrese	17	1977 - 93
Jo Bonnier	16	1956 - 71
Jack Brabham	16	1955 - 70
Jenson Button	16	2000 - 15
David Coulthard	15	1994 - 2008
Andrea De Cesaris	15	1980 - 94
Nigel Mansell	15	1980 - 95
Maurice Trintignant	15	1950 - 64
Jarno Trulli	15	1997 - 2011

133. Consecutive seasons of starting races *(Most)*

Rubens Barrichello	19	1993 - 2011
Graham Hill	18	1958 - 75
Riccardo Patrese	17	1977 - 93
Jo Bonnier	16	1956 - 71
Jack Brabham	16	1955 - 70
Jenson Button	16	2000 - 15
Michael Schumacher	16	1991 - 2006
David Coulthard	15	1994 - 2008
Andrea De Cesaris	15	1980 - 94
Maurice Trintignant	15	1950 - 64
Jarno Trulli	15	1997 - 2011

134. Races started by nationality

	drivers	races	starts		
Great Britain	146	919	3,778	Britain 1950	- Abu Dhabi 2015
Italy	84	782	2,934	Britain 1950	- Brazil 2011
France	70	800	2,563	Britain 1950	- Abu Dhabi 2015
United States	48	448	792	Monaco 1950	- Brazil 2015
Germany	46	718	1,945	Italy 1950	- Abu Dhabi 2015
Brazil	30	751	1,779	Italy 1951	- Abu Dhabi 2015
Switzerland	23	388	445	Britain 1950	- Brazil 2011
Argentina	22	248	337	Britain 1950	- San Marino 2001
Belgium	20	377	420	Britain 1950	- Italy 2012
Japan	17	401	553	Japan 1976	- Abu Dhabi 2014
South Africa	17	146	189	Britain 1961	- United States 1980
Netherlands	15	283	296	Netherlands 1952	- Abu Dhabi 2015
Australia	14	560	650	Belgium 1952	- Abu Dhabi 2015
Austria	14	554	664	Austria 1964	- Abu Dhabi 2010
Spain	13	368	542	Italy 1951	- Abu Dhabi 2015
Canada	11	258	261	United States 1961	- Germany 2006
Sweden	10	348	407	Italy 1956	- Abu Dhabi 2015
Finland	8	554	846	Sweden 1974	- Abu Dhabi 2015
New Zealand	8	186	348	Germany 1958	- Canada 1984
Mexico	6	196	240	Italy 1961	- Abu Dhabi 2015
Denmark	4	51	51	South Africa 1974	- Abu Dhabi 2014
Ireland	3	51	53	Britain 1950	- Caesars Palace 1982
Portugal	3	73	73	Portugal 1959	- Brazil 2006
Southern Rhodesia	3	9	15	South Africa 1962	- South Africa 1972
Uruguay	3	5	6	Britain 1952	- Argentina 1956
Colombia	2	115	115	United States West 1982	- United States 2006
India	2	57	57	Australia 2005	- Brazil 2012
Monaco	2	24	24	Britain 1950	- Hungary 1994
Morocco	2	1	2	Morocco 1958	
Russia	2	94	94	Bahrain 2010	- Abu Dhabi 2015
Venezuela	2	113	113	Brazil 1983	- Abu Dhabi 2015
Chile	1	24	24	San Marino 1981	- United States West 1983
Czech Republic	1	3	3	Italy 2001	- Japan 2001
Hungary	1	20	20	Hungary 2003	- Brazil 2004
Liechtenstein	1	10	10	France 1973	- Netherlands 1974
Malaysia	1	14	14	Italy 2001	- Japan 2002
Poland	1	76	76	Hungary 2006	- Abu Dhabi 2010
Thailand	1	19	19	Britain 1950	- Spain 1954
total	**657**	**924**	**20,758**		
Indianapolis 500					
United States	106 (a)	11	380	1950	- 1960
Italy	1 (b)	1	1	1952	
total	**107**	**11**	**381**		

(a) Three of these drivers participated in F1 races and are also included in the above table.
(b) Driver participated in F1 races and is also included in the above table.
Includes drivers who took over in a shared drive and were not on the starting grid (see section 171).
The following drivers were of dual nationality: Nano da Silva Ramos and Romain Grosjean are regarded as French in the above table, Ralph Firman as British, Hans Stuck as German, Ettore Chimeri and Alfonso Thiele as Italian and André Guelfi as Moroccan. Those from East Germany are included as German.

135. Seasons of starting races by nationality

Great Britain	66	1950 - 2015		Portugal	10	1959 - 2006
Germany	64	1950 - 2015		Southern Rhodesia	9	1962 - 72
France	61	1950 - 2015		Colombia	8	1982 - 2006
Italy	61	1950 - 2011		Ireland	7	1950 - 82
Brazil	51	1951 - 2015		Venezuela	7	1983 - 2015
Australia	47	1952 - 2015		Denmark	6	1974 - 2014
United States	44	1950 - 2015		Russia	6	2010 - 15
Belgium	43	1950 - 2012		Monaco	5	1950 - 94
Switzerland	41	1950 - 2011		Poland	5	2006 - 10
Austria	40	1964 - 2010		Thailand	5	1950 - 54
Finland	37	1974 - 2015		India	4	2005 - 12
Netherlands	37	1952 - 2015		Chile	3	1981 - 83
Sweden	35	1956 - 2015		Uruguay	3	1952 - 56
Spain	29	1951 - 2015		Hungary	2	2003 - 04
Argentina	27	1950 - 2001		Liechtenstein	2	1973 - 74
Canada	27	1961 - 2006		Malaysia	2	2001 - 02
Japan	27	1976 - 2014		Czech Republic	1	2001
Mexico	21	1961 - 2015		Morocco	1	1958
New Zealand	21	1958 - 84				
South Africa	19	1961 - 80				

Additional nations, China, Hong Kong and Israel have been represented by drivers who only appeared in practice sessions (see section 561).

136. Consecutive seasons of starting races by nationality *(Most)*

Great Britain	66	1950 - 2015		Germany	34	1982 - 2015
Brazil	46	1970 - 2015		Australia	27	1955 - 81
Italy	42	1970 - 2011		Finland	27	1989 - 2015
United States	40	1950 - 89		Switzerland	27	1961 - 87
France	39	1966 - 2004		Germany	24	1957 - 80

137. The only races where no British driver started

Whilst British drivers started during every season of Formula 1, there have been five races where there were none: Switzerland 1950 (only adhoc British participants that year), Belgium and Spain 1951 (again only adhoc British drivers), Monaco 1980 (the only regular British driver John Watson did not qualify) and United States 2005 (all the British drivers were among the Michelin runners who were withdrawn after the parade lap).

138. Drivers of the same nationality in a race *(Most)*

Britain	17	Britain 1952 (RACE RESULT- 3: Mike Hawthorn, 4: Dennis Poore, 5: Eric Thompson, 7: Reg Parnell, 8: Roy Salvadori, 9: Ken Downing, 10: Peter Whitehead, 12: Graham Whitehead, 15: Lance Macklin, 16: Kenneth McAlpine, 20: Eric Brandon, 21: Tony Crook, 22: Alan Brown, Retired: Peter Collins, Duncan Hamilton, Stirling Moss, David Murray)
Britain	16	Britain 1954
Britain	15	Britain 1953
Britain	15	Britain 1959
Britain	15	Britain 1961
Germany	14	Germany 1953
Britain	13	Britain 1956
Britain	13	Italy 1961
Germany	12	Germany 1952
Britain	12	Britain 1958
Britain	12	Germany 1958
Britain	12	Britain 1960
Britain	12	Germany 1966
Italian	12	Britain 1990
Italian	12	Hungary 1990

The record number of entrants of one nationality in a race is 20 British drivers at Britain 1959: Peter Ashdown, Chris Bristow, Tony Brooks, Ivor Bueb, Ian Burgess, Jack Fairman, Ron Flockhart, Keith Greene (nq), Graham Hill, Innes Ireland (ns), Stirling Moss, Brian Naylor, Mike Parkes (nq), Tim Parnell (nq), David Piper, Roy Salvadori, Alan Stacey, Henry Taylor, Mike Taylor, Trevor Taylor (nq). (nq) non-qualified, (ns) non-started.

139. Different nationalities of starters in a race

Most
16

1974: Sweden

1978: Britain, Austria, United States

1979: France, Britain, Germany, Austria, Netherlands

15

1972: South Africa

1974: Belgium

1978: Spain, Sweden, Netherlands

1979: Argentina, United States West, Canada

1980: Germany, United States

2006: Europe, Spain, Monaco, Britain, Canada, United States

Fewest
5

1951: Belgium

1953: Argentina

1960: Italy

6

1950: Belgium, France

1952: Netherlands

1954: Belgium, Italy

1955: Belgium, Netherlands, Italy

1956: Monaco

1957: France

1958: Argentina

1959: Netherlands

1969: France

1982: San Marino

2005: United States

Excludes Indianapolis 500.

140. Different nationalities of starters in a season

Most

19	1974 (Argentina, Australia, Austria, Belgium, Brazil, Canada, Denmark, Finland, France, Germany, Great Britain, Italy, Liechtenstein, Netherlands, New Zealand, South Africa, Sweden, Switzerland, United States)
18	1971, 77, 78
17	1972, 79
16	1963, 70, 73, 76, 80, 82, 2006

Fewest

10	1954, 55, 91, 99, 2008
11	1950, 53, 57, 90, 92, 93, 96, 2000, 09, 13

Total for each season

1950 - 11, 1951 - 13, 1952 - 13, 1953 - 11, 1954 - 10, 1955 - 10, 1956 - 12, 1957 - 11, 1958 - 13, 1959 - 13, 1960 - 13, 1961 - 14, 1962 - 14, 1963 - 16, 1964 - 15, 1965 - 13, 1966 - 12, 1967 - 15, 1968 - 15, 1969 - 14, 1970 - 16, 1971 - 18, 1972 - 17, 1973 - 16, 1974 - 19, 1975 - 15, 1976 - 16, 1977 - 18, 1978 - 18, 1979 - 17, 1980 - 16, 1981 - 15, 1982 - 16, 1983 - 15, 1984 - 14, 1985 - 13, 1986 - 14, 1987 - 12, 1988 - 12, 1989 - 12, 1990 - 11, 1991 - 10, 1992 - 11, 1993 - 11, 1994 - 14, 1995 - 12, 1996 - 11, 1997 - 12, 1998 - 12, 1999 - 10, 2000 - 11, 2001 - 13, 2002 - 12, 2003 - 14, 2004 - 13, 2005 - 14, 2006 - 16, 2007 - 12, 2008 - 10, 2009 - 11, 2010 - 13, 2011 - 14, 2012 - 13, 2013 - 11, 2014 - 13, 2015 - 13

Excludes Indianapolis 500.
For additional nations whose drivers did not start a race, see section 560.

141. Performance summary by nationality
(number of drivers)

	world champions	starters	winners	on pole position	point scorers
Great Britain	10	146	19	17	59
Italy	2	84	15	13	47
France	1	70	12	9	36
United States	2	48	5	4	16
Germany	2	46	7	8	20
Brazil	3	30	6	6	19
Switzerland	-	23	2	2	7
Argentina	1	22	3	3	7
Belgium	-	20	2	2	7
South Africa	1	17	1	1	3
Japan	-	17	-	-	7
Netherlands	-	15	-	-	5
Australia	2	14	4	3	5
Austria	2	14	3	3	7
Spain	1	13	1	1	8
Canada	1	11	2	2	2
Sweden	-	10	3	2	7

	world champions	starters	winners	on pole position	point scorers
Finland	3	8	4	4	7
New Zealand	1	8	2	2	4
Mexico	-	6	1	-	5
Denmark	-	4	-	-	2
Portugal	-	3	-	-	2
Ireland	-	3	-	-	1
Southern Rhodesia	-	3	-	-	1
Uruguay	-	3	-	-	-
Colombia	-	2	1	1	1
Venezuela	-	2	1	1	2
Russia	-	2	-	-	2
India	-	2	-	-	1
Monaco	-	2	-	-	1
Morocco	-	2	-	-	-
Poland	-	1	1	1	1
Chile	-	1	-	-	1
Hungary	-	1	-	-	1
Thailand	-	1	-	-	1
Czech Republic	-	1	-	-	-
Liechtenstein	-	1	-	-	-
Malaysia	-	1	-	-	-
total	**32**	**657**	**95**	**85**	**295**
Indianapolis 500					
United States (a)	-	106	10	11	35
Italy (b)	-	1	-	-	-
total	**-**	**107**	**10**	**11**	**35**

eg 146 British drivers have started a grand prix, of which 10 have become world champion, 19 have won races, 17 have achieved pole position and 59 have scored points.
(a) Includes three drivers who also started grands prix. They are also listed in the main table above.
(b) Relates to Alberto Ascari who also started grands prix. He is also listed in the main table above.

142. Driver entrants in a race *(Most)*
The record is 39, occurring in 13 of the 16 races during 1989.

143. Driver entrants in a season

Most

1952	76 (inc. 5 non-starters)	1954	55
1953	73 (inc. 2 non-starters)	1976	55
1974	62 (inc. 6 non-starters)	1958	54
1977	61 (inc. 12 non-starters)	1961	54
1960	58	1963	54
1959	56		

Fewest

2008	22	1999	24
2015	22	2003	24
1998	23	2014	24
2000	23	2004	25
2002	23	2009	25
2013	23	2012	25
1996	24		

Excludes drivers who only took part in practice, with no attempt to qualify for the race.

144. First time race starters

Most

(apart from the first race at Britain 1950, where there were 23 starters)

Germany 1952	13: Bill Aston, Marcel Balsa, Günther Bechem, Adolf Brudes, Willi Heeks, Theo Helfrich, Hans Klenk, Ernest Klodwig, Rudolf Krause, Helmut Niedermayr, Josef Peters, Fritz Riess, Rudolf Schoeller
Britain 1952	9: Gino Bianco, Eitel Cantoni, Tony Crook, Ken Downing, Kenneth McAlpine, Dennis Poore, Roy Salvadori, Eric Thompson, Graham Whitehead
Germany 1953	9: Kurt Adolff, Edgar Barth, Erwin Bauer, Theo Fitzau, Hans Herrmann, Oswald Karch, Ernest Loof, Rodney Nuckey, Wolf gang Seidel
Italy 1950	8: Clement Biondetti, Franco Comotti, Henri Louveau, Guy Mairesse, Paul Pietsch, Consalvo Sanesi, Dorino Serafini, Piero Taruffi
Monaco 1950	8: Alberto Ascari, José Froilán González, Robert Manzon, Franco Rol, Harry Schell, Raymond Sommer, Maurice Trintignant, Luigi Villoresi
Belgium 1952	8: Charles de Tornaco, Paul Frère, Tony Gaze, Mike Hawthorn, Roger Laurent, Arthur Legat, Robin Montgomerie-Charrington, Robert O'Brien
Switzerland 1952	8: Eric Brandon, Alan Brown, Peter Collins, Max De Terra, Lance Macklin, Hans Stuck, Toni Ulmen, Ken Wharton
Britain 1954	8: Don Beauman, Clemar Bucci, Ron Flockhart, Horace Gould, Leslie Marr, John Riseley-Prichard, Leslie Thorne, Bill Whitehouse
Germany 1966	7: Kurt Ahrens, Jean-Pierre Beltoise, Piers Courage, Hubert Hahne, Jacky Ickx, Alan Rees, Jo Schlesser
Argentina 1960	6: Roberto Bonomi, Ettore Chimeri, Antonio Creus, Nasif Estéfano. Alberto Rodríguez Larreta, Gino Munaron
Italy 1961	6: Roberto Bussinello, Roberto Lippi, Renato Pirocchi, Ricardo Rodríguez, Gaetano Starrabba, Nino Vaccarella
South Africa 1962	6: Mike Harris, Bruce Johnstone, Neville Lederle, John Love, Ernie Pieterse, Doug Serrurier (four South Africans and two Southern Rhodesians)

Overall by decade

1950s	207
1960s	128
1970s	117
1980s	70
1990s	59
2000s	49
2010s	27

Excludes Indianapolis 500.

by season (Most)

1950	46
1952	42
1953	26
1960	22
1961	21
1974	19
1975	18
1951	16
1962	16
1971	16

by season (Fewest)

1998	2
2008	2
2012	2
1985	3
1990	3
1986	4
1996	4
1999	4
2000	4
2004	4
2009	4

145. Age of drivers who started a race

Youngest

	years, days	
Max Verstappen	17y, 166d	Australia 2015
Jaime Alguersuari	19y, 125d	Hungary 2009
Mike Thackwell	19y, 182d	Canada 1980
Ricardo Rodríguez	19y, 208d	Italy 1961
Fernando Alonso	19y, 218d	Australia 2001
Esteban Tuero	19y, 320d	Australia 1998
Chris Amon	19y, 324d	Belgium 1963
Daniil Kvyat	19y, 324d	Australia 2014
Sebastian Vettel	19y, 349d	United States 2007
Jenson Button	20y, 53d	Australia 2000
Eddie Cheever	20y, 53d	South Africa 1978

Oldest

	years, days	
Louis Chiron	55y, 292d	Monaco 1955
Philippe Etançelin	55y, 191d	France 1952
Arthur Legat	54y, 232d	Belgium 1953
Luigi Fagioli	53y, 22d	France 1951
Adolf Brudes	52y, 293d	Germany 1952
Hans Stuck	52y, 260d	Italy 1953
Bill Aston	52y, 127d	Germany 1952
Clemente Biondetti	51y, 320d	Italy 1950
Louis Rosier	50y, 274d	Germany 1956
Rudolf Schoeller	50y, 98d	Germany 1952

Oldest to make their debut

	years, days	
Arthur Legat	53y, 234d	Belgium 1952
Philippe Etançelin	53y, 136d	Britain 1950
Adolf Brudes	52y, 293d	Germany 1952
Bill Aston	52y, 127d	Germany 1952
Luigi Fagioli	51y, 338d	Britain 1950
Clemente Biondetti	51y, 320d	Italy 1950
Hans Stuck	51y, 143d	Switzerland 1952
Louis Chiron	50y, 283d	Britain 1950
Rudolf Schoeller	50y, 98d	Germany 1952
Ernst Klodwig	49y, 72d	Germany 1952

146. Races started with the same constructor *(Most)*

Michael Schumacher	180	Ferrari	Australia 1996	- Brazil 2006
David Coulthard	150	McLaren	Australia 1996	- Brazil 2004
Felipe Massa	139	Ferrari	Bahrain 2006	- Brazil 2013
Jacques Laffite	132	Ligier	Brazil 1976	- Britain 1986 (a)
Mika Häkkinen	131	McLaren	Portugal 1993	- Japan 2001
Mark Webber	129	Red Bull	Australia 2007	- Brazil 2013
Nico Rosberg	115	Mercedes-Benz	Bahrain 2010	- Abu Dhabi 2015
Jenson Button	114	McLaren	Bahrain 2010	- Abu Dhabi 2015
Sebastian Vettel	113	Red Bull	Australia 2009	- Abu Dhabi 2014
Lewis Hamilton	110	McLaren	Australia 2007	- Brazil 2012
Alain Prost	107	McLaren	Argentina 1980	- Australia 1989
Nelson Piquet	106	Brabham	Canada 1978	- Australia 1985
Fernando Alonso	105	Renault	Australia 2003	- Brazil 2012
Rubens Barrichello	102	Ferrari	Australia 2000	- China 2005
Pierluigi Martini	102	Minardi	Brazil 1985	- Germany 1995
Fernando Alonso	96	Ferrari	Bahrain 2010	- Abu Dhabi 2014
Gerhard Berger	96	Ferrari	Brazil 1987	- Australia 1996
Ayrton Senna	96	McLaren	Brazil 1988	- Australia 1993
Nigel Mansell	95	Williams	Brazil 1985	- Australia 1994
Ralf Schumacher	94	Williams	Australia 1999	- Brazil 2004
Adrian Sutil	92	Force India	Australia 2008	- Brazil 2013
Elio De Angelis	90	Lotus	Argentina 1980	- Australia 1985
Kimi Räikkönen	90	Ferrari	Australia 2007	- Abu Dhabi 2015
Jarno Trulli	90	Toyota	Japan 2004	- Abu Dhabi 2009
Kimi Räikkönen	87	McLaren	Australia 2002	- Brazil 2006
Denny Hulme	86	McLaren	South Africa 1968	- United States 1974
Riccardo Patrese	81	Williams	Australia 1987	- Australia 1992
Jacques Villeneuve	81	BAR	Australia 1999	- United States 2003
Michele Alboreto	80	Ferrari	Brazil 1984	- Australia 1988
Jack Brabham	80	Brabham	Germany 1962	- Mexico 1970
Patrick Depailler	80	Tyrrell	France 1972	- Canada 1978

(a) Includes Talbot-Ligier.
For more information on drivers who started with each constructor, see section 674.

147. Consecutive races started with the same constructor *(Most)*
(ie started every race in the period)

David Coulthard	150	McLaren	Australia 1996	- Brazil 2004
Mark Webber	129	Red Bull	Australia 2007	- Brazil 2013
Michael Schumacher	124	Ferrari	Malaysia 1999	- Brazil 2006
Nico Rosberg	115	Mercedes-Benz	Bahrain 2010	- Abu Dhabi 2015
Sebastian Vettel	113	Red Bull	Australia 2009	- Abu Dhabi 2014
Lewis Hamilton	110	McLaren	Australia 2007	- Brazil 2012
Jenson Button	99	McLaren	Bahrain 2010	- China 2015
Fernando Alonso	96	Ferrari	Bahrain 2010	- Abu Dhabi 2014

Jacques Laffite	96	Ligier	Brazil 1976	- United States West 1982 (a)
Alain Prost	96	McLaren	Brazil 1984	- Australia 1989
Ayrton Senna	96	McLaren	Brazil 1988	- Australia 1993
Mika Häkkinen	91	McLaren	Australia 1996	- Europe 2001
Riccardo Patrese	81	Williams	Australia 1987	- Australia 1992
Michele Alboreto	80	Ferrari	Brazil 1984	- Australia 1988
Ralf Schumacher	80	Williams	Australia 1999	- Hungary 2003
Jarno Trulli	80	Toyota	France 2005	- Abu Dhabi 2009
awsedrty	78	Tyrrell	Argentina 1974	- Canada 1978
Felipe Massa	77	Ferrari	Bahrain 2010	- Brazil 2013
Adrian Sutil	73	Force India	Australia 2008	- Brazil 2011
Mario Andretti	72	Lotus	Sweden 1976	- United States 1980 (b)

(a) Includes Talbot-Ligier.
(b) Includes JPS Lotus.

148. Seasons of starting races with the same constructor *(Most)*

Michael Schumacher	11	Ferrari	1996 - 2006
Jack Brabham	9	Brabham	1962 - 70
Jim Clark	9	Lotus	1960 - 68
David Coulthard	9	McLaren	1996 - 2004
Mika Häkkinen	9	McLaren	1993 - 2001
Jacques Laffite	9	Ligier	1976 - 86 (a)
Pierluigi Martini	8	Minardi	1985 - 95 (a)
Felipe Massa	8	Ferrari	2006 - 13
Bruce McLaren	8	Cooper	1958 - 65
Nelson Piquet	8	Brabham	1978 - 85

(a) Missed some intervening seasons.

149. Races started exclusively for one constructor throughout their career *(Most)*

Jim Clark	72	Lotus	Netherlands 1960	- South Africa 1968
Paul Di Resta	58	Force India	Australia 2011	- Brazil 2013
Jean-Eric Vergne	58	Toro Rosso	Australia 2012	- Abu Dhabi 2014
Valtteri Bottas	56	Williams	Australia 2013	- Abu Dhabi 2015
Sébastien Buemi	55	Toro Rosso	Australia 2009	- Brazil 2011
Jaime Alguersuari	46	Toro Rosso	Hungary 2009	- Brazil 2011
Esteban Gutiérrez	38	Sauber	Australia 2013	- Abu Dhabi 2014
Max Chilton	35	Marussia	Australia 2013	- Russia 2014
Jules Bianchi	34	Marussia	Australia 2013	- Japan 2014
Gunnar Nilsson	31	JPS Lotus	South Africa 1976	- Japan 1977

At the end of 2012, Lewis Hamilton held the record of starts exclusively for one constructor (110 with McLaren), but it reverted to Jim Clark, once Lewis raced with Mercedes-Benz from the beginning of 2013.

150. Different constructors driven for during their career *(Most)*

Chris Amon	13	Amon, Brabham *, BRM, Cooper, Ensign, Ferrari, Lola, Lotus, March, Matra-Simca, Tecno, Tyrrell, Wolf-Williams *
Andrea De Cesaris	10	Alfa Romeo, Brabham, Dallara, Jordan, Ligier, McLaren, Minardi, Rial, Sauber, Tyrrell
Stefan Johansson	10	AGS *, Ferrari, Footwork, Ligier, McLaren, Onyx, Shadow *, Spirit, Toleman, Tyrrell
Stirling Moss	10	BRM, Connaught, Cooper, ERA, Ferguson, HWM, Lotus, Maserati, Mercedes-Benz, Vanwall
Maurice Trintignant	10	Aston Martin, BRM, Bugatti, Cooper, Ferrari (inc. Lancia-Ferrari), Gordini (inc. Simca-Gordini), Lola, Lotus, Maserati, Vanwall
Eddie Cheever	9	Alfa Romeo, Arrows, Hesketh, Lola, Osella, Renault, Talbot-Ligier, Theodore *, Tyrrell
Jacky Ickx	9	Brabham, Cooper, Ensign, Ferrari, Ligier, JPS Lotus, Matra, McLaren, Williams (as Iso-Marlboro & Wolf-Williams)
Roberto Moreno	9	AGS, Andrea Moda, Benetton, Coloni, EuroBrun, Forti, Jordan, Lotus *, Minardi
Jo Bonnier	8	Brabham, BRM, Cooper, Honda, Lotus, Maserati, McLaren, Porsche
Martin Brundle	8	Benetton, Brabham, Jordan, Ligier, McLaren, Tyrrell, Williams, Zakspeed
Hans Herrmann	8	Brabham, BRM, Cooper, Lotus *, Maserati, Mercedes-Benz, Porsche, Veritas
Jean-Pierre Jarier	8	ATS, Ligier (inc. Talbot-Ligier), JPS Lotus, March, Osella, Penske *, Shadow, Tyrrell *
Roy Salvadori	8	Aston Martin, BRM *, Connaught, Cooper, Ferrari, Lola, Maserati, Vanwall
Rolf Stommelen	8	Arrows, Brabham, Eifelland-March, Hesketh, Hill, Lola, Lotus, Surtees
John Surtees	8	BRM, Cooper, Ferrari, Honda, Lola, Lotus, McLaren, Surtees
Patrick Tambay	8	Ensign, Ferrari, Lola, McLaren, Renault, Talbot-Ligier, Surtees *, Theodore

* Non-qualifier/ Non-starter.

151. Different constructors driven for in a season *(Most)*

Alberto Ascari	3	1954	Maserati, Ferrari, Lancia
Jo Bonnier	3	1968	Cooper, McLaren, Honda
Olivier Gendebien	3	1961	Emeryson (nq), Ferrari, Lotus
Dan Gurney	3	1968	Eagle, Brabham, McLaren
Mike Hawthorn	3	1956	Maserati, BRM, Vanwall
Johnny Herbert	3	1994	Lotus, Ligier, Benetton
Jacky Ickx	3	1973	Ferrari, McLaren, Iso-Marlboro (Williams)
Jean-Pierre Jarier	3	1977	Penske, Shadow, Ligier
Geoff Lees	3	1980	Shadow, Ensign, Williams (nq)
Roberto Moreno	3	1991	Benetton, Jordan, Minardi
Stirling Moss	3	1952	HWM, ERA, Connaught
Nelson Piquet	3	1978	Ensign, McLaren, Brabham
Keke Rosberg	3	1978	Theodore, ATS, Wolf
Roy Salvadori	3	1957	BRM (nq), Vanwall, Cooper
Harry Schell	3	1955	Maserati, Ferrari, Vanwall
Maurice Trintignant	3	1958	Cooper, Maserati, BRM
Maurice Trintignant	3	1963	Lola, Lotus, BRM
John Watson	3	1975	Surtees, JPS Lotus, Penske

(nq) Non-qualifier.

152. Drove for two constructors in a race
(Stirling Moss at the 1961 British Grand Prix: Lotus and Ferguson)
Stirling Moss is the only driver to race for two constructors in the same race, at Britain 1961. He started in a Lotus 18/21 which retired after 44 laps (brake pipe failure), then took over Jack Fairman's Ferguson P99, but was disqualified on lap 57, having been push-started in the pit lane. In an interview with Jack Fairman in July 1997, who was 84 by that time, he recalled that day at Aintree where team manager Rob Walker had decided to enter not just a Lotus for Stirling Moss, but also the Ferguson for Jack. Fairman said "because he was Stirling, he decided he'd have a run in the Ferguson as well as his car [to see if he preferred it]. Moss opted for the Lotus" and Fairman said "I was resigned to drive the Ferguson". He explained that "the Ferguson was running beautifully in the rain, being the only four-wheel drive car out there. After a pit stop, I was going like bloody steam and beginning to catch up cars. I thought *Christ Almighty, if I can keep this up I could win this race.* Then suddenly coming down past the pits, I saw a come in signal. I thought that can't be for me, the car's going perfectly. Then I saw Rob Walker [the team manager] making violent signs. So I came into the pits and was scarcely out of the car when two blokes literally yanked me out and almost threw me on the ground. Stirling having retired his car, had walked down to the pits and Walker put Stirling in mine and they pushed him off to start. This was the first time in a major race, that push-starts had been disallowed. The car was disqualified a few laps later. A well known team owner was there at the time and said *Jack, I don't know how you controlled your temper. How on earth you kept yourself from hitting the silly bugger on the nose is beyond my comprehension".*
Asking Jack whether he was disappointed, he replied "not so much disappointed, bloody furious. I knew the way the car was going I had every chance of being in the first three and that would have been very good indeed on its first outing. I managed to control my temper and I had a lap to think about it and when Stirling came in, I was very close to punching him on the bloody nose when he got out. I often drove with Moss for one good reason - I was the only one daft enough to put up with his tantrums. Everything had to be done his way."

153. Races started as team-mates *(Most)*

Rubens Barrichello, Michael Schumacher	102	Australia 2000	- China 2005	(Ferrari)
David Coulthard, Mika Häkkinen	98	Australia 1996	- Japan 2001	(McLaren)
Sebastian Vettel, Mark Webber	94	Australia 2009	- Brazil 2013	(Red Bull)
Jean Alesi, Gerhard Berger	77	South Africa 1993	- Europe 1997	(Ferrari, Benetton)
Fernando Alonso, Felipe Massa	77	Bahrain 2010	- Brazil 2013	(Ferrari)
Juan Pablo Montoya, Ralf Schumacher	61	Australia 2001	- Brazil 2004	(Williams)
Elio De Angelis, Nigel Mansell	59	Austria 1980	- Portugal 1984	(Lotus)
Eddie Irvine, Michael Schumacher	58	Australia 1996	- Japan 1999	(Ferrari)
Nico Rosberg, Michael Schumacher	58	Bahrain 2010	- Brazil 2012	(Mercedes-Benz)
Jenson Button, Lewis Hamilton	58	Bahrain 2010	- Brazil 2012	(McLaren)
Lewis Hamilton, Nico Rosberg	57	Australia 2013	- Abu Dhabi 2015	(Mercedes-Benz)
Nick Heidfeld, Robert Kubica	57	Hungary 2006	- Abu Dhabi 2009	(BMW Sauber)
Niki Lauda, Clay Regazzoni	56	Argentina 1973	- Japan 1976	(BRM, Ferrari)
Ivan Capelli, Maurício Gugelmin	55	Brazil 1988	- Spain 1991	(March) (a)
Rubens Barrichello, Jenson Button	53	Bahrain 2006	- Brazil 2008	(Honda)
Ralf Schumacher, Jarno Trulli	53	Australia 2005	- Brazil 2007	(Toyota)
David Coulthard, Kimi Räikkönen	51	Australia 2002	- Brazil 2004	(McLaren)
Giancarlo Fisichella, Alexander Wurz	49	Australia 1998	- Malaysia 2000	(Benetton)
Gerhard Berger, Ayrton Senna	48	United States 1990	- Australia 1992	(McLaren)
Nigel Mansell, Riccardo Patrese	46	Brazil 1988	- Australia 1992	(Williams)

(a) Includes Leyton House in 1990 - 91.

154. Races started at the same circuit *(Most)*

Rubens Barrichello	19	Hungaroring	1993 - 2011
Rubens Barrichello	19	Interlagos	1993 - 2011
Rubens Barrichello	19	Monte-Carlo	1993 - 2011
Rubens Barrichello	19	Monza	1993 - 2011
Rubens Barrichello	19	Silverstone	1993 - 2011
Michael Schumacher	19	Catalunya	1991 - 2012
Michael Schumacher	19	Suzuka	1991 - 2012
Rubens Barrichello	18	Catalunya	1993 - 2011
Rubens Barrichello	18	Montréal	1993 - 2011
Michael Schumacher	18	Interlagos	1992 - 2012
Michael Schumacher	18	Monte-Carlo	1992 - 2012
Michael Schumacher	18	Montréal	1992 - 2012
Michael Schumacher	18	Silverstone	1992 - 2012

155. Races started with the same engine make *(Most)*

Michael Schumacher	180	Ferrari	Australia 1996	- Brazil 2006
Lewis Hamilton	167	Mercedes	Australia 2007	- Abu Dhabi 2015
David Coulthard	150	Mercedes	Australia 1996	- Brazil 2004
Emerson Fittipaldi	143	Ford Cosworth	Britain 1970	- United States 1980
Felipe Massa	139	Ferrari	Bahrain 2006	- Brazil 2013 (a)
Jean-Pierre Jarier	129	Ford Cosworth	Italy 1971	- South Africa 1983
Mark Webber	129	Renault	Australia 2007	- Brazil 2013
Ronnie Peterson	122	Ford Cosworth	Monaco 1970	- Italy 1978
Jenson Button	120	Honda	Australia 2003	- Abu Dhabi 2015
Nico Rosberg	115	Mercedes	Bahrain 2010	- Abu Dhabi 2015
John Watson	115	Ford Cosworth	Britain 1973	- Netherlands 1983
Jenson Button	113	Mercedes	Australia 2009	- Abu Dhabi 2014
Mika Häkkinen	113	Mercedes	Brazil 1995	- Japan 2001
Sebastian Vettel	113	Renault	Australia 2009	- Abu Dhabi 2014
Alan Jones	111	Ford Cosworth	Spain 1975	- Australia 1986
Fernando Alonso	105	Renault	Australia 2003	- Abu Dhabi 2009
Jochen Mass	105	Ford Cosworth	Britain 1973	- France 1982
Rubens Barrichello	102	Ferrari	Australia 2000	- China 2005
Mario Andretti	101	Ford Cosworth	United States 1968	- United States West 1982
Carlos Reutemann	100	Ford Cosworth	Argentina 1972	- Brazil 1982

(a) Felipe Massa started an additional 52 races (Australia 2002 - China 2005) with Petronas engines which were re-badged Ferrari engines.
Additionally, Jean Alesi used Ferrari engines re-badged as Acer and Petronas. Adding those in, would give him a Ferrari total of 123 (United States 1991 - Germany 2001).
For more information on drivers who started with each engine make, see section 968.

156. Races started with a turbocharged engine *(Most)*
(turbocharged engines were used from Britain 1977 to Australia 1988 and from Australia 2014)

Alain Prost	126	United States West 1981	- Australia 1988
René Arnoux	120	Argentina 1979	- Australia 1987
Nelson Piquet	106	South Africa 1982	- Australia 1988
Derek Warwick	99	Caesars Palace 1981	- Australia 1988
Riccardo Patrese	89	South Africa 1982	- Australia 1987
Michele Alboreto	80	Brazil 1984	- Australia 1988
Eddie Cheever	79	Brazil 1983	- Australia 1988
Ayrton Senna	78	Brazil 1984	- Australia 1988
Andrea De Cesaris	72	United States West 1983	- Australia 1987
Gergard Berger	68	Austria 1984	- Australia 1988
Nigel Mansell	68	Britain 1983	- Mexico 1987

157. Race retirements *(Most)*

		% of starts		
Andrea De Cesaris	149	71.63	Canada 1980	- Europe 1994
Riccardo Patrese	145	56.64	Belgium 1977	- Australia 1993
Michele Alboreto	102	52.58	San Marino 1981	- Australia 1994
Rubens Barrichello	97	30.03	South Africa 1993	- Germany 2011
Gerhard Berger	95	45.24	Austria 1984	- San Marino 1997
Nigel Mansell	93	49.73	Austria 1980	- Europe 1995
Jarno Trulli	90	35.71	Monaco 1997	- Singapore 2011
Jean Alesi	87	43.28	Britain 1989	- Japan 2001
Jacques Laffite	86	48.86	Germany 1974	- Britain 1986
Nelson Piquet	86	42.16	Germany 1978	- Hungary 1991
Eddie Cheever	84	63.64	South Africa 1978	- Australia 1989
Derek Warwick	84	57.53	Caesars Palace 1981	- Japan 1993
David Coulthard	81	32.93	Spain 1994	- Brazil 2008
Niki Lauda	80	46.78	Austria 1971	- Australia 1985
Johnny Herbert	78	48.45	Belgium 1989	- Malaysia 2000
Graham Hill	77	43.75	Monaco 1958	- Netherlands 1974
Giancarlo Fisichella	74	32.31	Australia 1996	- Turkey 2009
Mario Andretti	72	56.25	United States 1968	- Caesars Palace 1982
René Arnoux	70	46.98	Netherlands 1978	- Australia 1989
Martin Brundle	70	44.30	Portugal 1985	- Belgium 1996

Includes all retirements, even those where the driver was classified (completed 90% of full race distance).

158. Race retirements in a season *(Most)*

Andrea De Cesaris	16 of 16	1987	(Brabham BT56 - BMW)
Ivan Capelli	15 of 16	1989	(March 881, CG891 - Judd)
Alessandro Nannini	15 of 16	1987	(Minardi M187 - Motori Moderni)
Rubens Barrichello	15 of 17	1997	(Stewart SF-1 - Ford Cosworth)
Alex Caffi	14 of 16	1987	(Osella F1I - Alfa Romeo)
Andrea De Cesaris	14 of 16	1986	(Minardi M185B, M186 - Motori Moderni)
Piercarlo Ghinzani	14 of 16	1986	(Osella FA1G - Alfa Romeo)
Adrián Campos	13 of 16	1987	(Minardi M187 - Motori Moderni)
Eddie Cheever	13 of 16	1984	(Alfa Romeo 184T)
Andrea De Cesaris	13 of 16	1988	(Rial ARC1 - Ford Cosworth)
Pierluigi Martini	13 of 16	1985	(Minardi M185 - Ford Cosworth, Motori Moderni)
Alessandro Nannini	13 of 16	1986	(Minardi M185B - Motori Moderni)
Riccardo Patrese	13 of 16	1986	(Brabham BT54, BT55 - BMW)
Jacques Villeneuve	13 of 16	1999	(BAR 01 - Supertec)
Jan Magnussen	13 of 17	1997	(Stewart SF-1 - Ford Cosworth)

159. Race retirements at the same venue *(Most)*

grand prix

Andrea De Cesaris	12	Brazil	1981 - 93	(Jacarepaguá, 8; Interlagos, 4)
Andrea De Cesaris	12	Britain	1981 - 94	(Silverstone, 10; Brands Hatch, 2)
Andrea De Cesaris	12	San Marino	1982 - 94	(Imola)
Riccardo Patrese	12	Belgium	1977 - 90	(Spa-Francorchamps, 6; Zolder, 6)
Riccardo Patrese	12	Britain	1977 - 91	(Silverstone, 8; Brands Hatch, 4)
Rubens Barrichello	11	Brazil	1993 - 2007	(Interlagos)
Jo Bonnier	11	Britain	1957 - 69	(Silverstone, 5; Aintree, 3; Brands Hatch, 3)
Andrea De Cesaris	11	Belgium	1981 - 94	(Spa-Francorchamps, 8; Zolder, 3)
Riccardo Patrese	11	Canada	1977 - 93	(Montréal, 10; Mosport Park, 1)
Rubens Barrichello	10	Germany	1993 - 2011	(Hockenheim, 9; Nürburgring, 1)
Andrea De Cesaris	10	Canada	1980 - 94	(Montréal)
Graham Hill	10	Belgium	1958 - 72	(Spa-Francorchamps, 9; Nivelles-Baulers, 1)
Riccardo Patrese	10	Brazil	1982 - 93	(Jacarepaguá, 8; Interlagos, 2)
Riccardo Patrese	10	Germany	1977 - 92	(Hockenheim, 9; Nürburgring, 1)
Riccardo Patrese	10	Italy	1977 - 91	(Monza, 9; Imola, 1)
Riccardo Patrese	10	Monaco	1979 - 93	(Monte-Carlo)
Michael Schumacher	10	Australia	1991 - 2012	(Melbourne, 6; Adelaide, 4)

Andrea De Cesaris	12	Imola	1982 - 94
Rubens Barrichello	11	Interlagos	1993 - 2007
Andrea De Cesaris	10	Montréal	1980 - 94
Andrea De Cesaris	10	Silverstone	1981 - 94
Riccardo Patrese	10	Monte-Carlo	1979 - 93
Riccardo Patrese	10	Montréal	1979 - 93
Michele Alboreto	9	Monza	1981 - 94
Rubens Barrichello	9	Hockenheim	1993 - 2008
Andrea De Cesaris	9	Monte-Carlo	1981 - 92
Andrea De Cesaris	9	Monza	1981 - 94
Graham Hill	9	Monza	1959 - 71
Graham Hill	9	Spa-Francorchamps	1958 - 70
Riccardo Patrese	9	Hockenheim	1977 - 92
Riccardo Patrese	9	Monza	1977 - 91
Riccardo Patrese	9	Österreichring	1978 - 87
John Surtees	9	Monte-Carlo	1960 - 70
John Surtees	9	Monza	1961 - 72
Jarno Trulli	9	Montréal	1997 - 2010

160. Consecutive race retirements at the same venue *(Most)*

Andrea De Cesaris holds the record for the most consecutive retirements at the same grand prix, with 10 at Brazil 1984 to 93 and 10 at Britain 1985 to 94.

161. Race retirements on home soil *(Most)*

Andrea De Cesaris	21	Italy	1981 - 94 (a)	(Imola, 12; Monza, 9)
Riccardo Patrese	17	Italy	1977 - 93 (b)	(Monza, 9; Imola, 8)
Michele Alboreto	16	Italy	1981 - 94 (c)	(Monza, 9; imola, 7)
Mario Andretti	11	United States	1968 - 82 (d)	(Watkins Glen, 6; Long Beach, 3; Las Vegas, 2)
Rubens Barrichello	11	Brazil	1993 - 2007	(Interlagos)
Eddie Cheever	11	United States	1980 - 88 (e)	(Detroit, 5; Long Beach, 3; Dallas, 1; Las Vegas, 1; Watkins Glen, 1)
Heinz-Harald Frentzen	11	Germany	1994 - 2003 (f)	(Hockenheim, 6; Nürburgring, 5)
Ivan Capelli	10	Italy	1986 - 92 (g)	(Imola, 6; Monza, 4)
Jarno Trulli	9	Italy	1998 - 2010 (h)	(Monza, 5; Imola, 4)
Thierry Boutsen	8	Belgium	1983 - 93	(Spa-Francorchamps, 7; Zolder, 1)
Giancarlo Fisichella	8	Italy	1996 - 2008 (i)	(Imola, 6; Monza, 2)
Piercarlo Ghinzani	8	Italy	1983 - 88 (j)	(Monza, 5; Imola, 3)
Graham Hill	8	Britain	1958 - 73	(Silverstone, 5; Brands Hatch, 2; Aintree, 1)
Pierluigi Martini	8	Italy	1985 - 94 (j)	(Monza, 5; Imola, 3)

(a) 12 San Marino & 9 Italian Grands Prix. (b) 10 Italian & 7 San Marino Grands Prix. (c) 9 Italian & 7 San Marino Grands Prix.
(d) 6 United States, 3 United States West & 2 Caesars Palace Grands Prix. (e) 5 Detroit, 3 United States West, 1 Caesars Palace, 1 Dallas & 1 United States Grands Prix.
(f) 6 German & 5 European Grands Prix. (g) 6 San Marino & 4 Italian Grands Prix. (h) 5 Italian & 4 San Marino Grands Prix. (i) 6 San Marino & 2 Italian Grands Prix.
(j) 5 Italian & 3 San Marino Grands Prix.

162. Consecutive race retirements at home grand prix *(Most)*

Rubens Barrichello holds the record for the most consecutive retirements at a home grand prix, with 9 from 1995 to 2003, at Interlagos.

163. Race retirements before the end of the first lap *(Most)*

Jarno Trulli	14	Canada 1998	- Brazil 2009
Rubens Barrichello	13	Hungary 1993	- Belgium 2010
Andrea De Cesaris	12	United States West 1981	- Germany 1994
Patrick Tambay	10	Argentina 1979	- Mexico 1986
David Coulthard	9	Spain 1996	- Brazil 2008
Giancarlo Fisichella	9	Monaco 1996	- Turkey 2008
Jean-Pierre Jarier	9	Argentina 1974	- Europe 1983
Kimi Räikkönen	9	Malaysia 2001	- Austria 2015
Pedro de la Rosa	8	Britain 1999	- Monaco 2012
Mika Häkkinen	8	Monaco 1994	- Brazil 2001
Pierluigi Martini	8	Italy 1985	- Germany 1994

Includes cases where a driver retired during an initial race that was subject to a restart.
Excludes cases where car failed or was withdrawn before the race started.

164. First retirement in three consecutive races

Jackie Oliver	1969	Spain (oil line) & Monaco (accident) & Netherlands (gear selector) (BRM P133)
Jackie Oliver	1973	France (clutch) & Britain (accident *) & Netherlands (throttle jammed/ accident) (Shadow DN1 - Ford Cosworth)
Pedro Diniz	1998	Italy (brakes/ spin) & Luxembourg (hydraulics) & Japan (brakes/ spin) (Arrows A19)
Heinz-Harald Frentzen	2003	Austria (clutch *) & Monaco (accident) & Canada (electronics) (Sauber C22 - Petronas)

Retired at the first start (before the race was stopped and restarted).

165. Consecutive races started with a retirement *(Most)*

Andrea De Cesaris	22	Australia 1986	- Canada 1988	(Minardi, Brabham, Rial)
Andrea De Cesaris	18	France 1985	- Portugal 1986	(Ligier, Minardi)
Bertrand Gachot	18	Hungary 1992	- France 1995	(Venturi, Pacific)
Piercarlo Ghinzani	18	Britain 1985	- Hungary 1986	(Osella, Toleman)
Alex Caffi	17	Brazil 1987	- Mexico 1988	(Osella, Dallara)
Ivan Capelli	14	Italy 1990	- Germany 1991	(Leyton House)
Philippe Alliot	13	Portugal 1985	- Germany 1986	(RAM, Ligier)
Eddie Cheever	13	South Africa 1984	- Europe 1984	(Alfa Romeo)
Andrea De Cesaris	12	Brazil 1982	- Austria 1982	(Alfa Romeo)
Alessandro Nannini	12	Brazil 1986 (a)	- Portugal 1986	(Minardi)

Includes all retirements, even those where the driver was classified (completed 90% of full race distance).
(a) These were the first 12 races started in his Formula 1 career.

166. Consecutive races started without a retirement *(Most)*

Kimi Räikkönen	38	Hungary 2009	- Hungary 2013 (a)	(Ferrari F60, Lotus E20, E21 - Renault)
Nick Heidfeld	33	China 2007	- Italy 2009	(BMW Sauber F1.07, F1.08, F1.09 - BMW)
Fernando Alonso	29	China 2013	- Belgium 2014	(Ferrari F138, F14 T)
Valtteri Bottas	26	Canada 2014	- Japan 2015 (b)	(FW36, FW37 - Mercedes)
Nico Rosberg	27	Canada 2008	- Japan 2009	(Williams FW30, FW31 - Toyota)
Max Chilton	25	Australia 2013	- Monaco 2014	(Marussia MR02 - Cosworth, MR03 - Ferrari)
Felipe Massa	24	Malaysia 2012	- Spain 2013	(Ferrari F2012, F138)
Michael Schumacher	24	Hungary 2001	- Malaysia 2003	(Ferrari F2001, F2002)
Fernando Alonso	23	Europe 2011	- Hungary 2012	(Ferrari F150th Italia, F2012)
Rubens Barrichello	23	Spain 2005	- Britain 2006	(Ferrari F2005, Honda RA106)

(a) Not active for two years within the period. (b) Missed 1 race within the period.

167. Completed every race in a season without a retirement
(ie running at the finish although not necessarily on same lap as winner)

Kimi Räikkönen	20	2012	(Lotus E20 - Renault)
Max Chilton	19	2013	(Marussia MR02 - Cosworth)
Nick Heidfeld	18	2008	(BMW Sauber F1.08 - BMW)
Michael Schumacher	17	2002 (a)	(Ferrari F2001, F2002)
Richie Ginther	10	1964	(BRM P261)
Juan Manuel Fangio	8	1954 (b)	(Maserati 250F, Mercedes-Benz W196, W196 str.)
Dan Gurney	8	1961	(Porsche 718, 787)
Mike Hawthorn	8	1953 (b)	(Ferrari 500)
Maurice Trintignant	8	1959 (b)	(Cooper T51 - Climax)

(a) Also completed every lap that season (ie on same lap as winner in every race).
(b) Excludes Indianapolis 500.

168. Races in a season without a retirement *(Most)*

Kimi Räikkönen	20 of 20	2012	(Lotus E20 - Renault)
Max Chilton	19 of 19	2013	(Marussia MR02 - Cosworth)
Heikki Kovalainen	19 of 20	2012	(Caterham CT01 - Renault)
Felipe Massa	19 of 20	2012	(Ferrari F2012)
Daniel Ricciardo	19 of 20	2012	(Toro Rosso STR7 - Ferrari)
Nick Heidfeld	18 of 18	2008	(BMW Sauber F1.08 - BMW)
Fernando Alonso	18 of 19	2011	(Ferrari F150th Italia)
Fernando Alonso	18 of 19	2013	(Ferrari F138)
Valtteri Bottas	18 of 19	2014	(Williams FW36 - Mercedes)
Jenson Button	18 of 19	2013	(McLaren MP4-27 - Mercedes)
Lewis Hamilton	18 of 19	2013	(Mercedes-Benz F1 W04)
Lewis Hamilton	18 of 19	2015	(Mercedes-Benz F1 W06)
Kevin Magnussen	18 of 19	2014	(McLaren MP4-29 - Mercedes)
Felipe Massa	18 of 19	2010	(Ferrari F10)
Tiago Monteiro	18 of 19	2005	(Jordan EJ15, EJ15B - Toyota)
Sergio Pérez	18 of 19	2015	(Force India VJM08 – Mercedes)
Kimi Räikkönen	18 of 19	2014	(Ferrari F14 T)
Sebastian Vettel	18 of 19	2011	(Red Bull RB7 - Renault)
Sebastian Vettel	18 of 19	2013	(Red Bull RB9 - Renault)
Mark Webber	18 of 19	2011	(Red Bull RB7 - Renault)

169. Races started in which no points scored *(Most)*

Andrea De Cesaris	186	Michele Alboreto	147
Rubens Barrichello	183	Johnny Herbert	132
Riccardo Patrese	183	Jean Alesi	131
Jarno Trulli	180	Jenson Button	129
Giancarlo Fisichella	156	Olivier Panis	129

170. Consecutive races started with no points scored

Heikki Kovalainen	62	Japan 2009	- Brazil 2013	(McLaren, Lotus, Caterham)
Piercarlo Ghinzani	61	Britain 1984	- Australia 1989 (a)	(Osella, Toleman, Ligier, Zakspeed)
Ukyo Katayama	57	Germany 1994	- Europe 1997 (a)	(Tyrrell, Minardi)
Timo Glock	55	Bahrain 2010	- Brazil 2012	(Virgin, Marussia)
Luca Badoer	51	South Africa 1993	- Belgium 2009 (a)	(Lola, Minardi, Forti, Ferrari)
Jos Verstappen	46	Europe 1996	- Monaco 2000 (a)	(Footwork, Tyrrell, Stewart, Arrows)
Manfred Winkelhock	45	United States West 1982	- Germany 1985	(ATS, Brabham, RAM)
Aguri Suzuki	44	San Marino 1991	- San Marino 1995 (a)	(Lola, Footwork, Jordan, Ligier)
Nicola Larini	43	Spain 1987	- Pacific 1994 (a)	(Coloni, Osella, Ligier, Lamborghini, Ferrari)
Jonathan Palmer	41	Europe 1983	- Belgium 1987 (a)	(Williams, RAM, Zakspeed, Tyrrell)

(a) Includes race(s) with a retirement at the first start of a restarted race.

171. Shared cars

Last occasion of drivers sharing a car

United States 1964	Jim Clark started off in car no.1 (Lotus 25) and Mike Spence took over, retiring after 54 laps. Spence started in car no.2 (Lotus 33) with Clark taking over, but retired after 104 laps (placed 7th). Even though points were not awarded for shared cars by this time, the team decided that if Clark could take over and finish ahead of his main rivals, it would reduce the number of points they could score.

Won in a shared car

France 1951	Luigi Fagioli took over from Juan Manuel Fangio (Alfa Romeo 159)
Argentina 1956	Luigi Musso took over from Juan Manuel Fangio (Lancia-Ferrari D50)
Britain 1957	Tony Brooks took over from Stirling Moss (Vanwall VW4/57)

Others on the podium in a shared car

Italy 1950	2nd: Dorino Serfaini & Alberto Ascari (Ferrari 375)
France 1951	2nd: José Froilán González & Alberto Ascari (Ferrari 375)
Italy 1951	3rd: Felice Bonetto & Giuseppe Farina (Alfa Romeo 159)

Netherlands 1953	3rd: Felice Bonetto & José Froilán González (Maserati A6GCM)
Germany 1954	2nd: José Froilán González & Mike Hawthorn (Ferrari 625)
Italy 1954	3rd: Umberto Maglioli & José Froilán González (Ferrari 625)
Argentina 1955	2nd: José Froilán González & Giuseppe Farina & Maurice Trintignant (Ferrari 625)
Argentina 1955	3rd: Giuseppe Farina & Umberto Maglioli & Maurice Trintignant (Ferrari 625)
Monaco 1955	3rd: Jean Behra & Cesare Perdisa (Maserati 250F)
Belgium 1956	3rd: Cesare Perdisa & Stirling Moss (Maserati 250F)
Monaco 1956	2nd: Peter Collins & Juan Manuel Fangio (Lancia-Ferrari D50)
Britain 1956	2nd: Alfonso de Portago & Peter Collins (Lancia-Ferrari D50)
Italy 1956	2nd: Peter Collins & Juan Manuel Fangio (Lancia-Ferrari D50)
Argentina 1960	3rd: Maurice Trintignant & Stilring Moss (Cooper T51 - Climax)
Indianapolis 500	
1951	3rd: Jack McGarth & Manny Ayulo (Kurtis-Kraft 3000 - Offenhauser)
1953	3rd: Sam Hanks & Duane Carter (Kurtis-Kraft 4000 - Offenhauser)
1955	2nd: Tony Bettenhausen & Paul Russo (Kurtis-Kraft 500C - Offenhauser)

Achieved more than one top six placing in the same race by sharing a car

| Argentina 1955 | Giuseppe Farina (2nd & 3rd) & Maurice Trintignant (2nd & 3rd) (Ferrari 625) |
| Monaco 1956 | Juan Manuel Fangio (2nd & 4th) (Lancia-Ferrari D50) |

172. Took over in a shared drive and was not on the starting grid

Jo Bonnier	Italy 1956		**Indianapolis 500**	
Eugène Chaboud	France 1950		Manny Ayulo	1951
Alfonso de Portago	Argentina 1957		Bill Cantrell	1950
Ron Flockhart	Britain 1954		Jimmy Davies	1954
Paul Frère	Monaco 1955		Duke Dinsmore	1953
Gerino Gerini	Argentina 1956		Walt Faulkner	1954
Oscar González	Argentina 1956		Pat Flaherty	1954
Peter Hirt	France 1952		George Fonder	1954
Umberto Maglioli	Argentina 1955		Jackie Holmes	1953
Luigi Musso	Italy 1953		Bill Homeier	1955
André Pilette	Monaco 1956		Jimmy Jackson	1954
Tony Rolt	Britain 1950		Eddie Johnson	1953 & 54
Harry Schell	Argentina 1953		Danny Kladis	1954
Brian Shawe-Taylor	Britain 1950		Johnny Mantz	1953
Ottorino Volonterio	Spain 1954 & Italy 1957		Eddie Russo	1956
Wolfgang von Trips	Argentina 1957		Paul Russo	1955
Peter Walker	Britain 1955		Bob Scott	1954
			Marshall Teague	1954

173. Started a race, but was never on the starting grid in their career
Of Formula 1 drivers, Oscar González is the only driver to start a race, but never take a place on the grid. At his only race, he took over from Alberto Uría in a shared drive at Argentina 1956 (Maserati). Similarly, drivers racing at the Indianapolis 500 who were never on the starting grid were Bill Cantrell, Danny Kladis and Johnny Mantz.

174. Started a race unofficially
(all of the following are counted as a start, in the analyses)
Vern Schuppan (Ensign N174 - Ford Cosworth), Sweden 1974
Was first reserve, with only 25 cars being permitted in the race. Instead of pulling off when everyone else started he remained as the "26th" starter, but completed the race, finishing 12th and was disqualified.
Tim Schenken (JPS Lotus 76 - Ford Cosworth), United States 1974
Lined up on the grid as second reserve, having qualified 27th and should have pulled off before the start. Black-flagged after six laps and subsequently disqualified.
Wilson Fittipaldi (Copersucar FD02 - Ford Cosworth), South Africa 1975
Only 27th in qualifying, but lined up for the race as first reserve, in case one of the qualified cars did not appear. During the first lap, once he realised that all 26 cars had started, he withdrew.
Harald Ertl (Hesketh 308D - Ford Cosworth), France 1976
He was 29th fastest in qualifying for the 26 car grid and so was not eligible to race. He started the race, but before he was black-flagged, retired with driveshaft failure after four laps.
Hans Heyer (Penske PC4 - Ford Cosworth), Germany 1977
He had failed to qualify (27th fastest) for a 24 car grid, but nevertheless positioned himself at the back of the grid. He was popular with marshals who turned a blind eye to the situation. In any case he was in breach of the regulations by having raced in a supporting event within the previous 24 hours. His car suffered gear linkage failure after nine laps and was disqualified and banned from the next race. This was to be his only grand prix start.

175. Only ever started in the Formula 2 section of a grand prix

At six races, Formula 2 cars were permitted entry to boost the number of participants. They were not eligible for championship points. The races were Germany 1957, 58, 66, 67, 69 and Morocco 1958.

The following drivers only ever started in the world championship in the Formula 2 section of a grand prix:

Tom Bridger, Paul England, Dick Gibson, Christian Goethals, André Guelfi, Brian Hart, Robert La Caze, Xavier Perrot, François Picard, Peter Westbury.

176. Drivers who had a Formula 1 car named after them

Chris Amon (Amon)
Bill Aston (Aston-Butterworth)
Jean Behra (Behra-Porsche)
Jack Brabham (Brabham)
Alejandro de Tomaso (de Tomaso)
Paul Emery (Emeryson)
Emerson Fittipaldi (Fittipaldi)
Graham Hill (Hill)
Hans Klenk (Klenk)
Guy Ligier (Ligier)
Brian McGuire (McGuire)
Bruce McLaren (McLaren)

Arturo Merzario (Merzario)
Brian Naylor (John Brian Naylor, the 'JB' in JBW)
Roger Penske (Penske)
Alain Prost (Prost)
Hector Rebaque (Rebaque)
Alan Rees (the 'ar' in March)
Doug Serrurier (Louis Douglas Serrurier, LDS)
John Stephens (first half of Stebro name)
Jackie Stewart (Stewart)
John Surtees (Surtees)
Aguri Suzuki (Super Aguri)

177. Raced in a car of their name

Chris Amon	1974	Aldo Gordini	1951 (d)
Bill Aston	1952 (a)	Graham Hill	1975
Jack Brabham	1962, 63, 64, 65, 66, 67, 68, 69, 70	Bruce McLaren	1966, 67, 68, 69, 70
David Brabham	1990	Arturo Merzario	1978, 79
Paul Emery	1956 (b)	Hector Rebaque	1979
Wilson Fittipaldi	1975 (c)	John Surtees	1970, 71, 72
Emerson Fittipaldi	1976, 77, 78, 79, 80 (c)		

(a) As Aston-Butterworth. (b) As Emeryson. (c) Cars were named Copersucar 1975 - 79. (d) As Simca-Gordini.
Additionally there were two drivers who did not start races: Jean Behra, 1959 (as Behra-Porsche) and Brian McGuire, 1977.

Constructor name derivations. See section 653

178. Non-English British drivers

Northern Ireland
Kenny Acheson, Martin Donnelly, Eddie Irvine, Damien Magee, Desmond Titterington, John Watson

Scotland
Jim Clark, David Coulthard, Jim Crawford, Paul Di Resta, Johnny Dumfries, Ron Flockhart, Innes Ireland, Allan McNish, David Murray, Archie Scott Brown, Ian Stewart, Jackie Stewart, Jimmy Stewart, Leslie Thorne, Susie Wolff (p)

Wales
Jack Lewis, Tom Pryce, Alan Rees

(p) Practice only.

179. Interval between races started *(Longest)*

	years, days	races		
Jan Lammers	10y, 114d	165	Netherlands 1982 (Theodore)	- Japan 1992 (March)
Luca Badoer	9y, 296d	168	Japan 1999 (Minardi)	- Europe 2009 (Ferrari)
Pete Lovely	8y, 304d	88	United States 1960 (Cooper)	- Canada 1969 (Lotus)
André Pilette	7y, 349d	71	France 1956 (Gordini)	- Belgium 1964 (Scirocco)
Peter Revson	7y, 27d	79	Italy 1964 (Lotus)	- United States 1971 (Tyrrell)
Eppie Wietzes	7y, 26d	91	Canada 1967 (Lotus)	- Canada 1974 (Brabham)
Mike Hailwood	6y, 98d	73	Monaco 1965 (Lotus)	- Italy 1971 (Surtees)
Narain Karthikeyan	5y, 176d	91	China 2005 (Jordan)	- Malaysia 2011 (HRT)
Hans Herrmann	5y, 1d	47	Germany 1961 (Porsche)	- Germany 1966 (Brabham)
Wolfgang Seidel	4y, 317d	39	Germany 1953 (Veritas)	- Belgium 1958 (Maserati)

180. Interval between first & last races started *(Longest)*

	years, days	races		
Michael Schumacher	21y, 92d	367	Belgium 1991	- Brazil 2012
Rubens Barrichello	18y, 258d	325	South Africa 1993	- Brazil 2011
Graham Hill	16y, 253d	186	Monaco 1958	- Brazil 1975
Luca Badoer	16y, 169d	282	South Africa 1993	- Belgium 2009

	years, days	races		
Riccardo Patrese	16y, 169d	262	Monaco 1977	- Australia 1993
Jenson Button	15y, 262d	288	Australia 2000	- Abu Dhabi 2015
Jack Brabham	15y, 101d	150	Britain 1955	- Mexico 1970
Jo Bonnier	15y, 31d	152	Italy 1956	- United States 1971
Fernando Alonso	14y, 270d	271	Australia 2001	- Abu Dhabi 2015
Nigel Mansell	14y, 270d	230	Austria 1980	- Spain 1995
Kimi Räikkönen	14y, 270d	271	Australia 2001	- Abu Dhabi 2015

181. Interval between race starters of the same nationality *(Longest)*

	years, days	races		
Monaco	38y, 309d	506	Monaco 1955 (Louis Chiron)	- Brazil 1994 (Olivier Beretta)
Mexico	29y, 161d	483	Caesars Palace 1981 (Hector Rebaque)	- Australia 2011 (Sergio Pérez)
Portugal	29y, 6d	416	Italy 1964 (Mário Cabral)	- Italy 1993 (Pedro Lamy)
Ireland	27y, 2d	295	Britain 1951 (Joe Kelly)	- Britain 1978 (Derek Daly)
Venezuela	26y, 262d	443	Dallas 1984 (Johnny Cecotto)	- Australia 2011 (Pastor Maldonado)
Sweden	22y, 287d	393	Canada 1991 (Stefan Johansson)	- Australia 2014 (Marcus Ericsson)
Denmark	21y, 135d	337	Sweden 1974 (Tom Belsø)	- Pacific 1995 (Jan Magnussen)
Colombia	17y, 160d	277	Europe 1983 (Roberto Guerrero)	- Australia 2001 (Juan Pablo Montoya)
Belgium	16y, 183d	279	Portugal 1994 (Philippe Adams)	- Australia 2011 (Jérôme d'Ambrosio)
Switzerland	13y, 179d	226	Europe 1995 (Jean-Denis Delétraz)	- Australia 2009 (Sébastien Buemi)

182. Races started without ever finishing during their career *(Most)*

Alex Soler-Roig	6	South Africa 1971	- Spain 1972	(March, BRM)
Clemar Bucci	5	Britain 1954	- Argentina 1955	(Gordini, Maserati)
David Murray	4	Britain 1950	- Britain 1952	(Maserati, Cooper)
Piero Carini	3	France 1952	- Italy 1953	(Ferrari)
Andrea Chiesa	3	Mexico 1992	- France 1992	(Fondmetal)
Beppe Gabbiani	3	United States West 1981	- Belgium 1981	(Osella)
Hideki Noda	3	Europe 1994	- Australia 1994	(Larrousse)
Paul Pietsch	3	Italy 1950	- Germany 1952	(Maserati, Alfa Romeo, Veritas)
Tony Rolt	3	Britain 1950	- Britain 1955	(Connaught, ERA)

183. Races started on home soil but never a podium *(Most)*

Andrea De Cesaris	Italy/ San Marino	27	1981 - 94	(best: 3 x 6th)
Jarno Trulli	Italy/ San Marino	23	1997 - 2010	(best: 1 x 4th)
Jenson Button	Britain	16	2000 - 15	(best: 3 x 4th)
Pierluigi Martini	Italy/ San Marino	14	1985 - 95	(best: 1 x 4th)
Ivan Capelli	Italy/ San Marino	13	1986 - 92	(best: 1 x 5th)
Maurice Trintignant	France	13	1951 - 64	(best: 1 x 5th)
Mark Webber	Australia	12	2002 - 13	(best: 1 x 4th)
Thierry Boutsen	Belgium	11	1983 - 93	(best: 1 x 4th)
Piercarlo Ghinzani	Italy/ San Marino	10	1983 - 88	(best: 1 x 7th)
Bruno Giacomelli	Italy/ San Marino	10	1977 - 83	(best: 1 x 7th)
Jean-Pierre Jarier	France/ Switzerland	10	1973 - 83	(best: 1 x 5th)

San Marino Grand Prix on Italian soil and Switzerland on French soil.

184. Races started but never a win *(Most)*

Andrea De Cesaris	208
Nick Heidfeld	183
Martin Brundle	158
Derek Warwick	146
Jean-Pierre Jarier	134
Eddie Cheever	132
Adrian Sutil	128
Pierluigi Martini	118
Mika Salo	110
Philippe Alliot	109

185. Races started but never a podium *(Most)*

Adrian Sutil	128
Pierluigi Martini	118
Philippe Alliot	109
Pedro Diniz	98
Ukyo Katayama	95
Nico Hülkenberg	94
Jonathan Palmer	83
Marc Surer	82
Vitantonio Liuzzi	80
Piercarlo Ghinzani	76

186. Races started but never a pole position (Most)

Johnny Herbert	161
Martin Brundle	158
Olivier Panis	158
Eddie Irvine	146
Derek Warwick	146
Eddie Cheever	132
Adrian Sutil	128
Pierluigi Martini	118
Mika Salo	110
Philippe Alliot	109

187. Races started but never a front row (Most)

Johnny Herbert	161
Martin Brundle	158
Olivier Panis	158
Derek Warwick	146
Mika Salo	110
Philippe Alliot	109
Jos Verstappen	107
Pedro de la Rosa	105
Jochen Mass	105
Pedro Diniz	98

188. Races started but never a fastest lap (Most)

Johnny Herbert	161
Martin Brundle	158
Olivier Panis	158
Eddie Cheever	132
Pierluigi Martini	118
Mika Salo	110
Philippe Alliot	109
Elio De Angelis	108
Jos Verstappen	107
Jo Bonnier	104

189. Races started but never scored a point (Most)

Luca Badoer	51
Charles Pic	39
Max Chilton	35
Brett Lunger	34
Tora Takagi	32
Enrique Bernoldi	28
Mike Beuttler	28
Scott Speed	28
Ricardo Rosset	27
Rupert Keegan	25
Huub Rothengatter	25

190. Races started but never led (Most)

Martin Brundle	158
Eddie Cheever	132
Adrian Sutil	128
Philippe Alliot	109
Jos Verstappen	107

Pedro de la Rosa	105
Pedro Diniz	98
Ukyo Katayama	95
Jonathan Palmer	83
Marc Surer	82

191. Milestones: Number of races started

Rubens Barrichello	100th: San Marino 1999, 200th: San Marino 2005, 250th: Brazil 2007, 300th: Singapore 2010
Michael Schumacher	100th: Japan 1997, 200th: Europe 2004, 250th: Australia 2010, 300th: Singapore 2012
Fernando Alonso	100th: Italy 2007, 200th: China 2013, 250th: United States 2015
Jenson Button	100th: China 2005, 200th: Hungary 2011, 250th: Bahrain 2014
Riccardo Patrese	100th: San Marino 1984, 200th: Britain 1990, 250th: Germany 1993
Jarno Trulli	100th: Spain 2003, 200th: Australia 2009, 250th: India 2011
Jean Alesi	100th: Pacific 1995, 200th: United States 2001
Gerhard Berger	100th: United States 1991, 200th: San Marino 1997
David Coulthard	100th: Austria 2000, 200th: Monaco 2006
Andrea De Cesaris	100th: Portugal 1987, 200th: Canada 1994
Giancarlo Fisichella	100th: Europe 2002, 200th: Monaco 2008
Felipe Massa	100th: Belgium 2008, 200th: Britain 2014
Nelson Piquet	100th: Detroit 1985, 200th: Italy 1991
Kimi Räikkönen	100th: Turkey 2006, 200th: Canada 2014
Mark Webber	100th: Belgium 2007, 200th: Bahrain 2013

192. Milestones: Drivers to start a race

(eg Gabriele Tarquini was the 500th driver to start a race)

1st	Giuseppe Farina	Spain 1950		300th	Jacky Ickx	Germany 1966
50th	George Abecassis	Switzerland 1951		400th	Roelof Wunderink	Spain 1975
100th	Ernst Klodwig	Germany 1952		500th	Gabriele Tarquini	San Marino 1987
200th	David Piper	Britain 1959		600th	Justin Wilson	Australia 2003
250th	Lloyd Ruby	United States 1961				

Excludes Indianapolis 500.

Chapter 6: Winning Drivers

193. Wins

		% of starts		
Michael Schumacher	91	29.64	Belgium 1992 (Benetton)	- China 2006 (Ferrari)
Alain Prost	51	25.63	France 1981 (Renault)	- Germany 1993 (Williams)
Lewis Hamilton	43	25.75	Canada 2007 (McLaren)	- United States 2015 (Mercedes-Benz)
Sebastian Vettel	42	26.58	Italy 2008 (Toro Rosso)	- Singapore 2015 (Ferrari)
Ayrton Senna	41	25.47	Portugal 1985 (Lotus)	- Australia 1993 (McLaren)
Fernando Alonso	32	12.65	Hungary 2003 (Renault)	- Spain 2013 (Ferrari)
Nigel Mansell	31	16.58	Europe 1985 (Williams)	- Australia 1994 (William)
Jackie Stewart	27	27.27	Italy 1965 (BRM)	- Germany 1973 (Tyrrell)
Jim Clark	25	34.72	Belgium 1962 (Lotus)	- South Africa 1968 (Lotus)
Niki Lauda	25	14.62	Spain 1974 (Ferrari)	- Netherlands 1985 (McLaren)
Juan Manuel Fangio	24	47.06	Monaco 1950 (Alfa Romeo)	- Germany 1957 (Maserati) *
Nelson Piquet	23	11.27	United States West 1980 (Brabham)	- Canada 1991 (Benetton)
Damon Hill	22	19.13	Hungary 1993 (Williams)	- Belgium 1998 (Jordan)
Mika Häkkinen	20	12.42	Europe 1997 (McLaren)	- United States 2001 (McLaren)
Kimi Räikkönen	20	8.66	Malaysia 2003 (McLaren)	- Australia 2013 (Lotus)
Stirling Moss	16	24.24	Britain 1955 (Mercedes-Benz)	- Germany 1961 (Lotus) *
Jenson Button	15	5.28	Hungary 2006 (Honda)	- Brazil 2012 (McLaren)
Jack Brabham	14	11.11	Monaco 1959 (Cooper)	- South Africa 1970 (Brabham)
Emerson Fittipaldi	14	9.72	United States 1970 (Lotus)	- Britain 1975 (McLaren)
Graham Hill	14	7.95	Netherlands 1962 (BRM)	- Monaco 1969 (Lotus)
Nico Rosberg	14	7.57	China 2012 (Mercedes-Benz)	- Abu Dhabi 2015 (Mercedes-Benz)
Alberto Ascari	13	41.94	Germany 1951 (Ferrari)	- Switzerland 1953 (Ferrari)
David Coulthard	13	5.28	Portugal 1995 (Williams)	- Australia 2003 (McLaren)
Mario Andretti	12	9.38	South Africa 1971 (Ferrari)	- Netherlands 1978 (JPS Lotus)
Alan Jones	12	10.34	Austria 1977 (Shadow)	- Caesars Palace 1981 (Williams)
Carlos Reutemann	12	8.22	South Africa 1974 (Brabham)	- Belgium 1981 (Williams)
Rubens Barrichello	11	3.41	Germany 2000 (Ferrari)	- Italy 2009 (Brawn)
Felipe Massa	11	4.80	Turkey 2006 (Ferrari)	- Brazil 2008 (Ferrari)
Jacques Villeneuve	11	6.75	Europe 1996 (Williams)	- Luxembourg 1997 (Williams)
Gerhard Berger	10	4.76	Mexico 1986 (Benetton)	- Germany 1997 (Benetton)
James Hunt	10	10.87	Netherlands 1975 (Hesketh)	- Japan 1977 (McLaren)
Ronnie Peterson	10	8.13	France 1973 (JPS Lotus)	- Austria 1978 (JPS Lotus)
Jody Scheckter	10	8.93	Sweden 1974 (Tyrrell)	- Italy 1979 (Ferrari)
Mark Webber	9	4.19	Germany 2009 (Red Bull)	- Britain 2012 (Red Bull)
Denny Hulme	8	7.14	Monaco 1967 (Brabham)	- Argentina 1974 (McLaren)
Jacky Ickx	8	6.90	France 1968 (Ferrari)	- Germany 1972 (Ferrari)
René Arnoux	7	4.70	Brazil 1980 (Renault)	- Netherlands 1983 (Ferrari)
Juan Pablo Montoya	7	7.45	Italy 2001 (Williams)	- Brazil 2005 (McLaren)
Tony Brooks	6	15.79	Britain 1957 (Vanwall)	- Germany 1959 (Ferrari) *
Jacques Laffite	6	3.41	Sweden 1977 (Ligier)	- Canada 1981 (Talbot-Ligier)
Riccardo Patrese	6	2.34	Monaco 1982 (Brabham)	- Japan 1992 (Williams)
Jochen Rindt	6	10.00	United States 1969 (Lotus)	- Germany 1970 (Lotus)
Ralf Schumacher	6	3.33	San Marino 2001 (Williams)	- France 2003 (Williams)
John Surtees	6	5.41	Germany 1963 (Ferrari)	- Italy 1967 (Honda)
Gilles Villeneuve	6	8.96	Canada 1978 (Ferrari)	- Spain 1981 (Ferrari)
Michele Alboreto	5	2.58	Caesars Palace 1982 (Tyrrell)	- Germany 1985 (Ferrari)
Giuseppe Farina	5	15.15	Britain 1950 (Alfa Romeo)	- Germany 1953 (Ferrari)
Clay Regazzoni	5	3.79	Italy 1970 (Ferrari)	- Britain 1979 (Williams)
Keke Rosberg	5	4.39	Switzerland 1982 (Williams)	- Australia 1985 (Williams)
John Watson	5	3.29	Austria 1976 (Penske)	- United States West 1983 (McLaren)
Dan Gurney	4	4.65	France 1962 (Porsche)	- Belgium 1967 (Eagle)
Eddie Irvine	4	2.74	Australia 1999 (Ferrari)	- Malaysia 1999 (Ferrari)
Bruce McLaren	4	4.00	United States 1959 (Cooper)	- Belgium 1968 (McLaren)
Thierry Boutsen	3	1.84	Canada 1989 (Williams)	- Hungary 1990 (Williams)
Peter Collins	3	9.38	Belgium 1956 (Lancia-Ferrari)	- Britain 1958 (Ferrari)
Giancarlo Fisichella	3	1.31	Brazil 2003 (Jordan)	- Malaysia 2006 (Renault)
Heinz-Harald Frentzen	3	1.91	San Marino 1997 (Williams)	- Italy 1999 (Jordan)
Mike Hawthorn	3	6.67	France 1953 (Ferrari)	- France 1958 (Ferrari)

		% of starts		
Johnny Herbert	3	1.86	Britain 1995 (Benetton)	- Europe 1999 (Stewart)
Phil Hill	3	6.25	Italy 1960 (Ferrari)	- Italy 1961 (Ferrari)
Didier Pironi	3	4.29	Belgium 1980 (Ligier)	- Netherlands 1982 (Ferrari)
Daniel Ricciardo	3	3.41	Canada 2014 (Red Bull)	- Belgium 2014 (Red Bull)
Elio De Angelis	2	1.85	Austria 1982 (Lotus)	- San Marino 1985 (Lotus)
Patrick Depailler	2	2.11	Monaco 1978 (Tyrrell)	- Spain 1979 (Ligier)
José Froilán González	2	7.69	Britain 1951 (Ferrari)	- Britain 1954 (Ferrari)
Jean-Pierre Jabouille	2	4.08	France 1979 (Renault)	- Austria 1980 (Renault)
Peter Revson	2	6.67	Britain 1973 (McLaren)	- Canada 1973 (McLaren)
Pedro Rodríguez	2	3.64	South Africa 1967 (Cooper)	- Belgium 1970 (BRM)
Jo Siffert	2	2.08	Britain 1968 (Lotus)	- Austria 1971 (BRM)
Patrick Tambay	2	1.75	Germany 1982 (Ferrari)	- San Marino 1983 (Ferrari)
Maurice Trintignant	2	2.47	Monaco 1955 (Ferrari)	- Monaco 1958 (Cooper)
Wolfgang von Trips	2	7.41	Netherlands 1961 (Ferrari)	- Britain 1961 (Ferrari)
Jean Alesi	1	0.50	Canada 1995 (Ferrari)	
Giancarlo Baghetti	1	4.76	France 1961 (Ferrari)	
Lorenzo Bandini	1	2.38	Austria 1964 (Ferrari)	
Jean-Pierre Beltoise	1	1.16	Monaco 1972 (BRM)	
Jo Bonnier	1	0.96	Netherlands 1959 (BRM)	
Vittorio Brambilla	1	1.35	Austria 1975 (March)	
François Cevert	1	2.13	United States 1971 (Tyrrell)	
Luigi Fagioli	1	14.29	France 1951 (Alfa Romeo) *	
Peter Gethin	1	3.33	Italy 1971 (BRM)	
Richie Ginther	1	1.92	Mexico 1965 (Honda)	
Innes Ireland	1	2.00	United States 1961 (Lotus)	
Heikki Kovalainen	1	0.91	Hungary 2008 (McLaren)	
Robert Kubica	1	1.32	Canada 2008 (BMW Sauber)	
Pastor Maldonado	1	1.05	Spain 2012 (Williams)	
Jochen Mass	1	0.95	Spain 1975 (McLaren)	
Luigi Musso	1	4.17	Argentina 1956 (Lancia-Ferrari) *	
Alessandro Nannini	1	1.32	Japan 1989 (Benetton)	
Gunnar Nilsson	1	3.23	Belgium 1977 (JPS Lotus)	
Carlos Pace	1	1.39	Brazil 1975 (Brabham)	
Olivier Panis	1	0.63	Monaco 1996 (Ligier)	
Ludovico Scarfiotti	1	10.00	Italy 1966 (Ferrari)	
Piero Taruffi	1	5.56	Switzerland 1952 (Ferrari)	
Jarno Trulli	1	0.40	Monaco 2004 (Renault)	
Indianapolis 500				
Bill Vukovich	2	40.00	1953 (Kurtis-Kraft)	- 1954 (Kurtis-Kraft)
Jimmy Bryan	1	11.11	1958 (Salih)	
Pat Flaherty	1	16.67	1956 (Watson)	
Sam Hanks	1	12.50	1957 (Salih)	
Johnnie Parsons	1	11.11	1950 (Kurtis-Kraft)	
Jim Rathmann	1	10.00	1960 (Watson)	
Troy Ruttman	1	14.29	1952 (Kuzma)	
Bob Sweikert	1	20.00	1955 (Kurtis-Kraft)	
Lee Wallard	1	50.00	1951 (Kurtis-Kraft)	
Rodger Ward	1	10.00	1959 (Watson)	

* Shared drive(s) included (see section 171).

194. Percentage of races won *(Highest)*

	%	wins			%	wins
Juan Manuel Fangio	47.06	24		Jackie Stewart	27.27	27
Alberto Ascari	41.94	13		Lewis Hamilton	25.75	43
Jim Clark	34.72	25		Alain Prost	25.63	51
Michael Schumacher	29.64	91		Ayrton Senna	25.47	41
Sebastian Vettel	28.06	39		Stirling Moss	24.24	16

Excludes Indianapolis 500.

195. Winner age

Youngest

	years, days	
Sebastian Vettel	21y, 73d	Italy 2008
Fernando Alonso	22y, 26d	Hungary 2003
Bruce McLaren	22y, 104d	United States 1959
Lewis Hamilton	22y, 154d	Canada 2007
Kimi Räikkönen	23y, 157d	Malaysia 2003
Robert Kubica	23y, 184d	Canada 2008
Jacky Ickx	23y, 188d	France 1968
Michael Schumacher	23y, 240d	Belgium 1992
Emerson Fittipaldi	23y, 296d	United States 1970
Mike Hawthorn	24y, 86d	France 1953
Indianapolis 500		
Troy Ruttman	22y, 80d	1952

Oldest

	years, days	
Luigi Fagioli	53y, 22d	France 1951
Giuseppe Farina	46y, 276d	Germany 1953
Juan Manuel Fangio	46y, 41d	Germany 1957
Piero Taruffi	45y, 219d	Switzerland 1952
Jack Brabham	43y, 339d	South Africa 1970
Nigel Mansell	41y, 97d	Australia 1994
Maurice Trintignant	40y, 200d	Monaco 1958
Graham Hill	40y, 92d	Monaco 1969
Clay Regazzoni	39y, 312d	Britain 1979
Carlos Reutemann	39y, 35d	Belgium 1981
Indianapolis 500		
Sam Hanks	42y, 321d	1957
Lee Wallard	39y, 264d	1951

196. Wins in a season *(Most)*

Michael Schumacher	13 of 18	2004	(Ferrari F2004)
Sebastian Vettel	13 of 19	2013	(Red Bull RB9 - Renault)
Michael Schumacher	11 of 17	2002	(Ferrari F2001, F2002)
Lewis Hamilton	11 of 19	2014	(Mercedes-Benz F1 W05)
Sebastian Vettel	11 of 19	2011	(Renault RB7 - Renault)
Lewis Hamilton	10 of 19	2015	(Mercedes-Benz F1 W06)
Nigel Mansell	9 of 16	1992	(Williams FW14B - Renault)
Michael Schumacher	9 of 17	1995	(Benetton B195 - Renault)
Michael Schumacher	9 of 17	2000	(Ferrari F1 2000)
Michael Schumacher	9 of 17	2001	(Ferrari F2001)

All became world champion that season.

197. Wins in a season without becoming champion *(Most)*

Alain Prost	7	1984	(McLaren MP4/2 - TAG Porsche)
Alain Prost	7	1988	(McLaren MP4/4 - Honda)
Kimi Räikkönen	7	2005	(McLaren MP4-20 - Mercedes)
Michael Schumacher	7	2006	(Ferrari 248 F1)
Damon Hill	6	1994	(Williams FW16, FW16B - Renault)
Nigel Mansell	6	1987	(Williams FW11B - Honda)
Felipe Massa	6	2008	(Ferrari F2008)
Nico Rosberg	6	2015	(Mercedes-Benz F1 W06)
Michael Schumacher	6	1998	(Ferrari F300)
Ayrton Senna	6	1989	(McLaren MP4/5 - Honda)

198. Won all but one race of a season

Alberto Ascari is the only driver to achieve this, winning 6 out of the 7 grands prix in 1952 (Ferrari 500).

199. Consecutive wins *(Most)*

Alberto Ascari	9	Belgium 1952	- Belgium 1953	(Ferrari 500)
Sebastian Vettel	9	Belgium 2013	- Brazil 2013	(Red Bull RB9 - Renault)
Michael Schumacher	7	Europe 2004	- Hungary 2004	(Ferrari F2004)
Michael Schumacher	6	Italy 2000	- Malaysia 2001	(Ferrari F1 2000, F2001)
Jack Brabham	5	Netherlands 1960	- Portugal 1960	(Cooper T53 - Climax)
Jim Clark	5	Belgium 1965	- Germany 1965	(Lotus 25, 33 - Climax)
Lewis Hamilton	5	Italy 2014	- United States 2014	(Mercedes-Benz F1 W05)
Nigel Mansell	5	South Africa 1992	- San Marino 1992	(Williams FW14B - Renault)
Michael Schumacher	5	Australia 2004	- Spain 2004	(Ferrari F2004)
Fernando Alonso	4	Spain 2006	- Canada 2006	(Renault R26)
Jack Brabham	4	France 1966	- Germany 1966	(Brabham BT19 - Repco)

Jenson Button	4	Bahrain 2009	- Turkey 2009	(Brawn BGP 001 - Mercedes)
Jim Clark	4	Belgium 1963	- Britain 1963	(Lotus 25 - Climax)
Juan Manuel Fangio	4	Italy 1953	- France 1954	(Maserati A6GCM, 250F, Mercedes-Benz W196 str.)
Lewis Hamilton	4	Malaysia 2014	- Spain 2014	(Mercedes-Benz F1 W05)
Damon Hill	4	Australia 1995	- Argentina 1996	(Williams FW17B, FW18 - Renault)
Alain Prost	4	Canada 1993	- Germany 1993	(Williams FW15C - Renault)
Jochen Rindt	4	Netherlands 1970	- Germany 1970	(Lotus 72C - Ford Cosworth)
Michael Schumacher	4	Brazil 1994	- Monaco 1994	(Benetton B194 - Ford Cosworth)
Michael Schumacher	4	Brazil 2002	- Austria 2002	(Ferrari F2002)
Ayrton Senna	4	Britain 1988	- Belgium 1988	(McLaren MP4/4 - Honda)
Ayrton Senna	4	United States 1991	- Monaco 1991	(McLaren MP4/6 - Honda)
Sebastian Vettel	4	Brazil 2010	- Malaysia 2011	(Red Bull RB6, RB7 - Renault)
Sebastian Vettel	4	Singapore 2012	- India 2012	(Red Bull RB8 - Renault)

200. Won the season's opening race

Alain Prost	6	Renault 1982; McLaren 1984, 85, 87, 88; Williams 1993
Michael Schumacher	6	Benetton 1994, 95; Ferrari 2000, 01, 02, 04
Juan Manuel Fangio	5	Alfa Romeo 1951; Maserati 1954, 57; Mercedes-Benz 1955; Lancia-Ferrari 1956 (a)
Graham Hill	3	BRM 1962, 63, 64
Jackie Stewart	3	BRM 1966; Matra 1969; Tyrrell 1972
Fernando Alonso	2	Renault 2006; Ferrari 2010
Mario Andretti	2	Ferrari 1971; JPS Lotus 1978
Jack Brabham	2	Cooper 1959; Brabham 1970
Jenson Button	2	Brawn 2009; McLaren 2012
Jim Clark	2	Lotus 1965, 68
David Coulthard	2	McLaren 1997, 2003
Emerson Fittipaldi	2	JPS Lotus 1973; McLaren 1975
Lewis Hamilton	2	McLaren 2008; Mercedes-Benz 2015
Alan Jones	2	Williams 1980, 81
Nigel Mansell	2	Ferrari 1989; Williams 1992
Stirling Moss	2	Cooper 1958; Lotus 1961
Nelson Piquet	2	Brabham 1983; Williams 1986
Kimi Räikkönen	2	Ferrari 2007; Lotus 2013
Ayrton Senna	2	McLaren 1990, 91
Alberto Ascari	1	Ferrari 1953
Giuseppe Farina	1	Alfa Romeo 1950
Giancarlo Fisichella	1	Renault 2005
Mika Häkkinen	1	McLaren 1998
Damon Hill	1	Williams 1996
Denny Hulme	1	McLaren 1974
Eddie Irvine	1	Ferrari 1999
Jacques Laffite	1	Ligier 1979
Niki Lauda	1	Ferrari 1976
Bruce McLaren	1	Cooper 1960
Luigi Musso	1	Lancia-Ferrari 1956 (a)
Pedro Rodríguez	1	Cooper 1967
Nico Rosberg	1	Mercedes-Benz 2014
Jody Scheckter	1	Wolf 1977
Piero Taruffi	1	Ferrari 1952
Sebastian Vettel	1	Red Bull 2011

(a) Shared drive.

201. Won the opening race and became world champion that season

Michael Schumacher	6	1994, 95, 2000, 01, 02, 04	Giuseppe Farina	1	1950
Juan Manuel Fangio	5	1951, 54, 55, 56 (a), 57	Mika Häkkinen	1	1998
Lewis Hamilton	2	2008, 15	Graham Hill	1	1962
Alain Prost	2	1985, 93	Damon Hill	1	1996
Ayrton Senna	2	1990, 91	Alan Jones	1	1980
Fernando Alonso	1	2006	Nigel Mansell	1	1992
Mario Andretti	1	1978	Nelson Piquet	1	1983
Alberto Ascari	1	1953	Kimi Räikkönen	1	2007
Jack Brabham	1	1959	Jackie Stewart	1	1969
Jenson Button	1	2009	Sebastian Vettel	1	2011
Jim Clark	1	1965			

(a) Shared drive with Luigi Musso.

202. Opening race their only win of the season

Piero Taruffi	1952	(Ferrari)		Mario Andretti	1971	(Ferrari)
Luigi Musso	1956 (a)	(Ferrari)		Denny Hulme	1974	(McLaren)
Bruce McLaren	1960	(Cooper)		David Coulthard	2003	(McLaren)
Jackie Stewart	1966	(BRM)		Giancarlo Fisichella	2005	(Renault)
Pedro Rodríguez	1967	(Cooper)		Kimi Räikkönen	2013	(Lotus)
Jim Clark	1968	(Lotus)				
Jack Brabham	1970	(Brabham)				

(a) Shared drive with Juan Manuel Fangio.

203. Consecutive wins from the start of a season

Nigel Mansell	5	1992 (wc)	(Williams FW14B - Renault)
Michael Schumacher	5	2004 (a)(wc)	(Ferrari F2004)
Michael Schumacher	4	1994 (wc)	(Benetton B194 - Ford Cosworth)
Ayrton Senna	4	1991 (wc)	(McLaren MP4/6 - Honda)
Alberto Ascari	3	1953 (wc)	(Ferrari 500)
Juan Manuel Fangio	3	1954 (wc)	(Maserati 250F, Mercedes-Benz W196 str.)
Juan Manuel Fangio	3	1957 (wc)	(Maserati 250F)
Damon Hill	3	1996 (wc)	(Williams FW18 - Renault)
Michael Schumacher	3	2000 (wc)	(Ferrari F1 2000)
Jenson Button	2	2009 (wc)	(Brawn BGP 001 - Mercedes)
Emerson Fittipaldi	2	1973 (wc 2nd)	(JPS Lotus 72D - Ford Cosworth)
Mika Häkkinen	2	1998 (wc)	(McLaren MP4-13 - Mercedes)
Jacques Laffite	2	1979 (wc 4th)	(Ligier JS11 - Ford Cosworth)
Niki Lauda	2	1976 (wc 2nd)	(Ferrari 312T)
Alain Prost	2	1982 (wc 4th)	(Renault RE30B)
Michael Schumacher	2	2001 (wc)	(Ferrari F2001)
Jackie Stewart	2	1969 (wc)	(Matra MS10, MS80 - Ford Cosworth)
Sebastian Vettel	2	2011 (wc)	(Red Bull RB7 - Renault)

(a) Michael Schumacher is the only driver to win 7 out of the first 8 races in a season (in 2004).
(wc) World champion that season.
(wc 2nd) Finished 2nd in the championship that season.
(wc 4th) Finished 2nd in the championship that season.

204. Impressive starts to the season and became world champion
(apart from those at section 203)

Alberto Ascari	1952	won 6 of the first 7 races	(Ferrari 500)
Juan Manuel Fangio	1955	won 3 of the first 4 races	(Mercedes-Benz W196)
Jim Clark	1963	won 4 of the first 5 races	(Lotus 25 - Climax)
Jim Clark	1965	won 6 of the first 7 races	(Lotus 33, 25 - Climax)
Michael Schumacher	2002	won 5 of the first 6 races	(Ferrari F2001, F2002)
Fernando Alonso	2005	won 3 of the first 4 races	(Renault R25)
Lewis Hamilton	2014	won 4 of the first 5 races	(Mercedes-Benz F1 W05)
Lewis Hamilton	2015	won 3 of the first 4 races	(Mercedes-Benz F1 W06)

205. Impressive starts to the season, but failed to be champion
(apart from those at section 203)

Alain Prost	1988	won 3 of the first 4 races	(McLaren MP4/4 - Honda)
Ayrton Senna	1989	won 3 of the first 4 races	(McLaren MP4/5 - Honda)

The above finished 2nd in the championship that season.

206. Winner of the opening race who finished lowest in that season's championship

Jim Clark	1968	(11th in championship)	Pedro Rodríguez	1967	(6th)
Mario Andretti	1971	(8th)	Jenson Button	2012	(5th)
Jackie Stewart	1966	(7th)	Jack Brabham	1970	(5th)
Denny Hulme	1974	(7th)	Giancarlo Fisichella	2005	(5th)
David Coulthard	2003	(7th)	Kimi Räikkönen	2013	(5th)

207. Seasons of winning *(Most)*

Michael Schumacher	15	1992 - 2006	(Benetton, Ferrari)
Alain Prost	11	1981 - 93	(Renault, McLaren, Ferrari, Williams)
Nelson Piquet	10	1980 - 91	(Brabham, Williams, Benetton)
Ayrton Senna	9	1985 - 93	(Lotus, McLaren)
Fernando Alonso	9	2003 - 13	(Renault, McLaren, Ferrari)
Lewis Hamilton	9	2007 - 15	(McLaren, Mercedes-Benz)
Gerhard Berger	8	1986 - 97	(Benetton, Ferrari, McLaren)
David Coulthard	8	1995 - 2003	(Williams, McLaren)
Niki Lauda	8	1974 - 85	(Ferrari, Brabham, McLaren)
Nigel Mansell	8	1985 - 94	(Williams, Ferrari)
Kimi Räikkönen	8	2003 - 13	(McLaren, Ferrari, Lotus)
Jackie Stewart	8	1965 - 73	(BRM, Matra, March, Tyrrell)

208. Consecutive seasons of winning *(Most)*

Michael Schumacher	15	1992 - 2006	(Benetton, Ferrari)
Alain Prost	10	1981 - 90	(Renault, McLaren, Ferrari)
Ayrton Senna	9	1985 - 93	(Lotus, McLaren)
Lewis Hamilton	9	2007 - 15	(McLaren, Mercedes-Benz)
Nelson Piquet	8	1980 - 87	(Brabham, Williams)
Jim Clark	7	1962 - 68	(Lotus)
David Coulthard	7	1997 - 2003	(McLaren)
Stirling Moss	7	1955 - 61	(Mercedes-Benz, Maserati, Vanwall, Cooper, Lotus)
Jackie Stewart	6	1968 - 73	(Matra, March, Tyrrell)
Sebastian Vettel	6	2008 - 13	(Toro Rosso, Red Bull)

209. Wins by nationality

Argentina:	Juan Manuel Fangio, 24; Carlos Reutemann, 12; José Froilán González, 2
Australia:	Jack Brabham, 14; Alan Jones, 12; Mark Webber, 9; Daniel Ricciardo, 3
Austria:	Niki Lauda, 25; Gerhard Berger, 10; Jochen Rindt, 6
Belgium:	Jacky Ickx, 8; Thierry Boutsen, 3
Brazil:	Ayrton Senna, 41; Nelson Piquet, 23; Emerson Fittipaldi, 14; Rubens Barrichello, 11; Felipe Massa, 11; Carlos Pace, 1
Canada:	Jacques Villeneuve, 11; Gilles Villeneuve, 6
Colombia:	Juan Pablo Montoya, 7
Finland:	Mika Häkkinen, 20; Kimi Räikkönen, 20; Keke Rosberg, 5; Heikki Kovalainen, 1
France:	Alain Prost, 51; René Arnoux, 7; Jacques Laffite, 6; Didier Pironi, 3; Patrick Depailler, 2; Jean-Pierre Jabouille, 2; Patrick Tambay, 2; Maurice Trintignant, 2; Jean Alesi, 1; Jean-Pierre Beltoise, 1; François Cevert, 1; Olivier Panis, 1
Germany:	Michael Schumacher, 91; Sebastian Vettel, 42; Nico Rosberg, 14; Ralf Schumacher, 6; Heinz-Harald Frentzen, 3; Wolfgang von Trips, 2; Jochen Mass, 1
Great Britain:	Lewis Hamilton, 43; Nigel Mansell, 31; Jackie Stewart, 27; Jim Clark, 25; Damon Hill, 22; Stirling Moss, 16; Jenson Button, 15; Graham Hill, 14; David Coulthard, 13; James Hunt, 10; Tony Brooks, 6; John Surtees, 6; John Watson, 5; Eddie Irvine, 4; Peter Collins, 3; Mike Hawthorn, 3; Johnny Herbert, 3; Peter Gethin, 1; Innes Ireland, 1
Italy:	Alberto Ascari, 13; Riccardo Patrese, 6; Michele Alboreto, 5; Giuseppe Farina, 5; Giancarlo Fisichella, 3; Elio De Angelis, 2; Giancarlo Baghetti, 1; Lorenzo Bandini, 1; Vittorio Brambilla, 1; Luigi Fagioli, 1; Luigi Musso, 1; Alessandro Nannini, 1; Ludovico Scarfiotti, 1; Piero Taruffi, 1; Jarno Trulli, 1
Mexico:	Pedro Rodríguez, 2
New Zealand:	Denny Hulme, 8; Bruce McLaren, 4
Poland:	Robert Kubica, 1
South Africa:	Jody Scheckter, 10
Spain:	Fernando Alonso, 32
Sweden:	Ronnie Peterson, 10; Jo Bonnier, 1; Gunnar Nilsson, 1
Switzerland:	Clay Regazzoni, 5; Jo Siffert, 2
United States:	Mario Andretti, 12; Dan Gurney, 4; Phil Hill, 3; Peter Revson, 2; Richie Ginther, 1
Venezuela:	Pastor Maldonado, 1

Summary

	races	drivers		
Great Britain	247	19	France 1953 (Mike Hawthorn)	- United States 2015 (Lewis Hamilton) (a)
Germany	159	7	Netherlands 1961 (Wolfgang von Trips)	- Abu Dhabi 2015 (Nico Rosberg)
Brazil	101	6	United States 1970 (Emerson Fittipaldi)	- Italy 2009 (Rubens Barrichello)
France	79	12	Monaco 1955 (Maurice Trintignant)	- Monaco 1996 (Olivier Panis)
Finland	46	4	Switzerland 1982 (Keke Rosberg)	- Australia 2013 (Kimi Räikkönen)
Italy	43	15	Britain 1950 (Giuseppe Farina)	- Malaysia 2006 (Giancarlo Fisichella) (b)
Austria	41	3	United States 1969 (Jochen Rindt)	- Germany 1997 (Gerhard Berger)
Argentina	38	3	Monaco 1950 (Juan Manuel Fangio)	- Belgium 1981 (Carlos Reutemann) (b)

	races	drivers		
Australia	38	4	Monaco 1959 (Jack Brabham)	- Belgium 2014 (Daniel Ricciardo)
Spain	32	1	Hungary 2003 (Fernando Alonso)	- Spain 2013 (Fernando Alonso)
United States	22	5	Italy 1960 (Phil Hill)	- Netherlands 1978 (Mario Andretti)
Canada	17	2	Canada 1978 (Gilles Villeneuve)	- Luxembourg 1997 (Jacques Villeneuve)
New Zealand	12	2	United States 1959 (Bruce McLaren)	- Argentina 1974 (Denny Hulme)
Sweden	12	3	Netherlands 1959 (Jo Bonnier)	- Austria 1978 (Ronnie Peterson)
Belgium	11	2	France 1960 (Jacky Ickx)	- Hungary 1990 (Thierry Boutsen)
South Africa	10	1	Sweden 1974 (Jody Scheckter)	- Italy 1979 (Jody Scheckter)
Colombia	7	1	Italy 2001 (Juan Pablo Montoya)	- Brazil 2005 (Juan Pablo Montoya)
Switzerland	7	2	Britain 1968 (Jo Siffert)	- Britain 1979 (Clay Regazzoni)
Mexico	2	1	South Africa 1967 (Pedro Rodríguez)	- Belgium 1970 (Pedro Rodríguez)
Poland	1	1	Canada 2008 (Robert Kubica)	
Venezuela	1	1	Spain 2012 (Pastor Maldonado)	

Excludes Indianapolis 500. (a) In Britain 1957, two British drivers shared a car for the win (counted as one race). (b) Includes France 1951 and Argentina 1956, where an Italian and an Argentinian shared the win.

210. Seasons of winning by nationality

Great Britain	55	1953 - 2015	Spain	9	2003 - 13
Brazil	27	1970 - 2009	Belgium	7	1968 - 90
Germany	25	1961 - 2015	Switzerland	7	1968 - 79
France	21	1955 - 96	Sweden	6	1959 - 78
Italy	21	1950 - 2006	Canada	5	1978 - 97
Austria	18	1969 - 97	South Africa	5	1974 - 79
Finland	17	1983 - 2013	Colombia	4	2001 - 05
Australia	14	1959 - 2014	Mexico	2	1967 - 70
Argentina	13	1950 - 81	Poland	1	2008
United States	11	1960 - 78	Venezuela	1	2012
New Zealand	9	1959 - 74			

211. Consecutive seasons of winning by nationality *(Most)*

Great Britain	21	1953 - 73	Austria	6	1984 - 89
Germany	15	1992 - 2006	Argentina	5	1953 - 57
Great Britain	15	1989 - 2003	Austria	5	1974 - 78
Brazil	14	1980 - 93	Belgium	5	1968 - 72
France	14	1977 - 90	Finland	5	1997 - 2001
Great Britain	10	2006 - 15	South Africa	5	1974 - 79
Germany	8	2008 - 15			

212. Wins at the same venue *(Most)*

grand prix

Michael Schumacher	8	France	1994 - 2006	(Magny-Cours)
Michael Schumacher	7	Canada	1994 - 2004	(Montréal)
Michael Schumacher	7	San Marino	1994 - 2006	(Imola)
Alain Prost	6	Brazil	1982 - 90	(Jacarepaguá, 5; Interlagos, 1)
Alain Prost	6	France	1981 - 93	(Paul Ricard, 4; Dijon-Prenois, 1; Magny-Cours, 1)
Michael Schumacher	6	Belgium	1992 - 2002	(Spa-Francorchamps)
Michael Schumacher	6	Europe	1994 - 2006	(Nürburgring, 5; Jerez de la Frontera, 1)
Michael Schumacher	6	Japan	1995 - 2004	(Suzuka)
Michael Schumacher	6	Spain	1995 - 2004	(Catalunya)
Ayrton Senna	6	Monaco	1987 - 93	(Monte-Carlo)

circuit

Michael Schumacher	8	Magny-Cours	1994 - 2006		Alain Prost	5	Jacarepaguá	1982 - 88
Michael Schumacher	7	Imola	1994 - 2006		Alain Prost	5	Silverstone	1983 - 93
Michael Schumacher	7	Montréal	1994 - 2004		Michael Schumacher	5	Indianapolis	2000 - 06
Michael Schumacher	6	Catalunya	1995 - 2004		Michael Schumacher	5	Monte-Carlo	1994 - 2001
Michael Schumacher	6	Spa-Francorchamps	1992 - 2002		Michael Schumacher	5	Monza	1996 - 2006
Michael Schumacher	6	Suzuka	1995 - 2004		Michael Schumacher	5	Nürburgring	1995 - 2006 (a)
Ayrton Senna	6	Monte-Carlo	1987 - 93		Ayrton Senna	5	Spa-Francorchamps	1985 - 91
Graham Hill	5	Monte-Carlo	1963 - 69					

(a) European Grand Prix.

213. Consecutive wins at the same venue *(Most)*

grand prix

Ayrton Senna	5	Monaco	1989 - 93	(Monte-Carlo)
Jim Clark	4	Belgium	1962 - 65	(Spa-Francorchamps)
Jim Clark	4	Britain	1962 - 65	(Silverstone, 2; Aintree, 1; Brands Hatch, 1)
Juan Manuel Fangio	4	Argentina	1954 - 57	(Buenos Aires No.2)
Michael Schumacher	4	United States	2003 - 06	(Indianapolis)
Michael Schumacher	4	Spain	2001 - 04	(Catalunya)
Ayrton Senna	4	Belgium	1988 - 91	(Spa-Francorchamps)
Jim Clark	3	Netherlands	1963 - 65	(Zandvoort)
Juan Manuel Fangio	3	Germany	1954 - 57 (a)	(Nürburgring)
Juan Manuel Fangio	3	Italy	1953 - 55	(Monza)
Mika Häkkinen	3	Spain	1998 - 2000	(Catalunya)
Graham Hill	3	Monaco	1963 - 65	(Monte-Carlo)
Graham Hill	3	United States	1963 - 65	(Watkins Glen)
Felipe Massa	3	Turkey	2006 - 08	(Istanbul)
Alain Prost	3	France	1988 - 90	(Paul Ricard)
Alain Prost	3	Monaco	1984 - 86	(Monte-Carlo)
Kimi Räikkönen	3	Belgium	2004 - 07 (b)	(Spa-Francorchamps)
Nico Rosberg	3	Monaco	2013 - 15	(Monte-Carlo)
Michael Schumacher	3	Australia	2000 - 02	(Melbourne)
Michael Schumacher	3	Belgium	1995 - 97	(Spa-Francorchamps)
Michael Schumacher	3	Canada	2002 - 04	(Montréal)
Michael Schumacher	3	Japan	2000 - 02	(Suzuka)
Michael Schumacher	3	San Marino	2002 - 04	(Imola)
Ayrton Senna	3	Germany	1988 - 90	(Hockenheim)
Ayrton Senna	3	United States	1986 - 88	(Detroit)
Jackie Stewart	3	Spain	1969 - 71	(Montjuïc, 2; Jarama, 1)
Sebastian Vettel	3	India	2011 - 13	(Buddh)
Sebastian Vettel	3	Korea	2011 - 13	(Yeongam)
Sebastian Vettel	3	Singapore	2011 - 13	(Marina Bay)

(a) No German Grand Prix in 1955.
(b) No Belgian Grand Prix in 2006.

circuit

Ayrton Senna	5	Monte-Carlo	1989 - 93
Juan Manuel Fangio	4	Buenos Aires No.2	1954 - 57 (c)
Jim Clark	4	Spa-Francorchamps	1962 - 65
Ayrton Senna	4	Spa-Francorchamps	1988 - 91
Michael Schumacher	4	Indianapolis	2003 - 06
Michael Schumacher	4	Catalunya	2001 - 04
Juan Manuel Fangio	3	Monza	1953 - 55
Juan Manuel Fangio	3	Nürburgring	1954 - 57
Graham Hill	3	Monte-Carlo	1963 - 65
Graham Hill	3	Watkins Glen	1963 - 65
Jim Clark	3	Zandvoort	1963 - 65
Jim Clark	3	Silverstone	1963 - 67
Alain Prost	3	Monte-Carlo	1984 - 86
Ayrton Senna	3	Detroit	1986 - 88
Ayrton Senna	3	Hockenheim	1988 - 90
Alain Prost	3	Paul Ricard	1988 - 90
Michael Schumacher	3	Spa-Francorchamps	1995 - 97
Mika Häkkinen	3	Catalunya	1998 - 2000
Michael Schumacher	3	Melbourne	2000 - 02
Michael Schumacher	3	Suzuka	2000 - 02
Michael Schumacher	3	Imola	2002 - 04
Michael Schumacher	3	Montréal	2002 - 04
Kimi Räikkönen	3	Spa-Francorchamps	2004 - 07
Felipe Massa	3	Istanbul	2006 - 08
Sebastian Vettel	3	Buddh	2011 - 13
Sebastian Vettel	3	Marina Bay	2011 - 13
Sebastian Vettel	3	Yeongam	2011 - 13
Nico Rosberg	3	Monte-Carlo	2013 - 15

(c) Includes 1 shared drive.

214. Consecutive different winners at the same venue

grand prix

Germany	14	1972 - 85	France	8	1956 - 63
Belgium	11	1976 - 86	Germany	8	1996 - 2003
Mexico	11	1964 - 89 (a)	Italy	8	1966 - 73
Austria	9	1964 - 77 (a)	Italy	8	1975 - 82
Britain	9	1973 - 81	Netherlands	8	1953 - 63 (a)
Spain	9	2007 - 15	Netherlands	8	1976 - 83
Argentina	8	1974 - 95 (a)	United States	8	1969 - 76
Britain	8	2003 - 10	United States West	8	1976 - 83
Canada	8	1989 - 96			

(a) Race not held every year within the period.

Mexico City	11	1964 - 89 (a)		Monza	8	1966 - 73
Paul Ricard	10	1971 - 86 (a)		Monza	8	1975 - 83 (a)
Brands Hatch	9	1964 - 80 (a)		Österreichring	8	1970 - 77
Catalunya	9	2007 - 15		Silverstone	8	2003 - 10
Hockenheim	9	1970 - 84 (a)		Spa-Francorchamps	8	1965 - 86 (a)
Interlagos	9	1974 - 92 (a)		Watkins Glen	8	1969 - 76
Nürburgring	9	1972 - 96 (a)		Zandvoort	8	1953 - 63 (a)
Buenos Aires	8	1974 - 95 (a)		Zandvoort	8	1976 - 83
Hockenheim	8	1996 - 2003		Zolder	8	1976 - 84 (a)
Long Beach	8	1976 - 83				
Montréal	8	1989 - 96				

(a) Race not held every year within the period.

215. More than one win in a country during a season

Stirling Moss (Vanwall)	1957	Italy (Pescara & Monza)
Carlos Reutemann (Ferrari)	1978	United States (Long Beach & Watkins Glen)
Gilles Villeneuve (Ferrari)	1979	United States (Long Beach & Watkins Glen)
Alan Jones (Williams)	1981	United States (Long Beach & Caesars Palace)
Alain Prost (McLaren)	1984	Germany (Hockenheim & Nürburgring)
Michael Schumacher (Benetton)	1995	Germany (Hockenheim & Nürburgring)
Michael Schumacher (Benetton)	1995	Japan (Aida & Suzuka)
Mika Häkkinen (McLaren)	1998	Germany (Hockenheim & Nürburgring)
Michael Schumacher (Ferrari)	2000	Italy (Imola & Monza)
Michael Schumacher (Ferrari)	2003	Italy (Imola & Monza)
Michael Schumacher (Ferrari)	2004	Germany (Nürburgring & Hockenheim)
Fernando Alonso (Renault)	2005	Germany (Nürburgring & Hockenheim)
Michael Schumacher (Ferrari)	2006	Germany (Nürburgring & Hockenheim)
Michael Schumacher (Ferrari)	2006	Italy (Imola & Monza)
Sebastian Vettel (Red Bull)	2011	Spain (Catalunya & Valencia)

216. Wins on home soil

by country

Argentina

Buenos Aires No.2	4	Juan Manuel Fangio, 4

Austria

Österreichring	1	Niki Lauda, 1

Brazil

Interlagos	7	Emerson Fittipaldi, 2; Felipe Massa, 2; Ayrton Senna, 2; Carlos Pace, 1
Jacarepaguá	2	Nelson Piquet, 2

Britain

Aintree	3	Stirling Moss, 2 (a); Tony Brooks, 1 (a); Jim Clark, 1
Brands Hatch	3	Nigel Mansell, 2 (b); Jim Clark, 1
Silverstone	18	Jim Clark, 3; Lewis Hamilton, 3; Nigel Mansell, 3; David Coulthard, 2; Jackie Stewart, 2; Peter Collins, 1; Johnny Herbert, 1; Damon Hill, 1; James Hunt, 1; John Watson, 1

Canada

Montréal	1	Gilles Villeneuve, 1

France

Dijon-Prenois	2	Jean-Pierre Jabouille, 1; Alain Prost, 1
Magny-Cours	1	Alain Prost, 1
Paul Ricard	5	Alain Prost, 4; René Arnoux, 1

Germany

Hockenheim	6	Michael Schumacher, 4; Nico Rosberg, 1; Ralf Schumacher, 1
Nürburgring	7	Michael Schumacher, 5 (c); Ralf Schumacher, 1 (c); Sebastian Vettel, 1

Italy

Imola (d)	2	Elio De Angelis, 1; Riccardo Patrese, 1
Monza	4	Alberto Ascari, 2; Giuseppe Farina, 1; Ludovico Scarfiotti, 1

South Africa

Kyalami	1	Jody Scheckter, 1

Spain

Catalunya	2	Fernando Alonso, 2
Valencia (c)	1	Fernando Alonso, 1

United States

Long Beach (e)	1	Mario Andretti, 1

Excludes Indianapolis 500.
(a) Includes 1 shared drive. (b) 1 British & 1 European Grand Prix. (c) European Grand Prix. (d) San Marino Grand Prix. (e) United States West Grand Prix.

by driver

Michael Schumacher	9	Germany	1995 - 2006	(Nürburgring, 5; Hockenheim, 4)
Alain Prost	6	France	1981 - 93	(Paul Ricard, 4; Dijon-Prenois, 1; Magny-Cours, 1)
Jim Clark	5	Britain	1962 - 67	(Silverstone, 3; Aintree, 1; Brands Hatch, 1)
Nigel Mansell	5	Britain	1985 - 92	(Silverstone, 3; Brands Hatch, 2)
Juan Manuel Fangio	4	Argentina	1954 - 57	(Buenos Aires No.2)
Fernando Alonso	3	Spain	2006 - 13	(Catalunya, 2; Valencia, 1)
Lewis Hamilton	3	Britain	2008 - 15	(Silverstone)
Alberto Ascari	2	Italy	1951 - 52	(Monza)
David Coulthard	2	Britain	1999 - 2000	(Silverstone)
Emerson Fittipaldi	2	Brazil	1973 - 74	(Interlagos)
Felipe Massa	2	Brazil	2006 - 08	(Interlagos)
Stirling Moss	2	Britain	1955 - 57	(Aintree)
Nelson Piquet	2	Brazil	1983 - 86	(Jacarepaguá)
Ralf Schumacher	2	Germany	2001 - 03	(Hockenheim, 1; Nürburgring, 1)
Ayrton Senna	2	Brazil	1991 - 93	(Interlagos)
Jackie Stewart	2	Britain	1969 - 71	(Silverstone)
Mario Andretti	1	United States	1977	(Long Beach)
René Arnoux	1	France	1982	(Paul Ricard)
Tony Brooks	1	Britain	1957	(Aintree)
Peter Collins	1	Britain	1958	(Silverstone)
Elio De Angelis	1	Italy	1985	(Imola)
Giuseppe Farina	1	Italy	1950	(Monza)
Johnny Herbert	1	Britain	1995	(Silverstone)
Damon Hill	1	Britain	1994	(Silverstone)
James Hunt	1	Britain	1977	(Silverstone)
Jean-Pierre Jabouille	1	France	1979	(Dijon-Prenois)
Niki Lauda	1	Austria	1984	(Österreichring)
Carlos Pace	1	Brazil	1975	(Interlagos)
Riccardo Patrese	1	Italy	1990	(Imola)
Nico Rosberg	1	Germany	2014	(Hockenheim)
Ludovico Scarfiotti	1	Italy	1966	(Monza)
Jody Scheckter	1	South Africa	1975	(Kyalami)
Sebastian Vettel	1	Germany	2013	(Nürburgring)
Gilles Villeneuve	1	Canada	1978	(Montréal)
John Watson	1	Britain	1981	(Silverstone)

217. First win was on home soil

Tony Brooks	Britain 1957	(Aintree)		Stirling Moss	Britain 1955	(Aintree)
Johnny Herbert	Britain 1995	(Silverstone)		Carlos Pace	Brazil 1975	(Interlagos)
Jean-Pierre Jabouille	France 1979	(Dijon-Prenois)		Alain Prost	France 1981	(Dijon-Prenois)
Nigel Mansell	Europe 1985	(Brands Hatch)		Ludovico Scarfiotti	Italy 1966	(Monza)

218. Two wins on home soil in a season

Michael Schumacher is the only driver to do so, winning the German and European Grands Prix in 1995, 2004 and 2006.

219. Wins at the four classic circuits
(Monte-Carlo, Monza, Silverstone and Spa-Francorchamps)

all four

David Coulthard	Monte-Carlo (2), Monza (1), Silverstone (2), Spa-Francorchamps (1)
Juan Manuel Fangio	Monte-Carlo (2), Monza (3), Silverstone (1), Spa-Francorchamps (3)
Lewis Hamilton	Monte-Carlo (1), Monza (3), Silverstone (3), Spa-Francorchamps (2)
Alain Prost	Monte-Carlo (4), Monza (3), Silverstone (5), Spa-Francorchamps (2)
Michael Schumacher	Monte-Carlo (5), Monza (5), Silverstone (3), Spa-Francorchamps (6)
Ayrton Senna	Monte-Carlo (6), Monza (2), Silverstone (1), Spa-Francorchamps (5)
Sebastian Vettel	Monte-Carlo (1), Monza (3), Silverstone (1), Spa-Francorchamps (2)

three out of four

Fernando Alonso	Monte-Carlo (2), Monza (2), Silverstone (2)	Damon Hill	Monza (2), Silverstone (1), Spa-Francorchamps (3)
Alberto Ascari	Monza (2), Silverstone (2), Spa-Francorchamps (2)	Nigel Mansell	Monza (1), Silverstone (3), Spa-Francorchamps (1)
Jack Brabham	Monte-Carlo (1), Silverstone (1), Spa-Francorchamps (1)	Juan Pablo Montoya	Monte-Carlo (1), Monza (2), Silverstone (1)
Jim Clark	Monza (1), Silverstone (3), Spa-Francorchamps (4)	Kimi Räikkönen	Monte-Carlo (1), Silverstone (1), Spa-Francorchamps (4)
Giuseppe Farina	Monza (1), Silverstone (1), Spa-Francorchamps (1)	Jackie Stewart	Monte-Carlo (3), Monza (2), Silverstone (2)
Mika Häkkinen	Monte-Carlo (1), Silverstone (1), Spa-Francorchamps (1)		

220. Race starts taken to achieve their first win
(number of races includes the first race won)

Fewest

Giuseppe Farina	1	Britain 1950 (a)	
Giancarlo Baghetti	1	France 1961 (a)	
Juan Manuel Fangio	2	Monaco 1950 (a)	
Tony Brooks	3	Britain 1957 (b)	
Emerson Fittipaldi	4	United States 1970 (a)(b)	
Ludovico Scarfiotti	4	Italy 1966 (c)	
Jacques Villeneuve	4	Europe 1996 (a)	
José Froilán González	5	Britain 1951	
Clay Regazzoni	5	Italy 1970 (a)	
Lewis Hamilton	6	Canada 2007 (a)	
Luigi Fagioli	7	France 1951	
Piero Taruffi	7	Switzerland 1952	

Jackie Stewart	8	Italy 1965 (a)
Alberto Ascari	9	Germany 1951 (b)
Mike Hawthorn	9	France 1953
Jacky Ickx	9	France 1968
Bruce McLaren	9	United States 1959
Mario Andretti	10	South Africa 1971 (d)
Luigi Musso	10	Argentina 1956 (b)
Pedro Rodríguez	10	South Africa 1967

Excludes Indianapolis 500.
(a) First season to enter Formula 1.
(b) Additionally 1 race non-start before first win.
(c) Additionally 2 race non-starts before first win.
(d) Additionally excluded from one race before first win.

Most

Mark Webber	130	Germany 2009
Rubens Barrichello	124	Germany 2000
Jarno Trulli	117	Monaco 2004
Jenson Button	113	Hungary 2006
Nico Rosberg	111	China 2012
Giancarlo Fisichella	110	Brazil 2003
Mika Häkkinen	96	Europe 1997
Thierry Boutsen	95	Canada 1989
Jean Alesi	91	Canada 1995
Eddie Irvine	81	Australia 1999
Nigel Mansell	72	Europe 1985
Johnny Herbert	71	Britain 1995

Riccardo Patrese	71	Monaco 1982
Ralf Schumacher	70	San Marino 2001
Patrick Depailler	69	Monaco 1978
Felipe Massa	66	Turkey 2006
Alessandro Nannini	61	Japan 1989
Daniel Ricciardo	57	Canada 2014
Jo Siffert	57	Britain 1968
Elio De Angelis	54	Austria 1982
Patrick Tambay	53	Germany 1982
Heinz-Harald Frentzen	52	San Marino 1997

For most races started but never a win, see section 184.

221. Wins in their first season

Lewis Hamilton	4	2007
Jacques Villeneuve	4	1996
Juan Manuel Fangio	3	1950
Giuseppe Farina	3	1950
Giancarlo Baghetti	1	1961

Emerson Fittipaldi	1	1970
Juan Pablo Montoya	1	2001
Clay Regazzoni	1	1970
Jackie Stewart	1	1965

222. First win immediately followed by others
(including first win)

Damon Hill	3	Hungary 1993	- Italy 1993	(Williams FW15C - Renault)
Mika Häkkinen	3	Europe 1997	- Brazil 1998	(McLaren MP4-12, MP4-13 - Mercedes)
René Arnoux	2	Brazil 1980	- South Africa 1980	(Renault RE20)
Alberto Ascari	2	Germany 1951	- Italy 1951	(Ferrari 375)
Peter Collins	2	Belgium 1956	- France 1956	(Lancia-Ferrari D50)
Lewis Hamilton	2	Canada 2007	- United States 2007	(McLaren MP4-22 - Mercedes)
Nigel Mansell	2	Europe 1985	- South Africa 1985	(Williams FW10 - Honda)
Bruce McLaren	2	United States 1959	- Argentina 1960	(Cooper T51 - Climax)

First win was in their first title winning season. See section 111

223. Led every lap in the race of their first win

Jean-Pierre Beltoise	Monaco 1972
Richie Ginther	Mexico 1965
Juan Manuel Fangio	Monaco 1950
Damon Hill	Hungary 1993
Nelson Piquet	United States West 1980
Didier Pironi	Belgium 1980

Jody Scheckter	Sweden 1974
Ralf Schumacher	San Marino 2001
Ayrton Senna	Portugal 1985
Jacques Villeneuve	Europe 1996
Wolfgang von Trips	Netherlands 1961

224. 2nd places before their first win *(Most)*

Patrick Depailler	8	Ronnie Peterson	5	Dan Gurney	4
Richie Ginther	8	Alberto Ascari	4	Lewis Hamilton	4
Jean Alesi	6	Jenson Button	4	Damon Hill	4
Rubens Barrichello	5	David Coulthard	4	Eddie Irvine	4
Giancarlo Fisichella	5	Luigi Fagioli	4	John Surtees	4

225. Podiums before their first win

Most

Jean Alesi	15
Patrick Depailler	15
Mika Häkkinen	15
Eddie Irvine	15
Jenson Button	13
Richie Ginther	13
Rubens Barrichello	12
Giancarlo Fisichella	9
Ralf Schumacher	9
Ronnie Peterson	8

Fewest (no previous podiums)

Giancarlo Baghetti
Jo Bonnier
Jack Brabham
Vittorio Brambilla
Juan Manuel Fangio
Giuseppe Farina
Emerson Fittipaldi
Peter Gethin
Jean-Pierre Jabouille
Alan Jones
Pastor Maldonado
Pedro Rodríguez
Ludovico Scarfiotti
Sebastian Vettel

226. Pole positions before their first win *(Most)*

Jochen Rindt	7 *	David Coulthard	3 *	Jean-Pierre Jabouille	2 *
Ronnie Peterson	4	Juan Pablo Montoya	3 *	Niki Lauda	2 *
Rubens Barrichello	3	Fernando Alonso	2 *	John Surtees	2
Jenson Button	3	René Arnoux	2		

* Includes race of first win.

227. Won their final race

Luigi Fagioli	France 1951	shared car with Juan Manuel Fangio. This made him the oldest Formula 1 race winner (see section 195).
Jim Clark	South Africa 1968	killed in a Formula 2 race (Deutschland Trophäe) at Hockenheim, three months later and prior to the next Formula 1 race.

228. Wins in their final season

Alain Prost	7	1993		Jim Clark	1	1968
Jochen Rindt	5	1970		Peter Collins	1	1958
Jackie Stewart	5	1973		Luigi Fagioli	1	1951
Mika Häkkinen	2	2001		Mike Hawthorn	1	1958
Stirling Moss	2	1961		Denny Hulme	1	1974
Ronnie Peterson	2	1978		Niki Lauda	1	1985
Didier Pironi	2	1982		Gunnar Nilsson	1	1977
Wolfgang von Trips	2	1961		Nelson Piquet	1	1991
Gerhard Berger	1	1997		Jo Siffert	1	1971
Jack Brabham	1	1970				

229. Winning driver and car of the same nationality

There have been five nationalities of winning driver and car being the same.
The first occasions for each were:

American	Belgium 1967	Dan Gurney	Eagle T1G
British	Argentina 1958	Stirling Moss	Cooper T43
French	Sweden 1977	Jacques Laffite	Ligier JS7

Germany	Germany 2014	Nico Rosberg	Mercedes-Benz F1 W05
Italian	Britain 1950	Giuseppe Farina	Alfa Romeo 158

230. Wins from pole position

Michael Schumacher	40	Monaco 1994 (Benetton)	- France 2006 (Ferrari)
Ayrton Senna	29	Portugal 1985 (Lotus)	- Australia 1993 (McLaren)
Sebastian Vettel	28	Italy 2008 (Toro Rosso)	- Singapore 2015 (Ferrari)
Lewis Hamilton	25	Canada 2007 (McLaren)	- Italy 2015 (Mercedes-Benz)
Alain Prost	18	Netherlands 1981 (Renault)	- Germany 1993 (Williams)
Nigel Mansell	17	South Africa 1985 (Williams)	- Australia 1994 (Williams)

Jim Clark	15	Britain 1962 (Lotus)	- South Africa 1968 (Lotus)
Juan Manuel Fangio	15	Monaco 1950 (Alfa Romeo)	- Germany 1957 (Maserati) (a)
Fernando Alonso	14	Hungary 2003 (Renault)	- Germany 2012 (Ferrari)
Mika Häkkinen	10	Australia 1998 (McLaren)	- Belgium 2000 (McLaren)
Alberto Ascari	9	Germany 1951 (Ferrari)	- Britain 1953 (Ferrari)
Niki Lauda	9	Spain 1974 (Ferrari)	- Britain 1976 (Ferrari)
Nico Rosberg	9	China 2012 (Mercedes-Benz)	- Abu Dhabi 2015 (Mercedes-Benz)
Mario Andretti	8	Japan 1976 (JPS Lotus)	- Netherlands 1978 (JPS Lotus)
Felipe Massa	8	Turkey 2006 (Ferrari)	- Brazil 2008 (Ferrari)
Stirling Moss	8	Britain 1955 (Mercedes-Benz)	- Monaco 1961 (Lotus) (b)
Jackie Stewart	8	France 1969 (Matra)	- Germany 1973 (Tyrrell)
Damon Hill	7	Britain 1994 (Williams)	- Germany 1996 (Williams)
James Hunt	7	Spain 1976 (McLaren)	- United States 1977 (McLaren)
Jack Brabham	6	Britain 1959 (Cooper)	- Netherlands 1966 (Brabham)
Kimi Räikkönen	6	Spain 2005 (McLaren)	- Spain 2008 (Ferrari)
Rubens Barrichello	5	Hungary 2002 (Ferrari)	- China 2004 (Ferrari)
Gerhard Berger	5	Japan 1987 (Ferrari)	- Germany 1997 (Benetton)
Jenson Button	5	Australia 2009 (Brawn)	- Belgium 2012 (McLaren)
Nelson Piquet	5	United States West 1980 (Brabham)	- Italy 1987 (Williams)
Jacques Villeneuve	5	Brazil 1997 (Williams)	- Austria 1997 (Williams)
Emerson Fittipaldi	4	Belgium 1972 (JPS Lotus)	- Canada 1974 (McLaren)
Graham Hill	4	United States 1963 (BRM)	- Monaco 1968 (Lotus)
Jacky Ickx	4	Germany 1969 (Brabham)	- Germany 1972 (Ferrari)
John Surtees	4	Germany 1964 (Ferrari)	- Mexico 1966 (Cooper)
Mark Webber	4	Germany 2009 (Red Bull)	- Monaco 2012 (Red Bull)
Juan Pablo Montoya	3	Italy 2001 (Williams)	- Italy 2005 (McLaren)
Ronnie Peterson	3	Italy 1973 (JPS Lotus)	- Austria 1978 (JPS Lotus)
Carlos Reutemann	3	United States 1974 (Brabham)	- Belgium 1981 (Williams)
Jochen Rindt	3	United States 1969 (Lotus)	- Britain 1970 (Lotus)
René Arnoux	2	France 1982 (Renault)	- Canada 1983 (Ferrari)
Tony Brooks	2	France 1959 (Ferrari)	- Germany 1959 (Ferrari)
David Coulthard	2	Portugal 1995 (Williams)	- San Marino 1998 (McLaren)
Giancarlo Fisichella	2	Australia 2005 (Renault)	- Malaysia 2006 (Renault)
Phil Hill	2	Italy 1960 (Ferrari)	- Belgium 1961 (Ferrari)
Alan Jones	2	Canada 1979 (Williams)	- Argentina 1980 (Williams)
Jacques Laffite	2	Argentina 1979 (Ligier)	- Brazil 1979 (Ligier)
Riccardo Patrese	2	Mexico 1991 (Williams)	- Portugal 1991 (Williams)
Jody Scheckter	2	Sweden 1976 (Tyrrell)	- Monaco 1979 (Ferrari)
Michele Alboreto	1	Belgium 1984 (Ferrari)	
Jo Bonnier	1	Netherlands 1959 (BRM)	
Thierry Boutsen	1	Hungary 1990 (Williams)	
Giuseppe Farina	1	Britain 1950 (Alfa Romeo)	
José Froilán González	1	Britain 1951 (Ferrari)	
Mike Hawthorn	1	France 1958 (Ferrari)	
Jean-Pierre Jabouille	1	France 1979 (Renault)	
Pastor Maldonado	1	Spain 2012 (Williams)	
Clay Regazzoni	1	United States West 1976 (Ferrari)	
Ralf Schumacher	1	France 2003 (Williams)	
Jo Siffert	1	Austria 1971 (BRM)	
Jarno Trulli	1	Monaco 2004 (Renault)	
Gilles Villeneuve	1	United States West 1979 (Ferrari)	

Indianapolis 500

Pat Flaherty	1	1956 (Watson)
Bill Vukovich	1	1953 (Kurtis-Kraft)

(a) Includes France 1951 & Argentina 1956, where he started in a different car from which he finished the race.
(b) Includes Britain 1957, where he started in a different car from which he finished the race.

231. Consecutive races with a win from pole *(Most)*

Michael Schumacher	6	Italy 2000	- Malaysia 2001	(Ferrari F1 2000, F2001)
Alberto Ascari	5	Germany 1952	- Netherlands 1953	(Ferrari 500)
Nigel Mansell	5	South Africa 1992	- San Marino 1992	(Williams FW14B - Renault)
Fernando Alonso	4	Spain 2006	- Canada 2006	(Renault R26)
Ayrton Senna	4	United States 1991	- Monaco 1991	(McLaren MP4/6 - Honda)
Jack Brabham	3	Belgium 1960	- Britain 1960	(Cooper T53 - Climax)
Jim Clark	3	Netherlands 1963	- Britain 1963	(Lotus 25 - Climax)
Lewis Hamilton	3	China 2014	- Monaco 2014	(Mercedes-Benz F1 W05)
Nigel Mansell	3	France 1992	- Germany 1992	(Williams FW14B - Renault)
Nico Rosberg	3	Mexico 2015	- Abu Dhabi 2015	(Mercedes-Benz F1 W06)
Michael Schumacher	3	Australia 2004	- Bahrain 2004	(Ferrari F2004)
Michael Schumacher	3	San Marino 2003	- Austria 2003	(Ferrari F2002, F2003-GA)
Ayrton Senna	3	Germany 1988	- Belgium 1988	(McLaren MP4/4 - Honda)
Ayrton Senna	3	San Marino 1989	- Mexico 1989	(McLaren MP4/5 - Honda)
Sebastian Vettel	3	Abu Dhabi 2010	- Malaysia 2011	(Red Bull RB6, RB7 - Renault)
Sebastian Vettel	3	Belgium 2011	- Singapore 2011	(Red Bull RB7 - Renault)
Sebastian Vettel	3	Italy 2013	- Korea 2013	(Red Bull RB9 - Renault)

232. Wins from front row *(Most)*

Michael Schumacher	67	Brazil 1994	- Italy 2006
Sebastian Vettel	39	Italy 2008	- Singapore 2015
Lewis Hamilton	38	Canada 2007	- United States 2015
Ayrton Senna	34	Portugal 1985	- Australia 1993
Alain Prost	29	Netherlands 1981	- Germany 1993
Nigel Mansell	26	South Africa 1985	- Australia 1994
Juan Manuel Fangio	24	Monaco 1950	- Germany 1957 (a)
Jim Clark	20	Britain 1962	- South Africa 1968
Fernando Alonso	18	Hungary 2003	- Germany 2012
Damon Hill	18	Hungary 1993	- Japan 1996

(a) Includes France 1951 & Argentina 1956, where he started in a different car from which he finished the race.
(b) Includes Britain 1957, where he started in a different car from which he finished the race.

233. Wins from behind front row *(Most)*

Michael Schumacher	24	Belgium 1992	- China 2006
Alain Prost	22	France 1981	- Britain 1990
Nelson Piquet	16	Netherlands 1980	- Canada 1991
Fernando Alonso	14	Europe 2005	- Spain 2013
Niki Lauda	13	Sweden 1975	- Netherlands 1985
Jackie Stewart	11	Monaco 1966	- Belgium 1973
Kimi Räikkönen	10	Malaysia 2003	- Australia 2013
David Coulthard	8	Australia 1997	- Australia 2003
Denny Hulme	7	Monaco 1967	- Argentina 1974
Ayrton Senna	7	Britain 1988	- Monaco 1993

234. Winner from lowest grid position

John Watson	22nd	United States West 1983	(McLaren MP/1C - Ford Cosworth)
Rubens Barrichello	18th	Germany 2000	(Ferrari F1 2000)
Kimi Räikkönen	17th	Japan 2005	(McLaren MP4-20 - Mercedes)
John Watson	17th	Detroit 1982	(McLaren MP4B - Ford Cosworth)
Michael Schumacher	16th	Belgium 1995	(Benetton B195 - Renault)
Jackie Stewart	16th	South Africa 1973	(Tyrrell 006 - Ford Cosworth)
Fernando Alonso	15th	Singapore 2008	(Renault R28)
Jenson Button	14th	Hungary 2006	(Honda RA106)
Johnny Herbert	14th	Europe 1999	(Stewart SF-3 - Ford Cosworth)
Alan Jones	14th	Austria 1977	(Shadow DN8 - Ford Cosworth)
Olivier Panis	14th	Monaco 1996	(Ligier JS43 - Mugen Honda)
Indianapolis 500			
Bill Vukovich	19th	1954	(Kurtis-Kraft 500A - Offenhauser)
Bob Sweikert	14th	1955	(Kurtis-Kraft 500D - Offenhauser)

235. Different winners in a season

Most

1982	11	(René Arnoux, Niki Lauda, Didier Pironi, Alain Prost and John Watson achieved two each, whilst Michele Alboreto, Elio De Angelis, Riccardo Patrese, Nelson Piquet, Keke Rosberg and Patrick Tambay had one victory each)
1975	9	
1977	8	
1983	8	
1985	8	
2003	8	
2012	8	

Fewest

1950	2
1952	2
1954	3
1955	3
1957	3
1963	3
1988	3
2014	3
2015	3

Total for each season

1950 - 2, 1951 - 5, 1952 - 2, 1953 - 4, 1954 - 3, 1955 - 3, 1956 - 4, 1957 - 3, 1958 - 5, 1959 - 5, 1960 - 4, 1961 - 5, 1962 - 4, 1963 - 3, 1964 - 5, 1965 - 4, 1966 - 5, 1967 - 6, 1968 - 7, 1969 - 5, 1970 - 7, 1971 - 6, 1972 - 5, 1973 - 5, 1974 - 7, 1975 - 9, 1976 - 7, 1977 - 8, 1978 - 6, 1979 - 7, 1980 - 7, 1981 - 7, 1982 - 11, 1983 - 8, 1984 - 5, 1985 - 8, 1986 - 5, 1987 - 5, 1988 - 3, 1989 - 6, 1990 - 6, 1991 - 5, 1992 - 5, 1993 - 4, 1994 - 4, 1995 - 5, 1996 - 6, 1997 - 6, 1998 - 4, 1999 - 6, 2000 - 4, 2001 - 5, 2002 - 4, 2003 - 8, 2004 - 5, 2005 - 5, 2006 - 5, 2007 - 4, 2008 - 7, 2009 - 6, 2010 - 5, 2011 - 5, 2012 - 8, 2013 - 5, 2014 - 3, 2015 - 3

Excludes Indianapolis 500.

236. Different winners in consecutive races *(Most)*

France 1961 - France 1962	9	Baghetti, von Trips, Moss, Phil Hill, Ireland, Graham Hill, McLaren, Clark, Gurney
Monaco - Switzerland 1982	9	Patrese, Watson, Piquet, Pironi, Lauda, Arnoux, Tambay, De Angelis, Rosberg
Austria 1982 - San Marino 1983	8	De Angelis, Rosberg, Arnoux, Alboreto, Piquet, Watson, Prost, Tambay
Germany 1982 - France 1983	8	Tambay, De Angelis, Rosberg, Arnoux, Alboreto, Piquet, Watson, Prost
Monaco - Austria 1977	7	Scheckter, Nilsson, Laffite, Andretti, Hunt, Lauda, Jones
Italy 1982 - Monaco 1983	7	Arnoux, Alboreto, Piquet, Watson, Prost, Tambay, Rosberg
Abu Dhabi 2011 - Spain 2012	7	Hamilton, Webber, Button, Alonso, Rosberg, Vettel, Maldonado
Australia - Canada 2012	7	Button, Alonso, Rosberg, Vettel, Maldonado, Webber, Hamilton

237. Different winners from the start of a season *(Most)*

2012	7	Jenson Button, Fernando Alonso, Nico Rosberg, Sebastian Vettel, Pastor Maldonado, Mark Webber, Lewis Hamilton
1951	5	Juan Manuel Fangio, Giuseppe Farina, Luigi Fagioli (a), Froilán González, Alberto Ascari
1967	5	Pedro Rodríguez, Denny Hulme, Jim Clark, Dan Gurney, Jack Brabham
1975	5	Emerson Fittipaldi, Carlos Pace, Jody Scheckter, Jochen Mass, Niki Lauda
1983	5	Nelson Piquet, John Watson, Alain Prost, Patrick Tambay, Keke Rosberg
1961	4	Stirling Moss, Wolfgang Von Trips, Phil Hill, Giancarlo Baghetti
1962	4	Graham Hill, Bruce McLaren, Jim Clark, Dan Gurney
1970	4	Jack Brabham, Jackie Stewart, Jochen Rindt, Pedro Rodríguez
1972	4	Jackie Stewart, Denny Hulme, Emerson Fittipaldi, Jean-Pierre Beltoise
1974	4	Denny Hulme, Emerson Fittipaldi, Carlos Reutemann, Niki Lauda
1977	4	Jody Scheckter, Carlos Reutemann, Niki Lauda, Mario Andretti
2003	4	David Coulthard, Kimi Räikkönen, Giancarlo Fisichella, Michael Schumacher

(a) Shared drive with Juan Manuel Fangio.
Excludes Indianapolis 500.

238. First time winners in a season

Most

1982	5	Riccardo Patrese, Patrick Tambay, Elio De Angelis, Keke Rosberg, Michele Alboreto
1975	4	Carlos Pace, Jochen Mass, James Hunt, Vittorio Brambilla
1951	3	Luigi Fagioli, José Froilán González, Alberto Ascari
1959	3	Jack Brabham, Jo Bonnier, Bruce McLaren
1961	3	Wolfgang von Trips, Giancarlo Baghetti, Innes Ireland
1962	3	Graham Hill, Jim Clark, Dan Gurney
1971	3	Mario Andretti, Peter Gethin, François Cevert
1974	3	Carlos Reutemann, Niki Lauda, Jody Scheckter
1977	3	Gunnar Nilsson, Jacques Laffite, Alan Jones
1980	3	René Arnoux, Nelson Piquet, Didier Pironi
1995	3	Jean Alesi, Johnny Herbert, David Coulthard
2003	3	Kimi Räikkönen, Giancarlo Fisichella, Fernando Alonso
2008	3	Robert Kubica, Heikki Kovalainen, Sebastian Vettel

Fewest (none)

1954, 58, 83, 84, 87, 88, 90, 91, 94, 98, 2002, 05, 10, 11, 13, 15

Excludes Indianapolis 500.

239. Wins with the same constructor *(Most)*

Michael Schumacher	72	Ferrari	Spain 1996	- China 2006
Sebastian Vettel	38	Red Bull	China 2009	- Brazil 2013
Ayrton Senna	35	McLaren	San Marino 1988	- Australia 1993
Alain Prost	30	McLaren	Brazil 1984	- Italy 1989
Nigel Mansell	28	Williams	Europe 1985	- Australia 1994
Jim Clark	25	Lotus	Belgium 1962	- South Africa 1968
Lewis Hamilton	22	Mercedes-Benz	Hungary 2013	- United States 2015
Lewis Hamilton	21	McLaren	Canada 2007	- United States 2012
Damon Hill	21	Williams	Hungary 1993	- Japan 1996
Mika Häkkinen	20	McLaren	Europe 1997	- United States 2001

For complete list of winning drivers by constructor, see section 722.

240. Seasons of winning with the same constructor *(Most)*

Michael Schumacher	Ferrari	11	1996 - 2006		Alain Prost	McLaren	6	1984 - 89
Jim Clark	Lotus	7	1962 - 68		Ayrton Senna	McLaren	6	1988 - 93
David Coulthard	McLaren	7	1997 - 2003		Mika Häkkinen	McLaren	5	1997 - 2001
Lewis Hamilton	McLaren	6	2007 - 12		Denny Hulme	McLaren	5	1968 - 74
Nigel Mansell	Williams	6	1985 - 94		Sebastian Vettel	Red Bull	5	2009 - 13
Nelson Piquet	Brabham	6	1980 - 85					

241. Wins with the same engine make *(Most)*

Michael Schumacher	72	Ferrari	Spain 1996	- China 2006
Lewis Hamilton	43	Mercedes	Canada 2007	- United States 2015
Sebastian Vettel	38	Renault	China 2009	- Brazil 2013
Ayrton Senna	32	Honda	Monaco 1987	- Italy 1992
Jackie Stewart	25	Ford Cosworth	Netherlands 1968	- Germany 1973
Damon Hill	21	Renault	Hungary 1993	- Japan 1996
Mika Häkkinen	20	Mercedes	Europe 1997	- United States 2001
Jim Clark	19	Climax	Belgium 1962	- Germany 1965
Alain Prost	19	TAG Porsche	Brazil 1984	- Portugal 1987
Fernando Alonso	17	Renault	Hungary 2003	- Japan 2008

For complete list of winning drivers by engine make, see section 979.

242. Wins with a turbocharged engine
(turbocharged engines were used from Britain 1977 to Australia 1988 and from Australia 2014)

Alain Prost	35	France 1981	- Australia 1988	(McLaren - TAG Porsche, 19; Renault, 9; McLaren - Honda, 7)
Lewis Hamilton	21	Malaysia 2014	- United States 2015	(Mercedes-Benz)
Nelson Piquet	14	Canada 1982	- Italy 1987	(Brabham - BMW, 7; Williams - Honda, 7)
Ayrton Senna	14	Portugal 1985	- Japan 1988	(McLaren - Honda, 8; Lotus - Renault, 4; Lotus - Honda, 2)
Nigel Mansell	13	Europe 1985	- Mexico 1987	(Williams - Honda)
Nico Rosberg	11	Australia 2014	- Abu Dhabi 2015	(Mercedes-Benz)
René Arnoux	7	Brazil 1980	- Netherlands 1983	(Renault, 4; Ferrari, 3)
Niki Lauda	6	South Africa 1984	- Netherlands 1985	(McLaren - TAG Porsche)
Gergard Berger	4	Mexico 1986	- Italy 1988	(Benetton - BMW, 1; Ferrari, 3)
Michele Alboreto	3	Belgium 1984	- Germany 1985	(Ferrari)
Daniel Ricciardo	3	Canada 2014	- Belgium 2014	(Red Bull - Renault)
Keke Rosberg	3	Dallas 1984	- Australia 1985	(Williams - Honda)
Sebastian Vettel	3	Malaysia 2015	- Singapore 2015	(Ferrari)
Jean-Pierre Jabouille	2	France 1979	- Austria 1980	(Renault)
Didier Pironi	2	San Marino 1982	- Netherlands 1982	(Ferrari)
Patrick Tambay	2	Germany 1982	- San Marino 1983	(Ferrari)
Gilles Villeneuve	2	Monaco 1981	- Spain 1981	(Ferrari)
Elio De Angelis	1	San Marino 1985		(Lotus - Renault)
Riccardo Patrese	1	South Africa 1983		(Brabham - BMW)

243. First win for more than one constructor

3 constructors	
Dan Gurney	Porsche (France 1962), Brabham (France 1964), Eagle (Belgium 1967)
Stirling Moss	Vanwall (Britain 1957), Cooper (Argentina 1958), Lotus (Monaco 1960)
Jackie Stewart	Matra (Netherlands 1968), March (Spain 1970), Tyrrell (Spain 1971)
2 constructors	
Juan Manuel Fangio	Maserati (Italy 1953), Mercedes-Benz (France 1954)
Sebastian Vettel	Toro Rosso (Italy 2008), Red Bull (China 2009)

244. Races won without leading a lap!

Luigi Fagioli	France 1951	(shared drive in which Fangio took over the car)
Luigi Musso	Argentina 1956	(shared drive in which Fangio took over the car)
Tony Brooks	Britain 1957	(shared drive in which Moss took over the car)
Niki Lauda	Italy 1978	(inherited due to Andretti/ Villeneuve penalties) (a)
Alain Prost	Brazil 1982	(inherited due to Piquet/ Rosberg disqualifications) (b)
Elio De Angelis	San Marino 1985	(inherited due to Prost disqualification) (b)
Damon Hill	Belgium 1994	(inherited due to Michael Schumacher disqualification) (b)

(a) See section 554 for the circumstances.
(b) See section 552 for the circumstances.

245. Won, but never crossed the finishing line first in their career

For Luigi Fagioli and Luigi Musso, the above (at section 244) was their only win. So neither crossed the finishing line to victory in their world championship career. Additionally, Alessandro Nannini in Japan 1989 was handed the victory after Senna who was first across the line, had been disqualified for avoiding the chicane after the accident with Prost. Nannini never won another grand prix.

246. First across the finishing line, but not the winner

		winner
Howden Ganley (Iso-Marlboro - Ford Cosworth) (a)	Canada 1973	Peter Revson (McLaren - Ford Coswoth)
James Hunt (McLaren - Ford Cosworth) (b)	Britain 1976	Niki Lauda (Ferrari)
Mario Andretti (JPS Lotus - Ford Cosworth) (c)	Italy 1978	Niki Lauda (Brabham - Alfa Romeo)
Didier Pironi (Ligier - Ford Cosworth) (c)	Canada 1980	Alan Jones (Williams - Ford Cosworth)
Nelson Piquet (Brabham - Ford Cosworth) (b)	Brazil 1982	Alain Prost (Renault)
Alain Prost (McLaren - TAG Porsche) (b)	San Marino 1985	Elio De Angelis (Lotus - Renault)
Nelson Piquet (Williams - Honda) (d)	Mexico 1987	Nigel Mansell (Williams - Honda)
Ayrton Senna (McLaren - Honda) (b)	Japan 1989	Alessandro Nannini (Benetton - Ford Cosworth)
Gerhard Berger (McLaren - Honda) (c)	Canada 1990	Ayrton Senna (McLaren - Honda)
Michael Schumacher (Benetton - Ford Cosworth) (b)	Belgium 1994	Damon Hill (Williams - Renault)
Kimi Räikkönen (McLaren - Mercedes) (e)	Brazil 2003	Giancarlo Fisichella (Jordan - Ford Cosworth)
Lewis Hamilton (McLaren - Mercedes) (b)	Belgium 2008	Felipe Massa (Ferrari)

(a) Chequered flag was waved to indicate Ganley had won and his team's lap chart supported this. However, race officials declared Revson the winner (late pit stops had caused the confusion).
(b) Disqualified (see section 552 for the circumstances).
(c) Received a time penalty for an infringement (see section 554 for the circumstances).
(d) Race was in two parts with times aggregated due to an accident (although Piquet crossed the line first, Mansell won on aggregate).
(e) Initially declared the winner over 53 laps. The results were later amended to be over 54 laps, Fisichella winning and Kimi classified 2nd (the confusion arose after the race was stopped prematurely following Alonso's accident).

247. Race winner in own car

Jack Brabham (Brabham)	1966, 67, 70	Bruce McLaren (McLaren)	1968
Dan Gurney (Eagle)	1967		

248. Interval between wins

Shortest (won races a week apart)

Jim Clark	Netherlands	- France 1963 (a)	(Lotus)
Jim Clark	Britain	- Netherlands 1965	(Lotus)
Jack Brabham	Britain	- Netherlands 1966 (a)	(Brabham)
Jackie Stewart	Netherlands	- Germany 1973	(Tyrrell)
James Hunt	Canada	- United States 1976 (a)	(McLaren)
Alan Jones	Canada	- United States 1980	(Williams)
Nelson Piquet	Canada	- Detroit 1984 (a)	(Brabham)
Nigel Mansell	France	- Britain 1986	(Williams)
Nigel Mansell	France	- Britain 1987	(Williams)
Ayrton Senna	Canada	- Detroit 1988 (a)	(McLaren)
Alain Prost	Portugal	- Spain 1988	(McLaren)
Alain Prost	France	- Britain 1989	(McLaren)
Alain Prost	France	- Britain 1990	(Ferrari)
Nigel Mansell	France	- Britain 1991	(Williams)
Nigel Mansell	France	- Britain 1992 (a)	(Williams)
Alain Prost	France	- Britain 1993	(Williams)
Michael Schumacher	Pacific	- Japan 1995	(Benetton)
Damon Hill	Brazil	- Argentina 1996 (a)	(Williams)
Jacques Villeneuve	Austria	- Luxembourg 1997	(Williams)
Mika Häkkinen	Austria	- Germany 1998	(McLaren)
Eddie Irvine	Austria	- Germany 1999	(Ferrari)
Michael Schumacher	Europe	- France 2001 (a)	(Ferrari)
Michael Schumacher	France	- Germany 2002	(Ferrari)
Ralf Schumacher	Europe	- France 2003	(Williams)
Michael Schumacher	Canada	- United States 2004	(Ferrari)
Michael Schumacher	France	- Britain 2004	(Ferrari)
Lewis Hamilton	Canada	- United States 2007 (a)	(McLaren)
Kimi Räikkönen	France	- Britain 2007	(Ferrari)
Jenson Button	Australia	- Malaysia 2009 (a)	(Brawn)
Mark Webber	Spain	- Monaco 2010 (a)	(Red Bull)
Sebastian Vettel	Brazil	- Abu Dhabi 2010	(Red Bull)
Sebastian Vettel	Spain	- Monaco 2011	(Red Bull)
Sebastian Vettel	Japan	- Korea 2012	(Red Bull)
Sebastian Vettel	Korea	- Japan 2013	(Red Bull)
Sebastian Vettel	India	- Abu Dhabi 2013	(Red Bull)
Sebastian Vettel	United States	- Brazil 2013 (a)	(Red Bull)
Lewis Hamilton	Malaysia	- Bahrain 2014	(Mercedes-Benz)
Lewis Hamilton	Japan	- Russia 2014	(Mercedes-Benz)
Lewis Hamilton	China	- Bahrain 2015 (a)	(Mercedes-Benz)

(a) Additionally achieved pole position in both races.

Longest

	years, days	races		
Riccardo Patrese	6y, 210d	99	South Africa 1983 (Brabham)	- San Marino 1990 (Williams)
Bruce McLaren	6y, 6d	61	Monaco 1962 (Cooper)	- Belgium 1968 (McLaren)
Jack Brabham	5y, 323d	52	Portugal 1960 (Cooper)	- France 1966 (Brabham)
Mario Andretti	5y, 232d	82	South Africa 1971 (Ferrari)	- Japan 1976 (JPS Lotus)
John Watson	4y, 337d	76	Austria 1976 (Penske)	- Britain 1981 (McLaren)
Rubens Barrichello	4y, 331d	85	China 2004 (Ferrari)	- Europe 2009 (Brawn)
Johnny Herbert	4y, 16d	68	Italy 1995 (Benetton)	- Europe 1999 (Stewart)
Clay Regazzoni	3y, 332d	52	Italy 1970 (Ferrari)	- Germany 1974 (Ferrari)
Mike Hawthorn	3y, 255d	29	Spain 1954 (Ferrari)	- France 1958 (Ferrari)
Niki Lauda	3y, 206d	49	Italy 1978 (Brabham)	- United States West 1982 (McLaren)

Did not necessarily start every race during the period.

249. Interval between first & second wins

Shortest

	days			
Lewis Hamilton	7	Canada	- United States 2007 (a)	(McLaren)
Nigel Mansell	13	Europe	- South Africa 1985 (a)	(Williams)
Damon Hill	14	Hungary	- Belgium 1993 (a)	(Williams)
Giuseppe Farina	22	Britain	- Switzerland 1950	(Alfa Romeo)
Juan Manuel Fangio	28	Monaco	- Belgium 1950	(Alfa Romeo)
Peter Collins	28	Belgium	- France 1956 (a)	(Lancia-Ferrari)
René Arnoux	34	Brazil	- South Africa 1980 (a)	(Renault)
Jim Clark	34	Belgium	- Britain 1962	(Lotus)
Jody Scheckter	41	Sweden	- Britain 1974	(Tyrrell)
Alberto Ascari	49	Germany	- Italy 1951 (a)	(Ferrari)
Ronnie Peterson	49	France	- Austria 1973	(JPS Lotus)
Daniel Ricciardo	49	Canada	- Hungary 2014	(Red Bull)

(a) Consecutive races.

Longest

	years, days	races		
Mario Andretti	5y, 232d	82	South Africa 1971 (Ferrari)	- Japan 1976 (JPS Lotus)
John Watson	4y, 337d	76	Austria 1976 (Penske)	- Britain 1981 (McLaren)
Clay Regazzoni	3y, 332d	52	Italy 1970 (Ferrari)	- Germany 1974 (Ferrari)
Pedro Rodríguez	3y, 156d	37	South Africa 1967 (Cooper)	- Belgium 1970 (BRM)
Jo Siffert	3y, 26d	37	Britain 1968 (Lotus)	- Austria 1971 (BRM)
José Froilán González	3y, 3d	25	Britain 1951 (Ferrari)	- Britain 1954 (Ferrari)
Maurice Trintignant	2y, 361d	23	Monaco 1955 (Ferrari)	- Monaco 1958 (Cooper)
Elio De Angelis	2y, 263d	37	Austria 1982 (Lotus)	- San Marino 1985 (Lotus)
Jenson Button	2y, 235d	41	Hungary 2006 (Honda)	- Australia 2009 (Brawn)
Heinz-Harald Frentzen	2y, 61d	36	San Marino 1997 (Williams)	- France 1999 (Jordan)

250. Interval between first & last wins *(Longest)*

	years, days	races		
Michael Schumacher	14y, 32d	238	Belgium 1992	- China 2006
Alain Prost	12y, 20d	192	France 1981	- Germany 1993
Niki Lauda	11y, 119d	176	Spain 1974	- Netherlands 1985
Nelson Piquet	11y, 64d	173	United States West 1980	- Canada 1991
Jack Brabham	10y, 301d	109	Monaco 1959	- South Africa 1970
Gerhard Berger	10y, 288d	172	Mexico 1986	- Germany 1997
Riccardo Patrese	10y, 155d	168	Monaco 1982	- Japan 1992
Kimi Räikkönen	9y, 359d	180	Malaysia 2003	- Australia 2013
Fernando Alonso	9y, 261d	173	Hungary 2003	- Spain 2013
Rubens Barrichello	9y, 45d	159	Germany 2000	- Italy 2009

251. Interval between winners of the same nationality *(Longest)*

	years, days	races		
Australia	27y, 268d	455	Caesars Palace 1981 (Alan Jones)	- Germany 2009 (Mark Webber)
Germany	17y, 125d	274	Spain 1975 (Jochen Mass)	- Belgium 1992 (Michael Schumacher)
Belgium	16y, 323d	258	Germany 1972 (Jacky Ickx)	- Canada 1989 (Thierry Boutsen)
Argentina	16y, 238d	176	Germany 1957 (Juan Manuel Fangio)	- South Africa 1974 (Carlos Reutemann)
Canada	14y, 312d	236	Spain 1981 (Gilles Villeneuve)	- Europe 1996 (Jacques Villeneuve)
Sweden	14y, 31d	150	Netherlands 1959 (Jo Bonnier)	- France 1973 (Ronnie Peterson)
Germany	13y, 286d	155	Britain 1961 (Wolfgang von Trips)	- Spain 1975 (Jochen Mass)
France	13y, 138d	142	Monaco 1958 (Maurice Trintignant)	- United States 1971 (François Cevert)
Finland	11y, 357d	194	Australia 1985 (Keke Rosberg)	- Europe 1997 (Mika Häkkinen)
Italy	10y, 163d	169	Japan 1992 (Riccardo Patrese)	- Brazil 2003 (Giancarlo Fisichella)

252. Interval between first time winners *(Longest)*

2 years and 313 days, from Japan 1989 (22 October, Alessandro Nannini) until Belgium 1992 (30 August, Michael Schumacher).

253. Winning speed

Fastest

	km/h	mph		
Italy 2003	247.585	153.842	Michael Schumacher	(Ferrari F2003-GA)
Italy 2005	247.096	153.539	Juan Pablo Montoya	(McLaren MP4-20 - Mercedes)
Italy 2006	245.814	152.742	Michael Schumacher	(Ferrari 248 F1)
Italy 2004	244.374	151.847	Rubens Barrichello	(Ferrari F2004)
Italy 1971	242.615	150.754	Peter Gethin	(BRM P160)
Belgium 1970	241.308	149.942	Pedro Rodríguez	(BRM P153)
Italy 2002	241.090	149.806	Rubens Barrichello	(Ferrari F2002)
Italy 2009	241.000	149.750	Rubens Barrichello	(Brawn BGP 001 - Mercedes)
Italy 2010	240.849	149.657	Fernando Alonso	(Ferrari F10)
Italy 1993	239.144	148.597	Damon Hill	(Williams FW15C - Renault)

Slowest

	km/h	mph		
Canada 2011	74.864	46.518	Jenson Button (a)	(McLaren MP4-26 - Mercedes)
Monaco 1950	98.701	61.330	Juan Manuel Fangio	(Alfa Romeo 158)
Monaco 1984	100.775	62.619	Alain Prost	(McLaren MP4/2 - TAG Porsche)
Monaco 1972	102.756	63.849	Jean-Pierre Beltoise	(BRM P160B)
Monaco 1957	104.165	64.725	Juan Manuel Fangio	(Maserati 250F)
Monaco 1997	104.264	64.787	Michael Schumacher	(Ferrari F310B)
Monaco 1956	104.515	64.943	Stirling Moss	(Maserati 250F)
Monaco 1955	105.915	65.813	Maurice Trintignant	(Ferrari 625)
Monaco 1959	107.304	66.676	Jack Brabham	(Cooper T51 - Climax)
Monaco 1960	108.599	67.480	Stirling Moss	(Lotus 18 - Climax)

(a) The speed is low due to being based on the official data which includes the 2-hour stoppage time.

254. Winning margin

Largest

	1st	2nd
2 laps		
Spain 1969	Jackie Stewart (Matra)	Bruce McLaren (McLaren)
Australia 1995	Damon Hill (Williams)	Olivier Panis (Ligier)
1 lap		
Monaco 1950	Juan Manuel Fangio (Alfa Romeo)	Alberto Ascari (Ferrari)
Britain 1952	Alberto Ascari (Ferrari)	Piero Taruffi (Ferrari)
Argentina 1953	Alberto Ascari (Ferrari)	Luigi Villoresi (Ferrari)
Italy 1954	Juan Manuel Fangio (Mercedes-Benz)	Mike Hawthorn (Ferrari)
Britain 1956	Juan Manuel Fangio (Ferrari)	Alfonso de Portago/ Peter Collins (Ferrari)
Portugal 1959	Stirling Moss (Cooper)	Masten Gregory (Cooper)
France 1962	Dan Gurney (Porsche)	Tony Maggs (Cooper)
Netherlands 1963	Jim Clark (Lotus)	Dan Gurney (Brabham)
Monaco 1964	Graham Hill (BRM)	Richie Ginther (BRM)
Netherlands 1966	Jack Brabham (Brabham)	Graham Hill (BRM)
United States 1966	Jim Clark (Lotus)	Jochen Rindt (Cooper)
Monaco 1967	Denny Hulme (Brabham)	Graham Hill (Lotus)
Canada 1968	Denny Hulme (McLaren)	Bruce McLaren (McLaren)
Britain 1969	Jackie Stewart (Matra)	Jacky Ickx (Brabham)
Spain 1970	Jackie Stewart (March)	Bruce McLaren (McLaren)
Britain 1975	Emerson Fittipaldi (McLaren)	Carlos Pace (Brabham)
Japan 1976	Mario Andretti (JPS Lotus)	Patrick Depailler (Tyrrell)
Monaco 1982	Riccardo Patrese (Brabham)	Didier Pironi (Ferrari)
San Marino 1985	Elio De Angelis (Lotus)	Thierry Boutsen (Arrows)
Britain 1985	Alain Prost (McLaren)	Michele Alboreto (Ferrari)
Austria 1986	Alain Prost (McLaren)	Michele Alboreto (Ferrari)
Brazil 1994	Michael Schumacher (Benetton)	Damon Hill (Williams)
Indianapolis 500		
1 lap		
1950	Johnnie Parsons (Kurtis-Kraft)	Bill Holland (Deidt)

Smallest

	seconds	1st	2nd
Italy 1971	0.010s	Peter Gethin (BRM)	Ronnie Peterson (March)
United States 2002	0.011s	Rubens Barrichello (Ferrari)	Michael Schumacher (Ferrari) (a)
Spain 1986	0.014s	Ayrton Senna (Lotus)	Nigel Mansell (Williams)
Austria 1982	0.050s	Elio De Angelis (Lotus)	Keke Rosberg (Williams)
Italy 1969	0.080s	Jackie Stewart (Matra)	Jochen Rindt (Lotus)
France 1954	0.100s	Juan Manuel Fangio (Mercedes-Benz)	Karl Kling (Mercedes-Benz)
France 1961	0.100s	Giancarlo Baghetti (Ferrari)	Dan Gurney (Porsche)
Canada 2000	0.174s	Michael Schumacher (Ferrari)	Rubens Barrichello (Ferrari)
Austria 2002	0.182s	Michael Schumacher (Ferrari)	Rubens Barrichello (Ferrari) (a)
Britain 1955	0.200s	Stirling Moss (Mercedes-Benz)	Juan Manuel Fangio (Mercedes-Benz)
Italy 1967	0.200s	John Surtees (Honda)	Jack Brabham (Brabham)
Spain 1981	0.220s	Gilles Villeneuve (Ferrari)	Jacques Laffite (Ligier)
Monaco 1992	0.215s	Ayrton Senna (McLaren)	Nigel Mansell (Williams)
San Marino 2005	0.215s	Fernando Alonso (Renault)	Michael Schumacher (Ferrari)
Netherlands 1985	0.232s	Niki Lauda (McLaren)	Alain Prost (McLaren)
Italy 2002	0.255s	Rubens Barrichello (Ferrari)	Michael Schumacher (Ferrari)
Hungary 1990	0.288s	Thierry Boutsen (Williams)	Ayrton Senna (McLaren)
Singapore 2010	0.293s	Fernando Alonso (Ferrari)	Sebastian Vettel (Red Bull)
Europe 2002	0.294s	Rubens Barrichello (Ferrari)	Michael Schumacher (Ferrari)
Netherlands 1955	0.300s	Juan Manuel Fangio (Mercedes-Benz)	Stirling Moss (Mercedes-Benz)
France 1956	0.300s	Peter Collins (Lancia-Ferrari)	Eugenio Castellotti (Lancia-Ferrari)

(a) Stage-managed by Ferrari.

255. First and last winners of each decade

1950s	Giuseppe Farina (Alfa Romeo)	- Bruce McLaren (Cooper - Climax)
1960s	Bruce McLaren (Cooper - Climax)	- Denny Hulme (McLaren - Ford Cosworth)
1970s	Jack Brabham (Brabham - Ford Cosworth)	- Gilles Villeneuve (Ferrari)
1980s	Alan Jones (Williams - Ford Cosworth)	- Thierry Boutsen (Williams - Renault)
1990s	Ayrton Senna (McLaren - Honda)	- Mika Häkkinen (McLaren - Mercedes)
2000s	Michael Schumacher (Ferrari)	- Sebastian Vettel (Red Bull - Renault)
2010s	Sebastian Vettel (Red Bull - Renault)	

256. Wins but never a world championship *(Most)*

Stirling Moss	16	Rubens Barrichello	11	Mark Webber	9
Nico Rosberg	14	Felipe Massa	11	Jacky Ickx	8
David Coulthard	13	Gerhard Berger	10		
Carlos Reutemann	12	Ronnie Peterson	10		

Section 110 "Champions with the fewest wins in their career" highlights those who scored fewer wins than Stirling Moss.

257. Wins but never a pole position

Eddie Irvine	4	Giancarlo Baghetti	1	Jochen Mass	1
Bruce McLaren	4	Jean-Pierre Beltoise	1	Luigi Musso	1
Peter Collins	3	François Cevert	1	Alessandro Nannini	1
Johnny Herbert	3	Luigi Fagioli	1	Gunnar Nilsson	1
Daniel Ricciardo	3	Peter Gethin	1	Olivier Panis	1
Pedro Rodríguez	2	Richie Ginther	1	Ludovico Scarfiotti	1
Maurice Trintignant	2	Innes Ireland	1	Piero Taruffi	1

258. Wins but never a front row

Johnny Herbert	3	Jochen Mass	1	Olivier Panis	1
Giancarlo Baghetti	1	Alessandro Nannini	1		
Peter Gethin	1	Gunnar Nilsson	1		

259. Wins but never a fastest lap

Peter Collins	3	Peter Revson	2	Peter Gethin	1
Johnny Herbert	3	Wolfgang von Trips	2	Pastor Maldonado	1
Elio De Angelis	2	Jo Bonnier	1	Olivier Panis	1
Jean-Pierre Jabouille	2	Luigi Fagioli	1		

260. Milestones: Wins I

Michael Schumacher	25th: France 1997, 50th: France 2001, 75th: Spain 2004
Alain Prost	25th: Australia 1986, 50th: Britain 1993
Fernando Alonso	25th: Singapore 2010
Jim Clark	25th: South Africa 1968
Lewis Hamilton	25th: China 2014
Niki Lauda	25th: Netherlands 1985
Nigel Mansell	25th: Spain 1992
Ayrton Senna	25th: Belgium 1990
Jackie Stewart	25th: Monaco 1973
Sebastian Vettel	25th: Korea 2012

261. Milestones: Wins II

(eg winner of the 100th race was Graham Hill in a BRM P57)

1st	Giuseppe Farina (Alfa Romeo 158)	Britain 1950
100th	Graham Hill (BRM P57)	South Africa 1962
200th	Emerson Fittipaldi (JPS Lotus 72D)	Spain 1972
250th	Carlos Reutemann (Brabham BT44B)	Germany 1975
300th	Niki Lauda (Brabham BT46)	Italy 1978
400th	Nelson Piquet (Brabham BT54)	France 1985
500th	Ayrton Senna (McLaren MP4/6)	Belgium 1991
600th	Jacques Villeneuve (Williams FW19)	Austria 1997
700th	Michael Schumacher (Ferrari F2003-GA)	Italy 2003
750th	Michael Schumacher (Ferrari 248 F1)	France 2006
800th	Sebastian Vettel (Red Bull RB5)	Britain 2009
900th	Lewis Hamilton (Mercedes-Benz F1 W05)	Singapore 2014

Excludes Indianapolis 500.

262. Milestones: Wins III

(eg Luigi Musso was the 10th driver to achieve a win)

1st	Giuseppe Farina	Britain 1950	50th	Jacques Laffite	Sweden 1977
10th	Luigio Musso	Argentina 1956	60th	Patrick Tambay	Germany 1982
20th	Graham Hill	Netherlands 1962	70th	Damon Hill	Hungary 1993
30th	Jacky Ickx	France 1968	80th	Ralf Schumacher	San Marino 2001
40th	Peter Revson	Britain 1973	90th	Heikki Kovalainen	Hungary 2008

Excludes Indianapolis 500.

Chapter 7: Podium Drivers

263. Podium positions

		% of starts		
Michael Schumacher	155	50.49	Mexico 1992 (Benetton)	- Europe 2012 (Mercedes-Benz)
Alain Prost	106	53.27	Argentina 1981 (Renault)	- Australia 1993 (Williams)
Fernando Alonso	97	38.34	Malaysia 2003 (Renault)	- Hungary 2014 (Ferrari)
Lewis Hamilton	87	52.10	Australia 2007 (McLaren)	- Abu Dhabi 2015 (Mercedes-Benz)
Kimi Räikkönen	80	34.63	Australia 2002 (McLaren)	- Abu Dhabi 2015 (Ferrari)
Ayrton Senna	80	49.69	Monaco 1984 (Toleman)	- Australia 1993 (McLaren)
Sebastian Vettel	79	50.00	Italy 2008 (Toro Rosso)	- Brazil 2015 (Ferrari)
Rubens Barrichello	68	21.05	Pacific 1994 (Jordan)	- Italy 2009 (Brawn)
David Coulthard	62	25.20	Portugal 1994 (Williams)	- Canada 2008 (Red Bull)

		% of starts		
Nelson Piquet	60	29.41	Argentina 1980 (Brabham)	- Belgium 1991 (Benetton)
Nigel Mansell	59	31.55	Belgium 1981 (Lotus)	- Australia 1994 (Williams)
Niki Lauda	54	31.58	Argentina 1974 (Ferrari)	- Netherlands 1985 (McLaren)
Mika Häkkinen	51	31.68	Japan 1993 (McLaren)	- United States 2001 (McLaren)
Jenson Button	50	17.61	Malaysia 2004 (BAR)	- Australia 2014 (McLaren)
Gerhard Berger	48	22.86	San Marino 1986 (Benetton)	- Germany 1997 (Benetton)
Carlos Reutemann	45	30.82	France 1973 (Brabham)	- South Africa 1982 (Williams)
Jackie Stewart	43	43.43	Monaco 1965 (BRM)	- Austria 1973 (Tyrrell)
Damon Hill	42	36.52	Brazil 1993 (Williams)	- Belgium 1998 (Jordan)
Mark Webber	42	19.53	Monaco 2005 (Willlams)	- Brazil 2013 (Red Bull)
Felipe Massa	41	17.90	Europe 2006 (Ferrari)	- Italy 2015 (Williams)
Nico Rosberg	41	22.16	Australia 2008 (Williams)	- Abu Dhabi 2015 (Mercedes-Benz)
Riccardo Patrese	37	14.45	Sweden 1978 (Arrows)	- Hungary 1993 (Benetton)
Graham Hill	36	20.45	Netherlands 1960 (BRM)	- Monaco 1969 (Lotus)
Juan Manuel Fangio	35	68.63	Monaco 1950 (Alfa Romeo)	- Italy 1957 (Maserati) *
Emerson Fittipaldi	35	24.31	United States 1970 (Lotus)	- United States West 1980 (Fittipaldi)
Denny Hulme	33	29.46	France 1966 (Brabham)	- Austria 1974 (McLaren)
Jody Scheckter	33	29.46	Belgium 1974 (Tyrrell)	- Italy 1979 (Ferrari)
Jean Alesi	32	15.92	United States 1990 (Tyrrell)	- Belgium 1998 (Sauber)
Jim Clark	32	44.44	Portugal 1960 (Lotus)	- South Africa 1968 (Lotus)
Jacques Laffite	32	18.18	Germany 1975 (Williams)	- Detroit 1986 (Ligier)
Jack Brabham	31	24.60	Monaco 1959 (Cooper)	- Britain 1970 (Brabham)
Juan Pablo Montoya	30	31.91	Spain 2001 (Williams)	- Monaco 2006 (McLaren)
Clay Regazzoni	28	21.21	Austria 1970 (Ferrari)	- Canada 1979 (Williams)
Bruce McLaren	27	27.00	Britain 1959 (Cooper)	- Spain 1970 (McLaren)
Ralf Schumacher	27	15.00	Argentina 1997 (Jordan)	- Australia 2006 (Toyota)
Eddie Irvine	26	17.81	Canada 1995 (Jordan)	- Italy 2002 (Jaguar)
Ronnie Peterson	26	21.14	Monaco 1971 (March)	- Netherlands 1978 (JPS Lotus)
Jacky Ickx	25	21.55	Belgium 1968 (Ferrari)	- Spain 1975 (JPS Lotus)
Alan Jones	24	20.69	Austria 1977 (Shadow)	- Caesars Palace 1981 (Williams)
Stirling Moss	24	36.36	Belgium 1954 (Maserati)	- Germany 1961 (Lotus) *
John Surtees	24	21.62	Britain 1960 (Lotus)	- United States 1969 (BRM)
Michele Alboreto	23	11.86	San Marino 1982 (Tyrrell)	- Mexico 1989 (Tyrrell)
James Hunt	23	25.00	Netherlands 1973 (March)	- France 1978 (McLaren)
Jacques Villeneuve	23	14.11	Australia 1996 (Williams)	- Germany 2001 (BAR)
René Arnoux	22	14.77	France 1979 (Renault)	- Dallas 1984 (Ferrari)
John Watson	20	13.16	France 1976 (Penske)	- Netherlands 1983 (McLaren)
Mario Andretti	19	14.84	Spain 1970 (March)	- Italy 1982 (Ferrari)
Patrick Depailler	19	20.00	Sweden 1974 (Tyrrell)	- Spain 1979 (Ligier)
Giuseppe Farina	19	57.58	Britain 1950 (Alfa Romeo)	- Belgium 1955 (Ferrari) *
Giancarlo Fisichella	19	8.30	Canada 1997 (Jordan)	- Belgium 2009 (Force india)
Dan Gurney	19	22.09	Germany 1959 (Ferrari)	- Canada 1967 (Eagle)
Heinz-Harald Frentzen	18	11.47	Italy 1995 (Sauber)	- United States 2003 (Sauber)
Mike Hawthorn	18	40.00	Britain 1952 (Cooper)	- Morocco 1958 (Ferrari) *
Alberto Ascari	17	54.84	Monaco 1950 (Ferrari)	- Switzerland 1953 (Ferrari) *
Keke Rosberg	17	14.91	Argentina 1980 (Fittipaldi)	- Monaco 1986 (McLaren)
Phil Hill	16	33.33	Italy 1958 (Ferrari)	- Belgium 1962 (Ferrari)
Thierry Boutsen	15	9.20	San Marino 1985 (Arrows)	- Hungary 1990 (Williams)
José Froilán González	15	57.69	France 1951 (Ferrari)	- Argentina 1955 (Ferrari) *
Richie Ginther	14	26.92	Italy 1960 (Ferrari)	- Mexico 1965 (Honda)
François Cevert	13	27.66	France 1971 (Tyrrell)	- Germany 1973 (Tyrrell)
Nick Heidfeld	13	7.10	Brazil 2001 (Sauber)	- Malaysia 2011 (Renault)
Didier Pironi	13	18.57	Belgium 1979 (Tyrrell)	- France 1982 (Ferrari)
Jochen Rindt	13	21.67	Belgium 1966 (Cooper)	- Germany 1970 (Lotus)
Gilles Villeneuve	13	19.40	Austria 1978 (Ferrari)	- San Marino 1982 (Ferrari)
Stefan Johansson	12	15.19	Canada 1985 (Ferrari)	- Portugal 1989 (Onyx)
Robert Kubica	12	15.79	Italy 2006 (BMW Sauber)	- Belgium 2010 (Renault)
Chris Amon	11	11.46	Monaco 1967 (Ferrari)	- France 1972 (Matra-Simca)
Patrick Tambay	11	9.65	Britain 1982 (Ferrari)	- San Marino 1985 (Renault)
Jarno Trulli	11	4.37	Europe 1999 (Prost)	- Japan 2009 (Toyota)
Tony Brooks	10	26.32	Monaco 1957 (Vanwall)	- United States 1961 (BRM) *
Romain Grosjean	10	12.05	Bahrain 2012 (Lotus)	- Belgium 2015 (Lotus)
Daniel Ricciardo	10	11.36	Spain 2014 (Red Bull)	- Singapore 2015 (Red Bull)

		% of starts		
Jean Behra	9	16.98	Switzerland 1952 (Gordini)	- Netherlands 1958 (BRM) *
Martin Brundle	9	5.70	France 1992 (Benetton)	- Belgium 1995 (Ligier)
Eddie Cheever	9	6.82	Belgium 1982 (Talbot-Ligier)	- United States 1989 (Arrows)
Peter Collins	9	28.13	Monaco 1956 (Lancia-Ferrari)	- Britain 1958 (Ferrari) *
Elio De Angelis	9	8.33	Brazil 1980 (Lotus)	- Monaco 1985 (Lotus)
Alessandro Nannini	9	11.84	Britain 1988 (Benetton)	- Spain 1990 (Benetton)
Maurice Trintignant	9	11.11	Belgium 1954 (Ferrari)	- Argentina 1960 (Cooper) *
Lorenzo Bandini	8	19.05	Monaco 1962 (Ferrari)	- Belgium 1966 (Ferrari)
Jean-Pierre Beltoise	8	9.30	Netherlands 1968 (Matra)	- South Africa 1974 (BRM)
Valtteri Bottas	8	14.29	Austria 2014 (Williams)	- Mexico 2015 (Williams)
Jochen Mass	8	7.62	Brazil 1975 (McLaren)	- Canada 1977 (McLaren)
Peter Revson	8	26.67	South Africa 1972 (McLaren)	- Canada 1973 (McLaren)
Luigi Villoresi	8	25.81	Belgium 1951 (Ferrari)	- Italy 1953 (Ferrari)
Johnny Herbert	7	4.35	Spain 1995 (Benetton)	- Europe 1999 (Stewart)
Luigi Musso	7	29.17	Spain 1954 (Maserati)	- Monaco 1958 (Ferrari) *
Pedro Rodríguez	7	12.73	South Africa 1967 (Cooper)	- Netherlands 1971 (BRM)
Luigi Fagioli	6	85.71	Britain 1950 (Alfa Romeo)	- France 1951 (Alfa Romeo) *
Carlos Pace	6	8.33	Austria 1973 (Surtees)	- Argentina 1977 (Brabham)
Jo Siffert	6	6.25	United States 1964 (Brabham)	- United States 1971 (BRM)
Wolfgang von Trips	6	22.22	Italy 1957 (Lancia-Ferrari)	- Germany 1961 (Ferrari)
Andrea De Cesaris	5	2.40	Monaco 1982 (Alfa Romeo)	- Canada 1989 (Dallara)
Olivier Panis	5	3.16	Germany 1994 (Ligier)	- Spain 1997 (Prost)
Sergio Pérez	5	5.38	Malaysia 2012 (Sauber)	- Russia 2015 (Force India)
Piero Taruffi	5	27.78	Switzerland 1951 (Ferrari)	- Italy 1955 (Mercedes-Benz)
Innes Ireland	4	8.00	Netherlands 1960 (Lotus)	- United States 1961 (Lotus)
Heikki Kovalainen	4	3.60	Japan 2007 (Renault)	- Italy 2008 (McLaren)
Gunnar Nilsson	4	12.90	Spain 1976 (JPS Lotus)	- Britain 1977 (JPS Lotus)
Derek Warwick	4	2.74	South Africa 1984 (Renault)	- Germany 1984 (Renault)
Mark Blundell	3	4.92	South Africa 1993 (Ligier)	- Spain 1994 (Tyrrell)
Ivan Capelli	3	3.23	Belgium 1988 (March)	- France 1990 (Leyton House)
Eugenio Castellotti	3	21.43	Monaco 1955 (Lancia)	- France 1956 (Lancia-Ferrari)
Timo Glock	3	3.30	Hungary 2008 (Toyota)	- Singapore 2009 (Toyota)
Masten Gregory	3	7.89	Monaco 1957 (Maserati)	- Portugal 1959 (Cooper)
Jean-Pierre Jarier	3	2.24	Monaco 1974 (Shadow)	- Britain 1979 (Tyrrell)
Tony Maggs	3	12.00	France 1962 (Cooper)	- France 1963 (Cooper)
Alexander Wurz	3	4.35	Britain 1997 (Benetton)	- Canada 2007 (Williams)
Peter Arundell	2	18.18	Monaco 1964 (Lotus)	- Netherlands 1964 (Lotus)
Felice Bonetto	2	13.33	Italy 1951 (Alfa Romeo)	- Netherlands 1953 (Maserati) *
Piers Courage	2	7.14	Monaco 1969 (Brabham)	- United States 1969 (Brabham)
Teo Fabi	2	3.13	Detroit 1984 (Brabham)	- Austria 1987 (Benetton)
Rudi Fischer	2	28.57	Switzerland 1952 (Ferrari)	- Germany 1952 (Ferrari)
Olivier Gendebien	2	14.29	Belgium 1960 (Cooper)	- France 1960 (Cooper)
Mike Hailwood	2	4.00	Italy 1972 (Surtees)	- South Africa 1974 (McLaren)
Jean-Pierre Jabouille	2	4.08	France 1979 (Renault)	- Austria 1980 (Renault)
Karl Kling	2	18.18	France 1954 (Mercedes-Benz)	- Britain 1955 (Mercedes-Benz)
Stuart Lewis-Evans	2	14.29	Belgium 1958 (Vanwall)	- Portugal 1958 (Vanwall)
Umberto Maglioli	2	20.00	Italy 1954 (Ferrari)	- Argentina 1955 (Ferrari) *
Robert Manzon	2	7.14	Belgium 1952 (Gordini)	- France 1954 (Ferrari)
Onofré Marimón	2	18.18	Belgium 1953 (Maserati)	- Britain 1954 (Maserati)
Stefano Modena	2	2.86	Monaco 1989 (Brabham)	- Canada 1991 (Tyrrell)
Jackie Oliver	2	4.00	Mexico 1968 (Lotus)	- Canada 1973 (Shadow)
Mike Parkes	2	33.33	France 1966 (Ferrari)	- Italy 1966 (Ferrari)
Cesare Perdisa	2	28.57	Monaco 1955 (Maserati)	- Belgium 1956 (Maserati) *
Tom Pryce	2	4.76	Austria 1975 (Shadow)	- Brazil 1976 (Shadow)
Louis Rosier	2	5.26	Switzerland 1950 (Talbot-Lago)	- Belgium 1950 (Talbot-Lago)
Mika Salo	2	1.82	Germany 1999 (Ferrari)	- Italy 1999 (Ferrari)
Roy Salvadori	2	4.26	Britain 1958 (Cooper)	- Germany 1958 (Cooper)
Harry Schell	2	3.57	Pescara 1957 (Maserati)	- Netherlands 1958 (BRM)
Hans-Joachim Stuck	2	2.70	Germany 1977 (Brabham)	- Austria 1977 (Brabham)
Jos Verstappen	2	1.87	Hungary 1994 (Benetton)	- Belgium 1994 (Benetton)
Cliff Allison	1	6.25	Argentina 1960 (Ferrari)	
Bob Anderson	1	4.00	Austria 1964 Brabham)	
Michael Andretti	1	7.69	Italy 1993 (McLaren)	

		% of starts		
Richard Attwood	1	5.88	Monaco 1968 (BRM)	
Giancarlo Baghetti	1	4.76	France 1961 (Ferrari)	
Eric Bernard	1	2.22	Germany 1994 (Ligier)	
Lucien Bianchi	1	5.88	Monaco 1968 (Cooper)	
Jo Bonnier	1	0.96	Netherlands 1959 (BRM)	
Vittorio Brambilla	1	1.35	Austria 1975 (March)	
Louis Chiron	1	6.67	Monaco 1950 (Maserati)	
Pedro de la Rosa	1	0.95	Hungary 2006 (McLaren)	
Alfonso de Portago	1	20.00	Britain 1956 (Lancia-Ferrari) *	
Mark Donohue	1	7.14	Canada 1971 (McLaren)	
Ron Flockhart	1	7.69	Italy 1956 (Connaught)	
George Follmer	1	8.33	Spain 1973 (Shadow)	
Paul Frère	1	9.09	Belgium 1956 (Lancia-Ferrari)	
Peter Gethin	1	3.33	Italy 1971 (BRM)	
Bruno Giacomelli	1	1.45	Caesars Palace 1981 (Alfa Romeo)	
Maurício Gugelmin	1	1.35	Brazil 1989 (March)	
Hans Herrmann	1	5.56	Switzerland 1954 (Mercedes-Benz)	
Kamui Kobayashi	1	1.33	Japan 2012 (Sauber)	
Daniel Kvyat	1	2.70	Hungary 2015 (Red Bull)	
Nicola Larini	1	2.04	San Marino 1994 (Ferrari)	
J J Lehto	1	1.61	San Marino 1991 (Dallara)	
John Love	1	11.11	South Africa 1967 (Cooper)	
Kevin Magnussen	1	5.26	Australia 2014 (McLaren)	
Willy Mairesse	1	8.33	Italy 1960 (Ferrari)	
Pastor Maldonado	1	1.05	Spain 2012 (Williams)	
Carlos Menditéguy	1	10.00	Argentina 1957 (Maserati)	
Tiago Monteiro	1	2.70	United States 2005 (Jordan)	
Gianni Morbidelli	1	1.49	Australia 1995 (Footwork)	
Roberto Moreno	1	2.38	Japan 1990 (Benetton)	
Reg Parnell	1	16.67	Britain 1950 (Alfa Romeo)	
Henri Pescarolo	1	1.75	Monaco 1970 (Matra-Simca)	
Vitaly Petrov	1	1.75	Australia 2011 (Renault)	
Nelsinho Piquet	1	3.57	Germany 2008 (Renault)	
Brian Redman	1	8.33	Spain 1968 (Cooper)	
Takuma Sato	1	1.11	United States 2004 (BAR)	
Ludovico Scarfiotti	1	10.00	Italy 1966 (Ferrari)	
Tim Schenken	1	2.94	Austria 1971 (Brabham)	
Dorino Serafini	1	100.00	Italy 1950 (Ferrari) *	
Johnny Servoz-Gavin	1	8.33	Italy 1968 (Matra)	
Mike Spence	1	2.78	Mexico 1965 (Lotus)	
Rolf Stommelen	1	1.85	Austria 1970 (Brabham)	
Philippe Streiff	1	1.89	Australia 1985 (Ligier)	
Aguri Suzuki	1	1.56	Japan 1990 (Lola)	
Trevor Taylor	1	3.70	Netherlands 1962 (Lotus)	
Peter Whitehead	1	10.00	France 1950 (Ferrari)	
Reine Wisell	1	4.55	United States 1970 (Lotus)	
Indianapolis 500				
Sam Hanks	4	50.00	1952 (Kurtis-Kraft)	- 1957 (Salih) *
Jim Rathmann	4	40.00	1952 (Kurtis-Kraft)	- 1960 (Watson)
Jimmy Bryan	3	33.33	1954 (Kuzma)	- 1958 (Salih)
Jack McGrath	2	33.33	1951 (Kurtis-Kraft)	- 1954 (Kurtis-Kraft) *
Bill Vukovich	2	40.00	1953 (Kurtis-Kraft)	- 1954 (Kurtis-Kraft)
Rodger Ward	2	20.00	1959 (Watson)	- 1960 (Watson)
George Amick	1	100.00	1958 (Epperly)	
Manny Ayulo	1	25.00	1951 (Kutris Kraft) *	
Tony Bettenhausen	1	9.09	1955 (Kurtis-Kraft) *	
Johnny Boyd	1	16.67	1958 (Kurtis-Kraft)	
Duane Carter	1	12.50	1953 (Kurtis-Kraft) *	
Art Cross	1	25.00	1953 (Kurtis-Kraft)	
Jimmy Davies	1	25.00	1955 (Kurtis-Kraft)	
Pat Flaherty	1	16.67	1956 (Watson)	
Don Freeland	1	12.50	1956 (Phillips)	
Paul Goldsmith	1	33.33	1960 (Epperly)	

		% of starts		
Bill Holland	1	50.00	1950 (Deidt)	
Mike Nazaruk	1	33.33	1951 (Kurtis-Kraft)	
Johnnie Parsons	1	11.11	1950 (Kurtis-Kraft)	
Mauri Rose	1	50.00	1950 (Deidt)	
Paul Russo	1	12.50	1955 (Kurtis-Kraft) *	
Troy Ruttman	1	14.29	1952 (Kuzma)	
Bob Sweikert	1	20.00	1955 (Kurtis-Kraft)	
Johnny Thomson	1	12.50	1959 (Lesovsky)	
Lee Wallard	1	50.00	1951 (Kurtis-Kraft)	

Shared drive(s) included (see section 171).
At Argentina 1955, Farina and Trintignant finished 2nd and 3rd in shared cars (this is counted above as 1 podium for each driver).

264. Percentage of races with a podium *(Highest)*

	%	podiums				
Dorino Serafini	100.00	1		Alberto Ascari	54.84	17
Luigi Fagioli	85.71	6		Alain Prost	53.27	106
Juan Manuel Fangio	68.63	35		Lewis Hamilton	52.10	87
José Froilán González	57.69	15		Michael Schumacher	50.49	155
Giuseppe Farina	57.58	19		Sebastian Vettel	50.00	79

Excludes Indianapolis 500.

265. Podium driver age

Youngest

	years, days	
Sebastian Vettel	21y, 73d	Italy 2008
Daniil Kvyat	21y, 91d	Hungary 2015
Kevin Magnussen	21y, 162d	Australia 2014
Fernando Alonso	21y, 237d	Malaysia 2003
Robert Kubica	21y, 277d	Italy 2006
Ralf Schumacher	21y, 287d	Argentina 1997
Elio De Angelis	21y, 307d	Brazil 1980
Bruce McLaren	21y, 322d	Britain 1959
Rubens Barrichello	21y, 329d	Pacific 1994
Sergio Pérez	22y, 59d	Malaysia 2012
Indianapolis 500		
Troy Ruttmann	22y, 80d	1952

Oldest

	years, days	
Luigi Fagioli	53y, 22d	France 1951
Louis Chiron	50y, 291d	Monaco 1950
Felice Bonetto	49y, 363d	Netherlands 1953
Piero Taruffi	48y, 334d	Italy 1955
Giuseppe Farina	48y, 218d	Belgium 1955
Juan Manuel Fangio	46y, 76d	Italy 1957
Karl Kling	44y, 303d	Britain 1955
Louis Rosier	44y, 225d	Belgium 1950
Luigi Villoresi	44y, 120d	Italy 1953
Jack Brabham	44y, 107d	Britain 1970

266. Podiums in a season *(Most)*

Lewis Hamilton	17 of 19	2015 (wc)	(Mercedes-Benz F1 W06)
Michael Schumacher	17 of 17	2002 (wc)	(Ferrari F2001, F2002)
Sebastian Vettel	17 of 19	2011 (wc)	(Red Bull RB7 - Renault)
Lewis Hamilton	16 of 19	2014 (wc)	(Mercedes-Benz F1 W05)
Sebastian Vettel	16 of 19	2013 (wc)	(Red Bull RB9 - Renault)
Michael Schumacher	15 of 18	2004 (wc)	(Ferrari F2004)
Fernando Alonso	15 of 19	2005 (wc)	(Renault RS25)
Nico Rosberg	15 of 19	2014	(Mercedes-Benz F1 W05)
Nico Rosberg	15 of 19	2015	(Mercedes-Benz F1 W06)
Alain Prost	14 of 16	1988	(McLaren MP4/4 - Honda)
Michael Schumacher	14 of 17	2001 (wc)	(Ferrari F2001)
Fernando Alonso	14 of 18	2006 (wc)	(Renault R26)
Rubens Barrichello	14 of 18	2004	(Ferrari F2004)

(wc) World champion that season.

267. 2nd places in a season *(Most)*

Nico Rosberg	10	2014	(Mercedes-Benz F1 W05)
Fernando Alonso	7	2006 (wc)	(Renault R26)
Rubens Barrichello	7	2004	(Ferrari F2004)
Mika Häkkinen	7	2000	(McLaren MP4-15 - Mercedes)
Nelson Piquet	7	1987 (wc)	(Williams FW11B - Honda)
Alain Prost	7	1988	(McLaren MP4/4 - Honda)
Kimi Räikkönen	7	2003	(McLaren MP4-17D - Mercedes)
Nico Rosberg	7	2015	(Mercedes-Benz F1 W06)
François Cevert	6	1973	(Tyrrell 006 - Ford Cosworth)
David Coulthard	6	1998	(McLaren MP4-13 - Mercedes)
Lewis Hamilton	6	2015 (wc)	(Mercedes-Benz F1 W06)
Niki Lauda	6	1977 (wc)	(Ferrari 312T2)
Riccardo Patrese	6	1992	(Williams FW14B - Renault)
Alain Prost	6	1989 (wc)	(McLaren MP4/5 - Honda)
Kimi Räikkönen	6	2013	(Lotus E21 - Renault)

(wc) World champion that season.

268. Podium in all but one race of a season

Jim Clark	9	1963 (wc)	(Lotus 25 - Climax)
Juan Manuel Fangio	7	1954 (wc)	(Maserati 250F, Mercedes-Benz W196, W196 str.)
Alberto Ascari	6	1952 (wc)	(Ferrari 500)
Juan Manuel Fangio	6	1957 (wc)	(Maserati 250F)
Luigi Fagioli	5	1950	(Alfa Romeo 158)
Juan Manuel Fangio	5	1955 (wc)	(Mercedes-Benz W196, W196 str.)

(wc) World champion that season.

269. Consecutive podiums *(Most)*

Michael Schumacher	19	United States 2001	- Japan 2002	(Ferrari F2001, F2002)
Lewis Hamilton	16	Italy 2014	- Britain 2015	(Mercedes-Benz F1 W05, F1 W06)
Fernando Alonso	15	Turkey 2005	- Canada 2006	(Renault R25, R26)
Sebastian Vettel	11	Brazil 2010	- Britain 2011	(Red Bull RB6, RB7 - Renault)
Sebastian Vettel	11	Germany 2013	- Brazil 2013	(Red Bull RB9 - Renault)
Alberto Ascari	9	Belgium 1952	- Belgium 1953	(Ferrari 500)
Jim Clark	9	Belgium 1963	- South Africa 1963	(Lotus 25 - Climax)
Lewis Hamilton	9	Australia 2007	- Britain 2007	(McLaren MP4-22, MP4-23 - Mercedes)
Niki Lauda	9	Italy 1975	- Sweden 1976	(Ferrari 312T, 312T2)
Nelson Piquet	9	Monaco 1987	- Portugal 1987	(Williams FW11B - Honda)
Nico Rosberg	9	Australia 2015	- Britain 2015	(Mercedes-Benz F1 W06)
Michael Schumacher	9	Hungary 2000	- Brazil 2001	(Ferrari F1 2000, F2001)
Michael Schumacher	9	Europe 2004	- Italy 2004	(Ferrari F2004)

270. Consecutive podiums from the start of a season *(Most)*

Michael Schumacher	17	2002 (wc)	(Ferrari F2001, F2002)
Fernando Alonso	9	2006 (wc)	(Renault R26)
Lewis Hamilton	9	2007	(McLaren MP4-22 - Mercedes)
Lewis Hamilton	9	2015 (wc)	(Mercedes-Benz F1 W06)
Nico Rosberg	9	2015	(Mercedes-Benz F1 W06)
Sebastian Vettel	9	2011 (wc)	(Red Bull RB7 - Renault)
Jenson Button	7	2009 (wc)	(Brawn BGP 001 - Mercedes)
Niki Lauda	7	1976	(Ferrari 312T, 312T2)
Alain Prost	7	1988	(McLaren MP4/4 - Honda)
Michael Schumacher	7	1994 (wc)	(Benetton B194 - Ford Cosworth)

(wc) World champion that season.

271. Seasons of podiums *(Most)*

Michael Schumacher	16	1992 - 2012	(Benetton, Ferrari, Mercedes-Benz)
Nigel Mansell	13	1981 - 94	(Lotus, Williams, Ferrari)
Fernando Alonso	12	2003 - 14	(Renault, McLaren, Ferrari)
Rubens Barrichello	12	1994 - 2009	(Jordan, Stewart, Ferrari, Honda, Brawn)
Gerhard Berger	12	1986 - 97	(Benetton, Ferrari, McLaren)
David Coulthard	12	1994 - 2008	(Williams, McLaren, Red Bull)
Riccardo Patrese	12	1978 - 93	(Arrows, Brabham, Alfa Romeo, Williams, Benetton)
Alain Prost	12	1981 - 93	(Renault, McLaren, Ferrari, Williams)
Nelson Piquet	11	1980 - 91	(Brabham, Williams, Lotus, Benetton)
Kimi Räikkönen	11	2002 - 15	(McLaren, Ferrari, Lotus)

272. Consecutive seasons of podiums *(Most)*

Michael Schumacher	15	1992 - 2006	(Benetton, Ferrari)
Fernando Alonso	12	2003 - 14	(Renault, McLaren, Ferrari)
Gerhard Berger	12	1986 - 97	(Benetton, Ferrari, McLaren)
Nigel Mansell	12	1981 - 92	(Lotus, Williams, Ferrari)
Alain Prost	11	1981 - 91	(Renault, McLaren, Ferrari)
David Coulthard	10	1994 - 2003	(Williams, McLaren)
Ralf Schumacher	10	1997 - 2006	(Jordan, Williams, Toyota)
Ayrton Senna	10	1984 - 93	(Tolema, Lotus, McLaren)
Jean Alesi	9	1990 - 98	(Tyrrell, Ferrari, Benetton, Sauber)
Jim Clark	9	1960 - 68	(Lotus)
Mika Häkkinen	9	1993 - 2001	(McLaren)
Lewis Hamilton	9	2007 - 15	(McLaren, Mercedes-Benz)
Nelson Piquet	9	1980 - 88	(Brabham, Williams, Lotus)
Jackie Stewart	9	1965 - 73	(BRM, Matra, March, Tyrrell)

273. Podium positions by nationality

Argentina: Carlos Reutemann, 45; Juan Manuel Fangio, 35; José Froilán González, 15; Onofré Marimón, 2; Carlos Menditéguy, 1

Australia: Mark Webber, 42; Jack Brabham, 31; Alan Jones, 24; Daniel Ricciardo, 10; Tim Schenken, 1

Austria: Niki Lauda, 54; Gerhard Berger, 48; Jochen Rindt, 13; Alexander Wurz, 3

Belgium: Jacky Ickx, 25; Thierry Boutsen, 15; Olivier Gendebien, 2; Lucien Bianchi, 1; Paul Frère, 1; Willy Mairesse, 1

Brazil: Ayrton Senna, 80; Rubens Barrichello, 68; Nelson Piquet, 60; Felipe Massa, 41; Emerson Fittipaldi, 35; Carlos Pace, 6; Maurício Gugelmin, 1; Roberto Moreno, 1; Nelsinho Piquet, 1

Canada: Jacques Villeneuve, 23; Gilles Villeneuve, 13

Colombia: Juan Pablo Montoya, 30

Denmark: Kevin Magnussen, 1

Finland: Kimi Räikkönen, 80; Mika Häkkinen, 51; Keke Rosberg, 17; Valtteri Bottas, 8; Heikki Kovalainen, 4; Mika Salo, 2; J J Lehto, 1

France: Alain Prost, 106; Jean Alesi, 32; Jacques Laffite, 32; René Arnoux, 22; Patrick Depailler, 19; François Cevert, 13; Didier Pironi, 13; Patrick Tambay, 11; Romain Grosjean, 10; Jean Behra, 9; Maurice Trintignant, 9; Jean-Pierre Beltoise, 8; Olivier Panis, 5; Jean-Pierre Jarier, 3; Jean-Pierre Jabouille, 2; Robert Manzon, 2; Louis Rosier, 2; Eric Bernard, 1; Henri Pescarolo, 1; Johnny Servoz-Gavin, 1; Philippe Streiff, 1

Germany: Michael Schumacher, 155; Sebastian Vettel, 79; Nico Rosberg, 41; Ralf Schumacher, 27; Heinz-Harald Frentzen, 18; Nick Heidfeld, 13; Jochen Mass, 8; Wolfgang von Trips, 6; Timo Glock, 3; Karl Kling, 2; Hans-Joachim Stuck, 2; Hans Herrmann, 1; Rolf Stommelen, 1

Great Britain: Lewis Hamilton, 87; David Coulthard, 62; Nigel Mansell, 59; Jenson Button, 50; Jackie Stewart, 43; Damon Hill, 42; Graham Hill, 36; Jim Clark, 32; Eddie Irvine, 26; Stirling Moss, 24; John Surtees, 24; James Hunt, 23; John Watson, 20; Mike Hawthorn, 18; Tony Brooks, 10; Martin Brundle, 9; Peter Collins, 9; Johnny Herbert, 7; Innes Ireland, 4; Derek Warwick, 4; Mark Blundell, 3; Peter Arundell, 2; Piers Courage, 2; Mike Hailwood, 2; Stuart Lewis-Evans, 2; Jackie Oliver, 2; Tom Pryce, 2; Mike Parkes, 2; Roy Salvadori, 2; Cliff Allison, 1; Bob Anderson, 1; Richard Attwood, 1; Ron Flockhart, 1; Peter Gethin, 1; Reg Parnell, 1; Brian Redman, 1; Mike Spence, 1; Trevor Taylor, 1; Peter Whitehead, 1

Italy: Riccardo Patrese, 37; Michele Alboreto, 23; Giuseppe Farina, 19; Giancarlo Fisichella, 19; Alberto Ascari, 17; Jarno Trulli, 11; Elio De Angelis, 9; Alessandro Nannini, 9; Lorenzo Bandini, 8; Luigi Villoresi, 8; Luigi Musso, 7; Luigi Fagioli, 6; Andrea De Cesaris, 5; Piero Taruffi, 5; Ivan Capelli, 3; Eugenio Castellotti, 3; Felice Bonetto, 2; Teo Fabi, 2; Umberto Maglioli, 2; Stefano Modena, 2; Cesare Perdisa, 2; Giancarlo Baghetti, 1; Vittorio Brambilla, 1; Bruno Giacomelli, 1; Nicola Larini, 1; Gianni Morbidelli, 1; Ludovico Scarfiotti, 1; Dorino Serafini, 1

Japan: Kamui Kobayashi, 1; Takuma Sato, 1; Aguri Suzuki, 1

Mexico: Pedro Rodríguez, 7; Sergio Pérez, 5

Monaco: Louis Chiron, 1

Netherlands: Jos Verstappen, 2

New Zealand:	Denny Hulme, 33; Bruce McLaren, 27; Chris Amon, 11		
Poland:	Robert Kubica, 12		
Portugal:	Tiago Monteiro, 1		
Russia:	Daniil Kvyat, 1; Vitaly Petrov, 1		
South Africa:	Jody Scheckter, 33; Tony Maggs, 3		
Southern Rhodesia:	John Love, 1		
Spain:	Fernando Alonso, 97; Pedro de la Rosa, 1; Alfonso de Portago, 1		
Sweden:	Ronnie Peterson, 26; Stefan Johansson, 12; Gunnar Nilsson, 4; Jo Bonnier, 1; Reine Wisell, 1		
Switzerland:	Clay Regazzoni, 28; Jo Siffert, 6; Rudi Fischer, 2		
United States:	Mario Andretti, 19; Dan Gurney, 19; Phil Hill, 16; Richie Ginther, 14; Eddie Cheever, 9; Peter Revson, 8; Masten Gregory, 3; Harry Schell, 2; Michael Andretti, 1; Mark Donohue, 1; George Follmer, 1 Venezuela: Pastor Maldonado, 1		

Summary

	podium positions	races	drivers		
Great Britain	617	516	39	Britain 1950 (Reg Parnell)	- Abu Dhabi 2015 (Lewis Hamilton)
Germany	356	310	13	France 1954 (Karl Kling)	- Abu Dhabi 2015 (Nico Rosberg)
France	303	269	21	Switzerland 1950 (Louis Rosier)	- Belgium 2015 (Romain Grosjean)
Brazil	293	271	9	United States 1970 (Emerson Fittipaldi)	- Italy 2015 (Felipe Massa)
Italy	204	163	28	Britain 1950 (Luigi Fagioli)	- Japan 2009 (Jarno Trulli)
Finland	163	160	7	Argentina 1980 (Keke Rosberg)	- Abu Dhabi 2015 (Kimi Räikkönen)
Austria	118	118	4	Belgium 1966 (Jochen Rindt)	- Canada 2007 (Alexander Wurz)
Australia	108	108	5	Monaco 1959 (Jack Brabham)	- Singapore 2015 (Daniel Ricciardo)
Spain	99	99	3	Britain 1956 (Alfonso de Portago)	- Hungary 2014 (Fernando Alonso)
Argentina	98	86	5	Monaco 1950 (Juan Manuel Fangio)	- South Africa 1982 (Carlos Reutemann)
United States	93	84	11	Monaco 1957 (Masten Gregory)	- Italy 1993 (Michael Andretti)
New Zealand	71	67	3	Britain 1959 (Bruce McLaren)	- Austria 1974 (Denny Hulme)
Belgium	45	45	6	Belgium 1956 (Paul Frère)	- Hungary 1990 (Thierry Boutsen)
Sweden	44	43	5	Netherlands 1959 (Jo Bonnier)	- Portugal 1989 (Stefan Johansson)
Canada	36	36	2	Austria 1978 (Gilles Villeneuve)	- Germany 2001 (Jacques Villeneuve)
South Africa	36	36	2	France 1962 (Tony Maggs)	- Italy 1979 (Jody Scheckter)
Switzerland	36	36	3	Switzerland 1952 (Rudi Fischer)	- Canada 1979 (Clay Regazzoni)
Colombia	30	30	1	Spain 2001 (Juan Pablo Montoya)	- Monaco 2006 (Juan Pablo Montoya)
Mexico	12	12	2	South Africa 1967 (Pedro Rodríguez)	- Russia 2015 (Sergio Pérez)
Poland	12	12	1	Italy 2006 (Robert Kubica)	- Belgium 2010 (Robert Kubica)
Japan	3	3	3	Japan 1990 (Aguri Suzuki)	- Japan 2012 (Kamui Kobayashi)
Netherlands	2	2	1	Hungary 1994 (Jos Verstappen)	- Belgium 1994 (Jos Verstappen)
Russia	2	2	2	Australia 2011 (Vitaly Petrov)	- Hungary 2015 (Daniil Kvyat)
Denmark	1	1	1	Australia 2014 (Kevin Magnussen)	
Monaco	1	1	1	Monaco 1950 (Louis Chiron)	
Portugal	1	1	1	United States 2005 (Tiago Monteiro)	
Southern Rhodesia	1	1	1	South Africa 1967 (John Love)	
Venezuela	1	1	1	Spain 2012 (Pastor Maldonado)	

Excludes Indianapolis 500.
The podium positions total only counts 1 podium where two drivers of the same nationality shared a position.

274. Podium 1-2-3s by drivers of the same nationality

Italy 1950	I	1: Giuseppe Farina, 2: Dorino Serafini/ Alberto Ascari, 3: Luigi Fagioli
Belgium 1951	I	1: Giuseppe Farina, 2: Alberto Ascari, 3: Luigi Villoresi
France 1951	I	1: Luigi Fagioli, 2: Alberto Ascari, 3: Luigi Villoresi (a)
France 1952	I	1: Alberto Ascari, 2: Giuseppe Farina, 3: Piero Taruffi
Netherlands 1952	I	1: Alberto Ascari, 2: Giuseppe Farina, 3: Luigi Villoresi
Netherlands 1953	I	1: Alberto Ascari, 2: Giuseppe Farina, 3: Felice Bonetto (a)
Italy 1956	GB	1: Stirling Moss, 2: Peter Collins, 3: Ron Flockhart (a)
Belgium 1958	GB	1: Tony Brooks, 2: Mike Hawthorn, 3: Stuart Lewis-Evans
Britain 1958	GB	1: Peter Collins, 2: Mike Hawthorn, 3: Roy Salvadori
Portugal 1958	GB	1: Stirling Moss, 2: Mike Hawthorn, 3: Stuart Lewis-Evans
Britain 1963	GB	1: Jim Clark, 2: John Surtees, 3: Graham Hill
Netherlands 1964	GB	1: Jim Clark, 2: John Surtees, 3: Peter Arundell
Britain 1964	GB	1: Jim Clark, 2: Graham Hill, 3: John Surtees
South Africa 1965	GB	1: Jim Clark, 2: John Surtees, 3: Graham Hill
France 1965	GB	1: Jim Clark, 2: Jackie Stewart, 3: John Surtees
Britain 1965	GB	1: Jim Clark, 2: Graham Hill, 3: John Surtees

United States 1968	GB	1: Jackie Stewart, 2: Graham Hill, 3: John Surtees
South Africa 1980	F	1: René Arnoux, 2: Jacques Laffite, 3: Didier Pironi
France 1982	F	1: René Arnoux, 2: Alain Prost, 3: Didier Pironi
San Marino 1983	F	1: Patrick Tambay, 2: Alain Prost, 3: René Arnoux

Excludes Indianapolis 500.
(a) Whilst 1-2-3 were of the same nationality, another nationality of driver shared one of the cars on the podium.
It can be seen that in three consecutive British Grands Prix, British drivers achieved a complete podium, ie in 1963, 64 and 65.

by nationality

Great Britain (GB)	11	Italy 1956 United States 1968	(Stirling Moss, Peter Collins, Ron Flockhart) - (Jackie Stewart, Graham Hill, John Surtees)
Italy (I)	6	Italy 1950 Netherlands 1953	(Giuseppe Farina, Dorino Serafini/ Alberto Ascari, Luigi Fagioli) - (Alberto Ascari, Giuseppe Farina, Felice Bonetto)
France (F)	3	South Africa 1980 San Marino 1983	(René Arnoux, Jacques Laffite, Didier Pironi) - (Patrick Tambay, Alain Prost, René Arnoux)

Excludes Indianapolis 500.

by drivers (Most)

| Jim Clark, Graham Hill, John Surtees (GB) | 4 | Britain 1963 | - Britain 1965 |
| Giuseppe Farina, Alberto Ascari, Luigi Villoresi (I) | 2 | Belgium 1951 | - Netherlands 1952 |

275. Podium 1-2s by drivers of the same nationality

by nationality

Argentina: Juan Manuel Fangio, José Froilán González, 6
Brazil: Nelson Piquet, Ayrton Senna, 8;
Emerson Fittipaldi, Carlos Pace, 2;
Roberto Moreno, Nelson Piquet, 1
France: René Arnoux, Alain Prost, 3;
René Arnoux, Patrick Tambay, 3;
René Arnoux, Jacques Laffite, 2;
Alain Prost, Patrick Tambay, 2;
Patrick Depailler, Jacques Laffite, 1
Germany: Michael Schumacher, Ralf Schumacher, 5;
Heinz-Harald Frentzen, Michael Schumacher, 3;
Nico Rosberg, Sebastian Vettel, 3;
Heinz-Harald Frentzen, Ralf Schumacher, 1
Great Britain: Jim Clark, Graham Hill, 7;
Jim Clark, John Surtees, 5;
Graham Hill, Jackie Stewart, 4;
Jenson Button, Lewis Hamilton, 3;
Jim Clark, Jackie Stewart, 3;
Mike Hawthorn, Stirling Moss, 3;
Graham Hill, John Surtees, 3;
Tony Brooks, Mike Hawthorn, 2;
Peter Collins, Stirling Moss, 2;
David Coulthard, Damon Hill, 2;

David Coulthard, Eddie Irvine, 2;
Richard Attwood, Graham Hill, 1;
Tony Brooks, Roy Salvadori, 1;
Peter Collins, Mike Hawthorn, 1;
Piers Courage, Graham Hill, 1;
Graham Hill, Trevor Taylor, 1;
Innes Ireland, Stirling Moss, 1
Italy: Alberto Ascari, Giuseppe Farina, 8;
Alberto Ascari, Luigi Villoresi, 2;
Luigi Fagioli, Giuseppe Farina, 2;
Alberto Ascari, Luigi Fagioli, 1;
Alberto Ascari, Piero Taruffi, 1;
Andrea De Cesaris, Riccardo Patrese, 1;
Giuseppe Farina, Dorino Serafini, 1;
Alessandro Nannini, Riccardo Patrese, 1;
At Italy 1950, 2nd place was a shared drive between Ascari and Serafini, so both are counted here with winner Farina.
New Zealand: Denny Hulme, Bruce McLaren, 1
United States: Richie Ginther, Dan Gurney, 1;
Richie Ginther, Phil Hill, 1;
Dan Gurney, Phil Hill, 1

Excludes Indianapolis 500.

by drivers (Most)

Alberto Ascari, Giuseppe Farina (I)	8	Italy 1950	- Switzerland 1953
Nelson Piquet, Ayrton Senna (BR)	8	Brazil 1986	- Canada 1990
Jim Clark, Graham Hill (GB)	7	Belgium 1962	- South Africa 1968
Juan Manuel Fangio, José Froilán González (RA)	6	France 1951	- Argentina 1955
Jim Clark, John Surtees (GB)	5	Britain 1962	- South Africa 1965
Michael Schumacher, Ralf Schumacher (D)	5	Canada 2001	- Japan 2004
Graham Hill, Jackie Stewart (GB)	4	Italy 1965	- South Africa 1969
Mike Hawthorn, Stirling Moss (GB)	3	France 1958	- Morocco 1958
Graham Hill, John Surtees (GB)	3	Germany 1962	- United States 1964
Jim Clark, Jackie Stewart (GB)	3	Belgium 1965	- Netherlands 1965
René Arnoux, Alain Prost (F)	3	France 1982	- San Marino 1984
René Arnoux, Patrick Tambay (F)	3	Germany 1982	- Netherlands 1983
Heinz-Harald Frentzen, Michael Schumacher (D)	3	San Marino 1997	- Japan 1997
Jenson Button, Lewis Hamilton (GB)	3	China 2010	- Canada 2010
Nico Rosberg, Sebastian Vettel (D)	3	Monaco 2013	- Monaco 2015

Summary

Great Britain (GB)	42	Monaco 1956 (S Moss, P Collins)	- Canada 2010 (L Hamilton, J Button)	
Italy (I)	16	Britain 1950 (G Farina, L Fagioli)	- Japan 1989 (A Nannini, R Patrese)	
Germany (D)	12	San Marino 1997 (H-H Frentzen, M Schumacher)	- Monaco 2015 (N Rosberg, S Vettel)	
Brazil (BR)	11	Brazil 1975 (C Pace, E Fittipaldi)	- Japan 1990 (N Piquet, R Moreno)	
France (F)	11	Brazil 1979 (J Laffite, P Depailler)	- San Marino 1984 (A Prost, R Arnoux)	
Argentina (RA)	6	France 1951 (J M Fangio, J F González)	- Argentina 1955 (J M Fangio, J F González)	
United States (USA)	3	Italy 1960 (P Hill, R Ginther)	- Mexico 1965 (R Ginther, D Gurney)	
New Zealand (NZ)	1	Canada 1968 (D Hulme, B McLaren)		

Excludes Indianapolis 500.
Includes Italy 1955 where 1st and 2nd places on the podium were occupied by three drivers from Italy.
At France 1951, drivers from both Argentina and Italy finished 1st and 2nd in shared drives. Counted above for both countries.

276. Consecutive podium 1-2s by drivers of the same nationality

Great Britain	7	Belgium 1958 (1: Tony Brooks, 2: Mike Hawthorn)	- Morocco 1958 (1: Stirling Moss, 2: Mike Hawthorn)
Great Britain	6	Belgium 1965 (1: Jim Clark, 2: Jackie Stewart)	- Italy 1965 (1: Jackie Stewart, 2: Graham Hill)
Italy	5	Belgium 1952 (1: Alberto Ascari, 2: Giuseppe Farina)	- Netherlands 1952 (1: Alberto Ascari, 2: Giuseppe Farina)
Italy	3	Argentina 1953 (1: Alberto Ascari, 2: Luigi Villoresi)	- Belgium 1953 (1: Alberto Ascari, 2: Luigi Villoresi)
Argentina	2	France 1951 (1: Juan Manuel Fangio *, 2: José Froilán González *)	- Britain 1951 (1: José Froilán González, 2: Juan Manuel Fangio)
Argentina	2	Germany 1954 (1: Juan Manuel Fangio, 2: José Froilán González *)	- Switzerland 1954 (1: Juan Manuel Fangio, 2: José Froilán González)
Brazil	2	Germany 1986 (1: Nelson Piquet, 2: Ayrton Senna)	- Hungary 1986 (1: Nelson Piquet, 2: Ayrton Senna)
Brazil	2	Monaco 1987 (1: Ayrton Senna, 2: Nelson Piquet)	- Detroit 1987 (1: Ayrton Senna, 2: Nelson Piquet)
France	2	France 1982 (1: René Arnoux, 2: Alain Prost)	- Germany 1982 (1: Patrick Tambay, 2: René Arnoux)
France	2	Austria 1983 (1: Alain Prost, 2: René Arnoux)	- Netherlands 1983 (1: René Arnoux, 2: Patrick Tambay)
Great Britain	2	Britain 1962 (1: Jim Clark, 2: John Surtees)	- Germany 1962 (1: Graham Hill, 2: John Surtees)
Great Britain	2	Britain 1963 (1: Jim Clark, 2: John Surtees)	- Germany 1963 (1: John Surtees, 2: Jim Clark)
Great Britain	2	Britain 1964 (1: Jim Clark, 2: Graham Hill)	- Germany 1964 (1: John Surtees, 2: Graham Hill)
Great Britain	2	Britain 1999 (1: David Coulthard, 2: Eddie Irvine)	- Austria 1999 (1: Eddie Irvine, 2: David Coulthard)
Great Britain	2	Turkey 2010 (1: Lewis Hamilton, 2: Jenson Button)	- Canada 2010 (1: Lewis Hamilton, 2: Jenson Button)
Italy	2	Belgium 1951 (1: Giuseppe Farina, 2: Alberto Ascari)	- France 1951 (1: Luigi Fagioli *, 2: Alberto Ascari *)

* Shared with a driver of another nationality.

277. Races with at least two podium positions by drivers of the same nationality

by nationality

Great Britain	90	Monaco 1956 (1: S Moss, 2: P Collins)	- China 2012 (2: J Button, 3: L Hamilton)
Germany	46	San Marino 1997 (1: H-H Frentzen, 2: M Schumacher)	- Brazil 2015 (1: N Rosberg, 3: S Vettel)
Italy	35	Britain 1950 (1: G Farina, 2: L Fagioli)	- Canada 1991 (2: S Modena, 3: R Patrese)
France (a)	30	Monaco 1955 (1: M Trintignant, 3: J Behra)	- Spain 1997 (2: O Panis, 3: J Alesi)
Brazil	22	Brazil 1975 (1: C Pace, 2: E Fittipaldi)	- Germany 2008 (2: N Piquet, 3: F Massa)
Argentina	12	France 1951 (1: J M Fangio, 2: J F González)	- Argentina 1957 (1: J M Fangio, 3: C Menditéguy)
United States	9	Germany 1959 (2: D Gurney, 3: P Hill)	- Mexico 1965 (1: R Ginther, 2: D Gurney)
New Zealand	4	Monaco 1967 (1: D Hulme, 3: C Amon)	- Canada 1968 (1: D Hulme, 2: B McLaren)
Finland	3	Japan 2007 (2: H Kovalainen, 3: K Räikkönen)	- Hungary 2008 (1: H Kovalainen, 3: K Räikkönen)
Sweden	1	Belgium 1977 (1: G Nilsson, 3: R Peterson)	

(a) Excludes Argentina 1955, where Trintignant occupied two podium positions with a 2nd and a 3rd in shared cars.

278. Four drivers of the same nationality sharing a podium

The only occasion was in Italy 1950 with Giuseppe Farina (1st), Alberto Ascari and Dorino Serafini sharing a car (2nd) and Luigi Fagioli (3rd).

279. Podiums at the same venue *(Most)*

grand prix

Michael Schumacher	12	Canada	1992 - 2006	(Montréal)
Michael Schumacher	12	San Marino	1993 - 2006	(Imola)
Michael Schumacher	12	Spain	1992 - 2006	(Catalunya)
Alain Prost	11	France	1981 - 93	(Paul Ricard, 8; Magny-Cours, 2; Dijon-Prenois, 1)
Michael Schumacher	11	France	1993 - 2006	(Magny-Cours)
Michael Schumacher	10	Brazil	1992 - 2002	(Interlagos)
Michael Schumacher	9	Belgium	1992 - 2004	(Spa-Francorchamps)
Michael Schumacher	9	Europe	1994 - 2012	(Nürburgring, 7; Jerez de la Frontera, 1; Valencia, 1)
Michael Schumacher	9	Japan	1994 - 2004	(Suzuka)
Fernando Alonso	8	Brazil	2003 - 13	(Interlagos)
Michael Schumacher	8	Italy	1992 - 2006	(Monza)
Ayrton Senna	8	Monaco	1984 - 93	(Monte-Carlo)

Michael Schumacher	12	Catalunya	1992 - 2006
Michael Schumacher	12	Imola	1993 - 2006
Michael Schumacher	12	Montréal	1992 - 2006
Michael Schumacher	11	Magny-Cours	1993 - 2006
Michael Schumacher	10	Interlagos	1992 - 2002
Michael Schumacher	9	Spa-Francorchamps	1992 - 2004
Michael Schumacher	9	Suzuka	1994 - 2004
Fernando Alonso	8	Interlagos	2003 - 13
Alain Prost	8	Paul Ricard	1982 - 90
Michael Schumacher	8	Monza	1992 - 2006
Michael Schumacher	8	Nürburgring	1995 - 2006 (a)
Ayrton Senna	8	Monte-Carlo	1984 - 93

(a) 7 at European and 1 at Luxembourg Grands Prix.

280. Consecutive podiums at the same venue *(Most)*

Graham Hill	7	Monaco	1963 - 69	(Monte-Carlo)
Alain Prost	7	France	1985 - 91	(Paul Ricard, 6; Magny-Cours, 1)
Michael Schumacher	7	Canada	2000 - 06	(Montréal)
Michael Schumacher	7	United States	2000 - 06	(Indianapolis)
Ayrton Senna	7	Hungary	1986 - 92	(Hungaroring)
Sebastian Vettel	7	Japan	2009 - 15	(Suzuka)
Lewis Hamilton	6	China	2010 - 15	(Shanghai)
Alain Prost	6	Spain	1986 - 91	(Jerez de la Frontera, 5; Catalunya, 1)
Michael Schumacher	6	France	2001 - 06	(Magny-Cours)
Jim Clark	5	Netherlands	1963 - 67	(Zandvoort)
David Coulthard	5	Austria	1997 - 2001	(A1-Ring)
Juan Manuel Fangio	5	Italy	1953 - 57	(Monza)
Damon Hill	5	Hungary	1993 - 97	(Hungaroring)
Alain Prost	5	Portugal	1986 - 90	(Estoril)
Kimi Räikkönen	5	Britain	2003 - 07	(Silverstone)
Michael Schumacher	5	Brazil	1992 - 96	(Interlagos)
Michael Schumacher	5	Brazil	1998 - 2002	(Interlagos)
Michael Schumacher	5	San Marino	1996 - 2000	(Imola)
Michael Schumacher	5	San Marino	2002 - 06	(Imola)
Michael Schumacher	5	Spain	1992 - 96	(Catalunya)
Ayrton Senna	5	Germany	1986 - 90	(Hockenheim)
Ayrton Senna	5	Monaco	1989 - 93	(Monte-Carlo)
Sebastian Vettel	5	Singapore	2010 - 14	(Marina Bay)
Mark Webber	5	Britain	2009 - 13	(Silverstone)

281. Podiums on home soil *(Most)*

Michael Schumacher	14	Germany	1992 - 2006 (a)	(Hockenheim, 7; Nürburgring, 7)
Alain Prost	12	France	1981 - 93 (b)	(Paul Ricard, 8; Dijon-Prenois, 2; Magny-Cours, 2)
Fernando Alonso	9	Spain	2003 - 13 (c)	(Catalunya, 7; Valencia, 2)
Nigel Mansell	8	Britain	1983 - 92 (d)	(Silverstone, 5; Brands Hatch, 3)
Jim Clark	5	Britain	1962 - 67	(Silverstone, 3; Aintree, 1; Brands Hatch, 1)
Lewis Hamilton	5	Britain	2007 - 15	(Silverstone)
Felipe Massa	5	Brazil	2006 - 14	(Interlagos)
John Surtees	5	Britain	1960 - 65	(Silverstone, 3; Aintree, 1; Brands Hatch, 1)
Michele Alboreto	4	Italy	1982 - 88 (e)	(Imola, 2; Monza, 2)
Juan Manuel Fangio	4	Argentina	1954 - 57	(Buenos Aires No.2)
Emerson Fittipaldi	4	Brazil	1973 - 78	(Interlagos, 3; Jacarepaguá, 1)
Mike Hawthorn	4	Britain	1952 - 58	(Silverstone, 3; Aintree, 1)
Graham Hill	4	Britain	1963 - 66	(Silverstone, 2; Brands Hatch, 1)
Riccardo Patrese	4	Italy	1981 - 92 (f)	(Imola, 3; Monza, 1)
Nelson Piquet	4	Brazil	1983 - 88	(Jacarepaguá)
Carlos Reutemann	4	Argentina	1975 - 81	(Buenos Aires No.15)
Ayrton Senna	4	Brazil	1986 - 93	(Interlagos, 3; Jacarepaguá, 1)

(a) 7 German & 7 European Grands Prix. (b) 11 French & 1 Swiss Grands Prix.
(c) 7 Spanish & 2 European Grands Prix. (d) 6 British & 2 European Grands Prix.
(e) 2 Italian & 2 San Marino Grands Prix. (f) 3 San Marino & 1 Italian Grands Prix.

282. First podium was on home soil

Michele Alboreto	San Marino 1982	(Imola)		Kamui Kobayashi	Japan 2012	(Suzuka)
René Arnoux	France 1979	(Dijon-Prenois)		Nicola Larini	San Marino 1994	(Imola)
Felice Bonetto	Italy 1951	(Monza)		Umberto Maglioli	Italy 1954	(Monza)
François Cevert	France 1971	(Paul Ricard)		Carlos Menditéguy	Argentina 1957	(Buenos Aires No.2)
Louis Chiron	Monaco 1950	(Monte-Carlo)		Reg Parnell	Britain 1950	(Silverstone)
Rudi Fischer	Switzerland 1952	(Bremgarten)		Roy Salvadori	Britain 1958	(Silverstone)
Paul Frère	Belgium 1956	(Spa-Francorchamps)		Ludovico Scarfiotti	Italy 1966	(Monza)
Olivier Gendebien	Belgium 1960	(Spa-Francorchamps)		Dorino Serafini	Italy 1950	(Monza)
Maurício Gugelmin	Brazil 1989	(Jacarepaguá)		Hans-Joachim Stuck	Germany 1977	(Hockenheim)
Mike Hawthorn	Britain 1952	(Silverstone)		John Surtees	Britain 1960	(Silverstone)
Jacky Ickx	Belgium 1968	(Spa-Francorchamps)		Aguri Suzuki	Japan 1990	(Suzuka)
Jean-Pierre Jabouille	France 1979	(Dijon-Prenois)				

283. Two podiums on home soil in a season

Fernando Alonso: 2nd in the Spanish Grand Prix (Catalunya) & 1st in the European Grand Prix (Valencia) in 2012
Eddie Cheever: 2nd in the Detroit Grand Prix & 3rd at the Caesars Palace Grand Prix (Las Vegas) in 1982
Alain Prost: 2nd in the French Grand Prix (Paul Ricard) & 2nd in the Swiss Grand Prix (Dijon) in 1982
Michael Schumacher: 1st in the German Grand Prix (Hockenheim) & 1st in the European Grand Prix (Nürburgring) in 1995, 2004 and 06;
1st in the German Grand Prix (Hockenheim) & 2nd in the European Grand Prix (Nürburgring) in 2002

284. Race starts taken to achieve their first podium
(number of races includes the race of first podium)

Fewest

1st race

Peter Arundell	Monaco 1964 (a)	(placing: 3)		Jean Behra	Switzerland 1952 (d)	(placing: 3)
Alberto Ascari	Monaco 1950 (b)	(placing: 2)		Tony Brooks	Monaco 1957	(placing: 2)
Giancarlo Baghetti	France 1961 (b)	(placing: 1)		Eugenio Castellotti	Monaco 1955 (b)	(placing: 2)
Mark Donohue	Canada 1971 (b)	(placing: 3)		Louis Chiron	Monaco 1950 (b)	(placing: 3)
Luigi Fagioli	Britain 1950 (b)	(placing: 2)		Alfonso de Portago	Britain 1956 (b)(e)	(placing: 2)
Giuseppe Farina	Britain 1950 (b)	(placing: 1)		Juan Manuel Fangio	Monaco 1950 (b)	(placing: 1)
Masten Gregory	Monaco 1957 (b)	(placing: 3)		George Follmer	Spain 1973 (b)	(placing: 3)
Lewis Hamilton	Australia 2007 (b)	(placing: 3)		Dan Gurney	Germany 1959 (b)	(placing: 2)
Karl Kling	France 1954 (b)	(placing: 2)		Onofré Marimón	Belgium 1953	(placing: 3)
Kevin Magnussen	Australia 2014 (b)	(placing: 2)		Brian Redman	Spain 1968 (f)	(placing: 3)
Mike Parkes	France 1966 (c)	(placing: 2)		Jackie Stewart	Monaco 1965 (b)	(placing: 3)
Reg Parnell	Britain 1950 (b)	(placing: 3)		John Surtees	Britain 1960 (b)	(placing: 2)
Cesare Perdisa	Monaco 1955 (b)	(placing: 3)		Piero Taruffi	Switzerland 1951	(placing: 2)
Dorino Serafini	Italy 1950 (b)	(placing: 2)		Trevor Taylor	Netherlands 1962	(placing: 2)
Jacques Villeneuve	Australia 1996 (b)	(placing: 2)				
Peter Whitehead	France 1950 (a)(b)	(placing: 3)				
Reine Wisell	United States 1970 (b)	(placing: 3)				

Most

Martin Brundle	91	France 1992		Gianni Morbidelli	60	Australia 1995
Mika Salo	73	Germany 1999		Felipe Massa	57	Europe 2006
Jenson Button	68	Malaysia 2004		Mark Webber	56	Monaco 2005
Pedro de la Rosa	67	Hungary 2006		Kamui Kobayashi	55	Japan 2012
Johnny Herbert	67	Spain 1995		Daniel Ricciardo	55	Spain 2014

Excludes Indianapolis 500.
(a) Non-started 1 race before.
(b) First season to enter Formula 1.
(c) Non-qualified for 1 race before.
(d) Some sources state this to be his first race, but it is believed that he made his debut at Italy 1951 where he raced Maurice Trintignant's car wearing Trintignant's helmet (see section 558). Switzerland 1952 would therefore be Behra's second race.
(e) Shared drive.
(f) Entered an earlier season where he did not start.
For most races starts but never a podium, see section 185.

285. Podiums in their first season

Lewis Hamilton	12	2007		Mark Donohue	1	1971
Jacques Villeneuve	11	1996		Emerson Fittipaldi	1	1970
Luigi Fagioli	5	1950		George Follmer	1	1973
Jackie Stewart	5	1965		Richie Ginther	1	1960
Juan Pablo Montoya	4	2001		Masten Gregory	1	1957
Clay Regazzoni	4	1970		Mike Hawthorn	1	1952
Juan Manuel Fangio	3	1950		Karl Kling	1	1954
Giuseppe Farina	3	1950		Heikki Kovalainen	1	2007
Ayrton Senna	3	1984		Robert Kubica	1	2006
Eugenio Castellotti	2	1955		Kevin Magnussen	1	2014
Dan Gurney	2	1959		Willy Mairesse	1	1960
Phil Hill	2	1958		Tiago Monteiro	1	2005
James Hunt	2	1973		Olivier Panis	1	1994
Gunnar Nilsson	2	1976		Reg Parnell	1	1950
Louis Rosier	2	1950		Cesare Perdisa	1	1955
Jos Verstappen	2	1994		Nelsinho Piquet	1	2008
Michael Andretti	1	1993		Ralf Schumacher	1	1997
Alberto Ascari	1	1950		Dorino Serafini	1	1950
Giancarlo Baghetti	1	1961		John Surtees	1	1960
Louis Chiron	1	1950		Peter Whitehead	1	1950
Jim Clark	1	1960		Reine Wisell	1	1970
David Coulthard	1	1994		Alexander Wurz	1	1997
Alfonso de Portago	1	1956				

The following drivers achieved a podium in their first season of starting, but were active in an earlier season when they did not start:

Peter Arundell: 2 podiums in 1964 (did not start 1 race in 1963, his first season)
Mike Parkes: 2 podiums in 1966 (did not qualify for 1 race in 1959)
Brian Redman: 1 podium in 1968 (did not start 1 race in 1967)
Wolfgang von Trips: 1 podium in 1957 (did not start 1 race in 1956)

286. Podium in their first two or more races started

Lewis Hamilton	9	Australia 2007	- Britain 2007	(McLaren MP4-22 - Mercedes)
Peter Arundell	2	Monaco 1964	- Netherlands 1964	(Lotus 25 - Climax)

287. First podium immediately followed by others
(including first podium)

Lewis Hamilton	9	Australia	- Britain 2007	(McLaren MP4-22 - Mercedes)
José Froilán González	5	France	- Spain 1951	(Ferrari 375)
Jack Brabham	4	Monaco	- Britain 1959	(Cooper T51 - Climax)
Peter Collins	4	Monaco	- Britain 1956	(Lancia-Ferrari D50)
Jenson Button	3	Malaysia	- San Marino 2004	(BAR 006 - Honda)
Clay Regazzoni	3	Austria	- Canada 1970	(Ferrari 312B)
Jody Scheckter	3	Belgium	- Sweden 1974	(Tyrrell 007 - Ford Cosworth)
Michael Schumacher	3	Mexico	- Spain 1992	(Benetton B191B, B192 - Ford Cosworth)
Jackie Stewart	3	Monaco	- France 1965	(BRM P261)
Luigi Villoresi	3	Belgium	- Britain 1951	(Ferrari 375)
Fernando Alonso	2	Malaysia	- Brazil 2003	(Renault R23)
René Arnoux	2	France	- Britain 1979	(Renault RS10)
Peter Arundell	2	Monaco	- Netherlands 1964	(Lotus 25 - Climax)
Martin Brundle	2	France	- Britain 1992	(Benetton B192 - Ford Cosworth)
Olivier Gendebien	2	Britain	- France 1960	(Cooper T51 - Climax)
Dan Gurney	2	Germany	- Portugal 1959	(Ferrari Dino 246)
Damon Hill	2	Brazil	- Europe 1993	(Williams FW15C - Renault)
Phil Hill	2	Italy	- Morocco 1958	(Ferrari Dino 246)
Denny Hulme	2	France	- Britain 1966	(Brabham BT20 - Repco)
Stefan Johansson	2	Canada	- Detroit 1985	(Ferrari 156/85)
Louis Rosier	2	Switzerland	- Belgium 1950	(Talbot-Lago T26C-DA)
Roy Salvadori	2	Britain	- Germany 1958	(Cooper T45 - Climax)
Hans-Joachim Stuck	2	Germany	- Austria 1977	(Brabham BT45B - Alfa Romeo)
Jos Verstappen	2	Hungary	- Belgium 1994	(Benetton B194 - Ford Cosworth)
Derek Warwick	2	South Africa	- Belgium 1984	(Renault RE50)
John Watson	2	France	- Britain 1976	(Penske PC4 - Ford Cosworth)

288. Races where more than one driver achieved their maiden podium

Britain 1950	1: Giuseppe Farina (Alfa Romeo), 2: Luigi Fagioli (Alfa Romeo), 3: Reg Parnell (Alfa Romeo)
Monaco 1950	1: Juan Manuel Fangio (Alfa Romeo), 2: Alberto Ascari (Ferrari), 3: Louis Chiron (Maserati)
Switzerland 1952	2: Rudi Fischer (Ferrari), 3: Jean Behra (Gordini)
Belgium 1954	2: Maurice Trintignant (Ferrari), 3: Stirling Moss (Maserati)
Monaco 1955	2: Eugenio Castellotti (Lancia), 3: Cesare Perdisa (Maserati) (s)
Monaco 1957	2: Tony Brooks (Vanwall), 3: Masten Gregory (Maserati)
Netherlands 1960	2: Innes Ireland (Lotus), 3: Graham Hill (BRM)
Italy 1960	2: Richie Ginther (Ferrari), 3: Willy Mairesse (Ferrari)
France 1966	2: Mike Parkes (Ferrari), 3: Denny Hulme (Brabham)
South Africa 1967	1: Pedro Rodríguez (Cooper), 2: John Love (Cooper)
Monaco 1968	2: Richard Attwood (BRM), 3: Lucien Bianchi (Cooper)
Austria 1970	2: Clay Regazzoni (Ferrari), 3: Rolf Stommelen (Brabham)
United States 1970	1: Emerson Fittipaldi (Lotus), 3: Reine Wisell (Lotus)
Austria 1975	1: Vittorio Brambilla (March), 3: Tom Pryce (Shadow)
France 1979	1: Jean-Pierre Jabouille (Renault), 3: René Arnoux (Renault)
Argentina 1980	2: Nelson Piquet (Brabham), 3: Keke Rosberg (Fittipaldi)
Japan 1990	2: Roberto Moreno (Benetton), 3: Aguri Suzuki (Lola)
Germany 1994	2: Olivier Panis (Ligier), 3: Eric Bernard (Ligier)

(s) Shared drive.

289. Podium in their final race

Michael Andretti	Italy 1993	(3rd)	returned to CART IndyCar championship
Tony Brooks	United States 1961	(3rd)	retired from F1
Jim Clark	South Africa 1968	(1st)	killed in Formula 2 event, prior to next F1 race
Luigi Fagioli	France 1951	(1st)	his only race that year
Giuseppe Farina	Belgium 1955	(3rd)	retired from F1
Paul Frère	Belgium 1956	(2nd)	never had a regular drive
Mike Hawthorn	Morocco 1958	(2nd)	retired from F1
Onofré Marimón	Britain 1954	(3rd)	killed in qualifying for next F1 race, in Germany
Alessandro Nannini	Spain 1990	(3rd)	injured a week later in helicopter crash, ending F1 career
Didier Pironi	France 1982	(3rd)	injured in qualifying for next F1 race, in Germany, ending F1 career
Alain Prost	Australia 1993	(2nd)	retired from F1
Dorino Serafini	Italy 1950	(2nd)	only competed in this race
Jo Siffert	United States 1971	(2nd)	killed at the World Championship Victory Race, Brands Hatch, three weeks after end of season
Gilles Villeneuve	San Marino 1982	(2nd)	killed in qualifying for next F1 race, in Belgium
Mark Webber	Brazil 2013	(2nd)	retired from F1

290. Podiums in their final season *(Most)*

Alain Prost	12	1993		Jochen Rindt	5	1970
Jackie Stewart	8	1973		Jack Brabham	4	1970
Mark Webber	8	2013		Wolfgang von Trips	4	1961
François Cevert	7	1973		Mika Häkkinen	3	2001
Mike Hawthorn	7	1958		Robert Kubica	3	2010
Ronnie Peterson	7	1978		Alessandro Nannini	3	1990
Didier Pironi	6	1982		Nelson Piquet	3	1991

291. Podium from lowest grid position

	result	grid		
Onofré Marimón	3rd	28th	Britain 1954	(Maserati 250F)
Emerson Fittipaldi	3rd	24th	United States West 1980	(Fittipaldi F7 - Ford Cosworth)
Sebastian Vettel	3rd	24th	Abu Dhabi 2012	(Red Bull RB8 - Renault)
Niki Lauda	2nd	23rd	United States West 1983	(McLaren MP4/1C - Ford Cosworth)
Teo Fabi	3rd	23rd	Detroit 1984	(Brabham BT53 - BMW)
Ron Flockhart	3rd	23rd	Italy 1956	(Connaught B - Alta)
John Watson	1st	22nd	United States West 1983	(McLaren MP4/1C - Ford Cosworth)
Lewis Hamilton	3rd	22nd	Hungary 2014	(Mercedes-Benz F1 W05)
Kimi Räikkönen	3rd	22nd	Bahrain 2006	(McLaren MP4-21 - Mercedes)
Wolfgang von Trips	3rd	21st	France 1958	(Ferrari Dino 246)
John Watson	3rd	21st	Detroit 1983	(McLaren MP4/1C - Ford Cosworth)

	result	grid		
Indianapolis 500				
Jim Rathmann	2nd	32nd	1957	(Epperly - Offenhauser)
Don Freeland	3rd	26th	1956	(Phillips - Offenhauser)
Paul Goldsmith	3rd	26th	1960	(Epperly - Offenhauser)
George Amick	2nd	25th	1958	(Epperly - Offenhauser)

292. Different podium drivers in a season

Most

1982	18
1968	17
1970	15
1997	15
1974	14
1977	14
1994	14
2008	14

Fewest

1992	7
2000	7
2002	7
2011	7
1951	8
1953	8
1963	8
2007	8
2010	8
2013	8

Total for each season

1950 - 9, 1951 - 8, 1952 - 9, 1953 - 8, 1954 - 12, 1955 - 12, 1956 - 11, 1957 - 11, 1958 - 12, 1959 - 9, 1960 - 13, 1961 - 10, 1962 - 10, 1963 - 8, 1964 - 11, 1965 - 10, 1966 - 10, 1967 - 10, 1968 - 17, 1969 - 12, 1970 - 15, 1971 - 13, 1972 - 11, 1973 - 12, 1974 - 14, 1975 - 13, 1976 - 12, 1977 - 14, 1978 - 13, 1979 - 13, 1980 - 11, 1981 - 11, 1982 - 18, 1983 - 12, 1984 - 13, 1985 - 13, 1986 - 9, 1987 - 11, 1988 - 10, 1989 - 13, 1990 - 12, 1991 - 9, 1992 - 7, 1993 - 11, 1994 - 14, 1995 - 13, 1996 - 10, 1997 - 15, 1998 - 10, 1999 - 11, 2000 - 7, 2001 - 10, 2002 - 7, 2003 - 10, 2004 - 9, 2005 - 13, 2006 - 12, 2007 - 8, 2008 - 14, 2009 - 13, 2010 - 8, 2011 - 7, 2012 - 13, 2013 - 8, 2014 - 10, 2015 - 10

Excludes Indianapolis 500.

293. First time podium drivers in a season

Most

1950	9	Giuseppe Farina, Luigi Fagioli, Reg Parnell, Juan Manuel Fangio, Alberto Ascari, Louis Chiron, Louis Rosier, Peter Whitehead, Dorino Serafini
1960	8	Cliff Allison, Innes Ireland, Graham Hill, Olivier Gendebien, John Surtees, Jim Clark, Richie Ginther, Willy Mairesse
1968	7	Brian Redman, Richard Attwood, Lucien Bianchi, Jacky Ickx, Jean-Pierre Beltoise, Johnny Servoz-Gavin, Jackie Oliver
1954	6	Maurice Trintignant, Stirling Moss, Karl Kling, Hans Herrmann, Umberto Maglioli, Luigi Musso
1970	6	Mario Andretti, Henri Pescarolo, Rolf Stommelen, Clay Regazzoni, Emerson Fittipaldi, Reine Wisell
1994	6	Rubens Barrichello, Nicola Larini, Olivier Panis, Eric Bernard, Jos Verstappen, David Coulthard
1957	5	Carlos Menditéguy, Tony Brooks, Masten Gregory, Harry Schell, Wolfgang von Trips
1971	5	Ronnie Peterson, François Cevert, Tim Schenken, Peter Gethin, Mark Donohue

Fewest

None

1963, 83, 87, 98, 2000, 09, 10, 13

One

1953	Onofré Marimón
1961	Giancarlo Baghetti
1969	Piers Courage
1986	Gerhard Berger
1991	J J Lehto
1996	Jacques Villeneuve
2002	Kimi Räikkönen
2003	Fernando Alonso
2011	Vitaly Petrov
2015	Daniil Kvyat

Excludes Indianapolis 500.

294. Podiums with the same constructor *(Most)*

Michael Schumacher	116	Ferrari	Brazil 1996	- China 2006
Sebastian Vettel	65	Red Bull	China 2009	- Japan 2014
Alain Prost	63	McLaren	Brazil 1984	- Spain 1989
Rubens Barrichello	55	Ferrari	Australia 2000	- United States 2005
Ayrton Senna	55	McLaren	San Marino 1988	- Australia 1993
David Coulthard	51	McLaren	Europe 1996	- Japan 2003
Mika Häkkinen	51	McLaren	Japan 1993	- United States 2001
Lewis Hamilton	49	McLaren	Australia 2007	- United States 2012
Fernando Alonso	44	Ferrari	Bahrain 2010	- Hungary 2014
Nigel Mansell	43	Williams	Belgium 1985	- Australia 1994

For complete list of podium position drivers by constructor, see section 764.

295. 1-2-3 finishes with the same constructor

(from 1950 until the 1970s it was common for there to be more than two drivers running cars from the same constructor. Drivers are listed alphabetically)

Jack Brabham, Olivier Gendebien, Bruce McLaren	(Cooper)	2	Belgium 1960	- France 1960 (a)
Richie Ginther, Phil Hill, Wolfgang von Trips	(Ferrari)	2	Belgium 1961	- Britain 1961
Luigi Fagioli, Giuseppe Farina, Reg Parnell	(Alfa Romeo)	1	Britain 1950	
Alberto Ascari, Giuseppe Farina, Piero Taruffi	(Ferrari)	1	France 1952	
Alberto Ascari, Giuseppe Farina, Rudi Fischer	(Ferrari)	1	Germany 1952	
Alberto Ascari, Giuseppe Farina, Luigi Villoresi	(Ferrari)	1	Netherlands 1952	
Alberto Ascari, Giuseppe Farina, Mike Hawthorn	(Ferrari)	1	Switzerland 1953	
Juan Manuel Fangio, Karl Kling, Stirling Moss	(Mercedes-Benz)	1	Britain 1955	
Jean Behra, Juan Manuel Fangio, Carlos Menditéguy	(Maserati)	1	Argentina 1957	
Tony Brooks, Dan Gurney, Phil Hill	(Ferrari)	1	Germany 1959	
Richie Ginther, Phil Hill, Willy Mairesse	(Ferrari)	1	Italy 1960	

(a) Consecutive races (Brabham and McLaren were team-mates with the Cooper Car Co. whilst Gendebien was with Yeoman Credit Racing Team).

At the following races, the top four were with the same constructor

Alberto Ascari, Giuseppe Farina, Rudi Fischer, Piero Taruffi	Germany 1952	(Ferrari)
Juan Manuel Fangio, Karl Kling, Stirling Moss, Piero Taruffi	Britain 1955	(Mercedes-Benz)
Jean Behra, Juan Manuel Fangio, Carlos Menditéguy, Harry Schell	Argentina 1957	(Maserati)
Jack Brabham, Olivier Gendebien, Bruce McLaren, Henry Taylor	France 1960	(Cooper)
Richie Ginther, Olivier Gendebien, Phil Hill, Wolfgang von Trips	Belgium 1961	(Ferrari)

296. 1-2 finishes as team-mates *(Most)*

Rubens Barrichello, Michael Schumacher	24	Australia 2000	- United States 2005	(Ferrari)
Lewis Hamilton, Nico Rosberg	23	Malaysia 2014	- Abu Dhabi 2015	(Mercedes-Benz)
Sebastian Vettel, Mark Webber	16	China 2009	- Brazil 2013	(Red Bull)
Alain Prost, Ayrton Senna	14	San Marino 1988	- Belgium 1989	(McLaren)
David Coulthard, Mika Häkkinen	13	Europe 1997	- Austria 2000	(McLaren)
Nigel Mansell, Riccardo Patrese	8	Mexico 1991	- Britain 1992	(Williams)
Felipe Massa, Kimi Räikkönen	7	France 2007	- France 2008	(Ferrari)
Alberto Ascari, Giuseppe Farina	6	Belgium 1952	- Switzerland 1953	(Ferrari)
François Cevert, Jackie Stewart	6	France 1971	- Germany 1973	(Tyrrell)
Nigel Mansell, Nelson Piquet	6	Britain 1986	- Mexico 1987	(Williams)
Damon Hill, Jacques Villeneuve	6	Australia 1996	- Portugal 1996	(Williams)

297. Consecutive 1-2 finishes as team-mates *(Most)*

Rubens Barrichello, Michael Schumacher	5	Hungary 2002	- Japan 2002	(Ferrari F2002)
Lewis Hamilton, Nico Rosberg	5	Malaysia 2014	- Monaco 2014	(Mercedes-Benz F1 W05)
Lewis Hamilton, Nico Rosberg	4	Japan 2014	- Brazil 2014	(Mercedes-Benz F1 W05)
Lewis Hamilton, Nico Rosberg	4	United States 2015	- Abu Dhabi 2015	(Mercedes-Benz F1 W06)
Alan Jones, Carlos Reutemann	4	Canada 1980	- Brazil 1981	(Williams FW07B, FW07C - Ford Cosworth)
Alain Prost, Ayrton Senna	4	Mexico 1988	- France 1988	(McLaren MP4/4 - Honda)
Rubens Barrichello, Michael Schumacher	3	Europe 2004	- United States 2004	(Ferrari F2004)
David Coulthard, Mika Häkkinen	3	Europe 1997	- Brazil 1998	(McLaren MP4-12, MP4-13 - Mercedes)
Juan Manuel Fangio, Stirling Moss	3	Belgium 1955	- Britain 1955	(Mercedes-Benz W196)
Lewis Hamilton, Nico Rosberg	3	Canada 2015	- Britain 2015	(Mercedes-Benz F1 W06)
Nigel Mansell, Riccardo Patrese	3	South Africa 1992	- Brazil 1992	(Williams FW14B - Renault)
Alain Prost, Ayrton Senna	3	Germany 1988	- Belgium 1988	(McLaren MP4/4 - Honda)

298. 1-2 finishes as team-mates in a season *(Most)*

Lewis Hamilton, Nico Rosberg	12 of 19	2015	(Mercedes-Benz F1 W06)
Lewis Hamilton, Nico Rosberg	11 of 19	2014	(Mercedes-Benz F1 W05)
Alain Prost, Ayrton Senna	10 of 16	1988	(McLaren MP4/4 - Honda)
Rubens Barrichello, Michael Schumacher	9 of 17	2002	(Ferrari F2002)
Rubens Barrichello, Michael Schumacher	8 of 18	2004	(Ferrari F2004)
Nigel Mansell, Riccardo Patrese	6 of 16	1992	(Williams FW14B - Renault)
Damon Hill, Jacques Villeneuve	6 of 16	1996	(Williams FW18 - Renault)
David Coulthard, Mika Häkkinen	5 of 16	1998	(McLaren MP4-13 - Mercedes)
Alberto Ascari, Giuseppe Farina	4 of 7	1952	(Ferrari 500)

Mario Andretti, Ronnie Peterson	4 of 16	1978	(JPS Lotus 78, 79 - Ford Cosworth)
Niki Lauda, Alain Prost	4 of 16	1984	(McLaren MP4/2 - TAG Porsche)
Nigel Mansell, Nelson Piquet	4 of 16	1987	(Williams FW11B - Honda)
Alain Prost, Ayrton Senna	4 of 16	1989	(McLaren MP4/5 - Honda)
David Coulthard, Mika Häkkinen	4 of 17	2000	(McLaren MP4-15 - Mercedes)
Fernando Alonso, Lewis Hamilton	4 of 17	2007	(McLaren MP4-22 - Mercedes)
Felipe Massa, Kimi Räikkönen	4 of 17	2007	(Ferrari F2007)
Rubens Barrichello, Jenson Button	4 of 17	2009	(Brawn BGP 001 - Mercedes)
Sebastian Vettel, Mark Webber	4 of 17	2009	(Red Bull RB5 - Renault)
Sebastian Vettel, Mark Webber	4 of 19	2010	(Red Bull RB6 - Renault)
Sebastian Vettel, Mark Webber	4 of 19	2013	(Red Bull RB9 - Renault)

299. Podiums shared by team-mates *(Most)*

Rubens Barrichello, Michael Schumacher	38	Australia 2000	- United States 2005	(Ferrari)
Sebastian Vettel, Mark Webber	31	China 2009	- Brazil 2013	(Red Bull)
Lewis Hamilton, Nico Rosberg	27	Malaysia 2014	- Abu Dhabi 2015	(Mercedes-Benz)
David Coulthard, Mika Häkkinen	23	Australia 1997	- United States 2001	(McLaren)
Alain Prost, Ayrton Senna	15	San Marino 1988	- Spain 1989	(McLaren)
Eddie Irvine, Michael Schumacher	13	San Marino 1997	- Japan 1999	(Ferrari)
Gerhard Berger, Ayrton Senna	12	Brazil 1990	- Portugal 1992	(McLaren)
Nigel Mansell, Nelson Piquet	12	Canada 1986	- Mexico 1987	(Williams)
Nigel Mansell, Riccardo Patrese	12	Mexico 1991	- Belgium 1992	(Williams)
Felipe Massa, Kimi Räikkönen	12	Bahrain 2007	- Brazil 2008	(Ferrari)

300. Podiums in a season shared by team-mates *(Most)*

Lewis Hamilton, Nico Rosberg	15 of 19	2015	(Mercedes-Benz F1 W06)
Lewis Hamilton, Nico Rosberg	12 of 19	2014	(Mercedes-Benz F1 W05)
Rubens Barrichello, Michael Schumacher	11 of 18	2004	(Ferrari F2004)
Alain Prost, Ayrton Senna	10 of 16	1988	(McLaren MP4/4 - Honda)
Rubens Barrichello, Michael Schumacher	10 of 17	2002	(Ferrari F2002)
David Coulthard, Mika Häkkinen	9 of 17	2000	(McLaren MP4-15 - Mercedes)
Sebastian Vettel, Mark Webber	9 of 19	2011	(Red Bull RB7 - Renault)
Nigel Mansell, Riccardo Patrese	8 of 16	1992	(Williams FW14B - Renault)
Alan Jones, Carlos Reutemann	7 of 14	1980	(Williams FW07B - Ford Cosworth)
David Coulthard, Mika Häkkinen	7 of 16	1998	(McLaren MP4-13 - Mercedes)
Damon Hill, Jacques Villeneuve	7 of 16	1996	(Williams FW18 - Renault)
Nigel Mansell, Nelson Piquet	7 of 16	1986	(Williams FW11 - Honda)
Fernando Alonso, Lewis Hamilton	7 of 17	2007	(McLaren MP4-22 - Mercedes)
Rubens Barrichello, Michael Schumacher	7 of 17	2001	(Ferrari F2001)
Sebastian Vettel, Mark Webber	7 of 19	2010	(Red Bull RB6 - Renault)
Sebastian Vettel, Mark Webber	7 of 19	2013	(Red Bull RB9 - Renault)

Champions in the top placings in a race. See section 118

301. Identical top three in two consecutive races

Canada - United States 1980	1: Alan Jones (Williams), 2: Carlos Reutemann (Williams), 3: Didier Pironi (Ligier)
Germany - Hungary 1986	1: Nelson Piquet (Williams), 2: Ayrton Senna (Lotus), 3: Nigel Mansell (Williams)
Australia 1986 - Brazil 1987	1: Alain Prost (McLaren), 2: Nelson Piquet (Williams), 3: Stefan Johansson (Ferrari/ McLaren)
Canada - Detroit 1988	1: Ayrton Senna (McLaren), 2: Alain Prost (McLaren), 3: Thierry Boutsen (Benetton)
Belgium - Italy 1990	1: Ayrton Senna (McLaren), 2: Alain Prost (Ferrari), 3: Gerhard Berger (McLaren)
Mexico - Brazil 1992	1: Nigel Mansell (Williams), 2: Riccardo Patrese (Williams), 3: Michael Schumacher (Benetton)
France - Britain 1992	1: Nigel Mansell (Williams), 2: Riccardo Patrese (Williams), 3: Martin Brundle (Benetton)
Canada - France 1996	1: Damon Hill (Williams), 2: Jacques Villeneuve (Williams), 3: Jean Alesi (Benetton)
Malaysia 2000 - Australia 2001	1: Michael Schumacher (Ferrari), 2: David Coulthard (McLaren), 3: Rubens Barrichello (Ferrari)
Europe - Canada 2004	1: Michael Schumacher (Ferrari), 2: Rubens Barrichello (Ferrari), 3: Jenson Button (BAR)
Britain - Canada 2006	1: Fernando Alonso (Renault), 2: Michael Schumacher (Ferrari), 3: Kimi Räikkönen (McLaren)

302. Podium position, but had retired from the race

2nd

Carlos Pace (Brabham BT44B - Ford Cosworth)	Britain 1975	(multiple car accident on final lap)
Didier Pironi (Ferrari 126C2)	Monaco 1982	(electrics on final lap)

3rd

Jody Scheckter (Tyrrell 007 - Ford Cosworth)	Britain 1975	(multiple car accident on final lap)
Andrea De Cesaris (Alfa Romeo 182)	Monaco 1982	(out of fuel on final lap)
Elio De Angelis (Lotus 95T - Renault)	San Marino 1984	(out of fuel on final lap)
Andrea De Cesaris (Brabham BT56 - BMW)	Belgium 1987	(out of fuel on final lap)
Heinz-Harald Frentzen (Jordan 199 - Mugen Honda)	Brazil 1999	(out of fuel on final lap)

303. Only podium positions were wins

Jean-Pierre Jabouille	2	Vittorio Brambilla	1	Ludovico Scarfiotti	1
Giancarlo Baghetti	1	Peter Gethin	1	*Excludes Indianapolis 500.*	
Jo Bonnier	1	Pastor Maldonado	1		

304. Interval between podiums (Longest)

	years, days	races		
Alexander Wurz	7y, 285d	129	Britain 1997 (Benetton)	- San Marino 2005 (McLaren)
Michael Schumacher	5y, 267d	100	China 2006 (Ferrari)	- Europe 2012 (Mercedes-Benz)
Mario Andretti	5y, 176d	78	South Africa 1971 (Ferrari)	- Netherlands 1976 (JPS Lotus)
Eddie Cheever	5y, 0d	78	Italy 1983 (Renault)	- Italy 1988 (Arrows)
Jackie Oliver	4y, 324d	61	Mexico 1968 (Lotus)	- Canada 1973 (Shadow)
Jean-Pierre Jarier	4y, 281d	75	Monaco 1974 (Shadow)	- South Africa 1979 (Tyrrell)
Nick Heidfeld	3y, 353d	67	Brazil 2001 (Sauber)	- Malaysia 2005 (Williams)
Jarno Trulli	3y, 311d	65	Europe 1999 (Prost)	- Germany 2003 (Renault)
Jo Siffert	3y, 290d	38	United States 1964 (Brabham)	- Britain 1968 (Lotus)
Andrea De Cesaris	3y, 214d	51	South Africa 1983 (Alfa Romeo)	- Belgium 1987 (Brabham)

Did not necessarily start every race during the period.

305. Interval between first & last podiums (Longest)

	years, days	races		
Michael Schumacher	20y, 94d	348	Mexico 1992	- Europe 2012
Rubens Barrichello	15y, 149d	266	Pacific 1994	- Italy 2009
Riccardo Patrese	15y, 59d	238	Sweden 1978	- Hungary 1993
Kimi Räikkönen	13y, 271d	254	Australia 2002	- Abu Dhabi 2015
David Coulthard	13y, 257d	231	Portugal 1994	- Canada 2008
Nigel Mansell	13y, 180d	217	Belgium 1981	- Australia 1994
Alain Prost	12y, 209d	203	Argentina 1981	- Australia 1993
Mario Andretti	12y, 146d	186	Spain 1970	- Italy 1982
Giancarlo Fisichella	12y, 76d	211	Canada 1997	- Belgium 2009
Niki Lauda	11y, 224d	179	Argentina 1974	- Netherlands 1985
Nelson Piquet	11y, 224d	182	Argentina 1980	- Belgium 1991

306. Interval between podium drivers of the same nationality (Longest)

	years, days	races		
Spain	47y, 113d	645	Britain 1956 (Alfonso de Portago)	- Malaysia 2003 (Fernando Alonso)
Mexico	40y, 279d	659	Netherlands 1971 (Pedro Rodríguez)	- Malaysia 2012 (Sergio Pérez)
Australia	23y, 217d	380	Caesars Palace 1981 (Alan Jones)	- Monaco 2005 (Mark Webber)
Argentina	15y, 296d	164	Italy 1957 (Juan Manuel Fangio)	- France 1973 (Carlos Reutemann)
Germany	14y, 165d	222	Canada 1977 (Jochen Mass)	- Mexico 1992 (Michael Schumacher)
Canada	13y, 320d	221	San Marino 1982 (Gilles Villeneuve)	- Australia 1996 (Jacques Villeneuve)
Japan	13y, 243d	223	Japan 1990 (Aguri Suzuki)	- United States 2004 (Takuma Sato)
France	13y, 236d	235	Belgium 1998 (Jean Alesi)	- Bahrain 2012 (Romain Grosjean)
Switzerland	12y, 62d	109	Germany 1952 (Rudi Fischer)	- United States 1964 (Jo Siffert)
Sweden	11y, 126d	118	Netherlands 1959 (Jo Bonnier)	- United States 1970 (Reine Wisell)

307. Interval between first time podium drivers *(Longest)*

2 years and 194 days, from Italy 2008 (14 September, Sebastian Vettel) until Australia 2011 (27 March, Vitaly Petrov).

308. Podiums but never a world championship *(Most)*

Rubens Barrichello	68	Mark Webber	42	Jean Alesi	32
David Coulthard	62	Felipe Massa	41	Jacques Laffite	32
Gerhard Berger	48	Nico Rosberg	41		
Carlos Reutemann	45	Riccardo Patrese	37		

309. Podiums but never a win *(Most)*

Nick Heidfeld	13	Jean Behra	9	Luigi Villoresi	8
Stefan Johansson	12	Martin Brundle	9	Andrea De Cesaris	5
Chris Amon	11	Eddie Cheever	9		
Romain Grosjean	10	Valtteri Bottas	8		

310. 2nd places but never a win *(Most)*

Nick Heidfeld	8	Eugenio Castellotti	2	Tony Maggs	2
Stefan Johansson	4	Eddie Cheever	2	Mike Parkes	2
Chris Amon	3	Piers Courage	2	Sergio Pérez	2
Jean Behra	2	Andrea De Cesaris	2	Luigi Villoresi	2
Martin Brundle	2	Timo Glock	2	Derek Warwick	2
Ivan Capelli	2	Romain Grosjean	2		

311. Podiums but never a pole position *(Most)*

Bruce McLaren	27	Romain Grosjean	10	Peter Collins	9
Eddie Irvine	26	Daniel Ricciardo	10	Alessandro Nannini	9
Richie Ginther	14	Jean Behra	9	Maurice Trintignant	9
François Cevert	13	Martin Brundle	9		
Stefan Johansson	12	Eddie Cheever	9		

312. Podiums but never a front row *(Most)*

Martin Brundle	9	Olivier Panis	5	Mark Blundell	3
Alessandro Nannini	9	Sergio Pérez	5	Ivan Capelli	3
Jochen Mass	8	Gunnar Nilsson	4	Tony Maggs	3
Johnny Herbert	7	Derek Warwick	4	Alexander Wurz	3

313. Podiums but never a fastest lap *(Most)*

Stefan Johanson	12	Elio De Angelis	9	Wolfgang von Trips	6
Martin Brundle	9	Peter Revson	8	Olivier Panis	5
Eddie Cheever	9	Johnny Herbert	7		
Peter Collins	9	Luigi Fagioli	6		

314. Podiums but never led *(Most)*

Martin Brundle	9	Teo Fabi	2	Cesare Perdisa	2
Eddie Cheever	9	Rudi Fischer	2	Louis Rosier	2
Mark Blundell	3	Umberto Maglioli	2	Roy Salvadori	2
Tony Maggs	3	Robert Manzon	2	Jos Verstappen	2
Alexander Wurz	3	Onofré Marimón	2		
Peter Arundell	2	Stefano Modena	2		

315. Milestones: Podiums I

Michael Schumacher	50th: Canada 1997, 75th: Britain 2000, 100th: Brazil 2002, 125th: Bahrain 2004, 150th: France 2006
Alain Prost	50th: Belgium 1987, 75th: Britain 1989, 100th: France 1993
Fernando Alonso	50th: Singapore 2008: 75th: Spain 2012
Lewis Hamilton	50th: Malaysia 2013: 75th: Monaco 2015
Kimi Räikkönen	50th: Bahrain 2008: 75th: Hungary 2013
Ayrton Senna	50th: Germany 1990, 75th: Brazil 1993
Sebastian Vettel	50th: Monaco 2013, 75th: Singapore 2015
Rubens Barrichello	50th: United States 2004
Jenson Button	50th: Australia 2014
David Coulthard	50th: United States 2001
Mika Häkkinen	50th: Britain 2001
Niki Lauda	50th: Austria 1984
Nigel Mansell	50th: Spain 1992
Nelson Piquet	50th: Mexico 1987

316. Milestones: Podiums II
(eg the 1,000th podium position was achieved by Nelson Piquet in a Brabham BT40C)

1st	Giuseppe Farina (Alfa Romeo 158)	Britain 1950
500th	Jean-Pierre Beltoise (Matra MS80 - Ford Cosworth)	France 1969
1,000th	Nelson Piquet (Brabham BT49C - Ford Cosworth)	Argentina 1981
1,500th	Nelson Piquet (Benetton B191 - Ford Cosworth)	Belgium 1991
2,000th	Rubens Barrichello (Ferrari F2001)	Italy 2001
2,500th	Sebastian Vettel (Red Bull RB7 - Ford Cosworth)	Monaco 2011

Excludes Indianapolis 500.
The above is based on actual steps of the podium, ie three per race. So where drivers shared a podium position such as the shared drives at Argentina 1955, only one is counted. 2nd place at Brazil 1983 is counted, where after the disqualification, the position was left vacant.

317. Milestones: Podiums III
(eg Piero Taruffi was the 10th driver to achieve a podium position)

1st	Giuseppe Farina	Britain 1950	100th	Gunnar Nilsson	Spain 1976
10th	Piero Taruffi	Switzerland 1951	110th	Keke Rosberg	Argentina 1980
20th	Stirling Moss	Belgium 1954	120th	Ayrton Senna	Monaco 1984
30th	Ron Flockhart	Italy 1956	130th	Jean Alesi	United States 1990
40th	Jo Bonnier	Netherlands 1959	140th	Rubens Barrichello	Pacific 1994
50th	Willy Mairesse	Italy 1960	150th	Jacques Villeneuve	Australia 1996
60th	Jochen Rindt	Belgium 1966	160th	Jenson Button	Malaysia 2004
70th	Jacky Ickx	Belgium 1968	170th	Nelsinho Piquet	Germany 2008
80th	Reine Wisell	United States 1970	180th	Valtteri Bottas	Austria 2014
90th	James Hunt	Netherlands 1973			

Excludes Indianapolis 500.

Chapter 8: **Pole Position Drivers**

318. Pole positions

		% of starts		
Michael Schumacher	68	22.15	Monaco 1994 (Benetton)	- France 2006 (Ferrari) (a)
Ayrton Senna	65	40.37	Portugal 1985 (Lotus)	- San Marino 1994 (Williams)
Lewis Hamilton	49	29.34	Canada 2007 (McLaren)	- Italy 2015 (Mercedes-Benz)
Sebastian Vettel	46	29.11	Italy 2008 (Toro Rosso)	- Singapore 2015 (Ferrari)
Jim Clark	33	45.83	Monaco 1962 (Lotus)	- South Africa 1968 (Lotus)
Alain Prost	33	16.58	Germany 1981 (Renault)	- Japan 1993 (Williams)
Nigel Mansell	32	17.11	Dallas 1984 (Lotus)	- Australia 1994 (Williams)
Juan Manuel Fangio	29	56.86	Monaco 1950 (Alfa Romeo)	- Argentina 1958 (Maserati)
Mika Häkkinen	26	16.15	Luxembourg 1997 (McLaren)	- Belgium 2000 (McLaren)
Niki Lauda	24	14.04	South Africa 1974 (Ferrari)	- South Africa 1978 (Brabham)
Nelson Piquet	24	11.76	United States West 1980 (Brabham)	- Spain 1987 (Williams)
Fernando Alonso	22	9.36	Malaysia 2003 (Renault)	- Germany 2012 (Ferrari)
Nico Rosberg	22	11.89	China 2012 (Mercedes-Benz)	- Abu Dhabi 2015 (Mercedes-Benz)

		% of starts		
Damon Hill	20	17.39	France 1993 (Williams)	- Portugal 1996 (Williams)
Mario Andretti	18	14.06	United States 1968 (Lotus)	- Italy 1982 (Ferrari)
René Arnoux	18	12.08	Austria 1979 (Renault)	- Britain 1983 (Ferrari)
Jackie Stewart	17	17.17	Monaco 1969 (Matra)	- Germany 1973 (Tyrrell)
Felipe Massa	16	6.99	Turkey 2006 (Ferrari)	- Austria 2014 (Williams)
Stirling Moss	16	24.24	Britain 1955 (Mercedes-Benz)	- Monaco 1961 (Lotus)
Kimi Räikkönen	16	6.93	Europe 2003 (McLaren)	- France 2008 (Ferrari)
Alberto Ascari	14	45.16	Germany 1951 (Ferrari)	- Spain 1954 (Lancia)
Rubens Barrichello	14	4.33	Belgium 1994 (Jordan)	- Brazil 2009 (Brawn)
James Hunt	14	15.22	Brazil 1976 (McLaren)	- United States 1977 (McLaren)
Ronnie Peterson	14	11.38	Brazil 1973 (JPS Lotus)	- Austria 1978 (JPS Lotus)
Jack Brabham	13	10.32	Britain 1959 (Cooper)	- Spain 1970 (Brabham)
Graham Hill	13	7.39	Belgium 1962 (BRM)	- Britain 1968 (Lotus)
Jacky Ickx	13	11.21	Germany 1968 (Ferrari)	- Italy 1972 (Ferrari)
Juan Pablo Montoya	13	13.83	Germany 2001 (Williams)	- Belgium 2005 (McLaren)
Jacques Villeneuve	13	7.98	Australia 1996 (Williams)	- Europe 1997 (Williams)
Mark Webber	13	6.05	Germany 2009 (Red Bull)	- Abu Dhabi 2013 (Red Bull)
Gerhard Berger	12	5.71	Portugal 1987 (Ferrari)	- Germany 1997 (Benetton)
David Coulthard	12	4.88	Argentina 1995 (Williams)	- Monaco 2001 (McLaren)
Jochen Rindt	10	16.67	France 1968 (Brabham)	- Austria 1970 (Lotus)
Jenson Button	8	2.81	San Marino 2004 (BAR)	- Belgium 2012 (McLaren)
Riccardo Patrese	8	3.13	United States West 1981 (Arrows)	- Hungary 1992 (Williams)
John Surtees	8	7.21	Portugal 1960 (Lotus)	- Italy 1968 (Honda)
Jacques Laffite	7	3.98	Italy 1976 (Ligier)	- Spain 1981 (Talbot-Ligier)
Emerson Fittipaldi	6	4.17	Monaco 1972 (JPS Lotus)	- Canada 1974 (McLaren)
Phil Hill	6	12.50	Italy 1960 (Ferrari)	- Germany 1961 (Ferrari)
Jean-Pierre Jabouille	6	12.25	South Africa 1979 (Renault)	- South Africa 1980 (Renault)
Alan Jones	6	5.17	Britain 1979 (Williams)	- Germany 1980 (Williams)
Carlos Reutemann	6	4.11	Argentina 1972 (Brabham)	- Caesars Palace 1981 (Williams)
Ralf Schumacher	6	3.33	France 2001 (Williams)	- Japan 2005 (Toyota)
Chris Amon	5	5.21	Spain 1968 (Ferrari)	- France 1972 (Matra-Simca)
Giuseppe Farina	5	15.15	Britain 1950 (Alfa Romeo)	- Argentina 1954 (Ferrari)
Clay Regazzoni	5	3.79	Mexico 1970 (Ferrari)	- United States West 1976 (Ferrari)
Keke Rosberg	5	4.39	Britain 1982 (Williams)	- Germany 1986 (McLaren)
Patrick Tambay	5	4.39	United States West 1983 (Ferrari)	- France 1984 (Renault)
Giancarlo Fisichella	4	1.75	Austria 1998 (Benetton)	- Belgium 2009 (Force India)
Mike Hawthorn	4	8.89	Belgium 1958 (Ferrari)	- Morocco 1958 (Ferrari)
Didier Pironi	4	5.71	Monaco 1980 (Ligier)	- Germany 1982 (Ferrari) (a)
Jarno Trulli	4	1.59	Monaco 2004 (Renault)	- Bahrain 2009 (Toyota) (a)
Tony Brooks	3	7.90	Monaco 1958 (Vanwall)	- Germany 1959 (Ferrari)
Elio De Angelis	3	2.78	Europe 1983 (Lotus)	- Canada 1985 (Lotus)
Teo Fabi	3	4.69	Germany 1985 (Toleman)	- Italy 1986 (Benetton)
José Froilán González	3	11.54	Britain 1951 (Ferrari)	- Argentina 1955 (Ferrari)
Dan Gurney	3	3.49	Germany 1962 (Porsche)	- Belgium 1964 (Brabham)
Jean-Pierre Jarier	3	2.24	Argentina 1975 (Shadow)	- Canada 1978 (JPS Lotus) (a)
Jody Scheckter	3	2.68	Sweden 1976 (Tyrrell)	- Monaco 1979 (Ferrari)
Michele Alboreto	2	1.03	Belgium 1984 (Ferrari)	- Brazil 1985 (Ferrari)
Jean Alesi	2	1.00	Italy 1994 (Ferrari)	- Italy 1997 (Benetton)
Heinz-Harald Frentzen	2	1.27	Monaco 1997 (Williams)	- Europe 1999 (Jordan)
Stuart Lewis-Evans	2	14.29	Italy 1957 (Vanwall)	- Netherlands 1958 (Vanwall)
Jo Siffert	2	2.08	Mexico 1968 (Lotus)	- Austria 1971 (BRM)
Gilles Villeneuve	2	2.99	United States West 1979 (Ferrari)	- San Marino 1981 (Ferrari)
John Watson	2	1.32	Monaco 1977 (Brabham)	- France 1978 (Brabham)
Lorenzo Bandini	1	2.38	France 1966 (Ferrari)	
Jo Bonnier	1	0.96	Netherlands 1959 (BRM)	
Thierry Boutsen	1	0.61	Hungary 1990 (Williams)	
Vittorio Brambilla	1	1.35	Sweden 1975 (March)	
Eugenio Castellotti	1	7.14	Belgium 1955 (Lancia)	
Andrea De Cesaris	1	0.48	United States West 1982 (Alfa Romeo)	

		% of starts		
Patrick Depailler	1	1.05	Sweden 1974 (Tyrrell)
Bruno Giacomelli	1	1.45	United States 1980 (Alfa Romeo)
Nick Heidfeld	1	0.55	Europe 2005 (Williams)
Nico Hülkenberg	1	1.06	Brazil 2010 (Williams)
Denny Hulme	1	0.89	South Africa 1973 (McLaren)
Heikki Kovalainen	1	0.91	Britain 2008 (McLaren)
Robert Kubica	1	1.32	Bahrain 2008 (BMW Sauber)
Pastor Maldonado	1	1.05	Spain 2012 (Williams)
Carlos Pace	1	1.39	South Africa 1975 (Brabham)
Mike Parkes	1	16.67	Italy 1966 (Ferrari)
Tom Pryce	1	2.38	Britain 1975 (Shadow)
Peter Revson	1	3.33	Canada 1972 (McLaren)
Wolfgang von Trips	1	3.70	Italy 1961 (Ferrari)
Indianapolis 500			
Freddie Agabashian	1	12.50	1952 (Kurtis-Kraft)
Walt Faulkner	1	20.00	1950 (Kurtis-Kraft)
Pat Flaherty	1	16.67	1956 (Watson)
Jerry Hoyt	1	25.00	1955 (Stevens)
Jack McGrath	1	16.67	1954 (Kurtis-Kraft)
Duke Nalon	1	33.33	1951 (Kurtis-Kraft)
Pat O'Connor	1	20.00	1957 (Kurtis-Kraft)
Dick Rathmann	1	20.00	1958 (Watson)
Eddie Sachs	1	25.00	1960 (Ewing)
Johnny Thomson	1	12.50	1959 (Lesovsky)
Bill Vukovich	1	20.00	1953 (Kurtis-Kraft)

(a) Did not start one of the races (see section 351).
See section 360 for cases of drivers being stripped of their pole position with a penalty.
At France 1956, Peter Collins started from the pole position slot on the grid but it is known that Juan Manuel Fangio actually achieved the fastest time in qualifying. It is possible that Fangio was driving Collins' car when he set that time or that they just lined up on the grid incorrectly. Whatever the explanation, it is generally accepted that Fangio should be credited with pole position.

319. Percentage of races with a pole position *(Highest)*

	%	poles			%	poles
Juan Manuel Fangio	56.86	29		Sebastian Vettel	29.11	46
Jim Clark	45.83	33		Stirling Moss	24.24	16
Alberto Ascari	45.16	14		Michael Schumacher	22.15	68
Ayrton Senna	40.37	65		Damon Hill	17.39	20
Lewis Hamilton	29.34	49		Jackie Stewart	17.17	17

Excludes Indianapolis 500.

320. Pole position driver age

Youngest

	years, days	
Sebastian Vettel	21y, 73d	Italy 2008
Fernando Alonso	21y, 237d	Malaysia 2003
Rubens Barrichello	22y, 97d	Belgium 1994
Lewis Hamilton	22y, 154d	Canada 2007
Andrea De Cesaris	22y, 308d	United States West 1982
Nico Hülkenberg	23y, 80d	Brazil 2010
Robert Kubica	23y, 121d	Bahrain 2008
Jacky Ickx	23y, 216d	Germany 1968
Kimi Räikkönen	23y, 255d	Europe 2003
David Coulthard	24y, 13d	Argentina 1995

Oldest

	years, days	
Giuseppe Farina	47y, 79d	Argentina 1954
Juan Manuel Fangio	46y, 209d	Argentina 1958
Jack Brabham	44y, 17d	Spain 1970
Mario Andretti	42y, 196d	Italy 1982
Nigel Mansell	41y, 97d	Australia 1994
Carlos Reuteman	39y, 188d	Caesars Palace 1981
Graham Hill	39y, 156d	Britain 1968
Alain Prost	38y, 242d	Japan 1993
Riccardo Patrese	38y, 121d	Hungary 1992
Gerhard Berger	37y, 334d	Germany 1997
Indianapolis 500		
Fred Agabashian	38y, 283d	1952
Duke Nalon	38y, 89d	1951

321. Pole positions in a season *(Most)*

Sebastian Vettel	15 of 19	2011	(Red Bull RB7 - Renault)
Nigel Mansell	14 of 16	1992	(Williams FW14B - Renault)
Alain Prost	13 of 16	1993	(Williams FW15C - Renault)
Ayrton Senna	13 of 16	1988	(McLaren MP4/4 - Honda)
Ayrton Senna	13 of 16	1989 (a)	(McLaren MP4/5 - Honda)
Mika Häkkinen	11 of 16	1999	(McLaren MP4-14 - Mercedes)
Lewis Hamilton	11 of 19	2015	(Mercedes-Benz F1 W06)
Michael Schumacher	11 of 17	2001	(Ferrari F2001)
Nico Rosberg	11 of 19	2014 (a)	(Mercedes-Benz F1 W05)
Ayrton Senna	10 of 16	1990	(McLaren MP4/5B - Honda)
Jacques Villeneuve	10 of 17	1997	(Williams FW19 - Renault)
Sebastian Vettel	10 of 19	2010	(Red Bull RB6 - Renault)

All became world champion that season, except (a).

322. Pole position in all but one race of a season

Juan Manuel Fangio was the only driver to achieve this, achieving pole in 6 out of the 7 Grands Prix in 1956 (Lancia-Ferrari D50).

323. Consecutive pole positions *(Most)*

Ayrton Senna	8	Spain 1988	- United States 1989	(McLaren MP4/4, MP4/5 - Honda)
Lewis Hamilton	7	Monaco 2015	- Italy 2015	(Mercedes-Benz F1 W06)
Alain Prost	7	South Africa 1993	- Canada 1993	(Williams FW15C - Renault)
Michael Schumacher	7	Italy 2000	- Brazil 2001	(Ferrari F1 2000, F2001)
Ayrton Senna	7	Spain 1990	- Monaco 1991	(McLaren MP4/5B, MP4/6 - Honda)
Mika Häkkinen	6	Britain 1999	- Italy 1999	(McLaren MP4-14 - Mercedes)
Niki Lauda	6	Netherlands 1974	- Italy 1974	(Ferrari 312B3)
Nigel Mansell	6	South Africa 1992	- Monaco 1992	(Williams FW14B - Renault)
Stirling Moss	6	Portugal 1959	- Netherlands 1960	(Cooper T51, Lotus 18 - Climax)
Nico Rosberg	6	Japan 2015	- Abu Dhabi 2015	(Mercedes-Benz F1 W06)
Ayrton Senna	6	Brazil 1988	- Detroit 1988	(McLaren MP4/4 - Honda)
Ayrton Senna	6	Belgium 1989	- Australia 1989	(McLaren MP4/5 - Honda)

324. Pole in the season's opening race

Jim Clark	5	Lotus 1963, 64, 65, 66, 68
Ayrton Senna	5	Lotus 1986; McLaren 1988, 89, 91; Williams 1994
Lewis Hamilton	4	McLaren 2008, 12; Mercedes-Benz 2014, 15
Stirling Moss	4	Maserati 1957; Cooper 1959, 60; Lotus 1961
Michael Schumacher	4	Ferrari 2001, 03, 04, 06
Juan Manuel Fangio	3	Alfa Romeo 1951; Lancia-Ferrari 1956; Maserati 1958
Giuseppe Farina	3	Alfa Romeo 1950; Ferrari 1952, 54
Mika Häkkinen	3	McLaren 1998, 99, 2000
Sebastian Vettel	3	Red Bull 2010, 11, 13
Jack Brabham	2	Brabham 1967, 69
James Hunt	2	McLaren 1976, 77
Nigel Mansell	2	Williams 1987, 92
Jackie Stewart	2	March 1970; Tyrrell 1971
Jacques Villeneuve	2	Williams 1996, 97
Michele Alboreto	1	Ferrari 1985
Mario Andretti	1	JPS Lotus 1978
René Arnoux	1	Renault 1982
Alberto Ascari	1	Ferrari 1953
Rubens Barrichello	1	Ferrari 2002
Gerhard Berger	1	McLaren 1990
Jenson Button	1	Brawn 2009
Elio De Angelis	1	Lotus 1984
Giancarlo Fisichella	1	Renault 2005
José Froilán González	1	Ferrari 1955
Damon Hill	1	Williams 1995
Jean-Pierre Jarier	1	Shadow 1975

Alan Jones	1	Williams 1980
Jacques Laffite	1	Ligier 1979
Riccardo Patrese	1	Arrows 1981
Ronnie Peterson	1	JPS Lotus 1974
Alain Prost	1	Williams 1993
Kimi Räikkönen	1	Ferrari 2007
Clay Regazzoni	1	BRM 1973
Carlos Reutemann	1	Brabham 1972
Keke Rosberg	1	Williams 1983
John Surtees	1	Lola 1962

325. Pole in the opening race and became world champion that season

Lewis Hamilton	3	2008, 14, 15	Jenson Button	1	2009
Michael Schumacher	3	2001, 03, 04	Giuseppe Farina	1	1950
Sebastian Vettel	3	2010, 11, 13	James Hunt	1	1976
Jim Clark	2	1963, 65	Alan Jones	1	1980
Juan Manuel Fangio	2	1951, 56	Nigel Mansell	1	1992
Mika Häkkinen	2	1998, 99	Alain Prost	1	1993
Ayrton Senna	2	1988, 91	Kimi Räikkönen	1	2007
Mario Andretti	1	1978	Jackie Stewart	1	1971
Alberto Ascari	1	1953	Jacques Villeneuve	1	1997

326. Opening race their only pole of the season

Giuseppe Farina	1954	(Ferrari)	Clay Regazzoni	1973	(BRM)
José Froilán González	1955	(Ferrari)	Ronnie Peterson	1974	(JPS Lotus)
Juan Manuel Fangio	1958	(Maserati)	Riccardo Patrese	1981	(Arrows)
Stirling Moss	1961	(Lotus)	Keke Rosberg	1983	(Williams)
John Surtees	1962	(Lola)	Elio De Angelis	1984	(Lotus)
Jim Clark	1968	(Lotus)	Michele Alboreto	1985	(Ferrari)
Carlos Reutemann	1972	(Brabham)	Giancarlo Fisichella	2005	(Renault)

327. Consecutive pole positions from the start of a season *(Most)*

Alain Prost	7	1993 (wc)	(Williams FW15C - Renault)
Nigel Mansell	6	1992 (wc)	(Williams FW14B - Renault)
Ayrton Senna	6	1988 (wc)	(McLaren MP4/4 - Honda)
Mika Häkkinen	5	1999 (wc)	(McLaren MP4-14 - Mercedes)
Ayrton Senna	5	1989	(McLaren MP4/5 - Honda)
Juan Manuel Fangio	4	1956 (wc)	(Lancia-Ferrari D50)
Lewis Hamilton	4	2015 (wc)	(Mercedes-Benz F1 W06)
Ayrton Senna	4	1991 (wc)	(McLaren MP4/6 - Honda)
Sebastian Vettel	4	2011 (wc)	(Red Bull RB7 - Renault)
Jacques Villeneuve	4	1997 (wc)	(Williams FW19 - Renault)

(wc) World champion that season.

328. Seasons of pole positions *(Most)*

Michael Schumacher	13	1994 - 2006	(Benetton, Ferrari)
Ayrton Senna	10	1985 - 94	(Lotus, McLaren, Williams)
Lewis Hamilton	9	2007 - 15	(McLaren, Mercedes-Benz)
Alain Prost	9	1981 - 93	(Renault, McLaren, Williams)
Fernando Alonso	8	2003 - 12	(Renault, McLaren, Ferrari)
Juan Manuel Fangio	8	1950 - 58	(Alfa Romeo, Maserati, Mercedes-Benz, Ferrari)
Nigel Mansell	8	1984 - 94	(Lotus, Williams, Ferrari)
Nelson Piquet	8	1980 - 87	(Brabham, Williams)
Rubens Barrichello	7	1994 - 2009	(Jordan, Stewart, Ferrari, Brawn)
Gerhard Berger	7	1987 - 97	(Ferrari, McLaren, Benetton)
Jack Brabham	7	1959 - 70	(Cooper, Brabham)
Jim Clark	7	1962 - 68	(Lotus)
Stirling Moss	7	1955 - 61	(Mercedes-Benz, Maserati, Vanwall, Cooper, Lotus)
Sebastian Vettel	7	2008 - 15	(Toro Rosso, Red Bull, Ferrari)

329. Consecutive seasons of pole positions *(Most)*

Michael Schumacher	13	1994 - 2006	(Benetton, Ferrari)
Ayrton Senna	10	1985 - 94	(Lotus, McLaren, Williams)
Lewis Hamilton	9	2007 - 15	(McLaren, Mercedes-Benz)
Nelson Piquet	8	1980 - 87	(Brabham, Williams)
Jim Clark	7	1962 - 68	(Lotus)
Stirling Moss	7	1955 - 61	(Mercedes-Benz, Maserati, Vanwall, Cooper, Lotus)
Juan Manuel Fangio	6	1953 - 58	(Maserati, Mercedes-Benz, Ferrari)
Alain Prost	6	1981 - 86	(Renault, McLaren)
Kimi Räikkönen	6	2003 - 08	(McLaren, Ferrari)
Sebastian Vettel	6	2008 - 13	(Toro Rosso, Red Bull)

330. Pole positions by nationality

Argentina: Juan Manuel Fangio, 29; Carlos Reutemann, 6; José Froilán González, 3

Australia: Jack Brabham, 13; Mark Webber, 13; Alan Jones, 6

Austria: Niki Lauda, 24; Gerhard Berger, 12; Jochen Rindt, 10

Belgium: Jacky Ickx, 13; Thierry Boutsen, 1

Brazil: Ayrton Senna, 65; Nelson Piquet, 24; Felipe Massa, 16; Rubens Barrichello, 14; Emerson Fittipaldi, 6; Carlos Pace, 1

Canada: Jacques Villeneuve, 13; Gilles Villeneuve, 2

Colombia: Juan Pablo Montoya, 13

Finland: Mika Häkkinen, 26; Kimi Räikkönen, 16; Keke Rosberg, 5; Heikki Kovalainen, 1

France: Alain Prost, 33; René Arnoux, 18; Jacques Laffite, 7; Jean-Pierre Jabouille, 6; Patrick Tambay, 5; Didier Pironi, 4; Jean-Pierre Jarier, 3; Jean Alesi, 2; Patrick Depailler, 1

Germany: Michael Schumacher, 68; Sebastian Vettel, 46; Nico Rosberg, 22; Ralf Schumacher, 6; Heinz-Harald Frentzen, 2; Nick Heidfeld, 1; Nico Hülkenberg, 1; Wolfgang von Trips, 1

Great Britain: Lewis Hamilton, 49; Jim Clark, 33; Nigel Mansell, 32; Damon Hill, 20; Jackie Stewart, 17; Stirling Moss, 16; James Hunt, 14; Graham Hill, 13; David Coulthard, 12; Jenson Button, 8; John Surtees, 8; Mike Hawthorn, 4; Tony Brooks, 3; Stuart Lewis-Evans, 2; John Watson, 2; Mike Parkes, 1; Tom Pryce, 1

Italy: Alberto Ascari, 14; Riccardo Patrese, 8; Giuseppe Farina, 5; Giancarlo Fisichella, 4; Jarno Trulli, 4; Elio De Angelis, 3; Teo Fabi, 3; Michele Alboreto, 2; Lorenzo Bandini, 1; Vittorio Brambilla, 1; Eugenio Castellotti, 1; Andrea De Cesaris, 1; Bruno Giacomelli, 1

New Zealand: Chris Amon, 5; Denny Hulme, 1

Poland: Robert Kubica, 1

South Africa: Jody Scheckter, 3

Spain: Fernando Alonso, 22

Sweden: Ronnie Peterson, 14; Jo Bonnier, 1

Switzerland: Clay Regazzoni, 5; Jo Siffert, 2

United States: Mario Andretti, 18; Phil Hill, 6; Dan Gurney, 3; Peter Revson, 1

Venezuela: Pastor Maldonado, 1

Summary

	races	drivers		
Great Britain	235	17	Britain 1955 (Stirling Moss)	- Italy 2015 (Lewis Hamilton)
Germany	147	8	Italy 1961 (Wolfgang von Trips)	- Abu Dhabi 2015 (Nico Rosberg)
Brazil	126	6	Monaco 1972 (Emerson Fittipaldi)	- Austria 2014 (Felipe Massa)
France	79	9	Sweden 1974 (Patrick Depailler)	- Italy 1997 (Jean Alesi)
Finland	48	4	Britain 1982 (Keke Rosberg)	- Britain 2008 (Heikki Kovalainen)
Italy	48	13	Britain 1950 (Giuseppe Farina)	- Belgium 2009 (Giancarlo Fisichella)
Austria	46	3	France 1968 (Jochen Rindt)	- Germany 1997 (Gerhard Berger)
Argentina	38	3	Monaco 1950 (Juan Manuel Fangio)	- Caesars Palace 1981 (Carlos Reutemann)
Australia	32	3	Britain 1959 (Jack Brabham)	- Abu Dhabi 2013 (Mark Webber)
United States	28	4	Italy 1960 (Phil Hill)	- Italy 1982 (Mario Andretti)
Spain	22	1	Malaysia 2003 (Fernando Alonso)	- Germany 2012 (Fernando Alonso)
Canada	15	2	United States West 1979 (Gilles Villeneuve)	- Europe 1997 (Jacques Villeneuve)
Sweden	15	2	Netherlands 1959 (Jo Bonnier)	- Austria 1978 (Ronnie Peterson)
Belgium	14	2	Germany 1968 (Jacky Ickx)	- Hungary 1990 (Thierry Boutsen)
Colombia	13	1	Germany 2001 (Juan Pablo Montoya)	- Belgium 2005 (Juan Pablo Montoya)
Switzerland	7	2	Mexico 1968 (Jo Siffert)	- United States West 1976 (Clay Regazzoni)
New Zealand	6	2	Spain 1968 (Chris Amon)	- South Africa 1973 (Denny Hulme)
South Africa	3	1	Sweden 1976 (Jody Scheckter)	- Monaco 1979 (Jody Scheckter)
Poland	1	1	Bahrain 2008 (Robert Kubica)	
Venezuela	1	1	Spain 2012 (Pastor Maldonado)	

Excludes Indianapolis 500.

331. Pole positions at the same venue *(Most)*

grand prix

Michael Schumacher	8	Japan	1994 - 2004	(Suzuka)
Ayrton Senna	8	San Marino	1985 - 94	(Imola)
Michael Schumacher	7	Hungary	1994 - 2005	(Hungaroring)
Michael Schumacher	7	Spain	1994 - 2004	(Catalunya)
Michael Schumacher	6	Canada	1994 - 2001	(Montréal)
Ayrton Senna	6	Australia	1985 - 93	(Adelaide)
Ayrton Senna	6	Brazil	1986 - 94	(Interlagos, 3; Jacarepaguá, 3)
Jim Clark	5	Britain	1962 - 67	(Silverstone, 3; Aintree, 1; Brands Hatch, 1)
Juan Manuel Fangio	5	France	1950 - 57	(Reims/ Reims-Gueux, 4; Rouen-les-Essarts, 1)
Juan Manuel Fangio	5	Italy	1950 - 56	(Monza)
Lewis Hamilton	5	China	2007 - 15	(Shanghai)
Lewis Hamilton	5	Hungary	2007 - 15	(Hungaroring)
Michael Schumacher	5	Malaysia	1999 - 2004	(Sepang)
Michael Schumacher	5	San Marino	1995 - 2006	(Imola)
Ayrton Senna	5	Italy	1985 - 91	(Monza)
Ayrton Senna	5	Monte-Carlo	1985 - 91	(Monte-Carlo)

Additionally, Ayrton Senna had 5 poles in United States between 1985 and 91 (3 at Detroit and 2 at Phoenix), but only the Phoenix race was actually named the United States Grand Prix.

circuit

Michael Schumacher	8	Suzuka	1994 - 2004		Lewis Hamilton	5	Hungaroring	2007 - 15
Ayrton Senna	8	Imola	1985 - 94		Lewis Hamilton	5	Shanghai	2007 - 15
Michael Schumacher	7	Catalunya	1994 - 2004		Michael Schumacher	5	Imola	1995 - 2006
Michael Schumacher	7	Hungaroring	1994 - 2005		Michael Schumacher	5	Sepang	1999 - 2004
Michael Schumacher	6	Montréal	1994 - 2001		Ayrton Senna	5	Monte-Carlo	1985 - 91
Ayrton Senna	6	Adelaide	1985 - 93		Ayrton Senna	5	Monza	1985 - 91
Juan Manuel Fangio	5	Monza	1950 - 56					

332. Consecutive pole positions at the same venue *(Most)*

Ayrton Senna	7	San Marino	1985 - 91	(Imola)
Michael Schumacher	5	Spain	2000 - 04	(Catalunya)
Michael Schumacher	5	Japan	1998 - 2002	(Suzuka)
Jim Clark	4	Britain	1962 - 65	(Silverstone, 2; Aintree, 1; Brands Hatch, 1)
Juan Manuel Fangio	4	Monaco	1950 - 57	(Monte-Carlo) (a)
Stirling Moss	4	Britain	1955 - 58	(Aintree, 2; Silverstone, 2)
Michael Schumacher	4	Malaysia	1999 - 2002	(Sepang)
Ayrton Senna	4	Australia	1988 - 91	(Adelaide)
Ayrton Senna	4	Belgium	1988 - 91	(Spa-Francorchamps)
Ayrton Senna	4	Brazil	1988 - 91	(Interlagos, 2; Jacarepaguá, 2)
Ayrton Senna	4	Italy	1988 - 91	(Monza)
Ayrton Senna	4	Monaco	1988 - 91	(Monte-Carlo)
Sebastian Vettel	4	Japan	2009 - 12	(Suzuka)

(a) No Monaco Grand Prix in 1951 - 54.

333. More than one pole in a country during a season

Alain Prost (McLaren)	1982	United States (Detroit & Caesars Palace)
Nelson Piquet (Brabham)	1984	Italy (Imola & Monza)
Ayrton Senna (Lotus)	1985	Italy (Imola & Monza)
Ayrton Senna (McLaren)	1988	Italy (Imola & Monza)
Ayrton Senna (McLaren)	1989	Italy (Imola & Monza)
Ayrton Senna (McLaren)	1990	Italy (Imola & Monza)
Ayrton Senna (McLaren)	1991	Italy (Imola & Monza)
Nigel Mansell (Williams)	1992	Italy (Imola & Monza)
Alain Prost (Williams)	1993	Britain (Donington & Silverstone)
Alain Prost (Williams)	1993	Italy (Imola & Monza)
Michael Schumacher (Benetton)	1994	Spain (Catalunya & Jerez de la Frontera)
Damon Hill (Williams)	1996	Germany (Nürburgring & Hockenheim)
Jacques Villeneuve (Williams)	1997	Spain (Catalunya & Jerez de la Frontera)
Mika Häkkinen (McLaren)	1999	Italy (Imola & Monza)
David Coulthard (McLaren)	2000	Germany (Nürburgring & Hockenheim)
Michael Schumacher (Ferrari)	2003	Italy (Imola & Monza)
Michael Schumacher (Ferrari)	2004	Germany (Nürburgring & Hockenheim)

334. Pole positions on home soil

by country

Argentina

Buenos Aires	4	Juan Manuel Fangio, 2; José Froilán González, 1; Carlos Reutemann, 1

Austria

Österreichring	4	Niki Lauda, 3; Jochen Rindt, 1

Brazil

Interlagos	10	Rubens Barrichello, 3; Felipe Massa, 3; Ayrton Senna, 3; Emerson Fittipaldi, 1
Jacarepaguá	4	Ayrton Senna, 3; Nelson Piquet, 1

Britain

Aintree	3	Stirling Moss, 2; Jim Clark, 1
Brands Hatch	2	Jim Clark, 1; Graham Hill, 1
Silverstone	16	Jim Clark, 3; Lewis Hamilton, 3; Damon Hill, 3; Nigel Mansell, 3; Stirling Moss, 2; James Hunt, 1; Tom Pryce, 1

France

Dijon-Prenois	4	René Arnoux, 1; Jean-Pierre Jabouille, 1; Alain Prost, 1 (a); Patrick Tambay, 1
Paul Ricard	5	Alain Prost, 3; Jacques Laffite, 1; René Arnoux, 1

Germany

Hockenheim	4	Michael Schumacher, 2; Nico Rosberg, 1; Sebastian Vettel, 1
Nürburgring	5	Michael Schumacher, 3 (b); Heinz-Harald Frentzen, 1 (c); Nick Heidfeld, 1 (c)

Italy

Monza	4	Alberto Ascari, 2; Teo Fabi, 1; Riccardo Patrese, 1

Spain

Catalunya	1	Fernando Alonso, 1

Sweden

Anderstorp	1	Ronnie Peterson, 1

United States

Watkins Glen	2	Mario Andretti, 2

Excludes Indianapolis 500.
(a) Swiss Grand Prix.
(b) 2 European & 1 Luxembourg Grands Prix.
(c) European Grand Prix.

by driver

Ayrton Senna	6	Brazil	1986 - 94	(Interlagos, 3; Jacarepaguá, 3)
Jim Clark	5	Britain	1962 - 67	(Silverstone, 3; Aintree, 1; Brands Hatch, 1)
Michael Schumacher	5	Germany	1998 - 2004	(Nürburgring, 3; Hockenheim, 2)
Stirling Moss	4	Britain	1955 - 58	(Aintree, 2; Silverstone, 2)
Alain Prost	4	France	1982 - 89	(Paul Ricard, 3; Dijon-Prenois, 1)
Rubens Barrichello	3	Brazil	2003 - 09	(Interlagos)
Lewis Hamilton	3	Britain	2007 - 15	(Silverstone)
Damon Hill	3	Britain	1994 - 96	(Silverstone)
Niki Lauda	3	Austria	1974 - 77	(Österreichring)
Nigel Mansell	3	Britain	1990 - 92	(Silverstone)
Felipe Massa	3	Brazil	2006 - 08	(Interlagos)
Mario Andretti	2	United States	1968 - 78	(Watkins Glen)
René Arnoux	2	France	1981 - 82	(Dijon-Prenois, 1; Paul Ricard, 1)
Alberto Ascari	2	Italy	1952 - 53	(Monza)
Juan Manuel Fangio	2	Argentina	1956 - 58	(Buenos Aires No.2)
Fernando Alonso	1	Spain	2006	(Catalunya)
Teo Fabi	1	Italy	1986	(Monza)
Emerson Fittipaldi	1	Brazil	1974	(Interlagos)
Heinz-Harald Frentzen	1	Germany	1999	(Nürburgring)
José Froilán González	1	Argentina	1955	(Buenos Aires No.2)
Nick Heidfeld	1	Germany	2005	(Nürburgring)
Graham Hill	1	Britain	1968	(Brands Hatch)
James Hunt	1	Britain	1977	(Silverstone)
Jean-Pierre Jabouille	1	France	1979	(Dijon-Prenois)
Jacques Laffite	1	France	1980	(Paul Ricard)
Riccardo Patrese	1	Italy	1983	(Monza)
Ronnie Peterson	1	Sweden	1973	(Anderstorp)
Nelson Piquet	1	Brazil	1981	(Jacarepaguá)

Tom Pryce	1	Britain	1975	(Silverstone)
Carlos Reutemann	1	Argentina	1972	(Buenos Aires No.9)
Nico Rosberg	1	Germany	2014	(Hockenheim)
Jochen Rindt	1	Austria	1970	(Österreichring)
Patrick Tambay	1	France	1984	(Dijon-Prenois)
Sebastian Vettel	1	Germany	2010	(Hockenheim)

335. First pole position was on home soil

Mario Andretti	United States 1968	(Watkins Glen)	Tom Pryce	Britain 1975	(Silverstone)
Nick Heidfeld	Europe 2005	(Nürburgring)	Carlos Reutemann	Argentina 1972	(Buenos Aires No.9)
Stirling Moss	Britain 1955	(Aintree)			

336. Two poles on home soil in a season

Michael Schumacher is the only driver to achieve two poles in his home nation in a season, in 2004 at the European and German Grands Prix.

337. Races taken to achieve their first pole position
(number of races includes the race of first pole and all qualifying attempts)

Fewest

Mario Andretti	1 (a)	Stuart Lewis-Evans	6
Giuseppe Farina	1	Tony Brooks	8
Carlos Reutemann	1	Clay Regazzoni	8
Jacques Villeneuve	1	Patrick Depailler	9
Juan Manuel Fangio	2	Alberto Ascari	10
Eugenio Castellotti	3	David Coulthard	10
John Surtees	3	Jacky Ickx	11
Mike Parkes	5	Juan Pablo Montoya	12
José Froilán González	5	Peter Revson	15
Lewis Hamilton	6	Damon Hill	16

Most

Mark Webber	132	Jenson Button	71
Jarno Trulli	119	Felipe Massa	67
Thierry Boutsen	116	Jo Siffert	65
Nico Rosberg	111	Patrick Tambay	64
Mika Häkkinen	97	Alan Jones	61
Nick Heidfeld	91	Keke Rosberg	59
Denny Hulme	85	Heinz-Harald Frentzen	54
Jean Alesi	82	Nigel Mansell	54
Ralf Schumacher	76	Riccardo Patrese	53
Elio De Angelis	72	John Watson	52

(a) This was the first race he started. He did enter one earlier race, Italy 1968 but was excluded (in breach of regulations, having raced in another series in the United States within previous 24 hours).
Excludes Indianapolis 500.
For most races started but never a pole position, see section 186.

338. Pole positions in their first season
(first season defined as the first year to attempt qualification)

Lewis Hamilton	6	2007	Eugenio Castellotti	1	1955
Juan Manuel Fangio	4	1950	Nico Hülkenberg	1	2010
Juan Pablo Montoya	3	2001	Stuart Lewis-Evans	1	1957
Jacques Villeneuve	3	1996	Clay Regazzoni	1	1970
Giuseppe Farina	2	1950	Carlos Reutemann	1	1972
Mario Andretti	1	1968	John Surtees	1	1960

Mike Parkes achieved a pole in his first season of starting (in 1966), but made his debut in 1959, with a non-qualification.

339. First pole position immediately followed by others
(including first pole position)

Michael Schumacher	3	Monaco	- Canada 1994	(Benetton B194 - Ford Cosworth)
Ayrton Senna	3	Portugal	- Monaco 1985	(Lotus 97T - Renault)
René Arnoux	2	Austria	- Netherlands 1979	(Renault RS10)
Juan Manuel Fangio	2	Monaco	- Switzerland 1950	(Alfa Romeo 158)
Emerson Fittipaldi	2	Monaco	- Belgium 1972	(JPS Lotus 72D - Ford Cosworth)
Lewis Hamilton	2	Canada	- United States 2007	(McLaren MP4-22 - Mercedes)
Mike Hawthorn	2	Belgium	- France 1958	(Ferrari Dino 246)
James Hunt	2	Brazil	- South Africa 1976	(McLaren M23 - Ford Cosworth)
Jean-Pierre Jarier	2	Argentina	- Brazil 1975	(Shadow DN5 - Ford Cosworth)
Niki Lauda	2	South Africa	- Spain 1974	(Ferrari 312B3)

340. Front rows before their first pole

Most

Denny Hulme	19
Jackie Stewart	12
Mike Hawthorn	10
Stirling Moss	7
Graham Hill	6
Damon Hill	5
Jody Scheckter	5
Michael Schumacher	5
Jack Brabham	4
Felipe Massa	4
Jarno Trulli	4
Mark Webber	4
Alberto Ascari	3
Lorenzo Bandini	3
Gerhard Berger	3
Emerson Fittipaldi	3
Heinz-Harald Frentzen	3
Dan Gurney	3
Phil Hill	3
Kimi Räikkönen	3
Ralf Schumacher	3
Wolfgang von Trips	3

Fewest (no previous front rows)

Fernando Alonso	Stuart Lewis-Evans
Mario Andretti	Pastor Maldonado
Rubens Barrichello	Riccardo Patrese
Jo Bonnier	Carlos Reutemann
Thierry Boutsen	Peter Revson
Vittorio Brambilla	Keke Rosberg
Jenson Button	Ayrton Senna
Eugenio Castellotti	John Surtees
David Coulthard	Patrick Tambay
Elio De Angelis	Sebastian Vettel
Andrea De Cesaris	Jacques Villeneuve
Patrick Depailler	
Teo Fabi	
Giuseppe Farina	
Bruno Giacomelli	
Nick Heidfeld	
Nico Hülkenberg	
Jean-Pierre Jabouille	
Jean-Pierre Jarier	
Alan Jones	
Jacques Laffite	
Niki Lauda	

341. Pole position in their final race

Jim Clark	South Africa 1968	killed in Formula 2 event, prior to next F1 race
Mike Hawthorn	Morocco 1958	retired from F1
Didier Pironi	Germany 1982	non-starter: injured in qualifying, ending F1 career
Jochen Rindt	Austria 1970	killed in qualifying for next F1 race, in Italy
Ayrton Senna	San Marino 1994	killed in this race
Wolfgang von Trips	Italy 1961	killed in this race

342. Pole positions in their final season

Alain Prost	13	1993		Jack Brabham	1	1970
Mike Hawthorn	4	1958		Jim Clark	1	1968
Ronnie Peterson	3	1978		Juan Manuel Fangio	1	1958
Jochen Rindt	3	1970		Giancarlo Fisichella	1	2009
Ayrton Senna	3	1994		Stuart Lewis-Evans	1	1958
Jackie Stewart	3	1973		Stirling Moss	1	1961
Didier Pironi	2	1982		Keke Rosberg	1	1986
Mark Webber	2	2013		Jo Siffert	1	1971
Mario Andretti	1	1982		Wolfgang von Trips	1	1961
Gerhard Berger	1	1997				

343. Different pole position drivers in a season

Most

2005	9		1982	7
1968	8		1983	7
1985	8		1994	7
2009	8		2004	7
1976	7		2012	7
1980	7			
1981	7			

Fewest

1950	2		1988	3
1952	2		1989	3
1953	2		1992	3
1956	2		1993	3
1965	2		1996	3
1951	3		2002	3
1957	3		2011	3
1963	3		2014	3
1967	3		2015	3

Total for each season

1950 - 2, 1951 - 3, 1952 - 2, 1953 - 2, 1954 - 4, 1955 - 4, 1956 - 2, 1957 - 3, 1958 - 5, 1959 - 4, 1960 - 4, 1961 - 4, 1962 - 4, 1963 - 3, 1964 - 4, 1965 - 2, 1966 - 5, 1967 - 3, 1968 - 8, 1969 - 4, 1970 - 5, 1971 - 5, 1972 - 6, 1973 - 5, 1974 - 6, 1975 - 5, 1976 - 7, 1977 - 5, 1978 - 6, 1979 - 6, 1980 - 7, 1981 - 7, 1982 - 7, 1983 - 7, 1984 - 6, 1985 - 8, 1986 - 6, 1987 - 4, 1988 - 3, 1989 - 3, 1990 - 4, 1991 - 4, 1992 - 3, 1993 - 3, 1994 - 7, 1995 - 4, 1996 - 3, 1997 - 6, 1998 - 4, 1999 - 4, 2000 - 4, 2001 - 4, 2002 - 3, 2003 - 6, 2004 - 7, 2005 - 9, 2006 - 6, 2007 - 4, 2008 - 6, 2009 - 8, 2010 - 5, 2011 - 3, 2012 - 7, 2013 - 4, 2014 - 3, 2015 - 3

Excludes Indianapolis 500.

344. Different pole position drivers in consecutive races *(Most)*

Britain 1968 - South Africa 1969	7	Graham Hill, Ickx, Surtees, Rindt, Andretti, Siffert, Brabham
Austria 1972 - South Africa 1973	7	Fittipaldi, Ickx, Revson, Stewart, Regazzoni, Peterson, Hulme
Germany 1961 - Belgium 1962	6	Phil Hill, von Trips, Brabham, Surtees, Clark, Graham Hill
Britain - Italy 1982	6	Rosberg, Arnoux, Pironi, Piquet, Prost, Andretti
France - United States 2003	6	Ralf Schumacher, Barrichello, Montoya, Alonso, Michael Schumacher, Räikkönen
Europe - Italy 2003	6	Räikkönen, Ralf Schumacher, Barrichello, Montoya, Alonso, Michael Schumacher
Monaco - Britain 2004	6	Trulli, Michael Schumacher, Ralf Schumacher, Barrichello, Alonso, Räikkönen
Morocco 1958 - Britain 1959	5	Hawthorn, Moss, Bonnier, Brooks, Brabham
Netherlands - Italy 1968	5	Amon, Rindt, Graham Hill, Ickx, Surtees
United States 1968 - Monaco 1969	5	Andretti, Siffert, Brabham, Rindt, Stewart
South Africa - France 1980	5	Jabouille, Piquet, Jones, Pironi, Laffite
San Marino - France 1981	5	Villeneuve, Reutemann, Piquet, Laffite, Arnoux
Canada 1981 - United States West 1982	5	Piquet, Reutemann, Arnoux, Prost, De Cesaris
Britain - Italy 1985	5	Rosberg, Fabi, Prost, Piquet, Senna
Britain - Italy 1994	5	Damon Hill, Berger, Michael Schumacher, Barrichello, Alesi
Germany - Japan 2003	5	Montoya, Alonso, Michael Schumacher, Räikkönen, Barrichello
Canada - Germany 2004	5	Ralf Schumacher, Barrichello, Alonso, Räikkönen, Michael Schumacher
Monaco - France 2005	5	Räikkönen, Heidfeld, Button, Trulli, Alonso
Japan 2005 - Australia 2006	5	Ralf Schumacher, Alonso, Michael Schumacher, Fisichella, Button
Britain - Belgium 2009	5	Vettel, Webber, Alonso, Hamilton, Fisichella
Malaysia - Monaco 2012	5	Hamilton, Rosberg, Vettel, Maldonado, Webber

345. Different pole position drivers from the start of a season *(Most)*

1958	4	Juan Manuel Fangio, Tony Brooks, Stuart Lewis-Evans, Mike Hawthorn
1959	4	Stirling Moss, Jo Bonnier, Tony Brooks, Jack Brabham
1966	4	Jim Clark, John Surtees, Lorenzo Bandini, Jack Brabham
1972	4	Carlos Reutemann, Jackie Stewart, Jacky Ickx, Emerson Fittipaldi
1978	4	Mario Andretti, Ronnie Peterson, Niki Lauda, Carlos Reutemann
1983	4	Keke Rosberg, Patrick Tambay, Alain Prost, René Arnoux
2008	4	Lewis Hamilton, Felipe Massa, Robert Kubica, Kimi Räikkönen
1955	3	José Froilán González, Juan Manuel Fangio, Eugenio Castellotti
1962	3	John Surtees, Jim Clark, Graham Hill
1968	3	Jim Clark, Chris Amon, Graham Hill
1969	3	Jack Brabham, Jochen Rindt, Jackie Stewart
1973	3	Clay Regazzoni, Ronnie Peterson, Denny Hulme
1974	3	Ronnie Peterson, Emerson Fittipaldi, Niki Lauda
1982	3	René Arnoux, Alain Prost, Andrea De Cesaris
1984	3	Elio De Angelis, Nelson Piquet, Michele Alboreto
1995	3	Damon Hill, David Coulthard, Michael Schumacher
2002	3	Rubens Barrichello, Michael Schumacher, Juan Pablo Montoya
2003	3	Michael Schumacher, Fernando Alonso, Rubens Barrichello
2006	3	Michael Schumacher, Giancarlo Fisichella, Jenson Button

Excludes Indianapolis 500.

346. First time pole position drivers in a season *(Most)*

1968	5	Chris Amon, Jochen Rindt, Jacky Ickx, Mario Andretti, Jo Siffert
1975	4	Jean-Pierre Jarier, Carlos Pace, Vittorio Brambilla, Tom Pryce
1979	4	Jean-Pierre Jabouille, Gilles Villeneuve, Alan Jones, René Arnoux
1962	3	Jim Clark, Graham Hill, Dan Gurney
1972	3	Carlos Reutemann, Emerson Fittipaldi, Peter Revson
1976	3	James Hunt, Jody Scheckter, Jacques Laffite
1980	3	Nelson Piquet, Didier Pironi, Bruno Giacomelli
1994	3	Michael Schumacher, Rubens Barrichello, Jean Alesi
2008	3	Robert Kubica, Heikki Kovalainen, Sebastian Vettel

Fewest (none)
1952, 53, 54, 56, 63, 64, 65, 67, 71, 78, 86, 88, 89, 91, 92, 99, 2000, 02, 11, 13, 14, 15

Excludes Indianapolis 500.

347. Pole positions with the same constructor *(Most)*

Michael Schumacher	58	Ferrari	San Marino 1996	- France 2006
Ayrton Senna	46	McLaren	Brazil 1988	- Australia 1993
Sebastian Vettel	44	Red Bull	China 2009	- Brazil 2013
Jim Clark	33	Lotus	Monaco 1962	- South Africa 1968
Nigel Mansell	28	Williams	South Africa 1985	- Australia 1994
Mika Häkkinen	26	McLaren	Luxembourg 1997	- Belgium 2000
Lewis Hamilton	26	McLaren	Canada 2007	- Brazil 2012
Lewis Hamilton	23	Mercedes-Benz	China 2013	- Italy 2015
Niki Lauda	23	Ferrari	South Africa 1974	- Austria 1977
Nico Rosberg	22	Mercedes-Benz	China 2012	- Abu Dhabi 2015

For complete list of pole position drivers by constructor, see section 800.

348. Seasons of pole positions with the same constructor *(Most)*

Michael Schumacher	11	Ferrari	1996 - 2006		Ayrton Senna	6	McLaren	1988 - 93
Jim Clark	7	Lotus	1962 - 68		Fernando Alonso	5	Renault	2003 - 09
Lewis Hamilton	6	McLaren	2007 - 12		Alain Prost	5	McLaren	1984 - 89
Nigel Mansell	6	Williams	1985 - 94		Sebastian Vettel	5	Red Bull	2009 - 13
Nelson Piquet	6	Brabham	1980 - 85		Mark Webber	5	Red Bull	2009 - 13

349. Pole positions with the same engine make *(Most)*

Michael Schumacher	58	Ferrari	San Marino 1996	- France 2006
Lewis Hamilton	49	Mercedes	Canada 2007	- Italy 2015
Ayrton Senna	46	Honda	San Marino 1987	- Canada 1992
Sebastian Vettel	44	Renault	China 2009	- Brazil 2013
Mika Häkkinen	26	Mercedes	Luxembourg 1997	- Belgium 2000
Jim Clark	26	Climax	Monaco 1962	- Germany 1966
Niki Lauda	23	Ferrari	South Africa 1974	- Austria 1977
Alain Prost	23	Renault	Germany 1981	- Japan 1993
Nico Rosberg	22	Mercedes	China 2012	- Abu Dhabi 2015
Damon Hill	20	Renault	France 1993	- Portugal 1996

For complete list of pole position drivers by engine make, see section 1001.

350. Pole positions to race retirement *(Most)*

Ayrton Senna	22	San Marino 1985	- San Marino 1994
Jim Clark	15	Monaco 1962	- Canada 1967 (a)
Nigel Mansell	11	Dallas 1984	- Australia 1992
Mika Häkkinen	9	Luxembourg 1997	- Brazil 2000
Lewis Hamilton	8	China 2007	- Australia 2014
Ronnie Peterson	8	Brazil 1973	- Britain 1978
Nelson Piquet	8	Canada 1980	- Belgium 1986
Mario Andretti	7	United States 1968	- United States 1978
René Arnoux	7	Netherlands 1979	- Detroit 1983
Juan Manuel Fangio	7	Switzerland 1950	- Belgium 1956
Niki Lauda	7	South Africa 1974	- South Africa 1978
Michael Schumacher	7	San Marino 1995	- France 2000 (b)
Stirling Moss	7	Britain 1956	- Argentina 1960 (c)
Juan Pablo Montoya	7	Germany 2001	- Belgium 2005

(a) At United States 1964, Clark retired, took over team-mate's car and retired in that also (counted as 1 race).
(b) Plus 1 race non-started (engine failure on the parade lap).
(c) At Britain 1957, Moss retired and then took over his team-mate's car to win the race (counted here as a retirement from pole).

351. Pole position to race retirement before end of first lap

Jack Brabham	Monaco 1967	(Brabham BT19 - Repco): engine
Niki Lauda	Germany 1974	(Ferrari 312B3): accident
Niki Lauda	Spain 1975	(Ferrari 312T): accident
Mario Andretti	Belgium 1977	(JPS Lotus 78 - Ford Cosworth): accident
Ayrton Senna	Japan 1990	(McLaren MP4/5B - Honda): accident
Ayrton Senna	Pacific 1994	(Williams FW16 - Renault): accident
Michael Schumacher	Monaco 1996	(Ferrari F310): accident
Jacques Villeneuve	Australia 1997	(Williams FW19 - Renault): accident
Mika Häkkinen	Belgium 1998	(McLaren MP4-13 - Mercedes): accident
Rubens Barrichello	Australia 2002	(Ferrari F2001): accident
Indianapolis 500		
Dick Rathmann	1958	(Watson - Offenhauser): accident

failure before the race started

Jean-Pierre Jarier	Argentina 1975	(Shadow DN5 - Ford Cosworth): crown wheel & pinion failure on the parade lap
Didier Pironi	Germany 1982	(Ferrari 126C2): injury from accident in qualifying which ended his career
Michael Schumacher	France 1996	(Ferrari F310): engine failure on the parade lap
Jarno Trulli	United States 2005	(Toyota TF105): withdrawn on the parade lap along with all other Michelin runners, due to tyre safety concerns

352. Consecutive races with a pole position to retirement *(Most)*

Niki Lauda	3	Germany	- Italy 1974	(Ferrari 312B3)
Juan Pablo Montoya	3	Monaco	- Europe 2002	(Williams FW24 - BMW)
Ayrton Senna	3	Spain	- Australia 1990	(McLaren MP4/5B - Honda)
Ayrton Senna	3	Brazil	- San Marino 1994	(Williams FW16 - Renault)

353. Interval between pole positions

Shortest (pole in races a week apart)

Jim Clark	Netherlands	- France 1963 (a)	(Lotus)
Jack Brabham	Britain	- Netherlands 1966 (a)	(Brabham)
James Hunt	Canada	- United States 1976 (a)	(McLaren)
Alan Jones	Canada	- United States 1979	(Williams)
Alain Prost	Monaco	- Belgium 1983	(Renault)
René Arnoux	Detroit	- Canada 1983	(Ferrari)
Patrick Tambay	Germany	- Austria 1983	(Ferrari)
Nelson Piquet	Canada	- Detroit 1984 (a)	(Brabham)
Ayrton Senna	Canada	Detroit 1988 (a)	(McLaren)
Ayrton Senna	Mexico	- United States 1989	(McLaren)
Ayrton Senna	Portugal	- Spain 1989	(McLaren)
Nigel Mansell	France	- Britain 1990	(Ferrari)
Nigel Mansell	France	- Britain 1992 (a)	(Williams)
Damon Hill	France	- Britain 1994	(Williams)
David Coulthard	Portugal	- Europe 1995	(Williams)
Damon Hill	Brazil	- Argentina 1996 (a)	(Williams)
Mika Häkkinen	Austria	- Germany 1999	(McLaren)
Michael Schumacher	Europe	- France 2001 (a)	(Ferrari)
Fernando Alonso	France	- Britain 2005	(Renault)
Juan Pablo Montoya	Italy	- Belgium 2005	(McLaren)
Fernando Alonso	Europe	- Spain 2006	(Renault)
Kimi Räikkönen	Germany	- Hungary 2006	(McLaren)
Felipe Massa	Malaysia	- Bahrain 2007	(Ferrari)
Lewis Hamilton	Canada	- United States 2007 (a)	(McLaren)
Lewis Hamilton	Japan	- China 2007	(McLaren)
Lewis Hamilton	Japan	- China 2008	(McLaren)
Jenson Button	Australia	- Malaysia 2009 (a)	(Brawn)
Mark Webber	Spain	- Monaco 2010 (a)	(Red Bull)
Sebastian Vettel	Germany	- Hungary 2010	(Red Bull)
Sebastian Vettel	Malaysia	- China 2011	(Red Bull)
Lewis Hamilton	Australia	- Malaysia 2012	(McLaren)
Sebastian Vettel	Australia	- Malaysia 2013	(Red Bull)
Lewis Hamilton	Britain	- Germany 2013	(Mercedes-Benz)
Sebastian Vettel	United States	- Brazil 2013 (a)	(Red Bull)

Nico Rosberg	Germany	- Hungary 2014	(Mercedes-Benz)
Nico Rosberg	United States	- Brazil 2014	(Mercedes-Benz)
Lewis Hamilton	China	- Baharin 2015 (a)	(Mercedes-Benz)
Nico Rosberg	United States	- Mexico 2015	(Mercedes-Benz)

(a) Additionally won both races.

Longest

	years, days	races		
Mario Andretti	8y, 18d	108	United States 1968 (Lotus)	- Japan 1976 (JPS Lotus)
Giancarlo Fisichella	6y, 223d	108	Austria 1998 (Benetton)	- Australia 2005 (Renault)
Riccardo Patrese	5y, 336d	92	Italy 1983 (Brabham)	- Hungary 1989 (Williams)
Felipe Massa	5y, 232d	102	Brazil 2008 (Ferrari)	- Austria 2014 (Williams)
Rubens Barrichello	4y, 359d	88	Brazil 2004 (Ferrari)	- Brazil 2009 (Brawn)
Rubens Barrichello	4y, 303d	78	Belgium 1994 (Jordan)	- France 1999 (Stewart)
Jack Brabham	4y, 281d	43	United States 1961 (Cooper)	- Britain 1966 (Brabham)
Mario Andretti	3y, 346d	60	United States 1978 (JPS Lotus)	- Italy 1982 (Ferrari)
Jarno Trulli	3y, 311d	67	United States 2005 (Toyota)	- Bahrain 2009 (Toyota)
Jean-Pierre Jarier	3y, 255d	61	Brazil 1975 (Shadow)	- Canada 1978 (JPS Lotus)

Did not necessarily start every race during the period.

354. Interval between first & second poles

Shortest

	days		
Lewis Hamilton	7	Canada - United States 2007 (a)	(McLaren)
René Arnoux	14	Austria - Netherlands 1979 (a)	(Renault)
Juan Manuel Fangio	14	Monaco - Switzerland 1950 (a)	(Alfa Romeo)
Jean-Pierre Jarier	14	Argentina - Brazil 1975 (a)	(Shadow)
Michael Schumacher	14	Monaco - Spain 1994 (a)	(Benetton)
Ayrton Senna	14	Portugal - San Marino 1985 (a)	(Lotus)
Emerson Fittipaldi	21	Monaco - Belgium 1972 (a)	(JPS Lotus)
Mike Hawthorn	21	Belgium - France 1958 (a)	(Ferrari)
Chris Amon	28	Spain - Belgium 1968	(Ferrari)
Alain Prost	28	Germany - Netherlands 1981	(Renault)

(a) Consecutive grands prix.

Longest

	years, days	races		
Mario Andretti	8y, 18d	108	United States 1968 (Lotus)	- Japan 1976 (JPS Lotus)
Giancarlo Fisichella	6y, 223d	108	Austria 1998 (Benetton)	- Australia 2005 (Renault)
Rubens Barrichello	4y, 303d	78	Belgium 1994 (Jordan)	- France 1999 (Stewart)
José Froilán González	3y, 39d	27	Britain 1951 (Ferrari)	- Switzerland 1954 (Ferrari)
Jean Alesi	2y, 361d	50	Italy 1994 (Ferrari)	- Italy 1997 (Benetton)
Jo Siffert	2y, 285d	32	Mexico 1968 (Lotus)	- Austria 1971 (BRM)
Carlos Reutemann	2y, 256d	41	Argentina 1972 (Brabham)	- United States 1974 (Brabham)
Riccardo Patrese	2y, 180d	43	United States West 1981 (Arrows)	- Italy 1983 (Brabham)
Heinz-Harald Frentzen	2y, 138d	42	Monaco 1997 (Williams)	- Europe 1999 (Jordan)
Jacques Laffite	2y, 131d	37	Italy 1976 (Ligier)	- Argentina 1979 (Ligier)

355. Interval between first & last pole positions *(Longest)*

	years, days	races		
Rubens Barrichello	15y, 51d	260	Belgium 1994	- Brazil 2009
Mario Andretti	13y, 341d	200	United States 1968	- Italy 1982
Alain Prost	12y, 83d	195	Germany 1981	- Japan 1993
Michael Schumacher	12y, 62d	209	Monaco 1994	- France 2006
Riccardo Patrese	11y, 154d	184	United States West 1981	- Hungary 1992
Giancarlo Fisichella	11y, 35d	191	Austria 1998	- Belgium 2009
Jack Brabham	10y, 275d	106	Britain 1959	- Spain 1970
Nigel Mansell	10y, 128d	167	Dallas 1984	- Australia 1994
Gerhard Berger	9y, 310d	159	Portugal 1987	- Germany 1997
Carlos Reutemann	9y, 267d	148	Argentina 1972	- Caesars Palace 1981

356. Interval between pole position drivers of the same nationality *(Longest)*

	years, days	races		
Germany	32y, 247d	451	Italy 1961 (Wolfgang von Trips)	- Monaco 1994 (Michael Schumacher)
Australia	28y, 336d	475	Germany 1980 (Alan Jones)	- Germany 2009 (Mark Webber)
Belgium	17y, 336d	276	Italy 1972 (Jacky Ickx)	- Hungary 1990 (Thierry Boutsen)
Canada	14y, 312d	236	San Marino 1981 (Gilles Villeneuve)	- Australia 1996 (Jacques Villeneuve)
Sweden	14y, 109d	144	Netherlands 1959 (Jo Bonnier)	- Brazil 1973 (Ronnie Peterson)
Argentina	14y, 4d	144	Argentina 1958 (Juan Manuel Fangio)	- Argentina 1972 (Carlos Reutemann)
Finland	11y, 42d	180	Germany 1986 (Keke Rosberg)	- Italy 1997 (Mika Häkkinen)
Italy	11y, 28d	99	Belgium 1955 (Eugenio Castellotti)	- France 1966 (Lorenzo Bandini)
Austria	9y, 200d	148	South Africa 1978 (Niki Lauda)	- Portugal 1987 (Gerhard Berger)
Australia	9y, 86d	136	Spain 1970 (Jack Brabham)	- Britain 1979 (Alan Jones)

357. Interval between first time pole position drivers *(Longest)*

3 years and 332 days, from Germany 1962 (5 August, Graham Hill) until France 1966 (3 July, Lorenzo Bandini).

358. Pole position speed

Fastest

	km/h	mph		
Italy 2004	260.395	161.802	Rubens Barrichello	(Ferrari F2004)
Italy 2002	259.827	161.449	Juan Pablo Montoya	(Williams FW24 - BMW)
Britain 1985	258.983	160.925	Keke Rosberg	(Williams FW10 - Honda)
Italy 2003	257.584	160.055	Michael Schumacher	(Ferrari F2003-GA)
Italy 1991	257.415	159.951	Ayrton Senna	(McLaren MP4/6 - Honda)
Italy 2005	257.295	159.876	Juan Pablo Montoya	(McLaren MP4-20 - Mercedes)
Italy 1993	257.209	159.822	Alain Prost	(Williams FW15C - Renault)
Austria 1987	256.621	159.457	Nelson Piquet	(Williams FW11B - Honda)
Britain 1987	256.315	159.267	Nelson Piquet	(Williams FW11B - Honda)
Austria 1986	256.032	159.091	Teo Fabi	(Benetton B186 - BMW)

Slowest

	km/h	mph		
Monaco 1950	103.884	64.550	Juan Manuel Fangio	(Alfa Romeo 158)
Monaco 1956	108.865	67.646	Juan Manuel Fangio	(Lancia-Ferrari D50)
Monaco 1957	110.243	68.502	Juan Manuel Fangio	(Maserati 250F)
Monaco 1955	111.988	69.586	Juan Manuel Fangio	(Mercedes-Benz W196)
Monaco 1958	113.447	70.493	Tony Brooks	(Vanwall VW10/57)
Monaco 1959	113.675	70.634	Stirling Moss	(Cooper T51 - Climax)
Monaco 1961	114.248	70.991	Stirling Moss	(Lotus 18 - Climax)
Monaco 1960	117.570	73.055	Stirling Moss	(Lotus 18 - Climax)
Monaco 1962	118.679	73.744	Jim Clark	(Lotus 25 - Climax)
Monaco 1963	120.064	74.604	Jim Clark	(Lotus 25 - Climax)

359. Identical time as the pole time in qualifying

4 drivers		
Britain 1961	1m 58.8s	Phil Hill (Ferrari), Richie Ginther (Ferrari), Jo Bonnier (Porsche), Wolfgang von Trips (Ferrari)
3 drivers		
Europe 1997	1m 21.072s	Jacques Villeneuve (Williams), Michael Schumacher (Ferrari), Heinz-Harald Frentzen (Williams)
2 drivers		
Belgium 1950	4m 37s	Giuseppe Farina (Alfa Romeo), Juan Manuel Fangio (Alfa Romeo)
Britain 1952	1m 50s	Giuseppe Farina (Ferrari), Alberto Ascari (Ferrari)
Monaco 1955	1m 41.1s	Juan Manuel Fangio (Mercedes-Benz), Alberto Ascari (Lancia)
Britain 1956	1m 41s	Stirling Moss (Maserati), Juan Manuel Fangio (Lancia-Ferrari)
Portugal 1958	2m 34.2s	Stirling Moss (Vanwall), Mike Hawthorn (Ferrari)
Netherlands 1959	1m 36.0s	Jo Bonnier (BRM), Jack Brabham (Cooper)
Britain 1959	1m 58.0s	Jack Brabham (Cooper), Roy Salvadori (Aston Martin)
Netherlands 1961	1m 35.7s	Phil Hill (Ferrari), Wolfgang von Trips (Ferrari)

Canada 1968	1m 33.8s	Jochen Rindt (Brabham), Chris Amon (Ferrari)
South Africa 1970	1m 19.3s	Jackie Stewart (March), Chris Amon (March)
Britain 1970	1m 24.8s	Jochen Rindt (Lotus), Jack Brabham (Brabham)
Britain 1971	1m 18.1s	Clay Regazzoni (Ferrari), Jackie Stewart (Tyrrell)
Britain 1974	1m 19.7s	Niki Lauda (Ferrari), Ronnie Peterson (JPS Lotus)

Of the above, only Europe 1997 was measured to three decimal places.

360. Set time for pole position, but did not start from pole

Germany 1959	Cliff Allison (Ferrari): set the fastest time in qualifying, but being a reserve driver, was put on the penultimate row of the grid, in 14th place. Pole position: Tony Brooks (Ferrari)
Argentina 1975	Jean-Pierre Jarier (Shadow - Ford Cosworth): car failed on the parade lap (crown wheel & pinion failure)
Belgium 1981	Alan Jones (Williams - Ford Cosworth) set the fastest time, but this was removed as the side-pods of his car were declared illegal. He was unable to match that time later. Pole position: Carlos Reutemann (Williams - Ford Cosworth)
Germany 1982	Didier Pironi (Ferrari): injured in an accident during qualifying which ended his career
Italy 1986	Teo Fabi (Benetton - Ford Cosworth): difficulty firing-up engine on the parade lap. Started from the back of the grid
Brazil 1988	Ayrton Senna (McLaren - Honda): gearbox problems on the dummy grid. Started from the pit lane in the spare
Hungary 1993	Alain Prost (Williams - Renault): late to get away on the parade lap, due to a clutch problem. Had to start from the back of the grid
Portugal 1993	Damon Hill (Williams - Renault): late to get away on the parade lap, due to external starter becoming dislodged. Had to start from the back of the grid
France 1996	Michael Schumacher (Ferrari): suffered an engine failure on the parade lap
Japan 1998	Michael Schumacher (Ferrari): stalled on the dummy grid at the restart. Had to start from the back of the grid
Monaco 2001	David Coulthard (McLaren - Mercedes): an electrical problem stalled the engine on the dummy grid, meaning he had to start from the back of the grid
United States 2005	Jarno Trulli (Toyota): withdrawn on the parade lap along with all other Michelin runners, due to tyre safety concerns
Italy 2005	Kimi Räikkönen (McLaren - Mercedes): won pole position, but was given a 10-place penalty, due to an engine change. Pole position: Juan Pablo Montoya (McLaren - Mercedes)
Monaco 2006	Michael Schumacher (Ferrari): set fastest time in the third qualifying session, but had all times removed, demoting him to the back of the grid. He was accused of deliberately coming to a halt during the final lap of qualifying and preventing others from setting a faster time. Pole position: Fernando Alonso (Renault)
Hungary 2007	Fernando Alonso (McLaren - Mercedes): set fastest time in the third qualifying session, but received a five-place grid penalty for preventing Hamilton from recording a further lap time, by delaying him in the pit lane. Pole position: Lewis Hamilton (McLaren - Mercedes)
Spain 2012	Lewis Hamilton (McLaren - Mercedes): set fastest time in the third qualifying session, but had all times removed, demoting him to the back of the grid for having insufficient fuel to provide a sample. Pole position: Pastor Maldonado (Williams - Renault)
Monaco 2012	Michael Schumacher (Mercedes-Benz): set fastest time in the third qualifying session, but received a five-place grid penalty for causing an accident with Bruno Senna at the previous race, in Spain. Pole position: Mark Webber (Red Bull - Renault)

361. Pole positions but never a world championship *(Most)*

Nico Rosberg	22	Rubens Barrichello	14	Mark Webber	13
René Arnoux	18	Ronnie Peterson	14	Gerhard Berger	12
Felipe Massa	16	Jacky Ickx	13	David Coulthard	12
Stirling Moss	16	Juan Pablo Montoya	13		

362. Pole positions but never a win

Chris Amon	5	Eugenio Castellotii	1	Nico Hülkenberg	1
Teo Fabi	3	Andrea De Cesaris	1	Mike Parkes	1
Jean-Pierre Jarier	3	Bruno Giacomelli	1	Tom Pryce	1
Stuart Lewis-Evans	2	Nick Heidfeld	1		

363. Pole positions but never a podium

Nico Hülkenberg is the only driver to achieve a pole position but never reach the podium.

364. Pole positions but never a fastest lap

Jean-Pierre Jabouille	6	Eugenio Castellotti	1	Tom Pryce	1
Elio De Angelis	3	Bruno Giacomelli	1	Peter Revson	1
Stuart Lewis-Evans	2	Pastor Maldonado	1	Wolfgang von Trips	1
Jo Bonnier	1	Mike Parkes	1		

365. Pole positions but never led

Teo Fabi is the only driver to lead a race but never achieve a pole position (3 poles).

366. Milestones: Pole positions I

Michael Schumacher	25th: Monaco 2000, 50th: Japan 2002	Lewis Hamilton	25th: Abu Dhabi 2012
Ayrton Senna	25th: Belgium 1988, 50th: Spain 1990	Nigel Mansell	25th: Britain 1992
Jim Clark	25th: Monaco 1966	Alain Prost	25th: Spain 1993
Juan Manuel Fangio	25th: Monaco 1957	Sebastian Vettel	25th: Italy 2011
Mika Häkkinen	25th: Austria 2000		

367. Milestones: Pole positions II
(eg pole position in the 100th race was achieved by Jim Clark in a Lotus 25)

1st	Giuseppe Farina (Alfa Romeo 158)	Britain 1950
100th	Jim Clark (Lotus 25)	South Africa 1962
200th	Jacky Ickx (Ferrari 312B2)	Spain 1972
250th	Niki Lauda (Ferrari 312T)	Germany 1975
300th	Mario Andretti (JPS Lotus 79)	Italy 1978
400th	Keke Rosberg (Williams FW10)	France 1985
500th	Ayrton Senna (McLaren MP4/6)	Belgium 1991
600th	Jacques Villeneuve (Williams FW19)	Austria 1997
700th	Michael Schumacher (Ferrari F2003-GA)	Italy 2003
750th	Michael Schumacher (Ferrari 248 F1)	France 2006
800th	Sebastian Vettel (Red Bull RB5)	Britain 2009
900th	Lewis Hamilton (Mercedes-Benz F1 W05)	Singapore 2014

Excludes Indianapolis 500.

368. Milestones: Pole positions III
(eg Jo Bonnier was the 10th driver to achieve a pole position)

1st	Giuseppe Farina	Britain 1950
10th	Jo Bonnier	Netherlands 1959
20th	Chris Amon	Spain 1968
30th	Ronnie Peterson	Brazil 1973
40th	Jacques Laffite	Italy 1976
50th	Alain Prost	Germany 1981
60th	Thierry Boutsen	Hungary 1990
70th	Ralf Schumacher	France 2001
80th	Heikki Kovalainen	Britain 2008

Excludes Indianapolis 500.

Chapter 9: Front Row Drivers

369. Front row positions
(until 1973, starting grids could feature up to four cars on the front row, see section 59 "Starting grid formats")

		% of starts		
Michael Schumacher	116	37.79	Spain 1992 (Benetton)	- China 2012 (Mercedes-Benz) (a)
Lewis Hamilton	90	53.89	Bahrain 2007 (McLaren)	- Abu Dhabi 2015 (Mercedes-Benz)
Ayrton Senna	87	54.04	Portugal 1985 (Lotus)	- San Marino 1994 (Williams)
Alain Prost	86	43.22	Argentina 1981 (Renault)	- Australia 1993 (Williams)
Sebastian Vettel	70	44.30	Italy 2008 (Toro Rosso)	- Singapore 2015 (Ferrari)
Nigel Mansell	56	29.95	Monaco 1984 (Lotus)	- Australia 1994 (Williams)
Jim Clark	48	66.67	Monaco 1961 (Lotus)	- South Africa 1968 (Lotus)
Juan Manuel Fangio	48	94.12	Britain 1950 (Alfa Romeo)	- Argentina 1958 (Maserati)
Damon Hill	47	40.87	Brazil 1993 (Williams)	- Japan 1996 (Williams)
Nelson Piquet	44	21.57	United States 1979 (Brabham)	- Spain 1987 (Williams)
Graham Hill	42	23.86	Argentina 1960 (BRM)	- Netherlands 1969 (Lotus)

	% of starts			
Jackie Stewart	42	42.42	Belgium 1965 (BRM)	- Germany 1973 (Tyrrell)
Nico Rosberg	40	21.62	Malaysia 2010 (Mercedes-Benz)	- Abu Dhabi 2015 (Mercedes-Benz)
Mika Häkkinen	39	24.22	Monaco 1994 (McLaren)	- Britain 2001 (McLaren)
Jack Brabham	38	30.16	Monaco 1958 (Cooper)	- Britain 1970 (Brabham)
Fernando Alonso	37	14.62	Malaysia 2003 (Renault)	- Germany 2012 (Ferrari)
David Coulthard	37	15.04	Argentina 1995 (Williams)	- Brazil 2003 (McLaren)
Stirling Moss	37	56.06	Britain 1954 (Maserati)	- Germany 1961 (Lotus)
Mark Webber	37	17.21	Malaysia 2004 (Jaguar)	- United States 2013 (Red Bull)
René Arnoux	34	22.82	France 1979 (Renault)	- Belgium 1984 (Ferrari)
Rubens Barrichello	34	10.53	Belgium 1994 (Jordan)	- Brazil 2009 (Brawn) (a)
Kimi Räikkönen	34	14.72	Belgium 2002 (McLaren)	- Italy 2015 (Ferrari) (a)
Gerhard Berger	32	15.24	Belgium 1986 (Benetton)	- Germany 1997 (Benetton)
Niki Lauda	31	18.13	South Africa 1974 (Ferrari)	- United States West 1982 (McLaren)
Riccardo Patrese	28	10.94	United States West 1981 (Arrows)	- Japan 1992 (Williams)
Giuseppe Farina	27	81.82	Britain 1950 (Alfa Romeo)	- Belgium 1954 (Ferrari)
Felipe Massa	27	11.79	Bahrain 2006 (Ferrari)	- Austria 2014 (Williams)
Juan Pablo Montoya	26	27.66	Austria 2001 (Williams)	- Brazil 2005 (Williams)
Alberto Ascari	25	80.65	Italy 1950 (Ferrari)	- Monaco 1955 (Lancia)
Jacky Ickx	25	21.55	Belgium 1968 (Ferrari)	- Brazil 1973 (Ferrari)
Ronnie Peterson	25	20.33	Canada 1972 (March)	- Netherlands 1978 (JPS Lotus)
Mario Andretti	24	18.75	United States 1968 (Lotus)	- Italy 1982 (Ferrari)
Jenson Button	24	8.45	San Marino 2004 (BAR)	- Brazil 2012 (McLaren)
James Hunt	24	26.09	United States 1974 (Hesketh)	- Brazil 1978 (McLaren)
Denny Hulme	23	20.54	Britain 1966 (Brabham)	- Britain 1973 (McLaren)
Jacques Villeneuve	23	14.11	Australia 1996 (Williams)	- Italy 1998 (Williams)
Dan Gurney	22	25.58	Germany 1959 (Ferrari)	- Germany 1967 (Eagle)
Carlos Reutemann	22	15.07	Argentina 1972 (Brabham)	- Caesars Palace 1981 (Williams)
Clay Regazzoni	21	15.91	Austria 1970 (Ferrari)	- Monaco 1976 (Ferrari)
John Surtees	21	18.92	Portugal 1960 (Lotus)	- Italy 1968 (Honda)
Chris Amon	19	19.79	Mexico 1967 (Ferrari)	- Italy 1972 (Matra-Simca)
Ralf Schumacher	19	10.56	Brazil 2001 (Williams)	- Japan 2005 (Toyota)
Jochen Rindt	18	30.00	Belgium 1966 (Cooper)	- Austria 1970 (Lotus)
Mike Hawthorn	17	37.78	Netherlands 1952 (Cooper)	- Morocco 1958 (Ferrari)
Emerson Fittipaldi	16	11.11	United States 1971 (Lotus)	- United States 1975 (McLaren)
Jarno Trulli	15	5.95	Monaco 2000 (Jordan)	- Japan 2009 (Toyota) (a)
Alan Jones	13	11.21	Britain 1979 (Williams)	- Caesars Palace 1981 (Williams)
Jody Scheckter	13	11.61	South Africa 1973 (McLaren)	- Monaco 1979 (Ferrari)
Heinz-Harald Frentzen	12	7.64	Australia 1997 (Williams)	- Britain 2000 (Jordan)
José Froilán González	12	46.15	Monaco 1950 (Maserati)	- Argentina 1955 (Ferrari)
Tony Brooks	11	28.95	Britain 1957 (Vanwall)	- Belgium 1960 (Cooper)
Giancarlo Fisichella	11	4.80	Germany 1997 (Jordan)	- Belgium 2009 (Force India)
Jean-Pierre Jabouille	11	22.45	South Africa 1979 (Renault)	- Italy 1980 (Renault)
Jacques Laffite	11	6.25	Italy 1976 (Ligier)	- Spain 1981 (Talbot-Ligier)
John Watson	11	7.24	Austria 1976 (Penske)	- France 1981 (McLaren)
Jean Alesi	10	4.98	Canada 1994 (Ferrari)	- France 1999 (Sauber)
Jean Behra	10	18.87	Argentina 1955 (Maserati)	- Monaco 1959 (Ferrari)
Keke Rosberg	10	8.77	Britain 1982 (Williams)	- Germany 1986 (McLaren)
Phil Hill	9	18.75	France 1959 (Ferrari)	- Germany 1961 (Ferrari)
Patrick Tambay	9	7.89	United States West 1983 (Ferrari)	- France 1984 (Renault)
Peter Collins	8	25.00	Belgium 1956 (Lancia-Ferrari)	- Germany 1958 (Ferrari)
Richie Ginther	8	15.38	Italy 1960 (Ferrari)	- Netherlands 1965 (Honda)
Gilles Villeneuve	8	11.94	United States West 1978 (Ferrari)	- Brazil 1982 (Ferrari)
Eugenio Castellotti	7	50.00	Belgium 1955 (Lancia)	- Argentina 1957 (Lancia-Ferrari)
Patrick Depailler	7	7.37	Sweden 1974 (Tyrrell)	- Belgium 1979 (Ligier)
Bruce McLaren	7	7.00	Britain 1960 (Cooper)	- Italy 1968 (McLaren)
Carlos Pace	7	9.72	South Africa 1974 (Surtees)	- South Africa 1977 (Brabham)
Elio De Angelis	6	5.56	Europe 1983 (Lotus)	- Canada 1985 (Lotus)
Luigi Musso	6	25.00	Argentina 1956 (Lancia-Ferrari)	- France 1958 (Ferrari)
Didier Pironi	6	8.57	Brazil 1980 (Ligier)	- Germany 1982 (Ferrari) (a)
Lorenzo Bandini	5	11.90	Germany 1963 (BRM)	- Monaco 1967 (Ferrari)
Jo Bonnier	5	4.81	Netherlands 1959 (BRM)	- Germany 1961 (Porsche)
Heikki Kovalainen	5	4.50	Turkey 2008 (McLaren)	- Europe 2009 (McLaren)

		% of starts		
Stuart Lewis-Evans	5	35.71	Italy 1957 (Vanwall)	- Morocco 1958 (Vanwall)
Peter Revson	5	16.67	Canada 1972 (McLaren)	- Canada 1973 (McLaren)
Harry Schell	5	8.93	Spain 1954 (Maserati)	- United States 1959 (Cooper)
Jo Siffert	5	5.21	Canada 1968 (Lotus)	- Canada 1971 (BRM)
Luigi Villoresi	5	16.13	Switzerland 1951 (Ferrari)	- France 1953 (Ferrari)
Michele Alboreto	4	2.06	Brazil 1984 (Ferrari)	- Britain 1988 (Ferrari)
Luigi Fagioli	4	57.14	Britain 1950 (Alfa Romeo)	- France 1950 (Alfa Romeo)
Eddie Irvine	4	2.74	Luxembourg 1998 (Ferrari)	- Malaysia 1999 (Ferrari)
Robert Kubica	4	5.26	Australia 2008 (BMW Sauber)	- Monaco 2010 (Renault)
Piero Taruffi	4	22.22	Switzerland 1952 (Ferrari)	- Britain 1952 (Ferrari)
Wolfgang von Trips	4	14.81	Netherlands 1961 (Ferrari)	- Italy 1961 (Ferrari)
François Cevert	3	6.38	Canada 1971 (Tyrrell)	- Netherlands 1973 (Tyrrell)
Teo Fabi	3	4.69	Germany 1985 (Toleman)	- Italy 1986 (Benetton)
Innes Ireland	3	6.00	Argentina 1960 (Lotus)	- Britain 1962 (Lotus)
Jean-Pierre Jarier	3	2.24	Argentina 1975 (Shadow)	- Canada 1978 (JPS Lotus) (a)
Karl Kling	3	27.27	France 1954 (Mercedes-Benz)	- Italy 1955 (Mercedes-Benz)
Robert Manzon	3	10.71	Switzerland 1952 (Gordini)	- Germany 1952 (Gordini)
Daniel Ricciardo	3	3.41	Australia 2014 (Red Bull)	- Singapore 2015 (Red Bull)
Pedro Rodríguez	3	5.45	Spain 1968 (BRM)	- Netherlands 1971 (BRM)
Jean-Pierre Beltoise	2	2.33	Canada 1969 (Matra)	- France 1970 (Matra-Simca)
Valtteri Bottas	2	3.57	Austria 2014 (Williams)	- Germany 2014 (Williams)
Andrea De Cesaris	2	0.96	United States West 1982 (Alfa Romeo)	- Dertroit 1982 (Alfa Romeo)
Nick Heidfeld	2	1.09	Europe 2005 (Williams)	- Hungary 2007 (BMW Sauber)
Willy Mairesse	2	16.67	Italy 1960 (Ferrari)	- Belgium 1963 (Ferrari)
Pastor Maldonado	2	2.11	Spain 2012 (Williams)	- Singapore 2012 (Williams)
Mike Parkes	2	33.33	France 1966 (Ferrari)	- Italy 1966 (Ferrari)
Tom Pryce	2	4.76	Monaco 1975 (Shadow)	- Britain 1975 (Shadow)
Roy Salvadori	2	4.26	Britain 1958 (Cooper)	- Britain 1959 (Aston Martin)
Ludovico Scarfiotti	2	20.00	Germany 1966 (Ferrari)	- Italy 1966 (Ferrari)
Maurice Trintignant	2	2.47	Germany 1952 (Gordini)	- Italy 1952 (Gordini)
Felice Bonetto	1	6.67	France 1953 (Maserati)	
Thierry Boutsen	1	0.61	Hungary 1990 (Williams)	
Vittorio Brambilla	1	1.35	Sweden 1975 (March)	
Eddie Cheever	1	0.76	France 1983 (Renault)	
Olivier Gendebien	1	7.14	Belgium 1961 (Ferrari)	
Bruno Giacomelli	1	1.45	United States 1980 (Alfa Romeo)	
Timo Glock	1	1.10	Bahrain 2009 (Toyota)	
Masten Gregory	1	2.63	Portugal 1959 (Cooper)	
Romain Grosjean	1	1.20	Hungary 2012 (Lotus)	
Nico Hülkenberg	1	1.06	Brazil 2010 (Williams)	
Stefan Johansson	1	1.27	Germany 1985 (Ferrari)	
Kamui Kobayashi	1	1.33	Belgium 2012 (Sauber)	
Pierluigi Martini	1	0.85	United States 1990 (Minardi)	
Stefano Modena	1	1.43	Monaco 1991 (Tyrrell)	
Jackie Oliver	1	2.00	Britain 1968 (Lotus)	
Reg Parnell	1	16.67	Britain 1950 (Alfa Romeo)	
Ricardo Rodríguez	1	20.00	Italy 1961 (Ferrari)	
Consalvo Sanesi	1	20.00	Italy 1950 (Alfa Romeo)	
Takuma Sato	1	1.11	Europe 2004 (BAR)	
Johnny Servoz-Gavin	1	8.33	Monaco 1968 (Matra)	
Hans-Joachim Stuck	1	1.35	United States 1977 (Brabham)	
Adrian Sutil	1	0.78	Italy 2009 (Force India)	
Trevor Taylor	1	3.70	Belgium 1962 (Lotus)	
Indianapolis 500				
Jack McGrath	5	83.33	1951 (Kurtis-Kraft)	- 1955 (Kurtis-Kraft)
Freddie Agabashian	3	37.50	1950 (Kurtis-Kraft)	- 1953 (Kurtis-Kraft)
Jim Rathmann	3	30.00	1956 (Kurtis-Kraft)	- 1960 (Watson)
Eddie Sachs	3	75.00	1957 (Kuzma)	- 1960 (Ewing)
Pat O'Connor	2	40.00	1956 (Kurtis-Kraft)	- 1957 (Kurtis-Kraft)
Tony Bettenhausen	1	9.10	1955 (Kurtis-Kraft)	
Jimmy Bryan	1	11.11	1954 (Kuzma)	
Jimmy Daywalt	1	16.67	1954 (Kurtis-Kraft)	

	% of starts		
Ed Elisian	1	20.00	1958 (Watson)
Walt Faulkner	1	20.00	1950 (Kurtis-Kraft)
Pat Flaherty	1	16.67	1956 (Watson)
Jerry Hoyt	1	25.00	1955 (Stevens)
Andy Linden	1	14.29	1952 (Kurtis-Kraft)
Duke Nalon	1	33.33	1951 (Kurtis-Kraft)
Dick Rathmann	1	20.00	1958 (Watson)
Jimmy Reece	1	16.67	1958 (Watson)
Mauri Rose	1	50.00	1950 (Deidt)
Troy Ruttman	1	14.29	1957 (Watson)
Johnny Thomson	1	12.50	1959 (Lesovsky)
Bill Vukovich	1	20.00	1953 (Kurtis-Kraft)
Lee Wallard	1	50.00	1951 (Kurtis-Kraft)
Rodger Ward	1	10.00	1960 (Watson)

(a) Did not start one of the races (see section 405).

370. Percentage of races with a front row *(Highest)*

	%	front rows			%	front rows
Juan Manuel Fangio	94.12	48		Stirling Moss	56.06	37
Giuseppe Farina	81.82	27		Ayrton Senna	54.04	87
Alberto Ascari	80.65	25		Lewis Hamilton	53.89	90
Jim Clark	66.67	48		Eugenio Castellotti	50.00	7
Luigi Fagioli	57.14	4		José Froilán González	46.15	12

Excludes Indianapolis 500.

371. Front row driver age

Youngest

	years, days	
Ricardo Rodríguez	19y, 208d	Italy 1961
Sebastian Vettel	21y, 73d	Italy 2008
Fernando Alonso	21y, 237d	Malaysia 2003
Rubens Barrichello	22y, 97d	Belgium 1994
Lewis Hamilton	22y, 98d	Bahrain 2007
Andrea De Cesaris	22y, 308d	United States West 1982
Kimi Räikkönen	22y, 319d	Belgium 2002
Bruce McLaren	22y, 321d	Britain 1960
Jody Scheckter	23y, 33d	South Africa 1973
Nico Hülkenberg	23y, 80d	Brazil 2010

Oldest

	years, days	
Luigi Fagioli	52y, 23d	France 1950
Felice Bonetto	50y, 26d	France 1953
Giuseppe Farina	47y, 233d	Belgium 1954
Juan Manuel Fangio	46y, 209d	Argentina 1958
Piero Taruffi	45y, 281d	Britain 1952
Karl Kling	44y, 360d	Italy 1955
Jack Brabham	44y, 107d	Britain 1970
Luigi Villoresi	44y, 50d	France 1953
Michael Schumacher	43y, 103d	China 2012
Mario Andretti	42y, 196d	Italy 1982
Indianapolis 500		
Mauri Rose	44y, 4d	1950

372. Front rows in a season *(Most)*

Lewis Hamilton	18 of 19	2015 (wc)	(Mercedes-Benz F1 W06)
Sebastian Vettel	18 of 19	2011 (wc)	(Red Bull RB7 - Renault)
Damon Hill	16 of 16	1996 (wc)	(Williams FW18 - Renault)
Alain Prost	16 of 16	1993 (wc)	(Williams FW15C - Renault)
Ayrton Senna	16 of 16	1989	(McLaren MP4/5 - Honda)
Nigel Mansell	15 of 16	1992 (wc)	(Williams FW14B - Renault)
Ayrton Senna	15 of 16	1988 (wc)	(McLaren MP4/4 - Honda)
Lewis Hamilton	15 of 19	2014 (wc)	(Mercedes-Benz F1 W05)
Nico Rosberg	15 of 19	2014	(Mercedes-Benz F1 W05)
Sebastian Vettel	15 of 19	2013 (wc)	(Red Bull RB9 - Renault)

(wc) World champion that season.

373. Front row in every race of a season

Damon Hill	16	1996 (wc)	(Williams FW18 - Renault)
Alain Prost	16	1993 (wc)	(Williams FW15C - Renault)
Ayrton Senna	16	1989	(McLaren MP4/5 - Honda)
Alberto Ascari	8	1953 (wc)	(Maserati A6GCM)
Jack Brabham	8	1959 (wc)	(Cooper T51 - Climax)
Juan Manuel Fangio	8	1954 (wc)	(Maserati 250F, Mercedes-Benz W196, W196 str.)
Juan Manuel Fangio	7	1951 (wc)	(Alfa Romeo 159)
Juan Manuel Fangio	7	1956 (wc)	(Lancia-Ferrari D50)
Giuseppe Farina	7	1951	(Alfa Romeo 159)
Giuseppe Farina	7	1952	(Ferrari D500)
Juan Manuel Fangio	6	1950	(Alfa Romeo 158)
Juan Manuel Fangio	6	1955 (wc)	(Mercedes-Benz W196, W196 str.)
Giuseppe Farina	6	1950 (wc)	(Alfa Romeo 158)

(wc) World champion that season.

374. Front row in all but one race of a season

Lewis Hamilton	18	2015 (wc)	(Mercedes-Benz F1 W06)
Sebastian Vettel	18	2011 (wc)	(Red Bull RB7 - Renault)
Nigel Mansell	15	1992 (wc)	(Williams FW14B - Renault)
Ayrton Senna	15	1988 (wc)	(McLaren MP4/4 - Honda)
Jim Clark	9	1965 (wc)	(Lotus 33, 25 - Climax)
Jim Clark	8	1962	(Lotus 25 - Climax)
Juan Manuel Fangio	7	1953	(Maserati A6GCM)
Alberto Ascari	6	1952 (wc)	(Ferrari 500)
Juan Manuel Fangio	6	1957	(Maserati 250F)
Stirling Moss	5	1955	(Mercedes-Benz W196, W196 str.)

(wc) World champion that season.

375. Consecutive front rows *(Most)*

Juan Manuel Fangio	28	Britain 1953	- France 1957	(Maserati A6GCM, 250F, Mercedes-Benz W196 str., W196, Lancia-Ferrari D50)
Ayrton Senna	24	Germany 1988	- Australia 1989	(McLaren MP4/4, MP4/5 - Honda)
Giuseppe Farina	22	Britain 1950	- Netherlands 1953	(Alfa Romeo 158, 159, Ferrari 500)
Lewis Hamilton	20	Belgium 2014	- Italy 2015	(Mercedes-Benz F1 W05, F1 W06)
Damon Hill	17	Australia 1995	- Japan 1996	(Williams FW17B, FW18 - Renault)
Alain Prost	16	South Africa 1993	- Australia 1993	(Williams FW15C - Renault)
Nigel Mansell	15	Australia 1986	- Mexico 1987	(Williams FW11, FW11B - Honda)
Alberto Ascari	14	Belgium 1952	- Italy 1953	(Ferrari 500)
Sebastian Vettel	14	Singapore 2010	- Britain 2011	(Red Bull RB6, RB7 - Renault)
Juan Manuel Fangio	13	Britain 1950	- Spain 1951	(Alfa Romeo 158, 159)

376. Consecutive front rows from the start of a season *(Most)*
(not counting any into the following season)

Damon Hill	16	1996 (wc)	(Williams FW18 - Renault)
Alain Prost	16	1993 (wc)	(Williams FW15C - Renault)
Ayrton Senna	16	1989	(McLaren MP4/5 - Honda)
Nigel Mansell	14	1987	(Williams FW11B - Honda)
Lewis Hamilton	12	2015 (wc)	(Mercedes-Benz F1 W06)
Sebastian Vettel	9	2011 (wc)	(Red Bull RB7 - Renault)
Alberto Ascari	8	1953 (wc)	(Ferrari 500)
Jack Brabham	8	1959 (wc)	(Cooper T51 - Climax)
Juan Manuel Fangio	8	1954 (wc)	(Maserati 250F, Mercedes-Benz W196)
Graham Hill	8	1963	(BRM P57, P61)

(wc) World champion that season.

377. Seasons of front rows (Most)

Michael Schumacher	16	1992 - 2012	(Benetton, Ferrari, Mercedes-Benz)
Alain Prost	12	1981 - 93	(Renault, McLaren, Ferrari, Williams)
Jack Brabham	11	1958 - 70	(Cooper, Brabham)
Fernando Alonso	10	2003 - 12	(Renault, McLaren, Ferrari)
Gerhard Berger	10	1986 - 97	(Benetton, Ferrari, McLaren)
Kimi Räikkönen	10	2002 - 15	(McLaren, Ferrari, Lotus)
Ayrton Senna	10	1985 - 94	(Lotus, McLaren, Williams)
Rubens Barrichello	9	1994 - 2009	(Jordan, Stewart, Ferrari, Brawn)
Lewis Hamilton	9	2007 - 15	(McLaren, Mercedes-Benz)
Graham Hill	9	1960 - 69	(BRM, Lotus)
Nigel Mansell	9	1984 - 94	(Lotus, Williams, Ferrari)
Nelson Piquet	9	1979 - 87	(Brabham, Williams)
Carlos Reutemann	9	1972 - 81	(Brabham, Ferrari, Lotus, Williams)
Jackie Stewart	9	1965 - 73	(BRM, Matra, Tyrrell)
Mark Webber	9	2004 - 13	(Jaguar, Williams, Red Bull)

378. Consecutive seasons of front rows (Most)

Michael Schumacher	15	1992 - 2006	(Benetton, Ferrari)
Alain Prost	11	1981 - 91	(Renault, McLaren, Ferrari)
Fernando Alonso	10	2003 - 12	(Renault, McLaren, Ferrari)
Gerhard Berger	10	1986 - 97	(Benetton, Ferrari, McLaren)
Ayrton Senna	10	1985 - 94	(Lotus, McLaren, Williams)
Lewis Hamilton	9	2007 - 15	(McLaren, Mercedes-Benz)
Nelson Piquet	9	1979 - 87	(Brabham, Williams)
Jackie Stewart	9	1965 - 73	(BRM, Matra, Tyrrell)
Jim Clark	8	1961 - 68	(Lotus)
Denny Hulme	8	1966 - 73	(Brabham, McLaren)
Stirling Moss	8	1954 - 61	(Maserati, Mercedes-Benz, Vanwall, Cooper, Lotus)
Kimi Räikkönen	8	2002 - 09	(McLaren, Ferrari)
Sebastian Vettel	8	2008 - 15	(Toro Rosso, Red Bull, Ferrari)

379. Front rows by nationality

Argentina: Juan Manuel Fangio, 48; Carlos Reutemann, 22; José Froilán González, 12

Australia: Jack Brabham, 38; Mark Webber, 37; Alan Jones, 13; Daniel Ricciardo, 3

Austria: Gerhard Berger, 32; Niki Lauda, 31; Jochen Rindt, 18

Belgium: Jacky Ickx, 25; Willy Mairesse, 2; Thierry Boutsen, 1; Olivier Gendebien, 1

Brazil: Ayrton Senna, 87; Nelson Piquet, 44; Rubens Barrichello, 34; Felipe Massa, 27; Emerson Fittipaldi, 16; Carlos Pace, 7

Canada: Jacques Villeneuve, 23; Gilles Villeneuve, 8

Colombia: Juan Pablo Montoya, 26

Finland: Mika Häkkinen, 39; Kimi Räikkönen, 34; Keke Rosberg, 10; Heikki Kovalainen, 5; Valtteri Bottas, 2

France: Alain Prost, 86; René Arnoux, 34; Jean-Pierre Jabouille, 11; Jacques Laffite, 11; Jean Alesi, 10; Jean Behra, 10; Patrick Tambay, 9; Patrick Depailler, 7; Didier Pironi, 6; François Cevert, 3; Jean-Pierre Jarier, 3; Robert Manzon, 3; Jean-Pierre Beltoise, 2; Maurice Trintignant, 2; Romain Grosjean, 1; Johnny Servoz-Gavin, 1

Germany: Michael Schumacher, 116; Sebastian Vettel, 70; Nico Rosberg, 40; Ralf Schumacher, 19; Heinz-Harald Frentzen, 12; Wolfgang von Trips, 4; Karl Kling, 3; Nick Heidfeld, 2; Timo Glock, 1; Nico Hülkenberg, 1; Hans-Joachim Stuck, 1; Adrian Sutil, 1

Great Britain: Lewis Hamilton, 90; Nigel Mansell, 56; Jim Clark, 48; Damon Hill, 47; Graham Hill, 42; Jackie Stewart, 42; David Coulthard, 37; Stirling Moss, 37; Jenson Button, 24; James Hunt, 24; John Surtees, 21; Mike Hawthorn, 17; Tony Brooks, 11; John Watson, 11; Peter Collins, 8; Stuart Lewis-Evans, 5; Eddie Irvine, 4; Innes Ireland, 3; Mike Parkes, 2; Tom Pryce, 2; Roy Salvadori, 2; Jackie Oliver, 1; Reg Parnell, 1; Trevor Taylor, 1

Italy: Riccardo Patrese, 28; Giuseppe Farina, 27; Alberto Ascari, 25; Jarno Trulli, 15; Giancarlo Fisichella, 11; Eugenio Castellotti, 7; Elio De Angelis, 6; Luigi Musso, 6; Lorenzo Bandini, 5; Luigi Villoresi, 5; Michele Alboreto, 4; Luigi Fagioli, 4; Piero Taruffi, 4; Teo Fabi, 3; Andrea De Cesaris, 2; Ludovico Scarfiotti, 2; Felice Bonetto, 1; Vittorio Brambilla, 1; Bruno Giacomelli, 1; Pierluigi Martini, 1; Stefano Modena, 1; Consalvo Sanesi, 1

Japan: Kamui Kobayashi, 1; Takuma Sato, 1

Mexico: Pedro Rodríguez, 3; Ricardo Rodríguez, 1

New Zealand: Denny Hulme, 23; Chris Amon, 19; Bruce McLaren, 7

Poland: Robert Kubica, 4

South Africa: Jody Scheckter, 13

Spain: Fernando Alonso, 37

Sweden: Ronnie Peterson, 25; Jo Bonnier, 5; Stefan Johansson, 1

Switzerland: Clay Regazzoni, 21; Jo Siffert, 5

United States: Mario Andretti, 24; Dan Gurney, 22; Phil Hill, 9; Richie Ginther, 8; Peter Revson, 5; Harry Schell, 5; Eddie Cheever, 1; Masten Gregory, 1

Venezuela: Pastor Maldonado, 2

Summary

	front row positions	races	drivers		
Great Britain	536	431	24	Britain 1950 (Reg Parnell)	- Abu Dhabi 2015 (Lewis Hamilton)
Germany	270	252	12	France 1954 (Karl Kling)	- Abu Dhabi 2015 (Nico Rosberg)
Brazil	215	209	6	United States 1971 (Emerson Fittipaldi)	- Austria 2014 (Felipe Massa)
France	199	166	16	Switzerland 1952 (Robert Manzon)	- Hungary 2012 (Romain Grosjean)
Italy	160	122	22	Britain 1950 (Giuseppe Farina/ Luigi Fagioli)	- Japan 2009 (Jarno Trulli)
Australia	91	91	4	Monaco 1958 (Jack Brabham)	- Singapore 2015 (Daniel Ricciardo)
Finland	90	90	5	Britain 1982 (Keke Rosberg)	- Italy 2015 (Kimi Räikkönen)
Argentina	82	70	3	Britain 1950 (Juan Manuel Fangio)	- Caesars Palace 1981 (Carlos Reutemann)
Austria	81	81	3	Belgium 1966 (Jochen Rindt)	- Germany 1997 (Gerhard Berger)
United States	75	71	8	Spain 1954 (Harry Schell)	- France 1983 (Eddie Cheever)
New Zealand	49	46	3	Britain 1960 (Bruce McLaren)	- Britain 1973 (Denny Hulme)
Spain	37	37	1	Malaysia 2003 (Fernando Alonso)	- Germany 2012 (Fernando Alonso)
Canada	31	31	2	United States West 1978 (Gilles Villeneuve)	- Italy 1998 (Jacques Villeneuve)
Sweden	31	31	3	Netherlands 1959 (Jo Bonnier)	- Germany 1985 (Stefan Johansson)
Belgium	29	29	4	Italy 1960 (Willy Mairesse)	- Hungary 1990 (Thierry Boutsen)
Colombia	26	26	1	Austria 2001 (Juan Pablo Montoya)	- Brazil 2005 (Juan Pablo Montoya)
Switzerland	26	25	2	Canada 1968 (Jo Siffert)	- Monaco 1976 (Clay Regazzoni)
South Africa	13	13	1	South Africa 1973 (Jody Scheckter)	- Monaco 1979 (Jody Scheckter)
Mexico	4	4	2	Italy 1961 (Ricardo Rodríguez)	- Netherlands 1971 (Pedro Rodríguez)
Poland	4	4	1	Australia 2008 (Robert Kubica)	- Monaco 2010 (Robert Kubica)
Japan	2	2	2	Europe 2004 (Takuma Sato)	- Belgium 2012 (Kamui Kobayashi)
Venezuela	2	2	1	Spain 2012 (Pastor Maldonado)	- Singapore 2012 (Pastor Maldonado)

Excludes Indianapolis 500.

380. Starting grid top three by drivers of the same nationality
(included in section 381)

Belgium 1952	I	Alberto Ascari, Giuseppe Farina, Piero Taruffi (a)
France 1952	I	Alberto Ascari, Giuseppe Farina, Piero Taruffi (a)
Britain 1952	I	Giuseppe Farina, Alberto Ascari, Piero Taruffi (a)
Italy 1952	I	Alberto Ascari, Luigi Villoresi, Giuseppe Farina (a)
France 1953	I	Alberto Ascari, Felice Bonetto, Luigi Villoresi (a)
Italy 1957	GB	Stuart Lewis-Evans, Stirling Moss, Tony Brooks (a)
Netherlands 1958	GB	Stuart Lewis-Evans, Stirling Moss, Tony Brooks (a)
Germany 1958	GB	Mike Hawthorn, Tony Brooks, Stirling Moss (a)
Portugal 1958	GB	Stirling Moss, Mike Hawthorn, Stuart Lewis-Evans (a)
Italy 1958	GB	Stirling Moss, Tony Brooks, Mike Hawthorn (a)
Morocco 1958	GB	Mike Hawthorn, Stirling Moss, Stuart Lewis-Evans (a)
Argentina 1960	GB	Stirling Moss, Innes Ireland, Graham Hill (a)
Netherlands 1962	GB	John Surtees, Graham Hill, Jim Clark (a)
Britain 1962	GB	Jim Clark, John Surtees, Innes Ireland (a)
Monaco 1963	GB	Jim Clark, Graham Hill, John Surtees
Italy 1963	GB	John Surtees, Graham Hill, Jim Clark
United States 1963	GB	Graham Hill, Jim Clark, John Surtees
Mexico 1963	GB	Jim Clark, John Surtees, Graham Hill
Austria 1964	GB	Graham Hill, John Surtees, Jim Clark (a)
Belgium 1965	GB	Graham Hill, Jim Clark, Jackie Stewart (a)
Germany 1965	GB	Jim Clark, Jackie Stewart, Graham Hill (a)
Italy 1965	GB	Jim Clark, John Surtees, Jackie Stewart (a)
Monaco 1966	GB	Jim Clark, John Surtees, Jackie Stewart
Germany 1966	GB	Jim Clark, John Surtees, Jackie Stewart (a)
South Africa 1968	GB	Jim Clark, Graham Hill, Jackie Stewart (a)
France 1980	F	Jacques Laffite, René Arnoux, Didier Pironi
Canada 1982	F	Didier Pironi, René Arnoux, Alain Prost
France 1982	F	René Arnoux, Alain Prost, Didier Pironi
Germany 1982	F	Didier Pironi, Alain Prost, René Arnoux
Britain 1983	F	René Arnoux, Patrick Tambay, Alain Prost
France 1997	D	Michael Schumacher, Heinz-Harald Frentzen, Ralf Schumacher

Excludes Indianapolis 500.
(a) All were on the front row of the grid.

by nationality

Great Britain (GB)	20	Italy 1957	- South Africa 1968
France (F)	5	France 1980	- Britain 1983
Italy (I)	5	Belgium 1952	- France 1953
Germany (D)	1	France 1997	

by drivers (Most)

Jim Clark, Graham Hill, John Surtees (GB)	6	Netherlands 1962	- Monaco 1963
René Arnoux, Didier Pironi, Alain Prost (F)	3	Canada 1982	- Germany 1982
Alberto Ascari, Giuseppe Farina, Piero Taruffi (I)	3	Belgium 1952	- Britain 1952
Jim Clark, Graham Hill, Jackie Stewart (GB)	3	Belgium 1965	- South Africa 1968
Jim Clark, Jackie Stewart, John Surtees (GB)	3	Italy 1965	- Germany 1966
Tony Brooks, Mike Hawthorn, Stirling Moss (GB)	2	Germany 1958	- Italy 1958
Tony Brooks, Stuart Lewis-Evans, Stirling Moss (GB)	2	Italy 1957	- Netherlands 1958
Mike Hawthorn, Stuart Lewis-Evans, Stirling Moss (GB)	2	Portugal 1958	- Morocco 1958

381. Front row 1-2s by drivers of the same nationality

by nationality

Argentina Juan Manuel Fangio, José Froilán González, 4
Brazil Nelson Piquet, Ayrton Senna, 6
France René Arnoux, Alain Prost, 12;
René Arnoux, Jean-Pierre Jabouille, 6;
René Arnoux, Patrick Tambay, 4;
Patrick Depailler, Jacques Laffite, 4;
René Arnoux, Jacques Laffite, 1;
René Arnoux, Didier Pironi, 1;
Jean-Pierre Jabouille, Didier Pironi, 1;
Jacques Laffite, Didier Pironi, 1;
Didier Pironi, Alain Prost, 1;
Alain Prost, Patrick Tambay, 1
Germany Michael Schumacher, Ralf Schumacher, 8;
Nico Rosberg, Sebastian Vettel, 6;
Heinz-Harald Frentzen, Michael Schumacher, 2;
Nico Hülkenberg, Sebastian Vettel, 1;
Nico Rosberg, Michael Schumacher, 1
Great Britain Jim Clark, Graham Hill, 17;
Jim Clark, John Surtees, 10;
David Coulthard, Damon Hill, 6;
Jenson Button, Lewis Hamilton, 4;

Tony Brooks, Stirling Moss, 3;
Graham Hill, John Surtees, 3;
James Hunt, John Watson, 3;
Jim Clark, Jackie Stewart, 2;
Mike Hawthorn, Stirling Moss, 2;
Stuart Lewis-Evans, Stirling Moss, 2;
Tony Brooks, Mike Hawthorm, 1;
Damon Hill, Nigel Mansell, 1;
Graham Hill, Jackie Oliver, 1;
Innes Ireland, Stirling Moss, 1
Italy Alberto Ascari, Giuseppe Farina, 5;
Giancarlo Fisichella, Jarno Trulli, 2;
Alberto Ascari, Felice Bonetto, 1;
Alberto Ascari, Luigi Villoresi, 1;
Michele Alboreto, Elio De Angelis, 1;
Elio De Angelis, Riccardo Patrese, 1;
Luigi Fagioli, Giuseppe Farina, 1;
Giuseppe Farina, Piero Taruffi, 1
New Zealand Chris Amon, Denny Hulme, 1
United States Richie Ginther, Phil Hill, 2

by drivers (Most)

Jim Clark, Graham Hill (GB)	17	Monaco 1962	- South Africa 1968
Réne Arnoux, Alain Prost (F)	12	Britain 1981	- Canada 1983
Jim Clark, John Surtees (GB)	10	Britain 1962	- Mexico 1966
Michael Schumacher, Ralf Schumacher (D)	8	Brazil 2001	- Japan 2004
René Arnoux, Jean-Pierre Jabouille (F)	6	France 1979	- Italy 1980
David Coulthard, Damon Hill (GB)	6	Argentina 1995	- Australia 1995
Nelson Piquet, Ayrton Senna (BR)	6	Europe 1985	- Mexico 1986
Nico Rosberg, Sebastian Vettel (D)	6	Bahrain 2013	- Hungary 2014
Alberto Ascari, Giuseppe Farina (I)	5	Belgium 1952	- Netherlands 1952
René Arnoux, Patrick Tambay (F)	4	United States West 1983	- Austria 1983
Jenson Button, Lewis Hamilton (GB)	4	Australia 2012	- Brazil 2012
Patrick Depailler, Jacques Laffite (F)	4	Argentian 1979	- Belgium 1979
Juan Manuel Fangio, José Froilán González (RA)	4	Britain 1951	- Switzerland 1954

Summary

Great Britain (GB)	56	Italy 1957 (S Lewis-Evans, S Moss)	- Brazil 2012 (L Hamilton, J Button)
France (F)	32	Argentina 1979 (J Laffite, P Depailler)	- Austria 1983 (P Tambay, R Arnoux)
Germany (D)	18	Monaco 1997 (H-H Frentzen, M Schumacher)	- Hungary 2014 (S Vettel, N Rosberg)
Italy (I)	13	Britain 1950 (G Farina, L Fagioli)	- Belgium 2009 (G Fisichella, J Trulli)
Brazil (BR)	6	Europe 1985 (A Senna, N Piquet)	- Mexico 1986 (A Senna, N Piquet)
Argentina (RA)	4	Britain 1951 (J F González, J M Fangio)	- Switzerland 1954 (J F González, J M Fangio)
United States (USA)	2	Italy 1960 (P Hill, R Ginther)	- Britain 1961 (P Hill, R Ginther)
New Zealand (NZ)	1	France 1972 (C Amon, D Hulme)	

Excludes Indianapolis 500.

382. Consecutive front row 1-2s by drivers of the same nationality *(Most)*

Italy	7	Switzerland - Italy 1952	Alberto Ascari, Giuseppe Farina, 5; Giuseppe Farina, Piero Taruffi, 1; Alberto Ascari, Luigi Villoresi, 1
Great Britain	7	Belgium - United States 1965	Graham Hill, Jim Clark, 4; Jim Clark, Jackie Stewart, 2; Jim Clark, John Surtees, 1
Great Britain	4	Germany - Morocco 1958	Stirling Moss, Mike Hawthorn, 2; Mike Hawthorn, Tony Brooks, 1; Stirling Moss, Tony Brooks, 1
Great Britain	4	Germany - Mexico 1963	Jim Clark, John Surtees, 2; John Surtees, Graham Hill, 1; Graham Hill, Jim Clark, 1
France	4	Britain - Netherlands 1981	René Arnoux, Alain Prost, 4
France	4	Canada - Austria 1983	René Arnoux, Patrick Tambay, 3; René Arnoux, Alain Prost, 1
Great Britain	3	Britain - Austria 1964	Jim Clark, Graham Hill, 1; John Surtees, Jim Clark, 1; Graham Hill, John Surtees, 1
France	3	Austria - Italy 1980	René Arnoux, Jean-Pierre Jabouille, 3
Brazil	3	Brazil - San Marino 1986	Ayrton Senna, Nelson Piquet, 3
Great Britain	3	Portugal - Pacific 1995	David Coulthard, Damon Hill, 3
Germany	3	Canada - France 2001	Michael Schumacher, Ralf Schumacher, 3

383. Complete front rows by drivers of the same nationality
(included in section 381 - some early races had more than two cars on the front row)

Great Britain	36	Netherlands 1958 (S Lewis-Evans, S Moss, T Brooks)	- Brazil 2012 (L Hamilton, J Button)
France	32	Argentina 1979 (J Laffite, P Depailler)	- Austria 1983 (P Tambay, R Arnoux)
Germany	18	Monaco 1997 (H-H Frentzen, M Schumacher)	- Hungary 2014 (N Rosberg, S Vettel)
Italy	7	Britain 1952 (A Ascari, G Farina, P Taruffi)	- Belgium 2009 (G Fisichella, J Trulli)
Brazil	6	Europe 1985 (A Senna, N Piquet)	- Mexico 1986 (A Senna, N Piquet)
New Zealand	1	France 1972 (C Amon, D Hulme)	

Excludes Indianapolis 500.

384. Front rows at the same venue *(Most)*

grand prix

Michael Schumacher	10	Japan	1994 - 2006	(Suzukua)
Michael Schumacher	9	France	1995 - 2006	(Magny-Cours)
Michael Schumacher	8	Canada	1994 - 2005	(Montréal)
Michael Schumacher	8	Hungary	1994 - 2005	(Hungaroring)
Michael Schumacher	8	Monaco	1993 - 2001	(Monte-Carlo)
Michael Schumacher	8	San Marino	1994 - 2006	(Imola)
Michael Schumacher	8	Spain	1992 - 2004	(Catalunya)
Ayrton Senna	8	San Marino	1985 - 94	(Imola)
Juan Manuel Fangio	7	Italy	1950 - 57	(Monza)
Lewis Hamilton	7	Canada	2007 - 15	(Montréal)
Graham Hill	7	Netherlands	1962 - 69	(Zandvoort)
Alain Prost	7	Belgium	1982 - 93	(Spa-Francorchamps, 6; Zolder, 1)
Alain Prost	7	France	1982 - 93	(Paul Ricard, 5; Magny-Cours, 2)
Alain Prost	7	Germany	1981 - 93	(Hockenheim)
Alain Prost	7	Monaco	1983 - 93	(Monte-Carlo)
Michael Schumacher	7	Europe	1994 - 2006	(Nürburgring, 5; Jerez de la Frontera, 2)
Ayrton Senna	7	Australia	1985 - 93	(Adelaide)
Jackie Stewart	7	Germany	1965 - 73	(Nürburgring)

circuit

Michael Schumacher	10	Suzuka	1994 - 2006
Michael Schumacher	9	Magny-Cours	1995 - 2006
Michael Schumacher	8	Catalunya	1992 - 2004
Michael Schumacher	8	Hungaroring	1994 - 2005
Michael Schumacher	8	Imola	1994 - 2006
Michael Schumacher	8	Monte-Carlo	1993 - 2001
Michael Schumacher	8	Montréal	1994 - 2005
Ayrton Senna	8	Imola	1985 - 94
Juan Manuel Fangio	7	Monza	1950 - 57
Lewis Hamilton	7	Montréal	2007 - 15
Graham Hill	7	Zandvoort	1962 - 69
Alain Prost	7	Hockenheim	1981 - 93
Alain Prost	7	Monte-Carlo	1983 - 93
Ayrton Senna	7	Adelaide	1985 - 93
Jackie Stewart	7	Nürburgring	1965 - 73

385. Consecutive front rows at the same venue *(Most)*

Ayrton Senna	7	San Marino	1985 - 91	(Imola)
Jim Clark	6	Germany	1962 - 67	(Nürburgring)
Jim Clark	6	United States	1962 - 67	(Watkins Glen)
Juan Manuel Fangio	6	Argentina	1953 - 58	(Buenos Aires No.2)
Michael Schumacher	6	Japan	1997 - 2002	(Suzuka)
Ayrton Senna	6	Australia	1988 - 93	(Adelaide)
Alberto Ascari	5	Italy	1950 - 54	(Monza)
Jim Clark	5	Mexico	1963 - 67	(Mexico City)
Jim Clark	5	Netherlands	1962 - 66	(Zandvoort)
Juan Manuel Fangio	5	Italy	1953 - 57	(Monza)
Jacky Ickx	5	Germany	1968 - 72	(Nürburgring, 4; Hockenheim, 1)
Stirling Moss	5	Britain	1954 - 58	(Silverstone, 3; Aintree, 2)
Juan Pablo Montoya	5	Italy	2001 - 05	(Monza)
Michael Schumacher	5	Monaco	1993 - 97	(Monte-Carlo)
Michael Schumacher	5	Spain	2000 - 04	(Catalunya)
Ayrton Senna	5	Belgium	1988 - 92	(Spa-Francorchamps)
Ayrton Senna	5	Canada	1985 - 90 (a)	(Montréal)
Ayrton Senna	5	Germany	1987 - 91	(Hockenheim)
Ayrton Senna	5	Italy	1988 - 92	(Monza)
Ayrton Senna	5	Monaco	1987 - 91	(Monte-Carlo)
John Surtees	5	Germany	1962 66	(Nürburgring)
Sebastian Vettel	5	Japan	2009 - 13	(Suzuka)

(a) No Canadian Grand Prix in 1987.

386. Front rows on home soil *(Most)*

Michael Schumacher	11	Germany	1995 - 2006 (a)	(Nürburgring, 6; Hockenheim, 5)
Alain Prost	8	France	1982 - 93 (b)	(Paul Ricard, 5; Magny-Cours, 2; Dijon-Prenois, 1)
Juan Manuel Fangio	6	Argentina	1953 - 58	(Buenos Aires no.2)
Graham Hill	6	Britain	1960 - 68	(Silverstone, 4; Brands Hatch, 2)
Ayrton Senna	6	Brazil	1986 - 94	(Interlagos, 3; Jacarepaguá, 3)
René Arnoux	5	France	1979 - 82 (c)	(Dijon-Prenois, 3; Paul Ricard, 2)
Alberto Ascari	5	Italy	1950 - 54	(Monza)
Jim Clark	5	Britain	1962 - 67	(Silverstone, 3; Aintree, 1; Brands Hatch, 1)
Damon Hill	5	Britain	1993 - 96 (d)	(Silverstone, 4; Donington, 1)
Nigel Mansell	5	Britain	1986 - 92	(Silverstone, 4; Brands Hatch, 1)
Stirling Moss	5	Britain	1954 - 58	(Silverstone, 3; Aintree, 2)
Ralf Schumacher	5	Germany	2001 - 03 (e)	(Hockenheim, 3; Nürburgring, 2)

(a) 5 German, 5 European & 1 Luxembourg Grands Prix.
(b) 7 French & 1 Swiss Grands Prix.
(c) 4 French & 1 Swiss Grands Prix.
(d) 4 British & 1 European Grands Prix.
(e) 3 German & 2 European Grands Prix.

387. First front row was on home soil

Mario Andretti	United States 1968	(Watkins Glen)		Jackie Oliver	Britain 1968	(Brands Hatch)
René Arnoux	France 1979	(Dijon-Prenois)		Reg Parnell	Britain 1950	(Silverstone)
Alberto Ascari	Italy 1950	(Monza)		Carlos Reutemann	Argentina 1972	(Buenos Aires No.9)
Tony Brooks	Britain 1957	(Aintree)		Daniel Ricciardo	Australia 2014	(Melbourne)
Olivier Gendebien	Belgium 1961	(Spa-Francorchamps)		Roy Salvadori	Britain 1958	(Silverstone)
Nick Heidfeld	Europe 2005	(Nürburgring)		Consalvo Sanesi	Italy 1950	(Monza)
Jacky Ickx	Belgium 1968	(Spa-Francorchamps)		Jody Scheckter	South Africa 1973	(Kyalami)
Stirling Moss	Britain 1954	(Silverstone)				

388. Two front rows on home soil in a season

Heinz-Harald Frentzen:	German Grand Prix (Hockenheim) & European Grand Prix (Nürburgring) in 1999.
Damon Hill:	British Grand Prix (Silverstone) & European Grand Prix (Donington Park) in 1993.
Alain Prost:	French Grand Prix (Paul Ricard) & Swiss Grand Prix (Dijon) in 1982.
Michael Schumacher:	German Grand Prix (Hockenheim) & European Grand Prix (Nürburgring) in 2000, 04 & 06.
Ralf Schumacher:	German Grand Prix (Hockenheim) & European Grand Prix (Nürburgring) in 2001 & 02.

389. Races taken to achieve their first front row
(number of races includes the race of first front row and all qualifying attempts)

Fewest

1st race

Mario Andretti	United States 1968 (a)	(pole)
Liugi Fagioli	Britain 1950	(2nd on grid)
Juan Manuel Fangio	Britain 1950	(3rd on grid)
Giuseppe Farina	Britain 1950	(pole)
José Froilán González	Monaco 1950	(3rd on grid)
Karl Kling	France 1954	(2nd on grid)
Reg Parnell	Britain 1950	(4th on grid)
Carlos Reutemann	Argentina 1972	(pole)
Ricardo Rodríguez	Italy 1961	(2nd on grid)
Consalvo Sanesi	Italy 1950	(4th on grid)
Jacques Villeneuve	Australia 1996	(pole)

2nd race

Dan Gurney	Germany 1959	(3rd on grid)
Jody Scheckter	South Africa 1973	(3rd on grid)
Johnny Servoz-Gavin	Monaco 1968	(2nd on grid)
Mike Parkes	France 1966 (b)	(3rd on grid)

3rd race

Eugenio Castellotti	Belgium 1955	(pole)
Lewis Hamilton	Bahrain 2007	(2nd on grid)
Willy Mairesse	Italy 1960	(3rd on grid)
Jackie Stewart	Belgium 1965	(3rd on grid)
John Surtees	Portugal 1960	(pole)

Most

Thierry Boutsen	116	Hungary 1990
Nick Heidfeld	91	Europe 2005
Eddie Irvine	80	Luxembourg 1998
Jean Alesi	76	Canada 1994
Nico Rosberg	73	Malaysia 2010
Elio De Angelis	72	Europe 1983
Jenson Button	71	San Marino 2004
Ralf Schumacher	69	Brazil 2001
Patrick Tambay	64	United States West 1983
Jo Siffert	63	Canada 1968
Alan Jones	61	Britain 1979
Keke Rosberg	59	Britain 1982
Felipe Massa	54	Bahrain 2006
Stefano Modena	53	Monaco 1991
Riccardo Patrese	53	United States West 1981
Jarno Trulli	53	Monaco 2000
Kamui Kobayashi	52	Belgium 2012
Nigel Mansell	51	Monaco 1984
Eddie Cheever	50	France 1983
Heinz-Harald Frentzen	50	Australia 1997

For most races started but never a front row, see section 187.

(a) This was the first race he started. He did enter one earlier, race (Italy 1968), but was excluded (in breach of regulations, having raced in another series in the United States within previous 24 hours).
(b) This was the first race that he started (he had failed to qualify at Britain 1959).

390. Front rows in their first season
(first season is defined as the first year to attempt qualification)

Lewis Hamilton	12	2007		José Froilán González	1	1950
Jacques Villeneuve	9	1996		Dan Gurney	1	1959
Juan Manuel Fangio	6	1950		Mike Hawthorn	1	1952
Giuseppe Farina	6	1950		Nico Hülkenberg	1	2010
Juan Pablo Montoya	5	2001		Karl Kling	1	1954
Jackie Stewart	5	1965		Stuart Lewis-Evans	1	1957
Luigi Fagioli	4	1950		Willy Mairesse	1	1960
Clay Regazzoni	2	1970		Reg Parnell	1	1950
Mario Andretti	1	1968		Carlos Reutemann	1	1972
Alberto Ascari	1	1950		Ricardo Rodríguez	1	1961
Eugenio Castellotti	1	1955		Consalvo Sanesi	1	1950
Richie Ginther	1	1960		John Surtees	1	1960

Mike Parkes achieved two front rows in his first season of starting (in 1966), but made his debut in 1959, with a non-qualification.

391. Front row in the first two or more races of their career

Giuseppe Farina	22	Britain 1950	- Netherlands 1953	(Alfa Romeo 158, 159, Ferrari 500)
Juan Manuel Fangio	16	Britain 1950	- Belgium 1953	(Alfa Romeo 158, 159, Maserati A6GCM)

Excludes Indianapolis 500.

392. First front row immediately followed by others
(including first front row)

Giuseppe Farina	22	Britain 1950 - Netherlands 1953	(Alfa Romeo 158, 159, Ferrari 500)
Juan Manuel Fangio	13	Britain 1950 - Spain 1951	(Alfa Romeo 158, 159)
Ayrton Senna	6	Portugal - France 1985	(Lotus 97T - Renault)
Peter Collins	4	Belgium - Germany 1956	(Lancia-Ferrari D50)
Damon Hill	4	Brazil - Spain 1993	(Williams FW15C - Renault)
Alan Jones	4	Britain - Netherlands 1979	(Williams FW07 - Ford Cosworth)
Stirling Moss	4	Britain - Italy 1954	(Maserati 250F)
Piero Taruffi	4	Switzerland - Britain 1952	(Ferrari 500)
Jackie Stewart	3	Belgium - Britain 1965	(BRM P261)
Wolfgang von Trips	3	Netherlands - France 1961	(Ferrari 156)
Denny Hulme	2	Britain - Netherlands 1966	(Brabham BT20 - Repco)
Jean-Pierre Jarier	2	Argentina - Brazil 1975	(Shadow DN5 - Ford Cosworth)
Niki Lauda	2	South Africa - Spain 1974	(Ferrari 312B3)
Peter Revson	2	Canada - United States 1972	(McLaren M19C - Ford Cosworth)
Ludovico Scarfiotti	2	Germany - Italy 1966	(Ferrari 246, 312)
Luigi Villoresi	2	Switzerland - Belgium 1951	(Ferrari 375)

393. Races where more than one driver achieved their maiden front row

Britain 1950	1: Giuseppe Farina (Alfa Romeo), 2: Luigi Fagioli (Alfa Romeo), 3: Juan Manuel Fangio (Alfa Romeo), 4: Reg Parnell (Alfa Romeo) (4 car front row)
Italy 1950	2: Alberto Ascari (Ferrari), 4: Consalvo Sanesi (Alfa Romeo) (4 car front row)
Switzerland 1952	2: Piero Taruffi (Ferrari), 3 Robert Manzon (Gordini) (3 car front row)
Argentina 1960	2: Innes Ireland (Lotus), 3: Graham Hill (BRM) (4 car front row)
Italy 1960	2: Richie Ginther (Ferrari), 3: Willy Mairesse (Ferrari) (3 car front row)
Canada 1972	1: Peter Revson (McLaren), 3: Ronnie Peterson (March) (3 car front row)
South Africa 1974	1: Niki Lauda (Ferrari), 2: Carlos Pace (Surtees) (2 car front row)
Germany 1985	1: Teo Fabi (Toleman), 2: Stefan Johansson (Ferrari) (2 car front row)

394. Front row in their final race

Alberto Ascari	Monaco 1955	(2nd on grid)	killed at Monza, four days after this race
Lorenzo Bandini	Monaco 1967	(2nd)	killed in this race
Eugenio Castellotti	Argentina 1957	(4th)	killed two months later, prior to next F1 race
Jim Clark	South Africa 1968	(pole)	killed in Formula 2 event, prior to next F1 race
Peter Collins	Germany 1958	(4th)	killed in this race
Mike Hawthorn	Morocco 1958	(pole)	retired from F1
Karl Kling	Italy 1955	(3rd)	retired from F1
Stuart Lewis-Evans	Morocco 1958	(3rd)	died from injuries in this race
Luigi Musso	France 1958	(2nd)	killed in this race
Carlos Pace	South Africa 1977	(2nd)	killed in aircraft accident prior to next F1 race
Didier Pironi	Germany 1982	(pole)	non-starter: injured in qualifying, ending F1 career
Alain Prost	Australia 1993	(2nd)	retired from F1
Jochen Rindt	Austria 1970	(pole)	killed in qualifying for next F1 race, in Italy
Ayrton Senna	San Marino 1994	(pole)	killed in this race
Wolfgang von Trips	Italy 1961	(pole)	killed in this race

Excludes Indianapolis 500.

395. Front rows in their final season *(Most)*

Alain Prost	16	1993		Jackie Stewart	4	1973
Mike Hawthorn	8	1958		Wolfgang von Trips	4	1961
Ronnie Peterson	6	1978		Jack Brabham	3	1970
Jochen Rindt	5	1970		Mika Häkkinen	3	2001
Mark Webber	5	2013		Ayrton Senna	3	1994
Stuart Lewis-Evans	4	1958		Jo Siffert	3	1971

396. Different front row drivers in a season

Most

1968	14		1966	10
1960	12		1973	10
2009	12		1982	10
1958	11		2004	10
1975	11		2005	10
1959	10		2012	10
1961	10			

Fewest

1989	4		1996	5
1992	4		2007	5
1993	4		2011	5
1951	5		2015	5
1987	5			
1988	5			
1995	5			

Total for each season

1950 - 7, 1951 - 5, 1952 - 7, 1953 - 7, 1954 - 8, 1955 - 7, 1956 - 7, 1957 - 9, 1958 - 11, 1959 - 10, 1960 - 12, 1961 - 10, 1962 - 8, 1963 - 8, 1964 - 6, 1965 - 8, 1966 - 10, 1967 - 9, 1968 - 14, 1969 - 8, 1970 - 9, 1971 - 9, 1972 - 9, 1973 - 10, 1974 - 9, 1975 - 11, 1976 - 9, 1977 - 9, 1978 - 9, 1979 - 9, 1980 - 8, 1981 - 9, 1982 - 10, 1983 - 8, 1984 - 8, 1985 - 9, 1986 - 7, 1987 - 5, 1988 - 5, 1989 - 4, 1990 - 7, 1991 - 6, 1992 - 4, 1993 - 4, 1994 - 8, 1995 - 5, 1996 - 5, 1997 - 7, 1998 - 7, 1999 - 7, 2000 - 6, 2001 - 6, 2002 - 6, 2003 - 8, 2004 - 10, 2005 - 10, 2006 - 7, 2007 - 5, 2008 - 9, 2009 - 12, 2010 - 9, 2011 - 5, 2012 - 10, 2013 - 6, 2014 - 6, 2015 - 5

Excludes Indianapolis 500.

397. First time front row drivers in a season

Most

1950	7	Giuseppe Farina, Luigi Fagioli, Juan Manuel Fangio, Reg Parnell, José Froilán González, Alberto Ascari, Consalvo Sanesi
1960	6	Innes Ireland, Graham Hill, Bruce McLaren, John Surtees, Richie Ginther, Willy Mairesse
1968	6	Pedro Rodríguez, Johnny Serviz-Gavin, Jacky Ickx, Jackie Oliver, Jo Siffert, Mario Andretti
1952	4	Piero Taruffi, Robert Manzon, Maurice Trintignant, Mike Hawthorn
1959	4	Jo Bonnier, Phil Hill, Dan Gurney, Masten Gregory
1961	4	Jim Clark, Wolfgang von Trips, Olivier Gendebien, Ricardo Rodríguez
1966	4	Jochen Rindt, Mike Parkes, Denny Hulme, Ludovico Scarfiotti
1974	4	Niki Lauda, Carlos Pace, Patrick Depailler, James Hunt
1979	4	Jean-Pierre Jabouille, René Arnoux, Alan Jones, Nelson Piquet

Fewest (none)

1964, 87, 88, 89, 99, 2011, 13, 15

Excludes Indianapolis 500.

398. Front rows with the same constructor *(Most)*

Michael Schumacher	91	Ferrari	Argentina 1996	- Japan 2006
Sebastian Vettel	66	Red Bull	China 2009	- Hungary 2014
Ayrton Senna	61	McLaren	Brazil 1988	- Australia 1993
Nigel Mansell	51	Williams	Monaco 1985	- Australia 1994
Jim Clark	48	Lotus	Monaco 1961	- South Africa 1968
Lewis Hamilton	48	McLaren	Bahrain 2007	- Brazil 2012
Damon Hill	47	Williams	Brazil 1993	- Japan 1996
Alain Prost	43	McLaren	San Marino 1984	- Australia 1989
Lewis Hamilton	42	Mercedes-Benz	China 2013	- Abu Dhabi 2015
Nico Rosberg	40	Mercedes-Benz	Malaysia 2010	- Abu Dhabi 2015

For complete list of front row drivers by constructor, see section 844.

399. Front row 1-2s as team-mates *(Most)*
(until 1973, front rows could contain more than two cars)

Lewis Hamilton, Nico Rosberg	30	Spain 2013	- Abu Dhabi 2015	(Mercedes-Benz)
Alain Prost, Ayrton Senna	23	San Marino 1988	- Australia 1989	(McLaren)
Sebastian Vettel, Mark Webber	23	Australia 2010	- United States 2013	(Red Bull)
David Coulthard, Mika Häkkinen	18	Australia 1998	- San Marino 2001	(McLaren)
Rubens Barrichello, Michael Schumacher	15	Italy 2000	- Hungary 2004	(Ferrari)
Damon Hill, Alain Prost	12	Brazil 1993	- Portugal 1993	(Williams)
Nigel Mansell, Riccardo Patrese	12	Canada 1991	- Japan 1992	(Williams)
René Arnoux, Alain Prost	10	Britain 1981	- Caesars Palace 1982	(Renault)
Damon Hill, Jacques Villeneuve	9	Australia 1996	- Japan 1996	(Williams)
Juan Manuel Fangio, Giuseppe Farina	8	Monaco 1950	- Italy 1951	(Alfa Romeo)
Niki Lauda, Clay Regazzoni	8	Monaco 1974	- Monaco 1976	(Ferrari)
Nigel Mansell, Nelson Piquet	8	Britain 1986	- Spain 1987	(Williams)
Gerhard Berger, Ayrton Senna	8	Brazil 1990	- Australia 1991	(McLaren)

400. Consecutive front row 1-2s as team-mates *(Most)*

Lewis Hamilton, Nico Rosberg	9	Belgium 2014	- Australia 2015	(Mercedes-Benz F1 W05, F1 W06)
Alain Prost, Ayrton Senna	8	San Marino 1989	- Germany 1989	(McLaren MP4/5 - Honda)
Damon Hill, Alain Prost	8	Canada 1993	- Portugal 1993	(Williams FW15C - Renault)
Lewis Hamilton, Nico Rosberg	7	Spain 2015	- Belgium 2015	(Mercedes-Benz F1 W06)
Lewis Hamilton, Nico Rosberg	6	Japan 2015	- Abu Dhabi 2015	(Mercedes-Benz F1 W06)
Alain Prost, Ayrton Senna	6	Belgium 1988	- Australia 1988	(McLaren MP4/4 - Honda)
Alberto Ascari, Giuseppe Farina	5	Belgium 1952	- Netherlands 1952	(Ferrari 500)
Juan Manuel Fangio, Giuseppe Farina	4	Monaco 1950	- France 1950	(Alfa Romeo 158)
Mario Andretti, Ronnie Peterson	4	Britain 1978	- Netherlands 1978	(JPS Lotus 79 - Ford Cosworth)
René Arnoux, Alain Prost	4	Britain 1981	- Netherlands 1981	(Renault RE30)
Alain Prost, Ayrton Senna	4	San Marino 1988	- Canada 1988	(McLaren MP4/4 - Honda)
Nigel Mansell, Riccardo Patrese	4	France 1992	- Hungary 1992	(Williams FW14B - Renault)
Damon Hill, Alain Prost	4	Brazil 1993	- Spain 1993	(Williams FW15C - Renault)
Damon Hill, Jacques Villeneuve	4	Belgium 1996	- Japan 1996	(Williams FW18 - Renault)
David Coulthard, Mika Häkkinen	4	San Marino 1998	- Canada 1998	(McLaren MP4-13 - Mercedes)

401. Front row 1-2s as team-mates in a season *(Most)*

Lewis Hamilton, Nico Rosberg	15 of 19	2015	(Mercedes-Benz F1 W06)
Alain Prost, Ayrton Senna	12 of 16	1988	(McLaren MP4/4 - Honda)
Damon Hill, Alain Prost	12 of 16	1993	(Williams FW15C - Renault)
Lewis Hamilton, Nico Rosberg	12 of 19	2014	(Mercedes-Benz F1 W05)
Alain Prost, Ayrton Senna	11 of 16	1989	(McLaren MP4/5 - Honda)
Nigel Mansell, Riccardo Patrese	10 of 16	1992	(Williams FW14B - Renault)
Damon Hill, Jacques Villeneuve	9 of 16	1996	(Williams FW18 - Renault)
David Coulthard, Mika Häkkinen	9 of 16	1998	(McLaren MP4-13 - Mercedes)
Sebastian Vettel, Mark Webber	8 of 19	2010	(Red Bull RB6 - Renault)
Sebastian Vettel, Mark Webber	7 of 19	2011	(Red Bull RB7 - Renault)

402. Complete front row of drivers who had not won by that time

Britain 1950	Giuseppe Farina, Luigi Fagioli, Juan Manuel Fangio, Reg Parnell	Sweden 1975	Vittorio Brambilla, Patrick Depailler
		France 1979	Jean-Pierre Jabouille, René Arnoux
Italy 1960	Phil Hill, Richie Ginther, Willy Mairesse	Germany 1985	Teo Fabi, Stefan Johansson
Netherlands 1962	John Surtees, Graham Hill, Jim Clark	Austria 1986	Teo Fabi, Gerhard Berger
South Africa 1974	Niki Lauda, Carlos Pace	Malaysia 2003	Fernando Alonso, Jarno Trulli
Sweden 1974	Patrick Depailler, Jody Scheckter	Monaco 2004	Jarno Trulli, Jenson Button
Argentina 1975	Jean-Pierre Jarier, Carlos Pace	Britain 2008	Heikki Kovalainen, Mark Webber

403. Front rows to race retirement (Most)

Ayrton Senna	28	San Marino 1985	- San Marino 1994
Alain Prost	22	Britain 1981	- Italy 1993
Jim Clark	20	Monaco 1962	- Canada 1967
Nigel Mansell	20	Monaco 1984	- France 1994
Nelson Piquet	19	United States 1979	- Belgium 1987
Graham Hill	18	Argentina 1960	- Spain 1969
Michael Schumacher	18	Monaco 1993	- China 2012 (a)
Stirling Moss	17	Britain 1954	- Argentina 1960 (b)
René Arnoux	14	Netherlands 1979	- Detroit 1983
Mika Häkkinen	14	Monaco 1994	- Spain 2001

(a) Plus 1 race non-started (engine failure on the parade lap at France 1996).
(b) At Britain 1957, Moss retired and then took over his team-mate's car and won the race (counted here as a retirement).
Includes cases of retirements but classified (ie completed 90% of race distance).

404. Consecutive races with a front row to retirement (Most)

Alberto Ascari	4	Italy 1954	- Monaco 1955	(Ferrari 625, Lancia D50)
Jim Clark	4	Italy 1965	- Monaco 1966	(Lotus 33 - Climax)
Graham Hill	4	Netherlands 1967	- Britain 1967	(Lotus 49 - Ford Cosworth)
Niki Lauda	4	Germany 1974	- Canada 1974	(Ferrari 312B3)
Ayrton Senna	4	United States 1989	- Britain 1989	(McLaren MP4/5 - Honda)
Chris Amon	3	Germany 1968	- Canada 1968	(Ferrari 312)
René Arnoux	3	San Marino 1982	- Monaco 1982	(Renault RE30B)
Eugenio Castellotti	3	Germany 1956	- Argentina 1957	(Lancia-Ferrari D50, 801)
Juan Manuel Fangio	3	Argentina 1953	- Belgium 1953	(Maserati A6GCM)
Giuseppe Farina	3	Britain 1951	- Italy 1951	(Alfa Romeo 159)
Nigel Mansell	3	Japan 1992	- France 1994 (a)	(Williams FW14B, FW16 - Renault)
Juan Pablo Montoya	3	Monaco 2002	- Europe 2002	(Williams FW24 - BMW)
Stirling Moss	3	Britain 1954	- Switzerland 1954	(Maserati 250F)
Jochen Rindt	3	South Africa 1969	- Netherlands 1969 (a)	(Lotus 49B - Ford Cosworth)
Ayrton Senna	3	Spain 1990	- Australia 1990	(McLaren MP4/5B - Honda)
Ayrton Senna	3	Brazil 1994	- San Marino 1994	(Williams FW16B - Renault)
Jackie Stewart	3	Canada 1970	- Mexico 1970	(Tyrrell 001 - Ford Cosworth)
John Surtees	3	Germany 1965	- Monaco 1966 (a)	(Ferrari 1512, 312)

(a) Consecutive races started but not consecutive events.

405. Front row to race retirement before end of first lap

Giuseppe Farina	Monaco 1950	(Alfa Romeo 158): accident
José Froilán González	Monaco 1950	(Maserati 4CLT/48): accident/ fire
Peter Collins	Argentina 1958	(Ferrari Dino 246): driveshaft
Stirling Moss	Belgium 1958	(Vanwall VW10/57): valves
Tony Brooks	Italy 1959	(Ferrari Dino 246): clutch
Graham Hill	France 1960	(BRM P48): accident
Jack Brabham	Germany 1961	(Cooper T58 - Climax): throttle jammed/ accident
Lorenzo Bandini	Germany 1963	(BRM P57): accident
Graham Hill	Italy 1964	(BRM P261): clutch
Jackie Stewart	Belgium 1966	(BRM P261): accident/ injury
Jack Brabham	Monaco 1967	(Brabham BT19 - Repco): engine
Ronnie Peterson	Germany 1973	(JPS Lotus 72E - Ford Cosworth): distributor
Niki Lauda	Germany 1974	(Ferrari 312B3): accident
Niki Lauda	Spain 1975	(Ferrari 312T): accident
Niki Lauda	Germany 1976	(Ferrari 312T2): accident/ injury (a)
Mario Andretti	Belgium 1977	(JPS Lotus 78 - Ford Cosworth): accident
John Watson	Belgium 1977	(Brabham BT45B - Alfa Romeo): accident
Mario Andretti	Austria 1978	(JPS Lotus 79 - Ford Cosworth): accident

Riccardo Patrese	Britain 1982	(Brabham BT50 - BMW): stalled on grid/ accident
Ayrton Senna	France 1989	(McLaren MP4/5 - Honda): differential
Alain Prost	Australia 1989	(McLaren MP4/5 - Honda): withdrew (a)
Alain Prost	Japan 1990	(Ferrari 641/2): accident
Ayrton Senna	Japan 1990	(McLaren MP4/5B - Honda): accident
Ayrton Senna	Pacific 1994	(Williams FW16 - Renault): accident
Mika Häkkinen	Monaco 1994	(McLaren MP4/9 - Peugeot): accident
Jean Alesi	Germany 1994	(Ferrari 412T1B): electrics
Michael Schumacher	Monaco 1996	(Ferrari F310): accident
Jacques Villeneuve	Australia 1997	(Williams FW19 - Renault): accident
Heinz-Harald Frentzen	Britain 1997	(Williams FW19 - Renault): accident
Mika Häkkinen	Canada 1998	(McLaren MP4-13 - Mercedes): gearbox
Mika Häkkinen	Belgium 1998	(McLaren MP4-13 - Mercedes): accident
Michael Schumacher	Britain 1999	(Ferrari F399): accident/ injury (a)
Michael Schumacher	Germany 2000	(Ferrari F1 2000): accident
Rubens Barrichello	Italy 2000	(Ferrari F1 2000): accident
Rubens Barrichello	Australia 2002	(Ferrari F2001): accident
Indianapolis 500		
Ed Elisian	1958	(Watson - Offenhauser): accident
Dick Rathmann	1958	(Watson - Offenhauser): accident

(a) Race was stopped with the driver only starting the initial race and not the race proper (these situations are still regarded as race starts).

failure before the race started

Jean-Pierre Jarier	Argentina 1975	(Shadow DN5 - Ford Cosworth): crown wheel & pinion failure on the parade lap
Didier Pironi	Germany 1982	(Ferrari 126C2): injury from accident in qualifying which ended his career
Michael Schumacher	France 1996	(Ferrari F310): engine failure on the parade lap
Rubens Barrichello	Spain 2002	(Ferrari F2002): gearbox failure at start of the parade lap
Jarno Trulli	United States 2005	(Toyota TF105) &
Kimi Räikkönen	United States 2005	(McLaren MP4-20 - Mercedes): withdrawn on the parade lap along with all other Michelin runners, due to tyre safety concerns

406. Complete front row eliminated on first lap

| Belgium 1977 at Zolder: | pole-sitter Mario Andretti (JPS Lotus 78) and second on the grid, John Watson (Brabham BT45B) retired on the first lap when Andretti ran into Watson who had led from the first corner. |
| Japan 1990 at Suzuka: | Ayrton Senna (McLaren MP4/5B) in pole and Alain Prost (Ferrari 641/2) in second place came together at the first corner. |

Whilst two front row cars retired on the first lap at Monaco 1950 (José Froilán González & Giuseppe Farina) in an accident, the row consisted of three cars, of which pole-sitter Fangio went on to win the race.

407. Only front rows were pole positions

| Teo Fabi | 3 | Thierry Boutsen | 1 | Bruno Giacomelli | 1 |
| Jean-Pierre Jarier | 3 | Vittorio Brambilla | 1 | Nico Hülkenberg | 1 |

408. Interval between front rows *(Longest)*

	years, days	races		
Mario Andretti	7y, 251d	99	United States 1968 (Lotus)	- Sweden 1976 (JPS Lotus)
Giancarlo Fisichella	6y, 223d	108	Austria 1998 (Benetton)	- Australia 2005 (Renault)
Michael Schumacher	5y, 190d	94	Japan 2006 (Ferrari)	- China 2012 (Mercedes-Benz)
Riccardo Patrese	5y, 182d	82	Europe 1983 (Brabham)	- Brazil 1989 (Williams)
Rubens Barrichello	4y, 156d	73	Brazil 2004 (Ferrari)	- Australia 2009 (Brawn)
Bruce McLaren	4y, 79d	45	Netherlands 1963 (Cooper)	- Italy 1967 (McLaren)
Niki Lauda	4y, 31d	60	South Africa 1978 (Brabham)	- United States West 1982 (McLaren)
Mario Andretti	3y, 346d	60	United States 1978 (JPS Lotus)	- Italy 1982 (Ferrari)
Kimi Räikkönen	3y, 325d	72	Monaco 2009 (Ferrari)	- China 2013 (Lotus)
Jean-Pierre Jarier	3y, 255d	61	Brazil 1975 (Shadow)	- Canada 1978 (JPS Lotus)
Harry Schell	3y, 255d	29	Spain 1954 (Maserati)	- France 1958 (BRM)

Did not necessarily start every race during the period.

409. Interval between first & last front rows (Longest)

	years, days	races		
Michael Schumacher	19y, 348d	341	Spain 1992	- China 2012
Rubens Barrichello	15y, 51d	260	Belgium 1994	- Brazil 2009
Mario Andretti	13y, 341d	200	United States 1968	- Italy 1982
Kimi Räikkönen	13y, 5d	234	Belgium 2002	- Italy 2015
Alain Prost	12y, 209d	203	Argentina 1981	- Australia 1993
Jack Brabham	12y, 61d	125	Monaco 1958	- Britain 1970
Giancarlo Fisichella	12y, 34d	208	Germany 1997	- Belgium 2009
Riccardo Patrese	11y, 224d	188	United States West 1981	- Japan 1992
Gerhard Berger	11y, 63d	182	Belgium 1986	- Germany 1997
Nigel Mansell	10y, 163d	170	Monaco 1984	- Australia 1994

410. Interval between front row drivers of the same nationality (Longest)

	years, days	races		
Australia	23y, 210d	358	Caesars Palace 1981 (Alan Jones)	- Malaysia 2004 (Mark Webber)
Belgium	17y, 182d	272	Brazil 1973 (Jacky Ickx)	- Hungary 1990 (Thierry Boutsen)
Germany	16y, 22d	194	Italy 1961 (Wolfgang von Trips)	- United States 1977 (Hans-Joachim Stuck)
Germany	15y, 152d	225	United States 1977 (Hans-Joachim Stuck)	- Spain 1992 (Michael Schumacher)
Argentina	14y, 4d	144	Argentina 1958 (Juan Manuel Fangio)	- Argentina 1972 (Carlos Reutemann)
Canada	13y, 355d	223	Brazil 1982 (Gilles Villeneuve)	- Australia 1996 (Jacques Villeneuve)
France	13y, 32d	232	France 1999 (Jean Alesi)	- Hungary 2012 (Romain Grosjean)
Sweden	11y, 49d	119	Germany 1961 (Jo Bonnier)	- Canada 1972 (Ronnie Peterson)
France	9y, 16d	88	Monaco 1959 (Jean Behra)	- Monaco 1968 (Johnny Servoz-Gavin)
Australia	8y, 361d	131	Britain 1970 (Jack Brabham)	- Britain 1979 (Alan Jones)

411. Interval between first time front row drivers (Longest)

3 years and 290 days from Belgium 1986 (25 May, Gerhard Berger) until United States 1990 (11 March, Pierluigi Martini).

412. Front rows but never a world championship (Most)

Nico Rosberg	40	René Arnoux	34	Felipe Massa	27
David Coulthard	37	Rubens Barrichello	34	Juan Pablo Montoya	26
Stirling Moss	37	Gerhard Berger	32		
Mark Webber	37	Riccardo Patrese	28		

413. Front rows but never a win (Most)

Chris Amon	19	Harry Schell	5	Karl Kling	3
Jean Behra	10	Luigi Villoresi	5	Robert Manzon	3
Eugenio Castellotti	7	Teo Fabi	3		
Stuart Lewis-Evans	5	Jean-Pierre Jarier	3		

414. Front rows but never a podium

Nico Hülkenberg	1	Ricardo Rodríguez	1	Adrian Sutil	1
Pierluigi Martini	1	Canselvo Sanesi	1		

415. Front rows but never a pole position (Most)

Jean Behra	10	Luigi Musso	6	Eddie Irvine	4
Peter Collins	8	Harry Schell	5	Piero Taruffi	4
Richie Ginther	8	Luigi Villoresi	5		
Bruce McLaren	7	Luigi Fagioli	4		

416. Front rows but never led

Robert Manzon	3	Kamui Kobayashi	1	Consalvo Sanesi	1
Teo Fabi	3	Stefano Modena	1	Adrian Sutil	1
Roy Salvadori	2	Reg Parnell	1		
Eddie Cheever	1	Ricardo Rodríguez	1		

417. Milestones: Front rows I

Michael Schumacher	25th: Argentina 1996, 50th: Europe 2000, 75th: Brazil 2002, 100th: Germany 2004
Lewis Hamilton	25th: Abu Dhabi 2009, 50th: Spain 2013, 75th: China 2015
Alain Prost	25th: Germany 1984, 50th: Japan 1988, 75th: Spain 1993
Ayrton Senna	25th: San Marino 1988, 50th: Italy 1989, 75th: Japan 1991
Nigel Mansell	25th: Italy 1987, 50th: Belgium 1992
Sebastian Vettel	25th: Malaysia 2011, 50th: Australia 2013
Fernando Alonso	25th: Europe 2007
René Arnoux	25th: Caesars Palace 1982
Alberto Ascari	25th: Monaco 1955
Rubens Barrichello	25th: United States 2004
Gerhard Berger	25th: Australia 1991
Jack Brabham	25th: Britain 1966
Jim Clark	25th: Mexico 1964
David Coulthard	25th: Brazil 2000
Juan Manuel Fangio	25th: Germany 1954
Giuseppe Farina	25th: Italy 1953
Mika Häkkinen	25th: Hungary 1999
Damon Hill	25th: Britain 1995
Graham Hill	25th: Monaco 1965
Jacky Ickx	25th: Brazil 1973
Niki Lauda	25th: France 1976
Felipe Massa	25th: Bahrain 2010
Juan Pablo Montoya	25th: Belgium 2005
Stirling Moss	25th: Morocco 1958
Riccardo Patrese	25th: Germany 1992
Ronnie Peterson	25th: Netherlands 1978
Nelson Piquet	25th: Europe 1984
Kimi Räikkönen	25th: China 2007
Nico Rosberg	25th: Abu Dhabi 2014
Jackie Stewart	25th: Mexico 1970
Mark Webber	25th: India 2011

418. Milestones: Front rows II
(eg the 300th front row position was achieved by Jack Brabham)

1st	Giuseppe Farina (Alfa Romeo 158)	Britain 1950
100th	Mike Hawthorn (Ferrari 625)	Argentina 1954
200th	Tony Brooks (Vanwall VW7/57)	Netherlands 1958
300th	Jack Brabham (Cooper T58)	United States 1961
400th	Jim Clark (Lotus 33)	Netherlands 1965
500th	Jo Siffert (Lotus 49B)	Mexico 1968
600th	Emerson Fittipaldi (JPS Lotus 72D)	Belgium 1972
700th	Niki Lauda (Ferrari 312T)	France 1975
800th	Ronnie Peterson (JPS Lotus 79)	Austria 1978
900th	Alain Prost (Renault RE30B)	Brazil 1982
1,000th	Elio De Angelis (Lotus 97T)	Canada 1985
1,100th	Alain Prost (McLaren MP4/4)	France 1988
1,200th	Nigel Mansell (Williams FW14)	Germany 1991
1,300th	Rubens Barrichello (Jordan 194)	Belgium 1994
1,400th	Jacques Villeneuve (Williams FW19)	Belgium 1997
1,500th	Mika Häkkinen (McLaren MP4-15)	Belgium 2000
1,600th	Juan Pablo Montoya (Williams FW25)	Germany 2003
1,700th	Fernando Alonso (Renault R26)	Canada 2006
1,800th	Jenson Button (BGP 001)	Monaco 2009
1,900th	Lewis Hamilton (McLaren MP4-27)	Australia 2012
2,000th	Nico Rosberg (Mercedes-Benz F1 W05)	Belgium 2014

Excludes Indianapolis 500. Includes drivers who qualified on the front row but failed to take up their position (see section 405).

419. Milestones: Front rows III

1st	Giuseppe Farina	50th	Jackie Oliver	100th	Jacques Villeneuve
20th	Peter Collins	60th	Jody Scheckter	120th	Nico Rosberg
40th	Lorenzo Bandini	80th	Andrea De Cesaris		

Excludes Indianapolis 500.

Alberto Ascari (Ferrari 375 "Camelli") at Monza in the 1951 Italian Grand Prix - the second of his two victories that season (The GP Library).

Jose Froilán González whose most successful season was 1951, with the Ferrari 375 (The GP Library).

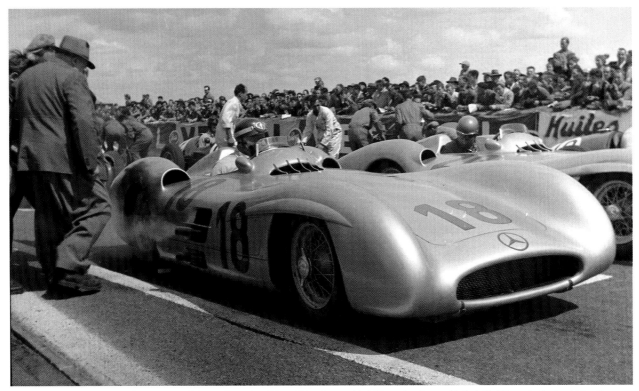

The start of the 1954 French Grand Prix at Reims, where Juan Manuel Fangio provided Mercedes-Benz with their first Formula 1 win, driving the W196 Streamliner (The GP Library).

The Gordini T16 of Jean Behra at Silverstone for the 1954 British Grand Prix. He was one of seven drivers to share fastest lap of the race (The GP Library).

Stirling Moss who achieved his first win at the 1955 British Grand Prix (Mercedes-Benz W196) (The GP Library).

Eugenio Castellotti (Lancia D50) in 1955 at Monaco, where he finished second, his best career result (The GP Library).

Juan Manuel Fangio in conversation with Enzo Ferrari in 1956. He achieved five wins for the team that season in the Lancia-Ferrari D50 (The GP Library).

Mike Hawthorn and Peter Collins sharing a joke at Aintree (1957 British Grand Prix). The following year, Hawthorn would be world champion, and Collins was killed at the German Grand Prix (The GP Library).

Stirling Moss and Mike Hawthorn at Silverstone in 1958. Hawthorn was second in a 1-2 with team-mate Peter Collins, whilst Moss' Vanwall retired with engine failure after 25 laps (The GP Library).

Jack Brabham at the 1960 Belgian Grand Prix. He won in the Cooper T53, the fourth victory of his career (The GP Library).

Wolfgang von Trips (Ferrari 156 "Sharknose") on his way to winning the 1961 British Grand Prix at Aintree (The GP Library).

American, Phil Hill, the 1961 world champion in a Ferrari (The GP Library).

Wolfgang von Trips in the Ferrari 156 and Dan Gurney (Porsche 718) preparing for the 1961 Italian Grand Prix. It was here that von Trips was killed on the second lap. Gurney finished second (The GP Library).

The Rodríguez brothers: Ricardo who began his career in 1961 and was killed the following year, and Pedro who made his debut in 1963. They are seen here with their father (The GP Library).

Graham Hill in the BRM P57, having problems at the start of the German Grand Prix in 1963. He achieved a couple of victories that season (The GP Library).

Swiss driver, Jo Siffert, in the Scuderia Filipinetti Lotus 24 - BRM (1963) (The GP Library).

Stirling Moss interviews Phil Hill, who was driving for Cooper (1964) (The GP Library).

Jim Clark (Lotus), the 1963 and 1965 world champion.

Jackie Stewart, who won the first of his three world titles in 1969.

Emerson Fittipaldi, world champion in 1972 and 1974.

Lotus team chief, Colin Chapman, chats to an unhappy Jochen Rindt and Dick Scammel, their Racing Manager in 1970 (The GP Library).

Mike Hailwood, who drove most of his races in a Surtees during the seasons 1971 to 1973.

Jean-Pierre Beltoise, who had one victory, Monaco in 1972, driving a BRM.

The BRM P160 of Pedro Rodríguez at the French Grand Prix of 1971. His final F1 outing, before suffering a fatal accident in a sports car race, just a week later (The GP Library).

Jochen Rindt (Lotus 72C) at the Austrian Grand Prix, which was to be his final race. Although he suffered an engine failure here, he had already won four races, and won the 1970 title posthumously (The GP Library).

Emerson Fittipaldi in the JPS Lotus 72D, which took him to his first world title. He is seen here at Monza (1972), where he achieved his fifth win of the season (The GP Library).

Francois Cevert (Tyrrell 006) at the 1973 Belgian Grand Prix (Zolder). One of his six second places that season (The GP Library).

Niki Lauda (Ferrari 312T) at the 1976 British Grand Prix. He won the race from pole position (The GP Library).

The start of the 1977 South African Grand Prix. James Hunt (McLaren, no.1) leads eventual winner, Niki Lauda (Ferrari, no.11) (The GP Library).

Jody Scheckter in 1979, the year he won the world championship (The GP Library).

Gilles Villeneuve, the Canadian who had six victories between 1978 and 1981 for Ferrari (The GP Library).

Nelson Piquet (Brabham BT52B - BMW turbo) at the 1983 Italian Grand Prix, which he won, on his way to his second world title (The GP Library).

Michele Alboreto (Ferrari 126C4) at the 1984 Austrian Grand Prix, where he finished third (The GP Library).

Martin Brundle (Tyrrell 015 - Renault) catching up with Derek Warwick (Brabham BT55 - BMW) at the 1986 Canadian Grand Prix (David Hayhoe).

Ayrton Senna (Lotus), on the grid for the start of the 1987 San Marino Grand Prix (David Hayhoe).

Alain Prost (McLaren) at the 1987 San Marino Grand Prix (David Hayhoe).

Nigel Mansell (Williams FW11B) leads Ayrton Senna (Lotus 99T) around Le Portier at the 1987 Monaco Grand Prix (Mansell retired, Senna won) (David Hayhoe).

Ayrton Senna at the 1987 British Grand Prix (Lotus 99T - Honda) (David Hayhoe).

Nelson Piquet (Lotus) at the 1988 British Grand Prix (David Hayhoe).

Riccardo Patrese (Williams) at the 1989 British Grand Prix (David Hayhoe).

Gerhard Berger (McLaren MP4/5B - Honda) finished third at Monaco in 1990 (David Hayhoe).

Ivan Capelli (Leyton House CG911 - Ilmor) in 1991 at Monaco (David Hayhoe).

Roberto Moreno (Benetton B191 - Ford Cosworth) at Monaco, 1991 (David Hayhoe).

Chapter 10: Fastest Lap Drivers

420. Fastest laps

		% of starts		
Michael Schumacher	77	25.08	Belgium 1992 (Benetton)	- Germany 2012 (Mercedes-Benz)
Kimi Räikkönen	42	18.18	Australia 2002 (McLaren)	- Canada 2015 (Ferrari)
Alain Prost	41	20.60	France 1981 (Renault)	- Japan 1993 (Williams)
Nigel Mansell	30	16.04	Europe 1983 (Lotus)	- Japan 1992 (Williams)
Jim Clark	28	38.89	Netherlands 1961 (Lotus)	- South Africa 1968 (Lotus)
Lewis Hamilton	28	16.77	Malaysia 2007 (McLaren)	- Abu Dhabi 2015 (Mercedes-Benz)
Mika Häkkinen	25	15.53	Italy 1997 (McLaren)	- Hungary 2001 (McLaren)
Sebastian Vettel	25	15.82	Britain 2009 (Red Bull)	- Russia 2015 (Ferrari)
Niki Lauda	24	14.04	Spain 1974 (Ferrari)	- Germany 1985 (McLaren)
Juan Manuel Fangio	23	45.10	Monaco 1950 (Alfa Romeo)	- Argentina 1958 (Maserati) *
Nelson Piquet	23	11.27	United States 1979 (Brabham)	- Mexico 1987 (Williams) *
Fernando Alonso	21	8.30	Canada 2003 (Renault)	- Abu Dhabi 2013 (Ferrari)
Gerhard Berger	21	10.00	Germany 1986 (Benetton)	- Germany 1997 (Benetton)
Damon Hill	19	16.52	Britain 1993 (Williams)	- Hungary 1996 (Williams)
Stirling Moss	19	28.79	Britain 1954 (Maserati)	- Monaco 1961 (Lotus) *
Ayrton Senna	19	11.80	Monaco 1984 (Toleman)	- Europe 1993 (McLaren)
Mark Webber	19	8.84	Hungary 2009 (Red Bull)	- Brazil 2013 (Red Bull)
David Coulthard	18	7.32	Germany 1994 (Williams)	- France 2002 (McLaren)
Rubens Barrichello	17	5.26	Australia 2000 (Ferrari)	- Spain 2009 (Brawn)

Felipe Massa	15	6.55	Spain 2006 (Ferrari)	- Canada 2014 (Williams)
Clay Regazzoni	15	11.36	Austria 1970 (Ferrari)	- Italy 1979 (Williams) *
Jackie Stewart	15	15.15	Germany 1968 (Matra)	- Italy 1973 (Tyrrell)
Nico Rosberg	14	7.57	Bahrain 2006 (Williams)	- Mexico 2015 (Mercedes-Benz)
Jacky Ickx	13	11.21	Germany 1969 (Brabham)	- Italy 1972 (Ferrari) *
Alan Jones	13	11.21	United States West 1978 (Williams)	- Netherlands 1981 (Williams)
Riccardo Patrese	13	5.08	Monaco 1982 (Brabham)	- Germany 1992 (Williams)
René Arnoux	12	8.05	France 1979 (Renault)	- Netherlands 1984 (Ferrari)
Alberto Ascari	12	38.71	Belgium 1952 (Ferrari)	- Spain 1954 (Lancia) *
Jack Brabham	12	9.52	Monaco 1959 (Cooper)	- Britain 1970 (Brabham) *
Juan Pablo Montoya	12	12.77	Europe 2001 (Williams)	- Turkey 2005 (McLaren)
Mario Andretti	10	7.81	South Africa 1971 (Ferrari)	- Italy 1978 (JPS Lotus)
Graham Hill	10	5.68	Britain 1960 (BRM)	- United States 1967 (Lotus)
John Surtees	10	9.01	Portugal 1960 (Lotus)	- Belgium 1968 (Honda)
Denny Hulme	9	8.04	Netherlands 1966 (Brabham)	- Belgium 1974 (McLaren) *
Ronnie Peterson	9	7.32	Spain 1973 (JPS Lotus)	- Austria 1978 (JPS Lotus)
Jacques Villeneuve	9	5.52	Australia 1996 (Williams)	- Austria 1997 (Williams)
Jenson Button	8	2.82	Malaysia 2009 (Brawn)	- India 2012 (McLaren)
James Hunt	8	8.70	Britain 1973 (March)	- Britain 1977 (McLaren)
Ralf Schumacher	8	4.44	Italy 1999 (Williams)	- Belgium 2005 (Toyota)
Gilles Villeneuve	8	11.94	Argentina 1978 (Ferrari)	- San Marino 1981 (Ferrari)
Jacques Laffite	7	3.98	Japan 1976 (Ligier)	- Europe 1985 (Ligier)
Emerson Fittipaldi	6	4.17	Argentina 1973 (JPS Lotus)	- United States 1975 (McLaren) *
Heinz-Harald Frentzen	6	3.82	Australia 1997 (Williams)	- Europe 1997 (Williams)
José Froilán González	6	23.08	Italy 1952 (Maserati)	- Italy 1954 (Ferrari) *
Dan Gurney	6	6.98	South Africa 1963 (Brabham)	- Germany 1967 (Eagle)
Mike Hawthorn	6	13.33	Britain 1954 (Ferrari)	- Portugal 1958 (Ferrari) *
Phil Hill	6	12.50	Italy 1958 (Ferrari)	- Germany 1961 (Ferrari) *
Carlos Reutemann	6	4.11	South Africa 1974 (Brabham)	- Italy 1981 (Williams)
Michele Alboreto	5	2.58	Caesars Palace 1982 (Tyrrell)	- Italy 1988 (Ferrari) *
Giuseppe Farina	5	15.15	Britain 1950 (Alfa Romeo)	- Italy 1951 (Alfa Romeo)
Carlos Pace	5	6.94	Germany 1973 (Surtees)	- South Africa 1975 (Brabham)
Didier Pironi	5	7.14	Britain 1980 (Ligier)	- Canada 1982 (Ferrari)
Jody Scheckter	5	4.46	France 1974 (Tyrrell)	- Japan 1977 (Wolf)
John Watson	5	3.29	South Africa 1977 (Brabham)	- Detroit 1983 (McLaren)
Jean Alesi	4	1.99	United States 1991 (Ferrari)	- Monaco 1996 (Benetton)
Jean-Pierre Beltoise	4	4.65	Spain 1968 (Matra)	- Monaco 1972 (BRM)
Patrick Depailler	4	4.21	Sweden 1974 (Tyrrell)	- Monaco 1979 (Ligier)
Daniel Ricciardo	4	4.55	Abu Dhabi 2014 (Red Bull)	- Singapore 2015 (Red Bull)
Jo Siffert	4	4.17	Britain 1968 (Lotus)	- Austria 1971 (BRM)
Chris Amon	3	3.13	Belgium 1970 (March)	- France 1972 (Matra-Simca)
Tony Brooks	3	7.89	Italy 1957 (Vanwall)	- Britain 1961 (BRM)
Richie Ginther	3	5.77	Monaco 1961 (Ferrari)	- Mexico 1966 (Honda)*
Jean-Pierre Jarier	3	2.24	Brazil 1975 (Shadow)	- United States 1978 (JPS Lotus)
Bruce McLaren	3	3.00	Britain 1959 (Cooper)	- Netherlands 1962 (Cooper) *
Sergio Pérez	3	3.23	Monaco 2012 (Sauber)	- Austria 2014 (Force India)
Jochen Rindt	3	5.00	Spain 1969 (Lotus)	- Monaco 1970 (Lotus)
Keke Rosberg	3	2.63	France 1985 (Williams)	- Australia 1985 (Williams)
Lorenzo Bandini	2	4.76	Monaco 1966 (Ferrari)	- France 1966 (Ferrari)
François Cevert	2	4.26	Germany 1971 (Tyrrell)	- Belgium 1973 (Tyrrell)
Teo Fabi	2	3.13	Italy 1986 (Benetton)	- San Marino 1987 (Benetton)
Giancarlo Fisichella	2	0.87	Spain 1997 (Jordan)	- Spain 2005 (Renault)
Nick Heidfeld	2	1.09	Malaysia 2008 (BMW Sauber)	- Germany 2008 (BMW Sauber)
Heikki Kovalainen	2	1.80	Australia 2008 (McLaren)	- Bahrain 2008 (McLaren)
Jochen Mass	2	1.90	France 1975 (McLaren)	- Spain 1976 (McLaren)
Alessandro Nannini	2	2.63	Germany 1988 (Benetton)	- San Marino 1990 (Benetton)
Patrick Tambay	2	1.75	Canada 1983 (Ferrari)	- South Africa 1984 (Renault)
Derek Warwick	2	1.37	Netherlands 1982 (Brabham)	- Detroit 1984 (Renault)
Richard Attwood	1	5.88	Monaco 1968 (BRM)	
Giancarlo Baghetti	1	4.76	Italy 1961 (Ferrari)	
Jean Behra	1	1.89	Britain 1954 (Gordini) *	

		% of starts		
Valtteri Bottas	1	1.79	Russia 2014 (Williams)	
Thierry Boutsen	1	0.61	Germany 1990 (Williams)	
Vittorio Brambilla	1	1.35	Austria 1975 (March)	
Andrea De Cesaris	1	0.48	Belgium 1983 (Alfa Romeo)	
Pedro de la Rosa	1	0.95	Bahrain 2005 (McLaren)	
Bertrand Gachot	1	2.13	Hungary 1991 (Jordan)	
Timo Glock	1	1.10	Europe 2009 (Toyota)	
Romain Grosjean	1	1.20	Spain 2012 (Lotus)	
Maurício Gugelmin	1	1.35	France 1989 (March)	
Esteban Gutiérrez	1	2.63	Spain 2013 (Sauber)	
Mike Hailwood	1	2.00	South Africa 1972 (Surtees)	
Brian Henton	1	5.26	Britain 1982 (Tyrrell)	
Hans Herrmann	1	5.56	France 1954 (Mercedes-Benz)	
Nico Hülkenberg	1	1.06	Singapore 2012 (Force India)	
Innes Ireland	1	2.00	Belgium 1960 (Lotus) *	
Eddie Irvine	1	0.68	Canada 1999 (Ferrari)	
Karl Kling	1	9.09	Germany 1954 (Mercedes-Benz)	
Kamui Kobayashi	1	1.33	China 2012 (Sauber)	
Robert Kubica	1	1.32	Canada 2010 (Renault)	
Onofré Marimón	1	9.09	Britain 1954 (Maserati) *	
Roberto Mières	1	5.88	Netherlands 1955 (Maserati)	
Roberto Moreno	1	2.38	Belgium 1991 (Benetton)	
Luigi Musso	1	4.17	France 1957 (Lancia-Ferrari)	
Satoru Nakajima	1	1.35	Australia 1989 (Lotus)	
Gunnar Nilsson	1	3.23	Belgium 1977 (JPS Lotus)	
Jackie Oliver	1	2.00	Italy 1968 (Lotus)	
Jonathan Palmer	1	1.20	Canada 1989 (Tyrrell)	
Henri Pescarolo	1	1.75	Italy 1971 (March)	
Vitaly Petrov	1	1.75	Turkey 2010 (Renault)	
Pedro Rodríguez	1	1.82	France 1968 (BRM)	
Ludovico Scarfiotti	1	10.00	Italy 1966 (Ferrari)	
Bruno Senna	1	2.17	Belgium 2012 (Williams)	
Marc Surer	1	1.22	Brazil 1981 (Ensign)	
Adrian Sutil	1	0.78	Italy 2009 (Force India)	
Piero Taruffi	1	5.56	Switzerland 1952 (Ferrari)	
Maurice Trintignant	1	1.23	United States 1959 (Cooper)	
Jarno Trulli	1	0.40	Bahrain 2009 (Toyota)	
Luigi Villoresi	1	3.23	Netherlands 1953 (Ferrari)	
Alexander Wurz	1	1.45	Argentina 1998 (Benetton)	
Indianapolis 500				
Bill Vukovich	3	60.00	1952 (Kurtis-Kraft)	- 1955 (Kurtis-Kraft)
Jim Rathmann	2	20.00	1957 (Epperly)	- 1960 (Watson)
Tony Bettenhausen	1	9.09	1958 (Epperly)	
Jack McGrath	1	16.67	1954 (Kurtis-Kraft)	
Johnnie Parsons	1	11.11	1950 (Kurtis-Kraft)	
Paul Russo	1	12.50	1956 (Kurtis-Kraft)	
Johnny Thomson	1	12.50	1959 (Levosky)	
Lee Wallard	1	50.00	1951 (Kurtis-Kraft)	

Fastest lap time for the Indianapolis 500 races is based on the driver's fastest leading lap.
* Includes one or more joint fastest laps (see section 422).

Situations of contention:

France 1953: the fastest lap is often shown as being shared by Juan Manuel Fangio (Maserati) and Alberto Ascari (Ferrari) in 2 min 41.1 sec. Further research suggests that it should probably be credited just to Fangio.

South Africa 1970: John Surtees (McLaren) is often credited with a 1 min 20.8 sec fastest lap time on lap 6 which was equalled by Jack Brabham (Brabham) later in the race. However, studying the lap times, it is unlikely that Surtees did such a time and that on lap 6 the time was actually 1 min 22.8 sec. Consequently, he has not been credited with fastest lap here.

Austria 1970: Jacky Ickx and Clay Regazzoni (Ferrari) have often both been credited with a fastest lap of 1 min 40.4 sec on lap 45. However, the lap chart shows that Regazzoni recorded the fastest lap (1 min 40.39 sec) on lap 51.

Japan 1976: although Masahiro Hasemi (Kojima) is often recorded as having set the fastest lap in 1 min 18.230 sec, records have since shown that it was Jacques Laffite (Ligier) who actually set the fastest lap in 1 min 19.97 sec. Laffite has been credited with it here.

421. Percentage of races with a fastest lap *(Highest)*

	%	fastest laps			%	fastest laps
Juan Manuel Fangio	45.10	23		José Froilán González	23.08	6
Jim Clark	38.89	28		Alain Prost	20.60	41
Alberto Ascari	38.71	12		Kimi Räikkönen	18.18	42
Stirling Moss	28.79	19		Lewis Hamilton	16.77	28
Michael Schumacher	25.08	77		Damon Hill	16.52	19

Excludes Indianapolis 500.

422. Joint fastest laps

Italy 1952	Alberto Ascari, José Froilán González
Britain 1953	Alberto Ascari, José Froilán González
Britain 1954	Alberto Ascari, Jean Behra, Juan Manuel Fangio, José Froilán González, Mike Hawthorn, Onofré Marimón, Stirling Moss
Britain 1959	Bruce McLaren, Stirling Moss
Belgium 1960	Jack Brabham, Phil Hill, Innes Ireland
Monaco 1961	Richie Ginther, Stirling Moss
Canada 1969	Jack Brabham, Jacky Ickx
Brazil 1973	Emerson Fittipaldi, Denny Hulme
Europe 1984	Michele Alboreto, Nelson Piquet

423. Fastest lap driver age

Youngest

	years, days	
Nico Rosberg	20y, 258d	Bahrain 2006
Esteban Gutiérrez	21y, 280d	Spain 2013
Fernando Alonso	21y, 321d	Canada 2003
Bruce McLaren	21y, 322d	Britain 1959
Sebastian Vettel	21y, 353d	Britain 2009
Lewis Hamilton	22y, 91d	Malaysia 2007
Sergio Pérez	22y, 122d	Monaco 2012
Kimi Räikkönen	22y, 137d	Australia 2002
David Coulthard	23y, 126d	Germany 1994
Michael Schumacher	23y, 240d	Belgium 1992

Oldest

	years, days	
Juan Manuel Fangio	46y, 209d	Argentina 1958
Piero Taruffi	45y, 219d	Switzerland 1952
Giuseppe Farina	44y, 321d	Italy 1951
Jack Brabham	44y, 107d	Britain 1970
Luigi Villoresi	44y, 22d	Netherlands 1953
Karl Kling	43y, 319d	Germany 1954
Michael Schumacher	43y, 201d	Germany 2012
Maurice Trintignant	42y, 43d	United States 1959
Jacques Laffite	41y, 319d	Europe 1985
Clay Regazzoni	40y, 4d	Italy 1979
Indianapolis 500		
Paul Russo	42y, 50d	1956
Tony Bettenhausen	41y, 260d	1958
Lee Wallard	39y, 264d	1951

424. Fastest laps in a season *(Most)*

Kimi Räikkönen	10 of 18	2008	(Ferrari F2008)
Michael Schumacher	10 of 18	2004 (wc)	(Ferrari F2004)
Kimi Räikkönen	10 of 19	2005	(McLaren MP4-20 - Mercedes)
Mika Häkkinen	9 of 17	2000	(McLaren MP4-15 - Mercedes)
Nigel Mansell	8 of 16	1992 (wc)	(Ferrari FW14B - Renault)
Michael Schumacher	8 of 16	1994 (wc)	(Benetton B194 - Ford Cosworth)
Michael Schumacher	8 of 17	1995 (wc)	(Benetton B195 - Renault)
Lewis Hamilton	8 of 19	2015 (wc)	(Mercedes-Benz F1 W06)
Nelson Piquet	7 of 16	1986	(Williams FW11 - Honda)
Alain Prost	7 of 16	1988	(McLaren MP4/4 - Honda)
Michael Schumacher	7 of 17	2002 (wc)	(Ferrari F2002)
Michael Schumacher	7 of 18	2006	(Ferrari 248 F1)
Lewis Hamilton	7 of 19	2014 (wc)	(Mercedes-Benz F1 W05)
Sebastian Vettel	7 of 19	2013 (wc)	(Red Bull RB9 - Renault)
Mark Webber	7 of 19	2011	(Red Bull RB7 - Renault)

(wc) World champion that season.

425. Fastest lap in all but one race of a season

Alberto Ascari (Ferrari 500) achieved this with fastest lap in 6 out of the 7 races of 1952 *(excludes Indianapolis 500)*.

426. Consecutive fastest laps *(Most)*

Alberto Ascari	7	Belgium 1952	- Argentina 1953	(Ferrari 500)
Kimi Räikkönen	6	Spain 2008	- Britain 2008	(Ferrari F2008)
Juan Manuel Fangio	5	France 1950	- France 1951	(Alfa Romeo 158, 159)
Michael Schumacher	5	Bahrain 2004	- Europe 2004	(Ferrari F2004)
Nigel Mansell	4	Canada 1991	- Britain 1991	(Williams FW14 - Renault)
Kimi Räikkönen	4	France 2005	- Hungary 2005	(McLaren MP4-20 - Mercedes)
Jackie Stewart	4	Monaco 1969	- Britain 1969	(Matra MS80 - Ford Cosworth)
Gilles Villeneuve	4	South Africa 1979	- Belgium 1979	(Ferrari 312T4)

427. Consecutive fastest laps from the start of a season

Juan Manuel Fangio	3	1951 (wc)	(Alfa Romeo 159)
Juan Manuel Fangio	3	1955 (wc)	(Mercedes-Benz W196)
Emerson Fittipaldi	3	1973	(JPS Lotus 72D - Ford Cosworth)
Gerhard Berger	2	1990	(McLaren MP4/5B - Honda)
Jack Brabham	2	1970	(Brabham BT33 - Ford Cosworth)
Juan Manuel Fangio	2	1956 (wc)	(Lancia-Ferrari D50)
Mika Häkkinen	2	1998 (wc)	(McLaren MP4-13 - Mercedes)
James Hunt	2	1977	(McLaren M23 - Ford Cosworth)
Jacques Laffite	2	1979	(Ligier JS11 - Ford Cosworth)
Alain Prost	2	1982	(Renault RE30B)
Clay Regazzoni	2	1974	(Ferrari 312B3)
Michael Schumacher	2	1994 (wc)	(Benetton B194 - Ford Cosworth)
Michael Schumacher	2	1995 (wc)	(Benetton B195 - Renault)

(wc) World champion that season.

428. Seasons of fastest laps *(Most)*

Michael Schumacher	16	1992 - 2012		Fernando Alonso	8	2003 - 13
Alain Prost	12	1981 - 93		David Coulthard	8	1994 - 2002
Kimi Räikkönen	11	2002 - 15		Juan Manuel Fangio	8	1950 - 58
Gerhard Berger	10	1986 - 97		Lewis Hamilton	8	2007 - 15
Niki Lauda	9	1974 - 85		Stirling Moss	8	1954 - 61
Nigel Mansell	9	1983 - 92		Nelson Piquet	8	1979 - 87
Ayrton Senna	9	1984 - 93				

429. Consecutive seasons of fastest laps *(Most)*

Michael Schumacher	15	1992 - 2006		Sebastian Vettel	7	2009 - 15
Alain Prost	11	1981 - 91		René Arnoux	6	1979 - 84
Nigel Mansell	8	1985 - 92		David Coulthard	6	1997 - 2002
Stirling Moss	8	1954 - 61		Juan Manuel Fangio	6	1953 - 58
Gerhard Berger	7	1986 - 92		Lewis Hamilton	6	2010 - 15
Kimi Räikkönen	7	2002 - 08		Nelson Piquet	6	1979 - 84
Ayrton Senna	7	1987 - 93				

430. Fastest laps by nationality

Argentina: Juan Manuel Fangio, 23; José Froilán González, 6; Carlos Reutemann, 6; Onofré Marimón, 1; Roberto Mières, 1

Australia: Mark Webber, 19; Alan Jones, 13; Jack Brabham, 12; Daniel Ricciardo, 4

Austria: Niki Lauda, 24; Gerhard Berger, 21; Jochen Rindt, 3; Alexander Wurz, 1

Belgium: Jacky Ickx, 13; Thierry Boutsen, 1

Brazil: Nelson Piquet, 23; Ayrton Senna, 19; Rubens Barrichello, 17; Felipe Massa, 15; Emerson Fittipaldi, 6; Carlos Pace, 5; Maurício Gugelmin, 1; Roberto Moreno, 1; Bruno Senna, 1

Canada: Jacques Villeneuve, 9; Gilles Villeneuve, 8

Colombia: Juan Pablo Montoya, 12

Finland: Kimi Räikkönen, 42; Mika Häkkinen, 25; Keke Rosberg, 3; Heikki Kovalainen, 2; Valtteri Bottas, 1

France:	Alain Prost, 41; René Arnoux, 12; Jacques Laffite, 7; Didier Pironi, 5; Jean Alesi, 4; Jean-Pierre Beltoise, 4; Patrick Depailler, 4; Jean-Pierre Jarier, 3; François Cevert, 2; Patrick Tambay, 2; Jean Behra, 1; Bertrand Gachot, 1; Romain Grosjean, 1; Henri Pescarolo, 1; Maurice Trintignant, 1		
Germany:	Michael Schumacher, 77; Sebastian Vettel, 25; Nico Rosberg, 14; Ralf Schumacher, 8; Heinz-Harald Frentzen, 6; Nick Heidfeld, 2; Jochen Mass, 2; Timo Glock, 1; Hans Herrmann, 1; Nico Hülkenberg, 1; Karl Kling, 1; Adrian Sutil, 1		
Great Britain:	Nigel Mansell, 30; Jim Clark, 28; Lewis Hamilton, 28; Damon Hill, 19; Stirling Moss, 19; David Coulthard, 18; Jackie Stewart, 15; Graham Hill, 10; John Surtees, 10; Jenson Button, 8; James Hunt, 8; Mike Hawthorn, 6; John Watson, 5; Tony Brooks, 3; Derek Warwick, 2; Richard Attwood, 1; Mike Hailwood, 1; Brian Henton, 1; Innes Ireland, 1; Eddie Irvine, 1; Jackie Oliver, 1; Jonathan Palmer, 1		
Italy:	Riccardo Patrese, 13; Alberto Ascari, 12; Michele Alboreto, 5; Giuseppe Farina, 5; Lorenzo Bandini, 2; Teo Fabi, 2; Giancarlo Fisichella, 2; Alessandro Nannini, 2; Giancarlo Baghetti, 1; Vittorio Brambilla, 1; Andrea De Cesaris, 1; Luigi Musso, 1; Ludovico Scarfiotti, 1; Piero Taruffi, 1; Jarno Trulli, 1; Luigi Villoresi, 1		
Japan:	Kamui Kobayashi, 1; Satoru Nakajima, 1		
Mexico:	Sergio Pérez, 3; Esteban Gutiérrez, 1; Pedro Rodríguez, 1		
New Zealand:	Denny Hulme, 9; Chris Amon, 3; Bruce McLaren, 3		
Poland:	Robert Kubica, 1		
Russia:	Vitaly Petrov, 1		
South Africa:	Jody Scheckter, 5		
Spain:	Fernando Alonso, 21; Pedro de la Rosa, 1		
Sweden:	Ronnie Peterson, 9; Gunnar Nilsson, 1		
Switzerland:	Clay Regazzoni, 15; Jo Siffert, 4; Marc Surer, 1		
United States:	Mario Andretti, 10; Dan Gurney, 6; Phil Hill, 6; Richie Ginther, 3		

Total for the drivers above do not equate to those in the following summary table where more than one driver of a nationality shared the fastest lap at Britain 1954 (nations affected are Great Britain, 1 extra and Argentina, 2 extra in this table).

Summary

	races	drivers		
Great Britain	215	22	Britain 1954 (Stirling Moss)	- Abu Dhabi 2015 (Lewis Hamilton)
Germany	139	12	France 1954 (Hans Herrmann)	- Mexico 2015 (Nico Rosberg)
France	89	15	Britain 1954 (Jean Behra)	- Spain 2012 (Romain Grosjean)
Brazil	88	9	Argentina 1973 (Emerson Fittipaldi)	- Canada 2014 (Felipe Massa)
Finland	73	5	France 1985 (Keke Rosberg)	- Canada 2015 (Kimi Räikkönen)
Italy	51	16	Britain 1950 (Giuseppe Farina)	- Bahrain 2009 (Jarno Trulli)
Austria	49	4	Spain 1969 (Jochen Rindt)	- Argentina 1998 (Alexander Wurz)
Australia	48	4	Monaco 1959 (Jack Brabham)	- Singapore 2015 (Daniel Ricciardo)
Argentina	35	5	Monaco 1950 (Juan Manuel Fangio)	- Italy 1981 (Carlos Reutemann)
United States	25	4	Italy 1958 (Phil Hill)	- Italy 1978 (Mario Andretti)
Spain	22	2	Canada 2003 (Fernando Alonso)	- Abu Dhabi 2013 (Fernando Alonso)
Switzerland	20	3	Britain 1968 (Jo Siffert)	- Brazil 1981 (Marc Surer)
Canada	17	2	Argentina 1978 (Gilles Villeneuve)	- Austria 1997 (Jacques Villeneuve)
New Zealand	15	3	Britain 1959 (Bruce McLaren)	- Belgium 1974 (Denny Hulme)
Belgium	14	2	Germany 1969 (Jacky Ickx)	- Germany 1990 (Thierry Boutsen)
Colombia	12	1	Europe 2001 (Juan Pablo Montoya)	- Turkey 2005 (Juan Pablo Montoya)
Sweden	10	2	Spain 1973 (Ronnie Peterson)	- Austria 1978 (Ronnie Peterson)
Mexico	5	3	France 1968 (Pedro Rodríguez)	- Austria 2014 (Sergio Pérez)
South Africa	5	1	France 1974 (Jody Scheckter)	- Japan 1977 (Jody Scheckter)
Japan	2	2	Australia 1989 (Satoru Nakajima)	- China 2012 (Kamui Kobayashi)
Poland	1	1	Canada 2010 (Robert Kubica)	
Russia	1	1	Turkey 2010 (Vitaly Petrov)	

Excludes Indianapolis 500.
At Britain 1954, where two British and three Argentinian drivers were among the drivers who had joint fastest lap, those nationalities have only been counted once each.

431. Fastest laps at the same venue *(Most)*

grand prix

Nigel Mansell	7	Britain	1986 - 92	(Silverstone, 6; Brands Hatch, 1)
Michael Schumacher	7	Spain	1993 - 2004	(Catalunya)
Alain Prost	6	Belgium	1985 - 93	(Spa-Francorchamps)
Michael Schumacher	6	Europe	1994 - 2006	(Nürburgring, 5; Jerez de la Frontera, 1)
Jim Clark	5	Netherlands	1961 - 67	(Zandvoort)
David Coulthard	5	France	1998 - 2002	(Magny-Cours)
Stirling Moss	5	Britain	1954 - 59	(Aintree, 3; Silverstone, 2)

Kimi Räikkönen	5	Australia	2002 - 13	(Melbourne)
Michael Schumacher	5	Australia	1992 - 2004	(Melbourne, 3; Adelaide, 2)
Michael Schumacher	5	Brazil	1993 - 2006	(Interlagos)
Michael Schumacher	5	France	1993 - 2006	(Magny-Cours)
Michael Schumacher	5	Germany	1993 - 2012	(Hockenheim)
Michael Schumacher	5	Monaco	1994 - 2006	(Monte-Carlo)
Michael Schumacher	5	San Marino	1998 - 2005	(Imola)

circuit

Michael Schumacher	7	Catalunya	1993 - 2004	
Nigel Mansell	6	Silverstone	1987 - 92	
Alain Prost	6	Spa-Francorchamps	1985 - 93	
Jim Clark	5	Zandvoort	1961 - 67	
David Coulthard	5	Magny-Cours	1998 - 2002	
Kimi Räikkönen	5	Melbourne	2002 - 13	
Michael Schumacher	5	Hockenheim	1993 - 2012	
Michael Schumacher	5	Imola	1998 - 2005	
Michael Schumacher	5	Interlagos	1993 - 2006	
Michael Schumacher	5	Magny-Cours	1993 - 2006	
Michael Schumacher	5	Monte-Carlo	1994 - 2006	
Michael Schumacher	5	Nürburgring	1995 - 2006 (a)	

(a) European Grand Prix.

432. Consecutive fastest laps at the same venue *(Most)*

Nigel Mansell	7	Britain	1986 - 92	(Silverstone, 6; Brands Hatch, 1)
David Coulthard	5	France	1998 - 2002	(Magny-Cours)
Juan Manuel Fangio	4	Monaco	1950 - 57 (a)	(Monte-Carlo)
Stirling Moss	4	Britain	1954 - 57	(Aintree, 2; Silverstone, 2)
Alberto Ascari	3	Britain	1952 - 54	(Silverstone)
Gerhard Berger	3	Portugal	1987 - 89	(Estoril)
Jim Clark	3	Netherlands	1963 - 65	(Zandvoort)
Jim Clark	3	United States	1962 - 64	(Watkins Glen)
Mika Häkkinen	3	Britain	1999 - 2001	(Silverstone)
Mika Häkkinen	3	Monaco	1998 - 2000	(Monte-Carlo)
Lewis Hamilton	3	Italy	2013 - 15	(Monza)
Damon Hill	3	Britain	1993 - 95	(Silverstone)
Phil Hill	3	Italy	1958 - 60	(Monza)
Nigel Mansell	3	France	1990 - 92	(Magny-Cours, 2; Paul Ricard, 1)
Stirling Moss	3	Netherlands	1958 - 60	(Zandvoort)
Alain Prost	3	Belgium	1985 - 87	(Spa-Francorchamps)
Michael Schumacher	3	Brazil	1993 - 95	(Interlagos)
Michael Schumacher	3	Canada	1993 - 95	(Montréal)
Michael Schumacher	3	Monaco	2004 - 06	(Monte-Carlo)
Michael Schumacher	3	San Marino	2003 - 05	(Imola)
Sebastian Vettel	3	United States	2012 - 14	(Austin)

(a) No Monaco Grand Prix in 1951 - 54.

433. Fastest laps on home soil *(Most)*

Michael Schumacher	10	Germany	1993 - 2012 (a)	(Hockenheim, 5; Nürburgring, 5)
Nigel Mansell	8	Britain	1983 - 92 (b)	(Silverstone, 6; Brands Hatch, 2)
Stirling Moss	5	Britain	1954 - 59	(Aintree, 3; Silverstone, 2)
Alain Prost	5	France	1981 - 88 (c)	(Dijon-Prenois, 3; Paul Ricard, 2)
Juan Manuel Fangio	3	Argentina	1955 - 58	(Buenos Aires No.2)
Damon Hill	3	Britain	1993 - 95	(Silverstone)
Nelson Piquet	3	Brazil	1983 - 87	(Jacarepaguá)
Jackie Stewart	3	Britain	1969 - 72	(Silverstone, 2; Brands Hatch, 1)
Jim Clark	2	Britain	1962 - 64	(Aintree, 1; Brands Hatch, 1)
Lewis Hamilton	2	Britain	2014 - 15	(Silverstone)
Mike Hawthorn	2	Britain	1954 - 58	(Silverstone)
Graham Hill	2	Britain	1960 - 65	(Silverstone)
James Hunt	2	Britain	1973 - 77	(Silverstone)
Riccardo Patrese	2	Italy	1983 - 92	(Imola) (d)

(a) 5 German & 5 European Grands Prix. (b) 7 British & 1 European Grands Prix. (c) 4 French & 1 Swiss Grands Prix. (d) San Marino Grand Prix.

434. First fastest lap was on home soil

René Arnoux	France 1979	(Dijon-Prenois)		James Hunt	Britain 1973	(Silverstone)
Giancarlo Baghetti	Italy 1961	(Monza)		Karl Kling	Germany 1954	(Nürburgring)
Teo Fabi	Italy 1986	(Monza)		Nigel Mansell	Europe 1983	(Brands Hatch)
Mike Hawthorn	Britain 1954 (a)	(Silverstone)		Stirling Moss	Britain 1954 (a)	(Silverstone)
Brian Henton	Britain 1982	(Brands Hatch)		Alain Prost	France 1981	(Dijon-Prenois)
Damon Hill	Britain 1993	(Silverstone)		Ludovico Scarfiotti	Italy 1966	(Monza)
Graham Hill	Britain 1960	(Silverstone)				

(a) Shared fastest lap.

435. Race starts taken to achieve their first fastest lap
(number of races includes the race of first fastest lap)

Fewest

Giuseppe Farina	1		Giancarlo Baghetti	3
Nico Rosberg	1		Phil Hill	3
Jacques Villeneuve	1		James Hunt	3
Juan Manuel Fangio	2		Karl Kling	3
Lewis Hamilton	2		John Surtees	3
Hans Herrmann	2			

Most

Jarno Trulli	203		Mika Häkkinen	92
Jenson Button	155		Keke Rosberg	89
Nick Heidfeld	134		Eddie Irvine	86
Mark Webber	131		Jonathan Palmer	74
Rubens Barrichello	114			
Thierry Boutsen	114			

For most races started but never a fastest lap, see section 188.

436. Fastest laps in their first season

Jacques Villeneuve	6	1996		Giancarlo Baghetti	1	1961
Juan Manuel Fangio	3	1950		Esteban Gutiérrez	1	2013
Giuseppe Farina	3	1950		Phil Hill	1	1958
Juan Pablo Montoya	3	2001		Karl Kling	1	1954
Clay Regazzoni	3	1970		Vitaly Petrov	1	2010
David Coulthard	2	1994		Nico Rosberg	1	2006
Lewis Hamilton	2	2007		Ayrton Senna	1	1984
James Hunt	2	1973		John Surtees	1	1960

437. First fastest lap immediately followed by others
(including first fastest lap)

Alberto Ascari	7	Belgium 1952	- Argentina 1953	(Ferrari 500)
Emerson Fittipaldi	3	Argentina 1973	- South Africa 1973	(JPS Lotus 72D - Ford Cosworth)
Clay Regazzoni	3	Austria 1970	- Canada 1970	(Ferrari 312B)
Carlos Pace	2	Germany 1973	- Austria 1973	(Surtees TS14A - Ford Cosworth)

438. Fastest lap in their final race

Jim Clark	South Africa 1968	killed in Formula 2 event, prior to next F1 race
Richie Ginther	Mexico 1966	retired from racing the following year after a non-qualification at Monaco
Onofré Marimón	Britain 1954	killed in qualifying for next F1 race, in Germany
Mark Webber	Brazil 2013	retired from F1

439. Fastest laps in their final season

Alain Prost	6	1993		Jim Clark	1	1968		Roberto Mières	1	1955
Mike Hawthorn	5	1958		Teo Fabi	1	1987		Stirling Moss	1	1961
Mark Webber	5	2013		Juan Manuel Fangio	1	1958		Alessandro Nannini	1	1990
Jack Brabham	4	1970		Richie Ginther	1	1966 (a)		Gunnar Nilsson	1	1977
Mika Häkkinen	3	2001		Brian Henton	1	1982		Jonathan Palmer	1	1989
Ronnie Peterson	3	1978		Denny Hulme	1	1974		Jochen Rindt	1	1970
Gerhard Berger	2	1997		Kamui Kobayashi	1	2012		Michael Schumacher	1	2012
Didier Pironi	2	1982		Robert Kubica	1	2010		Bruno Senna	1	2012
Tony Brooks	1	1961		Niki Lauda	1	1985		Jo Siffert	1	1971
François Cevert	1	1973		Onofré Marimón	1	1954		Jackie Stewart	1	1973

(a) Whilst 1966 was his final season of starting, he did enter a race in 1967 at which he non-qualified.

440. Different fastest lap drivers in a season

Most

				Fewest			
2012	12	2009	10	1950	2	1962	3
1975	10	1954	9	1951	2	1963	3
1976	10	1983	9	1956	2	1965	3
1981	10			1952	3	1994	3
1982	10			1955	3		

Total for each season

1950 - 2, 1951 - 2, 1952 - 3, 1953 - 4, 1954 - 9, 1955 - 3, 1956 - 2, 1957 - 4, 1958 - 4, 1959 - 6, 1960 - 7, 1961 - 7, 1962 - 3, 1963 - 3, 1964 - 5, 1965 - 3, 1966 - 6, 1967 - 4, 1968 - 8, 1969 - 5, 1970 - 5, 1971 - 7, 1972 - 6, 1973 - 7, 1974 - 8, 1975 - 10, 1976 - 10, 1977 - 8, 1978 - 7, 1979 - 7, 1980 - 6, 1981 - 10, 1982 - 10, 1983 - 9, 1984 - 8, 1985 - 7, 1986 - 5, 1987 - 6, 1988 - 6, 1989 - 8, 1990 - 7, 1991 - 8, 1992 - 5, 1993 - 4, 1994 - 3, 1995 - 5, 1996 - 5, 1997 - 7, 1998 - 4, 1999 - 5, 2000 - 4, 2001 - 5, 2002 - 5, 2003 - 6, 2004 - 4, 2005 - 7, 2006 - 5, 2007 - 4, 2008 - 5, 2009 - 10, 2010 - 7, 2011 - 6, 2012 - 12, 2013 - 7, 2014 - 8, 2015 - 5

Excludes Indianapolis 500.

441. Different fastest lap drivers in consecutive races *(Most)*

France - Germany 1954	9	Herrmann, Moss (a), González (a), Fangio (a), Hawthorn (a), Marimón (a), Behra (a), Ascari (a), Kling
Bahrain - Europe 2009	8	Trulli, Barrichello, Massa, Button, Vettel, Alonso, Webber, Glock
Britain 1960 - Netherlands 1961	7	Graham Hill, Surtees, Phil Hill, Brabham, Ginther (b), Moss (b), Clark
Germany 1971 - South Africa 1972	7	Cevert, Siffert, Pescarolo, Hulme, Ickx, Stewart, Hailwood
Brazil - Sweden 1977	7	Hunt, Watson, Lauda, Laffite, Scheckter, Nilsson, Andretti
Japan 1977 - Belgium 1978	7	Scheckter, Villeneuve, Reutemann, Andretti, Jones, Lauda, Peterson
United States West - Canada 1983	7	Lauda, Prost, Patrese, Piquet, De Cesaris, Watson, Tambay
San Marino - Germany 1983	7	Patrese, Piquet, De Cesaris, Watson, Tambay, Prost, Arnoux
Japan 2004 - Spain 2005	7	Barrichello, Montoya, Alonso, Räikkönen, de la Rosa, Michael Schumacher, Fisichella
Brazil 2011 - Monaco 2012	7	Webber, Button, Räikkönen, Kobayashi, Vettel, Grosjean, Pérez

(a) These seven drivers shared fastest lap in Britain 1954. (b) These two drivers shared fastest lap in Monaco 1961.

442. Different fastest lap drivers from the start of a season *(Most)*

1975	7	James Hunt, Jean-Pierre Jarier, Carlos Pace, Mario Andretti, Patrick Depailler, Clay Regazzoni, Niki Lauda
1978	6	Gilles Villeneuve, Carlos Reutemann, Mario Andretti, Alan Jones, Niki Lauda, Ronnie Peterson
2012	6	Jenson Button, Kimi Räikkönen, Kamui Kobayashi, Sebastian Vettel, Romain Grosjean, Sergio Pérez
1972	5	Jackie Stewart, Mike Hailwood, Jacky Ickx, Jean-Pierre Beltoise, Chris Amon
1981	5	Alan Jones, Marc Surer, Nelson Piquet, Jacques Villeneuve, Carlos Reutemann
2005	5	Fernando Alonso, Kimi Räikkönen, Pedro de la Rosa, Michael Schumacher, Giancarlo Fisichella
1953	4	Alberto Ascari, Luigi Villoresi, Jose Froilán González, Juan Manuel Fangio
1954	4	José Froilán González, Juan Manuel Fangio, Hans Herrmann, Stirling Moss
1964	4	Graham Hill, Jim Clark, Dan Gurney, Jack Brabham
1968	4	Jim Clark, Jean-Pierre Beltoise, Richard Attwood, John Surtees
1976	4	Jean-Pierre Jarier, Niki Lauda, Clay Regazzoni, Jochen Mass
1983	4	Nelson Piquet, Niki Lauda, Alain Prost, Riccardo Patrese
1984	4	Alain Prost, Patrick Tambay, René Arnoux, Nelson Piquet
1987	4	Nelson Piquet, Teo Fabi, Alain Prost, Ayrton Senna
1991	4	Jean Alesi, Nigel Mansell, Gerhard Berger, Alain Prost
2009	4	Nico Rosberg, Jenson Button, Rubens Barrichello, Jarno Trulli

Excludes Indianapolis 500.

443. First time fastest lap drivers in a season

Most

1954	6	Hans Herrmann, Jean Behra, Mike Hawthorn, Onofré Marimón, Stirling Moss, Karl Kling
1968	6	Jean-Pierre Beltoise, Richard Attwood, Pedro Rodríguez, Jo Siffert, Jackie Stewart, Jackie Oliver
2009	6	Jenson Button, Jarno Trulli, Sebastian Vettel, Mark Webber, Timo Glock, Adrian Sutil
2012	5	Kamui Kobayashi, Romain Grosjean, Sergio Pérez, Bruno Senna, Nico Hülkenberg
1973	4	Emerson Fittipaldi, Ronnie Peterson, James Hunt, Carlos Pace
1974	4	Carlos Reutemann, Niki Lauda, Patrick Depailler, Jody Scheckter
1982	4	Riccardo Patrese, Derek Warwick, Brian Henton, Michele Alboreto

Fewest (none)

1951, 56, 62, 64, 65, 67, 87, 95, 2004, 11, 15 *Excludes Indianapolis 500.*

444. Fastest laps with the same constructor *(Most)*

Michael Schumacher	53	Ferrari	Spain 1996	- Brazil 2006
Jim Clark	28	Lotus	Netherlands 1961	- South Africa 1968
Mika Häkkinen	25	McLaren	Italy 1997	- Hungary 2001
Alain Prost	24	McLaren	Brazil 1994	- Japan 1989
Sebastian Vettel	24	Red Bull	Britain 2009	- United States 2014
Nigel Mansell	23	Williams	Italy 1985	- Japan 1992
Michael Schumacher	23	Benetton	Belgium 1992	- Japan 1995
Damon Hill	19	Williams	Britain 1993	- Hungary 1996
Kimi Räikkönen	19	Ferrari	Australia 2007	- Canada 2015
Kimi Räikkönen	19	McLaren	Australia 2002	- Italy 2006
Mark Webber	19	Red Bull	Hungary 2009	- Brazil 2013

For complete list of fastest lap drivers by constructor, see section 874.

445. Fastest laps with the same engine make *(Most)*

Michael Schumacher	53	Ferrari	Spain 1996	- Brazil 2006
Lewis Hamilton	28	Mercedes	Malaysia 2007	- Abu Dhabi 2015
Mika Häkkinen	25	Mercedes	Italy 1997	- Hungary 2001
Sebastian Vettel	24	Renault	Britain 2009	- United States 2014
Jim Clark	23	Climax	Netherlands 1961	- Monaco 1967
Damon Hill	19	Renault	Britain 1993	- Hungary 1996
Kimi Räikkönen	19	Ferrari	Australia 2007	- Canada 2015
Kimi Räikkönen	19	Mercedes	Australia 2002	- Italy 2006
Mark Webber	19	Renault	Hungary 2009	- Brazil 2013
Rubens Barrichello	15	Ferrari	Australia 2000	- Japan 2004
Nigel Mansell	15	Renault	Europe 1983	- Japan 1992
Michael Schumacher	15	Ford Cosworth	Belgium 1992	- Australia 1994
Jackie Stewart	15	Ford Cosworth	Germany 1968	- Italy 1973

446. Interval between fastest laps *(Longest)*

	years, days	races		
Giancarlo Fisichella	7y, 348d	133	Spain 1997 (Jordan)	- Spain 2005 (Renault)
Riccardo Patrese	5y, 329d	92	San Marino 1983 (Brabham)	- Brazil 1989 (Renault)
Michael Schumacher	5y, 274d	100	Brazil 2006 (Ferrari)	- Germany 2012 (Mercedes-Benz)
Richie Ginther	5y, 127d	53	Belgium 1961 (Ferrari)	- Mexico 1966 (Honda)
Rubens Barrichello	4y, 191d	76	Japan 2004 (Ferrari)	- China 2009 (Brawn)
Jean Alesi	4y, 79d	68	United States 1991 (Ferrari)	- Monaco 1995 (Ferrari)
Denny Hulme	4y, 66d	51	Britain 1967 (Brabham)	- Canada 1971 (McLaren)
Mario Andretti	4y, 52d	56	South Africa 1971 (Ferrari)	- Spain 1975 (Parnelli)
Jacques Laffite	4y, 51d	65	Austria 1981 (Talbot-Ligier)	- Europe 1985 (Ligier)
John Watson	4y, 44d	64	Austria 1977 (Brabham)	- Canada 1981 (McLaren)

Did not necessarily start every race during the period.

447. Interval between first & last fastest laps *(Longest)*

	years, days	races		
Michael Schumacher	19y, 327d	340	Belgium 1992	- Germany 2012
Kimi Räikkönen	13y, 96d	242	Australia 2002	- Canada 2015
Alain Prost	12y, 111d	197	France 1981	- Japan 1993
Niki Lauda	11y, 98d	174	Spain 1974	- Germany 1985
Jack Brabham	11y, 69d	115	Monaco 1959	- Britain 1970
Gerhard Berger	11y, 0d	177	Germany 1986	- Germany 1997
Fernando Alonso	10y, 141d	190	Canada 2003	- Abu Dhabi 2013
Riccardo Patrese	10y, 64d	163	Monaco 1982	- Germany 1992
Nico Rosberg	9y, 234d	182	Bahrain 2006	- Mexico 2015
Rubens Barrichello	9y, 59d	161	Australia 2000	- Spain 2009

448. Interval between fastest lap drivers of the same nationality *(Longest)*

	years, days	races		
Mexico	43y, 325d	697	France 1968 (Pedro Rodríguez)	- Monaco 2012 (Sergio Pérez)
Australia	27y, 330d	459	Netherlands 1981 (Alan Jones)	- Hungary 2009 (Mark Webber)
Japan	22y, 162d	377	Australia 1989 (Satoru Nakajima)	- China 2012 (Kamui Kobayashi)

	years, days	races		
Finland	21y, 276d	190	Australia 1985 (Keke Rosberg)	- Italy 1997 (Mika Häkkinen)
Germany	20y, 339d	221	Germany 1954 (Karl Kling)	- France 1975 (Jochen Mass)
Belgium	17y, 322d	275	Italy 1972 (Jacky Ickx)	- Germany 1990 (Thierry Boutsen)
Germany	16y, 120d	260	Spain 1976 (Jochen Mass)	- Belgium 1992 (Michael Schumacher)
Argentina	16y, 70d	173	Argentina 1958 (Juan Manuel Fangio)	- South Africa 1974 (Carlos Reutemann)
France	15y, 360d	276	Monaco 1996 (Jean Alesi)	- Spain 2012 (Romain Grosjean)
Canada	14y, 312d	236	San Marino 1981 (Gilles Villeneuve)	- Australia 1996 (Jacques Villeneuve)

449. Interval between first time fastest lap drivers *(Longest)*

2 years and 145 days from South Africa 1963 (28 December, Dan Gurney) until Monaco 1966 (22 May, Lorenzo Bandini).

450. Fastest lap speed

Fastest

	km/h	mph		
Italy 2004	257.320	159.892	Rubens Barrichello	(Ferrari F2004)
Italy 2005	255.874	158.993	Kimi Räikkönen	(McLaren MP4-20 - Mercedes)
Italy 2003	254.848	158.356	Michael Schumacher	(Ferrari F2003-GA)
Italy 2006	252.604	156.961	Kimi Räikkönen	(McLaren MP4-21 - Mercedes)
Italy 2007	251.653	156.370	Fernando Alonso	(McLaren MP4-22 - Mercedes)
Italy 1993	249.835	155.241	Damon Hill	(Williams FW15C - Renault)
Italy 2002	249.289	154.901	Rubens Barrichello	(Ferrari F2002)
Italy 2010	247.861	154.014	Fernando Alonso	(Ferrari F10)
Italy 1971	247.016	153.489	Henri Pescarolo	(March 711 - Ford Cosworth)
Britain 1987	246.324	153.059	Nigel Mansell	(Williams FW11B - Honda)

Slowest

	km/h	mph		
Monaco 1950	103.135	64.085	Juan Manuel Fangio	(Alfa Romeo 158)
Monaco 1984	104.283	64.799	Ayrton Senna	(Toleman TG184 - Hart)
Monaco 1997	106.937	66.448	Michael Schumacher	(Ferrari F310B)
Monaco 1957	107.216	66.621	Juan Manuel Fangio	(Maserati 250F)
Monaco 1956	108.448	67.387	Juan Manuel Fangio	(Lancia-Ferrari D50)
Monaco 1955	110.566	68.703	Juan Manuel Fangio	(Mercedes-Benz W196)
Monaco 1958	112.545	69.932	Mike Hawthorn	(Ferrari Dino 246)
Monaco 1959	112.769	70.071	Jack Brabham	(Cooper T51 - Climax)
Monaco 1972	113.220	70.352	Jean-Pierre Beltoise	(BRM P160B)
Monaco 1961	117.570	73.055	Richie Ginther	(Ferrari 156) &
			Stirling Moss	(Lotus 18 - Climax)

451. Fastest laps but never a world championship *(Most)*

Gerhard Berger	21	Rubens Barrichello	17	Nico Rosberg	14
Stirling Moss	19	Felipe Massa	15	Riccardo Patrese	13
Mark Webber	19	Clay Regazzoni	15		
David Coulthard	18	Jacky Ickx	14		

452. Fastest laps but never a win *(Most)*

Chris Amon	3	Sergio Pérez	3	Nick Heidfeld	2
Jean-Pierre Jarier	3	Teo Fabi	2	Derek Warwick	2

453. Fastest laps but never a podium

Bertrand Gachot	1	Roberto Mières	1	Marc Surer	1
Esteban Gutiérrez	1	Satoru Nakajima	1	Adrian Sutil	1
Brian Henton	1	Jonathan Palmer	1		
Nico Hülkenberg	1	Bruno Senna	1		

454. Fastest laps but never a pole position *(Most)*

Jean-Pierre Beltoise	4	Bruce McLaren	3	Jochen Mass	2
Daniel Ricciardo	4	Sergio Pérez	3	Alessandro Nannini	2
Richie Ginther	3	François Cevert	2	Derek Warwick	2

455. Fastest laps but never scored a point

The only driver to achieve a fastest lap and yet never score a point was Brian Henton in Britain 1982.

456. Fastest laps but never led

Teo Fabi	2	Hans Herrmann	1	Jonathan Palmer	1
Richard Attwood	1	Kamui Kobayashi	1	Henri Pescarolo	1
Pedro de la Rosa	1	Onofré Marimón	1	Vitaly Petrov	1
Bertrand Gachot	1	Roberto Mières	1	Bruno Senna	1
Maurício Gugelmin	1	Roberto Moreno	1	Marc Surer	1
Brian Henton	1	Satoru Nakajima	1	Alexander Wurz	1

457. Milestones: Fastest laps I

Michael Schumacher	25th: Italy 1996, 50th: Belgium 2002, 75th: Turkey 2006
Jim Clark	25th: Canada 1967
Mika Häkkinen	25th: Hungary 2001
Lewis Hamilton	25th: Italy 2015
Nigel Mansell	25th: Monaco 1992
Alain Prost	25th: Hungary 1988
Kimi Räikkönen	25th: Brazil 2007
Sebastian Vettel	25th: Russia 2015

458. Milestones: Fastest laps II
(eg fastest lap in the 100th race was achieved by Jim Clark in a Lotus 25)

1st	Giuseppe Farina (Alfa Romeo 158)	Britain 1950
100th	Jim Clark (Lotus 25)	South Africa 1962
200th	Jacky Ickx (Ferrari 312B)	Spain 1972
250th	Clay Regazzoni (Ferrari 312T)	Germany 1975
300th	Mario Andretti (JPS Lotus 79)	Italy 1978
400th	Keke Rosberg (Williams FW10)	France 1985
500th	Roberto Moreno (Benetton B191)	Belgium 1991
600th	Jacques Villeneuve (Williams FW19)	Austria 1997
700th	Michael Schumacher (Ferrari F2003-GA)	Italy 2003
750th	Michael Schumacher (Ferrari 248 F1)	France 2006
800th	Sebastian Vettel (Red Bull RB5)	Britain 2009
900th	Lewis Hamilton (Mercedes-Benz F1 W05)	Singapore 2014

Excludes Indianapolis 500.

459. Milestones: Fastest laps III
(eg Innes Ireland was the 20th driver to achieve a fastest lap)

1st	Giuseppe Farina	Britain 1950	60th	René Arnoux	France 1979
20th	Innes Ireland	Belgium 1960	80th	Thierry Boutsen	Germany 1990
40th	Mario Andretti	South Africa 1971	100th	Felipe Massa	Spain 2006
50th	Patrick Depailler	Sweden 1974			

Excludes Indianapolis 500.

Chapter 11: Point Scoring Drivers

460. Points *(Most)*

		races		
Sebastian Vettel	1,896	124	United States 2007 (BMW Sauber)	- Abu Dhabi 2015 (Ferrari)
Lewis Hamilton	1,867	133	Australia 2007 (McLaren)	- Abu Dhabi 2015 (Mercedes-Benz)
Fernando Alonso	1,778	179	Australia 2003 (Renault)	- Hungary 2015 (McLaren)
Michael Schumacher (a)	1,566	221	Italy 1991 (Benetton)	- Brazil 2012 (Mercedes-Benz)
Jenson Button	1,214	155	Brazil 2000 (Williams)	- United States 2015 (McLaren)
Nico Rosberg	1,209.5	113	Bahrain 2006 (Williams)	- Abu Dhabi 2015 (Mercedes-Benz)
Kimi Räikkönen	1,174	154	Australia 2001 (Sauber)	- Abu Dhabi 2015 (Ferrari)
Felipe Massa	1,071	139	Malaysia 2002 (Sauber)	- Abu Dhabi 2015 (Williams)
Mark Webber	1,047.5	112	Australia 2002 (Minardi)	- Brazil 2013 (Red Bull)
Alain Prost	798.5	128	Argentina 1980 (McLaren)	- Australia 1993 (Williams)
Rubens Barrichello	658	140	Japan 1993 (Jordan)	- Canada 2011 (Williams)
Ayrton Senna	614	96	South Africa 1984 (Toleman)	- Australia 1993 (McLaren)
David Coulthard	535	121	Canada 1994 (Williams)	- Singapore 2008 (Red Bull)
Nelson Piquet	485.5	100	Netherlands 1979 (Brabham)	- Australia 1991 (Benetton)
Nigel Mansell	482	82	Belgium 1981 (Lotus)	- Australia 1994 (Williams)
Niki Lauda	420.5	73	Belgium 1973 (BRM)	- Netherlands 1985 (McLaren)
Mika Häkkinen	420	83	San Marino 1991 (Lotus)	- Japan 2001 (McLaren)
Gerhard Berger (b)	385	94	South Africa 1985 (Arrows)	- Europe 1997 (Benetton)
Daniel Ricciardo	360	42	China 2013 (Red Bull)	- Abu Dhabi 2015 (Red Bull)
Jackie Stewart	360	57	South Africa 1965 (BRM)	- Canada 1973 (Tyrrell)
Damon Hill	360	56	Brazil 1993 (Williams)	- Belgium 1999 (Jordan)
Ralf Schumacher	329	90	Argentina 1997 (Jordan)	- Hungary 2007 (Toyota)
Valtteri Bottas	326	31	United States 2013 (Williams)	- Brazil 2015 (Williams)
Carlos Reutemann	310	66	Canada 1972 (Brabham)	- South Africa 1982 (Williams)

		races		
Juan Pablo Montoya	307	57	Spain 2001 (Williams)	- Britain 2006 (McLaren)
Nico Hülkenberg	290	52	Malaysia 2010 (Williams)	- Abu Dhabi 2015 (Force India)
Graham Hill	289	59	Netherlands 1960 (BRM)	- Sweden 1974 (Lola)
Romain Grosjean	287	35	China 2012 (Lotus)	- Abu Dhabi 2015 (Lotus)
Emerson Fittipaldi	281	57	Germany 1970 (Lotus)	- Monaco 1980 (Fittipaldi)
Riccardo Patrese	281	73	Japan 1977 (Shadow)	- Italy 1993 (Benetton)
Juan Manuel Fangio	277.64	43	Monaco 1950 (Alfa Romeo)	- France 1958 (Maserati)
Giancarlo Fisichella	275	73	San Marino 1997 (Jordan)	- Belgium 2009 (Force India)
Jim Clark	274	40	Belgium 1960 (Lotus)	- South Africa 1968 (Lotus)
Robert Kubica	273	46	Italy 2006 (BMW Sauber)	- Abu Dhabi 2010 (Renault)
Sergio Pérez	266	47	Spain 2011 (Sauber)	- Abu Dhabi 2015 (Force India)
Jack Brabham	261	53	Monaco 1958 (Cooper)	- Britain 1970 (Brabham)
Nick Heidfeld	259	70	Australia 2001 (Sauber)	- Britain 2011 (Renault)
Jody Scheckter	255	53	Spain 1974 (Tyrrell)	- United States West 1980 (Ferrari)
Denny Hulme	248	61	France 1965 (Brabham)	- Canada 1974 (McLaren)
Jarno Trulli	246.5	72	Germany 1997 (Prost)	- Abu Dhabi 2009 (Toyota)
Jean Alesi	241	70	France 1989 (Tyrrell)	- Belgium 2001 (Jordan)
Jacques Villeneuve	235	53	Australia 1996 (Williams)	- Britain 2006 (BMW Sauber)
Jacques Laffite	228	59	Germany 1975 (Williams)	- France 1986 (Ligier)
Clay Regazzoni	212	52	Netherlands 1970 (Ferrari)	- Canada 1979 (Williams)
Ronnie Peterson	206	42	Monaco 1971 (March)	- Netherlands 1978 (JPS Lotus)
Alan Jones	206	39	Germany 1975 (Hill)	- Italy 1986 (Lola)
Bruce McLaren	196.5	50	Monaco 1959 (Cooper)	- Spain 1970 (McLaren)
Eddie Irvine	191	50	Japan 1993 (Jordan)	- Italy 2002 (Jaguar)
Stirling Moss	186.64	35	Belgium 1954 (Maserati)	- Germany 1961 (Lotus)
Michele Alboreto	186.5	47	Brazil 1982 (Tyrrell)	- Monaco 1994 (Minardi)

(a) In 1997, Michael Schumacher was disqualified from the championship for causing an accident with Jacques Villeneue in the European Grand Prix. However, his results and the points he scored during the season still stood, and are counted above.

461. Point scoring for drivers explained

Points have been distributed as follows:

1950 to 59	8, 6, 4, 3 and 2 points awarded to the first five finishers. The driver setting the fastest lap scored a point. Points were shared for joint fastest laps. Until 1957 where more than one driver shared a car, they shared the points (from 1958, points were only awarded to a driver who handled the car throughout). From 1956 where drivers shared cars and finished in a point scoring position in more than one car, only their best points score was taken into account (this only affected Fangio at Monaco 1956). Points were not awarded to a driver who retired. The Indianapolis 500 race featured as a round the world championship.
1960	8, 6, 4, 3, 2 and 1 point awarded to the first six finishers. No point awarded for fastest lap from now on. This was the final season featuring the Indianapolis 500 in the championship.
1961 to 90	9 points awarded to the winner, ie 9, 6, 4, 3, 2 and 1 point to the first six finishers. Drivers who completed 90% of the race distance were awarded points even if they retired.
1991 to 2002	as above, except 10 points now for a win.
2003 to 09	10 points awarded to the winner, with 8 for 2nd place, then 6, 5, 4, 3, 2, 1 down to 8th place.
2010 to present	25, 18, 15, 12, 10, 8, 6, 4, 2, 1 point awarded to the first 10 finishers.
2014 only	as above, but double points awarded in final race of the season.

Notes:

Although Formula 2 participants were permitted to run alongside Formula 1 cars in six races between 1957 and 69, they were ineligible for points.
Half points were awarded for races stopped before three-quarter distance was completed (see section 486 for the occasions).

Until 1990, drivers were only able to count points from a specific number of races towards their total each year, as follows:

1950 - best 4 from 7	1967 - best 5 from first 6, 4 from remaining 5	1984 - best 11 from 16
1951 - best 4 from 8	1968 - best 5 from first 6, 5 from remaining 6	1985 - best 11 from 16
1952 - best 4 from 8	1969 - best 5 from first 6, 4 from remaining 5	1986 - best 11 from 16
1953 - best 4 from 9	1970 - best 6 from first 7, 5 from remaining 6	1987 - best 11 from 16
1954 - best 5 from 9	1971 - best 5 from first 6, 4 from remaining 5	1988 - best 11 from 16
1955 - best 5 from 7	1972 - best 5 from first 6, 5 from remaining 6	1989 - best 11 from 16
1956 - best 5 from 8	1973 - best 7 from first 8, 6 from remaining 7	
1957 - best 5 from 8	1974 - best 7 from first 8, 6 from remaining 7	1990 - best 11 from 16
1958 - best 6 from 11	1975 - best 6 from first 7, 6 from remaining 7	
1959 - best 5 from 9	1976 - best 7 from first 8, 7 from remaining 8	*For point scoring for constructors explained, see section 883.*
1960 - best 6 from 10	1977 - best 8 from first 9, 7 from remaining 8	
1961 - best 5 from 8	1978 - best 7 from first 8, 7 from remaining 8	
1962 - best 5 from 9	1979 - best 4 from first 7, 4 from remaining 8	
1963 - best 6 from 10	1980 - best 5 from first 7, 5 from remaining 7	
1964 - best 6 from 10	1981 - best 11 from 15	
1965 - best 6 from 10	1982 - best 11 from 16	
1966 - best 5 from 9	1983 - best 11 from 15	

462. Point scoring races *(Most)*

		% of starts		
Michael Schumacher	221	71.99	Italy 1991 (Benetton)	- Brazil 2012 (Mercedes-Benz)
Fernando Alonso	179	70.75	Australia 2003 (Renault)	- Hungary 2015 (McLaren)
Jenson Button	155	54.58	Brazil 2000 (Williams)	- United States 2015 (McLaren)
Kimi Räikkönen	154	66.67	Australia 2001 (Sauber)	- Abu Dhabi 2015 (Ferrari)
Rubens Barrichello	140	43.34	Japan 1993 (Jordan)	- Canada 2011 (Williams)
Felipe Massa	139	60.70	Malaysia 2002 (Sauber)	- Abu Dhabi 2015 (Williams)
Lewis Hamilton	133	79.64	Australia 2007 (McLaren)	- Abu Dhabi 2015 (Mercedes-Benz)
Alain Prost	128	64.32	Argentina 1980 (McLaren)	- Australia 1993 (Williams)
Sebastian Vettel	124	78.48	United States 2007 (BMW Sauber)	- Abu Dhabi 2015 (Ferrari)
David Coulthard	121	49.19	Canada 1994 (Williams)	- Singapore 2008 (Red Bull)
Nico Rosberg	113	61.08	Bahrain 2006 (Williams)	- Abu Dhabi 2015 (Mercedes-Benz)
Mark Webber	112	52.09	Australia 2002 (Minardi)	- Brazil 2013 (Red Bull)
Nelson Piquet	100	49.02	Netherlands 1979 (Brabham)	- Australia 1991 (Benetton)
Ayrton Senna	96	59.63	South Africa 1984 (Toleman)	- Australia 1993 (McLaren)
Gerhard Berger	94	44.76	South Africa 1985 (Arrows)	- Europe 1997 (Benetton)
Ralf Schumacher	90	50.00	Argentina 1997 (Jordan)	- Hungary 2007 (Toyota)
Mika Häkkinen	83	51.55	San Marino 1991 (Lotus)	- Japan 2001 (McLaren)
Nigel Mansell	82	43.85	Belgium 1981 (Lotus)	- Australia 1994 (Williams)
Giancarlo Fisichella	73	31.88	San Marino 1997 (Jordan)	- Belgium 2009 (Force India)
Niki Lauda	73	42.69	Belgium 1973 (BRM)	- Netherlands 1985 (McLaren)
Riccardo Patrese	73	28.52	Japan 1977 (Shadow)	- Italy 1993 (Benetton)

463. Point scorer age

Youngest

	years, days	
Max Verstappen	17y, 180d	Malaysia 2015
Daniil Kvyat	19y, 324d	Australia 2014
Sebastian Vettel	19y, 349d	United States 2007
Jaime Alguersuari	20y, 12d	Malaysia 2010
Jenson Button	20y, 67d	Brazil 2000
Ricardo Rodríguez	20y, 123d	Belgium 1962
Sébastien Buemi	20y, 149d	Australia 2009
Carlos Sainz	20y, 195d	Australia 2015
Nico Rosberg	20y, 258d	Bahrain 2006
Chris Amon	20y, 309d	Netherlands 1964

Oldest

	years, days	
Philippe Etançelin	53y, 249d	Italy 1950
Luigi Fagioli	53y, 22d	France 1951
Louis Chiron	50y, 291d	Monaco 1950
Louis Rosier	50y, 274d	Germany 1956
Felice Bonetto	50y, 75d	Switzerland 1953
Piero Taruffi	48y, 334d	Italy 1955
Giuseppe Farina	48y, 218d	Belgium 1955
Chico Landi	48y, 192d	Argentina 1956
Luigi Villoresi	47y, 18d	Belgium 1956
Juan Manuel Fangio	47y, 12d	France 1958

464. Scored more points in a season than the champion

Graham Hill, 1964	Scored 41 points, whilst John Surtees scored 40. With only the best 6 scores counting, Hill had to drop 2, leaving him 1 point behind Surtees who dropped no points.
Alain Prost, 1988	Scored 105, against Ayrton Senna's 94. With only the best 11 scores counting, Prost had to drop 18, but Senna only had to drop 4. Senna's net points tally was therefore 90, compared to Prost's 87.

465. Points scored in a season *(Most)*

from 2010 with new points system			
Sebastian Vettel	397	2013 (wc)	(Red Bull RB9 - Renault)
Sebastian Vettel	392	2011 (wc)	(Red Bull RB7 - Renault)
Lewis Hamilton	384	2014 (wc)	(Mercedes-Benz F1 W05)
Lewis Hamilton	381	2015 (wc)	(Mercedes-Benz F1 W06)
Nico Rosberg	322	2015	(Mercedes-Benz F1 W06)
Nico Rosberg	317	2014	(Mercedes-Benz F1 W05)
Sebastian Vettel	281	2012 (wc)	(Red Bull RB8 - Renault)
Fernando Alonso	278	2012	(Ferrari F2012)
Sebastian Vettel	278	2015	(Ferrari SF15-T)
Jenson Button	270	2011	(McLaren MP4-26 - Mercedes)
before 2010			
Michael Schumacher	148	2004 (wc)	(Ferrari F2004)
Michael Schumacher	144	2002 (wc)	(Ferrari F2001, F2002)
Fernando Alonso	134	2006 (wc)	(Renault R26)

Fernando Alonso	133	2005 (wc)	(Renault R25)
Michael Schumacher	123	2001 (wc)	(Ferrari F2001)
Michael Schumacher	121	2006	(Ferrari 248 F1)
Rubens Barrichello	114	2004	(Ferrari F2004)
Kimi Räikkönen	112	2005	(McLaren MP4-20 - Mercedes)
Kimi Räikkönen	110	2007 (wc)	(Ferrari F2007)
Fernando Alonso	109	2007	(McLaren MP4-22 - Mercedes)
Lewis Hamilton	109	2007	(McLaren MP4-22 - Mercedes)

(wc) World champion that season.

466. Point scoring races in a season *(Most)*

Kimi Räikkönen	19 of 20	2012	(Lotus E20 - Renault)
Fernando Alonso	18 of 19	2011	(Ferrari F150th Italia)
Lewis Hamilton	18 of 19	2015 (wc)	(Mercedes-Benz F1 W06)
Sebastian Vettel	18 of 19	2011 (wc)	(Red Bull RB7 - Renault)
Sebastian Vettel	18 of 19	2013 (wc)	(Red Bull RB9 - Renault)
Mark Webber	18 of 19	2011	(Red Bull RB7 - Renault)
Fernando Alonso	18 of 20	2012	(Ferrari F2012)
Michael Schumacher	17 of 17	2002 (wc)	(Ferrari F2001, F2002)
Fernando Alonso	17 of 19	2013	(Ferrari F138)
Fernando Alonso	17 of 19	2014	(Ferrari F14 T)
Valtteri Bottas	17 of 19	2015	(Williams FW36 - Mercedes)
Jenson Button	17 of 19	2011	(McLaren MP4-26 - Mercedes)
Lewis Hamilton	17 of 19	2013	(Mercedes-Benz F1 W04)
Nico Rosberg	17 of 19	2015	(Mercedes-Benz F1 W06)
Sebastian Vettel	17 of 19	2015	(Ferrari SF15-T)
Mark Webber	17 of 19	2010	(Red Bull RB6 - Renault)
Sebastian Vettel	17 of 20	2012 (wc)	(Red Bull RB8 - Renault)

(wc) World champion that season.

467. Points scored in every race of a season

Michael Schumacher	17	2002	(Ferrari F2001, F2002)
Juan Manuel Fangio	8	1954	(Maserati 250F, Mercedes-Benz W196, W196 str.)
Juan Manuel Fangio	6	1955	(Mercedes-Benz W196, W196 str.)

All became world champion that season.

468. Points scored in all but one race of a season

from 2010 with new points system			
Kimi Räikkönen	19	2012	(Lotus E20 - Renault)
Fernando Alonso	18	2011	(Ferrari F150th Italia)
Lewis Hamilton	18	2015 (wc)	(Mercedes-Benz F1 W06)
Sebastian Vettel	18	2011 (wc)	(Red Bull RB7 - Renault)
Sebastian Vettel	18	2013 (wc)	(Red Bull RB9 - Renault)
Mark Webber	18	2011	(Red Bull RB7 - Renault)
before 2010			
Fernando Alonso	16	2007	(McLaren MP4-22 - Mercedes)
Jenson Button	16	2009 (wc)	(Brawn BGP 001 - Mercedes)
Michael Schumacher	15	2003 (wc)	(Ferrari F2002, F2003-GA)
Jim Clark	9	1963 (wc)	(Lotus 25 - Climax)
Mike Hawthorn	9	1958 (wc)	(Ferrari Dino 246)
Graham Hill	9	1965	(BRM P261)
Graham Hill	8	1962 (wc)	(BRM P57)
Alberto Ascari	7	1953 (wc)	(Ferrari 500)
Mike Hawthorn	7	1953	(Ferrari 500)
Alberto Ascari	6	1952 (wc)	(Ferrari 500)
Juan Manuel Fangio	6	1951 (wc)	(Alfa Romeo 159)

Juan Manuel Fangio	6	1956 (wc)	(Lancia-Ferrari D50)
Juan Manuel Fangio	6	1957 (wc)	(Maserati 250F)
Giuseppe Farina	6	1951	(Alfa Romeo 159)
Stirling Moss	6	1956	(Maserati 250F)
Luigi Fagioli	5	1950	(Alfa Romeo 158)

(wc) World champion that season.

469. Consecutive point scoring races *(Most)*

Kimi Räikkönen	27	Bahrain 2012 (Lotus E20)	- Hungary 2013 (Lotus E21)
Michael Schumacher	24	Hungary 2001 (Ferrari F2001)	- Malaysia 2003 (Ferrari F2002)
Fernando Alonso	23	Europe 2011 (Ferrari F150th Italia)	- Hungary 2012 (Ferrari F2012)
Juan Manuel Fangio	21	France 1953 (Maserati A6GCM)	- Monaco 1956 (Lancia-Ferrari D50)
Sebastian Vettel	21	Britain 2014 (Red Bull RB10)	- Hungary 2015 (Ferrari SF15-T)
Lewis Hamilton	19	Italy 2014 (Mercedes-Benz F1 W05)	- Italy 2015 (Mercedes-Benz F1 W06)
Sebastian Vettel	19	Brazil 2010 (Red Bull RB6)	- India 2011 (Red Bull RB7)
Fernando Alonso	18	Turkey 2005 (Renault R25)	- Germany 2006 (Renault R26)
Michael Schumacher	18	San Marino 2003 (Ferrari F2002)	- Spain 2004 (Ferrari F2004)
Fernando Alonso	17	China 2006 (Renault R26)	- Belgium 2007 (McLaren MP4-22)
Nico Rosberg	17	Belgium 2013 (Mercedes-Benz F1 W04)	- Austria 2014 (Mercedes-Benz F1 W05)

470. Consecutive point scoring races from the start of a season *(Most)*
(not counting any into the following season)

from 2010 with new points system			
Sebastian Vettel	17	2011 (wc)	(Red Bull RB7 - Renault)
Mark Webber	12	2011	(Red Bull RB7 - Renault)
Fernando Alonso	12	2014	(Ferrari F14 T)
Lewis Hamilton	12	2015 (wc)	(Mercedes-Benz F1 W06)
Fernando Alonso	11	2012	(Ferrari F2012)
Nico Rosberg	11	2015	(Mercedes-Benz F1 W06)
Nico Hülkenberg	10	2014	(Force India VJM07 - Mercedes)
Kimi Räikkönen	10	2013	(Lotus E21 - Renault)
Sebastian Vettel	10	2015	(Ferrari SF15-T)
Jenson Button	8	2011	(McLaren MP4-26 - Mercedes)
Nico Rosberg	8	2014	(Mercedes-Benz F1 W05)
Mark Webber	8	2010	(Red Bull RB6 - Renault)
before 2010			
Michael Schumacher	17	2002 (a)(wc)	(Ferrari F2001, F2002)
Fernando Alonso	14	2007	(McLaren MP4-22 - Mercedes)
Fernando Alonso	12	2006 (wc)	(Renault R26)
Rubens Barrichello	11	2004	(Ferrari F2004)
Jenson Button	11	2009 (wc)	(Brawn BGP 001 - Mercedes)
Ralf Schumacher	10	2003	(Williams FW25 - BMW)
Lewis Hamilton	9	2007 (wc)	(McLaren MP4-22 - Mercedes)
Graham Hill	9	1965	(BRM P261)
Jenson Button	8	2004	(BAR 006 - Honda)
Juan Manuel Fangio	8	1954 (a)(wc)	(Maserati 250F, Mercedes-Benz W196)

(a) Sequence continued into the following season. (wc) World champion that season.

471. Seasons of scoring points *(Most)*

Michael Schumacher	19	1991 - 2012	(Benetton, Ferrari, Mercedes-Benz)
Rubens Barrichello	18	1993 - 2011	(Jordan, Stewart, Ferrari, Honda, Brawn, Williams)
Jenson Button	16	2000 - 15	(Williams, Benetton, Renault, BAR, Honda, Brawn, McLaren)
Riccardo Patrese	16	1977 - 93	(Shadow, Arrows, Brabham, Alfa Romeo, Williams, Benetton)
David Coulthard	15	1994 - 2008	(Williams, McLaren, Red Bull)
Graham Hill	14	1960 - 74	(BRM, Lotus, Brabham, Lola)
Fernando Alonso	13	2003 - 15	(Renault, McLaren, Ferrari)
Gerhard Berger	13	1985 - 97	(Arrows, Benetton, Ferrari, McLaren)

Jack Brabham	13	1958 - 70	(Cooper, Brabham, Lotus)
Nigel Mansell	13	1981 - 94	(Lotus, Williams, Ferrari)
Felipe Massa	13	2002 - 15	(Sauber, Ferrari, Williams)
Nelson Piquet	13	1979 - 91	(Brabham, Williams, Lotus, Benetton)
Alain Prost	13	1980 - 93	(McLaren, Renault, Ferrari, Williams)
Kimi Räikkönen	13	2001 - 15	(Sauber, McLaren, Ferrari, Lotus)
Jarno Trulli	13	1997 - 2009	(Prost, Jordan, Renault, Toyota)

472. Consecutive seasons of scoring points *(Most)*

Jenson Button	16	2000 - 15	(Williams, Renault, BAR, Honda, Brawn, McLaren)
Michael Schumacher	16	1991 - 2006	(Benetton, Ferrari)
David Coulthard	15	1994 - 2008	(Williams, McLaren, Red Bull)
Rubens Barrichello	14	1993 - 2006	(Jordan, Stewart, Ferrari, Honda)
Fernando Alonso	13	2003 - 15	(Renault, McLaren, Renault, Ferrari, McLaren)
Gerhard Berger	13	1985 - 97	(Arrows, Benetton, Ferrari, McLaren)
Jack Brabham	13	1958 - 70	(Cooper, Brabham, Lotus)
Graham Hill	13	1960 - 72	(BRM, Lotus, Brabham)
Nelson Piquet	13	1979 - 91	(Brabham, Williams, Lotus, Benetton)
Jarno Trulli	13	1997 - 2009	(Prost, Jordan, Renault, Toyota)

473. Points scored by nationality

	points	races	drivers		
Great Britain	7,305.28	763	59	Britain 1950 (Reg Parnell)	- Abu Dhabi 2015 (Lewis Hamilton)
Germany	6,110.5	456	20	Switzerland 1953 (Hermann Lang)	- Abu Dhabi 2015 (Nico Rosberg, Sebastian Vettel, Nico Hülkenberg)
Brazil	3,323	490	19	Argentina 1956 (Chico Landi)	- Abu Dhabi 2015 (Felipe Massa)
France	2,673.47	461	36	Britain 1950 (Yves Giraud-Cabantous, Louis Rosier)	- Abu Dhabi 2015 (Romain Grosjean)
Finland	2,227.5	297	7	Argentina 1980 (Keke Rosberg)	- Abu Dhabi 2015 (Kimi Räikkönen)
Italy	2,019.8	408	47	Britain 1950 (Giuseppe Farina, Luigi Fagioli)	- Korea 2010 (Vitantonio Liuzzi)
Australia	1,881.5	240	5	Monaco 1958 (Jack Brabham)	- Abu Dhabi 2015 (Daniel Ricciardo)
Spain	1,878	200	8	Britain 1956 (Alfonso de Portago)	- United States 2015 (Carlos Sainz)
Austria	990.5	215	7	Germany 1965 (Jochen Rindt)	- Europe 2007 (Alexander Wurz)
United States	734	152	16	Belgium 1956 (Harry Schell)	- Italy 1993 (Michael Andretti)
Argentina	697.42	115	7	Monaco 1950 (Juan Manuel Fangio)	- South Africa 1982 (Carlos Reutemann)
New Zealand	537.5	120	4	Monaco 1959 (Bruce McLaren)	- Spain 1976 (Chris Amon)
Sweden	387	105	7	Morocco 1958 (Jo Bonnier)	- Italy 2015 (Marcus Ericsson)
Mexico	360	78	5	Belgium 1962 (Ricardo Rodríguez)	- Abu Dhabi 2015 (Sergio Pérez)
Belgium	357	93	7	Belgium 1952 (Paul Frère)	- Australia 1992 (Thierry Boutsen)
Switzerland	348	104	7	Switzerland 1951 (Emmanuel de Graffenried)	- Korea 2011 (Sébastien Buemi)
Canada	342	74	2	Belgium 1978 (Gilles Villeneuve)	- Britain 2006 (Jacques Villeneuve)
Colombia	307	57	1	Spain 2001 (Juan Pablo Montoya)	- Britain 2006 (Juan Pablo Montoya)
South Africa	282	62	3	Netherlands 1962 (Tony Maggs)	- United States West 1980 (Jody Scheckter)
Poland	273	46	1	Italy 2006 (Robert Kubica)	- Abu Dhabi 2010 (Robert Kubica)
Japan	209	64	7	San Marino 1987 (Satoru Nakajima)	- Brazil 2012 (Kamui Kobayashi)
Russia	167	32	2	China 2010 (Vitaly Petrov)	- Abu Dhabi 2015 (Daniil Kvyat)
Venezuela	77	15	2	United States West 1983 (Johnny Cecotto)	- Brazil 2015 (Pastor Maldonado)
Netherlands	76	24	5	Netherlands 1962 (Carel Godin de Beaufort)	- Brazil 2015 (Max Verstappen)
Denmark	56	13	2	Canada 1998 (Jan Magnussen)	- Brazil 2014 (Kevin Magnussen)
Ireland	15	8	1	Canada 1978 (Derek Daly)	- Caesars Palace 1982 (Derek Daly)
Portugal	8	3	2	Australia 1995 (Pedro Lamy)	- Belgium 2005 (Tiago Monteiro)
Thailand	8	3	1	Monaco 1950 ('B' Bira)	- France 1954 ('B' Bira)
Southern Rhodesia	6	1	1	South Africa 1967 (John Love)	
India	5	1	1	United States 2005 (Narain Karthikeyan)	
Monaco	4	1	1	Monaco 1950 (Louis Chiron)	
Chile	3	2	1	Netherlands 1981 (Eliseo Salazar)	- San Marino 1982 (Eliseo Salazar)
Hungary	1	1	1	United States 2004 (Zsolt Baumgartner)	

Of those who started races, drivers from the following nations have not scored points: Czech Republic, Liechtenstein, Malaysia, Morocco and Uruguay.
Yannick Dalmas (France) and Jo Gartner (Austria) are excluded. They finished a race in a point scoring position, but were not eligible for points (drove their team's second car, although only one car was registered for the season).

Indianapolis 500

| United States | 264 | 11 | 35 | 1950 - 1960 |

474. Drivers of the same nationality to score points in a race (Most)

Italy	5	Italy 1951	1: Alberto Ascari, 3: Felice Bonetto & Giuseppe Farina, 4: Luigi Villoresi, 5: Piero Taruffi
Britain	5	Netherlands 1964	1: Jim Clark, 2: John Surtees, 3: Peter Arundell, 4: Graham Hill, 6: Bob Anderson
Britain	5	South Africa 1965	1: Jim Clark, 2: John Surtees, 3: Graham Hill, 4: Mike Spence, 6: Jackie Stewart
Britain	5	Britain 1965	1: Jim Clark, 2: Graham Hill, 3: John Surtees, 4: Mike Spence, 5: Jackie Stewart
Germany	5	Britain 2010	3: Nico Rosberg, 7: Sebastian Vettel, 8: Adrian Sutil, 9: Michael Schumacher, 10: Nico Hülkenberg

Excludes Indianapolis 500.

475. Point scores at the same circuit (Most)

Michael Schumacher	Catalunya	17	1991 - 2011	Michael Schumacher	Suzuka	13	1994 - 2011
Michael Schumacher	Interlagos	16	1992 - 2012	Fernando Alonso	Melbourne	12	2003 - 14
Michael Schumacher	Montréal	14	1992 - 2011	Jenson Button	Suzuka	12	2000 - 14
Michael Schumacher	Monza	14	1991 - 2012	Michael Schumacher	Imola	12	1993 - 2006
Michael Schumacher	Hockenheim	13	1992 - 2012	Michael Schumacher	Magny-Cours	12	1993 - 2006
Michael Schumacher	Silverstone	13	1992 - 2012	Michael Schumacher	Spa-Francorchamps	12	1992 - 2012

476. First point was on home soil

Jean Alesi	France 1989	(Paul Ricard)	Neville Lederle	South Africa 1962	(East London)
René Arnoux	France 1979	(Dijon-Prenois)	Vitantonio Liuzzi	San Marino 2005	(Imola)
Lucien Bianchi	Belgium 1960	(Spa-Francorchamps)	Umberto Maglioli	Italy 1954	(Monza)
Giulio Cabianca	Italy 1960	(Monza)	Robert Manzon	France 1950	(Reims-Gueux)
Eugène Chaboud	France 1950	(Reims-Gueux)	Gerhard Mitter	Germany 1963	(Nürburgring)
Eddie Cheever	United States West 1981	(Long Beach)	Alessandro Nannini	San Marino 1988	(Imola)
Louis Chiron	Monaco 1950	(Monte-Carlo)	Reg Parnell	Britain 1950	(Silverstone)
Andrea De Cesaris	San Marino 1981	(Imola)	André Pilette	Belgium 1954	(Spa-Francorchamps)
Emmanuel de Graffenried	Switzerland 1951	(Bremgarten)	Dennis Poore	Britain 1952	(Silverstone)
Philippe Etançelin	France 1950	(Reims-Gueux)	Daniel Ricciardo	Australia 2012	(Melbourne)
Jack Fairman	Britain 1956	(Silverstone)	Pedro Rodríguez	Mexico 1964	(Mexico City)
Rudi Fischer	Switzerland 1952	(Bremgarten)	Roy Salvadori	Britain 1957	(Aintree)
Giancarlo Fisichella	San Marino 1997	(Imola)	Takuma Sato	Japan 2002	(Suzuka)
Paul Frère	Belgium 1952	(Spa-Francorchamps)	Giorgio Scarlatti	Italy 1957	(Monza)
Oscar Gálvez	Argentina 1953	(Buenos Aires No.2)	Dorino Serafini	Italy 1950	(Monza)
Carel Godin de Beaufort	Netherlands 1962	(Zandvoort)	John Surtees	Britan 1960	(Silverstone)
Horace Gould	Britain 1956	(Silverstone)	Eric Thompson	Britain 1952	(Silverstone)
Olivier Grouillard	France 1989	(Paul Ricard)	Maurice Trintignant	France 1952	(Rouen-les-Essarts)
Walt Hansgen	United States 1964	(Watkins Glen)	Gijs van Lennep	Netherlands 1973	(Zandvoort)
Nicola Larini	San Marino 1994	(Imola)	Mark Webber	Australia 2002	(Melbourne)

Excludes Indianapolis 500.

477. Race starts taken to score their first point
(number of races includes the race with the first point)

Fewest (first race start)

18 points: Kevin Magnussen, Australia 2014

10 points: Felipe Nasr, Australia 2015

9 points: Giancarlo Baghetti, France 1961; Giuseppe Farina, Britain 1950

6 points: Alberto Ascari, Monaco 1950; Luigi Fagioli, Britain 1950; Lewis Hamilton, Australia 2007; Karl Kling, France 1954; Mike Parkes, France 1966; Jacques Villeneuve, Australia 1996

4 points: Peter Arundell, Monaco 1964; Mark Donohue, Canada 1971; Masten Gregory, Monaco 1957; Reg Parnell, Britain 1950; Peter Whitehead, France 1950; Reine Wisell, United States 1970

3 points: Jean Alesi, France 1989; Vic Elford, France 1968; Yves Giraud-Cabantous, Britain 1950; Ignazio Giunti, Belgium 1970; Mike Hawthorn, Belgium 1952; Johnny Herbert, Brazil 1989; Innes Ireland, Netherlands 1959; Stuart Lewis-Evans, Monaco 1957; Dennis Poore, Britain 1952; Clay Regazzoni, Netherlands 1970; Dorino Serafini, Italy 1950; Raymond Sommer, Monaco 1950; Ken Wharton, Switzerland 1952

2 points: Felice Bonetto, Switzerland 1950; Sébastien Bourdais, Australia 2008; Alan Brown, Switzerland 1952; Sébastien Buemi, Australia 2009; Paul Frère, Belgium 1952; Oscar Gálvez, Argentina 1953; Olivier Gendebien, Argentina 1956; Timo Glock, Canada 2004; Daniil Kvyat, Australia 2014; Hermann Lang, Switzerland 1953; Cesare Perdisa, Monaco 1955; Nico Rosberg, Bahrain 2006; Louis Rosier, Britain 1950; Carlos Sainz, Australia 2015; Eric Thompson, Britain 1952; Mark Webber, Australia 2002

1.5 points: Gerino Gerini, Argentina 1956

1 point: Lucien Bianchi, Belgium 1960; Pedro de la Rosa, Australia 1999; Paul Di Resta, Australia 2011; George Follmer, South Africa 1973; Richie Ginther, Monaco 1960; Eddie Irvine, Japan 1993; Neville Lederle, South Africa 1962; Vitantonio Liuzzi, San Marino 2005; Arturo Merzario, Britain 1972; Alain Prost, Argentina 1980; Kimi Räikkönen, Australia 2001; Ludovico Scarfiotti, Netherlands 1963; Jackie Stewart, South Africa 1965; Sebastian Vettel, United States 2007

A further 12 Indianapolis 500 drivers scored point(s) in their first world championship race.

Most

Nicola Larini	44	San Marino 1994
Jonathan Palmer	42	Monaco 1987
Philippe Alliot	32	Mexico 1986
Alessandro Nannini	32	San Marino 1988
Alex Caffi	31	Monaco 1989

Ukyo Katayama	31	Brazil 1994
Harry Schell	26	Belgium 1956
Jules Bianchi	25	Monaco 2014
Jan Magnussen	25	Canada 1998
Pedro Diniz	24	Spain 1996

For most races started but never scored a point, see section 189.

478. Points scored in each of a driver's first two or more races

	races	points			
Lewis Hamilton	9	70	Australia 2007	- Britain 2007	(McLaren MP4-22 - Mercedes)
Jackie Stewart	6	25	South Africa 1965	- Netherlands 1965	(BRM P261)
Richie Ginther	6	20	Monaco 1960	- Belgium 1961 (a)	(Ferrari Dino 246MP, Dino 246, 156)
Kevin Magnussen	2	20	Australia 2014	- Malaysia 2014	(McLaren MP4-29 - Mercedes)
Carlos Sainz	2	6	Australia 2015	- Malaysia 2015	(Toro Rosso STR10 - Renault)
Peter Arundell	2	8	Monaco 1964	- Netherlands 1964	(Lotus 25 - Climax)
Clay Regazzoni	2	6	Netherlands 1970	- Britain 1970 (a)	(Ferrari 312B)
George Follmer	2	5	South Africa 1973	- Spain 1973	(Shadow DN1 - Ford Cosworth)
Daniil Kvyat	2	3	Australia 2014	- Malaysia 2014	(Toro Rosso STR9 - Renault)
Alain Prost	2	3	Argentina 1980	- Brazil 1980	(McLaren M29 - Ford Cosworth)
Paul Di Resta	2	2	Australia 2011	- Malaysia 2011	(Force India VJM04 - Mercedes)

(a) Not consecutive events (ie he missed races inbetween).

479. Points scored in their first season *(Most)*
(excluding 1950, the first season of the championship)

	points	races	season	position	
Lewis Hamilton	109	15 of 17	2007	2nd	(McLaren MP4-22 - Mercedes)
Jacques Villeneuve	78	11 of 16	1996	2nd	(Williams FW18 - Renault)
Kevin Magnussen	55	12 of 19	2014	11th	(McLaren MP4-29 - Mercedes)
Max Verstappen	49	10 of 19	2015	12th	(Toro Rosso STR10 - Renault)
Jackie Stewart	34	7 of 10	1965	3rd	(BRM P261)
Clay Regazzoni	33	6 of 8	1970	3rd	(Ferrari 312B)
Juan Pablo Montoya	31	5 of 17	2001	6th	(Williams FW23 - BMW)
Heikki Kovalainen	30	11 of 17	2007	7th	(Renault R27)
Paul Di Resta	27	8 of 19	2011	13th	(Force India VJM04 - Mercedes)
Felipe Nasr	27	6 of 19	2015	13th	(Sauber C34 - Ferrari)
Vitaly Petrov	27	5 of 19	2010	13th	(Renault R30)
Nico Hülkenberg	22	7 of 19	2010	14th	(Williams FW32 - Cosworth)
Carlos Sainz	18	7 of 19	2015	15th	(Toro Rosso STR10 - Renault)
Jean-Eric Vergne	16	4 of 20	2012	17th	(Toro Rosso STR7 - Ferrari)
David Coulthard	14	5 of 8	1994	8th	(Williams FW16, FW16B - Renault)
James Hunt	14	4 of 8	1973	8th	(March 731 - Ford Cosworth)
Ayrton Senna	13	5 of 15	1984	9th	(Toleman TG183B, TG184 - Hart)
Dan Gurney	13	3 of 4	1959	7th	(Ferrari Dino 246)
Jenson Button	12	6 of 17	2000	8th	(Williams FW22 - BMW)
Eugenio Castellotti	12	3 of 6	1955	3rd	(Lancia D50, Ferrari 555, 625)
Karl Kling	12	3 of 6	1954	5th	(Mercedes-Benz W196, W196 str.)
Emerson Fittipaldi	12	2 of 6	1970	10th	(Lotus 49C, 72C - Ford Cosworth)

Excludes Indianapolis 500.

480. Different point scorers in a season

Most

1989	29		1991	24
1982	26		2005	24
1970	25		1964	22
1994	25		1971	22
1968	24		1993	22

Fewest

1953	12		1958	16
1951	13		1965	16
1959	14		1996	16
1950	16		2000	16
1952	16			

Excludes Indianapolis 500.

Total for each season

1950 - 16, 1951 - 13, 1952 - 16, 1953 - 12, 1954 - 20, 1955 - 17, 1956 - 21, 1957 - 17, 1958 - 16, 1959 - 14, 1960 - 21, 1961 - 17, 1962 - 19, 1963 - 17, 1964 - 22, 1965 - 16, 1966 - 20, 1967 - 21, 1968 - 24, 1969 - 18, 1970 - 25, 1971 - 22, 1972 - 21, 1973 - 21, 1974 - 20, 1975 - 21, 1976 - 20, 1977 - 21, 1978 - 21, 1979 - 21, 1980 - 21, 1981 - 21, 1982 - 26, 1983 - 20, 1984 - 20, 1985 - 20, 1986 - 19, 1987 - 21, 1988 - 17, 1989 - 29, 1990 - 18, 1991 - 24, 1992 - 19, 1993 - 22, 1994 - 25, 1995 - 18, 1996 - 16, 1997 - 20, 1998 - 17, 1999 - 18, 2000 - 16, 2001 - 18, 2002 - 18, 2003 - 20, 2004 - 20, 2005 - 24, 2006 - 19, 2007 - 19, 2008 - 18, 2009 - 19, 2010 - 19, 2011 - 19, 2012 - 18, 2013 - 18, 2014 - 17, 2015 - 18   *Excludes Indianapolis 500.*

481. First time point scorers in a season

Most

1950	16		1989	8
1956	11		1964	7
1970	11		1968	7
1952	9		1974	7
1954	9		1991	7
1960	8			

Fewest

1969	0		1999	2
1976	1		2000	2
1998	1		2006	2
1961	2		2009	2
1990	2		2013	2
1996	2			

Excludes Indianapolis 500.

482. Seasons of scoring points with the same constructor *(Most)*

Michael Schumacher	Ferrari	11	1996 - 2006
Jack Brabham	Brabham	9	1962 - 70
Jim Clark	Lotus	9	1960 - 68
David Coulthard	McLaren	9	1996 - 2004
Mika Häkkinen	McLaren	9	1993 - 2001
Jacques Laffite	Ligier	9	1976 - 86
Felipe Massa	Ferrari	8	2006 - 13

Graham Hill	BRM	7	1960 - 66
Denny Hulme	McLaren	7	1968 - 74
Nigel Mansell	Williams	7	1985 - 94
Bruce McLaren	Cooper	7	1959 - 65
Nelson Piquet	Brabham	7	1979 - 85
Alain Prost	McLaren	7	1980 - 89
Mark Webber	Red Bull	7	2007 - 13

483. Point scoring races with the same constructor *(Most)*

	constructor	races	points		
Michael Schumacher	Ferrari	145	1,066	Brazil 1996	- Brazil 2006
Felipe Massa	Ferrari	103	789	Malaysia 2006	- Brazil 2013
Sebastian Vettel	Red Bull	96	1,577	China 2009	- Abu Dhabi 2014
Nico Rosberg	Mercedes-Benz	88	1,134	Bahrain 2010	- Abu Dhabi 2015
Mark Webber	Red Bull	87	978.5	United States 2007	- Brazil 2013
David Coulthard	McLaren	87	412	Europe 1996	- Italy 2004
Fernando Alonso	Ferrari	86	1,190	Bahrain 2010	- Abu Dhabi 2014
Lewis Hamilton	McLaren	82	913	Australia 2007	- United States 2012
Jenson Button	McLaren	78	887	Bahrain 2010	- United States 2015
Mika Häkkinen	McLaren	76	407	Japan 1993	- Japan 2001

For more information on point scoring drivers with each constructor, see section 894.

484. Points scored with the same constructor *(Most)*

Sebastian Vettel	Red Bull	1,577	China 2009	- Abu Dhabi 2014
Fernando Alonso	Ferrari	1,190	Bahrain 2010	- Abu Dhabi 2014
Nico Rosberg	Mercedes-Benz	1,134	Bahrain 2010	- Abu Dhabi 2015
Michael Schumacher	Ferrari	1,066	Brazil 1996	- Brazil 2006
Mark Webber	Red Bull	978.5	United States 2007	- Brazil 2013
Lewis Hamilton	Mercedes-Benz	954	Australia 2013	- Abu Dhabi 2015
Lewis Hamilton	McLaren	913	Australia 2007	- United States 2012
Jenson Button	McLaren	887	Bahrain 2010	- United States 2015
Felipe Massa	Ferrari	789	Malaysia 2006	- Brazil 2013
Fernando Alonso	Renault	468	Australia 2003	- Singapore 2009

485. Scored points with more than one constructor in a season

Reg Parnell	1951	Ferrari (a), BRM
Alberto Ascari	1954	Maserati, Lancia
Juan Manuel Fangio	1954	Maserati, Mercedes-Benz
Eugenio Castellotti	1955	Lancia, Ferrari
Stuart Lewis-Evans	1957	Connaught, Vanwall
Stirling Moss	1957	Maserati, Vanwall
Jean Behra	1958	Maserati, BRM
Stirling Moss	1958	Cooper, Vanwall
Stirling Moss	1959	Cooper, BRM
Phil Hill	1960	Ferrari, Cooper
Jack Brabham	1962	Lotus, Brabham
Lorenzo Bandini	1963	BRM, Ferrari

Jo Bonnier	1964	Cooper, Brabham
Richie Ginther	1966	Cooper, Honda
John Surtees	1966	Ferrari, Cooper
Jo Bonnier	1968	McLaren, Honda
John Surtees	1970	McLaren, Surtees
Jacky Ickx	1973	Ferrari, McLaren
Carlos Pace	1974	Surtees, Brabham
Mark Donohue	1975	Penske, March
Mario Andretti	1976	Parnelli, Lotus (b)
Andrea De Cesaris	1994	Jordan, Sauber
Jean Alesi	2001	Prost, Jordan
Sebastian Vettel	2007	BMW (c), Toro Rosso

(a) As Thin Wall Special. (b) As JPS Lotus. (c) As BMW Sauber.

486. Half points awarded (shortened races)

Spain 1975	five spectators killed when Rolf Stommelen crashed	Australia 1991	heavy rain
Austria 1975	heavy rain	Malaysia 2009	heavy rain
Monaco 1984	heavy rain		

487. Interval between point scores (Longest)

	years, days	races		
Lucien Bianchi	7y, 342d	75	Belgium 1960 (Cooper)	- Monaco 1968 (Cooper)
Mike Hailwood	7y, 118d	84	Monaco 1964 (Lotus)	- Italy 1971 (Surtees)
Hans Herrmann	5y, 232d	51	Argentina 1955 (Mercedes-Benz)	- Italy 1960 (Porsche)
Louis Rosier	5y, 49d	45	Belgium 1951 (Talbot-Lago)	- Germany 1956 (Maserati)
Rolf Stommelen	5y, 15d	71	Britain 1971 (Surtees)	- Germany 1976 (Brabham)
Alan Jones	4y, 304d	75	Caesars Palace 1981 (Williams)	- Austria 1986 (Lola)
Maurice Trintignant	4y, 234d	43	United States 1959 (Cooper)	- Germany 1964 (BRM)
Alex Wurz	4y, 226d	75	Italy 2000 (Benetton)	- San Marino 2005 (McLaren)
Aguri Suzuki	4y, 142d	72	United States 1991 (Lola)	- Germany 1995 (Ligier)
Jacky Ickx	4y, 78d	68	Spain 1975 (JPS Lotus)	- Britain 1979 (Ligier)

Did not necessarily start every race during the period.

488. Interval between first & last point scores (Longest)

	years, days	races		
Michael Schumacher	21y, 78d	366	Italy 1991 (Benetton)	- Brazil 2012 (Mercedes-Benz)
Rubens Barrichello	17y, 231d	299	Japan 1993 (Jordan)	- Canada 2011 (Williams)
Riccardo Patrese	15y, 324d	248	Japan 1977 (Shadow)	- Italy 1993 (Benetton)
Jenson Button	15y, 213d	284	Brazil 2000 (Williams)	- United States 2015 (McLaren)
Kimi Räikkönen	14y, 270d	271	Australia 2001 (Sauber)	- Abu Dhabi 2015 (Ferrari)
David Coulthard	14y, 108d	246	Canada 1994 (Williams)	- Singapore 2008 (Red Bull)
Graham Hill	14y, 3d	154	Netherlands 1960 (BRM)	- Sweden 1974 (Lola)
Alain Prost	13y, 298d	219	Argentina 1980 (McLaren)	- Australia 1993 (Williams)
Felipe Massa	13y, 257d	253	Malaysia 2002 (Sauber)	- Abu Dhabi 2015 (Williams)
Nigel Mansell	13y, 180d	217	Belgium 1981 (Lotus)	- Australia 1994 (Williams)

489. Interval between point scorers of the same nationality (Longest)

	years, days	races		
Spain	32y, 184d	419	Argentina 1957 (Alfonso de Portago)	- Britain 1989 (Luis Sala)
Mexico	29y, 265d	490	Netherlands 1981 (Hector Rebaque)	- Spain 2011 (Sergio Pérez)
Venezuela	28y, 154d	476	United States West 1983 (Johnny Cecotto)	- Belgium 2011 (Pastor Maldonado)
Sweden	25y, 172d	436	Portugal 1989 (Stefan Johansson)	- Australia 2015 (Marcus Ericsson)
Switzerland	23y, 202d	388	Italy 1985 (Marc Surer)	- Australia 2009 (Sébastien Buemi)
Netherlands	19y, 11d	297	Germany 1975 (Gijs van Lennep)	- Hungary 1994 (Jos Verstappen)
Denmark	15y, 282d	277	Canada 1998 (Jan Magnussen)	- Australia 2014 (Kevin Magnussen)
Australia	15y, 177d	248	Italy 1986 (Alan Jones)	- Australia 2002 (Mark Webber)
Brazil	14y, 192d	143	Argentina 1956 (Chico Landi)	- Germany 1970 (Emerson Fittipaldi)
Canada	13y, 320d	221	San Marino 1982 (Gilles Villeneuve)	- Australia 1996 (Jacques Villeneuve)

490. Points but never a world championship (Most)

Nico Rosberg	1,209.5	David Coulthard	535	Valtteri Bottas	326
Felipe Massa	1,071	Gerhard Berger	385	Carlos Reutemann	310
Mark Webber	1,047.5	Daniel Ricciardo	360		
Rubens Barrichello	658	Ralf Schumacher	329		

491. Points but never a win (Most)

Valtteri Bottas	326	Nick Heidfeld	259	Daniil Kvyat	103
Nico Hülkenberg	290	Kamui Kobayashi	125	Martin Brundle	98
Romain Grosjean	287	Adrian Sutil	124		
Sergio Pérez	266	Paul Di Resta	121		

492. Points but never a podium *(Most)*

Nico Hülkenberg	290	Max Verstappen	49	Felipe Nasr	27
Adrian Sutil	124	Bruno Senna	33	Vitantonio Liuzzi	26
Paul Di Resta	121	Jaime Alguersuari	31		
Jean-Eric Vergne	51	Sébastien Buemi	29		

493. Points but never a pole position *(Most)*

Daniel Ricciardo	360	Bruce McLaren	196.5	Paul Di Resta	121
Valtteri Bottas	326	Eddie Irvine	191	Richie Ginther	107
Romain Grosjean	287	Kamui Kobayashi	125		
Sergio Pérez	266	Adrian Sutil	124		

494. Milestones: Points scored

Fernando Alonso	500th: France 2008, 1,000th: Italy 2011, 1,500th: Belgium 2013
Lewis Hamilton	500th: Australia 2011, 1,000th: Britain 2013, 1,500th: Australia 2015
Michael Schumacher	500th: Germany 1998, 1,000th: Europe 2003, 1,500th: Japan 2011
Sebastian Vettel	500th: Monaco 2011, 1,000th: India 2012, 1,500th: Canada 2014
Jenson Button	500th: Singapore 2010, 1,000th: Australia 2013
Felipe Massa	500th: Europe 2011, 1,000th: Austria 2015
Kimi Räikkönen	500th: Britain 2008, 1,000th: Belgium 2014
Nico Rosberg	500th: Italy 2013, 1,000th: Monaco 2015
Mark Webber	500th: Canada 2011, 1,000th: Abu Dhabi 2013
Rubens Barrichello	500th: Monaco 2006
David Coulthard	500th: Australia 2006
Alain Prost	500th: Japan 1988
Ayrton Senna	500th: Monaco 1992

495. Milestones: Point scoring drivers
(eg Johnny Herbert was the 200th driver to score points)

1st	Giuseppe Farina	Britain 1950	150th	Tony Brise	Sweden 1975
50th	Nano da Silva Ramos	Monaco 1956	200th	Johnny Herbert	Brazil 1989
100th	Richard Attwood	Italy 1965	250th	Mark Webber	Australia 2002

Excludes Indianapolis 500.

496. Milestones: Point scoring races

Michael Schumacher	50th: Germany 1996, 100th: Australia 2001, 150th: San Marino 2004, 200th: Japan 2010
Fernando Alonso	50th: France 2006, 100th: Germany 2010, 150th: Britain 2013
Jenson Button	50th: Spain 2006, 100th: Canada 2011, 150th: Brazil 2014
Kimi Räikkönen	50th: Europe 2006, 100th: Canada 2012, 150th: Singapore 2015
Rubens Barrichello	50th: Germany 2001, 100th: Brazil 2005
David Coulthard	50th: Monaco 2000, 100th: Belgium 2004
Lewis Hamilton	50th: Korea 2010, 100th: Malaysia 2014
Felipe Massa	50th: Japan 2008, 100th: Brazil 2012
Nelson Piquet	50th: Britain 1986, 100th: Australia 1991
Alain Prost	50th: Monaco 1986, 100th: France 1990
Nico Rosberg	50th: Japan 2011, 100th: Bahrain 2015
Sebastian Vettel	50th: Belgium 2011, 100th: Belgium 2014
Mark Webber	50th: Malaysia 2010, 100th: Bahrain 2013

Chapter 12: Race Leading Drivers

Based on actual laps led, even where a disqualification or other penalty was later applied and also where times were aggregated.
All distances led are calculated as complete laps, based on the leader at the end of each lap (actual distances in the lead are not recorded for the official results).

497. Laps led *(Most)*

	laps	races	km	miles		
Michael Schumacher	5,094	142	24,054	14,946	Belgium 1992 (Benetton)	- Japan 2011 (Mercedes-Benz)
Ayrton Senna	2,931	86	13,430	8,345	Portugal 1985 (Lotus)	- San Marino 1994 (Williams)
Alain Prost	2,683	84	12,477	7,753	France 1981 (Renault)	- Australia 1993 (Williams)
Sebastian Vettel	2,614	70	13,749	8,543	Japan 2007 (Toro Rosso)	- Singapore 2015 (Ferrari)
Lewis Hamilton	2,424	85	12,336	7,665	Australia 2007 (McLaren)	- Abu Dhabi 2015 (Mercedes-Benz)
Nigel Mansell	2,057	55	9,501	5,904	Monaco 1984 (Lotus)	- Australia 1994 (Williams)
Jim Clark	1,942	43	10,121	6,289	Netherlands 1962 (Lotus)	- South Africa 1968 (Lotus)
Jackie Stewart	1,918	51	9,173	5,700	Monaco 1965 (BRM)	- Canada 1973 (Tyrrell)
Fernando Alonso	1,767	84	8,640	5,369	Malaysia 2003 (Renault)	- Hungary 2014 (Ferrari)
Nelson Piquet	1,633	59	7,757	4,820	United States West 1980 (Brabham)	- Belgium 1991 (Benetton)
Niki Lauda	1,591	41	7,062	4,388	Canada 1973 (BRM)	- Australia 1985 (McLaren)
Mika Häkkinen	1,489	48	7,194	4,470	San Marino 1994 (McLaren)	- United States 2001 (McLaren)
Damon Hill	1,363	45	6,338	3,938	Brazil 1993 (Williams)	- Britain 1999 (Jordan)

	laps	races	km	miles		
Juan Manuel Fangio	1,348	38	9,322	5,792	Britain 1950 (Alfa Romeo)	- Argentina 1958 (Maserati)
Stirling Moss	1,181	31	6,369	3,958	Italy 1954 (Maserati)	- United States 1961 (Lotus)
Kimi Räikkönen	1,166	66	5,930	3,685	France 2002 (McLaren)	- Hungary 2015 (Ferrari)
Graham Hill	1,105	32	4,764	2,960	Britain 1960 (BRM)	- Netherlands 1969 (Lotus)
Nico Rosberg	1,044	42	4,846	3,011	Singapore 2008 (Williams)	- Abu Dhabi 2015 (Mercedes-Benz)
Felipe Massa	936	42	4,534	2,817	Brazil 2004 (Sauber)	- Britain 2015 (Williams)
Alberto Ascari	925	21	5,887	3,658	Italy 1950 (Ferrari)	- Argentina 1955 (Lancia)
David Coulthard	897	62	4,210	2,616	Belgium 1994 (Williams)	- Canada 2008 (Red Bull)
Rubens Barrichello	854	51	4,152	2,580	Portugal 1994 (Jordan)	- Brazil 2009 (Brawn)
Jack Brabham	825	28	4,540	2,821	Monaco 1959 (Cooper)	- Britain 1970 (Brabham)
Mario Andretti	798	22	3,573	2,220	South Africa 1971 (Ferrari)	- United States 1978 (JPS Lotus)
Jenson Button	762	42	3,885	2,414	United States 2003 (BAR)	- Hungary 2014 (McLaren)
Gerhard Berger	754	33	3,718	2,310	Austria 1986 (Benetton)	- Germany 1997 (Williams)
Ronnie Peterson	707	28	3,313	2,059	Italy 1971 (March)	- Austria 1978 (JPS Lotus)
Jody Scheckter	675	23	2,855	1,774	South Africa 1973 (McLaren)	- Italy 1979 (Ferrari)
James Hunt	666	24	3,363	2,090	Argentina 1975 (Hesketh)	- Spain 1978 (McLaren)
Carlos Reutemann	650	19	3,314	2,059	Argentina 1974 (Brabham)	- Belgium 1981 (Williams)
Jacques Villeneuve	633	20	2,965	1,842	Australia 1996 (Williams)	- Europe 1997 (Williams)
Mark Webber	611	29	2,777	1,726	United States 2003 (Jaguar)	- India 2013 (Red Bull)
Juan Pablo Montoya	605	32	2,965	1,843	Brazil 2001 (Williams)	- San Marino 2006 (McLaren)
Alan Jones	589	24	2,847	1,769	Austria 1977 (Shadow)	- Caesars Palace 1981 (Williams)
Riccardo Patrese	566	29	2,559	1,590	South Africa 1978 (Arrows)	- Australia 1992 (Williams)
Gilles Villeneuve	534	18	2,254	1,401	United States West 1978 (Ferrari)	- San Marino 1982 (Ferrari)
Jacky Ickx	529	19	3,122	1,940	France 1968 (Ferrari)	- Spain 1975 (JPS Lotus)
Keke Rosberg	512	20	2,165	1,345	Belgium 1982 (Williams)	- Australia 1986 (McLaren)
René Arnoux	506	25	2,565	1,594	Italy 1979 (Renault)	- Detroit 1986 (Ligier)
Emerson Fittipaldi	478	18	2,235	1,389	United States 1970 (Lotus)	- Britain 1975 (McLaren)
Denny Hulme	436	18	1,920	1,193	Italy 1966 (Brabham)	- Argentina 1974 (McLaren)
Ralf Schumacher	401	21	1,936	1,203	Europe 1999 (Williams)	- France 2006 (Toyota)
Jochen Rindt	387	12	1,898	1,180	Belgium 1966 (Cooper)	- Germany 1970 (Lotus)
Clay Regazzoni	360	20	1,851	1,150	Germany 1970 (Ferrari)	- Britain 1979 (Williams)
Giuseppe Farina	338	14	2,664	1,655	Britain 1950 (Alfa Romeo)	- Belgium 1954 (Ferrari)
John Surtees	307	16	2,117	1,316	Portugal 1960 (Lotus)	- Italy 1968 (Honda)
Didier Pironi	295	10	1,240	771	Belgium 1980 (Ligier)	- Netherlands 1982 (Ferrari)
John Watson	287	10	1,238	770	Austria 1976 (Penske)	- United States West 1983 (McLaren)
Jacques Laffite	283	14	1,519	944	Sweden 1977 (Ligier)	- Detroit 1986 (Ligier)
José Froilán González	272	9	1,525	948	Britain 1951 (Ferrari)	- Argentina 1956 (Maserati)

498. Races led *(Most)*

		% of starts
Michael Schumacher	142	46.25
Ayrton Senna	86	53.42
Lewis Hamilton	85	50.90
Fernando Alonso	84	33.20
Alain Prost	84	42.21
Sebastian Vettel	70	44.30
Kimi Räikkönen	66	28.57
David Coulthard	62	25.20
Nelson Piquet	59	28.92
Nigel Mansell	55	29.41
Rubens Barrichello	51	15.79
Jackie Stewart	51	51.52
Mika Häkkinen	48	29.81
Damon Hill	45	39.13
Jim Clark	43	59.72
Jenson Button	42	14.79
Felipe Massa	42	18.34
Nico Rosberg	42	22.70
Niki Lauda	41	23.98
Juan Manuel Fangio	38	74.51

499. Distance led *(Longest)*

	km	miles
Michael Schumacher	24,054	14,946
Sebastian Vettel	13,749	8,543
Ayrton Senna	13,430	8,345
Alain Prost	12,477	7,753
Lewis Hamilton	12,336	7,665
Jim Clark	10,121	6,289
Nigel Mansell	9,501	5,904
Juan Manuel Fangio	9,322	5,792
Jackie Stewart	9,173	5,700
Fernando Alonso	8,640	5,369
Nelson Piquet	7,757	4,820
Mika Häkkinen	7,194	4,470
Niki Lauda	7,062	4,388
Stirling Moss	6,369	3,958
Damon Hill	6,338	3,938
Kimi Räikkönen	5,930	3,685
Alberto Ascari	5,887	3,658
Nico Rosberg	4,846	3,011
Graham Hill	4,764	2,960
Jack Brabham	4,540	2,821

500. Race leader age

Youngest

	years, days	
Sebastian Vettel	20y, 89d	Japan 2007
Sébastien Buemi	21y, 225d	Canada 2010
Fernando Alonso	21y, 237d	Malaysia 2003
Robert Kubica	21y, 277d	Italy 2006
Esteban Gutiérrez	21y, 280d	Spain 2013
Sergio Pérez	22y, 59d	Malaysia 2012
Lewis Hamilton	22y, 70d	Australia 2007
Bruce McLaren	22y, 104d	United States 1959
Rubens Barrichello	22y, 125d	Portugal 1994
Kimi Räikkönen	22y, 277d	France 2002
Indianapolis 500		
Jimmy Davies	21y, 285d	1951
Troy Ruttman	22y, 80d	1952

Oldest

	years, days	
Luigi Fagioli	52y, 9d	Belgium 1950
Felice Bonetto	48y, 35d	Britain 1951
Giuseppe Farina	47y, 233d	Belgium 1954
Juan Manuel Fangio	46y, 209d	Argentina 1958
Piero Taruffi	45y, 219d	Switzerland 1952
Jack Brabham	44y, 107d	Britain 1970
Karl Kling	43y, 354d	Italy 1954
Raymond Sommer	43y, 291d	Belgium 1950
Michael Schumacher	42y, 279d	Japan 2011
Jacques Laffite	42y, 213d	Detroit 1986
Indianapolis 500		
Mauri Rose	44y, 4d	1950
Paul Russo	43y, 50d	1957
Sam Hanks	42y, 321d	1957

501. Races led in a season *(Most)*

Sebastian Vettel	18 of 19	2013	(Red Bull RB9 - Renault)
Lewis Hamilton	17 of 19	2015	(Mercedes-Benz F1 W06)
Sebastian Vettel	17 of 19	2011	(Red Bull RB7 - Renault)
Michael Schumacher	16 of 18	2004	(Ferrari F2004)
Alain Prost	15 of 16	1993	(Williams FW15C - Renault)
Fernando Alonso	15 of 18	2006	(Renault R26)
Lewis Hamilton	15 of 19	2014	(Mercedes-Benz F1 W05)
Nico Rosberg	15 of 19	2014 (a)	(Mercedes-Benz F1 W05)
Nigel Mansell	14 of 16	1992	(Williams FW14B - Renault)
Ayrton Senna	14 of 16	1990	(McLaren MP4/5B - Honda)
Michael Schumacher	14 of 17	1995	(Benetton B195 - Renault)
Michael Schumacher	14 of 17	2000	(Ferrari F1-2000)
Nico Rosberg	14 of 19	2015 (a)	(Mercedes-Benz F1 W06)

All became world champion that season, except (a).

502. Led in every race of a season

Jackie Stewart	11	1969	(Matra MS10, MS80 - Ford Cosworth)
Juan Manuel Fangio	7	1951	(Alfa Romeo 159)
Juan Manuel Fangio	6	1955	(Mercedes-Benz W196, W196 str.)

All became world champion that season.

503. Led in all but one race of a season

Sebastian Vettel	18	2013	(Red Bull RB9 - Renault)
Alain Prost	15	1993	(Williams FW15C - Renault)
Jim Clark	9	1963	(Lotus 25 - Climax)
Graham Hill	8	1962	(BRM P57)
Alberto Ascari	7	1953	(Ferrari 500)
Alberto Ascari	6	1952	(Ferrari 500)
Juan Manuel Fangio	5	1950 (a)	(Alfa Romeo 158)
Giuseppe Farina	5	1950	(Alfa Romeo 158)

All became world champion that season, except (a).

504. Laps led in a season *(Most)*

	laps	%		
Sebastian Vettel	739 of 1,133	65.23	2011	(Renault RB7 - Renault)
Nigel Mansell	693 of 1,036	66.89	1992	(Williams FW14B - Renault)
Sebastian Vettel	684 of 1,131	60.48	2013	(Red Bull RB9 - Renault)

	laps	%		
Michael Schumacher	683 of 1,122	60.87	2004	(Ferrari F2004)
Michael Schumacher	629 of 1,046	60.13	1994	(Benetton B194 - Ford Cosworth)
Lewis Hamilton	587 of 1,149	51.09	2015	(Mercedes-Benz F1 W06)
Mika Häkkinen	576 of 1,015	56.75	1998	(McLaren MP4-13 - Mercedes)
Michael Schumacher	558 of 1,090	51.19	2002	(Ferrari F2001, F2002)
Ayrton Senna	553 of 1,031	53.64	1988	(McLaren MP4/4 - Honda)
Michael Schumacher	548 of 1,074	51.02	2000	(Ferrari F1 2000)

All became world champion that season.

505. Distance led in a season *(Longest)*

	km	miles		
Sebastian Vettel	3,794	2,358	2011	(Renault RB7 - Renault)
Sebastian Vettel	3,637	2,260	2013	(Red Bull RB9 - Renault)
Michael Schumacher	3,356	2,086	2004	(Ferrari F2004)
Nigel Mansell	3,289	2,044	1992	(Williams FW14B - Renault)
Lewis Hamilton	3,095	1,923	2015	(Mercedes-Benz F1 W06)
Michael Schumacher	2,764	1,718	2002	(Ferrari F2001, F2002)
Jim Clark	2,759	1,714	1963	(Lotus 25 - Climax)
Michael Schumacher	2,742	1,704	1994	(Benetton B194 - Ford Cosworth)
Mika Häkkinen	2,708	1,683	1998	(McLaren MP4-13 - Mercedes)
Lewis Hamilton	2,675	1,662	2014	(Mercedes-Benz F1 W05)

506. Percentage of laps led in driver's title winning season

Highest

	%	laps		
Alberto Ascari	77.85	348 of 447	1952 (a)	(Ferrari 500)
Alberto Ascari	77.43	415 of 536	1953 (a)	(Ferrari 500)
Jim Clark	71.47	506 of 708	1963	(Lotus 25 - Climax)
Nigel Mansell	66.89	693 of 1,036	1992	(Williams FW14B - Renault)
Juan Manuel Fangio	65.47	309 of 472	1955 (a)	(Mercedes-Benz W196, W196 str.)
Sebastian Vettel	65.23	739 of 1,133	2011	(Renault RB7 - Renault)
Michael Schumacher	60.87	683 of 1,122	2004	(Ferrari F2004)
Sebastian Vettel	60.48	684 of 1,131	2013	(Red Bull RB9 - Renault)
Michael Schumacher	60.13	629 of 1,046	1994	(Benetton B194 - Ford Cosworth)
Mika Häkkinen	56.75	576 of 1,015	1998	(McLaren MP4-13 - Mercedes)

(a) Total laps for the season excludes Indianapolis 500.

Lowest

	%	laps		
Keke Rosberg	7.55	80 of 1,060	1982	(Williams FW08 - Ford Cosworth)
Emerson Fittipaldi	7.87	77 of 979	1974	(McLaren M23 - Ford Cosworth)
John Surtees	12.33	89 of 722	1964	(Ferrari 158)
Alain Prost	15.90	166 of 1,044	1986	(McLaren MP4/2C - TAG Porsche)
Niki Lauda	16.78	190 of 1,132	1977	(Ferrari 312T2)
Niki Lauda	16.78	168 of 1,001	1984	(McLaren MP4/2 - TAG Porsche)
Alain Prost	17.25	178 of 1,032	1985	(McLaren MP4/2B - TAG Porsche)
Jody Scheckter	17.44	170 of 975	1979	(Ferrari 312T4)
Nelson Piquet	18.53	187 of 1,009	1987	(Williams FW11B - Honda)
Jochen Rindt	18.76	172 of 917	1970	(Lotus 49C, 72C - Ford Cosworth)

507. Percentage of laps led in a season without becoming champion *(Highest)*

	%	laps				%	laps	
Stirling Moss	47.86	224 of 468	1956 (a)		Jim Clark	42.79	267 of 624	1962
Ayrton Senna	46.87	487 of 1,039	1989		Nico Rosberg	42.59	483 of 1,134	2014
Juan Manuel Fangio	45.78	179 of 391	1950 (a)		Ronnie Peterson	40.39	393 of 973	1973
Jim Clark	44.60	322 of 722	1964		Jackie Stewart	39.75	320 of 805	1972
Alain Prost	43.65	450 of 1,031	1988		Stirling Moss	39.53	234 of 592	1958 (a)

(a) Total laps for the season excludes Indianapolis 500.

508. Laps led with the same constructor *(Most)*

		laps led	races led		
Michael Schumacher	Ferrari	3,934	111	San Marino 1996	- Japan 2006
Ayrton Senna	McLaren	2,392	60	San Marino 1988	- Australia 1993
Sebastian Vettel	Red Bull	2,386	64	China 2009	- Singapore 2014
Jim Clark	Lotus	1,942	43	Netherlands 1962	- South Africa 1968
Nigel Mansell	Williams	1,880	46	Europe 1985	- Australia 1994
Alain Prost	McLaren	1,507	45	Brazil 1984	- Japan 1989
Mika Häkkinen	McLaren	1,489	48	San Marino 1994	- United States 2001
Lewis Hamilton	McLaren	1,276	48	Australia 2007	- Brazil 2012
Damon Hill	Williams	1,274	42	Brazil 1993	- Japan 1996
Niki Lauda	Ferrari	1,167	27	South Africa 1974	- Netherlands 1977

For more information on race leading drivers by constructor, see section 933.

509. Races of leading every lap

Ayrton Senna	19	Portugal 1985 (Lotus)	- Australia 1991 (McLaren)
Jim Clark	13	Britain 1962 (Lotus)	- Germany 1965 (Lotus)
Sebastian Vettel	13	Japan 2009 (Red Bull)	- Singapore 2015 (Ferrari)
Michael Schumacher	11	Pacific 1994 (Benetton)	- Japan 2004 (Ferrari)
Jackie Stewart	11	Germany 1968 (Matra)	- Germany 1973 (Tyrrell)
Nigel Mansell	9	Portugal 1986 (Williams)	- Portugal 1992 (Williams)
Alberto Ascari	7	France 1952 (Ferrari)	- Britain 1953 (Ferrari)
Lewis Hamilton	7	Hungary 2007 (McLaren)	- Japan 2015 (Mercedes-Benz)
Alain Prost	7	Italy 1981 (Renault)	- France 1989 (McLaren)
Niki Lauda	6	Netherlands 1974 (Ferrari)	- Monaco 1976 (Ferrari)
Mario Andretti	5	Spain 1977 (JPS Lotus)	- Netherlands 1978 (JPS Lotus)
Jack Brabham	5	Britain 1959 (Cooper)	- Germany 1966 (Brabham)
Juan Manuel Fangio	5	Monaco 1950 (Alfa Romeo)	- Germany 1956 (Ferrari)
Stirling Moss	5	Monaco 1956 (Maserati)	- Germany 1961 (Lotus)
Damon Hill	4	Hungary 1993 (Williams)	- Japan 1996 (Williams)
Mika Häkkinen	4	Brazil 1998 (McLaren)	- Hungary 1999 (McLaren)
Nelson Piquet	4	United States West 1980 (Brabham)	- Detroit 1984 (Brabham)
Carlos Reutemann	4	Austria 1974 (Brabham)	- Brazil 1981 (Williams)
Nico Rosberg	4	Monaco 2013 (Mercedes-Benz)	- Germany 2014 (Mercedes-Benz)
Fernando Alonso	3	France 2005 (Renault)	- Singapore 2010 (Ferrari)
David Coulthard	3	San Marino 1998 (McLaren)	- Monaco 2002 (McLaren)
Kimi Räikkönen	3	Spain 2005 (McLaren)	- Turkey 2005 (McLaren)
Clay Regazzoni	3	Germany 1974 (Ferrari)	- United States West 1976 (Ferrari)
Jody Scheckter	3	Sweden 1974 (Tyrrell)	- Monaco 1979 (Ferrari)
Mark Webber	3	Spain 2010 (Red Bull)	- Britain 2010 (Red Bull)
Gerhard Berger	2	Australia 1987 (Ferrari)	- Germany 1994 (Ferrari)
Jenson Button	2	Australia 2009 (Brawn)	- Belgium 2012 (McLaren)
James Hunt	2	Germany 1976 (McLaren)	- Japan 1977 (McLaren)
Alan Jones	2	Germany 1979 (Williams)	- Caesars Palace 1981 (Williams)
Ronnie Peterson	2	Italy 1973 (JPS Lotus)	- United States 1973 (JPS Lotus)
Ralf Schumacher	2	San Marino 2001 (Williams)	- France 2003 (Williams)
Michele Alboreto	1	Belgium 1984 (Ferrari)	
René Arnoux	1	Italy 1982 (Renault)	
Rubens Barrichello	1	Europe 2002 (Ferrari)	
Jean-Pierre Beltoise	1	Monaco 1972 (BRM)	
Thierry Boutsen	1	Hungary 1990 (Williams)	
Tony Brooks	1	France 1959 (Ferrari)	
Peter Collins	1	Britain 1958 (Ferrari)	
Patrick Depailler	1	Spain 1979 (Ligier)	
Emerson Fittipaldi	1	Brazil 1973 (JPS Lotus)	
José Froilán González	1	Britain 1954 (Ferrari)	
Richie Ginther	1	Mexico 1965 (Honda)	
Mike Hawthorn	1	France 1958 (Ferrari)	

Graham Hill	1	Italy 1962 (BRM)
Jacky Ickx	1	Germany 1972 (Ferrari)
Jacques Laffite	1	Brazil 1979 (Ligier)
Juan Pablo Montoya	1	Italy 2005 (McLaren)
Didier Pironi	1	Belgium 1980 (Ligier)
Keke Rosberg	1	Monaco 1983 (Williams)
Jo Siffert	1	Austria 1971 (BRM)
Jacques Villeneuve	1	Europe 1996 (Williams)
Gilles Villeneuve	1	United States West 1979 (Ferrari)
Wolfgang von Trips	1	Netherlands 1961 (Ferrari)

510. Consecutive races led *(Most)*

Lewis Hamilton	18	Hungary 2014	- Britain 2015	(Mercedes-Benz F1 W05, F1 W06)
Jackie Stewart	17	United States 1968	- Belgium 1970	(Matra MS10, MS80, March 701 - Ford Cosworth)
Michael Schumacher	15	Australia 2004	- Italy 2004	(Ferrari F2004)
Sebastian Vettel	13	Japan 2010	- Britain 2011	(Red Bull RB6, RB7 - Renault)
Sebastian Vettel	13	Canada 2013	- Brazil 2013	(Red Bull RB9 - Renault)
Ayrton Senna	12	Spain 1989	- Germany 1990	(McLaren MP4/5, MP4/5B - Honda)
Michael Schumacher	12	Europe 1994	- Germany 1995	(Benetton B194 - Ford Cosworth, B195 - Renault)
Fernando Alonso	12	China 2005	- France 2006	(Renault R25, R26)
Michael Schumacher	11	Malaysia 1999	- France 2000	(Ferrari F399, F1 2000)
Jim Clark	10	Netherlands 1967	- South Africa 1968	(Lotus 49 - Ford Cosworth)
Alain Prost	10	South Africa 1993	- Germany 1993	(Williams FW15C - Renault)

511. Consecutive laps led *(Most)*

Alberto Ascari	304	Belgium 1952 (lap 2)	- Netherlands 1952 (end) (5 races)	(Ferrari 500)
Ayrton Senna	264	Britain 1988 (lap 14)	- Italy 1988 (lap 49) (5 races)	(McLaren MP4/4 - Honda)
Ayrton Senna	237	San Marino 1989 (lap 1)	- United States 1989 (lap 33) (4 races)	(McLaren MP4/5 - Honda)
Nigel Mansell	235	Brazil 1992 (lap 32)	- Monaco 1992 (lap 70) (4 races)	(Williams FW14B - Renault)
Alberto Ascari	231	Italy 1952 (lap 37)	- Netherlands 1953 (end) (3 races)	(Ferrari 500)
Sebastian Vettel	205	Singapore 2012 (lap 23)	- India 2012 (end) (4 races)	(Red Bull RB8 - Renault)
Jim Clark	186	Mexico 1963 (lap 1)	- Monaco 1964 (lap 36) (3 races)	(Lotus 25 - Climax)
Jim Clark	165	Belgium 1963 (lap 1)	- France 1963 (end) (3 races)	(Lotus 25 - Climax)
Kimi Räikkönen	162	Spain 2005 (lap 1)	- Europe 2005 (lap 18) (3 races)	(McLaren MP4-20 - Mercedes)
Mark Webber	159	Spain 2010 (lap 1)	- Turkey 2010 (lap 15) (3 races)	(Red Bull RB6 - Renault)

512. Seasons of leading races *(Most)*

Michael Schumacher	16	1992 - 2011	(Benetton, Ferrari, Mercedes-Benz)
David Coulthard	13	1994 - 2008	(Williams, McLaren, Red Bull)
Fernando Alonso	12	2003 - 14	(Renault, McLaren, Ferrari)
Alain Prost	12	1981 - 93	(Renault, McLaren, Ferrari, Williams)
Rubens Barrichello	11	1994 - 2009	(Jordan, Stewart, Ferrari, Honda, Brawn)
Gerhard Berger	11	1986 - 97	(Benetton, Ferrari, McLaren, Benetton)
Felipe Massa	11	2004 - 15	(Sauber, Ferrari, Williams)
Kimi Räikkönen	11	2002 - 15	(McLaren, Ferrari, Lotus)
Jenson Button	10	2003 - 14	(BAR, Honda, Brawn, McLaren)
Nelson Piquet	10	1980 - 91	(Brabham, Williams, Benetton)
Ayrton Senna	10	1985 - 94	(Lotus, McLaren, Williams)

513. Consecutive seasons of leading races *(Most)*

Michael Schumacher	15	1992 - 2006		Felipe Massa	10	2006 - 15
Fernando Alonso	12	2003 - 14		Lewis Hamilton	9	2007 - 15
Alain Prost	11	1981 - 91		Denny Hulme	9	1966 - 74
David Coulthard	10	1994 - 2003		Jackie Stewart	9	1965 - 73
Ayrton Senna	10	1985 - 94		Sebastian Vettel	9	2007 - 15

514. Laps led by nationality

	laps	races	km	miles	drivers		
Great Britain	15,722	453	78,960	49,063	28	France 1953 (M Hawthorn)	- Abu Dhabi 2015 (L Hamilton)
Germany	9,602	276	46,890	29,136	15	France 1954 (K Kling)	- Abu Dhabi 2015 (N Rosberg)
Brazil	6,913	249	32,557	20,230	9	United States 1970 (E Fittipaldi)	- Britain 2015 (F Massa)
France	5,132	174	24,071	14,957	18	Belgium 1950 (R Sommer)	- United States 2013 (R Grosjean)
Finland	3,216	149	15,534	9,653	6	Belgium 1982 (K Rosberg)	- Hungary 2015 (K Räikkönen)
Italy	2,909	128	16,482	10,241	23	Britain 1950 (G Farina)	- Belgium 2009 (G Fisichella)
Austria	2,732	86	12,679	7,878	3	Belgium 1966 (J Rindt)	- Germany 1997 (G Berger)
Argentina	2,309	85	14,314	8,895	4	Britain 1950 (J M Fangio)	- Belgium 1981 (C Reutemann)
Australia	2,104	60	10,613	6,595	4	Monaco 1959 (J Brabham)	- United States 2015 (D Ricciardo)
Spain	1,767	84	8,640	5,368	1	Malaysia 2003 (F Alonso)	- Hungary 2014 (F Alonso)
United States	1,381	56	7,878	4,895	7	Spain 1954 (H Schell)	- United States 1978 (M Andretti)
Canada	1,167	38	5,218	3,243	2	United States West 1978 (G Villeneuve)	- Europe 1997 (J Villeneuve)
Sweden	870	35	3,969	2,466	4	Netherlands 1959 (J Bonnier)	- Belgium 1986 (S Johansson)
Belgium	698	26	3,855	2,395	4	Belgium 1961 (O Gendebien)	- Hungary 1990 (T Boutsen)
South Africa	675	23	2,855	1,774	1	South Africa 1973 (J Scheckter)	- Italy 1979 (J Scheckter)
New Zealand	660	26	2,958	1,838	3	United States 1959 (B McLaren)	- Argentina 1974 (D Hulme)
Colombia	605	32	2,965	1,843	1	Brazil 2001 (J P Montoya)	- San Marino 2006 (J P Montoya)
Switzerland	460	25	2,376	1,476	3	Britain 1968 (J Siffert)	- Canada 2010 (S Buemi)
Mexico	111	12	712	442	3	South Africa 1967 (P Rodríguez)	- Austria 2014 (S Pérez)
Poland	74	8	337	209	1	Italy 2006 (R Kubica)	- Japan 2008 (R Kubica)
Venezuela	37	1	172	107	1	Spain 2012 (P Maldonado)	
Southern Rhodesia	13	1	53	33	1	South Africa 1967 (J Love)	
Japan	2	1	10	6	1	Europe 2004 (T Sato)	

515. Races led at the same circuit *(Most)*

Michael Schumacher	11	Imola	1994 - 2006
Michael Schumacher	11	Suzuka	1994 - 2011
Michael Schumacher	10	Catalunya	1994 - 2006
Michael Schumacher	10	Magny-Cours	1994 - 2006
Michael Schumacher	10	Montréal	1994 - 2004
Michael Schumacher	10	Spa-Francorchamps	1992 - 2004
Ayrton Senna	9	Monte-Carlo	1985 - 93
Michael Schumacher	9	Monte-Carlo	1993 - 2004
Michael Schumacher	8	Monza	1996 - 2006
Michael Schumacher	8	Silverstone	1994 - 2004

516. First race led was on home soil

Alberto Ascari	Italy 1950	(Monza)	Luigi Musso	Italy 1956	(Monza)
Gerhard Berger	Austria 1986	(Österreichring)	Jackie Oliver	Britain 1968	(Brands Hatch)
Olivier Gendebien	Belgium 1961	(Spa-Francorchamps)	Carlos Pace	Brazil 1975	(Silverstone)
Nick Heidfeld	Europe 2005	(Nürburgring)	Alain Prost	France 1981	(Dijon-Prenois)
Johnny Herbert	Britain 1995	(Silverstone)	Carlos Reutemann	Argentina 1974	(Buenos Aires No.15)
Graham Hill	Britain 1960	(Silverstone)	Ludovico Scarfiotti	Italy 1966	(Monza)
Nicola Larini	San Marino 1994	(Imola)	Jody Scheckter	South Africa 1973	(Kyalami)
Willy Mairesse	Belgium 1962	(Spa-Francorchamps)	Ralf Schumacher	Europe 1999	(Nürburgring)
Felipe Massa	Brazil 2004	(Interlagos)	Markus Winkelhock	Europe 2007	(Nürburgring)
Carlos Mendítéguy	Argentina 1956	(Buenos Aires No.2)			

517. Race starts taken to lead a lap
(number of races includes the first race led)

Fewest

Giancarlo Baghetti	1	France 1961
Luigi Fagioli	1	Britain 1950
Juan Manuel Fangio	1	Britain 1950
Giuseppe Farina	1	Britain 1950
Lewis Hamilton	1	Australia 2007
Karl Kling	1	France 1954
Jacques Villeneuve	1	Australia 1996
Markus Winkelhock	1	Europe 2007
Dan Gurney	2	Germany 1959
Jody Scheckter	2	South Africa 1973
Johnny Servoz-Gavin	2	Monaco 1968
Jackie Stewart	2	Monaco 1965

Most

Nick Heidfeld	91	Europe 2005
Adrian Sutil	91	Australia 2013
Mika Salo	73	Germany 1999
Thierry Boutsen	71	Mexico 1987
Johnny Herbert	71	Britain 1995
Jenson Button	65	United States 2003
Alessandro Nannini	61	Japan 1989
Daniel Ricciardo	57	Canada 2014
Jo Siffert	57	Britain 1968
Elio de Angelis	54	Austria 1982

For most races started but never led, see section 190.

518. Led in their first two or more races started

Lewis Hamilton	7	Australia 2007	- United States 2007	(McLaren MP4-22 - Mercedes)
Juan Manuel Fangio	5	Britain 1950	- France 1950	(Alfa Romeo 158)

519. Laps led in their first season *(Most)*

	laps	races	km	miles	
Lewis Hamilton	321	12	1,447	899	2007
Jacques Villeneuve	285	9	1,369	851	1996
Giuseppe Farina	197	5	1,248	776	1950
Juan Manuel Fangio	179	5	1,067	663	1950
Juan Pablo Montoya	122	9	634	394	2001
Jackie Stewart	45	2	246	153	1965
Jarno Trulli	37	1	160	99	1997
Clay Regazzoni	37	4	214	133	1970
John Surtees	25	1	185	115	1960
Richie Ginther	24	1	240	149	1960

520. Led in their final race

Lorenzo Bandini	Monaco 1967	killed in this race
Eugenio Castellotti	Argentina 1957	killed two months later, prior to next F1 race
Jim Clark	South Africa 1968	killed in Formula 2 event, prior to next F1 race
Peter Collins	Germany 1958	killed in this race
Richie Ginther	Mexico 1966	failed to qualify for one further race, then retired from F1
Niki Lauda	Australia 1985	retired from F1
Stirling Moss	United States 1961	retired from F1, following serious injury at Goodwood pre-1962 season
Alain Prost	Australia 1993	retired from F1
Keke Rosberg	Australia 1986	retired from F1
Ayrton Senna	San Marino 1994	killed in this race
Jackie Stewart	Canada 1973	retired from F1 after qualifying for next F1 event, in United States
Gilles Villeneuve	San Marino 1982	killed in qualifying for next F1 race, in Belgium
Markus Winkelhock	Europe 2007	his only F1 race - no further drive available

521. Laps led in their first season *(Most)*

	laps	races	km	miles	
Alain Prost	431	15	2,095	1,302	1993
Jackie Stewart	214	6	1,088	676	1973
Jochen Rindt	172	5	819	509	1970
Wolfgang von Trips	156	4	787	489	1961
Stirling Moss	132	3	726	452	1961
Mike Hawthorn	125	6	822	511	1958
Jack Brabham	124	3	460	286	1970
Mika Häkkinen	110	3	525	326	2001
Keke Rosberg	86	4	396	246	1986
Peter Collins	83	3	518	322	1958

Drivers leading in a race *(Most)*. See section 68

522. Percentage of race led, but did not win *(Highest)*

	race	%	laps led	winner
Nigel Mansell	Canada 1991	98.55	68 of 69	Nelson Piquet
Michael Schumacher	Belgium 1994	97.73	43 of 44	Damon Hill (a)
Ronnie Peterson	Sweden 1973	97.50	78 of 80	Denny Hulme
Rubens Barrichello	Austria 2002	97.18	69 of 71	Michael Schumacher (b)
Sebastian Vettel	Canada 2011	97.14	68 of 70	Jenson Button
Jim Clark	Mexico 1964	96.92	63 of 65	Dan Gurney
Alain Prost	Switzerland 1982	96.25	77 of 80	Keke Rosberg
Ayrton Senna	Italy 1988	96.08	49 of 51	Gerhard Berger
Nelson Piquet	Britain 1987	95.39	62 of 65	Nigel Mansell
Jody Scheckter	United States West 1977	95.00	76 of 80	Mario Andretti
Mario Andretti	Canada 1977	95.00	76 of 80	Jody Scheckter
Mario Andretti	Sweden 1977	94.44	68 of 72	Jacques Laffite
John Watson	France 1977	93.75	75 of 80	Mario Andretti
Ayrton Senna	San Marino 1985	93.33	56 of 60	Elio De Angelis (c)
Michael Schumacher	United States 2002	93.15	68 of 73	Rubens Barrichello (b)
Carlos Reutemann	Argentina 1974	92.45	49 of 53	Denny Hulme
Nigel Mansell	Hungary 1987	92.11	70 of 76	Nelson Piquet
Niki Lauda	Britain 1974	92.00	69 of 75	Jody Scheckter
Keke Rosberg	Belgium 1982	91.43	64 of 70	John Watson
Gerhard Berger	Portugal 1987	91.43	64 of 70	Alain Prost

(a) Michael Schumacher originally won, but was disqualified for illegal skid block wear, handing the victory to Damon Hill who had not led during the race.
(b) Stage-managed by Ferrari.
(c) Elio de Angelis hadn't led any laps but inherited the win upon Alain Prost's disqualification.

523. Led every lap of a race except the final one

The only occasion was in Canada 1991 where Nigel Mansell (Williams - Renault) retired officially from a gearbox/ engine failure on the 69th lap, although it is thought that he accidentally switched off the engine while waving to the crowd. Nelson Piquet (Benetton - Ford Cosworth) took over the lead to win the race.

524. Leader at the finish was not leading at the start of the final lap

	leader at the finish	leader at the start of the final lap
Italy 1953	Juan Manuel Fangio (Maserati)	Alberto Ascari (Ferrari), retired (accident)/ not classified
France 1954	Juan Manuel Fangio (Mercedes-Benz)	Karl Kling (Mercedes-Benz), finished 2nd
United States 1959	Bruce McLaren (Cooper) *	Jack Brabham (Cooper), finished 4th
France 1961	Giancarlo Baghetti (Ferrari)	Dan Gurney (Porsche), finished 2nd
Belgium 1964	Jim Clark (Lotus) *	Graham Hill (BRM), retired (fuel pump)/ classified 5th
Italy 1967	John Surtees (Honda) *	Jim Clark (Lotus), finished 3rd
Belgium 1968	Bruce McLaren (McLaren) *	Jackie Stewart (Matra), low fuel, delayed In pits/ classified 4th
Monaco 1970	Jochen Rindt (Lotus) *	Jack Brabham (Brabham), finished 2nd
Britain 1970	Jochen Rindt (Lotus)	Jack Brabham (Brabham), finished 2nd
Italy 1971	Peter Gethin (BRM)	Ronnie Peterson (March), finished 2nd
Spain 1975	Jochen Mass (McLaren)	Jacky Ickx (JPS Lotus), finished 2nd
France 1977	Mario Andretti (JPS Lotus) *	John Watson (Brabham), finished 2nd
South Africa 1978	Ronnie Peterson (JPS Lotus) *	Patrick Depailler (Tyrrell), finished 2nd
San Marino 1982	Didier Pironi (Ferrari)	Gilles Villeneuve (Ferrari), finished 2nd
Monaco 1982	Riccardo Patrese (Brabham)	Didier Pironi (Ferrari), retired (battery/ fuel injection)/ classified 2nd
Canada 1991	Nelson Piquet (Benetton) *	Nigel Mansell (Williams), retired (gearbox/engine)/ classified 6th
Japan 1991	Gerhard Berger (McLaren)	Ayrton Senna (McLaren), finished 2nd
Hungary 1997	Jacques Villeneuve (Williams) *	Damon Hill (Arrows), finished 2nd
Europe 1997	Mika Häkkinen (McLaren) *	Jacques Villeneuve (Williams), finished 3rd
Spain 2001	Michael Schumacher (Ferrari)	Mika Häkkinen (McLaren), retired (clutch)/ classified 9th
Austria 2002	Michael Schumacher (Ferrari)	Rubens Barrichello (Ferrari), finished 2nd
United States 2002	Rubens Barrichello (Ferrari)	Michael Schumacher (Ferrari), finished 2nd
Brazil 2003	Giancarlo Fisichella (Jordan) *	Kimi Räikkönen (McLaren), finished 2nd
Europe 2005	Fernando Alonso (Renault)	Kimi Räikkönen (McLaren), retired (tyre/accident)/classified 11th
Japan 2005	Kimi Räikkönen (McLaren)	Giancarlo Fisichella (Renault), finished 2nd
Canada 2011	Jenson Button (McLaren) *	Sebastian Vettel (Red Bull), finished 2nd

* The final lap was the only lap he led in the race.

525. Different leaders within the first five laps *(Most)*

4 drivers	
Italy 1966	Lorenzo Bandini, Mike Parkes, John Surtees, Jack Brabham (within 4 first laps)
3 drivers	
France 1956	Peter Collins, Eugenio Castellotti, Juan Manuel Fangio (within first 4 laps)
Germany 1958	Stirling Moss, Mike Hawthorn, Peter Collins (5)
Belgium 1962	Graham Hill, Trevor Taylor, Willy Mairesse (4)
Germany 1963	Richie Ginther, John Surtees, Jim Clark (4)
Germany 1964	Jim Clark, John Surtees, Dan Gurney (4)
Belgium 1966	John Surtees, Lorenzo Bandini, Jochen Rindt (4)
France 1967	Graham Hill, Jack Brabham, Jim Clark (5)
Belgium 1970	Chris Amon, Jackie Stewart, Pedro Rodríguez (5)
Italy 1970	Jacky Ickx, Pedro Rodríguez, Jackie Stewart (5)
Netherlands 1980	Alan Jones, René Arnoux, Jacques Laffite (3)
Italy 1980	René Arnoux, Jean-Pierre Jabouille, Nelson Piquet (4)
Canada 1989	Alain Prost, Ayrton Senna, Riccardo Patrese (4)
Belgium 1992	Ayrton Senna, Nigel Mansell, Riccardo Patrese (4)
Malaysia 2001	Michael Schumacher, Jarno Trulli, David Coulthard (4)
Italy 2002	Ralf Schumacher, Juan Pablo Montoya, Rubens Barrichello (5)

526. Different leaders within the final five laps *(Most)*

3 drivers	
Belgium 1964	Dan Gurney, Graham Hill, Jim Clark (within final 4 laps)
Italy 1971	Mike Hailwood, Peter Gethin, Ronnie Peterson (5)
Spain 1975	Rolf Stommelen, Jochen Mass, Jacky Ickx (5)
Monaco 1982	Alain Prost, Riccardo Patrese, Didier Pironi (4)
San Marino 1985	Ayrton Senna, Stefan Johansson, Alain Prost (5)
Brazil 2003	David Coulthard, Kimi Räikkönen, Giancarlo Fisichella (3)

527. Different leaders in a season

Most				Fewest			
1975	15	2003	13	1988	4	1992	5
2008	15	2009	13	1950	5	1993	5
1968	13	2012	13	1952	5	2000	5
1977	13	2013	13	1953	5		
1982	13			1964	5		

Total for each season
1950 - 5, 1951 - 6, 1952 - 5, 1953 - 5, 1954 - 9, 1955 - 6, 1956 - 9, 1957 - 9, 1958 - 8, 1959 - 9, 1960 - 10, 1961 - 10, 1962 - 6, 1963 - 6, 1964 - 5, 1965 - 6, 1966 - 10, 1967 - 10, 1968 - 13, 1969 - 7, 1970 - 11, 1971 - 12, 1972 - 8, 1973 - 11, 1974 - 8, 1975 - 15, 1976 - 8, 1977 - 13, 1978 - 11, 1979 - 8, 1980 - 9, 1981 - 10, 1982 - 13, 1983 - 10, 1984 - 9, 1985 - 9, 1986 - 9, 1987 - 7, 1988 - 4, 1989 - 9, 1990 - 10, 1991 - 7, 1992 - 5, 1993 - 5, 1994 - 10, 1995 - 8, 1996 - 8, 1997 - 11, 1998 - 6, 1999 - 11, 2000 - 5, 2001 - 7, 2002 - 6, 2003 - 13, 2004 - 11, 2005 - 11, 2006 - 11, 2007 - 12, 2008 - 15, 2009 - 13, 2010 - 8, 2011 - 8, 2012 - 13, 2013 - 13, 2014 - 10, 2015 - 7
Excludes Indianapolis 500.

528. First time leaders in a season

Most
1975	7	James Hunt, Jean-Pierre Jarier, Carlos Pace, Rolf Stommelen, Jochen Mass, Vittorio Brambilla, Tom Pryce
1968	6	Jean-Pierre Beltoise, Chris Amon, Johnny Servoz-Gavin, Jacky Ickx, Jackie Oliver, Jo Siffert
1950	5	Giuseppe Farina, Luigi Fagioli, Juan Manuel Fangio, Raymond Sommer, Alberto Ascari
1959	5	Jack Brabham, Jo Bonnier, Masten Gregory, Dan Gurney, Bruce McLaren
1971	5	Mario Andretti, Ronnie Peterson, François Cevert, Mike Hailwood, Peter Gethin
1982	5	Andrea De Cesaris, Keke Rosberg, Patrick Tambay, Elio De Angelis, Michele Alboreto
2012	5	Sergio Pérez, Paul Di Resta, Romain Grosjean, Pastor Maldonado, Nico Hülkenberg

Fewest (none)
1955, 63, 72, 83, 91, 98, 2000, 09, 11, 15
Excludes Indianapolis 500.

529. Interval between races led *(Longest)*

	years, days	races		
Bruce McLaren	6y, 6d	61	Monaco 1962 (Cooper)	- Belgium 1968 (McLaren)
Riccardo Patrese	5y, 162d	81	South Africa 1983 (Brabham)	- Brazil 1989 (Williams)
Derek Warwick	5y, 85d	85	Brazil 1984 (Renault)	- Canada 1989 (Arrows)
Michael Schumacher	5y, 1d	87	Japan 2006 (Ferrari)	- Japan 2011 (Mercedes-Benz)
Jean Behra	4y, 205d	39	Belgium 1952 (Gordini)	- Argentina 1957 (Maserati)
Mario Andretti	4y, 52d	56	South Africa 1971 (Ferrari)	- Spain 1975 (Parnelli)
Johnny Herbert	4y, 16d	68	Italy 1995 (Benetton)	- Europe 1999 (Stewart)
Niki Lauda	3y, 262d	53	Britain 1978 (Brabham)	- United States West 1982 (McLaren)
Rubens Barrichello	3y, 213d	56	Italy 1995 (Jordan)	- Brazil 1999 (McLaren)
Giancarlo Fisichella	3y, 192d	56	Europe 1999 (Benetton)	- Brazil 2003 (Jordan)

Did not necessarily start every race during the period.

530. Interval between first & last race led *(Longest)*

	years, days	races		
Michael Schumacher	19y, 40d	326	Belgium 1992 (Benetton)	- Japan 2011 (Mercedes-Benz)
Rubens Barrichello	15y, 23d	258	Portugal 1994 (Jordan)	- Brazil 2009 (Brawn)
Riccardo Patrese	14y, 249d	232	South Africa 1978 (Arrows)	- Australia 1992 (Williams)
David Coulthard	13y, 285d	233	Belgium 1994 (Williams)	- Canada 2008 (Red Bull)
Kimi Räikkönen	13y, 5d	235	France 2002 (McLaren)	- Hungary 2015 (Ferrari)
Alain Prost	12y, 125d	198	France 1981 (Renault)	- Australia 1993 (Williams)
Niki Lauda	12y, 41d	186	Canada 1973 (BRM)	- Australia 1985 (McLaren)
Giancarlo Fisichella	12y, 34d	208	Germany 1997 (Jordan)	- Belgium 2009 (Force India)
Jarno Trulli	11y, 217d	196	Austria 1997 (Prost)	- Bahrain 2009 (Toyota)
Nelson Piquet	11y, 148d	179	United States West 1980 (Brabham)	- Belgium 1991 (Benetton)

531. Interval between race leaders of the same nationality *(Longest)*

	years, days	races		
Mexico	40y, 279d	659	Netherlands 1971 (Pedro Rodríguez)	- Malaysia 2012 (Sergio Pérez)
Switzerland	30y, 334d	506	Britain 1979 (Clay Regazzoni)	- Canada 2010 (Sébastien Buemi)
Australia	21y, 346d	355	Caesars Palace 1981 (Alan Jones)	- United States 2003 (Mark Webber)
Argentina	15y, 359d	171	Argentina 1958 (Juan Manuel Fangio)	- Argentina 1974 (Carlos Reutemann)
Germany	14y, 333d	233	United States 1977 (Hans-Joachim Stuck)	- Belgium 1992 (Michael Schumacher)
Canada	13y, 320d	221	San Marino 1982 (Gilles Villeneuve)	- Australia 1996 (Jacques Villeneuve)
Germany	13y, 286d	155	Britain 1961 (Wolfgang Von Trips)	- Spain 1975 (Rolf Stommelen)
Belgium	12y, 174d	196	Spain 1975 (Jacky Ickx)	- Mexico 1987 (Thierry Boutsen)
France	11y, 35d	191	Italy 1997 (Jean Alesi)	- Japan 2008 (Sébastien Bourdais)
Sweden	10y, 65d	108	France 1961 (Jo Bonnier)	- Italy 1971 (Ronnie Peterson)

532. Laps led but never a world championship *(Most)*

	laps	races
Stirling Moss	1,181	31
Nico Rosberg	1,044	42
Felipe Massa	936	42
David Coulthard	897	62
Rubens Barrichello	854	51
Gerhard Berger	754	33
Ronnie Peterson	707	28
Carlos Reutemann	650	19
Mark Webber	611	29
Juan Pablo Montoya	605	32

533. Laps led but never a win *(Most)*

	laps	races
Chris Amon	183	7
Jean Behra	107	7
Jean-Pierre Jarier	79	3
Ivan Capelli	46	2
Nico Hülkenberg	43	3
Romain Grosjean	40	7
Carlos Menditéguy	39	1
Jackie Oliver	36	3
Andrea De Cesaris	32	2
Bruno Giacomelli	31	1

534. Laps led but never a podium

	laps	races
Nico Hülkenberg	43	3
Cristiano da Matta	17	1
Adrian Sutil	11	1
Markus Winkelhock	6	1
Raymond Sommer	5	1
Paul Di Resta	4	2
Sébastien Bourdais	3	1
Esteban Gutiérrez	2	1
Sébastien Buemi	1	1
Pierluigi Martini	1	1
Antônio Pizzonia	1	1

535. Laps led but never a pole position *(Most)*

	laps	races
Eddie Irvine	157	8
François Cevert	129	5
Peter Collins	127	7
Richie Ginther	116	8
Jean Behra	107	7
Jean-Pierre Beltoise	101	4
Pedro Rodríguez	86	7
Daniel Ricciardo	79	5
Maurice Trintignant	78	3
Ludovico Scarfiotti	55	1

536. Laps led but never a fastest lap *(Most)*

	laps	races
Jean-Pierre Jabouille	180	7
Wolfgang von Trips	156	4
Jo Bonnier	139	4
Peter Collins	127	7
Peter Revson	63	2

	laps	races
Ivan Capelli	46	2
Johnny Herbert	44	4
Carlos Menditéguy	39	1
Pastor Maldonado	37	1
Bruno Giacomelli	31	1

537. Milestones: Races led

Michael Schumacher	50th: France 1998, 100th: Italy 2002
Fernando Alonso	50th: Japan 2008
Rubens Barrichello	50th: Italy 2009
David Coulthard	50th: France 2001
Lewis Hamilton	50th: China 2013
Nigel Mansell	50th: Belgium 1992
Nelson Piquet	50th: Germany 1987
Alain Prost	50th: Canada 1988
Kimi Räikkönen	50th: Japan 2008
Ayrton Senna	50th: United States 1990
Jackie Stewart	50th: Germany 1973
Sebastian Vettel	50th: China 2013

538. Milestones: Race leading drivers
(eg Tony Brooks was the 20th driver to lead a race)

1st	Giuseppe Farina	Britain 1950
20th	Tony Brooks	Italy 1957
40th	Jochen Rindt	Belgium 1966
60th	Jody Scheckter	South Africa 1973
80th	René Arnoux	Italy 1979
100th	Michael Schumacher	Belgium 1992
120th	Jenson Button	United States 2003
140th	Adrian Sutil	Australia 2013

Excludes Indianapolis 500.

539. Milestones: Laps led

Michael Schumacher	1,000th: Britain 1995, 2,000th: Malaysia 1999, 3,000th: Hungary 2001, 4,000th: Australia 2004, 5,000th: Germany 2006
Lewis Hamilton	1,000th: Abu Dhabi 2011, 2,000th: Bahrain 2015
Nigel Mansell	1,000th: Portugal 1990, 2,000th: Japan 1992
Alain Prost	1,000th: Monaco 1985, 2,000th: Britain 1989
Ayrton Senna	1,000th: Italy 1988, 2,000th: Australia 1990
Sebastian Vettel	1,000th: Europe 2011, 2,000th: Belgium 2013
Fernando Alonso	1,000th: Malaysia 2007
Jim Clark	1,000th: Britain 1964
Mika Häkkinen	1,000th: Japan 1999
Damon Hill	1,000th: Monaco 1996
Graham Hill	1,000th: Mexico 1968
Niki Lauda	1,000th: South Africa 1977
Juan Manuel Fangio	1,000th: France 1956
Stirling Moss	1,000th: United States 1960
Nelson Piquet	1,000th: Detroit 1984
Kimi Räikkönen	1,000th: Belgium 2008
Nico Rosberg	1,000th: Brazil 2015
Jackie Stewart	1,000th: United States 1970

Chapter 13: Miscellaneous Driver Facts

Win/ pole position doubles *(Most).* See section 230

Consecutive win/ pole position doubles *(Most).* See section 231

540. Pole position/ fastest lap doubles *(Most)*

Michael Schumacher	27	Monaco 1994 (Benetton)	- France 2006 (Ferrari)
Jim Clark	18	Monaco 1962 (Lotus)	- South Africa 1968 (Lotus)
Juan Manuel Fangio	16	Monaco 1950 (Alfa Romeo)	- Argentina 1958 (Maserati) (a)
Alain Prost	15	Brazil 1982 (Renault)	- Japan 1993 (Williams)
Sebastian Vettel	12	Britain 2009 (Red Bull)	- United States 2013 (Red Bull)
Nigel Mansell	11	Germany 1987 (Williams)	- Japan 1992 (Williams)
Ayrton Senna	11	Portugal 1985 (Lotus)	- Italy 1991 (McLaren)
Mika Häkkinen	10	Australia 1998 (McLaren)	- San Marino 2000 (McLaren)
Lewis Hamilton	10	Japan 2007 (McLaren)	- Italy 2015 (Mercedes-Benz)
Alberto Ascari	9	Belgium 1952 (Ferrari)	- Spain 1954 (Lancia)
Damon Hill	9	Portugal 1993 (Williams)	- Germany 1996 (Williams)
Jacky Ickx	9	Germany 1969 (Brabham)	- Italy 1972 (Ferrari)

(a) Includes four races where he drove two cars in a race to achieve this.

541. Consecutive pole position/ fastest lap doubles *(Most)*

Juan Manuel Fangio	5	France 1950	- France 1951	(Alfa Romeo 158, 159)
Alberto Ascari	4	Germany 1952	- Argentina 1953	(Ferrari 500)
Jim Clark	3	United States 1964	- South Africa 1965	(Lotus 25, 33 - Climax)
Michael Schumacher	3	Monaco 1994	- Canada 1994	(Benetton B194 - Ford Cosworth)

542. Win/ pole position/ fastest lap trebles *(Most)*

Michael Schumacher	22	Monaco 1994 (Benetton - Ford Cosworth)	- France 2006 (Ferrari)
Jim Clark	11	Britain 1962 (Lotus - Climax)	- South Africa 1968 (Lotus - Ford Cosworth)
Juan Manuel Fangio	9	Monaco 1950 (Alfa Romeo)	- Germany 1957 (Maserati) (a)
Lewis Hamilton	9	Japan 2007 (McLaren)	- Italy 2015 (Mercedes-Benz)
Alain Prost	8	Brazil 1982 (Renault)	- San Marino 1993 (Williams - Renault)
Sebastian Vettel	8	Britain 2009 (Red Bull - Renault)	- United States 2013 (Red Bull - Renault)
Alberto Ascari	7	Belgium 1952 (Ferrari)	- Britain 1953 (Ferrari)
Ayrton Senna	7	Portugal 1985 (Lotus - Renault)	- Italy 1990 (McLaren - Honda)
Fernando Alonso	5	Britain 2006 (Renault)	- Singapore 2010 (Ferrari)
Mika Häkkinen	5	Australia 1998 (McLaren - Mercedes)	- Brazil 1999 (McLaren - Mercedes)
Damon Hill	5	Britain 1994 (Williams - Renault)	- Germany 1996 (Williams - Renault)
Nigel Mansell	5	Britain 1991 (Williams - Renault)	- Britain 1992 (Williams - Renault)

(a) Includes two races where he drove two cars in a race to achieve this.

543. Consecutive win/ pole position/ fastest lap trebles *(Most)*

Alberto Ascari	4	Germany 1952	- Argentina 1953	(Ferrari 500)
Fernando Alonso	2	Italy 2010	- Singapore 2010	(Ferrari F10)
Alberto Ascari	2	Belgium 1952	- France 1952	(Ferrari 500)
Jack Brabham	2	Belgium 1960	- France 1960	(Cooper T53 - Climax)
Jim Clark	2	Netherlands 1963	- France 1963	(Lotus 25 - Climax)
Jim Clark	2	Mexico 1967	- South Africa 1968	(Lotus 49 - Ford Cosworth)
Mika Häkkinen	2	Australia 1998	- Brazil 1998	(McLaren MP4-13 - Mercedes)
Mika Häkkinen	2	Spain 1998	- Monaco 1998	(McLaren MP4-13 - Mercedes)
Lewis Hamilton	2	Italy 2014	- Singapore 2014	(Mercedes-Benz F1 W05)
Jacques Laffite	2	Argentina 1979	- Brazil 1979	(Ligier JS11 - Ford Cosworth)
Nigel Mansell	2	France 1992	- Britain 1992	(Williams FW14B - Renault)
Felipe Massa	2	Bahrain 2007	- Spain 2007	(Ferrari F2007)
Michael Schumacher	2	United States 2006	- France 2006	(Ferrari 248 F1)
Sebastian Vettel	2	Singapore 2013	- Korea 2013	(Red Bull RB9 - Renault)

544. Win/ pole position/ fastest lap trebles and also led every lap *(Most)*

Jim Clark	8	Britain 1962 (Lotus)	- Germany 1965 (Lotus)
Alberto Ascari	5	France 1952 (Ferrari)	- Britain 1953 (Ferrari)
Michael Schumacher	5	Monaco 1994 (Benetton)	- Hungary 2004 (Ferrari)
Nigel Mansell	4	Britain 1991 (Williams)	- Britain 1992 (Williams)
Ayrton Senna	4	Portugal 1985 (Lotus)	- Italy 1990 (McLaren)
Jackie Stewart	4	France 1969 (Matra)	- United States 1972 (Tyrrell)
Sebastian Vettel	4	India 2011 (Red Bull)	- Korea 2013 (Red Bull)
Nelson Piquet	3	United States West 1980 (Brabham)	- Canada 1984 (Brabham)
Jack Brabham	2	Belgium 1960 (Cooper)	- Britain 1966 (Brabham)
Juan Manuel Fangio	2	Monaco 1950 (Alfa Romeo)	- Germany 1956 (Lancia)
Mika Häkkinen	2	Brazil 1998 (McLaren)	- Monaco 1998 (McLaren)
Lewis Hamilton	2	Malaysia 2014	- Italy 2015 (Mercedes-Benz)

545. Maiden pole & maiden to win at the same race

	pole position	winner
Britain 1950	Giuseppe Farina	Giuseppe Farina
Monaco 1950	Juan Manuel Fangio	Juan Manuel Fangio
Britain 1951	José Froilán González	José Froilán González
Germany 1951	Alberto Ascari	Alberto Ascari
Britain 1955	Stirling Moss	Stirling Moss
Netherlands 1959	Jo Bonnier	Jo Bonnier
Italy 1960	Phil Hill	Phil Hill
Belgium 1962 (a)	Graham Hill	Jim Clark
Italy 1966 (a)	Mike Parkes	Ludovico Scarfiotti
France 1968 (a)	Jochen Rindt	Jacky Ickx
Monaco 1972 (a)	Emerson Fittipaldi	Jean-Pierre Beltoise
South Africa 1974 (a)	Niki Lauda	Carlos Reutemann
Sweden 1974 (a)	Patrick Depailler	Jody Scheckter
United States West 1980	Nelson Piquet	Nelson Piquet
Portugal 1985	Ayrton Senna	Ayrton Senna
Malaysia 2003 (a)	Fernando Alonso	Kimi Räikkönen
Monaco 2004	Jarno Trulli	Jarno Trulli
Turkey 2006	Felipe Massa	Felipe Massa
Canada 2007	Lewis Hamilton	Lewis Hamilton
Italy 2008	Sebastian Vettel	Sebastian Vettel
Germany 2009	Mark Webber	Mark Webber
China 2012	Nico Rosberg	Nico Rosberg
Spain 2012	Pastor Maldonado	Pastor Maldonado

(a) Race where different drivers claimed their first pole and first win.

546. Drivers of the same nationality in the top six *(Most)*

British	6	Britain 1957 (1: Tony Brooks/ Stirling Moss, 3: Mike Hawthorn, 4: Peter Collins, 5: Roy Salvadori, 6: Bob Gerard)
French	5	France 1950 (4: Robert Manzon, 5: Philippe Etançelin/ Eugène Chaboud, 6: Charles Pozzi/ Louis Rosier)
Italian	5	Italy 1951 (1: Alberto Ascari, 3: Felice Bonetto/ Giuseppe Farina, 4: Luigi Villoresi, 5: Piero Taruffi)
British	5	Netherlands 1964 (1: Jim Clark, 2: John Surtees, 3: Peter Arundell, 4: Graham Hill, 6: Bob Anderson)
British	5	South Africa 1965 (1: Jim Clark, 2: John Surtees, 3: Graham Hill, 4: Mike Spence, 6: Jackie Stewart)
British	5	Britain 1965 (1: Jim Clark, 2: Graham Hill, 3: John Surtees, 4th: Mike Spence, 5: Jackie Stewart)

547. Top six finishers in same order as the eventual table for the season

This has only happened once, at Monaco 1973.

Race result

1st	Jackie Stewart	Tyrrell - Ford Cosworth	78 laps
2nd	Emerson Fittipaldi	Lotus - Ford Cosworth	78
3rd	Ronnie Peterson	Lotus - Ford Cosworth	77
4th	François Cevert	Tyrrell - Ford Cosworth	77
5th	Peter Revson	McLaren - Ford Cosworth	76
6th	Denny Hulme	McLaren - Ford Cosworth	76

Final drivers' championship table

1st	Jackie Stewart	71
2nd	Emerson Fittipaldi	55
3rd	Ronnie Peterson	52
4th	François Cevert	47
5th	Peter Revson	38
6th	Denny Hulme	26

548. Best race finishes of those eliminated in the first qualifying session

(from 2006 when the new qualifying format was introduced)

Valtteri Bottas	2nd	Britain 2014	Mark Webber	3rd	China 2011
Nelsinho Piquet	2nd	Germany 2008	Alexander Wurz	3rd	Canada 2007
Rubens Barrichello	3rd	Britain 2008	Heikki Kovalainen	4th	Canada 2007
Romain Grosjean	3rd	India 2013	Jarno Trulli	4th	United States 2006
Lewis Hamilton	3rd	Brazil 2009	Sebastian Vettel	4th	Brazil 2009
Lewis Hamilton	3rd	Hungary 2014	Sebastian Vettel	4th	Abu Dhabi 2015
Kimi Räikkönen	3rd	Bahrain 2006	Mark Webber	4th	Europe 2012

549. Consecutive finishes in the same position (excluding wins) *(Most)*

(see section 199 for consecutive wins)

4 x 2nd	Lewis Hamilton	Malaysia	- Monaco 2007
4 x 2nd	Nelson Piquet	Monaco	- Britain 1987
4 x 2nd	Nico Rosberg	Malaysia	- Spain 2014
4 x 3rd	Heinz-Harald Frentzen	Belgium	- Luxembourg 1997
4 x 4th	Mark Webber	Australia	- Bahrain 2012
4 x 7th	Michele Alboreto	Monaco	- Britain 1992

550. Disqualifications *(Most)*

Stefan Bellof	11	Brazil 1984	- Netherlands 1984 (a)
Martin Brundle	8	Brazil 1984	- Austria 1987 (a)
Stefan Johansson	4	Britain 1984	- Canada 1989 (a)
Niki Lauda	3	Canada 1972	- Germany 1983
Stirling Moss	3	France 1959	- Britain 1961
Mika Salo	3	Europe 1996	- Australia 2000
Takuma Sato	3	San Marino 2005	- China 2006
Michael Schumacher	3	Britain 1994	- Canada 2004
Ayrton Senna	3	Australia 1987	- Japan 1989
John Watson	3	Argentina 1975	- South Africa 1983

(a) Includes Tyrrell team disqualifications in 1984 (found to have added water and lead shot late in races to satisfy the minimum weight limit).

551. Disqualifications in a race *(Most)*

The most disqualifications in a race was four in Canada 2004, all for having illegal brake ducts:
Ralf Schumacher & Juan Pablo Montoya (Williams FW26 - BMW); Cristiano da Matta & Olivier Panis (Toyota TF104).

552. Disqualified from a point scoring position

driver (car - engine)	race	position	circumstances
Bruce Halford (Maserati)	Germany 1956	5th	received a push-started after spin
Stirling Moss (Lotus - Climax)	Portugal 1960	5th	drove in wrong direction after spin
James Hunt (McLaren - Ford Cosworth)	Britain 1976	1st	took short-cut back to the pits after the initial race was stopped
Nelson Piquet (Brabham - Ford Cosworth)	Brazil 1982	1st	car under the minimum weight limit
Keke Rosberg (Williams - Ford Cosworth)	Brazil 1982	2nd	car under the minimum weight limit
Gilles Villeneuve (Ferrari)	United States West 1982	3rd	illegal two-part rear wing
Manfred Winkelhock (ATS - Ford Cosworth)	San Marino 1982	6th	car under the minimum weight limit
Niki Lauda (McLaren - Ford Cosworth)	Belgium 1982	3rd	car under the minimum weight limit
Keke Rosberg (Williams - Ford Cosworth)	Brazil 1983	2nd	received a push-start in the pit lane
Niki Lauda (McLaren - Ford Cosworth)	Germany 1983	5th	reversed in the pit lane
Martin Brundle (Tyrrell - Ford Cosworth)	Brazil 1984	5th	(a)
Stefan Bellof (Tyrrell - Ford Cosworth)	Belgium 1984	6th	(a)
Stefan Bellof (Tyrrell - Ford Cosworth)	San Marino 1984	5th	(a)
Stefan Bellof (Tyrrell - Ford Cosworth)	Monaco 1984	3rd	(a)
Martin Brundle (Tyrrell - Ford Cosworth)	Detroit 1984	2nd	(a)
Alain Prost (McLaren - TAG Porsche)	San Marino 1985	1st	car under the minimum weight limit
Ayrton Senna (Lotus - Honda)	Australia 1987	2nd	had oversized front brake cooling ducts
Thierry Boutsen (Benetton - Ford Cosworth)	Belgium 1988	3rd	fuel irregularities
Alessandro Nannini (Benetton - Ford Cosworth)	Belgium 1988	4th	fuel irregularities
Ayrton Senna (McLaren - Honda)	Japan 1989	1st	used chicane escape road after accident with Alain Prost
Christian Fittipaldi (Footwork - Ford Cosworth)	Canada 1994	6th	car under the minimum weight limit
Michael Schumacher (Benetton - Ford Cosworth)	Britain 1994	2nd	overtook on the parade lap & ignored a stop-go penalty
Michael Schumacher (Benetton - Ford Cosworth)	Belgium 1994	1st	illegal skid block wear
Mika Häkkinen (McLaren - Mercedes)	Belgium 1997	3rd	fuel irregularities in practice
Jacques Villeneuve (Williams - Renault)	Japan 1997	5th	failed to slow down under waved yellow flags in practice
Mika Salo (Sauber - Petronas)	Australia 2000	6th	front wing infringement
David Coulthard (McLaren - Mercedes)	Brazil 2000	2nd	front wing end-plates lower than permitted

driver (car - engine)	race	position	circumstances
Ralf Schumacher (Williams - BMW)	Canada 2004	2nd	brake duct infringements
Juan Pablo Montoya (Williams - BMW)	Canada 2004	5th	brake duct infringements
Christiano da Matta (Toyota)	Canada 2004	8th	brake duct infringements
Jenson Button (BAR - Honda)	San Marino 2005	3rd	car under the minimum weight limit
Takuma Sato (BAR - Honda)	San Marino 2005	5th	car under the minimum weight limit
Robert Kubica (BMW Sauber - BMW)	Hungary 2006	7th	car under the minimum weight limit
Rubens Barrichello (Honda)	Australia 2008	6th	exited the pit lane under a red light
Lewis Hamilton (McLaren - Mercedes)	Australia 2009	4th	misled the race stewards re Jarno Trulli's overtake
Sergio Pérez (Sauber - Ferrari)	Australia 2011	7th	illegal upper rear wing dimensions
Kamui Kobayashi (Sauber - Ferrari)	Australia 2011	8th	illegal upper rear wing dimensions
Daniel Ricciardo (Red Bull - Renault)	Australia 2014	3rd	breach of fuel flow regulations
Felipe Massa (Williams - Mercedes)	Brazil 2015	8th	rear tyre temperature in excess of limit

In the above races, lower positions were promoted into disqualified slots, except at Brazil 1983, where 2nd place remained vacant.
(a) The Tyrrell team was disqualified from all placings in 1984 (found to have added water and lead shot late in races to satisfy the minimum weight limit).

553. Excluded from results due to alleged breach, but later reinstated
Carroll Shelby & Masten Gregory (Maserati)
Italy 1958 (for sharing a car, but reinstated receiving no points)
Graham Hill (BRM)
France 1963 (for being push-started on the grid, but later reinstated with a 1-minute penalty which kept him in 3rd place. However, the FIA withheld points)
Jochen Rindt (Lotus - Ford Cosworth)
Britain 1970 (for rear wing being too high)
James Hunt (McLaren - Ford Cosworth)
Spain 1976 (for car being too wide)
Jacques Laffite (Ligier - Matra)
Spain 1976 (for rear aerofoil irregularities)
John Watson (Penske - Ford Cosworth)
France 1976 (for rear aerofoil irregularities)
Thierry Boutsen (Williams - Renault) & Alex Caffi (Dallara - Ford Cosworth)
San Marino 1989 (for changing tyres in the pit lane prior to the restart)
Eddie Irvine & Michael Schumacher (Ferrari)
Malaysia 1999 (for illegal bargeboards)
Jarno Trulli (Jordan - Honda)
United States 2001 (for worn underbody plank)
Jarno Trulli (Toyota)
Australia 2009 (for overtaking behind the safety car, but reinstated after it was judged that Hamilton had misled the stewards)

554. Penalty from a point scoring position
(where position was affected/ apart from disqualifications at section 552)

driver (car - engine)	race	original	eventual	circumstances
Jean Behra (Maserati)	France 1957	5th	6th	final lap was too slow, after pushing the car, 1 lap penalty
Chris Amon (Ferrari)	Mexico 1967	5th	9th	final lap was too slow, 1 lap penalty
Jean-Pierre Jarier (Shadow - Ford Cosworth)	Spain 1975	3rd	4th	overtook under yellow flags, 1 lap penalty
Mario Andretti (JPS Lotus - Ford Cosworth)	Italy 1978	1st	6th	jumped the start, 1-minute penalty
Gilles Villeneuve (Ferrari)	Italy 1978	2nd	7th	jumped the start, 1-minute penalty
Didier Pironi (Ligier - Ford Cosworth)	Canada 1980	1st	3rd	jumped the restart, 1-minute penalty
Gerhard Berger (McLaren - Honda)	Canada 1990	1st	4th	jumped the start, 1-minute penalty
Olivier Panis (BAR - Honda)	Australia 2001	4th	7th	overtook under yellow flags, 25-second penalty
Ralf Schumacher (Toyota)	San Marino 2005	6th	9th	unsafe release from pit stop, 25-second penalty
Scott Speed (Toro Rosso - Cosworth)	Australia 2006	8th	9th	overtook under yellow flags, 25-second penalty
Vitantonio Liuzzi (Toro Rosso - Ferrari)	Japan 2007	8th	9th	overtook under yellow flags, 25-second penalty
Lewis Hamilton (McLaren - Mercedes)	Belgium 2008	1st	3rd	gained advantage by cutting the chicane, 25-second penalty
Timo Glock (Toyota)	Belgium 2008	8th	9th	overtook under yellow flags, 25-second penalty
Sébastien Bourdais (Toro Rosso - Ferrari)	Japan 2008	6th	10th	left the pits into the path of Massa, 25-second penalty
Heikki Kovalainen (McLaren -Mercedes)	Brazil 2009	9th	12th	unsafe release from pit stop, 25-second penalty
Michael Schumacher (Ferrari)	Monaco 2010	6th	12th	overtook under safety car conditions, 20-second penalty
Sébastien Buemi (Toro Rosso - Ferrari)	Europe 2010	8th	9th	speeding while safety car was deployed, 5-second penalty
Pedro de la Rosa (BMW Sauber - Ferrari)	Europe 2010	10th	12th	speeding while safety car was deployed, 5-second penalty
Jaime Alguersuari (Toro Rosso - Ferrari)	Belgium 2010	10th	13th	left the track and gained an advantage, 20-second penalty

driver (car - engine)	race	original	eventual	circumstances
Adrian Sutil (Force India - Mercedes)	Singapore 2010	8th	9th	left the track and gained an advantage, 20-second penalty
Nico Hülkenberg (Williams - Cosworth)	Singapore 2010	9th	10th	left the track and gained an advantage, 20-second penalty
Lewis Hamilton (McLaren - Mercedes)	Malaysia 2011	7th	8th	made more than one change of direction to defend position, 20-second penalty
Pastor Maldonado (Williams - Renault)	Europe 2012	10th	12th	caused accident with Hamilton, 20-second penalty
Sebastian Vettel (Red Bull - Renault)	Germany 2012	2nd	5th	left the track and gained an advantage, 20-second penalty
Mark Webber (Red Bull - Renault)	Singapore 2012	10th	11th	left the track and gained an advantage, 20-second penalty
Jules Bianchi (Marussia - Ferrari)	Monaco 2014	8th	9th	took a race penalty under the safety car, 5-second penalty
Kevin Magnussen (McLaren - Mercedes)	Belgium 2014	6th	12th	forced Alonso off the track, 20-second penalty
Kevin Magnussen (McLaren - Mercedes)	Italy 2014	7th	10th	forced Bottas off the track, 5-second penalty
Kimi Räikkönen (Ferrari)	Russia 2015	5th	8th	caused accident with Bottas, 30-second penalty
Fernando Alonso (McLaren - Honda)	Russia 2015	10th	11th	failed to respect the track limits, 5-second penalty
Carlos Sainz (Toro Rosso - Renault)	United States 2015	6th	7th	speeding in the pit lane, 5-second penalty

555. Incurred a penalty before, during and after a race

Lewis Hamilton (McLaren - Mercedes), Monaco 2011

before:	best qualifying time erased, for cutting the chicane.
during:	drive-through penalty, for causing an accident with Felipe Massa.
after:	20-seconds added to final time, for causing an accident with Pastor Maldonado.

Pastor Maldonado (Williams - Cosworth), Abu Dhabi 2011

before:	10-place grid penalty, for replacing the engine which exceeded his season engine quota.
during:	drive-through penalty, for ignoring blue flags.
after:	30-seconds added to final time, for ignoring blue flags again.

556. Biggest grid penalties

70-places for Jenson Button (McLaren - Honda) at the 2015 Mexican Grand Prix. This was on a 20-car grid! For 2015, penalties were given for the use of extra power unit elements above the permitted four for the season. In Mexico, Button had to sit out qualifying, due to engine problems. So he started at the back of the grid, in any case.

In the 2015 Belgian Grand Prix, Button's team-mate Fernando Alonso was given a 55-place grid penalty in similar circumstances. There were several other such penalties, totalling up to 50-places on the grid, during the season.

557. Point scoring position, but not eligible for points
(apart from disqualifications at section 552 or demoted with a penalty at section 554)

driver(s), (car - engine)	race	finishing position
Johnny Claes/ Juan Manuel Fangio (Maserati)	Belgium 1953	3rd (a)
Alberto Ascari (Ferrari)	Italy 1953	3rd (a)
Juan Manuel Fangio (Lancia-Ferrari)	Monaco 1956	4th (b)
Peter Collins (Lancia-Ferrari)	Britain 1957	4th (c)
Bruce McLaren (Cooper - Climax)	Germany 1958	5th overall (d)
Cliff Allison (Lotus - Climax)	Germany 1958	5th in F1 section (e)
Masten Gregory/ Carroll Shelby (Maserati)	Italy 1958	4th (f)
Maurice Trintignant/ Stirling Moss (Cooper - Climax)	Argentina 1960	3rd (f)
Graham Hill (BRM)	Belgium 1960	3rd (a)
Jackie Oliver (Lotus - Ford Cosworth)	Germany 1967	5th (d)
Henri Pescarolo (Matra - Ford Cosworth)	Germany 1969	5th (d)
Richard Attwood (Brabham - Ford Cosworth)	Germany 1969	6th (d)
Jo Gartner (Osella - Alfa Romeo)	Italy 1984	5th (g)
Gerhard Berger (ATS - BMW)	Italy 1984	6th (g)
Yannick Dalmas (Lola - Ford Cosworth)	Australia 1987	5th (g)

(a) Retired and was not classified - would have been classified if the car had not retired (from 1961 such cases were eligible for points).
(b) Only eligible for points for shared drive in his other car to 2nd place.
(c) Completed insufficient distance (only three laps) in the shared drive.
(d) Formula 2 car, so ineligible for points.
(e) Finished behind Formula 2 cars, in 10th place overall.
(f) Shared drives no longer eligible for points.
(g) The constructor had not submitted an entry for a second car that season.

558. Serious breaches of regulations which were not subjected to a penalty
(went unnoticed or were argued out of a penalty)

Jean Behra (Simca-Gordini), Italy 1951
Allegedly drove in the race impersonating Maurice Trintignant who was suffering from indigestion (and wearing his helmet), so that the team would not lose starting money.

Mike Hawthorn (Ferrari), Portugal 1958
Hawthorn encountered a problem and restarted his car, illegally driving in the wrong direction. Moss backed him up by telling the stewards that Hawthorn had been on the pavement when he made the manoeuvre and so was not in breach of the regulations. No action was taken against Hawthorn (who stood to lose his 7 points) and consequently, win the championship by 1 point over Moss.

Harry Schell (Cooper - Climax), United States 1959
Qualified third using a short-cut. Tony Brooks (Ferrari) should have started third instead.

Jochen Rindt (Lotus - Ford Cosworth), Britain 1970
Disqualified from 1st place when the scrutineers found that if the struts on the rear wing had not been bent, the wing would have been too high. After an argument, the struts were straightened and refitted, and he was reinstated. The wing probably had been illegal during the race.

Vittorio Brambilla (March - Ford Cosworth), Sweden 1975
Started from pole position. Allegedly a team member cut the timing beam by waving a hand in front of the car before Brambilla's car got to the line. Patrick Depailler (Tyrrell - Ford Cosworth) probably recorded the real pole position time.

James Hunt (McLaren - Ford Cosworth), Spain 1976
On measuring the car after the race it was found to be wider than the legal limit and so Hunt was disqualified. McLaren appealed by stating that measuring after the race with tyres warm and inflated was inappropriate. Two months later Hunt was reinstated as the winner.

Ayrton Senna (McLaren - Honda), Japan 1990
At the first corner, Senna moved over and crashed into his rival Alain Prost (Ferrari). He had been unhppy about the accident with Prost in Japan 1989 (when they were team-mates) that deprived him of the title. He was also unhappy that pole at this race was on the dirty side of the track.

Michael Schumacher & Eddie Irvine (Ferrari), Malaysia 1999
They finished 1st and 2nd but were disqualified for a discrepancy in the oversize bargeboards on their cars. After appeal, the disqualifications were overturned with the FIA stating that the dimensions fell within an allowable 5 mm tolerance.

Fernando Alonso (Renault), Singapore 2008
Nelsinho Piquet was asked by his team to crash on purpose, in order to bring out the safety car and bunch up the field to give Fernando Alonso an easy chance of winning the race, which he did. Although the result stood, there was a fine for the team.

559. Non-starters

	Nat	Date of birth	Date of death	Races	First - last
Giovanna AMATI	I	20 Jul 1962		3	South Africa - Brazil 1992
Michael BARTELS	D	8 Mar 1968		4	Germany - Spain 1991
Azdrúbal BAYARDO	ROU	26 Dec 1922	9 Jul 2006	1	France 1959
Enrico BERTAGGIA	I	19 Sep 1964		6	Belgium - Australia 1989
Juan Manuel BORDEU	RA	28 Jan 1934	24 Nov 1990	1	France 1961
Gary BRABHAM	AUS	29 Mar 1961		2	United States - Brazil 1990
Tino BRAMBILLA	I	31 Jan 1934		2	Italy 1963 - Italy 1969
Gianfranco BRANCATELLI	I	18 Jan 1950		3	Spain - Monaco 1979
Oscar CABALÉN	RA	4 Feb 1924	25 Aug 1967	1	Argentina 1960
Phil CADE	USA	12 Jun 1916	28 Aug 2001	1	United States 1959
Colin CHAPMAN	GB	19 May 1928	16 Dec 1982	1	France 1956
Pedro CHAVES	P	27 Feb 1965		13	United States - Portugal 1991
Kevin COGAN	USA	31 Mar 1956		2	Canada 1980 - United States West 1981
Alberto COLOMBO	I	23 Feb 1946		3	Belgium - Italy 1978
Alberto CRESPO	RA	16 Jan 1930	14 Aug 1991	1	Italy 1952
Alain de CHANGY	B	5 Feb 1922	5 Aug 1994	1	Monaco 1959
Bernard de DRYVER	B	19 Sep 1952		2	Belgium 1977 - Belgium 1978
Giovanni De RIU	I	10 Mar 1925	11 Dec 2008	1	Italy 1954
Frank DOCHNAL	USA	8 Oct 1920	7 Jul 2010	1	Mexico 1963
Piero DUSIO	I	13 Oct 1899	7 Nov 1975	1	Italy 1952
Bernie ECCLESTONE	GB	28 Oct 1930		1	Netherlands 1958
Carlo FACETTI	I	26 Jun 1935		1	Italy 1974
Willie FERGUSON	ZA	6 Mar 1940	19 May 2007	1	South Africa 1972
Ludwig FISCHER	D	17 Dec 1915	8 Mar 1991	1	Germany 1952
Carlo FRANCHI. See "GIMAX"					
Giorgio FRANCIA	I	8 Nov 1947		2	Italy 1977 - Spain 1981
Hiroshi FUSHIDA	J	10 Mar 1946		2	Netherlands - Britain 1975
Divina GALICA	GB	13 Aug 1944		3	Britain 1976 - Brazil 1978
"GIMAX"	I	1 Jan 1938		1	Italy 1978

	Nat	Date of birth	Date of death	Races	First - last
Helm GLÖCKLER	D	13 Jan 1909	18 Dec 1993	1	Germany 1953
Brian GUBBY	GB	17 Apr 1934		1	Britain 1965
Naoki HATTORI	J	13 Jun 1966		2	Japan - Australia 1991
Tom JONES	USA	26 Apr 1943	29 May 2015	1	Canada 1967
Juan JOVER	E	23 Nov 1923	28 Jun 1960	1	Spain 1951
Ken KAVANAGH	AUS	12 Dec 1923		2	Monaco - Belgium 1958
David KENNEDY	IRL	15 Jan 1953		7	Argentina - France 1980
Bruce KESSLER	USA	23 Mar 1936		1	Monaco 1958
Mikko KOZAROWITSKY	FIN	17 May 1948		2	Sweden - Britain 1977
Willi KRAKAU	D	4 Dec 1911	26 Apr 1995	1	Germany 1952
Kurt KUHNKE	D	30 Apr 1910	8 Feb 1969	1	Germany 1963
Masami KUWASHIMA	J	14 Sep 1950		1	Japan 1976
Claudio LANGES	I	20 Jul 1960		14	United States - Spain 1990
Ricardo LONDOÑO	CO	8 Aug 1949	18 Jul 2009	1	Brazil 1981
Jean LUCIENBONNET	F	7 Jan 1923	19 Aug 1962	1	Monaco 1959
Perry McCARTHY	GB	3 Mar 1961		7	Spain - Belgium 1992
Brian McGUIRE	AUS	13 Dec 1945	29 Aug 1977	1	Britain 1977
Harry MERKEL	D	10 Jan 1918	11 Feb 1995	1	Germany 1952
Bill MOSS	GB	4 Sep 1933	13 Jan 2010	1	Britain 1959
Jac NELLEMAN	DK	19 Apr 1944		1	Sweden 1976
Alfredo PIÁN	RA	21 Oct 1912	25 Jul 1990	1	Monaco 1950
Ernesto PRINOTH	I	15 Apr 1923	26 Nov 1981	1	Italy 1962
Clive PUZEY	RSR	11 Jul 1941		1	South Africa 1965
Ken RICHARDSON	GB	21 Aug 1911	27 Jun 1997	1	Italy 1951
Alan ROLLINSON	GB	15 May 1943		1	Britain 1965
Jean-Claude RUDAZ	CH	7 Jul 1942		1	Italy 1964
Günther SEIFERT	D	18 Oct 1937		1	Germany 1962
Vincenzo SOSPIRI	I	9 Oct 1966		1	Australia 1997
Stephen SOUTH	GB	19 Feb 1952		1	United States West 1980
Otto STUPPACHER	A	3 Mar 1947	13 Aug 2001	3	Italy - United States 1976
Andy SUTCLIFFE	GB	9 May 1947	13 Jul 2015	1	Britain 1977
Luigi TARAMAZZO	I	5 May 1932	15 Feb 2004	1	Monaco 1958
Dennis TAYLOR	GB	12 Jun 1921	2 Jun 1962	1	Britain 1959
André TESTUT	F	13 Apr 1926	24 Sep 2005	2	Monaco 1958 - Monaco 1959
Tony TRIMMER	GB	24 Jan 1943		6	Germany 1975 - Britain 1978
Jacques VILLENEUVE Sr.	CDN	4 Nov 1953		3	Canada 1981 - Canada 1983
Volker WEIDLER	D	18 Mar 1962		10	Brazil - Hungary 1989
Ted WHITEAWAY	GB	1 Nov 1928	18 Oct 1995	1	Monaco 1955
Desiré WILSON	ZA	26 Nov 1953		1	Britain 1980
Joachim WINKELHOCK	D	24 Oct 1960		7	Brazil - France 1989
Emilio ZAPICO	E	21 May 1944	6 Aug 1996	1	Spain 1976

Excludes Indianapolis 500.
For key to nationalities, see foot of section 125.

560. Non-starting nationalities
(number of nationalities each season, other than those in section 140, whose drivers did not qualify or did not start races)
1956 - 2, 1958 - 1, 1959 - 1, 1961 - 1, 1962 - 1, 1964 - 1, 1969 - 1, 1970 - 1, 1973 - 1, 1975 - 1, 1976 - 2, 1977 - 1, 1978 - 1, 1980 - 2, 1981 - 2, 1982 - 1, 1983 - 1, 1989 - 2, 1990 - 1, 1991 - 1

561. Drivers who only ever entered practice
(with no intention of qualifying for the race)

	Nat	Date of birth	Date of death	Races	First - last
Michael AMMERMÜLLER	D	14 Feb 1986		3	China - Brazil 2006
Matteo BOBBI	I	2 Jul 1978		1	San Marino 2003
Ryan BRISCOE	AUS	24 Sep 1981		6	Hungary - Brazil 2004
James CALADO	GB	13 Jun 1989		5	Italy - Brazil 2013
Jan CHAROUZ	CZ	17 Jul 1987		1	Brazil 2011
Dani CLOS	E	23 Oct 1988		6	Spain - Korea 2012
Fairuz FAUZY	MAL	24 Oct 1982		5	Malaysia - Abu Dhabi 2010

	Nat	Date of birth	Date of death	Races	First - last
Adderly FONG	HK	2 Mar 1990		1	Abu Dhabi 2014
Robin FRIJNS	NL	7 Aug 1991		2	Bahrain - Britain 2014
Rodolfo GONZÁLEZ	YV	14 May 1986		9	Bahrain - Brazil 2013
Neel JANI	CH	8 Dec 1983		18	Bahrain - Brazil 2006
Daniel JUNCADELLA	E	7 May 1991		3	Britain - Brazil 2014
Fabio LEIMER	CH	17 Apr 1989		1	Hungary 2015
Bas LEINDERS	B	16 Jul 1975		17	Malaysia - Brazil 2004
Pedro LLANO	RA		10 Apr 1968	1	Argentina 1960
MA Qing Hua	CHN	25 Dec 1987		5	Italy 2012 - China 2013
Raffaele MARCIELLO	I	17 Dec 1994		4	Malaysia – United States 2015
Giorgio MONDINI	CH	19 Jul 1980		9	Malaysia - Italy 2006
Satoshi MOTOYAMA	J	4 Mar 1971		1	Japan 2003
Chanoch NISSANY	IL	29 Jul 1963		1	Hungary 2005
Esteban OCON	F	17 Sep 1996		1	Abu Dhabi 2014
Jolyon PALMER	GB	20 Jan 1991		13	China – Abu Dhabi 2015
Julio POLA	YV	23 Mar 1916	5 Apr 1974	1	Argentina 1960
Alexandre PRÉMAT	F	5 Apr 1982		1	China 2006
Luiz RAZIA	BR	4 Apr 1989		2	China - Brazil 2011
Sergey SIROTKIN	RUS	27 Aug 1995		1	Russia 2014
Enrico TOCCACELO	I	12 Dec 1978		3	Turkey - Belgium 2005
Davide VALSECCHI	I	24 Jan 1987		1	Malaysia 2011
Ernesto VISO	YV	19 Mar 1985		1	Brazil 2006
Robert WICKENS	CDN	13 Mar 1989		1	Abu Dhabi 2011
Björn WIRDHEIM	S	4 Apr 1980		18	United States 2003 - Brazil 2004
Susie WOLFF	GB	6 Dec 1982		4	Britain 2014 - Britain 2015

For key to nationalities, see foot of section 125.

562. Non-qualifications *(Most)*
(includes non-pre-qualifications)

Gabriele Tarquini	40	Detroit 1988	- Australia 1991	(Coloni, AGS, Fomet)
Bertrand Gachot	37	Brazil 1989	- Australia 1994	(Onyx, Rial, Coloni, Lola, Pacific)
Roberto Moreno	32	Netherlands 1982	- Belgium 1992	(Lotus, Coloni, EuroBrun, Andrea Moda)
Piercarlo Ghinzani	31	Monaco 1981	- Japan 1989	(Osella, Zakspeed)
Arturo Merzario	26	Monaco 1975	- United States 1979	(Williams, March, Merzario)
Bernd Schneider	25	Brazil 1988	- Spain 1990	(Zakspeed, Arrows)
Yannick Dalmas	24	Canada 1988	- Australia 1990	(Lola, AGS)
Stefan Johansson	24	Argentina 1980	- Britain 1991	(Shadow, Tyrrell, Ligier, Onyx, AGS, Footwork)
Eric van de Poele	24	United States 1991	- Germany 1992	(Lamborghini, Brabham)
Nicola Larini	23	Italy 1987	- Japan 1991	(Coloni, Osella, Lamborghini)

Excludes cases where driver was excluded from the event for breach of regulations.

The history of pre-qualifying. See section 960.

563. Final race featuring pre-qualifying
The last time there was pre-qualifying was at Hungary 1992. Five drivers took part, with Perry McCarthy (Andrea Moda), being the only one to non-pre-qualify.

564. Failed to qualify for every race in a season
Aguri Suzuki was the only driver to non-pre-qualify in every race during a season (16 races for Zakspeed in 1989). Bertrand Gachot failed in all 16 races of 1990 for Coloni (10 pre-qualifying and 6 qualifying).

565. Consecutive non-qualifications *(Most)*

Bertrand Gachot	18	Japan 1989	- Australia 1990	(Rial, Coloni)
Aguri Suzuki	16	Brazil 1989	- Australia 1989	(Zakspeed)
Gabriele Tarquini	16	Britain 1989	- France 1990	(AGS)
Yannick Dalmas	14	Monaco 1989	- United States 1990 (a)	(Lola, AGS)
Claudio Langes	14	United States 1990	- Spain 1990 (b)	(EuroBrun)
Pedro Chaves	13	United States 1991	- Portugal 1991 (b)	(Coloni)

Pierre-Henri Raphanel	13	Mexico 1989	- Australia 1989	(Coloni, Rial)
Bernd Schneider	13	San Marino 1989	- Spain 1989	(Zakspeed)
Eric van de Poele	13	Monaco 1991	- Australia 1991	(Lamborghini)
Fabrizio Barbazza	12	San Marino 1991	- Spain 1991	(AGS)
Gregor Foitek	12	Brazil 1989	- Spain 1989 (c)	(EuroBrun, Rial)
Bruno Giacomelli	12	San Marino 1990	- Spain 1990	(Life)

(a) Includes Portugal 1989 where he was excluded (tyre infringement before qualifying). Did not enter one of the events within the period.
(b) This was every race entered during his career.
(c) Did not enter two events within the period.

566. Unsuccessful qualifying attempts for drivers who never started a race *(Most)*

Claudio Langes	14	EuroBrun, 1990
Pedro Chaves	13	Coloni, 1991
Volker Weidler	10	Rial, 1989 (a)
David Kennedy	7	Shadow, 1980
Perry McCarthy	7	Andrea Moda, 1992 (b)
Joachim Winkelhock	7	AGS, 1989
Enrico Bertaggia	6	Coloni, 1989
Tony Trimmer	6	Maki, 1975 - 76; Surtees, 1977; McLaren, 1978
Michael Bartels	4	Lotus, 1991
Giovanna Amati	3	Brabham, 1992
Gianfranco Brancatelli	3	Kauhsen, 1979; Merzario, 1979
Alberto Colombo	3	ATS, 1978; Merzario, 1978
Divina Galica	3	Surtees, 1976; Hesketh, 1978
Otto Stuppacher	3	Tyrrell, 1976
Jacques Villeneuve Sr.	3	Arrows, 1981; RAM March, 1983

(a) Includes Germany 1989, where he was excluded for mechanics working on his car away for the pit lane during practice.
(b) Includes Germany 1992, where he was excluded for missing a weight check.

567. Grand Prix drivers who non-qualified at the Indianapolis 500 (1950 - 60)
(when the Indianapolis 500 was within the world championship)
Chuck Daigh, Jorge Daponte, Juan Manuel Fangio, Giuseppe Farina, John Fitch, Rob Schroeder.

568. Banned from racing
Ken Richardson (BRM P15), Italy 1951
It was discovered that he did not possess the correct racing licence due to his lack of experience. So even though he had qualified in 10th position, he was not allowed to start the race. He never entered another grand prix.
Lella Lombardi (Brabham BT44B - Ford Cosworth), Germany 1976
On the Friday evening, her car was impounded by police following Loris Kessel being dropped by the team in favour of her. It was Kessel who had brought Tissot watch sponsorship to the team and he consequently filed a law suit against the team, resulting in Lombardi's car being impounded.
Karl Oppitzhauser (March 761 - Ford Cosworth), Austria 1976
Otto Stuppacher (March 761 - Ford Cosworth), Austria 1976
Both for lack of experience in single-seater racing.
Hans Heyer (Penske PC4 - Ford Cosworth), Austria 1977
Started illegally at the previous race in Germany after failing to qualify.
Riccardo Patrese (Arrows A1 - Ford Cosworth), United States 1978
Not initially banned, but other drivers blamed Patrese, at the time, for the multiple pile-up at the start of the Italian Grand Prix, which killed Ronnie Peterson. They refused to race with him at this next race, so he was forced to stand aside.
Ricardo Londoño (Ensign N180B - Ford Cosworth), Brazil 1981
Super-licence refused due to his lack of racing experience.
Emilio de Villota (Williams FW07 - Ford Cosworth), Spain 1981
A new ruling prevented private entries from taking part.
Nigel Mansell (Ferrari 640), Spain 1989
Reversed in the pit lane in Portugal, after overshooting his pit and ignored the resulting black disqualification flags - meanwhile Mansell, in an attempt to overtake Senna on the 49th lap, caused a crash, sending both cars out. He was banned from the following race in Spain.
Eddie Irvine (Jordan 194 - Hart), Pacific, San Marino & Monaco 1994
Dangerous driving. Caused an accident on the 35th lap of the Brazilian Grand Prix, involving Verstappen, Bernard and Brundle, resulting in the three race ban.
Mika Häkkinen (McLaren MP4/9 - Peugeot), Hungary 1994
Dangerous driving. Caused a multi-car accident at the first corner of the German Grand Prix and was banned from the next race.

Michael Schumacher (Benetton B194 - Ford Cosworth), Italy & Portugal 1994

Illegally refuelled during a stop-go penalty and also ignored the subsequent black flag. His punishment of a two race ban and disqualification from that race was confirmed after an appeal. The stop-go penalty had been issued for passing Hill twice on the parade lap.

Jenson Button & Takuma Sato (BAR 007 - Honda), Monaco & Spain 2005

A constructor's ban for running cars which were able to race below the minimum legal weight limit in San Marino.

Yuji Ide (Super Aguri SA05 - Honda), Europe 2006

Had his super licence withdrawn due to erratic driving during the first four races of 2006. He was therefore unable to compete beyond San Marino.

Romain Grosjean (Lotus E20 - Renault), Italy 2012

Dangerous driving. Caused an accident with Hamilton at the start in Belgium which also took out Pérez and Alonso. This resulted in the one race ban.

Additionally, Jacques Villeneuve (Williams FW19 - Renault) was handed a one race ban after ignoring yellow flags in qualifying at Japan 1997. He was permitted to participate in that race under appeal. Withdrawing the appeal, he was disqualified from his 5th place finish.

569. Female drivers

Maria Teresa De Filippis	Maserati, Behra-Porsche	1958 - 59	3 races started + 2 non-qualifications
Lella Lombardi (a)	Brabham, March, Williams	1974 - 76	12 races started + 5 non-starts/non-qualifications
Divina Galica	Surtees, Hesketh	1976 - 78	3 non-qualifications
Desiré Wilson	Williams	1980	1 non-qualification
Giovanna Amati	Brabham	1992	3 non-qualifications
Susie Wolff	Williams	2014 - 15	practice at 4 races

(a) The only female to score world championship points, finishing 6th in Spain 1975 (half a point due to the race being stopped early).

570. Relatives in grands prix

father/ son

Mario/ Michael Andretti
Jack/ David & *Gary* Brabham
Wilson/ Christian Fittipaldi
Graham/ Damon Hill
Jan/ Kevin Magnussen
Satoru/ Kazuki Nakajima
Reg/ Tim Parnell
Nelson/ Nelsinho Piquet
André/ Teddy Pilette
Keke/ Nico Rosberg
Hans/ Hans-Joachim Stuck
Jos/ Max Verstappen
Gilles/ Jacques Villeneuve
Manfred/ Markus Winkelhock

father-in-law/ son-in-law

Emerson Fittipaldi/ Max Papis

brothers

David/ *Gary* Brabham
Tino/ Vittorio Brambilla
Corrado/ Teo Fabi
Emerson/ Wilson Fittipaldi
Pedro/ Ricardo Rodríguez
Ian/ Jody Scheckter
Michael/ Ralf Schumacher
Jackie/ Jimmy Stewart
Gilles/ *Jacques (Sr.)* Villeneuve
Graham/ Peter Whitehead (half brothers)
Joachim/ Manfred Winkelhock

uncle/ nephew

Emerson/ Christian Fittipaldi
Jo/ Jean-Louis Schlesser
Ayrton/ Bruno Senna
Jacques (Sr.)/ Jacques Villeneuve
Joachim/ Markus Winkelhock

great-uncle/ grand-nephew

Lucien/ Jules Bianchi

cousins

José Dolhem/ Didier Pironi

brothers-in-law

Jean-Pierre Beltoise/ François Cevert
David Brabham/ Mike Thackwell
Jean-Pierre Jabouille/ Jacques Laffite
Tony Maggs/ Mike Spence

Italicised drivers did not start a race.

571. Brothers together

on the starting grid together

Michael/ Ralf Schumacher	Australia 1997 - Brazil 2006	(157 races)
Emerson/ Wilson Fittipaldi	Spain 1972 - United States 1975	(35 races)
Ian/ Jody Scheckter	South Africa 1974 - Canada 1977	(18 races)
Graham/ Peter Whitehead	Britain 1952	(1 race)

on the front row of the grid together

Michael/ Ralf Schumacher	Brazil 2001 - Japan 2004	(8 races)

on the podium together

Michael and Ralf Schumacher have been the only brothers on the podium together, at the following 16 races:

1998	Italy
2000	Australia, Belgium, Italy
2001	Canada (a), France (a)
2002	Malaysia, Brazil (a), San Marino, Monaco, Germany, Hungary
2003	Canada (a), France
2004	Japan (a)
2005	Hungary

(a) Achieved a 1-2 finish.

scored points in the same race

Michael/ Ralf Schumacher	France 1997 - Turkey 2006	(66 races)
Emerson/ Wilson Fittipaldi	Argentina 1973- Germany 1973	(2 races)

572. Father versus son performances

race winners

Of the twelve father and son drivers in the history of Formula 1, six fathers and three sons have been race winners -

Fathers: Mario Andretti, Jack Brabham, Graham Hill, Nelson Piquet, Keke Rosberg and Gilles Villeneuve.

Sons: Damon Hill, Nico Rosberg and Jacques Villeneuve.

Each of the above sons have won more races than their father, Damon eight more than Graham, Jacques five more than Gilles and Nico nine more than Keke. However, Graham Hill did achieve two world championship titles compared to Damon's one. Keke also became a world champion, not yet achieved by Nico.

won a grand prix which his father had won

Damon Hill	Italy (1993, 94: Williams - Renault)	Graham (1962: BRM)
	Spain (1994: Williams - Renault)	Graham (1968: Lotus - Ford Cosworth) (a)
	Germany (1996: Williams - Renault)	Graham (1962: BRM) (b)
Nico Rosberg	Australia (2014: Mercedes-Benz)	Keke (1985: Williams - Honda) (c)
Nico Rosberg	Monaco (2013, 14, 15: Mercedes-Benz)	Keke (1983: Williams - Ford Cosworth)
Jacques Villeneuve	Spain (1997: Williams - Renault)	Gilles (1981: Ferrari) (d)

(a) Graham at Jarama, Damon at Catalunya.
(b) Graham at Nürburgring, Damon at Hockenheim.
(c) Keke at Adelaide, Nico at Melbourne.
(d) Gilles at Jarama, Jacques at Catalunya.

Additional occasion where a son won a race in the same country as his father:
Italy - Damon Hill won at San Marino in 1995 & 96 (Williams - Renault)

pole position at a grand prix where his father had pole

Jacques Villeneuve	San Marino (1997: Williams - Renault)	Gilles (1981: Ferrari)
Damon Hill	France (1993, 94, 95: Williams - Renault)	Graham (1967: Lotus - Ford Cosworth) (a)
Damon Hill	Britain (1994, 95, 96: Williams - Renault)	Graham (1968: Lotus - Ford Cosworth) (b)
Damon Hill	Monaco (1995: Williams - Renault)	Graham (1965: BRM, 68: Lotus - Ford Cosworth)
Nico Rosberg	Brazil (2014, 15: Mercedes-Benz)	Keke (1983: Williams - Ford Cosworth) (c)
Nico Rosberg	Germany (2014: Mercedes-Benz)	Keke (1986: McLaren - TAG Porsche) (d)
Nico Rosberg	Britain (2014: Mercedes-Benz)	Keke (1982: Williams - Ford Cosworth, 85: Williams - Honda) (e)

(a) Graham at Bugatti au Mans, Damon at Magny-Cours.
(b) Graham at Brands Hatch, Damon at Silverstone.
(c) Keke at Jacarepaguá, Nico at Interlagos.
(d) Both at Hockenheim.
(e) Keke at Brands Hatch & Silverstone, Nico at Silverstone.

573. Drove three or more different car models during a race weekend

4 car models	
Monaco 1957:	Peter Collins, in practice sessions drove the Cooper T43, Ferrari Dino 156 and Lancia-Ferrari D50. In the race he drove a Lancia-Ferrari 801.
3 car models	
Monaco 1959:	Stirling Moss drove a Cooper T51 - BRM and the works BRM P25 in practice. He raced a Cooper T51 - Climax.
Belgium 1961:	Willy Mairesse drove an Emeryson 1002 and a Lotus 21 in practice, and a Lotus 18 in the race.
Italy 1961:	John Surtees drove the Cooper T55 and T56 in practice and raced the T53.
Italy 1964:	Lorenzo Bandini practiced in a Ferrari 156 and a 1512. For the race, he drove the 158. These three each had different configurations of engine, 156 fitted with V6, 158 fitted with V8 and 1512 fitted with flat 12.
Britain 1969:	Graham Hill drove a Brabham BT26 and Lotus 63 in practice. In the race he drove a Lotus 49.

574. Murdered Formula 1 drivers

Jackie Pretorius, 30 March 2009 in Midrand, Johannesburg, South Africa, aged 74. He was attacked by intruders to his home and died later in hospital. His wife, Shirley had been killed in similar circumstances at the same house in 2003. Formula 1 career: first appeared at South Africa 1965 where he failed to pre-qualify and raced in 1968, 71 and 73 at South Africa, retiring twice and being non-classified in the other.

Ricardo Londoño was shot on 18 July 2009 in San Bernardo del Viento, Colombia. He was 59. Formula 1 career: only appearance was at Brazil 1981 where his super-licence was refused resulting in exclusion from the event.

575. Kidnapped Formula 1 drivers

Juan Manuel Fangio was kidnapped by Cuban rebels on 23 February 1958 at Hotel Lincoln in Havana. He was there to race in the non-championship Cuban Grand Prix which he had won the year before. On the eve of the race, Fangio walked into the lobby on his way to dinner to be confronted by a man wearing a leather jacket and brandishing a pistol. He was taken away, but treated very well in a furnished apartment as he sympathised with the rebels' case. The second in command to Fidel Castro who was leading the guerrilla forces, gave Fangio a personal apology and supplied a radio for him to listen to the race, although Fangio said he didn't feel in the mood for it.

Giovanna Amati, prior to her racing career, when she was 15, was kidnapped. It occurred in February 1978 in Italy when three gangsters took her out of a car she was sitting in near her parents' villa and drove her away in a van. Giovanna was kept in a wooden cage for 75 days and physically and mentally abused. She was not released until an 800 million-lire ransom was paid. The money was raised by her father using funds from his theatre's box office takings from the film "Star Wars" and her mother sold some of her jewelry and got her servants to lend some money too.

Hans Herrmann, was kidnapped after he had retired from racing, on 13 December 1991. He was taken from his home in Maichingen, near Stuttgart in Germany, put in the boot of his Mercedes 500 and driven to a car park. Once a ransom was paid, he was released. The police never found the perpetrators.

576. Track invaders

1953: Argentina (Buenos Aires no.2)
On lap 32, a spectator attempted to cross the track, causing Giuseppe Farina to lose control, his Ferrari ploughing into the crowd and killing 13 spectators. The race continued.

1962: France (Rouen-les-Essarts)
A long line of gendarmes who had formed up shoulder-to-shoulder by the finishing line caused a massive shunt. Maurice Trintignant had to swerve to avoid Surtees and went into the path of Trevor Taylor who was finishing at high speed. Both cars were written-off but the drivers were luckily unscathed.

1992: Britain (Silverstone)
Mansell-Mania erupted following Nigel's victory, with a track invasion as the cars negotiated their slowing down lap. Mansell's car nudged one of the spectators. Mansell didn't complain - he enjoyed the celebration.

2000: Germany (Hockenheim)
A disgruntled Mercedes worker, 47-year old Frenchman Robert Sehli, got onto the track before the first chicane, by cutting a hole in the fence. It was on lap 24 of the race, to protest about being sacked because of his physical disability. The safety car was deployed and cost Mika Häkkinen victory. The massive 34-second lead that the two McLarens held over Rubens Barrichello was instantly negated and it provided Barrichello's first Formula 1 victory.

2003: Britain (Silverstone)
On the 12th lap, Neil Horan, a 56-year old former Irish Roman Catholic priest climbed over the fence and ran across the track on Hangar Straight. He was wearing a kilt and waving a banner "Read The Bible, The Bible is always right" and promoted his religious belief that the end of the world is near. Several cars had to swerve to avoid him and it required a safety car period.

2015: China (Shanghai)
An unidentified Chinese fan ran across the main straight, towards the pits, during second practice on the Friday. He jumped over the pit wall and into the Ferrari garage, demanding a drive in a Formula 1 car. He reportedly shouted at team personnel "I want a car. I have got a ticket".

2015: Singapore (Marina Bay)
On the 37th lap of the race, a 27-year old British national, Yogvitam Pravin Dhokia, walked along the side of the track and took photographs. He had appeared through a gap in the fencing and walked along Esplanade Drive straight.

Chapter 14: Driver Successes Outside The F1 World Championship

577. GP2 Series

champions

Timo Glock	1	2007		Pastor Maldonado	1	2010
Romain Grosjean	1	2011		Jolyon Palmer (p)	1	2014
Lewis Hamilton	1	2006		Giorgio Pantano	1	2008
Nico Hülkenberg	1	2009		Nico Rosberg	1	2005
Fabio Leimer (p)	1	2013		Davide Valsecchi (p)	1	2012

winners

	GP2 wins		best GP2 season	best F1 race result
Pastor Maldonado	10	(2007 - 10)	1st (2010)	1st (2012)
Romain Grosjean	9	(2008 - 11)	1st (2011)	2nd (2012 - 13)
Giorgio Pantano	9	(2006 - 08)	1st (2008)	13th (2004)

	GP2 wins		best GP2 season	best F1 race result
Timo Glock	7	(2006 - 07)	1st (2007)	2nd (2008 - 09)
Jolyon Palmer (p)	7	(2012 - 14)	1st (2014)	-
Davide Valsecchi (p)	7	(2008 - 12)	1st (2012)	-
Lucas Di Grassi	5	(2007 - 09)	2nd (2007)	14th (2010)
Lewis Hamilton	5	(2006)	1st (2006)	1st (2007 - 15)
Nico Hülkenberg	5	(2009)	1st (2009)	4th (2012 - 13)
Heikki Kovalainen	5	(2005)	2nd (2005)	1st (2008)
Fabio Leimer (p)	5	(2010 -13)	1st (2013)	-
Sergio Pérez	5	(2010)	2nd (2010)	2nd (2012)
Nelsinho Piquet	5	(2005 - 06)	2nd (2006)	2nd (2008)
Luiz Razia (p)	5	(2009 - 12)	2nd (2012)	-
Nico Rosberg	5	(2005)	1st (2005)	1st (2012 - 15)
Giedo van der Garde	5	(2009 - 12)	5th (2011)	14th (2013)
James Calado (p)	4	(2012 - 13)	3rd (2013)	-
Esteban Gutiérrez	4	(2011 - 12)	3rd (2012)	7th (2013)
Felipe Nasr	4	(2014)	3rd (2014)	5th (2015)
Vitaly Petrov	4	(2007 - 09)	2nd (2009)	3rd (2011)
Alexander Rossi	4	(2013 - 15)	2nd (2015)	- (2015)
Gianmaria Bruni	3	(2005 - 06)	7th (2006)	14th (2004)
Marcus Ericsson	3	(2010 - 13)	6th (2013)	8th (2015)
Charles Pic	3	(2010 - 11)	4th (2011)	12th (2012)
Bruno Senna	3	(2007 - 08)	2nd (2008)	6th (2012)
Sébastien Buemi	2	(2008)	6th (2008)	7th (2009)
Karun Chandhok	2	(2007 - 08)	10th (2008)	14th (2010)
Max Chilton	2	(2012)	4th (2012)	13th (2014)
Neel Jani (p)	2	(2005)	7th (2005)	-
Ernesto Viso (p)	2	(2006)	6th (2006)	-
Michael Ammermüller (p)	1	(2006)	11th (2006)	-
Jules Bianchi	1	(2011)	3rd (2011)	9th (2014)
Daniel Clos (p)	1	(2010)	4th (2010)	-
Jérôme d'Ambrosio	1	(2010)	9th (2009)	13th (2012)
Robin Frijns (p)	1	(2013)	15th (2013)	-
Kamui Kobayashi	1	(2008)	16th (2008, 09)	3rd (2012)
Raffaele Marciello (p)	1	(2014)	7th (2015)	-
Sergey Sirotkin (p)	1	(2015)	3rd (2015)	-

non-winners

	best GP2 race result	best GP2 season	best F1 race result
Fairuz Fauzy (p)	5th (2011)	18th (2011)	-
Rodolfo González (p)	4th (2010)	21st (2010)	-
Ma Qing Hua (p)	21st (2013)	- (2013)	-
Giorgio Mondini (p)	13th (2005)	- (2005)	-
Kazuki Nakajima	2nd (2007)	5th (2007)	6th (2008)
Antônio Pizzonia	8th (2007)	27th (2007)	7th (2004 - 05)
Scott Speed	2nd (2005)	3rd (2005)	9th (2006 - 07)
Sakon Yamamoto	4th (2008)	23rd (2008)	12th (2007)

(p) Only practiced in Formula 1.

578. GP2 Asia Series (2008 - 11)

champions

Romain Grosjean	2	2008, 11		Kamui Kobayashi	1	2008/09

winners

Roman Grosjean	5	2008, 11		Sébastein Buemi	1	2008
Kamui Kobayashi	4	2008, 08/09		Daniel Clos (p)	1	2011
Davide Valsecchi (p)	4	2008/09, 09/10		Fairuz Fauzy	1	2008
Sergio Pérez	2	2008/09		Nico Hülkenberg	1	2008/09
Vitaly Petrov	2	2008, 08/09		Charles Pic	1	2009/10
Jules Bianchi	1	2011		Luiz Razia (p)	1	2008/09

(p) Only practiced in Formula 1.
There were two seasons which straddled two years, 2008/09 and 2009/10.

579. International Formula 3000 (1985 - 2004) champions

Jean Alesi	1989		Vitantonio Liuzzi	2004
Luca Badoer	1992		Stefano Modena	1987
Jean-Christophe Boullion	1994		Juan Pablo Montoya	1998
Sébastien Bourdais	2002		Roberto Moreno	1988
Ivan Capelli	1986		Olivier Panis	1993
Erik Comas	1990		Vincenzo Sospiri (nq)	1995
Christian Danner	1985		Justin Wilson	2001
Christian Fittipaldi	1991		Björn Wirdheim (p)	2003
Nick Heidfeld	1999		Ricardo Zonta	1997

(nq) Non-qualifier in Formula 1, (p) Only practiced in Formula 1.
Of the 20 Formula 3000 champions, Jörg Müller and Bruno Junqueira were the only two not to enter Formula 1.

580. British Formula 3000 (1989 - 96) champions

Gary Brabham	1989		Pedro Chaves	1990

Both were non-qualifiers in Formula 1.

581. Auto GP/ Euro Formula 3000 champions

Romain Grosjean	2010		Felipe Massa	2001

Auto GP (2010 onwards).

582. European Formula 2 (1967 - 84) champions

René Arnoux	1977		Jean-Pierre Jarier	1973
Jean-Pierre Beltoise	1968		Jacques Laffite	1975
Patrick Depailler	1974		Geoff Lees	1981
Corrado Fabi	1982		Jonathan Palmer	1983
Bruno Giacomelli	1978		Ronnie Peterson	1971
Mike Hailwood	1972		Clay Regazzoni	1970
Brian Henton	1980		Johnny Servoz-Gavin	1969
Jacky Ickx	1967		Marc Surer	1979
Jean-Pierre Jabouille	1976		Mike Thackwell	1984

583. Japanese Championship Super Formula champions

Marco Apicella	1994		Satoshi Motoyama (p)	1998, 2001, 03, 05
Pedro de la Rosa	1997		Kazuki Nakajima	2012, 14
Ralph Firman	2002		Satoru Nakajima	1981, 82, 84, 85, 86
Masahiro Hasemi	1980		Ralf Schumacher	1996
Kazuyoshi Hoshino	1975, 77, 78, 87, 90, 93		Aguri Suzuki	1988
Ukyo Katayama	1991		Toshio Suzuki	1995
Geoff Lees	1983		Tora Takagi	2000
André Lotterer	2011		Noritake Takahara	1974, 76

(p) Only practiced in Formula 1.
All-Japan Formula 2000 (1973 - 77), All-Japan Formula 2 (1978 - 86), Japanese Formula 3000 (1987 - 95), Formula Nippon (1996 - 2012), Japanese Championship Super Formula (2013 onwards).

584. GP3 Series champions

Valtteri Bottas	2011		Daniil Kvyat	2013
Esteban Gutiérrez	2010			

585. European Formula 3 champions

Michele Alboreto	1980	Jan Lammers	1978
Mauro Baldi	1981	Oscar Larrauri	1982
Jules Bianchi	2009	Raffaele Marciello (p)	2013
Ryan Briscoe (p)	2003	Pierluigi Martini	1983
Alex Caffi	1985	Roberto Merhi	2011 (a)(c)
Ivan Capelli	1984	Stefano Modena	1986
Anthony Davidson	2001	Gianni Morbidelli	1989
Paul Di Resta	2006	Esteban Ocon (p)	2014
Piercarlo Ghinzani	1977	Riccardo Patrese	1976
Romain Grosjean	2007	Larry Perkins	1975
Lewis Hamilton	2005	Alain Prost	1979
Nico Hülkenberg	2008	Joachim Winkelhock	1988
Daniel Juncadella (p)	2012 (a)(b)	Alessandro Zanardi	1990

European F3 Cup (1975), European F3 Championship (1976 - 84 and 2012 onwards), F3 European Cup (1985 - 2002), F3 Euro Series (2003 - 12), F3 International Trophy (2011).
(a) F3 Euro Series.
(b) European F3 Championship.
(c) F3 International Trophy.
(p) Only practiced in Formula 1.

586. British Formula 3 (1951 - 2014) champions
(until 1978 there was more than one championship for most seasons)

Jaime Alguersuari	2008	Gunnar Nilsson	1975 (BP F3)
Peter Arundell	1963 (Express & Star Formula Junior/BARC F Junior)	Carlos Pace	1970 (Forward Trust F3)
Rubens Barrichello	1991	Jonathan Palmer	1981
David Brabham	1989	Nelsinho Piquet	2004
Eric Brandon	1951 (Autosport F3)	Nelson Piquet	1978 (BP F3)
Tony Brise	1973 (Lombard North/John Player Euro F3)	Antônio Pizzonia	2000
Tommy Byrne	1982	Daniel Ricciardo	2009
Jim Clark	1960 * (John Davy F Junior/Motor Racing F Junior)	Takuma Sato	2001
Derek Daly	1977 (BP F3)	Tim Schenken	1968 (Lombank F3)
Johnny Dumfries	1984	Ayrton Senna	1983
Ralph Firman	1996	Chico Serra	1979
Emerson Fittipaldi	1969 (Lombank F3)	Stephen South (nq)	1977 (Vandervell F3)
Bruno Giacomelli	1976 (Shellsport F3)	Jackie Stewart	1964 (Express & Star F3)
Maurício Gugelmin	1985	Henry Taylor	1955 (JAP F3)
Mika Häkkinen	1990	Trevor Taylor	1958 (BRSCC F3), 60 * (M Racing F Junior), 61 (M Racing F Junior)
Brian Henton	1974 (Lombard N F3/Forward Trust F3)	Tony Trimmer (nq)	1970 (Shellsport F3)
Johnny Herbert	1987	Jean-Eric Vergne	2010
Stefan Johansson	1980	Rikky von Opel	1972 (Lombard N F3)
Rupert Keegan	1976 (BP F3)	Dave Walker	1970 (Lombank F3), 71 (Shellsport/Forward Trust F3)
J J Lehto	1988	Derek Warwick	1978 (Vandervell F3)
Les Leston	1954 (BRSCC National F3)	Roger Williamson	1971 (Lombard N F3), 72 (Forward Trust F3), 72 (Shellsport F3)
Jan Magnussen	1994		
Bill Moss (nq)	1961 (J Davy F Junior)		
Felipe Nasr	2011		

* Tied.
(nq) Non-qualifier in Formula 1.

587. Macau "Grand Prix" single-seater race winners

Enrico Bertaggia (nq)	1988 (Formula 3)	Roberto Moreno	1982 (F Pacific)
David Brabham	1989 (F3)	Riccardo Patrese	1977, 78 (F Pacific)
David Coulthard	1991 (F3)	Alexandre Prémat (p)	2004 (F3)
Lucas Di Grassi	2005 (F3)	Dieter Quester	1970 (Formula Libre)
Martin Donnelly	1987 (F3)	Takuma Sato	2001 (F3)
Ralph Firman	1996 (F3)	Michael Schumacher	1990 (F3)
Maurício Gugelmin	1985 (F3)	Ralf Schumacher	1995 (F3)
Daniel Juncadella (p)	2011 (F3)	Vern Schuppan	1974, 76 (F Pacific)
Geoff Lees	1979, 80 (Formula Pacific)	Ayrton Senna	1983 (F3)

(nq) Non-qualifier in Formula 1.
(p) Only practiced in Formula 1.

588. Monaco Formula 3 "Grand Prix" (1950 - 2005) winners

Peter Arundell	1961, 62		Michael May	1959
Richard Attwood	1963		Stirling Moss	1950
Mauro Baldi	1980		Henri Pescarolo	1967
Jean-Pierre Beltoise	1966		Ronnie Peterson	1969
Enrico Bertaggia (nq)	1988		Didier Pironi	1977
Ivan Capelli	1984		Alain Prost	1979
Yannick Dalmas	1986		Tom Pryce	1974
Elio De Angelis	1978		Pierre-Henri Raphanel	1985
Patrick Depailler	1972		Peter Revson	1965
Giancarlo Fisichella	1994		Jackie Stewart	1964
Bruno Giacomelli	1976		Henry Taylor	1960
Lewis Hamilton	2005		Tony Trimmer (nq)	1970
Nick Heidfeld	1997		Dave Walker	1971
Jacques Laffite	1973		Renzo Zorzi	1975

Monaco Junior (1950 - 63).
(nq) Non-qualifier in Formula 1.

589. Masters of Formula 3 race winners

Jules Bianchi	2008		Daniel Juncadella (p)	2012
Valtteri Bottas	2009, 10		Christian Klien	2003
David Coulthard	1991		Pedro Lamy	1992
Paul Di Resta	2006		Alexandre Prémat (p)	2004
Norberto Fontana	1995		Takuma Sato	2001
Lewis Hamilton	2005		Jos Verstappen	1993
Nico Hülkenberg	2007		Max Verstappen	2014

All above races held at Zandvoort circuit, Netherlands except 2007 which was at Zolder, Belgium.
(p) Only practiced in Formula 1.

590. French Formula 3 (1964 - 2002) champions

Jean Alesi	1987		Franck Lagorce	1992
Jean-Pierre Beltoise	1965		Miche Leclère	1972
Sébastien Bourdais	1999		François Mazet	1969
François Cevert	1968		Henri Pescarolo	1967
Erik Comas	1988		Alain Prost	1978 *, 79
Yannick Dalmas	1986		Pierre-Henri Raphanel	1985
Patrick Depailler	1971		Jean-Louis Schlesser	1978 *
Jean-Marc Gounon	1989		Johnny Servoz-Gavin	1966
Olivier Grouillard	1984		Philippe Streiff	1981
Jacques Laffite	1973			

* Tied.

591. German Formula 3 (1950 - 2014) champions

Christijan Albers	1999		Michael Schumacher	1990
Norberto Fontana	1995		Jarno Trulli	1996
Giorgio Francia (nq)	1974		Jos Verstappen	1993
Nick Heidfeld	1997		Volker Weidler (nq)	1985
Pedro Lamy	1992		Karl Wendlinger	1989
Giorgio Pantano	2000		Joachim Winkelhock	1988
Bernd Schneider	1987			

(nq) Non-qualifier in Formula 1.

592. Italian Formula 3 (1964 - 2012) champions

Enrico Bertaggia (nq)	1987	Franco Forini	1985
Tino Brambilla (nq)	1966	"Geki"	1964
Vittorio Brambilla	1972	Piercarlo Ghinzani	1979
Ivan Capelli	1983	Nicola Larini	1986
Alberto Colombo	1974	Gianni Morbidelli	1989
Andrea De Adamich	1965	Emanuele Naspetti	1988
Elio De Angelis	1977	Riccardo Patrese	1976
Giancarlo Fisichella	1994	Siegfried Stohr	1978

(nq) Non-qualifier in Formula 1.

593. Japanese Formula 3 champions

Pedro de la Rosa	1995	Adrian Sutil	2006
Marcus Ericsson	2009	Toshio Suzuki	1979
Naoki Hattori (nq)	1990		

(nq) Non-qualifier in Formula 1.

594. Brazilian Formula 3 champions

Cristiano da Matta	1994	Ricardo Zonta	1995
Christian Fittipaldi	1989		

595. Formula 3 Sudamericana (1987 - 2013) champions

Christian Fittipaldi	1990	Luiz Razia (p)	2006
Nelsinho Piquet	2002	Ricardo Zonta	1995

(p) Only practiced in Formula 1.

596. Formula Renault 3.5 Series champions

Robert Kubica	2005	Carlos Sainz	2014
Kevin Magnussen	2013	Giedo van der Garde	2008

597. Formula Renault 2.0 UK (1989 - 2011) champions

Pedro de la Rosa	1992	Antônio Pizzonia	1999
Lewis Hamilton	2003	Kimi Räikkönen	2000

598. GM Lotus Euroseries (1988 - 99) champions

Rubens Barrichello	1990	Pedro Lamy	1991
Mika Häkkinen	1988	Bas Leinders (p)	1996

(p) Only practiced in Formula 1.

599. Formula Vauxhall (1988 - 97) champions

Luciano Burti	1997	Vincenzo Sospiri (nq)	1990
Allan McNish	1988		

(nq) Non-qualifier in Formula 1.

600. Formula Palmer Audi (1998 - 2010) champion

Justin Wilson	1998

(nq) Non-qualifier in Formula 1.

601. Formula Ford Festival winners

Julian Bailey	1982		Geoff Lees	1975
Jenson Button	1998		Jan Magnussen	1992
Tommy Byrne	1981		Robert Moreno	1980
Derek Daly	1976		Roland Ratzenberger	1986
Anthony Davidson	2000		Chico Serra	1977
Johnny Herbert	1985		Vincenzo Sospiri (nq)	1988
Eddie Irvine	1987		Mark Webber	1996

(nq) Non-qualifier in Formula 1

602. Pre-Formula 1 major single-seater grand prix winners (1906 - 49)

Alberto Ascari	1949		Louis Rosier	1949
Louis Chiron	1928 - 49		Raymond Sommer	1936
Emmanuel de Graffenried	1949		Hans Stuck	1934 - 35
Luigi Fagioli	1933 - 35		Luigi Villoresi	1948
Giuseppe Farina	1940 - 48		Peter Whitehead	1949
Hermann Lang	1937 - 39			

603. A1 GP World Cup of Motorsport (2005/06 - 2008/09) champions

Nico Hülkenberg	2006/07 (a)		Alexandre Prémat (p)	2005/06 (c)
Neel Jani (p)	2007/08 (b)			

Each season straddled two years.
(a) On behalf of Germany. (b) On behalf of Switzerland. (c) On behalf of France. (p) Only practiced in Formula 1.

604. World Touring Car (WTCC) champion

Gabriele Tarquini	2009

605. British Touring Car (BTCC) champions

Jim Clark	1964		Gabriele Tarquini	1994
Frank Gardner	1967, 68, 73		Joachim Winkelhock	1993
John Love	1962			

British Saloon Car Championship until 1986.

606. German Touring Car (DTM) champions

Paul Di Resta	2010		Hans-Joachim Stuck	1990
Nicola Larini	1993		Eric van de Poele	1987
Bernd Schneider	1995, 2000, 01, 03, 06			

607. IndyCar

Indianapolis 500 drivers (1950 - 60) who won the race in other years

A J Foyt	1961, 64, 67, 77		Mauri Rose	1941, 47, 48
Bill Holland	1949		Rodger Ward	1962

Indianapolis 500 winners

Mario Andretti (a)	1969		Bobby Rahal	1986
Eddie Cheever	1998		Troy Ruttman	1952
Jim Clark (a)	1965		Danny Sullivan	1985
Mark Donohue	1972		Bobby Unser	1968, 75, 81
Emerson Fittipaldi (a)	1989, 93		Jacques Villeneuve (a)	1995
Graham Hill (a)	1966		Rodger Ward	1959, 62
Juan Pablo Montoya	2000, 15			

(a) Also a Formula 1 world champion.

Formula 1 and IndyCar race winners

	Formula 1	IndyCar
Mario Andretti	1971 - 78	1965 - 93
Jim Clark	1962 - 68	1963 - 65
Emerson Fittipaldi	1970 - 75	1985 - 95
Dan Gurney	1962 - 67	1967 - 70
Graham Hill	1962 - 69	1966

	Formula 1	IndyCar
Nigel Mansell	1985 - 94	1993
Juan Pablo Montoya	2001	1999 - 2015
Peter Revson	1973	1969
Jacques Villeneuve	1996 - 97	1994 - 95

Formula 1 non-winners who won an IndyCar race

Michael Andretti	1986 - 2002 (a)
Mark Blundell	1997 (a)
Sébastien Bourdais	2003 - 15 (a)(b)
Ryan Briscoe	2008 - 12 (b)
Ronnie Bucknum	1968 (c)
Eddie Cheever	1997 - 2001 (b)
Cristiano da Matta	2000 - 05 (a)
Mark Donohue	1971 - 72 (c)
Robert Doornbos	2007 (a)
Teo Fabi	1983 - 89 (a)
Christian Fittipaldi	1999 - 2000 (a)
George Follmer	1969 (c)
Roberto Guerrero	1987 (a)
Maurício Gugelmin	1997 (a)
Roberto Moreno	2000 - 01 (a)

Danny Ongais	1977 - 78 (c)
Max Papis	2000 - 01 (a)
Bobby Rahal	1982 - 92 (a)
Hector Rebaque	1982 (a)
Lloyd Ruby	1961 - 70 (c)
Troy Ruttman	1952 (d)
Eliseo Salazar	1997 (b)
Takuma Sato	2013 (b)
Danny Sullivan	1984 - 93 (a)
Bobby Unser	1966 - 81 (a)(c)
Jacques Villeneuve Sr.	1985 (a)
Rodger Ward	1953 - 66 (c)(d)
Justin Wilson	2005 - 12 (a)(b)
Alex Zanardi	1996 - 98 (a)

(a) CART/ Fedex/ Champ Car (1979 - 2007).
(b) Indy Racing League (1996 - 2002), IndyCar Series (2003 onwards).
(c) USAC National Championship (1956 - 79).
(d) AAA National Championship Car (until 1955).

Formula 1 drivers who won an IndyCar championship

Mario Andretti	1965 (a), 66 (a), 69 (a), 84 (b)
Michael Andretti	1991 (b)
Sébastien Bourdais	2004 (b), 05 (b), 06 (b), 07 (b)
Cristiano da Matta	2002 (b)
Emerson Fittipaldi	1989 (b)
Nigel Mansell	1993 (b)
Juan Pablo Montoya	1999 (b)

Bobby Rahal	1986 (b), 87 (b), 92 (b)
Danny Sullivan	1988 (b)
Bobby Unser	1968 (a), 74 (a)
Jacques Villeneuve	1995 (b)
Rodger Ward	1959 (a), 62 (a)
Alessandro Zanardi	1997 (b), 98 (b)

(a) USAC National Championship (1956 - 79).
(b) PPG IndyCar World Series (1980 - 96), PPG CART World Series (1997), FedEx Championship Series (1998 - 2002), Champ Car World Series (2003 - 07).

Formula 1 and IndyCar world champions

	Formula 1	IndyCar
Mario Andretti	1978	1965, 66, 69, 84
Emerson Fittipaldi	1972, 74	1989

	Formula 1	IndyCar
Nigel Mansell	1992	1993
Jacques Villeneuve	1997	1995

Formula 1 and IndyCar champion simultaneously

Nigel Mansell has been the only driver to hold the Formula 1 and IndyCar titles simultaneously. This he achieved for seven days in 1993. On 19 September he won the IndyCar title at Nazareth in Pennsylvania while he was still the reigning F1 champion. His F1 title reign ended on 26 September, when Prost clinched the 1993 title at the Portuguese Grand Prix.

AAA & USAC National champions who competed in the Formula 1 World Championship

Henry Banks	1950
Tony Bettenhausen	1951, 58
Jimmy Bryan	1954, 56, 57
A J Foyt	1960, 61, 63, 64, 67, 75, 79
Sam Hanks	1953

Johnnie Parsons	1949
Mauri Rose	1936
Chick Stevenson	1952
Bob Sweikert	1955
Rodger Ward	1959, 62

AAA National Championship (until 1955), USAC National Championship (1956 onwards).

608. Indy Lights champions

Fabrizio Barbazza	1986 (a)			Cristiano da Matta	1998 (b)	

(a) CART American Racing Series. (b) CART Firestone/PPG/Dayton Indy Lights Series.

609. NASCAR Sprint Cup Series race winners

Dan Gurney	5 wins	1963 - 68 (a)		Mario Andretti	1 win	1967 (a)
Juan Pablo Montoya	2 wins	2008 - 10		Mark Donohue	1 win	1973 (b)

(a) Grand National Series. (b) Winston Cup Series.

610. World Sportscar/ Endurance/ GT/ GT1 champions

Julian Bailey	2000 (GT) *		Jan Lammers	2002 (SC) *, 03 (SC) *
Mauro Baldi	1990 (WSP) *		André Lotterer	2012 (WEC) *
Michael Bartels (nq)	2006 (GT) *, 08 (GT) *, 09 (GT) *, 10 (GT1) *		Allan McNish	2013 (WEC) *
Derek Bell	1985 (WSP) *, 86 (WEC) *		Jean-Louis Schlesser	1989 (WSP) *, 90 (WSP) *
Stefan Bellof	1984 (WEC)		Bernd Schneider	1997 (GT)
Olivier Beretta	1999 (GT) *		Vincenzo Sospiri	1998 (ISR) *, 99 (SRWC) *
Raul Boesel	1987 (WSP) *		Hans-Joachim Stuck	1985 (WEC) *
Martin Brundle	1988 (WSP) *		Derek Warwick	1992 (WSC) *
Sébastien Buemi	2014 (WEC) *		Mark Webber	2015 (WEC) *
Yannick Dalmas	1992 (WSC) *		Karl Wendlinger	1999 (GT) *
Anthony Davidson	2014 (WEC) *		Markus Winkelhock	2012 (GT1) *
Teo Fabi	1991 (WSC)		Ricardo Zonta	1998 (GT) *
Jacky Ickx	1982 (WEC), 83 (WEC)			

* Joint champion.
(nq) Non-qualifier in Formula 1.
GT - GT Championship (1997 - 2009).
GT1 - GT1 Championship (2010 - 12).
SC - Sports Car Championship (2001 - 03).
SRWC - Sports Racing World Cup (1999 - 2000).
WEC - World Endurance Championship (1981 - 85 & 2012 onwards).
WSC - World Sports Car Championship (1991 - 92).
WSP - World Sports Prototype Championship (1986 - 90).

611. Super GT (Japan) champions

David Brabham	1996 *		Ralph Firman	2007 *
Erik Comas	1998 *, 99		André Lotterer	2006 *, 09 *
Pedro de la Rosa	1997 *		Tora Takagi	2005 *

All-Japan Grand Touring Car Championship until 2004.
* Joint champion.

612. European Le Mans Series champions

Jean-Christophe Boullion	2005 *, 06 *		Pedro Lamy	2007 *
Tomáš Enge	2009 *		Alexandre Prémat (p)	2008 *
Johnny Herbert	2004 *		Stéphane Sarrazin	2007 *, 10

Le Mans Endurance Series until 2005, Le Mans Series 2006 - 11.
* Joint champion.
(p) Only practiced in Formula 1.

613. American Le Mans Series (1999 - 2013) champions

David Brabham	2009 *, 10 *		Allan McNish	2000, 06 *, 07 *
J J Lehto	2004 *		Emanuele Pirro	2001, 05 *

* Joint champion.

614. Grand-Am Rolex Sports Car Series (2000 - 13) champion

Max Papis	2004

Joint champion.

615. United SportsCar champion

Christian Fittipaldi	2014, 15

Joint champion.

616. Can-Am Challenge (1966 - 86) champions

Mark Donohue	1973		Jackie Oliver	1974
George Follmer	1972		Peter Revson	1971
Denny Hulme	1968, 70		John Surtees	1966
Jacky Ickx	1979		Patrick Tambay	1977, 80
Alan Jones	1978		Jacques Villeneuve Sr. (nq)	1983
Bruce McLaren	1967, 69			

(nq) Non-qualifier in Formula 1.

617. IMSA GT (1971 - 98) champion

Brian Redman	1981

618. Tasman Cup (1964 - 75) champions

Chris Amon	1969		Bruce McLaren	1964
Warwick Brown	1975		Graham McRae	1971, 72, 73
Jim Clark	1965, 67, 68		Jackie Stewart	1966
Peter Gethin	1974			

619. Le Mans 24 hours winners

Michele Alboreto	1997		Jan Lammers	1988
Chris Amon	1966		Hermann Lang	1952
Richard Attwood	1970		Gérard Larrousse	1973, 74
Mauri Baldi	1994		J J Lehto	1995, 2005
Lorenzo Bandini	1963		André Lotterer	2011, 12, 14
Paolo Barilla	1985		Helmut Marko	1971
Derek Bell	1975, 81, 82, 86, 87		Pierluigi Martini	1999
Lucien Bianchi	1968		Jochen Mass	1989
Mark Blundell	1992		Bruce McLaren	1966
Martin Brundle	1990		Allan McNish	1998, 2008, 13
David Brabham	2009		Jackie Oliver	1969
Ivor Bueb	1955, 57		Henri Pescarolo	1972, 73, 74, 84
Eugène Chaboud	1938		Didier Pironi	1978
Yannick Dalmas	1992, 94, 95, 99		Emanuele Pirro	2000, 01, 02, 06, 07
Johnny Dumfries	1988		Fritz Riess	1952
Philippe Etançelin	1934		Jochen Rindt	1965
Ron Flockhart	1956, 57		Pedro Rodríguez	1968
A J Foyt	1967		Tony Rolt	1953
Paul Frère	1960		Louis Rosier	1950
Bertrand Gachot	1991		Roy Salvadori	1959
Olivier Gendebien	1958, 60, 61, 62		Ludovico Scarfiotti	1963
Marc Gené	2009		Vern Schuppan	1983
José Froilán González	1954		Carroll Shelby	1959
Masten Gregory	1965		Raymond Sommer	1932, 33
Dan Gurney	1967		Hans-Joachim Stuck	1986, 87
Duncan Hamilton	1953		Maurice Trintignant	1954
Mike Hawthorn	1955		Nino Vaccarella	1964
Johnny Herbert	1991		Gijs van Lennep	1971, 76
Hans Herrmann	1970		Peter Walker	1951
Graham Hill	1972		Derek Warwick	1992
Phil Hill	1958, 61, 62		Peter Whitehead	1951
Nico Hülkenberg	2015		Joachim Winkelhock	1999
Jacky Ickx	1969, 75, 76, 77, 81, 82		Alexander Wurz	1996, 2009
Stefan Johansson	1997			

All were shared drives.

620. Won the Le Mans 24 hours whilst active in Formula 1

1950	Louis Rosier		1967	Dan Gurney
1951	Peter Whitehead		1968	Lucien Bianchi & Pedro Rodríguez
1954	José Froilán González & Maurice Trintignant		1969	Jacky Ickx & Jackie Oliver
1955	Mike Hawthorn		1971	Gijs van Lennep
1957	Ivor Bueb & Ron Flockhart		1972	Graham Hill & Henri Pescarolo
1958	Olivier Gendebien & Phil Hill		1973	Henri Pescarolo
1959	Roy Salvadori & Carroll Shelby		1974	Gerard Larrousse & Henri Pescarolo
1960	Olivier Gendebien		1975	Jacky Ickx
1961	Olivier Gendebien & Phil Hill		1976	Jacky Ickx
1962	Phil Hill		1978	Didier Pironi
1965	Masten Gregory & Jochen Rindt		1991	Bertrand Gachot & Johnny Herbert
1966	Bruce McLaren		2015	Nico Hülkenburg

Other drivers were active in Formula 1 during their Le Mans winning season but not during the same time of the year.

621. Formula 1 world title, Indianapolis 500 and Le Mans 24 hours "Triple Crown"

Achieved only by Graham Hill (Formula 1 in 1962 and 68, Indianapolis in 1966 and Le Mans in 1972). Dan Gurney won the Indianapolis 500, Le Mans and was a Formula 1 winner but did not win the title.

622. Daytona 24 hours winners

Chris Amon	1967		Leo Kinnunen	1970
Mario Andretti	1972		Jan Lammers	1988, 90
Mauro Baldi	1998, 2002		Giovanni Lavaggi	1995
Lorenzo Bandini	1967		Juan Pablo Montoya	2007, 08, 13
Derek Bell	1986, 87, 89		Jackie Oliver	1971
Olivier Beretta	2000		Danny Ongais	1979
Raoul Boesel	1988		Max Papis	2002
Sébastien Bourdais	2014		Henri Pescarolo	1991
Thierry Boutsen	1985		Bobby Rahal	1981
Martin Brundle	1988		Brian Redman	1970, 76, 81
Mark Donohue	1969		Pedro Rodríguez	1970, 71
Vic Elford	1968		Lloyd Ruby	1966
Christian Fittipaldi	2004, 14		Jo Siffert	1968
A J Foyt	1983, 85		Rolf Stommelen	1968, 78, 80, 82
Masahiro Hasemi	1992		Toshio Suzuki	1992
Hans Herrmann	1968		Karl Wendlinger	2000
Kazuyoshi Hoshino	1992		Justin Wilson	2012
Jacky Ickx	1972			

All were shared drives.

623. Spa 24 hours winners

Michael Bartels	2005, 06, 08		Jean-Pierre Jarier	1993
Gerhard Berger	1985		Leslie Johnson	1948
Sébastien Bourdais	2002		Jean Lucas	1949
David Brabham	1991		Jochen Mass	1972
Johnny Cecotto	1990		Teddy Pilette	1978
Louis Chiron	1933		Dieter Quester	1973, 86, 88
Christian Danner	1992		Stéphane Sarrazin	2008
Jean-Denis Delétraz	2007		Bernd Schneider	1989, 2013
Giuseppe Farina	1953		Alex Soler-Roig	1971
Christian Fittipaldi	1993		Raymond Sommer	1936
Hubert Hahne	1966		Hans-Joachim Stuck	1972
Naoki Hattori (nq)	1991		Marc Surer	1985
Mike Hawthorn	1953		Eric van de Poele	1987, 98, 2005, 06, 08
Hans Heyer	1982, 83, 84		Joachim Winkelhock (nq)	1995
Jacky Ickx	1966		Markus Winkelhock	2014

All were shared drives.
(nq) Non-qualifier in Formula 1.

624. Mille Miglia (1927 - 57) winners

Alberto Ascari	1954		Stirling Moss	1955
Clemente Biondetti	1938, 47, 48, 49		Piero Taruffi	1957
Eugenio Castellotti	1956		Luigi Villoresi	1951

625. Motorcycle 500cc world championship

world championship titles

John Surtees	4	1956, 58, 59, 60	(MV Agusta)		Mike Hailwood	4	1962, 63, 64, 65	(MV Agusta)

point scorers

Bob Anderson	1958 - 59	(Norton)		Ken Kavanagh (ns)	1951 - 59	(Norton, Moto Guzzi)
Johnny Cecotto *	1976 - 80	(Yamha)		Nello Pagani *	1949 - 55	(Gilera, MV Agusta)
Paddy Driver	1959 - 65	(Norton, Matchless)		John Surtees *	1952 - 60	(Norton, MV Agusta)
Mike Hailwood *	1960 - 67	(Norton, MV Agusta, Honda)				

* Motorcycle 500cc race winners.
(nq) Non-starter in Formula 1.

626. Formula 1 car and motorcycle 500cc world champion

Only John Surtees has achieved this. He won the 500cc motorcycle championship four times (1956, 58, 59 and 60) and in a Formula 1 car, won the World Championship in 1964.

Chapter 15: World Champion Constructors

627. World champions

year	constructor	nat	point scoring drivers (in order of total points scored for the constructor)
1958	Vanwall	GB	Stirling Moss, Tony Brooks, Stuart Lewis-Evans (a)
1959	Cooper - Climax	GB	Jack Brabham, Maurice Trintignant (a), Stirling Moss, Bruce McLaren, Masten Gregory (a)
1960	Cooper - Climax	GB	Jack Brabham, Bruce McLaren, Olivier Gendebien (a), Tony Brooks (a), Henry Taylor (a), Lucien Bianchi (a), Phil Hill (a)
1961	Ferrari	I	Phil Hill, Wolfgang von Trips, Richie Ginther (a), Giancarlo Baghetti, Olivier Gendebien (a)
1962	BRM	GB	Graham Hill, Richie Ginther (a)
1963	Lotus - Climax	GB	Jim Clark, Trevor Taylor (a)
1964	Ferrari	I	John Surtees, Lorenzo Bandini, Pedro Rodríguez (a)
1965	Lotus - Climax	GB	Jim Clark, Mike Spence (a)
1966	Brabham - Repco	GB - AUS	Jack Brabham, Denny Hulme (a)
1967	Brabham - Repco	GB - AUS	Denny Hulme, Jack Brabham, Guy Ligier (a)
1968	Lotus - Ford Cosworth	GB	Graham Hill, Jo Siffert, Jim Clark, Jackie Oliver
1969	Matra - Ford Cosworth	F - GB	Jackie Stewart, Jean-Pierre Beltoise, Johnny Servoz-Gavin (a)
1970	Lotus - Ford Cosworth	GB	Jochen Rindt, Emerson Fittipaldi, Graham Hill, Reine Wisell (a), John Miles
1971	Tyrrell - Ford Cosworth	GB	Jackie Stewart, François Cevert
1972	Lotus - Ford Cosworth	GB	Emerson Fittipaldi
1973	Lotus - Ford Cosworth	GB	Emerson Fittipaldi, Ronnie Peterson
1974	McLaren - Ford Cosworth	GB	Emerson Fittipaldi, Denny Hulme, Mike Hailwood
1975	Ferrari	I	Niki Lauda, Clay Regazzoni
1976	Ferrari	I	Niki Lauda, Clay Regazzoni
1977	Ferrari	I	Niki Lauda, Carlos Reutemann
1978	Lotus - Ford Cosworth	GB	Mario Andretti, Ronnie Peterson, Hector Rebaque (a)
1979	Ferrari	I	Jody Scheckter, Gilles Villenueve
1980	Williams - Ford Cosworth	GB	Alan Jones, Carlos Reutemann
1981	Williams - Ford Cosworth	GB	Carlos Reutemann, Alan Jones
1982	Ferrari	I	Didier Pironi, Patrick Tambay, Gilles Villeneuve, Mario Andretti
1983	Ferrari	I	René Arnoux, Patrick Tambay

year	constructor	nat	point scoring drivers (in order of total points scored for the constructor)
1984	McLaren - TAG Porsche	GB - D	Niki Lauda, Alain Prost
1985	McLaren - TAG Porsche	GB - D	Alain Prost, Niki Lauda
1986	Williams - Honda	GB - J	Nigel Mansell, Nelson Piquet
1987	Williams - Honda	GB - J	Nelson Piquet, Nigel Mansell
1988	McLaren - Honda	GB - J	Alain Prost, Ayrton Senna
1989	McLaren - Honda	GB - J	Alain Prost, Ayrton Senna
1990	McLaren - Honda	GB - J	Ayrton Senna, Gerhard Berger
1991	McLaren - Honda	GB - J	Ayrton Senna, Gerhard Berger
1992	Williams - Renault	GB - F	Nigel Mansell, Riccardo Patrese
1993	Williams - Renault	GB - F	Alain Prost, Damon Hill
1994	Williams - Renault	GB - F	Damon Hill, David Coulthard, Nigel Mansell (b)
1995	Benetton - Renault	GB - F	Michael Schumacher, Johnny Herbert
1996	Williams - Renault	GB - F	Damon Hill, Jacques Villeneuve
1997	Williams - Renault	GB - F	Jacques Villeneuve, Heinz-Harald Frentzen
1998	McLaren - Mercedes	GB - D	Mika Häkkinen, David Coulthard
1999	Ferrari	I	Eddie Irvine, Michael Schumacher, Mika Salo
2000	Ferrari	I	Michael Schumacher, Rubens Barrichello
2001	Ferrari	I	Michael Schumacher, Rubens Barrichello
2002	Ferrari	I	Michael Schumacher, Rubens Barrichello
2003	Ferrari	I	Michael Schumacher, Rubens Barrichello
2004	Ferrari	I	Michael Schumacher, Rubens Barrichello
2005	Renault	F	Fernando Alonso, Giancarlo Fisichella
2006	Renault	F	Fernando Alonso, Giancarlo Fisichella
2007	Ferrari (c)	I	Kimi Räikkönen, Felipe Massa
2008	Ferrari	I	Felipe Massa, Kimi Räikkönen
2009	Brawn - Mercedes	GB - D	Jenson Button, Rubens Barrichello
2010	Red Bull - Renault	A/GB - F	Sebastian Vettel, Mark Webber
2011	Red Bull - Renault	A/GB - F	Sebastian Vettel, Mark Webber
2012	Red Bull - Renault	A/GB - F	Sebastian Vettel, Mark Webber
2013	Red Bull - Renault	A/GB - F	Sebastian Vettel, Mark Webber
2014	Mercedes-Benz	D/GB	Lewis Hamilton, Nico Rosberg
2015	Mercedes-Benz	D/GB	Lewis Hamilton, Nico Rosberg

In 1972, 73 and 78, Lotus cars were named JPS Lotus.
(a) Scored points but with only the best result at each race or a certain number of races counting, their points became irrelevant for the constructors' championship.
(b) The season began with Ayrton Senna as the main driver for Williams, but he had scored no points at the time of his death.
(c) McLaren scored the most points in 2007 but were stripped all their constructors' championship points, due to the spying scandal.

628. Constructors' championship titles

Ferrari	16	1961 - 2008		Renault	2	2005 - 06
Williams	9	1980 - 97		Benetton	1	1995
McLaren	8	1974 - 98		Brawn	1	2009
Lotus	7	1963 - 78		BRM	1	1962
Red Bull	4	2010 - 13		Matra	1	1969
Brabham	2	1966 - 67		Tyrrell	1	1971
Cooper	2	1959 - 60		Vanwall	1	1958
Mercedes-Benz	2	2014 - 15				

629. Drivers' championship titles
(see section 74 for a chronological list of world champions)

Ferrari	15	1952 - 2007		Benetton	2	1994 - 95
McLaren	12	1974 - 2008		Cooper	2	1959 - 60
Williams	7	1980 - 97		Maserati	2	1954 - 57 (a)
Lotus	6	1963 - 78		Renault	2	2005 - 06
Brabham	4	1966 - 83		Tyrrell	2	1971 - 73
Mercedes-Benz	4	1954 - 2015 (a)		Brawn	1	2009
Red Bull	4	2010 - 13		BRM	1	1962
Alfa Romeo	2	1950 - 51		Matra	1	1969

(a) Juan Manuel Fangio drove Maserati and Mercedes-Benz cars to his 1954 title.

630. Back-to-back constructors' titles

Ferrari	6	1999 - 2004		Ferrari	2	2007 - 08
McLaren	4	1988 - 91		Lotus	2	1972 - 73
Red Bull	4	2010 - 13		McLaren	2	1984 - 85
Ferrari	3	1975 - 77		Mercedes-Benz	2	2014 - 15
Williams	3	1992 - 94		Renault	2	2005 - 06
Brabham	2	1966 - 67		Williams	2	1980 - 81
Cooper	2	1959 - 60		Williams	2	1986 - 87
Ferrari	2	1982 - 83		Williams	2	1996 - 97

631. Back-to-back drivers' titles

Ferrari	5	2000 - 04	(Michael Schumacher)
McLaren	4	1988 - 91	(Ayrton Senna, 3; Alain Prost, 1)
Red Bull	4	2010 - 13	(Sebastian Vettel)
McLaren	3	1984 - 86	(Alain Prost, 2; Niki Lauda, 1)
Alfa Romeo	2	1950 - 51	(Giuseppe Farina, 1; Juan Manuel Fangio, 1)
Benetton	2	1994 - 95	(Michael Schumacher)
Brabham	2	1966 - 67	(Jack Brabham, 1; Denny Hulme, 1)
Cooper	2	1959 - 60	(Jack Brabham)
Ferrari	2	1952 - 53	(Alberto Ascari)
McLaren	2	1998 - 99	(Mika Häkkinen)
Mercedes-Benz	2	1954 - 55	(Juan Manuel Fangio)
Mercedes-Benz	2	2014 - 15	(Lewis Hamilton)
Renault	2	2005 - 06	(Fernando Alonso)
Williams	2	1992 - 93	(Nigel Mansell, 1; Alain Prost, 1)
Williams	2	1996 - 97	(Damon Hill, 1; Jacques Villeneuve, 1)

632. Constructors' championship decided in final race of the season

1962 South Africa	1964 Mexico	1968 Mexico	1973 United States	1974 United States	1982 Caesars Palace
1983 South Africa	1985 Australia	1991 Australia	1994 Australia	1998 Japan	1999 Japan
2000 Malaysia	2003 Japan	2005 China	2006 Brazil	2008 Brazil	

633. Races remaining after championship was decided (Most)

		(world champion)				(world champion)
2004	5	(Ferrari)		2014	4	(Mercedes-Benz)
1960	4	(Cooper - Climax)		2015	4	(Mercedes-Benz)
1993	4	(Williams - Renault)		1961	3	(Ferrari)
1996	4	(Williams - Renault)		2007	3	(Ferrari)
2001	4	(Ferrari)		2011	3	(Red Bull - Renault)
2002	4	(Ferrari)		2013	3	(Red Bull - Renault)

634. Constructors' world championship runner-up

Ferrari	16	(1958, 59, 66, 70, 74, 78, 84, 85, 88, 90, 96, 97, 98, 2006, 12, 15)
McLaren	14	- Ford Cosworth (1968, 76, 82, 93), - TAG Porsche (1986, 87), - Honda (1992), - Mercedes (1999, 2000, 01, 05, 08, 10, 11)
Williams	6	- Ford Cosworth (1979), - Renault (1989, 91, 95), - BMW (2002, 03)
Lotus	5	- Climax (1960, 61, 62), - Ford Cosworth (1967, 77)
BRM	4	(1963, 64, 65, 71)
Brabham	3	- Ford Cosworth (1969, 75, 81)
Red Bull	2	- Renault (2009, 14)
Tyrrell	2	- Ford Cosworth (1972, 73)
BAR	1	- Honda (2004)
Benetton	1	- Ford Cosworth (1994)
BMW Sauber	1	(2007)
Ligier	1	- Ford Cosworth (1980)
Mercedes-Benz	1	(2013)
Renault	1	(1983)

635. No wins in the season before winning the title

BRM	1961	(P48/57 - Climax) - only podium 1 x 3rd
	1962	champion (P57)
Brabham	1965	(BT11 - Climax, BRM) - only podiums 2 x 2nd
	1966	champion (BT19, 20 - Repco)
Tyrrell	1970	(001 - Ford Cosworth) - only present as a constructor for three races (no points)
		did win a race as a team with a March 701 - Ford Cosworth
	1971	champion (003, 002, 001 - Ford Cosworth)
Lotus	1971	(72D, 72C - Ford Cosworth) - only podium 1 x 2nd
	1972	champion (72D - Ford Cosworth)
Brawn	2008	(operated as Honda, RA108) - only podium 1 x 3rd
	2009	champion (BGP 001 - Mercedes)

636. No wins in the season after winning the title

Vanwall	1958	champion (1957 model)
	1959	(1959 model) - only 1 entry which was a retirement
Cooper	1960	champion (mainly T51, T53 - Climax)
	1961	(T55, T53 - Climax) - only podium 1 x 3rd
Ferrari	1961	champion (156)
	1962	(156) - only podium 1 x 2nd
Ferrari	1964	champion (158, 156, 1512)
	1965	(158, 1512) - only podiums 2 x 2nd
Brabham	1967	champion (mainly BT24 - Repco)
	1968	(BT24, BT26, BT20 - Repco) - only podiums 2 x 3rd
Matra	1969	champion (MS80, MS10 - Ford Cosworth)
	1970	(Matra-Simca MS120 - Matra) - only podiums 3 x 3rd
Lotus	1970	champion (Lotus 72C, 49C - Ford Cosworth)
	1971	(Lotus 72D, 72C - Ford Cosworth) - only podium 1 x 2nd
Lotus	1978	champion (JPS Lotus 78, 79 - Ford Cosworth)
	1979	(mainly Lotus 79 - Ford Cosworth) - only podiums 2 x 2nd
Ferrari	1979	champion (312T4)
	1980	(312T5) - best results 3 x 5th
Williams	1987	champion (FW11B - Honda)
	1988	(FW12 - Judd) - only podiums 2 x 2nd
Benetton	1995	champion (BT195 - Renault)
	1996	(B196 - Renault) - only podiums 5 x 2nd
Williams	1997	champion (FW19 - Renault)
	1998	(FW20 - Mecachrome) - only podiums 3 x 3rd
Renault	2006	champion (R26)
	2007	(R27) - only podium 1 x 2nd

637. Non-operational in the season after winning the title

Alfa Romeo	1952	withdrew, due to the new formula being too expensive.
Mercedes-Benz	1956	withdrew, not to return as a constructor until after 2010.
Brawn	2010	Brawn - Mercedes, the 2009 champion was not operating in 2010 but as Mercedes-Benz, best results were 3 x 3rd places, finishing the championship in 4th.

638. Championship title winning margin

Narrowest (net points)

1964	3	1962	6	1961	8
1999	4	1970	7	1974	8
1982	5	1958	8	1985	8
2006	5	1959	8		

Widest (net points)

from 2010 with new points system	
2014	304
2015	275
2013	236
2011	153
before 2010	
2004	143
1988	134

2002	129
1996	105
2007	103
1984	86
1993	84
2001	77
1992	65
1989	64

639. Seasons where the champion was beaten in terms of total wins

	champion	beaten by
1977	Ferrari, 4	Lotus, 5
1982	Ferrari, 3	McLaren, 4; Renault, 4
1994	Williams, 7	Benetton, 8

1999	Ferrari, 6	McLaren, 7
2005	Renault, 8	McLaren, 10
2006	Renault, 8	Ferrari, 9

Scored more points in a season than the champion. See section 884

640. Fewest wins in their championship title winning season

Ferrari	3 of 16	1982
Ferrari	3 of 10	1964
Ferrari	4 of 17	1977
Ferrari	4 of 15	1983
McLaren - Ford Cosworth	4 of 15	1974

Williams - Ford Cosworth	4 of 15	1981
Brabham - Repco	4 of 11	1967
Brabham - Repco	4 of 9	1966
BRM	4 of 9	1962

641. Fewest poles in their championship title winning season

BRM	1 of 9	1962
Ferrari	2 of 17	1977
McLaren - TAG Porsche	2 of 16	1985
Ferrari	2 of 15	1979
McLaren - Ford Cosworth	2 of 15	1974

Williams - Ford Cosworth	2 of 15	1981
Brabham - Repco	2 of 11	1967
Matra - Ford Cosworth	2 of 11	1969
Ferrari	2 of 10	1964

642. Drivers' and constructors' championships achieved by different teams in a season

	driver's team	constructor
1958	Ferrari	Vanwall
1973	Tyrrell - Ford Cosworth	Lotus - Ford Cosworth
1976	McLaren - Ford Cosworth	Ferrari
1981	Brabham - Ford Cosworth	Williams - Ford Cosworth
1982	Williams - Ford Cosworth	Ferrari

1983	Brabham - BMW	Ferrari
1986	McLaren - TAG Porsche	Williams - Honda
1994	Benetton - Ford Cosworth	Williams - Renault
1999	McLaren - Mercedes	Ferrari
2008	McLaren - Mercedes	Ferrari

643. Drivers for the same constructor, finishing in the top positions in the drivers' championship

Top 4			
Ferrari	1952	1: Alberto Ascari, 2: Giuseppe Farina, 3: Piero Taruffi, 4: Rudi Fischer	(500)
Top 3			
Alfa Romeo	1950	1: Giuseppe Farina, 2: Juan Manuel Fangio, 3: Luigi Fagioli	(158)
Top 2			
Mercedes-Benz	1955	1: Juan Manuel Fangio, 2: Stirling Moss	(W196, W196 str.)
Cooper	1960	1: Jack Brabham, 2: Bruce McLaren	(T53, T51 - Climax)
Ferrari	1961	1: Phil Hill, 2: Wolfgang von Trips	(156)
Brabham	1967	1: Denny Hulme, 2: Jack Brabham	(BT24, BT20, BT19 - Repco)
Lotus	1978	1: Mario Andretti, 2: Ronnie Peterson	(79, 78 - Ford Cosworth)
Ferrari	1979	1: Jody Scheckter, 2: Jacques Villeneuve	(312T4, 312T3)
McLaren	1984	1: Niki Lauda, 2: Alain Prost	(MP4/2 - TAG Porsche)
Williams	1987	1: Nelson Piquet, 2: Nigel Mansell	(FW11B - Honda)
McLaren	1988	1: Ayrton Senna, 2: Alain Prost	(MP4/4 - Honda)
McLaren	1989	1: Alain Prost, 2: Ayrton Senna	(MP4/5 - Honda)
Williams	1992	1: Nigel Mansell, 2: Riccardo Patrese	(FW14B - Renault)

Williams	1996	1: Damon Hill, 2: Jacques Villeneuve	(FW18 - Renault)
Williams	1997	1: Jacques Villeneuve, 2: Heinz-Harald Frentzen	(FW19 - Renault)
Ferrari	2002	1: Michael Schumacher, 2: Rubens Barrichello	(F2001, F2002)
Ferrari	2004	1: Michael Schumacher, 2: Rubens Barrichello	(F2004)
Mercedes-Benz	2014	1: Lewis Hamilton, 2: Nico Rosberg	(F1 W05)
Mercedes-Benz	2015	1: Lewis Hamilton, 2: Nico Rosberg	(F1 W06)

644. World champion drivers by constructor

Alfa Romeo:	Juan Manuel Fangio, 1; Giuseppe Farina, 1
Benetton:	Michael Schumacher, 2
Brabham:	Nelson Piquet, 2; Jack Brabham, 1; Denny Hulme, 1
Brawn:	Jenson Button, 1
BRM:	Graham Hill, 1
Cooper:	Jack Brabham, 2
Ferrari:	Michael Schumacher, 5; Alberto Ascari, 2; Niki Lauda, 2; Juan Manuel Fangio, 1; Mike Hawthorn, 1; Phil Hill, 1; Kimi Räikkönen, 1; Jody Scheckter, 1; John Surtees, 1
Lotus:	Jim Clark, 2; Mario Andretti, 1; Emerson Fittipaldi, 1; Graham Hill, 1; Jochen Rindt, 1
Maserati:	Juan Manuel Fangio, 2 (a)
Matra:	Jackie Stewart, 1
McLaren:	Alain Prost, 3; Ayrton Senna, 3; Mika Häkkinen, 2; Emerson Fittipaldi, 1; Lewis Hamilton, 1; James Hunt, 1; Niki Lauda, 1
Mercedes-Benz:	Juan Manuel Fangio, 2 (a); Lewis Hamilton, 2
Red Bull:	Sebastian Vettel, 4
Renault:	Fernando Alonso, 2
Tyrrell:	Jackie Stewart, 2
Williams:	Damon Hill, 1; Alan Jones, 1; Nigel Mansell, 1; Nelson Piquet, 1; Alain Prost, 1; Keke Rosberg, 1; Jaques Villeneuve, 1

Summary

	no of drivers				
Ferrari	9		Brawn	1	
McLaren	7		BRM	1	
Williams	7		Cooper	1	
Lotus	5		Maserati	1	(a)
Brabham	3		Matra	1	
Alfa Romeo	2		Red Bull	1	
Mercedes-Benz	2 (a)		Renault	1	
Benetton	1		Tyrrell	1	

(a) Juan Manuel Fangio drove Maserati and Mercedes-Benz cars to his 1954 title.

645. Interval between constructors' titles *(Longest)*

Ferrari	16 years	1983 - 99		Lotus	5 years	1973 - 78
Ferrari	11 years	1964 - 75		Williams	5 years	1981 - 86
McLaren	10 years	1974 - 84		Williams	5 years	1987 - 92
McLaren	7 years	1991 - 98				

646. Interval between drivers' titles *(Longest)*

Mercedes-Benz	59 years	1955 (Juan Manuel Fangio)	- 2014 (Lewis Hamilton)
Ferrari	21 years	1979 (Jody Scheckter)	- 2000 (Michael Schumacher)
Brabham	14 years	1967 (Denny Hulme)	- 1981 (Nelson Piquet)
Ferrari	11 years	1964 (Phil Hill)	- 1975 (Niki Lauda)
McLaren	9 years	1999 (Mika Häkkinen)	- 2008 (Lewis Hamilton)
McLaren	8 years	1976 (James Hunt)	- 1984 (Niki Lauda)
McLaren	7 years	1991 (Ayrton Senna)	- 1998 (Mika Häkkinen)
Lotus	6 years	1972 (Emerson Fittipaldi)	- 1978 (Mario Andretti)
Williams	5 years	1982 (Keke Rosberg)	- 1987 (Nelson Piquet)
Williams	5 years	1987 (Nelson Piquet)	- 1992 (Nigel Mansell)

647. Milestones: Constructors' world champions

Ferrari	5th: 1977, 10th: 2000, 15th: 2007		McLaren	5th: 1991
Lotus	5th: 1972		Williams	5th: 1992

648. Milestones: Drivers' world champions

Ferrari	5th: 1961, 10th: 2000, 15th: 2007		Lotus	5th: 1972
McLaren	5th: 1984, 10th: 1999		Williams	5th: 1993

Chapter 16: Race Starting Constructors

649. Grand prix constructors

	Races	(Cars)	W	Pod	PP	FR	FL	First start	Last start
AFM	4	(7)	-	-	-	-	-	Switzerland 1952	- Italy 1953
AGS	47	(48)	-	-	-	-	-	Italy 1986	- Monaco 1991
Alfa Romeo	110	(234)	10	26	12	35	14	Britain 1950	- Australia 1985
Alfa Special	2	(2)	-	-	-	-	-	South Africa 1963	- South Africa 1965
Alta	5	(6)	-	-	-	-	-	Britain 1950	- Britain 1952
Amon	1	(1)	-	-	-	-	-	Spain 1974	
Andrea Moda	1	(1)	-	-	-	-	-	Monaco 1992	
Arrows	382	(724)	-	9	1	1	-	Brazil 1978	- Germany 2002
Arrows	*291*	*(552)*	-	*8*	*1*	*1*	-	*Brazil 1978*	*- Germany 2002*
Footwork	*91*	*(172)*	-	*1*	-	-	-	*United States 1991*	*- Japan 1996*
Aston-Butterworth	2	(2)	-	-	-	-	-	Belgium 1952	- Germany 1952
Aston Martin	5	(10)	-	-	-	1	-	Netherlands 1959	- Britain 1960
ATS (Germany)	89	(107)	-	-	-	-	-	Argentina 1978	- Portugal 1984
ATS (Italy)	6	(11)	-	-	-	-	-	Belgium 1963	- Italy 1964
ATS	*5*	*(10)*	-	-	-	-	-	*Belgium 1963*	*- Mexico 1963*
Derrington-Francis	*1*	*(1)*	-	-	-	-	-	*Italy 1964*	
BAR	117	(231)	-	15	2	8	-	Australia 1999	- China 2005
Bellasi	2	(2)	-	-	-	-	-	Austria 1970	- Italy 1971
Benetton	260	(519)	27	102	15	33	36	Brazil 1986	- Japan 2001
BMW (a)	70	(140)	1	17	1	4	2	Bahrain 2006	- Abu Dhabi 2009
BMW specials	2	(6)	-	-	-	-	-	Germany 1952	- Germany 1953

	Races	(Cars)	W	Pod	PP	FR	FL	First start	Last start
Brabham	394	(932)	35	124	39	105	41	Germany 1962	Hungary 1992
Brawn	17	(34)	8	15	5	9	4	Australia 2009	- Abu Dhabi 2009
BRM	197	(522)	17	61	11	57	15	Britain 1951	- South Africa 1977
BRM	*184*	*(509)*	*17*	*61*	*11*	*57*	*15*	*Britain 1951*	*- United States 1974*
Stanley-BRM	*13*	*(13)*	*-*	*-*	*-*	*-*	*-*	*Argentina 1975*	*- South Africa 1977*
BRP	13	(18)	-	-	-	-	-	Belgium 1963	- Mexico 1964
Bugatti	1	(1)	-	-	-	-	-	France 1956	
Caterham	56	(110)	-	-	-	-	-	Australia 2012	- Abu Dhabi 2014
Coloni	13	(14)	-	-	-	-	-	Spain 1987	- Portugal 1989
Connaught	17	(49)	-	1	-	-	-	Britain 1952	- United States 1959
Connew	1	(1)	-	-	-	-	-	Austria 1972	
Cooper	129	(499)	16	58	11	40	14	Monaco 1950	- Monaco 1969
Dallara	78	(133)	-	2	-	-	-	San Marino 1988	- Australia 1992
de Tomaso	10	(12)	-	-	-	-	-	France 1961	- United States 1970
Eagle	25	(32)	1	2	-	5	2	Belgium 1966	- Canada 1969
Emeryson	4	(4)	-	-	-	-	-	Britain 1956	- Italy 1962
EMW	1	(1)	-	-	-	-	-	Germany 1953	
ENB	1	(1)	-	-	-	-	-	Germany 1962	
Ensign	99	(116)	-	-	-	-	1	France 1973	- Italy 1982
Boro	*6*	*(6)*	*-*	*-*	*-*	*-*	*-*	*Spain 1976*	*- Netherlands 1977*
Ensign	*99*	*(110)*	*-*	*-*	*-*	*-*	*1*	*France 1973*	*- Italy 1982*
ERA	7	(12)	-	-	-	-	-	Britain 1950	- Netherlands 1952
EuroBrun	14	(19)	-	-	-	-	-	Brazil 1988	- San Marino 1990
Ferguson	1	(1)	-	-	-	-	-	Britain 1961	
Ferrari (b)	907	(2,001)	224	696	208	470	233	Monaco 1950	- Abu Dhabi 2015
Ferrari	*896*	*(1,942)*	*219*	*679*	*202*	*446*	*228*	*Monaco 1950*	*- Abu Dhabi 2015*
Lancia-Ferrari	*14*	*(57)*	*5*	*17*	*6*	*24*	*5*	*Argentina 1956*	*- Italy 1957*
Thin Wall Special	*2*	*(2)*	*-*	*-*	*-*	*-*	*-*	*France 1951*	*- Britain 1951*
Fittipaldi	104	(123)	-	3	-	-	-	Argentina 1975	- Italy 1982
Copersucar	*72*	*(75)*	*-*	*1*	*-*	*-*	*-*	*Argentina 1975*	*- United States 1979*
Fittipaldi	*32*	*(48)*	*-*	*2*	*-*	*-*	*-*	*Argentina 1980*	*- Italy 1982*
Force India	150	(298)	-	3	1	2	3	Australia 2008	- Abu Dhabi 2015
Forti	23	(44)	-	-	-	-	-	Brazil 1995	- France 1996
Frazer Nash	4	(4)	-	-	-	-	-	Switzerland 1952	- Netherlands 1952
Gilby	3	(3)	-	-	-	-	-	Britain 1961	- Britain 1963
Gordini	40	(127)	-	2	-	5	1	Monaco 1950	- Italy 1956
Gordini	*33*	*(99)*	*-*	*2*	*-*	*5*	*1*	*Switzerland 1952*	*- Italy 1956*
Simca-Gordini	*14*	*(28)*	*-*	*-*	*-*	*-*	*-*	*Monaco 1950*	*- Belgium 1953*
Hesketh	52	(73)	1	7	-	2	1	South Africa 1974	- South Africa 1978
Hill	10	(19)	-	-	-	-	-	Spain 1975	- United States 1975
Honda	88	(152)	3	9	2	6	2	Germany 1964	- Brazil 2008
HRT	56	(112)	-	-	-	-	-	Bahrain 2010	- Brazil 2012
HWM	14	(43)	-	-	-	-	-	Switzerland 1951	- France 1954
Jaguar	85	(170)	-	2	-	1	-	Australia 2000	- Brazil 2004
JBW	5	(5)	-	-	-	-	-	Britain 1959	- Italy 1961
Jordan	250	(491)	4	19	2	9	2	United States 1991	- China 2005
Klenk	1	(1)	-	-	-	-	-	Germany 1954	
Kojima	2	(3)	-	-	-	-	-	Japan 1976	- Japan 1977
Kurtis-Kraft (b)	1	(1)	-	-	-	-	-	United States 1959	
Lamborghini	6	(6)	-	-	-	-	-	United States 1991	- Australia 1991
Lancia	4	(10)	-	1	2	4	1	Spain 1954	- Belgium 1955
Larrousse	48	(93)	-	-	-	-	-	South Africa 1992	- Australia 1994
Larrousse	*32*	*(63)*	*-*	*-*	*-*	*-*	*-*	*South Africa 1993*	*- Australia 1994*
Venturi-Larrousse	*16*	*(30)*	*-*	*-*	*-*	*-*	*-*	*South Africa 1992*	*- Australia 1992*
LDS	5	(6)	-	-	-	-	-	South Africa 1962	- South Africa 1968
Lec	3	(3)	-	-	-	-	-	Belgium 1977	- France 1977
Ligier (c)	326	(578)	9	50	9	19	10	Brazil 1976	- Japan 1996
Ligier	*296*	*(521)*	*7*	*39*	*8*	*18*	*9*	*Brazil 1976*	*- Japan 1996*
Talbot-Ligier	*30*	*(57)*	*2*	*11*	*1*	*1*	*1*	*United States West 1981*	*- Caesars Palace 1982*
Lola	149	(245)	-	3	1	3	-	Netherlands 1962	- Portugal 1993
Lotus	606	(1,464)	81	197	107	178	76	Monaco 1958	- Abu Dhabi 2015
JPS Lotus (Team Lotus)	*105*	*(208)*	*29*	*56*	*34*	*56*	*22*	*Argentina 1972*	*- Canada 1978*
Lotus (Team Lotus)	*401*	*(1,029)*	*50*	*116*	*73*	*120*	*49*	*Monaco 1958*	*- Australia 1994*

	Races	(Cars)	W	Pod	PP	FR	FL	First start	Last start
Lotus (ex Renault)	*77*	*(153)*	*2*	*25*	*-*	*2*	*5*	*Australia 2012*	*- Abu Dhabi 2015*
Lotus (Malaysia) (d)	*38*	*(74)*	*-*	*-*	*-*	*-*	*-*	*Bahrain 2010*	*- Brazil 2011*
Lyncar	1	(1)	-	-	-	-	-	Britain 1975	
March	227	(557)	3	22	5	12	7	South Africa 1970	- Australia 1992
Eifelland-March	*8*	*(8)*	*-*	*-*	*-*	*-*	*-*	*South Africa 1972*	*- Austria 1972*
Leyton House	*30*	*(57)*	*-*	*1*	*-*	*-*	*-*	*United States 1990*	*- Australia 1991*
March	*197*	*(492)*	*3*	*21*	*5*	*12*	*7*	*South Africa 1970*	*- Australia 1992*
Martini	4	(4)	-	-	-	-	-	Belgium 1978	- Netherlands 1978
Marussia	111	(216)	-	-	-	-	-	Bahrain 2010	- Abu Dhabi 2015
Marussia	*73*	*(143)*	*-*	*-*	*-*	*-*	*-*	*Australia 2012*	*- Abu Dhabi 2015*
Virgin	*38*	*(73)*	*-*	*-*	*-*	*-*	*-*	*Bahrain 2010*	*- Brazil 2011*
Maserati (b)	68	(368)	9	37	10	39	15	Britain 1950	- United States 1960
Maserati	*67*	*(358)*	*9*	*37*	*10*	*39*	*15*	*Britain 1950*	*- United States 1960*
Maserati-Milano	*4*	*(4)*	*-*	*-*	*-*	*-*	*-*	*Switzerland 1950*	*- France 1951*
Maserati-Platé	*3*	*(6)*	*-*	*-*	*-*	*-*	*-*	*Switzerland 1952*	*- Britain 1952*
Matra	62	(118)	9	21	4	17	12	Germany 1966	- United States 1972
Matra	*28*	*(64)*	*9*	*16*	*2*	*11*	*10*	*Germany 1966*	*- Mexico 1969*
Matra-Simca	*34*	*(54)*	*-*	*5*	*2*	*6*	*2*	*South Africa 1970*	*- United States 1972*
McLaren	780	(1,611)	182	485	155	336	152	Monaco 1966	- Abu Dhabi 2015
Mercedes-Benz	127	(269)	45	95	53	103	38	France 1954	- Abu Dhabi 2015
Merzario	10	(10)	-	-	-	-	-	Argentina 1978	- United States West 1979
Midland	18	(36)	-	-	-	-	-	Bahrain 2006	- Brazil 2006
Minardi	340	(634)	-	-	-	1	-	Brazil 1985	- China 2005
Onyx	17	(25)	-	1	-	-	-	Mexico 1989	- Germany 1990
Monteverdi	*1*	*(2)*	*-*	*-*	*-*	*-*	*-*	*Germany 1990*	
Onyx	*16*	*(23)*	*-*	*1*	*-*	*-*	*-*	*Mexico 1989*	*- Mexico 1990*
OSCA	4	(6)	-	-	-	-	-	Italy 1951	- Italy 1953
Osella	151	(191)	-	-	-	-	-	South Africa 1980	- Italy 1992
Fomet	*6*	*(6)*	*-*	*-*	*-*	*-*	*-*	*Mexico 1991*	*- Japan 1991*
Fondmetal	*13*	*(19)*	*-*	*-*	*-*	*-*	*-*	*South Africa 1992*	*- Italy 1992*
Osella	*132*	*(166)*	*-*	*-*	*-*	*-*	*-*	*South Africa 1980*	*- Australia 1990*
Pacific	22	(40)	-	-	-	-	-	Brazil 1994	- Australia 1995
Parnelli	16	(16)	-	-	-	-	1	Canada 1974	- United States West 1976
Penske	40	(44)	1	3	-	1	-	Canada 1974	- Canada 1977
Porsche	33	(73)	1	5	1	3	-	Germany 1957	- Netherlands 1964
Behra-Porsche	*2*	*(2)*	*-*	*-*	*-*	*-*	*-*	*Argentina 1960*	*- Italy 1960*
Porsche	*32*	*(71)*	*1*	*5*	*1*	*3*	*-*	*Germany 1957*	*- Netherlands 1964*
Prost (c)	83	(164)	-	3	-	-	-	Australia 1997	- Japan 2001
Protos	1	(2)	-	-	-	-	-	Germany 1967	
RAM	31	(54)	-	-	-	-	-	Brazil 1983	- Europe 1985
RAM	*28*	*(51)*	*-*	*-*	*-*	*-*	*-*	*Brazil 1984*	*- Europe 1985*
RAM March	*3*	*(3)*	*-*	*-*	*-*	*-*	*-*	*Brazil 1983*	*- South Africa 1983*
Rebaque	1	(1)	-	-	-	-	-	Canada 1979	
Red Bull	203	(404)	50	119	57	103	47	Australia 2005	- Abu Dhabi 2015
Renault	300	(581)	35	100	51	91	31	Britain 1977	- Brazil 2011
Rial	20	(20)	-	-	-	-	-	Brazil 1988	- Canada 1989
Sauber (a)	330	(654)	-	10	-	3	3	South Africa 1993	- Abu Dhabi 2015
BMW Sauber	*19*	*(37)*	*-*	*-*	*-*	*-*	*-*	*Bahrain 2010*	*- Abu Dhabi 2010*
Sauber	*311*	*(617)*	*-*	*10*	*-*	*3*	*3*	*South Africa 1993*	*- Abu Dhabi 2015*
Scarab	2	(3)	-	-	-	-	-	Belgium 1960	- United States 1960
Scirocco	5	(7)	-	-	-	-	-	Belgium 1963	- Belgium 1964
Shadow	104	(211)	1	7	3	4	2	South Africa 1973	- South Africa 1980
Shannon	1	(1)	-	-	-	-	-	Britain 1966	
Simtek	21	(37)	-	-	-	-	-	Brazil 1994	- Monaco 1995
Spirit	23	(23)	-	-	-	-	-	Britain 1983	- San Marino 1985
Spyker	17	(34)	-	-	-	-	-	Australia 2007	- Brazil 2007
Stebro	1	(1)	-	-	-	-	-	United States 1963	
Stewart	49	(97)	1	5	1	1	-	Australia 1997	- Japan 1999
Super Aguri	39	(78)	-	-	-	-	-	Bahrain 2006	- Spain 2008
Surtees	118	(224)	-	2	-	1	3	Britain 1970	- Canada 1978
Talbot-Lago	13	(80)	-	2	-	-	-	Britain 1950	- Spain 1951
Tec-Mec	1	(1)	-	-	-	-	-	United States 1959	
Tecno	11	(11)	-	-	-	-	-	Germany 1969	- Netherlands 1973

	Races	(Cars)	W	Pod	PP	FR	FL	First start	Last start
Theodore	34	(43)	-	-	-	-	-	South Africa 1978	- Europe 1983
Token	3	(3)	-	-	-	-	-	Belgium 1974	- Austria 1974
Toleman	57	(94)	-	3	1	1	2	Italy 1981	- Australia 1985
Toro Rosso	185	(370)	1	1	1	1	-	Bahrain 2006	- Abu Dhabi 2015
Toyota	139	(276)	-	13	3	11	3	Australia 2002	- Abu Dhabi 2009
Trojan	6	(6)	-	-	-	-	-	Spain 1974	- Italy 1974
Tyrrell	430	(842)	23	77	14	33	20	Canada 1970	- Japan 1998
Vanwall	28	(64)	9	13	7	22	6	Britain 1954	- France 1960
Veritas	6	(18)	-	-	-	-	-	Switzerland 1951	- Germany 1953
Williams (e)	692	(1,345)	114	310	128	270	133	Britain 1972	- Abu Dhabi 2015
Iso-Marlboro	*30*	*(50)*	*-*	*-*	*-*	*-*	*-*	*Argentina 1973*	*- United States 1974*
Politoys	*1*	*(1)*	*-*	*-*	*-*	*-*	*-*	*Britain 1972*	
Williams	*649*	*(1,276)*	*114*	*310*	*128*	*270*	*133*	*Argentina 1975*	*- Abu Dhabi 2015*
Wolf-Williams	*13*	*(18)*	*-*	*-*	*-*	*-*	*-*	*Brazil 1976*	*- Japan 1976*
Wolf	47	(52)	3	13	1	3	2	Argentina 1977	- United States 1979
Zakspeed	53	(83)	-	-	-	-	-	Portugal 1985	- Japan 1989

Key to column headings:

W - Wins, Pod - Podium positions, PP - Pole positions, FR - Front row positions, FL - Fastest laps.

(a) Includes BMW Sauber only until 2009. Whilst the cars were still named BMW Sauber in 2010, the cars were operated by Sauber.
(b) Also started Indianapolis 500 race(s) in the world championship, so also has an entry in section 650.
(c) Whilst the 1997 cars were named Prost, the team was still in effect Ligier with a model number in the Ligier sequence. They are included here under Prost nevertheless.
(d) The constructor became Caterham from the beginning of 2012.
(e) In Brazil 1976, a Williams and a Wolf-Williams started, hence the total races being one out.

Several constructors have changed their name, chiefly for the purpose of marketing. Those affected are shown above in italics.
As is now common practice, drivers retiring on the formation lap are not counted as having started. Where races have been subject to a restart, those retiring during an initial race are included as having started.
For constructors which never started a race, see section 959.
"Fastest laps" relates to the number of races, so where for example, 2 Brabhams shared fastest lap in Canada 1969, this is counted as 1.

Constructor name changes (apart from those shown in above table)
BAR became Honda from 2006, Brawn in 2009 and Mercedes-Benz from 2010.
Jordan became Midland for 2006, Spyker in 2007 and Force India from 2008.
The Lotus name was used under licence in 2010 & 2011 for the Malaysian outfit run by Tony Fernades (becoming Caterham from 2012).
Minardi became Toro Rosso from 2006.
Stewart became Jaguar from 2000 and Red Bull from 2005.
Toleman became Benetton from 1996, Renault from 2002 and Lotus from 2012 until 2015.

650. Indianapolis 500 constructors (1950 - 60)

	Races	(Cars)	W	Pod	PP	FR	FL	First - Last start
Adams	1	(1)	-	-	-	-	-	1950
Bromme	4	(4)	-	-	-	-	-	1951 - 54
Christensen	2	(2)	-	-	-	-	-	1959 - 60
Deidt	3	(8)	-	2	-	1	-	1950 - 52
Del Roy-Allen	1	(1)	-	-	-	-	-	1953
Dunn	3	(3)	-	-	-	-	-	1957 - 59
Eddie Allen	2	(2)	-	-	-	-	-	1954 - 55
Elder	1	(1)	-	-	-	-	-	1959
Epperly	5	(11)	-	3	-	-	2	1955 - 60
Ewing	2	(3)	-	-	1	1	-	1950 - 60
Ferrari	1	(1)	-	-	-	-	-	1952
Kurtis-Kraft	11	(193)	5	16	6	18	7	1950 - 60
Kuzma	10	(35)	1	3	-	3	-	1951 - 60
Langley	1	(1)	-	-	-	-	-	1950
Lesovsky	9	(15)	-	1	1	1	1	1950 - 60
Marchese	2	(2)	-	-	-	-	-	1950 - 51
Maserati	2	(3)	-	-	-	-	-	1950 - 51
Meskowski	1	(2)	-	-	-	-	-	1960

	Races	(Cars)	W	Pod	PP	FR	FL	First - Last start
Moore	3	(3)	-	-	-	-	-	1950 - 59
Nichels	2	(2)	-	-	-	-	-	1950 - 54
Olson	1	(1)	-	-	-	-	-	1950
Pankratz	2	(2)	-	-	-	-	-	1954 - 55
Phillips	7	(7)	-	1	-	-	-	1954 - 60
Rae	1	(1)	-	-	-	-	-	1950
Rassey	1	(1)	-	-	-	-	-	1950
Salih	4	(5)	2	2	-	-	-	1957 - 60
Schroeder	4	(6)	-	-	-	-	-	1951 - 55
Silnes	3	(4)	-	-	-	-	-	1950 - 55
Silnes-Pawl	1	(1)	-	-	-	-	-	1951
Silnes-Sherman	2	(2)	-	-	-	-	-	1951 - 52
Stevens	7	(10)	-	-	1	1	-	1950 - 56
Trevis	4	(6)	-	-	-	-	-	1951 - 60
Turner	1	(1)	-	-	-	-	-	1953
Watson	9	(22)	3	5	2	8	1	1950 - 60
Wetteroth	1	(1)	-	-	-	-	-	1950

Fastest lap at the Indianapolis 500 relates to the fastest leading lap of the race.

651. Races started *(Most)*

Ferrari	907	Monaco 1950	- Abu Dhabi 2015 (a)
McLaren	780	Monaco 1966	- Abu Dhabi 2015
Williams	692	Britain 1972	- Abu Dhabi 2015
Lotus	606	Monaco 1958	- Abu Dhabi 2015
Tyrrell	430	Canada 1970	- Japan 1998
Brabham	394	Germany 1962	- Hungary 1992
Arrows	382	Brazil 1978	- Germany 2002
Minardi	340	Brazil 1985	- China 2005
Sauber	330	South Africa 1993	- Abu Dhabi 2015
Ligier	326	Brazil 1976	- Japan 1996

(a) Excludes 1 race started at the Indianapolis 500.

652. Car starts *(Most)*

Ferrari	2,001	Monaco 1950	- Abu Dhabi 2015
McLaren	1,611	Monaco 1966	- Abu Dhabi 2015
Lotus	1,464	Monaco 1958	- Abu Dhabi 2015
Williams	1,345	Britain 1972	- Abu Dhabi 2015
Brabham	932	Germany 1962	- Hungary 1992
Tyrrell	842	Canada 1970	- Japan 1998
Arrows	724	Brazil 1978	- Germany 2002
Sauber	654	South Africa 1993	- Abu Dhabi 2015
Minardi	634	Brazil 1985	- China 2005
Renault	581	Britain 1977	- Brazil 2011

653. Constructor name derivations

AFM	Alex von Falkenhausen Motorenbau (German automotive engineer)
AGS	Automobiles Gonfaronnaises Sportives (Gonfaron, France)
Alfa Romeo	Societa Anonima Lombarda Fabbrica Automobili (ALFA), Nicola Romeo (Italian engineer) took over.
Alta	"al" came "aluminium block", the main feature of the engines and the "ta" from founder Geoffrey Taylor
Amon	Chris Amon (New Zealand racing driver)
Andrea Moda	Andrea Sassetti (Italian shoe designer)
Arrows	Name initials: Franco Ambrosio, Alan Rees, Jackie Oliver, Dave Wass and Tony Southgate
Arzani-Volpini *	Egidio Arzani (Italian engine builder) and Gianpaolo Volpini (Italian car designer)
Aston-Butterworth	Bill Aston (test pilot, motorcycle and car racer) and Archie Butterworth (engineer)
Aston Martin	Aston Clinton hill-climb in Buckinghamshire and Lionel Martin (car dealer & hill-climb driver)
ATS (Germany)	Auto Technisches Spezialzubehör

ATS (Italy)	Automobili Turismo e Sport
BAR	British American Racing (British American Tobacco)
Behra-Porsche	Jean Behra (racing driver) & see Porsche
Bellasi	Guglielmo Bellasi (Italian racing driver & engineer)
Benetton	Luciano, Gilberto and Carlo Benetton (Italian luxury fashion)
BMW	Bayerische Motoren Werke (Bavaria)
Brabham	Jack Brabham (Australian racing driver)
Brawn	Ross Brawn (Formula 1 engineer)
BRM	British Racing Motors
BRP	British Racing Partnership
Bugatti	Ettore Bugatti (Italian artist & engineer)
Caterham	car manufacturer originating in Caterham, Surrey, England
Cisitalia *	Compagnia Industriale Sportiva Italia
Coloni	Enzo Coloni (Italian racing driver)
Connew	Peter Connew (draughtsman)
Cooper	Charles Cooper (motorsport mechanic & designer) & son, John Cooper
Copersucar	Brazilian sugar marketing organisation
Dallara	Gianpaolo Dallara (Italian aeronautical engineer)
de Tomaso	Alejandro de Tomaso (Argentinian racing driver & industrialist)
Derrington-Francis	Vic Derrington (British engine tuner), Alf Francis (Polish-born, British mechanic)
Eifelland-March	Eifelland caravan manufacturing company (from Eifel mountains in Germany) (& see March)
Emeryson	Paul Emery (racing driver & car designer)
EMW	Eisenacher Motoren Werke (Eisenach, Germany)
ENB	Equipe Nationale Belge (Belgium)
ERA	English Racing Automobiles
EuroBrun	Walter Brun (Swiss slot machine magnate & racing driver)
Ferguson	Henry George "Harry" Ferguson (Irish engineer)
Ferrari	Enzo Ferrari (Italian racing driver & entrepreneur)
Fittipaldi	Wilson and Emerson Fittipaldi (Brazilian racing drivers)
Fomet	British subsidiary of Fondmetal
Fondmetal	Italian wheel manufacturer
Footwork	Japanese logistics company
Force India	Indian businessman, Vijay Mallya
Forti	Guido Forti (Italian racing driver)
Frazer Nash	Archie Frazer Nash (cyclecar and sportscar manufacturer)
Fry *	Joseph "Joe" Fry (racing driver)
Gilby	Gilby Engineering Company
Gordini	Amédée Gordini (Italian-born, French engineer)
Hesketh	Lord Alexander Hesketh (peer, politician & stock broker)
Hill	Graham Hill (racing driver)
Honda	Soichiro Honda (Japanese engineer)
HRT	Hispania Racing Team from Spain
HWM	Hersham and Walton Motors
Iso-Marlboro	Iso-Rivolta (Italian sports cars), Marlboro (cigarettes)
Jaguar	associated with agility, pace and elegance of the jungle cat
JBW	John Brian Naylor (racing driver) and Fred Wilkinson (mechanic)
Jordan	Eddie Jordan (racing driver)
JPS Lotus	John Player Special (cigarettes)
Kauhsen *	Willibald "Willi" Kauhsen (German sports car entrant & driver)
Klenk	Hans Klenk (German racing driver)
Kojima	Matsuhisa Kojima (Japanese moto-cross rider)
Kurtis-Kraft	Frank Kurtis (American car designer and builder)
Lamborghini	Ferruccio Lamborghini (Italian manufacturer of agricultural equipment)
Lancia	Gianni Lancia (Italian engineer and industrialist)
Larrousse	Gérard Larrousse (French rally driver)
LDS	Louis Douglas Serrurier (speedway champion & racing driver)
Lec	Longford Engineering Company Ltd (refrigerator & freezer manufacturer)
Leyton House	Japanese real estate company
Life *	The founder, Ernesto Vito's surname, 'Vita' being Italian for 'Life'
Ligier	Guy Ligier (French motorcycle and car racer)
Lotus	lotus flower (the hypnotic effect which was akin to the long days of car building)

Lyncar	Lyn and Carol (wives of the founders Martin Slater and Graham Coaker)
Maki *	Masao Ono and Kenji Mimura (the engineer/founder and the designer)
March	Initials of the founders: Max Mosley, Alan Rees, Graham Coaker and Robin Herd
Martini	Renato "Tico" Martini (Italian kart builder & race instructor)
Marussia	Russian sports car manufacturer
Maserati	Alfieri Maserati (Italian automotive engineer)
Matra-Simca	Société Industrielle de Mécanique et Carrosserie Automobile (& see Matra)
Matra	Mécanique Aviation Traction
McGuire *	Brian McGuire (Australian racing driver)
McLaren	Bruce McLaren (New Zealand racing driver)
Mercedes-Benz	Mercédès Jellinek (daughter of Emil Jellinek, Austrian car designer & entrepreneur) and Karl Benz (engineer)
Merzario	Arturo Merzario (Italian racing driver)
Midland	Midland Resources Holding Ltd (trading & investment)
Milano *	Scuderia Milano (Italian racing team from Milan)
Minardi	Giancarlo Minardi (FIAT car dealer)
Monteverdi	Peter Monteverdi (Swiss prestige car manufacturer)
OSCA	Officine Specializzate Costruzioni Automobili
Osella	Vincenzo "Enzo" Osella (sports car driver & car designer)
Parnelli	Rufus Parnell "Parnelli" Jones (American racing driver)
Penske	Roger Penske (American engineer & entrepreneur)
Politoys	Italian toy manufacturer
Porsche	Ferdinand "Ferry" Porsche (Austrian automotive engineer & entrepreneur)
Prost	Alain Prost (French racing driver)
RAM	Mick Ralph (engineer), John MacDonald (engineer & racing driver)
RAM March	see RAM & March
Rebaque	Hector Rebaque (Mexican racing driver)
Red Bull	Red Bull energy drinks (Austria)
Renault	Renault brothers: Louis (engineer), Marcel (racing driver) and Fernand
Rial	German light alloy wheel and rim producer
Sauber	Peter Sauber (Swiss car salesman & racing driver)
Scarab	The Egyptian "good luck" beetle
Shadow	"The Shadow", an American radio drama series
Simca-Gordini	Société Industrielle de Mécanique et Carrosserie Automobile (& see Gordini)
Simtek	Simulation Technology (racing car design & engineering)
Spyker	Jacobus & Hendrik-Jan Spijker (Dutch coach & carriage builders)
Stanley-BRM	Louis Stanley (journalist & BRM chairman) (& see BRM)
Stebro	John Stephens and Peter Broeker (Canadian engineers)
Stewart	Jackie Stewart (racing driver)
Super Aguri	Aguri Suzuki (Japanese racing driver)
Surtees	John Surtees (motorcycle and car racer)
Talbot-Lago	Charles Chetwynd-Talbot (British peer & businessman) and Antonio "Tony" Lago (engineer)
Talbot-Ligier	Charles Chetwynd-Talbot (British peer & businessman) (& see Ligier)
Tec-Mec	Studio Tecnica Meccanica (Italy)
Tecno	Tecnokart (Italian go-kart builder)
Theodore	Theodore "Teddy" Yip (Indonesian businessman)
Thin Wall Special	Thinwall bearings (see Vanwall) - an adapted Ferrari
Token	Tony Vlassopulos (Greek shipbroker) and Ken Grob (Lloyds underwriter)
Toleman	Norman Edward "Ted" Toleman (businessman)
Toro Rosso	Italian Red Bull team
Toyota	Toyota (Japanese city of the car manufacturer's headquarters)
Tyrrell	Ken Tyrrell (racing driver)
Vanwall	"Van" from Guy Anthony "Tony" Vandervell (engineer and businessman) & "wall" from Thinwall bearings
Venturi-Larrousse	Venturi sports cars (from France-Monaco) & see Larrousse
Virgin	Virgin Group (entertainment & travel)
Williams	Frank Williams (racing driver and mechanic)
Wolf	Walter Wolf (Canadian oil drilling equipment supplier)
Zakspeed	Erich Zakowski (German mechanic)

* Non-starter (see section 959).

See Section 176 for "Drivers who had a Formula 1 car named after them" and 177 for those who "Raced in a car of their name".

654. Consecutive races started (Most)

Ferrari	564	Italy 1982	- Abu Dhabi 2015
Williams	378	Belgium 1982	- Canada 2005
McLaren	361	Belgium 1983	- Canada 2005
Benetton	260	Brazil 1986	- Japan 2001
Brabham	251	United States 1962	- United States West 1982
Jordan	250	United States 1991	- China 2005
McLaren	195	France 2005	- Abu Dhabi 2015
Red Bull	195	France 2005	- Abu Dhabi 2015
Williams	195	France 2005	- Abu Dhabi 2015
Toro Rosso	185	Bahrain 2006	- Abu Dhabi 2015
Arrows	178	Portugal 1991	- Britain 2002
Tyrrell	174	Canada 1988	- Japan 1998
McLaren	172	Netherlands 1970	- United States West 1982
Tyrrell	164	Argentina 1974	- Germany 1984
Minardi	157	Belgium 1992	- San Marino 2002
Lotus (a)	151	Canada 1970	- Argentina 1981
Force India	150	Australia 2008	- Abu Dhabi 2015
Ligier	119	Belgium 1989	- Japan 1996
Renault	118	France 2005	- Brazil 2011
Lotus	117	Belgium 1982	- Hungary 1989

(a) Includes JPS Lotus.

655. Cars of the same constructor in a race (Most)

Cooper	12	Britain 1959	Maserati	11	Italy 1957
Cooper	12	Britain 1960	Cooper	10	Germany 1958
Cooper	12	United States 1960	Cooper	10	France 1960
Lotus	11	Britain 1961	Maserati	10	Spain 1954
Maserati	11	Britain 1956	Maserati	10	Italy 1956
Maserati	11	Germany 1956	Maserati	10	Pescara 1957

Excludes Indianapolis 500.

656. The last time a constructor had more than three cars in a race
McLaren (five) in Italy 1978:

>   Patrick Tambay, 5th;
>   Nelson Piquet, 9th;
>   Bruno Giacomelli, 14th;
>   James Hunt, retired after 19 laps (distributor failure);
>   Brett Lunger, retired at first start (accident/ did not start restarted race)

657. The last time a constructor had three cars in a race
Renault in Germany 1985:

>   Derek Warwick, retired after 25 laps (ignition failure);
>   Patrick Tambay, retired after 19 laps (spin);
>   François Hesnault, retired after 8 laps (clutch failure)

658. Different constructor entrants in a race
Most
20
Belgium 1978:   Arrows, ATS, Brabham, Copersucar, Ensign, Ferrari, Hesketh (nq), Ligier, Lotus (inc JPS Lotus), March (nq), Martini, McLaren, Merzario (nq), Renault, Shadow, Surtees, Theodore (nq), Tyrrell, Williams, Wolf
Brazil to Australia 1989 (16 races)
            AGS, Arrows, Benetton, Brabham, Coloni, Dallara, EuroBrun, Ferrari, Ligier, Lola, Lotus, March, McLaren, Minardi, Onyx, Osella, Rial, Tyrrell, Williams, Zakspeed
19
South Africa and Monaco 1978 (2 races)
            Arrows, ATS, Brabham, Ensign (nq), Ferrari, Fittipaldi (as Copersucar), Hesketh, Ligier, Lotus (inc JPS Lotus), Martini, McLaren, Merzario, Renault, Shadow, Surtees, Theodore, Tyrrell, Williams, Wolf
United States to Hungary 1990 (10 races)
            AGS, Arrows, Benetton, Brabham, Coloni, Dallara, EuroBrun, Ferrari, Life, Ligier, Lola, Lotus, March (as Leyton House), McLaren, Minardi, Onyx, Osella, Tyrrell, Williams

Fewest
2

Argentina 1956	Ferrari (inc. Lancia-Ferrari), Maserati
Argentina 1957	Ferrari (inc. Lancia-Ferrari), Maserati

3

Belgium 1951	Alfa Romeo, Ferrari, Talbot-Lago
Argentina 1954	Ferrari, Gordini, Maserati
Belgium 1954	Ferrari, Gordini, Maserati
Germany 1956	Ferrari (inc Lancia-Ferrari), Gordini, Maserati
Italy 1957	Ferrari (as Lancia-Ferrari), Maserati, Vanwall
Argentina 1958	Cooper, Ferrari, Maserati

(nq) Did not qualify.

659. Different constructor starters in a race

Most
18

Canada 1989	AGS, Arrows, Benetton, Brabham, Coloni, Dallara, Ferrari, Ligier, Lola, Lotus, March, McLaren, Minardi, Onyx, Osella, Rial, Tyrrell, Williams (additionally EuroBrun and Zakspeed did not pre-qualify)

17

Monaco 1988	Arrows, Benetton, Coloni, Dallara, EuroBrun, Ferrari, Ligier, Lola, Lotus, March, McLaren, Minardi, Osella, Rial, Tyrrell, Williams, Zakspeed (additionally AGS did not start)

Fewest
2

Argentina 1956	Ferrari (inc. Lancia-Ferrari), Maserati
Argentina 1957	Ferrari (inc. Lancia-Ferrari), Maserati

3

Belgium 1951	Alfa Romeo, Ferrari, Talbot-Lago
Argentina 1954	Ferrari, Gordini, Maserati
Belgium 1954	Ferrari, Gordini, Maserati
Germany 1956	Ferrari (inc. Lancia-Ferrari), Gordini, Maserati
Italy 1957	Ferrari (as Lancia-Ferrari), Maserati, Vanwall
Argentina 1958	Cooper, Ferrari, Maserati
United States 2005	Ferrari, Jordan, Minardi

Excludes Indianapolis 500.

660. First time starters in a race *(Most)*
(apart from Britain 1950, where there were five constructors starting)

Switzerland 1952   4
AFM, Frazer Nash, Gordini (previously Simca-Gordini), Maserati-Platé (the first race for Maserati-Platé but Maserati had appeared before)

Bahrain 2006   4
BMW Sauber, Midland, Super Aguri, Toro Rosso

Monaco 1950   3
Cooper, Ferrari, Simca-Gordini

Belgium 1963   3
ATS (Italy), BRP, Scirocco

Argentina 1975   3
Copersucar, Stanley-BRM (had previously been BRM), Williams (previously Iso-Marlboro)

Switzerland 1951   2
HWM, Veritas

United States 1959   2
Kurtis-Kraft, Tec-Mec

Britain 1961   2
Ferguson, Gilby

Germany 1962   2
Brabham, ENB

South Africa 1970
March, Matra-Simca (previously Matra)

Canada 1974   2
Parnelli, Penske

Spain 1974   2
Amon, Trojan

Brazil 1976   2
Ligier, Wolf-Williams (was Williams in 1975)

Argentina 1978   2
ATS (Germany), Merzario

Brazil 1988   2
EuroBrun, Rial

United States 1991   2
Footwork (previously Arrows), Jordan, Lamborghini

South Africa 1992   2
Fondmetal (previously Osella), Venturi-Larrousse

South Africa 1993   2
Larrousse (previously Venturi-Larrousse), Sauber

Brazil 1994   2
Pacific, Simtek

Australia 1997   2
Prost (previously Ligier), Stewart

Bahrain 2010   2
HRT, Virgin

Australia 2012   2
Caterham (previously Lotus), Marussia (previously Virgin)

661. Seasons of starting races *(Most)*

Ferrari	66	1950 - 2015		Tyrrell	29	1970 - 98
McLaren	50	1966 - 2015		Arrows	25	1978 - 2002
Lotus	43	1958 - 2015		BRM	23	1951 - 77
Williams	43	1972 - 2015		Ligier	21	1976 - 96
Brabham	30	1962 - 92		Minardi	21	1985 - 2005

662. Consecutive seasons of starting races *(Most)*

Ferrari	66	1950 - 2015		Brabham	26	1962 - 87
McLaren	50	1966 - 2015		Arrows	25	1978 - 2002
Lotus	37	1958 - 94		BRM	22	1956 - 77
Williams	38	1978 - 2015		Ligier	21	1976 - 96
Tyrrell	29	1970 - 98		Minardi	21	1985 - 2005

663. Race retirements *(Most)*
(number of cars)

		% of starts		
Lotus	685	46.79	Monaco 1958	- Abu Dhabi 2015
Ferrari	640	31.98	Monaco 1950	- Mexico 2015 (a)
McLaren	528	32.77	Monaco 1966	- Mexico 2015
Brabham	494	53.00	Germany 1962	- Spain 1991
Williams	437	32.49	Britain 1972	- United States 2015
Arrows	377	52.07	South Africa 1978	- Germany 2002
Tyrrell	368	43.71	Canada 1970	- Japan 1998
Minardi	343	54.10	Brazil 1985	- Brazil 2005
March	301	54.04	South Africa 1970	- Australia 1992
Ligier	280	48.44	Brazil 1976	- Japan 1996

Includes all retirements even if classified (completed 90% of the race distance).
(a) Excludes 1 Indianapolis 500 race started.

664. Percentage of race retirements *(Most)*
(constructors with ten or more cars starting)

Highest

	%					
Merzario	90.00	9 of 10		Osella	76.96	147 of 191
de Tomaso	83.33	10 of 12		Toleman	72.34	68 of 94
ATS (Italy)	81.82	9 of 11		RAM	72.22	39 of 54
Tecno	81.82	9 of 11		Lancia	70.00	7 of 10
Pacific	80.00	32 of 40		Rial	70.00	14 of 20

Lowest

Brawn	5.88	2 of 34		Caterham	20.91	23 of 110
BMW	15.71	22 of 140		Force India	23.49	70 of 298
Mercedes-Benz	18.22	49 of 269		Porsche	24.66	18 of 73
Red Bull	19.06	77 of 404		Toyota	28.26	78 of 276
Marussia	20.37	44 of 216		Toro Rosso	29.46	109 of 370

Other current constructors

Ferrari	31.98	640 of 2,001		Sauber	35.02	229 of 654
Williams	32.49	437 of 1,345		Lotus	46.79	685 of 1,464
McLaren	32.77	528 of 1,611				

The only constructors to record no retirements are ENB, Ferguson and Stebro, which only started one race each, although the Ferguson was disqualified for a push-start (explained in section 152).

665. Race retirements in a season *(Most)*

March	36 of 53	1976	(761 - Ford Cosworth)
March	31 of 60	1970	(701 - Ford Cosworth)
Cooper	31 of 74	1960	(T43, T45, T51, T53 - Castellotti, Climax, Maserati)
Minardi	28 of 31	1987	(M187 - Motori Moderni)
Stewart	28 of 34	1997	(SF-1 - Ford Cosworth)
Lotus	28 of 57	1962	(18/21, 24, 25 - BRM, Climax)
Maserati	28 of 57	1954	(250F, A6GCM)
Minardi	27 of 29	1986	(185B, 186 - Motori Moderni)
Brabham	27 of 32	1987	(BT56 - BMW)
Lotus	27 of 47	1969	(49B, 63 - Ford Cosworth)
Lotus	27 of 55	1961	(18, 18/21, 21 - Climax, Maserati)
Maserati	27 of 60	1956	(250F)

666. Race retirements at the same venue *(Most)*

grand prix
(total number of cars)

Lotus	68	Germany	1958 - 2014 (a)
Lotus	60	Britain	1958 - 2015 (a)
Ferrari	59	Italy	1950 - 2014 (b)
Lotus	57	Italy	1959 - 2015 (a)
Ferrari	56	Belgium	1951 - 2015 (b)
Lotus	51	Monaco	1958 - 2015 (a)
Lotus	50	Belgium	1958 - 2015 (a)
Ferrari	49	Monaco	1950 - 2013 (b)
Ferrari	47	Germany	1952 - 2013 (b)
Lotus	47	United States	1959 - 2015 (c)

Relates to the country's national grand prix.

circuit

Ferrari	58	Monza	1950 - 2014 (b)
Lotus	56	Monza	1959 - 2015 (a)
Ferrari	51	Spa-Francorchamps	1951 - 2015 (b)
Lotus	51	Monte-Carlo	1958 - 2015 (a)
Ferrari	49	Monte-Carlo	1950 - 2013 (b)
Lotus	40	Nürburgring	1958 - 85 (a) (d)
Lotus	40	Watkins Glen	1961 - 79 (a)
Brabham	39	Monza	1963 - 90
McLaren	39	Monte-Carlo	1966 - 2015
Brabham	38	Monte-Carlo	1963 - 91
McLaren	38	Monza	1967 - 2015
Williams	38	Monte-Carlo	1973 - 2014

(a) Includes JPS Lotus.
(b) Includes Lancia-Ferrari.
(c) Excludes 1 Dallas, 7 Detroit, 3 Caesars Palace (Las Vegas) and 8 United States West (Long Beach) Grands Prix.
(d) Includes 2 European Grand Prix.

667. Race retirements before the end of first lap *(Most)*
(excludes retirements on the parade lap and other race non-starts)

McLaren	52	Monaco 1968	- Britain 2015
Ferrari	41	Italy 1951	- Austria 2015 (a)
Lotus	38	Italy 1961	- Abu Dhabi 2015
Sauber	36	Europe 1993	- Russia 2015
Tyrrell	36	Italy 1972	- Belgium 1998 (a)
Williams	33	Argentina 1973	- Germany 2014
Arrows	32	Netherlands 1978	- Malaysia 2000
Jordan	32	France 1991	- Belgium 2004
Minardi	30	Italy 1985	- Belgium 2004
Brabham	29	Britain 1964	- Japan 1990

Includes cases where a car did not take the restart following a race being abandoned.
(a) Includes 1 disqualification.

668. Consecutive races without a retirement *(Most)*

Ferrari	18	(36 cars)	Hungary 2013	- Austria 2014	(F138, F14 T)
McLaren	16	(32 cars)	Japan 2006	- Belgium 2007	(MP4-21, MP4-22 - Mercedes)
Mercedes-Benz	16	(32 cars)	Japan 2014	- Belgium 2015	(F1 W05, F1 W06)
Caterham	15	(30 cars)	Germany 2012	- Bahrain 2013	(CT01, CT03 - Renault)
Red Bull	14	(28 cars)	Brazil 2010	- Belgium 2011	(RB6, RB7 - Renault)
McLaren	13	(26 cars)	Germany 2013	- Malaysia 2014	(MP4-28, MP4-29 - Mercedes)
Williams	12	(28 cars)	France 1980	- San Marino 1981 (a)	(FW07, FW07B, FW07C - Ford Cosworth)
McLaren	11	(22 cars)	San Marino 2000	- Belgium 2000	(MP4-15 - Mercedes)
Renault	11	(22 cars)	Malaysia 2006	- Germany 2006	(R26)
Williams	11	(22 cars)	France 2008	- Brazil 2008	(FW30 - Toyota)
Williams	11	(22 cars)	Malaysia 2015	- Italy 2015	(FW37 - Mercedes)

(a) All above are free of non-starts apart from this one. There were some non-qualifiers during the period for Williams, but with three or four cars entered for most races, there were always at least two starters per race.

669. All cars of a constructor, retired from the race before end of first lap
(only cases where a constructor was at the start of the race with two or more cars)

Monaco 1950	Simca-Gordini	Roberto Manzon, Maurice Trintignant
Belgium 1966	BRM	Bob Bondurant, Graham Hill, Jackie Stewart
Belgium 1966	Lotus	Jim Clark, Mike Spence (a)
Britain 1973	Surtees	Mike Hailwood *, Jochen Mass *, Carlos Pace *
Germany 1976	March	Ronnie Peterson, Hans-Joachim Stuck *
Monaco 1980	Tyrrell	Derek Daly, Jean-Pierre Jarier
Belgium 1981	Arrows	Riccardo Patrese *, Siegfried Stohr *
Belgium 1982	ATS	Eliseo Salazar, Manfred Winkelhock
Canada 1982	Osella	Jean-Pierre Jarier *, Riccardo Paletti *
Austria 1982	Alfa Romeo	Andrea De Cesaris, Bruno Giacomelli
Monaco 1984	Renault	Patrick Tambay, Derek Warwick
South Africa 1985	Alfa Romeo	Eddie Cheever, Riccardo Patrese
Britain 1986	Osella	Allen Berg *, Piercarlo Ghinzani *
San Marino 1989	Lola	Philippe Alliot (& Yannick Dalmas on the dummy grid)
Japan 1989	Minardi	Paolo Barilla, Luis Sala
Hungary 1992	Ligier	Thierry Boutsen, Erik Comas
Italy 1993	Footwork	Aguri Suzuki, Derek Warwick
Italy 1993	Jordan	Marco Apicella, Rubens Barrichello
Germany 1994	Jordan	Rubens Barrichello, Eddie Irvine
Germany 1994	Lotus	Johnny Herbert, Alessandro Zanardi
Germany 1994	Minardi	Michele Alboreto, Pierluigi Martini
Germany 1994	Sauber	Andrea De Cesaris, Heinz-Harald Frentzen
Hungary 1994	Jordan	Rubens Barrichello, Eddie Irvine
Monaco 1995	Simtek	Mimmo Schiattarella *, Jos Verstappen *
Monaco 1996	Minardi	Giancarlo Fisichella, Pedro Lamy
Belgium 1996	Sauber	Heinz-Harald Frentzen, Johnny Herbert
Luxembourg 1997	Jordan	Giancarlo Fisichella, Ralf Schumacher
Italy 2000	Jordan	Heinz-Harald Frentzen, Jarno Trulli
Belgium 2001	Sauber	Nick Heidfeld, Kimi Räikkönen*
Australia 2002	Sauber	Nick Heidfeld, Felipe Massa
Hungary 2005	Red Bull	David Coulthard, Christian Klien
United States 2006	McLaren	Juan Pablo Montoya, Kimi Räikkönen
Spain 2009	Toro Rosso	Sébastien Bourdais, Sébastien Buemi
Canada 2014	Marussia	Jules Bianchi, Max Chilton
Australia 2015	Lotus	Romain Grosjean, Pastor Maldonado
Britain 2015	Lotus	Romain Grosjean, Pastor Maldonado

(a) Another Lotus, driven by Peter Arundell, did not start the race.
* Retired after the first start which was aborted and so did not make it to the grid for the restarted race.
At Monaco 1974, Carlos Pace retired his Surtees on the first lap. The other Surtees, driven by Jochen Mass did not start due to shortage of parts.
At United States West 1979, neither Renaults started the race (René Arnoux - universal joint and Jean-Pierre Jabouille - accident/ injury).
At United States 2005, 14 drivers from the 7 Michelin teams, withdrew on the parade lap due to tyre safety concerns.

For consecutive races with all cars of a constructor not qualifying, see section 962.

670. Four-wheel drive cars

First

Ferguson P99 with a Climax, 4-cylinder engine (driven by Jack Fairman/ Stirling Moss): Britain 1961.

Last

Lotus 56B with a Pratt & Whitney turbine engine (driven by Emerson Fittipaldi): Italy 1971.

671. Rear/ front-engined cars

First rear-engined car

Cooper T12 with a JAP V2 engine (driven by Harry Schell): Monaco 1950.

Last front-engined car

Ferguson P99 with a 4-cylinder Climax engine (driven by Jack Fairman/ Stirling Moss): Britain 1961.

For rear/ front-engined car winners, see section 721.

672. Six-wheeled cars

The only six-wheeled car to start a grand prix was the Tyrrell P34:

First race

Spain 1976, driven by Patrick Depailler.

Last race

Japan 1977, driven by Ronnie Peterson and Patrick Depailler.

Top placings for the P34

1st = 1 (Jody Scheckter at Sweden 1976), 2nd = 9, 3rd = 4, 4th = 4, 5th = 3, 6th = 3.

Other six-wheeled Formula 1 cars, the March 2-4-0 (tested in 1977) and Williams FW08B (1982) were only experimental and never entered a race.

673. Oldest car to ever race in the world championship

A 1935 ERA type A in Monaco 1950 (chassis number 4A) driven by Bob Gerard, finishing 6th.

674. Race starting drivers by constructor

	drivers	most starts
Lotus	116	Elio De Angelis, 90
Cooper	100	Bruce McLaren, 64
Ferrari	94	Michael Schumacher, 180
Maserati	80	Harry Schell, 21
Brabham	75	Nelson Piquet, 106
BRM	59	Graham Hill, 64
Williams	56	Nigel Mansell, 95
McLaren	54	David Coulthard, 150
March	47	Ivan Capelli, 74
Tyrrell	45	Patrick Depailler, 80
Minardi	37	Pierluigi Martini, 102
Arrows	33	Derek Warwick, 63
Jordan	30	Rubens Barrichello, 64
Surtees	30	Vittorio Brambilla, 29
Ligier	28	Jacques Laffite, 132
Connaught	26	Kenneth McAlpine, 7
Ensign	26	Clay Regazzoni, 19
Gordini	26	Robert Manzon, 23
Sauber	25	Heinz-Harald Frentzen, 65
Lola	24	Philippe Alliot, 46
Renault	20	Fernando Alonso, 105
Osella	18	Piercarlo Ghinzani, 47
Talbot-Lago	18	Louis Rosier, 13
Alfa Romeo	17	Bruno Giacomelli, 49
Benetton	17	Michael Schumacher, 68
Shadow	17	Jean-Pierre Jarier, 44
Veritas	15	Theo Helfrich, 2; Arthur Legat, 2; Toni Ulmen, 2
HWM	14	Lance Macklin, 12
Porsche	14	Carel Godin de Beaufort, 26
Hesketh	12	James Hunt, 27
ATS (Germany)	11	Manfred Winkelhock, 38
Toro Rosso	11	Jean-Eric Vergne, 58
Vanwall	11	Tony Brooks, 16

	drivers	most starts
Mercedes-Benz	10	Nico Rosberg, 115
Larrousse	9	Erik Comas, 31
Marussia	9	Timo Glock, 55
Prost	9	Olivier Panis, 42
Theodore	9	Roberto Guerrero, 13
Toyota	9	Jarno Trulli, 90
Caterham	8	Heikki Kovalainen, 20
Honda	8	Rubens Barrichello, 53; Jenson Button, 53
HRT	8	Narain Karthikeyan, 27
Jaguar	8	Eddie Irvine, 50
Matra	8	Jean-Pierre Beltoise, 46
Red Bull	8	Mark Webber, 129
Toleman	8	Derek Warwick, 26
BAR	7	Jacques Villeneuve, 81
ERA	7	Bob Gerard, 3; Cuth Harrison, 3; Stirling Moss, 3
Penske	7	John Watson, 17
AGS	6	Philippe Streiff, 15
Dallara	6	J J Lehto, 31
de Tomaso	6	Piers Courage, 4; Tim Schenken, 4
Fittipaldi	6	Emerson Fittipaldi, 74
Force India	6	Adrian Sutil, 92
RAM	6	Philippe Alliot, 26
Simtek	6	David Brabham, 16
Zakspeed	6	Jonathan Palmer, 23
AFM	5	Hans Stuck, 3
Eagle	5	Dan Gurney, 24
Hill	5	Tony Brise, 9
Pacific	5	Bertrand Gachot, 16; Andrea Montermini, 16
Super Aguri	5	Takuma Sato, 39
Alta	4	Geoffrey Crossley, 2; Joe Kelly, 2
BMW	4	Nick Heidfeld, 70
BMW specials	4	Ernst Klodwig, 2; Rudolf Krause, 2
Coloni	4	Gabriele Tarquini, 8
Forti	4	Pedro Diniz, 17; Roberto Moreno, 17
Lancia	4	Alberto Ascari, 3; Eugenio Castellotti, 3; Luigi Villoresi, 3
Onyx	4	Stefan Johansson, 8
Spyker	4	Adrian Sutil, 17
Stewart	4	Rubens Barrichello, 49
Tecno	4	Chris Amon, 4; Nanni Galli, 4
Wolf	4	Jody Scheckter, 33
Aston Martin	3	Roy Salvadori, 5
ATS (Italy)	3	Giancarlo Baghetti, 5; Phil Hill, 5
Emeryson	3	Tony Settember, 2
EuroBrun	3	Stefano Modena, 10
Kojima	3	Masahiro Hasemi, 1; Kazuyoshi Hoshino, 1; Noritake Takahara, 1
OSCA	3	Elie Bayol, 3
Scirocco	3	Tony Settember, 4
Spirit	3	Mauro Baldi, 10
Aston-Butterworth	2	Bill Aston, 1; Robin Montgomerie-Charrington, 1
Brawn	2	Rubens Barrichello, 17; Jenson Button, 17
BRP	2	Innes Ireland, 12
Ferguson	2	Jack Fairman, 1; Stirling Moss, 1
Frazer Nash	2	Ken Wharton, 3
Gilby	2	Keith Greene, 2
Lamborghini	2	Nicola Larini, 5
LDS	2	Sam Tingle, 4
Midland	2	Christijan Albers, 18; Tiago Monteiro, 18
Protos	2	Kurt Ahrens, 1; Brian Hart, 1
Rial	2	Andrea De Cesaris, 16
Scarab	2	Chuck Daigh, 2
Token	2	Ian Ashley, 2
Alfa Special	1	Peter De Klerk, 2
Amon	1	Chris Amon, 1
Andrea Moda	1	Roberto Moreno, 1
Bellasi	1	Silvio Moser, 2
Bugatti	1	Maurice Trintignant, 1
Connew	1	François Migault, 1

	drivers	most starts
EMW	1	Edgar Barth, 1
ENB	1	Lucien Bianchi, 1
JBW	1	Brian Naylor, 5
Klenk	1	Theo Helfrich, 1
Kurtis-Kraft	1	Rodger Ward, 1
Lec	1	David Purley, 3
Lyncar	1	John Nicholson, 1
Martini	1	René Arnoux, 4
Merzario	1	Arturo Merzario, 10
Parnelli	1	Mario Andretti, 16
Rebaque	1	Hector Rebaque, 1
Shannon	1	Trevor Taylor, 1
Stebro	1	Peter Broeker, 1
Tec-Mec	1	Fritz d'Orey, 1
Trojan	1	Tim Schenken, 6

675. Races started with the same engine make *(Most)*
(excludes retirements on the parade lap and other race non-starts)

Ferrari	907	Ferrari	Monaco 1950	- Abu Dhabi 2015 (a)
McLaren	351	Mercedes-Benz	Brazil 1995	- Abu Dhabi 2014
Tyrrell	310	Cosworth	Canada 1970	- Japan 1998 (b)
Renault	300	Renault	Britain 1977	- Brazil 2011
Lotus	277	Cosworth	Germany 1966	- Abu Dhabi 2010 (c)
McLaren	236	Cosworth	Spain 1968	- Australia 1993 (b)
Williams	201	Cosworth	Britain 1972	- Brazil 2011 (c)
Minardi	198	Cosworth	Brazil 1985	- China 2005 (c)
BRM	189	BRM	Britain 1951	- South Africa 1977
Williams	185	Renault	Brazil 1989	- Brazil 2013 (d)

(a) Includes Lancia-Ferrari. (b) As Ford Cosworth. (c) Includes Ford Cosworth. (d) An additional 16 races were with Mecachrome and another 16 with Supertec, Renault-based engines, within the period.
For complete list of race starting constructors by engine make, see section 969.

Overall
(number of races)

AFM: BMW, 2; Bristol, 2; Küchen, 1
AGS: Ford Cosworth, 45; Motori Moderni, 2
Alfa Romeo: Alfa Romeo, 110
Alfa Special: Alfa Romeo, 2
Alta: Alta, 5
Amon: Ford Cosworth, 1
Andrea Moda: Judd, 1
Arrows: Ford Cosworth, 158; BMW, 45; Hart, 33; Arrows, 32; Megatron, 32; Mugen Honda, 32; Asiatech, 17; Supertec, 17; Yamaha, 17; Porsche, 4
Aston-Butterworth: Butterworth, 2
Aston Martin: Aston Martin, 5
ATS (Germany): Ford Cosworth, 60; BMW, 29
ATS (Italy): ATS, 6
BAR: Honda, 101; Supertec, 16
Bellasi: Ford Cosworth, 2
Benetton: Ford Cosworth, 128; Renault, 67; Playlife, 49; BMW, 16
BMW: BMW, 70
BMW specials: BMW, 2
Brabham: Ford Cosworth, 133; BMW, 91; Alfa Romeo, 62; Climax, 47; Judd, 35; Repco, 33; BRM, 24; Yamaha, 16; Ford, 3
Brawn: Mercedes-Benz, 17
BRM: BRM, 189; Climax, 8
BRP: BRM, 13
Bugatti: Bugatti, 1
Caterham: Renault, 56
Coloni: Ford Cosworth, 13
Connaught: Lea-Francis, 10; Alta, 7
Connew: Ford Cosworth, 1
Cooper: Climax, 81; Maserati, 44; Bristol, 17; BRM, 11; Alta, 5; Castellotti, 3; Ferrari, 3; Alfa Romeo, 1; ATS, 1; Borgward, 1; Ford, 1; JAP, 1; OSCA, 1
Dallara: Ford Cosworth, 46; Ferrari, 16; Judd, 16
de Tomaso: Ford Cosworth, 8; OSCA, 2; Conrero, 1
Eagle: Weslake, 16; Climax, 10
Emeryson: Climax, 3; Alta, 1
EMW: EMW, 1
ENB: Maserati, 1
Ensign: Ford Cosworth, 99
ERA: ERA, 4; Bristol, 3

EuroBrun: Ford Cosworth, 12; Judd, 2
Ferguson: Climax, 1
Ferrari: Ferrari, 907 (inc. Lancia-Ferrari); Jaguar, 1
Fittipaldi: Ford Cosworth, 104
Force India: Mercedes-Benz, 132; Ferrari, 18
Forti: Ford Cosworth, 23
Frazer Nash: Bristol, 4
Gilby: BRM, 2; Climax, 1
Gordini: Gordini, 40
Hesketh: Ford Cosworth, 52
Hill: Ford Cosworth, 10
Honda: Honda, 88
HRT: Cosworth, 56
HWM: Alta, 14
Jaguar: Ford Cosworth, 85
JBW: Maserati, 4; Climax, 1
Jordan: Ford Cosworth, 50; Peugeot, 50; Mugen Honda, 49; Honda, 34; Hart, 32; Toyota, 19, Yamaha, 16
Klenk: BMW, 1
Kojima: Ford Cosworth, 2
Kurtis-Kraft: Offenhauser, 1
Lamborghini: Lamborghini, 6
Lancia: Lancia, 4
Larrousse: Lamborghini, 32; Ford Cosworth, 16
LDS: Alfa Romeo, 3; Climax, 1; Repco, 1
Lec: Ford Cosworth, 3
Ligier: Renault, 95; Matra, 79; Ford Cosworth, 74; Mugen Honda, 33; Lamborghini, 16; Megatron, 15; Judd, 14
Lola: Ford Cosworth, 78; Lamborghini, 32; Climax, 18; Ferrari, 14; Hart, 6; BMW, 2
Lotus: Ford Cosworth/ Cosworth, 277; Renault, 139; Climax, 82; BRM, 48; Honda, 32; Judd, 31; Mercedes-Benz, 19; Lamborghini, 16;
                     Mugen Honda, 16; Pratt & Whitney, 3; Ford, 1; Maserati, 1
Lyncar: Ford Cosworth, 1
March: Ford Cosworth, 149; Judd, 46; Ilmor, 32; Alfa Romeo, 9
Martini: Ford Cosworth, 4
Marussia: Cosworth, 77; Ferrari, 34
Maserati: Maserati, 68 (inc. Milano and Platé); OSCA, 1
Matra: Matra, 44; Ford Cosworth, 28; BRM, 1
McLaren: Mercedes-Benz, 351; Ford Cosworth, 236; Honda, 99; TAG Porsche, 68; Peugeot, 16; BRM, 13; Alfa Romeo, 4; Ford, 3; Serenissima, 1
Mercedes-Benz: Mercedes-Benz, 127
Merzario: Ford Cosworth, 10
Midland: Toyota, 18
Minardi: Ford Cosworth/ Cosworth, 198; Motori Moderni, 44; European, 17; Fondmetal, 17; Hart, 17; Asiatech, 16; Ferrari, 16; Lamborghini, 15
Onyx: Ford Cosworth, 17
OSCA: OSCA, 4
Osella: Alfa Romeo, 76; Ford Cosworth, 75
Pacific: Ford Cosworth, 17; Ilmor, 5
Parnelli: Ford Cosworth, 16
Penske: Ford Cosworth, 40
Porsche: Porsche, 33
Prost: Peugeot, 49; Acer, 17; Mugen Honda, 17
Protos: Ford Cosworth, 1
RAM: Hart, 28; Ford Cosworth, 3
Rebaque: Ford Cosworth, 1
Red Bull: Renault, 167; Cosworth, 18; Ferrari, 18
Renault: Renault, 300
Rial: Ford Cosworth, 20
Sauber: Petronas, 151; Ferrari, 115; Ford Cosworth, 33; Ilmor, 16; Mercedes-Benz, 15
Scarab: Scarab, 2
Scirocco: BRM, 4; Climax, 1
Shadow: Ford Cosworth, 104; Matra, 2
Shannon: Climax, 1
Simtek: Ford Cosworth, 21
Spirit: Hart, 17; Honda, 6
Spyker: Ferrari, 17
Stebro: Ford, 1
Stewart: Ford Cosworth, 49
Super Aguri: Honda, 39
Surtees: Ford Cosworth, 118
Talbot-Lago: Talbot-Lago, 13
Tec-Mec: Maserati, 1
Tecno: Tecno, 10; Ford Cosworth, 1
Theodore: Ford Cosworth, 34
Token: Ford Cosworth, 3
Toleman: Hart, 57
Toro Rosso: Ferrari, 129; Renault, 38; Cosworth, 18
Toyota: Toyota, 139
Trojan: Ford Cosworth, 6
Tyrrell: Ford Cosworth, 310; Yamaha, 65; Renault, 26; Honda, 16; Ilmor, 16

Vanwall:	Vanwall, 28
Veritas:	Veritas, 6
Williams:	Ford Cosworth/ Cosworth, 201; Renault, 185; BMW, 103; Honda, 65; Toyota, 52; Mercedes-Benz, 38; Judd, 16; Mecachrome, 16; Supertec, 16
Wolf:	Ford Cosworth, 47
Zakspeed:	Zakspeed, 51; Yamaha, 2

676. Interval between races started *(Longest)*

	years, days	races		
Mercedes-Benz	54y, 184d	773	Italy 1955 (J M Fangio, K Kling, S Moss, P Taruffi)	- Bahrain 2010 (N Rosberg, M Schumacher)
Honda	37y, 129d	578	Mexico 1968 (J Bonnier, J Surtees)	- Bahrain 2006 (R Barrichello, J Button)
Alfa Romeo	27y, 197d	304	Spain 1951 (F Bonetto, E de Graffenried, J M Fangio, G Farina)	- Belgium 1979 (B Giacomelli)
Renault	16y, 120d	261	Australia 1985 (P Tambay, D Warwick)	- Australia 2002 (J Button, J Trulli)
Lotus	15y, 121d	257	Australia 1994 (M Salo, A Zanardi)	- Bahrain 2010 (H Kovalainen, J Trulli)
Lola	10y, 191d	163	South Africa 1975 (R Stomellen)	- Italy 1985 (A Jones)
de Tomaso	8y, 178d	84	Italy 1961 (R Bussinello, R Lippi, N Vaccarella)	- South Africa 1970 (P Courage)
Emeryson	5y, 310d	49	Britain 1956 (P Emery)	- Netherlands 1962 (W Seidel)
Lola	5y, 162d	67	Germany 1968 (H Hahne)	- Argentina 1974 (G Edwards, G Hill)
BRM	5y, 0d	42	Britain 1951 (R Parnell, P Walker)	- Britain 1956 (T Brooks, R Flockhart, M Hawthorn)

677. Interval between first & last races started *(Longest)*

	years, days	races		
Ferrari	65y, 192d	933	Monaco 1950	- Abu Dhabi 2015
Mercedes-Benz	61y, 148d	899	France 1954	- Abu Dhabi 2015
Lotus	57y, 195d	869	Monaco 1958	- Abu Dhabi 2015
McLaren	49y, 191d	793	Monaco 1966	- Abu Dhabi 2015
Honda	44y, 92d	676	Germany 1964	- Brazil 2008
Williams	43y, 137d	720	Britain 1972	- Abu Dhabi 2015
Alfa Romeo	35y, 174d	419	Britain 1950	- Australia 1985
Renault	34y, 134d	568	Britain 1977	- Brazil 2011
Lola	31y, 129d	443	Netherlands 1962	- Portugal 1993
Brabham	30y, 11d	419	Germany 1962	- Hungary 1992

678. Races started but never a win *(Most)*

Arrows	382		Force India	150		BAR	117
Minardi	340		Lola	149		Marussia	111
Sauber	330		Toyota	139			
Osella	151		Surtees	118			

679. Races started but never a podium *(Most)*

Minardi	340		ATS (Germany)	89		Larrousse	48
Osella	151		Caterham	56		AGS	47
Marussia	111		HRT	56			
Ensign	99		Zakspeed	53			

680. Races started but never a pole position *(Most)*

Minardi	340		Marussia	111		Jaguar	85
Sauber	330		Fittipaldi	104		Prost	83
Osella	151		Ensign	99			
Surtees	118		ATS (Germany)	89			

681. Races started but never a front row *(Most)*

Osella	151		ATS (Germany)	89		HRT	56
Marussia	111		Prost	83		Zakspeed	53
Fittipaldi	104		Dallara	78			
Ensign	99		Caterham	56			

682. Races started but never a fastest lap *(Most)*

Arrows	382	Lola	149	ATS (Germany)	89
Minardi	340	BAR	117	Jaguar	85
Toro Rosso	185	Marussia	111		
Osella	151	Fittipaldi	104		

683. Races started but never scored a point *(Most)*

Caterham	56	Spirit	23	EuroBrun	14
HRT	56	Pacific	22	Coloni	13
RAM	31	Simtek	21		
Forti	23	Midland	18		

684. Races started but never led *(Most)*

Osella	151	Ensign	99	Caterham	56
Lola	149	ATS (Germany)	89	HRT	56
Marussia	111	Dallara	78		
Fittipaldi	104	Toleman	57		

685. Milestones: Number of races started

Ferrari (a)	100th: Italy 1963, 200th: South Africa 1973, 250th: Netherlands 1976, 300th: Italy 1979, 400th: France 1986, 500th: Belgium 1992, 600th: Italy 1998, 700th: Italy 2004, 750th: Europe 2007, 800th: Canada 2010, 900th: Italy 2015
McLaren	100th: Brazil 1975, 200th: Germany 1981, 250th: Portugal 1984, 300th: San Marino 1988, 400th: Canada 1994, 500th: Canada 2000, 600th: Europe 2006, 700th: Korea 2011, 750th: Austria 2014
Lotus (b)	100th: Germany 1968, 200th: Monaco 1976, 250th: Monaco 1979, 300th: Italy 1982, 400th: Mexico 1989, 500th: Europe 2010, 600th: Singapore 2015
Williams (c)	100th: Canada 1980, 200th: France 1987, 250th: Britain 1990, 300th: Germany 1993, 400th: Belgium 1999, 500th: Germany 2005, 600th: Turkey 2011
Tyrrell	100th: United States 1977, 200th: Canada 1984, 250th: Spain 1987, 300th: Australia 1990, 400th: Argentina 1997
Arrows (d)	100th: Netherlands 1984, 200th: Canada 1991, 250th: Belgium 1994, 300th: Belgium 1997
Brabham	100th: United States 1971, 200th: Germany 1978, 250th: South Africa 1982, 300th: Canada 1985
Ligier (e)	100th: Canada 1982, 200th: Brazil 1989, 250th: San Marino 1992, 300th: France 1995
Minardi	100th: Britain 1991, 200th: Belgium 1997, 250th: Belgium 2000, 300th: Hungary 2003
Renault	100th: Detroit 1984, 200th: Britain 2006, 250th: Spain 2009, 300th: Brazil 2011
Sauber (f)	100th: San Marino 1999, 200th: Bahrain 2005, 250th: Korea 2011, 300th: Austria 2014
Benetton	100th: Spain 1992, 200th: Monaco 1998, 250th: Monaco 2001
Jordan	100th: Argentina 1997, 200th: Brazil 2003, 250th: China 2005
March (g)	100th: United States West 1977, 200th: Canada 1991
Red Bull	100th: Hungary 2010, 200th: United States 2015
Alfa Romeo	100th: Detroit 1985
BAR	100th: Japan 2004
BRM (h)	100th: Belgium 1968
Cooper	100th: Britain 1966
Fittipaldi (i)	100th: Netherlands 1982
Force India	100th: Canada 2013
Lola	100th: Italy 1989
Marussia (j)	100th: Austria 2015
Mercedes-Benz	100th: Hungary 2014
Osella (k)	100th: Austria 1987
Shadow	100th: Netherlands 1979
Surtees	100th: United States 1977
Toro Rosso	100th: Hungary 2011
Toyota	100th: Italy 2007

(a) Includes Lancia-Ferrari & Thin Wall Special/ excludes Indianapolis 500. (b) Includes JPS Lotus. (c) Includes Iso-Marlboro, Politoys & Wolf-Williams. (d) Includes Footwork. (e) Includes Talbot-Ligier. (f) Includes BMW Sauber in 2010. (g) Includes Eifelland-March & Leyton House. (h) Includes Stanley-BRM. (i) Includes Copersucar. (j) Includes Virgin. (k) Includes Fomet & Fondmetal.

Chapter 17: Winning Constructors

686. Wins

		drivers		
Ferrari (a)	224	38	Britain 1951 (José Froilán González)	- Singapore 2015 (Sebastian Vettel)
McLaren	182	19	Belgium 1968 (Bruce McLaren)	- Brazil 2012 (Jenson Button)
Williams	114	16	Britain 1979 (Clay Regazzoni)	- Spain 2012 (Pastor Maldonado)
Lotus (b)	81	13	Monaco 1960 (Stirling Moss)	- Australia 2013 (Kimi Räikkönen)
Red Bull	50	3	China 2009 (Sebastian Vettel)	- Belgium 2014 (Daniel Ricciardo)
Mercedes-Benz	45	4	France 1954 (Juan Manuel Fangio)	- Abu Dhabi 2015 (Nico Rosberg)
Brabham	35	9	France 1964 (Dan Gurney)	- France 1985 (Nelson Piquet)
Renault	35	6	France 1979 (Jean-Pierre Jabouille)	- Japan 2008 (Fernando Alonso)
Benetton	27	5	Mexico 1986 (Gerhard Berger)	- Germany 1997 (Gerhard Berger)
Tyrrell	23	5	Spain 1971 (Jackie Stewart)	- Detroit 1983 (Michele Alboreto)
BRM	17	7	Netherlands 1959 (Jo Bonnier)	- Monaco 1972 (Jean-Pierre Beltoise)
Cooper	16	6	Argentina 1958 (Stirling Moss)	- South Africa 1967 (Pedro Rodríguez)
Alfa Romeo	10	3	Britain 1950 (Giuseppe Farina)	- Spain 1951 (Juan Manuel Fangio)

drivers				
Ligier (c)	9	4	Sweden 1977 (Jacques Laffite)	- Monaco 1996 (Olivier Panis)
Maserati	9	2	Italy 1953 (Juan Manuel Fangio)	- Germany 1957 (Juan Manuel Fangio)
Matra	9	1	Netherlands 1968 (Jackie Stewart)	- Italy 1969 (Jackie Stewart)
Vanwall	9	2	Britain 1957 (Stirling Moss, Tony Brooks)	- Morocco 1958 (Stirling Moss)
Brawn	8	2	Australia 2009 (Jenson Button)	- Italy 2009 (Rubens Barrichello)
Jordan	4	3	Belgium 1998 (Damon Hill)	- Brazil 2003 (Giancarlo Fisichella)
Honda	3	3	Mexico 1965 (Richie Ginther)	- Hungary 2006 (Jenson Button)
March	3	3	Spain 1970 (Jackie Stewart)	- Italy 1976 (Ronnie Peterson)
Wolf	3	1	Argentina 1977 (Jody Scheckter)	- Canada 1977 (Jody Scheckter)
BMW (d)	1	1	Canada 2008 (Rubert Kubica)	
Eagle	1	1	Belgium 1967 (Dan Gurney)	
Hesketh	1	1	Netherlands 1975 (James Hunt)	
Penske	1	1	Austria 1976 (John Watson)	
Porsche	1	1	France 1962 (Dan Gurney)	
Shadow	1	1	Austria 1977 (Alan Jones)	
Stewart	1	1	Europe 1999 (Johnny Herbert)	
Toro Rosso	1	1	Italy 2008 (Sebastian Vettel)	
Indianapolis 500				
Kurtis-Kraft	5	4	1950 (Johnnie Parsons)	- 1955 (Bob Sweikert)
Watson	3	3	1956 (Pat Flaherty)	- 1960 (Jim Rathmann)
Salih	2	2	1957 (Sam Hanks)	- 1958 (Jimmy Bryan)
Kuzma	1	1	1952 (Troy Ruttman)	

(a) Includes Lancia-Ferrari. (b) Includes JPS Lotus. (c) Includes Talbot-Ligier. (d) As BMW Sauber.

687. Percentage of races won *(Highest)*

	%	wins
Brawn	47.06	8
Mercedes-Benz	35.43	45
Vanwall	32.14	9
Ferrari	24.70	224
Red Bull	24.63	50

	%	wins
McLaren	23.33	182
Williams	16.47	114
Matra	14.52	9
Lotus	13.37	81
Maserati	13.24	9

688. Wins in a season *(Most)*

Mercedes-Benz	16 of 19	2014	(F1 W05)	(Lewis Hamilton, 11; Nico Rosberg, 5)
Mercedes-Benz	16 of 19	2015	(F1 W06)	(Lewis Hamilton, 10; Nico Rosberg, 6)
McLaren	15 of 16	1988	(MP4/4 - Honda)	(Ayrton Senna, 8; Alain Prost, 7)
Ferrari	15 of 17	2002	(F2001, F2002)	(Michael Schumacher, 11; Rubens Barrichello, 4)
Ferrari	15 of 18	2004	(F2004)	(Michael Schumacher, 13; Rubens Barrichello, 2)
Red Bull	13 of 19	2013	(RB9 - Renault)	(Sebastian Vettel)
McLaren	12 of 16	1984	(MP4/2 - TAG Porsche)	(Alain Prost, 7; Niki Lauda, 5)
Williams	12 of 16	1996	(FW18 - Renault)	(Damon Hill, 8; Jacques Villeneuve, 4)
Red Bull	12 of 19	2011	(RB7 - Renault)	(Sebastian Vettel, 11; Mark Webber, 1)
Benetton	11 of 17	1995	(B195 - Renault)	(Michael Schumacher, 9; Johnny Herbert, 2)

All became world champion constructor that season.

689. Wins in a season without becoming constructors' champion *(Most)*

McLaren	10 of 19	2005	(MP4-20 - Mercedes)	(Kimi Räikkönen, 7; Juan Pablo Montoya, 3)
Ferrari	9 of 18	2006	(248-F1)`	(Michael Schumacher, 7; Felipe Massa, 2)
Benetton	8 of 16	1994	(B194 - Ford Cosworth)	(Michael Schumacher)
McLaren	8 of 17	2007 (a)	(MP4-22 - Mercedes)	(Lewis Hamilton, 4; Fernando Alonso, 4)
McLaren	7 of 16	1999	(MP4-14 - Mercedes)	(Mika Häkkinen, 5; David Coulthard, 2)
Williams	7 of 16	1991	(FW14 - Renault)	(Nigel Mansell, 5; Riccardo Patrese, 2)
McLaren	7 of 17	2000	(MP4-15 - Mercedes)	(Mika Häkkinen, 4; David Coulthard, 3)
McLaren	7 of 20	2012	(MP4-27 - Mercedes)	(Lewis Hamilton, 4; Jenson Button, 3)
Ferrari	6 of 16	1990	(641, 641/2)	(Alain Prost, 5; Nigel Mansell, 1)
Ferrari	6 of 16	1998	(F300)	(Michael Schumacher)
McLaren	6 of 16	1976	(M23 - Ford Cosworth)	(James Hunt)
Red Bull	6 of 17	2009	(RB5 - Renault)	(Sebastian Vettel 4; Mark Webber 2)
McLaren	6 of 18	2008	(MP4-23 - Mercedes)	(Lewis Hamilton 5; Heikki Kovalainen 1)
McLaren	6 of 19	2011	(MP4-26 - Mercedes)	(Jenson Button 3; Lewis Hamilton 3)

(a) In 2007, McLaren were stripped of all their constructors' championship points, due to the spying scandal.

690. Won every race of a season

Ferrari	7	1952	(Ferrari 500)	(Alberto Ascari, 6; Piero Taruffi, 1)
Alfa Romeo	6	1950	(Alfa Romeo 158)	(Giuseppe Farina, 3; Juan Manuel Fangio, 3)

691. Won all but one race of a season

McLaren	15	1988	(MP4/4 - Honda)	(Ayrton Senna, 8; Alain Prost, 7)
Ferrari	7	1953	(500)	(Alberto Ascari, 5, Giuseppe Farina, 1; Mike Hawthorn, 1)
Mercedes-Benz	5	1955	(W196, W196 str.)	(Juan Manuel Fangio, 4; Stirling Moss, 1)

692. Consecutive wins (Most)

Ferrari	14	Switzerland 1952	- Switzerland 1953	(500)
McLaren	11	Brazil 1988	- Belgium 1988	(MP4/4 - Honda)
Ferrari	10	Canada 2002	- Japan 2002	(F2002)
Alfa Romeo	9	Britain 1950	- France 1951	(158, 159)
Red Bull	9	Belgium 2013	- Brazil 2013	(RB9 - Renault)
Ferrari	8	Italy 2003	- Spain 2004	(F2003-GA, F2004)
McLaren	8	Britain 1984	- Brazil 1985	(MP4/2, MP4/2B - TAG Porsche)
Mercedes-Benz	8	Italy 2014	- Australia 2015	(F1 W05, F1 W06)
Ferrari	7	Europe 2004	- Hungary 2004	(F2004)
Mercedes-Benz	7	China 2015	- Britain 2015	(F1 W06)
Williams	7	Canada 1993	- Italy 1993	(FW15C - Renault)

693. Won the seasons's opening race

Ferrari	13	Piero Taruffi 1952; Alberto Ascari 1953; Juan Manuel Fangio, Luigi Musso 1956 (a); Mario Andretti 1971; Niki Lauda 1976; Nigel Mansell 1989; Eddie Irvine 1999; Michael Schumacher 2000, 01, 02, 04; Kimi Räikkönen 2007; Fernando Alonso 2010
McLaren	13	Denny Hulme 1974; Emerson Fittipaldi 1975; Alain Prost 1984, 85, 87, 88; Ayrton Senna 1990, 91; David Coulthard 1997, 2003; Mika Häkkinen 1998; Lewis Hamilton 2008; Jenson Button 2012
Lotus	6	Stirling Moss 1961; Jim Clark 1965, 68; Emerson Fittipaldi 1973 (b); Mario Andretti 1978 (b); Kimi Räikkönen 2013
Williams	6	Alan Jones 1980, 81; Nelson Piquet 1986; Nigel Mansell 1992; Alain Prost 1993; Damon Hill 1996
BRM	4	Graham Hill 1962, 63, 64; Jackie Stewart 1966
Cooper	4	Stirling Moss 1958; Jack Brabham 1959; Bruce McLaren 1960; Pedro Rodríguez 1967
Mercedes-Benz	3	Juan Manuel Fangio 1955; Nico Rosberg 2014; Lewis Hamilton 2015
Renault	3	Alain Prost 1982; Giancarlo Fisichella 2005; Fernando Alonso 2006
Alfa Romeo	2	Giuseppe Farina 1950; Juan Manuel Fangio 1951
Benetton	2	Michael Schumacher 1994, 95
Brabham	2	Jack Brabham 1970; Nelson Piquet 1983
Maserati	2	Juan Manuel Fangio 1954, 57
Brawn	1	Jenson Button 2009
Ligier	1	Jacques Laffite 1979
Matra	1	Jackie Stewart 1969
Red Bull	1	Sebastian Vettel 2011
Tyrrell	1	Jackie Stewart 1972
Wolf	1	Jody Scheckter 1977

(a) As Lancia-Ferrari, shared drive. (b) As JPS Lotus.

694. Opening race their only win of the season

BRM	1966	(P261)	(Jackie Stewart)	Brabham	1970	(BT33 - Ford Cosworth)	(Jack Brabham)
Cooper	1967	(T81 - Maserati)	(Pedro Rodríguez)	Lotus	2013	(E21 - Renault)	(Kimi Räikkönen)

695. Won the opening race and became constructors' champion that season

Benetton - Renault	1995	McLaren - Honda	1988, 90, 91
Brawn - Mercedes	2009	McLaren - Mercedes	1998
BRM	1962	McLaren - TAG Porsche	1984, 85
Cooper - Climax	1959, 60	Mercedes-Benz	2014, 15
Ferrari	1976, 99, 2000, 01, 02, 04, 07	Red Bull - Renault	2011
Lotus - Climax	1965	Renault	2005, 06
Lotus - Ford Cosworth	1968, 73, 78	Williams - Ford Cosworth	1980, 81
Matra - Ford Cosworth	1969	Williams - Honda	1986
McLaren - Ford Cosworth	1974	Williams - Renault	1992, 93, 96

696. Consecutive wins from the start of a season *(Most)*
(not counting any into the following season)

McLaren	11	1988 (wc)	(MP4/4 - Honda)	(Ayrton Senna, 7; Alain Prost, 4)
Ferrari	7	1952 (a)	(500)	(Alberto Ascari, 6; Piero Taruffi, 1)
Ferrari	7	1953	(500)	(Alberto Ascari, 5; Giuseppe Farina, 1; Mike Hawthorn, 1)
Alfa Romeo	6	1950 (a)	(158)	(Juan Manuel Fangio, 3; Giuseppe Farina, 3)
Mercedes-Benz	6	2014 (wc)	(F1 W05)	(Lewis Hamilton, 4; Nico Rosberg, 2)
Ferrari	5	2004 (wc)	(F2004)	(Michael Schumacher)
Williams	5	1992 (wc)	(FW14B - Renault)	(Nigel Mansell)
Williams	5	1996 (wc)	(FW18 - Renault)	(Damon Hill, 4; Jacques Villeneuve, 1)
Benetton	4	1994	(B194 - Ford Cosworth)	(Michael Schumacher)
McLaren	4	1991 (wc)	(MP4/5B - Honda)	(Ayrton Senna)
Renault	4	2005 (wc)	(R25)	(Fernando Alonso, 3; Giancarlo Fisichella, 1)

(a) Sequence continued into the following season.
(wc) World champion constructor that season.

697. Impressive starts to the season and became champion
(apart from those in section 696)

Cooper	1960	won 6 of the first 7 races	(T51, T53 - Climax)
Ferrari	1961	won 4 of the first 5 races	(156)
Lotus	1963	won 4 of the first 5 races	(25 - Climax)
Lotus	1965	won 6 of the first 7 races	(33 - Climax)
Matra	1969	won 5 of the first 6 races	(MS10, MS80 - Ford Cosworth)
Ferrari	1976	won 5 of the first 6 races	(312T, 312T2)
McLaren	1984	won 5 of the first 6 races	(MP4/2 - TAG Porsche)
McLaren	1989	won 7 of the first 9 races	(MP4/5 - Honda)
McLaren	1998	won 5 of the first 6 races	(MP4-13 - Mercedes)
Ferrari	2002	won 5 of the first 6 races	(F2001, F2002)
Renault	2006	won 7 of the first 9 races	(R26)
Ferrari	2008	won 4 of the first 5 races	(F2008)
Brawn	2009	won 6 of the first 7 races	(BGP 001 - Mercedes)
Red Bull	2011	won 5 of the first 6 races	(RB7 - Renault)
Mercedes-Benz	2015	won 8 of the first 9 races	(F1 W06)

698. Impressive starts to the season, but failed to be champion

Lotus	1964	won 2 of the first 3 races	(25 - Climax)
Ferrari	1978	won 2 of the first 4 races	(312T2, T3)
Ligier	1979	won the first 2 races	(JS11 - Ford Cosworth)
Renault	1980	won 2 of the first 3 races	(RE20)
Brabham	1981	won 2 of the first 4 races	(BT49C - Ford Cosworth)
Renault	1982	won the first 2 races	(RE30B)
Lotus	1985	won 2 of the first 3 races	(97T - Renault)
McLaren	1986	won 2 of the first 4 races	(MP4/2 - TAG Porsche)
McLaren	1987	won 2 of the first 3 races	(MP4/3 - TAG Porsche)
McLaren	1993	won 2 of the first 3 races	(MP4/8 - Ford Cosworth)
Benetton	1994	won the first 4 races	(B194 - Ford Cosworth)
Williams	1995	won 2 of the first 3 races	(FW17 - Renault)
McLaren	2003	won the first 2 races	(MP4-17D - Mercedes)

699. Winner of the opening race which finished lowest in that season's championship

BRM	1966	(4th in championship)		McLaren - Ford Cosworth	1975	(3rd)
Brabham - Ford Cosworth	1970	(4th)		Ligier - Ford Cosworth	1979	(3rd)
Wolf - Ford Cosworth	1977	(4th)		Renault	1982	(3rd)
McLaren - Mercedes	1997	(4th)		Brabham - BMW	1983	(3rd)
Lotus - Renault	2013	(4th)		Ferrari	1989	(3rd)
Cooper - Climax	1958	(3rd)		McLaren - Mercedes	2003	(3rd)
Cooper - Maserati	1967	(3rd)		Ferrari	2010	(3rd)
Ferrari	1971	(3rd)		McLaren - Mercedes	2012	(3rd)

700. Seasons of winning *(Most)*

Ferrari	53	1951 - 2015		Benetton	9	1986 - 97
McLaren	36	1968 - 2012		BRM	9	1959 - 72
Lotus	23	1960 - 2013		Tyrrell	9	1971 - 83
Williams	23	1979 - 2012		Cooper	6	1958 - 67
Brabham	14	1964 - 85		Mercedes-Benz	6	1954 - 2015
Renault	10	1979 - 2008		Red Bull	6	2009 - 14

701. Consecutive seasons of winning *(Most)*

Ferrari	20	1994 - 2013		Ferrari	6	1974 - 79
McLaren	13	1981 - 93		JPS Lotus	6	1972 - 78
Lotus	11	1960 - 70		McLaren	6	1972 - 77
Williams	9	1979 - 87		McLaren	6	2000 - 05
Williams	9	1989 - 97		McLaren	6	2007 - 12
Benetton	7	1989 - 95		Red Bull	6	2009 - 14
Brabham	6	1980 - 85		Tyrrell	6	1971 - 76
Ferrari	6	1951 - 56 (a)				

(a) As Lancia-Ferrari in 1956.

702. Wins at the same venue *(Most)*

grand prix

Ferrari	21	Germany	1951 - 2012 (a)	(Hockenheim, 11; Nürburgring, 9; AVUS, 1)
Ferrari	18	Italy	1951 - 2010	(Monza)
Ferrari	17	France	1952 - 2008 (a)	(Magny-Cours, 8; Reims, 5; Paul Ricard, 2; Rouen-les-Essarts, 2)
Ferrari	16	Belgium	1952 - 2009 (a)	(Spa-Francorchamps, 12; Zolder, 4)
Ferrari	16	Britain	1951 - 2011	(Silverstone, 13; Brands Hatch, 2; Aintree, 1)
McLaren	15	Monaco	1984 - 2008	(Monte-Carlo)
McLaren	14	Belgium	1968 - 2012	(Spa-Francorchamps, 12; Nivelles-Baulers, 1; Zolder, 1)
McLaren	14	Britain	1973 - 2008	(Silverstone, 12; Brands Hatch, 2)
McLaren	13	Canada	1968 - 2012	(Montréal, 9; Mosport Park, 3; Mont-Tremblant, 1)
Ferrari	12	Spain	1954 - 2013	(Catalunya, 8; Jarama, 2; Jerez de la Fontera, 1; Pedralbes, 1)
McLaren	12	Brazil	1974 - 2012	(Interlagos, 8; Jacarepaguá, 4)

circuit

Ferrari	18	Monza	1951 - 2010
McLaren	15	Monte-Carlo	1984 - 2008
Ferrari	14	Nürburgring	1951 - 2006 (a)(b)
Ferrari	13	Silverstone	1951 - 2011
Ferrari	12	Spa-Francorchamps	1952 - 2009 (a)
McLaren	12	Silverstone	1973 - 2008
Ferrari	11	Hockenheim	1977 - 2012
McLaren	11	Hungaroring	1988 - 2012
McLaren	11	Spa-Francorchamps	1968 - 2012
Ferrari	10	Montréal	1978 - 2004
McLaren	10	Monza	1968 - 2012

(a) As Lancia-Ferrari in one race.
(b) Includes 5 European Grands Prix.

703. Consecutive wins at the same venue *(Most)*

McLaren	Monaco	6	1988 - 93	(Monte-Carlo)
Ferrari	Japan	5	2000 - 04	(Suzuka)
Ferrari	United States	5	2002 - 06	(Indianapolis)
McLaren	Belgium	5	1987 - 91	(Spa-Francorchamps)
BRM	Monaco	4	1963 - 66	(Monte-Carlo)
Ferrari	Australia	4	1999 - 2002	(Melbourne)
Ferrari	Britain	4	1951 - 54	(Silverstone)
Ferrari	Spain	4	2001 - 04	(Catalunya)
Lotus	Belgium	4	1962 - 65	(Spa-Francorchamps)
Lotus	Britain	4	1962 - 65	(Silverstone, 2; Aintree, 1; Brands Hatch, 1)
Williams	Britain	4	1991 - 94	(Silverstone)
Williams	Spain	4	1991 - 94	(Catalunya)

704. Races taken to achieve their first win
(number of races relates to those started and includes the first race won)

Alfa Romeo	1	McLaren	14	Ligier	24
Brawn	1	Vanwall	14	Maserati	25 (a)
Mercedes-Benz	1	Benetton	15	Renault	25
Wolf	1	BRM	16	BMW	42
March	2	Brabham	17	Stewart	47
Tyrrell	5	Lotus	19	Toro Rosso	49
Ferrari	9 (a)	Porsche	20 (b)	Shadow	69
Matra	10 (b)	Hesketh	21	Red Bull	74
Honda	11	Cooper	23 (c)	Williams	81
Eagle	12	Penske	23	Jordan	127

(a) Excludes Indianapolis 500. (b) In 2 races, the constructor only ran Formula 2 cars. (c) In 1 race, the constructor only ran Formula 2 cars. For most races started but never a win, see section 678.

705. 2nd places before their first win

Ferrari	5	McLaren	1	Lotus	0
BMW	4	Stewart	1	March	0
Maserati	4	Tyrrell	1	Matra	0
Brabham	3	Vanwall	1	Mercedes-Benz	0
Porsche	3	Alfa Romeo	0	Penske	0
Williams	3	Benetton	0	Red Bull	0
Jordan	2	Brawn	0	Renault	0
BRM	1	Cooper	0	Shadow	0
Hesketh	1	Eagle	0	Toro Rosso	0
Ligier	1	Honda	0	Wolf	0

706. Races with a podium position before their first win

BMW	8	Red Bull	3	Alfa Romeo	0
Maserati	8	Stewart	3	Brawn	0
Ferrari	6	Penske	2	Eagle	0
Brabham	5	Benetton	1	Honda	0
Jordan	5	BRM	1	Lotus	0
Shadow	5	Cooper	1	Matra	0
Hesketh	4	March	1	Mercedes-Benz	0
Williams	4	McLaren	1	Renault	0
Ligier	3	Tyrrell	1	Toro Rosso	0
Porsche	3	Vanwall	1	Wolf	0

707. Pole positions before their first win

Shadow	3	Stewart	1	Williams	1 *
Renault	2 *	Alfa Romeo	1 *	Cooper	0
Benetton	2	Brawn	1 *	Eagle	0
Brabham	2	BRM	1 *	Hesketh	0
Maserati	2	Ferrari	1 *	Honda	0
Tyrrell	2	Lotus	1 *	Matra	0
BMW	1	Mercedes-Benz	1 *	McLaren	0
Jordan	1	Red Bull	1 *	Penske	0
Ligier	1	Toro Rosso	1 *	Porsche	0
March	1	Vanwall	1 *	Wolf	0

* Includes the pole achieved in the race of that first win.

708. Led every lap in the race of their first win

Williams	Britain 1979	(FW07 - Ford Cosworth)	(Alan Jones, Clay Regazzoni)
Alfa Romeo	Britain 1950	(158)	(Giuseppe Farina, Luigi Fagioli, Juan Manuel Fangio)
Mercedes-Benz	France 1954	(W196 str.)	(Karl Kling, Juan Manuel Fangio)
Brawn	Australia 2009	(BGP 001 - Mercedes)	(Jenson Button)
Honda	Mexico 1965	(RA272 - Honda)	(Richie Ginther)
March	Spain 1970	(701 - Ford Cosworth)	(Jackie Stewart)

709. Wins in their first season

Brawn	8 of 17	2009	(BGP 001 - Mercedes)	(Jenson Button, 6; Rubens Barrichello, 2)
Alfa Romeo	6 of 6	1950	(158)	(Juan Manuel Fangio, 3; Giuseppe Farina, 3)
Mercedes-Benz	4 of 9	1954	(W196, W196 str.)	(Juan Manuel Fangio)
Wolf	3 of 17	1977	(WR1 - Ford Cosworth)	(Jody Scheckter)
March	1 of 13	1970	(701 - Ford Cosworth)	(Jackie Stewart)
Benetton	1 of 16	1986	(B186 - BMW)	(Gerhard Berger)

710. First win immediately followed by others
(including first win)

Alfa Romeo	9	Britain 1950 - France 1951	(158, 159)	(Luigi Fagioli, Juan Manuel Fangio, Giuseppe Farina)
Williams	4	Britain - Netherlands 1979	(FW07 - Ford Cosworth)	(Clay Regazzoni, Alan Jones)
Ferrari	3	Britain - Italy 1951	(375)	(José Froilán González, Alberto Ascari)
Maserati	3	Italy 1953 - Belgium 1954	(A6GCM, 250F)	(Juan Manuel Fangio)
Brawn	2	Australia - Malaysia 2009	(BGP 001 - Mercedes)	(Jenson Button)
Cooper	2	Argentina - Monaco 1958	(T34, T45 - Climax)	(Stirling Moss, Maurice Trintignant)
Tyrrell	2	Spain - Monaco 1971	(003 - Ford Cosworth)	(Mario Andretti, Jackie Stewart)

711. Wins in their final season

Brawn	8	2009	(BGP 001 - Mercedes)	(Jenson Button, 6; Rubens Barrichello, 2)
Ligier	1	1996	(JS43 - Mugen Honda)	(Olivier Panis)
Stewart	1	1999	(SF-3 - Ford Cosworth)	(Johnny Herbert)

712. More than one win in a country during a season

Vanwall	1957	Italy	Stirling Moss (Pescara & Monza)
Ferrari	1978	United States	Carlos Reutemann (Long Beach & Watkins Glen)
Ferrari	1979	United States	Gilles Villeneuve (Long Beach & Watkins Glen)
Williams	1981	United States	Alan Jones (Long Beach & Caesars Palace)
McLaren	1982	United States	Niki Lauda (Long Beach) & John Watson (Detroit)
McLaren	1984	Germany	Alain Prost (Hockenheim & Nürburgring)
McLaren	1984	Italy	Alain Prost (Imola) & Niki Lauda (Monza)
Williams	1987	Italy	Nigel Mansell (Imola) & Nelson Piquet (Moza)
McLaren	1989	Italy	Ayrton Senna (Imola) & Alain Prost (Monza)
Williams	1993	Italy	Alain Prost (Imola) & Damon Hill (Monza)
Benetton	1995	Germany	Michael Schumacher (Hockenheim & Nürburgring)
Benetton	1995	Japan	Michael Schumacher (Aida & Suzuka)
Williams	1996	Germany	Jacques Villeneuve (Nürburgring) & Damon Hill (Hockenheim)
McLaren	1998	Germany	Mika Häkkinen (Hockenheim & Nürburgring)
Ferrari	2000	Italy	Michael Schumacher (Imola & Monza)
Ferrari	2000	Germany	Ferrari (Nürburgring & Hockenheim)
Williams	2001	Italy	Williams (Imola & Monza)
Ferrari	2002	Germany	Rubens Barrichello (Nürburgring) & Michael Schumacher (Hockenheim)
Ferrari	2002	Italy	Michael Schumacher (Imola) & Rubens Barrichello (Monza)
Ferrari	2003	Italy	Michael Schumacher (Imola & Monza)
Williams	2003	Germany	Ralf Schumacher (Nürburgring) & Juan Pablo Montoya (Hockenheim)
Ferrari	2004	Germany	Michael Schumacher (Nürburgring & Hockenheim)
Ferrari	2004	Italy	Michael Schumacher (Imola) & Rubens Barrichello (Monza)
Renault	2005	Germany	Fernando Alonso (Nürburgring & Hockenheim)
Ferrari	2006	Germany	Michael Schumacher (Nürburgring & Hockenheim)
Ferrari	2006	Italy	Michael Schumacher (Imola & Monza)
Ferrari	2008	Spain	Kimi Räikkönen (Catalunya) & Felipe Massa (Valencia)
Brawn	2009	Spain	Jenson Button (Catalunya) & Rubens Barrichello (Valencia)
Red Bull	2010	Spain	Mark Webber (Catalunya) & Sebastian Vettel (Valencia)
Red Bull	2011	Spain	Sebastian Vettel (Catalunya & Valencia)

713. Races with a win & pole position
(not necessarily the same car from pole to the win)

Ferrari (a)	124	Britain 1951	- Singapore 2015
McLaren	90	Brazil 1974	- Brazil 2012
Williams	70	Britain 1979	- Spain 2012
Lotus (b)	47	Monaco 1960	- Detroit 1986
Mercedes-Benz	41	France 1954	- Abu Dhabi 2015
Red Bull	38	China 2009	- Brazil 2013
Renault	24	France 1979	- Canada 2006
Brabham	11	Britain 1966	- Detroit 1984
Cooper	10	Monaco 1959	- Mexico 1966
Tyrrell	10	Monaco 1971	- Sweden 1976
Alfa Romeo	9	Britain 1950	- France 1951
Benetton	7	Monaco 1994	- Germany 1997
BRM	5	Netherlands 1959	- Austria 1971
Maserati	5	Belgium 1954	- Germany 1957
Vanwall	5	Britain 1957	- Italy 1958
Brawn	4	Australia 2009	- Monaco 2009
Ligier	3	Argentina 1979	- Spain 1979
Matra	1	France 1969	
Toro Rosso	1	Italy 2008	
Indianapolis 500			
Kurtis-Kraft	4	1950	- 1954
Watson	1	1956	

(a) Includes Lancia-Ferrari.
(b) Includes JPS Lotus.

714. Consecutive races with a win & pole position *(Most)*

Alfa Romeo	9	Britain 1950	- France 1951	(158, 159)
Ferrari	9	Switzerland 1952	- Netherlands 1953	(500)
Mercedes-Benz	8	Italy 2014	- Australia 2015	(F1 W05, F1 W06)
Red Bull	8	Italy 2013	- Brazil 2013	(RB9 - Renault)
McLaren	7	Brazil 1988	- France 1988	(MP4/4 - Honda)
Mercedes-Benz	7	China 2015	- Britain 2015	(F1 W06)
Williams	7	Canada 1993	- Italy 1993	(FW15C - Renault)
Ferrari	6	Italy 2000	- Malaysia 2001	(F1 2000, F2001)
Mercedes-Benz	6	Australia 2014	- Monaco 2014	(F1 W05)
Mercedes-Benz	6	Japan 2015	- Abu Dhabi 2015	(F1 W06)
Williams	6	France 1987	- Italy 1987	(FW11B - Honda)

Winner from lowest grid position. See section 234

715. Different winners in a season

Most

1982	7	Renault, McLaren, Ferrari, Brabham, Lotus, Williams, Tyrrell
1975	6	McLaren, Brabham, Tyrrell, Ferrari, Hesketh, March
1976	6	Ferrari, McLaren, Tyrrell, Penske, March, JPS Lotus
1977	6	Wolf, Ferrari, JPS Lotus, Ligier, McLaren, Shadow
1981	6	Williams, Brabham, Ferrari, Renault, McLaren, Talbot-Ligier
1983	6	Brabham, McLaren, Renault, Ferrari, Williams, Tyrrell
2012	6	McLaren, Ferrari, Mercedes-Benz, Red Bull, Williams, Lotus
1966	5	BRM, Ferrari, Brabham, Lotus, Cooper
1967	5	Cooper, Brabham, Lotus, Eagle, Honda
1970	5	Brabham, March, Lotus, BRM, Ferrari
1972	5	Tyrrell, McLaren, JPS Lotus, BRM, Ferrari
1974	5	McLaren, Brabham, Ferrari, JPS Lotus, Tyrrell
1985	5	McLaren, Lotus, Ferrari, Williams, Brabham
2003	5	McLaren, Jordan, Ferrari, Williams, Renault
2008	5	McLaren, Ferrari, BMW Sauber, Toro Rosso, Renault

1950	1	Alfa Romeo
1952	1	Ferrari
1951	2	Alfa Romeo, Ferrari
1953	2	Ferrari, Maserati
1955	2	Mercedes-Benz, Ferrari
1956	2	Lancia-Ferrari, Maserati
1957	2	Maserati, Vanwall

1961	2	Lotus, Ferrari
1988	2	McLaren, Ferrari
2000	2	Ferrari, McLaren
2007	2	Ferrari, McLaren
2014	2	Mercedes-Benz, Red Bull
2015	2	Mercedes-Benz, Ferrari

Total for each season

1950 - 1, 1951 - 2, 1952 - 1, 1953 - 2, 1954 - 3, 1955 - 2, 1956 - 2, 1957 - 2, 1958 - 3, 1959 - 3, 1960 - 3, 1961 - 2, 1962 - 4, 1963 - 3, 1964 - 4, 1965 - 3, 1966 - 5, 1967 - 5, 1968 - 4, 1969 - 4, 1970 - 5, 1971 - 3, 1972 - 5, 1973 - 3, 1974 - 5, 1975 - 6, 1976 - 6, 1977 - 6, 1978 - 4, 1979 - 4, 1980 - 4, 1981 - 6, 1982 - 7, 1983 - 6, 1984 - 4, 1985 - 5, 1986 - 4, 1987 - 4, 1988 - 2, 1989 - 4, 1990 - 4, 1991 - 3, 1992 - 3, 1993 - 3, 1994 - 3, 1995 - 3, 1996 - 3, 1997 - 4, 1998 - 3, 1999 - 4, 2000 - 2, 2001 - 3, 2002 - 3, 2003 - 5, 2004 - 4, 2005 - 3, 2006 - 3, 2007 - 2, 2008 - 5, 2009 - 4, 2010 - 3, 2011 - 3, 2012 - 6, 2013 - 4, 2014 - 2, 2015 - 2

Excludes Indianapolis 500.

716. Different winners in consecutive races *(Most)*

Germany 1982 - United States West 1983	7	Ferrari, Lotus, Williams, Renault, Tyrrell, Brabham, McLaren
Caesars Palace 1982 - Monaco 1983	6	Tyrrell, Brabham, McLaren, Renault, Ferrari, Williams
Mexico 1969 - Belgium 1970	5	McLaren, Brabham, March, Lotus, BRM
South Africa - Sweden 1974	5	Brabham, Ferrari, McLaren, JPS Lotus, Ferrari
Britain - Canada 1974	5	Tyrrell, Ferrari, Brabham, JPS Lotus, McLaren
Netherlands - Austria 1975	5	Hesketh, Ferrari, McLaren, Brabham, March
Sweden - Austria 1977	5	Ligier, JPS Lotus, McLaren, Ferrari, Shadow
Austria - Canada 1977	5	Shadow, Ferrari, JPS Lotus, McLaren, Wolf
Spain - Austria 1981	5	Ferrari, Renault, McLaren, Brabham, Talbot-Ligier
Britain - Switzerland 1982	5	McLaren, Renault, Ferrari, Lotus, Williams
San Marino - France 1985	5	Lotus, McLaren, Ferrari, Williams, Brabham
Australia - Spain 2012	5	McLaren, Ferrari, Mercedes-Benz, Red Bull, Williams

717. Different winners from the start of a season *(Most)*

1983	5	Brabham, McLaren, Renault, Ferrari, Williams
2012	5	McLaren, Ferrari, Mercedes-Benz, Red Bull, Williams
1962	4	BRM, Cooper, Lotus, Porsche
1967	4	Cooper, Brabham, Lotus, Eagle
1970	4	Brabham, March, Lotus, BRM
1972	4	Tyrrell, McLaren, JPS Lotus, BRM
1959	3	Cooper, BRM, Ferrari

1966	3	BRM, Ferrari, Brabham
1975	3	McLaren, Brabham, Tyrrell
1986	3	Williams, Lotus, McLaren
1990	3	McLaren, Ferrari, Williams
2010	3	Ferrari, McLaren, Red Bull
2013	3	Lotus, Red Bull, Ferrari

718. First time winners in a season *(Most)*

1977	3	Wolf, Ligier, Shadow
1968	2	McLaren, Matra
1979	2	Renault, Williams

2008	2	BMW, Toro Rosso
2009	2	Brawn, Red Bull

719. Races won without leading a lap!

Of the seven cases shown at section 244, only the following constructors had none of their cars leading during a race that they won:

Brabham	Italy 1978	Niki Lauda inherited the win due to Andretti/ Villeneuve penalties. See section 554.
Renault	Brazil 1982	Alain Prost inherited the win due to Piquet/ Rosberg disqualifications. See section 552.

720. First win for nationality of constructor

Italy	Britain 1950	(Alfa Romeo)	(Giuseppe Farina)
Germany	France 1954	(Mercedes-Benz)	(Juan Manuel Fangio)
Great Britain	Britain 1957	(Vanwall)	(Tony Brooks, Stirling Moss)
Japan	Mexico 1965	(Honda)	(Richie Ginther)
United States	Belgium 1967	(Eagle)	(Dan Gurney)
France	Netherlands 1968	(Matra)	(Jackie Stewart)
Canada	Argentina 1977	(Wolf) (a)	(Jody Scheckter)
Austria	China 2009	(Red Bull) (b)	(Sebastian Vettel)

(a) Joint Canadian/ British. (b) Joint Austrian/ British.

721. Rear/ front-engined car winners

First rear-engined winner

Cooper T43 with a 4-cylinder Climax engine (driven by Stirling Moss): Argentina 1958.

Last front-engined winner

Ferrari Dino 246 with V6 engine (driven by Phil Hill): Italy 1960.

722. Winning drivers by constructor

Alfa Romeo: Juan Manuel Fangio, 6; Giuseppe Farina, 4; Luigi Fagioli, 1

Benetton: Michael Schumacher, 19; Nelson Piquet, 3; Gerhard Berger, 2; Johnny Herbert, 2; Alessandro Nannini, 1

BMW *(as BMW Sauber):*   Robert Kubica, 1

Brabham: Nelson Piquet, 13; Jack Brabham, 7; Carlos Reutemann, 4; Dan Gurney, 2; Denny Hulme, 2; Jacky Ickx, 2; Niki Lauda, 2; Riccardo Patrese, 2; Carlos Pace, 1

Brawn: Jenson Button, 6; Rubens Barrichello, 2

BRM: Graham I Iill, 10; Jackie Stewart, 2; Jean-Pierre Beltoise, 1; Jo Bonnier, 1; Peter Gethin, 1; Pedro Rodríguez, 1; Jo Siffert, 1

Cooper: Jack Brabham, 7; Bruce McLaren, 3; Stirling Moss, 3; Pedro Rodríguez, 1; John Surtees, 1; Maurice Trintignant, 1

Eagle: Dan Gurney, 1

Ferrari: Michael Schumacher, 72; Niki Lauda, 15; Alberto Ascari, 13; Fernando Alonso, 11; Felipe Massa, 11; Rubens Barrichello, 9; Kimi Räikkönen, 9; Jacky Ickx, 6; Gilles Villeneuve, 6; Gerhard Berger, 5; Alain Prost, 5; Carlos Reutemann, 5; Eddie Irvine, 4; Clay Regazzoni, 4; John Surtees, 4; Michele Alboreto, 3; René Arnoux, 3; Juan Manuel Fangio, 3 (a); Mike Hawthorn, 3; Phil Hill, 3; Nigel Mansell, 3; Jody Scheckter, 3; Peter Collins, 3 (a); Sebastian Vettel, 3; Tony Brooks, 2; José Froilán González, 2; Didier Pironi, 2; Patrick Tambay, 2; Wolfgang von Trips, 2; Jean Alesi, 1; Mario Andretti, 1; Giancarlo Baghetti, 1; Lorenzo Bandini, 1; Giuseppe Farina, 1; Luigi Musso, 1 (a); Ludovico Scarfiotti, 1; Piero Taruffi, 1; Maurice Trintignant, 1
(a) Inc. Lancia-Ferrari.

Hesketh: James Hunt, 1

Honda: Jenson Button, 1; Richie Ginther, 1; John Surtees, 1

Jordan: Heinz-Harald Frentzen, 2; Giancarlo Fisichella, 1; Damon Hill, 1

Ligier: Jacques Laffite, 6 (inc. Talbot-Ligier); Patrick Depailler, 1; Olivier Panis, 1; Didier Pironi, 1

Lotus: Jim Clark, 25; Mario Andretti, 11 (a); Emerson Fittipaldi, 9 (a); Ronnie Peterson, 9 (a); Jochen Rindt, 6; Ayrton Senna, 6; Graham Hill, 4; Stirling Moss, 4; Elio De Angelis, 2; Kimi Räikkönen, 2; Innes Ireland, 1; Gunnar Nilsson, 1 (a); Jo Siffert, 1
(a) Inc. JPS Lotus.

March: Vittorio Brambilla, 1; Ronnie Peterson, 1; Jackie Stewart, 1

Maserati: Juan Manuel Fangio, 7; Stirling Moss, 2

Matra: Jackie Stewart, 9

McLaren: Ayrton Senna, 35; Alain Prost, 30; Lewis Hamilton, 21; Mika Häkkinen, 20; David Coulthard, 12; James Hunt, 9; Kimi Räikkönen, 9; Jenson Button, 8; Niki Lauda, 8; Denny Hulme, 6; Emerson Fittipaldi, 5; Fernando Alonso, 4; John Watson, 4; Gerhard Berger, 3; Juan Pablo Montoya, 3; Peter Revson, 2; Heikki Kovalainen, 1; Jochen Mass, 1; Bruce McLaren, 1

Mercedes-Benz: Lewis Hamilton, 22; Nico Rosberg, 14; Juan Manuel Fangio, 8; Stirling Moss, 1

Penske: John Watson, 1

Porsche: Dan Gurney, 1

Red Bull: Sebastian Vettel, 38; Mark Webber, 9; Daniel Ricciardo, 3

Renault: Fernando Alonso, 17; Alain Prost, 9; René Arnoux, 4; Giancarlo Fisichella, 2; Jean-Pierre Jabouille, 2; Jarno Trulli, 1

Shadow: Alan Jones, 1

Stewart: Johnny Herbert, 1

Toro Rosso: Sebastian Vettel, 1

Tyrrell: Jackie Stewart, 15; Jody Scheckter, 4; Michele Alboreto, 2; François Cevert, 1; Patrick Depailler, 1

Vanwall: Stirling Moss, 6; Tony Brooks, 4

Williams: Nigel Mansell, 28; Damon Hill, 21; Alan Jones, 11; Jacques Villeneuve, 11; Nelson Piquet, 7; Alain Prost, 7; Ralf Schumacher, 6; Keke Rosberg, 5; Juan Pablo Montoya, 4; Riccardo Patrese, 4; Thierry Boutsen, 3; Carlos Reutemann, 3; David Coulthard, 1; Heinz-Harald Frentzen, 1; Pastor Maldonado, 1; Clay Regazzoni, 1

Wolf: Jody Scheckter, 3

The total for some constructors is higher than in section 686 "Wins", due to drivers sharing a car. Those affected are Alfa Romeo, Ferrari and Vanwall.

723. Wins with the same engine make *(Most)*

Ferrari	224	Ferrari	Britain 1951 (José Froilán González)	-	Singapore 2015 (Sebastian Vettel)
McLaren	78	Mercedes	Australia 1997 (David Coulthard)	-	Belgium 2012 (Lewis Hamilton)
Williams	64	Renault	Canada 1989 (Thierry Boutsen)	-	Spain 2012 (Pastor Maldonado)
Red Bull	50	Renault	China 2009 (Sebastian Vettel)	-	Belgium 2014 (Daniel Ricciardo)
Lotus	47	Ford Cosworth	Netherlands 1967 (Jim Clark)	-	Austria 1982 (Elio De Angelis)
Mercedes-Benz	45	Mercedes	France 1954 (Juan Manuel Fangio)	-	Abu Dhabi 2015 (Nico Rosberg)
McLaren	44	Honda	Brazil 1988 (Alain Prost)	-	Australia 1992 (Gerhard Berger)
McLaren	35	Ford Cosworth	Belgium 1968 (Bruce McLaren)	-	Australia 1993 (Ayrton Senna)
Renault	35	Renault	France 1979 (Jean-Pierre Jabouille)	-	Japan 2008 (Fernando Alonso)
McLaren	25	TAG Porsche	Brazil 1984 (Alain Prost)	-	Portugal 1987 (Alain Prost)

For complete list of winning constructors by engine make, see section 980.

Overall

Alfa Romeo:	Alfa Romeo, 10
Benetton:	Ford Cosworth, 14; Renault, 12; BMW, 1
BMW:	BMW, 1
Brabham:	Ford Cosworth, 15; BMW, 8; Repco, 8; Alfa Romeo, 2; Climax, 2
Brawn:	Mercedes-Benz, 8
BRM:	BRM, 17
Cooper:	Climax, 14; Maserati, 2
Eagle:	Weslake, 1
Ferrari:	Ferrari, 224
Hesketh:	Ford Cosworth, 1
Honda:	Honda, 3
Jordan:	Mugen Honda, 3; Ford Cosworth, 1
Ligier:	Ford Cosworth, 5; Matra, 3 (as Talbot-Ligier); Mugen Honda, 1
Lotus:	Ford Cosworth, 47; Climax, 24; Renault, 7; Honda, 2; BRM, 1
March:	Ford Cosworth, 3

Maserati:	Maserati, 9
Matra:	Ford Cosworth, 9
McLaren:	Mercedes-Benz, 78; Honda, 44; Ford Cosworth, 35; TAG Porsche, 25
Mercedes-Benz:	Mercedes-Benz, 45
Penske:	Ford Cosworth, 1
Porsche:	Porsche, 1
Red Bull:	Renault, 50
Renault:	Renault, 35
Shadow:	Ford Cosworth, 1
Stewart:	Ford Cosworth, 1
Toro Rosso:	Ferrari, 1
Tyrrell:	Ford Cosworth, 23
Vanwall:	Vanwall, 9
Williams:	Renault, 64; Honda, 23; Ford Cosworth, 17; BMW, 10
Wolf:	Ford Cosworth, 3

724. Interval between wins (Longest)

	years, days	races		
Mercedes-Benz (a)	56y, 217d	813	Italy 1955 (Juan Manuel Fangio)	- China 2012 (Nico Rosberg)
Honda (a)	38y, 330d	604	Italy 1967 (John Surtees)	- Hungary 2006 (Jenson Button)
Lotus (a)	25y, 136d	435	Detroit 1987 (Ayrton Senna)	- Abu Dhabi 2012 (Kimi Räikkönen)
Renault (a)	20y, 10d	326	Austria 1983 (Alain Prost)	- Hungary 2003 (Fernando Alonso)
Ligier (b)	14y, 235d	231	Canada 1981 (Jacques Laffite)	- Monaco 1996 (Olivier Panis)
Williams	7y, 202d	132	Brazil 2004 (Juan Pablo Montoya)	- Spain 2012 (Pastor Maldonado)
March	5y, 120d	76	Spain 1970 (Jackie Stewart)	- Austria 1975 (Vittorio Brambilla)
Cooper	4y, 142d	46	Monaco 1962 (Bruce McLaren)	- Mexico 1966 (John Surtees)
Tyrrell	4y, 141d	71	Monaco 1978 (Patrick Depailler)	- Caesars Palace 1982 (Michele Alboreto)
Brabham	4y, 23d	53	South Africa 1970 (Jack Brabham)	- South Africa 1974 (Carlos Reutemann)

(a) Not present throughout the period.
(b) As Talbot-Ligier at Canada 1981.

725. Interval between first & second wins

Shortest

	days		
Brawn	7	Australia 2009 (Jenson Button)	- Malaysia 2009 (Jenson Button) (a)
Alfa Romeo	8	Britain 1950 (Giuseppe Farina)	- Monaco 1950 (Juan Manuel Fangio) (a)
Ferrari	15	Britain 1951 (José Froilán González)	- Germany 1951 (Alberto Ascari) (a)
Williams	15	Britain 1979 (Clay Regazzoni)	- Germany 1979 (Alan Jones) (a)
Mercedes-Benz	28	France 1954 (Juan Manuel Fangio)	- Germany 1954 (Juan Manuel Fangio)
Vanwall	29	Britain 1957 (Stirling Moss, Tony Brooks)	- Pescara 1957 (Stirling Moss)
Tyrrell	35	Spain 1971 (Jackie Stewart)	- Monaco 1971 (Jackie Stewart) (a)
Matra	42	Netherlands 1968 (Jackie Stewart)	- Germany 1968 (Jackie Stewart)
Red Bull	63	China 2009 (Sebastian Vettel)	- Britain 2009 (Sebastian Vettel)
McLaren	91	Belgium 1968 (Bruce McLaren)	- Italy 1968 (Denny Hulme)

(a) Consecutive races.

Longest

	years, days	races		
March	5y, 120d	76	Spain 1970 (Jackie Stewart)	- Austria 1975 (Vittorio Brambilla)
Benetton	3y, 10d	48	Mexico 1986 (Gerhard Berger)	- Japan 1989 (Alessandro Nannini)
BRM	2y, 354d	25	Netherlands 1959 (Jo Bonnier)	- Netherlands 1962 (Graham Hill)
Honda	1y, 321d	18	Mexico 1965 (Richie Ginther)	- Italy 1967 (John Surtees)
Ligier	1y, 216d	26	Sweden 1977 (Jacques Laffite)	- Argentina 1979 (Jacques Laffite)

726. Interval between first & last wins *(Longest)*

	years, days	races		
Ferrari	64y, 68d	917	Britain 1951	- Singapore 2015
Mercedes-Benz	61y, 148d	899	France 1954	- Abu Dhabi 2015
Lotus	52y, 292d	793	Monaco 1960	- Australia 2013
McLaren	44y, 169d	713	Belgium 1968	- Brazil 2012
Honda	40y, 286d	622	Mexico 1965	- Hungary 2006
Williams	32y, 304d	541	Britain 1979	- Spain 2012
Renault	29y, 103d	480	France 1979	- Japan 2008
Brabham	21y, 9d	286	France 1964	- France 1985
Ligier	18y, 335d	299	Sweden 1977	- Monaco 1996
BRM	12y, 349d	134	Netherlands 1959	- Monaco 1972

727. Interval between first time winners *(Longest)*

11 years and 322 days, from Mexico 1986 (12 October, Benetton) until Belgium 1998 (30 August, Jordan).

728. Wins but never a constructors' championship *(Most)*

Alfa Romeo	10 (a)	Jordan	4	Wolf	3
Ligier	9	Honda	3		
Maserati	9 (a)	March	3		

(a) All achieved before constructors' championship established.

729. Wins but never a drivers' championship *(Most)*

Ligier	9	Jordan	4	March	3
Vanwall	9	Honda	3	Wolf	3

730. Wins but never a pole position

Eagle	1	Hesketh	1	Penske	1

731. Wins but never a fastest lap

Penske	1	Stewart	1
Porsche	1	Toro Rosso	1

Winning speed *(Fastest/ Slowest).* See section 253
Winning margin *(Largest/ Smallest).* See section 254
First and last winners of each decade. See section 255

732. Milestones: Wins

Ferrari	25th: Germany 1956, 50th: Spain 1974, 100th: France 1990, 150th: Canada 2002, 200th: China 2007
McLaren	25th: United States West 1982, 50th: Monaco 1986, 100th: Brazil 1993, 150th: Monaco 2007
Williams	25th: Canada 1986, 50th: Portugal 1991, 100th: Britain 1997
Lotus	25th: United States 1966, 50th: Spain 1973
Red Bull	25th: Korea 2011, 50th: Belgium 2014
Benetton	25th: Pacific 1995
Brabham	25th: San Marino 1981
Mercedes-Benz	25th: Japan 2014
Renault	25th: China 2005

Chapter 18: Podium Constructors

733. Podium positions

		races	drivers		
Ferrari (a)	696	521	56	Monaco 1950 (Alberto Ascari)	- Abu Dhabi 2015 (Kimi Räikkönen)
McLaren	485	391	29	Spain 1968 (Denny Hulme)	- Australia 2014 (Kevin Magnussen, Jenson Button)
Williams	310	241	23	Germany 1975 (Jacques Laffite)	- Mexico 2015 (Valtteri Bottas)
Lotus (b)	197	177	24	Monaco 1960 (Stirling Moss)	- Belgium 2015 (Romain Grosjean)
Brabham	124	106	20	Belgium 1963 (Dan Gurney)	- Monaco 1989 (Stefano Modena)
Red Bull	119	85	5	Monaco 2006 (David Coulthard)	- Singapore 2015 (Daniel Ricciardo)
Benetton	102	94	14	San Marino 1986 (Gerhard Berger)	- Belgium 2001 (Giancarlo Fisichella)
Renault	100	88	14	France 1979 (Jean-Pierre Jabouille, René Arnoux)	- Malaysia 2011 (Nick Heidfeld)
Mercedes-Benz	95	61	8	France 1954 (Juan Manuel Fangio, Karl Kling)	- Abu Dhabi 2015 (Nico Rosberg, Lewis Hamilton)
Tyrrell	77	66	11	South Africa 1971 (Jackie Stewart)	- Spain 1994 (Mark Blundell)
BRM	61	53	14	Netherlands 1958 (Harry Schell, Jean Behra)	- South Africa 1974 (Jean-Pierre Beltoise)
Cooper	58	41	15	Britain 1952 (Mike Hawthorn)	- Monaco 1968 (Lucien Bianchi)
Ligier (c)	50	45	9	Belgium 1976 (Jacques Laffite)	- Monaco 1996 (Olivier Panis)
Maserati	37	28	13	Monaco 1950 (Louis Chiron)	- Italy 1957 (Juan Manuel Fangio)
Alfa Romeo	26	18	8	Britain 1950 (Giuseppe Farina, Luigi Fagioli, Reg Parnell)	- Italy 1984 (Riccardo Patrese)
March (d)	22	21	8	South Africa 1970 (Jackie Stewart)	- France 1990 (Ivan Capelli)
Matra (e)	21	17	5	Netherlands 1968 (Jackie Stewart, Jean-Pierre Beltoise)	- France 1972 (Chris Amon)

	races	drivers			
Jordan	19	17	7	Pacific 1994 (Rubens Barrichello)	- United States 2005 (Tiago Monteiro)
BMW (f)	17	16	2	Hungary 2006 (Nick Heidfeld)	- Brazil 2009 (Robert Kubica)
BAR	15	15	3	Spain 2001 (Jacques Villeneuve)	- Belgium 2005 (Jenson Button)
Brawn	15	11	2	Australia 2009 (Jenson Button, Rubens Barrichello)	- Abu Dhabi 2009 (Jenson Button)
Toyota	13	13	3	Malaysia 2005 (Jarno Trulli)	- Japan 2009 (Jarno Trulli)
Vanwall	13	11	3	Monaco 1957 (Tony Brooks)	- Morocco 1958 (Stirling Moss)
Wolf	13	13	1	Argentina 1977 (Jody Scheckter)	- Canada 1978 (Jody Scheckter)
Sauber	10	10	6	Italy 1995 (Heinz-Harald Frentzen)	- Japan 2012 (Kamui Kobayashi)
Arrows (g)	9	9	5	Sweden 1978 (Riccardo Patrese)	- Hungary 1997 (Damon Hill)
Honda	9	9	4	Mexico 1965 (Richie Ginther)	- Britain 2008 (Rubens Barrichello)
Hesketh	7	7	1	Sweden 1974 (James Hunt)	- Austria 1975 (James Hunt)
Shadow	7	7	5	Spain 1973 (George Follmer)	- Italy 1977 (Alan Jones)
Porsche	5	5	1	France 1961 (Dan Gurney)	- Germany 1962 (Dan Gurney)
Stewart	5	4	2	Monaco 1997 (Rubens Barrichello)	- Europe 1999 (Johnny Herbert, Rubens Barrichello)
Fittipaldi (h)	3	3	2	Brazil 1978 (Emerson Fittipaldi)	- United States West 1980 (Emerson Fittipaldi)
Force India	3	3	2	Belgium 2009 (Giancarlo Fisichella)	- Russia 2015 (Sergio Pérez)
Lola	3	3	2	Britain 1962 (John Surtees)	- Japan 1990 (Aguri Suzuki)
Penske	3	3	1	France 1976 (John Watson)	- Austria 1976 (John Watson)
Prost	3	3	2	Brazil 1997 (Olivier Panis)	- Europe 1999 (Jarno Trulli)
Toleman	3	3	1	Monaco 1984 (Ayrton Senna)	- Portugal 1984 (Ayrton Senna)
Dallara	2	2	2	Canada 1989 (Andrea De Cesaris)	- San Marino 1991 (J J Lehto)
Eagle	2	2	1	Belgium 1967 (Dan Gurney)	- Canada 1967 (Dan Gurney)
Gordini	2	2	2	Switzerland 1952 (Jean Behra)	- Belgium 1952 (Robert Manzon)
Jaguar	2	2	1	Monaco 2001 (Eddie Irvine)	- Italy 2002 (Eddie Irvine)
Surtees	2	2	2	Italy 1972 (Mike Hailwood)	- Austria 1973 (Carlos Pace)
Talbot-Lago	2	2	1	Switzerland 1950 (Louis Rosier)	- Belgium 1950 (Louis Rosier)
Connaught	1	1	1	Italy 1956 (Ron Flockhart)	
Lancia	1	1	1	Monaco 1955 (Eugenio Castellotti)	
Onyx	1	1	1	Portugal 1989 (Stefan Johansson)	
Toro Rosso	1	1	1	Italy 2008 (Sebastian Vettel)	

Indianapolis 500

Kurtis-Kraft	16	8	15	1950 (Johnnie Parsons)	- 1958 (Johnny Boyd)
Watson	5	3	3	1956 (Pat Flaherty)	- 1960 (Jim Rathmann, Rodger Ward)
Epperly	3	3	3	1957 (Jim Rathmann)	- 1960 (Paul Goldsmith)
Kuzma	3	3	2	1952 (Troy Ruttman)	- 1957 (Jimmy Bryan)
Deidt	2	1	2	1950 (Bill Holland, Mauri Rose)	
Salih	2	2	2	1957 (Sam Hanks)	- 1958 (Jimmy Bryan)
Lesovsky	1	1	1	1959 (Johnny Thomson)	
Phillips	1	1	1	1956 (Don Freeland)	

At Brazil 1983, 2nd place was not allocated after Keke Rosberg in a Williams was disqualified and lower positions were not adjusted.
(a) Includes Lancia-Ferrari.
(b) Includes JPS Lotus.
(c) Includes Talbot-Ligier.
(d) Includes Leyton House.
(e) Includes Matra-Simca.
(f) As BMW Sauber.
(g) Includes Footwork.
(h) Includes Copersucar.

734. Percentage of races with a podium position *(Highest)*

	%	races with a podium		%	
Brawn	64.71	11	Maserati	41.18	28
Ferrari	57.44	521	Vanwall	39.29	11
McLaren	50.13	391	Benetton	36.15	94
Mercedes-Benz	48.03	61	Williams	34.83	241
Red Bull	41.87	85	Cooper	31.78	41

735. Podium positions in a season (Most)

Mercedes-Benz	32	2015 (wc)	(F1 W06)	(Lewis Hamilton, 17; Nico Rosberg, 15)
Mercedes-Benz	31	2014 (wc)	(F1 W05)	(Lewis Hamilton, 16; Nico Rosberg, 15)
Ferrari	29	2004 (wc)	(F2004)	(Michael Schumacher, 15; Rubens Barrichello, 14)
Ferrari	27	2002 (wc)	(F2001, F2002)	(Michael Schumacher, 17; Rubens Barrichello, 10)
Red Bull	27	2011 (wc)	(RB7 - Renault)	(Sebastian Vettel, 17; Mark Webber, 10)
McLaren	25	1988 (wc)	(MP4/4 - Honda)	(Alain Prost, 14; Ayrton Senna, 11)
Ferrari	24	2001 (wc)	(F2001)	(Michael Schumacher, 14; Rubens Barrichello, 10)
McLaren	24	2007 (a)	(MP4-22 - Mercedes)	(Fernando Alonso, 12; Lewis Hamilton, 12)
Red Bull	24	2013 (wc)	(RB9 - Renault)	(Sebastian Vettel, 16; Mark Webber, 8)
Ferrari	22	2007 (wc)	(F2007)	(Kimi Räikkönen, 12; Felipe Massa, 10)
McLaren	22	2000	(MP4-15 - Mercedes)	(David Coulthard, 11; Mika Häkkinen, 11)
Williams	22	1993 (wc)	(FW15C - Renault)	(Alain Prost, 12; Damon Hill, 10)

(a) In 2007, McLaren were stripped of all their constructors' championship points, due to the spying scandal.
(wc) World champion constructor that season.

736. Races in a season with a podium position (Most)

Mercedes-Benz	19 of 19	2014 (wc)	(F1 W05)	(Lewis Hamilton, 16; Nico Rosberg, 15)
Ferrari	18 of 18	2004 (wc)	(F2004)	(Michael Schumacher, 15; Rubens Barrichello, 14)
Red Bull	18 of 19	2011 (wc)	(RB7 - Renault)	(Sebastian Vettel, 17; Mark Webber, 10)
Ferrari	17 of 17	2000 (wc)	(F1 2000)	(Michael Schumacher, 12; Rubens Barrichello, 9)
Ferrari	17 of 17	2001 (wc)	(F2001)	(Michael Schumacher, 14; Rubens Barrichello, 10)
Ferrari	17 of 17	2002 (wc)	(F2001, F2002)	(Michael Schumacher, 17; Rubens Barrichello, 10)
McLaren	17 of 17	2007 (a)	(MP4-22 - Mercedes)	(Fernando Alonso, 12; Lewis Hamilton, 12)
Mercedes-Benz	17 of 19	2015 (wc)	(F1 W06)	(Lewis Hamilton, 17; Nico Rosberg, 15)
Red Bull	17 of 19	2013 (wc)	(RB9 - Renault)	(Sebastian Vettel, 16; Mark Webber, 8)
Williams	16 of 16	1993 (wc)	(FW15C - Renault)	(Alain Prost, 12; Damon Hill, 10)
Ferrari	16 of 17	2007 (wc)	(F2007)	(Kimi Räikkönen, 12; Felipe Massa, 10)
McLaren	16 of 19	2011	(MP4-26 - Mercedes)	(Jenson Button, 12; Lewis Hamilton, 6)

(a) In 2007, McLaren were stripped of all their constructors' championship points, due to the spying scandal.
(wc) World champion constructor that season.

737. Podium in every race of a season

Mercedes-Benz	19	2014 (wc)	(F1 W05)	(L Hamilton, N Rosberg)
Ferrari	18	2004 (wc)	(F2004)	(R Barrichello, M Schumacher)
Ferrari	17	2000 (wc)	(F1 2000)	(R Barrichello, M Schumacher)
Ferrari	17	2001 (wc)	(F2001)	(R Barrichello, M Schumacher)
Ferrari	17	2002 (wc)	(F2001, F2002)	(R Barrichello, M Schumacher)
McLaren	17	2007 (a)	(MP4-22 - Mercedes)	(F Alonso, L Hamilton)
Williams	16	1993 (wc)	(FW15C - Renault)	(D Hill, A Prost)
Ferrari	8	1953	(500)	(A Ascari, G Farina, M Hawthorn, L Villoresi)
Ferrari	8	1954	(625)	(G Farina, J F González, M Hawthorn, U Maglioli, R Manzon, M Trintignant)
Alfa Romeo	7	1951	(159)	(F Bonetto, L Fagioli, J M Fangio, G Farina)
Ferrari	7	1951	(375)	(A Ascari, J F González, P Taruffi, L Villoresi)
Ferrari	7	1952	(500)	(A Ascari, G Farina, R Fischer, P Taruffi, L Villoresi)
Lancia-Ferrari	7	1956	(D50)	(E Castellotti, P Collins, A de Portago, J M Fangio, P Frère, L Musso)
Maserati	7	1956	(250F)	(J Behra, M Hawthorn, S Moss, C Perdisa)
Alfa Romeo	6	1950	(158)	(L Fagioli, J M Fangio, G Farina, R Parnell)

(a) In 2007, McLaren were stripped of all their constructors' championship points, due to the spying scandal.
(wc) World champion constructor that season.

738. Podium in all but one race of a season

Red Bull	18	2011 (wc)	(RB7 - Renault)	(S Vettel, M Webber)
Ferrari	16	2007 (wc)	(F2007)	(F Massa, K Räikkönen)
McLaren	15	1988 (wc)	(MP4/4 - Honda)	(A Prost, A Senna)
BRM	9	1965	(P261)	(G Hill, J Stewart)
Lotus	9	1963 (wc)	(25 - Climax)	(J Clark)
Cooper	8	1960 (wc)	(T51, T53 - Climax)	(J Brabham, O Gendebien, B McLaren, S Moss, M Trintignant)
Cooper	7	1959 (wc)	(T51 - Climax)	(J Brabham, M Gregory, B McLaren, S Moss, M Trintignant)
Ferrari	7	1961 (wc)	(156)	(G Baghetti, R Ginther, P Hill, W von Trips)
Maserati	6	1957	(250F)	(J Behra, J M Fangio, M Gregory, C Menditéguy, H Schell)
Mercedes-Benz	5	1955	(W196, W196 str.)	(J M Fangio, K Kling, S Moss, P Taruffi)

(wc) World champion constructor that season.

739. Consecutive races with a podium *(Most)*

Ferrari	53	Malaysia 1999	- Japan 2002	(F399, F1 2000, F2001, F2002)
Ferrari	35	France 1950	- Belgium 1955	(125, 375, 500, 625, 555)
Mercedes-Benz	28	Australia 2014	- Britain 2015	(F1 W05, F1 W06)
Ferrari	22	Italy 2003	- Australia 2005	(F2003-GA, F2004, F2004M)
McLaren	19	Australia 2007	- Malaysia 2008	(MP4-22, MP4-23 - Mercedes)
Red Bull	19	Brazil 2010	- India 2011	(RB6, RB7 - Renault)
Renault	17	Turkey 2005	- France 2006	(R25, R26)
Williams	17	South Africa 1993	- Brazil 1994	(FW15C, FW16 - Renault)
Red Bull	14	Monaco 2013	- Brazil 2013	(RB9 - Renault)
Alfa Romeo	13	Britain 1950	- Spain 1951	(158, 159)
McLaren	13	Germany 2011	- China 2012	(MP4-26, MP4-27 - Mercedes)
McLaren	13	United States 1990	- Portugal 1990	(MP4/5B - Honda)

740. Consecutive races with a podium from the start of a season *(Most)*
(not counting any into the following season)

Mercedes-Benz	19	2014	(F1 W05)	(Lewis Hamilton, Nico Rosberg)
Ferrari	18	2004 (a)	(F2004)	(Rubens Barrichello, Michael Schumacher)
Ferrari	17	2000 (a)	(F1 2000)	(Rubens Barrichello, Michael Schumacher)
Ferrari	17	2001 (a)	(F2001)	(Rubens Barrichello, Michael Schumacher)
Ferrari	17	2002	(F2001, F2002)	(Rubens Barrichello, Michael Schumacher)
McLaren	17	2007 (a)	(MP4-22 - Mercedes)	(Fernando Alonso, Lewis Hamilton)
Red Bull	17	2011	(RB7 - Renault)	(Mark Webber, Sebastian Vettel)
Williams	16	1993 (a)	(FW15C - Renault)	(Damon Hill, Alain Prost)
McLaren	13	1990 (a)	(MP4/5B - Honda)	(Gerhard Berger, Ayrton Senna)
McLaren	11	1988 (a)	(MP4/4 - Honda)	(Alain Prost, Ayrton Senna)
Renault	11	2006	(R26)	(Fernando Alonso, Giancarlo Fisichella)

(a) Sequence continued into the following season.
All above became world champion constructor that season, apart from McLaren in 2007, being stripped of all their points, due to the spying scandal.

741. Seasons of podiums *(Most)*

Ferrari	64	1950 - 2015		Benetton	16	1986 - 2001
McLaren	45	1968 - 2014		BRM	16	1958 - 74
Williams	34	1975 - 2015		Renault	16	1979 - 2011
Lotus	32	1960 - 2015		Tyrrell	15	1971 - 94
Brabham	22	1963 - 89		Ligier	13	1976 - 96

742. Consecutive seasons of podiums *(Most)*

Ferrari	35	1981 - 2015		Benetton	16	1986 - 2001
McLaren	32	1981 - 2012		BRM	15	1958 - 72
Lotus	29	1960 - 88		McLaren	12	1968 - 79
Williams	28	1978 - 2005		Cooper	11	1958 - 68
Ferrari	23	1950 - 72		Red Bull	10	2006 - 15

743. Podium positions at the same venue *(Most)*

grand prix

Ferrari	65	Italy	1950 - 2015 (a)	(Monza)
Ferrari	52	Britain	1951 - 2015 (a)	(Silverstone, 40; Brands Hatch, 7; Aintree, 5)
Ferrari	51	Germany	1951 - 2012 (a)	(Nürburgring, 26; Hockenheim, 22; AVUS, 3)
Ferrari	49	Monaco	1950 - 2015 (a)	(Monte-Carlo)
Ferrari	48	France	1950 - 2008 (a)	(Magny-Cours, 20; Reims, 10; Rouen-les-Essarts, 6; Paul Ricard, 5; Dijon-Prenois, 3; Reims-Gueux, 3; Clermont-Ferrand, 1)
Ferrari	45	Belgium	1951 - 2013 (a)	(Spa-Francorchamps, 36; Zolder, 8; Nivelles-Baulers, 1)
Ferrari	35	Spain	1951 - 2015	(Catalunya, 22; Jarama, 7; Jerez de la Frontera, 3; Pedralbes, 2; Montjuïc, 1)
McLaren	33	Britain	1969 - 2010	(Silverstone, 27; Brands Hatch, 6)
Ferrari	32	Canada	1970 - 2013	(Montréal, 29; Mont-Tremblant, 2; Mosport Park, 1)
McLaren	31	Brazil	1973 - 2012	(Interlagos, 23; Jacarepaguá, 8)

circuit

Ferrari	65	Monza	1950 - 2015 (a)		Ferrari	29	Montréal	1978 - 2013
Ferrari	49	Monte-Carlo	1950 - 2015 (a)		McLaren	27	Silverstone	1969 - 2010
Ferrari	41	Nürburgring	1951 - 2011 (a) (b)		McLaren	26	Monte-Carlo	1975 - 2011
Ferrari	40	Silverstone	1951 - 2015 (a)		McLaren	26	Monza	1968 - 2012
Ferrari	36	Spa-Francorchamps	1951 - 2013 (a)		McLaren	25	Spa-Francorchamps	1968 - 2012

(a) Includes Lancia-Ferrari. (b) Includes 14 European and 1 Luxembourg Grands Prix.

744. Consecutive podiums at the same venue *(Most)*

Ferrari	13	San Marino	1994 - 2006	(Imola)
Ferrari	12	Italy	1950 - 61	(Pescara)
Ferrari	10	Canada	1997 - 2006	(Montréal)
Ferrari	10	Europe	2000 - 09	(Nürburgring, 8; Valencia, 2)
Ferrari	10	United States	1991 - 2012 (a)	(Indianapolis, 8; Phoenix, 1, Austin, 1)
Williams	10	Hungary	1989 - 98	(Hungaroring)
Ferrari	9	France	1950 - 59 (b)	(Reims, 5; Reims-Gueux, 2; Rouen-les-Essarts, 2)
Ferrari	9	France	2000 - 08	(Magny-Cours)
McLaren	9	Italy	1989 - 97	(Monza)
Ferrari	9	Japan	1996 - 2004	(Suzuka)

(a) No United States Grand Prix in 1992 - 99 and 2008 - 11. (b) No French Grand Prix in 1955.

745. Races taken to achieve their first podium
(number of races relates to those started and includes the first podium)

Alfa Romeo	1	Tyrrell	4	Honda	11	Renault	25
Brawn	1	Brabham	5	Eagle	12	Surtees	28
Ferrari	1	Cooper	5	McLaren	12	Force India	30
March	1	Hesketh	5	Porsche	12	Toleman	34
Mercedes-Benz	1	Ligier	5	Vanwall	12	BAR	38
Wolf	1	Lola	5	BMW	13	Williams	41
Maserati	2	Stewart	5	Connaught	14	Fittipaldi	43
Prost	2	Arrows	7	Lotus	19	Sauber	43
Shadow	2	BRM	7	Dallara	20	Toro Rosso	49
Benetton	3	Gordini	8	Penske	20	Jordan	50
Lancia	3	Matra	10	Jaguar	24	Toyota	53
Talbot-Lago	3	Onyx	10	Red Bull	25		

For most races started but never a podium, see section 679.

746. Races with a podium in their first season
(number of podium positions in brackets)

Brawn	11	(15)	2009	(BGP 001 - Mercedes)	(Jenson Button, 9; Rubens Barrichello, 6)
Wolf	9	(9)	1977	(WR1, WR2 - Ford Cosworth)	(Jody Scheckter)
March	7	(8)	1970	(701 - Ford Cosworth)	(Jackie Stewart, 4; Chris Amon, 3; Mario Andretti, 1)
Alfa Romeo	6	(12)	1950	(158)	(Luigi Fagioli, 5; Juan Manuel Fangio, 3; Giuseppe Farina, 3; Reg Parnell, 1)
Mercedes-Benz	5	(7)	1954	(W196 str., W196)	(Juan Manuel Fangio, 5; Hans Herrmann, 1; Karl Kling, 1)
Ferrari	3	(4)	1950	(125, 375)	(Alberto Ascari, 2; Dorino Serafini, 1; Peter Whitehead, 1)
Hesketh	3	(3)	1974	(308 - Ford Cosworth)	(James Hunt)

Ligier	3	(3)	1976	(JS5 - Matra)	(Jacques Laffite)
Benetton	2	(2)	1986	(B186 - BMW)	(Gerhard Berger)
Lola	2	(2)	1962	(Mk 4 - Climax)	(John Surtees)
Prost	2	(2)	1997	(JS45 - Mugen Honda)	(Olivier Panis)
Shadow	2	(2)	1973	(DN1 - Ford Cosworth)	(George Follmer, 1; Jackie Oliver, 1)
Talbot-Lago	2	(2)	1950	(T26-DA)	(Louis Rosier)
Arrows	1	(1)	1978	(FA1 - Ford Cosworth)	(Riccardo Patrese)
Maserati	1	(1)	1950	(4CLT/48)	(Louis Chiron)
Onyx	1	(1)	1989	(ORE-1 - Ford Cosworth)	(Stefan Johansson)
Stewart	1	(1)	1997	(SF-1 - Ford Cosworth)	(Rubens Barrichello)

747. First race with a podium immediately followed by others
(including first podium position)

Alfa Romeo	13	Britain 1950 - Spain 1951	(158, 159)
Brawn	8	Australia - Britain 2009	(BGP 001 - Mercedes)
Tyrrell	3	South Africa - Monaco 1971	(001, 003 - Ford Cosworth)
Brabham	2	Belgium - Netherlands 1963	(BT7 - Climax)
Lola	2	Britain - Germany 1962	(Mk 4 - Climax)
Lotus	2	Monaco - Netherlands 1960	(Lotus 18 - Climax)
March	2	South Africa - Spain 1970	(701 - Ford Cosworth)
Matra	2	Netherlands - France 1968	(MS10 - Ford Cosworth, MS11)
Penske	2	France - Britain 1976	(PC4 - Ford Cosworth)
Renault	2	France - Britain 1979	(RS10)
Toyota	2	Malaysia - Bahrain 2005	(TF105)

748. Podium in their final race

Brawn	Abu Dhabi 2009	(BGP 001 - Mercedes)	(Jenson Button)

Brawn became Mercedes-Benz from 2010.

749. Podium positions in their final season

Brawn	15	2009	(BGP 001- Mercedes)	(Jenson Button, 9; Rubens Barrichello, 6)
Toyota	5	2009	(TF109)	(Jarno Trulli, 3; Timo Glock, 2)
Stewart	4	1999	(SF-3 - Ford Cosworth)	(Rubens Barrichello, 3; Johnny Herbert, 1)
BAR	2	2005	(007 - Honda)	(Jenson Button)
BMW	2	2009	(BMW Sauber F1.09)	(Nick Heidfeld, 1; Robert Kubica, 1)
Renault	2	2011	(R31)	(Nick Heidfeld, 1; Vitaly Petrov, 1)
Benetton	1	2001	(B201 - Renault)	(Giancarlo Fisichella)
Honda	1	2008	(RA108)	(Rubens Barrichello)
Jordan	1	2005	(EJ15 - Toyota)	(Tiago Monteiro)
Lancia	1	1955	(D50)	(Eugenio Castellotti)
Ligier	1	1996	(JS43 - Mugen Honda)	(Olivier Panis)
Matra (a)	1	1972	(MS120D)	(Chris Amon)

(a) As Matra-Simca.

Podium from lowest grid position. See section 291

750. Different podium constructors in a season

Most

1978	10	JPS Lotus, Brabham, Tyrrell, Ferrari, Copersucar, Wolf, Ligier, Arrows, McLaren, Williams
1989	10	Ferrari, McLaren, March, Benetton, Brabham, Williams, Tyrrell, Arrows, Dallara, Onyx
1975	9	McLaren, Hesketh, Brabham, Tyrrell, JPS Lotus, Ferrari, March, Shadow, Williams
1981	9	Williams, Brabham, Arrows, Renault, Talbot-Ligier, Lotus, Ferrari, McLaren, Alfa Romeo
1982	9	Renault, Williams, McLaren, Lotus, Brabham, Ferrari, Tyrrell, Talbot-Ligier, Alfa Romeo
1997	9	McLaren, Ferrari, Williams, Benetton, Prost, Jordan, Stewart, Benetton, Arrows, Sauber
2008	9	McLaren, BMW Sauber, Williams, Ferrari, Red Bull, Toyota, Honda, Renault, Toro Rosso
1968	8	Lotus, Brabham, McLaren, Cooper, BRM, Ferrari, Matra, Honda
1971	8	Ferrari, Tyrrell, Matra-Simca, March, BRM, Lotus, Brabham, McLaren
1972	8	Tyrrell, McLaren, Ferrari, JPS Lotus, BRM, Matra-Simca, March, Surtees
1974	8	McLaren, Ferrari, JPS Lotus, Brabham, BRM, Tyrrell, Shadow, Hesketh

1976	8	Ferrari, Shadow, McLaren, Tyrrell, JPS Lotus, Ligier, Penske, March
1977	8	Wolf, Brabham, Ferrari, McLaren, Tyrrell, JPS Lotus, Ligier, Shadow
1983	8	Brabham, McLaren, Williams, Ferrari, Renault, Tyrrell, Alfa Romeo, Lotus
1984	8	McLaren, Williams, Lotus, Renault, Ferrari, Toleman, Brabham, Alfa Romeo
1985	8	McLaren, Ferrari, Lotus, Renault, Arrows, Brabham, Ligier, Williams
1995	8	Benetton, Williams, Ferrari, Jordan, Ligier, McLaren, Sauber, Footwork
2009	8	Brawn, Toyota, BMW Sauber, Red Bull, Ferrari, McLaren, Force India, Renault

Fewest

1951	2	Alfa Romeo, Ferrari
1953	2	Ferrari, Maserati
1954	3	Maserati, Ferrari, Mercedes-Benz
1956	3	Lancia-Ferrari, Maserati, Connaught
1957	3	Maserati, Vanwall, Lancia-Ferrari
1959	3	Cooper, Ferrari, BRM
1950	4	Alfa Romeo, Ferrari, Maserati, Talbot-Lago
1952	4	Ferrari, Gordini, Cooper, Maserati
1955	4	Mercedes-Benz, Ferrari, Lancia, Maserati
1958	4	Cooper, Ferrari, Vanwall, BRM
1960	4	Cooper, Ferrari, Lotus, BRM
1992	4	Williams, McLaren, Benetton, Ferrari
2002	4	Ferrari, Williams, McLaren, Jaguar
2011	4	Red Bull, McLaren, Renault, Ferrari
2013	4	Lotus, Ferrari, Red Bull, Mercedes-Benz

Excludes Indianapolis 500.

751. First time podium constructors in a season *(Most)*

1950	4	Alfa Romeo, Ferrari, Maserati, Talbot-Lago	1989	2	Dallara, Onyx
1952	2	Gordini, Cooper	1997	2	Prost, Stewart
1968	2	McLaren, Matra	2001	2	BAR, Jaguar
1971	2	Tyrrell, March	2006	2	Red Bull, BMW (a)
1976	2	Ligier, Penske	2009	2	Brawn, Force India
1978	2	Fittipaldi, Arrows			

(a) As BMW Sauber.

752. 1-2 finishes

Constructor		First	Last
Ferrari (a)	81	Italy 1951 (Alberto Ascari, José Froilán González)	- Germany 2010 (Fernando Alonso, Felipe Massa)
McLaren	47	Canada 1968 (Denny Hulme, Bruce McLaren)	- Canada 2010 (Lewis Hamilton, Jenson Button)
Williams	33	Germany 1979 (Alan Jones, Clay Regazzoni)	- France 2003 (Ralf Schumacher, Juan Pablo Montoya)
Mercedes-Benz	28	France 1954 (Juan Manuel Fangio, Karl Kling)	- Abu Dhabi 2015 (Nico Rosberg, Lewis Hamilton)
Red Bull	16	China 2009 (Sebastian Vettel, Mark Webber)	- Brazil 2013 (Sebastian Vettel, Mark Webber)
Brabham	8	Britain 1966 (Jack Brabham, Denny Hulme)	- Canada 1982 (Nelson Piquet, Riccardo Patrese)
Lotus (b)	8	United States 1960 (Stirling Moss, Innes Ireland)	- Netherlands 1978 (Mario Andretti, Ronnie Peterson)
Tyrrell	8	France 1971 (Jackie Stewart, François Cevert)	- Sweden 1976 (Jody Scheckter, Patrick Depailler)
Cooper	6	Portugal 1959 (Stirling Moss, Masten Gregory)	- South Africa 1967 (Pedro Rodríguez, John Love)
BRM	5	Italy 1962 (Graham Hill, Richie Ginther)	- Italy 1965 (Jackie Stewart, Graham Hill)
Alfa Romeo	4	Britain 1950 (Giuseppe Farina, Luigi Fagioli)	- France 1950 (Juan Manuel Fangio, Luigi Fagioli)
Brawn	4	Australia 2009 (Jenson Button, Rubens Barrichello)	- Italy 2009 (Rubens Barrichello, Jenson Button)
Benetton	2	Japan 1990 (Nelson Piquet, Roberto Moreno)	- Spain 1995 (Michael Schumacher, Johnny Herbert)
Matra	2	Netherlands 1968 (Jackie Stewart, Jean-Pierre Beltoise)	- France 1969 (Jackie Stewart, Jean-Pierre Beltoise)
Renault	2	France 1982 (René Arnoux, Alain Prost)	- Malaysia 2006 (Giancarlo Fisichella, Fernando Alonso)
BMW (c)	1	Canada 2008 (Robert Kubica, Nick Heidfeld)	
Jordan	1	Belgium 1998 (Damon Hill, Ralf Schumacher)	
Ligier	1	Brazil 1979 (Jacques Laffite, Patrick Depailler)	
Maserati	1	Argentina 1957 (Juan Manuel Fangio, Jean Behra)	

Excludes Indianapolis 500. (a) Includes Lancia-Ferrari. (b) Includes JPS Lotus. (c) As BMW Sauber.
For driver 1-2 finishes as team-mates, see section 296.

753. Consecutive 1-2 finishes *(Most)*

Ferrari	6	Switzerland 1952	- Netherlands 1952	(500)
Ferrari	5	Hungary 2002	- Japan 2002	(F2002)
Mercedes-Benz	5	Malaysia 2014	- Monaco 2014	(F1 W05)
McLaren	4	Mexico 1988	- France 1988	(MP4/4 - Honda)
Mercedes-Benz	4	Belgium 1955	- Italy 1955	(W196, W196 str.)
Mercedes-Benz	4	Japan 2014	- Brazil 2014	(F1 W05)
Mercedes-Benz	4	United States 2015	- Abu Dhabi 2015	(F1 W06)
Williams	4	Canada 1980	- Brazil 1981	(FW07B, FW07C - Ford Cosworth)
Alfa Romeo	3	Switzerland 1950	- France 1950	(158)
Ferrari	3	Argentina 1953	- Belgium 1953	(500)
Lancia-Ferrari	3	Bolgium 1956	- Britain 1956	(D50)
Ferrari	3	Europe 2004	- United States 2004	(F2004)
McLaren	3	Germany 1988	- Belgium 1988	(MP4/4 - Honda)
McLaren	3	Europe 1997	- Brazil 1998	(MP4-12, MP4-13 - Mercedes)
Mercedes-Benz	3	Canada 2015	- Britain 2015	(F1 W06)
Williams	3	South Africa 1992	- Brazil 1992	(FW14B - Renault)

For driver consecutive 1-2 finishes as team-mates, see section 297.

754. 1-2 finishes in a season *(Most)*

Mercedes-Benz	12 of 19	2015	(F1 W06)	(Lewis Hamilton, Nico Rosberg)
Mercedes-Benz	11 of 19	2014	(F1 W05)	(Lewis Hamilton, Nico Rosberg)
McLaren	10 of 16	1988	(MP4/4 - Honda)	(Alain Prost, Ayrton Senna)
Ferrari	9 of 17	2002	(F2002)	(Rubens Barrichello, Michael Schumacher)
Ferrari	8 of 18	2004	(F2004)	(Rubens Barrichello, Michael Schumacher)
Ferrari	6 of 7	1952	(500)	(Alberto Ascari, Giuseppe Farina, Rudi Fischer, Piero Taruffi)
Williams	6 of 16	1992	(FW14B - Renault)	(Nigel Mansell, Riccardo Patrese)
Williams	6 of 16	1996	(FW18 - Renault)	(Damon Hill, Jacques Villeneuve)
McLaren	5 of 16	1998	(MP4/4 - Honda)	(David Coulthard, Mika Häkkinen)

755. 1-2 finish in all but one race of a season

Ferrari	6	1952	(Ferrari 500)	(Alberto Ascari, Giuseppe Farina, Piero Taruffi, Rudi Fischer)

756. 1-2 finish in the first race of the season

1950	Alfa Romeo	(158)	(1: Giuseppe Farina, 2: Luigi Fagioli)
1952	Ferrari	(500)	(1: Piero Taruffi, 2: Rudi Fischer)
1953	Ferrari	(500)	(1: Alberto Ascari, 2: Luigi Villoresi)
1957	Maserati	(250F)	(1: Juan Manuel Fangio, 2: Jean Behra)
1963	BRM	(P57)	(1: Graham Hill, 2: Richie Ginther)
1964	BRM	(P261)	(1: Graham Hill, 2: Richie Ginther)
1967	Cooper	(T81 - Maserati, T79 - Climax)	(1: Pedro Rodríguez, 2: John Love)
1968	Lotus (wc)	(49 - Ford Cosworth)	(1: Jim Clark, 2: Graham Hill)
1981	Williams (wc)	(FW07C - Ford Cosworth)	(1: Alan Jones, 2: Carlo Reutemann)
1992	Williams (wc)	(FW14B - Renault)	(1: Nigel Mansell, 2: Riccardo Patrese)
1996	Williams (wc)	(FW18 - Renault)	(1: Damon Hill, 2: Jacques Villeneuve)
1998	McLaren (wc)	(MP4-13 - Mercedes)	(1: Mika Häkkinen, 2: David Coulthard)
2000	Ferrari (wc)	(F1 2000)	(1: Michael Schumacher, 2: Rubens Barrichello)
2004	Ferrari (wc)	(F2004)	(1: Michael Schumacher, 2: Rubens Barrichello)
2009	Brawn (wc)	(BGP 001 - Mercedes)	(1: Jenson Button, 2: Rubens Barrichello)
2010	Ferrari	(F10)	(1: Fernando Alonso, 2: Felipe Massa)
2015	Mercedes-Benz (wc)	(F1 W06)	(1: Lewis Hamilton, 2: Nico Rosberg)

(wc) World champion constructor that season.

757. Consecutive 1-2 finishes from the start of a season
(not counting any into the following season)

Ferrari	6	1952 (a)	(500)	(Alberto Ascari, Giuseppe Farina, Piero Taruffi, Rudi Fischer)
Ferrari	3	1953	(500)	(Alberto Ascari, Luigi Villoresi, Giuseppe Farina)
Williams	3	1992 (wc)	(FW14B - Renault)	(Nigel Mansell, Riccardo Patrese)
Williams	2	1981 (wc)	(FW07 - Ford Cosworth)	(Alan Jones, Carlos Reutemann)
McLaren	2	1998 (wc)	(MP4-13 - Mercedes)	(Mika Häkkinen, David Coulthard)

(a) Sequence continued into the following season.
(wc) World champion constructor that season.

758. 1-2 finish in the race of their first win

Alfa Romeo	Britain 1950	(158)	(1: Giuseppe Farina, 2: Luigi Fagioli)
Mercedes-Benz	France 1954	(W196 str.)	(1: Juan Manuel Fangio, 2: Karl Kling)
Matra	Netherlands 1968	(MS10 - Ford Cos., MS11 - Matra)	(1: Jackie Stewart, 2: Jean-Pierre Beltoise)
Jordan	Belgium 1998	(198 - Mugen Honda)	(1: Damon Hill, 2: Ralf Schumacher)
BMW	Canada 2008	(BMW Sauber F1.08 - BMW)	(1: Robert Kubica, 2: Nick Heidfeld)
Brawn	Australia 2009	(BGP 001 - Mercedes)	(1: Jenson Button, 2: Rubens Barrichello)
Red Bull	China 2009	(RB5 - Renault)	(1: Sebastian Vettel, 2: Mark Webber)

759. Complete podiums
(occurred in the early days, where teams ran more than two cars in a race)

Ferrari	8	France 1952	- Britain 1961 (a)		Maserati	1	Argentina 1957
Cooper	2	Belgium 1960	- France 1960		Mercedes-Benz	1	Britain 1955
Alfa Romeo	1	Britain 1950					

(a) The 1961 British Grand Prix, was the last time that a single constructor's cars filled a podium (Wolfgang von Trips, Phil Hill and Richie Ginther). After that it became rarer for constructors to run more than two cars in a race.
For driver 1-2-3 finishes with the same constructor, see section 295.

760. Complete podiums in a season

Ferrari	3 of 7	1952	France	- Netherlands	(500)
Ferrari	2 of 8	1961	Belgium	- Britain	(156)
Cooper	2 of 9	1960	Belgium	- France	(T51, T53 - Climax)

761. Consecutive complete podiums

Cooper	2	Belgium 1960	- France 1960	(T51, T53 - Climax)
Ferrari	2	Germany 1952	- Netherlands 1952	(500)

762. Two or more cars on the podium

Ferrari (a)	167	Belgium 1951	- Singapore 2015	BRM	8	Netherlands 1958	- Monaco 1966
McLaren	94	Canada 1968	- Australia 2014	Maserati	8	France 1953	- Pescara 1957
Williams	69	Germany 1979	- Abu Dhabi 2014	Alfa Romeo	7	Britain 1950	- Spain 1951
Red Bull	34	China 2009	- Hungary 2015	Ligier	5	Brazil 1979	- Germany 1994
Mercedes-Benz	33	France 1954	- Abu Dhabi 2015	Brawn	4	Australia 2009	- Italy 2009
Lotus (b)	20	Britain 1960	- Korea 2013	Matra	4	Netherlands 1968	- Italy 1969
Brabham	18	France 1964	- Detroit 1984	Jordan	2	Canada 1995	- Belgium 1998
Cooper	15	Germany 1958	- South Africa 1967	Vanwall	2	Belgium 1958	- Portugal 1958
Renault	12	France 1979	- Japan 2006	BMW Sauber	1	Canada 2008	
Tyrrell	11	France 1971	- Sweden 1976	March	1	Spain 1970	
Benetton	8	Japan 1990	- Britain 1997	Stewart	1	Europe 1999	

Excludes Indianapolis 500.
(a) Includes Lancia-Ferrari.
(b) Includes JPS Lotus.

763. Percentage of races in a season, featuring three different constructors on the podium

Highest				Lowest		
1977	88.24	(15 of 17)		1958	0.00	(0 of 10)
1994	81.25	(13 of 16)		1953	0.00	(0 of 8)
1963	80.00	(8 of 10)		1959	0.00	(0 of 8)
1981	80.00	(12 of 15)		1951	0.00	(0 of 7)
1965	70.00	(7 of 10)		1952	0.00	(0 of 7)
1962	66.67	(6 of 9)		1956	0.00	(0 of 7)
1971	63.64	(7 of 11)		1955	0.00	(0 of 6)
1976	62.50	(10 of 16)		2015	10.53	(2 of 19)
1982	62.50	(10 of 16)		1966	11.11	(1 of 9)
1985	62.50	(10 of 16)		1954	12.50	(1 of 8)
				1998	12.50	(2 of 16)

Excludes Indianapolis 500.

764. Podium position drivers by constructor

Alfa Romeo: Juan Manuel Fangio, 8; Giuseppe Farina, 7; Luigi Fagioli, 6; Andrea De Cesaris, 3; Felice Bonetto, 1; Bruno Giacomelli, 1; Reg Parnell, 1; Riccardo Patrese, 1

Arrows: Riccardo Patrese, 4; Eddie Cheever, 2; Thierry Boutsen, 1; Damon Hill, 1; Gianni Morbidelli, 1 (as Footwork)

BAR: Jenson Button, 12; Jacques Villeneuve, 2; Takuma Sato, 1

Benetton: Michael Schumacher, 38; Jean Alesi, 13; Alessandro Nannini, 9; Giancarlo Fisichella, 7; Nelson Piquet, 7; Gerhard Berger, 6; Thierry Boutsen, 6; Martin Brundle, 5; Johnny Herbert, 4; Riccardo Patrese, 2; Jos Verstappen, 2; Teo Fabi, 1; Roberto Moreno, 1; Alexander Wurz, 1

BMW *(as BMW Sauber):* Robert Kubica, 9; Nick Heidfeld, 8

Brabham: Nelson Piquet, 29; Jack Brabham, 21; Denny Hulme, 12; Carlos Reutemann, 12; Dan Gurney, 10; Niki Lauda, 7; Riccardo Patrese, 6; Jacky Ickx, 5; Carlos Pace, 5; John Watson, 4; Piers Courage, 2; Jochen Rindt, 2; Hans-Joachim Stuck, 2; Bob Anderson, 1; Andrea De Cesaris, 1; Teo Fabi, 1; Stefano Modena, 1; Tim Schenken, 1; Jo Siffert, 1; Rolf Stommelen, 1

Brawn: Jenson Button, 9; Rubens Barrichello, 6

BRM: Graham Hill, 26; Richie Ginther, 9; Jackie Stewart, 8; Pedro Rodríguez, 6; Jean-Pierre Beltoise, 2; Jo Siffert, 2; Richard Attwood, 1; Jean Behra, 1; Jo Bonnier, 1; Tony Brooks, 1; Peter Gethin, 1; Stirling Moss, 1; Harry Schell, 1; John Surtees, 1

Connaught: Ron Flockhart, 1

Cooper: Bruce McLaren, 20; Jack Brabham, 10; Maurice Trintignant, 5; Stirling Moss, 4; Tony Maggs, 3; Jochen Rindt, 3; John Surtees, 3; Olivier Gendebien, 2; Masten Gregory, 2; Roy Salvadori, 2; Lucien Bianchi, 1; Mike Hawthorn, 1; John Love, 1; Brian Redman, 1; Pedro Rodríguez, 1

Dallara: Andrea De Cesaris, 1; J J Lehto, 1

Eagle: Dan Gurney, 2

Ferrari: Michael Schumacher, 116; Rubens Barrichello, 55; Fernando Alonso, 44; Felipe Massa, 36; Niki Lauda, 32; Kimi Räikkönen, 29; Gerhard Berger, 24; Eddie Irvine, 23; Clay Regazzoni, 23; Michele Alboreto, 19; Alberto Ascari, 17; Jean Alesi, 16; Mike Hawthorn, 16 (a); Phil Hill, 16; Jacky Ickx, 16; Alain Prost, 14; Carlos Reutemann, 13; John Surtees, 13; Sebastian Vettel, 13; Gilles Villeneuve, 13; Giuseppe Farina, 12; René Arnoux, 11; José Froilán González, 11; Nigel Mansell, 11; Peter Collins, 9 (a); Lorenzo Bandini, 8; Patrick Tambay, 8; Luigi Villoresi, 8; Chris Amon, 6; Stefan Johansson, 6; Didier Pironi, 6; Jody Scheckter, 6; Wolfgang von Trips, 6 (a); Juan Manuel Fangio, 5 (a); Luigi Musso, 5 (a); Tony Brooks, 4; Richie Ginther, 4; Piero Taruffi, 4; Maurice Trintignant, 4; Mario Andretti, 2; Eugenio Castellotti, 2 (a); Rudi Fischer, 2; Dan Gurney, 2; Umberto Maglioli, 2; Mike Parkes, 2; Mika Salo, 2; Cliff Allison, 1; Giancarlo Baghetti, 1; Alfonso de Portago, 1 (a); Paul Frère, 1 (a); Nicola Larini, 1; Willy Mairesse, 1; Robert Manzon, 1; Ludovico Scarfiotti, 1; Dorino Serafini, 1; Peter Whitehead, 1
(a) Inc. Lancia-Ferrari.

Fittipaldi: Emerson Fittipaldi, 2 (as Copersucar); Keke Rosberg, 1

Force India: Sergio Pérez, 2; Giancarlo Fisichella, 1

Gordini: Jean Behra, 1; Robert Manzon, 1

Hesketh: James Hunt, 7

Honda: John Surtees, 4; Jenson Button, 3; Rubens Barrichello, 1; Richie Ginther, 1

Jaguar: Eddie Irvine, 2

Jordan: Heinz-Harald Frentzen, 8; Giancarlo Fisichella, 3; Ralf Schumacher, 3; Rubens Barrichello, 2; Damon Hill, 1; Eddie Irvine, 1; Tiago Monteiro, 1

Lancia: Eugenio Castellotti, 1

Ligier: Jacques Laffite, 31 (a); Didier Pironi, 5; Eddie Cheever, 3 (a); Olivier Panis, 3; Mark Blundell, 2; Martin Brundle, 2; Patrick Depailler, 2; Eric Bernard, 1; Philippe Streiff, 1
(a) Inc. Talbot-Ligier.

Lola: John Surtees, 2; Aguri Suzuki, 1

Lotus: Jim Clark, 32; Ayrton Senna, 22; Emerson Fittipaldi, 20 (a); Ronnie Peterson, 18 (a); Mario Andretti, 16 (a); Kimi Räikkönen, 15; Romain Grosjean, 10; Graham Hill, 10; Elio De Angelis, 9;; Jochen Rindt, 8; Nigel Mansell, 5; Innes Ireland, 4; Stirling Moss, 4; Gunnar Nilsson, 4 (a); Carlos Reutemann, 4; Jacky Ickx, 3 (a); Nelson Piquet, 3; Jo Siffert, 3; Peter Arundell, 2; Jackie Oliver, 1; Mike Spence, 1; John Surtees, 1; Trevor Taylor, 1; Reine Wisell, 1
(a) Inc. JPS Lotus.

March:	Ronnie Peterson, 7; Jackie Stewart, 4; Chris Amon, 3; Ivan Capelli, 3 (inc. Leyton House); James Hunt, 2; Mario Andretti, 1; Vittorio Brambilla, 1; Maurício Gugelmin, 1
Maserati:	Juan Manuel Fangio, 12; Jean Behra, 7; Stirling Moss, 5; José Froilán González, 4; Onofré Marimón, 2; Luigi Musso, 2; Cesare Perdisa, 2; Felice Bonetto, 1; Louis Chiron, 1; Masten Gregory, 1; Mike Hawthorn, 1; Carlos Mendítéguy, 1; Harry Schell, 1
Matra:	Jackie Stewart, 11; Jean-Pierre Beltoise, 6 (a); Chris Amon, 2 (a); Henri Pescarolo, 1 (a); Johnny Servoz-Gavin, 1 (a) Inc. Matra-Simca.
McLaren:	Alain Prost, 63; Ayrton Senna, 55; David Coulthard, 51; Mika Häkkinen, 51; Lewis Hamilton, 49; Kimi Räikkönen, 36; Jenson Button, 26; Denny Hulme, 21; Gerhard Berger, 18; Niki Lauda, 15; James Hunt, 14; Emerson Fittipaldi, 13; John Watson, 13; Fernando Alonso, 12; Jochen Mass, 8; Peter Revson, 8; Bruce McLaren, 7; Juan Pablo Montoya, 7; Stefan Johansson, 5; Heikki Kovalainen, 3; Martin Brundle, 2; Michael Andretti, 1; Pedro de la Rosa, 1; Mark Donohue, 1; Mike Hailwood, 1; Jacky Ickx, 1; Kevin Magnussen, 1; Keke Rosberg, 1; Alexander Wurz, 1
Mercedes-Benz:	Nico Rosberg, 39; Lewis Hamilton, 38; Juan Manuel Fangio, 10; Stirling Moss, 3; Karl Kling, 2; Hans Herrmann, 1; Michael Schumacher, 1; Piero Taruffi, 1
Onyx:	Stefan Johansson, 1
Penske:	John Watson, 3
Porsche:	Dan Gurney, 5
Prost:	Olivier Panis, 2; Jarno Trulli, 1
Red Bull:	Sebastian Vettel, 65; Mark Webber, 41; Daniel Ricciardo, 10; David Coulthard, 2; Daniil Kvyat, 1
Renault:	Fernando Alonso, 41; Alain Prost, 17; René Arnoux, 11; Giancarlo Fisichella, 8; Eddie Cheever, 4; Derek Warwick, 4; Robert Kubica, 3; Patrick Tambay, 3; Jarno Trulli, 3; Jean-Pierre Jabouille, 2; Nick Heidfeld, 1; Heikki Kovalainen, 1; Vitaly Petrov, 1; Nelsinho Piquet, 1
Sauber:	Sergio Pérez, 3; Heinz-Harald Frentzen, 2; Johnny Herbert, 2; Jean Alesi, 1; Nick Heidfeld, 1; Kamui Kobayashi, 1
Shadow:	Alan Jones, 2; Tom Pryce, 2; George Follmer, 1; Jean-Pierre Jarier, 1; Jackie Oliver, 1
Stewart:	Rubens Barrichello, 4; Johnny Herbert, 1
Surtees:	Mike Hailwood, 1; Carlos Pace, 1
Talbot-Lago:	Louis Rosier, 2
Toleman:	Ayrton Senna, 3
Toro Rosso:	Sebastian Vettel, 1
Toyota:	Jarno Trulli, 7; Timo Glock, 3; Ralf Schumacher, 3
Tyrrell:	Jackie Stewart, 20; Patrick Depailler, 17; Jody Scheckter, 14; François Cevert, 13; Michele Alboreto, 4; Jean Alesi, 2; Jean-Pierre Jarier, 2; Didier Pironi, 2; Mark Blundell, 1; Stefano Modena, 1; Ronnie Peterson, 1
Vanwall:	Stirling Moss, 7; Tony Brooks, 5; Stuart Lewis-Evans, 2
Williams:	Nigel Mansell, 43; Damon Hill, 40; Riccardo Patrese, 24; Juan Pablo Montoya, 23; Alan Jones, 22; Nelson Piquet, 21; Ralf Schumacher, 21; Jacques Villeneuve, 21; Carlos Reutemann, 16; Keke Rosberg, 15; Alain Prost, 12; David Coulthard, 9; Valtteri Bottas, 8; Thierry Boutsen, 8; Heinz-Harald Frentzen, 8; Felipe Massa, 5; Clay Regazzoni, 5; Nick Heidfeld, 3; Nico Rosberg, 2; Jacques Laffite, 1; Pastor Maldonado, 1; Mark Webber, 1; Alexander Wurz, 1
Wolf:	Jody Scheckter, 13

The total for some constructors is higher than in section 733 "Podium positions", due to drivers sharing a car. Those affected are Alfa Romeo, Cooper, Ferrari, Maserati and Vanwall.

765. Races with a podium with the same engine make *(Most)*

Ferrari	521	Ferrari	Monaco 1950 (Alberto Ascari)	- Abu Dhabi 2015 (Kimi Räikkönen)
McLaren	185	Mercedes	Italy 1995 (Mika Häkkinen)	- Australia 2014 (Kevin Magnussen, Jenson Button)
Williams	107	Renault	Mexico 1989 (Riccardo Patrese)	- Spain 2012 (Pastor Maldonado) (a)
McLaren	90	Ford Cosworth	Spain 1968 (Denny Hulme)	- Australia 1993 (Ayrton Senna)
Renault	88	Renault	France 1979 (Jean-Pierre Jabouille, René Arnoux)	- Malaysia 2011 (Nick Heidfeld)
Lotus	85	Ford Cosworth	Netherlands 1967 (Jim Clark)	- Austria 1982 (Elio De Angelis)
Red Bull	84	Renault	Europe 2007 (Mark Webber)	- Singapore 2015 (Daniel Ricciardo)
McLaren	64	Honda	Brazil 1988 (Alain Prost)	- Australia 1992 (Gerhard Berger)
Tyrrell	64	Ford Cosworth	South Africa 1971 (Jackie Stewart)	- Monaco 1990 (Jean Alesi)
Mercedes-Benz	61	Mercedes	France 1954 (Juan Manuel Fangio, Karl Kling)	- Abu Dhabi 2015 (Nico Rosberg, Lewis Hamilton)

(a) There were three additional wins with Mecachrome and three with Supertec, Renault-based engines, within the period.

766. Interval between podiums *(Longest)*

	years, days	races		
Mercedes-Benz (a)	54y, 205d	775	Italy 1955 (J M Fangio, P Taruffi)	- Malaysia 2010 (N Rosberg)
Honda (a)	37y, 164d	580	United States 1968 (J Surtees)	- Malaysia 2006 (J Button)
Alfa Romeo (a)	29y, 354d	342	Spain 1951 (G Farina, J M Fangio)	- Caesars Palace 1981 (B Giacomelli)
Lola (a)	28y, 77d	391	Germany 1962 (J Surtees)	- Japan 1990 (A Suzuki)
Lotus (a)	23y, 161d	394	Australia 1988 (N Piquet)	- Bahrain 2012 (K Räikkönen, R Grosjean)
Renault (a)	17y, 322d	292	San Marino 1985 (P Tambay)	- Malaysia 2003 (F Alonso)
March (a)	11y, 351d	186	Italy 1976 (R Peterson)	- Belgium 1988 (I Capelli)
Sauber (b)	8y, 179d	148	United States 2003 (H-H Frentzen)	- Malaysia 2012 (S Pérez)
Ligier	6y, 265d	106	Detroit 1986 (J Laffite)	- South Africa 1993 (M Blundell)
Arrows (c)	6y, 161d	108	United States 1989 (E Cheever)	- Australia 1995 (G Morbidelli)

(a) Not present throughout the period. (b) BMW controlled the operation as BMW Sauber from 2006 to 2009. (c) Australia 1995, as Footwork.

767. Interval between first & last podiums *(Longest)*

	years, days	races		
Ferrari	65y, 192d	932	Monaco 1950	- Abu Dhabi 2015
Mercedes-Benz	61y, 148d	899	France 1954	- Abu Dhabi 2015
Lotus	55y, 86d	841	Monaco 1960	- Belgium 2015
McLaren	44y, 197d	715	Spain 1968	- Australia 2014
Honda	42y, 256d	653	Mexico 1965	- Britain 2008
Williams	40y, 261d	672	Germany 1975	- Mexico 2015
Alfa Romeo	34y, 119d	401	Britain 1950	- Italy 1984
Renault	31y, 283d	520	France 1979	- Malaysia 2011
Lola	28y, 92d	392	Britain 1962	- Japan 1990
Brabham	25y, 332d	358	Belgium 1963	- Monaco 1989

768. Interval between first time podium constructors *(Longest)*

4 years and 338 days from France 1979 (1 July, Renault) until Monaco 1984 (3 June, Toleman).

769. Podium positions but never a constructors' championship *(Most)*

Ligier	50	March	22	BAR	15
Maserati	37 (a)	Jordan	19	Toyota	13
Alfa Romeo	26 (b)	BMW	17	Wolf	13

(a) All achieved before constructors' championship established. (b) 21 achieved before constructors' championship established.

770. Podium positions but never a drivers' championship *(Most)*

Ligier	50	BAR	15	Sauber	10
March	22	Toyota	13	Arrows	9
Jordan	19	Vanwall	13	Honda	9
BMW	17	Wolf	13		

771. Podium positions but never a win *(Most)*

BAR	15	Force India	3	Gordini	2
Toyota	13	Lola	3	Jaguar	2
Sauber	10	Prost	3	Surtees	2
Arrows	9	Toleman	3	Talbot-Lago	2
Fittipaldi	3	Dallara	2		

772. Podium positions but never a pole position *(Most)*

Sauber	10	Prost	3	Jaguar	2
Hesketh	7	Dallara	2	Surtees	2
Fittipaldi	3	Eagle	2	Talbot-Lago	2
Penske	3	Gordini	2		

773. Milestones: Podium positions

Ferrari	50th: Argentina 1954, 100th: Germany 1959, 200th: Netherlands 1975, 250th: Monaco 1979, 300th: Germany 1985, 400th: Japan 1997, 500th: Hungary 2002, 600th: China 2007
McLaren	50th: Spain 1975, 100th: Canada 1984, 200th: Germany 1990, 250th: Belgium 1994, 300th: Hungary 1999, 400th: Spain 2007
Williams	50th: Switzerland 1982, 100th: Britain 1988, 200th: Belgium 1995, 250th: Belgium 2000, 300th: Germany 2014
Lotus	50th: Monaco 1968, 100th: Italy 1974, 150th: Netherlands 1985
Benetton	50th: Portugal 1993, 100th: Monaco 2000
Brabham	50th: Mexico 1969, 100th: United States West 1982
Red Bull	50th: Europe 2011, 100th: Abu Dhabi 2013
Renault	50th: France 2004, 100th: Malaysia 2011
BRM	50th: Belgium 1968
Cooper	50th: Belgium 1965
Ligier	50th: Monaco 1996
Mercedes-Benz	50th: Hungary 2014
Tyrrell	50th: Sweden 1976

Michele Alboreto (Footwork) at June 1991's Silverstone test session (David Hayhoe).

Jordan team-mates, Stefano Modena and Maurício Gugelmin at the 1992 British Grand Prix (David Hayhoe).

Ayrton Senna (McLaren) at Silverstone in 1992 (David Hayhoe).

Nigel Mansell (Williams) at the British Grand Prix in 1992, his world title season (David Hayhoe).

Johnny Herbert (Lotus 107B - Ford Cosworth), fourth at Donington Park in the 1993 European Grand Prix (David Hayhoe).

Damon Hill (Williams) at Donington Park for the 1993 European Grand Prix (David Hayhoe).

Gerhard Berger (Ferrari) at the 1994 Hungarian Grand Prix (Proaction).

Johnny Herbert (Sauber C15 - Ford Cosworth) at the 1996 British Grand Prix, where he finished 9th (David Hayhoe).

Martin Brundle (McLaren MP4/9 - Peugeot) at the 1994 Hungarian Grand Prix, 1994 (Proaction).

Jacques Villeneuve in the Williams FW19 - Renault, at Silverstone in 1997 (David Hayhoe).

Ralf Schumacher (Jordan 197 - Peugeot) at the 1997 British Grand Prix (David Hayhoe).

Podium at the 1999 European Grand Prix (Nürburgring): Jackie Stewart (Jaguar team principal), Jarno Trulli (2nd), Johnny Herbert (1st) and Rubens Barrichello (3rd) (David Hayhoe).

Mika Häkkinen (McLaren), 1999 European Grand Prix (Nürburgring) (David Hayhoe).

Launch of BAR's 2000 car, the 002 at London's Queen Elizabeth Conference Centre (David Hayhoe).

Eddie Irvine (Jaguar R1) at the Silverstone test in April 2000 (David Hayhoe).

Michael Schumacher at Ferrari's F1 2000 launch in Maranello (David Hayhoe).

Jacques Villeneuve at the launch of the 2002 BAR 004 at the Brackley factory (David Hayhoe).

Jenson Button in 2002, at the Renault RS202 launch in Guyancourt, Paris (David Hayhoe).

Mark Webber (Jaguar) at Silverstone in 2003 (David Hayhoe).

Launch of the Ferrari F2005 in Maranello (February 2005) (David Hayhoe).

Kimi Räikkönen (McLaren) at the 2004 British Grand Prix (David Hayhoe).

David Coulthard (McLaren) at the 2004 British Grand Prix (David Hayhoe).

Jarno Trulli tries out the newly launched Renault R24 around Piazza Castelnuovo in Palermo, Sicily in 2004 (David Hayhoe).

Jarno Trulli (Toyota TF105) at June's Silverstone test session in 2005 (David Hayhoe).

The Williams FW27 - BMW, launched at Valencia airport in 2005 (David Hayhoe).

The 2006 British Grand Prix podium featuring winner Alonso, with Remi Matin (Renault engineer), Michael Schumacher and Räikkönen (David Hayhoe).

Sebastian Vettel, then BMW Sauber's reserve driver, at the 2007 British Grand Prix (David Hayhoe).

Kimi Räikkönen (Ferrari F2007) at Silverstone in 2007 (David Hayhoe).

Vitantonio Liuzzi (Toro Rosso STR2) at Silverstone testing in 2007 (David Hayhoe).

Felipe Massa (Ferrari) at the 2008 British Grand Prix (David Hayhoe).

Nelsinho Piquet (Renault) at the 2008 British Grand Prix (David Hayhoe).

The 2008 British Grand Prix podium: winner Hamilton, Heidfeld (2nd) and Barrichello (3rd) with McLaren team chief Martin Whitmarsh (David Hayhoe).

The Honda RA108 launch at their Brackley factory in 2008 (David Hayhoe).

Fernando Alonso (Renault R28 launch at Renault Square.com in Paris, 2008) (David Hayhoe).

Rubens Barrichello (Honda) at the 2008 British Grand Prix (David Hayhoe).

Robert Kubica (BMW Sauber F1.09). The 2009 launch at Valencia's Circuit Ricardo Tormo (David Hayhoe).

Sebastian Vettel (Red Bull RB7 - Renault), on his way to second place at the 2011 British Grand Prix (David Woollard).

Lewis Hamilton (McLaren MP4-26 - Mercedes) in practice for the 2011 British Grand Prix (David Woollard).

Michael Schumacher (Mercedes-Benz F1 W03) - the 2012 British Grand Prix (David Woollard).

Fernando Alonso in the Ferrari F2012 - the British Grand Prix, where he finished 2nd to Mark Webber (David Woollard).

Romain Grosjean, in his second season at Lotus, in 2013 (Team Lotus).

Jules Bianchi (2014), the first driver to score points for Marussia (Marussia F1 Team).

Jules Bianchi (Marussia) finished 14th here at the 2014 British Grand Prix (David Woollard).

Valtteri Bottas (Williams) at the 2015 British Grand Prix (Jakob Ebrey Photography).

Nico Rosberg (Mercedes-Benz) at the 2015 British Grand Prix (Jakob Ebrey Photography).

Sergio Pérez (Force India VJM08 - Mercedes) at the 2015 British Grand Prix (David Woollard).

Daniel Ricciardo (Red Bull) at the 2015 British Grand Prix (Red Bull Racing/Getty Images).

Max Verstappen (Toro Rosso) in 2015, the youngest driver to ever start a Formula 1 race (Scuderia Toro Rosso/Getty Images).

Chapter 19: Pole Position Constructors

774. Pole positions

		drivers		
Ferrari (a)	208	32	Britain 1951 (José Froilán González)	- Singapore 2015 (Sebastian Vettel)
McLaren	155	16	Canada 1972 (Peter Revson)	- Brazil 2012 (Lewis Hamilton)
Williams	128	19	Britain 1979 (Alan Jones)	- Austria 2014 (Felipe Massa)
Lotus (b)	107	13	Monaco 1960 (Stirling Moss)	- San Marino 1987 (Ayrton Senna)
Red Bull	57	2	China 2009 (Sebastian Vettel)	- Brazil 2013 (Sebastian Vettel)
Mercedes-Benz	53	4	France 1954 (Juan Manuel Fangio)	- Abu Dhabi 2015 (Nico Rosberg)
Renault	51	7	South Africa 1979 (Jean-Pierre Jabouille)	- Hungary 2009 (Fernando Alonso)
Brabham	39	10	Netherlands 1964 (Dan Gurney)	- Netherlands 1985 (Nelson Piquet)
Benetton	15	5	Austria 1986 (Teo Fabi)	- Austria 1998 (Giancarlo Fisichella)
Tyrrell	14	3	Canada 1970 (Jackie Stewart)	- Sweden 1976 (Jody Scheckter)
Alfa Romeo	12	4	Britain 1950 (Giuseppe Farina)	- United States West 1982 (Andrea De Cesaris)
BRM	11	4	Netherlands 1959 (Jo Bonnier)	- Argentina 1973 (Clay Regazzoni)
Cooper	11	3	Monaco 1959 (Stirling Moss)	- Mexico 1966 (John Surtees)
Maserati	10	2	Belgium 1953 (Juan Manuel Fangio)	- Argentina 1958 (Juan Manuel Fangio)
Ligier (c)	9	2	Italy 1976 (Jacques Laffite)	- Spain 1981 (Jacques Laffite)
Vanwall	7	3	Britain 1957 (Stirling Moss)	- Italy 1958 (Stirling Moss)
Brawn	5	2	Australia 2009 (Jenson Button)	- Brazil 2009 (Rubens Barrichello)
March	5	3	South Africa 1970 (Jackie Stewart)	- Netherlands 1976 (Ronnie Peterson)
Matra (d)	4	2	Monaco 1969 (Jackie Stewart)	- France 1972 (Chris Amon)
Shadow	3	2	Argentina 1975 (Jean-Pierre Jarier)	- Britain 1975 (Tom Pryce)

			drivers	
Toyota	3	2	United States 2005 (Jarno Trulli)	- Bahrain 2009 (Jarno Trulli)
BAR	2	1	San Marino 2004 (Jenson Button)	- Canada 2005 (Jenson Button)
Honda	2	2	Italy 1968 (John Surtees)	- Australia 2006 (Jenson Button)
Jordan	2	2	Belgium 1994 (Rubens Barrichello)	- Europe 1999 (Heinz-Harald Frentzen)
Lancia	2	2	Spain 1954 (Alberto Ascari)	- Belgium 1955 (Eugenio Castellotti)
Arrows	1	1	United States West 1981 (Riccardo Patrese)	
BMW (e)	1	1	Bahrain 2008 (Robert Kubica)	
Force India	1	1	Belgium 2009 (Giancarlo Fisichella)	
Lola	1	1	Netherlands 1962 (John Surtees)	
Porsche	1	1	Germany 1962 (Dan Gurney)	
Stewart	1	1	France 1999 (Rubens Barrichello)	
Toleman	1	1	Germany 1985 (Teo Fabi)	
Toro Rosso	1	1	Italy 2008 (Sebastian Vettel)	
Wolf	1	1	Germany 1977 (Jody Scheckter)	
Indianapolis 500				
Kurtis-Kraft	6	6	1950 (Walt Faulkner)	- 1957 (Pat O'Connor)
Watson	2	2	1956 (Pat Flaherty)	- 1958 (Dick Rathmann)
Ewing	1	1	1960 (Eddie Sachs)	
Lesovsky	1	1	1959 (Johnny Thomson)	
Stevens	1	1	1955 (Jerry Hoyt)	

Includes cases where cars did not start the race (see section 351).
(a) Includes Lancia-Ferrari.
(b) Includes JPS Lotus.
(c) Includes Talbot-Ligier.
(d) Includes Matra-Simca.
(e) As BMW Sauber.

775. Percentage of races with a pole position *(Highest)*

	%	pole positions			%	pole positions
Lancia	50.00	2		Ferrari	22.93	208
Mercedes-Benz	41.73	53		McLaren	19.87	155
Brawn	29.41	5		Williams	18.50	128
Red Bull	28.08	57		Lotus	17.66	107
Vanwall	25.00	7		Renault	17.00	51

776. Pole positions in a season *(Most)*

Mercedes-Benz	18 of 19	2014	(F1 W05)	(Nico Rosberg, 11; Lewis Hamilton, 7)
Mercedes-Benz	18 of 19	2015	(F1 W06)	(Lewis Hamilton, 11; Nico Rosberg, 7)
Red Bull	18 of 19	2011	(RB7 - Renault)	(Sebastian Vettel, 15; Mark Webber, 3)
McLaren	15 of 16	1988	(MP4/4 - Honda)	(Ayrton Senna, 13; Alain Prost, 2)
McLaren	15 of 16	1989	(MP4/5 - Honda)	(Ayrton Senna, 13; Alain Prost, 2)
Williams	15 of 16	1992	(FW14B - Renault)	(Nigel Mansell, 14; Riccardo Patrese, 1)
Williams	15 of 16	1993	(FW15C - Renault)	(Alain Prost, 13; Damon Hill, 2)
Red Bull	15 of 19	2010	(RB6 - Renault)	(Sebastian Vettel, 10; Mark Webber, 5)
JPS Lotus	12 of 16	1978	(78, 79 - Ford Cosworth)	(Mario Andretti, 8; Ronnie Peterson, 3, Jean-Pierre Jarier, 1)
McLaren	12 of 16	1990	(MP4/5B - Honda)	(Ayrton Senna, 10; Gerhard Berger, 2)
McLaren	12 of 16	1998	(MP4-13 - Mercedes)	(Mika Häkkinen, 9; David Coulthard, 3)
Williams	12 of 16	1987	(FW11B - Honda)	(Nigel Mansell, 8; Nelson Piquet, 4)
Williams	12 of 16	1996	(FW18 - Renault)	(Damon Hill, 9; Jacques Villeneuve, 3)
Williams	12 of 17	1995 (a)	(FW17, FW17B - Renault)	(Damon Hill, 7; David Coulthard, 5)
Ferrari	12 of 18	2004	(F2004)	(Michael Schumacher, 8; Rubens Barrichello, 4)

All became world champion constructor that season, except (a).

777. Pole position in every race of a season

Ferrari	7	1952	(Ferrari 500)	(Alberto Ascari, 5; Giuseppe Farina, 2)
Alfa Romeo	6	1950	(Alfa Romeo 158)	(Juan Manuel Fangio, 4; Giuseppe Farina, 2)

Excludes Indianapolis 500.

778. Pole position in all but one race of a season

Mercedes-Benz	18	2014	(F1 W05)	(Nico Rosberg, 11; Lewis Hamilton, 7)
Mercedes-Benz	18	2015	(F1 W06)	(Lewis Hamilton, 11; Nico Rosberg, 7)
Red Bull	18	2011	(RB7 - Renault)	(Sebastian Vettel, 15; Mark Webber, 3)
McLaren	15	1988	(MP4/4 - Honda)	(Ayrton Senna, 13; Alain Prost, 2)
McLaren	15	1989	(MP4/5 - Honda)	(Ayrton Senna, 13; Alain Prost, 2)
Williams	15	1992	(FW14B - Renault)	(Nigel Mansell, 14; Riccardo Patrese, 1)
Williams	15	1993	(FW15C - Renault)	(Alain Prost, 13; Damon Hill, 2)
Lancia-Ferrari	6	1956 (a)	(D50)	(Juan Manuel Fangio, 6)

All became world champion constructor that season, except (a) - no constructors' championship until 1958.

779. Consecutive pole positions *(Most)*

Williams	24	France 1992	- Japan 1993	(FW14B, FW15C - Renault)
Mercedes-Benz	23	Britain 2014	- Italy 2015	(F1 W05, F1 W06)
McLaren	17	Germany 1988	- Germany 1989	(MP4-4, MP4-5 - Honda)
Red Bull	16	Abu Dhabi 2010	- Japan 2011	(RB6, RB7 - Renault)
McLaren	12	Belgium 1989	- Mexico 1990	(MP4-5, MP4-5B - Honda)
Ferrari	10	Spain 1951	- Netherlands 1953	(375, 500)
Lotus	10	Netherlands 1967	- South Africa 1968	(49 - Ford Cosworth)
Williams	10	Belgium 1996	- Spain 1997	(FW18, FW19 - Renault)
Alfa Romeo	9	Britain 1950	- France 1951	(158, 159)
McLaren	9	Australia 1998	- Britain 1998	(MP4-13 - Mercedes)
Williams	9	Belgium 1987	- Italy 1987	(FW11B - Honda)

780. Pole in the season's opening race

Ferrari	12	Giuseppe Farina 1952, 54; Alberto Ascari 1953; José Froilán González 1955; Juan Manuel Fangio 1956 (a); Michele Alboreto 1985; Michael Schumacher 2001, 03, 04, 06; Rubens Barrichello 2002; Kimi Räikkönen 2007
McLaren	11	James Hunt 1976, 77; Ayrton Senna 1988, 89, 91; Gerhard Berger 1990; Mika Häkkinen 1998, 99, 2000; Lewis Hamilton 2008, 12
Lotus	10	Stirling Moss 1961; Jim Clark 1963, 64, 65, 66, 68; Ronnie Peterson 1974 (b); Mario Andretti 1978 (b); Elio De Angelis 1984; Ayrton Senna 1986
Williams	9	Alan Jones 1980; Keke Rosberg 1983; Nigel Mansell 1987, 92; Alain Prost 1993; Ayrton Senna 1994; Damon Hill 1995; Jacques Villeneuve 1996, 97
Brabham	3	Jack Brabham 1967, 69; Carlos Reutemann 1972
Red Bull	3	Sebastian Vettel 2010, 11, 13
Alfa Romeo	2	Giuseppe Farina 1950; Juan Manuel Fangio 1951
Cooper	2	Stirling Moss 1959, 60
Maserati	2	Stirling Moss 1957; Juan Manuel Fangio 1958
Mercedes-Benz	2	Lewis Hamilton 2014, 15
Renault	2	René Arnoux 1982; Giancarlo Fisichella 2005
Arrows	1	Riccardo Patrese 1981
Brawn	1	Jenson Button 2009
BRM	1	Clay Regazzoni 1973
Ligier	1	Jacques Laffite 1979
Lola	1	Stirling Moss 1962
March	1	Jackie Stewart 1970
Shadow	1	Jean-Pierre Jarier 1975
Tyrrell	1	Jackie Stewart 1971

(a) As Lancia-Ferrari.
(b) As JPS Lotus.

781. Opening race their only pole of the season

Ferrari	1955	(José Froilán González)	BRM	1973	(Clay Regazzoni)
Maserati	1958	(Juan Manuel Fangio)	JPS Lotus	1974	(Ronnie Peterson)
Lotus	1961	(Stirling Moss)	Arrows	1981	(Riccardo Patrese)
Lola	1962	(John Surtees)	Williams	1983	(Keke Rosberg)
Brabham	1972	(Carlos Reutemann)	Ferrari	1985	(Michele Alboreto)

782. Consecutive pole positions from the start of a season *(Most)*
(not counting any into the following season)

Red Bull	15	2011 (wc)	(RB7 - Renault)	(Sebastian Vettel, 12; Mark Webber, 3)
Williams	15	1993 (wc)	(FW15C - Renault)	(Alain Prost, 13; Damon Hill, 2)
Mercedes-Benz	12	2015 (wc)	(F1 W06)	(Lewis Hamilton, 11; Nico Rosberg, 1)
McLaren	9	1989 (wc)	(MP4/5 - Honda)	(Ayrton Senna, 7; Alain Prost, 2)
McLaren	9	1998 (wc)	(MP4-13 - Mercedes)	(Mika Häkkinen, 6; David Coulthard, 3)
Ferrari	7	1952 (a)	(500)	(Alberto Ascari, 5; Giuseppe Farina, 2)
McLaren	7	1988 (wc)	(MP4/4 - Honda)	(Ayrton Senna, 6; Alain Prost, 1)
Mercedes-Benz	7	2014 (wc)	(F1 W05)	(Lewis Hamilton, 4; Nico Rosberg, 3)
Red Bull	7	2010 (wc)	(RB6 - Renault)	(Mark Webber, 4; Sebastian Vettel, 3)
Alfa Romeo	6	1950 (a)	(158)	(Juan Manuel Fangio, 4; Giuseppe Farina, 2)
McLaren	6	1990 (wc)	(MP4/5B - Honda)	(Ayrton Senna, 4; Gerhard Berger, 2)
Williams	6	1992 (wc)	(FW14B - Renault)	(Nigel Mansell, 6)
Williams	6	1997 (wc)	(FW19 - Renault)	(Jacques Villeneuve, 5; Heinz-Harald Frentzen, 1)

(a) Sequence continued into the following season.
(wc) World champion constructor that season.

783. Seasons of pole positions *(Most)*

Ferrari	49	1951 - 2015	Brabham	17	1964 - 85	Tyrrell	6	1970 - 76
McLaren	29	1972 - 2012	Renault	11	1979 - 2009	Benetton	5	1986 - 96
Williams	25	1979 - 2014	BRM	7	1959 - 73	Maserati	5	1953 - 58
Lotus	22	1960 - 87	Mercedes-Benz	6	1954 - 2015	Red Bull	5	2009 - 13

784. Consecutive seasons of pole positions *(Most)*

Ferrari	15	1994 - 2008	Ferrari	6	1974 - 79	McLaren	5	1997 - 2001
Lotus	11	1960 - 70	McLaren	6	1988 - 93	Red Bull	5	2009 - 13
McLaren	10	2003 - 12	Renault	6	1979 - 84	Tyrrell	5	1970 - 74
Williams	9	1989 - 97	Brabham	5	1966 - 70	Williams	5	1979 - 83
Brabham	6	1980 - 85	Ferrari	5	1981 - 85	Williams	5	2001 - 05
Ferrari	6	1951 - 56	Lotus	5	1983 - 87			

785. Pole positions at the same venue *(Most)*

grand prix

Ferrari	19	Germany	1951 - 2012 (a)	(Nürburgring, 11; Hockenheim, 7; AVUS, 1)
Ferrari	19	Italy	1952 - 2010 (a)	(Monza)
Ferrari	17	France	1952 - 2008 (a)	(Magny-Cours, 6; Reims, 6; Paul Ricard, 2; Clermont-Ferrand, 1; Dijon-Prenois, 1; Rouen-les-Essarts, 1)
Ferrari	15	Britain	1951 - 2012	(Silverstone, 11; Brands Hatch, 3; Aintree, 1)
Ferrari	13	Belgium	1952 - 2007 (a)	(Spa-Francorchamps, 9; Zolder, 3; Nivelles-Baulers, 1)
Ferrari	13	Spain	1951 - 2008	(Catalunya, 7; Jarama, 3; Montjuïc, 2; Pedralbes, 1)
Williams	13	Britain	1979 - 2002	(Silverstone, 11; Brands Hatch, 2)
McLaren	12	Germany	1976 - 2008	(Hockenheim, 11; Nürburgring, 1)
McLaren	11	Belgium	1985 - 2012	(Spa-Francorchamps)
McLaren	11	Brazil	1974 - 2012	(Interlagos, 9; Jacarepaguá, 2)
McLaren	11	Canada	1972 - 2010	(Montréal, 8; Mosport Park, 3)
McLaren	11	Italy	1977 - 2012	(Monza)
McLaren	11	Monaco	1984 - 2007	(Monte-Carlo)

circuit

Ferrari	19	Monza	1952 - 2010 (a)	Ferrari	9	Monte-Carlo	1956 - 2008 (a)
Ferrari	15	Nürburgring	1951 - 2007 (a)(b)	Ferrari	9	Spa-Francorchamps	1952 - 2007 (a)
Ferrari	11	Silverstone	1951 - 2012	Ferrari	9	Suzuka	1987 - 2006
McLaren	11	Hockenheim	1984 - 2008	Lotus	9	Monte-Carlo	1960 - 85 (c)
McLaren	11	Monte-Carlo	1984 - 2007	McLaren	9	Imola	1988 - 2005
McLaren	11	Monza	1977 - 2012	McLaren	9	Interlagos	1974 - 2012
McLaren	11	Spa-Francorchamps	1985 - 2012	Williams	9	Hockenheim	1980 - 2003
Williams	11	Silverstone	1979 - 2002				

(a) Includes Lancia-Ferrari. (b) Includes European and Luxembourg Grands Prix. (c) Includes JPS Lotus.

786. Consecutive pole positions at the same venue *(Most)*

Ferrari	7	Japan	1998 - 2004	(Suzuka)		Lotus	5	Monaco	1960 - 64	(Monte-Carlo)
Williams	7	Britain	1991 - 97	(Silverstone)		Red Bull	5	Japan	2009 - 13	(Suzuka)
Williams	6	Brazil	1992 - 97	(Interlagos)		Williams	5	France	1991 - 95	(Magny-Cours)
Ferrari	5	Spain	2000 - 04	(Catalunya)						

787. Races taken to achieve their first pole position
(number of races includes the race of first pole and all qualifying attempts)

Alfa Romeo	1	Ligier	13	Shadow	28	Toyota	60
Brawn	1	Brabham	15	Force India	30	Toleman	63
Lancia	1	Vanwall	15	Honda	32	McLaren	69
Lola	1	BRM	18	Cooper	33	Red Bull	75
March	1	Lotus	19	BMW	38	BAR	87
Mercedes-Benz	1	Maserati	20	Stewart	40	Williams	88
Tyrrell	1	Matra	20	Arrows	45		
Ferrari	9	Renault	22	Toro Rosso	49		
Wolf	11	Porsche	23	Jordan	59		

For races started but never a pole position, see section 680.

788. Races with a front row position before their first pole *(Most)*

McLaren	13	Porsche	2	BAR	0	Renault	0
Brabham	5	Toyota	2	Brawn	0	Shadow	0
Matra	5	Benetton	1	Force India	0	Stewart	0
BRM	4	Lotus	1	Jordan	0	Toleman	0
Ferrari	4	Red Bull	1	Lancia	0	Toro Rosso	0
Cooper	3	Vanwall	1	Ligier	0	Tyrrell	0
Maserati	3	Wolf	1	Lola	0	Williams	0
BMW	2	Alfa Romeo	0	March	0		
Honda	2	Arrows	0	Mercedes-Benz	0		

789. Pole positions in their first season

Alfa Romeo	6 of 6	1950	(158)	(Juan Manuel Fangio, 4; Giuseppe Farina, 2)
Brawn	5 of 17	2009	(BGP 001 - Mercedes)	(Jenson Button, 4; Rubens Barrichello, 1)
Mercedes-Benz	4 of 8	1954	(W196 str., W196)	(Juan Manuel Fangio)
March	3 of 13	1970	(701 - Ford Cosworth)	(Jackie Stewart)
Benetton	2 of 16	1986	(B186 - BMW)	(Teo Fabi)
Lancia	1 of 8	1954	(D50)	(Alberto Ascari)
Lola	1 of 9	1962	(Mk 4 - Climax)	(John Surtees)
Tyrrell	1 of 13	1970	(001 - Ford Cosworth)	(Jackie Stewart)
Ligier	1 of 16	1976	(JS5 - Matra)	(Jacques Laffite)
Wolf	1 of 17	1977	(WR2 - Ford Cosworth)	(Jody Scheckter)

790. First pole position immediately followed by others
(including first pole position)

Alfa Romeo	9	Britain 1950 - France 1951	(158, 159)
Mercedes-Benz	3	France - Germany 1954	(W196 str., W196)
Benetton	2	Austria - Italy 1986	(B186 - BMW)
Brabham	2	Netherlands - Belgium 1964	(BT7 - Climax)
Brawn	2	Australia - Malaysia 2009	(BGP 001 - Mercedes)
Ferrari	2	Britain - Germany 1951	(375)
Lotus	2	Monaco - Netherlands 1960	(18 - Climax)
Shadow	2	Argentina - Brazil 1975	(DN5 - Ford Cosworth)

791. Pole position in their final race

| Lancia | Belgium 1955 | (Lancia D50) | (Eugenio Castellotti) |

The only constructor to achieve pole in the final race they started. Lancia did enter a later race but withdrew due to tyre safety concerns.

792. Pole positions in their final season

Brawn	5	2009	(BGP 001 - Mercedes)	(Jenson Button, 4; Rubens Barrichello, 1)
BAR	1	2005	(007 - Honda)	(Jenson Button)
Lancia	1	1955	(D50)	(Eugenio Castellotti)
Matra (a)	1	1972	(MS120D)	(Chris Amon)
Stewart	1	1999	(SF-3 - Ford Cosworth)	(Rubens Barrichello)
Toleman	1	1985	(TG185 - Hart)	(Teo Fabi)
Toyota	1	2009	(TF109)	(Jarno Trulli)

(a) As Matra-Simca.

793. More than one pole in a country during a season

Renault	1982	United States	Alain Prost (Detroit & Caesars Palace)
Renault	1982	France	René Arnoux (Paul Ricard) & Alain Prost (Dijon-Prenois)
Ferrari	1983	United States	Patrick Tambay (Long Beach) & René Arnoux (Detroit)
Brabham	1984	Italy	Nelson Piquet (Imola & Monza)
Lotus	1985	Italy	Ayrton Senna (Imola & Monza)
McLaren	1988	Italy	Ayrton Senna (Imola & Monza)
McLaren	1989	Italy	Ayrton Senna (Imola & Monza)
McLaren	1990	Italy	Ayrton Senna (Imola & Monza)
McLaren	1991	Italy	Ayrton Senna (Imola & Monza)
Williams	1992	Italy	Nigel Mansell (Imola & Monza)
Williams	1993	Britain	Alain Prost (Donington & Silverstone)
Williams	1993	Italy	Alain Prost (Imola & Monza)
Benetton	1994	Spain	Michael Schumacher (Catalunya & Jerez de la Frontera)
Williams	1995	Germany	Damon Hill (Hockenheim) & David Coulthard (Nürburgring)
Williams	1996	Germany	Damon Hill (Nürburgring & Hockenheim)
Williams	1997	Spain	Jacques Villeneuve (Catalunya & Jerez de la Frontera)
McLaren	1999	Italy	Mika Häkkinen (Imola & Monza)
McLaren	2000	Germany	David Coulthard (Nürburgring & Hockenheim)
Ferrari	2003	Italy	Michael Schumacher (Imola & Monza)
Ferrari	2004	Germany	Michael Schumacher (Nürburgring & Hockenheim)
McLaren	2005	Italy	Kimi Räikkönen (Imola) & Juan Pablo Montoya (Monza)
Ferrari	2008	Spain	Kimi Räikkönen (Catalunya) & Felipe Massa (Valencia)
Red Bull	2010	Spain	Mark Webber (Catalunya) & Sebastian Vettel (Valencia)
Red Bull	2011	Spain	Mark Webber (Catalunya) & Sebastian Vettel (Valencia)

794. Different pole position constructors in a season

Most

1972	6	Brabham, Tyrrell, Ferrari, JPS Lotus, Matra-Simca, McLaren
1976	6	McLaren, Ferrari, Tyrrell, March, Ligier, JPS Lotus
1981	6	Arrows, Brabham, Ferrari, Williams, Talbot-Ligier
1985	6	Ferrari, Lotus, Williams, Toleman, McLaren, Brabham
2005	6	Renault, McLaren, Williams, BAR, Toyota, Ferrari
2009	6	Brawn, Red Bull, Toyota, Renault, McLaren, Force India
1970	5	March, Brabham, Lotus, Ferrari, Tyrrell
1974	5	JPS Lotus, McLaren, Ferrari, Tyrrell, Brabham
1977	5	McLaren, Ferrari, JPS Lotus, Brabham, Wolf
1980	5	Williams, Renault, Brabham, Ligier, Alfa Romeo
1982	5	Renault, Alfa Romeo, Ferrari, Williams, Brabham
1983	5	Williams, Ferrari, Renault, Brabham, Lotus
1984	5	Lotus, Brabham, Ferrari, Renault, McLaren
2004	5	Ferrari, BAR, Renault, Williams, McLaren
2012	5	McLaren, Mercedes-Benz, Red Bull, Williams, Ferrari

Fewest

1950	1	Alfa Romeo		1992	2	Williams, McLaren
1952	1	Ferrari		1993	2	Williams, McLaren
1951	2	Alfa Romeo, Ferrari		1996	2	Williams, Ferrari
1953	2	Ferrari, Maserati		2000	2	McLaren, Ferrari
1956	2	Lancia-Ferrari, Maserati		2002	2	Ferrari, Williams
1957	2	Maserati, Vanwall		2007	2	Ferrari, McLaren
1965	2	Lotus, BRM		2011	2	Red Bull, McLaren
1967	2	Brabham, Lotus		2013	2	Red Bull, Mercedes-Benz
1988	2	McLaren, Ferrari		2014	2	Mercedes-Benz, Williams
1989	2	McLaren, Williams		2015	2	Mercedes-Benz, Ferrari
1991	2	McLaren, Williams				

Total for each season

1950 - 1, 1951 - 2, 1952 - 1, 1953 - 2, 1954 - 4, 1955 - 3, 1956 - 2, 1957 - 2, 1958 - 3, 1959 - 3, 1960 - 3, 1961 - 3, 1962 - 4, 1963 - 3, 1964 - 4, 1965 - 2, 1966 - 4, 1967 - 2, 1968 - 4, 1969 - 3, 1970 - 5, 1971 - 4, 1972 - 6, 1973 - 4, 1974 - 5, 1975 - 4, 1976 - 6, 1977 - 5, 1978 - 3, 1979 - 4, 1980 - 5, 1981 - 6, 1982 - 5, 1983 - 5, 1984 - 5, 1985 - 6, 1986 - 4, 1987 - 3, 1988 - 2, 1989 - 2, 1990 - 3, 1991 - 2, 1992 - 2, 1993 - 2, 1994 - 4, 1995 - 3, 1996 - 2, 1997 - 4, 1998 - 3, 1999 - 4, 2000 - 2, 2001 - 3, 2002 - 2, 2003 - 4, 2004 - 5, 2005 - 6, 2006 - 4, 2007 - 2, 2008 - 4, 2006 - 6, 2010 - 4, 2011 - 2, 2012 - 5, 2013 - 2, 2014 - 2, 2015 - 2

Excludes Indianapolis 500.

795. Different pole position constructors in consecutive races *(Most)*

Italy 1961	- Belgium 1962	5	Ferrari, Cooper, Lola, Lotus, BRM
Austria 1972	- Argentina 1973	5	Lotus, Ferrari, McLaren, Tyrrell, BRM
San Marino	- France 1981	5	Ferrari, Williams, Brabham, Talbot-Ligier, Renault
Britain	- Italy 1985	5	Williams, Toleman, McLaren, Brabham, Lotus
Monaco	- France 2005	5	McLaren, Williams, BAR, Toyota, Renault

796. Different pole position constructors from the start of a season *(Most)*

1972	4	Brabham, Tyrrell, Ferrari, JPS Lotus		1962	3	Lola, Lotus, BRM
2006	3	Ferrari, Renault, Honda		1969	3	Brabham, Lotus, Matra
2008	3	McLaren, Ferrari, BMW Sauber		1973	3	BRM, JPS Lotus, McLaren
1954	3	Ferrari, Maserati, Mercedes-Benz		1974	3	JPS Lotus, McLaren, Ferrari
1955	3	Ferrari, Mercedes-Benz, Lancia		1983	3	Williams, Ferrari, Renault
1959	3	Cooper, BRM, Ferrari		1984	3	Lotus, Brabham, Ferrari

797. First time pole position constructors in a season *(Most)*

2009	3	Brawn, Red Bull, Force India		1970	2	March, Tyrrell
1954	2	Mercedes-Benz, Lancia		1979	2	Renault, Williams
1959	2	Cooper, BRM		2008	2	BMW (a), Toro Rosso
1962	2	Lola, Porsche				

(a) As BMW Sauber.

798. Pole positions to race retirement *(Most)*

Lotus	47	Portugal 1960	- Portugal 1986
Ferrari	41	Switzerland 1952	- Malaysia 2008 (a)
McLaren	41	Brazil 1976	- Brazil 2012
Williams	38	Britain 1979	- Italy 2002
Brabham	18	Netherlands 1964	- Italy 1984
Renault	13	South Africa 1979	- Hungary 2009
Vanwall	6	Britain 1957	- Italy 1958
Alfa Romeo	5	Switzerland 1950	- United States West 1982
Benetton	4	Austria 1986	- Austria 1998
Cooper	4	Monaco 1959	- United States 1961
March	4	Monaco 1970	- Netherlands 1976
Mercedes-Benz	4	Monaco 1955	- Russia 2015

(a) Plus 2 races where the pole car did not start the race (see section 351).

Pole position to race retirement before end of first lap. See section 351

799. Consecutive races with a pole position to retirement *(Most)*

Ferrari	3	Germany	- Italy 1974	(312B3)	(Niki Lauda)
McLaren	3	Spain	- Australia 1990	(MP4/5B - Honda)	(Ayrton Senna)
Renault	3	San Marino	- Monaco 1982	(RE30B)	(René Arnoux, 2; Alain Prost, 1)
Williams	3	Brazil	- San Marino 1994	(FW16 - Renault)	(Ayrton Senna)
Williams	3	Monaco	- Europe 2002	(FW24 - BMW)	(Juan Pablo Montoya)

(a) Plus 2 races where the pole car did not start the race (see section 351).

800. Pole position drivers by constructor

Alfa Romeo: Juan Manuel Fangio, 8; Giuseppe Farina, 2; Andrea De Cesaris, 1; Bruno Giacomelli, 1

Arrows: Riccardo Patrese, 1

BAR: Jenson Button, 2

Benetton: Michael Schumacher, 10; Teo Fabi, 2; Jean Alesi, 1; Gerhard Berger, 1; Giancarlo Fisichella, 1

BMW *(as BMW Sauber)*: Robert Kubica, 1

Brabham: Nelson Piquet, 18; Jack Brabham, 8; Dan Gurney, 2; Jacky Ickx, 2; Carlos Reutemann, 2; Jochen Rindt, 2; John Watson, 2; Niki Lauda, 1; Carlos Pace, 1; Riccardo Patrese, 1

Brawn: Jenson Button, 4; Rubens Barrichello, 1

BRM: Graham Hill, 8; Jo Bonnier, 1; Clay Regazzoni, 1; Jo Siffert, 1

Cooper: Jack Brabham, 5; Stirling Moss, 5; John Surtees, 1

Ferrari: Michael Schumacher, 58; Niki Lauda, 23; Felipe Massa, 15; Alberto Ascari, 13; Rubens Barrichello, 11; Jacky Ickx, 11; Gerhard Berger, 7; Juan Manuel Fangio, 6 (as Lancia-Ferrari); Phil Hill, 6; Kimi Räikkönen, 5; Fernando Alonso, 4; René Arnoux, 4; Mike Hawthorn, 4; Clay Regazzoni, 4; John Surtees, 4; Patrick Tambay, 4; Chris Amon, 3; Giuseppe Farina, 3; José Froilán González, 3; Nigel Mansell, 3; Michele Alboreto, 2; Tony Brooks, 2; Didier Pironi, 2; Carlos Reutemann, 2; Gilles Villeneuve, 2; Jean Alesi, 1; Mario Andretti, 1; Lorenzo Bandini, 1; Mike Parkes, 1; Jody Scheckter, 1; Sebastian Vettel, 1; Wolfgang von Trips, 1

Force India: Giancarlo Fisichella, 1

Honda: Jenson Button, 1; John Surtees, 1

Jordan: Rubens Barrichello, 1; Heinz-Harald Frentzen, 1

Lancia: Alberto Ascari, 1; Eugenio Castellotti, 1

Ligier: Jacques Laffite, 7 (inc. Talbot-Ligier); Didier Pironi, 2

Lola: John Surtees, 1

Lotus: Jim Clark, 33; Mario Andretti, 17 (a); Ayrton Senna, 16; Ronnie Peterson, 13 (a); Jochen Rindt, 8; Graham Hill, 5; Emerson Fittipaldi, 4 (a); Stirling Moss, 4; Elio De Angelis, 3; Jean-Pierre Jarier, 1 (a); Nigel Mansell, 1; Jo Siffert, 1; John Surtees, 1
(a) Inc. JPS Lotus.

March: Jackie Stewart, 3; Vittorio Brambilla, 1; Ronnie Peterson, 1

Maserati: Juan Manuel Fangio, 8; Stirling Moss, 2

Matra: Chris Amon, 2 (as Matra-Simca); Jackie Stewart, 2

McLaren: Ayrton Senna, 46; Mika Häkkinen, 26; Lewis Hamilton, 26; James Hunt, 14; Kimi Räikkönen, 11; Alain Prost, 10; David Coulthard, 7; Gerhard Berger, 4; Fernando Alonso, 2; Emerson Fittipaldi, 2; Juan Pablo Montoya, 2; Jenson Button, 1; Denny Hulme, 1; Heikki Kovalainen, 1; Peter Revson, 1; Keke Rosberg, 1

Mercedes-Benz: Lewis Hamilton, 23; Nico Rosberg, 22; Juan Manuel Fangio, 7; Stirling Moss, 1

Porsche: Dan Gurney, 1

Red Bull: Sebastian Vettel, 44; Mark Webber, 13

Renault: Fernando Alonso, 16; René Arnoux, 14; Alain Prost, 10; Jean-Pierre Jabouille, 6; Giancarlo Fisichella, 2; Jarno Trulli, 2; Patrick Tambay, 1

Shadow: Jean-Pierre Jarier, 2; Tom Pryce, 1

Stewart: Rubens Barrichello, 1

Toleman: Teo Fabi, 1

Toro Rosso: Sebastian Vettel, 1

Toyota: Jarno Trulli, 2; Ralf Schumacher, 1

Tyrrell: Jackie Stewart, 12; Patrick Depailler, 1; Jody Scheckter, 1

Vanwall: Stirling Moss, 4; Stuart Lewis-Evans, 2; Tony Brooks, 1

Williams: Nigel Mansell, 28; Damon Hill, 20; Alain Prost, 13; Jacques Villeneuve, 13; Juan Pablo Montoya, 11; Alan Jones, 6; Riccardo Patrese, 6; Nelson Piquet, 6; David Coulthard, 5; Ralf Schumacher, 5; Keke Rosberg, 4; Ayrton Senna, 3; Carlos Reutemann, 2; Thierry Boutsen, 1; Heinz-Harald Frentzen, 1; Nick Heidfeld, 1; Nico Hülkenberg, 1; Pastor Maldonado, 1; Felipe Massa, 1

Wolf: Jody Scheckter, 1

801. Pole positions with the same engine make *(Most)*

Ferrari	208	Ferrari	Britain 1951 (José Froilán González)	- Singapore 2015 (Sebastian Vettel)
Williams	80	Renault	Hungary 1989 (Riccardo Patrese)	- Spain 2012 (Pastor Maldonado)
McLaren	76	Mercedes	Luxembourg 1997 (Mika Häkkinen)	- Brazil 2012 (Lewis Hamilton)
Red Bull	57	Renault	China 2009 (Sebastian Vettel)	- Brazil 2013 (Sebastian Vettel)
Lotus	56	Ford Cosworth	Netherlands 1967 (Graham Hill)	- Canada 1978 (Jean-Pierre Jarier)
McLaren	53	Honda	Brazil 1988 (Ayrton Senna)	- Canada 1992 (Ayrton Senna)
Mercedes-Benz	53	Mercedes	France 1954 (Juan Manuel Fangio)	- Abu Dhabi 2015 (Nico Rosberg)
Renault	51	Renault	South Africa 1979 (Jean-Pierre Jabouille)	- Hungary 2009 (Fernando Alonso)
Lotus	31	Climax	Monaco 1960 (Stirling Moss)	- Germany 1966 (Jim Clark)
Lotus	19	Renault	Europe 1983 (Elio De Angelis)	- Mexico 1986 (Ayrton Senna)
McLaren	19	Ford Cosworth	Canada 1972 (Peter Revson)	- Australia 1993 (Ayrton Senna)
Williams	19	Honda	France 1985 (Keke Rosberg)	- Mexico 1987 (Nigel Mansell)

For complete list of pole position constructors by engine make, see section 1002.

Overall

Alfa Romeo: Alfa Romeo, 12
Arrows: Ford Cosworth, 1
BAR: Honda, 2
Benetton: Ford Cosworth, 6; Renault, 6; BMW, 2; Playlife, 1
BMW: BMW, 1
Brabham: Ford Cosworth, 14; BMW, 13; Repco, 7; Alfa Romeo, 3; Climax, 2
Brawn: Mercedes-Benz, 5
BRM: BRM, 11
Cooper: Climax, 10; Maserati, 1
Ferrari: Ferrari, 208
Force India: Mercedes-Benz, 1
Honda: Honda, 2
Jordan: Hart, 1; Mugen Honda, 1
Lancia: Lancia, 2
Ligier: Ford Cosworth, 7; Matra, 2
Lola: Climax, 1
Lotus: Ford Cosworth, 56; Climax, 31; Renault, 19; Honda, 1
March: Ford Cosworth, 5
Maserati: Maserati, 10
Matra: Ford Cosworth, 2; Matra, 2
McLaren: Mercedes-Benz, 76; Honda, 53; Ford Cosworth, 19; TAG Porsche, 7
Mercedes-Benz: Mercedes-Benz, 53
Porsche: Porsche, 1
Red Bull: Renault, 57
Renault: Renault, 51
Shadow: Ford Cosworth, 3
Stewart: Ford Cosworth, 1
Toleman: Hart, 1
Toro Rosso: Ferrari, 1
Toyota: Toyota, 3
Tyrrell: Ford Cosworth, 14
Vanwall: Vanwall, 7
Williams: Renault, 80; Honda, 19; BMW, 17; Cosworth, 11 (inc. Ford Cosworth); Mercedes-Benz, 1
Wolf: Ford Cosworth, 1

802. Interval between pole positions *(Longest)*

	years, days	races		
Mercedes-Benz (a)	56y, 217d	813	Italy 1955 (Juan Manuel Fangio)	- China 2012 (Nico Rosberg)
Honda (a)	37y, 206d	583	Italy 1968 (John Surtees)	- Australia 2006 (Jenson Button)
Alfa Romeo (a)	29y, 19d	328	Italy 1951 (Juan Manuel Fangio)	- United States 1980 (Bruno Giacomelli)
Renault (a)	18y, 307d	306	France 1984 (Patrick Tambay)	- Malaysia 2003 (Fernando Alonso)
Benetton	7y, 250d	119	Italy 1986 (Teo Fabi)	- Monaco 1994 (Michael Schumacher)
McLaren	6y, 245d	99	United States 1977 (James Hunt)	- Monaco 1984 (Alain Prost)
BRM	5y, 316d	65	United States 1965 (Graham Hill)	- Austria 1971 (Jo Siffert)
Williams	5y, 162d	100	Europe 2005 (Nick Heidfeld)	- Brazil 2010 (Nico Hülkenberg)
Jordan	5y, 29d	85	Belgium 1994 (Rubens Barrichello)	- Europe 1999 (Heinz-Harld Frentzen)
Cooper	5y, 15d	48	United States 1961 (Jack Brabham)	- Mexico 1966 (John Surtees)

(a) Not present throughout the period.

803. Interval between first & second pole positions

Shortest

	days		
Brawn	7	Australia 2009 (Jenson Button)	- Malaysia 2009 (Jenson Button) (a)
Mercedes-Benz	7	France 1954 (Juan Manuel Fangio)	- Britain 1954 (Juan Manuel Fangio) (a)
Alfa Romeo	8	Britain 1950 (Giuseppe Farina)	- Monaco 1950 (Juan Manuel Fangio) (a)
Lotus	8	Monaco 1960 (Stirling Moss)	- Netherlands 1960 (Stirling Moss) (a)
Shadow	14	Argentina 1975 (Jean-Pierre Jarier)	- Brazil 1975 (Jean-Pierre Jarier) (a)
Ferrari	15	Britain 1951 (José Froilán González)	- Germany 1951 (Alberto Ascari) (a)
Benetton	21	Austria 1986 (Teo Fabi)	- Italy 1986 (Teo Fabi) (a)
Brabham	21	Netherlands 1964 (Dan Gurney)	- Belgium 1964 (Dan Gurney) (a)
Matra	49	Monaco 1969 (Jackie Stewart)	- France 1969 (Jackie Stewart)
Red Bull	49	China 2009 (Sebastian Vettel)	- Turkey 2009 (Sebastian Vettel)

(a) Consecutive grands prix.

Longest

	years, days	races		
Honda	37y, 206d	583	Italy 1968 (John Surtees)	- Australia 2006 (Jenson Button)
Jordan	5y, 29d	85	Belgium 1994 (Rubens Barrichello)	- Europe 1999 (Heinz-Harald Frentzen)
BRM	3y, 17d	27	Netherlands 1959 (Jo Bonnier)	- Belgium 1962 (Graham Hill)
Ligier	2y, 131d	37	Italy 1976 (Jacques Laffite)	- Argentina 1979 (Jacques Laffite)
BAR	1y 48d	22	San Marino 2004 (Jenson Button)	- Canada 2005 (Jenson Button)

804. Interval between first & last pole positions *(Longest)*

	years, days	races		
Ferrari	64y, 68d	917	Britain 1951	- Singapore 2015
Mercedes-Benz	61y, 148d	899	France 1954	- Abu Dhabi 2015
McLaren	40y, 65d	659	Canada 1972	- Brazil 2012
Honda	37y, 206d	583	Italy 1968	- Australia 2006
Williams	34y, 343d	583	Britain 1979	- Austria 2014
Alfa Romeo	31y, 326d	359	Britain 1950	- United States West 1982
Renault	30y, 145d	497	South Africa 1979	- Hungary 2009
Lotus	26y, 339d	352	Monaco 1960	- San Marino 1987
Brabham	21y, 93d	292	Netherlands 1964	- Netherlands 1985
BRM	13y, 242d	143	Netherlands 1959	- Argentina 1973

805. Interval between first time pole position constructors *(Longest)*

8 years and 11 days, from Austria 1986 (17 August, Benetton) until Belgium 1994 (28 August, Jordan).

806. Pole positions but never a constructors' championship *(Most)*

Alfa Romeo	12 (a)	Shadow	3	Jordan	2		
Maserati	10 (b)	Toyota	3	Lancia	2 (b)		
Ligier	9	BAR	2				
March	5	Honda	2				

(a) 10 achieved before constructors' championship established.
(b) 9 achieved before constructors' championship established.

807. Pole positions but never a win

Toyota	3	Arrows	1	Toleman	1
BAR	2	Force India	1		
Lancia	2	Lola	1		

808. Pole positions but never a fastest lap

BAR	2	Lola	1	Stewart	1
Arrows	1	Porsche	1	Toro Rosso	1

809. Pole positions but never led

Lola	1	Toleman	1

Pole position speed *(Fastest/ Slowest)*. See section 358

Identical time as the pole time in qualifying. See section 359

810. Milestones: Pole positions

Ferrari	25th: Italy 1956, 50th: Germany 1970, 100th: Austria 1983, 150th: Malaysia 2002, 200th: France 2008
McLaren	25th: Germany 1986, 50th: Belgium 1989, 100th: Germany 1999, 150th: Hungary 2012
Lotus	25th: France 1965, 50th: United States 1969, 100th: Spain 1986
Williams	25th: Hungary 1987, 50th: Portugal 1992, 100th: Argentina 1997
Mercedes-Benz	25th: Britain 2014, 50th: United States 2015
Red Bull	25th: Spain 2011, 50th: Italy 2013
Renault	25th: France 1982, 50th: China 2006
Brabham	25th: Monaco 1981

Chapter 20: Front Row Constructors

811. Front row positions

	races		drivers			
Ferrari (a)	470	361	47	Italy 1950 (Alberto Ascari)	- Singapore 2015 (Sebastian Vettel)
McLaren	336	270	20	Italy 1967 (Bruce McLaren)	- Brazil 2012 (Lewis Hamilton, Jenson Button)
Williams	270	208	21	Britain 1979 (Alan Jones)	- Germany 2014 (Valtteri Bottas)
Lotus (b)	178	158	19	Argentina 1960 (Innes Ireland)	- China 2013 (Kimi Räikkönen)
Brabham	105	95	12	Belgium 1963 (Dan Gurney)	- South Africa 1985 (Nelson Piquet)
Mercedes-Benz	103	64	6	France 1954 (Juan Manuel Fangio, Karl Kling)	- Abu Dhabi 2015 (Nico Rosberg, Lewis Hamilton)
Red Bull	103	80	3	Britain 2008 (Mark Webber)	- Singapore 2015 (Daniel Ricciardo)
Renault	91	69	9	South Africa 1979 (Jean-Pierre Jabouille)	- Monaco 2010 (Robert Kubica)
BRM	57	51	12	Britain 1956 (Mike Hawthorn)	- Argentina 1973 (Clay Regazzoni)
Cooper	40	29	10	Netherlands 1952 (Mike Hawthorn)	- Mexico 1966 (John Surtees)
Maserati	39	32	7	Monaco 1950 (José Froilán González)	- Argentina 1958 (Juan Manuel Fangio, Jean Behra)
Alfa Romeo	35	16	7	Britain 1950 (Giuseppe Farina, Luigi Fagioli, Juan Manuel Fangio, Reg Parnell)	- Detroit 1982 (Andrea De Cesaris)
Benetton	33	32	5	Belgium 1986 (Gerhard Berger)	- Austria 1998 (Giancarlo Fisichella)
Tyrrell	33	30	5	Canada 1970 (Jackie Stewart)	- Monaco 1991 (Stefano Modena)

	races	drivers			
Vanwall	22	12	3	Monaco 1957 (Stirling Moss)	- Morocco 1958 (Stirling Moss, Stuart Lewis-Evans)
Ligier (c)	19	14	3	Italy 1976 (Jacques Laffite)	- Spain 1981 (Jacques Laffite)
Matra (d)	17	17	4	South Africa 1968 (Jackie Stewart)	- Italy 1972 (Chris Amon)
March	12	9	4	South Africa 1970 (Jackie Stewart, Chris Amon)	- Canada 1976 (Ronnie Peterson)
Toyota	11	10	3	Australia 2005 (Jarno Trulli)	- Japan 2009 (Jarno Trulli)
Brawn	9	8	2	Australia 2009 (Jenson Button, Rubens Barrichello)	- Brazil 2009 (Rubens Barrichello)
Jordan	9	9	4	Belgium 1994 (Rubens Barrichello)	- Belgium 2000 (Jarno Trulli)
BAR	8	8	2	San Marino 2004 (Jenson Button)	- Japan 2005 (Jenson Button)
Honda	6	6	3	Britain 1965 (Richie Ginther)	- San Marino 2006 (Jenson Button)
Eagle	5	5	1	Britain 1966 (Dan Gurney)	- Germany 1967 (Dan Gurney)
Gordini	5	4	2	Switzerland 1952 (Robert Manzon)	- Italy 1952 (Maurice Trintignant)
BMW (e)	4	4	2	Hungary 2007 (Nick Heidfeld)	- Canada 2008 (Robert Kubica)
Lancia	4	4	2	Spain 1954 (Alberto Ascari)	- Belgium 1955 (Eugenio Castellotti)
Shadow	4	4	2	Argentina 1975 (Jean-Pierre Jarier)	- Britain 1975 (Tom Pryce)
Lola	3	3	1	Netherlands 1962 (John Surtees)	- Germany 1962 (John Surtees)
Porsche	3	3	2	Britain 1961 (Jo Bonnier)	- Germany 1962 (Dan Gurney)
Sauber	3	3	2	Austria 1998 (Jean Alesi)	- Belgium 2012 (Kamui Kobayashi)
Wolf	3	3	1	Monaco 1977 (Jody Scheckter)	- Canada 1978 (Jody Scheckter)
Force India	2	2	2	Belgium 2009 (Giancarlo Fisichella)	- Italy 2009 (Adrian Sutil)
Hesketh	2	2	1	United States 1974 (James Hunt)	- Austria 1975 (James Hunt)
Arrows	1	1	1	United States West 1981 (Riccardo Patrese)	
Aston Martin	1	1	1	Britain 1959 (Roy Salvadori)	
Jaguar	1	1	1	Malaysia 2004 (Mark Webber)	
Minardi	1	1	1	United States 1990 (Pierluigi Martini)	
Penske	1	1	1	Austria 1976 (John Watson)	
Stewart	1	1	1	France 1999 (Rubens Barrichello)	
Surtees	1	1	1	South Africa 1974 (Carlos Pace)	
Toleman	1	1	1	Germany 1985 (Teo Fabi)	
Toro Rosso	1	1	1	Italy 2008 (Sebastian Vettel)	
Indianapolis 500					
Kurtis-Kraft	18	8	12	1950 (Walt Faulkner)	- 1957 (Pat O'Connor)
Watson	8	5	7	1956 (Pat Flaherty)	- 1960 (Rodger Ward)
Kuzma	3	3	2	1954 (Jimmy Bryan)	- 1959 (Eddie Sachs)
Deidt	1	1	1	1950 (Mauri Rose)	
Stevens	1	1	1	1955 (Jerry Hoyt)	
Lesovsky	1	1	1	1959 (Johnny Thomson)	
Ewing	1	1	1	1960 (Eddie Sachs)	

Includes cases where drivers did not start the race (see section 405).
(a) Includes Lancia-Ferrari. (b) Includes JPS Lotus. (c) Includes Talbot-Ligier. (d) Includes Matra-Simca. (e) As BMW Sauber.

812. Percentage of races with a front row position *(Highest)*

	%	races with a front row		%	races with a front row
Lancia	100.00	4	Ferrari	39.80	362
Mercedes-Benz	50.39	64	Red Bull	39.41	80
Maserati	47.06	32	McLaren	34.62	270
Brawn	47.06	8	Williams	30.06	208
Vanwall	42.86	12	Matra	27.42	17

813. Front row positions in a season *(Most)*

Mercedes-Benz	33 of 38	2015	(F1 W06)	(Lewis Hamilton, 18; Nico Rosberg, 15)
Mercedes-Benz	30 of 38	2014	(F1 W05)	(Lewis Hamilton, 15; Nico Rosberg, 15)
Williams	28 of 32	1993	(FW15C - Renault)	(Alain Prost, 16; Damon Hill, 12)
McLaren	27 of 32	1988	(MP4/4 - Honda)	(Ayrton Senna, 15; Alain Prost, 12)
McLaren	27 of 32	1989	(MP4/5 - Honda)	(Ayrton Senna, 16; Alain Prost, 11)
Williams	26 of 32	1992	(FW14B - Renault)	(Nigel Mansell, 15; Riccardo Patrese, 11)
Red Bull	26 of 38	2010	(RB6 - Renault)	(Sebastian Vettel, 14; Mark Webber, 12)
Red Bull	26 of 38	2011	(RB7 - Renault)	(Sebastian Vettel, 18; Mark Webber, 8)
Williams	25 of 32	1996	(FW18 - Renault)	(Damon Hill, 16; Jacques Villeneuve, 9)
McLaren	22 of 32	1998	(MP4-13 - Mercedes)	(Mika Häkkinen, 12; David Coulthard, 10)

All became world champion constructor that season.

814. Races in a season with a front row position *(Most)*

Red Bull	19 of 19	2011	(RB7 - Renault)	(Sebastian Vettel, Mark Webber)
Mercedes-Benz	18 of 19	2014	(F1 W05)	(Lewis Hamilton, Nico Rosberg)
Mercedes-Benz	18 of 19	2015	(F1 W06)	(Lewis Hamilton, Nico Rosberg)
Red Bull	18 of 19	2010	(RB6 - Renault)	(Sebastian Vettel, Mark Webber)
McLaren	16 of 16	1989	(MP4/5 -Honda)	(Alain Prost, Ayrton Senna)
Williams	16 of 16	1992	(FW14B - Renault)	(Nigel Mansell, Riccardo Patrese)
Williams	16 of 16	1993	(FW15C - Renault)	(Damon Hill, Alain Prost)
Williams	16 of 16	1996	(FW18 - Renault)	(Damon Hill, Jacques Villeneuve)
McLaren	16 of 17	2007 (a)	(MP4-22 - Mercedes)	(Fernando Alonso, Lewis Hamilton)
Williams	16 of 17	1997	(FW19 - Renault)	(Heinz-Harald Frentzen, Jacques Villeneuve)
Ferrari	16 of 18	2004	(F2004)	(Rubens Barrichello, Michael Schumacher)

All became world champion constructor that season, except (a).
(a) In 2007, McLaren were stripped of all their constructors' championship points, due to the spying scandal.

815. Front row in every race of a season
(apart from those in section 814)

Lotus	15	1973 (wc)	(72D, 72E - Ford Cosworth)	(E Fittipaldi, R Peterson)
Lotus	9	1962	(24, 25 - Climax)	(J Clark, I Ireland, T Taylor)
Cooper	8	1959 (wc)	(T51 - Climax)	(J Brabham, M Gregory, S Moss, H Schell)
Ferrari	8	1953	(500)	(A Ascari, G Farina, M Hawthorn, L Villoresi)
Maserati	8	1953	(A6GCM)	(F Bonetto, J M Fangio, J F González)
Maserati	8	1954	(250F)	(A Ascari, J M Fangio, S Moss, H Schell)
Alfa Romeo	7	1951	(159)	(J M Fangio, G Farina)
Ferrari	7	1951	(375)	(A Ascari, J F González, L Villoresi)
Ferrari	7	1952	(500)	(A Ascari, G Farina, P Taruffi, L Villoresi)
Ferrari	7	1956	(D50)	(E Castellotti, P Collins, J M Fangio, L Musso)
Maserati	7	1957	(250F)	(J Behra, J M Fangio, S Moss)
Alfa Romeo	6	1950	(158)	(L Fagioli, J M Fangio, G Farina, R Parnell, C Sanesi)
Mercedes-Benz	6	1955	(W196, W196 str.)	(J M Fangio, K Kling, S Moss)

(wc) World champion constructor that season. No constructors' championship until 1958.

816. Front row in all but one race of a season

Mercedes-Benz	18	2014 (wc)	(F1 W05)	(L Hamilton, N Rosberg)
Red Bull	18	2010 (wc)	(RB6 - Renault)	(S Vettel, M Webber)
Mercedes-Benz	18	2015 (wc)	(F1 W06)	(L Hamilton, N Rosberg)
McLaren	16	2007 (a)	(MP4-22 - Mercedes)	(F Alonso, L Hamilton)
Williams	16	1997 (wc)	(FW19 - Renault)	(H-H Frentzen, J Villeneuve)
McLaren	15	1988 (wc)	(MP4/4 - Honda)	(A Prost, A Senna)
Brabham	9	1964	(BT7 - Climax)	(J Brabham, D Gurney)
Lotus	9	1965 (wc)	(25, 33 - Climax)	(J Clark)
BRM	8	1962 (wc)	(P57)	(R Ginther, G Hill)
Cooper	8	1960 (wc)	(T51, T53 - Climax)	(J Brabham, T Brooks, B McLaren, S Moss)
Ferrari	7	1954	(625, 553)	(A Ascari, G Farina, J F González, M Hawthorn)
Ferrari	7	1961 (wc)	(156)	(O Gendebien, R Ginther, P Hill, R Rodríguez, W von Trips)

(a) In 2007, McLaren were stripped of all their constructors' championship points, due to the spying scandal.
(wc) World champion constructor that season.

817. Consecutive races with a front row *(Most)*

Williams	35	South Africa 1992	- San Marino 1994	(FW14B, FW15C, FW16 - Renault)
McLaren	33	Germany 1988	- Germany 1990	(MP4/4, MP4/5, MP4/5B - Honda)
Williams	26	Australia 1995	- Britain 1997	(FW17B, FW18, FW19 - Renault)
Ferrari	25	Italy 1950	- Belgium 1954	(375, 500, 625, 553)
Red Bull	24	Singapore 2010	- Brazil 2011	(RB6, RB7 - Renault)
Mercedes-Benz	23	Britain 2014	- Italy 2015	(F1 W05, F1 W06)
Maserati	17	Argentina 1953	- Argentina 1955	(A6GCM, 250F)
Red Bull	17	Singapore 2009	- Belgium 2010	(RB5, RB6, RB7 - Renault)
Williams	17	Portugal 1986	- Mexico 1987	(FW11, FW11B - Honda)
Ferrari	16	Netherlands 1970	- Germany 1971	(312B, 312B2)
JPS Lotus	16	Argentina 1973	- Argentina 1974	(72D, 72E - Ford Cosworth)

818. Consecutive races with a front row from the start of a season (Most)

(not counting any into the following season)

Red Bull	19	2011	(RB7 - Renault)	(Sebastian Vettel, Mark Webber)
McLaren	16	1989 (a)	(MP4/5 - Honda)	(Alain Prost, Ayrton Senna)
Williams	16	1992 (a)	(FW14B - Renault)	(Nigel Mansell, Riccardo Patrese)
Williams	16	1993 (a)	(FW15C - Renault)	(Damon Hill, Alain Prost)
Williams	16	1996 (a)	(FW18 - Renault)	(Damon Hill, Jacques Villeneuve)
JPS Lotus	15	1973 (a)	(72D, 72E - Ford Cosworth)	(Emerson Fittipaldi, Ronnie Peterson)
Williams	14	1987	(FW11B - Honda)	(Nigel Mansell, Nelson Piquet)
McLaren	13	2007	(MP4-22 - Mercedes)	(Fernando Alonso, Lewis Hamilton)
Red Bull	13	2010	(RB6 - Renault)	(Sebastian Vettel, Mark Webber)
Mercedes-Benz	12	2015	(F1 W06)	(Lewis Hamilton, Nico Rosberg)

(a) Sequence continued into the following season.
All above became world champion constructor that season, apart from McLaren in 2007, being stripped of all their points, due to the spying scandal.

819. Seasons of front rows (Most)

Ferrari	60	1950 - 2015		Renault	13	1979 - 2010
McLaren	41	1967 - 2012		Benetton	8	1986 - 98
Williams	29	1979 - 2014		Cooper	8	1952 - 66
Lotus	26	1960 - 2013		Red Bull	8	2008 - 15
Brabham	21	1963 - 85		Tyrrell	8	1970 - 91
BRM	15	1956 - 73				

820. Consecutive seasons of front rows (Most)

Williams	22	1979 - 98		Ferrari	12	1950 - 61
Ferrari	20	1994 - 2013		McLaren	12	1967 - 78
Ferrari	17	1963 - 79		BRM	11	1958 - 68
Lotus	15	1960 - 74		McLaren	10	1984 - 94
McLaren	16	1997 - 2012		Brabham	9	1977 - 85

821. Front row positions at the same venue (Most)

grand prix

Ferrari	49	Italy	1950 - 2015 (a)	(Monza)
Ferrari	45	Germany	1951 - 2012 (a)	(Nürburgring, 30; Hockenheim, 13; AVUS, 2)
Ferrari	43	France	1951 - 2008 (a)	(Reims/ Reims-Gueux, 16; Magny-Cours, 13; Rouen-les-Essarts, 6; Paul Ricard, 5; Clermont-Ferrand, 2; Dijon-Prenois, 1)
Ferrari	36	Belgium	1951 - 2008 (a)	(Spa-Francorchamps, 28; Zolder, 6; Nivelles-Baulers, 2)
Ferrari	34	Britain	1951 - 2012 (a)	(Silverstone, 27; Brands Hatch, 5; Aintree, 2)
Ferrari	29	Monaco	1956 - 2009 (a)	(Monte-Carlo)
Ferrari	26	Spain	1951 - 2012	(Catalunya, 12; Montjuïc, 5; Jarama, 4; Pedralbes, 3; Jerez de la Frontera, 2)
McLaren	24	Italy	1967 - 2012	(Monza)
McLaren	23	Belgium	1972 - 2012	(Spa-Francorchamps, 21; Nivelles-Baulers, 1; Zolder, 1)
McLaren	23	Canada	1972 - 2012	(Montréal, 17; Mosport Park, 6)

circuit

Ferrari	49	Monza	1950 - 2015 (a)		McLaren	24	Monza	1967 - 2012
Ferrari	38	Nürburgring	1951 - 2007 (a)(b)		McLaren	21	Spa-Francorchamps	1985 - 2012
Ferrari	29	Monte-Carlo	1956 - 2009 (a)		McLaren	19	Interlagos	1974 - 2012
Ferrari	28	Spa-Francorchamps	1951 - 2008 (a)		McLaren	19	Monte-Carlo	1984 - 2011
Ferrari	27	Silverstone	1951 - 2012 (a)		Williams	18	Montréal	1979 - 2004

Excludes Indianapolis 500.
(a) Includes Lancia-Ferrari.
(b) Includes European and Luxembourg Grands Prix.

822. Consecutive front rows at the same venue *(Most)*

Williams	12	Hungary	1986 - 97	(Hungaroring)
Ferrari	9	Germany	1951 - 61 (a)	(Nürburgring, 8; AVUS, 1)
Lotus	9	Netherlands	1962 - 70	(Zandvoort)
Ferrari	8	Japan	1997 - 2004	(Suzuka)
Ferrari	7	Britain	1998 - 2004	(Silverstone)
Lotus	7	Germany	1961 - 67	(Nürburgring)
McLaren	7	Australia	1987 - 93	(Adelaide)
McLaren	7	Italy	2005 - 11	(Monza)
Williams	7	Brazil	1991 - 97	(Interlagos)
Williams	7	Britain	1991 - 97	(Silverstone)
Williams	7	France	1991 - 97	(Magny-Cours)

(a) No German Grand Prix in 1955 and 1960.

823. Races taken to achieve their first front row
(number of races includes the race of first front row and all qualifying attempts)

Alfa Romeo	1	Benetton	5	Vanwall	13	Toro Rosso	49
Brawn	1	Brabham	5	Porsche	14	Toyota	52
Lancia	1	Ferrari	5	Lotus	18	Jordan	59
Lola	1	Cooper	6	Renault	22	Red Bull	63
March	1	Matra	6	Penske	23	Toleman	63
Mercedes-Benz	1	Wolf	6	Shadow	28	Jaguar	69
Tyrrell	1	Honda	7	BMW	29	Minardi	81
Aston Martin	2	Gordini	8	Force India	30	BAR	87
Maserati	2	McLaren	10	Stewart	40	Williams	88
Eagle	3	Hesketh	13	Arrows	45	Sauber	92
BRM	4	Ligier	13	Surtees	48		

For most races started but never a front row, see section 681.

824. Races with a front row in their first season
(number of front row positions in brackets)

Brawn	8	(9)	2009	(BGP 001 - Mercedes)	(Jenson Button, 5; Rubens Barrichello, 4)
Alfa Romeo	6	(18)	1950	(158)	(Juan Manuel Fangio, 6; Giuseppe Farina, 6; Luigi Fagioli, 4; Reg Parnell, 1; Consalvo Sanesi, 1)
Mercedes-Benz	6	(7)	1954	(W196 str., W196)	(Juan Manuel Fangio, 6; Karl Kling, 1)
March	5	(8)	1970	(701 - Ford Cosworth)	(Jackie Stewart, 5; Chris Amon, 3)
Benetton	3	(4)	1986	(B186 - BMW)	(Gerhard Berger, 2; Teo Fabi, 2)
Lola	3	(3)	1962	(Mk 4 - Climax)	(John Surtees)
Tyrrell	3	(3)	1970	(001 - Ford Cosworth)	(Jackie Stewart)
Wolf	2	(2)	1977	(WR1, WR2 - Ford Cosworth)	(Jody Scheckter)
Aston Martin	1	(1)	1959	(DBR4)	(Roy Salvadori)
Eagle	1	(1)	1966	(T1G - Climax)	(Dan Gurney)
Ferrari	1	(1)	1950	(375)	(Alberto Ascari)
Hesketh	1	(1)	1974	(308 - Ford Cosworth)	(James Hunt)
Lancia	1	(1)	1954	(D50)	(Alberto Ascari)
Ligier	1	(1)	1976	(JS5 - Matra)	(Jacques Laffite)
Maserati	1	(1)	1950	(4CLT/48)	(José Froilán González)

825. First race with a front row immediately followed by others
(including first front row position)

Ferrari	25	Italy 1950 - Belgium 1954	(375, 500, 625, 553)
Alfa Romeo	13	Britain 1950 - Spain 1951	(158, 159)
Mercedes-Benz	12	France 1954 - Italy 1955	(W196 str., W196)
March	5	South Africa - Netherlands 1970	(701 - Ford Cosworth)
Lancia	4	Spain 1954 - Belgium 1955	(D50)
Tyrrell	4	Canada 1970 - South Africa 1971	(001 - Ford Cosworth)
Williams	4	Britain - Netherlands 1979	(FW07 - Ford Cosworth)
Lotus	3	Argentina - Netherlands 1960	(18 - Climax)
Brawn	2	Australia - Malaysia 2009	(BGP 001 - Mercedes)
Force India	2	Belgium - Italy 2009	(VJM02 - Mercedes)

Honda	2	Britain - Netherlands 1965	(RA272)
Porsche	2	Britain - Germany 1961	(718)
Shadow	2	Argentina - Brazil 1975	(DN5 - Ford Cosworth)
Toyota	2	Australia - Malaysia 2005	(TF105)

826. Front row in their final race

| Lancia | Belgium 1955 | (Lancia D50) | (Eugenio Castellotti) |

Final race started (did enter a later race but withdrew due to tyre safety concerns).

827. Front row positions in their final season

Brawn	9	2009	(BGP 001 - Mercedes)	(Jenson Button, 5; Rubens Barrichello, 4)
Toyota	5	2009	(TF109)	(Jarno Trulli, 4; Timo Glock, 1)
BAR	4	2005	(007 - Honda)	(Jenson Button)
Lancia	3	1955	(D50)	(Alberto Ascari, 2; Eugenio Castellotti, 1)
Matra	2	1972	(MS120D)	(Chris Amon)
Stewart	1	1999	(SF-3 - Ford Cosworth)	(Rubens Barrichello)
Toleman	1	1985	(TG185 - Hart)	(Teo Fabi)

828. Different front row constructors in a season

Most

1970	8	March, Brabham, McLaren, Lotus, Ferrari, Matra-Simca, BRM, Tyrrell
1968	7	Lotus, Matra, Ferrari, BRM, McLaren, Brabham, Honda
1972	7	Brabham, Tyrrell, Ferrari, JPS Lotus, McLaren, Matra-Simca, March
1974	7	JPS Lotus, Ferrari, McLaren, Brabham, Surtees, Tyrrell, Hesketh
1975	7	Shadow, Brabham, McLaren, Ferrari, March, Tyrrell, Hesketh
1976	7	McLaren, Ferrari, Tyrrell, JPS Lotus, Penske, March, Ligier
1981	7	Arrows, Williams, Brabham, Renault, Ferrari, Talbot-Ligier, McLaren
2008	7	McLaren, BMW Sauber, Ferrari, Renault, Red Bull, Toro Rosso, Toyota
2009	7	Brawn, Toyota, Red Bull, Renault, Ferrari, McLaren, Force India
2012	7	McLaren, Mercedes-Benz, Red Bull, Williams, Ferrari, Lotus, Sauber

Fewest

1951	2	Alfa Romeo, Ferrari	1993	3	Williams, McLaren, Benetton
1953	2	Ferrari, Maserati	1995	3	Williams, Benetton, Ferrari
2002	2	Ferrari, Williams	2000	3	McLaren, Ferrari, Jordan
1950	3	Alfa Romeo, Maserati, Ferrari	2001	3	Ferrari, Williams, McLaren
1952	3	Ferrari, Gordini, Cooper	2002	3	Ferrari, Williams, McLaren
1956	3	Lancia-Ferrari, Maserati, BRM	2007	3	Ferrari, McLaren, BMW Sauber
1957	3	Maserati, Lancia-Ferrari, Vanwall	2011	3	Red Bull, McLaren, Ferrari
1988	3	McLaren, Williams, Ferrari	2014	3	Mercedes-Benz, Red Bull, Williams
1989	3	McLaren, Williams, Ferrari	2015	3	Mercedes-Benz, Ferrari, Red Bull
1992	3	Williams, McLaren, Benetton			

Excludes Indianapolis 500.

829. First time front row constructors in a season *(Most)*

1950	3	Alfa Romeo, Maserati, Ferrari	1976	2	Penske, Ligier
1952	2	Gordini, Cooper	1979	2	Renault, Williams
1954	2	Mecedes-Benz, Lancia	2004	2	Jaguar, BAR
1970	2	March, Tyrrell	2008	2	Red Bull, Toro Rosso
1974	2	Surtees, Hesketh	2009	2	Brawn, Force India

830. Complete front rows

(in the early days, some grids featured more than two cars and teams ran more than two cars, so the following races could include up to four cars on the grid - the final race with more than two cars on the front row was Netherlands 1973).
(included in section 836 "Front row 1-2s")

McLaren	62	Germany 1986 (K Rosberg, A Prost)	- Brazil 2012 (L Hamilton, J Button)
Williams	62	Caesars Palace 1981 (C Reutemann, A Jones)	- Austria 2014 (F Massa, V Bottas)
Ferrari (a)	55	Belgium 1952 (A Ascari, G Farina, P Taruffi)	- France 2008 (K Räikkönen, F Massa)
Mercedes-Benz	33	Netherlands 1955 (J M Fangio, S Moss, K Kling)	- Abu Dhabi 2015 (N Rosberg, L Hamilton)
Red Bull	23	Australia 2010 (S Vettel, M Webber)	- United States 2013 (S Vettel, M Webber)
Renault	22	France 1979 (J-P Jabouille, R Arnoux)	- China 2006 (F Alonso, G Fisichella)
Lotus (b)	9	United States 1967 (G Hill, J Clark)	- Canada 1985 (E De Angelis, A Senna)
Ligier	5	Argentina 1979 (J Laffite, P Depailler)	- Britain 1980 (D Pironi, J Laffite)
Alfa Romeo	4	Britain 1950 (G Farina, L Fagioli, J M Fangio, R Parnell)	- France 1950 (J M Fangio, G Farina, L Fagioli)
Brabham	4	South Africa 1967 (J Brabham, D Hulme)	- Austria 1982 (N Piquet, R Patrese)
Cooper	2	Portugal 1959 (S Moss, J Brabham, M Gregory)	- United States 1959 (S Moss, J Brabham, H Schell)
Benetton	1	Austria 1986 (T Fabi, G Berger)	
Brawn	1	Australia 2009 (J Button, R Barrichello)	
March	1	Monaco 1970 (J Stewart, C Amon)	
Toyota	1	Bahrain 2009 (J Trulli, T Glock)	
Tyrrell	1	Sweden 1974 (P Depailler, J Scheckter)	
Vanwall	1	Netherlands 1958 (S Lewis-Evans, S Moss, T Brooks)	

(a) Includes Lancia-Ferrari.
(b) Includes JPS Lotus.

831. Complete front rows involving more than two cars from the same constructor

(included in section 830)

Ferrari (a)	8	Belgium 1952	- France 1961 (all were 3-car rows)
Alfa Romeo	4	Britain 1950	- France 1950 (1 x 4-car row, 3 x 3-car rows)
Cooper	2	Portugal 1959	- United States 1959 (both were 3-car rows)
Mercedes-Benz	2	Netherlands 1955	- Italy 1955 (both were 3-car rows)
Vanwall	1	Netherlands 1958 (3-car row)	

(a) Includes Lancia-Ferrari.

832. Last occasion with three cars from the same constructor on the front row

This was France 1961 for Ferrari (model 156) with Phil Hill, Wolfgang von Trips and Richie Ginther.

833. Four car complete front row for a constructor

The only occasion was at Britain 1950 for Alfa Romeo (model 158) with Giuseppe Farina, Luigi Fagioli, Juan Manuel Fangio and Reg Parnell.

834. Consecutive complete front rows *(Most)*

(included in section 837 "Consecutive front row 1-2s")

Mercedes-Benz	9	Belgium 2014	- Australia 2015	(F1 W05, F1 W06)
Mercedes-Benz	7	Spain 2015	- Belgium 2015	(F1 W06)
McLaren	8	San Marino 1989	- Germany 1989	(MP4/5 - Honda)
Williams	8	Canada 1993	- Portugal 1993	(FW15C - Renault)
McLaren	6	Belgium 1988	- Australia 1988	(MP4/4 - Honda)
Williams	5	Belgium 1996	- Australia 1997	(FW18, FW19 - Renault)
JPS Lotus	4	Britain 1978	- Netherlands 1978	(79 - Ford Cosworth)
McLaren	4	San Marino 1988	- Canada 1988	(MP4/4 - Honda)
McLaren	4	San Marino 1998	- Canada 1998	(MP4-13 - Mercedes)
Renault	4	Britain 1981	- Netherlands 1981	(RE30)
Williams	4	France 1992	- Hungary 1992	(FW14B - Renault)
Williams	4	Brazil 1993	- Spain 1993	(FW15C - Renault)

835. Complete front rows in a season *(Most)*

(included in section 838 "Front row 1-2s in a season")

Mercedes-Benz	15 of 19	2015	(F1 W06)	(L Hamilton, N Rosberg)
McLaren	12 of 16	1988	(MP4/4 - Honda)	(A Prost, A Senna)
Williams	12 of 16	1993	(FW15C - Renault)	(D Hill, A Prost)
Mercedes-Benz	12 of 19	2014	(F1 W05)	(L Hamilton, N Rosberg)
McLaren	11 of 16	1989	(MP4/5 - Honda)	(A Prost, A Senna)

Williams	10 of 16	1992	(FW14B - Renault)	(N Mansell, R Patrese)
McLaren	9 of 16	1998	(MP4-13 - Mercedes)	(D Coulthard, M Häkkinen)
Williams	9 of 16	1996	(FW18 - Renault)	(D Hill, J Villeneuve)
Red Bull	8 of 19	2010	(RB6 - Renault)	(M Webber, S Vettel)
Red Bull	7 of 19	2011	(RB7 - Renault)	(M Webber, S Vettel)

All became world champion constructor that season.

836. Front row 1-2s
(Some of the following were not complete front rows, due to front rows in the early days often featuring more than two cars. The final race with more than two cars on the front row was Netherlands 1973).

Ferrari (a)	70	Germany 1951 (A Ascari, J F González)	- France 2008 (K Räikkönen, F Massa)
McLaren	63	Canada 1972 (P Revson, D Hulme)	- Brazil 2012 (L Hamilton, J Button)
Williams	62	Caesars Palace 1981 (C Reutemann, A Jones)	- Austria 2014 (F Massa, V Bottas)
Mercedes-Benz	35	France 1954 (J M Fangio, K Kling)	- Abu Dhabi 2015 (N Rosberg, L Hamilton)
Red Bull	23	Australia 2010 (S Vettel, M Webber)	- United States 2013 (S Vettel, M Webber)
Renault	22	France 1979 (J-P Jabouille, R Arnoux)	- China 2006 (F Alonso, G Fisichella)
Lotus (b)	14	Britain 1967 (J Clark, G Hill)	- Canada 1985 (E De Angelis, A Senna)
Alfa Romeo	9	Britain 1950 (G Farina, L Fagioli)	- Italy 1951 (J M Fangio, G Farina)
Brabham	6	Britain 1966 (J Brabham, D Hulme)	- Austria 1982 (N Piquet, R Patrese)
Ligier	5	Argentina 1979 (J Laffite, P Depailler)	- Britain 1980 (D Pironi, J Laffite)
Cooper	3	Portugal 1959 (S Moss, J Brabham)	- Belgium 1960 (J Brabham, T Brooks)
Vanwall	3	Italy 1957 (S Lewis-Evans, S Moss)	- Italy 1958 (S Moss, T Brooks)
March	2	South Africa 1970 (J Stewart, C Amon)	- Monaco 1970 (J Stewart, C Amon)
Maserati	2	Argentina 1957 (S Moss, J M Fangio)	- France 1957 (J M Fangio, J Behra)
Benetton	1	Austria 1986 (T Fabi, G Berger)	
Brawn	1	Australia 2009 (J Button, R Barrichello)	
Toyota	1	Bahrain 2009 (J Trulli, T Glock)	
Tyrrell	1	Sweden 1974 (P Depailler, J Scheckter)	

(a) Includes Lancia-Ferrari. (b) Includes JPS Lotus.
For "Complete front rows" which includes races with more than two cars on the front row, see section 830.

837. Consecutive front row 1-2s *(Most)*

Mercedes-Benz	9	Belgium 2014	- Australia 2015	(F1 W05, F1 W06)
McLaren	8	San Marino 1989	- Germany 1989	(MP4/5 - Honda)
Williams	8	Canada 1993	- Portugal 1993	(FW15C - Renault)
Ferrari	7	Switzerland 1952	- Italy 1952	(500)
Mercedes-Benz	7	Spain 2015	- Belgium 2015	(F1 W06)
McLaren	6	Belgium 1988	- Australia 1988	(MP4/4 - Honda)
Mercedes-Benz	6	Japan 2015	- Abu Dhabi 2015	(F1 W06)
Alfa Romeo	5	Britain 1950	- France 1950	(158)
Williams	5	Belgium 1996	- Australia 1997	(FW18, FW19 - Renault)
Ferrari	4	Netherlands 1961	- Britain 1961	(156)
JPS Lotus	4	Britain 1978	- Netherlands 1978	(79 - Ford Cosworth)
McLaren	4	San Marino 1988	- Canada 1988	(MP4/4 - Honda)
McLaren	4	San Marino 1998	- Canada 1998	(MP4-13 - Mercedes)
Renault	4	Britain 1981	- Netherlands 1981	(RE30)
Williams	4	France 1992	- Hungary 1992	(FW14B - Renault)
Williams	4	Brazil 1993	- Spain 1993	(FW15C - Renault)

838. Front row 1-2s in a season *(Most)*

Mercedes-Benz	15 of 19	2015 (wc)	(F1 W06)	(L Hamilton, N Rosberg)
McLaren	12 of 16	1988 (wc)	(MP4/4 - Honda)	(A Prost, A Senna)
Williams	12 of 16	1993 (wc)	(FW15C - Renault)	(D Hill, A Prost)
Mercedes-Benz	12 of 19	2014 (wc)	(F1 W05)	(L Hamilton, N Rosberg)
McLaren	11 of 16	1989 (wc)	(MP4/5 - Honda)	(A Prost, A Senna)
Williams	10 of 16	1992 (wc)	(FW14B - Renault)	(N Mansell, R Patrese)
McLaren	9 of 16	1998 (wc)	(MP4-13 - Mercedes)	(D Coulthard, M Häkkinen)
Williams	9 of 16	1996 (wc)	(FW18 - Renault)	(D Hill, J Villeneuve)
Red Bull	8 of 19	2010 (wc)	(RB6 - Renault)	(S Vettel, M Webber)
Ferrari	7 of 7	1952 (a)	(500)	(A Ascari, G Farina, P Taruffi, L Villoresi)
Red Bull	7 of 19	2011 (wc)	(RB7 - Renault)	(S Vettel, M Webber)

(a) Not complete front rows. (wc) World champion constructor that season. No constructors' championship until 1958.

839. Front row 1-2 in the first race of the season

1950	Alfa Romeo	(158)	(1: Giuseppe Farina, 2: Luigi Fagioli)
1951	Alfa Romeo	(159)	(1: Juan Manuel Fangio, 2: Giuseppe Farina)
1952	Ferrari	(500)	(1: Giuseppe Farina, 2: Piero Taruffi)
1954	Ferrari	(625)	(1: Giuseppe Farina, 2: Jose Froilán González)
1956	Lancia-Ferrari	(D50)	(1: Juan Manuel Fangio, 2: Eugenio Castellotti)
1957	Maserati	(250F)	(1: Stirling Moss, 2: Juan Manuel Fangio)
1967	Brabham (wc)	(BT20 - Repco)	(1: Jack Brabham, 2: Denny Hulme)
1968	Lotus (wc)	(49 - Ford Cosworth)	(1: Jim Clark, 2: Graham Hill)
1970	March	(701 - Ford Cosworth)	(1: Jackie Stewart, 2: Chris Amon)
1979	Ligier	(JS11 - Ford Cosworth)	(1: Jacques Laffite, 2: Patrick Depailler)
1987	Williams (wc)	(FW11B - Honda)	(1: Nigel Mansell, 2: Nelson Piquet)
1996	Williams (wc)	(FW18 - Renault)	(1: Jacques Villeneuve, 2: Damon Hill)
1997	Williams (wc)	(FW19 - Renault)	(1: Jacques Villeneuve, 2: Heinz-Harald Frentzen)
1998	McLaren (wc)	(MP4-13 - Mercedes)	(1: Mika Häkkinen, 2: David Coulthard)
1999	McLaren	(MP4-14 - Mercedes)	(1: Mika Häkkinen, 2: David Coulthard)
2000	McLaren	(MP4-15 - Mercedes)	(1: David Coulthard, 2: Mika Häkkinen)
2001	Ferrari (wc)	(F2001)	(1: Michael Schumacher, 2: Rubens Barrichello)
2002	Ferrari (wc)	(F2001)	(1: Rubens Barrichello, 2: Michael Schumacher)
2003	Ferrari (wc)	(F2002)	(1: Michael Schumacher, 2: Rubens Barrichello)
2004	Ferrari (wc)	(F2004)	(1: Michael Schumacher, 2: Rubens Barrichello)
2006	Ferrari	(248 F1)	(1: Michael Schumacher, 2: Felipe Massa)
2009	Brawn (wc)	(BGP 001 - Mercedes)	(1: Jenson Button, 2: Rubens Barrichello)
2012	McLaren	(MP4-27 - Mercedes)	(1: Lewis Hamilton, 2: Jenson Button)
2013	Red Bull (wc)	(RB9 - Renault)	(1: Sebastian Vettel, 2: Mark Webber)
2015	Mercedes-Benz (wc)	(F1 W06)	(1: Lewis Hamilton, 2: Nico Rosberg)

(wc) World champion constructor that season.

840. Consecutive front row 1-2s from the start of a season

Ferrari	7	1952	(500)	(Alberto Ascari, Giuseppe Farina, Piero Taruffi, Luigi Villoresi)
Alfa Romeo	5	1950	(158)	(Luigi Fagioli, Juan Manuel Fangio, Giuseppe Farina)
Alfa Romeo	3	1951	(159)	(Juan Manuel Fangio, Giuseppe Farina)
McLaren	3	1999	(MP4-14 - Mercedes)	(David Coulthard, Mika Häkkinen)
Ferrari	2	2001 (wc)	(F2001)	(Rubens Barrichello, Michael Schumacher)
Ligier	2	1979	(JS11 - Ford Cosworth)	(Patrick Depailler, Jacques Laffite)
McLaren	2	1998 (wc)	(MP4-13 - Mercedes)	(David Coulthard, Mika Häkkinen)
McLaren	2	2000	(MP4-15 - Mercedes)	(David Coulthard, Mika Häkkinen)
McLaren	2	2012	(MP4-27 - Mercedes)	(Jenson Button, Lewis Hamilton)

(wc) World champion constructor that season.

841. Front row 1-2 in the race of their first pole position

Alfa Romeo	Britain 1950	(158)	(1: Giuseppe Farina, 2: Luigi Fagioli)
Benetton	Austria 1986	(B186 - BMW)	(1: Teo Fabi, 2: Gerhard Berger)
Mercedes-Benz	France 1954	(W196 str.)	(1: Juan Manuel Fangio, 2: Karl Kling)
March	South Africa 1970	(701 - Ford Cosworth)	(1: Jackie Stewart, 2: Chris Amon)
McLaren	Canada 1972	(M19C - Ford Cosworth)	(1: Peter Revson, 2: Denny Hulme)
Brawn	Australia 2009	(BGP 001 - Mercedes)	(1: Jenson Button, 2: Rubens Barrichello)

842. Front rows to race retirement *(Most)*

Ferrari	125	Italy 1950	- Canada 2011 (a)	Renault	29	South Africa 1979	- Hungary 2009
McLaren	87	Italy 1967	- Brazil 2012 (b)	BRM	24	Britain 1956	- Italy 1970
Williams	79	Britain 1979	- Singapore 2012	Maserati	16	Monaco 1950	- Britain 1957
Lotus	73	Portugal 1960	- Portugal 1986	Cooper	14	Monaco 1959	- France 1966
Brabham	47	Britain 1963	- South Africa 1985	Alfa Romeo	13	Britain 1950	- Detroit 1982

(a) Excludes three races where a front row car did not start (see section 405).
(b) Excludes one race where a front row car did not start (see section 405).

Front row to race retirement before end of first lap. See section 405

843. Consecutive races with a front row to retirement

Lotus	6	Netherlands 1967	- Canada 1967	(49 - Ford Cosworth)	(Graham Hill, 4; Jim Clark, 2)
Lancia-Ferrari	5	Britain 1956	- Monaco 1957	(D50, 801)	(Eugenio Castellotti, 3; Peter Collins, 3; Luigi Musso, 1)
Brabham	4	South Africa 1963	- Belgium 1964	(BT7 - Climax)	(Jack Brabham, 2; Dan Gurney, 2)
Ferrari	4	Germany 1974	- Canada 1974	(312B3)	(Niki Lauda)
Lancia	4	Spain 1954	- Belgium 1955	(D50)	(Alberto Ascari, 3; Eugenio Castellotti, 1)
Lotus	4	Italy 1965	- Monaco 1966	(33 - Climax)	(Jim Clark)
Maserati	4	Argentina 1953	- France 1953	(A6GCM)	(Juan Manuel Fangio, 3; José Froilán González, 1; Felice Bonetto, 1)
Maserati	4	France 1954	- Switzerland 1954	(250F)	(Stirling Moss, 3; Alberto Ascari, 1)
McLaren	4	United States 1989	- Britain 1989	(MP4/5 - Honda)	(Ayrton Senna, 4; Alain Prost, 1)
Williams	4	Italy 1992	- Australia 1992	(FW14B - Renault)	(Nigel Mansell, 3; Riccardo Patrese, 1)

844. Front row drivers by constructor

Alfa Romeo: Juan Manuel Fangio, 13; Giuseppe Farina, 13; Luigi Fagioli, 4; Andrea De Cesaris, 2; Bruno Giacomelli, 1; Reg Parnell, 1; Consalvo Sanesi, 1

Arrows: Riccardo Patrese, 1

Aston Martin: Roy Salvadori, 1

BAR: Jenson Button, 7; Takuma Sato, 1

Benetton: Michael Schumacher, 24; Gerhard Berger, 4; Jean Alesi, 2; Teo Fabi, 2; Giancarlo Fisichella, 1

BMW (as BMW Sauber): Robert Kubica, 3; Nick Heidfeld, 1

Brabham: Nelson Piquet, 30; Jack Brabham, 20; Dan Gurney, 13; John Watson, 9; Carlos Reutemann, 7; Denny Hulme, 6; Carlos Pace, 6; Riccardo Patrese, 5; Jochen Rindt, 4; Jacky Ickx, 3; Niki Lauda, 1; Hans-Joachim Stuck, 1

Brawn: Jenson Button, 5; Rubens Barrichello, 4

BRM: Graham Hill, 30; Jackie Stewart, 8; Jo Bonnier, 3; Pedro Rodríguez, 3; Harry Schell, 3; Jo Siffert, 3; Dan Gurney, 2; Lorenzo Bandini, 1; Jean Behra, 1; Richie Ginther, 1; Mike Hawthorn, 1; Clay Regazzoni, 1

Cooper: Jack Brabham, 18; Stirling Moss, 7; Bruce McLaren, 5; John Surtees, 3; Tony Brooks, 2; Masten Gregory, 1; Mike Hawthorn, 1; Jochen Rindt, 1; Roy Salvadori, 1; Harry Schell, 1

Eagle: Dan Gurney, 5

Ferrari: Michael Schumacher, 91; Niki Lauda, 29; Rubens Barrichello, 27; Felipe Massa, 26; Jacky Ickx, 22; Alberto Ascari, 21; Clay Regazzoni, 20; Gerhard Berger, 15; Mike Hawthorn, 15 (a); Giuseppe Farina, 14; Kimi Räikkönen, 13; John Surtees, 13; Chris Amon, 11; René Arnoux, 9; José Froilán González, 9; Phil Hill, 9; Peter Collins, 8 (a); Alain Prost, 8; Patrick Tambay, 8; Gilles Villeneuve, 8; Fernando Alonso, 7; Juan Manuel Fangio, 7 (a); Carlos Reutemann, 7; Jean Alesi, 6; Eugenio Castellotti, 6 (a); Luigi Musso, 6 (a); Richie Ginther, 5; Luigi Villoresi, 5; Michele Alboreto, 4; Lorenzo Bandini, 4; Eddie Irvine, 4; Piero Taruffi, 4; Wolfgang von Trips, 4; Tony Brooks, 3; Nigel Mansell, 3; Sebastian Vettel, 3; Willy Mairesse, 2; Mike Parkes, 2; Didier Pironi, 2; Ludovico Scarfiotti, 2; Jody Scheckter, 2; Mario Andretti, 1; Jean Behra, 1; Olivier Gendebien, 1; Dan Gurney, 1; Stefan Johansson, 1; Ricardo Rodríguez, 1
(a) Inc. Lancia-Ferrari.

Force India: Giancarlo Fisichella, 1; Adrian Sutil, 1

Gordini: Robert Manzon, 3; Maurice Trintignant, 2

Hesketh: James Hunt, 2

Honda: Jenson Button, 3; Richie Ginther, 2; John Surtees, 1

Jaguar: Mark Webber, 1

Jordan: Heinz-Harald Frentzen, 4; Rubens Barrichello, 2; Jarno Trulli, 2; Giancarlo Fisichella, 1

Lancia: Alberto Ascari, 3; Eugenio Castellotti, 1

Ligier: Jacques Laffite, 11 (inc. Talbot-Ligier); Patrick Depailler, 4; Didier Pironi, 4

Lola: John Surtees, 3

Lotus: Jim Clark, 48; Mario Andretti, 23 (a); Ayrton Senna, 23; Ronnie Peterson, 22 (a); Jochen Rindt, 13; Emerson Fittipaldi, 12 (a); Graham Hill, 12; Elio De Angelis, 6; Stirling Moss, 5; Innes Ireland, 3; Nigel Mansell, 2; Jo Siffert, 2; Romain Grosjean, 1; Jean-Pierre Jarier, 1 (a); Jackie Oliver, 1; Kimi Räikkönen, 1; Carlos Reutemann, 1; John Surtees, 1; Trevor Taylor, 1
(a) Inc. JPS Lotus.

March: Jackie Stewart, 5; Chris Amon, 3; Ronnie Peterson, 3; Vittorio Brambilla, 1

Maserati: Juan Manuel Fangio, 16; Stirling Moss, 9; Jean Behra, 8; José Froilán González, 3; Alberto Ascari, 1; Felice Bonetto, 1; Harry Schell, 1

Matra: Jackie Stewart, 9; Chris Amon, 5 (a); Jean-Pierre Beltoise, 2 (a); Johnny Servoz-Gavin, 1
(a) Inc. Matra-Simca.

McLaren: Ayrton Senna, 61; Lewis Hamilton, 48; Alain Prost, 43; Mika Häkkinen, 39; David Coulthard, 30; James Hunt, 22; Kimi Räikkönen, 20; Denny Hulme, 17; Gerhard Berger, 13; Fernando Alonso, 9; Jenson Button, 9; Heikki Kovalainen, 5; Peter Revson, 5; Emerson Fittipaldi, 4; Juan Pablo Montoya, 4; Bruce McLaren, 2; Jody Scheckter, 2; Niki Lauda, 1; Keke Rosberg, 1; John Watson, 1

Mercedes-Benz: Lewis Hamilton, 42; Nico Rosberg, 40; Juan Manuel Fangio, 12; Stirling Moss, 5; Karl Kling, 3; Michael Schumacher, 1

Minardi: Pierluigi Martini, 1

Penske: John Watson, 1

Porsche: Jo Bonnier, 2; Dan Gurney, 1

Red Bull: Sebastian Vettel, 66; Mark Webber, 34; Daniel Ricciardo, 3

Renault: René Arnoux, 25; Fernando Alonso, 21; Alain Prost, 19; Jean-Pierre Jabouille, 11; Giancarlo Fisichella, 8; Jarno Trulli, 4; Eddie Cheever, 1; Robert Kubica, 1; Patrick Tambay, 1

Sauber: Jean Alesi, 2; Kamui Kobayashi, 1

Shadow: Jean-Pierre Jarier, 2; Tom Pryce, 2

Stewart:	Rubens Barrichello, 1
Surtees:	Carlos Pace, 1
Toleman:	Teo Fabi, 1
Toro Rosso:	Sebastian Vettel, 1
Toyota:	Jarno Trulli, 9; Timo Glock, 1; Ralf Schumacher, 1
Tyrrell:	Jackie Stewart, 20; Jody Scheckter, 6; François Cevert, 3; Patrick Depailler, 3; Stefano Modena, 1
Vanwall:	Stirling Moss, 11; Tony Brooks, 6; Stuart Lewis-Evans, 5
Williams:	Nigel Mansell, 51; Damon Hill, 47; Jacques Villeneuve, 23; Juan Pablo Montoya, 22; Riccardo Patrese, 22; Ralf Schumacher, 18; Alain Prost, 16; Nelson Piquet, 14; Alan Jones, 13; Keke Rosberg, 9; Heinz-Harald Frentzen, 8; David Coulthard, 7; Carlos Reutemann, 7; Ayrton Senna, 3; Valtteri Bottas, 2; Pastor Maldonado, 2; Mark Webber, 2; Thierry Boutsen, 1; Nick Heidfeld, 1; Nico Hülkenberg, 1; Felipe Massa, 1
Wolf:	Jody Scheckter, 3

845. Races with a front row position with the same engine make *(Most)*

Ferrari	361	Ferrari	Italy 1950 (Alberto Ascari)	- Singapore 2015 (Sebastian Vettel)
McLaren	133	Mercedes	Austria 1997 (Mika Häkkinen)	- Brazil 2012 (Lewis Hamilton, Jenson Button)
Williams	105	Renault	Brazil 1989 (Riccardo Patrese)	- Singapore 2012 (Pastor Maldonado) (a)
Lotus	80	Ford Cosworth	Netherlands 1967 (Graham Hill)	- United States West 1979 (Carlos Reutemann)
Red Bull	80	Renault	Britain 2008 (Mark Webber)	- Singapore 2015 (Daniel Ricciardo)
Renault	69	Renault	South Africa 1979 (Jean-Pierre Jabouille)	- Monaco 2010 (Robert Kubica)
Mercedes-Benz	64	Mercedes	France 1954 (Juan Manuel Fangio, Karl Kling)	- Abu Dhabi 2015 (Nico Rosberg, Lewis Hamilton)
McLaren	63	Honda	Brazil 1988 (Ayrton Senna)	- Australia 1992 (Ayrton Senna)
McLaren	52	Ford Cosworth	Spain 1968 (Denny Hulme)	- Australia 1993 (Ayrton Senna)
BRM	50	BRM	Britain 1956 (Mike Hawthorn)	- Argentina 1973 (Clay Regazzoni)

(a) An additional front row position with Mecachrome, Renault-based engine, within the period.

846. Interval between front rows *(Longest)*

	years, days	races		
Mercedes-Benz (a)	54y, 205d	775	Italy 1955 (Juan Manuel Fangio, Stirling Moss, Karl Kling)	- Malaysia 2010 (Nico Rosberg)
Honda (a)	37y, 192d	582	Italy 1968 (John Surtees)	- Malaysia 2006 (Jenson Button)
Alfa Romeo (a)	28y, 343d	327	Spain 1951 (Juan Manuel Fangio, Giuseppe Farina)	- United States 1980 (Bruno Giacomelli)
Lotus (a)	25y, 3d	425	Germany 1987 (Ayrton Senna)	- Hungary 2012 (Romain Grosjean)
Renault (a)	18y, 307d	306	France 1984 (Patrick Tambay)	- Malaysia 2003 (Fernando Alonso, Jarno Trulli)
Tyrrell	14y, 214d	225	United States 1976 (Jody Scheckter)	- Monaco 1991 (Stefano Modena)
Cooper	5y, 274d	44	Netherlands 1952 (Mike Hawthorn)	- Monaco 1958 (Jack Brabham)
Benetton	5y, 239d	87	Italy 1986 (Teo Fabi)	- Spain 1992 (Michael Schumacher)
Lotus	4y, 170d	70	United States West 1979 (Carlos Reutemann)	- Europe 1983 (Elio De Angelis)
Williams	4y, 163d	81	Monaco 2006 (Mark Webber)	- Brazil 2010 (Nico Hülkenberg)

(a) Not present throughout the period.

847. Interval between first & last front rows *(Longest)*

	years, days	races		
Ferrari	65y, 17d	922	Italy 1950	- Singapore 2015
Mercedes-Benz	61y, 148d	899	France 1954	- Abu Dhabi 2015
Lotus	53y, 66d	796	Argentina 1960	- China 2013
McLaren	45y, 76d	719	Italy 1967	- Brazil 2012
Honda	40y, 287d	618	Britain 1965	- San Marino 2006
Williams	35y, 6d	585	Britain 1979	- Germany 2014
Alfa Romeo	32y, 24d	363	Britain 1950	- Detroit 1982
Renault	31y, 74d	510	South Africa 1979	- Monaco 2010
Brabham	22y, 132d	306	Belgium 1963	- South Africa 1985
Tyrrell	20y, 234d	309	Canada 1970	- Monaco 1991

848. Interval between first time front row constructors *(Longest)*

4 years and 268 days from France 1999 (27 June, Stewart) until Malaysia 2004 (21 March, Jaguar).

849. Front row positions but never a constructors' championship *(Most)*

Maserati	39 (a)	Toyota	11	Eagle	5
Alfa Romeo	35 (b)	Jordan	9	Gordini	5 (a)
Ligier	19	BAR	8		
March	12	Honda	6		

(a) All achieved before constructors' championship established.
(b) 32 achieved before constructors' championship established.

850. Front row positions but never a win

Toyota	11	Sauber	3	Minardi	1
BAR	8	Force India	2	Surtees	1
Gordini	5	Arrows	1	Toleman	1
Lancia	4	Aston Martin	1		
Lola	3	Jaguar	1		

(a) All achieved before constructors' championship established.
(b) 32 achieved before constructors' championship established.

851. Front row positions but never a podium

Aston Martin	1	Minardi	1

852. Front row positions but never a pole position

Eagle	5	Hesketh	2	Minardi	1
Gordini	5	Aston Martin	1	Penske	1
Sauber	3	Jaguar	1	Surtees	1

853. Front row positions but never led

Lola	3	Aston Martin	1	Toleman	1

854. Milestones: Front row positions

Ferrari	50th: Argentina 1954, 100th: Germany 1959, 150th: Britain 1968, 200th: Canada 1974, 250th: Belgium 1983, 300th: Argentina 1996, 400th: France 2004
McLaren	50th: Canada 1977, 100th: Japan 1988, 150th: United States 1991, 200th: Brazil 1999, 250th: Spain 2005, 300th: Europe 2009
Williams	50th: Brazil 1987, 100th: Canada 1992, 150th: Britain 1994, 200th: Australia 1997, 250th: France 2003
Lotus	50th: Mexico 1966, 100th: Belgium 1973, 150th: Dallas 1984
Brabham	50th: Austria 1974, 100th: Europe 1984
Mercedes-Benz	50th: Canada 2014, 100th: Brazil 2015
Red Bull	50th: Britain 2011, 100th: China 2014
BRM	50th: Germany 1967
Renault	50th: Caesars Palace 1982

Chapter 21: Fastest Lap Constructors

855. Fastest laps

		drivers			
Ferrari (a)	233	35	Switzerland 1952 (Piero Taruffi)	- Russia 2015 (Sebastian Vettel) *
McLaren	152	19	Canada 1971 (Denny Hulme)	- Malaysia 2013 (Sergio Pérez) *
Williams	133	19	United States West 1978 (Alan Jones)	- Russia 2014 (Valtteri Bottas)
Lotus (b)	76	18	Netherlands 1960 (Stirling Moss)	- India 2013 (Kimi Räikkönen) *
Red Bull	47	3	Britain 2009 (Sebastian Vettel)	- Singapore 2015 (Daniel Ricciardo)
Brabham	41	10	South Africa 1963 (Dan Gurney)	- Europe 1984 (Nelson Piquet) *
Mercedes-Benz	38	7	France 1954 (Hans Herrmann)	- Abu Dhabi 2015 (Lewis Hamilton) *
Benetton	36	7	Germany 1986 (Gerhard Berger)	- Argentina 1998 (Alexander Wurz)
Renault	31	8	France 1979 (René Arnoux)	- Canada 2010 (Robert Kubica)
Tyrrell	20	8	Monaco 1971 (Jackie Stewart)	- Canada 1989 (Jonathan Palmer)
BRM	15	7	France 1959 (Stirling Moss)	- Monaco 1972 (Jean-Pierre Beltoise) *
Maserati	15	6	Italy 1952 (José Froilán González)	- Argentina 1958 (Juan Manuel Fangio) *
Alfa Romeo	14	3	Britain 1950 (Giuseppe Farina)	- Belgium 1983 (Andrea De Cesaris)
Cooper	14	5	Monaco 1959 (Jack Brabham)	- United States 1966 (John Surtees) *
Matra (c)	12	3	Spain 1968 (Jean-Pierre Beltoise)	- France 1972 (Chris Amon)
Ligier (d)	10	3	Japan 1976 (Jacques Laffite)	- Europe 1985 (Jacques Laffite)
March	7	6	Belgium 1970 (Chris Amon)	- France 1989 (Maurício Gugelmin)
Vanwall	6	2	Britain 1957 (Stirling Moss)	- Morocco 1958 (Stirling Moss)
Brawn	4	2	Malaysia 2009 (Jenson Button)	- Turkey 2009 (Jenson Button)
Force India	3	3	Italy 2009 (Adrian Sutil)	- Austria 2014 (Sergio Pérez)
Sauber	3	3	China 2012 (Kamui Kobayashi)	- Spain 2013 (Esteban Gutiérrez)
Surtees	3	2	South Africa 1972 (Mike Hailwood)	- Austria 1973 (Carlos Pace)
Toyota	3	3	Belgium 2005 (Ralf Schumacher)	- Europe 2009 (Timo Glock)
BMW (e)	2	1	Malaysia 2008 (Nick Heidfeld)	- Germany 2008 (Nick Heidfled)
Eagle	2	1	Belgium 1967 (Dan Gurney)	- Germany 1967 (Dan Gurney)

		drivers			
Honda	2	2	Mexico 1966 (Richie Ginther)	- Belgium 1968 (John Surtees)	
Jordan	2	2	Hungary 1991 (Bertrand Gachot)	- Spain 1997 (Giancarlo Fisichella)	
Shadow	2	1	Brazil 1975 (Jean-Pierre Jarier)	- Brazil 1976 (Jean-Pierre Jarier)	
Toleman	2	2	Netherlands 1982 (Derek Warwick)	- Monaco 1984 (Ayrton Senna)	
Wolf	2	1	Monaco 1977 (Jody Scheckter)	- Japan 1977 (Jody Scheckter)	
Ensign	1	1	Brazil 1981 (Marc Surer)		
Gordini	1	1	Britain 1954 (Jean Behra) *		
Hesketh	1	1	Argentina 1975 (James Hunt)		
Lancia	1	1	Spain 1954 (Alberto Ascari)		
Parnelli	1	1	Spain 1975 (Mario Andretti)		
Indianapolis 500					
Kurtis-Kraft	7	5	1950 (Johnnie Parsons)	- 1956 (Paul Russo)	
Epperly	2	2	1957 (Jim Rathmann)	- 1958 (Tony Bettenhausen)	
Lesovsky	1	1	1959 (Johnny Thomson)		
Watson	1	1	1960 (Jim Rathmann)		

Fastest lap at the Indianapolis 500 relates to the fastest leading lap of the race.
Relates to number of races, so where for example, 2 Brabhams shared fastest lap in Canada 1969, this is counted as 1.
* Includes joint fastest lap(s) with another constructor (see section 857).
(a) Includes Lancia-Ferrari.
(b) Includes JPS Lotus.
(c) Includes Matra-Simca.
(d) Includes Talbot-Ligier.
(e) As BMW Sauber.
For explanation about situations that have been in doubt over the years, see footnote at section 420.

856. Percentage of races with a fastest lap *(Highest)*

	%	fastest laps			%	fastest laps
Mercedes-Benz	29.92	38		Maserati	22.06	15
Ferrari	25.69	233		Vanwall	21.43	6
Lancia	25.00	1		McLaren	19.49	152
Brawn	23.53	4		Matra	19.35	12
Red Bull	23.15	47		Williams	19.22	133

857. Joint fastest laps

Italy 1952	Ferrari, Maserati		Monaco 1961	Ferrari, Lotus
Britain 1953	Ferrari, Maserati		Canada 1969	2 x Brabham
Britain 1954	2 x Ferrari, Gordini, 3 x Maserati, Mercedes-Benz		Brazil 1973	JPS Lotus, McLaren
Britain 1959	BRM, Cooper		Europe 1984	Brabham, Ferrari
Belgium 1960	Cooper, Ferrari, Lotus			

858. Fastest laps in a season *(Most)*

Ferrari	14 of 18	2004	(F2004)	(Michael Schumacher, 10; Rubens Barrichello, 4)
Ferrari	13 of 18	2008	(F2008)	(Kimi Räikkönen, 10; Felipe Massa, 3)
Mercedes-Benz	13 of 19	2015	(F1 W06)	(Lewis Hamilton, 8; Nico Rosberg, 5)
Ferrari	12 of 17	2002	(F2002)	(Michael Schumacher, 7; Rubens Barrichello, 5)
Ferrari	12 of 17	2007	(F2007)	(Felipe Massa, 6; Kimi Räikkönen, 6)
McLaren	12 of 17	2000 (a)	(MP4-15 - Mercedes)	(Mika Häkkinen, 9; David Coulthard, 3)
McLaren	12 of 19	2005 (a)	(MP4-20 - Mercedes)	(Kimi Räikkönen, 10; Pedro de la Rosa, 1; Juan Pablo Monyota, 1)
Mercedes-Benz	12 of 19	2014	(F1 W05)	(Lewis Hamilton, 7; Nico Rosberg, 5)
Red Bull	12 of 19	2013	(RB9 - Renault)	(Sebastian Vettel, 7; Mark Webber, 5)
Williams	11 of 16	1986	(FW11 - Honda)	(Nelson Piquet, 7; Nigel Mansell, 4)
Williams	11 of 16	1992	(FW14B - Renault)	(Nigel Mansell, 8; Riccardo Patrese, 3)
Williams	11 of 16	1996	(FW18 - Renault)	(Jacques Villeneuve, 6; Damon Hill, 5)

All became world champion constructor that season, except (a).

859. Fastest lap in every race of a season

Alfa Romeo	7	1951	(Alfa Romeo 159)	(Juan Manuel Fangio, 5; Giuseppe Farina, 2)
Ferrari	7	1952	(Ferrari 500)	(Alberto Ascari, 6; José Froilán González, 1; Piero Taruffi, 1) (a)
Alfa Romeo	6	1950	(Alfa Romeo 158)	(Juan Manuel Fangio, 3 Giuseppe Farina, 3)

(a) Includes joint fastest lap in Italy for Ascari and González.

860. Fastest lap in all but one race of a season

Mercedes-Benz	5	1955	(W196, W196 str.)	(Juan Manuel Fangio, 3; Stirling Moss, 2)

861. Consecutive fastest laps *(Most)*

Alfa Romeo	13	Britain 1950	- Spain 1951	(158, 159)
Ferrari	9	Switzerland 1952	- Netherlands 1953	(500)
Ferrari	9	Bahrain 2004	- Britain 2004	(F2004)
Ferrari	8	Germany 1970	- Spain 1971	(312B)
Mercedes-Benz	7	Britain 2014	- Japan 2014	(F1 W05)
Ferrari	6	Germany 2002	- Japan 2002	(F2002)
Ferrari	6	United States 2007	- Turkey 2007	(F2007)
Ferrari	6	Spain 2008	- Britain 2008	(F2008)
Ferrari	6	Hungary 2008	- Japan 2008	(F2008)
McLaren	6	San Marino 1988	- France 1988	(MP4/4 - Honda)
McLaren	6	France 1999	- Belgium 1999	(MP4-14 - Mercedes)
McLaren	6	France 2005	- Italy 2005	(MP4-20 - Mercedes)
Williams	6	Hungary 1993	- Australia 1993	(FW15C - Renault)

862. Consecutive fastest laps from the start of a season *(Most)*
(not counting any into the following season)

Alfa Romeo	7	1951	(159)	(Juan Manuel Fangio, 5; Giuseppe Farina, 2)
Ferrari	7	1952 (a)	(500)	(Alberto Ascari, 6; Piero Taruffi, 1)
Alfa Romeo	6	1950 (a)	(158)	(Juan Manuel Fangio, 3; Giuseppe Farina, 3)
JPS Lotus	4	1973 (wc)	(72D, 72E - Ford Cosworth)	(Emerson Fittipaldi, 3; Ronnie Peterson, 1)
Mercedes-Benz	4	2014 (wc)	(F1 W05)	(Nico Rosberg, 3; Lewis Hamilton, 1)
Ferrari	3	1966	(246, 312)	(Lorenzo Bandini, 2; John Surtees, 1)
Mercedes-Benz	3	1955	(W196)	(Juan Manuel Fangio, 3)
Mercedes-Benz	3	2015 (wc)	(F1 W06)	(Lewis Hamilton, 2; Nico Rosberg, 1)
Williams	3	1986 (wc)	(FW11 - Honda)	(Nelson Piquet, 2; Nigel Mansell, 1)

(a) Sequence continued into the following season.
(wc) World champion constructor that season.

863. Seasons of fastest laps *(Most)*

Ferrari	51	1952 - 2015		Renault	11	1979 - 2010
McLaren	36	1971 - 2013		BRM	9	1959 - 72
Williams	26	1978 - 2014		Tyrrell	9	1971 - 89
Lotus	21	1960 - 2013		Maserati	7	1952 - 58
Brabham	17	1963 - 84		Red Bull	7	2009 - 15
Benetton	12	1986 - 98				

864. Consecutive seasons of fastest laps *(Most)*

Ferrari	21	1995 - 2015		Maserati	9	1952 - 58
McLaren	13	1981 - 93		Brabham	8	1977 - 84
Williams	13	1985 - 97		McLaren	7	1971 - 77
McLaren	12	1997 - 2008		Red Bull	7	2009 - 15
Benetton	9	1990 - 98		Tyrrell	7	1971 - 77

865. Fastest laps at the same venue *(Most)*

grand prix

Ferrari	19	Britain	1952 - 2011 (a)		Ferrari	10	Netherlands	1952 - 84
Ferrari	19	Italy	1952 - 2010		Ferrari	10	San Marino	1981 - 2005
Ferrari	17	Belgium	1952 - 2008		McLaren	10	Brazil	1973 - 2012
Ferrari	17	Germany	1952 - 2013 (b)		McLaren	10	France	1973 - 2005
Ferrari	17	Monaco	1956 - 2014 (b)		McLaren	10	Monaco	1986 - 2007
Ferrari	14	France	1952 - 2008 (b)		Williams	10	Brazil	1986 - 2004
Ferrari	14	Spain	1971 - 2008		Williams	10	Britain	1979 - 96
McLaren	11	Canada	1971 - 2011		Williams	10	Germany	1980 - 2003
McLaren	11	Italy	1984 - 2011					

circuit

Ferrari	19	Monza	1952 - 2010		Ferrari	10	Imola	1981 - 2005
Ferrari	17	Silverstone	1952 - 2011		Ferrari	10	Zandvoort	1952 - 84
Ferrari	17	Monte-Carlo	1956 - 2014 (b)		Williams	10	Hockenheim	1980 - 2003
Ferrari	15	Nürburgring	1952 - 2013 (b)(c)		McLaren	10	Monte-Carlo	1986 - 2007
Ferrari	13	Spa-Francorchamps	1952 - 2008		McLaren	10	Montréal	1981 - 2011
McLaren	11	Monza	1984 - 2011					

Where a constructor had more than one car sharing the fastest lap in a race (eg Ferrari at Britain 1954), this is counted as 1.
(a) Britain 1954 where two Ferraris achieved joint fastest lap, is counted as 1.
(b) Includes Lancia-Ferrari.
(c) Includes European Grand Prix.

866. Consecutive fastest laps at the same venue *(Most)*

Ferrari	6	United States	2002 - 07	(Indianapolis)
Williams	6	Britain	1991 - 96	(Silverstone)
McLaren	5	France	1998 - 2002	(Magny-Cours)
Ferrari	4	Italy	1958 - 61	(Monza)
Ferrari	4	San Marino	2002 - 05	(Imola)
Ferrari	4	Spain	2001 - 04	(Catalunya)
Benetton	4	Argentina	1995 - 98	(Buenos Aires No.6)
McLaren	4	Austria	1998 - 2001	(A1-Ring)
McLaren	4	Monaco	1998 - 2001	(Monte-Carlo)
Mercedes-Benz	4	Italy	2012 - 15	(Monza)
Williams	4	Portugal	1993 - 96	(Estoril)

867. Races taken to achieve their first fastest lap
(number of races relates to those started and includes the first fastest lap)

Alfa Romeo	1	Matra	7 (a)	Ligier	16	Cooper	33 (b)
Lancia	1	Benetton	10	BRM	17	BMW	39
Mercedes-Benz	1	Jordan	10	Maserati	17	McLaren	55
Brawn	2	Eagle	12	Lotus	20	Williams	60
March	4	Brabham	13	Surtees	20	Toyota	66
Parnelli	6	Ferrari	13	Renault	25	Ensign	79
Toleman	6	Hesketh	14	Gordini	26	Red Bull	79
Tyrrell	6	Honda	14	Shadow	29	Sauber	256
Wolf	6	Vanwall	14	Force India	31		

(a) Includes 2 races where they only entered Formula 2 cars.
(b) Includes 1 race where they only entered Formula 2 cars.
For most races started but never a fastest lap, see section 682.

868. Fastest laps in their first season

Alfa Romeo	6	1950	(158)	(Juan Manuel Fangio, 3; Giuseppe Farina, 3)
Brawn	4	2009	(BGP 001 - Mercedes)	(Rubens Barrichello, 2; Jenson Button, 2)
Mercedes-Benz	4	1954	(W196 str., W196)	(Juan Manuel Fangio, 2; Hans Herrmann, 1; Karl Kling, 1)
Benetton	3	1986	(B186 - BMW)	(Gerhard Berger, 2; Teo Fabi, 1)
Wolf	2	1977	(WR1, WR3 - Ford Cosworth)	(Jody Scheckter)
Jordan	1	1991	(191 - Ford Cosworth)	(Bertrand Gachot)
Lancia	1	1954	(D50)	(Alberto Ascari)
Ligier	1	1976	(JS5 - Matra)	(Jacques Laffite)
March	1	1970	(701 - Ford Cosworth)	(Chris Amon)

869. Fastest laps in their final season

Brawn	4	2009	(BGP 001 - Mercedes)	(Rubens Barrichello, 2; Jenson Button, 2)
Matra (a)	2	1972	(Matra MS120D)	(Chris Amon)
Toyota	2	2009	(TF109)	(Timo Glock, 1; Jarno Trulli, 1)

(a) As Matra-Simca.

870. Different fastest lap constructors in a season

Most

1975	8	Hesketh, Shadow, Brabham, Parnelli, Tyrrell, Ferrari, McLaren, March
1976	7	Shadow, Ferrari, McLaren, JPS Lotus, Tyrrell, March, Ligier
1977	7	McLaren, Brabham, Ferrari, Ligier, Wolf, JPS Lotus, Tyrrell
1981	7	Williams, Ensign, Brabham, Ferrari, Renault, Talbot-Ligier, McLaren
2009	7	Williams, Brawn, Toyota, Ferrari, Red Bull, Renault, Force India
2012	7	McLaren, Lotus, Sauber, Red Bull, Mercedes-Benz, Williams, Force India
1972	6	Tyrrrell, Surtees, Ferrari, BRM, Matra-Simca, McLaren
1982	6	Renault, McLaren, Ferrari, Brabham, Toleman, Tyrrell
1983	6	Brabham, McLaren, Renault, Alfa Romeo, Ferrari, Lotus
1989	6	Williams, McLaren, Ferrari, Tyrrell, March, Lotus
2013	6	Lotus, McLaren, Red Bull, Sauber, Ferrari, Mercedes-Benz

Fewest

1950	1	Alfa Romeo
1951	1	Alfa Romeo
1952	2	Ferrari, Maserati
1953	2	Ferrari, Maserati
1955	2	Mercedes-Benz, Maserati
1956	2	Lancia-Ferrari, Maserati
1994	2	Benetton, Williams
2000	2	Ferrari, McLaren
2007	2	Ferrari, McLaren

Total for each season

1950 - 1, 1951 - 1, 1952 - 2, 1953 - 2, 1954 - 5, 1955 - 2, 1956 - 2, 1957 - 3, 1958 - 3, 1959 - 3, 1960 - 4, 1961 - 4, 1962 - 3, 1963 - 3, 1964 - 4, 1965 - 3, 1966 - 4, 1967 - 3, 1968 - 4, 1969 - 3, 1970 - 4, 1971 - 5, 1972 - 6, 1973 - 5, 1974 - 5, 1975 - 8, 1976 - 7, 1977 - 7, 1978 - 4, 1979 - 5, 1980 - 4, 1981 - 7, 1982 - 6, 1983 - 6, 1984 - 5, 1985 - 5, 1986 - 3, 1987 - 5, 1988 - 4, 1989 - 6, 1990 - 4, 1991 - 5, 1992 - 3, 1993 - 3, 1994 - 2, 1995 - 3, 1996 - 3, 1997 - 5, 1998 - 3, 1999 - 3, 2000 - 2, 2001 - 3, 2002 - 3, 2003 - 4, 2004 - 3, 2005 - 4, 2006 - 4, 2007 - 2, 2008 - 3, 2009 - 7, 2010 - 4, 2011 - 3, 2012 - 7, 2013 - 6, 2014 - 5, 2015 - 3

Excludes Indianapolis 500.

871. Different fastest lap constructors in consecutive races *(Most)*

Austria 1971 - South Africa 1972	6	BRM, March, McLaren, Ferrari, Tyrrell, Surtees
Argentina - Belgium 1975	6	Hesketh, Shadow, Brabham, Parnelli, Tyrrell, Ferrari
Brazil - Belgium 1977	6	McLaren, Brabham, Ferrari, Ligier, Wolf, JPS Lotus
Belgium - Britain 1982	6	McLaren, Brabham, Renault, Ferrari, Toleman, Tyrrell
Italy 1966 - Monaco 1967	5	Ferrari, Cooper, Honda, Brabham, Lotus
Germany - United States 1971	5	Tyrrell, BRM, March, McLaren, Ferrari
Argentina - Belgium 1972	5	Tyrrell, Surtees, Ferrari, BRM, Matra-Simca
Austria 1973 - Argentina 1974	5	Surtees, Tyrrell, JPS Lotus, March, Ferrari
Netherlands - Japan 1976	5	Ferrari, March, Tyrrell, McLaren, Ligier
Detroit - France 1982	5	Renault, Ferrari, Toleman, Tyrrell, Brabham
Monaco - Britain 1983	5	Brabham, Alfa Romeo, McLaren, Ferrari, Renault
Europe 1983 - Belgium 1984	5	Lotus, Brabham, McLaren, Renault, Ferrari
South Africa - Monaco 1984	5	Renault, Ferrari, Brabham, McLaren, Toleman
Argentina - Canada 1997	5	Benetton, Williams, Ferrari, Jordan, McLaren

872. Different fastest lap constructors from the start of a season *(Most)*

1975	6	Hesketh, Shadow, Brabham, Parnelli, Tyrrell, Ferrari	1964	3	BRM, Lotus, Brabham
1972	5	Tyrrell, Surtees, Ferrari, BRM, Matra-Simca	1983	3	Brabham, McLaren, Renault
1968	4	Lotus, Matra, BRM, Honda	1985	3	McLaren, Lotus, Ferrari
1981	4	Williams, Ensign, Brabham, Ferrari	1991	3	Ferrari, Williams, McLaren
1984	4	McLaren, Renault, Ferrari, Brabham	1993	3	Williams, Benetton, McLaren
1987	4	Williams, Benetton, McLaren, Lotus	2001	3	Ferrari, McLaren, Williams
2012	4	McLaren, Lotus, Sauber, Red Bull	2006	3	Williams, Renault, McLaren
1954	3	Ferrari, Maserati, Mercedes-Benz	2013	3	Lotus, McLaren, Red Bull
1958	3	Maserati, Ferrari, Vanwall			

873. First time fastest lap constructors in a season *(Most)*

1954	3	Mercedes-Benz, Gordini, Lancia	1952	2	Ferrari, Maserati
1975	3	Hesketh, Shadow, Parnelli	1959	2	Cooper, BRM
2009	3	Brawn, Red Bull, Force India	1971	2	Tyrrell, McLaren

874. Fastest lap drivers by constructor

Alfa Romeo: Juan Manuel Fangio, 8; Giuseppe Farina, 5; Andrea De Cesaris, 1

Benetton: Michael Schumacher, 23; Gerhard Berger, 5; Jean Alesi, 2; Teo Fabi, 2; Alessandro Nannini, 2; Roberto Moreno, 1; Alexander Wurz, 1

BMW *(as BMW Sauber):* Nick Heidfeld, 2

Brabham: Nelson Piquet, 12; Jack Brabham, 7; Dan Gurney, 4; Niki Lauda, 4; Denny Hulme, 3; Jacky Ickx, 3; Carlos Pace, 3; Riccardo Patrese, 3; John Watson, 2; Carlos Reutemann, 1

Brawn: Rubens Barrichello, 2; Jenson Button, 2

BRM: Graham Hill, 8; Stirling Moss, 2; Richard Attwood, 1; Jean-Pierre Beltoise, 1; Tony Brooks, 1; Pedro Rodríguez, 1; Jo Siffert, 1

Cooper: Jack Brabham, 5; Bruce McLaren, 3; Stirling Moss, 3; John Surtees, 2; Maurice Trintignant, 1

Eagle: Dan Gurney, 2

Ensign: Marc Surer, 1

Ferrari: Michael Schumacher, 53; Kimi Räikkönen, 19; Rubens Barrichello, 15; Felipe Massa, 14; Clay Regazzoni, 13; Niki Lauda, 12; Alberto Ascari, 10; Jacky Ickx, 10; Gerhard Berger, 9; Fernando Alonso, 8; Gilles Villeneuve, 8; Mike Hawthorn, 6; Phil Hill, 6; Nigel Mansell, 6; John Surtees, 6; Michele Alboreto, 4; René Arnoux, 4; Juan Manuel Fangio, 4 (a); José Froilán González, 3; Didier Pironi, 3; Alain Prost, 3; Jean Alesi, 2; Lorenzo Bandini, 2; Richie Ginther, 2; Carlos Reutemann, 2; Mario Andretti, 1; Giancarlo Baghetti, 1; Tony Brooks, 1; Eddie Irvine, 1; Luigi Musso, 1 (a); Ludovico Scarfiotti, 1; Patrick Tambay, 1; Piero Taruffi, 1; Sebastian Vettel, 1; Luigi Villoresi, 1
(a) As Lancia-Ferrari.

Force India: Nico Hülkenberg, 1; Sergio Pérez, 1; Adrian Sutil, 1

Gordini: Jean Behra, 1

Hesketh: James Hunt, 1

Honda: Richie Ginther, 1; John Surtees, 1

Jordan: Giancarlo Fisichella, 1; Bertrand Gachot, 1

Lancia: Alberto Ascari, 1

Ligier: Jacques Laffite, 7 (inc. Talbot-Ligier); Didier Pironi, 2; Patrick Depailler, 1

Lotus: Jim Clark, 28; Mario Andretti, 8 (a); Ronnie Peterson, 7 (a); Ayrton Senna, 6; Emerson Fittipaldi, 5 (a); Kimi Räikkönen, 4; Jochen Rindt, 3; Jo Siffert, 3; Graham Hill, 2; Stirling Moss, 2; Romain Grosjean, 1; Innes Ireland, 1; Jean-Pierre Jarier, 1 (a); Nigel Mansell, 1; Satoru Nakajima, 1; Gunnar Nilsson, 1 (a); Jackie Oliver, 1; John Surtees, 1
(a) As JPS Lotus.

March: James Hunt, 2; Chris Amon, 1; Vittorio Brambilla, 1; Maurício Gugelmin, 1; Henri Pescarolo, 1; Ronnie Peterson, 1

Maserati: Juan Manuel Fangio, 6; Stirling Moss, 5; José Froilán González, 3; Alberto Ascari, 1; Onofré Marimón, 1; Roberto Mières, 1

Matra: Jackie Stewart, 7; Jean-Pierre Beltoise, 3; Chris Amon, 2 (as Matra-Simca)

McLaren: Mika Häkkinen, 25; Alain Prost, 24; Kimi Räikkönen, 19; David Coulthard, 14; Lewis Hamilton, 12; Ayrton Senna, 12; Niki Lauda, 8; Gerhard Berger, 7; Jenson Button, 6; Denny Hulme, 6; James Hunt, 5; Fernando Alonso, 3; John Watson, 3; Heikki Kovalainen, 2; Jochen Mass, 2; Pedro de la Rosa, 1; Emerson Fittipaldi, 1; Juan Pablo Montoya, 1; Sergio Pérez, 1

Mercedes-Benz: Lewis Hamilton, 16; Nico Rosberg, 12; Juan Manuel Fangio, 5; Stirling Moss, 2; Hans Herrmann, 1; Karl Kling, 1; Michael Schumacher, 1

Parnelli: Mario Andretti, 1

Red Bull: Sebastian Vettel, 24; Mark Webber, 19; Daniel Ricciardo, 4

Renault: Fernando Alonso, 10; René Arnoux, 8; Alain Prost, 8; Giancarlo Fisichella, 1; Robert Kubica, 1; Vitaly Petrov, 1; Patrick Tambay, 1; Derek Warwick, 1

Sauber: Esteban Gutiérrez, 1; Kamui Kobayashi, 1; Sergio Pérez, 1

Shadow: Jean-Pierre Jarier, 2

Surtees: Carlos Pace, 2; Mike Hailwood, 1

Toleman: Ayrton Senna, 1; Derek Warwick, 1

Toyota: Timo Glock, 1; Ralf Schumacher, 1; Jarno Trulli, 1

Tyrrell:	Jackie Stewart, 8; Patrick Depailler, 3; Jody Scheckter, 3; François Cevert, 2; Michele Alboreto, 1; Brian Henton, 1; Jonathan Palmer, 1; Ronnie Peterson, 1
Vanwall:	Stirling Moss, 5; Tony Brooks, 1
Williams:	Nigel Mansell, 23; Damon Hill, 19; Alan Jones, 13; Juan Pablo Montoya, 11; Nelson Piquet, 11; Riccardo Patrese, 10; Jacques Villeneuve, 9; Ralf Schumacher, 7; Heinz-Harald Frentzen, 6; Alain Prost, 6; David Coulthard, 4; Carlos Reutemann, 3; Keke Rosberg, 3; Clay Regazzoni, 2; Nico Rosberg, 2; Valtteri Bottas, 1; Thierry Boutsen, 1; Felipe Massa, 1; Bruno Senna, 1
Wolf:	Jody Scheckter, 2

The total for some constructors is higher than in section 855 "Fastest laps", due to races where their drivers achieved joint fastest lap. Those affected are Brabham (1 extra), Ferrari (2) and Maserati (2). Section 857 lists races with joint fastest laps.

875. Fastest laps with the same engine make *(Most)*

Ferrari	233	Ferrari	Switzerland 1952 (Piero Taruffi)	- Russia 2015 (Sebastian Vettel)
McLaren	84	Mercedes	Canada 1997 (David Coulthard)	- Malaysia 2013 (Sergio Pérez)
Williams	70	Renault	Brazil 1989 (Riccardo Patrese)	- Belgium 2012 (Bruno Senna) (a)
Red Bull	47	Renault	Britain 2009 (Sebastian Vettel)	- Singapore 2015 (Daniel Ricciardo)
Lotus	36	Ford Cosworth	Netherlands 1967 (Jim Clark)	- United States 1978 (Jean-Pierre Jarier)
Renault	31	Renault	France 1979 (René Arnoux)	- Canada 2010 (Robert Kubica)
McLaren	30	Honda	San Marino 1988 (Alain Prost)	- Portugal 1992 (Ayrton Senna)
Lotus	27	Climax	Netherlands 1960 (Stirling Moss)	- Monaco 1967 (Jim Clark)
Williams	22	Honda	France 1985 (Keke Rosberg)	- Mexico 1987 (Nelson Piquet)

(a) An additional fastest lap with a Supertec, Renault-based engine, within the period.

876. Interval between fastest laps *(Longest)*

	years, days	races		
Mercedes-Benz (a)	56y, 287d	818	Italy 1955 (Stirling Moss)	- Europe 2012 (Nico Rosberg)
Alfa Romeo (a)	31y, 206d	364	Spain 1951 (Juan Manuel Fangio)	- Belgium 1983 (Andrea De Cesaris)
Lotus (a)	22y, 141d	376	Australia 1989 (Satoru Nakajima)	- Malaysia 2012 (Kimi Räikkönen)
Renault (a)	18y, 356d	309	Detroit 1984 (Derek Warwick)	- Canada 2003 (Fernando Alonso)
March (a)	12y, 300d	198	Italy 1976 (Ronnie Peterson)	- France 1989 (Maurício Gugelmin)
Tyrrell	6y, 266d	101	Caesars Palace 1982 (Michele Alboreto)	- Canada 1989 (Jonathan Palmer)
Jordan	5y, 287d	93	Hungary 1991 (Bertrand Gachot)	- Spain 1997 (Giancarlo Fisichella)
Lotus (b)	4y, 359d	75	United States 1978 (Jean-Pierre Jarier)	- Europe 1983 (Nigel Mansell)
Tyrrell	4y, 289d	72	United States 1977 (Ronnie Peterson)	- Britain 1982 (Brian Henton)
McLaren	4y, 73d	66	Britain 1977 (James Hunt)	- Canada 1981 (John Watson)

(a) Not present throughout the period.
(b) As JPS Lotus at United States 1978.

877. Interval between first & last fastest laps *(Longest)*

	years, days	races		
Ferrari	63y, 146d	915	Switzerland 1952	- Russia 2015
Mercedes-Benz	61y, 148d	899	France 1954	- Abu Dhabi 2015
Lotus	53y, 143d	806	Netherlands 1960	- India 2013
McLaren	41y, 186d	673	Canada 1971	- Malaysia 2013
Williams	36y, 193d	612	United States West 1978	- Russia 2014
Alfa Romeo	33y, 9d	378	Britain 1950	- Belgium 1983
Renault	30y, 347d	507	France 1979	- Canada 2010
Brabham	20y, 284d	282	South Africa 1963	- Europe 1984
March	19y, 32d	287	Belgium 1970	- France 1989
Tyrrell	18y, 26d	274	Monaco 1971	- Canada 1989

878. Interval between first time fastest lap constructors *(Longest)*

14 years and 31 days from Hungary 1991 (11 August, Jordan) until Belgium 2005 (11 September, Toyota).

879. Fastest laps but never a win

Force India	3	Toyota	3	Gordini	1
Sauber	3	Toleman	2	Lancia	1
Surtees	3	Ensign	1	Parnelli	1

880. Fastest laps but never a pole position

Sauber	3	Ensign	1	Parnelli	1
Surtees	3	Gordini	1		
Eagle	2	Hesketh	1		

Fastest lap speed *(Fastest/ Slowest).* See section 450

881. Milestones: Fastest laps

Ferrari	25th: Portugal 1958, 50th: United States 1970, 100th: San Marino 1985, 150th: Austria 2002, 200th: Europe 2007
McLaren	25th: Austria 1984, 50th: United States 1989, 100th: Malaysia 2000, 150th: India 2012
Williams	25th: San Marino 1986, 50th: Mexico 1991, 100th: Portugal 1996
Lotus	25th: Germany 1965, 50th: Netherlands 1974
Benetton	25th: Canada 1995
Brabham	25th: Britain 1978
Mercedes-Benz	25th: Brazil 2014
Red Bull	25th: Hungary 2012
Renault	25th: Britain 2006

Chapter 22: Point Scoring Constructors

882. Points

	for drivers' championship	for constructors' championship	races		
Ferrari (a)	7,164.27	6,262.5	724	Monaco 1950	- Abu Dhabi 2015
McLaren	5,358.5	5,040.5	610	Britain 1966	- United States 2015
Williams (b)	3,344	3,338	439	Netherlands 1973	- Abu Dhabi 2015
Red Bull	3,052.5	3,052.5	161	Australia 2005	- Abu Dhabi 2015
Mercedes-Benz	2,424.14	2,285	118	France 1954	- Abu Dhabi 2015
Lotus (c)	2,220	2,074	317	Belgium 1958	- Abu Dhabi 2015
Renault	1,318	1,318	190	United States 1978	- Brazil 2011
Brabham	983	864	184	United States 1962	- Japan 1991
Benetton	861.5	851.5	166	Brazil 1986	- Belgium 2001
Tyrrell	711	621	157	South Africa 1971	- Monaco 1997
Force India	627	627	86	Belgium 2009	- Abu Dhabi 2015
BRM	537.5	433	100	Britain 1951	- Belgium 1974
Sauber (d)	502	502	135	South Africa 1993	- United States 2015
Cooper	494.5	342	83	Switzerland 1952	- Canada 1968
Ligier (e)	388	388	102	United States West 1976	- Italy 1996
Maserati (f)	313.42	6	39	Monaco 1950	- France 1958
BMW (g)	308	308	56	Malaysia 2006	- Abu Dhabi 2009
Jordan	291	291	91	Canada 1991	- Belgium 2005
Toyota	278.5	278.5	68	Australia 2002	- Abu Dhabi 2009
Toro Rosso	266	266	75	United States 2006	- Brazil 2015
BAR	227	227	53	Australia 2000	- China 2005
Alfa Romeo	214	50	30	Britain 1950	- Europe 1984
March (h)	193	181.5	55	South Africa 1970	- Canada 1992
Matra (i)	184	163	38	South Africa 1968	- Canada 1972
Brawn	172	172	17	Australia 2009	- Abu Dhabi 2009
Arrows (j)	167	167	76	United States West 1978	- Monaco 2002
Honda	156	154	35	Belgium 1965	- Britain 2008
Vanwall	108	57	14	Belgium 1956	- Morocco 1958

	for drivers' championship	for constructors' championship	races		
Wolf	79	79	15	Argentina 1977	- Canada 1978
Shadow	68.5	67.5	26	South Africa 1973	- United States 1979
Surtees	54	53	22	Canada 1970	- Austria 1978
Porsche	50	48	16	Italy 1960	- United States 1963
Jaguar	49	49	22	Monaco 2000	- Belgium 2004
Hesketh	48	48	12	Sweden 1974	- United States 1975
Stewart	47	47	11	Monaco 1997	- Malaysia 1999
Fittipaldi (k)	44	44	19	United States West 1976	- Belgium 1982
Lola	43	43	19	Monaco 1962	- Mexico 1991
Minardi	38	38	19	Detroit 1988	- United States 2005
Prost	35	35	16	Australia 1997	- Germany 2001
Gordini (l)	30.14	-	12	France 1950	- Monaco 1956
Toleman	26	26	10	Netherlands 1983	- Portugal 1984
Talbot-Lago	25	-	6	Britain 1950	- Belgium 1951
Penske	23	23	7	Sweden 1975	- United States West 1977
Ensign	19	19	12	Germany 1975	- Netherlands 1981
Connaught	17	-	4	Britain 1952	- Monaco 1957
Eagle	17	17	4	France 1966	- Canada 1967
Dallara	15	15	6	Monaco 1989	- San Marino 1992
BRP	11	11	5	Netherlands 1963	- United States 1964
Lancia	9	-	2	Spain 1954	- Monaco 1955
ATS (Germany)	7	7	4	United States 1979	- San Marino 1982
Larrousse (m)	6	6	5	Monaco 1992	- Germany 1994
Onyx	6	6	2	France 1989	- Portugal 1989
Parnelli	6	6	3	Sweden 1975	- South Africa 1976
Rial	6	6	2	Detroit 1988	- United States 1989
Osella	5	5	2	San Marino 1982	- Dallas 1984
Super Aguri	4	4	2	Spain 2007	- Canada 2007
Frazer Nash	3	-	1	Switzerland 1952	
Hill	3	3	2	Sweden 1975	- Germany 1975
AGS	2	2	2	Australia 1987	- Mexico 1989
HWM	2	-	1	Belgium 1952	
Marussia	2	2	1	Monaco 2014	
Theodore	2	2	2	United States West 1981	- United States West 1983
Zakspeed	2	2	1	San Marino 1987	
Spyker	1	1	1	Japan 2007	
Tecno	1	1	1	Belgium 1973	
Indianapolis 500					
Kurtis-Kraft	127	-	9	1950	- 1958
Epperly	44	-	4	1957	- 1960
Watson	36	-	3	1956	- 1960
Kuzma	24	-	5	1952	- 1957
Deidt	10	-	1	1950	
Lesovsky	10	-	3	1952	- 1960
Phillips	7	-	2	1956	- 1960
Silnes-Sherman	3	-	1	1951	
Salih	2	-	2	1957	- 1958
Schroeder	2	-	1	1951	
Trevis	1	-	1	1960	

(a) Includes 126.5 Lancia-Ferrari and 3 Thin Wall Special points. (b) Includes 6 Iso-Marlboro points. (c) Includes 438 JPS Lotus points. (d) Includes 44 BMW Sauber points in 2010. (e) Includes 64 Talbot-Ligier points (f) Includes 2 Maserati-Milano points. (g) As BMW Sauber until 2009. BMW Sauber points (44) in 2010 are included with Sauber. (h) Includes 8 Leyton House points. (i) Includes 46 Matra-Simca points. (j) Includes 25 Footwork points. (k) Includes 32 Copersucar points. (l) Includes 5 Simca-Gordini points. (m) Includes 1 Venturi-Larrousse point.

Constructors' championship points are often different from those scored by drivers, due to the championship not commencing until 1958 or a constructor only being able to score points for their highest placed car (see section 883).
In 2007, McLaren were stripped of all their constructor's points (218), due to the spying scandal - that involved acquiring technical information from Ferrari and passing information to Renault. The points were not redistributed to other constructors. McLaren's drivers retained their points.
At Australia 1987, Lola was not awarded the two points for fifth place as the constructor had not submitted an entry for a second car that season. For the same reason, points were not awarded at Italy 1984 to ATS (5th) and Osella (6th).

883. Point scoring for constructors explained

Points have been distributed as follows:

1958 to 59	8, 6, 4, 3 and 2 points awarded to the first five finishers (excluding Indianapolis 500 races). Only scored points for their highest placed car in each race. No points for fastest lap or for shared drives.
1960 to 61	as above, except 1 point awarded for 6th place.
1962 to 90	9 points awarded to the winner, ie 9, 6, 4, 3, 2 and 1 point to the first six finishers. Until 1978, constructors were only awarded points for their highest placed car in each race. In 1966 and 67, cars running at the finish which were unclassified (were not within a certain percentage of the winning time) received no points even if they finished in the top six.
1991 to 2002	as above, but 10 points for a win.
2003 to 09	10 points awarded to the winner, with 8 for 2nd place, then 6, 5, 4, 3, 2, 1 down to 8th place.
2010 to present	25, 18, 15, 12, 10, 8, 6, 4, 2, 1 point awarded to the first 10 finishers.
2014 only	as above, but double points awarded in final race of the season.

Formula 2 participants were permitted to run alongside Formula 1 cars in six races but were ineligible for points.
Different car/engine combinations have been treated as separate constructors.
Half points were awarded for races stopped before three-quarter distance was completed (see section 486).
Until 1978, constructors were only able to count points from a specific number of races towards their total each year, as follows:

1958	- best 6 from 11	1967	- best 5 from first 6, 4 from remaining 5
1959	- best 5 from 9	1968	- best 5 from first 6, 5 from remaining 6
1960	- best 6 from 10	1969	- best 5 from first 6, 4 from remaining 5
1961	- best 5 from 8	1970	- best 6 from first 7, 5 from remaining 6
1962	- best 5 from 9	1971	- best 5 from first 6, 4 from remaining 5
1963	- best 6 from 10	1972	- best 5 from first 6, 5 from remaining 6
1964	- best 6 from 10	1973	- best 7 from first 8, 6 from remaining 7
1965	- best 6 from 10	1974	- best 7 from first 8, 6 from remaining 7
1966	- best 5 from 9	1975	- best 6 from first 7, 6 from remaining 7
		1976	- best 7 from first 8, 7 from remaining 8
		1977	- best 8 from first 9, 7 from remaining 8
		1978	- best 7 from first 8, 7 from remaining 8

For point scoring for drivers explained, see section 461.

884. Scored more points in a season than the champion

BRM	1964	Scored 51, whilst Ferrari scored only 49. The best six scores counted, meaning BRM dropped 9, but Ferrari only 4. This left BRM with only 42 points compared to Ferrari's 45.
BRM	1965	Scored 61, whilst Lotus - Climax scored 58. Only the six best scores counted, which meant that BRM had to drop 16, but Lotus - Climax only 4. Net points were Lotus - Climax, 54 and BRM, 45.

885. Points scored in a season *(Most)*

from 2010 with new points system				
Mercedes-Benz	703	2015 (wc)	(F1 W06)	(Lewis Hamilton, 381; Nico Rosberg, 322)
Mercedes-Benz	701	2014 (wc)	(F1 W05)	(Lewis Hamilton, 384; Nico Rosberg, 317)
Red Bull	650	2011 (wc)	(RB7 - Renault)	(Sebastian Vettel, 392; Mark Webber, 258)
Red Bull	596	2013 (wc)	(RB9 - Renault)	(Sebastian Vettel, 397; Mark Webber, 199)
Red Bull	498	2010 (wc)	(RB6 - Renault)	(Sebastian Vettel, 256; Mark Webber, 242)
McLaren	497	2011	(MP4-26 - Mercedes)	(Jenson Button, 270; Lewis Hamilton, 227)
Red Bull	460	2012 (wc)	(RB8 - Renault)	(Sebastian Vettel, 281; Mark Webber, 179)
McLaren	454	2010	(MP4-25 - Mercedes)	(Lewis Hmailton, 240; Jenson Button, 214)
Ferrari	428	2015	(SF15-T)	(Sebastian Vettel, 278; Kimi Räikkönen, 150)
Red Bull	405	2014	(RB10 - Renault)	(Daniel Ricciardo, 238; Sebastian Vettel, 167)
before 2010				
Ferrari	262	2004 (wc)	(F2004)	(Michael Schumacher, 148; Rubens Barrichello, 114)
Ferrari	221	2002 (wc)	(F2001, F2002)	(Michael Schumacher, 144; Rubens Barrichello, 77)
Renault	206	2006 (wc)	(R26)	(Fernando Alonso, 134; Giancarlo Fisichella, 72)
Ferrari	204	2007 (wc)	(F2007)	(Kimi Räikkönen, 110; Felipe Massa, 94)
Ferrari	201	2006	(248 F1)	(Michael Schumacher, 121; Felipe Massa, 80)
McLaren	199	1988 (a)(wc)	(MP4/4 - Honda)	(Alain Prost, 105; Ayrton Senna, 94)
Renault	191	2005 (wc)	(R25)	(Fernando Alonso, 133; Giancarlo Fisichella, 58)
McLaren	182	2005	(MP4-20 - Mercedes)	(Kimi Räikkönen, 112; Juan Pablo Montoya, 60; Alexander Wurz, 6; Pedro de la Rosa, 4)
Ferrari	179	2001 (wc)	(F2001)	(Michael Schumacher, 123; Rubens Barrichello, 56)
Williams	175	1996 (wc)	(FW18 - Renault)	(Damon Hill, 97; Jacques Villeneuve, 78)

(a) Prost had to drop 4 points and Senna, 18, with only the best scores counting.
(wc) World champion constructor that season.
Additionally, McLaren scored 218 points in 2007 (MP4-22 - Mercedes) but were stripped of all constructors' championship points (see footnote to section 882).

The sections below, relate to points scored for the drivers' world championship unless otherwise stated.

886. Consecutive point scoring races (Most)

Ferrari	81	Germany 2010	- Singapore 2014	(F10, F150th italia, F2012, F138, F14 T)
McLaren	64	Bahrain 2010	- Monaco 2013	(MP4-25, MP4-26, MP4-27, MP4-28 - Mercedes)
Mercedes-Benz	58	Brazil 2012	- Abu Dhabi 2015	(F1 W03, F1 W04, F1 W05, F1 W06)
Ferrari	55	Malaysia 1999	- Malaysia 2003	(F399, F1 2000, F2001, F2002)
Ferrari	46	San Marino 2006	- Italy 2008	(248 F1, F2007, F2008)
Lotus	38	Australia 2012	- United States 2013	(E20, E21 - Renault)
Ferrari	37	Belgium 1950	- Netherlands 1955	(275, 125, 375, 375 Thin Wall, 500, 625, 553, 555)
BMW Sauber	34	Australia 2007	- China 2008	(F1.07, F1.08)
Ferrari	33	San Marino 2003	- Malaysia 2005	(F2002, F2003-GA, F2004, F2004M)
Red Bull	33	Brazil 2010	- Belgium 2012	(RB6, RB7, RB8 - Renault)

887. Consecutive point scoring races from the start of a season (Most)

from 2010 with new points system			
Ferrari	20	2012 (a)	(F2012)
McLaren	20	2012 (a)	(MP4-27 - Mercedes)
Lotus	20	2012 (a)	(E20 - Renault)
Ferrari	19	2011 (a)	(F150th Italia)
Ferrari	19	2013 (a)	(F138)
McLaren	19	2010 (a)	(MP4-25 - Mercedes)
McLaren	19	2011 (a)	(MP4-26 - Mercedes)
Mercedes-Benz	19	2013 (a)	(F1 W04)
Mercedes-Benz	19	2014 (wc)	(F1 W05)
Mercedes-Benz	19	2015 (wc)	(F1 W06)
Red Bull	19	2011 (a)(wc)	(RB7 - Renault)
Red Bull	19	2013 (wc)	(RB9 - Renault)
Williams	19	2014	(FW36 - Mercedes)
before 2010			
Ferrari	18	2004 (a)(wc)	(F2004)
BMW Sauber	17	2007 (a)	(F1.07 - BMW)
BMW Sauber	17	2008	(F1.08 - BMW)
Brawn	17	2009 (wc)	(BGP 001 - Mercedes)
McLaren	17	2007 (b)	(MP4-22 - Mercedes)
Ferrari	17	2000 (a)(wc)	(F1 2000)
Ferrari	17	2001 (a)(wc)	(F2001)
Ferrari	17	2002 (a)(wc)	(F2001, F2002)
Ferrari	17	2007 (a)(wc)	(F2007)
Benetton	16	1992	(B191B, B192 - Ford Cosworth)
Williams	16	1993 (a)	(FW15C - Renault)

(a) Sequence continued into the following season.
(b) In 2007, McLaren were stripped of all constructors' championship points (see footnote to section 882).
(wc) World Champion constructor that season.

888. Seasons of scoring points (Most)

Ferrari	66	1950 - 2015	Brabham	29	1962 - 91	Renault	18	1978 - 2011
McLaren	50	1966 - 2015	Tyrrell	25	1971 - 97	Sauber	18	1993 - 2015 (a)
Williams	41	1973 - 2015	Arrows	24	1978 - 2002			
Lotus	40	1958 - 2015	BRM	18	1951 - 74			

(a) Excludes BMW Sauber (2006 - 2009).

889. Consecutive seasons of scoring points (Most)

Ferrari	66	1950 - 2015	Brabham	26	1962 - 87	Arrows	13	1978 - 90
McLaren	50	1966 - 2015	BRM	17	1958 - 74	Sauber	13	1993 - 2005
Lotus	36	1958 - 93	Benetton	16	1986 - 2001	Tyrrell	13	1971 - 83
Williams	38	1978 - 2015	Jordan	15	1991 - 2005			

890. Races taken to score their first point

(number of races relates to those started and includes the race with the first point)

Fewest (first race)

Alfa Romeo	Britain 1950	(Giuseppe Farina, Luigi Fagioli, Reg Parnell), 19 points
Benetton	Brazil 1986	(Gerhard Berger), 1 point
Brawn	Australia 2009	(Jenson Button, Rubens Barrichello), 18 points
BRM	Britain 1951	(Reg Parnell), 2 points
Connaught	Britain 1952	(Dennis Poore, Eric Thompson), 5 points
Ferrari	Monaco 1950	(Alberto Ascari, Raymond Sommer), 9 points
Frazer Nash	Switzerland 1952	(Ken Wharton), 3 points
Lancia	Spain 1954	(Alberto Ascari), 1 point
March	South Africa 1970	(Jackie Stewart), 4 points
Mercedes-Benz	France 1954	(Juan Manuel Fangio, Karl Kling, Hans Hermann), 15 points
Prost	Australia 1997	(Olivier Panis), 2 points
Red Bull	Australia 2005	(David Coulthard, Christian Klien), 7 points
Sauber	South Africa 1993	(J J Lehto), 2 points
Shadow	South Africa 1973	(George Follmer), 1 point
Talbot-Lago	Britain 1950	(Yves Giraud-Cabantous, Louis Rosier), 5 points
Toyota	Australia 2002	(Mika Salo), 1 point
Wolf	Argentina 1977	(Jody Scheckter), 9 points

Most

Marussia (a)	83	Monaco 2014	(Jules Bianchi)
Minardi	52	Detroit 1988	(Pierluigi Martini)
Force India	30	Belgium 2009	(Giancarlo Fisichella)
Zakspeed	27	San Marino 1987	(Martin Brundle)
Toleman	25	Netherlands 1983	(Derek Warwick)
ATS (Germany)	24	United States 1979	(Hans-Joachim Stuck)
Osella	24	San Marino 1982	(Jean-Pierre Jarier)
Super Aguri	22	Spain 2007	(Takuma Sato)
BAR	17	Australia 2000	(Jacques Villeneuve)
Dallara	17	Monaco 1989	(Alex Caffi)
Renault	17	United States 1978	(Jean-Pierre Jabouille)

(a) The cars were named Virgin during 2010 and 2011.
For most races started but never scored a point, see section 683.

891. Points scored in their first season *(Most)*

	points	races	season	constructors' championship (a)	
Brawn	172	17 of 17	2009	1st	(BGP 001 - Mercedes)
Alfa Romeo	89	6 of 6	1950	-	(158)
Mercedes-Benz	60.14	6 of 8	1954	-	(W196 str., W196)
March	55	10 of 13	1970	3rd	(701 - Ford Cosworth)
Wolf	55	9 of 17	1977	4th	(WR1, WR2 - Ford Cosworth)
BMW	36	12 of 18	2006	5th	(BMW Sauber F1.06)
Red Bull	34	11 of 19	2005	7th	(RB1 - Cosworth)
Ferrari	21	4 of 6	1950	-	(125, 275, 375)
Prost	21	8 of 17	1997	6th	(JS45 - Mugen Honda)
Talbot-Lago	20	5 of 6	1950	-	(T26C-DA, T26C)
Ligier	20	5 of 16	1976	6th	(JS5 - Matra)

Excludes Indianapolis 500.
(a) No constructors' championship until 1958.

892. Different point scorers in a season

Most

1989	16	1975	13	1981	13	1987	13
1978	14	1976	13	1982	13	1992	13

Fewest

1953	3	1959	4	1956	5	1961	5
1951	4	1950	5	1957	5		
1955	4	1954	5	1960	5		

Total for each season

1950 - 5, 1951 - 4, 1952 - 7, 1953 - 3, 1954 - 5, 1955 - 4, 1956 - 5, 1957 - 5, 1958 - 6, 1959 - 4, 1960 - 5, 1961 - 5, 1962 - 7, 1963 - 7, 1964 - 6, 1965 - 6, 1966 - 8, 1967 - 8, 1968 - 8, 1969 - 6, 1970 - 8, 1971 - 9, 1972 - 9, 1973 - 11, 1974 - 12, 1975 - 13, 1976 - 13, 1977 - 12, 1978 - 14, 1979 - 12, 1980 - 11, 1981 - 13, 1982 - 13, 1983 - 11, 1984 - 11, 1985 - 9, 1986 - 10, 1987 - 13, 1988 - 10, 1989 - 16, 1990 - 10, 1991 - 12, 1992 - 13, 1993 - 11, 1994 - 11, 1995 - 10, 1996 - 9, 1997 - 10, 1998 - 9, 1999 - 10, 2000 - 9, 2001 - 10, 2002 - 11, 2003 - 9, 2004 - 10, 2005 - 10, 2006 - 9, 2007 - 10 (a), 2008 - 9, 2009 - 10, 2010 - 9, 2011 - 9, 2012 - 9, 2013 - 9, 2014 - 9, 2015 - 9

Excludes Indianapolis 500.
(a) Excludes McLaren who were stripped of all their constructors' championship points, due to the spying scandal.

893. First time point scorers in a season *(Most)*

| 1950 | 5 | 1952 | 4 | 1975 | 4 | 1973 | 3 |

894. Point scoring drivers by constructor

	drivers	most races of scoring points
Ferrari	66	Michael Schumacher, 145
Lotus	44	Elio De Angelis, 42
McLaren	39	David Coulthard, 87
Williams	34	Nigel Mansell, 55; Ralf Schumacher, 55
Brabham	31	Nelson Piquet, 45
Cooper	28	Bruce McLaren, 34
Maserati	27	Juan Manuel Fangio, 15
BRM	26	Graham Hill, 36
Tyrrell	23	Patrick Depailler, 31
Sauber	22	Kamui Kobayashi, 26
Arrows	19	Derek Warwick, 16
Jordan	18	Heinz-Harald Frentzen, 20
Ligier	18	Jacques Laffite, 50
Benetton	17	Michael Schumacher, 45
March	16	Ronnie Peterson, 14
Renault	16	Fernando Alonso, 75
Alfa Romeo	13	Juan Manuel Fangio, 10; Giuseppe Farina, 10
Minardi	11	Pierluigi Martini, 8
Shadow	10	Tom Pryce, 9
Toro Rosso	10	Sébastien Buemi, 15
Surtees	9	Mike Hailwood, 5
Mercedes-Benz	8	Nico Rosberg, 88
Ensign	7	Clay Regazzoni, 3; Patrick Tambay, 3
Lola	7	John Surtees, 5
Red Bull	7	Sebastian Vettel, 96
Toyota	7	Jarno Trulli, 36
Force India	6	Nico Hülkenberg, 35
Gordini	6	Robert Manzon, 4
Honda	6	Jenson Button, 15
BAR	5	Jenson Button, 32
Connaught	5	Jack Fairman, 2
Dallara	5	Alex Caffi, 2; Pierluigi Martini, 2
Jaguar	5	Mark Webber, 11
Matra	5	Jean-Pierre Beltoise, 18
Porsche	5	Dan Gurney, 8
ATS	4	Slim Borgudd, 1; Eliseo Salazar, 1; Hans-Joachim Stuck, 1; Manfred Winkelhock, 1
BMW	4	Nick Heidfeld, 41
Prost	4	Olivier Panis, 7
Talbot-Lago	4	Louis Rosier, 5
Toleman	4	Ayrton Senna, 5
Vanwall	4	Stirling Moss, 9
Fittipaldi	3	Emerson Fittipaldi, 16
Lancia	3	Alberto Ascari, 1; Eugenio Castellotti, 1; Luigi Villoresi, 1
Larrousse	3	Erik Comas, 3
Penske	3	John Watson, 5
Stewart	3	Rubens Barrichello, 10
AGS	2	Roberto Moreno, 1; Gabriele Tarquini, 1
Brawn	2	Jenson Button, 16

	drivers	most races of scoring points
BRP	2	Innes Ireland, 4
Hill	2	Tony Brise, 1; Alan Jones, 1
Osella	2	Piercarlo Ghinzani, 1; Jean-Pierre Jarier, 1
Rial	2	Christian Danner, 1; Andrea De Cesaris, 1
Theodore	2	Johnny Cecotto, 1; Patrick Tambay, 1
Eagle	1	Dan Gurney, 4
Frazer Nash	1	Ken Wharton, 1
Hesketh	1	James Hunt, 12
HWM	1	Paul Frère, 1
Marussia	1	Jules Bianchi, 1
Onyx	1	Stefan Johansson, 2
Parnelli	1	Mario Andretti, 3
Spyker	1	Adrian Sutil, 1
Super Aguri	1	Takuma Sato, 2
Tecno	1	Chris Amon, 1
Wolf	1	Jody Scheckter, 15
Zakspeed	1	Martin Brundle, 1
Indianapolis 500		
Kurtis-Kraft	23	Bill Vukovich, 19
Epperly	4	Jim Rathmann, 9
Kuzma	4	Jimmy Bryan, 10
Watson	3	Jim Rathmann, 14; Rodger Ward, 14
Deidt	2	Bill Holland, 3; Mauri Rose, 1
Lesovsky	2	Johnny Thomson, 7
Phillips	2	Don Freeland, 4
Salih	2	Jimmy Bryan, 8; Sam Hanks, 8
Schroeder	1	Bobby Ball, 2
Silnes-Sherman	1	Andy Linden, 3
Trevis	1	Eddie Johnson, 1

895. Point scoring races with the same engine make *(Most)*

Ferrari	724	Ferrari	Monaco 1950	- Abu Dhabi 2015
McLaren	302	Mercedes	Brazil 1995	- Abu Dhabi 2014
Renault	190	Renault	United States 1978	- Brazil 2011
McLaren	166	Ford Cosworth	Spain 1968	- Australia 1993
Lotus	143	Ford Cosworth	Netherlands 1967	- Belgium 1993
Red Bull	143	Renault	Spain 2007	- Abu Dhabi 2015
Williams	138	Renault	San Marino 1989	- United States 2013 (a)
Tyrrell	133	Ford Cosworth	South Africa 1971	- Monaco 1997
Mercedes-Benz	118	Mercedes	France 1954	- Abu Dhabi 2015
BRM	97	BRM	Britain 1951	- Belgium 1974

*(a) An additional 12 races of scoring points with Mecachrome and further 11 with Supertec, Renault-based engines, within the period.
Sauber scored points in 102 races with Petronas (re-badged Ferrari) plus Ferrari engines, from Australia 1997 to Brazil 2013.*

896. Interval between point scores *(Longest)*

	years, days	races		
Mercedes-Benz (a)	54y, 184d	773	Italy 1955 (Juan Manuel Fangio, Piero Taruffi, Stirling Moss)	- Bahrain 2010 (Nico Rosberg, Michael Schumacher)
Honda (a)	37y, 129d	578	Mexico 1968 (Jo Bonnier)	- Bahrain 2006 (Jenson Button)
Alfa Romeo (a)	28y, 77d	314	Spain 1951 (Juan Manuel Fangio, Giuseppe Farina, Felice Bonetto)	- Argentina 1980 (Bruno Giacomelli)
Lotus (a)	18y, 202d	315	Belgium 1993 (Johnny Herbert)	- Australia 2012 (Kimi Räikkönen)
Renault (a)	16y, 183d	265	Belgium 1985 (Derek Warwick)	- Malaysia 2002 (Jenson Button)
Lola (a)	12y, 69d	190	Sweden 1974 (Graham Hill)	- Austria 1986 (Alan Jones, Patrick Tambay)
Lola (a)	11y, 308d	134	Germany 1962 (John Surtees)	- Sweden 1974 (Graham Hill)
March (a)	10y, 233d	161	United States 1976 (Hans-Joachim Stuck)	- Monaco 1987 (Ivan Capelli)
BRM (a)	6y, 308d	54	Britain 1951 (Reg Parnell)	- Monaco 1958 (Harry Schell)
Cooper	4y, 337d	39	Netherlands 1952 (Mike Hawthorn)	- Britain 1957 (Roy Salvadori)

(a) Not present throughout the period.

897. Interval between first & last point scores (Longest)

	years, days	races		
Ferrari	65y, 192d	933	Monaco 1950 (A Ascari, R Sommer)	- Abu Dhabi 2015 (K Räikkönen, S Vettel)
Mercedes -Benz	61y, 148d	899	France 1954 (J M Fangio, K Kling, H Herrmann)	- Abu Dhabi 2015 (N Rosberg, L Hamilton)
Lotus	57y, 167d	866	Belgium 1958 (C Allison)	- Abu Dhabi 2015 (R Grosjean)
McLaren	49y, 101d	787	Britain 1966 (B McLaren)	- United States 2015 (J Button)
Honda	43y, 23d	660	Belgium 1965 (R Ginther)	- Britain 2008 (R Barrichello)
Williams	42y, 123d	705	Netherlands 1973 (G van Lennep)	- Abu Dhabi 2015 (F Massa)
Alfa Romeo	34y, 147d	402	Britain 1950 (G Farina, L Fagioli, R Parnell)	- Europe 1984 (R Patrese)
Renault	33y, 57d	546	United States 1978 (J-P Jabouille)	- Brazil 2011 (V Petrov)
Brabham	29y, 13d	405	United States 1962 (J Brabham)	- Japan 1991 (M Brundle)
Lola	29y, 13d	402	Monaco 1962 (J Surtees)	- Mexico 1991 (E Bernard)

898. Points but never a constructors' championship (Most)
(based on constructors' championship points)

Force India	627		BMW	308		Toro Rosso	266
Sauber	502		Jordan	291		BAR	227
Ligier	388		Toyota	278.5		March	181.5

899. Points but never a win (Most)
(based on drivers' championship points)

Force India	627		Arrows	167		Lola	43
Sauber	502		Surtees	54		Minardi	38
Toyota	278.5		Jaguar	49			
BAR	227		Fittipaldi	44			

900. Points but never a podium (Most)
(based on drivers' championship points)

Minardi	38		Larrousse	6		Super Aguri	4
Ensign	19		Parnelli	6		Hill	3
BRP	11		Rial	6			
ATS (Germany)	7		Osella	5			

901. Points but never a pole position (Most)
(based on drivers' championship points)

Sauber	502		Fittipaldi	44		Penske	23
Surtees	54		Minardi	38		Talbot-Lago	25
Jaguar	49		Prost	35			
Hesketh	48		Gordini	30.14			

902. Milestones: Points scored

Constructors' championship

Ferrari	1,000th: United States 1979, 2,000th: Brazil 1997, 3,000th: Canada 2003, 4,000th: China 2008, 5,000th: Britain 2012, 6,000th: Canada 2015
McLaren	1,000th: Mexico 1986, 2,000th: Australia 1997, 3,000th: Italy 2005, 4,000th: Canada 2011, 5,000th: Abu Dhabi 2014
Williams	1,000th: Germany 1991, 2,000th: Britain 2000, 3,000th: Brazil 2014
Red Bull	1,000th: Canada 2011, 2,000th: Monaco 2013, 3,000th: Japan 2015
Lotus	1,000th: Belgium 1981, 2,000th: China 2015
Mercedes-Benz	1,000th: China 2014, 2,000th: Belgium 2015
Renault	1,000th: Hungary 2008

Drivers' championship

Ferrari	1,000th: United States 1964, 2,000th: France 1982, 3,000th: Australia 1998, 4,000th: Australia 2004, 5,000th: Bahrain 2010, 6,000th: Singapore 2012, 7,000th: Italy 2015
McLaren	1,000th: Belgium 1985, 2,000th: Europe 1994, 3,000th: Spain 2005, 4,000th: Hungary 2010, 5,000th: United States 2012
Red Bull	1,000th: Canada 2011, 2,000th: Monaco 2013, 3,000th: Japan 2015
Williams	1,000th: Germany 1991, 2,000th: Japan 1999, 3,000th: Brazil 2014
Lotus	1,000th: United States West 1978, 2,000th: Hungary 2013
Mercedes-Benz	1,000th: United States 2013, 2,000th: Canada 2015
Renault	1,000th: Hungary 2008

903. Milestones: Point scoring races

Ferrari	100th: United States 1964, 200th: Monaco 1977, 250th: Netherlands 1982, 300th: Portugal 1986, 400th: San Marino 1996, 500th: Italy 2002, 600th: Brazil 2008, 700th: Belgium 2014
McLaren	100th: South Africa 1977, 200th: Brazil 1987, 250th: Belgium 1990, 300th: Italy 1994, 400th: Monaco 2002, 500th: Italy 2008, 600th: Singapore 2014
Williams	100th: Detroit 1987, 200th: San Marino 1995, 250th: Italy 1998, 300th: Australia 2003, 400th: India 2012
Lotus	100th: Italy 1972, 200th: Netherlands 1984, 250th: Canada 1990, 300th: Abu Dhabi 2013
Benetton	50th: Australia 1990, 100th: Europe 1994, 150th: France 1998
Brabham	50th: France 1969, 100th: Germany 1976, 150th: Switzerland 1982
Renault	50th: France 1985, 100th: Britain 2005, 150th: Japan 2008
Red Bull	50th: Abu Dhabi 2009, 100th: Singapore 2012, 150th: Canada 2015
Tyrrell	50th: United States 1975, 100th: Britain 1981, 150th: Belgium 1994
BRM	50th: Britain 1965, 100th: Belgium 1974
Ligier	50th: Austria 1982, 100th: Spain 1996
Mercedes-Benz	50th: Bahrain 2012, 100th: Australia 2015
Sauber	50th: Canada 2001, 100th Singapore 2011

Chapter 23: Race Leading Constructors

Based on actual laps led, even where a disqualification or other penalty was later applied and also where times were aggregated.
All distances led are calculated as complete laps, based on the leader at the end of each lap (actual distances in the lead are not recorded for the official results).

904. Laps led

	laps	races	km	miles		
Ferrari (a)	13,863	416	72,118	44,812	Italy 1950 (Alberto Ascari)	- Singapore 2015 (Sebastian Vettel)
McLaren	10,584	322	50,383	31,307	Belgium 1968 (Denny Hulme)	- Hungary 2014 (Jenson Button)
Williams	7,589	225	35,267	21,914	Belgium 1979 (Alan Jones)	- Britain 2015 (Felipe Massa)
Lotus (b)	5,623	160	26,852	16,685	Argentina 1960 (Innes Ireland)	- United States 2013 (Romain Grosjean)
Red Bull	3,075	82	15,810	9,824	Europe 2005 (David Coulthard)	- United States 2015 (Daniel Ricciardo)
Mercedes-Benz	2,757	60	14,771	9,178	France 1954 (Karl Kling)	- Abu Dhabi 2015 (Nico Rosberg)
Brabham	2,721	91	13,240	8,227	Britain 1963 (Jack Brabham)	- France 1985 (Nelson Piquet)
Renault	2,514	88	12,150	7,549	South Africa 1979 (Jean-Pierre Jabouille)	- Singapore 2009 (Fernando Alonso)
Benetton	1,527	55	7,248	4,504	Austria 1986 (Gerhard Berger)	- Europe 1999 (Giancarlo Fisichella)
Tyrrell	1,493	38	6,737	4,186	Canada 1970 (Jackie Stewart)	- United States 1990 (Jean Alesi)
BRM	1,347	40	6,099	3,790	Britain 1956 (Mike Hawthorn)	- Canada 1973 (Jean-Pierre Beltoise)
Cooper	830	23	4,546	2,825	Argentina 1958 (Stirling Moss)	- South Africa 1967 (Pedro Rodríguez)
Maserati	826	21	4,723	2,935	Italy 1952 (José Froilán González)	- Argentina 1958 (Juan Manuel Fangio)
Alfa Romeo	701	16	4,793	2,978	Britain 1950 (Giuseppe Farina)	- Belgium 1983 (Andrea De Cesaris)
Matra	668	23	3,610	2,243	South Africa 1968 (Jackie Stewart)	- France 1972 (Chris Amon)
Ligier (c)	565	18	2,628	1,633	Sweden 1977 (Jacques Laffite)	- Monaco 1996 (Olivier Panis)
Brawn	405	11	1,957	1,216	Australia 2009 (Jenson Button)	- Brazil 2009 (Rubens Barrichello)

	laps	races	km	miles		
Vanwall	371	12	2,784	1,730	Italy 1956 (Harry Schell)	- Morocco 1958 (Stirling Moss)
March (d)	339	17	1,499	932	South Africa 1970 (Jackie Stewart)	- France 1990 (Ivan Capelli)
Wolf	214	9	815	506	Argentina 1977 (Jody Scheckter)	- Britain 1978 (Jody Scheckter)
Arrows	127	4	495	308	South Africa 1978 (Riccardo Patrese)	- Hungary 1997 (Damon Hill)
Jordan	113	12	629	391	Portugal 1994 (Rubens Barrichello)	- Brazil 2003 (Giancarlo Fisichella)
Honda	111	11	623	387	Netherlands 1965 (Richie Ginther)	- Canada 2008 (Rubens Barrichello)
BMW (e)	98	13	450	279	Italy 2006 (Robert Kubica)	- Japan 2008 (Robert Kubica)
Hesketh	88	5	396	246	Argentina 1975 (James Hunt)	- Austria 1975 (James Hunt)
Stewart	84	3	363	226	Brazil 1999 (Rubens Barrichello)	- Europe 1999 (Rubens Barrichello)
BAR	81	10	416	259	United States 2003 (Jenson Button)	- Japan 2005 (Jenson Button)
Toyota	66	11	341	212	Britain 2003 (Cristiano da Matta)	- Bahrain 2009 (Jarno Trulli)
Force India	65	7	306	190	Belgium 2009 (Giancarlo Fisichella)	- Brazil 2014 (Nico Hülkenberg)
Toro Rosso	56	4	315	196	Japan 2007 (Sebastian Vettel)	- Canada 2010 (Sébastien Buemi)
Shadow	50	4	335	208	Canada 1973 (Jackie Oliver)	- Austria 1977 (Alan Jones)
Penske	45	1	266	165	Austria 1976 (John Watson)	
Prost	37	1	160	99	Austria 1997 (Jarno Trulli)	
Sauber	25	7	133	83	United States 2003 (Heinz-Harald Frentzen)	- Spain 2013 (Esteban Gutiérrez)
Porsche	20	3	172	107	France 1961 (Jo Bonnier)	- Germany 1962 (Dan Gurney)
Lancia	20	2	95	59	Spain 1954 (Alberto Ascari)	- Argentina 1955 (Alberto Ascari)
Eagle	19	3	330	205	Belgium 1967 (Dan Gurney)	- Italy 1967 (Dan Gurney)
Parnelli	10	1	38	24	Spain 1975 (Mario Andretti)	
Surtees	9	2	46	28	Italy 1971 (Mike Hailwood)	- Belgium 1977 (Vittorio Brambilla)
Hill	8	1	30	19	Spain 1975 (Rolf Stommelen)	
Spyker	6	1	31	19	Europe 2007 (Markus Winkelhock)	
Talbot-Lago	5	1	71	44	Belgium 1950 (Raymond Sommer)	
Jaguar	2	1	8	5	United States 2003 (Mark Webber)	
Gordini	1	1	14	9	Belgium 1952 (Jean Behra)	
Minardi	1	1	4	3	Portugal 1989 (Pierluigi Martini)	
Indianapolis 500						
Kurtis-Kraft	1,068	9	4,297	2,670	1950 - 1958	
Watson	460	4	1,851	1,150	1956 - 1960	
Salih	275	2	1,106	687	1957 - 1958	
Kuzma	143	6	575	357	1952 - 1958	
Epperly	66	2	266	165	1957 - 1958	
Lesovsky	50	2	201	125	1959 - 1960	
Silnes-Pawl	25	1	101	62	1951	
Deidt	23	1	93	58	1950	
Ewing	21	1	84	52	1960	
Phillips	7	2	28	17	1955 - 1956	

(a) Includes Lancia-Ferrari. (b) Includes JPS Lotus. (c) Includes Talbot-Ligier. (d) Includes Leyton House. (e) As BMW Sauber.

905. Races led *(Most)*

		% of races started				
Ferrari	416	45.87		Renault	88	29.33
McLaren	322	41.28		Red Bull	82	40.39
Williams	225	32.51		Mercedes-Benz	60	47.24
Lotus	160	26.40		Benetton	55	21.15
Brabham	91	23.10		BRM	40	20.30

906. Distance led *(Longest)*

	km	miles			km	miles
Ferrari	72,118	44,812		Mercedes-Benz	14,771	9,178
McLaren	50,383	31,307		Brabham	13,240	8,227
Williams	35,267	21,914		Renault	12,150	7,549
Lotus	26,852	16,685		Benetton	7,248	4,504
Red Bull	15,810	9,824		Tyrrell	6,737	4,186

907. Races led in a season *(Most)*

Mercedes-Benz	19 of 19	2014 (wc)	(F1 W05)	(Lewis Hamilton, 15; Nico Rosberg, 15)
Red Bull	19 of 19	2011 (wc)	(RB7 - Renault)	(Sebastian Vettel, 17; Mark Webber, 3)

Ferrari	18 of 18	2004 (wc)	(F2004)	(Michael Schumacher, 16; Rubens Barrichello, 8)
Red Bull	18 of 19	2013 (wc)	(RB9 - Renault)	(Sebastian Vettel, 18; Mark Webber, 5)
Mercedes-Benz	17 of 19	2015 (wc)	(F1 W06)	(Lewis Hamilton, 17; Nico Rosberg, 14)
McLaren	16 of 16	1988 (wc)	(MP4/4 - Honda)	(Ayrton Senna, 12; Alain Prost, 9)
Williams	16 of 16	1993 (wc)	(FW15C - Renault)	(Alain Prost, 15; Damon Hill, 10)
Williams	16 of 16	1996 (wc)	(FW18 - Renault)	(Damon Hill, 12; Jacques Villeneuve, 9)
Ferrari	16 of 17	2002 (wc)	(F2001, F2002)	(Michael Schumacher, 13; Rubens Barrichello, 11)
McLaren	16 of 17	2000	(MP4-15 - Mercedes)	(Mika Häkkinen, 12; David Coulthard, 9)

(wc) World champion constructor that season.

908. Led in every race of a season
(apart from those in section 907)

Matra	11	1969 (wc)	(MS10, MS80 - Ford Cosworth)	(Jackie Stewart)
Ferrari	8	1953	(500)	(Alberto Ascari, 7; Giuseppe Farina, 3; Mike Hawthorn, 2)
Alfa Romeo	7	1951	(159)	(Juan Manuel Fangio, 7; Giuseppe Farina, 3; Felice Bonetto, 1)
Ferrari	7	1952	(500)	(Alberto Ascari, 6; Giuseppe Farina, 1; Piero Taruffi, 1)
Alfa Romeo	6	1950	(158)	(Juan Manuel Fangio, 5; Giuseppe Farina, 5; Luigi Fagioli, 3)
Mercedes-Benz	6	1955	(W196, W196 str.)	(Juan Manuel Fangio, 6; Stirling Moss, 3)

(wc) World champion constructor that season (no championship pre-1958).

909. Led in all but one race of a season
(apart from those in section 907)

Lotus	9	1963 (wc)	(25 - Climax)	(Jim Clark)
BRM	8	1962 (wc)	(P57)	(Graham Hill)
Cooper	8	1960 (wc)	(T51, T53 - Climax)	(Jack Brabham, 7; Bruce McLaren, 1; Stirling Moss, 1)
Cooper	7	1959 (wc)	(T51 - Climax)	(Stirling Moss, 5; Jack Brabham, 4; Masten Gregory, 2)
Lancia-Ferrari	6	1956	(D50)	(Juan Manuel Fangio, 5; Peter Collins, 2; Eugenio Castellotti, 2; Luigi Musso, 1)
Maserati	6	1957	(250F)	(Juan Manuel Fangio, 5; Jean Behra, 3)

(wc) World champion constructor that season (no championship pre-1958).

910. Laps led in a season *(Most)*

	laps	%		
McLaren	1,003 of 1,031	97.28	1988	(MP4/4 - Honda)
Mercedes-Benz	978 of 1,134	86.24	2014	(F1 W05)
Mercedes-Benz	936 of 1,149	81.46	2015	(F1 W06)
Williams	867 of 1,036	83.69	1992	(FW14B - Renault)
Ferrari	865 of 1,090	79.36	2002	(F2001, F2002)
Red Bull	798 of 1,133	70.43	2011	(RB7 - Renault)
Ferrari	785 of 1,122	69.96	2004	(F2004)
Williams	765 of 1,014	75.44	1996	(FW18 - Renault)
Red Bull	753 of 1,131	66.58	2013	(RB9 - Renault)
McLaren	745 of 1,039	71.70	1989	(MP4/5 - Honda)

All became world champion constructor that season.

911. Distance led in a season *(Longest)*

	km	miles		
Mercedes-Benz	4,922	3,058	2014	(F1 W05)
Mercedes-Benz	4,704	2,923	2015	(F1 W06)
McLaren	4,622	2,872	1988	(MP4/4 - Honda)
Ferrari	4,209	2,616	2002	(F2001, F2002)
Williams	4,098	2,547	1992	(FW14B - Renault)
Red Bull	4,064	2,525	2011	(RB7 - Renault)
Red Bull	4,001	2,486	2013	(RB9 - Renault)
Ferrari	3,892	2,418	2004	(F2004)
Williams	3,556	2,210	1996	(FW18 - Renault)
McLaren	3,515	2,184	1989	(MP4/5 - Honda)

All became world champion constructor that season.

912. Percentage of laps led in a season *(Highest)*

	%	laps led		
Alfa Romeo	98.21	384 of 391	1950 (a)	(158)
McLaren	97.28	1,003 of 1,031	1988 (wc)	(MP4/4 - Honda)
Ferrari	91.72	410 of 447	1952 (a)	(500)
Mercedes-Benz	89.19	421 of 472	1955 (a)	(W196, W196 str.)
Ferrari	86.38	463 of 536	1953	(500)
Mercedes-Benz	86.24	978 of 1,134	2014 (wc)	(F1 W05)
Williams	83.69	867 of 1,036	1992 (wc)	(FW14B - Renault)
Mercedes-Benz	81.46	936 of 1,149	2015 (wc)	(F1 W06)
Ferrari	79.36	865 of 1,090	2002 (wc)	(F2001, F2002)
Williams	75.44	765 of 1,014	1996 (wc)	(FW18 - Renault)

(a) Total laps for the season excludes Indianapolis 500.
(wc) World champion constructor that season (no championship pre-1958).

913. Percentage of laps led in constructor's title winning season

Lowest

	%	laps led		
McLaren	8.07	79 of 979	1974	(M23 - Ford Cosworth)
Ferrari	13.87	147 of 1,060	1982	(126C2)
Ferrari	18.37	208 of 1,132	1977	(312T2)
Lotus	19.63	180 of 917	1970	(49C, 72C - Ford Cosworth)
Ferrari	20.50	148 of 722	1964	(158, 156)
Williams	22.05	196 of 889	1980	(FW07, FW07B - Ford Cosworth)
McLaren	22.38	231 of 1,032	1985	(MP4/2B - TAG Porsche)
Williams	28.11	294 of 1,046	1994	(FW16, FW16B - Renault)
Ferrari	28.83	271 of 940	1983	(126C2B, 126C3)
Lotus	29.81	240 of 805	1972	(72D - Ford Cosworth)

914. Percentage of laps led in a season without becoming constructors' champion

Highest

	%	laps led		
Benetton	60.13	629 of 1,046	1994	(B194 - Ford Cosworth)
Lotus	54.60	439 of 804	1967	(49 - Ford Cosworth)
McLaren	52.80	528 of 1,000	1999	(MP4-14 - Mercedes)
McLaren	50.17	592 of 1,180	2005	(MP4-20 - Mercedes)
McLaren	49.20	524 of 1,065	2007 (a)	(MP4-22 - Mercedes)
Williams	46.89	527 of 1,124	1995	(FW17, FW17B - Renault)
Ferrari	45.73	520 of 1,137	2006	(248 F1)
Lotus	44.60	322 of 722	1964	(25, 33 - Climax)
Lotus	43.59	272 of 624	1962	(24, 25 - Climax)
Renault	43.58	462 of 1,060	1982	(RE30B)

(a) In 2007, McLaren were stripped of all their constructors' championship points, due to the spying scandal.

915. Races of leading every lap

Ferrari (a)	67	Switzerland 1952 (G Farina, P Taruffi)	- Singapore 2015 (S Vettel)
McLaren	61	Germany 1976 (J Hunt)	- Belgium 2012 (J Button)
Williams	47	Britain 1979 (A Jones, C Regazzoni)	- France 2003 (R Schumacher)
Lotus (b)	31	Germany 1961 (S Moss)	- Belgium 1985 (A Senna)
Mercedes-Benz	30	France 1954 (K Kling, J M Fangio)	- Abu Dhabi 2015 (L Hamilton, N Rosberg)
Red Bull	19	Britain 2009 (S Vettel, M Webber)	- Brazil 2013 (S Vettel)
Brabham	11	Britain 1966 (J Brabham)	- Detroit 1984 (N Piquet)
Tyrrell	8	Monaco 1971 (J Stewart)	- Sweden 1974 (J Scheckter)
Renault	7	South Africa 1980 (J P Jabouille, R Arnoux)	- Britain 2006 (F Alonso, G Fisichella)
Alfa Romeo	5	Britain 1950 (G Farina, L Fagioli, J M Fangio)	- Switzerland 1951 (J M Fangio, G Farina)
Cooper	5	Britain 1959 (J Brabham)	- Belgium 1960 (J Brabham)
Benetton	4	Pacific 1994 (M Schumacher)	- Spain 1995 (M Schumacher)

Ligier	4	Argentina 1979 (P Depailler, J Laffite)	- Belgium 1980 (D Pironi)
Matra	4	Germany 1968 (J Stewart)	- France 1969 (J Stewart)
BRM	3	Italy 1962 (G Hill)	- Monaco 1972 (J-P Beltoise)
Vanwall	2	Netherlands 1958 (S Moss)	- Morocco 1958 (S Moss)
Brawn	1	Australia 2009 (J Button)	
Honda	1	Mexico 1965 (R Ginther)	
March	1	Spain 1970 (J Stewart)	
Maserati	1	Monaco 1956 (S Moss)	
Wolf	1	Monaco 1977 (J Scheckter)	

(a) Includes Lancia-Ferrari.
(b) Includes JPS Lotus.

916. Consecutive races led *(Most)*

Williams	31	France 1995	- San Marino 1997	(FW17, FW17B, FW18, FW19 - Renault)
McLaren	28	Brazil 1988	- Italy 1989	(MP4/4, MP4/5 - Honda)
Mercedes-Benz	28	Australia 2014	- Britain 2015	(F1 W05, F1 W06)
Williams	26	Belgium 1986	- Mexico 1987	(FW11, FW11B - Honda)
Williams	26	France 1992	- Brazil 1994	(FW14B, FW15C, FW16 - Renault)
Red Bull	24	Japan 2010	- Australia 2012	(RB6, RB7, RB8 - Renault)
Ferrari	23	Belgium 1951	- Belgium 1954	(375, 500, 625, 553)
Ferrari	22	Italy 2003	- Australia 2005	(F2003-GA, F2004, F2004M)
Ferrari	18	Canada 2002	- Canada 2003	(F2002, F2003-GA)
Ferrari	16	Monaco 1975	- Monaco 1976	(312T, 312T2)
Renault	14	Brazil 2005	- France 2006	(R25, R26)

917. Consecutive laps led *(Most)*

Mercedes-Benz	413	Australia 2014 (lap 1)	- Canada 2014 (lap 45)	(F1 W05, F1 W06)
McLaren	477	Brazil 1988 (lap 1)	- France 1988 (end)	(MP4/4 - Honda)
Williams	419	Canada 1993 (lap 1)	- Italy 1993 (end)	(FW15C - Renault)
Williams	407	South Africa 1992 (lap 1)	- Monaco 1992 (lap 70)	(FW14B - Renault)
Ferrari	340	Italy 1975 (lap 1)	- Spain 1976 (lap 31)	(312T, 312T2)
Ferrari	304	Belgium 1952 (lap 2)	- Netherlands 1952 (end)	(500)
McLaren	282	San Marino 1989 (lap 1)	- Canada 1989 (lap 3)	(MP4/5 - Honda)
Mercedes-Benz	276	Belgium 1955 (lap 1)	- Italy 1955 (end)	(W196, W196 str.)
McLaren	264	Britain 1988 (lap 14)	- Italy 1988 (lap 49)	(MP4/4 - Honda)
Mercedes-Benz	233	Spain 2015 (lap 17)	- Austria 2015 (lap 35)	(F1 W06)

918. Seasons of leading races *(Most)*

Ferrari	64	1950 - 2015	BRM	15	1956 - 73
McLaren	45	1968 - 2014	Benetton	13	1986 - 99
Williams	30	1979 - 2015	Renault	13	1979 - 2009
Lotus	25	1960 - 2013	Tyrrell	11	1970 - 90
Brabham	17	1963 - 85	Red Bull	9	2005 - 14

919. Consecutive seasons of leading races *(Most)*

McLaren	34	1981 - 2014	Lotus	11	1960 - 70
Ferrari	23	1950 - 72	McLaren	11	1968 - 78
Ferrari	23	1993 - 2015	Williams	9	1979 - 87
Ferrari	18	1974 - 91	Williams	9	1989 - 97
Benetton	11	1989 - 99	Red Bull	8	2007 - 14

920. Races led at the same circuit (Most)

Ferrari (a)	38	Monza	1950 - 2013		Ferrari (a)	22	Nürburgring	1951 - 2011
Ferrari (a)	25	Spa-Francorchamps	1951 - 2011		McLaren	19	Silverstone	1973 - 2012
Ferrari	25	Monte-Carlo	1955 - 2012		Ferrari	18	Montréal	1978 - 2012
Ferrari (a)	23	Silverstone	1951 - 2012		McLaren	17	Hungaroring	1988 - 2014
McLaren	23	Monza	1968 - 2012		McLaren	17	Monte-Carlo	1984 - 2011

(a) Includes Lancia-Ferrari.

921. Races taken to lead a lap
(number of races relates to those started and includes the first race led)

Fewest

Alfa Romeo	1	March	1	Arrows	2
Brawn	1	Mercedes-Benz	1	BRM	2
Hill	1	Tyrrell	1		
Lancia	1	Wolf	1		

Most

Sauber	178	Jaguar	66	Force India	30
BAR	82	Jordan	61	Toyota	28
Williams	78	Stewart	35		
Minardi	73	Toro Rosso	33		

For most races started but never led, see section 684.

922. Led in their first two or more races started

Alfa Romeo	13	Britain 1950	- Spain 1951	(158, 159)
Brawn	7	Australia 2009	- Turkey 2009	(BGP 001 - Mercedes)
March	4	South Africa 1970	- Belgium 1970	(701 - Ford Cosworth)
Tyrrell	2	Canada 1970	- United States 1970	(001 - Ford Cosworth)

923. Laps led in their first season

	laps	races	km	miles		
Brawn	405	11	1,957	1,216	2009	(BGP 001 - Mercedes)
Alfa Romeo	384	6	2,364	1,469	1950	(158)
Wolf	198	7	748	465	1977	(WR1, WR2, WR3 - Ford Cosworth)
Mercedes-Benz	168	4	1,608	999	1954	(W196 str., W196)
March	157	5	623	387	1970	(701 - Ford Cosworth)
Tyrrell	113	2	436	271	1970	(001 - Ford Cosworth)
Benetton	66	3	341	212	1986	(B186 - BMW)
Arrows	37	1	152	94	1978	(FA1 - Ford Cosworth)
Prost	37	1	160	99	1997	(JS45 - Mugen Honda)
Hill	8	1	30	19	1975	(GH1 - Ford Cosworth)
Lancia	7	1	44	27	1954	(D50)
Spyker	6	1	31	19	2007	(F8-VII - Ferrari)
BMW	5	1	29	18	2006	(BMW Sauber F1.06)
Talbot-Lago	5	1	71	44	1950	(T26C)
Ferrari	2	1	13	8	1950	(375)
Red Bull	2	2	11	7	2005	(RB1 - Cosworth)

924. Laps led in their final season

	laps	races	km	miles		
Brawn	405	11	1,957	1,216	2009	(BGP 001 - Mercedes)
Stewart	84	3	363	226	1999	(SF-3 - Ford Cosworth)
Matra	19	1	153	95	1972	(Matra-Simca MS120D)
Ligier	16	1	53	33	1996	(JS43 - Mugen Honda)
Lancia	13	1	51	32	1955	(D50)
Toyota	13	2	70	44	2009	(TF109)
BAR	9	2	48	30	2005	(007 - Honda)
Hill	8	1	30	19	1975	(GH1 - Ford Cosworth)
Honda	7	1	31	19	2008	(RA108)
Spyker	6	1	31	19	2007	(F8-VII - Ferrari)

925. Percentage of race led, but did not win (Highest)

		%	laps led	winner
Williams	Canada 1991	98.55	68 of 69	Benetton
Lotus	Sweden 1973	97.50	78 of 80	McLaren
Renault	Switzerland 1982	97.50	78 of 80	Williams
Red Bull	Canada 2011	97.14	68 of 70	McLaren
Lotus	Mexico 1964	96.92	63 of 65	Brabham
McLaren	Italy 1988	96.08	49 of 51	Ferrari
Renault	Monaco 1982	96.05	73 of 76	Brabham
Lotus	Canada 1977	95.00	76 of 80	Wolf
Wolf	United States West 1977	95.00	76 of 80	Lotus
Lotus	Sweden 1977	94.44	68 of 72	Ligier
Ferrari	Portugal 1987	94.29	66 of 70	McLaren
Brabham	France 1977	93.75	75 of 80	Lotus
Lotus	San Marino 1985	93.33	56 of 60	McLaren
Ferrari	Belgium 2008	93.18	41 of 44	McLaren
Mercedes-Benz	Canada 2014	92.86	65 of 70	Red Bull
Brabham	Argentina 1974	92.45	49 of 53	McLaren
Ferrari	Britain 1974	92.00	69 of 75	Tyrrell
Williams	Belgium 1982	91.43	64 of 70	McLaren
Williams	Monaco 1992	89.74	70 of 78	McLaren
Lotus	Britain 1985	89.23	58 of 65	McLaren

Additionally, in Belgium 1994, Benetton originally won, having led 43 of 44 laps (97.73%), but was disqualified for illegal skid block wear, handing the victory to Williams.

926. Led every lap of a race except the final one

Apart from Canada 1991 where the Williams - Renault of Nigel Mansell retired on the final lap after leading every lap until then, there has been no other race where a constructors' cars have led every lap except the final one.

927. Leader at the finish was not leading at the start of the final lap

	leader at the finish	leader at the start of the final lap
Italy 1953	Maserati (Juan Manuel Fangio)	Ferrari (Alberto Ascari), retired (accident), not classified
France 1961	Ferrari (Giancarlo Baghetti)	Porsche (Dan Gurney), finished 2nd
Belgium 1964	Lotus (Jim Clark) *	BRM (Graham Hill), retired (fuel pump), classified 5th
Italy 1967	Honda (John Surtees) *	Lotus (Jim Clark), finished 3rd
Belgium 1968	McLaren (Bruce McLaren)	Matra (Jackie Stewart), low fuel, delayed in pits, classified 4th
Monaco 1970	Lotus (Jochen Rindt) *	Brabham (Jack Brabham), finished 2nd
Britain 1970	Lotus (Jochen Rindt)	Brabham (Jack Brabham), finished 2nd
Italy 1971	BRM (Peter Gethin)	March (Ronnie Peterson), finished 2nd
Spain 1975	McLaren (Jochen Mass)	JPS Lotus (Jacky Ickx), finished 2nd
France 1977	JPS Lotus (Mario Andretti) *	Brabham (John Watson), finished 2nd
South Africa 1978	JPS Lotus (Ronnie Peterson)	Tyrrell (Patrick Depailler), finished 2nd
Monaco 1982	Brabham (Riccardo Patrese)	Ferrari (Didier Pironi), retired (battery/ fuel injection), classified 2nd
Canada 1991	Benetton (Nelson Piquet) *	Williams (Nigel Mansell), retired (gearbox/engine), classified 6th
Hungary 1997	Williams (Jacques Villeneuve)	Arrows (Damon Hill), finished 2nd
Europe 1997	McLaren (Mika Häkkinen) *	Williams (Jacques Villeneuve), finished 3rd
Spain 2001	Ferrari (Michael Schumacher)	McLaren (Mika Häkkinen), retired (clutch), classified 9th
Brazil 2003	Jordan (Giancarlo Fisichella) *	McLaren (Kimi Räikkönen), finished 2nd
Europe 2005	Renault (Fernando Alonso)	McLaren (Kimi Räikkönen), retired (front tyre/ suspension/accident), classified 11th
Japan 2005	McLaren (Kimi Räikkönen)	Renault (Giancarlo Fisichella), finished 2nd
Canada 2011	McLaren (Jenson Button) *	Red Bull (Sebastian Vettel), finished 2nd

* The final lap was the only lap led by this constructor in the race.

928. Different leaders in a season

Most

1975	10	1970	8	2009	8
2003	9	1977	8	2012	8
2008	9	1982	8		

Fewest

1951	2	1957	3	2000	3
1953	2	1959	3	2002	3
1950	3	1988	3		
1952	3	1992	3		

Total for each season

1950 - 3, 1951 - 2, 1952 - 3, 1953 - 2, 1954 - 4, 1955 - 4, 1956 - 4, 1957 - 3, 1958 - 5, 1959 - 3, 1960 - 4, 1961 - 4, 1962 - 5, 1963 - 4, 1964 - 4, 1965 - 5, 1966 - 6, 1967 - 7, 1968 - 6, 1969 - 5, 1970 - 8, 1971 - 7, 1972 - 7, 1973 - 5, 1974 - 5, 1975 - 10, 1976 - 6, 1977 - 8, 1978 - 7, 1979 - 4, 1980 - 6, 1981 - 7, 1982 - 8, 1983 - 7, 1984 - 6, 1985 - 5, 1986 - 6, 1987 - 5, 1988 - 3, 1989 - 6, 1990 - 6, 1991 - 4, 1992 - 3, 1993 - 4, 1994 - 5, 1995 - 5, 1996 - 5, 1997 - 7, 1998 - 4, 1999 - 6, 2000 - 3, 2001 - 4, 2002 - 3, 2003 - 9, 2004 - 6, 2005 - 7, 2006 - 7, 2007 - 7, 2008 - 9, 2009 - 8, 2010 - 5, 2011 - 4, 2012 - 8, 2013 - 7, 2014 - 6, 2015 - 4

Excludes Indianapolis 500.

929. Leaders in a race *(Most)*

Italy 1971	6	Ferrari, March, Tyrrell, Surtees, BRM, Matra
Spain 1975	6	Hesketh, Parnelli, Hill, Brabham, McLaren, JPS Lotus
Britain 1975	6	Brabham, Ferrari, Shadow, Tyrrell, Hesketh, McLaren
Japan 2005	6	Toyota, Renault, BAR, Red Bull, Ferrari, McLaren
Canada 1973	5	JPS Lotus, BRM, Tyrrell, Shadow, McLaren
Belgium 1977	5	Wolf, McLaren, Surtees, Ferrari, JPS Lotus
Italy 1995	5	Williams, Ferrari, Jordan, McLaren, Benetton
Europe 1999	5	Jordan, McLaren, Williams, Benetton, Stewart
United States 2003	5	McLaren, Ferrari, Jaguar, BAR, Sauber
Brazil 2004	5	McLaren, Ferrari, Sauber, Renault, Williams
Canada 2008	5	McLaren, BMW Sauber, Honda, Red Bull, Toyota
Japan 2008	5	BMW Sauber, Renault, Toyota, Toro Rosso, Ferrari
Australia 2013	5	Red Bull, Ferrari, Mercedes-Benz, Force India, Lotus
China 2013	5	Mercedes-Benz, Ferrari, Sauber, McLaren, Red Bull
Spain 2013	5	Mercedes-Benz, Sauber, Ferrari, Red Bull, Lotus

930. Different leaders within the first five laps *(Most)*

3 constructors	
Belgium 1962	BRM, Lotus, Ferrari (within the first 4 laps)
Germany 1963	BRM, Ferrari, Lotus (4)
Germany 1964	Lotus, Ferrari, Brabham (4)
Italy 1966	Ferrari, Cooper, Brabham (4)
Italy 1970	Ferrari, BRM, March (5)
Netherlands 1980	Williams, Renault, Ligier (3)
Malaysia 2001	Ferrari, Jordan, McLaren (4)

931. Different leaders within the final five laps *(Most)*

3 constructors	
Belgium 1964	Brabham, BRM, Lotus (within the first 4 laps)
Italy 1971	Surtees, BRM, March (5)
Spain 1975	Hill, McLaren, JPS Lotus (5)
Monaco 1982	Renault, Brabham, Ferrari (4)
San Marino 1985	Lotus, Ferrari, McLaren (5)

932. First time leaders in a season *(Most)*

2003	4	Toyota, Jaguar, BAR, Sauber	1968	2	Matra, McLaren
1950	3	Alfa Romeo, Talbot-Lago, Ferrari	1970	2	March, Tyrrell
1975	3	Hesketh, Parnelli, Hill	1977	2	Wolf, Ligier
1952	2	Gordini, Maserati	1979	2	Renault, Williams
1954	2	Mercedes-Benz, Lancia	2007	2	Spyker, Toro Rosso
1956	2	BRM, Vanwall	2009	2	Brawn, Force India

933. Race leading drivers by constructor

	drivers	most laps led			drivers	most laps led
Ferrari (a)	50	Michael Schumacher, 3,934		Vanwall	4	Stirling Moss, 324
Williams	24	Nigel Mansell, 1,880		Arrows	3	Damon Hill, 62
McLaren	21	Ayrton Senna, 2,392		Toro Rosso	3	Sebastian Vettel, 52
Lotus (b)	20	Jim Clark, 1,942		BAR	2	Jenson Button, 79
BRM	14	Graham Hill, 729		BMW (e)	2	Robert Kubica, 74
Brabham	12	Nelson Piquet, 1,153		Brawn	2	Jenson Button, 280
Renault	10	Fernando Alonso, 1,033		Porsche	2	Dan Gurney, 19
Cooper	9	Jack Brabham, 406		Stewart	2	Rubens Barrichello, 67
Benetton	8	Michael Schumacher, 1,157		Surtees	2	Mike Hailwood, 5
Alfa Romeo	6	Juan Manuel Fangio, 359		Eagle	1	Dan Gurney, 19
Maserati	6	Juan Manuel Fangio, 389		Gordini	1	Jean Behra, 1
Mercedes-Benz	6	Lewis Hamilton, 1,148		Hesketh	1	James Hunt, 88
Tyrrell	6	Jackie Stewart, 994		Hill	1	Rolf Stommelen, 8
Force India	5	Nico Hülkenberg, 35		Jaguar	1	Mark Webber, 2
Jordan	5	Heinz-Harald Frentzen, 73		Lancia	1	Alberto Ascari, 20
Ligier (c)	5	Jacques Laffite, 264		Minardi	1	Pierluigi Martini, 1
March (d)	5	Jackie Stewart, 154		Parnelli	1	Mario Andretti, 10
Sauber	5	Sergio Pérez, 12		Penske	1	John Watson, 45
Honda	4	Richie Ginther, 68		Prost	1	Jarno Trulli, 37
Matra	4	Jackie Stewart, 622		Spyker	1	Markus Winkelhock, 6
Red Bull	4	Sebastian Vettel, 2,386		Talbot-Lago	1	Raymond Sommer, 5
Shadow	4	Jean-Pierre Jarier, 30		Wolf	1	Jody Scheckter, 214
Toyota	4	Jarno Trulli, 22				

Excludes Indianapolis 500.
(a) Includes Lancia-Ferrari. (b) Includes JPS Lotus. (c) Includes Talbot-Ligier. (d) Includes Leyton House. (e) As BMW Sauber.

934. Laps led with the same engine make *(Most)*

	engine	laps	races	km	miles		
Ferrari	Ferrari	13,863	416	72,118	44,812	Italy 1950	- Singapore 2015
McLaren	Mercedes	4,913	171	24,063	14,952	Italy 1995	- Hungary 2014
Williams	Renault	4,271	106	19,951	12,396	Brazil 1989	- Spain 2012
Red Bull	Renault	3,073	80	15,799	9,817	Europe 2007	- United States 2015
McLaren	Honda	3,036	62	13,943	8,664	Brazil 1988	- Australia 1992
Lotus	Ford Cosworth	3,030	80	13,609	8,456	Netherlands 1967	- Austria 1982
Mercedes-Benz	Mercedes	2,757	60	14,771	9,178	France 1954	- Abu Dhabi 2015
Renault	Renault	2,514	88	12,150	7,549	South Africa 1979	- Singapore 2009
Lotus	Climax	1,839	39	9,764	6,067	Argentina 1960	- Netherlands 1966
Williams	Honda	1,548	41	7,051	4,381	South Africa 1984	- Mexico 1987

935. Interval between races led *(Longest)*

	years, days	races		
Mercedes-Benz (a)	54y, 219d	776	Italy 1955 (Juan Manuel Fangio)	- China 2010 (Nico Rosberg)
Honda (a)	37y, 185d	581	Italy 1968 (John Surtees)	- Bahrain 2006 (Jenson Button)
Alfa Romeo (a)	28y, 343d	327	Spain 1951 (Juan Manuel Fangio)	- United States 1980 (Bruno Giacomelli)
Lotus (a)	24y, 173d	411	Japan 1987 (Ayrton Senna)	- Bahrain 2012 (Romain Grosjean)
Renault (a)	18y, 195d	297	Italy 1984 (Patrick Tambay)	- Malaysia 2003 (Fernando Alonso)
March (a)	12y, 27d	189	Canada 1976 (Ronnie Peterson)	- Japan 1988 (Ivan Capelli)
Ligier	9y, 332d	160	Detroit 1986 (Jacques Laffite)	- Monaco 1996 (Olivier Panis)
Arrows	8y, 95d	131	United States West 1981 (Riccardo Patrese)	- Canada 1989 (Derek Warwick)
Arrows	8y, 53d	134	Canada 1989 (Derek Warwick)	- Hungary 1997 (Damon Hill)
Sauber (b)	7y, 153d	129	Brazil 2004 (Felipe Massa)	- Malaysia 2012 (Sergio Pérez)

(a) Not present throughout the period.
(b) BMW controlled the operation as BMW Sauber from 2006 to 2009.

936. Interval between first & last race led *(Longest)*

	years, days	races		
Ferrari	65y, 17d	922	Italy 1950	- Singapore 2015
Mercedes-Benz	61y, 148d	899	France 1954	- Abu Dhabi 2015
Lotus	53y, 283d	811	Argentina 1960	- United States 2013
McLaren	46y, 48d	743	Belgium 1968	- Hungary 2014
Honda	42y, 326d	655	Netherlands 1965	- Canada 2008
Williams	36y, 53d	606	Belgium 1979	- Britain 2015
Alfa Romeo	33y, 9d	378	Britain 1950	- Belgium 1983
Renault	30y, 208d	501	South Africa 1979	- Singapore 2009
Brabham	21y, 352d	295	Britain 1963	- France 1985
March	20y, 123d	306	South Africa 1970	- France 1990

937. Laps led but never a win

	laps	races			
Arrows	127	4	Surtees	9	2
BAR	81	10	Hill	8	1
Toyota	66	11	Spyker	6	1
Force India	65	7	Talbot-Lago	5	1
Prost	37	1	Jaguar	2	1
Sauber	25	7	Gordini	1	1
Lancia	20	2	Minardi	1	1
Parnelli	10	1			

938. Laps led but never a podium

	laps	races			
Parnelli	10	1	Spyker	6	1
Hill	8	1	Minardi	1	1

939. Milestones: Races led

Ferrari	50th: Germany 1959, 100th: Belgium 1974, 200th: Germany 1994, 250th: Brazil 2000, 300th: Austria 2003, 400th: Europe 2012
McLaren	50th: San Marino 1984, 100th: Mexico 1989, 200th: Germany 2000, 300th: Spain 2011
Williams	50th: France 1986, 100th: Hungary 1992, 200th: San Marino 2003
Lotus	25th: Belgium 1964, 50th: South Africa 1968, 100th: Spain 1977, 150th: Spain 2012
Brabham	25th: Germany 1969, 50th: United States 1977, 75th: Canada 1983
Red Bull	25th: Japan 2010, 50th: Monaco 2012, 75th: Abu Dhabi 2013
Renault	25th: Germany 1982, 50th: Belgium 2004, 75th: France 2006
Benetton	25th: Belgium 1994, 50th: Brazil 1997
Mercedes-Benz	25th: Australia 2014, 50th: Canada 2015
BRM	25th: Italy 1965
Tyrrell	25th: Sweden 1974

940. Milestones: Laps led

Ferrari	1,000th: Italy 1953, 2,500th: Monaco 1965, 5,000th: United States 1978, 7,500th: Europe 1997, 10,000th: Belgium 2002, 12,500th: Malaysia 2008
McLaren	1,000th: Japan 1977, 2,500th: Monaco 1988, 5,000th: Hungary 1991, 7,500th: Malaysia 2000, 10,000th: Spain 2011
Williams	1,000th: Detroit 1985, 2,500th: Canada 1989, 5,000th: Brazil 1995, 7,500th: Spain 2012
Lotus	1,000th: Mexico 1963, 2,000th: France 1967, 2,500th: Monaco 1968, 5,000th: Portugal 1985
Red Bull	1,000th: Abu Dhabi 2010, 2,000th: Singapore 2012, 2,500th: Germany 2013, 3,000th: Hungary 2014
Brabham	1,000th: Austria 1974, 2,000th: France 1982, 2,500th: Canada 1984
Mercedes-Benz	1,000th: Bahrain 2014, 1,500th: Italy 2014, 2,000th: Spain 2015, 2,500th: Russia 2015
Renault	1,000th: France 1983, 2,000th: Austria 2006, 2,500th: Hungary 2009
Benetton	1,000th: Monaco 1995, 1,500th: Canada 1998
BRM	1,000th: Monaco 1966
Tyrrell	1,000th: Belgium 1973

Chapter 24: Car Models

Statistics for models include derivatives of those models, ie Williams FW14 includes FW14B.

941. Races started *(Most)*

McLaren M23	80	South Africa 1973	- Italy 1978		Maserati 250F	43	Argentina 1954	- United States 1960
Lotus 72	74	Spain 1970	- United States 1975		Williams FW07	43	Spain 1979	- United States West 1982
Lotus 25	49	Netherlands 1962	- Netherlands 1967		McLaren MP4	42	Argentina 1981	- South Africa 1983
McLaren MP4/2	48	Brazil 1984	- Australia 1986		Lotus 49	41	Netherlands 1967	- Austria 1970
BRM P160	47	South Africa 1971	- Britain 1974		Tyrrell 020	41	United States 1991	- Britain 1993

942. Car starts *(Most)*

Maserati 250F	248	Argentina 1954	- United States 1960		Cooper T51	110	Monaco 1959	- South Africa 1963
McLaren M23	166	South Africa 1973	- Italy 1978		Lotus 25	101	Netherlands 1962	- Netherlands 1967
Lotus 72	149	Spain 1970	- United States 1975		McLaren MP4/2	95	Brazil 1984	- Australia 1986
BRM P160	121	South Africa 1971	- Britain 1974		March 761	90	Brazil 1976	- Japan 1977
Lotus 49	113	Netherlands 1967	- Austria 1970		Williams FW07	90	Spain 1979	- United States West 1982

943. Wins *(Most)*

McLaren MP4/2	22	Brazil 1984	- Australia 1986		Mercedes-Benz F1 W05	16	Australia 2014	- Abu Dhabi 2014
Lotus 72	20	Netherlands 1970	- Italy 1974		Mercedes-Benz F1 W06	16	Australia 2015	- Abu Dhabi 2015
Williams FW11	18	Brazil 1986	- Mexico 1987		Ferrari F2002	15	Brazil 2002	- San Marino 2003
Williams FW14	17	Mexico 1991	- Japan 1992		Ferrari F2004	15	Australia 2004	- Japan 2004
McLaren M23	16	Sweden 1973	- United States 1976		McLaren MP4/4	15	Brazil 1988	- Australia 1988
McLaren MP4/5	16	San Marino 1989	- Italy 1990		Williams FW07	15	Britain 1979	- Caesars Palace 1981

944. Podium positions *(Most)*

McLaren MP4/2	42	Brazil 1984	- Australia 1986		Williams FW14	38	Brazil 1991	- Japan 1992
Williams FW07	42	Monaco 1979	- United States West 1982		McLaren MP4/5	36	Brazil 1989	- Portugal 1990
Lotus 72	39	Netherlands 1970	- Spain 1975		Ferrari 500	33	Switzerland 1952	- Italy 1953
McLaren M23	38	Sweden 1973	- Sweden 1977		Mercedes-Benz F1 W06	32	Australia 2015	- Abu Dhabi 2015
Williams FW11	37	Brazil 1986	- Mexico 1987		Mercedes-Benz F1 W05	31	Australia 2014	- Abu Dhabi 2014

945. Pole positions *(Most)*

McLaren MP4/5	27	Brazil 1989	- Australia 1990
Williams FW14	21	Canada 1991	- Australia 1992
Lotus 49	19	Netherlands 1967	- United States 1969
Lotus 25	18	Monaco 1962	- France 1965
Mercedes-Benz F1 W05	18	Australia 2014	- Abu Dhabi 2014

Mercedes-Benz F1 W06	18	Australia 2015	- Abu Dhabi 2015
Red Bull RB7	18	Australia 2011	- Brazil 2011
Lotus 72	17	Netherlands 1970	- Argentina 1974
Renault RE30	16	France 1981	- Caesars Palace 1982
Williams FW11	16	Belgium 1986	- Mexico 1987

946. Front row positions *(Most)*

Williams FW14	39	Brazil 1991	- Australia 1992
Ferrari 500	35	Switzerland 1952	- Italy 1953
Williams FW11	35	Brazil 1986	- Mexico 1987
Lotus 49	33	Netherlands 1967	- Belgium 1970
Mercedes-Benz F1 W06	33	Australia 2015	- Abu Dhabi 2015
Alfa Romeo 158, 159	32	Britain 1950	- Spain 1951

Lotus 72	31	Netherlands 1970	- Britain 1974
Mercedes-Benz F1 W05	30	Australia 2014	- Abu Dhabi 2014
Renault RE30	29	France 1981	- Brazil 1983
Maserati 250F	28	Argentina 1954	- Argentina 1958
Williams FW15C	28	South Africa 1993	- Australia 1993

947. Fastest laps *(Most)*

Williams FW14	19	Brazil 1991	- Japan 1992
Williams FW11	18	Brazil 1986	- Mexico 1987
McLaren MP4/2	16	Brazil 1984	- Belgium 1986
Williams FW07	16	Britain 1979	- Italy 1981
Ferrari F2002	15	San Marino 2002	- San Marino 2003
Ferrari F2004	14	Australia 2004	- Japan 2004

Lotus 25	14	Monaco 1962	- France 1965
Lotus 49	14	Netherlands 1967	- Monaco 1970
Alfa Romeo 158, 159	13	Britain 1950	- Spain 1951
Ferrari F2008	13	Spain 2008	- Brazil 2008
McLaren MP4/5	13	San Marino 1989	- Italy 1990
Mercedes-Benz F1 W06	13	Australia 2015	- Abu Dhabi 2015

948. Points *(Most)*

from 2010 with new points system		
Mercedes-Benz F1 W06	703	2015
Mercedes-Benz F1 W05	701	2014
Red Bull RB7	650	2011
Red Bull RB9	596	2013
Red Bull RB6	498	2010
McLaren MP4-26	497	2011
Red Bull RB8	460	2012
McLaren MP4-25	454	2010
Red Bull RB10	405	2014
Ferrari F2012	400	2012

before 2010		
McLaren MP4/2	329.5	1984 - 86
McLaren M23	319	1973 - 78
Williams FW07	300	1979 - 82
Lotus 72	295	1970 - 75
Williams FW14	289	1991 - 92
Williams FW11	278	1986 - 87
Ferrari F2004	272	2004 - 05
McLaren MP4/5	262	1989 - 90
Ferrari 500	243	1952 - 57
Ferrari F2002	239	2002 - 03

Chapter 25: Miscellaneous Constructor Facts

Win/ pole position doubles (Most) See section 713
Consecutive win/ pole position doubles (Most) See section 714

949. Win/ pole position/ fastest lap trebles (Most)
(not necessarily the same car to achieve each)

Ferrari (a)	86	Switzerland 1952	- Singapore 2010
Williams	52	Britain 1979	- Germany 2003
McLaren	51	Spain 1976	- Brazil 2012
Lotus (b)	26	Monaco 1961	- Portugal 1985
Mercedes-Benz	26	France 1954	- Abu Dhabi 2015

Red Bull	22	Britain 2009	- Brazil 2013
Renault	11	France 1979	- Britain 2006
Alfa Romeo	9	Britain 1950	- France 1951
Brabham	9	Britain 1966	- Canada 1984
Cooper	7	Monaco 1959	- France 1960

(a) Includes Lancia-Ferrari. (b) Includes JPS Lotus.

950. Consecutive win/ pole position/ fastest lap trebles (Most)

Alfa Romeo	9	Britain 1950	- France 1951	(158, 159)
Ferrari	9	Switzerland 1952	- Netherlands 1953	(500)
McLaren	6	San Marino 1988	- France 1988	(MP4/4 - Honda)
Williams	5	France 1987	- Austria 1987	(FW11B - Honda)
Mercedes-Benz	4	Australia 2014	- China 2014	(F1 W05)
Mercedes-Benz	4	United States 2015	- Abu Dhabi 2015	(F1 W06)
Williams	4	Mexico 1991	- Germany 1991	(FW14 - Renault)
Ferrari	3	San Marino 2002	- Austria 2002	(F2002)
Ferrari	3	Germany 2002	- Belgium 2002	(F2002)
Ferrari	3	San Marino 2003	- Austria 2003	(F2003-GA)
Ferrari	3	Italy 2004	- Japan 2004	(F2004)
Lotus	3	United States 1967	- South Africa 1968	(49 - Ford Cosworth)
Red Bull	3	Singapore 2013	- Japan 2013	(RB9 - Renault)
McLaren	3	Spain 1988	- Australia 1988	(MP4/4 - Honda)
Mercedes-Benz	3	Italy 2014	- Japan 2014	(F1 W05)
Williams	3	Brazil 1992	- San Marino 1992	(FW14B - Renault)

Williams	3	France 1992	- Germany 1992	(FW14B - Renault)
Williams	3	Hungary 1993	- Italy 1993	(FW15C - Renault)
Williams	3	Australia 1995	- Brazil 1996	(FW17B, FW18 - Renault)

951. Win/ pole position/ fastest lap trebles and also led every lap (Most)
(not necessarily the same car to achieve each)

Ferrari (a)	40	Switzerland 1952	- Singapore 2010	Red Bull	11	Britain 2009	- Brazil 2013
McLaren	33	Austria 1985	- China 2008	Brabham	6	Britain 1966	- Canada 1984
Williams	32	Britain 1979	- France 2003	Alfa Romeo	5	Britain 1950	- Switzerland 1951
Mercedes-Benz	19	France 1954	- Abu Dhabi 2015	Tyrrell	5	Monaco 1971	- Sweden 1974
Lotus (b)	16	Britain 1962	- Portugal 1985	Cooper	4	Britain 1959	- Belgium 1960

(a) Includes Lancia-Ferrari. (b) includes JPS Lotus.

952. The same constructor in each of the top four finishing positions

Ferrari	Germany 1952	(500)	(1: Alberto Ascari, 2: Giuseppe Farina, 3: Rudi Fischer, 4: Piero Taruffi)
Mercedes-Benz	Britain 1955	(W196)	(1: Stirling Moss, 2: Juan Manuel Fangio, 3: Karl Kling, 4: Piero Taruffi)
Maserati	Argentina 1957	(250F)	(1: Juan Manuel Fangio, 2: Jean Behra, 3: Carlos Menditéguy, 4: Harry Schell)
Cooper	France 1960	(T53, T51 - Climax)	(1: Jack Brabham, 2: Olivier Gendebien, 3: Bruce McLaren, 4: Henry Taylor)
Ferrari	Belgium 1961	(156)	(1: Phil Hill, 2: Wolfgang von Trips, 3: Richie Ginther, 4: Olivier Gendebien)

Excludes Indianapolis 500.

953. Different constructors in each of the top finishing positions

Top 14	
Britain 1981	1: McLaren, 2: Williams, 3: Talbot-Ligier, 4: Tyrrell, 5: Brabham, 6: ATS, 7: March,8: Osella, 9: Renault, 10: Arrows, 11: Theodore, retired: Alfa Romeo, retired: Fittipaldi, black-flagged/ withdrew: Lotus.
Top 12	
Austria 1978	1: JPS Lotus, 2: Tyrrell, 3: Ferrari, 4: Copersucar, 5: Ligier, 6: Surtees, 7: Brabham, 8: McLaren, 9: Martini, not classified: Shadow, not classified: Wolf, disqualified: Ensign.
Top 10	
Germany 1975	1: Brabham, 2: Williams, 3: Ferrari, 4: Shadow, 5: Hill, 6: Ensign, 7: March, 8: Hesketh, 9: Tyrrell, 10: Parnelli
Portugal 1989	1: Ferrari, 2: McLaren, 3: Onyx, 4: Benetton, 5: Minardi, 6: Tyrrell, 7: Lotus, 8: Brabham, 9: Lola, 10: March

954. Finished the race in pairs

Top 8		
Argentina 1957	Maserati	1: Juan Manuel Fangio, 2: Jean Behra
	Maserati	3: Carlos Menditéguy, 4: Harry Schell
	Lancia-Ferrari	5: Alfonso de Portago, 6: Wolfgang von Trips
	Maserati	7: Jo Bonnier, 8: Stirling Moss
Mexico 1988	McLaren	1: Alain Prost, 2: Ayrton Senna
	Ferrari	3: Gerhard Berger, 4: Michele Alboreto
	Arrows	5: Derek Warwick, 6: Eddie Cheever
	Benetton	7: Alessandro Nannini, 8: Thierry Boutsen
Top 6		
France 1960	Cooper	1: Jack Brabham, 2: Olivier Gendebien
	Cooper	3: Bruce McLaren, 4: Henry Taylor
	Lotus	5: Jim Clark, 6: Ron Flockhart
Netherlands 1974	Ferrari	1: Niki Lauda, 2: Clay Regazzoni
	McLaren	3: Emerson Fittipaldi, 4: Mike Hailwood
	Tyrrell	5: Jody Scheckter, 6: Patrick Depailler
France 1996	Williams	1: Damon Hill, 2: Jacques Villeneuve
	Benetton	3: Jean Alesi, 4: Gerhard Berger
	McLaren	5: Mika Häkkinen, 6: David Coulthard
United States 2005	Ferrari	1: Michael Schumacher, 2: Rubens Barrichello
	Jordan	3: Tiago Monteiro, 4: Narain Karthikeyan
	Minardi	5: Christijan Albers, 6: Patrick Friesacher
China 2009	Red Bull	1: Sebastian Vettel, 2: Mark Webber
	Brawn	3: Jenson Button, 4: Rubens Barrichello
	McLaren	5: Heikki Kovalainen, 6: Lewis Hamilton
Italy 2014	Mercedes-Benz	1: Lewis Hamilton, 2: Nico Rosberg

	Williams	3: Felipe Massa, 4: Valtteri Bottas
	Red Bull	5: Daniel Ricciardo, 6: Sebastian Vettel
China 2015	Mercedes-Benz	1: Lewis Hamilton, 2: Nico Roserg
	Ferrari	3: Sebastian Vettel, 4: Kimi Räikkönen
	Williams	5: Felipe Massa, 6: Valtteri Bottas

Excludes Indianapolis 500.

955. Different constructors in each of the top grid positions

Top 8	
Monaco 1986	1: McLaren, 2: Williams, 3: Lotus, 4: Ferrari, 5: Benetton, 6: Brabham, 7: Ligier, 8: Lola
Japan 2009	1: Red Bull, 2: Toyota, 3: McLaren, 4: BMW Sauber, 5: Ferrari, 6: Brawn, 7: Williams, 8: Force India
Brazil 2009	1: Brawn, 2: Red Bull, 3: Force India, 4: Toyota, 5: Ferrari, 6: Toro Rosso, 7: Williams, 8: BMW Sauber
Top 7	
Austria 1998	1: Benetton, 2: Sauber, 3: McLaren, 4: Ferrari, 5: Stewart, 6: Arrows, 7: Willams
France 1999	1: Stewart, 2: Sauber, 3: Prost, 4: McLaren, 5: Jordan, 6: Ferrari, 7: Benetton
Top 6	
Britain 1969	1: Lotus, 2: Matra, 3: McLaren, 4: Brabham, 5: Ferrari, 6: BRM
France 1972	1: Matra, 2: McLaren, 3: Tyrrell, 4: Ferrari, 5: Surtees, 6: BRM
Britain 1972	1: Ferrari, 2: JPS Lotus, 3: McLaren, 4: Tyrrell, 5: Surtees, 6: BRM
Austria 1972	1: JPS Lotus, 2: Ferrari, 3: Tyrrell, 4: McLaren, 5: Brabham, 6: Matra
Argentina 1974	1: JPS Lotus, 2: Ferrari, 3: McLaren, 4: Shadow, 5: March, 6: Brabham
Britain 1974	1: Ferrari, 2: JPS Lotus, 3: Tyrrell, 4: Brabham, 5: Shadow, 6: Hesketh
United States 1975	1: Ferrari, 2: McLaren, 3: Brabham, 4: Shadow, 5: Parnelli, 6: March
Austria 1976	1: McLaren, 2: Penske, 3: March, 4: JPS Lotus, 5: Ligier, 6: Shadow
Netherlands 1976	1: March, 2: McLaren, 3: Shadow, 4: Penske, 5: Ferrari, 6: JPS Lotus
Japan 1976	1: JPS Lotus, 2: McLaren, 3: Ferrari, 4: Penske, 5: Tyrrell, 6: Brabham
South Africa 1977	1: McLaren, 2: Brabham, 3: Ferrari, 4: Tyrrell, 5: Wolf, 6: JPS Lotus
Canada 1978	1: JPS Lotus, 2: Wolf, 3: Ferrari, 4: Brabham, 5: Williams, 6: Fittipaldi
Monaco 1985	1: Lotus, 2: Williams, 3: Ferrari, 4: Alfa Romeo, 5: McLaren, 6: Arrows
Germany 1985	1: Toleman, 2: Ferrari, 3: McLaren, 4: Williams, 5: Lotus, 6: Brabham
Netherlands 1985	1: Brabham, 2: Williams, 3: McLaren, 4: Lotus, 5: Toleman, 6: Renault
China 2004	1: Ferrari, 2: McLaren, 3: BAR, 4: Sauber, 5: Williams, 6: Renault

956. On the starting grid in pairs
(based on races with two by two grids)

Top 10		
Singapore 2011	Red Bull	1: Sebastian Vettel, 2: Mark Webber
	McLaren	3: Jenson Button, 4: Lewis Hamilton
	Ferrari	5: Fernando Alonso, 6: Felipe Massa
	Mercedes-Benz	7: Nico Rosberg, 8: Michael Schumacher
	Force India	9: Adrian Sutil, 10: Paul Di Resta
Top 8		
France 1988	McLaren	1: Alain Prost, 2: Ayrton Senna
	Ferrari	3: Gerhard Berger, 4: Michele Alboreto
	Benetton	5: Thierry Boutsen, 6: Alessandro Nannini
	Lotus	7: Nelson Piquet, 8: Satoru Nakajima
Australia 1991	McLaren	1: Ayrton Senna, 2: Gerhard Berger
	Williams	3: Nigel Mansell, 4: Riccardo Patrese
	Benetton	5: Nelson Piquet, 6: Michael Schumacher
	Ferrari	7: Jean Alesi, 8: Gianni Morbidelli
San Marino 1992	Williams	1: Nigel Mansell, 2: Riccardo Patrese
	McLaren	3: Ayrton Senna, 4: Gerhard Berger
	Benetton	5: Michael Schumacher, 6: Martin Brundle
	Ferrari	7: Jean Alesi, 8: Ivan Capelli
Europe 2002	Williams	1: Juan Pablo Montoya, 2: Ralf Schumacher
	Ferrari	3: Michael Schumacher, 4: Rubens Barrichello
	McLaren	5: David Coulthard, 6: Kimi Räikkönen
	Renault	7: Jarno Trulli, 8: Jenson Button
Japan 2002	Ferrari	1: Michael Schumacher, 2: Rubens Barrichello
	McLaren	3: David Coulthard, 4: Kimi Räikkönen
	Williams	5: Ralf Schumacher, 6: Juan Pablo Montoya
	Jordan	7: Takuma Sato, 8: Giancarlo Fisichella
Japan 2006	Ferrari	1: Felipe Massa, 2: Michael Schumacher

Toyota	3: Ralf Schumacher, 4: Jarno Trulli
Renault	5: Fernando Alonso, 6: Giancarlo Fischella
Honda	7: Jenson Button, 8: Rubens Barrichello

957. Disqualifications *(Most)*

Tyrrell (a)	27	United States West 1979 (Didier Pironi)	- Spain 1996 (Mika Salo)
McLaren (b)	11	Britain 1976 (James Hunt)	- Australia 2009 (Felipe Massa)
Lotus (c)	10	Portugal 1960 (Stirling Moss)	- Australia 1987 (Ayrton Senna)
Williams	8	Brazil 1982 (Keke Rosberg)	- Brazil 2015 (Felipe Massa)
Ferrari	7	Argentina 1954 (Mike Hawthorn)	- Canada 2007 (Felipe Massa)
Benetton	6	Belgium 1988 (Thierry Boutsen, Alessandro Nannini)	- Belgium 1994 (Michael Schumacher)
Arrows (d)	5	Germany 1978 (Rolf Stommelen)	- Australia 2002 (Enrique Bernoldi, Heinz-Harald Frentzen)
Fnsign (e)	4	Sweden 1974 (Vern Schuppan)	- Austria 1978 (Derek Daly)
March	4	Germany 1971 (Mike Beuttler)	- United States 1989 (Mauricio Gugelmin)
Sauber	4	France 1996 (Johnny Herbert)	- Australia 2011 (Kamui Kobayashi, Sergio Pérez)

(a) Includes Tyrrell team disqualifications in 1984 (added water and lead shot late in the race to satisfy the minimum weight limit).
(b) Excludes 2007, when McLaren were stripped of all their constructors' championship points, due to the spying scandal. They were not disqualified from individual races and the drivers were unaffected. (c) Includes JPS Lotus. (d) Includes Footwork. (e) Includes Boro.

Disqualified from a point scoring position. See section 552
Excluded from results due to alleged breach, but later reinstated. See section 553

958. Penalty from a point scoring position
Other than the disqualifications and penalties for drivers (in sections 552 and 554) which also affected the constructor, in the following races, drivers retained their points, while the constructor's were removed.

Benetton - Renault (Michael Schumacher)	Brazil 1995	finished 1st, but no constructor points due to fuel irregularities
Williams - Renault (David Coulthard)	Brazil 1995	finished 2nd, but no constructor points due to fuel irregularities
McLaren - Mercedes (Mika Häkkinen)	Austria 2000	finished 1st, but no constructor points due to a missing seal on the black box
McLaren - Mercedes (Fernando Alonso, Lewis Hamilton)	2007 season	all constructor points were removed due to the spying scandal that involved acquiring technical information from Ferrari and passing it to Renault

Point scoring position, but not eligible for points. See section 557

959. Race non-starters
(number of races entered)

Life	14	United States 1990	- Spain 1990	(Bruno Giacomelli, 12; Gary Brabham, 2)
Maki	8	Germany 1974	- Japan 1976	(Tony Trimmer, 4; Hiroshi Fushida, 2; Howden Ganley, 2)
Kauhsen	2	Spain 1979	- Belgium 1979	(Gianfranco Brancatelli)
Arzani-Volpini	1	Italy 1955		(Luigi Piotti)
Cisitalia	1	Italy 1952		(Piero Dusio)
Fry	1	Britain 1959		(Mike Parkes)
McGuire	1	Britain 1977		(Brian McGuire)
Milano	1	Italy 1950		(Felice Bonetto)

960. The history of pre-qualifying
Because of the dangers of having too many cars on the track at the same time in qualifying sessions, a pre-qualifying session was held for teams with the worst record over the previous six months and the new teams.

The first occasion was South Africa 1965. It wasn't until Britain 1977 that pre-qualifying occurred again, followed by several races between 1978 and 83. It was held on the first day of practice.

It was re-introduced in 1988 for 13 of the 16 events when there were 31 entrants, one more than permitted in qualifying. It was run concurrently with the first practice session for the newest teams, featuring Coloni, Dallara (entered by BMS Scuderia Italia), EuroBrun and Rial. The slowest car was eliminated. For the second half of the season (from Germany), the teams were re-assessed, based on their first half of the season performances. This meant that the following would now participate: Coloni, EuroBrun and Osella.

1989: The number of entrants reached 39, resulting in a separate one hour pre-qualifying session at all sixteen races. 13 cars were to fight for four places. Those having to pre-qualify were: Brazil to Britain - AGS (one of their two cars), Brabham, Coloni (one of their two cars), Dallara (one of their two cars), EuroBrun, Onyx, Osella, Rial (one of their two cars) and Zakspeed; From Germany, Brabham, Dallara and Rial were exempt, while AGS (both cars), Coloni (both cars) and Lola were included in pre-qualifying.

1990: The pre-qualifying teams started off as AGS, Coloni, EuroBrun, Life, Lola and Osella. For the second half of the season (from Germany), Ligier joined the pre-qualifiers, replacing Lola which was now exempt, based on their performances so far in the season.

1991: Those having to pre-qualify began as Coloni, Dallara, Fomet (Fondmetal) Jordan and Lamborghini, for the first half of the season. From Germany, it was to be AGS, Brabham, Coloni, Fomet (Fondmetal) and Footwork.

1992: Pre-qualifying featured Andrea Moda, Footwork, Fondmetal and Venturi-Larrousse, from the season start. After the Canadian Grand Prix, Footwork was exempt. By 1993, with many small teams having withdrawn, those sessions were unnecessary. Hungary 1992 featured the final session.

961. Races with a non-qualification/ non-pre-qualification *(Most)*
(number of cars in brackets)

Osella (a)	84	(98)	Argentina 1980	- Germany 1992		Brabham	46	(59)	Italy 1964	- Germany 1992
Coloni	55	(67)	Italy 1987	- Australia 1991		Arrows (d)	46	(57)	Britain 1978	- France 2002
March (b)	52	(82)	Spain 1970	- Britain 1992		Ensign (e)	41	(42)	France 1974	- France 1982
AGS	48	(74)	Italy 1987	- Spain 1991		EuroBrun	38	(53)	San Marino 1988	- Spain 1990
Lotus (c)	47	(67)	Monaco 1959	- San Marino 1992		Tyrrell	32	(34)	Netherlands 1976	- Japan 1998

(a) Includes Fomet & Fondetal.
(b) Includes Leyton House.
(c) Includes JPS Lotus.
(d) Includes Footwork.
(e) Includes Boro.

962. Consecutive races with all cars of a constructor not qualifying *(Most)*

Coloni	34	Spain 1989	- Australia 1991 (a)	(FC189, FC189C, C4 - Ford Cosworth, FC189B - Subaru)
EuroBrun	16	Brazil 1989	- Australia 1989	(ER188B, ER189 - Judd)
Life	14	United States 1990	- Spain 1990 (b)	(L190 - Life, Judd)
Zakspeed	13	San Marino 1989	- Spain 1989	(891 - Yamaha)
EuroBrun	11	Monaco 1990	- Spain 1990	(ER189, ER189B - Judd)
RAM March	11	France 1983	- Europe 1983 (a)	(01 - Ford Cosworth)
AGS	10	Britain 1989	- United States 1990	(JH23B, JH24 - Ford Cosworth)
AGS	10	Canada 1991	- Spain 1991	(JH25, JH25B, JH27 - Ford Cosworth)
Pacific	10	France 1994	- Australia 1994	(PR01 - Ilmor)
Rial	10	France 1989	- Australia 1989	(ARC2 - Ford Cosworth)

(a) Did not enter one of the races within the period.
(b) These were all the races they ever entered.

963. All cars of a constructor failed to qualify or start in a season
(includes non-pre-qualifications)

BMW specials	1969	1 race	(3 cars)	(BMW 269 - BMW)
Cisitalia	1952	1 race	(1 car)	(Cisitalia 246 - Cisitalia)
Coloni	1990	16 races	(16 cars)	(Coloni FC189B - Subaru, FC189C - Ford Cosworth)
Coloni	1991	15 races	(15 cars)	(Coloni C4 - Ford Cosworth)
de Tomaso	1962	1 race	(2 cars)	(de Tomaso 801, F1 - OSCA)
de Tomaso	1963	1 race	(1 car)	(de Tomaso F1 - Ferrari)
Emeryson	1961	2 races	(3 cars)	(Emeryson (61) - Maserati, Climax)
EuroBrun	1989	16 races	(16 cars)	(EuroBrun ER188B, ER189 - Judd)
Fry	1959	1 race	(1 car)	(Fry - Climax)
HWM	1955	1 race	(1 car)	(HWM (53) - Alta)
Kauhsen	1979	2 races	(2 cars)	(Kauhsen WK - Ford Cosworth)
Life	1990	14 races	(14 cars)	(Life L190 - Life, Judd)
Lola	1997	1 race	(2 cars)	(Lola T97/30 - Ford Cosworth)
Lyncar	1974	1 race	(1 car)	(Lyncar 006 - Ford Cosworth)
Maki	1974	2 races	(2 cars)	(Maki F101 - Ford Cosworth)
Maki	1975	5 races	(5 cars)	(Maki F101C - Ford Cosworth)
Maki	1976	1 race	(1 car)	(Maki F102A - Ford Cosworth)
March	1978	1 race	(1 car)	(March 781S - Ford Cosworth)
McGuire	1977	1 race	(1 car)	(McGuire BM1 - Ford Cosworth) (a)
OSCA	1958	1 race	(2 cars)	(OSCA - OSCA)
Williams	1977	1 race	(1 car)	(Williams FW04 - Ford Cosworth)

(a) A modified Williams FW04.

964. Banned from racing

Tyrrell - Ford Cosworth, Italy - Portugal 1984 (3 races): team banned from the final three races of the season (drivers Stefan Bellof and Stefan Johansson) and disqualified from earlier rounds after breaching regulations (found to have added water and lead shot late in races to satisfy the minimum weight limit).

BAR - Honda, Monaco - Spain 2005 (2 races): team banned for running cars which were able to race below the minimum legal weight limit in San Marino. Jenson Button and Takuma Sato were the drivers.

Chapter 26: Engines

(excluding Indianapolis 500)
Coventry Climax engines are referred to as Climax and Gurney-Weslake as Weslake.

965. Constructors' championships

Ferrari	16	1961, 64, 75 - 77, 79, 82, 83, 99 - 2004, 07, 08
Renault	12	1992 - 97, 2005, 06, 10 - 13
Ford Cosworth	10	1968 - 74, 78, 80. 81
Honda	6	1986 - 91
Climax	4	1959, 60, 63, 65

Mercedes-Benz	4	1998, 2009, 14, 15
Repco	2	1966, 67
TAG Porsche	2	1984, 85
Vanwall	1	1958
BRM	1	1962

966. Drivers' championships

Ferrari	15	1952, 53, 56, 58, 61, 64, 75, 77, 79, 2000 - 04, 07
Ford Cosworth	13	1968 - 74, 76, 78, 80 - 82, 94
Renault	11	1992, 93, 95 - 97, 2005, 06, 10 - 13
Mercedes-Benz	8	1954 *, 55, 98, 99, 2008, 09, 14, 15
Honda	5	1987 - 91
Climax	4	1959, 60, 63, 65

TAG Porsche	3	1984 - 86
Alfa Romeo	2	1950, 51
Maserati	2	1954 *, 57
Repco	2	1966, 67
BMW	1	1983
BRM	1	1962

Juan Manuel Fangio used both Maserati & Mercedes-Benz engines in his 1954 championship title winning season.

967. Races started *(Most)*

	races	cars		
Ferrari (a)	909	2,743	Monaco 1950 (Ferrari)	- Abu Dhabi 2015 (Ferrari, Marussia, Sauber)
Cosworth (b)	682	6,300	Germany 1966 (Brabham, Lotus, Matra)	- Brazil 2013 (Marussia)
Renault	557	2,106	Britain 1977 (Renault)	- Abu Dhabi 2015 (Red Bull, Toro Rosso)
Mercedes-Benz	397	1,407	France 1954 (Mercedes-Benz)	- Abu Dhabi 2015 (Force India, Lotus, Mercedes-Benz, Williams)
Honda	359	920	Germany 1964 (Honda)	- Abu Dhabi 2015 (McLaren)
BMW	269	682	Germany 1952 (AFM, BMW)	- Abu Dhabi 2009 (BMW Sauber)
Alfa Romeo	214	476	Britain 1950 (Alfa Romeo)	- Japan 1987 (Osella)
BRM	189	706	Britain 1951 (BRM)	- South Africa 1977 (Stanley-BRM)
Petronas (c)	151	301	Australia 1997 (Sauber)	- China 2005 (Sauber)
Mugen Honda	147	291	South Africa 1992 (Footwork)	- Malaysia 2000 (Jordan)
Hart	145	329	Italy 1981 (Toleman)	- Europe 1997 (Minardi)
Toyota	140	454	Australia 2002 (Toyota)	- Abu Dhabi 2009 (Toyota, Williams)
Matra	125	175	Monaco 1968 (Matra)	- Caesars Palace 1982 (Talbot-Ligier)
Yamaha	116	221	Brazil 1989 (Zaakspeed)	- Europe 1997 (Arrows)
Peugeot	115	228	Brazil 1994 (McLaren)	- Malaysia 2000 (Prost)
Maserati (d)	108	501	Britain 1950 (Maserati)	- Monaco 1969 (Cooper)
Climax	97	724	Monaco 1957 (Cooper)	- Canada 1969 (Brabham, Eagle)
Lamborghini	80	207	Brazil 1989 (Lola)	- Australia 1993 (Larrousse)
Judd	68	284	Brazil 1988 (Ligier, March, Williams)	- Hungary 1992 (Brabham)
TAG Porsche	68	134	Netherlands 1983 (McLaren)	- Australia 1987 (McLaren)

(a) Includes Lancia-Ferrari.
(b) As Ford Cosworth until 2004.
(c) Re-badged Ferrari engine.
(d) Includes Maserati-Milano and Maserati-Platé.

Totals, adding in re-badged engines

	races	cars	
Ferrari (including Acer, Castellotti and Petronas)	909	3,082	Monaco 1950 (Ferrari) - Abu Dhabi 2015 (Ferrari, Marussia, Sauber)
Renault (including Mecachrome, Playlife and Supertec)	606	2,333	Britain 1977 (Renault) - Abu Dhabi 2015 (Red Bull, Toro Rosso)
Alfa Romeo (including Conrero)	225	488	Britain 1950 (Alfa Romeo) - Japan 1987 (Osella)
BMW (including Megatron)	301	774	Germany 1952 (AFM, BMW) - Abu Dhabi 2009 (BMW Sauber)

Engine re-badging

Acer, Castellotti and Petronas were re-badged Ferrari
Conrero was a re-badged Alfa Romeo
EMW was developed from the BMW
Mecachrome assembled engines designed by Renault
Megatron was a re-badged BMW
Osella was a re-badged Alfa Romeo
Playlife and Supertec were designed by Renault
Sauber was a re-badged Ilmor

968. Race starting drivers by engine make

	drivers	most races started
Cosworth (a)	300	Emerson Fittipaldi, 143
Ferrari (b)	125	Michael Schumacher, 180
Maserati (c)	110	Jo Bonnier, 28
Climax	100	Jack Brabham, 72
BRM	84	Graham Hill, 58
Renault	63	Mark Webber, 129
Alfa Romeo	41	Bruno Giacomelli, 49
Mercedes-Benz	38	Lewis Hamilton, 167
BMW	35	Nick Heidfeld, 83
Hart	33	Rubens Barrichello, 31
Honda	32	Jenson Button, 120
Alta	31	Lance Macklin, 12
Gordini (d)	26	Roberto Manzon, 23
Judd	21	Ivan Capelli, 45
Talbot-Lago	18	Johnny Claes, 13; Louis Rosier, 13
Lamborghini	17	Philippe Alliot, 29; Erik Comas, 29
Lea-Francis	17	Kenneth McAlpine, 6
Mugen Honda	17	Olivier Panis, 43
Bristol	16	Ken Wharton, 9
Porsche	16	Carel Godin de Beaufort, 26
Toyota	15	Jarno Trulli, 90
Veritas	15	Theo Helfrich, 2; Arthur Legat, 2; Toni Ulmen, 2
Petronas	13	Felipe Massa, 52
Peugeot	11	Rubens Barrichello, 33
Repco	11	Jack Brabham, 31
Vanwall	11	Tony Brooks, 16
Yamaha	11	Ukyo Katayama, 64
Ilmor	9	Karl Wendlinger, 16
Matra	8	Jacques Laffite, 79
Ford	7	Bruce McLaren, 3
OSCA	7	Elie Bayol, 3
Supertec	7	Pedro de la Rosa, 17; Jos Verstappen, 17
ERA	6	Bob Gerard, 3; Cuth Harrison, 3
Zakspeed	6	Jonathan Palmer, 23

Acer	5	Jean Alesi, 12
Asiatech	5	Enrique Bernoldi, 17; Jos Verstappen, 17
Motori Moderni	5	Alessandro Nannini, 30
TAG Porsche	5	Alain Prost, 64
Arrows	4	Pedro de la Rosa, 16; Pedro Diniz, 16; Mika Salo, 16; Tora Takagi, 16
ATS (Italy)	4	Giancarlo Baghetti, 5; Phil Hill, 5
Lancia	4	Alberto Ascari, 3; Eugenio Castellotti, 3; Luigi Villoresi, 3
Megatron	4	Eddie Cheever, 32; Derek Warwick, 32
Weslake	4	Dan Gurney, 17
Aston Martin	3	Roy Salvadori, 5
European	3	Fernando Alonso, 17
Pratt & Whitney	3	Emerson Fittipaldi, 1; Dave Walker, 1; Reine Wisell, 1
Tecno	3	Chris Amon, 4; Nanni Galli, 4
Borgward	2	Chris Bristow, 1; Ivor Bueb, 1
Butterworth	2	Bill Aston, 1; Robin Montgomerie-Charrington, 1
Castellotti	2	Gino Munaron, 3
Conrero	2	Roberto Bussinello, 1; Nino Vaccarella, 1
Fondmetal	2	Marc Gené, 17; Gastón Mazzacane, 17
Mecachrome	2	Heinz-Harald Frentzen, 16; Jacques Villeneuve, 16
Playlife	2	Giancarlo Fisichella, 49; Alexander Wurz, 49
Sauber	2	J J Lehto, 16; Karl Wendlinger, 16
Scarab	2	Chuck Daigh, 2
Bugatti	1	Maurice Trintignant, 1
EMW	1	Edgar Barth, 1
Jaguar	1	Clemente Biondetti, 1
JAP	1	Harry Schell, 1
Küchen	1	Hans Stuck, 1
Offenhauser	1	Rodger Ward, 1
Osella	1	Nicola Larini, 10
Serenissima	1	Bruce McLaren, 1

(a) Includes Ford Cosworth. (b) Includes Lancia-Ferrari. (c) Includes Maserati-Milano and Maserati-Platé. (d) Includes Simca-Gordini.

969. Race starting constructors by engine make
(number of races started)

Acer: Prost, 17
Alfa Romeo: Alfa Romeo, 110; Osella, 66; Brabham, 62; March, 9; McLaren, 4; LDS, 3; Alfa Special, 2; Cooper, 1
Alta: HWM, 14; Connaught, 7; Alta, 5; Cooper, 5; Emeryson, 1
Arrows: Arrows, 32
Asiatech: Arrows, 17; Minardi, 16
Aston Martin: Aston Martin, 5
ATS (Italy): ATS (Italy), 6; Cooper, 1
BMW: Williams, 103; Brabham, 91; BMW, 70; Arrows, 45; ATS (Germany), 29; Benetton, 16; AFM, 2; BMW specials, 2; Lola, 2; Klenk, 1
Borgward: Cooper, 1
Bristol: Cooper, 17; Frazer Nash, 4; ERA, 3; AFM, 2
BRM: BRM, 189; Lotus, 48; Brabham, 24; BRP, 13; McLaren, 13; Cooper, 11; Scirocco, 4; Gilby, 2; Matra, 1
Bugatti: Bugatti, 1
Butterworth: Aston-Butterworth, 2
Castellotti: Cooper, 3
Climax: Lotus, 82; Cooper, 81; Brabham, 47; Lola, 18; Eagle, 10; BRM, 8; Emeryson, 3; Ferguson, 1; Gilby, 1; JBW, 1; LDS, 1; Scirocco, 1; Shannon, 1
Conrero: De Tomaso, 1
Cosworth (a): Tyrrell, 310; Lotus, 277; McLaren, 236; Williams, 201; Minardi, 198; Arrows, 158; March, 149; Brabham, 133; Benetton, 128; Surtees, 118; Fittipaldi, 104; Shadow, 104; Ensign, 99; Jaguar, 85; Lola, 78; Marussia, 77; Osella, 75; Ligier, 74; ATS (Germany), 60; HRT, 56; Hesketh, 52; Jordan, 50; Stewart, 49; Wolf, 47; Dallara, 46; AGS, 45; Penske, 40; Theodore, 34; Sauber, 33; Matra, 28; Forti, 23; Simtek, 21; Rial, 20; Red Bull, 18; Toro Rosso, 18; Onyx, 17; Pacific, 17; Larrousse, 16; Parnelli, 16; Coloni, 13; EuroBrun, 12; Hill, 10; Merzario, 10; De Tomaso, 8; Trojan, 6; Martini, 4; Lec, 3; RAM, 3; Token, 3; Bellasi, 2; Kojima, 2; Amon, 1; Connew, 1; Lyncar, 1; Protos, 1; Rebaque, 1; Tecno, 1
EMW: EMW, 1

ERA:	ERA, 4
European:	Minardi, 17
Ferrari:	Ferrari (inc. Lancia-Ferrari), 907; Toro Rosso, 129; Sauber, 115; Marussia, 34; Force India, 18; Red Bull, 18; Spyker, 17; Dallara, 16; Minardi, 16; Lola, 14; Cooper, 3
Fondmetal:	Minardi, 17
Ford:	Brabham, 3; McLaren, 3; Cooper, 1; Lotus, 1; Stebro, 1
Gordini:	Gordini, 40 (includes Simca-Gordini)
Hart:	Toleman, 57; Arrows, 33; Jordan, 32; RAM, 28; Minardi, 17; Spirit, 17; Lola, 6
Honda:	BAR, 101; McLaren, 99; Honda, 88; Williams, 65; Super Aguri, 39; Jordan, 34; Lotus, 32; Tyrrell, 16; Spirit, 6
Ilmor:	March, 32; Tyrrell, 16; Pacific, 5
Jaguar:	Ferrari, 1
JAP:	Cooper, 1
Judd:	March, 46; Brabham, 35; Lotus, 31; Dallara, 16; Williams, 16; Ligier, 14; EuroBrun, 2; Andrea Moda, 1
Küchen:	AFM, 1
Lamborghini:	Larrousse, 32; Lola, 32; Ligier, 16; Lotus, 16; Minardi, 15; Lamborghini, 6
Lancia:	Lancia, 4
Lea-Francis:	Connaught, 10
Maserati:	Maserati (a), 68; Cooper, 44; JBW, 4; ENB, 1; Lotus, 1; Tec-Mec, 1
	(a) Includes Maserati-Milano and Platé engines.
Matra:	Ligier, 79; Matra, 44; Shadow, 2
Mecachrome:	Williams, 16
Megatron:	Arrows, 32; Ligier, 15
Mercedes-Benz:	McLaren, 351; Force India, 132; Mercedes-Benz, 127; Williams, 38; Lotus, 19; Brawn, 17; Sauber, 15
Motori Moderni:	Minardi, 44; AGS, 2
Mugen Honda:	Jordan, 49; Ligier, 33; Arrows, 32; Prost, 17; Lotus, 16
Offenhauser:	Kurtis-Kraft, 1
OSCA:	OSCA, 4; De Tomaso, 2; Cooper, 1; Maserati, 1
Osella:	Osella, 12
Petronas:	Sauber, 151
Peugeot:	Jordan, 50; Prost, 49; McLaren, 16
Playlife:	Benetton, 49
Porsche:	Porsche, 33; Arrows, 4
Pratt & Whitney:	Lotus, 3
Renault:	Renault, 300; Williams, 185; Red Bull, 167; Lotus, 139; Ligier, 95; Benetton, 67; Caterham, 58; Toro Rosso, 38; Tyrrell, 26
Repco:	Brabham, 33; LDS, 1
Sauber:	Sauber, 16
Scarab:	Scarab, 2
Serenissima:	McLaren, 1
Supertec:	Arrows, 17; BAR, 16; Williams, 16
TAG Porsche:	McLaren, 68
Talbot:	Talbot-Lago, 13
Tecno:	Tecno, 10
Toyota:	Toyota, 139; Williams, 52; Jordan, 19; Midland, 18
Vanwall:	Vanwall, 28
Veritas:	Veritas, 6
Weslake:	Eagle, 18
Yamaha:	Tyrrell, 65; Arrows, 17; Brabham, 16; Jordan, 16; Zakspeed, 2
Zakspeed:	Zakspeed, 51

(a) Includes Ford Cosworth

970. Races started by engine type

configuration/ cylinders							
V8	654	Switzerland 1952	- Brazil 2013	8	17	France 1954	- Italy 1956
V12	378	Switzerland 1950	- Australia 1995	H16	16	France 1966	- South Africa 1968
V10	300	Brazil 1989	- Brazil 2006	8 supercharged	13	Britain 1950	- Spain 1951
V6 turbo	210	Britain 1977	- Abu Dhabi 2015	4 supercharged	12	Britain 1950	- Spain 1951
Flat 12	169	United States 1964	- United States 1980	V12 supercharged	8	Monaco 1950	- Italy 1951
4	115	Switzerland 1951	- Canada 1969	Flat 8	7	Netherlands 1962	- United States 1962
4 turbo	110	Italy 1981	- Australia 1989	6 supercharged	4	Britain 1950	- Britain 1951
V8 turbo	86	Brazil 1983	- Japan 1988	Turbine	3	Netherlands 1971	- Italy 1971
6	75	Britain 1950	- United States 1960	V2	1	Monaco 1950	
V6	58	Argentina 1958	- Italy 1966	V16 supercharged	1	Britain 1951	
Flat 4	35	Belgium 1952	- Netherlands 1964				

971. Races started but never a win (Most)

Petronas	151	Yamaha	116	Judd	68	Motori Moderni	44
Hart	145	Peugeot	115	Zakspeed	51		
Toyota	140	Lamborghini	80	Playlife	49		

972. Milestones: Number of races started

Ferrari	100th: Germany 1963, 200th: Argentina 1973, 250th: Britain 1976, 500th: Germany 1992, 750th: France 2007, 800th: Monaco 2010, 900th: Hungary 2015
Cosworth/ Ford Cosworth	100th: United States 1974, 200th: France 1981, 250th: Netherlands 1984, 500th: Malaysia 2000
Renault	100th: Detroit 1984, 200th: Belgium 1992, 250th: Europe 1995, 500th: Brazil 2012
BMW	100th: Britain 2000, 200th: Bahrain 2006, 250th: Japan 2008
Honda	100th: Austria 1987, 200th: Italy 2000, 250th: Hungary 2003
Mercedes-Benz	100th: France 1999, 200th: Monaco 2005, 250th: Bahrain 2008
Alfa Romeo	100th: France 1980, 200th: Australia 1986
BRM	100th: Mexico 1968
Hart	100th: Monaco 1995
Maserati	100th: France 1967
Matra	100th: Belgium 1981
Mugen Honda	100th: Brazil 1998
Petronas	100th: Australia 2003
Peugeot	100th: Brazil 2000
Toyota	100th: Turkey 2007
Yamaha	100th: Australia 1997

973. Wins

Ferrari (a)	225	Britain 1951 (J F González/ Ferrari)	- Singapore 2015 (S Vettel/ Ferrari)
Ford Cosworth	176	Netherlands 1967 (J Clark/ Lotus)	- Brazil 2003 (G Fisichella/ Jordan)
Renault	168	France 1979 (J-P Jabouille/ Renault)	- Belgium 2014 (D Ricciardo/ Red Bull)
Mercedes-Benz	131	France 1954 (J M Fangio/ Mercedes-Benz)	- Abu Dhabi 2015 (N Rosberg/ Mercedes-Benz)
Honda	72	Mexico 1965 (R Ginther/ Honda)	- Hungary 2006 (J Button/ Honda)
Climax	40	Argentina 1958 (S Moss/ Cooper)	- Germany 1965 (J Clark/ Lotus)
TAG Porsche	25	Brazil 1984 (A Prost/ McLaren)	- Portugal 1987 (A Prost/ McLaren)
BMW	20	Canada 1982 (N Piquet/ Brabham)	- Canada 2008 (R Kubica/ BMW Sauber)
BRM	18	Netherlands 1959 (J Bonnier/ BRM)	- Monaco 1972 (J-P Beltoise/ BRM)
Alfa Romeo	12	Britain 1950 (G Farina/ Alfa Romeo)	- Italy 1978 (N Lauda/ Brabham)
Maserati	11	Italy 1953 (J M Fangio/ Maserati)	- South Africa 1967 (P Rodríguez/ Cooper)
Vanwall	9	Britain 1957 (S Moss, T Brooks/ Vanwall)	- Morocco 1958 (S Moss/ Vanwall)
Repco	8	France 1966 (J Brabham/ Brabham)	- Canada 1967 (J Brabham/ Brabham)
Mugen Honda	4	Monaco 1996 (O Panis/ Ligier)	- Italy 1999 (H-H Frentzen/ Jordan)
Matra	3	Sweden 1977 (J Laffite/ Ligier)	- Canada 1981 (J Laffite/ Talbot-Ligier)
Porsche	1	France 1962 (D Gurney/ Porsche)	
Weslake	1	Belgium 1967 (D Gurney/ Eagle)	

(a) Includes Lancia-Ferrari.

974. Wins in a season *(Most)*

Mercedes-Benz	16 of 19	2014	(Mercedes-Benz)
Mercedes-Benz	16 of 19	2015	(Mercedes-Benz)
Renault	16 of 17	1995	(Benetton, 15; Williams, 5)
Ford Cosworth	15 of 15	1973	(JPS Lotus, 7; Tyrrell, 5; McLaren, 3)
Honda	15 of 16	1988	(McLaren)
Ferrari	15 of 17	2002	(Ferrari)
Ferrari	15 of 18	2004	(Ferrari)
Renault	14 of 19	2013	(Lotus, Red Bull)
Ford Cosworth	12 of 15	1974	(McLaren, 4; Brabham, 3; JPS Lotus, 3; Tyrrell, 2)
Renault	12 of 16	1996	(Williams)
TAG Porsche	12 of 16	1984	(McLaren)
Ford Cosworth	12 of 17	1977	(JPS Lotus, 5; McLaren, 3; Wolf, 3; Shadow, 1)
Renault	12 of 19	2011	(Red Bull)

975. Won every race of a season

Ford Cosworth	15	1973	(JPS Lotus, 7; Tyrrell, 5; McLaren, 3)	Ferrari	7	1952	(Ferrari)
Ford Cosworth	11	1969	(Matra, 6; Brabham, 2; Lotus, 2; McLaren, 1)	Alfa Romeo	6	1950	(Alfa Romeo)

976. Won all but one race of a season

Renault	16	1995	(Benetton, 11; Williams, 5)	Climax	8	1960	(Cooper, 6; Lotus, 2)
Honda	15	1988	(McLaren)	Ferrari	7	1953	(Ferrari)
Ford Cosworth	11	1968	(Lotus, 5; Matra, 3; McLaren, 3)	Mercedes-Benz	5	1955	(Mercedes-Benz)

977. Consecutive wins *(Most)*

Ford Cosworth	22	Austria 1972	- South Africa 1974	(Brabham, JPS Lotus, McLaren, Tyrrell)
Ford Cosworth	20	Britain 1968	- Monaco 1970	(Brabham, Lotus, March, Matra, McLaren)
Renault	16	France 1995	- San Marino 1996	(Benetton, Williams)
Ferrari	14	Switzerland 1952	- Switzerland 1953	(Ferrari)
Honda	11	Brazil 1988	- Belgium 1988	(McLaren)
Climax	10	Portugal 1959	- Portugal 1960	(Cooper, Lotus)
Ferrari	10	Canada 2002	- Japan 2002	(Ferrari)
Alfa Romeo	9	Britain 1950	- France 1951	(Alfa Romeo)
Ford Cosworth	9	Netherlands 1980	- Belgium 1981	(Brabham, Williams)
Renault	9	Belgium 2013	- Brazil 2013	(Red Bull)

978. Different winning engines in a season

Most

1967	5	Maserati, Repco, Ford Cosworth, Weslake, Honda
1985	5	TAG Porsche, Renault, Ferrari, Honda, BMW
2003	5	Mercedes-Benz, Ford Cosworth, Ferrari, BMW, Renault

Fewest

1950	1	Alfa Romeo
1952	1	Ferrari
1969	1	Ford Cosworth
1973	1	Ford Cosworth

979. Winning drivers by engine make

Alfa Romeo: Juan Manuel Fangio, 6 (a); Giuseppe Farina, 4; Niki Lauda, 2; Luigi Fagioli, 1 (a)

BMW: Nelson Piquet, 7; Ralf Schumacher, 6; Juan Pablo Montoya, 4; Gerhard Berger, 1; Robert Kubica, 1; Riccardo Patrese, 1

BRM: Graham Hill, 10; Jackie Stewart, 2; Jean-Pierre Beltoise, 1; Jo Bonnier, 1; Jim Clark, 1; Peter Gethin, 1; Pedro Rodríguez, 1; Jo Siffert, 1

Climax: Jim Clark, 19; Jack Brabham, 7; Stirling Moss, 7; Bruce McLaren, 3; Dan Gurney, 2; Innes Ireland, 1; Maurice Trintignant, 1

Cosworth (b): Jackie Stewart, 25; Emerson Fittipaldi, 14; Alan Jones, 12; Mario Andretti, 11; James Hunt, 10; Ronnie Peterson, 10; Michael Schumacher, 10; Nelson Piquet, 9; Carlos Reutemann, 7; Jody Scheckter, 7; Denny Hulme, 6; Jochen Rindt, 6; Jim Clark, 5; Ayrton Senna, 5; John Watson, 5; Graham Hill, 4; Jacques Laffite, 4; Michele Alboreto, 3; Patrick Depailler, 3; Jacky Ickx, 2; Niki Lauda, 2; Peter Revson, 2; Keke Rosberg, 2; Jack Brabham, 1; Vittorio Brambilla, 1; François Cevert, 1; Elio De Angelis, 1; Giancarlo Fisichella, 1; Johnny Herbert, 1; Jochen Mass, 1; Bruce McLaren, 1; Alessandro Nannini, 1; Gunnar Nilsson, 1; Carlos Pace, 1; Riccardo Patrese, 1; Didier Pironi, 1; Clay Regazzoni, 1; Jo Siffert, 1

Ferrari: Michael Schumacher, 72; Niki Lauda, 15; Alberto Ascari, 13; Fernando Alonso, 11; Felipe Massa, 11; Rubens Barrichello, 9; Kimi Räikkönen, 9; Jacky Ickx, 6; Gilles Villeneuve, 6; Gerhard Berger, 5; Alain Prost, 5; Carlos Reutemann, 5; Eddie Irvine, 4; Clay Regazzoni, 4; John Surtees, 4; Sebastian Vettel, 4; Michele Alboreto, 3; René Arnoux, 3; Peter Collins, 3 (c); Juan Manuel Fangio, 3 (a)(c); Mike Hawthorn, 3; Phil Hill, 3; Nigel Mansell, 3; Jody Scheckter, 3; Tony Brooks, 2; José Froilán González, 2; Didier Pironi, 2; Patrick Tambay, 2; Wolfgang von Trips, 2; Jean Alesi, 1; Mario Andretti, 1; Giancarlo Baghetti, 1; Lorenzo Bandini, 1; Giuseppe Farina, 1; Luigi Musso, 1 (a)(c); Ludovico Scarfiotti, 1; Piero Taruffi, 1; Maurice Trintignant, 1

Honda: Ayrton Senna, 32; Nigel Mansell, 13; Alain Prost, 11; Nelson Piquet, 7; Gerhard Berger, 3; Keke Rosberg, 3; Jenson Button, 1; Richie Ginther, 1; John Surtees, 1

Maserati: Juan Manuel Fangio, 7; Stirling Moss, 2; Pedro Rodríguez, 1; John Surtees, 1

Matra: Jacques Laffite, 3

Mercedes-Benz: Lewis Hamilton, 43; Mika Häkkinen, 20; Jenson Button, 14; Nico Rosberg, 14; David Coulthard, 12; Kimi Räikkönen, 9; Juan Manuel Fangio, 8; Fernando Alonso, 4; Juan Pablo Montoya, 3; Rubens Barrichello, 2; Heikki Kovalainen, 1; Stirling Moss, 1

Mugen Honda: Heinz-Harald Frentzen, 2; Damon Hill, 1; Olivier Panis, 1

Porsche: Dan Gurney, 1

Renault: Sebastian Vettel, 38; Damon Hill, 21; Fernando Alonso, 17; Alain Prost, 16; Nigel Mansell, 15; Jacques Villeneuve, 11; Michael Schumacher, 9; Mark Webber, 9; René Arnoux, 4; Riccardo Patrese, 4; Ayrton Senna, 4; Thierry Boutsen, 3; Daniel Ricciardo, 3; Giancarlo Fisichella, 2; Johnny Herbert, 2; Jean-Pierre Jabouille, 2; Kimi Räikkönen, 2; Gerhard Berger, 1; David Coulthard, 1; Elio De Angelis, 1; Heinz-Harald Frentzen, 1; Pastor Maldonado, 1; Jarno Trulli, 1

Repco: Jack Brabham, 6; Denny Hulme, 2

TAG Porsche: Alain Prost, 19; Niki Lauda, 6

Vanwall: Stirling Moss, 6 (a); Tony Brooks, 4 (a)

Weslake: Dan Gurney, 1

(a) Includes 1 shared car.
(b) As Ford Cosworth.
(c) Includes Lancia-Ferrari.

980. Winning constructors by engine make

Alfa Romeo:	Alfa Romeo, 10; Brabham, 2
BMW:	Williams, 10; Brabham, 8; Benetton, 1; BMW Sauber, 1
BRM:	BRM, 17; Lotus, 1
Climax:	Lotus, 24; Cooper, 14; Brabham, 2
Cosworth (a):	Lotus, 47; McLaren, 35; Tyrrell, 23; Williams, 17; Brabham, 15; Benetton, 14; Matra, 9; Ligier, 5; March, 3; Wolf, 3; Hesketh, 1; Jordan, 1; Penske, 1; Shadow, 1; Stewart, 1
Ferrari:	Ferrari, 224 (inc. Lancia-Ferrari); Toro Rosso, 1
Honda:	McLaren, 44; Williams, 23; Honda, 3; Lotus, 2
Maserati:	Maserati, 9; Cooper, 2
Matra:	Ligier, 3
Mercedes-Benz:	McLaren, 78; Mercedes-Benz, 45; Brawn, 8
Mugen Honda:	Jordan, 3; Ligier, 1
Porsche:	Porsche, 1
Renault:	Williams, 64; Red Bull, 50; Renault, 35; Benetton, 12; Lotus, 7
Repco:	Brabham, 8
TAG Porsche:	McLaren, 25
Vanwall:	Vanwall, 9
Weslake:	Eagle, 1

(a) As Ford Cosworth

981. Number of winning drivers and constructors by engine make

	drivers	constructors							
Ferrari (a)	39	2	Climax	7	3	TAG Porsche	2	1
Ford Cosworth	38	15	BMW	6	4	Vanwall	2	1
Renault	23	5	Alfa Romeo	4	2	Matra	1	1
Mercedes-Benz	12	3	Maserati	4	2	Porsche	1	1
Honda	9	4	Mugen Honda	3	2	Weslake	1	1
BRM	8	2	Repco	2	1			

(a) Includes Lancia-Ferrari.
For driver wins with the same engine make, see section 241.
For driver wins with a turbocharged engine, see section 242.
For constructor wins with the same engine make, see section 723.

982. Wins by engine type

configuration/cylinders

V8	370	Argentina 1956 (L Musso, J M Fangio/ Lancia-Ferrari)	- Brazil 2013 (S Vettel/ Red Bull - Renault)
V10	239	San Marino 1989 (A Senna/ McLaren - Honda)	- China 2005 (F Alonso/ Renault)
V6 turbo	138	France 1979 (J-P Jabouille/ Renault)	- Abu Dhabi 2015 (N Rosberg/ Mercedes-Benz)
4	45	Switzerland 1952 (P Taruffi/ Ferrari)	- United States 1961 (I Ireland/ Lotus - Climax)
V12	42	Britain 1951 (J F González/ Ferrari)	- Canada 1995 (J Alesi/ Ferrari)
Flat 12	39	Austria 1970 (J Ickx/ Ferrari)	- United States 1979 (G Villeneuve/ Ferrari)
V6	12	France 1958 (M Hawthorn/ Ferrari)	- Austria 1964 (L Bandini/ Ferrari)
8 supercharged	10	Britain 1950 (G Farina/ Alfa Romeo)	- Spain 1951 (J M Fangio/ Alfa Romeo)
4 turbo	9	Canada 1982 (N Piquet/ Brabham - BMW)	- Mexico 1986 (G Berger/ Benetton - BMW)
6	9	Italy 1953 (J M Fangio/ Maserati)	- Germany 1957 (J M Fangio/ Maserati)
8	9	France 1954 (J M Fangio/ Mercedes-Benz)	- Italy 1955 (J M Fangio/ Mercedes-Benz)
Flat 8	1	France 1962 (D Gurney/ Porsche)	
H16	1	United States 1966 (J Clark/ Lotus - BRM)	

983. Wins but never a pole position

Weslake	1

984. Wins but never a fastest lap

Mugen Honda	4
Porsche	1

985. Milestones: Wins

Ferrari	50th: Spain 1974, 100th: France 1990, 150th: Canada 2002, 200th: China 2007
Ford Cosworth	50th: Canada 1972, 100th: Monaco 1977, 150th: Austria 1982
Renault	50th: Belgium 1993, 100th: Bahrain 2005, 150th: India 2012
Mercedes-Benz	25th: Britain 1999, 50th: Italy 2005, 100th: Australia 2014
Honda	25th: Italy 1987, 50th: Belgium 1989
Climax	25th: France 1963
TAG Porsche	25th: Portugal 1987

986. Podium positions
(number of races in brackets)

Ferrari (a)	702	(524)	Monaco 1950 (A Ascari/ Ferrari)	- Abu Dhabi 2015 (K Räikkönen/ Ferrari)
Ford Cosworth	535	(291)	Netherlands 1967 (J Clark/ Lotus)	- Brazil 2003 (G Fisichella/ Jordan)
Renault	453	(312)	France 1979 (J-P Jabouille, R Arnoux/ Renault)	- Singapore 2015 (D Ricciardo/ Red Bull)
Mercedes-Benz	358	(253)	France 1954 (J M Fangio, K Kling/ Mercedes-Benz)	- Abu Dhabi 2015 (N Rosberg, L Hamilton/ Mercedes-Benz)
Honda	174	(123)	Mexico 1965 (R Ginther/ Honda)	- Britain 2008 (R Barrichello/ Honda)
Climax	104	(63)	Argentina 1958 (S Moss/ Cooper)	- South Africa 1967 (J Love/ Cooper)
BMW	86	(76)	Canada 1982 (N Piquet/ Brabham)	- Brazil 2009 (R Kubica/ BMW Sauber)
BRM	65	(55)	Netherlands 1958 (H Schell, J Behra/ BRM)	- South Africa 1974 (J-P Beltoise/ BRM)
TAG Porsche	54	(44)	Brazil 1984 (A Prost/ McLaren)	- Japan 1987 (S Johansson/ McLaren)
Maserati	44	(33)	Monaco 1950 (L Chiron/ Maserari)	- South Africa 1967 (P Rodríguez/ Cooper)
Alfa Romeo	40	(30)	Britain 1950 (G Farina, L Fagioli, R Parnell/ Alfa Romeo)	- Italy 1984 (R Patrese/ Alfa Romeo)
Repco	25	(17)	France 1966 (J Brabham, D Hulme/ Brabham)	- Germany 1968 (J Rindt/ Brabham)
Matra	24	(24)	Netherlands 1968 (J-P Beltoise/ Matra)	- Caesars Palace 1982 (E Cheever/ Talbot-Ligier)
Toyota	17	(17)	Malaysia 2005 (J Trulli/ Toyota)	- Japan 2009 (J Trulli/ Toyota)
Mugen Honda	16	(15)	Belgium 1995 (M Brundle/ Ligier)	- United States 2000 (H-H Frentzen/ Jordan)
Peugeot	14	(13)	San Marino 1994 (M Häkkinen/ McLaren)	- Europe 1999 (J Trulli/ Prost)
Vanwall	13	(11)	Monaco 1957 (T Brooks/ Vanwall)	- Morocco 1958 (S Moss/ Vanwall)
Judd	8	(8)	Britain 1988 (N Mansell/ Williams)	- San Marino 1991 (J J Lehto/ Dallara)
Playlife	6	(6)	Monaco 1998 (G Fisichella/ Benetton)	- Canada 2000 (G Fisichella/ Benetton)
Hart	5	(5)	Monaco 1984 (A Senna/ Toleman)	- Australia 1995 (G Morbidelli/ Footwork)
Porsche	5	(5)	France 1961 (D Gurney/ Porsche)	- Germany 1962 (D Gurney/ Porsche)
Petronas	4	(4)	Hungary 1997 (J Herbert/ Sauber)	- United States 2003 (H-H Frentzen/ Sauber)
Mecachrome	3	(3)	Australia 1998 (H-H Frentzen/ Williams)	- Hungary 1998 (J Villeneuve/ Williams)
Supertec	3	(3)	Australia 1999 (R Schumacher/ Williams)	- Italy 1999 (R Schumacher/ Williams)
Gordini	2	(2)	Switzerland 1952 (J Behra/ Gordini)	- Belgium 1952 (R Manzon/ Gordini)
Talbot-Lago	2	(2)	Switzerland 1950 (L Rosier/ Talbot-Lago)	- Belgium 1950 (L Rosier/ Talbot-Lago)
Weslake	2	(2)	Belgium 1967 (D Gurney/ Eagle)	- Canada 1967 (D Gurney/ Eagle)
Yamaha	2	(2)	Spain 1994 (M Blundell/ Tyrrell)	- Hungary 1997 (D Hill/ Arrows)
Alta	1	(1)	Italy 1956 (R Flockhart/ Connaught)	
Bristol	1	(1)	Britain 1952 (M Hawthorn/ Cooper)	
Lamborghini	1	(1)	Japan 1990 (A Suzuki/ Lola)	
Lancia	1	(1)	Monaco 1955 (E Castellotti/ Lancia)	
Megatron	1	(1)	Italy 1988 (E Cheever/ Arrows)	

(a) Includes Lancia-Ferrari.

987. Podium positions in a season *(Most)*

Ford Cosworth	45	1973	(JPS Lotus, 15; Tyrrell, 15; McLaren, 8; Brabham, 2; March, 2; Shadow, 2; Surtees, 1)
Mercedes-Benz	43	2014	(Mercedes-Benz, 31; Williams, 9; McLaren, 2; Force India, 1)
Ford Cosworth	38	1980	(Williams, 18; Ligier, 10; Brabham, 6; Fittipaldi, 2; Arrows, 1; Lotus, 1)
Renault	38	2013	(Red Bull, 24; Lotus 14)
Mercedes-Benz	38	2015	(Mercedes-Benz, 32; Williams, 4; Force India, 1; Lotus, 1)
Ford Cosworth	32	1974	(McLaren, 10; Tyrrell, 7; JPS Lotus, 6; Brabham, 5; Hesketh, 3; Shadow, 1)
Ford Cosworth	32	1976	(Tyrrell, 12; McLaren, 10; JPS Lotus, 5; Penske, 3; March, 1; Shadow, 1)
Renault	32	1995	(Williams, 17; Benetton, 15)
Ford Cosworth	31	1969	(Matra, 10; Brabham, 9; Lotus, 7; McLaren, 5)
Ford Cosworth	31	1975	(McLaren, 10; Brabham, 9; Hesketh, 4; Tyrrell, 4; JPS Lotus, 1; March, 1; Shadow, 1)
Renault	31	1996	(Williams, 21; Benetton, 10)

988. Races in a season with a podium *(Most)*

Mercedes-Benz	19 of 19	2014	(Mercedes-Benz, McLaren, Force India, Williams)
Renault	19 of 19	2013	(Lotus, Red Bull)
Ferrari	18 of 18	2004	(Ferrari)
Renault	18 of 19	2011	(Red Bull, Renault)
Ferrari	17 of 17	2000	(Ferrari)
Ferrari	17 of 17	2001	(Ferrari)
Ferrari	17 of 17	2002	(Ferrari)
Ford Cosworth	17 of 17	1977	(Wolf, McLaren, Tyrrell, JPS Lotus, Shadow)
Mercedes-Benz	17 of 17	2007	(McLaren)
Mercedes-Benz	17 of 19	2015	(Mercedes-Benz, Williams, Lotus, Force India)

989. Podium in every race of a season
(apart from those in section 988)

Ford Cosworth	15	1973	(JPS Lotus, Tyrrell, McLaren, Shadow, Brabham, March)
Ford Cosworth	15	1974	(McLaren, JPS Lotus, Brabham, Tyrrell, Shadow, Hesketh)
Ford Cosworth	15	1981	(Williams, Brabham, Arrows, Lotus, McLaren)
Ford Cosworth	14	1975	(McLaren, Hesketh, Brabham, Tyrrell, JPS Lotus, Williams, March, Shadow)
Ford Cosworth	14	1980	(Williams, Brabham, Fittipaldi, Lotus, Ligier, Arrows)
Ford Cosworth	13	1970	(Brabham, McLaren, March, Lotus)
Ford Cosworth	12	1968	(Lotus, McLaren, Matra)
Ford Cosworth	12	1972	(Tyrrell, McLaren, JPS Lotus, March, Surtees)
Ford Cosworth	11	1969	(Matra, Lotus, McLaren, Brabham)
Climax	10	1963	(Cooper, Lotus, Brabham)
Climax	9	1962	(Lotus, Cooper, Lola)
Ferrari	8	1953	(Ferrari)
Ferrari	8	1954	(Ferrari)
Alfa Romeo	7	1951	(Alfa Romeo)
Ferrari	7	1951	(Ferrari)
Ferrari	7	1952	(Ferrari)
Lancia-Ferrari	7	1956	(Lancia-Ferrari)
Maserati	7	1956	(Maserati)
Alfa Romeo	6	1950	(Alfa Romeo)

990. Different podium engine makes in a season

Most

1967	8	Maserati, Climax, Honda, Repco, BRM, Ferrari, Ford Cosworth, Weslake,
1997	8	Mercedes-Benz, Ferrari, Renault, Ford Cosworth, Mugen Honda, Peugeot, Yamaha, Petronas
1984	7	TAG Porsche, Honda, Renault, Ferrari, Hart, BMW, Alfa Romeo
1995	7	Renault, Ferrari, Peugeot, Mugen Honda, Mercedes-Benz, Ford Cosworth, Hart
1999	7	Ferrari, Mugen Honda, Supertec, Mercedes-Benz, Ford Cosworth, Playlife, Peugeot
2001	7	Ferrari, Mercedes-Benz, Petronas, BMW, Honda, Ford Cosworth, Renault

Fewest

1973	1	Ford Cosworth		1975	2	Ford Cosworth, Ferrari
1951	2	Alfa Romeo, Ferrari		1980	2	Ford Cosworth, Renault
1953	2	Ferrari, Maserati				

991. Complete podiums in a season *(Most)*

Ford Cosworth	15 of 15	1973		Climax	5 of 9	1960
Ford Cosworth	10 of 14	1980		Renault	5 of 16	1996
Ford Cosworth	9 of 11	1969		Renault	5 of 19	2013
Mercedes-Benz	8 of 19	2014		Ford Cosworth	4 of 13	1970
Ford Cosworth	7 of 12	1972		Ford Cosworth	4 of 15	1979
Ford Cosworth	6 of 14	1975		Ford Cosworth	4 of 16	1976
Ford Cosworth	6 of 15	1974		Mercedes-Benz	4 of 19	2015

992. The same engine make in each of the top finishing positions

Top 6			
Ford Cosworth	24	South Africa 1969	- United States West 1982
Climax	1	France 1960	
Top 5			
Ford Cosworth	33	South Africa 1969	- United States West 1982
Climax	2	France 1960	- Britain 1960
Mercedes-Benz	1	Russia 2014	
Top 4			
Ford Cosworth	54	South Africa 1969	- United States West 1982
Mercedes-Benz	5	Britain 1955	- Brazil 2014
Climax	3	France 1960	- United States 1960

Renault	3	France 1996	- Bahrain 2012
Ferrari	2	Germany 1952	- Belgium 1961
Honda	1	Britain 1987	
Maserati	1	Argentina 1957	

Top 3

Ford Cosworth	77	Mexico 1968	- Detroit 1983
Renault	17	France 1995	- United States 2013
Mercedes-Benz	15	Britain 1955	- Mexico 2015
Climax	8	Belgium 1960	- Belgium 1964
Ferrari (a)	8	France 1952	- Britain 1961
Honda	4	Britain 1987	- Australia 1988
Alfa Romeo	1	Britain 1950	
Maserati	1	Argentina 1957	

Top 2

Ford Cosworth	108	United States 1967	- Japan 1990
Ferrari (a)	82	Italy 1951	- Malaysia 2012
Mercedes-Benz	59	France 1954	- Abu Dhabi 2015
Renault	56	France 1982	- Brazil 2013
Honda	29	South Africa 1985	- Japan 1991
Climax	16	Portugal 1959	- Belgium 1964
TAG Porsche	7	South Africa 1984	- Belgium 1987
Alfa Romeo	5	Britain 1950	- Italy 1978
BRM	5	Italy 1962	- Italy 1965
BMW	4	Malaysia 2002	- Canada 2008
Repco	4	Britain 1966	- Canada 1967
Maserati	1	Argentina 1957	
Mugen Honda	1	Belgium 1998	

(a) Includes Lancia-Ferrari.
Additionally, at Italy 1960, the top five were Ferrari although 4th place was Castellotti, a re-badged Ferrari engine.
The most classified finishers with the same engine make in all of the top positions, was 16 by Ford Cosworth in Germany 1973.

993. Different engine make in each of the top finishing positions

Top 8

Japan 1992	1: Renault, 2: Honda, 3: Ford Cosworth, 4: Ilmor, 5: Ferrari, 6: Lamborghini, 7: Yamaha, 8: Mugen Honda

Top 7

Brazil 1994	1: Ford Cosworth, 2: Renault, 3: Ferrari, 4: Hart, 5: Yamaha, 6: Mercedes-Benz, 7: Mugen Honda
Europe 1994	1: Ford Cosworth, 2: Renault, 3: Peugeot, 4: Hart, 5: Ferrari, 6: Mercedes-Benz, 7: Yamaha
San Marino 1999	1: Ferrari, 2: Mercedes-Benz, 3: Ford Cosworth, 4: Mugen Honda, 5: Playlife, 6: Petronas, 7: Supertec
Italy 2000	1: Ferrari, 2: Mercedes-Benz, 3: BMW, 4: Supertec, 5: Playlife, 6: Honda, 7: Petronas
Canada 2001	1: BMW, 2: Ferrari, 3: Mercedes-Benz, 4: Petronas, 5: Acer, 6: Ford Cosworth, 7: Honda
Monaco 2004	1: Renault, 2: Honda, 3: Ferrari, 4: BMW, 5: Petronas, 6: Toyota, 7: Ford Cosworth
Belgium 2005	1: Mercedes-Benz, 2: Renault, 3: Honda, 4: BMW, 5: Ferrari, 6: Petronas, 7: Toyota

Top 6

San Marino 1994	1: Ford Cosworth, 2: Ferrari, 3: Peugeot, 4: Mercedes-Benz, 5: Yamaha, 6: Renault
Australia 1995	1: Renault, 2: Mugen Honda, 3: Hart, 4: Mercedes-Benz, 5: Yamaha, 6: Ford Cosworth
Hungary 1997	1: Renault, 2: Yamaha, 3: Petronas, 4: Ferrari, 5: Peugeot, 6: Mugen Honda
Australia 1999	1: Ferrari, 2: Mugen Honda, 3: Supertec, 4: Playlife, 5: Ford Cosworth, 6: Arrows
Canada 1999	1: Mercedes-Benz, 2: Playlife, 3: Ferrari, 4: Supertec, 5: Ford Cosworth, 6: Petronas
Australia 2002	1: Ferrari, 2: BMW, 3: Mercedes-Benz, 4: Ford Cosworth, 5: Asiatech, 6: Toyota
Monaco 2002	1: Mercedes-Benz, 2: Ferrari, 3: BMW, 4: Renault, 5: Honda, 6: Ford Cosworth
Germany 2004	1: Ferrari, 2: Honda, 3: Renault, 4: Mercedes-Benz, 5: BMW, 6: Ford Cosworth
San Marino 2005	1: Renault, 2: Ferrari, 3: Mercedes-Benz, 4: Petronas, 5: Toyota, 6: BMW
Canada 2007	1: Mercedes-Benz, 2: BMW, 3: Toyota, 4: Renault, 5: Ferrari, 6: Honda

The last time that as many as five different engine makes filled the top six finishing positions was Japan 2009, with BMW, Ferrari, Mercedes-Benz, Renault and Toyota.

994. Podium positions but never a win *(Most)*

Toyota	17	Playlife	6	Mecachrome	3	Talbot-Lago	2
Peugeot	14	Hart	5	Supertec	3	Yamaha	2
Judd	8	Petronas	4	Gordini	2		

995. Pole positions

Renault	213	South Africa 1979 (J-P Jabouille/ Renault)	- Brazil 2013 (S Vettel/ Red Bull)
Ferrari (a)	209	Britain 1951 (J F González/ Ferrari)	- Singapore 2015 (S Vettel/ Ferrari)
Cosworth (b)	140	Netherlands 1967 (G Hill/ Lotus)	- Brazil 2010 (N Hülkenberg/ Williams)
Mercedes-Benz	136	France 1954 (J M Fangio/ Mercedes-Benz)	- Abu Dhabi 2015 (N Rosberg/ Mercedes-Benz)
Honda	77	Italy 1968 (J Surtees/ Honda)	- Australia 2006 (J Button/ Honda)
Climax	44	Monaco 1959 (S Moss/ Cooper)	- Germany 1966 (J Clark/ Lotus)
BMW	33	Austria 1982 (N Piquet/ Brabham)	- Bahrain 2008 (R Kubica/ BMW Sauber)
Alfa Romeo	15	Britain 1950 (G Farina/ Alfa Romeo)	- United States West 1982 (A De Cesaris/ Alfa Romeo)
BRM	11	Netherlands 1959 (J Bonnier/ BRM)	- Argentina 1973 (C Regazzoni/ BRM)
Maserati	11	Belgium 1953 (J M Fangio/ Maserati)	- Mexico 1966 (J Surtees/ Cooper)
Repco	7	Britain 1966 (J Brabham/ Brabham)	- Canada 1968 (J Rindt/ Brabham)
TAG Porsche	7	Monaco 1984 (A Prost/ McLaren)	- Germany 1986 (K Rosberg/ McLaren)
Vanwall	7	Britain 1957 (S Moss/ Vanwall)	- Italy 1958 (S Moss/ Vanwall)
Matra	4	Italy 1971 (C Amon/ Matra-Simca)	- Spain 1981 (J Laffite/ Talbot-Ligier)
Toyota	3	United States 2005 (J Trulli/ Toyota)	- Bahrain 2009 (J Trulli/ Toyota)
Hart	2	Germany 1985 (T Fabi/ Toleman)	- Belgium 1994 (R Barrichello/ Jordan)
Lancia	2	Spain 1954 (A Ascari/ Lancia)	- Belgium 1955 (E Castellotti/ Lancia)
Mugen Honda	1	Europe 1999 (H-H Frentzen/ Jordan)	
Playlife	1	Austria 1998 (G Fisichella/ Benetton)	
Porsche	1	Germany 1962 (D Gurney/ Porsche)	

Includes cases where cars did not make it to the starting grid (see section 351).
(a) Includes Lancia-Ferrari.
(b) As Ford Cosworth until 2004.

996. Pole positions in a season *(Most)*

Mercedes-Benz	19 of 19	2014	(Mercedes-Benz, 18; Williams, 1)
Renault	18 of 19	2011	(Red Bull)
Mercedes-Benz	18 of 19	2015	(Mercedes-Benz)
Renault	16 of 17	1995	(Benetton, 12; Williams, 4)
Honda	15 of 16	1988	(McLaren)
Honda	15 of 16	1989	(McLaren)
Renault	15 of 16	1992	(Williams)
Renault	15 of 16	1993	(Williams)
Renault	15 of 19	2010	(Red Bull)
Ford Cosworth	14 of 15	1973	(JPS Lotus, 10; Tyrrell, 3; McLaren, 1)
Ford Cosworth	14 of 17	1977	(JPS Lotus, 7; McLaren, 6; Wolf, 1)

997. Pole position in every race of a season

Mercedes-Benz	19	2014	(Mercedes-Benz, 18; Williams, 1)
Ford Cosworth	11	1969	(Lotus, 5; Brabham, 4; Matra, 2)
Ferrari	7	1952	(Ferrari)
Alfa Romeo	6	1950	(Alfa Romeo)

998. Pole position in all but one race of a season
(apart from those in section 996)

Climax	8	1960	(Cooper, Lotus)
Lancia-Ferrari	6	1956	(Lancia-Ferrari)

999. Consecutive pole positions *(Most)*

Mercedes-Benz	31	Australia 2014	- Italy 2015	(Mercedes-Benz, Williams)
Renault	24	France 1992	- Japan 1993	(Williams)
Ford Cosworth	18	United States 1968	- Netherlands 1970	(Brabham, Lotus, March, Matra)
Honda	17	Germany 1988	- Germany 1989	(McLaren)
Ford Cosworth	16	Brazil 1973	- Brazil 1974	(JPS Lotus, McLaren, Tyrrell)
Renault	16	Abu Dhabi 2010	- Japan 2011	(Red Bull)
Honda	12	Australia 1986	- Italy 1987	(Lotus, Williams)
Honda	12	Belgium 1989	- Mexico 1990	(McLaren)
Renault	11	Australia 1994	- Hungary 1995	(Benetton, Williams)
Climax	10	Portugal 1959	- Portugal 1960	(Cooper, Lotus)
Ferrari	10	Spain 1951	- Netherlands 1953	(Ferrari)
Ford Cosworth	10	Netherlands 1967	- South Africa 1968	(Lotus)
Renault	10	Italy 1995	- Europe 1996	(Benetton, Williams)
Renault	10	Belgium 1996	- Spain 1997	(Williams)

1000. Different pole position engine makes in a season

Most

1985	6	Ferrari, Renault, Honda, Hart, TAG Porsche, BMW
2005	6	Renault, Mercedes-Benz, BMW, Honda, Toyota, Ferrari
1982	5	Renault, Alfa Romeo, Ferrari, Ford Cosworth, BMW
2004	5	Ferrari, Honda, Renault, BMW, Mercedes-Benz

Fewest

1950	1	Alfa Romeo
1952	1	Ferrari
1969	1	Ford Cosworth
2014	1	Mercedes-Benz

1001. Pole position drivers by engine make

Alfa Romeo: Juan Manuel Fangio, 8; Giuseppe Farina, 2; John Watson, 2; Andrea De Cesaris, 1; Bruno Giacomelli, 1; Niki Lauda, 1

BMW: Nelson Piquet, 12; Juan Pablo Montoya, 11; Ralf Schumacher, 5; Teo Fabi, 2; Nick Heidfeld, 1; Robert Kubica, 1; Riccardo Patrese, 1

BRM: Graham Hill, 8; Jo Bonnier, 1; Clay Regazzoni, 1; Jo Siffert, 1

Climax: Jim Clark, 26; Stirling Moss, 9; Jack Brabham, 5; Dan Gurney, 2; John Surtees, 2

Cosworth (a): Mario Andretti, 17; Jackie Stewart, 17; James Hunt, 14; Ronnie Peterson, 14; Jochen Rindt, 8; Jim Clark, 7; Emerson Fittipaldi, 6; Alan Jones, 6; Nelson Piquet, 6; Michael Schumacher, 6; Graham Hill, 5; Jacques Laffite, 5; Carlos Reutemann, 4; Jack Brabham, 3; Jean-Pierre Jarier, 3; Jacky Ickx, 2; Didier Pironi, 2; Keke Rosberg, 2; Jody Scheckter, 2; Rubens Barrichello, 1; Vittorio Brambilla, 1; Patrick Depailler, 1; Nico Hülkenberg, 1; Denny Hulme, 1; Carlos Pace, 1; Riccardo Patrese, 1; Tom Pryce, 1; Peter Revson, 1; Ayrton Senna, 1; Jo Siffert, 1

Ferrari: Michael Schumacher, 58; Niki Lauda, 23; Felipe Massa, 15; Alberto Ascari, 13; Rubens Barrichello, 11; Jacky Ickx, 11; Gerhard Berger, 7; Juan Manuel Fangio, 6 (as Lancia-Ferrari); Phil Hill, 6; Kimi Räikkönen, 5; Fernando Alonso, 4; René Arnoux, 4; Mike Hawthorn, 4; Clay Regazzoni, 4; John Surtees, 4; Patrick Tambay, 4; Chris Amon, 3; Giuseppe Farina, 3; José Froilán González, 3; Nigel Mansell, 3; Michele Alboreto, 2; Tony Brooks, 2; Didier Pironi, 2; Carlos Reutemann, 2; Sebastian Vettel, 2; Gilles Villeneuve, 2; Jean Alesi, 1; Mario Andretti, 1; Lorenzo Bandini, 1; Mike Parkes, 1; Jody Scheckter, 1; Wolfgang von Trips, 1

Hart: Rubens Barrichello, 1; Teo Fabi, 1

Honda: Ayrton Senna, 46; Nigel Mansell, 11; Nelson Piquet, 6; Gerhard Berger, 4; Alain Prost, 4; Jenson Button, 3; Keke Rosberg, 2; John Surtees, 1

Lancia: Alberto Ascari, 1; Eugenio Castellotti, 1

Maserati: Juan Manuel Fangio, 8; Stirling Moss, 2; John Surtees, 1

Matra: Chris Amon, 2; Jacques Laffite, 2

Mercedes-Benz: Lewis Hamilton, 49; Mika Häkkinen, 26; Nico Rosberg, 22; Kimi Räikkönen, 11; David Coulthard, 7; Juan Manuel Fangio, 7; Jenson Button, 5; Fernando Alonso, 2; Juan Pablo Montoya, 2; Rubens Barrichello, 1; Giancarlo Fisichella, 1; Heikki Kovalainen, 1; Felipe Massa, 1; Stirling Moss, 1

Mugen Honda: Heinz-Harald Frentzen, 1

Playlife: Giancarlo Fisichella, 1

Porsche: Dan Gurney, 1

Renault: Sebastian Vettel, 44; Alain Prost, 23; Damon Hill, 20; Nigel Mansell, 18; Ayrton Senna, 18; Fernando Alonso, 16; René Arnoux, 14; Jacques Villeneuve, 13; Mark Webber, 13; Jean-Pierre Jabouille, 6; Riccardo Patrese, 6; David Coulthard, 5; Michael Schumacher, 4; Elio De Angelis, 3; Giancarlo Fisichella, 2; Jarno Trulli, 2; Jean Alesi, 1; Gerhard Berger, 1; Thierry Boutsen, 1; Heinz-Harald Frentzen, 1; Pastor Maldonado, 1; Patrick Tambay, 1

Repco: Jack Brabham, 5; Jochen Rindt, 2

TAG Porsche: Alain Prost, 6; Keke Rosberg, 1

Toyota: Jarno Trulli, 2; Ralf Schumacher, 1

Vanwall: Stirling Moss, 4; Stuart Lewis-Evans, 2; Tony Brooks, 1

(a) Includes Ford Cosworth

1002. Pole position constructors by engine make

Alfa Romeo:	Alfa Romeo, 12; Brabham, 3
BMW:	Williams, 17; Brabham, 13; Benetton, 2; BMW, 1
BRM:	BRM, 11
Climax:	Lotus, 31; Cooper, 10; Brabham, 2; Lola, 1
Cosworth (a):	Lotus, 56; McLaren, 19; Brabham, 14; Tyrrell, 14; Williams, 11; Ligier, 7; Benetton, 6; March, 5; Shadow, 3; Matra, 2; Arrows, 1; Stewart, 1; Wolf, 1
Ferrari:	Ferrari, 208 (inc. Lancia-Ferrari); Toro Rosso, 1
Hart:	Jordan, 1; Toleman, 1
Honda:	McLaren, 53; Williams, 19; BAR, 2; Honda, 2; Lotus, 1
Lancia:	Lancia, 2
Maserati:	Maserati, 10; Cooper, 1
Matra:	Ligier, 2; Matra, 2
Mercedes-Benz:	McLaren, 76; Mercedes-Benz, 53; Brawn, 5; Force India, 1; Williams, 1
Mugen Honda:	Jordan, 1
Playlife:	Benetton, 1
Porsche:	Porsche, 1
Renault:	Williams, 80; Red Bull, 57; Renault, 51; Lotus, 19; Benetton, 6
Repco:	Brabham, 7
TAG Porsche:	McLaren, 7
Toyota:	Toyota, 3
Vanwall:	Vanwall, 7

(a) Includes Ford Cosworth

1003. Number of pole position drivers and constructors by engine make

	drivers	constructors							
Ferrari (a)	32	2	Climax	5	4	Repco	2	1
Cosworth (b)	30	13	BRM	4	1	TAG Porsche	2	1
Renault	22	5	Maserati	3	2	Toyota	2	1
Mercedes-Benz	14	5	Vanwall	3	1	Mugen Honda	1	1
Honda	8	5	Hart	2	2	Playlife	1	1
BMW	7	4	Lancia	2	1	Porsche	1	1
Alfa Romeo	6	2	Matra	2	2			

(a) Includes Lancia-Ferrari. (b) Includes Ford Cosworth.
For driver pole positions with the same engine make, see section 349.
For constructor pole positions with the same engine make, see section 801.

1004. Pole positions by engine type

configuration/cylinders			
V8	340	Spain 1954 (A Ascari/ Lancia)	- Brazil 2013 (S Vettel/ Red Bull - Renault)
V10	257	Brazil 1989 (A Senna/ McLaren - Honda)	- China 2005 (F Alonso/ Renault)
V6 turbo	148	South Africa 1979 (J-P Jabouille/ Renault)	- Abu Dhabi 2015 (N Rosberg/ Mercedes-Benz)
Flat 12	44	France 1970 (J Ickx/ Ferrari)	- Monaco 1979 (J Scheckter/ Ferrari)
4	38	Switzerland 1952 (G Farina/ Ferrari)	- Monaco 1961 (S Moss/ Lotus - Climax)
V12	38	Britain 1951 (J F González/ Ferrari)	- Belgium 1995 (G Berger/ Ferrari)
4 turbo	16	Austria 1982 (N Piquet/ Brabham - BMW)	- Italy 1986 (T Fabi/ Benetton - BMW)
V6	14	Belgium 1958 (M Hawthorn/ Ferrari)	- Italy 1963 (J Surtees/ Ferrari)
6	10	Belgium 1953 (J M Fangio/ Maserati)	- Argentina 1958 (J M Fangio/ Maserati)
8 supercharged	10	Britain 1950 (G Farina/ Alfa Romeo)	- Italy 1951 (J M Fangio/ Alfa Romeo)
8	8	France 1954 (J M Fangio/ Mercedes-Benz)	- Italy 1955 (J M Fangio/ Mercedes-Benz)
Flat 8	1	Germany 1962 (D Gurney/ Porsche)	

1005. Pole positions but never a win

Toyota	3	Lancia	2
Hart	2	Playlife	1

1006. Milestones: Pole positions

Ferrari	50th: Germany 1970, 100th: Austria 1983, 150th: Malaysia 2002, 200th: France 2008
Renault	50th: Mexico 1986, 100th: Canada 1995, 150th: Spain 2006, 200th: Korea 2012
Cosworth/ Ford Cosworth	50th: Belgium 1973, 100th: Sweden 1978
Mercedes-Benz	50th: Italy 2005, 100th: Australia 2014
Honda	50th: Japan 1989

1007. Front row positions
(number of races in brackets)

Ferrari (a)	472	(359)	Italy 1950 (A Ascari/ Ferrari)	- Singapore 2015 (S Vettel/ Ferrari)
Renault	388	(280)	South Africa 1979 (J-P Jabouille/ Renault)	- Singapore 2015 (D Ricciardo/ Red Bull)
Cosworth (b)	304	(203)	Netherlands 1967 (G Hill/ Lotus)	- Brazil 2010 (N Hülkenberg/ Williams)
Mercedes-Benz	280	(189)	France 1954 (J M Fangio, K Kling/ Mercedes-Benz)	- Abu Dhabi 2015 (N Rosberg, L Hamilton/ Mercedes-Benz)
Honda	160	(116)	Britain 1965 (R Ginther/ Honda)	- San Marino 2006 (J Button/ Honda)
Climax	106	(63)	Monaco 1958 (J Brabham/ Cooper)	- Germany 1966 (J Clark/ Lotus)
BMW	75	(67)	South Africa 1982 (N Piquet/ Brabham)	- Canada 2008 (R Kubica/ BMW Sauber)
BRM	60	(54)	Britain 1956 (M Hawthorn/ BRM)	- Argentina 1973 (C Regazzoni/ BRM)
Alfa Romeo	47	(28)	Britain 1950 (G Farina, L Fagioli, J M Fangio, R Parnell/ Alfa Romeo)	- Detroit 1982 (A De Cesaris/ Alfa Romeo)
Maserati	43	(36)	Monaco 1950 (J F González/ Maserati)	- Mexico 1966 (J Surtees/ Cooper)
Vanwall	22	(12)	Monaco 1957 (S Moss/ Vanwall)	- Morocco 1958 (S Moss, S Lewis-Evans/ Vanwall)
TAG Porsche	21	(20)	San Marino 1984 (A Prost/ McLaren)	- Australia 1987 (A Prost/ McLaren)
Repco	19	(15)	Britain 1966 (J Brabham, D Hulme/ Brabham)	- Canada 1968 (J Rindt/ Brabham)
Toyota	11	(10)	Australia 2005 (J Trulli/ Toyota)	- Japan 2009 (J Trulli/ Toyota)
Matra	10	(10)	France 1970 (J-P Beltoise/ Matra-Simca)	- Spain 1981 (J Laffite/ Talbot-Ligier)
Mugen Honda	6	(6)	Germany 1999 (H-H Frentzen/ Jordan)	- Belgium 2000 (J Trulli/ Jordan)
Gordini	5	(4)	Switzerland 1952 (R Manzon/ Gordini)	- Italy 1952 (M Trintignant/ Gordini)
Lancia	4	(4)	Spain 1954 (A Ascari/ Lancia)	- Belgium 1955 (E Castellotti/ Lancia)
Weslake	4	(4)	Netherlands 1967 (D Gurney/ Eagle)	- Germany 1967 (D Gurney/ Eagle)
Peugeot	3	(3)	Monaco 1994 (M Häkkinen/ McLaren)	- Germany 1997 (G Fisichella/ Jordan)
Porsche	3	(3)	Britain 1961 (J Bonnier/ Porsche)	- Germany 1962 (D Gurney/ Porsche)
Hart	2	(2)	Germany 1985 (T Fabi/ Toleman)	- Belgium 1994 (R Barrichello/ Jordan)
Judd	2	(2)	Brazil 1988 (N Mansell/ Williams)	- Hungary 1988 (N Mansell/ Williams)
Petronas	2	(2)	Austria 1998 (J Alesi/ Sauber)	- France 1999 (J Alesi/ Sauber)
Aston Martin	1	(1)	Britain 1959 (R Salvadori/ Aston Martin)	
Bristol	1	(1)	Netherlands 1952 (M Hawthorn/ Cooper)	
Mecachrome	1	(1)	Italy 1998 (J Villeneuve/ Williams)	
Playlife	1	(1)	Austria 1998 (G Fisichella/ Benetton)	

Includes cases where cars did not make it to the starting grid (see section 405).
(a) Includes Lancia-Ferrari.
(b) As Ford Cosworth until 2004.

1008. Front row positions in a season *(Most)*

Ford Cosworth	33 of 35	1973	(JPS Lotus, 17; McLaren, 9; Tyrrell, 6; Brabham, 1)
Mercedes-Benz	33 of 38	2014	(Mercedes-Benz, 30; Williams, 3)
Mercedes-Benz	33 of 38	2015	(Mercedes-Benz, 30; Williams, 3)
Renault	29 of 34	1995	(Williams, 19; Benetton, 10)
Renault	28 of 32	1993	(Williams)
Honda	27 of 32	1988	(McLaren)
Honda	27 of 32	1989	(McLaren)
Renault	27 of 38	2010	(Red Bull, 26; Renault, 1)
Ford Cosworth	26 of 28	1969	(Lotus, 10; Matra, 6; McLaren, 5; Brabham, 5)
Renault	26 of 32	1992	(Williams)
Renault	26 of 32	1996	(Williams, 25; Benetton, 1)
Renault	26 of 38	2011	(Red Bull)

1009. Races in a season with a front row position *(Most)*

Mercedes-Benz	19 of 19	2014	(Mercedes-Benz, Williams)	Renault	16 of 16	1992	(Williams)
Mercedes-Benz	19 of 19	2015	(Mercedes-Benz, Williams)	Renault	16 of 16	1993	(Williams)
Renault	19 of 19	2011	(Red Bull)	Renault	16 of 16	1996	(Williams, Benetton)
Renault	18 of 19	2010	(Red Bull, Renault)	Renault	16 of 17	1995	(Williams, Benetton)
Ford Cosworth	17 of 17	1977	(McLaren, JPS Lotus, Wolf)	Mercedes-Benz	16 of 17	2007	(McLaren)
Renault	17 of 17	1997	(Williams, Benetton)	Ferrari	16 of 18	2004	(Ferrari)
Honda	16 of 16	1989	(McLaren)	Renault	16 of 19	2013	(Red Bull, Lotus)

1010. Front row position in every race of a season
(apart from those in section 1009)

Ford Cosworth	15	1973	(JPS Lotus, McLaren, Tyrrell, Brabham)
Ford Cosworth	11	1969	(Brabham, Lotus, McLaren, Matra)
Climax	10	1964	(Lotus, Brabham)
Climax	10	1965	(Lotus, Brabham)
Climax	9	1962	(Lola, Lotus, Cooper)
Climax	8	1959	(Cooper)
Ferrari	8	1953	(Ferrari)
Maserati	8	1953	(Maserati)

Maserati	8	1954	(Maserati)
Alfa Romeo	7	1951	(Alfa Romeo)
Ferrari	7	1951	(Ferrari)
Ferrari	7	1952	(Ferrari)
Lancia-Ferrari	7	1956	(Lancia-Ferrari)
Maserati	7	1957	(Maserati)
Alfa Romeo	6	1950	(Alfa Romeo)
Mercedes-Benz	6	1955	(Mercedes-Benz)

1011. Complete front rows
(includes some three and four-car front rows)

Renault	107	France 1979	- United States 2013
Ford Cosworth	73	United States 1967	- Caesars Palace 1981 (a)
Mercedes-Benz	67	Netherlands 1955	- Abu Dhabi 2015 (b)
Ferrari (c)	55	Belgium 1952	- France 2008 (d)
Honda	44	Britain 1986	- Australia 1991
Climax	10	Portugal 1959	- Mexico 1965 (e)

BMW	8	Austria 1982	- Germany 2003
Alfa Romeo	4	Britain 1950	- France 1950 (f)
Repco	1	South Africa 1967	
TAG Porsche	1	Germany 1986	
Toyota	1	Bahrain 2009	
Vanwall	1	Netherlands 1958 (g)	

(a) Includes 16 x three-car front rows.
(b) Includes 2 x three-car front rows.
(c) Includes Lancia-Ferrari.
(d) Includes 8 x three-car front rows.
(e) Includes 6 x three-car front rows.
(f) Includes 3 x three-car and 1 x four-car front rows.
(g) Three-car front row.

1012. Complete front rows in a season *(Most)*
(all were 2-car front rows unless stated)

Mercedes-Benz	15 of 19	2015	(Mercedes-Benz)
Mercedes-Benz	14 of 19	2014	(Mercedes-Benz, Williams)
Ford Cosworth	13 of 15	1973 (a)	(Brabham, Lotus, McLaren, Tyrrell)
Renault	13 of 17	1995	(Benetton, Williams)
Honda	12 of 16	1988	(McLaren)

Renault	12 of 16	1993	(Williams)
Honda	11 of 16	1989	(McLaren)
Honda	10 of 16	1987	(Lotus, Williams)
Renault	10 of 16	1992	(Williams)
Renault	10 of 16	1996	(Benetton, Williams)

(a) Includes 4 x 3-car front rows.
(b) Includes 5 x 3-car front rows.

1013. Different front row position engine makes in a season

Most

1985	6	Ferrari, Honda, Renault, TAG Porsche, BMW, Hart
2004	6	Ferrari, Ford Cosworth, Honda, BMW, Renault, Mercedes-Benz
2005	6	Toyota, Renault, Ferrari, Mercedes-Benz, BMW, Honda
1958	5	Maserati, Ferrari, Vanwall, BRM, Climax
1966	5	Climax, Ferrari, Maserati, BRM, Repco
1967	5	Repco, Ferrari, Ford Cosworth, Weslake, BRM
1968	5	Ford Cosworth, Ferrari, BRM, Repco, Honda
1982	5	Renault, BMW, Ferrari, Alfa Romeo, Ford Cosworth
1984	5	Renault, Ferrari, BMW, Honda, TAG Porsche
1994	5	Renault, Ford Cosworth, Peugeot, Ferrari, Hart
1998	5	Mercedes-Benz, Ferrari, Playlife, Petronas, Mecachrome
1999	5	Mercedes-Benz, Ferrari, Ford Cosworth, Petronas, Mugen Honda
2006	5	Ferrari, Renault, Honda, Cosworth, Mercedes-Benz
2008	5	Mercedes-Benz, BMW, Ferrari, Renault, Toyota

Fewest

1951	2	Alfa Romeo, Ferrari
1953	2	Ferrari, Maserati
1969	2	Ford Cosworth, Ferrari
1974	2	Ford Cosworth, Ferrari

1975	2	Ford Cosworth, Ferrari
1993	2	Renault, Ford Cosworth
1995	2	Renault, Ferrari
2014	2	Mercedes-Benz, Renault

1014. Front row 1-2s

Renault	107	France 1979	- United States 2013		BMW	8	Austria 1982	- Germany 2003
Ford Cosworth	79	Britain 1967	- Caesars Palace 1981		Repco	3	Britain 1966	- South Africa 1967
Ferrari (a)	70	Germany 1951	- France 2008		Vanwall	3	Italy 1957	- Italy 1958
Mercedes-Benz	69	France 1954	- Abu Dhabi 2014		Maserati	2	Argentina 1957	- France 1957
Honda	44	Britain 1986	- Australia 1991		TAG Porsche	1	Germany 1986	
Climax	16	Portugal 1959	- Mexico 1965		Toyota	1	Bahrain 2009	
Alfa Romeo	9	Britain 1950	- Italy 1951					

(a) Includes Lancia-Ferrari.

1015. The same engine make in each of the top six grid positions

United States 1961	Climax		Britain 1973	Ford Cosworth
Germany 1969	Ford Cosworth		Netherlands 1973	Ford Cosworth
Italy 1969	Ford Cosworth		Italy 1973	Ford Cosworth
Canada 1969	Ford Cosworth		Canada 1973	Ford Cosworth
United States 1969	Ford Cosworth		United States 1973	Ford Cosworth
Mexico 1969	Ford Cosworth		Canada 1977	Ford Cosworth
Canada 1972	Ford Cosworth		Argentina 1980	Ford Cosworth
Sweden 1973	Ford Cosworth		Italy 2014	Mercedes-Benz
France 1973	Ford Cosworth			

1016. Different engine make in each of the top grid positions

Top 7	
Austria 1998	1: Playlife, 2: Petronas, 3: Mercedes-Benz, 4: Ferrari, 5: Ford Cosworth, 6: Arrows, 7: Mecachrome
France 1999	1: Ford Cosworth, 2: Petronas, 3: Peugeot, 4: Mercedes-Benz, 5: Mugen Honda, 6: Ferrari, 7: Playlife
Top 6	
Monaco 1985	1: Renault, 2: Honda, 3: Ferrari, 4: Alfa Romeo, 5: TAG Porsche, 6: BMW
Germany 1985	1: Hart, 2: Ferrari, 3: TAG Porsche, 4: Honda, 5: Renault, 6: BMW
China 2004	1: Ferrari, 2: Mercedes-Benz, 3: Honda, 4: Petronas, 5: BMW, 6: Renault

The last time that as many as four different engine makes filled the top six grid positions was Brazil 2010, with Cosworth, Ferrari, Mercedes-Benz and Renault.

1017. Front row positions but never a win

Toyota	11		Hart	2		Bristol	1
Gordini	5		Judd	2		Mecachrome	1
Lancia	4		Petronas	2		Playlife	1
Peugeot	3		Aston Martin	1			

1018. Fastest laps

Ferrari (a)(b)	236	Switzerland 1952 (P Taruffi/ Ferrari)	- Russia 2015 (S Vettel/ Ferrari)
Renault	171	France 1979 (R Arnoux/ Renault)	- Singapore 2015 (D Ricciardo/ Red Bull)
Cosworth (c)	160	Netherlands 1967 (J Clark/ Lotus)	- Bahrain 2006 (N Rosberg/ Williams)
Mercedes-Benz	131	France 1954 (H Herrmann/ Mercedes-Benz)	- Abu Dhabi 2015 (L Hamilton/ Mercedes-Benz)
Honda	57	Mexico 1966 (R Ginther/ Honda)	- Portugal 1992 (A Senna/ McLaren)
Climax (a)	44	Monaco 1959 (J Brabham/ Cooper)	- Monaco 1967 (J Clark/ Lotus)
BMW (a)	33	France 1982 (R Patrese/ Brabham)	- Germany 2008 (N Heidfeld/ BMW Sauber)
Alfa Romeo	20	Britain 1950 (G Farina/ Alfa Romeo)	- Belgium 1983 (A De Cesaris/ Alfa Romeo)
TAG Porsche	18	Brazil 1984 (A Prost/ McLaren)	- Japan 1987 (A Prost/ McLaren)
Maserati (a)	17	Italy 1952 (J F González/ Maserati)	- United States 1966 (J Surtees/ Cooper)
BRM (a)	14	France 1959 (S Moss/ BRM)	- Monaco 1972 (J-P Beltoise/ BRM)
Matra	6	Netherlands 1968 (J-P Beltoise/ Matra)	- Austria 1981 (J Laffite/ Talbot-Ligier)
Vanwall	6	Britain 1957 (S Moss/ Vanwall)	- Morocco 1958 (S Moss/ Vanwall)
Repco	4	Britain 1966 (J Brabham/ Brabham)	- Britain 1967 (D Hulme/ Brabham)
Toyota	4	Belgium 2005 (R Schumacher/ Toyota)	- Europe 2009 (T Glock/ Toyota)
Judd	3	Britain 1988 (N Mansell/ Williams)	- Australia 1989 (S Nakajima/ Lotus)
Hart	2	Netherlands 1982 (D Warwick/ Toleman)	- Monaco 1984 (A Senna/ Toleman)
Weslake	2	Belgium 1967 (D Gurney/ Eagle)	- Germany 1967 (D Gurney/ Eagle)
Gordini (a)	1	Britain 1954 (J Behra/ Gordini)	

Lancia	1	Spain 1954 (A Ascari/ Lancia)
Peugeot	1	Spain 1997 (G Fisichella/ Jordan)
Playlife	1	Argentina 1998 (A Wurz/ Benetton)
Supertec	1	Italy 1999 (R Schumacher/ Williams)

Relates to the number of races, so where for example, 2 cars with a Ford Cosworth engine achieved joint fastest lap in Canada 1969, this is counted as 1.
(a) Includes joint fastest lap(s) with another engine make.
(b) Includes Lancia-Ferrari.
(c) As Ford Cosworth for all of these races except Bahrain 2006.

1019. Fastest laps in a season *(Most)*

Ford Cosworth	15 of 15	1973	(JPS Lotus, 7 *; McLaren, 3 *; Surtees, 2; March, 2; Tyrrell, 2)
Mercedes-Benz	15 of 19	2014	(Mercedes-Benz, 12; Williams, 2; Force India, 1)
Renault	14 of 16	1996	(Williams, 11; Benetton, 3)
Renault	14 of 17	1995	(Benetton, 8; Williams, 6)
Ferrari	14 of 18	2004	(Ferrari)
Renault	14 of 19	2013	(Red Bull, 12; Lotus, 2)
Ferrari	13 of 18	2008	(Ferrari)
Mercedes-Benz	13 of 19	2015	(Mercedes-Benz, 12; Force India, 1)
Ferrari	12 of 17	2002	(Ferrari)
Ferrari	12 of 17	2007	(Ferrari)
Mercedes-Benz	12 of 17	2000	(McLaren)
Mercedes-Benz	12 of 19	2005	(McLaren)

* JPS Lotus and McLaren had one joint fastest lap.

1020. Fastest lap in every race of a season

Ford Cosworth	15	1973	(JPS Lotus, 7 *; McLaren, 3 *; Surtees, 2; March, 2; Tyrrell, 2)
Ford Cosworth	11	1969	(Matra, 6; Brabham, 3; Lotus, 2)
Ferrari	7	1952 (a)	(Ferrari)
Alfa Romeo	7	1951	(Alfa Romeo)
Alfa Romeo	6	1950	(Alfa Romeo)

* JPS Lotus and McLaren had one joint fastest lap.
(a) In Italy, fastest lap was shared with Maserati.

1021. Consecutive fastest laps *(Most)*

Ford Cosworth	21	Britain 1968	- Belgium 1970	(Brabham, Lotus, March, Matra)
Ford Cosworth	17	Canada 1972	- United States 1973	(JPS Lotus, March, McLaren, Surtees, Tyrrell)
Alfa Romeo	13	Britain 1950	- Spain 1951 (a)	(Alfa Romeo)
Renault	11	Portugal 1995	- Monaco 1996	(Benetton, Williams)
Mercedes-Benz	10	Canada 2014	- Russia 2014	(Williams, Force India, Mercedes-Benz)
Ferrari	9	Switzerland 1952	- Netherlands 1953	(Ferrari)
Ferrari	9	Bahrain 2004	- Britain 2004	(Ferrari)
Ferrari	8	Germany 1970	- Spain 1971	(Ferrari)
Honda	8	Monaco 1987	- Italy 1987	(Lotus, Williams)

1022. Different fastest lap engine makes in a season

Most

1954	5	Ferrari, Maserati, Mercedes-Benz, Gordini, Lancia	1984	5	TAG Porsche, Renault, Ferrari, BMW, Hart
1982	5	Renault, Ford Cosworth, Ferrari, Hart, BMW	1989	5	Renault, Honda, Ferrari, Ford Cosworth, Judd
1983	5	BMW, Ford Cosworth, Renault, Alfa Romeo, Ferrari			

Fewest

| 1950 | 1 | Alfa Romeo | 1969 | 1 | Ford Cosworth |
| 1951 | 1 | Alfa Romeo | 1973 | 1 | Ford Cosworth |

1023. Fastest laps but never a win

| Toyota | 4 | Hart | 2 | Lancia | 1 | Playlife | 1 |
| Judd | 3 | Gordini | 1 | Peugeot | 1 | Supertec | 1 |

1024. Milestones: Fastest laps

Ferrari	50th: United States 1970, 100th: San Marino 1985, 150th: Austria 2002, 200th: Europe 2007
Renault	50th: San Marino 1993, 100th: Hungary 1997, 150th: Abu Dhabi 2012
Cosworth/ Ford Cosworth	50th: Sweden 1973, 100th: Austria 1978, 150th: France 1993
Mercedes-Benz	50th: Australia 2003, 100th: India 2012
Honda	50th: Italy 1990

1025. Laps led
Based on actual laps led, even where a disqualification or other penalty was later applied and also where times were aggregated.
All distances led are calculated as complete laps, based on the leader at the end of each lap (actual distances in the lead are not recorded for the official results).

	laps	races	km	miles		
Ferrari (a)	13,947	420	72,585	45,102	Italy 1950	- Singapore 2015
Renault	11,113	300	54,070	33,598	South Africa 1979	- United States 2015
Cosworth (b)	10,684	232	49,233	30,592	Netherlands 1967	- Monaco 2006
Mercedes-Benz	8,194	234	41,382	25,713	France 1954	- Abu Dhabi 2015
Honda	4,885	126	22,485	13,972	Netherlands 1965	- Canada 2008
Climax	2,739	57	14,702	9,135	Argentina 1958	- South Africa 1967
BMW	1,735	79	8,337	5,181	Canada 1982	- Japan 2008
BRM	1,400	41	6,296	3,912	Britain 1956	- Canada 1973
TAG Porsche	1,106	33	5,173	3,214	Brazil 1984	- Portugal 1987
Alfa Romeo	967	25	5,953	3,699	Britain 1950	- Belgium 1983
Maserati	914	25	5,340	3,318	Italy 1952	- South Africa 1967
Repco	500	14	2,417	1,502	France 1966	- Italy 1967
Vanwall	371	12	2,784	1,730	Italy 1956	- Morocco 1958
Mugen Honda	153	9	765	476	Monaco 1996	- Britain 2000
Matra	122	7	679	422	France 1970	- Canada 1981
Toyota	93	12	487	302	Britain 2003	- Belgium 2009
Yamaha	62	1	246	153	Hungary 1997	
Judd	46	2	177	110	Japan 1988	- France 1990
Playlife	28	2	124	77	Canada 1998	- Europe 1999
Peugeot	21	5	117	73	San Marino 1994	- Germany 1997
Lancia	20	2	95	59	Spain 1954	- Argentina 1955
Porsche	20	3	172	107	France 1961	- Germany 1962
Weslake	19	3	330	205	Belgium 1967	- Italy 1967
Supertec	8	1	36	23	Europe 1999	
Talbot-Lago	5	1	71	44	Belgium 1950	
Hart	3	1	13	8	Portugal 1994	
Petronas	3	2	13	8	United States 2003	- Brazil 2004
Gordini	1	1	14	9	Belgium 1952	

(a) Includes Lancia-Ferrari.
(b) Includes Ford Cosworth.

1026. Races led *(Most)*

Ferrari	420		Honda	126		TAG Porsche	33
Renault	300		BMW	79		Alfa Romeo	25
Mercedes-Benz	234		Climax	57		Maserati	25
Cosworth	232		BRM	41			

1027. Distance led *(Longest)*

	km	miles			km	miles			km	miles
Ferrari	72,585	45,102		Honda	22,485	13,972		Alfa Romeo	5,953	3,699
Renault	54,070	33,598		Climax	14,702	9,135		Maserati	5,340	3,318
Cosworth	49,233	30,592		BMW	8,337	5,181				
Mercedes-Benz	41,382	25,713		BRM	6,296	3,912				

1028. Milestones: Turbo engines (1977 - 88)
(turbo engines returned in Australia 2014)

First race for a turbo-engined car: Britain 1977 (Jean-Pierre Jabouille/ Renault)

Last race for a turbo-engined car: Australia 1988 (9 drivers started)

First race in which turbo-powered cars filled all top six finishing positions: Italy 1983
(BMW, Ferrari, Renault, Ferrari, Renault, Hart engines)

Last race in which turbo-powered cars filled all top six finishing positions: Mexico 1988
(2 Honda, 2 Ferrari, 2 Megatron engines)

First all turbo race: Austria 1984

Last all turbo race: Australia 1986

First constructors' title: 1982 (Ferrari)

Last constructors' title: 1988 (McLaren/ Honda)

First drivers' title: 1983 (Nelson Piquet/ BMW)

Last drivers' tltle: 1988 (Ayrton Senna/ Honda)

First turbo win: France 1979 (Jean-Pierre Jabouille/ Renault)

Last turbo win: Australia 1988 (Alain Prost/ Honda)

First turbo 1-2-3: France 1982 (René Arnoux, Alain Prost/ Renault & Didier Pironi/ Ferrari)

Last turbo 1-2-3: Australia 1988 (Alain Prost, Ayrton Senna, Nelson Piquet/ Honda)

First pole position: South Africa 1979 (Jean-Pierre Jabouille/ Renault)

Last pole position: Australia 1988 (Ayrton Senna/ Honda)

First fastest lap: France 1979 (René Arnoux/ Renault)

Last fastest lap: Australia 1988 (Alain Prost/ Honda)

First points: United States 1978 (Jean-Pierre Jabouille/ Renault), 4th

Last points: Australia 1988 (Alain Prost, Ayrton Senna, Nelson Piquet/ Honda), 1st, 2nd, 3rd

Chapter 27: Tyres

(excluding Indianapolis 500)

1029. Races started

Goodyear	495	Belgium 1960	- Japan 1998		Firestone	110	Monaco 1966	- Argentina 1975
Pirelli	299	Britain 1950	- Abu Dhabi 2015		Englebert	32	Belgium 1950	- Morocco 1958
Bridgestone	244	Japan 1976	- Abu Dhabi 2010		Avon	22	San Marino 1981	- Switzerland 1982
Michelin	215	Britain 1977	- Brazil 2006		Continental	13	France 1954	- Argentina 1958
Dunlop	120	Monaco 1958	- Japan 1977					

1030. Wins

Goodyear	368	Mexico 1965 (Richie Ginther/ Honda)	- Italy 1998 (Michael Schumacher/ Ferrari)
Bridgestone	175	Australia 1998 (Mika Häkkinen/ McLaren)	- Abu Dhabi 2010 (Sebastian Vettel/ Red Bull)
Pirelli	140	Britain 1950 (Giuseppe Farina/ Alfa Romeo)	- Abu Dhabi 2015 (Nico Rosberg/ Mercedes-Benz)
Michelin	102	Brazil 1978 (Carlos Reutemann/ Ferrari)	- Japan 2006 (Fernando Alonso/ Renault)
Dunlop	83	Monaco 1958 (Maurice Trintignant/ Cooper)	- Belgium 1970 (Pedro Rodríguez/ BRM)
Firestone	38	Italy 1966 (Ludovico Scarfiotti/ Ferrari)	- Italy 1972 (Emerson Fittipaldi/ JPS Lotus)
Continental	10	France 1954 (Juan Manuel Fangio/ Mercedes-Benz)	- Argentina 1958 (Stirling Moss/ Cooper)
Englebert	8	Monaco 1955 (Maurice Trintignant/ Ferrari)	- Britain 1958 (Peter Collins/ Ferrari)

1031. Milestones: Wins

Goodyear	50th: Monaco 1974, 100th: Germany 1977, 150th: Canada 1983, 200th: Australia 1987, 250th: Brazil 1991, 300th: Spain 1994, 350th: Spain 1997
Bridgestone	50th: France 2001, 100th: Germany 2006, 150th: Europe 2009
Michelin	50th: Monaco 1984, 100th: Canada 2006
Pirelli	50th: Monaco 2012, 100th: Abu Dhabi 2013

Avon is the only tyre manufacturer to compete in the world championship, but achieve no wins or pole positions.

1032. Pole positions

Goodyear	358	Britain 1966 (Jack Brabham/ Brabham)	- Japan 1998 (Michael Schumacher/ Ferrari)
Bridgestone	168	Australia 1998 (Mika Häkkinen/ McLaren)	- Abu Dhabi 2010 (Sebastian Vettel/ Red Bull)
Pirelli	143	Britain 1950 (Giuseppe Farina/ Alfa Romeo)	- Abu Dhabi 2015 (Nico Rosberg / Mercedes-Benz)
Michelin	111	United States West 1978 (Carlos Reutemann/ Ferrari)	- China 2006 (Fernando Alonso/ Renault)
Dunlop	76	Monaco 1958 (Tony Brooks/ Vanwall)	- Canada 1970 (Jackie Stewart/ Tyrrell)
Firestone	49	Monaco 1966 (Jim Clark/ Lotus)	- Argentina 1973 (Clay Regazzoni/ BRM)
Englebert	11	Argentina 1955 (José Froilán González/ Ferrari)	- Morocco 1958 (Mike Hawthorn/ Ferrari)
Continental	8	France 1954 (Juan Manuel Fangio/ Mercedes-Benz)	- Italy 1955 (Juan Manuel Fangio/ Mercedes-Benz)

1033. Milestones: Pole positions

Goodyear	50th: Austria 1974, 100th: Japan 1977, 150th: Brazil 1985, 200th: France 1988, 250th: Germany 1991, 300th: Belgium 1994, 350th: Belgium 1997
Bridgestone	50th: San Marino 2001, 100th: Bahrain 2007, 150th: Bahrain 2010
Michelin	50th: Detroit 1984, 100th: China 2005
Pirelli	50th: China 2011, 100th: Korea 2013
Dunlop	50th: Monaco 1964

1034. Fastest laps

Goodyear	361	Mexico 1965 (Dan Gurney/ Brabham)	- Japan 1998 (Michael Schumacher/ Ferrari)
Bridgestone	170	Australia 1998 (Mika Häkkinen/ McLaren)	- Abu Dhabi 2010 (Lewis Hamilton/ McLaren)
Pirelli	147	Britain 1950 (Giuseppe Farina/ Alfa Romeo)	- Abu Dhabi 2015 (Lewis Hamilton/ Mercedes-Benz)
Michelin	108	Argentina 1978 (Gilles Villeneuve/ Ferrari)	- Japan 2006 (Fernando Alonso/ Renault)
Dunlop	78	Netherlands 1958 (Stirling Moss/ Vanwall)	- Italy 1969 (Jean-Pierre Beltoise/ Matra)
Firestone	42	Monaco 1966 (Lorenzo Bandini/ Ferrari)	- United States 1973 (James Hunt/ March)
Englebert	12	Britain 1954 (Jean Behra/ Gordini)	- Italy 1958 (Phil Hill/ Ferrari)
Continental	9	France 1954 (Hans Herrmann/ Mercedes-Benz)	- Italy 1955 (Stirling Moss/ Mercedes-Benz)

1035. Milestones: Fastest laps

Goodyear	50th: France 1974, 100th: Italy 1977, 150th: Europe 1984, 200th: Detroit 1988, 250th: Britain 1991, 300th: Belgium 1994, 350th: Belgium 1997
Bridgestone	50th: Britain 2001, 100th: Australia 2007, 150th: Brazil 2009
Michelin	50th: Monaco 1984, 100th: China 2005
Pirelli	50th: Italy 1986, 100th: Hungary 2013
Dunlop	50th: Belgium 1964

Appendix 1 In Memoriam

Drivers who have died from motor racing injuries

Grand Prix race starters

Driver	Nat	Car	Formula	Event	Place
1950					
Joe Fry	GB	Freikaiserwagen	Non-F1	Hill-climb	Blandford Camp, Dorset, England
Raymond Sommer	F	Cooper	Non-F1	Haute Garonne Grand Prix F3 race	Cadours, nr Toulouse, France
1952					
Luigi Fagioli	I	Lancia	Non-F1	Monaco sportscar Grand Prix	Monte-Carlo, Monaco
1953					
Charles de Tornaco	B	Ferrari	Non-F1	Modena Grand Prix (F2)	Modena Aerautodrome, Italy
Felice Bonetto	I	Lancia	Non-F1	Carrera Panamericana race	Silao, Mexico
1954					
Guy Mairesse	F	Talbot-Lago	Non-F1	Coupe de Paris practice	Montlhéry, nr Paris, France
Onofré Marimón	RA	Maserati	F1 practice	German Grand Prix	Nürburgring, West Germany
1955					
Alberto Ascari	I	Ferrari	Non-F1	Sportscar testing	Monza, Italy
Pierre Levegh	F	Mercedes-Benz	Non-F1	Le Mans 24 hours race	Le Mans, France
Don Beauman	GB	Connaught	Non-F1	Leinster trophy sportscar race	Rathnew, County Wicklow, Ireland
1956					
Louis Rosier	F	Ferrari	Non-F1	Coupe de Salon sportscar race	Montlhéry, nr Paris, France
1957					
Ken Wharton	GB	Ferrari	Non-F1	Sportscar race	Ardmore, New Zealand
Eugenio Castellotti	I	Ferrari	F1 testing		Modena Aerautodrome, Italy
Alfonso de Portago	E	Ferrari	Non-F1	Mille Miglia sports car race	between Goito and Guidizzolo, Italy
Piero Carini	I	Ferrari	Non-F1	Sportscar race	St Etienne, France
Bill Whitehouse	GB	Cooper	Non-F1	Coupe de Vitesse F2 race	Reims, France
Herbert MacKay-Fraser	USA	Lotus	Non-F1	Coupe de Vitesse F2 race	Reims, France
1958					
Archie Scott Brown	GB	Lister	Non-F1	Sportscar race	Spa-Francorchamps, Belgium
Erwin Bauer	D	Ferrari	Non-F1	1,000 km sportscar race	Nürburgring, West Germany
Luigi Musso	I	Ferrari	F1 race	French Grand Prix	Reims, France
Peter Collins	GB	Ferrari	F1 race	German Grand Prix	Nürburgring, West Germany
Peter Whitehead	GB	Jaguar	Non-F1	Tour de France Automobile	Lasalle, nr Nîmes, France
Stuart Lewis-Evans	GB	Vanwall	F1 race	Moroccan Grand Prix	Casablanca, Morocco
1959					
Jean Behra	F	Porsche	Non-F1	Berlin sportscar Grand Prix race	AVUS, Berlin, West Germany
Ivor Bueb	GB	Cooper	Non-F1	Auvergne Trophy F2 race	Clermont-Ferrand, France
1960					
Harry Blanchard	USA	Porsche	Non-F1	1,000 km sportscar race	Buenos Aires, Argentina
Ettore Chimeri	I	Ferrari	Non-F1	Sportscar practice	Havana, Cuba
Harry Schell	USA	Cooper	Other F1	International trophy practice	Silverstone, England
Chris Bristow	GB	Cooper	F1 race	Belgian Grand Prix	Spa-Francorchamps, Belgium
Alan Stacey	GB	Lotus	F1 race	Belgian Grand Prix	Spa-Francorchamps, Belgium
1961					
Giulio Cabianca	I	Cooper	Non-F1	Intercontinental testing	Modena Aerautodrome, Italy
Wolfgang von Trips	D	Ferrari	F1 race	Italian Grand Prix	Monza, Italy

Driver	Nat	Car	Formula	Event	Place
1962					
Peter Ryan	CDN	Lotus	Non-F1	Coupe de Vitesse des Juniors race	Reims, France
Ricardo Rodríguez	MEX	Lotus	Other F1	Mexican Grand Prix practice	Mexico City, Mexico
1964					
Tim Mayer	USA	Cooper	Non-F1	Tasman championship race practice	Longford, Tasmania, Australia
Carel Godin de Beaufort	NL	Porsche	F1 practice	German Grand Prix	Nürburgring, West Germany
1966					
Walt Hansgen	USA	Ford	Non-F1	Le Mans 24 hours testing	Le Mans, France
John Taylor	GB	Brabham	F1 race	German Grand Prix	Nürburgring, West Germany
1967					
Lorenzo Bandini	I	Ferrari	F1 race	Monaco Grand Prix	Monte-Carlo, Monaco
"Geki"	I	Matra	Non-F1	Italian F3 race	Caserta, nr Naples, Italy
Bob Anderson	GB	Brabham	F1 testing		Silverstone, England
Georges Berger	B	Porsche	Non-F1	Endurance race	Nürburgring, West Germany
Ian Raby	GB	Brabham	Non-F1	Formula 2 race	Zandvoort, Netherlands
1968					
Jim Clark	GB	Lotus	Non-F1	European Formula 2 race	Hockenheim, West Germany
Mike Spence	GB	Lotus	Non-F1	Indianapolis 500 practice	Indianapolis, United States
Ludovico Scarfiotti	I	Porsche	Non-F1	Mountain climb	Rossfeld, West Germany
Jo Schlesser	F	Honda	F1 race	French Grand Prix	Rouen, France
1969					
Lucien Bianchi	B	Alfa Romeo	Non-F1	Le Mans 24 hours testing	Le Mans, France
Paul Hawkins	AUS	Lola	Non-F1	Tourist Trophy race	Oulton Park, England
Moises Solana	MEX	McLaren	Non-F1	Hill-climb	Valle de Bravo, Mexico
Gerhard Mitter	D	BMW	F1 practice	German Grand Prix	Nürburgring, West Germany
1970					
Bruce McLaren	NZ	McLaren	Non-F1	Can-Am car testing	Goodwood, England
Piers Courage	GB	De Tomaso	F1 race	Dutch Grand Prix	Zandvoort, Netherlands
Jochen Rindt	A	Lotus	F1 qualifying	Italian Grand Prix	Monza, Italy
1971					
Ignazio Giunti	I	Ferrari	Non-F1	1,000 km sportscar race	Buenos Aires, Argentina
Pedro Rodríguez	MEX	Ferrari	Non-F1	Interserie sportscar race	Norisring, West Germany
Jo Siffert	CH	BRM	Other F1	Rothmans Victory race	Brands Hatch, England
1972					
Jo Bonnier	S	Lola	Non-F1	Le Mans 24 hours race	Le Mans, France
1973					
Roger Williamson	GB	March	F1 race	Dutch Grand Prix	Zandvoort, Netherlands
François Cevert	F	Tyrrell	F1 qualifying	United States Grand Prix	Watkins Glen, United States
Nasif Estéfano	RA	Ford	Non-F1	Turismo Carretara	Aimogasta, Argentina
1974					
Peter Revson	USA	Shadow	F1 testing		Kyalami, South Africa
Silvio Moser	CH	Lola	Non-F1	1,000 km sportscar race	Monza, Italy
Helmut Koinigg	A	Surtees	F1 race	United States Grand Prix	Watkins Glen, United States
1975					
Mark Donohue	USA	March	F1 practice	Austrian Grand Prix	Österreichring, Austria
1977					
Tom Pryce	GB	Shadow	F1 race	South African Grand Prix	Kyalami, South Africa
1978					
Ronnie Peterson	S	Lotus	F1 race	Italian Grand Prix	Monza, Italy
1980					
Patrick Depailler	F	Alfa Romeo	F1 testing		Hockenheim, West Germany
1982					
Gilles Villeneuve	CDN	Ferrari	F1 qualifying	Belgian Grand Prix	Zolder, Belgium
Riccardo Paletti	I	Osella	F1 race	Canadian Grand Prix	Montréal, Canada
1983					
Rolf Stommelen	D	Porsche	Non-F1	IMSA sportscar race	Riverside, California, United States
1985					
Manfred Winkelhock	D	Porsche	Non-F1	Sportscar race (World Endurance)	Mosport, Ontario, Canada
Stefan Bellof	D	Porsche	Non-F1	Sportscar race (World Endurance)	Spa-Francorchamps, Belgium

Driver	Nat	Car	Formula	Event	Place
1986					
Elio De Angelis	I	Brabham	F1 testing		Paul Ricard, France
Jo Gartner	A	Porsche	Non-F1	Le Mans 24 hours race	Le Mans, France
1994					
Roland Ratzenberger	A	Simtek	F1 qualifying	San Marino Grand Prix	Imola, Italy
Ayrton Senna	BR	Williams	F1 race	San Marino Grand Prix	Imola, Italy
2001					
Michele Alboreto	I	Audi	Non-F1	Sports car testing	Lausitz, Germany
2015					
Jules Bianchi	F	Marussia	F1 race	Japanese Grand Prix (2014)	Suzuka, Japan
Justin Wilson	GB	Dallara	Non-F1	IndyCar race	Pocono, Pennsylvania, United States

Additionally the following grand prix non-starters died from racing injuries:

Jean Lucienbonnet at Enna, Sicily, Italy in 1962 during a Formula Junior race; Brian McGuire at Brands Hatch, England in 1977 during practice for a Shellsport championship race; Dennis Taylor at Monte-Carlo, Monaco in 1962 during the Grand Prix Monaco-Junior race.

Ricardo Rodríguez was the youngest world championship driver to be killed racing, at the age of 20.
A total of 17 drivers have lost their lives from accidents in world championship grand prix races, whilst a further 8 have died during practice and qualifying sessions.
Nürburgring has claimed the most lives among grand prix drivers with a total of seven, two more than Le Mans and Monza.
16 grand prix drivers have died at the wheel of a Ferrari, with Lotus and Porsche resulting in eight driver fatalities each.

Indianapolis 500 race starters
(those who raced in the Formula 1 World Championship 1950 - 60)

Driver	Nat	Event	Place (all United States)
1951			
Walt Brown	USA	Sprint car race	Williams Grove, Pennsylvania
Cecil Green	USA	Sprint car qualifying	Winchester, Indiana
Bill Mackey	USA	Sprint car qualifying	Winchester, Indiana
1952			
Johnny McDowell	USA	Championship car race	Milwaukee, Wisconsin
Jim Rigsby	USA	Sprint car race	Dayton, Ohio
Bill Schindler	USA	Sprint car race	Allentown, Pennsylvania
Joe James	USA	Championship car race	San Jose, California
1953			
Chet Miller	USA	Indianapolis 500 practice	Indianapolis, Indiana
Carl Scarborough	USA	Indianapolis 500 race	Indianapolis, Indiana
1954			
Bobby Ball	USA	Midget car race	Gardena, California
Bob Scott	USA	Championship car race	Darlington, South Carolina
1955			
Larry Crockett	USA	Sprint car race	Langhorne, Pennsylvania
Mike Nazaruk	USA	Sprint car race	Langhorne, Pennsylvania
Manny Ayulo	USA	Indianapolis 500 practice	Indianapolis, Indiana
Bill Vukovich	USA	Indianapolis 500 race	Indianapolis, Indiana
Jerry Hoyt	USA	Sprint car race	Oklahoma City, Oklahoma
Jack McGrath	USA	Championship car race	Phoenix, Arizona
1956			
Walt Faulkner	USA	Stock car qualifying	Valleso, California
Bob Sweikert	USA	Sprint car race	Salem, Indiana
1957			
Keith Andrews	USA	Indianapolis 500 practice	Indianapolis, Indiana
1958			
Pat O'Connor	USA	Indianapolis 500 race	Indianapolis, Indiana
George Fonder	USA	Midget car race	Hartfield, Pennsylvania
Art Bisch	USA	Championship car race	Lakewood, Atlanta, Georgia
Jimmy Reece	USA	Championship car race	Trenton, New Jersey
1959			
Marshall Teague	USA	Championship car testing	Daytona Beach, Florida
George Amick	USA	Championship car race	Daytona Beach, Florida
Jerry Unser	USA	Indianapolis 500 practice	Indianapolis, Indiana
Ed Elisian	USA	Championship car race	Milwaukee, Wisconsin
1960			
Al Herman	USA	Midget car race	West Haven, Connecticut
Jimmy Bryan	USA	Championship car race	Langhorne, Pennsylvania
Johnny Thomson	USA	Sprint car race	Allentown, Pennsylvania

Driver	Nat	Event	Place (all United States)
1961			
Tony Bettenhausen	USA	Indianapolis 500 practice	Indianapolis, Indiana
Al Keller	USA	Championship car race	Phoenix, Arizona
1962			
Shorty Templeman	USA	Midget car race	Marion, Ohio
1964			
Eddie Sachs	USA	Indianapolis 500 race	Indianapolis, Indiana
1966			
Jimmy Davies	USA	Midget car race	Santa Fe, Illinois
Jud Larson	USA	Sprint car race	Reading, Pennsylvania
Don Branson	USA	Sprint car race	Gardena, California
1988			
Cal Niday	USA	Antique car race	Willow Springs, California

Additionally the following Indianapolis 500 non-starters died from racing injuries:
Tony Bonadies at Williams Grove, Pennsylvania in 1964 (Midget car race); Wally Campbell at Salem, Indiana in 1954 (Sprint car practice); Bob Cortner at Indianapolis in 1959 (Indianapolis 500 qualifying); Van Johnson at Williams Grove, Pennsylvania in 1959 (USAC IndyCar race); Frank Luptow at Lakewood, Atlanta, Georgia in 1952 (National Stock car race); Jim Packard at Fairfield, Illinois in 1960 (Midget car race qualifying); Gordon Reid at Dayton, Ohio in 1952 (Sprint car race); Chuck Rodee at Indianapolis in 1966 (Indianapolis 500 qualifying).

Members of the public and race officials who have died from motor racing injuries
(during Formula 1 world championship events)

Argentina 1953 (Buenos Aires no.2)	13 spectators were killed when Giuseppe Farina's Ferrari crashed into the crowd, after swerving to avoid a spectator who was on the track.
Netherlands 1960 (Zandvoort)	A spectator who was in a prohibited area, was killed by Dan Gurney's BRM which suffered brake failure and crashed on the seventh lap.
Italy 1961 (Monza)	15 spectators were killed in the accident between Wolfgang von Trips and Jim Clark, which claimed the life of von Trips who was driving a Ferrari.
Monaco 1962 (Monte-Carlo)	A marshal, Ange Baldoni, was killed from being hit by a right rear wheel from Richie Ginther's BRM, which was involved in an accident with three Lotuses and Dan Gurney's Porsche on the first lap.
Spain 1975 (Montjuïc)	Five spectators were killed when Rolf Stommelen's Hill crashed into a public area.
South Africa 1977 (Kyalami)	A 19-year old race marshal, Frederick Jansen van Vuuren was killed by Tom Pryce's Shadow on the 23rd lap, as he crossed the track to attend to the other Shadow of Renzo Zorzi which had retired from engine failure and caught fire.
Japan 1977 (Fuji)	On lap six, a marshal and a photographer were killed by debris from Gilles Villeneuve's Ferrari which collided with Ronnie Peterson's Tyrrell and cartwheeled off the track. The drivers escaped uninjured.
Belgium 1981 (Zolder)	During Friday practice, Giovanni Amedeo, a mechanic from the Osella team, fell off the pit wall into the path of Carlos Reutemann's Williams. He died in hospital, having suffered a fractured skull.
Italy 2000 (Monza)	Paolo Gislimberti, a 33-year old fire marshal was killed by being hit by a loose wheel from Heinz-Harald Frentzen's Jordan, after a first lap accident involving several cars.
Australia 2001 (Melbourne)	Graham Beveridge, a track marshal was killed on the fifth lap, by a wheel from Jacques Villenueve's BAR which hit him in the chest. The BAR had been in an accident with Ralf Schumacher's Williams.
Canada 2013 (Montréal)	Mark Robinson, a track marshal was driven over by a recovery vehicle which was attending to Esteban Gutiérrez's Sauber, after the end of the race. He died later in hospital.

Appendix 2 Development of Formula 1 Regulations

The Fédération Internationale de l'Automobile (FIA), the governing body of international motorsport has continually revised and added regulations in the interests of safety and to promote a spectacle. Safety has been a priority, requiring speed reduction, as the latest technology has been embraced, producing increasingly faster cars. In recent years, economy and energy conservation have been added to the equation, whilst still encouraging team and driver rivalry and maintaining the show. Here is a selection of notable regulations over the years.

1950 FORMULA 1 DRIVERS' WORLD CHAMPIONSHIP ESTABLISHED
1.5-LITRE SUPERCHARGED or 4.5-LITRE UNSUPERCHARGED ENGINES
RACE LENGTH: MINIMUM 300 KM or 3 HOURS
Maximum capacities of 1.5-litres for supercharged and 4.5-litres for unsupercharged engines. No fuel, weight or dimension restrictions. Races must be a minimum distance of 300 km (186.4 miles) or a duration of 3 hours.

1952 FORMULA 2 (1952 - 53)
500cc SUPERCHARGED or 2-LITRE UNSUPERCHARGED ENGINES
Maximum capacities lowered to 500cc for supercharged and 2-litres for unsupercharged engines (Formula 2 regulations). Crash helmets made compulsory.

1954 FORMULA 1 REGULATIONS RETURN
750cc SUPERCHARGED or 2.5-LITRE UNSUPERCHARGED ENGINES
RACE LENGTH: MINIMUM 500 KM or 3 HOURS
Formula 1 returns with maximum capacities of 750cc for supercharged and 2.5-litres for unsupercharged engines. Races must be a minimum distance of 500 km (310.7 miles) or a duration of 3 hours.

1958 FORMULA 1 CONSTRUCTORS' WORLD CHAMPIONSHIP ESTABLISHED
RACE LENGTH: MINIMUM 300 KM or 2 HOURS, MAXIMUM 500 KM
AVIATION FUEL ONLY
Aviation fuel with an octane rating of 130 now compulsory (alcohol based fuel brews banned). Races must be a minimum distance of 300 km (186.4 miles) or a duration of 2 hours, but must not exceed 500 km (310.7 miles).
(regulations from 1950 to 1960 did not apply to Indianapolis 500 races)

1961 1.3 to 1.5-LITRE UNSUPERCHARGED ENGINES
MINIMUM WEIGHT LIMIT
COMMERCIAL FUEL ONLY
Only unsupercharged engines allowed, of between 1.3 and 1.5-litres. The first weight limit regulation: a minimum dry weight limit of 450 kg (992 lb) (including wheels, oil and coolant, but excluding fuel, tyres, tools and spare wheels). Commercial fuel compulsory, with a maximum octane rating of 100. Fuel tank must be of the flexible aircraft safety type with fire protection. Cars to be fitted with a self-starter, separate emergency braking system, anti-roll bar and standardised seat-belt anchorage. The bodywork must enclose the cockpit or the wheels. No oil replenishment during the race.

1963 FLAG SIGNALLING
Flag signalling code established.

1966 1.5-LITRE SUPERCHARGED or 3-LITRE UNSUPERCHARGED ENGINES
RACE LENGTH: MINIMUM 300 KM, MAXIMUM 400 KM
Engine capacities amended to allow supercharged engines up to a maximum of 1.5-litres as well as normally aspirated engines of 3-litres. Initial minimum dry weight limit raised to 500 kg (1,102 lb). Maximum bodywork height and width restrictions ban the use of dangerous high wings. Races must be a minimum distance of 300 km (186.4 miles), but must not exceed 400 km (248.5 miles).

1969   Maximum rear wing overhang 110 cm (3.6 ft). Maximum width of coachwork ahead of front wheels 150 cm (4.9 ft) and maximum height 80 cm (2.6 ft) above the lowest part of car body. Limits put on aerodynamic aids. Movable aerofoils banned. An exception to the race distance requirement - Monaco allowed to fix a minimum distance of 250 km (155.3 miles).

1970
Safety bladder fuel cell tanks compulsory and to be included in a minimum dry weight limit of 530 kg (1,168 lb).

1971   RACE LENGTH: MINIMUM 250 KM, MAXIMUM 325 KM
Race distance now to be a minimum of 250 km (155.3 miles) at all circuits, and must not exceed 325 km (201.9 miles).

1972
Engines to have a maximum of 12 cylinders (there hadn't been any with 16 cylinders since 1968). Overall car width 130 cm (4.3 ft) maximum to accommodate a "deformable structure" containing no fuel, fuel lines or electric power. A fifteen watt, red rear light mandatory. Initial minimum dry weight limit increased to 550 kg (1,213 lb) to allow for thicker outer skin of the monocoque.

1973   RACE LENGTH: 200 MILES or 2 HOURS
        NUMBERS ALLOCATED TO CARS FOR THE SEASON
Maximum fuel capacity of 250 litres (55 gallons). Initial minimum dry weight limit increased to 575 kg (1,268 lb), to allow for compulsory "deformable structure", fuel tank protection devices. Numbers assigned to cars for the season, with number 1 being allocated to the reigning world champion. Race distance to be 200 miles (321.9 km) or a duration of 2 hours, whichever is the shorter.

1974   TWO BY TWO STARTING GRIDS
Restriction on rear wing overhang to 1 metre (3.3 ft) behind the rear axle line. Self-sealing fuel lines mandatory. Starting grid for all races must be two by two and staggered.

1976   TALL AIRBOXES BANNED
New restrictions limiting rear wing overhang to 80 cm (2.6 ft), front overhang to 120 cm (3.9 ft), overall car width to 215 cm (7.1 ft), maximum wheel width to 53 cm (20.9 inches) and rear wheel/tyre diameter to 33 cm (13 inches). Tall airboxes banned from the Spanish Grand Prix. Additional forward roll-over bar now required.

1977   RACE LENGTH: MINIMUM 250 KM, MAXIMUM 200 MILES or 2 HOURS
        RACES TO BE STARTED BY RED AND GREEN LIGHTS (replacing flag system)
Engine airboxes permitted to a maximum height of 95 cm (3.1 ft) above the ground. All races now started by means of a green light being displayed, within ten seconds of a red light appearing (this system replaced the flag which was raised and dropped to indicate the start of a race). Race distance to be a maximum of 200 miles (321.9 km) or a duration of 2 hours, and be a minimum of 250 km (155.3 miles).

1979
Further rigid dimensional requirements including maximum overall car length of 5 metres (16.4 ft).

1981   1.5-LITRE TURBO or 3-LITRE NON-TURBO ENGINES
        RACE LENGTH: MINIMUM 250 KM, MAXIMUM 320 KM or 2 HOURS
        GROUND-EFFECT CHASSIS DESIGNS LIMITED
All teams must enter their own cars but are permitted to acquire engine and gearbox from an independent manufacturer. Maximum capacities of 1.5-litres for turbocharged and 3-litres for non-turbocharged engines. Ban on sliding aerodynamic skirts - consistent 6 cm (2.4 inches) ground clearance required, to limit ground-effect. Reinforced "Survival cell" extending to the front of the driver's feet introduced. Initial minimum dry weight limit increased to 585 kg (1,290 lb) for turbocharged and 580 kg (1,279 lb) for normally aspirated cars. Race distance to be a maximum of 320 km (198.8 miles) or a duration of 2 hours, and be a minimum of 250 km (155.3 miles).

1982
Rotary, diesel and gas turbine engines banned. Rigid skirts and ride height restrictions removed (it had been difficult to police). Additional driver survival cell cockpit protection requirements featuring compulsory pedal box of 30 cm (11.8 inches) length. Initial minimum dry weight limit now 580 kg (1,279 lb) for all cars.

1983   GROUND-EFFECT CHASSIS OUTLAWED
Cars required to have a flat undertray, and side skirts are banned, reducing ground-effect to near zero. Maximum rear wing width reduced to 100 cm (3.3 ft), rear wing overhang to 60 cm (2 ft) and maximum wing height increased to 100 cm above the ground to improve drivers' vision. Pedal box length must be 50 cm (19.7 inches). Cars with more than four wheels and those with four-wheel drive banned. Initial minimum dry weight limit reduced to 540 kg (1,191 lb).

1984   REFUELLING BANNED DURING RACES
        RACE LENGTH: MINIMUM 300 KM, MAXIMUM 320 KM or 2 HOURS
Refuelling during races now banned. Maximum fuel capacity reduced to 220 litres (48 gallons) with fuel tank required to be in the centre of the car, between driver and engine. Race distance to be a maximum of 320 km (198.8 miles) or a duration of 2 hours. The minimum distance to be covered is 300 km (186.4 miles). The exception is Monaco, being allowed to fix a minimum distance of 260 km (161.6 miles).

1985
Rear wing-size limits. Mandatory crush-box on the car nose. Side step winglets banned.

1986   1.5-LITRE TURBO ENGINES ONLY
To reduce speed, a maximum fuel capacity reduction to 195 litres (43 gallons). 1.5-litre turbocharged engines only permitted.

1987   3.5-LITRE NORMALLY ASPIRATED ENGINES PERMITTED
Normally aspirated engines permitted again, of 3.5-litres with a minimum weight of 500 kg (1,102 lb), instead of the 540 kg limit for turbocharged cars. Engines may have up to 12 cylinders, oval pistons being banned. Fuel limit remained at 195 litres for turbocharged cars, but no limit for those with normally aspirated engines. Pop-off valves compulsory to limit boost pressure to 4.0 bar (to limit turbo power). Normally aspirated cars have their own championship, in which they can gain points towards two new competitions, the Colin Chapman Trophy for constructors and Jim Clark Trophy for drivers. Teams using turbo engines allowed to change engines once in the season to a normally aspirated unit, but those with non-turbos may not switch to turbos. Super-soft, sticky qualifying tyres banned.

1988
Fuel tankage restricted to 150 litres (33 gallons) for cars with turbocharged engines. Also, pop-off valves to allow only 2.5 bar (was 4.0) of boost pressure, further limiting turbo power. No fuel capacity restriction for normally aspirated 3.5-litre engine cars. Driver's feet must be behind front wheel axis, there must be larger mirrors and a quickly detachable steering wheel. No separate normally aspirated competitions (they existed only in 1987).

1989   3.5-LITRE ATMOSPHERIC (NON-TURBO) ENGINES ONLY
RACE LENGTH: MINIMUM 305 KM, MAXIMUM 2 HOURS
Turbocharged engines banned (they had first appeared in 1977). Only atmospheric 3.5-litre engines now permitted. Overhead air intakes allowed again. No maximum amount of fuel, although in-race refuelling remains banned. All drivers subject to dope testing. Race distance to be a minimum of 305 km (189.5 miles), unless the 2 hour maximum time has elapsed. The exception is Monaco, being allowed to fix a minimum distance of 260 km (161.6 miles).

1991
Front wing narrowed from 150 cm (4.9 ft) to 140 cm (4.2 ft). Rear overhang reduced from 60 cm (2 ft) to 50 cm (19.7 inches). Minimum weight limit of cars increased from 500 to 505 kg (1,113 lb).

1993   COMMERCIALLY AVAILABLE UNLEADED FUEL ONLY
SAFETY CAR OFFICIALLY INTRODUCED
To reduce the grip and the speed of cars, the complete wheel width, car width, front overhang and rear wing height further reduced. Distance of front wing endplates above the flat bottom increased. Fuel restricted to the unleaded type, available to the general public. The "Safety Car" officially introduced at every race, to be used for bad weather or obstructions. During safety car periods, only backmarkers are allowed to overtake, to unlap themselves (such unlapping was to be banned from 2010). Pit lane maximum speed limit of 50 km/h (31.1 mph) introduced for the free practice sessions.

1994   REFUELLING RETURNS
BAN ON ELECTRONIC DRIVER AIDS
UNDER CAR SKID BLOCKS MANDATORY
PIT LANE SPEED LIMIT DURING THE RACE
Refuelling during races reintroduced (it had been outlawed from 1984). Ban on electronic driver aids such as active suspension, ABS, traction control, launch control and automatic gearboxes. Additional safety measures introduced during the season including: reducing the size of front wing endplates and rear diffusers; the addition of a 10 mm wooden plank fitted (skid block) to the undertray, to further limit ground-effect; and airbox adjustments. Pit lane maximum speed limit introduced for warm-up and the race, at 120 km/h (74.6 mph). The speed limit throughout practice, now 80 km/h (49.7 mph).

1995   3-LITRE ENGINES ONLY
Engine capacity reduced from 3.5-litres to 3-litres (still up to 12 cylinders allowed). Better cockpit protection required, also higher sidepods, to reduce downforce. An additional 50 mm (1.6 ft) stepped flat bottom and smaller front and rear wings required. Overall car height lowered to 95 cm (3.1 ft). No bodywork permitted above the rear wheels. Increase in the length that the chassis must extend beyond the driver's feet from 15 to 30 cm (5.9 to 11.8 inches). Minimum dry weight limit of cars of 595 kg (1,312 lb) to apply to car and driver together.

1996   RACES STARTED BY FIVE RED LIGHTS (instead of a red and a green light)
NEW CAR NUMBERING SYSTEM (in order of team's position in the previous season)
Front wing endplates to be no more than 10 mm thick, to prevent tyre damage to other cars. Sharp nosecones banned. Cockpit sides raised further, for increased driver head protection. Minimum dry weight limit of the car and driver is increased to 600 kg (1,323 lb). The race start now indicated by five red lights turning on sequentially and going out simultaneously. Car numbers now allocated with the reigning champion in number 1, his team-mate in number 2, and the rest of the teams numbered in order of their finishing position in the previous season.

1998   GROOVED TYRES ONLY (ie SLICKS OUTLAWED)
Grooved tyres mandatory, to replace slicks which had existed since 1971 (four grooves required on the rear and three on the front tyres), to reduce cornering speeds. Cockpit dimensions increased. Width of car reduced from 2 metres to 1.8 metres (5.9 ft). Single fuel bladder mandatory and the fuel connector to be covered.

1999
Number of grooves on front tyres increased from three to four. Flexible wings banned. Each wheel to be tethered to the car by a cable.

2000   3-LITRE V10 ENGINES ONLY
Only 10 cylinder, normally aspirated engines up to 3-litres permitted (all engines had been V10s in 1998 and 99). Towards the end of the season, a ban introduced on the use of cooled fuel during a race.

2001   ELECTRONIC DRIVER AIDS NOW PERMITTED
Electronic driver aids including traction control, launch control and fully automatic transmission permitted from the Spanish Grand Prix (they had been outlawed from 1994). Rear wings must have no more than three elements. Pit lane speed limit reduced to 60 km/h (37.3 mph) in practice and 80 km/h (49.7 mph) during warm up and the race (60 km/h throughout, in Monaco).

2002
Power-assisted steering systems must be controlled manually. Team orders banned after Ferrari's actions in Austria, where Rubens Barrichello was handed victory by team-mate, Michael Schumacher.

2003
Bi-directional telemetry banned. HANS (head and neck safety) system, now mandatory. Teams (except the top three in the previous season's Constructors' Championship) permitted to run a third car in a private testing session at each event. This makes way for an in-season reduction of testing sessions.

2004   ENGINES TO LAST FOR AN ENTIRE RACE WEEKEND
LAUNCH CONTROL & AUTOMATIC TRANSMISSION BANNED
Engines required to last for the entire weekend of a race meeting with an engine change resulting in a 10-place grid penalty (or relegation to the back of the grid, if engine changed after qualifying). Multi-element rear wings banned and two-element wings mandatory. Launch control and fully automatic transmission banned again (had been legal from 2001 to 03). Traction control still permitted. Air ducts for front and rear brake cooling to be lower. Minimum dry weight limit (including driver and fuel) set at 605 kg (1,334 lb) during qualifying and at 600 kg (1,323 lb) at all other times. Teams now permitted to run a third car during the first day of free practice, instead of a separate private testing session. Pit lane speed limit remains at 60 km/h (37.3 mph) in free practice and increased to 100 km/h (62.1 mph) for the remainder of the event.

2005   TYRE CHANGES BANNED DURING QUALIFYING AND THE RACE
ENGINES TO LAST FOR TWO CONSECUTIVE RACE WEEKENDS
Each driver may use no more than one engine for every two event period. Should a driver change an engine during the first of those events, there will be a 10-place grid penalty at both events. If there is a change during the second event, the penalty will apply for that second event. An engine change after qualifying, puts a driver at the back of the starting grid for the race. Penalties are waived, where a driver fails to finish the race for reasons beyond the control of the team or driver. No tyre changes during qualifying and the race, apart from times of puncture or wet weather. Tyre usage for each driver for an event, now limited to four sets of dry-weather (down from 40), four sets of wet-weather (down from 28) and three sets of extreme-weather. Further changes to dimensions of front and rear wings and the car nose, to make overtaking easier. Higher noses required and rear diffuser size reduced, in order to limit downforce. From this season, when a race is stopped, timekeeping will keep running and the race restarted behind the safety car (procedure didn't need to be used until the 2007 European Grand Prix, see chapter 3, section 55).

2006   2.4-LITRE, V8 ENGINES ONLY
TYRE CHANGES PERMITTED, BUT LIMITED
Engine capacity limited to 2.4-litres (previously 3-litres) and the number of cylinders allowed, reduced from ten to eight. All engines must weigh at least 95 kg (209 lb). Tyre changes now permitted throughout each event. Each driver permitted 14 sets per race weekend (seven sets of dry-weather, four sets of wet-weather and three sets of extreme-weather tyres). Restrictions to aerodynamic devices.

2007   SINGLE TYRE SUPPLIER: BRIDGESTONE
DRIVERS MUST USE BOTH AVAILABLE TYRE COMPOUNDS IN EACH RACE
Bridgestone becomes the single contracted tyre supplier after the withdrawal of Michelin. Four compounds of tyre to be produced, two types being available at each race. Drivers must use both the hardest (called "prime") and softest ("option") specification tyre during each race. The limit of sets of tyres for each driver, now 14 dry, 5 wet and 4 extreme-weather (similar for 2008 and 2009). A rev limit of 19,000 rpm introduced and rear wing structure strengthened to prevent flexing. Cockpit warning lights mandatory for the track information system. Teams not allowed to run a third car in free practice, but they can choose to run a third driver in one of their two cars on the first day. Engine change restrictions now only apply on the days of qualifying and the race. Pit lane speed limit remains at 60 km/h (37.3 mph) in free practice, and reduced from 100 to 80 km/h (49.7 mph) for the remainder of the event.

2008   TRACTION CONTROL BANNED
GEARBOXES TO LAST FOR FOUR EVENTS
Gearboxes to last for four consecutive events (otherwise a grid penalty of 5-places). The penalty is waived, where a driver fails to finish the race for reasons beyond the control of the team or driver. Traction control banned for the second and final time (it had been legal since 2001) with all teams using a standard electronic control unit. Sidewalls of the softer tyres now painted green, in order to display the compound. Spare cars no longer permitted.

2009 KERS (Kinetic Energy Recovery System)
ENGINES LIMITED TO EIGHT PER CAR FOR THE SEASON (for race and qualifying)
AERODYNAMIC CHANGES TO FURTHER ASSIST OVERTAKING
SLICK TYRES PERMITTED

Each driver limited to eight race/qualifying engines for the whole season (a 10-place grid penalty is imposed every time an additional one is used). Engines to have a rev limiter set at 18,000 rpm (down from 19,000 rpm), to reduce engine wear. Slick tyres now permitted (keeping to narrow track dimensions) - they had been outlawed since 1998. Front wing maximum width increased from 1,400 mm to 1,800 mm and minimum height reduced from 150 mm to 75 mm. Adjustable flaps in the front wing to be adjusted by drivers up to twice per lap. A reduction of rear wing width from 1,000 mm to 750 mm and an increase in height from 800 mm to 950 mm. The rear diffuser must be longer and higher, and variable front aerodynamic devices permitted (with limited in-car control by driver). These measures are to protect cars from the airflow of the car in front, thus assisting overtaking. Winglets and aerodynamic additions on sidepods banned. The introduction of KERS to store some of the energy normally lost under braking, and convert it into a temporary horsepower increase of around 80 bhp - it can be used for 6.6 seconds per lap by drivers for overtaking (not yet compulsory). Ban on in-season testing, and Formula 1 factories to close for six weeks during the season, to reduce costs. Pit lane speed limit now 60 km/h (37.3 mph) in free practice, and returns to 100 km/h (62.1 mph) for the remainder of the event.

2010 REFUELLING BANNED DURING RACES

In-race refuelling banned again (it had been legal since 1994). Narrower front tyres introduced to improve balance. For each race weekend, each car allocated a maximum of eleven sets of dry-weather tyres (6 "prime" and 5 "option"), four sets of intermediate and three sets of wet-weather tyres. Teams agree not to use KERS (introduced in 2009), in order to allow all teams time to develop and perfect their own systems. Lifting of the ban on team orders from the German Grand Prix onwards, although there is a disrepute clause for the misuse of it. Backmarkers no longer able to unlap themselves behind the safety car. Minimum dry weight limit increased to 620 kg (1,367 lb), to accommodate the KERS system and heavier drivers.

2011 DRS (Drag Reduction System)
GEARBOXES TO LAST FOR FIVE EVENTS
SINGLE TYRE SUPPLIER: PIRELLI

Pirelli becomes the single tyre supplier, replacing Bridgestone. Gearbox life now extended from four to five events. Each driver is allowed one penalty free gearbox change for the season. Double-diffusers banned, with teams required to use simple, single-piece diffusers. The "F-duct" system (the process of a driver directing airflow over the rear wing) is banned, in conjunction with banning shark fins from being connected to the rear wing. Adjustable front wings also banned. Driver adjustable rear wing, known as DRS (Drag Reduction System) introduced to increase straight-line speed and help overtaking. It can be freely used in practice and qualifying, but in the race, only when a driver is within one second of the car in front, and can only be activated in the designated zone of the circuit. The DRS wing must immediately close under braking. DRS is banned during the first two laps of each race and when a track is declared wet. From the Canadian Grand Prix, there will be two DRS zones at most circuits. Teams agree to re-introduce KERS (see 2009), with minimum dry weight limit of cars increasing to 640 kg (1,411 lb), to offset the weight of the KERS device. Doubling of the number of wheel tethers (cables connecting wheel hubs to the bodywork).

2012

The penalty-free gearbox change (see 2011), no longer permitted. Exhaust tail pipes raised. Complete ban of off-throttle blown diffusers (a means of blowing exhaust gases over the car to improve downforce). A re-profiling of the car's nose, lowering the maximum height. Races capped at four hours (including stoppage time in adverse weather), following the long stoppage time in Canada, 2011. Limited in-season testing permitted.

2013

DRS use (see 2011) now applies to the designated zones during free practice and qualifying, in addition to the race. The double-DRS system banned. Minimum car weight without fuel, increased to 642 kg (1,415 lb), to allow for heavier tyres. From the Hungarian Grand Prix, the pit lane speed limit reduced to 80 km/h (49.7 mph) for the entire event.

2014 HYBRID TURBO 1.6-LITRE, V6 ENGINES ONLY
POWER UNITS LIMITED TO FIVE PER CAR FOR THE SEASON
NEW CAR NUMBERING SYSTEM (drivers to choose)

All cars must have hybrid turbocharged 1.6-litre capacity, V6 engines with 8-speed gearbox (turbos last ran in 1988). Engines "power units" must have ERS-K (previously known as KERS) integrated into them. Five power units per car are permitted for the entire season (down from eight engines). Grid penalties are imposed at the first event at which an additional element is used (from five to ten grid places). Replacing a complete power unit above the quota, forces a driver to start the race from the pit lane. Engines to have a rev limiter set at 15,000 rpm (down from 18,000 rpm). Maximum fuel allowed during the race is 100 kg maximum mass, also a fuel flow limit of 100 kg per hour above 10,500 rpm. Electronic braking devices permitted, to assist with the braking of the rear wheels. Lower car noses return (not seen since 2008). Minimum car weight limit increased from 642 kg to 690 kg (1,521 lb), to cater for the heavier battery, the ERS, their cooling systems and the latest tyres. From the Singapore Grand Prix, a restriction on pit-to-car communications, banning any radio transmissions between driver and team or pit boards displaying information that is related to the performance of the driver or their car, such as discussing sector times relative to other cars. Teams permitted to run up to four drivers during the two practice sessions on the first day (in a maximum of two cars). Introduction of the "Virtual Safety Car" after the Japanese Grand Prix. This is for where there is danger which does not warrant the proper safety car - drivers must reduce speed as indicated, during the process. For each race weekend, each car allocated 12 sets of dry-weather tyres (7 of "prime" and 5 of "option" specification), 4 sets of intermediate and 3 sets of wet-weather tyres. Penalty points system introduced for dangerous driving. Car numbering changed with drivers choosing their preferred number to use for the rest of their careers. Number 1 would continue to be reserved for the reigning world champion each season, should he wish to use it.

**2015   POWER UNITS LIMITED TO FOUR OF EACH ELEMENT, PER CAR FOR THE SEASON
GEARBOXES TO LAST FOR SIX EVENTS**

Each car now restricted to using four of each power unit element during the season. This increased during the season to five for new engine manufacturers, namely Honda (penalties outlined below). The overall weight of the power unit must be a minimum of 145 kg (320 lb). The Energy Store must be installed wholly within the survival cell and must weigh between 20 kg (44 lb) and 25 kg (55 lb). Each driver may use no more than one gearbox for six consecutive events (penalties outlined below). For each race weekend, each car allocated 13 sets of dry-weather tyres (7 of "prime" and 6 of "option"), 4 sets of intermediate and 3 sets of wet-weather tyres. Colours on tyres changed to orange markings (hard compound), white (medium), yellow (soft) and red (super-soft). For wet conditions, green (intermediate tyres) and blue (full wet tyres). Car nose regulations from 2014, relaxed to make them lower and thus more attractive, following criticism. Front and rear interconnected suspension systems banned. Titanium skid blocks on the underside of cars made mandatory. From the Belgian Grand Prix, teams not allowed pit-to-car communication relating to the start of the race. Minimum car weight increased to 702 kg (1,548 lb). Drivers must be at least 18-years old to qualify for a super-licence, to race in F1.

Current power unit and gearbox penalties:

Power unit - Each driver is permitted to use only four of each of the six power unit elements during a season. Grid penalties are imposed for drivers using more than this quota. The six elements are: internal combustion engine (ICE); motor generator unit-kinetic (MGU-K); motor generator unit-heat (MGU-H); energy store (ES); turbocharger (TC); and control electronics (CE). The penalties imposed for using additional elements are: the first time a fifth of any of the elements is used, a ten-place grid penalty; the first time a fifth of any of the remaining elements is used, a five-place grid penalty; the first time a sixth of any of the elements is used, a ten-place grid penalty, and so on. Gearbox - Every additional gearbox used above the quota of one for each six race sequence, results in a five-place grid penalty at that race and an additional five places at each race where a further gearbox is used. Unless the driver fails to finish the race (or is unable to start the race for reasons other than a penalty imposed by the stewards), the gearbox fitted to the car at the end of the event, must remain for the remainder of the six race sequence. Any driver who failed to finish the race at the first, second, third, fourth or fifth of the six events, may start the following event with a different gearbox without a penalty being incurred.

Point scoring systems are explained at sections 461 (for drivers) and 883 (for constructors).
For the history of car numbering, see chapter 2.
For the history of the "Safety Car", see chapter 3, section 52.
For the history of Pre-Qualifying, see chapter 25, section 960.

Appendix 3 Development of Formula 1 Qualifying Procedures

Starting grids for races have been decided by different methods over the years. In the early days, there were often numerous or lengthy practice sessions, to identify fastest and slowest, whilst now there's the strictly regulated, knock-out qualifying hour. These pages provide a guide to systems in place since the establishment of Formula 1.

"Day 1" relates to Friday (apart from Monaco which is traditionally held on Thursday, to allow for other formula events on Friday), "Day 2" is Saturday and "Day 3" Sunday. Until 1985, occasional races, such as the British Grand Prix at Silverstone, were held on Saturday, meaning that practice days fell on Thursday (Day 1) and Friday (Day 2).

1950

Prior to 1976, there was no ruling on the schedule of qualifying. At some grands prix, there were as many as six sessions, simply named "Practice", usually being held during the two days preceding the race, although at some events, they began as early as Wednesday. Normally all sessions counted towards starting grid positions for the race, those positions being determined by each driver's fastest lap time. There were exceptions, such as at Monaco 1950, where first practice decided the top three, and the rest of the grid was decided the following day. From 1969, the regulations required at least three periods of practice of at least 1 hour each. The maximum number of cars permitted to start each race was 26 (the limit at Monaco was 16 for many years, between 1972 and 1974 it was relaxed, and in 1975 the limit was 18). The warm-up on race day morning became a regular feature from 1972.

An example from 1968 (the United States Grand Prix) -

Day 1 - pm:	1st PRACTICE - 4 hours (both timed)
Day 2 - pm:	2nd PRACTICE - 4 hours (both timed)
Day 3 - pm:	RACE

An example from 1975 (the French Grand Prix) -

Day 1 - am & pm:	1st & 2nd PRACTICE - 1 hour 30 minutes each (both timed)
Day 2 - pm & pm:	3rd & 4th PRACTICE - 1 hour 30 minutes + 1 hour (both timed)
Day 3 - am:	WARM-UP (untimed practice) - 45 minutes
Day 3 - pm:	RACE

1976

Whilst there was still no specific schedule, the FIA introduced a minimum length of practice (ie timed sessions). Practice had to total at least 2 hours, the time being divided into two equal parts by a minimum interval of 4 hours. Should the two sessions take place on different days, each session could be divided and there had to be an interval of at least 1 hour between the two parts. Each session or division of a session had to last a minimum of 1 hour. With this new ruling, and given that overall practice was normally in excess of the 2 hours, circuits made one or more sessions untimed (day two's morning session was usually untimed). The starting grid at each event would be based on the order of the fastest time achieved by each driver, taking all timed practice sessions into account. The maximum number of cars permitted to start each race was 26 (the limit at Monaco was 20 during this period).

Typical timetable (the 1977 Swedish Grand Prix) -

Day 1 - am & pm:	1st & 2nd PRACTICE - 1 hour 30 minutes & 1 hour (both timed)
Day 2 - am & pm:	3rd & 4th PRACTICE - 1 hour 30 minutes (untimed) & 1 hour (timed)
Day 3 - am:	WARM-UP (untimed practice) - 30 minutes
Day 3 - pm:	RACE

From Argentina 1978 (until Austria 1997) there were often acclimatisation practice sessions, for the new circuits and those which had been significantly modified. Those sessions were normally held on the Thursday, the day prior to normal practice.

1980

This was the first season where the FIA laid down a standardised schedule to grand prix practice. The 2 hour minimum timed practice period remained, with practice sessions officially becoming known as "Official Timed Practice" and "Untimed Practice". All laps covered during the two timed sessions, determined each driver's position on the starting grid. The maximum number of cars permitted to start each race was 26 (20 at Monaco until 1986).

Timetable

Day 1 - am:	1st UNTIMED PRACTICE - 1 hour 30 minutes
Day 1 - pm:	1st OFFICIAL TIMED PRACTICE - 1 hour
Day 2 - am:	2nd UNTIMED PRACTICE - 1 hour 30 minutes
Day 2 - pm:	2nd OFFICIAL TIMED PRACTICE - 1 hour
Day 3 - am:	WARM-UP (untimed practice) - 30 minutes
Day 3 - pm:	RACE

The number of cars allowed in Official Timed Practice was limited to 30, so pre-qualifying was necessary where the number exceeded that. The following procedure was used: 26 places in Official Timed Practice were reserved for constructors with the best record over the previous two half-seasons. The remaining four places were made available to those who were fastest in Pre-Qualifying Practice. That session would take place within the first Untimed Practice (34 cars maximum). The fastest four of those not automatically eligible for Official Timed Practice, would be allowed to progress to the remaining practice sessions.

- At Monaco, until 1986, the limit was 26 cars in Official Timed Practice, where 22 places were reserved for constructors based on their performance in the previous two half-seasons.
- The use of treaded tyres (for wet or damp conditions) was unlimited. Otherwise each driver could use a maximum of 8 tyres during each timed practice session. The race number of each driver and a letter indicating the location of the race, were painted on the outer face of tyres, to identify tyre usage. Different colour paints were used for each session.

1989

There was a change of terminology for 1989: "Official Timed Practice" became known as "Qualifying Practice", whilst "Untimed Practice" became "Free Practice". A separate 1 hour "Pre-Qualifying Practice" was required for most of the races during this period, as the number of entrants exceeded the number permitted in Free Practice. The starting grid was drawn up in the order of the fastest time achieved by each driver taking both qualifying practice sessions into account, the fastest starting from pole position. There remained a limit of 26 cars which could take part in each race.

Timetable

Day 1 - am:	PRE-QUALIFYING PRACTICE (if necessary) - 1 hour;
	1st FREE PRACTICE - 1 hour 30 minutes
Day 1 - pm:	1st QUALIFYING PRACTICE - 1 hour
Day 2 - am:	2nd FREE PRACTICE - 1 hour 30 minutes
Day 2 - pm:	2nd QUALIFYING PRACTICE - 1 hour
Day 3 - am:	WARM-UP (free practice) - 30 minutes
Day 3 - pm:	RACE

(At the South African Grand Prix in 1993, the first race of the season, all practice sessions were trimmed to 45 minutes each).

Throughout this period, the number of cars entered usually exceeded the maximum number that was allowed in Free Practice (34). So, when necessary, a separate 1 hour Pre-Qualifying Practice session was held on the first morning. 26 cars would be exempt (those from constructors with the best record over the previous two half-seasons). The four fastest in Pre-Qualifying would advance to Free and Qualifying Practice. Otherwise, with 34 cars or fewer entered, the procedure for 1988, was used. After Hungary 1992, there was no requirement for pre-qualifying, with the number of entrants being fewer.
For the history of Pre-Qualifying, see Chapter 25, section 960.

- From 1993, there was a 12 lap limit in each of the two Qualifying Practice sessions, and a limit of 23 laps per driver in each Free Practice (completing more laps resulted in all times for a driver being cancelled).
- The previous limit of 8 tyres per driver during each Qualifying Practice remained, and there was a limit of 12 per driver during Pre-Qualifying Practice.

1994

The qualifying system from 1993 remained. However, Free Practice was divided up into four sessions, still amounting to 3 hours in total. Pre-Qualifying was no longer required.

Timetable

Day 1 - am:	1st & 2nd FREE PRACTICE - 45 minutes each
Day 1 - pm:	1st QUALIFYING PRACTICE - 1 hour
Day 2 - am:	3rd & 4th FREE PRACTICE - 45 minutes each
Day 2 - pm:	2nd QUALIFYING PRACTICE - 1 hour
Day 3 - am:	WARM-UP (free practice) - 30 minutes
Day 3 - pm:	RACE

- There was still the 12 lap limit for each driver in each Qualifying Practice, and also the 23 lap limit per driver per day in Free Practice.
- From 1994, there was no specific limit to the number of tyres used for qualifying. Instead, there was a limit of 28 tyres for the duration of the event (except for treaded tyres on a wet or damp track).

1996
Qualifying was amended with the Friday session abolished in favour of a single session on Saturday afternoon. The starting grid for the race was drawn up in the order of the fastest time achieved by each driver in Qualifying Practice (all laps counting). The two Free Practice sessions on the first day were extended to one hour each.

Timetable

Day 1 - am:	1st FREE PRACTICE - 1 hour
Day 1 - pm:	2nd FREE PRACTICE - 1 hour
Day 2 - am:	3rd & 4th FREE PRACTICE - 45 minutes each
Day 2 - pm:	QUALIFYING PRACTICE - 1 hour
Day 3 - am:	WARM-UP (free practice) - 30 minutes
Day 3 - pm:	RACE

- Each driver was still limited to 12 laps in Qualifying Practice. The number of laps allowed on each day of Free Practice increased from 23 to 30.
- Prior to qualifying, each driver had to nominate which specification of tyre he would use for the remainder of the weekend.
- Since 1996, there has been an increasing limitation on the use of tyres: a certain number limited for use on the first day; and limits on the number that could be used during qualifying and the race.

2003
For 2003, it was a return to Friday and Saturday afternoon qualifying. However, in both, each driver would complete just one single timed lap. Saturday's lap times would determine the starting grid order. Free Practice on the first day was reduced to a single 1 hour session and there was no limit to the number of laps covered by each driver. A private test session on the first day, enabled teams to run a third car. Warm-up was brought forward to the day before the race.

Timetable

Day 1 - am:	Private Test - 2 hours;
	1st FREE PRACTICE - 1 hour
Day 1 - pm:	1st QUALIFYING PRACTICE - 1 hour
Day 2 - am:	2nd & 3rd FREE PRACTICE - 45 minutes each
Day 2 - pm:	WARM-UP (free practice) - 15 minutes;
	2nd QUALIFYING PRACTICE - 1 hour
Day 3 - pm:	RACE

The two sessions of qualifying (Friday and Saturday afternoons):
1) During this session, each driver will be permitted to complete only one timed lap. Each will leave the pit lane to complete this lap in the order of the current drivers' World Championship standings. At the first race of the year, this order will be determined by the finishing order of the 2002 Championship. Any new drivers will be arranged in numerical order. Each driver will be able to complete his lap whilst no other car is on the track.
2) During this session, each driver will be permitted to complete only one timed lap. Each will complete this lap in the reverse order of times achieved during the first qualifying session (the slowest driver going first). Each driver will be able to complete his lap whilst no other car is on the track.

- The grid will be drawn up in the order of the fastest time achieved by each driver in the second session. The fastest driver will start the race from pole position on the grid.
- Fuel may not be added to nor removed from a car during a qualifying practice session.
- Prior to the second qualifying practice, each driver must nominate which specification of tyre he will use for the remainder of the event.

2004
Qualifying remained as single timed laps, but was now in a two part session on Saturday afternoon. Each driver's time from the second part, determined their grid position. Free Practice was back to four sessions and there was no longer a warm-up. Each team (except those finishing in the top four in 2003) was permitted to run a third car for their reserve drivers during both Free Practice sessions on the first day.

Timetable

Day 1 - am:	1st FREE PRACTICE - 1 hour
Day 1 - pm:	2nd FREE PRACTICE - 1 hour
Day 2 - am:	3rd & 4th FREE PRACTICE - 45 minutes each
Day 2 - pm:	1st & 2nd QUALIFYING PRACTICE
Day 3 - pm:	RACE

The qualifying practice session comprised two parts on the Saturday afternoon, separated by two minutes:
1) Each driver will carry out a single timed lap in the order they were classified at the end of the previous race (the best going first). Any drivers who were not classified will be arranged according to the number of laps they completed during that race, the one with the most laps going first. At the first race of the year, the order of the last race of 2003 will be used. Any new drivers will be arranged in numerical order.

2) Each driver will carry out a single timed lap. The running order for the second part will be determined by the times achieved in the first part, with the slowest driver going first.

- The grid will be drawn up in the order of the fastest time achieved by each driver in the second part of qualifying. The fastest driver will start the race from pole position on the grid.
- If a car stops on the circuit, the driver concerned will not be permitted to take any further part in that part of the session.
- Fuel may not be added to nor removed from a car between the start of the second part of qualifying practice and the start of the race.
- Prior to the second part of qualifying practice, each driver must nominate which specification of tyre he will use for the remainder of the event.

2005

There was a revised qualifying format for 2005, the season starting off with qualifying split over two days. Each driver did one timed lap each day (one on Saturday afternoon and one on Sunday morning), and had their times from the two sessions aggregated, to determine their grid position for the race. That was for the first six races, until the Monaco Grand Prix. From the European Grand Prix, there was a single qualifying session on the Saturday. There remained four Free Practice sessions and each team (except those finishing in the top four in 2004) was permitted to run a third car for their reserve drivers during both of those sessions on the first day.

Timetable (until the Monaco Grand Prix)

Day 1 - am:	1st FREE PRACTICE - 1 hour
Day 1 - pm:	2nd FREE PRACTICE - 1 hour
Day 2 - am:	3rd & 4th FREE PRACTICE - 45 minutes each
Day 2 - pm:	PRE-QUALIFYING PRACTICE
Day 3 - am:	QUALIFYING PRACTICE
Day 3 - pm:	RACE

The two sessions of qualifying on Saturday and Sunday (until the Monaco Grand Prix):
1) Each driver will carry out a single timed lap. The running sequence for this session will be the previous race classification reversed (the lowest going first). Drivers who were not classified will be arranged according to the number of laps they completed, the one with the most laps going last. At the first race of the year, the order of the last race of 2004 will be used. Any new drivers will be arranged in numerical order.
2) The running sequence for the timed lap in the second session will be the first session order reversed (the slowest going first).

- The grid will be drawn up in the order of the fastest aggregate time achieved by each driver, taking into account both qualifying practice sessions. The fastest driver will start the race from pole position on the grid.
- If a car stops on the circuit, the driver concerned will not be permitted to take any further part in that session.
- Fuel may not be added to nor removed from a car between the start of the second qualifying practice and the start of the race.
- Prior to the second day of practice, each driver must nominate which specification of tyre he will use for the remainder of the event. One set of dry-weather tyres must be used for both of the qualifying sessions, all reconnaissance laps and the entire race. Only a punctured or damaged tyre may be changed.

Timetable (from the European Grand Prix)

Day 1 - am:	1st FREE PRACTICE - 1 hour
Day 1 - pm:	2nd FREE PRACTICE - 1 hour
Day 2 - am:	3rd & 4th FREE PRACTICE - 45 minutes each
Day 2 - pm:	QUALIFYING PRACTICE
Day 3 - pm:	RACE

From the European Grand Prix, one qualifying session on Saturday afternoon:
During the session, each driver will carry out a single timed lap, the running sequence being the reverse order of their classification at the previous race (the lowest going first). Drivers who were not classified will be arranged according to the number of laps they completed, the one with the most laps going last. Any new drivers will be arranged in numerical order.

2006

A major change to the qualifying format, a one hour session split into a three-stage knock-out, with the slowest cars being excluded after each of the first two periods, leaving a final period for the fastest ten. The grid was drawn up with those excluded in the first period, occupying the lowest grid positions, and so on, with the top ten positions being occupied by those reaching the third period, the fastest, occupying pole position. Free Practice became three 1 hour sessions - in 2007, those on the first day were extended to 1 hour 30 minutes each. Teams (for 2006, except those finishing the previous season in the top four) were permitted to use their reserve drivers in additional cars during both Free Practice sessions on the first day. From 2007, a third car was no longer permitted.

Timetable

Day 1 - am:	1st FREE PRACTICE (P1) - 1 hour
Day 1 - pm:	2nd FREE PRACTICE (P2) - 1 hour
Day 2 - am:	3rd FREE PRACTICE (P3) - 1 hour
Day 2 - pm:	QUALIFYING PRACTICE (Q1, Q2 & Q3) - 1 hour in three periods
	(15 + 15 + 20 minutes until United States, 15 + 15 + 15 minutes from France onwards)
Day 3 - pm:	RACE

The three-stage Saturday afternoon qualifying session (based on an entry of 24 cars):

Q1) All cars will be permitted on the track and at the end of this period, the slowest 7 cars, taking into account only laps which were completed before the end of the period, will be prohibited from taking any further part in the session. Lap times achieved by the 17 remaining cars will then be deleted.

Q2) The 17 remaining cars will be permitted on the track and at the end of this period, the slowest 7 cars, taking into account only laps which were completed before the end of the period, will be prohibited from taking any further part in the session. Lap times achieved by the 10 remaining cars will then be deleted.

Q3) The 10 remaining cars will be permitted on the track.

The procedure can be adjusted as follows: When 22 cars are entered, 6 are excluded after each of the first two periods of qualifying. When 20 are entered, 5 are excluded after each of the first two periods. Throughout 2006, there were 22 entrants. This rose to 24 in 2010, was back to 22 in 2013, and had decreased to 20 entrants by 2014.

- The grid will be drawn up as follows (based on 24 cars):
i) The last 7 positions will be occupied by the cars eliminated during the first period of qualifying, the fastest in 18th position.
ii) The next 7 positions will be occupied by the cars eliminated during the second period of qualifying, the fastest in 11th position.
iii) The top ten positions will be occupied by the cars which took part in the third period of qualifying, the fastest starting the race from pole position on the grid.

- Any driver whose car stops on the circuit during the qualifying session, will not be permitted to take any further part in the session.
- Fuel: 2006 and 2007 - "Fuel may not be added to nor removed from any car eligible to take part in Q3, during that qualifying period. Fuel used during Q3 may be replaced on the day of the race. Otherwise there is to be no refuelling between the end of qualifying and the start of the race." For 2008 and 2009 fuel used in Q3 could not be replaced prior to the start of the race. With the in-race refuelling ban from 2010, cars were able to run in Q3 on a low fuel load, and later, be refuelled for the start of the race.
- Tyres: Until 2009, tyre changes were permitted during qualifying and the race. Between 2010 and 2013, cars which had run in Q3, had to start the race fitted with the same tyres on which the driver set his grid time. From 2014, the tyres used by cars running in Q3 could not be used again in the event. Instead those ten drivers in Q3, had to start the race fitted with the tyres with which the driver set his fastest time during Q2. These rulings related to when dry-weather tyres were used. Should the tyres be confirmed to be damaged, they were allowed to be replaced.
- From the German Grand Prix of 2006, in Q1 and Q2, the times of all laps begun at the end of the period, were recorded.
- From the start of 2008, the first period of qualifying was extended to 20 minutes, while the final period was shortened to 10 minutes.
- From 2014, the first period of qualifying would be 18 minutes (instead of 20), with the final period being 12 minutes (instead of 10).

Currently
The three-stage knock-out procedure established in 2006 remains, the slowest cars being excluded after each of the first two periods, leaving a final period for the fastest ten. The grid is drawn up with those excluded in the first period, occupying the lowest grid positions, and so on, with the top ten positions being occupied by those reaching the third period, the fastest, occupying pole position. There are three Free Practice sessions, two of 1 hour 30 minutes and one of 1 hour. Teams are permitted to use their reserve drivers during both Free Practice sessions on the first day.

Timetable

Day 1 - am:	1st FREE PRACTICE (P1) - 1 hour 30 minutes	
Day 1 - pm:	2nd FREE PRACTICE (P2) - 1 hour 30 minutes	
Day 2 - am:	3rd FREE PRACTICE (P3) - 1 hour	
Day 2 - pm:	QUALIFYING PRACTICE (Q1, Q2 & Q3) - 1 hour in three periods (18 + 15 + 12 minutes)	
Day 3 - pm:	RACE	

The three-stage Saturday afternoon qualifying session (based on an entry of 22 cars):

Q1) All cars will be permitted on the track and at the end of this period, the slowest 6 cars, will be prohibited from taking any further part in the session. Lap times achieved by the 16 remaining cars will then be deleted.

Q2) The 16 remaining cars will be permitted on the track and at the end of this period, the slowest 6 cars, will be prohibited from taking any further part in the session. Lap times achieved by the 10 remaining cars will then be deleted.

Q3) The 10 remaining cars will be permitted on the track.

The procedure can be adjusted as follows: When 20 cars are entered (as was the case throughout 2015), 5 are excluded after Q1. When 24 are entered, 7 are excluded after Q1.

- The grid will be drawn up as follows (based on 22 cars):
i) The last 6 positions will be occupied by the cars eliminated during the first period of qualifying, the fastest in 17th position.
ii) The next 6 positions will be occupied by the cars eliminated during the second period of qualifying, the fastest in 11th position.
iii) The top ten positions will be occupied by the cars which took part in the third period of qualifying, the fastest starting the race from pole position on the grid.

- Any driver whose car stops on the circuit during the qualifying session, will not be permitted to take any further part in the session.
- Cars are permitted to be refuelled prior to the race.
- Tyres: One set of "option" specification tyres may only be used during Q3, by those cars that qualified for Q3, and must be returned before the start of the race. One set of "option" specification tyres, which were allocated to cars which did not qualify for Q3, may be used during the race. At the start of the race each car which qualified for Q3 must be fitted with the tyres with which the driver set his fastest time during Q2. This will only apply if dry-weather tyres are used to set the fastest time in Q2 and if dry-weather tyres are used at the start of the race.

Appendix 4 Race Results: Quick Reference Guide

Engine configurations:

4, 6, 8	- straight / in-line
F4, F8, F12	- flat or boxer
H16	- double flat
V6, V8, V10, V12	- V formation
s	- supercharged
t	- turbocharged

1950

Date	RACE (Circuit)	Car & model -
Position	Driver	Engine & configuration

1) 13 May - BRITAIN (Silverstone)

1/ PP/ FL)	Giuseppe Farina	Alfa Romeo 158 - 8s
2)	Luigi Fagioli	Alfa Romeo 158 - 8s
3)	Reg Parnell	Alfa Romeo 158 - 8s

2) 21 May - MONACO (Monte-Carlo)

1/ PP/ FL)	Juan Manuel Fangio	Alfa Romeo 158 - 8s
2)	Alberto Ascari	Ferrari 125 - V12s
3)	Louis Chiron	Maserati 4CLT/48 - 4s

3) 30 May - INDIANAPOLIS 500 (Indianapolis)

1/ FL)	Johnnie Parsons	Kurtis-Kraft - Offenhauser 4
2)	Bill Holland	Deidt - Offenhauser 4
3)	Mauri Rose	Deidt - Offenhauser 4
PP)	Walt Faulkner	Kurtis-Kraft 2000 - Offenhauser 4

4) 4 Jun - SWITZERLAND (Bremgarten)

1/ FL)	Giuseppe Farina	Alfa Romeo 158 - 8s
2)	Luigi Fagioli	Alfa Romeo 158 - 8s
3)	Louis Rosier	Talbot-Lago T26C-DA - 6
PP)	Juan Manuel Fangio	Alfa Romeo 158 - 8s

5) 18 Jun - BELGIUM (Spa-Francorchamps)

1)	Juan Manuel Fangio	Alfa Romeo 158 - 8s
2)	Luigi Fagioli	Alfa Romeo 158 - 8s
3)	Louis Rosier	Talbot-Lago T26C-DA - 6
PP/ FL)	Giuseppe Farina	Alfa Romeo 158 - 8s

6) 2 Jul - FRANCE (Reims-Gueux)

1/ PP/ FL)	Juan Manuel Fangio	Alfa Romeo 158 - 8s
2)	Luigi Fagioli	Alfa Romeo 158 - 8s
3)	Peter Whitehead	Ferrari 125 - V12s

7) 3 Sep - ITALY (Monza)

1)	Giuseppe Farina	Alfa Romeo 158 - 8s
2=)	Dorino Serafini &	
2=)	Albert Ascari	Ferrari 375 - V12
3)	Luigi Fagioli	Alfa Romeo 158 - 8s
PP/ FL)	Juan Manuel Fangio	Alfa Romeo 158 - 8s

Drivers' championship

1) Giuseppe Farina   30
2) Juan Manuel Fangio   27
3) Luigi Fagioli   24

1951

1) 27 May - SWITZERLAND (Bremgarten)

1/ PP/ FL)	Juan Manuel Fangio	Alfa Romeo 159 - 8s
2)	Piero Taruffi	Ferrari 375 - V12
3)	Giuseppe Farina	Alfa Romeo 159 - 8s

2) 30 May - INDIANAPOLIS 500 (Indianapolis)

1/ FL)	Lee Wallard	Kurtis-Kraft - Offenhauser 4
2)	Mike Nazaruk	Kurtis-Kraft - Offenhauser 4
3=)	Jack McGrath &	
3=)	Manny Ayulo	Kurtis-Kraft 3000 - Offenhauser 4
PP)	Duke Nalon	Kurtis-Kraft - Novi 8s

3) 17 Jun - BELGIUM (Spa-Francorchamps)

1)	Giuseppe Farina	Alfa Romeo 159 - 8s
2)	Alberto Ascari	Ferrari 375 - V12
3)	Luigi Villoresi	Ferrari 375 - V12
PP/ FL)	Juan Manuel Fangio	Alfa Romeo 159 - 8s

4) 1 Jul - FRANCE (Reims-Gueux)

1=)	Luigi Fagioli &	
1=/ FL)	Juan Manuel Fangio	Alfa Romeo 159 - 8s
2=)	José Froilán González &	
2=)	Alberto Ascari	Ferrari 375 - V12
3)	Luigi Villoresi	Ferrari 375 - V12
PP)	Juan Manuel Fangio	Alfa Romeo 159 - 8s

5) 14 Jul - BRITAIN (Silverstone)

1/ PP)	José Froilán González	Ferrari 375 - V12
2)	Juan Manuel Fangio	Alfa Romeo 159 - 8s
3)	Luigi Villoresi	Ferrari 375 - V12
FL)	Giuseppe Farina	Alfa Romeo 159 - 8s

6) 29 Jul - GERMANY (Nürburgring)

1/ PP)	Alberto Ascari	Ferrari 375 - V12
2/ FL)	Juan Manuel Fangio	Alfa Romeo 159 - 8s
3)	José Froilán González	Ferrari 375 - V12

7) 16 Sep - ITALY (Monza)

1)	Alberto Ascari	Ferrari 375 - V12
2)	José Froilán González	Ferrari 375 - V12
3=)	Felice Bonetto &	
3=/ FL)	Giuseppe Farina	Alfa Romeo 159 - 8s
PP)	Juan Manuel Fangio	Alfa Romeo 159 - 8s

8) 28 Oct - SPAIN (Pedralbes)

1/ FL)	Juan Manuel Fangio	Alfa Romeo 159 - 8s
2)	José Froilán González	Ferrari 375 - V12
3)	Giuseppe Farina	Alfa Romeo 159 - 8s
PP)	Alberto Ascari	Ferrari 375 - V12

Drivers' championship
1) Juan Manuel Fangio   31
2) Alberto Ascari   25
3) José Froilán González 24

1952

1) 18 May - SWITZERLAND (Bremgarten)

1/ FL)	Piero Taruffi	Ferrari 500 - 4
2)	Rudi Fischer	Ferrari 500 - 4
3)	Jean Behra	Gordini T16 - 6
PP)	Giuseppe Farina	Ferrari 500 - 4

2) 30 May - INDIANAPOLIS 500 (Indianapolis)

1)	Troy Ruttman	Kuzma - Offenhauser 4
2)	Jim Rathmann	Kurtis-Kraft 3000 - Offenhauser 4
3)	Sam Hanks	Kurtis-Kraft 3000 - Offenhauser 4
PP)	Freddie Agabashian	Kurtis-Kraft - Cummins 6s
FL)	Bill Vukovich	Kurtis-Kraft 500A - Offenhauser 4

3) 22 Jun - BELGIUM (Spa-Francorchamps)

1/ PP/ FL)	Alberto Ascari	Ferrari 500 - 4
2)	Giuseppe Farina	Ferrari 500 - 4
3)	Robert Manzon	Gordini T16 - 6

4) 6 Jul - FRANCE (Rouen-les-Essarts)

1/ PP/ FL)	Alberto Ascari	Ferrari 500 - 4
2)	Giuseppe Farina	Ferrari 500 - 4
3)	Piero Taruffi	Ferrari 500 - 4

5) 19 Jul - BRITAIN (Silverstone)

1/ FL)	Alberto Ascari	Ferrari 500 - 4
2)	Piero Taruffi	Ferrari 500 - 4
3)	Mike Hawthorn	Cooper T20 - Bristol 6
PP)	Giuseppe Farina	Ferrari 500 - 4

6) 3 Aug - GERMANY (Nürburgring)

1/ PP/ FL)	Alberto Ascari	Ferrari 500 - 4
2)	Giuseppe Farina	Ferrari 500 - 4
3)	Rudi Fischer	Ferrari 500 - 4

7) 17 Aug - NETHERLANDS (Zandvoort)

1/ PP/ FL)	Alberto Ascari	Ferrari 500 - 4
2)	Giuseppe Farina	Ferrari 500 - 4
3)	Luigi Villoresi	Ferrari 500 - 4

8) 7 Sep - ITALY (Monza)

1/ PP/ FL)	Alberto Ascari	Ferrari 500 - 4
2/ FL)	José Froilán González	Maserati A6GCM - 6
3)	Luigi Villoresi	Ferrari 500 - 4

Drivers' championship
1) Alberto Ascari   36
2) Giuseppe Farina   24
3) Piero Taruffi   22

1953

1) 18 Jan - ARGENTINA (Buenos Aires No.2)

1/ PP/ FL)	Alberto Ascari	Ferrari 500 - 4
2)	Luigi Villoresi	Ferrari 500 - 4
3)	José Froilán González	Maserati A6GCM - 6

2) 30 May - INDIANAPOLIS 500 (Indianapolis)

1/ PP/ FL)	Bill Vukovich	Kurtis-Kraft 500A - Offenhauser 4
2)	Art Cross	Kurtis-Kraft 4000 - Offenhauser 4
3=)	Sam Hanks &	
3=)	Duane Carter	Kurtis-Kraft 4000 - Offenhauser 4

3) 7 Jun - NETHERLANDS (Zandvoort)

1/ PP)	Alberto Ascari	Ferrari 500 - 4
2)	Giuseppe Farina	Ferrari 500 - 4
3=)	Felice Bonetto &	
3=)	José Froilán González	Maserati A6GCM - 6
FL)	Luigi Villoresi	Ferrari 500 - 4

4) 21 Jun - BELGIUM (Spa-Francorchamps)

1)	Alberto Ascari	Ferrari 500 - 4
2)	Luigi Villoresi	Ferrari 500 - 4
3)	Onofré Marimón	Maserati A6GCM - 6
PP)	Juan Manuel Fangio	Maserati A6GCM - 6
FL)	José Froilán González	Maserati A6GCM - 6

5) 5 Jul - FRANCE (Reims)

1)	Mike Hawthorn	Ferrari 500 - 4
2/ FL)	Juan Manuel Fangio	Maserati A6GCM - 6
3)	José Froilán González	Maserati A6GCM - 6
PP)	Alberto Ascari	Ferrari 500 - 4

6) 18 Jul - BRITAIN (Silverstone)

1/ PP/ FL)	Alberto Ascari	Ferrari 500 - 4
2)	Juan Manuel Fangio	Maserati A6GCM - 6
3)	Giuseppe Farina	Ferrari 500 - 4
FL)	José Froilán González	Maserati A6GCM - 6

7) 2 Aug - GERMANY (Nürburgring)

1)	Giuseppe Farina	Ferrari 500 - 4
2)	Juan Manuel Fangio	Maserati A6GCM - 6
3)	Mike Hawthorn	Ferrari 500 - 4
PP/ FL)	Alberto Ascari	Ferrari 500 - 4

8) 23 Aug - SWITZERLAND (Bremgarten)

1/ FL)	Alberto Ascari	Ferrari 500 - 4
2)	Giuseppe Farina	Ferrari 500 - 4
3)	Mike Hawthorn	Ferrari 500 - 4
PP)	Juan Manuel Fangio	Maserati A6GCM - 6

9) 13 Sep - ITALY (Monza)

1/ FL)	Juan Manuel Fangio	Maserati A6GCM - 6
2)	Giuseppe Farina	Ferrari 500 - 4
3)	Luigi Villoresi	Ferrari 500 - 4
PP)	Alberto Ascari	Ferrari 500 - 4

Drivers' championship
1) Albert Ascari   34.5
2) Juan Manuel Fangio   28
3) Giuseppe Farina   26

1954

1) 17 Jan - ARGENTINA (Buenos Aires No.2)

1)	Juan Manuel Fangio	Maserati 250F - 6
2/ PP)	Giuseppe Farina	Ferrari 625 - 4
3/ FL)	José Froilán González	Ferrari 625 - 4

2) 31 May - INDIANAPOLIS 500 (Indianapolis)

1)	Bill Vukovich	Kurtis-Kraft 500A - Offenhauser 4
2)	Jimmy Bryan	Kuzma - Offenhauser 4
3/ PP/ FL)	Jack McGrath	Kurtis-Kraft 500C - Offenhauser 4

3) 20 Jun - BELGIUM (Spa-Francorchamps)

1/ PP/ FL)	Juan Manuel Fangio	Maserati 250F - 6
2)	Maurice Trintignant	Ferrari 625 - 4
3)	Stirling Moss	Maserati 250F - 6

4) 4 Jul - FRANCE (Reims)

1/ PP)	Juan Manuel Fangio	Mercedes-Benz W196 str. - 8
2)	Karl Kling	Mercedes-Benz W196 str. - 8
3)	Robert Manzon	Ferrari 625 - 4
FL)	Hans Herrmann	Mercedes-Benz W196 str. - 8

5) 17 Jul - BRITAIN (Silverstone)

1/ FL)	José Froilán González	Ferrari 625 - 4
2/ FL)	Mike Hawthorn	Ferrari 625 - 4
3/ FL)	Onofré Marimón	Maserati 250F - 6
PP/ FL)	Juan Manuel Fangio	Mercedes-Benz W196 str. - 8
FL)	Alberto Ascari	Maserati 250F - 6
FL)	Jean Behra	Gordini T16 - 6
FL)	Stirling Moss	Maserati 250F - 6

Seven drivers jointly achieved the fastest lap.

6) 1 Aug - GERMANY (Nürburgring)

1/ PP)	Juan Manuel Fangio	Mercedes-Benz W196 - 8
2=)	José Froilán González &	
2=)	Mike Hawthorn	Ferrari 625 - 4
3)	Maurice Trintignant	Ferrari 625 - 4
FL)	Karl Kling	Mercedes-Benz W196 - 8

7) 22 Aug - SWITZERLAND (Bremgarten)

1/ FL)	Juan Manuel Fangio	Mercedes-Benz W196 - 8
2/ PP)	José Froilán González	Ferrari 625 - 4
3)	Hans Herrmann	Mercedes-Benz W196 - 8

8) 5 Sep - ITALY (Monza)

1/ PP)	Juan Manuel Fangio	Mercedes-Benz W196 str. - 8
2)	Mike Hawthorn	Ferrari 625 - 4
3=)	Umberto Maglioli &	
3=/ FL)	José Froilán González	Ferrari 625 - 4

9) 24 Oct - SPAIN (Pedralbes)

1)	Mike Hawthorn	Ferrari 553 - 4
2)	Luigi Musso	Maserati 250F - 6
3)	Juan Manuel Fangio	Mercedes-Benz W196 - 8
PP/ FL)	Alberto Ascari	Lancia D50 - V8

Drivers' championship
1) Juan Manuel Fangio   42
2) José Froilán González 25.14
3) Mike Hawthorn   24.64

1955

1) 16 Jan - ARGENTINA (Buenos Aires No.2)

1/ FL)	Juan Manuel Fangio	Mercedes-Benz W196 - 8
2=/ PP)	José Froilán González &	
2=)	Giuseppe Farina &	
2=)	Maurice Trintignant	Ferrari 625 - 4
3=)	Giuseppe Farina &	
3=)	Umberto Maglioli &	
3=)	Maurice Trintignant	Ferrari 625 - 4

2) 22 May - MONACO (Monte-Carlo)

1)	Maurice Trintignant	Ferrari 625 - 4
2)	Eugenio Castellotti	Lancia D50 - V8
3=)	Jean Behra &	
3=)	Cesare Perdisa	Maserati 250F - 6
PP/ FL)	Juan Manuel Fangio	Mercedes-Benz W196 - 8

3) 30 May - INDIANAPOLIS 500 (Indianapolis)

1)	Bob Sweikert	Kurtis-Kraft 500D - Offenhauser 4
2=)	Tony Bettenhausen &	
2=)	Paul Russo	Kurtis-Kraft 500C - Offenhauser 4
3)	Jimmy Davies	Kurtis-Kraft 500B - Offenhauser 4
PP)	Jerry Hoyt	Stevens - Offenhauser 4
FL)	Bill Vukovich	Kurtis-Kraft 500C - Offenhauser 4

4) 5 Jun - BELGIUM (Spa-Francorchamps)

1/ FL)	Juan Manuel Fangio	Mercedes-Benz W196 - 8
2)	Stirling Moss	Mercedes-Benz W196 - 8
3)	Giuseppe Farina	Ferrari 555 - 4
PP)	Eugenio Castellotti	Lancia D50 - V8

5) 19 Jun - NETHERLANDS (Zandvoort)

1/ PP)	Juan Manuel Fangio	Mercedes-Benz W196 - 8
2)	Stirling Moss	Mercedes-Benz W196 - 8
3)	Luigi Musso	Maserati 250F - 6
FL)	Roberto Mières	Maserati 250F - 6

6) 16 Jul - BRITAIN (Aintree)

1/ PP/ FL)	Stirling Moss	Mercedes-Benz W196 - 8
2)	Juan Manuel Fangio	Mercedes-Benz W196 - 8
3)	Karl Kling	Mercedes-Benz W196 - 8

7) 11 Sep - ITALY (Monza)

1/ PP)	Juan Manuel Fangio	Mercedes-Benz W196 str. - 8
2)	Piero Taruffi	Mercedes-Benz W196 - 8
3)	Eugenio Castellotti	Ferrari 555 - 4
FL)	Stirling Moss	Mercedes-Benz W196 str. - 8

Drivers' championship
1) Juan Manuel Fangio   40
2) Stirling Moss   23
3) Eugenio Castellotti   12

1956

1) 22 Jan - ARGENTINA (Buenos Aires No.2)

1=)	Luigi Musso &	
1=/ FL)	Juan Manuel Fangio	Lancia-Ferrari D50 - V8
2)	Jean Behra	Maserati 250F - 6
3)	Mike Hawthorn	Maserati 250F - 6
PP)	Juan Manuel Fangio	Lancia-Ferrari D50 - V8

2) 13 May - MONACO (Monte-Carlo)

1)	Stirling Moss	Maserati 250F - 6
2=)	Peter Collins &	
2=/ PP/ FL)	Juan Manuel Fangio	Lancia-Ferrari D50 - V8
3)	Jean Behra	Maserati 250F - 6

3) 30 May - INDIANAPOLIS 500 (Indianapolis)

1/ PP)	Pat Flaherty	Watson - Offenhauser 4
2)	Sam Hanks	Kurtis-Kraft 500C - Offenhauser 4
3)	Don Freeland	Phillips - Offenhauser 4
FL)	Paul Russo	Kurtis-Kraft - Novi 8s

4) 3 Jun - BELGIUM (Spa-Francorchamps)

1)	Peter Collins	Lancia-Ferrari D50 - V8
2)	Paul Frère	Lancia-Ferrari D50 - V8
3=)	Cesare Perdisa &	
3=/ FL)	Stirling Moss	Maserati 250F - 6
PP)	Juan Manuel Fangio	Lancia-Ferrari D50 - V8

5) 1 Jul - FRANCE (Reims)

1)	Peter Collins	Lancia-Ferrari D50 - V8
2)	Eugenio Castellotti	Lancia-Ferrari D50 - V8
3)	Jean Behra	Maserati 250F - 6
PP/ FL)	Juan Manuel Fangio	Lancia-Ferrari D50 - V8

6) 14 Jul - BRITAIN (Silverstone)

1)	Juan Manuel Fangio	Lancia-Ferrari D50 - V8
2=)	Alfonso de Portago &	
2=)	Peter Collins	Lancia-Ferrari D50 - V8
3)	Jean Behra	Maserati 250F - 6
PP/ FL)	Stirling Moss	Maserati 250F - 6

7) 5 Aug - GERMANY (Nürburgring)

1/ PP/ FL)	Juan Manuel Fangio	Lancia-Ferrari D50 - V8
2)	Stirling Moss	Maserati 250F - 6
3)	Jean Behra	Maserati 250F - 6

8) 2 Sep - ITALY (Monza)

1/ FL)	Stirling Moss	Maserati 250F - 6
2=)	Peter Collins &	
2=/PP)	Juan Manuel Fangio	Lancia-Ferrari D50 - V8
3)	Ron Flockhart	Connaught B - Alta 4

Drivers' championship
1) Juan Manuel Fangio   30
2) Stirling Moss   27
3) Peter Collins   25

1957

1) 13 Jan - ARGENTINA (Buenos Aires No.2)

1)	Juan Manuel Fangio	Maserati 250F - 6
2)	Jean Behra	Maserati 250F - 6
3)	Carlos Menditéguy	Maserati 250F - 6
PP/ FL)	Stirling Moss	Maserati 250F - 6

2) 19 May - MONACO (Monte-Carlo)

1/ PP/ FL)	Juan Manuel Fangio	Maserati 250F - 6
2)	Tony Brooks	Vanwall VW7/57 - 4
3)	Masten Gregory	Maserati 250F - 6

3) 30 May - INDIANAPOLIS 500 (Indianapolis)

1)	Sam Hanks	Salih - Offenhauser 4
2/ FL)	Jim Rathmann	Epperly - Offenhauser 4
3)	Jimmy Bryan	Kuzma - Offenhauser 4
PP)	Pat O'Connor	Kurtis-Kraft 500G - Offenhauser 4

4) 7 Jul - FRANCE (Rouen-les-Essarts)

1/ PP)	Juan Manuel Fangio	Maserati 250F - 6
2/ FL)	Luigi Musso	Lancia-Ferrari 801 - V8
3)	Peter Collins	Lancia-Ferrari 801 - V8

5) 20 Jul - BRITAIN (Aintree)

1=)	Tony Brooks &	
1=/ PP/ FL)	Stirling Moss	Vanwall VW4/57 - 4
2)	Luigi Musso	Lancia-Ferrari 801 - V8
3)	Mike Hawthorn	Lancia-Ferrari 801 - V8

6) 4 Aug - GERMANY (Nürburgring)

1/ PP/ FL)	Juan Manuel Fangio	Maserati 250F - 6
2)	Mike Hawthorn	Lancia-Ferrari 801 - V8
3)	Peter Collins	Lancia-Ferrari 801 - V8

7) 18 Aug - PESCARA (Pescara)

1/ FL)	Stirling Moss	Vanwall VW5/57 - 4
2/ PP)	Juan Manuel Fangio	Maserati 250F - 6
3)	Harry Schell	Maserati 250F - 6

8) 8 Sep - ITALY (Monza)

1)	Stirling Moss	Vanwall VW5/57 - 4
2)	Juan Manuel Fangio	Maserati 250F - 6
3)	Wolfgang von Trips	Lancia-Ferrari 801 - V8
PP)	Stuart Lewis-Evans	Vanwall VW7/57 - 4
FL)	Tony Brooks	Vanwall VW6/57 - 4

Drivers' championship
1) Juan Manuel Fangio   40
2) Stirling Moss   25
3) Luigi Musso   16

1958

1) 19 Jan - ARGENTINA (Buenos Aires No.2)

1)	Stirling Moss	Cooper T43 - Climax 4
2)	Luigi Musso	Ferrari Dino 246 - V6
3)	Mike Hawthorn	Ferrari Dino 246 - V6
PP/ FL)	Juan Manuel Fangio	Maserati 250F - 6

2) 18 May - MONACO (Monte-Carlo)

1)	Maurice Trintignant	Cooper T45 - Climax 4
2)	Luigi Musso	Ferrari Dino 246 - V6
3)	Peter Collins	Ferrari Dino 246 - V6
PP)	Tony Brooks	Vanwall VW10/57 - 4
FL)	Mike Hawthorn	Ferrari Dino 246 - V6

3) 26 May - NETHERLANDS (Zandvoort)

1/ FL)	Stirling Moss	Vanwall VW10/57 - 4
2)	Harry Schell	BRM P25 - 4
3)	Jean Behra	BRM P25 - 4
PP)	Stuart Lewis-Evans	Vanwall VW5/57 - 4

4) 30 May - INDIANAPOLIS 500 (Indianapolis)

1)	Jimmy Bryan	Salih - Offenhauser 4
2)	George Amick	Epperly - Offenhauser 4
3)	Johnny Boyd	Kurtis-Kraft 500G - Offenhauser 4
PP)	Dick Rathmann	Watson - Offenhauser 4
FL)	Tony Bettenhausen	Epperly - Offenhauser 4

5) 15 Jun - BELGIUM (Spa-Francorchamps)

1)	Tony Brooks	Vanwall VW5/57 - 4
2/ PP/ FL)	Mike Hawthorn	Ferrari Dino 246 - V6
3)	Stuart Lewis-Evans	Vanwall VW4/57 - 4

6) 6 Jul - FRANCE (Reims)

1/ PP/ FL)	Mike Hawthorn	Ferrari Dino 246 - V6
2)	Stirling Moss	Vanwall VW10/57 - 4
3)	Wolfgang von Trips	Ferrari Dino 246 - V6

7) 19 Jul - BRITAIN (Silverstone)

1)	Peter Collins	Ferrari Dino 246 - V6
2/ FL)	Mike Hawthorn	Ferrari Dino 246 - V6
3)	Roy Salvadori	Cooper T45 - Climax 4
PP)	Stirling Moss	Vanwall VW10/57 - 4

8) 3 Aug - GERMANY (Nürburgring)

1)	Tony Brooks	Vanwall VW4/57 - 4
2)	Roy Salvadori	Cooper T45 - Climax 4
3)	Maurice Trintignant	Cooper T45 - Climax 4
PP)	Mike Hawthorn	Ferrari Dino 246 - V6
FL)	Stirling Moss	Vanwall VW10/57 - 4

9) 24 Aug - PORTUGAL (Porto)

1/ PP)	Stirling Moss	Vanwall VW10/57 4
2/ FL)	Mike Hawthorn	Ferrari Dino 246 - V6
3)	Stuart Lewis-Evans	Vanwall VW6/57 - 4

10) 7 Sep - ITALY (Monza)

1)	Tony Brooks	Vanwall VW5/57 - 4
2)	Mike Hawthorn	Ferrari Dino 246 - V6
3/ FL)	Phil Hill	Ferrari Dino 246 - V6
PP)	Stirling Moss	Vanwall VW10/57 - 4

11) 19 Oct - MOROCCO (Ain-Diab)

1/ FL)	Stirling Moss	Vanwall VW10/57 - 4
2/ PP)	Mike Hawthorn	Ferrari Dino 246 - V6
3)	Phil Hill	Ferrari Dino 246 - V6

Drivers' championship

1) Mike Hawthorn	42
2) Stirling Moss	41
3) Tony Brooks	24

Constructors' championship

1) Vanwall	48
2) Ferrari	40
3) Cooper - Climax	31

1959

1) 10 May - MONACO (Monte-Carlo)

1/ FL)	Jack Brabham	Cooper T51 - Climax 4
2)	Tony Brooks	Ferrari Dino 246 - V6
3)	Maurice Trintignant	Cooper T51 - Climax 4
PP)	Stirling Moss	Cooper T51 - Climax 4

2) 30 May - INDIANAPOLIS 500 (Indianapolis)

1)	Rodger Ward	Watson - Offenhauser 4
2)	Jim Rathmann	Watson - Offenhauser 4
3/ PP/ FL)	Johnny Thomson	Lesovsky - Offenhauser 4

3) 31 May - NETHERLANDS (Zandvoort)

1/ PP)	Jo Bonnier	BRM P25 - 4
2)	Jack Brabham	Cooper T51 - Climax 4
3)	Masten Gregory	Cooper T51 - Climax 4
FL)	Stirling Moss	Cooper T51 - Climax 4

4) 5 Jul - FRANCE (Reims)

1/ PP)	Tony Brooks	Ferrari Dino 246 - V6
2)	Phil Hill	Ferrari Dino 246 - V6
3)	Jack Brabham	Cooper T51 - Climax 4
FL)	Stirling Moss	BRM P25 - 4

5) 18 Jul - BRITAIN (Aintree)

1/ PP)	Jack Brabham	Cooper T51 - Climax 4
2/ FL)	Stirling Moss	BRM P25 - 4
3/ FL)	Bruce McLaren	Cooper T51 - Climax 4

6) 2 Aug - GERMANY (AVUS)

1/ PP/ FL)	Tony Brooks	Ferrari Dino 246 - V6
2)	Dan Gurney	Ferrari Dino 246 - V6
3)	Phil Hill	Ferrari Dino 246 - V6

Cliff Allison (Ferrari Dino 246 - V6) set the fastest time in practice, but being a reserve driver, was not eligible for pole position.

7) 23 Aug - PORTUGAL (Monsanto Park)

1/ PP/ FL)	Stirling Moss	Cooper T51 - Climax 4
2)	Masten Gregory	Cooper T51 - Climax 4
3)	Dan Gurney	Ferrari Dino 246 - V6

8) 13 Sep - ITALY (Monza)

1/ PP)	Stirling Moss	Cooper T51 - Climax 4
2/ FL)	Phil Hill	Ferrari Dino 246 - V6
3)	Jack Brabham	Cooper T51 - Climax 4

9) 12 Dec - UNITED STATES (Sebring)

1)	Bruce McLaren	Cooper T51 - Climax 4
2/ FL)	Maurice Trintignant	Cooper T51 - Climax 4
3)	Tony Brooks	Ferrari Dino 246 - V6
PP)	Stirling Moss	Cooper T51 - Climax 4

Drivers' championship

1) Jack Brabham	31
2) Tony Brooks	27
3) Stirling Moss	25.5

Constructors' championship

1) Cooper - Climax	40
2) Ferrari	32
3) BRM	18

1960

1) 7 Feb - ARGENTINA (Buenos Aires No.2)

1)	Bruce McLaren	Cooper T51 - Climax 4
2)	Cliff Allison	Ferrari Dino 246 - V6
3=)	Maurice Trintignant &	
3=)	Stirling Moss	Cooper T51 - Climax 4
PP/ FL)	Stirling Moss	Cooper T51 - Climax 4

2) 29 May - MONACO (Monte-Carlo)

1/ PP)	Stirling Moss	Lotus 18 - Climax 4
2/ FL)	Bruce McLaren	Cooper T53 - Climax 4
3)	Phil Hill	Ferrari Dino 246 - V6

3) 30 May - INDIANAPOLIS 500 (Indianapolis)

1/ FL)	Jim Rathmann	Watson - Offenhauser 4
2)	Rodger Ward	Watson - Offenhauser 4
3)	Paul Goldsmith	Epperly - Offenhauser 4
PP)	Eddie Sachs	Ewing - Offenhauser 4

4) 6 Jun - NETHERLANDS (Zandvoort)

1)	Jack Brabham	Cooper T53 - Climax 4
2)	Innes Ireland	Lotus 18 - Climax 4
3)	Graham Hill	BRM P48 - 4
PP/ FL)	Stirling Moss	Lotus 18 - Climax 4

5) 19 Jun - BELGIUM (Spa-Francorchamps)

1/ PP/ FL)	Jack Brabham	Cooper T53 - Climax 4
2)	Bruce McLaren	Cooper T53 - Climax 4
3)	Olivier Gendebien	Cooper T51 - Climax 4
FL)	Phil Hill	Ferrari Dino 246 - V6
FL)	Innes Ireland	Lotus 18 - Climax 4

6) 3 Jul - FRANCE (Reims)

1/ PP/ FL)	Jack Brabham	Cooper T53 - Climax 4
2)	Olivier Gendebien	Cooper T51 - Climax 4
3)	Bruce McLaren	Cooper T53 - Climax 4

7) 16 Jul - BRITAIN (Silverstone)

1/ PP)	Jack Brabham	Cooper T53 - Climax 4
2)	John Surtees	Lotus 18 - Climax 4
3)	Innes Ireland	Lotus 18 - Climax 4
FL)	Graham Hill	BRM P48 - 4

8) 14 Aug - PORTUGAL (Porto)

1)	Jack Brabham	Cooper T53 - Climax 4
2)	Bruce McLaren	Cooper T53 - Climax 4
3)	Jim Clark	Lotus 18 - Climax 4
PP/ FL)	John Surtees	Lotus 18 - Climax 4

9) 4 Sep - ITALY (Monza)

1/ PP/ FL)	Phil Hill	Ferrari Dino 246 - V6
2)	Richie Ginther	Ferrari Dino 246 - V6
3)	Willy Mairesse	Ferrari Dino 246 - V6

10) 20 Nov - UNITED STATES (Riverside)

1/ PP)	Stirling Moss	Lotus 18 - Climax 4
2)	Innes Ireland	Lotus 18 - Climax 4
3)	Bruce McLaren	Cooper T53 - Climax 4
FL)	Jack Brabham	Cooper T53 - Climax 4

Drivers' championship

1) Jack Brabham	43
2) Bruce McLaren	34
3) Stirling Moss	19

Constructors' championship

1) Cooper - Climax	48
2) Lotus - Climax	34
3) Ferrari	26

1961

1) 14 May - MONACO (Monte-Carlo)

1/ PP/ FL)	Stirling Moss	Lotus 18 - Climax 4
2/ FL)	Richie Ginther	Ferrari 156 - V6
3)	Phil Hill	Ferrari 156 - V6

2) 22 May - NETHERLANDS (Zandvoort)

1)	Wolfgang von Trips	Ferrari 156 - V6
2/ PP)	Phil Hill	Ferrari 156 - V6
3/ FL)	Jim Clark	Lotus 21 - Climax 4

3) 18 Jun - BELGIUM (Spa-Francorchamps)

1/ PP)	Phil Hill	Ferrari 156 - V6
2)	Wolfgang von Trips	Ferrari 156 - V6
3/ FL)	Richie Ginther	Ferrari 156 - V6

4) 2 Jul - FRANCE (Reims)

1)	Giancarlo Baghetti	Ferrari 156 - V6
2)	Dan Gurney	Porsche 718 - F4
3)	Jim Clark	Lotus 21 - Climax 4
PP/ FL)	Phil Hill	Ferrari 156 - V6

5) 15 Jul - BRITAIN (Aintree)

1)	Wolfgang von Trips	Ferrari 156 - V6
2/ PP)	Phil Hill	Ferrari 156 - V6
3)	Richie Ginther	Ferrari 156 - V6
FL)	Tony Brooks	BRM P48/57 - Climax 4

6) 6 Aug - GERMANY (Nürburgring)

1)	Stirling Moss	Lotus 18/21 - Climax 4
2)	Wolfgang von Trips	Ferrari 156 - V6
3/ PP/ FL)	Phil Hill	Ferrari 156 - V6

7) 10 Sep - ITALY (Monza)

1)	Phil Hill	Ferrari 156 - V6
2)	Dan Gurney	Porsche 718 - F4
3)	Bruce McLaren	Cooper T55 - Climax 4
PP)	Wolfgang von Trips	Ferrari 156 - V6
FL)	Giancarlo Baghetti	Ferrari 156 - V6

8) 8 Oct - UNITED STATES (Watkins Glen)

1)	Innes Ireland	Lotus 21 - Climax 4
2)	Dan Gurney	Porsche 718 - F4
3)	Tony Brooks	BRM P48/57 - Climax 4
PP/ FL)	Jack Brabham	Cooper T58 - Climax V8

Drivers' championship

1) Phil Hill	34
2) Wolfgang von Trips	33
3) Stirling Moss	21

Constructors' championship

1) Ferrari	40
2) Lotus - Climax	32
3) Porsche	22

1962

1) 20 May - NETHERLANDS (Zandvoort)

1)	Graham Hill	BRM P57 - V8
2)	Trevor Taylor	Lotus 24 - Climax V8
3)	Phil Hill	Ferrari 156 - V6
PP)	John Surtees	Lola Mk 4 - Climax V8
FL)	Bruce McLaren	Cooper T60 - Climax V8

2) 3 Jun - MONACO (Monte-Carlo)

1)	Bruce McLaren	Cooper T60 - Climax V8
2)	Phil Hill	Ferrari 156 - V6
3)	Lorenzo Bandini	Ferrari 156 - V6
PP/ FL)	Jim Clark	Lotus 25 - Climax V8

3) 17 Jun - BELGIUM (Spa-Francorchamps)

1/ FL)	Jim Clark	Lotus 25 - Climax V8
2/ PP)	Graham Hill	BRM P57 - V8
3)	Phil Hill	Ferrari 156 - V6

4) 8 Jul - FRANCE (Rouen-les-Essarts)

1)	Dan Gurney	Porsche 804 - F8
2)	Tony Maggs	Cooper T60 - Climax V8
3)	Richie Ginther	BRM P57 - V8
PP)	Jim Clark	Lotus 25 - Climax V8
FL)	Graham Hill	BRM P57 - V8

5) 21 Jul - BRITAIN (Aintree)

1/ PP/ FL)	Jim Clark	Lotus 25 - Climax V8
2)	John Surtees	Lola Mk 4 - Climax V8
3)	Bruce McLaren	Cooper T60 - Climax V8

6) 5 Aug - GERMANY (Nürburgring)

1/ FL)	Graham Hill	BRM P57 - V8
2)	John Surtees	Lola Mk 4 - Climax V8
3/ PP)	Dan Gurney	Porsche 804 - F8

7) 16 Sep - ITALY (Monza)

1/ FL)	Graham Hill	BRM P57 - V8
2)	Richie Ginther	BRM P57 - V8
3)	Bruce McLaren	Cooper T60 - Climax V8
PP)	Jim Clark	Lotus 25 - Climax V8

8) 7 Oct - UNITED STATES (Watkins Glen)

1/ PP/ FL)	Jim Clark	Lotus 25 - Climax V8
2)	Graham Hill	BRM P57 - V8
3)	Bruce McLaren	Cooper T60 - Climax V8

9) 29 Dec - SOUTH AFRICA (East London)

1)	Graham Hill	BRM P57 - V8
2)	Bruce McLaren	Cooper T60 - Climax V8
3)	Tony Maggs	Cooper T60 - Climax V8
PP/ FL)	Jim Clark	Lotus 25 - Climax V8

Drivers' championship

1) Graham Hill	42
2) Jim Clark	30
3) Bruce McLaren	27

Constructors' championship

1) BRM	42
2) Lotus - Climax	36
3) Cooper - Climax	29

1963

1) 26 May - MONACO (Monte-Carlo)

1)	Graham Hill	BRM P57 - V8
2)	Richie Ginther	BRM P57 - V8
3)	Bruce McLaren	Cooper T66 - Climax V8
PP)	Jim Clark	Lotus 25 - Climax V8
FL)	John Surtees	Ferrari 156 - V6

2) 9 Jun - BELGIUM (Spa-Francorchamps)

1/ FL)	Jim Clark	Lotus 25 - Climax V8
2)	Bruce McLaren	Cooper T66 - Climax V8
3)	Dan Gurney	Brabham BT7 - Climax V8
PP)	Graham Hill	BRM P57 - V8

3) 23 Jun - NETHERLANDS (Zandvoort)

1/ PP/ FL)	Jim Clark	Lotus 25 - Climax V8
2)	Dan Gurney	Brabham BT7 - Climax V8
3)	John Surtees	Ferrari 156 - V6

4) 30 Jun - FRANCE (Reims)

1/ PP/ FL)	Jim Clark	Lotus 25 - Climax V8
2)	Tony Maggs	Cooper T66 - Climax V8
3)	Graham Hill	BRM P61 - V8

Graham Hill received no points due to being push-started on the grid.

5) 20 Jul - BRITAIN (Silverstone)

1/ PP)	Jim Clark	Lotus 25 - Climax V8
2/ FL)	John Surtees	Ferrari 156 - V6
3)	Graham Hill	BRM P57 - V8

6) 4 Aug - GERMANY (Nürburgring)

1/ FL)	John Surtees	Ferrari 156 - V6
2/ PP)	Jim Clark	Lotus 25 - Climax V8
3)	Richie Ginther	BRM P57 - V8

7) 8 Sep - ITALY (Monza)

1/ FL)	Jim Clark	Lotus 25 - Climax V8
2)	Richie Ginther	BRM P57 - V8
3)	Bruce McLaren	Cooper T66 - Climax V8
PP)	John Surtees	Ferrari 156 - V6

8) 6 Oct - UNITED STATES (Watkins Glen)

1/ PP)	Graham Hill	BRM P57 - V8
2)	Richie Ginther	BRM P57 - V8
3/ FL)	Jim Clark	Lotus 25 - Climax V8

9) 27 Oct - MEXICO (Mexico City)

1/ PP/ FL)	Jim Clark	Lotus 25 - Climax V8
2)	Jack Brabham	Brabham BT7 - Climax V8
3)	Richie Ginther	BRM P57 - V8

10) 28 Dec - SOUTH AFRICA (East London)

1/ PP)	Jim Clark	Lotus 25 - Climax V8
2/ FL)	Dan Gurney	Brabham BT7 - Climax V8
3)	Graham Hill	BRM P57 - V8

Drivers' championship		**Constructors' championship**	
1) Jim Clark	54	1) Lotus - Climax	54
2) Graham Hill	29	2) BRM	36
3) Richie Ginther	29	3) Brabham - Climax	28

1964

1) 10 May - MONACO (Monte-Carlo)

1/ FL)	Graham Hill	BRM P261 - V8
2)	Richie Ginther	BRM P261 - V8
3)	Peter Arundell	Lotus 25 - Climax V8
PP)	Jim Clark	Lotus 25 - Climax V8

2) 24 May - NETHERLANDS (Zandvoort)

1/ FL)	Jim Clark	Lotus 25 - Climax V8
2)	John Surtees	Ferrari 158 - V8
3)	Peter Arundell	Lotus 25 - Climax V8
PP)	Dan Gurney	Brabham BT7 - Climax V8

3) 14 Jun - BELGIUM (Spa-Francorchamps)

1)	Jim Clark	Lotus 25 - Climax V8
2)	Bruce McLaren	Cooper T73 - Climax V8
3)	Jack Brabham	Brabham BT7 - Climax V8
PP/ FL)	Dan Gurney	Brabham BT7 - Climax V8

4) 28 Jun - FRANCE (Rouen-les-Essarts)

1)	Dan Gurney	Brabham BT7 - Climax V8
2)	Graham Hill	BRM P261 - V8
3/ FL)	Jack Brabham	Brabham BT7 - Climax V8
PP)	Jim Clark	Lotus 25 - Climax V8

5) 11 Jul - BRITAIN (Brands Hatch)

1/ PP/ FL)	Jim Clark	Lotus 25 - Climax V8
2)	Graham Hill	BRM P261 - V8
3)	John Surtees	Ferrari 158 - V8

6) 2 Aug - GERMANY (Nürburgring)

1/ PP/ FL)	John Surtees	Ferrari 158 - V8
2)	Graham Hill	BRM P261 - V8
3)	Lorenzo Bandini	Ferrari 156 - V6

7) 23 Aug - AUSTRIA (Zeltweg)

1)	Lorenzo Bandini	Ferrari 156 - V6
2)	Richie Ginther	BRM P261 - V8
3)	Bob Anderson	Brabham BT11 - Climax V8
PP)	Graham Hill	BRM P261 - V8
FL)	Dan Gurney	Brabham BT7 - Climax V8

8) 6 Sep - ITALY (Monza)

1/ PP/ FL)	John Surtees	Ferrari 158 - V8
2)	Bruce McLaren	Cooper T73 - Climax V8
3)	Lorenzo Bandini	Ferrari 158 - V8

9) 4 Oct - UNITED STATES (Watkins Glen)

1)	Graham Hill	BRM P261 - V8
2)	John Surtees	Ferrari 158 - V8
3)	Jo Siffert	Brabham BT11 - BRM V8
PP/FL)	Jim Clark	Lotus 25 - Climax V8

10) 25 Oct - MEXICO (Mexico City)

1)	Dan Gurney	Brabham BT7 - Climax V8
2)	John Surtees	Ferrari 158 - V8
3)	Lorenzo Bandini	Ferrari 1512 - F12
PP/ FL)	Jim Clark	Lotus 33 - Climax V8

Drivers' championship		**Constructors' championship**	
1) John Surtees	40	1) Ferrari	45
2) Graham Hill	39	2) BRM	42
3) Jim Clark	32	3) Lotus - Climax	37

1965

1) 1 Jan - SOUTH AFRICA (East London)

1/ PP/ FL)	Jim Clark	Lotus 33 - Climax V8
2)	John Surtees	Ferrari 158 - V8
3)	Graham Hill	BRM P261 - V8

2) 30 May - MONACO (Monte-Carlo)

1/ PP/ FL)	Graham Hill	BRM P261 - V8
2)	Lorenzo Bandini	Ferrari 1512 - F12
3)	Jackie Stewart	BRM P261 - V8

3) 13 Jun - BELGIUM (Spa-Francorchamps)

1/ FL)	Jim Clark	Lotus 33 - Climax V8
2)	Jackie Stewart	BRM P261 - V8
3)	Bruce McLaren	Cooper T77 - Climax V8
PP)	Graham Hill	BRM P261 - V8

4) 27 Jun - FRANCE (Clermont-Ferrand)

1/ PP/ FL)	Jim Clark	Lotus 25 - Climax V8
2)	Jackie Stewart	BRM P261 - V8
3)	John Surtees	Ferrari 158 - V8

5) 10 Jul - BRITAIN (Silverstone)

1/ PP)	Jim Clark	Lotus 33 - Climax V8
2/ FL)	Graham Hill	BRM P261 - V8
3)	John Surtees	Ferrari 1512 - F12

6) 18 Jul - NETHERLANDS (Zandvoort)

1/ FL)	Jim Clark	Lotus 33 - Climax V8
2)	Jackie Stewart	BRM P261 - V8
3)	Dan Gurney	Brabham BT11 - Climax V8
PP)	Graham Hill	BRM P261 - V8

7) 1 Aug - GERMANY (Nürburgring)

1/ PP/ FL)	Jim Clark	Lotus 33 - Climax V8
2)	Graham Hill	BRM P261 - V8
3)	Dan Gurney	Brabham BT11 - Climax V8

8) 12 Sep - ITALY (Monza)

1)	Jackie Stewart	BRM P261 - V8
2)	Graham Hill	BRM P261 - V8
3)	Dan Gurney	Brabham BT11 - Climax V8
PP/ FL)	Jim Clark	Lotus 33 - Climax V8

9) 3 Oct - UNITED STATES (Watkins Glen)

1/ PP/ FL)	Graham Hill	BRM P261 - V8
2)	Dan Gurney	Brabham BT11 - Climax V8
3)	Jack Brabham	Brabham BT11 - Climax V8

10) 24 Oct - MEXICO (Mexico City)

1)	Richie Ginther	Honda RA272 - V12
2/ FL)	Dan Gurney	Brabham BT11 - Climax V8
3)	Mike Spence	Lotus 33 - Climax V8
PP)	Jim Clark	Lotus 33 - Climax V8

Drivers' championship		Constructors' championship	
1) Jim Clark	54	1) Lotus - Climax	54
2) Graham Hill	40	2) BRM	45
3) Jackie Stewart	33	3) Brabham - Climax	27

1966

1) 22 May - MONACO (Monte-Carlo)

1)	Jackie Stewart	BRM P261 - V8
2/ FL)	Lorenzo Bandini	Ferrari 246 - V6
3)	Graham Hill	BRM P261 - V8
PP)	Jim Clark	Lotus 33 - Climax V8

2) 12 Jun - BELGIUM (Spa-Francorchamps)

1/ PP/ FL)	John Surtees	Ferrari 312 - V12
2)	Jochen Rindt	Cooper T81 - Maserati V12
3)	Lorenzo Bandini	Ferrari 246 - V6

3) 3 Jul - FRANCE (Reims)

1)	Jack Brabham	Brabham BT19 - Repco V8
2)	Mike Parkes	Ferrari 312 - V12
3)	Denny Hulme	Brabham BT20 - Repco V8
PP/ FL)	Lorenzo Bandini	Ferrari 312 - V12

4) 16 Jul - BRITAIN (Brands Hatch)

1/ PP/ FL)	Jack Brabham	Brabham BT19 - Repco V8
2)	Denny Hulme	Brabham BT20 - Repco V8
3)	Graham Hill	BRM P261 - V8

5) 24 Jul - NETHERLANDS (Zandvoort)

1/ PP)	Jack Brabham	Brabham BT19 - Repco V8
2)	Graham Hill	BRM P261 - V8
3)	Jim Clark	Lotus 33 - Climax V8
FL)	Denny Hulme	Brabham BT20 - Repco V8

6) 7 Aug - GERMANY (Nürburgring)

1)	Jack Brabham	Brabham BT19 - Repco V8
2/ FL)	John Surtees	Cooper T81 - Maserati V12
3)	Jochen Rindt	Cooper T81 - Maserati V12
PP)	Jim Clark	Lotus 33 - Climax V8

7) 4 Sep - ITALY (Monza)

1/ FL)	Lodovico Scarfiotti	Ferrari 312 - V12
2/ PP)	Mike Parkes	Ferrari 312 - V12
3)	Denny Hulme	Brabham BT20 - Repco V8

8) 2 Oct - UNITED STATES (Watkins Glen)

1)	Jim Clark	Lotus 43 - BRM H16
2)	Jochen Rindt	Cooper T81 - Maserati V12
3/ FL)	John Surtees	Cooper T81 - Maserati V12
PP)	Jack Brabham	Brabham BT20 - Repco V8

9) 23 Oct - MEXICO (Mexico City)

1/ PP)	John Surtees	Cooper T81 - Maserati V12
2)	Jack Brabham	Brabham BT20 - Repco V8
3)	Denny Hulme	Brabham BT20 - Repco V8
FL)	Richie Ginther	Honda RA273 - V12

Drivers' championship		Constructors' championship	
1) Jack Brabham	42	1) Brabham - Repco	42
2) John Surtees	28	2) Ferrari	31
3) Jochen Rindt	22	3) Cooper - Maserati	30

1967

1) 2 Jan - SOUTH AFRICA (Kyalami)

1)	Pedro Rodríguez	Cooper T81 - Maserati V12
2)	John Love	Cooper T79 - Climax 4
3)	John Surtees	Honda RA273 - V12
PP)	Jack Brabham	Brabham BT20 - Repco V8
FL)	Denny Hulme	Brabham BT20 - Repco V8

2) 7 May - MONACO (Monte-Carlo)

1)	Denny Hulme	Brabham BT20 - Repco V8
2)	Graham Hill	Lotus 33 - BRM V8
3)	Chris Amon	Ferrari 312 - V12
PP)	Jack Brabham	Brabham BT19 - Repco V8
FL)	Jim Clark	Lotus 33 - Climax V8

3) 4 Jun - NETHERLANDS (Zandvoort)

1/ FL)	Jim Clark	Lotus 49 - Ford Cosworth V8
2)	Jack Brabham	Brabham BT19 - Repco V8
3)	Denny Hulme	Brabham BT20 - Repco V8
PP)	Graham Hill	Lotus 49 - Ford Cosworth V8

4) 18 Jun - BELGIUM (Spa-Francorchamps)

1/ FL)	Dan Gurney	Eagle T1G - Weslake V12
2)	Jackie Stewart	BRM P83 - H16
3)	Chris Amon	Ferrari 312 - V12
PP)	Jim Clark	Lotus 49 - Ford Cosworth V8

5) 2 Jul - FRANCE (Bugatti au Mans)

1)	Jack Brabham	Brabham BT24 - Repco V8
2)	Denny Hulme	Brabham BT24 - Repco V8
3)	Jackie Stewart	BRM P261 - V8
PP/ FL)	Graham Hill	Lotus 49 - Ford Cosworth V8

6) 15 Jul - BRITAIN (Silverstone)

1/ PP)	Jim Clark	Lotus 49 - Ford Cosworth V8
2/ FL)	Denny Hulme	Brabham BT24 - Repco V8
3)	Chris Amon	Ferrari 312 - V12

7) 6 Aug - GERMANY (Nürburgring)

1)	Denny Hulme	Brabham BT24 - Repco V8
2)	Jack Brabham	Brabham BT24 - Repco V8
3)	Chris Amon	Ferrari 312 - V12
PP)	Jim Clark	Lotus 49 - Ford Cosworth V8
FL)	Dan Gurney	Eagle T1G - Weslake V12

8) 27 Aug - CANADA (Mosport Park)

1)	Jack Brabham	Brabham BT24 - Repco V8
2)	Denny Hulme	Brabham BT24 - Repco V8
3)	Dan Gurney	Eagle T1G - Weslake V12
PP/ FL)	Jim Clark	Lotus 49 - Ford Cosworth V8

9) 10 Sep - ITALY (Monza)

1)	John Surtees	Honda RA300 - V12
2)	Jack Brabham	Brabham BT24 - Repco V8
3/ PP/ FL)	Jim Clark	Lotus 49 - Ford Cosworth V8

10) 1 Oct - UNITED STATES (Watkins Glen)

1)	Jim Clark	Lotus 49 - Ford Cosworth V8
2/ PP/ FL)	Graham Hill	Lotus 49 - Ford Cosworth V8
3)	Denny Hulme	Brabham BT24 - Repco V8

11) 22 Oct - MEXICO (Mexico City)

1/ PP/ FL)	Jim Clark	Lotus 49 - Ford Cosworth V8
2)	Jack Brabham	Brabham BT24 - Repco V8
3)	Denny Hulme	Brabham BT24 - Repco V8

Drivers' championship

1) Denny Hulme	51
2) Jack Brabham	46
3) Jim Clark	41

Constructors' championship

1) Brabham - Repco	63
2) Lotus - Ford Cosworth	44
3) Cooper - Maserati	28

1968

1) 1 Jan - SOUTH AFRICA (Kyalami)

1/ PP/ FL)	Jim Clark	Lotus 49 - Ford Cosworth V8
2)	Graham Hill	Lotus 49 - Ford Cosworth V8
3)	Jochen Rindt	Brabham BT24 - Repco V8

2) 12 May - SPAIN (Jarama)

1)	Graham Hill	Lotus 49 - Ford Cosworth V8
2)	Denny Hulme	McLaren M7A - Ford Cosworth V8
3)	Brian Redman	Cooper T86B - BRM V12
PP)	Chris Amon	Ferrari 312 - V12
FL)	Jean-Pierre Beltoise	Matra MS10 - Ford Cosworth V8

3) 26 May - MONACO (Monte-Carlo)

1/ PP)	Graham Hill	Lotus 49B - Ford Cosworth V8
2/ FL)	Richard Attwood	BRM P126 - V12
3)	Lucien Bianchi	Cooper T86B - BRM V12

4) 9 Jun - BELGIUM (Spa-Francorchamps)

1)	Bruce McLaren	McLaren M7A - Ford Cosworth V8
2)	Pedro Rodríguez	BRM P133 - V12
3)	Jacky Ickx	Ferrari 312 - V12
PP)	Chris Amon	Ferrari 312 - V12
FL)	John Surtees	Honda RA301 - V12

5) 23 Jun - NETHERLANDS (Zandvoort)

1)	Jackie Stewart	Matra MS10 - Ford Cosworth V8
2/ FL)	Jean-Pierre Beltoise	Matra MS11 - V12
3)	Pedro Rodríguez	BRM P133 - V12
PP)	Chris Amon	Ferrari 312 - V12

6) 7 Jul - FRANCE (Rouen-les-Essarts)

1)	Jacky Ickx	Ferrari 312 - V12
2)	John Surtees	Honda RA301 - V12
3)	Jackie Stewart	Matra MS10 - Ford Cosworth V8
PP)	Jochen Rindt	Brabham BT26 - Repco V8
FL)	Pedro Rodríguez	BRM P133 - V12

7) 20 Jul - BRITAIN (Brands Hatch)

1/ FL)	Jo Siffert	Lotus 49B - Ford Cosworth V8
2)	Chris Amon	Ferrari 312 - V12
3)	Jacky Ickx	Ferrari 312 - V12
PP)	Graham Hill	Lotus 49B - Ford Cosworth V8

8) 4 Aug - GERMANY (Nürburgring)

1/ FL)	Jackie Stewart	Matra MS10 - Ford Cosworth V8
2)	Graham Hill	Lotus 49B - Ford Cosworth V8
3)	Jochen Rindt	Brabham BT26 - Repco V8
PP)	Jacky Ickx	Ferrari 312 - V12

9) 8 Sep - ITALY (Monza)

1)	Denny Hulme	McLaren M7A - Ford Cosworth V8
2)	Johnny Servoz-Gavin	Matra MS10 - Ford Cosworth V8
3)	Jacky Ickx	Ferrari 312 - V12
PP)	John Surtees	Honda RA301 - V12
FL)	Jackie Oliver	Lotus 49B - Ford Cosworth V8

10) 22 Sep - CANADA (Mont-Tremblant)

1)	Denny Hulme	McLaren M7A - Ford Cosworth V8
2)	Bruce McLaren	McLaren M7A - Ford Cosworth V8
3)	Pedro Rodríguez	BRM P133 - V12
PP)	Jochen Rindt	Brabham BT26 - Repco V8
FL)	Jo Siffert	Lotus 49B - Ford Cosworth V8

11) 6 Oct - UNITED STATES (Watkins Glen)

1/ FL)	Jackie Stewart	Matra MS10 - Ford Cosworth V8
2)	Graham Hill	Lotus 49B - Ford Cosworth V8
3)	John Surtees	Honda RA301 - V12
PP)	Mario Andretti	Lotus 49B - Ford Cosworth V8

12) 3 Nov - MEXICO (Mexico City)

1)	Graham Hill	Lotus 49B - Ford Cosworth V8
2)	Bruce McLaren	McLaren M7A - Ford Cosworth V8
3)	Jackie Oliver	Lotus 49B - Ford Cosworth V8
PP/ FL)	Jo Siffert	Lotus 49B - Ford Cosworth V8

Drivers' championship

1) Graham Hill	48
2) Jackie Stewart	36
3) Denny Hulme	33

Constructors' championship

1) Lotus - Ford Cosworth	62
2) McLaren - Ford Cosworth	49
3) Matra - Ford Cosworth	45

1969

1) 1 Mar - SOUTH AFRICA (Kyalami)
1/ FL)	Jackie Stewart	Matra MS10 - Ford Cosworth V8
2)	Graham Hill	Lotus 49B - Ford Cosworth V8
3)	Denny Hulme	McLaren M7A - Ford Cosworth V8
PP)	Jack Brabham	Brabham BT26A - Ford Cosworth V8

2) 4 May - SPAIN (Montjuïc)
1)	Jackie Stewart	Matra MS80 - Ford Cosworth V8
2)	Bruce McLaren	McLaren M7C - Ford Cosworth V8
3)	Jean-Pierre Beltoise	Matra MS80 - Ford Cosworth V8
PP/ FL)	Jochen Rindt	Lotus 49B - Ford Cosworth V8

3) 18 May - MONACO (Monte-Carlo)
1)	Graham Hill	Lotus 49B - Ford Cosworth V8
2)	Piers Courage	Brabham BT26A - Ford Cosworth V8
3)	Jo Siffert	Lotus 49B - Ford Cosworth V8
PP/ FL)	Jackie Stewart	Matra MS80 - Ford Cosworth V8

4) 21 Jun - NETHERLANDS (Zandvoort)
1/ FL)	Jackie Stewart	Matra MS80 - Ford Cosworth V8
2)	Jo Siffert	Lotus 49B - Ford Cosworth V8
3)	Chris Amon	Ferrari 312 - V12
PP)	Jochen Rindt	Lotus 49B - Ford Cosworth V8

5) 6 Jul - FRANCE (Clermont-Ferrand)
1/ PP/ FL)	Jackie Stewart	Matra MS80 - Ford Cosworth V8
2)	Jean-Pierre Beltoise	Matra MS80 - Ford Cosworth V8
3)	Jacky Ickx	Brabham BT26A - Ford Cosworth V8

6) 19 Jul - BRITAIN (Silverstone)
1/ FL)	Jackie Stewart	Matra MS80 - Ford Cosworth V8
2)	Jacky Ickx	Brabham BT26A - Ford Cosworth V8
3)	Bruce McLaren	McLaren M7C - Ford Cosworth V8
PP)	Jochen Rindt	Lotus 49B - Ford Cosworth V8

7) 3 Aug - GERMANY (Nürburgring)
1/ PP/ FL)	Jacky Ickx	Brabham BT26A - Ford Cosworth V8
2)	Jackie Stewart	Matra MS80 - Ford Cosworth V8
3)	Bruce McLaren	McLaren M7C - Ford Cosworth V8

8) 7 Sep - ITALY (Monza)
1)	Jackie Stewart	Matra MS80 - Ford Cosworth V8
2/ PP)	Jochen Rindt	Lotus 49B - Ford Cosworth V8
3/ FL)	Jean-Pierre Beltoise	Matra MS80 - Ford Cosworth V8

9) 20 Sep - CANADA (Mosport Park)
1/ PP/ FL)	Jacky Ickx	Brabham BT26A - Ford Cosworth V8
2/ FL)	Jack Brabham	Brabham BT26A - Ford Cosworth V8
3)	Jochen Rindt	Lotus 49B - Ford Cosworth V8

10) 5 Oct - UNITED STATES (Watkins Glen)
1/ PP/ FL)	Jochen Rindt	Lotus 49B - Ford Cosworth V8
2)	Piers Courage	Brabham BT26A - Ford Cosworth V8
3)	John Surtees	BRM P139 - V12

11) 19 Oct - MEXICO (Mexico City)
1)	Denny Hulme	McLaren M7A - Ford Cosworth V8
2/ FL)	Jacky Ickx	Brabham BT26A - Ford Cosworth V8
3/ PP)	Jack Brabham	Brabham BT26A - Ford Cosworth V8

Drivers' championship		Constructors' championship	
1) Jackie Stewart	63	1) Matra - Ford Cosworth	66
2) Jacky Ickx	37	2) Brabham - Ford Cosworth	49
3) Bruce McLaren	26	3) Lotus - Ford Cosworth	47

1970

1) 7 Mar - SOUTH AFRICA (Kyalami)
1/ FL)	Jack Brabham	Brabham BT33 - Ford Cosworth V8
2)	Denny Hulme	McLaren M14A - Ford Cosworth V8
3/ PP)	Jackie Stewart	March 701 - Ford Cosworth V8

2) 19 Apr - SPAIN (Jarama)
1)	Jackie Stewart	March 701 - Ford Cosworth V8
2)	Bruce McLaren	McLaren M14A - Ford Cosworth V8
3)	Mario Andretti	March 701 - Ford Cosworth V8
PP/ FL)	Jack Brabham	Brabham BT33 - Ford Cosworth V8

3) 10 May - MONACO (Monte-Carlo)
1/ FL)	Jochen Rindt	Lotus 49C - Ford Cosworth V8
2)	Jack Brabham	Brabham BT33 - Ford Cosworth V8
3)	Henri Pescarolo	Matra-Simca MS120 - V12
PP)	Jackie Stewart	March 701 - Ford Cosworth V8

4) 7 Jun - BELGIUM (Spa-Francorchamps)
1)	Pedro Rodríguez	BRM P153 - V12
2/ FL)	Chris Amon	March 701 - Ford Cosworth V8
3)	Jean-Pierre Beltoise	Matra-Simca MS120 - V12
PP)	Jackie Stewart	March 701 - Ford Cosworth V8

5) 21 Jun - NETHERLANDS (Zandvoort)
1/ PP)	Jochen Rindt	Lotus 72C - Ford Cosworth V8
2)	Jackie Stewart	March 701 - Ford Cosworth V8
3/ FL)	Jacky Ickx	Ferrari 312B - F12

6) 5 Jul - FRANCE (Clermont-Ferrand)
1)	Jochen Rindt	Lotus 72C - Ford Cosworth V8
2)	Chris Amon	March 701 - Ford Cosworth V8
3/ FL)	Jack Brabham	Brabham BT33 - Ford Cosworth V8
PP)	Jacky Ickx	Ferrari 312B - F12

7) 18 Jul - BRITAIN (Brands Hatch)
1/ PP)	Jochen Rindt	Lotus 72C - Ford Cosworth V8
2/ FL)	Jack Brabham	Brabham BT33 - Ford Cosworth V8
3)	Denny Hulme	McLaren M14D - Ford Cosworth V8

8) 2 Aug - GERMANY (Hockenheim)
1)	Jochen Rindt	Lotus 72C - Ford Cosworth V8
2/ PP/ FL)	Jacky Ickx	Ferrari 312B - F12
3)	Denny Hulme	McLaren M14A - Ford Cosworth V8

9) 16 Aug - AUSTRIA (Österreichring)

1)	Jacky Ickx	Ferrari 312B - F12
2/ FL)	Clay Regazzoni	Ferrari 312B - F12
3)	Rolf Stommelen	Brabham BT33 - Ford Cosworth V8
PP)	Jochen Rindt	Lotus 72C - Ford Cosworth V8

10) 6 Sep - ITALY (Monza)

1/ FL)	Clay Regazzoni	Ferrari 312B - F12
2)	Jackie Stewart	March 701 - Ford Cosworth V8
3)	Jean-Pierre Beltoise	Matra-Simca MS120 - V12
PP)	Jacky Ickx	Ferrari 312B - F12

11) 20 Sep - CANADA (Mont-Tremblant)

1)	Jacky Ickx	Ferrari 312B - F12
2/ FL)	Clay Regazzoni	Ferrari 312B - F12
3)	Chris Amon	March 701 - Ford Cosworth V8
PP)	Jackie Stewart	Tyrrell 001 - Ford Cosworth V8

12) 4 Oct - UNITED STATES (Watkins Glen)

1)	Emerson Fittipaldi	Lotus 72C - Ford Cosworth V8
2)	Pedro Rodríguez	BRM P153 - V12
3)	Reine Wisell	Lotus 72C - Ford Cosworth V8
PP/ FL)	Jacky Ickx	Ferrari 312B - F12

13) 25 Oct - MEXICO (Mexico City)

1/ FL)	Jacky Ickx	Ferrari 312B - F12
2/ PP)	Clay Regazzoni	Ferrari 312B - F12
3)	Denny Hulme	McLaren M14A - Ford Cosworth V8

Drivers' championship

1) Jochen Rindt	45
2) Jacky Ickx	40
3) Clay Regazzoni	33

Constructors' championship

1) Lotus - Ford Cosworth	59
2) Ferrari	52
3) March - Ford Cosworth	48

1971

1) 6 Mar - SOUTH AFRICA (Kyalami)

1/ FL)	Mario Andretti	Ferrari 312B - F12
2/ PP)	Jackie Stewart	Tyrrell 001 - Ford Cosworth V8
3)	Clay Regazzoni	Ferrari 312B - F12

2) 18 Apr - SPAIN (Montjuïc)

1)	Jackie Stewart	Tyrrell 003 - Ford Cosworth V8
2/ PP/ FL)	Jacky Ickx	Ferrari 312B - F12
3)	Chris Amon	Matra-Simca MS120B - V12

3) 23 May - MONACO (Monte-Carlo)

1/ PP/ FL)	Jackie Stewart	Tyrrell 003 - Ford Cosworth V8
2)	Ronnie Peterson	March 711 - Ford Cosworth V8
3)	Jacky Ickx	Ferrari 312B2 - F12

4) 20 Jun - NETHERLANDS (Zandvoort)

1/ PP/ FL)	Jacky Ickx	Ferrari 312B2 - F12
2)	Pedro Rodríguez	BRM P160 - V12
3)	Clay Regazzoni	Ferrari 312B2 - F12

5) 4 Jul - FRANCE (Paul Ricard)

1/ PP/ FL)	Jackie Stewart	Tyrrell 003 - Ford Cosworth V8
2)	François Cevert	Tyrrell 002 - Ford Cosworth V8
3)	Emerson Fittipaldi	Lotus 72D - Ford Cosworth V8

6) 17 Jul - BRITAIN (Silverstone)

1/ FL)	Jackie Stewart	Tyrrell 003 - Ford Cosworth V8
2)	Ronnie Peterson	March 711 - Ford Cosworth V8
3)	Emerson Fittipaldi	Lotus 72D - Ford Cosworth V8
PP)	Clay Regazzoni	Ferrari 312B2 - F12

7) 1 Aug - GERMANY (Nürburgring)

1/ PP)	Jackie Stewart	Tyrrell 003 - Ford Cosworth V8
2/ FL)	François Cevert	Tyrrell 002 - Ford Cosworth V8
3)	Clay Regazzoni	Ferrari 312B2 - F12

8) 15 Aug - AUSTRIA (Österreichring)

1/ PP/ FL)	Jo Siffert	BRM P160 - V12
2)	Emerson Fittipaldi	Lotus 72D - Ford Cosworth V8
3)	Tim Schenken	Brabham BT33 - Ford Cosworth V8

9) 5 Sep - ITALY (Monza)

1)	Peter Gethin	BRM P160 - V12
2)	Ronnie Peterson	March 711 - Ford Cosworth V8
3)	François Cevert	Tyrrell 002 - Ford Cosworth V8
PP)	Chris Amon	Matra-Simca MS120B - V12
FL)	Henri Pescarolo	March 711 - Ford Cosworth V8

10) 19 Sep - CANADA (Mosport Park)

1/ PP)	Jackie Stewart	Tyrrell 003 - Ford Cosworth V8
2)	Ronnie Peterson	March 711 - Ford Cosworth V8
3)	Mark Donohue	McLaren M19A - Ford Cosworth V8
FL)	Denny Hulme	McLaren M19A - Ford Cosworth V8

11) 3 Oct - UNITED STATES (Watkins Glen)

1)	François Cevert	Tyrrell 002 - Ford Cosworth V8
2)	Jo Siffert	BRM P160 - V12
3)	Ronnie Peterson	March 711 - Ford Cosworth V8
PP)	Jackie Stewart	Tyrrell 003 - Ford Cosworth V8
FL)	Jacky Ickx	Ferrari 312B - F12

Drivers' championship

1) Jackie Stewart	62
2) Ronnie Peterson	33
3) François Cevert	26

Constructors' championship

1) Tyrrell - Ford Cosworth	73
2) BRM	36
3) Ferrari	33

1972

1) 23 Jan - ARGENTINA (Buenos Aires No.9)

1/ FL)	Jackie Stewart	Tyrrell 003 - Ford Cosworth V8
2)	Denny Hulme	McLaren M19A - Ford Cosworth V8
3)	Jacky Ickx	Ferrari 312B2 - F12
PP)	Carlos Reutemann	Brabham BT34 - Ford Cosworth V8

2) 4 Mar - SOUTH AFRICA (Kyalami)

1)	Denny Hulme	McLaren M19A - Ford Cosworth V8
2)	Emerson Fittipaldi	JPS Lotus 72D - Ford Cosworth V8
3)	Peter Revson	McLaren M19A - Ford Cosworth V8
PP)	Jackie Stewart	Tyrrell 003 - Ford Cosworth V8
FL)	Mike Hailwood	Surtees TS9B - Ford Cosworth V8

3) 1 May - SPAIN (Jarama)

1)	Emerson Fittipaldi	JPS Lotus 72D - Ford Cosworth V8
2/ PP/ FL)	Jacky Ickx	Ferrari 312B2 - F12
3)	Clay Regazzoni	Ferrari 312B2 - F12

4) 14 May - MONACO (Monte-Carlo)

1/ FL)	Jean-Pierre Beltoise	BRM P160B - V12
2)	Jacky Ickx	Ferrari 312B2 - F12
3/ PP)	Emerson Fittipaldi	JPS Lotus 72D - Ford Cosworth V8

5) 4 Jun - BELGIUM (Nivelles-Baulers)

1/ PP)	Emerson Fittipaldi	JPS Lotus 72D - Ford Cosworth V8
2)	François Cevert	Tyrrell 002 - Ford Cosworth V8
3)	Denny Hulme	McLaren M19C - Ford Cosworth V8
FL)	Chris Amon	Matra-Simca MS120C - V12

6) 2 Jul - FRANCE (Clermont-Ferrand)

1)	Jackie Stewart	Tyrrell 003 - Ford Cosworth V8
2)	Emerson Fittipaldi	JPS Lotus 72D - Ford Cosworth V8
3/ PP/ FL)	Chris Amon	Matra-Simca MS120D - V12

7) 15 Jul - BRITAIN (Brands Hatch)

1)	Emerson Fittipaldi	JPS Lotus 72D - Ford Cosworth V8
2/ FL)	Jackie Stewart	Tyrrell 003 - Ford Cosworth V8
3)	Peter Revson	McLaren M19A - Ford Cosworth V8
PP)	Jacky Ickx	Ferrari 312B2 - F12

8) 30 Jul - GERMANY (Nürburgring)

1/ PP/ FL)	Jacky Ickx	Ferrari 312B2 - F12
2)	Clay Regazzoni	Ferrari 312B2 - F12
3)	Ronnie Peterson	March 721G - Ford Cosworth V8

9) 13 Aug - AUSTRIA (Österreichring)

1/ PP)	Emerson Fittipaldi	JPS Lotus 72D - Ford Cosworth V8
2/ FL)	Denny Hulme	McLaren M19C - Ford Cosworth V8
3)	Peter Revson	McLaren M19C - Ford Cosworth V8

10) 10 Sep - ITALY (Monza)

1)	Emerson Fittipaldi	JPS Lotus 72D - Ford Cosworth V8
2)	Mike Hailwood	Surtees TS9B - Ford Cosworth V8
3)	Denny Hulme	McLaren M19C - Ford Cosworth V8
PP/ FL)	Jacky Ickx	Ferrari 312B2 - F12

11) 24 Sep - CANADA (Mosport Park)

1/ FL)	Jackie Stewart	Tyrrell 005 - Ford Cosworth V8
2/ PP)	Peter Revson	McLaren M19C - Ford Cosworth V8
3)	Denny Hulme	McLaren M19C - Ford Cosworth V8

12) 8 Oct - UNITED STATES (Watkins Glen)

1/ PP/ FL)	Jackie Stewart	Tyrrell 005 - Ford Cosworth V8
2)	François Cevert	Tyrrell 006 - Ford Cosworth V8
3)	Denny Hulme	McLaren M19C - Ford Cosworth V8

Drivers' championship

1) Emerson Fittipaldi	61
2) Jackie Stewart	45
3) Denny Hulme	39

Constructors' championship

1) Lotus - Ford Cosworth	61
2) Tyrrell - Ford Cosworth	51
3) McLaren - Ford Cosworth	47

1973

1) 28 Jan - ARGENTINA (Buenos Aires No.9)

1/ FL)	Emerson Fittipaldi	JPS Lotus 72D - Ford Cosworth V8
2)	François Cevert	Tyrrell 006 - Ford Cosworth V8
3)	Jackie Stewart	Tyrrell 005 - Ford Cosworth V8
PP)	Clay Regazzoni	BRM P160D - V12

2) 11 Feb - BRAZIL (Interlagos)

1/ FL)	Emerson Fittipaldi	JPS Lotus 72D - Ford Cosworth V8
2)	Jackie Stewart	Tyrrell 005 - Ford Cosworth V8
3/ FL)	Denny Hulme	McLaren M19C - Ford Cosworth V8
PP)	Ronnie Peterson	JPS Lotus 72D - Ford Cosworth V8

3) 3 Mar - SOUTH AFRICA (Kyalami)

1)	Jackie Stewart	Tyrrell 006 - Ford Cosworth V8
2)	Peter Revson	McLaren M19C - Ford Cosworth V8
3/ FL)	Emerson Fittipaldi	JPS Lotus 72D - Ford Cosworth V8
PP)	Denny Hulme	McLaren M23 - Ford Cosworth V8

4) 29 Apr - SPAIN (Montjuïc)

1)	Emerson Fittipaldi	JPS Lotus 72E - Ford Cosworth V8
2)	François Cevert	Tyrrell 006 - Ford Cosworth V8
3)	George Follmer	Shadow DN1 - Ford Cosworth V8
PP/ FL)	Ronnie Peterson	JPS Lotus 72E - Ford Cosworth V8

5) 20 May - BELGIUM (Zolder)

1)	Jackie Stewart	Tyrrell 006 - Ford Cosworth V8
2/ FL)	François Cevert	Tyrrell 006 - Ford Cosworth V8
3)	Emerson Fittipaldi	JPS Lotus 72E - Ford Cosworth V8
PP)	Ronnie Peterson	JPS Lotus 72E - Ford Cosworth V8

6) 3 Jun - MONACO (Monte-Carlo)

1/ PP)	Jackie Stewart	Tyrrell 006 - Ford Cosworth V8
2/ FL)	Emerson Fittipaldi	JPS Lotus 72E - Ford Cosworth V8
3)	Ronnie Peterson	JPS Lotus 72E - Ford Cosworth V8

7) 17 Jun - SWEDEN (Anderstorp)

1/ FL)	Denny Hulme	McLaren M23 - Ford Cosworth V8
2/ PP)	Ronnie Peterson	JPS Lotus 72E - Ford Cosworth V8
3)	François Cevert	Tyrrell 006 - Ford Cosworth V8

8) 1 Jul - FRANCE (Paul Ricard)

1)	Ronnie Peterson	JPS Lotus 72E - Ford Cosworth V8
2)	François Cevert	Tyrrell 006 - Ford Cosworth V8
3)	Carlos Reutemann	Brabham BT42 - Ford Cosworth V8
PP)	Jackie Stewart	Tyrrell 006 - Ford Cosworth V8
FL)	Denny Hulme	McLaren M23 - Ford Cosworth V8

9) 14 Jul - BRITAIN (Silverstone)

1)	Peter Revson	McLaren M23 - Ford Cosworth V8
2/ PP)	Ronnie Peterson	JPS Lotus 72E - Ford Cosworth V8
3)	Denny Hulme	McLaren M23 - Ford Cosworth V8
FL)	James Hunt	March 731 - Ford Cosworth V8

10) 29 Jul - NETHERLANDS (Zandvoort)

1)	Jackie Stewart	Tyrrell 006 - Ford Cosworth V8
2)	François Cevert	Tyrrell 006 - Ford Cosworth V8
3)	James Hunt	March 731 - Ford Cosworth V8
PP/ FL)	Ronnie Peterson	JPS Lotus 72E - Ford Cosworth V8

11) 5 Aug - GERMANY (Nürburgring)
1/ PP)	Jackie Stewart	Tyrrell 006 - Ford Cosworth V8
2)	François Cevert	Tyrrell 006 - Ford Cosworth V8
3)	Jacky Ickx	McLaren M23 - Ford Cosworth V8
FL)	Carlos Pace	Surtees TS14A - Ford Cosworth V8

12) 19 Aug - AUSTRIA (Österreichring)
1)	Ronnie Peterson	JPS Lotus 72E - Ford Cosworth V8
2)	Jackie Stewart	Tyrrell 006 - Ford Cosworth V8
3/ FL)	Carlos Pace	Surtees TS14A - Ford Cosworth V8
PP)	Emerson Fittipaldi	JPS Lotus 72E - Ford Cosworth V8

13) 9 Sep - ITALY (Monza)
1/ PP)	Ronnie Peterson	JPS Lotus 72E - Ford Cosworth V8
2)	Emerson Fittipaldi	JPS Lotus 72E - Ford Cosworth V8
3)	Peter Revson	McLaren M23 - Ford Cosworth V8
FL)	Jackie Stewart	Tyrrell 006 - Ford Cosworth V8

14) 23 Sep - CANADA (Mosport Park)
1)	Peter Revson	McLaren M23 - Ford Cosworth V8
2/ FL)	Emerson Fittipaldi	JPS Lotus 72E - Ford Cosworth V8
3)	Jackie Oliver	Shadow DN1 - Ford Cosworth V8
PP)	Ronnie Peterson	JPS Lotus 72E - Ford Cosworth V8

15) 7 Oct - UNITED STATES (Watkins Glen)
1/ PP)	Ronnie Peterson	JPS Lotus 72E - Ford Cosworth V8
2/ FL)	James Hunt	March 731 - Ford Cosworth V8
3)	Carlos Reutemann	Brabham BT42 - Ford Cosworth V8

Drivers' championship			Constructors' championship	
1) Jackie Stewart	71		1) Lotus - Ford Cosworth	92
2) Emerson Fittipaldi	55		2) Tyrrell - Ford Cosworth	82
3) Ronnie Peterson	52		3) McLaren - Ford Cosworth	58

1974

1) 13 Jan - ARGENTINA (Buenos Aires No.15)
1)	Denny Hulme	McLaren M23 - Ford Cosworth V8
2)	Niki Lauda	Ferrari 312B3 - F12
3/ FL)	Clay Regazzoni	Ferrari 312B3 - F12
PP)	Ronnie Peterson	JPS Lotus 72E - Ford Cosworth V8

2) 27 Jan - BRAZIL (Interlagos)
1/ PP)	Emerson Fittipaldi	McLaren M23 - Ford Cosworth V8
2/ FL)	Clay Regazzoni	Ferrari 312B3 - F12
3)	Jacky Ickx	JPS Lotus 72E - Ford Cosworth V8

3) 30 Mar - SOUTH AFRICA (Kyalami)
1/ FL)	Carlos Reutemann	Brabham BT44 - Ford Cosworth V8
2)	Jean-Pierre Beltoise	BRM P201 - V12
3)	Mike Hailwood	McLaren M23 - Ford Cosworth V8
PP)	Niki Lauda	Ferrari 312B3 - F12

4) 28 Apr - SPAIN (Jarama)
1/ PP/ FL)	Niki Lauda	Ferrari 312B3 - F12
2)	Clay Regazzoni	Ferrari 312B3 - F12
3)	Emerson Fittipaldi	McLaren M23 - Ford Cosworth V8

5) 12 May - BELGIUM (Nivelles-Baulers)
1)	Emerson Fittipaldi	McLaren M23 - Ford Cosworth V8
2)	Niki Lauda	Ferrari 312B3 - F12
3)	Jody Scheckter	Tyrrell 007 - Ford Cosworth V8
PP)	Clay Regazzoni	Ferrari 312B3 - F12
FL)	Denny Hulme	McLaren M23 - Ford Cosworth V8

6) 26 May - MONACO (Monte-Carlo)
1/ FL)	Ronnie Peterson	JPS Lotus 72E - Ford Cosworth V8
2)	Jody Scheckter	Tyrrell 007 - Ford Cosworth V8
3)	Jean-Pierre Jarier	Shadow DN3 - Ford Cosworth V8
PP)	Niki Lauda	Ferrari 312B3 - F12

7) 9 Jun - SWEDEN (Anderstorp)
1)	Jody Scheckter	Tyrrell 007 - Ford Cosworth V8
2/ PP/ FL)	Patrick Depailler	Tyrrell 007 - Ford Cosworth V8
3)	James Hunt	Hesketh 308 - Ford Cosworth V8

8) 23 Jun - NETHERLANDS (Zandvoort)
1/ PP)	Niki Lauda	Ferrari 312B3 - F12
2)	Clay Regazzoni	Ferrari 312B3 - F12
3)	Emerson Fittipaldi	McLaren M23 - Ford Cosworth V8
FL)	Ronnie Peterson	JPS Lotus 72E - Ford Cosworth V8

9) 7 Jul - FRANCE (Dijon-Prenois)
1)	Ronnie Peterson	JPS Lotus 72E - Ford Cosworth V8
2/ PP)	Niki Lauda	Ferrari 312B3 - F12
3)	Clay Regazzoni	Ferrari 312B3 - F12
FL)	Jody Scheckter	Tyrrell 007 - Ford Cosworth V8

10) 20 Jul - BRITAIN (Brands Hatch)
1)	Jody Scheckter	Tyrrell 007 - Ford Cosworth V8
2)	Emerson Fittipaldi	McLaren M23 - Ford Cosworth V8
3)	Jacky Ickx	JPS Lotus 72E - Ford Cosworth V8
PP/ FL)	Niki Lauda	Ferrari 312B3 - F12

11) 4 Aug - GERMANY (Nürburgring)
1)	Clay Regazzoni	Ferrari 312B3 - F12
2/ FL)	Jody Scheckter	Tyrrell 007 - Ford Cosworth V8
3)	Carlos Reutemann	Brabham BT44 - Ford Cosworth V8
PP)	Niki Lauda	Ferrari 312B3 - F12

12) 18 Aug - AUSTRIA (Österreichring)
1)	Carlos Reutemann	Brabham BT44 - Ford Cosworth V8
2)	Denny Hulme	McLaren M23 - Ford Cosworth V8
3)	James Hunt	Hesketh 308 - Ford Cosworth V8
PP)	Niki Lauda	Ferrari 312B3 - F12
FL)	Clay Regazzoni	Ferrari 312B3 - F12

13) 8 Sep - ITALY (Monza)
1)	Ronnie Peterson	JPS Lotus 72E - Ford Cosworth V8
2)	Emerson Fittipaldi	McLaren M23 - Ford Cosworth V8
3)	Jody Scheckter	Tyrrell 007 - Ford Cosworth V8
PP)	Niki Lauda	Ferrari 312B3 - F12
FL)	Carlos Pace	Brabham BT44 - Ford Cosworth V8

14) 22 Sep - CANADA (Mosport Park)
1/ PP)	Emerson Fittipaldi	McLaren M23 - Ford Cosworth V8
2)	Clay Regazzoni	Ferrari 312B3 - F12
3)	Ronnie Peterson	JPS Lotus 72E - Ford Cosworth V8
FL)	Niki Lauda	Ferrari 312B3 - F12

15) 6 Oct - UNITED STATES (Watkins Glen)
1/ PP)	Carlos Reutemann	Brabham BT44 - Ford Cosworth V8
2/ FL)	Carlos Pace	Brabham BT44 - Ford Cosworth V8
3)	James Hunt	Hesketh 308 - Ford Cosworth V8

Drivers' championship
1) Emerson Fittipaldi 55
2) Clay Regazzoni 52
3) Jody Scheckter 45

Constructors' championship
1) McLaren - Ford Cosworth 73
2) Ferrari 65
3) Tyrrell - Ford Cosworth 52

1975

1) 12 Jan - ARGENTINA (Buenos Aires No.15)
1)	Emerson Fittipaldi	McLaren M23 - Ford Cosworth V8
2/ FL)	James Hunt	Hesketh 308B - Ford Cosworth V8
3)	Carlos Reutemann	Brabham BT44B - Ford Cosworth V8
PP)	Jean-Pierre Jarier	Shadow DN5 - Ford Cosworth V8

Jean-Pierre Jarier did not start (crown wheel & pinion failure on the parade lap).

2) 26 Jan - BRAZIL (Interlagos)
1)	Carlos Pace	Brabham BT44B - Ford Cosworth V8
2)	Emerson Fittipaldi	McLaren M23 - Ford Cosworth V8
3)	Jochen Mass	McLaren M23 - Ford Cosworth V8
PP/ FL)	Jean-Pierre Jarier	Shadow DN5 - Ford Cosworth V8

3) 1 Mar - SOUTH AFRICA (Kyalami)
1)	Jody Scheckter	Tyrrell 007 - Ford Cosworth V8
2)	Carlos Reutemann	Brabham BT44B - Ford Cosworth V8
3)	Patrick Depailler	Tyrrell 007 - Ford Cosworth V8
PP/ FL)	Carlos Pace	Brabham BT44B - Ford Cosworth V8

4) 27 Apr - SPAIN (Montjuïc)
1)	Jochen Mass	McLaren M23 - Ford Cosworth V8
2)	Jacky Ickx	JPS Lotus 72E - Ford Cosworth V8
3)	Carlos Reutemann	Brabham BT44B - Ford Cosworth V8
PP)	Niki Lauda	Ferrari 312T - F12
FL)	Mario Andretti	Parnelli VPJ4 - Ford Cosworth V8

Race was stopped early, due to accident and fatalities. Half points awarded.
Jean-Pierre Jarier (Shadow DN5 - Ford Cosworth V8) finished 3rd, but was given a 1 lap penalty for overtaking under yellow flags - classified 4th.

5) 11 May - MONACO (Monte-Carlo)
1/ PP)	Niki Lauda	Ferrari 312T - F12
2)	Emerson Fittipaldi	McLaren M23 - Ford Cosworth V8
3)	Carlos Pace	Brabham BT44B - Ford Cosworth V8
FL)	Patrick Depailler	Tyrrell 007 - Ford Cosworth V8

6) 25 May - BELGIUM (Zolder)
1/ PP)	Niki Lauda	Ferrari 312T - F12
2)	Jody Scheckter	Tyrrell 007 - Ford Cosworth V8
3)	Carlos Reutemann	Brabham BT44B - Ford Cosworth V8
FL)	Clay Regazzoni	Ferrari 312T - F12

7) 8 Jun - SWEDEN (Anderstorp)
1/ FL)	Niki Lauda	Ferrari 312T - F12
2)	Carlos Reutemann	Brabham BT44B - Ford Cosworth V8
3)	Clay Regazzoni	Ferrari 312T - F12
PP)	Vittorio Brambilla	March 751 - Ford Cosworth V8

8) 22 Jun - NETHERLANDS (Zandvoort)
1)	James Hunt	Hesketh 308B - Ford Cosworth V8
2/ PP/ FL)	Niki Lauda	Ferrari 312T - F12
3)	Clay Regazzoni	Ferrari 312T - F12

9) 6 Jul - FRANCE (Paul Ricard)
1/ PP)	Niki Lauda	Ferrari 312T - F12
2)	James Hunt	Hesketh 308B - Ford Cosworth V8
3/ FL)	Jochen Mass	McLaren M23 - Ford Cosworth V8

10) 19 Jul - BRITAIN (Silverstone)
1)	Emerson Fittipaldi	McLaren M23 - Ford Cosworth V8
2/ret)	Carlos Pace	Brabham BT44B - Ford Cosworth V8
3/ret)	Jody Scheckter	Tyrrell 007 - Ford Cosworth V8
PP)	Tom Pryce	Shadow DN5 - Ford Cosworth V8
FL)	Clay Regazzoni	Ferrari 312T - F12

11) 3 Aug - GERMANY (Nürburgring)
1)	Carlos Reutemann	Brabham BT44B - Ford Cosworth V8
2)	Jacques Laffite	Williams FW04 - Ford Cosworth V8
3/ PP)	Niki Lauda	Ferrari 312T - F12
FL)	Clay Regazzoni	Ferrari 312T - F12

12) 17 Aug - AUSTRIA (Österreichring)
1/ FL)	Vittorio Brambilla	March 751 - Ford Cosworth V8
2)	James Hunt	Hesketh 308B - Ford Cosworth V8
3)	Tom Pryce	Shadow DN5 - Ford Cosworth V8
PP)	Niki Lauda	Ferrari 312T - F12

Race was stopped early, due to heavy rain. Half points awarded.

13) 7 Sep - ITALY (Monza)
1/ FL)	Clay Regazzoni	Ferrari 312T - F12
2)	Emerson Fittipaldi	McLaren M23 - Ford Cosworth V8
3/ PP)	Niki Lauda	Ferrari 312T - F12

14) 5 Oct - UNITED STATES (Watkins Glen)

1/ PP)	Niki Lauda	Ferrari 312T - F12
2/ FL)	Emerson Fittipaldi	McLaren M23 - Ford Cosworth V8
3)	Jochen Mass	McLaren M23 - Ford Cosworth V8

Drivers' championship			Constructors' championship	
1) Niki Lauda	64.5		1) Ferrari	72.5
2) Emerson Fittipaldi	45		2) Brabham - Ford Cosworth	54
3) Carlos Reutemann	37		3) McLaren - Ford Cosworth	53

1976

1) 25 Jan - BRAZIL (Interlagos)

1)	Niki Lauda	Ferrari 312T - F12
2)	Patrick Depailler	Tyrrell 007 - Ford Cosworth V8
3)	Tom Pryce	Shadow DN5 - Ford Cosworth V8
PP)	James Hunt	McLaren M23 - Ford Cosworth V8
FL)	Jean-Pierre Jarier	Shadow DN5 - Ford Cosworth V8

2) 6 Mar - SOUTH AFRICA (Kyalami)

1/ FL)	Niki Lauda	Ferrari 312T - F12
2/ PP)	James Hunt	McLaren M23 - Ford Cosworth V8
3)	Jochen Mass	McLaren M23 - Ford Cosworth V8

3) 28 Mar - UNITED STATES WEST (Long Beach)

1/ PP/ FL)	Clay Regazzoni	Ferrari 312T - F12
2)	Niki Lauda	Ferrari 312T - F12
3)	Patrick Depailler	Tyrrell 007 - Ford Cosworth V8

4) 2 May - SPAIN (Jarama)

1/ PP)	James Hunt	McLaren M23 - Ford Cosworth V8
2)	Niki Lauda	Ferrari 312T2 - F12
3)	Gunnar Nilsson	JPS Lotus 77 - Ford Cosworth V8
FL)	Jochen Mass	McLaren M23 - Ford Cosworth V8

5) 16 May - BELGIUM (Zolder)

1/ PP/ FL)	Niki Lauda	Ferrari 312T2 - F12
2)	Clay Regazzoni	Ferrari 312T2 - F12
3)	Jacques Laffite	Ligier JS5 - Matra V12

6) 30 May - MONACO (Monte-Carlo)

1/ PP)	Niki Lauda	Ferrari 312T2 - F12
2)	Jody Scheckter	Tyrrell P34 - Ford Cosworth V8
3)	Patrick Depailler	Tyrrell P34 - Ford Cosworth V8
FL)	Clay Regazzoni	Ferrari 312T2 - F12

7) 13 Jun - SWEDEN (Anderstorp)

1/ PP)	Jody Scheckter	Tyrrell P34 - Ford Cosworth V8
2)	Patrick Depailler	Tyrrell P34 - Ford Cosworth V8
3)	Niki Lauda	Ferrari 312T2 - F12
FL)	Mario Andretti	JPS Lotus 77 - Ford Cosworth V8

8) 4 Jul - FRANCE (Paul Ricard)

1/ PP)	James Hunt	McLaren M23 - Ford Cosworth V8
2)	Patrick Depailler	Tyrrell P34 - Ford Cosworth V8
3)	John Watson	Penske PC4 - Ford Cosworth V8
FL)	Niki Lauda	Ferrari 312T2 - F12

9) 18 Jul - BRITAIN (Brands Hatch)

1/ PP/ FL)	Niki Lauda	Ferrari 312T2 - F12
2)	Jody Scheckter	Tyrrell P34 - Ford Cosworth V8
3)	John Watson	Penske PC4 - Ford Cosworth V8

James Hunt (McLaren M23 - Ford Cosworth V8) finished 1st, but was disqualified for taking a short-cut back to the pits after the initial race was stopped. He also recorded fastest lap, but this was removed.

10) 1 Aug - GERMANY (Nürburgring)

1/ PP)	James Hunt	McLaren M23 - Ford Cosworth V8
2/ FL)	Jody Scheckter	Tyrrell P34 - Ford Cosworth V8
3)	Jochen Mass	McLaren M23 - Ford Cosworth V8

11) 15 Aug - AUSTRIA (Österreichring)

1)	John Watson	Penske PC4 - Ford Cosworth V8
2)	Jacques Laffite	Ligier JS5 - Matra V12
3)	Gunnar Nilsson	JPS Lotus 77 - Ford Cosworth V8
PP/ FL)	James Hunt	McLaren M23 - Ford Cosworth V8

12) 29 Aug - NETHERLANDS (Zandvoort)

1)	James Hunt	McLaren M23 - Ford Cosworth V8
2/ FL)	Clay Regazzoni	Ferrari 312T2 - F12
3)	Mario Andretti	JPS Lotus 77 - Ford Cosworth V8
PP)	Ronnie Peterson	March 761 - Ford Cosworth V8

13) 12 Sep - ITALY (Monza)

1/ FL)	Ronnie Peterson	March 761 - Ford Cosworth V8
2)	Clay Regazzoni	Ferrari 312T2 - F12
3/ PP)	Jacques Laffite	Ligier JS5 - Matra V12

14) 3 Oct - CANADA (Mosport Park)

1/ PP)	James Hunt	McLaren M23 - Ford Cosworth V8
2/ FL)	Patrick Depailler	Tyrrell P34 - Ford Cosworth V8
3)	Mario Andretti	JPS Lotus 77 - Ford Cosworth V8

15) 10 Oct - UNITED STATES (Watkins Glen)

1/ PP/ FL)	James Hunt	McLaren M23 - Ford Cosworth V8
2)	Jody Scheckter	Tyrrell P34 - Ford Cosworth V8
3)	Niki Lauda	Ferrari 312T2 - F12

16) 24 Oct - JAPAN (Fuji)

1/ PP)	Mario Andretti	JPS Lotus 77 - Ford Cosworth V8
2)	Patrick Depailler	Tyrrell P34 - Ford Cosworth V8
3)	James Hunt	McLaren M23 - Ford Cosworth V8
FL)	Jacques Laffite	Ligier JS5 - Matra V12

Drivers' championship			Constructors' championship	
1) James Hunt	69		1) Ferrari	83
2) Niki Lauda	68		2) McLaren - Ford Cosworth	74
3) Jody Scheckter	49		3) Tyrrell - Ford Cosworth	71

1977

1) 9 Jan - ARGENTINA (Buenos Aires No.15)

1)	Jody Scheckter	Wolf WR1 - Ford Cosworth V8
2)	Carlos Pace	Brabham BT45 - Alfa Romeo F12
3)	Carlos Reutemann	Ferrari 312T2 - F12
PP/ FL)	James Hunt	McLaren M23 - Ford Cosworth V8

2) 23 Jan - BRAZIL (Interlagos)
1)	Carlos Reutemann	Ferrari 312T2 - F12
2/ PP/ FL)	James Hunt	McLaren M23 - Ford Cosworth V8
3)	Niki Lauda	Ferrari 312T2 - F12

3) 5 Mar - SOUTH AFRICA (Kyalami)
1)	Niki Lauda	Ferrari 312T2 - F12
2)	Jody Scheckter	Wolf WR1 - Ford Cosworth V8
3)	Patrick Depailler	Tyrrell P34 - Ford Cosworth V8
PP)	James Hunt	McLaren M23 - Ford Cosworth V8
FL)	John Watson	Brabham BT45 - Alfa Romeo F12

4) 3 Apr - UNITED STATES WEST (Long Beach)
1)	Mario Andretti	JPS Lotus 78 - Ford Cosworth V8
2/ PP/ FL)	Niki Lauda	Ferrari 312T2 - F12
3)	Jody Scheckter	Wolf WR1 - Ford Cosworth V8

5) 8 May - SPAIN (Jarama)
1/ PP)	Mario Andretti	JPS Lotus 78 - Ford Cosworth V8
2)	Carlos Reutemann	Ferrari 312T2 - F12
3)	Jody Scheckter	Wolf WR2 - Ford Cosworth V8
FL)	Jacques Laffite	Ligier JS7 - Matra V12

6) 22 May - MONACO (Monte-Carlo)
1/ FL)	Jody Scheckter	Wolf WR1 - Ford Cosworth V8
2)	Niki Lauda	Ferrari 312T2 - F12
3)	Carlos Reutemann	Ferrari 312T2 - F12
PP)	John Watson	Brabham BT45B - Alfa Romeo F12

7) 5 Jun - BELGIUM (Zolder)
1/ FL)	Gunnar Nilsson	JPS Lotus 78 - Ford Cosworth V8
2)	Niki Lauda	Ferrari 312T2 - F12
3)	Ronnie Peterson	Tyrrell P34 - Ford Cosworth V8
PP)	Mario Andretti	JPS Lotus 78 - Ford Cosworth V8

8) 19 Jun - SWEDEN (Anderstorp)
1)	Jacques Laffite	Ligier JS7 - Matra V12
2)	Jochen Mass	McLaren M23 - Ford Cosworth V8
3)	Carlos Reutemann	Ferrari 312T2 - F12
PP/ FL)	Mario Andretti	JPS Lotus 78 - Ford Cosworth V8

9) 3 Jul - FRANCE (Dijon-Prenois)
1/ PP/ FL)	Mario Andretti	JPS Lotus 78 - Ford Cosworth V8
2)	John Watson	Brabham BT45B - Alfa Romeo F12
3)	James Hunt	McLaren M26 - Ford Cosworth V8

10) 16 Jul - BRITAIN (Silverstone)
1/ PP/ FL)	James Hunt	McLaren M26 - Ford Cosworth V8
2)	Niki Lauda	Ferrari 312T2 - F12
3)	Gunnar Nilsson	JPS Lotus 78 - Ford Cosworth V8

11) 31 Jul - GERMANY (Hockenheim)
1/ FL)	Niki Lauda	Ferrari 312T2 - F12
2/ PP)	Jody Scheckter	Wolf WR2 - Ford Cosworth V8
3)	Hans-Joachim Stuck	Brabham BT45B - Alfa Romeo F12

12) 14 Aug - AUSTRIA (Österreichring)
1)	Alan Jones	Shadow DN8 - Ford Cosworth V8
2/ PP)	Niki Lauda	Ferrari 312T2 - F12
3)	Hans-Joachim Stuck	Brabham BT45B - Alfa Romeo F12
FL)	John Watson	Brabham BT45B - Alfa Romeo F12

13) 28 Aug - NETHERLANDS (Zandvoort)
1/ FL)	Niki Lauda	Ferrari 312T2 - F12
2)	Jacques Laffite	Ligier JS7 - Matra V12
3)	Jody Scheckter	Wolf WR2 - Ford Cosworth V8
PP)	Mario Andretti	JPS Lotus 78 - Ford Cosworth V8

14) 11 Sep - ITALY (Monza)
1/ FL)	Mario Andretti	JPS Lotus 78 - Ford Cosworth V8
2)	Niki Lauda	Ferrari 312T2 - F12
3)	Alan Jones	Shadow DN8 - Ford Cosworth V8
PP)	James Hunt	McLaren M26 - Ford Cosworth V8

15) 2 Oct - UNITED STATES (Watkins Glen)
1/ PP)	James Hunt	McLaren M26 - Ford Cosworth V8
2)	Mario Andretti	JPS Lotus 78 - Ford Cosworth V8
3)	Jody Scheckter	Wolf WR2 - Ford Cosworth V8
FL)	Ronnie Peterson	Tyrrell P34 - Ford Cosworth V8

16) 9 Oct - CANADA (Mosport Park)
1)	Jody Scheckter	Wolf WR1 - Ford Cosworth V8
2)	Patrick Depailler	Tyrrell P34 - Ford Cosworth V8
3)	Jochen Mass	McLaren M26 - Ford Cosworth V8
PP/ FL)	Mario Andretti	JPS Lotus 78 - Ford Cosworth V8

17) 23 Oct - JAPAN (Fuji)
1)	James Hunt	McLaren M26 - Ford Cosworth V8
2)	Carlos Reutemann	Ferrari 312T2 - F12
3)	Patrick Depailler	Tyrrell P34 - Ford Cosworth V8
PP)	Mario Andretti	JPS Lotus 78 - Ford Cosworth V8
FL)	Jody Scheckter	Wolf WR3 - Ford Cosworth V8

Drivers' championship		Constructors' championship	
1) Niki Lauda	72	1) Ferrari	95
2) Jody Scheckter	55	2) Lotus - Ford Cosworth	62
3) Mario Andretti	47	3) McLaren - Ford Cosworth	60

1978

1) 15 Jan - ARGENTINA (Buenos Aires No.15)
1/ PP)	Mario Andretti	JPS Lotus 78 - Ford Cosworth V8
2)	Niki Lauda	Brabham BT45C - Alfa Romeo F12
3)	Patrick Depailler	Tyrrell 008 - Ford Cosworth V8
FL)	Gilles Villeneuve	Ferrari 312T2 - F12

2) 29 Jan - BRAZIL (Jacarepaguá)
1/ FL)	Carlos Reutemann	Ferrari 312T2 - F12
2)	Emerson Fittipaldi	Copersucar F5A - Ford Cosworth V8
3)	Niki Lauda	Brabham BT45C - Alfa Romeo F12
PP)	Ronnie Peterson	JPS Lotus 78 - Ford Cosworth V8

3) 4 Mar - SOUTH AFRICA (Kyalami)

1)	Ronnie Peterson	JPS Lotus 78 - Ford Cosworth V8
2)	Patrick Depailler	Tyrrell 008 - Ford Cosworth V8
3)	John Watson	Brabham BT46 - Alfa Romeo F12
PP)	Niki Lauda	Brabham BT46 - Alfa Romeo F12
FL)	Mario Andretti	JPS Lotus 78 - Ford Cosworth V8

4) 2 Apr - UNITED STATES WEST (Long Beach)

1/ PP)	Carlos Reutemann	Ferrari 312T3 - F12
2)	Mario Andretti	JPS Lotus 78 - Ford Cosworth V8
3)	Patrick Depailler	Tyrroll 008 Ford Cosworth V8
FL)	Alan Jones	Williams FW06 - Ford Cosworth V8

5) 7 May - MONACO (Monte-Carlo)

1)	Patrick Depailler	Tyrrell 008 - Ford Cosworth V8
2/ FL)	Niki Lauda	Brabham BT46 - Alfa Romeo F12
3)	Jody Scheckter	Wolf WR1 - Ford Cosworth V8
PP)	Carlos Reutemann	Ferrari 312T3 - F12

6) 21 May - BELGIUM (Zolder)

1/ PP)	Mario Andretti	JPS Lotus 79 - Ford Cosworth V8
2/ FL)	Ronnie Peterson	JPS Lotus 78 - Ford Cosworth V8
3)	Carlos Reutemann	Ferrari 312T3 - F12

7) 4 Jun - SPAIN (Jarama)

1/ PP/ FL)	Mario Andretti	JPS Lotus 79 - Ford Cosworth V8
2)	Ronnie Peterson	JPS Lotus 79 - Ford Cosworth V8
3)	Jacques Laffite	Ligier JS9 - Matra V12

8) 17 Jun - SWEDEN (Anderstorp)

1/ FL)	Niki Lauda	Brabham BT46B - Alfa Romeo F12
2)	Riccardo Patrese	Arrows FA1 - Ford Cosworth V8
3)	Ronnie Peterson	JPS Lotus 79 - Ford Cosworth V8
PP)	Mario Andretti	JPS Lotus 79 - Ford Cosworth V8

9) 2 Jul - FRANCE (Paul Ricard)

1)	Mario Andretti	JPS Lotus 79 - Ford Cosworth V8
2)	Ronnie Peterson	JPS Lotus 79 - Ford Cosworth V8
3)	James Hunt	McLaren M26 - Ford Cosworth V8
PP)	John Watson	Brabham BT46 - Alfa Romeo F12
FL)	Carlos Reutemann	Ferrari 312T3 - F12

10) 16 Jul - BRITAIN (Brands Hatch)

1)	Carlos Reutemann	Ferrari 312T3 - F12
2/ FL)	Niki Lauda	Brabham BT46 - Alfa Romeo F12
3)	John Watson	Brabham BT46 - Alfa Romeo F12
PP)	Ronnie Peterson	JPS Lotus 79 - Ford Cosworth V8

11) 30 Jul - GERMANY (Hockenheim)

1/ PP)	Mario Andretti	JPS Lotus 79 - Ford Cosworth V8
2)	Jody Scheckter	Wolf WR5 - Ford Cosworth V8
3)	Jacques Laffite	Ligier JS9 - Matra V12
FL)	Ronnie Peterson	JPS Lotus 79 - Ford Cosworth V8

12) 13 Aug - AUSTRIA (Österreichring)

1/ PP/ FL)	Ronnie Peterson	JPS Lotus 79 - Ford Cosworth V8
2)	Patrick Depailler	Tyrrell 008 - Ford Cosworth V8
3)	Gilles Villeneuve	Ferrari 312T3 - F12

13) 27 Aug - NETHERLANDS (Zandvoort)

1/ PP)	Marlo Andretti	JPS Lotus 79 - Ford Cosworth V8
2)	Ronnie Peterson	JPS Lotus 79 - Ford Cosworth V8
3/ FL)	Niki Lauda	Brabham BT46 - Alfa Romeo F12

14) 10 Sep - ITALY (Monza)

1)	Niki Lauda	Brabham BT46 - Alfa Romeo F12
2)	John Watson	Brabham BT46 - Alfa Romeo F12
3)	Carlos Reutemann	Ferrari 312T3 - F12
PP/ FL)	Mario Andretti	JPS Lotus 79 - Ford Cosworth V8

Mario Andretti (JPS Lotus 79 - Ford Cosworth V8) and Gilles Villeneuve (Ferrari 312T3 - F12), finished 1st and 2nd, but were both given a 1-minute penalty for jumping the start, placing them 6th and 7th respectively.

15) 1 Oct - UNITED STATES (Watkins Glen)

1)	Carlos Reutemann	Ferrari 312T3 - F12
2)	Alan Jones	Williams FW06 - Ford Cosworth V8
3)	Jody Scheckter	Wolf WR6 - Ford Cosworth V8
PP)	Mario Andretti	JPS Lotus 79 - Ford Cosworth V8
FL)	Jean-Pierre Jarier	JPS Lotus 79 - Ford Cosworth V8

16) 8 Oct - CANADA (Montréal)

1)	Gilles Villeneuve	Ferrari 312T3 - F12
2)	Jody Scheckter	Wolf WR6 - Ford Cosworth V8
3)	Carlos Reutemann	Ferrari 312T3 - F12
PP)	Jean-Pierre Jarier	JPS Lotus 79 - Ford Cosworth V8
FL)	Alan Jones	Williams FW06 - Ford Cosworth V8

Drivers' championship		Constructors' championship	
1) Mario Andretti	64	1) Lotus - Ford Cosworth	86
2) Ronnie Peterson	51	2) Ferrari	58
3) Carlos Reutemann	48	3) Brabham - Alfa Romeo	53

1979

1) 21 Jan - ARGENTINA (Buenos Aires No.15)

1/ PP/ FL)	Jacques Laffite	Ligier JS11 - Ford Cosworth V8
2)	Carlos Reutemann	Lotus 79 - Ford Cosworth V8
3)	John Watson	McLaren M28 - Ford Cosworth V8

2) 4 Feb - BRAZIL (Interlagos)

1/ PP/ FL)	Jacques Laffite	Ligier JS11 - Ford Cosworth V8
2)	Patrick Depailler	Ligier JS11 - Ford Cosworth V8
3)	Carlos Reutemann	Lotus 79 - Ford Cosworth V8

3) 3 Mar - SOUTH AFRICA (Kyalami)

1/ FL)	Gilles Villeneuve	Ferrari 312T4 - F12
2)	Jody Scheckter	Ferrari 312T4 - F12
3)	Jean-Pierre Jarier	Tyrrell 009 - Ford Cosworth V8
PP)	Jean-Pierre Jabouille	Renault RS01 - V6t

4) 8 Apr - UNITED STATES WEST (Long Beach)

1/ PP/ FL)	Gilles Villeneuve	Ferrari 312T4 - F12
2)	Jody Scheckter	Ferrari 312T4 - F12
3)	Alan Jones	Williams FW06 - Ford Cosworth V8

5) 29 Apr - SPAIN (Jarama)

1)	Patrick Depailler	Ligier JS11 - Ford Cosworth V8
2)	Carlos Reutemann	Lotus 79 - Ford Cosworth V8
3)	Mario Andretti	Lotus 80 - Ford Cosworth V8
PP)	Jacques Laffite	Ligier JS11 - Ford Cosworth V8
FL)	Gilles Villeneuve	Ferrari 312T4 - F12

6) 13 May - BELGIUM (Zolder)

1)	Jody Scheckter	Ferrari 312T4 - F12
2/ PP)	Jacques Laffite	Ligier JS11 - Ford Cosworth V8
3)	Didier Pironi	Tyrrell 009 - Ford Cosworth V8
FL)	Gilles Villeneuve	Ferrari 312T4 - F12

7) 27 May - MONACO (Monte-Carlo)

1/ PP)	Jody Scheckter	Ferrari 312T4 - F12
2)	Clay Regazzoni	Williams FW07 - Ford Cosworth V8
3)	Carlos Reutemann	Lotus 79 - Ford Cosworth V8
FL)	Patrick Depailler	Ligier JS11 - Ford Cosworth V8

8) 1 Jul - FRANCE (Dijon-Prenois)

1/ PP)	Jean-Pierre Jabouille	Renault RS10 - V6t
2)	Gilles Villeneuve	Ferrari 312T4 - F12
3/ FL)	René Arnoux	Renault RS10 - V6t

9) 14 Jul - BRITAIN (Silverstone)

1/ FL)	Clay Regazzoni	Williams FW07 - Ford Cosworth V8
2)	René Arnoux	Renault RS10 - V6t
3)	Jean-Pierre Jarier	Tyrrell 009 - Ford Cosworth V8
PP)	Alan Jones	Williams FW07 - Ford Cosworth V8

10) 29 Jul - GERMANY (Hockenheim)

1)	Alan Jones	Williams FW07 - Ford Cosworth V8
2)	Clay Regazzoni	Williams FW07 - Ford Cosworth V8
3)	Jacques Laffite	Ligier JS11 - Ford Cosworth V8
PP)	Jean-Pierre Jabouille	Renault RS10 - V6t
FL)	Gilles Villeneuve	Ferrari 312T4 - F12

11) 12 Aug - AUSTRIA (Österreichring)

1)	Alan Jones	Williams FW07 - Ford Cosworth V8
2)	Gilles Villeneuve	Ferrari 312T4 - F12
3)	Jacques Laffite	Ligier JS11 - Ford Cosworth V8
PP/ FL)	René Arnoux	Renault RS10 - V6t

12) 26 Aug - NETHERLANDS (Zandvoort)

1)	Alan Jones	Williams FW07 - Ford Cosworth V8
2)	Jody Scheckter	Ferrari 312T4 - F12
3)	Jacques Laffite	Ligier JS11 - Ford Cosworth V8
PP)	René Arnoux	Renault RS10 - V6t
FL)	Gilles Villeneuve	Ferrari 312T4 - F12

13) 9 Sep - ITALY (Monza)

1)	Jody Scheckter	Ferrari 312T4 - F12
2)	Gilles Villeneuve	Ferrari 312T4 - F12
3/ FL)	Clay Regazzoni	Williams FW07 - Ford Cosworth V8
PP)	Jean-Pierre Jabouille	Renault RS10 - V6t

14) 30 Sep - CANADA (Montréal)

1/ PP/ FL)	Alan Jones	Williams FW07 - Ford Cosworth V8
2)	Gilles Villeneuve	Ferrari 312T4 - F12
3)	Clay Regazzoni	Williams FW07 - Ford Cosworth V8

15) 7 Oct - UNITED STATES (Watkins Glen)

1)	Gilles Villeneuve	Ferrari 312T4 - F12
2)	René Arnoux	Renault RS10 - V6t
3)	Didier Pironi	Tyrrell 009 - Ford Cosworth V8
PP)	Alan Jones	Williams FW07 - Ford Cosworth V8
FL)	Nelson Piquet	Brabham BT49 - Ford Cosworth V8

Drivers' championship		Constructors' championship	
1) Jody Scheckter	51	1) Ferrari	113
2) Gilles Villeneuve	47	2) Williams - Ford Cosworth	75
3) Alan Jones	40	3) Ligier - Ford Cosworth	61

1980

1) 13 Jan - ARGENTINA (Buenos Aires No.15)

1/ PP/ FL)	Alan Jones	Williams FW07 - Ford Cosworth V8
2)	Nelson Piquet	Brabham BT49 - Ford Cosworth V8
3)	Keke Rosberg	Fittipaldi F7 - Ford Cosworth V8

2) 27 Jan - BRAZIL (Interlagos)

1/ FL)	René Arnoux	Renault RE20 - V6t
2)	Elio De Angelis	Lotus 81 - Ford Cosworth V8
3)	Alan Jones	Williams FW07B - Ford Cosworth V8
PP)	Jean-Pierre Jabouille	Renault RE20 - V6t

3) 1 Mar - SOUTH AFRICA (Kyalami)

1/ FL)	René Arnoux	Renault RE20 - V6t
2)	Jacques Laffite	Ligier JS11/15 - Ford Cosworth V8
3)	Didier Pironi	Ligier JS11/15 - Ford Cosworth V8
PP)	Jean-Pierre Jabouille	Renault RE20 - V6t

4) 30 Mar - UNITED STATES WEST (Long Beach)

1/ PP/ FL)	Nelson Piquet	Brabham BT49 - Ford Cosworth V8
2)	Riccardo Patrese	Arrows A3 - Ford Cosworth V8
3)	Emerson Fittipaldi	Fittipaldi F7 - Ford Cosworth V8

5) 4 May - BELGIUM (Zolder)

1)		Didier Pironi	Ligier JS11/15 - Ford Cosworth V8
2/ PP)		Alan Jones	Williams FW07B - Ford Cosworth V8
3)		Carlos Reutemann	Williams FW07B - Ford Cosworth V8
FL)		Jacques Laffite	Ligier JS11/15 - Ford Cosworth V8

6) 18 May - MONACO (Monte-Carlo)

1/ FL)	Carlos Reutemann	Williams FW07B - Ford Cosworth V8
2)	Jacques Laffite	Ligier JS11/15 - Ford Cosworth V8
3)	Nelson Piquet	Brabham BT49 - Ford Cosworth V8
PP)	Didier Pironi	Ligier JS11/15 - Ford Cosworth V8

7) 29 Jun - FRANCE (Paul Ricard)

1/ FL)	Alan Jones	Williams FW07B - Ford Cosworth V8
2)	Didier Pironi	Ligier JS11/15 - Ford Cosworth V8
3/ PP)	Jacques Laffite	Ligier JS11/15 - Ford Cosworth V8

8) 13 Jul - BRITAIN (Brands Hatch)

1)	Alan Jones	Williams FW07B - Ford Cosworth V8
2)	Nelson Piquet	Brabham BT49 - Ford Cosworth V8
3)	Carlos Reutemann	Williams FW07B - Ford Cosworth V8
PP/ FL)	Didier Pironi	Ligier JS11/15 - Ford Cosworth V8

9) 10 Aug - GERMANY (Hockenheim)

1)	Jacques Laffite	Ligier JS11/15 - Ford Cosworth V8
2)	Carlos Reutemann	Williams FW07B - Ford Cosworth V8
3/ PP/ FL)	Alan Jones	Williams FW07B - Ford Cosworth V8

10) 17 Aug - AUSTRIA (Österreichring)

1)	Jean-Pierre Jabouille	Renault RE20 - V6t
2)	Alan Jones	Williams FW07B - Ford Cosworth V8
3)	Carlos Reutemann	Williams FW07B - Ford Cosworth V8
PP/ FL)	René Arnoux	Renault RE20 - V6t

11) 31 Aug - NETHERLANDS (Zandvoort)

1)	Nelson Piquet	Brabham BT49 - Ford Cosworth V8
2/ PP/ FL)	René Arnoux	Renault RE20 - V6t
3)	Jacques Laffite	Ligier JS11/15 - Ford Cosworth V8

12) 14 Sep - ITALY (Imola)

1)	Nelson Piquet	Brabham BT49 - Ford Cosworth V8
2/ FL)	Alan Jones	Williams FW07B - Ford Cosworth V8
3)	Carlos Reutemann	Williams FW07B - Ford Cosworth V8
PP)	René Arnoux	Renault RE20 - V6t

13) 28 Sep - CANADA (Montréal)

1)	Alan Jones	Williams FW07B - Ford Cosworth V8
2)	Carlos Reutemann	Williams FW07B - Ford Cosworth V8
3/ FL)	Didier Pironi	Ligier JS11/15 - Ford Cosworth V8
PP)	Nelson Piquet	Brabham BT49 - Ford Cosworth V8

Didier Pironi finished 1st, but was given a 1-minute penalty for jumping the second start.

14) 5 Oct - UNITED STATES (Watkins Glen)

1/ FL)	Alan Jones	Williams FW07B - Ford Cosworth V8
2)	Carlos Reutemann	Williams FW07B - Ford Cosworth V8
3)	Didier Pironi	Ligier JS11/15 - Ford Cosworth V8
PP)	Bruno Giacomelli	Alfa Romeo 179 - V12

Drivers' championship		Constructors' championship	
1) Alan Jones	67	1) Williams - Ford Cosworth	120
2) Nelson Piquet	54	2) Brabham - Ford Cosworth	66
3) Carlos Reutemann	42	3) Renault	55

1981

1) 15 Mar - UNITED STATES WEST (Long Beach)

1/ FL)	Alan Jones	Williams FW07C - Ford Cosworth V8
2)	Carlos Reutemann	Williams FW07C - Ford Cosworth V8
3)	Nelson Piquet	Brabham BT49C - Ford Cosworth V8
PP)	Riccardo Patrese	Arrows A3 - Ford Cosworth V8

2) 29 Mar - BRAZIL (Jacarepaguá)

1)	Carlos Reutemann	Williams FW07C - Ford Cosworth V8
2)	Alan Jones	Williams FW07C - Ford Cosworth V8
3)	Riccardo Patrese	Arrows A3 - Ford Cosworth V8
PP)	Nelson Piquet	Brabham BT49C - Ford Cosworth V8
FL)	Marc Surer	Ensign N180B - Ford Cosworth V8

3) 12 Apr - ARGENTINA (Buenos Aires No.15)

1/ PP/ FL)	Nelson Piquet	Brabham BT49C - Ford Cosworth V8
2)	Carlos Reutemann	Williams FW07C - Ford Cosworth V8
3)	Alain Prost	Renault RE20B - V6t

4) 3 May - SAN MARINO (Imola)

1)	Nelson Piquet	Brabham BT49C - Ford Cosworth V8
2)	Riccardo Patrese	Arrows A3 - Ford Cosworth V8
3)	Carlos Reutemann	Williams FW07C - Ford Cosworth V8
PP/ FL)	Gilles Villeneuve	Ferrari 126CK - V6t

5) 17 May - BELGIUM (Zolder)

1/ PP/ FL)	Carlos Reutemann	Williams FW07C - Ford Cosworth V8
2)	Jacques Laffite	Talbot-Ligier JS17 - Matra V12
3)	Nigel Mansell	Lotus 81 - Ford Cosworth V8

Alan Jones (Williams FW07C - Ford Cosworth V8) set the fastest time in qualifying, but this was removed as the side-pods of his car were declared illegal. He was unable to match that time later.

6) 31 May - MONACO (Monte-Carlo)

1)	Gilles Villeneuve	Ferrari 126CK - V6t
2/ FL)	Alan Jones	Williams FW07C - Ford Cosworth V8
3)	Jacques Laffite	Talbot-Ligier JS17 - Matra V12
PP)	Nelson Piquet	Brabham BT49C - Ford Cosworth V8

7) 21 Jun - SPAIN (Jarama)

1)	Gilles Villeneuve	Ferrari 126CK - V6t
2/ PP)	Jacques Laffite	Talbot-Ligier JS17 - Matra V12
3)	John Watson	McLaren MP4 - Ford Cosworth V8
FL)	Alan Jones	Williams FW07C - Ford Cosworth V8

8) 5 Jul - FRANCE (Dijon-Prenois)

1/ FL)	Alain Prost	Renault RE30 - V6t
2)	John Watson	McLaren MP4 - Ford Cosworth V8
3)	Nelson Piquet	Brabham BT49C - Ford Cosworth V8
PP)	René Arnoux	Renault RE30 - V6t

9) 18 Jul - BRITAIN (Silverstone)

1)	John Watson	McLaren MP4 - Ford Cosworth V8
2)	Carlos Reutemann	Williams FW07C - Ford Cosworth V8
3)	Jacques Laffite	Talbot-Ligier JS17 - Matra V12
PP/ FL)	René Arnoux	Renault RE30 - V6t

10) 2 Aug - GERMANY (Hockenheim)

1)	Nelson Piquet	Brabham BT49C - Ford Cosworth V8
2/ PP)	Alain Prost	Renault RE30 - V6t
3)	Jacques Laffite	Talbot-Ligier JS17 - Matra V12
FL)	Alan Jones	Williams FW07C - Ford Cosworth V8

11) 16 Aug - AUSTRIA (Österreichring)

1/ FL)	Jacques Laffite	Talbot-Ligier JS17 - Matra V12
2/ PP)	René Arnoux	Renault RE30 - V6t
3)	Nelson Piquet	Brabham BT49C - Ford Cosworth V8

12) 30 Aug - NETHERLANDS (Zandvoort)

1/ PP)	Alain Prost	Renault RE30 - V6t
2)	Nelson Piquet	Brabham BT49C - Ford Cosworth V8
3/ FL)	Alan Jones	Williams FW07C - Ford Cosworth V8

13) 13 Sep - ITALY (Monza)

1)	Alain Prost	Renault RE30 - V6t
2)	Alan Jones	Williams FW07C - Ford Cosworth V8
3/ FL)	Carlos Reutemann	Williams FW07C - Ford Cosworth V8
PP)	René Arnoux	Renault RE30 - V6t

14) 27 Sep - CANADA (Montréal)

1)	Jacques Laffite	Talbot-Ligier JS17 - Matra V12
2/ FL)	John Watson	McLaren MP4 - Ford Cosworth V8
3)	Gilles Villeneuve	Ferrari 126CK - V6t
PP)	Nelson Piquet	Brabham BT49C - Ford Cosworth V8

15) 17 Oct - CAESARS PALACE (Las Vegas)

1)	Alan Jones	Williams FW07C - Ford Cosworth V8
2)	Alain Prost	Renault RE30 - V6t
3)	Bruno Giacomelli	Alfa Romeo 179C - V12
PP)	Carlos Reutemann	Williams FW07C - Ford Cosworth V8
FL)	Didier Pironi	Ferrari 126CK - V6t

Drivers' championship

1) Nelson Piquet	50
2) Carlos Reutemann	49
3) Alan Jones	46

Constructors' championship

1) Williams - Ford Cosworth	95
2) Brabham - Ford Cosworth	61
3) Renault	54

1982

1) 23 Jan - SOUTH AFRICA (Kyalami)

1/ FL)	Alain Prost	Renault RE30B - V6t
2)	Carlos Reutemann	Williams FW07C - Ford Cosworth V8
3/ PP)	René Arnoux	Renault RE30B - V6t

2) 21 Mar - BRAZIL (Jacarepaguá)

1/ PP/ FL)	Alain Prost	Renault RE30B - V6t
2)	John Watson	McLaren MP4B - Ford Cosworth V8
3)	Nigel Mansell	Lotus 91 - Ford Cosworth V8

Nelson Piquet (Brabham BT49C - Ford Cosworth V8) and Keke Rosberg (Williams FW08 - Ford Cosworth V8) finished 1st and 2nd respectively, but were disqualified for cars being under the minimum weight limit. Piquet also recorded fastest lap, but this was removed.

3) 4 Apr - UNITED STATES WEST (Long Beach)

1/ FL)	Niki Lauda	McLaren MP4B - Ford Cosworth V8
2)	Keke Rosberg	Williams FW07C - Ford Cosworth V8
3)	Riccardo Patrese	Brabham BT49C - Ford Cosworth V8
PP)	Andrea De Cesaris	Alfa Romeo 182 - V12

Gilles Villeneuve (Ferrari 126C2 - V6t) finished 3rd, but was disqualified for having an illegal rear wing.

4) 25 Apr - SAN MARINO (Imola)

1/ FL)	Didier Pironi	Ferrari 126C2 - V6t
2)	Gilles Villeneuve	Ferrari 126C2 - V6t
3)	Michele Alboreto	Tyrrell 011 - Ford Cosworth V8
PP)	René Arnoux	Renault RE30B - V6t

5) 9 May - BELGIUM (Zolder)

1/ FL)	John Watson	McLaren MP4B - Ford Cosworth V8
2)	Keke Rosberg	Williams FW08 - Ford Cosworth V8
3)	Eddie Cheever	Talbot-Ligier JS17B - Matra V12
PP)	Alain Prost	Renault RE30B - V6t

Niki Lauda (McLaren MP4B - Ford Cosworth V8) finished 3rd, but was disqualified for car being under the minimum weight limit.

6) 23 May - MONACO (Monte-Carlo)

1/ FL)	Riccardo Patrese	Brabham BT49D - Ford Cosworth V8
2/ret)	Didier Pironi	Ferrari 126C2 - V6t
3/ret)	Andrea De Cesaris	Alfa Romeo 182 - V12
PP)	René Arnoux	Renault RE30B - V6t

7) 6 Jun - DETROIT (Detroit)

1)	John Watson	McLaren MP4B - Ford Cosworth V8
2)	Eddie Cheever	Talbot-Ligier JS17B - Matra V12
3)	Didier Pironi	Ferrari 126C2 - V6t
PP/ FL)	Alain Prost	Renault RE30B - V6t

8) 13 Jun - CANADA (Montréal)

1)	Nelson Piquet	Brabham BT50 - BMW 4t
2)	Riccardo Patrese	Brabham BT49D - Ford Cosworth V8
3)	John Watson	McLaren MP4B - Ford Cosworth V8
PP/ FL)	Didier Pironi	Ferrari 126C2 - V6t

9) 3 Jul - NETHERLANDS (Zandvoort)

1)	Didier Pironi	Ferrari 126C2 - V6t
2)	Nelson Piquet	Brabham BT50 - BMW 4t
3)	Keke Rosberg	Williams FW08 - Ford Cosworth V8
PP)	René Arnoux	Renault RE30B - V6t
FL)	Derek Warwick	Toleman TG181C - Hart 4t

10) 18 Jul - BRITAIN (Brands Hatch)

1)	Niki Lauda	McLaren MP4B - Ford Cosworth V8
2)	Didier Pironi	Ferrari 126C2 - V6t
3)	Patrick Tambay	Ferrari 126C2 - V6t
PP)	Keke Rosberg	Williams FW08 - Ford Cosworth V8
FL)	Brian Henton	Tyrrell 011 - Ford Cosworth V8

11) 25 Jul - FRANCE (Paul Ricard)

1/ PP)	René Arnoux	Renault RE30B - V6t
2)	Alain Prost	Renault RE30B - V6t
3)	Didier Pironi	Ferrari 126C2 - V6t
FL)	Riccardo Patrese	Brabham BT50 - BMW 4t

12) 8 Aug - GERMANY (Hockenheim)

1)	Patrick Tambay	Ferrari 126C2 - V6t
2)	René Arnoux	Renault RE30B - V6t
3)	Keke Rosberg	Williams FW08 - Ford Cosworth V8
PP)	Didier Pironi	Ferrari 126C2 - V6t
FL)	Nelson Piquet	Brabham BT50 - BMW 4t

Didier Pironi did not start (injury from accident in qualifying which ended his career).

13) 15 Aug - AUSTRIA (Österreichring)

1)	Elio De Angelis	Lotus 91 - Ford Cosworth V8
2)	Keke Rosberg	Williams FW08 - Ford Cosworth V8
3)	Jacques Laffite	Talbot-Ligier JS19 - Matra V12
PP/ FL)	Nelson Piquet	Brabham BT50 - BMW 4t

14) 29 Aug - SWITZERLAND (Dijon-Prenois)

1)	Keke Rosberg	Williams FW08 - Ford Cosworth V8
2/ PP/ FL)	Alain Prost	Renault RE30B - V6t
3)	Niki Lauda	McLaren MP4B - Ford Cosworth V8

15) 12 Sep - ITALY (Monza)

1/ FL)	René Arnoux	Renault RE30B - V6t
2)	Patrick Tambay	Ferrari 126C2 - V6t
3/ PP)	Mario Andretti	Ferrari 126C2 - V6t

16) 25 Sep - CAESARS PALACE (Las Vegas)

1/ FL)	Michele Alboreto	Tyrrell 011 - Ford Cosworth V8
2)	John Watson	McLaren MP4B - Ford Cosworth V8
3)	Eddie Cheever	Talbot-Ligier JS19 - Matra V12
PP)	Alain Prost	Renault RE30B - V6t

Drivers' championship		Constructors' championship	
1) Keke Rosberg	44	1) Ferrari	74
2) Didier Pironi	39	2) McLaren - Ford Cosworth	69
3) John Watson	39	3) Renault	62

1983

1) 13 Mar - BRAZIL (Jacarepaguá)

1/ FL)	Nelson Piquet	Brabham BT52 - BMW 4t
3)	Niki Lauda	McLaren MP4/1C - Ford Cosworth V8
PP)	Keke Rosberg	Williams FW08C - Ford Cosworth V8

Keke Rosberg finished 2nd, but was disqualified for a push-start in the pits. 2nd place remained vacant.

2) 27 Mar - UNITED STATES WEST (Long Beach)

1)	John Watson	McLaren MP4/1C - Ford Cosworth V8
2/ FL)	Niki Lauda	McLaren MP4/1C - Ford Cosworth V8
3)	René Arnoux	Ferrari 126C2B - V6t
PP)	Patrick Tambay	Ferrari 126C2B - V6t

3) 17 Apr - FRANCE (Paul Ricard)

1/ PP/ FL)	Alain Prost	Renault RE40 - V6t
2)	Nelson Piquet	Brabham BT52 - BMW 4t
3)	Eddie Cheever	Renault RE40 - V6t

4) 1 May - SAN MARINO (Imola)

1)	Patrick Tambay	Ferrari 126C2B - V6t
2)	Alain Prost	Renault RE40 - V6t
3/ PP)	René Arnoux	Ferrari 126C2B - V6t
FL)	Riccardo Patrese	Brabham BT52 - BMW 4t

5) 15 May - MONACO (Monte-Carlo)

1)	Keke Rosberg	Williams FW08C - Ford Cosworth V8
2/ FL)	Nelson Piquet	Brabham BT52 - BMW 4t
3/ PP)	Alain Prost	Renault RE40 - V6t

6) 22 May - BELGIUM (Spa-Francorchamps)

1/ PP)	Alain Prost	Renault RE40 - V6t
2)	Patrick Tambay	Ferrari 126C2B - V6t
3)	Eddie Cheever	Renault RE40 - V6t
FL)	Andrea De Cesaris	Alfa Romeo 183T - V8t

7) 5 Jun - DETROIT (Detroit)

1)	Michele Alboreto	Tyrrell 011 - Ford Cosworth V8
2)	Keke Rosberg	Williams FW08C - Ford Cosworth V8
3/ FL)	John Watson	McLaren MP4/1C - Ford Cosworth V8
PP)	René Arnoux	Ferrari 126C2B - V6t

8) 12 Jun - CANADA (Montréal)

1/ PP)	René Arnoux	Ferrari 126C2B - V6t
2)	Eddie Cheever	Renault RE40 - V6t
3/ FL)	Patrick Tambay	Ferrari 126C2B - V6t

9) 16 Jul - BRITAIN (Silverstone)

1/ FL)	Alain Prost	Renault RE40 - V6t
2)	Nelson Piquet	Brabham BT52B - BMW 4t
3)	Patrick Tambay	Ferrari 126C3 - V6t
PP)	René Arnoux	Ferrari 126C3 - V6t

10) 7 Aug - GERMANY (Hockenheim)

1/ FL)	René Arnoux	Ferrari 126C3 - V6t
2)	Andrea De Cesaris	Alfa Romeo 183T - V8t
3)	Riccardo Patrese	Brabham BT52B - BMW 4t
PP)	Patrick Tambay	Ferrari 126C3 - V6t

11) 14 Aug - AUSTRIA (Österreichring)

1/ FL)	Alain Prost	Renault RE40 - V6t
2)	René Arnoux	Ferrari 126C3 - V6t
3)	Nelson Piquet	Brabham BT52B - BMW 4t
PP)	Patrick Tambay	Ferrari 126C3 - V6t

12) 28 Aug - NETHERLANDS (Zandvoort)

1/ FL)	René Arnoux	Ferrari 126C3 - V6t
2)	Patrick Tambay	Ferrari 126C3 - V6t
3)	John Watson	McLaren MP4/1C - Ford Cosworth V8
PP)	Nelson Piquet	Brabham BT52B - BMW 4t

13) 11 Sep - ITALY (Monza)

1/ FL)	Nelson Piquet	Brabham BT52B - BMW 4t
2)	René Arnoux	Ferrari 126C3 - V6t
3)	Eddie Cheever	Renault RE40 - V6t
PP)	Riccardo Patrese	Brabham BT52B - BMW 4t

14) 25 Sep - EUROPE (Brands Hatch)

1)	Nelson Piquet	Brabham BT52B - BMW 4t
2)	Alain Prost	Renault RE40 - V6t
3/ FL)	Nigel Mansell	Lotus 94T - Renault V6t
PP)	Elio De Angelis	Lotus 94T - Renault V6t

15) 15 Oct - SOUTH AFRICA (Kyalami)

1)	Riccardo Patrese	Brabham BT52B - BMW 4t
2)	Andrea De Cesaris	Alfa Romeo 183T - V8t
3/ FL)	Nelson Piquet	Brabham BT52B - BMW 4t
PP)	Patrick Tambay	Ferrari 126C3 - V6t

Drivers' championship		Constructors' championship	
1) Nelson Piquet	59	1) Ferrari	89
2) Alain Prost	57	2) Renault	79
3) René Arnoux	49	3) Brabham - BMW	72

1984

1) 25 Mar - BRAZIL (Jacarepaguá)

1/ FL)	Alain Prost	McLaren MP4/2 - TAG Porsche V6t
2)	Keke Rosberg	Williams FW09 - Honda V6t
3/ PP)	Elio De Angelis	Lotus 95T - Renault V6t

2) 7 Apr - SOUTH AFRICA (Kyalami)

1)	Niki Lauda	McLaren MP4/2 - TAG Porsche V6t
2)	Alain Prost	McLaren MP4/2 - TAG Porsche V6t
3)	Derek Warwick	Renault RE50 - V6t
PP)	Nelson Piquet	Brabham BT53 - BMW 4t
FL)	Patrick Tambay	Renault RE50 - V6t

3) 29 Apr - BELGIUM (Zolder)

1/ PP)	Michele Alboreto	Ferrari 126C4 - V6t
2)	Derek Warwick	Renault RE50 - V6t
3/ FL)	René Arnoux	Ferrari 126C4 - V6t

4) 6 May - SAN MARINO (Imola)

1)	Alain Prost	McLaren MP4/2 - TAG Porsche V6t
2)	René Arnoux	Ferrari 126C4 - V6t
3/ret)	Elio De Angelis	Lotus 95T - Renault V6t
PP/ FL)	Nelson Piquet	Brabham BT53 - BMW 4t

5) 20 May - FRANCE (Dijon-Prenois)

1)	Niki Lauda	McLaren MP4/2 - TAG Porsche V6t
2/ PP)	Patrick Tambay	Renault RE50 - V6t
3)	Nigel Mansell	Lotus 95T - Renault V6t
FL)	Alain Prost	McLaren MP4/2 - TAG Porsche V6t

6) 3 Jun - MONACO (Monte-Carlo)

1/ PP)	Alain Prost	McLaren MP4/2 - TAG Porsche V6t
2/ FL)	Ayrton Senna	Toleman TG184 - Hart 4t
3)	René Arnoux	Ferrari 126C4 - V6t

Race was stopped early, due to heavy rain. Half points awarded.
Stefan Bellof (Tyrrell 012 - Ford Cosworth V8) finished 1st, but was disqualified for the Tyrrell weight deception scandal.

7) 17 Jun - CANADA (Montréal)

1/ PP/ FL)	Nelson Piquet	Brabham BT53 - BMW 4t
2)	Niki Lauda	McLaren MP4/2 - TAG Porsche V6t
3)	Alain Prost	McLaren MP4/2 - TAG Porsche V6t

8) 24 Jun - DETROIT (Detroit)

1/ PP)	Nelson Piquet	Brabham BT53 - BMW 4t
2)	Elio De Angelis	Lotus 95T - Renault V6t
3)	Teo Fabi	Brabham BT53 - BMW 4t
FL)	Derek Warwick	Renault RE50 - V6t

Martin Brundle (Tyrrell 012 - Ford Cosworth V8) finished 2nd, but was disqualified for the Tyrrell weight deception scandal.

9) 8 Jul - DALLAS (Dallas)

1)	Keke Rosberg	Williams FW09 - Honda V6t
2)	René Arnoux	Ferrari 126C4 - V6t
3)	Elio De Angelis	Lotus 95T - Renault V6t
PP)	Nigel Mansell	Lotus 95T - Renault V6t
FL)	Niki Lauda	McLaren MP4/2 - TAG Porsche V6t

10) 22 Jul - BRITAIN (Brands Hatch)

1/ FL)	Niki Lauda	McLaren MP4/2 - TAG Porsche V6t
2)	Derek Warwick	Renault RE50 - V6t
3)	Ayrton Senna	Toleman TG184 - Hart 4t
PP)	Nelson Piquet	Brabham BT53 - BMW 4t

11) 5 Aug - GERMANY (Hockenheim)

1/ PP/ FL)	Alain Prost	McLaren MP4/2 - TAG Porsche V6t
2)	Niki Lauda	McLaren MP4/2 - TAG Porsche V6t
3)	Derek Warwick	Renault RE50 - V6t

12) 19 Aug - AUSTRIA (Österreichring)

1/ FL)	Niki Lauda	McLaren MP4/2 - TAG Porsche V6t
2/ PP)	Nelson Piquet	Brabham BT53 - BMW 4t
3)	Michele Alboreto	Ferrari 126C4 - V6t

13) 26 Aug - NETHERLANDS (Zandvoort)

1/ PP)	Alain Prost	McLaren MP4/2 - TAG Porsche V6t
2)	Niki Lauda	McLaren MP4/2 - TAG Porsche V6t
3)	Nigel Mansell	Lotus 95T - Renault V6t
FL)	René Arnoux	Ferrari 126C4 - V6t

14) 9 Sep - ITALY (Monza)

1/ FL)	Niki Lauda	McLaren MP4/2 - TAG Porsche V6t
2)	Michele Alboreto	Ferrari 126C4 - V6t
3)	Riccardo Patrese	Alfa Romeo 184T - V8t
PP)	Nelson Piquet	Brabham BT53 - BMW 4t

15) 7 Oct - EUROPE (Nürburgring)

1)	Alain Prost	McLaren MP4/2 - TAG Porsche V6t
2/ FL)	Michele Alboreto	Ferrari 126C4 - V6t
3/ PP/ FL)	Nelson Piquet	Brabham BT53 - BMW 4t

16) 21 Oct - PORTUGAL (Estoril)

1)	Alain Prost	McLaren MP4/2 - TAG Porsche V6t
2/ FL)	Niki Lauda	McLaren MP4/2 - TAG Porsche V6t
3)	Ayrton Senna	Toleman TG184 - Hart 4t
PP)	Nelson Piquet	Brabham BT53 - BMW 4t

Drivers' championship

1) Niki Lauda	72
2) Alain Prost	71.5
3) Elio De Angelis	34

Constructors' championship

1) McLaren - TAG Porsche	143.5
2) Ferrari	57.5
3) Lotus - Renault	47

1985

1) 7 Apr - BRAZIL (Jacarepaguá)

1/ FL)	Alain Prost	McLaren MP4/2B - TAG Porsche V6t
2/ PP)	Michele Alboreto	Ferrari 156/85 - V6t
3)	Elio De Angelis	Lotus 97T - Renault V6t

2) 21 Apr - PORTUGAL (Estoril)

1/ PP/ FL)	Ayrton Senna	Lotus 97T - Renault V6t
2)	Michele Alboreto	Ferrari 156/85 - V6t
3)	Patrick Tambay	Renault RE60 - V6t

3) 5 May - SAN MARINO (Imola)

1)	Elio De Angelis	Lotus 97T - Renault V6t
2)	Thierry Boutsen	Arrows A8 - BMW 4t
3)	Patrick Tambay	Renault RE60 - V6t
PP)	Ayrton Senna	Lotus 97T - Renault V6t
FL)	Michele Alboreto	Ferrari 156/85 - V6t

Alain Prost (McLaren MP4/2B - TAG Porsche V6t) finished 1st, but was disqualified for car being under the minimum weight limit.

4) 19 May - MONACO (Monte-Carlo)

1)	Alain Prost	McLaren MP4/2B - TAG Porsche V6t
2/ FL)	Michele Alboreto	Ferrari 156/85 - V6t
3)	Elio De Angelis	Lotus 97T - Renault V6t
PP)	Ayrton Senna	Lotus 97T - Renault V6t

5) 16 Jun - CANADA (Montréal)

1)	Michele Alboreto	Ferrari 156/85 - V6t
2)	Stefan Johansson	Ferrari 156/85 - V6t
3)	Alain Prost	McLaren MP4/2B - TAG Porsche V6t
PP)	Elio De Angelis	Lotus 97T - Renault V6t
FL)	Ayrton Senna	Lotus 97T - Renault V6t

6) 23 Jun - DETROIT (Detroit)

1)	Keke Rosberg	Williams FW10 - Honda V6t
2)	Stefan Johansson	Ferrari 156/85 - V6t
3)	Michele Alboreto	Ferrari 156/85 - V6t
PP/ FL)	Ayrton Senna	Lotus 97T - Renault V6t

7) 7 Jul - FRANCE (Paul Ricard)

1)	Nelson Piquet	Brabham BT54 - BMW 4t
2/ PP/ FL)	Keke Rosberg	Williams FW10 - Honda V6t
3)	Alain Prost	McLaren MP4/2B - TAG Porsche V6t

8) 21 Jul - BRITAIN (Silverstone)

1/ FL)	Alain Prost	McLaren MP4/2B - TAG Porsche V6t
2)	Michele Alboreto	Ferrari 156/85 - V6t
3)	Jacques Laffite	Ligier JS25 - Renault V6t
PP)	Keke Rosberg	Williams FW10 - Honda V6t

9) 4 Aug - GERMANY (Nürburgring)

1)	Michele Alboreto	Ferrari 156/85 - V6t
2)	Alain Prost	McLaren MP4/2B - TAG Porsche V6t
3)	Jacques Laffite	Ligier JS25 - Renault V6t
PP)	Teo Fabi	Toleman TG185 - Hart 4t
FL)	Niki Lauda	McLaren MP4/2B - TAG Porsche V6t

10) 18 Aug - AUSTRIA (Österreichring)

1/ PP/ FL)	Alain Prost	McLaren MP4/2B - TAG Porsche V6t
2)	Ayrton Senna	Lotus 97T - Renault V6t
3)	Michele Alboreto	Ferrari 156/85 - V6t

11) 25 Aug - NETHERLANDS (Zandvoort)

1)	Niki Lauda	McLaren MP4/2B - TAG Porsche V6t
2/ FL)	Alain Prost	McLaren MP4/2B - TAG Porsche V6t
3)	Ayrton Senna	Lotus 97T - Renault V6t
PP)	Nelson Piquet	Brabham BT54 - BMW 4t

12) 8 Sep - ITALY (Monza)

1)	Alain Prost	McLaren MP4/2B - TAG Porsche V6t
2)	Nelson Piquet	Brabham BT54 - BMW 4t
3/ PP)	Ayrton Senna	Lotus 97T - Renault V6t
FL)	Nigel Mansell	Williams FW10 - Honda V6t

13) 15 Sep - BELGIUM (Spa-Francorchamps)

1)	Ayrton Senna	Lotus 97T - Renault V6t
2)	Nigel Mansell	Williams FW10 - Honda V6t
3/ PP/ FL)	Alain Prost	McLaren MP4/2B - TAG Porsche V6t

14) 6 Oct - EUROPE (Brands Hatch)

1)	Nigel Mansell	Williams FW10 - Honda V6t
2/ PP)	Ayrton Senna	Lotus 97T - Renault V6t
3)	Keke Rosberg	Williams FW10 - Honda V6t
FL)	Jacques Laffite	Ligier JS25 - Renault V6t

15) 19 Oct - SOUTH AFRICA (Kyalami)

1/ PP)	Nigel Mansell	Williams FW10 - Honda V6t
2/ FL)	Keke Rosberg	Williams FW10 - Honda V6t
3)	Alain Prost	McLaren MP4/2B - TAG Porsche V6t

16) 3 Nov - AUSTRALIA (Adelaide)

1/ FL)	Keke Rosberg	Williams FW10 - Honda V6t
2)	Jacques Laffite	Ligier JS25 - Renault V6t
3)	Philippe Streiff	Ligier JS25 - Renault V6t
PP)	Ayrton Senna	Lotus 97T - Renault V6t

Drivers' championship

1) Alain Prost	73
2) Michele Alboreto	53
3) Keke Rosberg	40

Constructors' championship

1) McLaren - TAG Porsche	90
2) Ferrari	82
3) Williams - Honda	71

1986

1) 23 Mar - BRAZIL (Jacarepaguá)

1/ FL)	Nelson Piquet	Williams FW11 - Honda V6t
2/ PP)	Ayrton Senna	Lotus 98T - Renault V6t
3)	Jacques Laffite	Ligier JS27 - Renault V6t

2) 13 Apr - SPAIN (Jerez de la Frontera)

1/ PP)	Ayrton Senna	Lotus 98T - Renault V6t
2/ FL)	Nigel Mansell	Williams FW11 - Honda V6t
3)	Alain Prost	McLaren MP4/2C - TAG Porsche V6t

3) 27 Apr - SAN MARINO (Imola)

1)	Alain Prost	McLaren MP4/2C - TAG Porsche V6t
2/ FL)	Nelson Piquet	Williams FW11 - Honda V6t
3)	Gerhard Berger	Benetton B186 - BMW 4t
PP)	Ayrton Senna	Lotus 98T - Renault V6t

4) 11 May - MONACO (Monte-Carlo)

1/ PP/ FL)	Alain Prost	McLaren MP4/2C - TAG Porsche V6t
2)	Keke Rosberg	McLaren MP4/2C - TAG Porsche V6t
3)	Ayrton Senna	Lotus 98T - Renault V6t

5) 25 May - BELGIUM (Spa-Francorchamps)

1)	Nigel Mansell	Williams FW11 - Honda V6t
2)	Ayrton Senna	Lotus 98T - Renault V6t
3)	Stefan Johansson	Ferrari F1-86 - V6t
PP)	Nelson Piquet	Williams FW11 - Honda V6t
FL)	Alain Prost	McLaren MP4/2C - TAG Porsche V6t

6) 15 Jun - CANADA (Montréal)

1/ PP)	Nigel Mansell	Williams FW11 - Honda V6t
2)	Alain Prost	McLaren MP4/2C - TAG Porsche V6t
3/ FL)	Nelson Piquet	Williams FW11 - Honda V6t

7) 22 Jun - DETROIT (Detroit)

1/ PP)	Ayrton Senna	Lotus 98T - Renault V6t
2)	Jacques Laffite	Ligier JS27 - Renault V6t
3)	Alain Prost	McLaren MP4/2C - TAG Porsche V6t
FL)	Nelson Piquet	Williams FW11 - Honda V6t

8) 6 Jul - FRANCE (Paul Ricard)

1/ FL)	Nigel Mansell	Williams FW11 - Honda V6t
2)	Alain Prost	McLaren MP4/2C - TAG Porsche V6t
3)	Nelson Piquet	Williams FW11 - Honda V6t
PP)	Ayrton Senna	Lotus 98T - Renault V6t

9) 13 Jul - BRITAIN (Brands Hatch)

1/ FL)	Nigel Mansell	Williams FW11 - Honda V6t
2/ PP)	Nelson Piquet	Williams FW11 - Honda V6t
3)	Alain Prost	McLaren MP4/2C - TAG Porsche V6t

10) 27 Jul - GERMANY (Hockenheim)

1)	Nelson Piquet	Williams FW11 - Honda V6t
2)	Ayrton Senna	Lotus 98T - Renault V6t
3)	Nigel Mansell	Williams FW11 - Honda V6t
PP)	Keke Rosberg	McLaren MP4/2C - TAG Porsche V6t
FL)	Gerhard Berger	Benetton B186 - BMW 4t

11) 10 Aug - HUNGARY (Hungaroring)

1/ FL)	Nelson Piquet	Williams FW11 - Honda V6t
2/ PP)	Ayrton Senna	Lotus 98T - Renault V6t
3)	Nigel Mansell	Williams FW11 - Honda V6t

12) 17 Aug - AUSTRIA (Österreichring)

1)	Alain Prost	McLaren MP4/2C - TAG Porsche V6t
2)	Michele Alboreto	Ferrari F1-86 - V6t
3)	Stefan Johansson	Ferrari F1-86 - V6t
PP)	Teo Fabi	Benetton B186 - BMW 4t
FL)	Gerhard Berger	Benetton B186 - BMW 4t

13) 7 Sep - ITALY (Monza)

1)	Nelson Piquet	Williams FW11 - Honda V6t
2)	Nigel Mansell	Williams FW11 - Honda V6t
3)	Stefan Johansson	Ferrari F1-86 - V6t
PP/ FL)	Teo Fabi	Benetton B186 - BMW 4t

14) 21 Sep - PORTUGAL (Estoril)

1/ FL)	Nigel Mansell	Williams FW11 - Honda V6t
2)	Alain Prost	McLaren MP4/2C - TAG Porsche V6t
3)	Nelson Piquet	Williams FW11 - Honda V6t
PP)	Ayrton Senna	Lotus 98T - Renault V6t

15) 12 Oct - MEXICO (Mexico City)

1)	Gerhard Berger	Benetton B186 - BMW 4t
2)	Alain Prost	McLaren MP4/2C - TAG Porsche V6t
3/ PP)	Ayrton Senna	Lotus 98T - Renault V6t
FL)	Nelson Piquet	Williams FW11 - Honda V6t

16) 26 Oct - AUSTRALIA (Adelaide)

1)	Alain Prost	McLaren MP4/2C - TAG Porsche V6t
2/ FL)	Nelson Piquet	Williams FW11 - Honda V6t
3)	Stefan Johansson	Ferrari F1-86 - V6t
PP)	Nigel Mansell	Williams FW11 - Honda V6t

Drivers' championship
1) Alain Prost	72
2) Nigel Mansell	70
3) Nelson Piquet	69

Constructors' championship
1) Williams - Honda	141
2) McLaren - TAG Porsche	96
3) Lotus - Renault	58

1987

1) 12 Apr - BRAZIL (Jacarepaguá)

1)	Alain Prost	McLaren MP4/3 - TAG Porsche V6t
2/ FL)	Nelson Piquet	Williams FW11B - Honda V6t
3)	Stefan Johansson	McLaren MP4/3 - TAG Porsche V6t
PP)	Nigel Mansell	Williams FW11B - Honda V6t

2) 3 May - SAN MARINO (Imola)

1)	Nigel Mansell	Williams FW11B - Honda V6t
2/ PP)	Ayrton Senna	Lotus 99T - Honda V6t
3)	Michele Alboreto	Ferrari F1-87 - V6t
FL)	Teo Fabi	Benetton B187 - Ford Cosworth V6t

3) 17 May - BELGIUM (Spa-Francorchamps)

1/ FL)	Alain Prost	McLaren MP4/3 - TAG Porsche V6t
2)	Stefan Johansson	McLaren MP4/3 - TAG Porsche V6t
3/ret)	Andrea De Cesaris	Brabham BT56 - BMW 4t
PP)	Nigel Mansell	Williams FW11B - Honda V6t

4) 31 May - MONACO (Monte-Carlo)

1/ FL)	Ayrton Senna	Lotus 99T - Honda V6t
2)	Nelson Piquet	Williams FW11B - Honda V6t
3)	Michele Alboreto	Ferrari F1-87 - V6t
PP)	Nigel Mansell	Williams FW11B - Honda V6t

5) 21 Jun - DETROIT (Detroit)

1/ FL)	Ayrton Senna	Lotus 99T - Honda V6t
2)	Nelson Piquet	Williams FW11B - Honda V6t
3)	Alain Prost	McLaren MP4/3 - TAG Porsche V6t
PP)	Nigel Mansell	Williams FW11B - Honda V6t

6) 5 Jul - FRANCE (Paul Ricard)
1/ PP)	Nigel Mansell	Williams FW11B - Honda V6t
2/ FL)	Nelson Piquet	Williams FW11B - Honda V6t
3)	Alain Prost	McLaren MP4/3 - TAG Porsche V6t

7) 12 Jul - BRITAIN (Silverstone)
1/ FL)	Nigel Mansell	Williams FW11B - Honda V6t
2/ PP)	Nelson Piquet	Williams FW11B - Honda V6t
3)	Ayrton Senna	Lotus 99T - Honda V6t

8) 26 Jul - GERMANY (Hockenheim)
1)	Nelson Piquet	Williams FW11B - Honda V6t
2)	Stefan Johansson	McLaren MP4/3 - TAG Porsche V6t
3)	Ayrton Senna	Lotus 99T - Honda V6t
PP/ FL)	Nigel Mansell	Williams FW11B - Honda V6t

9) 9 Aug - HUNGARY (Hungaroring)
1/ FL)	Nelson Piquet	Williams FW11B - Honda V6t
2)	Ayrton Senna	Lotus 99T - Honda V6t
3)	Alain Prost	McLaren MP4/3 - TAG Porsche V6t
PP)	Nigel Mansell	Williams FW11B - Honda V6t

10) 16 Aug - AUSTRIA (Österreichring)
1/ FL)	Nigel Mansell	Williams FW11B - Honda V6t
2/ PP)	Nelson Piquet	Williams FW11B - Honda V6t
3)	Teo Fabi	Benetton B187 - Ford Cosworth V6t

11) 6 Sep - ITALY (Monza)
1/ PP)	Nelson Piquet	Williams FW11B - Honda V6t
2/ FL)	Ayrton Senna	Lotus 99T - Honda V6t
3)	Nigel Mansell	Williams FW11B - Honda V6t

12) 20 Sep - PORTUGAL (Estoril)
1)	Alain Prost	McLaren MP4/3 - TAG Porsche V6t
2/ PP/ FL)	Gerhard Berger	Ferrari F1-87 - V6t
3)	Nelson Piquet	Williams FW11B - Honda V6t

13) 27 Sep - SPAIN (Jerez de la Frontera)
1)	Nigel Mansell	Williams FW11B - Honda V6t
2)	Alain Prost	McLaren MP4/3 - TAG Porsche V6t
3)	Stefan Johansson	McLaren MP4/3 - TAG Porsche V6t
PP)	Nelson Piquet	Williams FW11B - Honda V6t
FL)	Gerhard Berger	Ferrari F1-87 - V6t

14) 18 Oct - MEXICO (Mexico City)
1/ PP)	Nigel Mansell	Williams FW11B - Honda V6t
2/ FL)	Nelson Piquet	Williams FW11B - Honda V6t
3)	Riccardo Patrese	Brabham BT56 - BMW 4t

15) 1 Nov - JAPAN (Suzuka)
1/ PP)	Gerhard Berger	Ferrari F1-87 - V6t
2)	Ayrton Senna	Lotus 99T - Honda V6t
3)	Stefan Johansson	McLaren MP4/3 - TAG Porsche V6t
FL)	Alain Prost	McLaren MP4/3 - TAG Porsche V6t

16) 15 Nov - AUSTRALIA (Adelaide)
1/ PP/ FL)	Gerhard Berger	Ferrari F1-87 - V6t
2)	Michele Alboreto	Ferrari F1-87 - V6t
3)	Thierry Boutsen	Benetton B187 - Ford Cosworth V6t

Ayrton Senna (Lotus 99T - Honda V6t) finished 2nd, but was disqualified for illegal front brake cooling duct dimensions.

Drivers' championship
1)	Nelson Piquet	73
2)	Nigel Mansell	61
3)	Ayrton Senna	57

Constructors' championship
1)	Williams - Honda	137
2)	McLaren - TAG Porsche	76
3)	Lotus - Honda	64

1988

1) 3 Apr - BRAZIL (Jacarepaguá)
1)	Alain Prost	McLaren MP4/4 - Honda V6t
2/ FL)	Gerhard Berger	Ferrari F1-87/88C - V6t
3)	Nelson Piquet	Lotus 100T - Honda V6t
PP)	Ayrton Senna	McLaren MP4/4 - Honda V6t

2) 1 May - SAN MARINO (Imola)
1/ PP)	Ayrton Senna	McLaren MP4/4 - Honda V6t
2/ FL)	Alain Prost	McLaren MP4/4 - Honda V6t
3)	Nelson Piquet	Lotus 100T - Honda V6t

3) 15 May - MONACO (Monte-Carlo)
1)	Alain Prost	McLaren MP4/4 - Honda V6t
2)	Gerhard Berger	Ferrari F1-87/88C - V6t
3)	Michele Alboreto	Ferrari F1-87/88C - V6t
PP/ FL)	Ayrton Senna	McLaren MP4/4 - Honda V6t

4) 29 May - MEXICO (Mexico City)
1/ FL)	Alain Prost	McLaren MP4/4 - Honda V6t
2/ PP)	Ayrton Senna	McLaren MP4/4 - Honda V6t
3)	Gerhard Berger	Ferrari F1-87/88C - V6t

5) 12 Jun - CANADA (Montréal)
1/ PP/ FL)	Ayrton Senna	McLaren MP4/4 - Honda V6t
2)	Alain Prost	McLaren MP4/4 - Honda V6t
3)	Thierry Boutsen	Benetton B188 - Ford Cosworth V8

6) 19 Jun - DETROIT (Detroit)
1/ PP)	Ayrton Senna	McLaren MP4/4 - Honda V6t
2/ FL)	Alain Prost	McLaren MP4/4 - Honda V6t
3)	Thierry Boutsen	Benetton B188 - Ford Cosworth V8

7) 3 Jul - FRANCE (Paul Ricard)
1/ PP/ FL)	Alain Prost	McLaren MP4/4 - Honda V6t
2)	Ayrton Senna	McLaren MP4/4 - Honda V6t
3)	Michele Alboreto	Ferrari F1-87/88C - V6t

8) 10 Jul - BRITAIN (Silverstone)
1)	Ayrton Senna	McLaren MP4/4 - Honda V6t
2/ FL)	Nigel Mansell	Williams FW12 - Judd V8
3)	Alessandro Nannini	Benetton B188 - Ford Cosworth V8
PP)	Gerhard Berger	Ferrari F1-87/88C - V6t

9) 24 Jul - GERMANY (Hockenheim)
1/ PP)	Ayrton Senna	McLaren MP4/4 - Honda V6t
2)	Alain Prost	McLaren MP4/4 - Honda V6t
3)	Gerhard Berger	Ferrari F1-87/88C - V6t
FL)	Alessandro Nannini	Benetton B188 - Ford Cosworth V8

10) 7 Aug - HUNGARY (Hungaroring)
1/ PP)	Ayrton Senna	McLaren MP4/4 - Honda V6t
2/ FL)	Alain Prost	McLaren MP4/4 - Honda V6t
3)	Thierry Boutsen	Benetton B188 - Ford Cosworth V8

11) 28 Aug - BELGIUM (Spa-Francorchamps)
1/ PP)	Ayrton Senna	McLaren MP4/4 - Honda V6t
2)	Alain Prost	McLaren MP4/4 - Honda V6t
3)	Ivan Capelli	March 881 - Judd V8
FL)	Gerhard Berger	Ferrari F1-87/88C - V6t

Thierry Boutsen (Benetton B188 - Ford Cosworth V8) finished 3rd, but was disqualified for using illegal fuel.

12) 11 Sep - ITALY (Monza)

1)	Gerhard Berger	Ferrari F1-87/88C - V6t
2/ FL)	Michele Alboreto	Ferrari F1-87/88C - V6t
3)	Eddie Cheever	Arrows A10B - Megatron 4t
PP)	Ayrton Senna	McLaren MP4/4 - Honda V6t

13) 25 Sep - PORTUGAL (Estoril)

1/ PP)	Alain Prost	McLaren MP4/4 - Honda V6t
2)	Ivan Capelli	March 881 - Judd V8
3)	Thierry Boutsen	Benetton B188 - Ford Cosworth V8
FL)	Gerhard Berger	Ferrari F1-87/88C - V6t

14) 2 Oct - SPAIN (Jerez de la Frontera)

1/ FL)	Alain Prost	McLaren MP4/4 - Honda V6t
2)	Nigel Mansell	Williams FW12 - Judd V8
3)	Alessandro Nannini	Benetton B188 - Ford Cosworth V8
PP)	Ayrton Senna	McLaren MP4/4 - Honda V6t

15) 30 Oct - JAPAN (Suzuka)

1/ PP/ FL)	Ayrton Senna	McLaren MP4/4 - Honda V6t
2)	Alain Prost	McLaren MP4/4 - Honda V6t
3)	Thierry Boutsen	Benetton B188 - Ford Cosworth V8

16) 13 Nov - AUSTRALIA (Adelaide)

1/ FL)	Alain Prost	McLaren MP4/4 - Honda V6t
2/ PP)	Ayrton Senna	McLaren MP4/4 - Honda V6t
3)	Nelson Piquet	Lotus 100T - Honda V6t

Drivers' championship

1) Ayrton Senna	90
2) Alain Prost	87
3) Gerhard Berger	41

Constructors' championship

1) McLaren - Honda	199
2) Ferrari	65
3) Benetton - Ford Cosworth	39

1989

1) 26 Mar - BRAZIL (Jacarepaguá)

1)	Nigel Mansell	Ferrari 640 - V12
2)	Alain Prost	McLaren MP4/5 - Honda V10
3)	Mauricio Gugelmin	March 881 - Judd V8
PP)	Ayrton Senna	McLaren MP4/5 - Honda V10
FL)	Riccardo Patrese	Williams FW12C - Renault V10

2) 23 Apr - SAN MARINO (Imola)

1/ PP)	Ayrton Senna	McLaren MP4/5 - Honda V10
2/ FL)	Alain Prost	McLaren MP4/5 - Honda V10
3)	Alessandro Nannini	Benetton B188 - Ford Cosworth V8

3) 7 May - MONACO (Monte-Carlo)

1/ PP)	Ayrton Senna	McLaren MP4/5 - Honda V10
2/ FL)	Alain Prost	McLaren MP4/5 - Honda V10
3)	Stefano Modena	Brabham BT58 - Judd V8

4) 28 May - MEXICO (Mexico City)

1/ PP)	Ayrton Senna	McLaren MP4/5 - Honda V10
2)	Riccardo Patrese	Williams FW12C - Renault V10
3)	Michele Alboreto	Tyrrell 018 - Ford Cosworth V8
FL)	Nigel Mansell	Ferrari 640 - V12

5) 4 Jun - UNITED STATES (Phoenix)

1)	Alain Prost	McLaren MP4/5 - Honda V10
2)	Riccardo Patrese	Williams FW12C - Renault V10
3)	Eddie Cheever	Arrows A11 - Ford Cosworth V8
PP/ FL)	Ayrton Senna	McLaren MP4/5 - Honda V10

6) 18 Jun - CANADA (Montréal)

1)	Thierry Boutsen	Williams FW12C - Renault V10
2)	Riccardo Patrese	Williams FW12C - Renault V10
3)	Andrea De Cesaris	Dallara 189 - Ford Cosworth V8
PP)	Alain Prost	McLaren MP4/5 - Honda V10
FL)	Jonathan Palmer	Tyrrell 018 - Ford Cosworth V8

7) 9 Jul - FRANCE (Paul Ricard)

1/ PP)	Alain Prost	McLaren MP4/5 - Honda V10
2)	Nigel Mansell	Ferrari 640 - V12
3)	Riccardo Patrese	Williams FW12C - Renault V10
FL)	Mauricio Gugelmin	March CG891 - Judd V8

8) 16 Jul - BRITAIN (Silverstone)

1)	Alain Prost	McLaren MP4/5 - Honda V10
2/ FL)	Nigel Mansell	Ferrari 640 - V12
3)	Alessandro Nannini	Benetton B189 - Ford Cosworth V8
PP)	Ayrton Senna	McLaren MP4/5 - Honda V10

9) 30 Jul - GERMANY (Hockenheim)

1/ PP/ FL)	Ayrton Senna	McLaren MP4/5 - Honda V10
2)	Alain Prost	McLaren MP4/5 - Honda V10
3)	Nigel Mansell	Ferrari 640 - V12

10) 13 Aug - HUNGARY (Hungaroring)

1/ FL)	Nigel Mansell	Ferrari 640 - V12
2)	Ayrton Senna	McLaren MP4/5 - Honda V10
3)	Thierry Boutsen	Williams FW12C - Renault V10
PP)	Riccardo Patrese	Williams FW12C - Renault V10

11) 27 Aug - BELGIUM (Spa-Francorchamps)

1/ PP)	Ayrton Senna	McLaren MP4/5 - Honda V10
2/ FL)	Alain Prost	McLaren MP4/5 - Honda V10
3)	Nigel Mansell	Ferrari 640 - V12

12) 10 Sep - ITALY (Monza)

1/ FL)	Alain Prost	McLaren MP4/5 - Honda V10
2)	Gerhard Berger	Ferrari 640 - V12
3)	Thierry Boutsen	Williams FW12C - Renault V10
PP)	Ayrton Senna	McLaren MP4/5 - Honda V10

13) 24 Sep - PORTUGAL (Estoril)

1/ FL)	Gerhard Berger	Ferrari 640 - V12
2)	Alain Prost	McLaren MP4/5 - Honda V10
3)	Stefan Johansson	Onyx ORE-1 - Ford Cosworth V8
PP)	Ayrton Senna	McLaren MP4/5 - Honda V10

14) 1 Oct - SPAIN (Jerez de la Frontera)

1/ PP/ FL)	Ayrton Senna	McLaren MP4/5 - Honda V10
2)	Gerhard Berger	Ferrari 640 - V12
3)	Alain Prost	McLaren MP4/5 - Honda V10

15) 22 Oct - JAPAN (Suzuka)

1)	Alessandro Nannini	Benetton B189 - Ford Cosworth V8
2)	Riccardo Patrese	Williams FW13 - Renault V10
3)	Thierry Boutsen	Williams FW13 - Renault V10
PP)	Ayrton Senna	McLaren MP4/5 - Honda V10
FL)	Alain Prost	McLaren MP4/5 - Honda V10

Ayrton Senna finished 1st, but was disqualified for using the chicane's escape road to rejoin the circuit after the accident with Prost. He also recorded fastest lap, but this was removed.

16) 5 Nov - AUSTRALIA (Adelaide)

	1)	Thierry Boutsen	Williams FW13 - Renault V10
	2)	Alessandro Nannini	Benetton B189 - Ford Cosworth V8
	3)	Riccardo Patrese	Williams FW13 - Renault V10
	PP)	Ayrton Senna	McLaren MP4/5 - Honda V10
	FL)	Satoru Nakajima	Lotus 101 - Judd V8

Drivers' championship

1) Alain Prost	76
2) Ayrton Senna	60
3) Riccardo Patrese	40

Constructors' championship

1) McLaren - Honda	141
2) Williams - Renault	77
3) Ferrari	59

1990

1) 11 Mar - UNITED STATES (Phoenix)

	1)	Ayrton Senna	McLaren MP4/5B - Honda V10
	2)	Jean Alesi	Tyrrell 018 - Ford Cosworth V8
	3)	Thierry Boutsen	Williams FW13B - Renault V10
	PP/ FL)	Gerhard Berger	McLaren MP4/5B - Honda V10

2) 25 Mar - BRAZIL (Interlagos)

	1)	Alain Prost	Ferrari 641 - V12
	2/ FL)	Gerhard Berger	McLaren MP4/5B - Honda V10
	3/ PP)	Ayrton Senna	McLaren MP4/5B - Honda V10

3) 13 May - SAN MARINO (Imola)

	1)	Riccardo Patrese	Williams FW13B - Renault V10
	2)	Gerhard Berger	McLaren MP4/5B - Honda V10
	3/ FL)	Alessandro Nannini	Benetton B190 - Ford Cosworth V8
	PP)	Ayrton Senna	McLaren MP4/5B - Honda V10

4) 27 May - MONACO (Monte-Carlo)

	1/ PP/ FL)	Ayrton Senna	McLaren MP4/5B - Honda V10
	2)	Jean Alesi	Tyrrell 019 - Ford Cosworth V8
	3)	Gerhard Berger	McLaren MP4/5B - Honda V10

5) 10 Jun - CANADA (Montréal)

	1/ PP)	Ayrton Senna	McLaren MP4/5B - Honda V10
	2)	Nelson Piquet	Benetton B190 - Ford Cosworth V8
	3)	Nigel Mansell	Ferrari 641/2 - V12
	FL)	Gerhard Berger	McLaren MP4/5B - Honda V10

Gerhard Berger finished 1st, but was given a 1-minute penalty for jumping the start - classified 4th.

6) 24 Jun - MEXICO (Mexico City)

	1/ FL)	Alain Prost	Ferrari 641/2 - V12
	2)	Nigel Mansell	Ferrari 641/2 - V12
	3/ PP)	Gerhard Berger	McLaren MP4/5B - Honda V10

7) 8 Jul - FRANCE (Paul Ricard)

	1)	Alain Prost	Ferrari 641/2 - V12
	2)	Ivan Capelli	Leyton House CG901 - Judd V8
	3)	Ayrton Senna	McLaren MP4/5B - Honda V10
	PP/ FL)	Nigel Mansell	Ferrari 641/2 - V12

8) 15 Jul - BRITAIN (Silverstone)

	1)	Alain Prost	Ferrari 641/2 - V12
	2)	Thierry Boutsen	Williams FW13B - Renault V10
	3)	Ayrton Senna	McLaren MP4/5B - Honda V10
	PP/ FL)	Nigel Mansell	Ferrari 641/2 - V12

9) 29 Jul - GERMANY (Hockenheim)

	1/ PP)	Ayrton Senna	McLaren MP4/5B - Honda V10
	2)	Alessandro Nannini	Benetton B190 - Ford Cosworth V8
	3)	Gerhard Berger	McLaren MP4/5B - Honda V10
	FL)	Thierry Boutsen	Williams FW13B - Renault V10

10) 12 Aug - HUNGARY (Hungaroring)

	1/ PP)	Thierry Boutsen	Williams FW13B - Renault V10
	2)	Ayrton Senna	McLaren MP4/5B - Honda V10
	3)	Nelson Piquet	Benetton B190 - Ford Cosworth V8
	FL)	Riccardo Patrese	Williams FW13B - Renault V10

11) 26 Aug - BELGIUM (Spa-Francorchamps)

	1/ PP)	Ayrton Senna	McLaren MP4/5B - Honda V10
	2/ FL)	Alain Prost	Ferrari 641/2 - V12
	3)	Gerhard Berger	McLaren MP4/5B - Honda V10

12) 9 Sep - ITALY (Monza)

	1/ PP/ FL)	Ayrton Senna	McLaren MP4/5B - Honda V10
	2)	Alain Prost	Ferrari 641/2 - V12
	3)	Gerhard Berger	McLaren MP4/5B - Honda V10

13) 23 Sep - PORTUGAL (Estoril)

	1/ PP)	Nigel Mansell	Ferrari 641/2 - V12
	2)	Ayrton Senna	McLaren MP4/5B - Honda V10
	3)	Alain Prost	Ferrari 641/2 - V12
	FL)	Riccardo Patrese	Williams FW13B - Renault V10

14) 30 Sep - SPAIN (Jerez de la Frontera)

	1)	Alain Prost	Ferrari 641/2 - V12
	2)	Nigel Mansell	Ferrari 641/2 - V12
	3)	Alessandro Nannini	Benetton B190 - Ford Cosworth V8
	PP)	Ayrton Senna	McLaren MP4/5B - Honda V10
	FL)	Riccardo Patrese	Williams FW13B - Renault V10

15) 21 Oct - JAPAN (Suzuka)

	1)	Nelson Piquet	Benetton B190 - Ford Cosworth V8
	2)	Roberto Moreno	Benetton B190 - Ford Cosworth V8
	3)	Aguri Suzuki	Lola 90 - Lamborghini V12
	PP)	Ayrton Senna	McLaren MP4/5B - Honda V10
	FL)	Riccardo Patrese	Williams FW13B - Renault V10

16) 4 Nov - AUSTRALIA (Adelaide)

	1)	Nelson Piquet	Benetton B190 - Ford Cosworth V8
	2/ FL)	Nigel Mansell	Ferrari 641/2 - V12
	3)	Alain Prost	Ferrari 641/2 - V12
	PP)	Ayrton Senna	McLaren MP4/5B - Honda V10

Drivers' championship

1) Ayrton Senna	78
2) Alain Prost	71
3) Nelson Piquet	43

Constructors' championship

1) McLaren - Honda	121
2) Ferrari	110
3) Benetton - Ford Cosworth	71

1991

1) 10 Mar - UNITED STATES (Phoenix)

	1/ PP)	Ayrton Senna	McLaren MP4/6 - Honda V12
	2)	Alain Prost	Ferrari 642 - V12
	3)	Nelson Piquet	Benetton B190B - Ford Cosworth V8
	FL)	Jean Alesi	Ferrari 642 - V12

2) 24 Mar - BRAZIL (Interlagos)

	1/ PP)	Ayrton Senna	McLaren MP4/6 - Honda V12
	2)	Riccardo Patrese	Williams FW14 - Renault V10
	3)	Gerhard Berger	McLaren MP4/6 - Honda V12
	FL)	Nigel Mansell	Williams FW14 - Renault V10

3) 28 Apr - SAN MARINO (Imola)

	1/ PP)	Ayrton Senna	McLaren MP4/6 - Honda V12
	2/ FL)	Gerhard Berger	McLaren MP4/6 - Honda V12
	3)	J J Lehto	Dallara 191 - Judd V10

4) 12 May - MONACO (Monte-Carlo)
1/ PP)	Ayrton Senna	McLaren MP4/6 - Honda V12
2)	Nigel Mansell	Williams FW14 - Renault V10
3)	Jean Alesi	Ferrari 642 - V12
FL)	Alain Prost	Ferrari 642 - V12

5) 2 Jun - CANADA (Montréal)
1)	Nelson Piquet	Benetton B191 - Ford Cosworth V8
2)	Stefano Modena	Tyrrell 020 - Honda V10
3/ PP)	Riccardo Patrese	Williams FW14 - Renault V10
FL)	Nigel Mansell	Williams FW14 - Renault V10

6) 16 Jun - MEXICO (Mexico City)
1/ PP)	Riccardo Patrese	Williams FW14 - Renault V10
2/ FL)	Nigel Mansell	Williams FW14 - Renault V10
3)	Ayrton Senna	McLaren MP4/6 - Honda V12

7) 7 Jul - FRANCE (Magny-Cours)
1/ FL)	Nigel Mansell	Williams FW14 - Renault V10
2)	Alain Prost	Ferrari 643 - V12
3)	Ayrton Senna	McLaren MP4/6 - Honda V12
PP)	Riccardo Patrese	Williams FW14 - Renault V10

8) 14 Jul - BRITAIN (Silverstone)
1/ PP/ FL)	Nigel Mansell	Williams FW14 - Renault V10
2)	Gerhard Berger	McLaren MP4/6 - Honda V12
3)	Alain Prost	Ferrari 643 - V12

9) 28 Jul - GERMANY (Hockenheim)
1/ PP)	Nigel Mansell	Williams FW14 - Renault V10
2/ FL)	Riccardo Patrese	Williams FW14 - Renault V10
3)	Jean Alesi	Ferrari 643 - V12

10) 11 Aug - HUNGARY (Hungaroring)
1/ PP)	Ayrton Senna	McLaren MP4/6 - Honda V12
2)	Nigel Mansell	Williams FW14 - Renault V10
3)	Riccardo Patrese	Williams FW14 - Renault V10
FL)	Bertrand Gachot	Jordan 191 - Ford Cosworth V8

11) 25 Aug - BELGIUM (Spa-Francorchamps)
1/ PP)	Ayrton Senna	McLaren MP4/6 - Honda V12
2)	Gerhard Berger	McLaren MP4/6 - Honda V12
3)	Nelson Piquet	Benetton B191 - Ford Cosworth V8
FL)	Roberto Moreno	Benetton B191 - Ford Cosworth V8

12) 8 Sep - ITALY (Monza)
1)	Nigel Mansell	Williams FW14 - Renault V10
2/ PP/ FL)	Ayrton Senna	McLaren MP4/6 - Honda V12
3)	Alain Prost	Ferrari 643 - V12

13) 22 Sep - PORTUGAL (Estoril)
1/ PP)	Riccardo Patrese	Williams FW14 - Renault V10
2)	Ayrton Senna	McLaren MP4/6 - Honda V12
3)	Jean Alesi	Ferrari 643 - V12
FL)	Nigel Mansell	Williams FW14 - Renault V10

14) 29 Sep - SPAIN (Catalunya)
1)	Nigel Mansell	Williams FW14 - Renault V10
2)	Alain Prost	Ferrari 643 - V12
3/ FL)	Riccardo Patrese	Williams FW14 - Renault V10
PP)	Gerhard Berger	McLaren MP4/6 - Honda V12

15) 20 Oct - JAPAN (Suzuka)
1/ PP)	Gerhard Berger	McLaren MP4/6 - Honda V12
2/ FL)	Ayrton Senna	McLaren MP4/6 - Honda V12
3)	Riccardo Patrese	Williams FW14 - Renault V10

16) 3 Nov - AUSTRALIA (Adelaide)
1/ PP)	Ayrton Senna	McLaren MP4/6 - Honda V12
2)	Nigel Mansell	Williams FW14 - Renault V10
3/ FL)	Gerhard Berger	McLaren MP4/6 - Honda V12

Race was stopped early, due to heavy rain. Half points awarded.

Drivers' championship		Constructors' championship	
1) Ayrton Senna	96	1) McLaren - Honda	139
2) Nigel Mansell	72	2) Williams - Renault	125
3) Riccardo Patrese	53	3) Ferrari	55.5

1992

1) 1 Mar - SOUTH AFRICA (Kyalami)
1/ PP/ FL)	Nigel Mansell	Williams FW14B - Renault V10
2)	Riccardo Patrese	Williams FW14B - Renault V10
3)	Ayrton Senna	McLaren MP4/6B - Honda V12

2) 22 Mar - MEXICO (Mexico City)
1/ PP)	Nigel Mansell	Williams FW14B - Renault V10
2)	Riccardo Patrese	Williams FW14B - Renault V10
3)	Michael Schumacher	Benetton B191B - Ford Cosworth V8
FL)	Gerhard Berger	McLaren MP4/6B - Honda V12

3) 5 Apr - BRAZIL (Interlagos)
1/ PP)	Nigel Mansell	Williams FW14B - Renault V10
2/ FL)	Riccardo Patrese	Williams FW14B - Renault V10
3)	Michael Schumacher	Benetton B191B - Ford Cosworth V8

4) 3 May - SPAIN (Catalunya)
1/ PP/ FL)	Nigel Mansell	Williams FW14B - Renault V10
2)	Michael Schumacher	Benetton B192 - Ford Cosworth V8
3)	Jean Alesi	Ferrari F92A - V12

5) 17 May - SAN MARINO (Imola)
1/ PP)	Nigel Mansell	Williams FW14B - Renault V10
2/ FL)	Riccardo Patrese	Williams FW14B - Renault V10
3)	Ayrton Senna	McLaren MP4/7A - Honda V12

6) 31 May - MONACO (Monte-Carlo)
1)	Ayrton Senna	McLaren MP4/7A - Honda V12
2/ PP/ FL)	Nigel Mansell	Williams FW14B - Renault V10
3)	Riccardo Patrese	Williams FW14B - Renault V10

7) 14 Jun - CANADA (Montréal)
1/ FL)	Gerhard Berger	McLaren MP4/7A - Honda V12
2)	Michael Schumacher	Benetton B192 - Ford Cosworth V8
3)	Jean Alesi	Ferrari F92A - V12
PP)	Ayrton Senna	McLaren MP4/7A - Honda V12

8) 5 Jul - FRANCE (Magny-Cours)
1/ PP/ FL)	Nigel Mansell	Williams FW14B - Renault V10
2)	Riccardo Patrese	Williams FW14B - Renault V10
3)	Martin Brundle	Benetton B192 - Ford Cosworth V8

9) 12 Jul - BRITAIN (Silverstone)
1/ PP/ FL)	Nigel Mansell	Williams FW14B - Renault V10
2)	Riccardo Patrese	Williams FW14B - Renault V10
3)	Martin Brundle	Benetton B192 - Ford Cosworth V8

10) 26 Jul - GERMANY (Hockenheim)
1/ PP)	Nigel Mansell	Williams FW14B - Renault V10
2)	Ayrton Senna	McLaren MP4/7A - Honda V12
3)	Michael Schumacher	Benetton B192 - Ford Cosworth V8
FL)	Riccardo Patrese	Williams FW14B - Renault V10

11) 16 Aug - HUNGARY (Hungaroring)

1)	Ayrton Senna	McLaren MP4/7A - Honda V12
2/ FL)	Nigel Mansell	Williams FW14B - Renault V10
3)	Gerhard Berger	McLaren MP4/7A - Honda V12
PP)	Riccardo Patrese	Williams FW14B - Renault V10

12) 30 Aug - BELGIUM (Spa-Francorchamps)

1/ FL)	Michael Schumacher	Benetton B192 - Ford Cosworth V8
2/ PP)	Nigel Mansell	Williams FW14B - Renault V10
3)	Riccardo Patrese	Williams FW14B - Renault V10

13) 13 Sep - ITALY (Monza)

1)	Ayrton Senna	McLaren MP4/7A - Honda V12
2)	Martin Brundle	Benetton B192 - Ford Cosworth V8
3)	Michael Schumacher	Benetton B192 - Ford Cosworth V8
PP/ FL)	Nigel Mansell	Williams FW14B - Renault V10

14) 27 Sep - PORTUGAL (Estoril)

1/ PP)	Nigel Mansell	Williams FW14B - Renault V10
2)	Gerhard Berger	McLaren MP4/7A - Honda V12
3/ FL)	Ayrton Senna	McLaren MP4/7A - Honda V12

15) 25 Oct - JAPAN (Suzuka)

1)	Riccardo Patrese	Williams FW14B - Renault V10
2)	Gerhard Berger	McLaren MP4/7A - Honda V12
3)	Martin Brundle	Benetton B192 - Ford Cosworth V8
PP/ FL)	Nigel Mansell	Williams FW14B - Renault V10

16) 8 Nov - AUSTRALIA (Adelaide)

1)	Gerhard Berger	McLaren MP4/7A - Honda V12
2/ FL)	Michael Schumacher	Benetton B192 - Ford Cosworth V8
3)	Martin Brundle	Benetton B192 - Ford Cosworth V8
PP)	Nigel Mansell	Williams FW14B - Renault V10

Drivers' championship		**Constructors' championship**	
1) Nigel Mansell	108	1) Williams - Renault	164
2) Riccardo Patrese	56	2) McLaren - Honda	99
3) Michael Schumacher	53	3) Benetton - Ford Cosworth	91

1993

1) 14 Mar - SOUTH AFRICA (Kyalami)

1/ PP/ FL)	Alain Prost	Williams FW15C - Renault V10
2)	Ayrton Senna	McLaren MP4/8 - Ford Cosworth V8
3)	Mark Blundell	Ligier JS39 - Renault V10

2) 28 Mar - BRAZIL (Interlagos)

1)	Ayrton Senna	McLaren MP4/8 - Ford Cosworth V8
2)	Damon Hill	Williams FW15C - Renault V10
3/ FL)	Michael Schumacher	Benetton B192B - Ford Cosworth V8
PP)	Alain Prost	Williams FW15C - Renault V10

3) 11 Apr - EUROPE (Donington Park)

1/ FL)	Ayrton Senna	McLaren MP4/8 - Ford Cosworth V8
2)	Damon Hill	Williams FW15C - Renault V10
3/ PP)	Alain Prost	Williams FW15C - Renault V10

4) 25 Apr - SAN MARINO (Imola)

1/ PP/ FL)	Alain Prost	Williams FW15C - Renault V10
2)	Michael Schumacher	Benetton B193B - Ford Cosworth V8
3)	Martin Brundle	Ligier JS39 - Renault V10

5) 9 May - SPAIN (Catalunya)

1/ PP)	Alain Prost	Williams FW15C - Renault V10
2)	Ayrton Senna	McLaren MP4/8 - Ford Cosworth V8
3/ FL)	Michael Schumacher	Benetton B193B - Ford Cosworth V8

6) 23 May - MONACO (Monte-Carlo)

1)	Ayrton Senna	McLaren MP4/8 - Ford Cosworth V8
2)	Damon Hill	Williams FW15C - Renault V10
3)	Jean Alesi	Ferrari F93A - V12
PP/ FL)	Alain Prost	Williams FW15C - Renault V10

7) 13 Jun - CANADA (Montréal)

1/ PP)	Alain Prost	Williams FW15C - Renault V10
2/ FL)	Michael Schumacher	Benetton B193B - Ford Cosworth V8
3)	Damon Hill	Williams FW15C - Renault V10

8) 4 Jul - FRANCE (Magny-Cours)

1)	Alain Prost	Williams FW15C - Renault V10
2/ PP)	Damon Hill	Williams FW15C - Renault V10
3/ FL)	Michael Schumacher	Benetton B193B - Ford Cosworth V8

9) 11 Jul - BRITAIN (Silverstone)

1/ PP)	Alain Prost	Williams FW15C - Renault V10
2)	Michael Schumacher	Benetton B193B - Ford Cosworth V8
3)	Riccardo Patrese	Benetton B193B - Ford Cosworth V8
FL)	Damon Hill	Williams FW15C - Renault V10

10) 25 Jul - GERMANY (Hockenheim)

1/ PP)	Alain Prost	Williams FW15C - Renault V10
2/ FL)	Michael Schumacher	Benetton B193B - Ford Cosworth V8
3)	Mark Blundell	Ligier JS39 - Renault V10

11) 15 Aug - HUNGARY (Hungaroring)

1)	Damon Hill	Williams FW15C - Renault V10
2)	Riccardo Patrese	Benetton B193B - Ford Cosworth V8
3)	Gerhard Berger	Ferrari F93A - V12
PP/ FL)	Alain Prost	Williams FW15C - Renault V10

12) 29 Aug - BELGIUM (Spa-Francorchamps)

1)	Damon Hill	Williams FW15C - Renault V10
2)	Michael Schumacher	Benetton B193B - Ford Cosworth V8
3/ PP/ FL)	Alain Prost	Williams FW15C - Renault V10

13) 12 Sep - ITALY (Monza)

1/ FL)	Damon Hill	Williams FW15C - Renault V10
2)	Jean Alesi	Ferrari F93A - V12
3)	Michael Andretti	McLaren MP4/8 - Ford Cosworth V8
PP)	Alain Prost	Williams FW15C - Renault V10

14) 26 Sep - PORTUGAL (Estoril)

1)	Michael Schumacher	Benetton B193B - Ford Cosworth V8
2)	Alain Prost	Williams FW15C - Renault V10
3/ PP/ FL)	Damon Hill	Williams FW15C - Renault V10

15) 24 Oct - JAPAN (Suzuka)

1)	Ayrton Senna	McLaren MP4/8 - Ford Cosworth V8
2/ PP/ FL)	Alain Prost	Williams FW15C - Renault V10
3)	Mika Häkkinen	McLaren MP4/8 - Ford Cosworth V8

16) 7 Nov - AUSTRALIA (Adelaide)

1/ PP)	Ayrton Senna	McLaren MP4/8 - Ford Cosworth V8
2)	Alain Prost	Williams FW15C - Renault V10
3/ FL)	Damon Hill	Williams FW15C - Renault V10

Drivers' championship		Constructors' championship	
1) Alain Prost	99	1) Williams - Renault	168
2) Ayrton Senna	73	2) McLaren - Ford Cosworth	84
3) Damon Hill	69	3) Benetton - Ford Cosworth	72

1994

1) 27 Mar - BRAZIL (Interlagos)

1/ FL)	Michael Schumacher	Benetton B194 - Ford Cosworth V8
2)	Damon Hill	Williams FW16 - Renault V10
3)	Jean Alesi	Ferrari 412T1 - V12
PP)	Ayrton Senna	Williams FW16 - Renault V10

2) 17 Apr - PACIFIC (Aida)

1/ FL)	Michael Schumacher	Benetton B194 - Ford Cosworth V8
2)	Gerhard Berger	Ferrari 412T1 - V12
3)	Rubens Barrichello	Jordan 194 - Hart V10
PP)	Ayrton Senna	Williams FW16 - Renault V10

3) 1 May - SAN MARINO (Imola)

1)	Michael Schumacher	Benetton B194 - Ford Cosworth V8
2)	Nicola Larini	Ferrari 412T1 - V12
3)	Mika Häkkinen	McLaren MP4/9 - Peugeot V10
PP)	Ayrton Senna	Williams FW16 - Renault V10
FL)	Damon Hill	Williams FW16 - Renault V10

4) 15 May - MONACO (Monte-Carlo)

1/ PP/ FL)	Michael Schumacher	Benetton B194 - Ford Cosworth V8
2)	Martin Brundle	McLaren MP4/9 - Peugeot V10
3)	Gerhard Berger	Ferrari 412T1 - V12

5) 29 May - SPAIN (Catalunya)

1)	Damon Hill	Williams FW16 - Renault V10
2/ PP/ FL)	Michael Schumacher	Benetton B194 - Ford Cosworth V8
3)	Mark Blundell	Tyrrell 022 - Yamaha V10

6) 12 Jun - CANADA (Montréal)

1/ PP/ FL)	Michael Schumacher	Benetton B194 - Ford Cosworth V8
2)	Damon Hill	Williams FW16 - Renault V10
3)	Jean Alesi	Ferrari 412T1 - V12

7) 3 Jul - FRANCE (Magny-Cours)

1)	Michael Schumacher	Benetton B194 - Ford Cosworth V8
2/ PP/ FL)	Damon Hill	Williams FW16 - Renault V10
3)	Gerhard Berger	Ferrari 412T1B - V12

8) 10 Jul - BRITAIN (Silverstone)

1/ PP/ FL)	Damon Hill	Williams FW16 - Renault V10
2)	Jean Alesi	Ferrari 412T1B - V12
3)	Mika Häkkinen	McLaren MP4/9 - Peugeot V10

Michael Schumacher (Benetton B194 - Ford Cosworth V8) finished 2nd, but was disqualified for overtaking on the parade lap and ignoring stop-go penalty.

9) 31 Jul - GERMANY (Hockenheim)

1/ PP)	Gerhard Berger	Ferrari 412T1B - V12
2)	Olivier Panis	Ligier JS39B - Renault V10
3)	Éric Bernard	Ligier JS39B - Renault V10
FL)	David Coulthard	Williams FW16B - Renault V10

10) 14 Aug - HUNGARY (Hungaroring)

1/ PP/ FL)	Michael Schumacher	Benetton B194 - Ford Cosworth V8
2)	Damon Hill	Williams FW16B - Renault V10
3)	Jos Verstappen	Benetton B194 - Ford Cosworth V8

11) 28 Aug - BELGIUM (Spa-Francorchamps)

1/ FL)	Damon Hill	Williams FW16B - Renault V10
2)	Mika Häkkinen	McLaren MP4/9 - Peugeot V10
3)	Jos Verstappen	Benetton B194 - Ford Cosworth V8
PP)	Rubens Barrichello	Jordan 194 - Hart V10

Michael Schumacher (Benetton B194 - Ford Cosworth V8) finished 1st, but was disqualified for illegal skid block wear.

12) 11 Sep - ITALY (Monza)

1/ FL)	Damon Hill	Williams FW16B - Renault V10
2)	Gerhard Berger	Ferrari 412T1B - V12
3)	Mika Häkkinen	McLaren MP4/9 - Peugeot V10
PP)	Jean Alesi	Ferrari 412T1B - V12

13) 25 Sep - PORTUGAL (Estoril)

1)	Damon Hill	Williams FW16B - Renault V10
2/ FL)	David Coulthard	Williams FW16B - Renault V10
3)	Mika Häkkinen	McLaren MP4/9 - Peugeot V10
PP)	Gerhard Berger	Ferrari 412T1B - V12

14) 16 Oct - EUROPE (Jerez de la Frontera)

1/ PP/ FL)	Michael Schumacher	Benetton B194 - Ford Cosworth V8
2)	Damon Hill	Williams FW16B - Renault V10
3)	Mika Häkkinen	McLaren MP4/9 - Peugeot V10

15) 6 Nov - JAPAN (Suzuka)

1/ FL)	Damon Hill	Williams FW16B - Renault V10
2/ PP)	Michael Schumacher	Benetton B194 - Ford Cosworth V8
3)	Jean Alesi	Ferrari 412T1B - V12

16) 13 Nov - AUSTRALIA (Adelaide)

1/ PP)	Nigel Mansell	Williams FW16B - Renault V10
2)	Gerhard Berger	Ferrari 412T1B - V12
3)	Martin Brundle	McLaren MP4/9 - Peugeot V10
FL)	Michael Schumacher	Benetton B194 - Ford Cosworth V8

Drivers' championship		Constructors' championship	
1) Michael Schumacher	92	1) Williams - Renault	118
2) Damon Hill	91	2) Benetton - Ford Cosworth	103
3) Gerhard Berger	41	3) Ferrari	71

1995

1) 26 Mar - BRAZIL (Interlagos)

1/ FL)	Michael Schumacher	Benetton B195 - Renault V10
2)	David Coulthard	Williams FW17 - Renault V10
3)	Gerhard Berger	Ferrari 412T2 - V12
PP)	Damon Hill	Williams FW17 - Renault V10

2) 9 Apr - ARGENTINA (Buenos Aires No.6)

1)	Damon Hill	Williams FW17 - Renault V10
2)	Jean Alesi	Ferrari 412T2 - V12
3/ FL)	Michael Schumacher	Benetton B195 - Renault V10
PP)	David Coulthard	Williams FW17 - Renault V10

3) 30 Apr - SAN MARINO (Imola)

1)	Damon Hill	Williams FW17 - Renault V10
2)	Jean Alesi	Ferrari 412T2 - V12
3/ FL)	Gerhard Berger	Ferrari 412T2 - V12
PP)	Michael Schumacher	Benetton B195 - Renault V10

4) 14 May - SPAIN (Catalunya)

1/ PP)	Michael Schumacher	Benetton B195 - Renault V10
2)	Johnny Herbert	Benetton B195 - Renault V10
3)	Gerhard Berger	Ferrari 412T2 - V12
FL)	Damon Hill	Williams FW17 - Renault V10

5) 28 May - MONACO (Monte-Carlo)

1)	Michael Schumacher	Benetton B195 - Renault V10
2/ PP)	Damon Hill	Williams FW17 - Renault V10
3)	Gerhard Berger	Ferrari 412T2 - V12
FL)	Jean Alesi	Ferrari 412T2 - V12

6) 11 Jun - CANADA (Montréal)

1)	Jean Alesi	Ferrari 412T2 - V12
2)	Rubens Barrichello	Jordan 195 - Peugeot V10
3)	Eddie Irvine	Jordan 195 - Peugeot V10
PP/ FL)	Michael Schumacher	Benetton B195 - Renault V10

7) 2 Jul - FRANCE (Magny-Cours)

1/ FL)	Michael Schumacher	Benetton B195 - Renault V10
2/ PP)	Damon Hill	Williams FW17 - Renault V10
3)	David Coulthard	Williams FW17 - Renault V10

8) 16 Jul - BRITAIN (Silverstone)

1)	Johnny Herbert	Benetton B195 - Renault V10
2)	Jean Alesi	Ferrari 412T2 - V12
3)	David Coulthard	Williams FW17 - Renault V10
PP/ FL)	Damon Hill	Williams FW17 - Renault V10

9) 30 Jul - GERMANY (Hockenheim)

1/ FL)	Michael Schumacher	Benetton B195 - Renault V10
2)	David Coulthard	Williams FW17 - Renault V10
3)	Gerhard Berger	Ferrari 412T2 - V12
PP)	Damon Hill	Williams FW17 - Renault V10

10) 13 Aug - HUNGARY (Hungaroring)

1/ PP/ FL)	Damon Hill	Williams FW17 - Renault V10
2)	David Coulthard	Williams FW17 - Renault V10
3)	Gerhard Berger	Ferrari 412T2 - V12

11) 27 Aug - BELGIUM (Spa-Francorchamps)

1)	Michael Schumacher	Benetton B195 - Renault V10
2)	Damon Hill	Williams FW17 - Renault V10
3)	Martin Brundle	Ligier JS41 - Mugen Honda V10
PP)	Gerhard Berger	Ferrari 412T2 - V12
FL)	David Coulthard	Williams FW17 - Renault V10

12) 10 Sep - ITALY (Monza)

1)	Johnny Herbert	Benetton B195 - Renault V10
2)	Mika Häkkinen	McLaren MP4/10B - Mercedes V10
3)	Heinz-Harald Frentzen	Sauber C14 - Ford Cosworth V8
PP)	David Coulthard	Williams FW17 - Renault V10
FL)	Gerhard Berger	Ferrari 412T2 - V12

13) 24 Sep - PORTUGAL (Estoril)

1/ PP/ FL)	David Coulthard	Williams FW17 - Renault V10
2)	Michael Schumacher	Benetton B195 - Renault V10
3)	Damon Hill	Williams FW17 - Renault V10

14) 1 Oct - EUROPE (Nürburgring)

1/ FL)	Michael Schumacher	Benetton B195 - Renault V10
2)	Jean Alesi	Ferrari 412T2 - V12
3/ PP)	David Coulthard	Williams FW17B - Renault V10

15) 22 Oct - PACIFIC (Aida)

1/ FL)	Michael Schumacher	Benetton B195 - Renault V10
2/ PP)	David Coulthard	Williams FW17B - Renault V10
3)	Damon Hill	Williams FW17B - Renault V10

16) 29 Oct - JAPAN (Suzuka)

1/ PP/ FL)	Michael Schumacher	Benetton B195 - Renault V10
2)	Mika Häkkinen	McLaren MP4/10B - Mercedes V10
3)	Johnny Herbert	Benetton B195 - Renault V10

17) 12 Nov - AUSTRALIA (Adelaide)

1/ PP/ FL)	Damon Hill	Williams FW17B - Renault V10
2)	Olivier Panis	Ligier JS41 - Mugen Honda V10
3)	Gianni Morbidelli	Footwork FA16 - Hart V8

Drivers' championship

1) Michael Schumacher	102
2) Damon Hill	69
3) David Coulthard	49

Constructors' championship

1)Benetton - Renault	137
2) Williams - Renault	112
3) Ferrari	73

1996

1) 10 Mar - AUSTRALIA (Melbourne)

1)	Damon Hill	Williams FW18 - Renault V10
2/ PP/ FL)	Jacques Villeneuve	Williams FW18 - Renault V10
3)	Eddie Irvine	Ferrari F310 - V10

2) 31 Mar - BRAZIL (Interlagos)

1/ PP/ FL)	Damon Hill	Williams FW18 - Renault V10
2)	Jean Alesi	Benetton B196 - Renault V10
3)	Michael Schumacher	Ferrari F310 - V10

3) 7 Apr - ARGENTINA (Buenos Aires No.6)

1/ PP)	Damon Hill	Williams FW18 - Renault V10
2)	Jacques Villeneuve	Williams FW18 - Renault V10
3/ FL)	Jean Alesi	Benetton B196 - Renault V10

4) 28 Apr - EUROPE (Nürburgring)

1)	Jacques Villeneuve	Williams FW18 - Renault V10
2)	Michael Schumacher	Ferrari F310 - V10
3)	David Coulthard	McLaren MP4/11 - Mercedes V10
PP/ FL)	Damon Hill	Williams FW18 - Renault V10

5) 5 May - SAN MARINO (Imola)

1/ FL)	Damon Hill	Williams FW18 - Renault V10
2/ PP)	Michael Schumacher	Ferrari F310 - V10
3)	Gerhard Berger	Benetton B196 - Renault V10

6) 19 May - MONACO (Monte-Carlo)

1)	Olivier Panis	Ligier JS43 - Mugen Honda V10
2)	David Coulthard	McLaren MP4/11B - Mercedes V10
3)	Johnny Herbert	Sauber C15 - Ford Cosworth V10
PP)	Michael Schumacher	Ferrari F310 - V10
FL)	Jean Alesi	Benetton B196 - Renault V10

7) 2 Jun - SPAIN (Catalunya)

1/ FL)	Michael Schumacher	Ferrari F310 - V10
2)	Jean Alesi	Benetton B196 - Renault V10
3)	Jacques Villeneuve	Williams FW18 - Renault V10
PP)	Damon Hill	Williams FW18 - Renault V10

8) 16 Jun - CANADA (Montréal)

1/ PP)	Damon Hill	Williams FW18 - Renault V10
2/ FL)	Jacques Villeneuve	Williams FW18 - Renault V10
3)	Jean Alesi	Benetton B196 - Renault V10

9) 30 Jun - FRANCE (Magny-Cours)

1)	Damon Hill	Williams FW18 - Renault V10
2/ FL)	Jacques Villeneuve	Williams FW18 - Renault V10
3)	Jean Alesi	Benetton B196 - Renault V10
PP)	Michael Schumacher	Ferrari F310 - V10

Michael Schumacher did not start (engine failure on the parade lap).

10) 14 Jul - BRITAIN (Silverstone)

1/ FL)	Jacques Villeneuve	Williams FW18 - Renault V10
2)	Gerhard Berger	Benetton B196 - Renault V10
3)	Mika Häkkinen	McLaren MP4/11B - Mercedes V10
PP)	Damon Hill	Williams FW18 - Renault V10

11) 28 Jul - GERMANY (Hockenheim)

1/ PP/ FL)	Damon Hill	Williams FW18 - Renault V10
2)	Jean Alesi	Benetton B196 - Renault V10
3)	Jacques Villeneuve	Williams FW18 - Renault V10

12) 11 Aug - HUNGARY (Hungaroring)

1)	Jacques Villeneuve	Williams FW18 - Renault V10
2/ FL)	Damon Hill	Williams FW18 - Renault V10
3)	Jean Alesi	Benetton B196 - Renault V10
PP)	Michael Schumacher	Ferrari F310 - V10

13) 25 Aug - BELGIUM (Spa-Francorchamps)

1)	Michael Schumacher	Ferrari F310 - V10
2/ PP)	Jacques Villeneuve	Williams FW18 - Renault V10
3)	Mika Häkkinen	McLaren MP4/11B - Mercedes V10
FL)	Gerhard Berger	Benetton B196 - Renault V10

14) 8 Sep - ITALY (Monza)

1/ FL)	Michael Schumacher	Ferrari F310 - V10
2)	Jean Alesi	Benetton B196 - Renault V10
3)	Mika Häkkinen	McLaren MP4/11B - Mercedes V10
PP)	Damon Hill	Williams FW18 - Renault V10

15) 22 Sep - PORTUGAL (Estoril)

1/ FL)	Jacques Villeneuve	Williams FW18 - Renault V10
2/ PP)	Damon Hill	Williams FW18 - Renault V10
3)	Michael Schumacher	Ferrari F310 - V10

16) 13 Oct - JAPAN (Suzuka)

1)	Damon Hill	Williams FW18 - Renault V10
2)	Michael Schumacher	Ferrari F310 - V10
3)	Mika Häkkinen	McLaren MP4/11B - Mercedes V10
PP/ FL)	Jacques Villeneuve	Williams FW18 - Renault V10

Drivers' championship

1) Damon Hill	97
2) Jacques Villeneuve	78
3) Michael Schumacher	59

Constructors' championship

1) Williams - Renault	175
2) Ferrari	70
3) Benetton - Renault	68

1997

1) 9 Mar - AUSTRALIA (Melbourne)

1)	David Coulthard	McLaren MP4-12 - Mercedes V10
2)	Michael Schumacher	Ferrari F310B - V10
3)	Mika Häkkinen	McLaren MP4-12 - Mercedes V10
PP)	Jacques Villeneuve	Williams FW19 - Renault V10
FL)	Heinz-Harald Frentzen	Williams FW19 - Renault V10

2) 30 Mar - BRAZIL (Interlagos)

1/ PP/ FL)	Jacques Villeneuve	Williams FW19 - Renault V10
2)	Gerhard Berger	Benetton B197 - Renault V10
3)	Olivier Panis	Prost JS45 - Mugen Honda V10

3) 13 Apr - ARGENTINA (Buenos Aires No.6)

1/ PP)	Jacques Villeneuve	Williams FW19 - Renault V10
2)	Eddie Irvine	Ferrari F310B - V10
3)	Ralf Schumacher	Jordan 197 - Peugeot V10
FL)	Gerhard Berger	Benetton B197 - Renault V10

4) 27 Apr - SAN MARINO (Imola)

1/ FL)	Heinz-Harald Frentzen	Williams FW19 - Renault V10
2)	Michael Schumacher	Ferrari F310B - V10
3)	Eddie Irvine	Ferrari F310B - V10
PP)	Jacques Villeneuve	Williams FW19 - Renault V10

5) 11 May - MONACO (Monte-Carlo)

1/ FL)	Michael Schumacher	Ferrari F310B - V10
2)	Rubens Barrichello	Stewart SF-1 - Ford Cosworth V10
3)	Eddie Irvine	Ferrari F310B - V10
PP)	Heinz-Harald Frentzen	Williams FW19 - Renault V10

6) 25 May - SPAIN (Catalunya)

1/ PP)	Jacques Villeneuve	Williams FW19 - Renault V10
2)	Olivier Panis	Prost JS45 - Mugen Honda V10
3)	Jean Alesi	Benetton B197 - Renault V10
FL)	Giancarlo Fisichella	Jordan 197 - Peugeot V10

7) 15 Jun - CANADA (Montréal)

1/ PP)	Michael Schumacher	Ferrari F310B - V10
2)	Jean Alesi	Benetton B197 - Renault V10
3)	Giancarlo Fisichella	Jordan 197 - Peugeot V10
FL)	David Coulthard	McLaren MP4-12 - Mercedes V10

8) 29 Jun - FRANCE (Magny-Cours)

1/ PP/ FL)	Michael Schumacher	Ferrari F310B - V10
2)	Heinz-Harald Frentzen	Williams FW19 - Renault V10
3)	Eddie Irvine	Ferrari F310B - V10

9) 13 Jul - BRITAIN (Silverstone)

1/ PP)	Jacques Villeneuve	Williams FW19 - Renault V10
2)	Jean Alesi	Benetton B197 - Renault V10
3)	Alexander Wurz	Benetton B197 - Renault V10
FL)	Michael Schumacher	Ferrari F310B - V10

10) 27 Jul - GERMANY (Hockenheim)

1/ PP/ FL)	Gerhard Berger	Benetton B197 - Renault V10
2)	Michael Schumacher	Ferrari F310B - V10
3)	Mika Häkkinen	McLaren MP4-12 - Mercedes V10

11) 10 Aug - HUNGARY (Hungaroring)

1)	Jacques Villeneuve	Williams FW19 - Renault V10
2)	Damon Hill	Arrows A18 - Yamaha V10
3)	Johnny Herbert	Sauber C16 - Petronas V10
PP)	Michael Schumacher	Ferrari F310B - V10
FL)	Heinz-Harald Frentzen	Williams FW19 - Renault V10

12) 24 Aug - BELGIUM (Spa-Francorchamps)

1)	Michael Schumacher	Ferrari F310B - V10
2)	Giancarlo Fisichella	Jordan 197 - Peugeot V10
3)	Heinz-Harald Frentzen	Williams FW19 - Renault V10
PP/ FL)	Jacques Villeneuve	Williams FW19 - Renault V10

Mika Häkkinen (McLaren MP4-12 - Mercedes V10) finished 3rd, but was disqualified for using illegal fuel.

13) 7 Sep - ITALY (Monza)

1)	David Coulthard	McLaren MP4-12 - Mercedes V10
2/ PP)	Jean Alesi	Benetton B197 - Renault V10
3)	Heinz-Harald Frentzen	Williams FW19 - Renault V10
FL)	Mika Häkkinen	McLaren MP4-12 - Mercedes V10

14) 21 Sep - AUSTRIA (A1-Ring)

1/ PP/ FL)	Jacques Villeneuve	Williams FW19 - Renault V10
2)	David Coulthard	McLaren MP4-12 - Mercedes V10
3)	Heinz-Harald Frentzen	Williams FW19 - Renault V10

15) 28 Sep - LUXEMBOURG (Nürburgring)

1)	Jacques Villeneuve	Williams FW19 - Renault V10
2)	Jean Alesi	Benetton B197 - Renault V10
3/ FL)	Heinz-Harald Frentzen	Williams FW19 - Renault V10
PP)	Mika Häkkinen	McLaren MP4-12 - Mercedes V10

16) 12 Oct - JAPAN (Suzuka)

1)	Michael Schumacher	Ferrari F310B - V10
2/ FL)	Heinz-Harald Frentzen	Williams FW19 - Renault V10
3)	Eddie Irvine	Ferrari F310B - V10
PP)	Jacques Villeneuve	Williams FW19 - Renault V10

17) 26 Oct - EUROPE (Jerez de la Frontera)

1)	Mika Häkkinen	McLaren MP4-12 - Mercedes V10
2)	David Coulthard	McLaren MP4-12 - Mercedes V10
3/ PP)	Jacques Villeneuve	Williams FW19 - Renault V10
FL)	Heinz-Harald Frentzen	Williams FW19 - Renault V10

Drivers' championship

1) Jacques Villeneuve 81
2) Heniz-Harald Frentzen 42
3) David Coulthard 36

Constructors' championship

1) Williams - Renault 123
2) Ferrari 102
3) Benetton - Renault 67

Michael Schumacher was disqualified from the championship for causing an accident with Jacques Villeneue in the European Grand Prix. His results during the season still stood, however.

1998

1) 8 Mar - AUSTRALIA (Melbourne)

1/ PP/ FL)	Mika Häkkinen	McLaren MP4-13 - Mercedes V10
2)	David Coulthard	McLaren MP4-13 - Mercedes V10
3)	Heinz-Harald Frentzen	Williams FW20 - Mecachrome V10

2) 29 Mar - BRAZIL (Interlagos)

1/ PP/ FL)	Mika Häkkinen	McLaren MP4-13 - Mercedes V10
2)	David Coulthard	McLaren MP4-13 - Mercedes V10
3)	Michael Schumacher	Ferrari F300 - V10

3) 12 Apr - ARGENTINA (Buenos Aires No.6)

1)	Michael Schumacher	Ferrari F300 - V10
2)	Mika Häkkinen	McLaren MP4-13 - Mercedes V10
3)	Eddie Irvine	Ferrari F300 - V10
PP)	David Coulthard	McLaren MP4-13 - Mercedes V10
FL)	Alexander Wurz	Benetton B198 - Playlife V10

4) 26 Apr - SAN MARINO (Imola)

1/ PP)	David Coulthard	McLaren MP4-13 - Mercedes V10
2/ FL)	Michael Schumacher	Ferrari F300 - V10
3)	Eddie Irvine	Ferrari F300 - V10

5) 10 May - SPAIN (Catalunya)

1/ PP/ FL)	Mika Häkkinen	McLaren MP4-13 - Mercedes V10
2)	David Coulthard	McLaren MP4-13 - Mercedes V10
3)	Michael Schumacher	Ferrari F300 - V10

6) 24 May - MONACO (Monte-Carlo)

1/ PP/ FL)	Mika Häkkinen	McLaren MP4-13 - Mercedes V10
2)	Giancarlo Fisichella	Benetton B198 - Playlife V10
3)	Eddie Irvine	Ferrari F300 - V10

7) 7 Jun - CANADA (Montréal)

1/ FL)	Michael Schumacher	Ferrari F300 - V10
2)	Giancarlo Fisichella	Benetton B198 - Playlife V10
3)	Eddie Irvine	Ferrari F300 - V10
PP)	David Coulthard	McLaren MP4-13 - Mercedes V10

8) 28 Jun - FRANCE (Magny-Cours)

1)	Michael Schumacher	Ferrari F300 - V10
2)	Eddie Irvine	Ferrari F300 - V10
3/ PP)	Mika Häkkinen	McLaren MP4-13 - Mercedes V10
FL)	David Coulthard	McLaren MP4-13 - Mercedes V10

9) 12 Jul - BRITAIN (Silverstone)

1/ FL)	Michael Schumacher	Ferrari F300 - V10
2/ PP)	Mika Häkkinen	McLaren MP4-13 - Mercedes V10
3)	Eddie Irvine	Ferrari F300 - V10

10) 26 Jul - AUSTRIA (A1-Ring)

1)	Mika Häkkinen	McLaren MP4-13 - Mercedes V10
2/ FL)	David Coulthard	McLaren MP4-13 - Mercedes V10
3)	Michael Schumacher	Ferrari F300 - V10
PP)	Giancarlo Fisichella	Benetton B198 - Playlife V10

11) 2 Aug - GERMANY (Hockenheim)

1/ PP)	Mika Häkkinen	McLaren MP4-13 - Mercedes V10
2/ FL)	David Coulthard	McLaren MP4-13 - Mercedes V10
3)	Jacques Villeneuve	Williams FW20 - Mecachrome V10

12) 16 Aug - HUNGARY (Hungaroring)

1/ FL)	Michael Schumacher	Ferrari F300 - V10
2)	David Coulthard	McLaren MP4-13 - Mercedes V10
3)	Jacques Villeneuve	Williams FW20 - Mecachrome V10
PP)	Mika Häkkinen	McLaren MP4-13 - Mercedes V10

13) 30 Aug - BELGIUM (Spa-Francorchamps)

1)	Damon Hill	Jordan 198 - Mugen Honda V10
2)	Ralf Schumacher	Jordan 198 - Mugen Honda V10
3)	Jean Alesi	Sauber C17 - Petronas V10
PP)	Mika Häkkinen	McLaren MP4-13 - Mercedes V10
FL)	Michael Schumacher	Ferrari F300 - V10

14) 13 Sep - ITALY (Monza)

1/ PP)	Michael Schumacher	Ferrari F300 - V10
2)	Eddie Irvine	Ferrari F300 - V10
3)	Ralf Schumacher	Jordan 198 - Mugen Honda V10
FL)	Mika Häkkinen	McLaren MP4-13 - Mercedes V10

15) 27 Sep - LUXEMBOURG (Nürburgring)

1/ FL)	Mika Häkkinen	McLaren MP4-13 - Mercedes V10
2/ PP)	Michael Schumacher	Ferrari F300 - V10
3)	David Coulthard	McLaren MP4-13 - Mercedes V10

16) 1 Nov - JAPAN (Suzuka)

1)	Mika Häkkinen	McLaren MP4-13 - Mercedes V10
2)	Eddie Irvine	Ferrari F300 - V10
3)	David Coulthard	McLaren MP4-13 - Mercedes V10
PP/ FL)	Michael Schumacher	Ferrari F300 - V10

Drivers' championship

1) Mika Häkkinen	100
2) Michael Schumacher	86
3) David Coulthard	56

Constructors' championship

1) McLaren - Mercedes	156
2) Ferrari	133
3) Williams - Mechachrome	38

1999

1) 7 Mar - AUSTRALIA (Melbourne)

1)	Eddie Irvine	Ferrari F399 - V10
2)	Heinz-Harald Frentzen	Jordan 199 - Mugen Honda V10
3)	Ralf Schumacher	Williams FW21 - Supertec V10
PP)	Mika Häkkinen	McLaren MP4-14 - Mercedes V10
FL)	Michael Schumacher	Ferrari F399 - V10

2) 11 Apr - BRAZIL (Interlagos)

1/ PP/ FL)	Mika Häkkinen	McLaren MP4-14 - Mercedes V10
2)	Michael Schumacher	Ferrari F399 - V10
3/ret)	Heinz-Harald Frentzen	Jordan 199 - Mugen Honda V10

3) 2 May - SAN MARINO (Imola)

1/ FL)	Michael Schumacher	Ferrari F399 - V10
2)	David Coulthard	McLaren MP4-14 - Mercedes V10
3)	Rubens Barrichello	Stewart SF-3 - Ford Cosworth V10
PP)	Mika Häkkinen	McLaren MP4-14 - Mercedes V10

4) 16 May - MONACO (Monte-Carlo)

1)	Michael Schumacher	Ferrari F399 - V10
2)	Eddie Irvine	Ferrari F399 - V10
3/ PP/ FL)	Mika Häkkinen	McLaren MP4-14 - Mercedes V10

5) 30 May - SPAIN (Catalunya)

1/ PP)	Mika Häkkinen	McLaren MP4-14 - Mercedes V10
2)	David Coulthard	McLaren MP4-14 - Mercedes V10
3/ FL)	Michael Schumacher	Ferrari F399 - V10

6) 13 Jun - CANADA (Montréal)

1)	Mika Häkkinen	McLaren MP4-14 - Mercedes V10
2)	Giancarlo Fisichella	Benetton B199 - Playlife V10
3/ FL)	Eddie Irvine	Ferrari F399 - V10
PP)	Michael Schumacher	Ferrari F399 - V10

7) 27 Jun - FRANCE (Magny-Cours)

1)	Heinz-Harald Frentzen	Jordan 199 - Mugen Honda V10
2)	Mika Häkkinen	McLaren MP4-14 - Mercedes V10
3/ PP)	Rubens Barrichello	Stewart SF-3 - Ford Cosworth V10
FL)	David Coulthard	McLaren MP4-14 - Mercedes V10

8) 11 Jul - BRITAIN (Silverstone)

1)	David Coulthard	McLaren MP4-14 - Mercedes V10
2)	Eddie Irvine	Ferrari F399 - V10
3)	Ralf Schumacher	Williams FW21 - Supertec V10
PP/ FL)	Mika Häkkinen	McLaren MP4-14 - Mercedes V10

9) 25 Jul - AUSTRIA (A1-Ring)

1)	Eddie Irvine	Ferrari F399 - V10
2)	David Coulthard	McLaren MP4-14 - Mercedes V10
3/ PP/ FL)	Mika Häkkinen	McLaren MP4-14 - Mercedes V10

10) 1 Aug - GERMANY (Hockenheim)

1)	Eddie Irvine	Ferrari F399 - V10
2)	Mika Salo	Ferrari F399 - V10
3)	Heinz-Harald Frentzen	Jordan 199 - Mugen Honda V10
PP)	Mika Häkkinen	McLaren MP4-14 - Mercedes V10
FL)	David Coulthard	McLaren MP4-14 - Mercedes V10

11) 15 Aug - HUNGARY (Hungaroring)

1/ PP)	Mika Häkkinen	McLaren MP4-14 - Mercedes V10
2/ FL)	David Coulthard	McLaren MP4-14 - Mercedes V10
3)	Eddie Irvine	Ferrari F399 - V10

12) 29 Aug - BELGIUM (Spa-Francorchamps)

1)	David Coulthard	McLaren MP4-14 - Mercedes V10
2/ PP/ FL)	Mika Häkkinen	McLaren MP4-14 - Mercedes V10
3)	Heinz-Harald Frentzen	Jordan 199 - Mugen Honda V10

13) 12 Sep - ITALY (Monza)

1)	Heinz-Harald Frentzen	Jordan 199 - Mugen Honda V10
2/ FL)	Ralf Schumacher	Williams FW21 - Supertec V10
3)	Mika Salo	Ferrari F399 - V10
PP)	Mika Häkkinen	McLaren MP4-14 - Mercedes V10

14) 26 Sep - EUROPE (Nürburgring)

1)	Johnny Herbert	Stewart SF-3 - Ford Cosworth V10
2)	Jarno Trulli	Prost AP02 - Peugeot V10
3)	Rubens Barrichello	Stewart SF-3 - Ford Cosworth V10
PP)	Heinz-Harald Frentzen	Jordan 199 - Mugen Honda V10
FL)	Mika Häkkinen	McLaren MP4-14 - Mercedes V10

15) 17 Oct - MALAYSIA (Sepang)

1)	Eddie Irvine	Ferrari F399 - V10
2/ PP/ FL)	Michael Schumacher	Ferrari F399 - V10
3)	Mika Häkkinen	McLaren MP4-14 - Mercedes V10

16) 31 Oct - JAPAN (Suzuka)

	1)	Mika Häkkinen	McLaren MP4-14 - Mercedes V10
	2/ PP/ FL)	Michael Schumacher	Ferrari F399 - V10
	3)	Eddie Irvine	Ferrari F399 - V10

Drivers' championship

1) Mika Häkkinen	76
2) Eddie Irvine	74
3) Heinz-Harald Frentzen	54

Constructors' championship

1) Ferrari	128
2) McLaren - Mercedes	124
3) Jordan - Mugen Honda	61

2000

1) 12 Mar - AUSTRALIA (Melbourne)

	I)	Michael Schumacher	Ferrari F1 2000 - V10
	2/ FL)	Rubens Barrichello	Ferrari F1 2000 - V10
	3)	Ralf Schumacher	Williams FW22 - BMW V10
	PP)	Mika Häkkinen	McLaren MP4-15 - Mercedes V10

2) 26 Mar - BRAZIL (Interlagos)

	1/ FL)	Michael Schumacher	Ferrari F1 2000 - V10
	2)	Giancarlo Fisichella	Benetton B200 - Playlife V10
	3)	Heinz-Harald Frentzen	Jordan EJ10 - Mugen Honda V10
	PP)	Mika Häkkinen	McLaren MP4-15 - Mercedes V10

David Coulthard (McLaren MP4-15 - Mercedes V10) finished 2nd, but was disqualified for the front wing end-plates being too low.

3) 9 Apr - SAN MARINO (Imola)

	1)	Michael Schumacher	Ferrari F1 2000 - V10
	2/ PP/ FL)	Mika Häkkinen	McLaren MP4-15 - Mercedes V10
	3)	David Coulthard	McLaren MP4-15 - Mercedes V10

4) 23 Apr - BRITAIN (Silverstone)

	1)	David Coulthard	McLaren MP4-15 - Mercedes V10
	2/ FL)	Mika Häkkinen	McLaren MP4-15 - Mercedes V10
	3)	Michael Schumacher	Ferrari F1 2000 - V10
	PP)	Rubens Barrichello	Ferrari F1 2000 - V10

5) 7 May - SPAIN (Catalunya)

	1/ FL)	Mika Häkkinen	McLaren MP4-15 - Mercedes V10
	2)	David Coulthard	McLaren MP4-15 - Mercedes V10
	3)	Rubens Barrichello	Ferrari F1 2000 - V10
	PP)	Michael Schumacher	Ferrari F1 2000 - V10

6) 21 May - EUROPE (Nürburgring)

	1/ FL)	Michael Schumacher	Ferrari F1 2000 - V10
	2)	Mika Häkkinen	McLaren MP4-15 - Mercedes V10
	3/ PP)	David Coulthard	McLaren MP4-15 - Mercedes V10

7) 4 Jun - MONACO (Monte-Carlo)

	1)	David Coulthard	McLaren MP4-15 - Mercedes V10
	2)	Rubens Barrichello	Ferrari F1 2000 - V10
	3)	Giancarlo Fisichella	Benetton B200 - Playlife V10
	PP)	Michael Schumacher	Ferrari F1 2000 - V10
	FL)	Mika Häkkinen	McLaren MP4-15 - Mercedes V10

8) 18 Jun - CANADA (Montréal)

	1/ PP)	Michael Schumacher	Ferrari F1 2000 - V10
	2)	Rubens Barrichello	Ferrari F1 2000 - V10
	3)	Giancarlo Fisichella	Benetton B200 - Playlife V10
	FL)	Mika Häkkinen	McLaren MP4-15 - Mercedes V10

9) 2 Jul - FRANCE (Magny-Cours)

	1/ FL)	David Coulthard	McLaren MP4-15 - Mercedes V10
	2)	Mika Häkkinen	McLaren MP4-15 - Mercedes V10
	3)	Rubens Barrichello	Ferrari F1 2000 - V10
	PP)	Michael Schumacher	Ferrari F1 2000 - V10

10) 16 Jul - AUSTRIA (A1-Ring)

	1/ PP)	Mika Häkkinen	McLaren MP4-15 - Mercedes V10
	2/ FL)	David Coulthard	McLaren MP4-15 - Mercedes V10
	3)	Rubens Barrichello	Ferrari F1 2000 - V10

11) 30 Jul - GERMANY (Hockenheim)

	1/ FL)	Rubens Barrichello	Ferrari F1 2000 - V10
	2)	Mika Häkkinen	McLaren MP4-15 - Mercedes V10
	3/ PP)	David Coulthard	McLaren MP4-15 - Mercedes V10

12) 13 Aug - HUNGARY (Hungaroring)

	1/ FL)	Mika Häkkinen	McLaren MP4-15 - Mercedes V10
	2/ PP)	Michael Schumacher	Ferrari F1 2000 - V10
	3)	David Coulthard	McLaren MP4-15 - Mercedes V10

13) 27 Aug - BELGIUM (Spa-Francorchamps)

	1/ PP)	Mika Häkkinen	McLaren MP4-15 - Mercedes V10
	2)	Michael Schumacher	Ferrari F1 2000 - V10
	3)	Ralf Schumacher	Williams FW22 - BMW V10
	FL)	Rubens Barrichello	Ferrari F1 2000 - V10

14) 10 Sep - ITALY (Monza)

	1/ PP)	Michael Schumacher	Ferrari F1 2000 - V10
	2/ FL)	Mika Häkkinen	McLaren MP4-15 - Mercedes V10
	3)	Ralf Schumacher	Williams FW22 - BMW V10

15) 24 Sep - UNITED STATES (Indianapolis)

	1/ PP)	Michael Schumacher	Ferrari F1 2000 - V10
	2)	Rubens Barrichello	Ferrari F1 2000 - V10
	3)	Heinz-Harald Frentzen	Jordan EJ10 - Mugen Honda V10
	FL)	David Coulthard	McLaren MP4-15 - Mercedes V10

16) 8 Oct - JAPAN (Suzuka)

	1/ PP)	Michael Schumacher	Ferrari F1 2000 - V10
	2/ FL)	Mika Häkkinen	McLaren MP4-15 - Mercedes V10
	3)	David Coulthard	McLaren MP4-15 - Mercedes V10

17) 22 Oct - MALAYSIA (Sepang)

	1/ PP)	Michael Schumacher	Ferrari F1 2000 - V10
	2)	David Coulthard	McLaren MP4-15 - Mercedes V10
	3)	Rubens Barrichello	Ferrari F1 2000 - V10
	FL)	Mika Häkkinen	McLaren MP4-15 - Mercedes V10

Drivers' championship

1) Michael Schumacher	108
2) Mika Häkkinen	89
3) David Coulthard	73

Constructors' championship

1) Ferrari	170
2) McLaren - Mercedes	152
3) Williams - BMW	36

2001

1) 4 Mar - AUSTRALIA (Melbourne)
    1/ PP/ FL)   Michael Schumacher   Ferrari F2001 - V10
    2)   David Coulthard   McLaren MP4-16 - Mercedes V10
    3)   Rubens Barrichello   Ferrari F2001 - V10

2) 18 Mar - MALAYSIA (Sepang)
    1/ PP)   Michael Schumacher   Ferrari F2001 - V10
    2)   Rubens Barrichello   Ferrari F2001 - V10
    3)   David Coulthard   McLaren MP4-16 - Mercedes V10
    FL)   Mika Häkkinen   McLaren MP4-16 - Mercedes V10

3) 1 Apr - BRAZIL (Interlagos)
    1)   David Coulthard   McLaren MP4-16 - Mercedes V10
    2/ PP)   Michael Schumacher   Ferrari F2001 - V10
    3)   Nick Heidfeld   Sauber C20 - Petronas V10
    FL)   Ralf Schumacher   Williams FW23 - BMW V10

4) 15 Apr - SAN MARINO (Imola)
    1/ FL)   Ralf Schumacher   Williams FW23 - BMW V10
    2/ PP)   David Coulthard   McLaren MP4-16 - Mercedes V10
    3)   Rubens Barrichello   Ferrari F2001 - V10

5) 29 Apr - SPAIN (Catalunya)
    1/ PP/ FL)   Michael Schumacher   Ferrari F2001 - V10
    2)   Juan Pablo Montoya   Williams FW23 - BMW V10
    3)   Jacques Villeneuve   BAR 003 - Honda V10

6) 13 May - AUSTRIA (A1-Ring)
    1/ FL)   David Coulthard   McLaren MP4-16 - Mercedes V10
    2/ PP)   Michael Schumacher   Ferrari F2001 - V10
    3)   Rubens Barrichello   Ferrari F2001 - V10

7) 27 May - MONACO (Monte-Carlo)
    1)   Michael Schumacher   Ferrari F2001 - V10
    2)   Rubens Barrichello   Ferrari F2001 - V10
    3)   Eddie Irvine   Jaguar R2 - Ford Cosworth V10
    PP/ FL)   David Coulthard   McLaren MP4-16 - Mercedes V10

8) 10 Jun - CANADA (Montréal)
    1/ FL)   Ralf Schumacher   Williams FW23 - BMW V10
    2/ PP)   Michael Schumacher   Ferrari F2001 - V10
    3)   Mika Häkkinen   McLaren MP4-16 - Mercedes V10

9) 24 Jun - EUROPE (Nürburgring)
    1/ PP)   Michael Schumacher   Ferrari F2001 - V10
    2/ FL)   Juan Pablo Montoya   Williams FW23 - BMW V10
    3)   David Coulthard   McLaren MP4-16 - Mercedes V10

10) 1 Jul - FRANCE (Magny-Cours)
    1)   Michael Schumacher   Ferrari F2001 - V10
    2/ PP)   Ralf Schumacher   Williams FW23 - BMW V10
    3)   Rubens Barrichello   Ferrari F2001 - V10
    FL)   David Coulthard   McLaren MP4-16 - Mercedes V10

11) 15 Jul - BRITAIN (Silverstone)
    1/ FL)   Mika Häkkinen   McLaren MP4-16 - Mercedes V10
    2/ PP)   Michael Schumacher   Ferrari F2001 - V10
    3)   Rubens Barrichello   Ferrari F2001 - V10

12) 29 Jul - GERMANY (Hockenheim)
    1)   Ralf Schumacher   Williams FW23 - BMW V10
    2)   Rubens Barrichello   Ferrari F2001 - V10
    3)   Jacques Villeneuve   BAR 003 - Honda V10
    PP/ FL)   Juan Pablo Montoya   Williams FW23 - BMW V10

13) 19 Aug - HUNGARY (Hungaroring)
    1/ PP)   Michael Schumacher   Ferrari F2001 - V10
    2)   Rubens Barrichello   Ferrari F2001 - V10
    3)   David Coulthard   McLaren MP4-16 - Mercedes V10
    FL)   Mika Häkkinen   McLaren MP4-16 - Mercedes V10

14) 2 Sep - BELGIUM (Spa-Francorchamps)
    1/ FL)   Michael Schumacher   Ferrari F2001 - V10
    2)   David Coulthard   McLaren MP4-16 - Mercedes V10
    3)   Giancarlo Fisichella   Benetton B201 - Renault V10
    PP)   Juan Pablo Montoya   Williams FW23 - BMW V10

15) 16 Sep - ITALY (Monza)
    1/ PP)   Juan Pablo Montoya   Williams FW23 - BMW V10
    2)   Rubens Barrichello   Ferrari F2001 - V10
    3/ FL)   Ralf Schumacher   Williams FW23 - BMW V10

16) 30 Sep - UNITED STATES (Indianapolis)
    1)   Mika Häkkinen   McLaren MP4-16 - Mercedes V10
    2/ PP)   Michael Schumacher   Ferrari F2001 - V10
    3)   David Coulthard   McLaren MP4-16 - Mercedes V10
    FL)   Juan Pablo Montoya   Williams FW23 - BMW V10

17) 14 Oct - JAPAN (Suzuka)
    1/ PP)   Michael Schumacher   Ferrari F2001 - V10
    2)   Juan Pablo Montoya   Williams FW23 - BMW V10
    3)   David Coulthard   McLaren MP4-16 - Mercedes V10
    FL)   Ralf Schumacher   Williams FW23 - BMW V10

Drivers' championship
1) Michael Schumacher   123
2) David Coulthard   65
3) Rubens Barrichello   56

Constructors' championship
1) Ferrari   179
2) McLaren - Mercedes   102
3) Williams - BMW   80

2002

1) 3 Mar - AUSTRALIA (Melbourne)
    1)   Michael Schumacher   Ferrari F2001 - V10
    2)   Juan Pablo Montoya   Williams FW24 - BMW V10
    3/ FL)   Kimi Räikkönen   McLaren MP4-17 - Mercedes V10
    PP)   Rubens Barrichello   Ferrari F2001 - V10

2) 17 Mar - MALAYSIA (Sepang)
    1)   Ralf Schumacher   Williams FW24 - BMW V10
    2/ FL)   Juan Pablo Montoya   Williams FW24 - BMW V10
    3/ PP)   Michael Schumacher   Ferrari F2001 - V10

3) 31 Mar - BRAZIL (Interlagos)
    1)   Michael Schumacher   Ferrari F2002 - V10
    2)   Ralf Schumacher   Williams FW24 - BMW V10
    3)   David Coulthard   McLaren MP4-17 - Mercedes V10
    PP/ FL)   Juan Pablo Montoya   Williams FW24 - BMW V10

4) 14 Apr - SAN MARINO (Imola)
    1/ PP)   Michael Schumacher   Ferrari F2002 - V10
    2/ FL)   Rubens Barrichello   Ferrari F2002 - V10
    3)   Ralf Schumacher   Williams FW24 - BMW V10

5) 28 Apr - SPAIN (Catalunya)
1/ PP/ FL)	Michael Schumacher	Ferrari F2002 - V10
2)	Juan Pablo Montoya	Williams FW24 - BMW V10
3)	David Coulthard	McLaren MP4-17 - Mercedes V10

6) 12 May - AUSTRIA (A1-Ring)
1/ FL)	Michael Schumacher	Ferrari F2002 - V10
2/ PP)	Rubens Barrichello	Ferrari F2002 - V10
3)	Juan Pablo Montoya	Williams FW24 - BMW V10

7) 26 May - MONACO (Monte-Carlo)
1)	David Coulthard	McLaren MP4-17 - Mercedes V10
2)	Michael Schumacher	Ferrari F2002 - V10
3)	Ralf Schumacher	Williams FW24 - BMW V10
PP)	Juan Pablo Montoya	Williams FW24 - BMW V10
FL)	Rubens Barrichello	Ferrari F2002 - V10

8) 9 Jun - CANADA (Montréal)
1)	Michael Schumacher	Ferrari F2002 - V10
2)	David Coulthard	McLaren MP4-17 - Mercedes V10
3)	Rubens Barrichello	Ferrari F2002 - V10
PP/ FL)	Juan Pablo Montoya	Williams FW24 - BMW V10

9) 23 Jun - EUROPE (Nürburgring)
1)	Rubens Barrichello	Ferrari F2002 - V10
2/ FL)	Michael Schumacher	Ferrari F2002 - V10
3)	Kimi Räikkönen	McLaren MP4-17 - Mercedes V10
PP)	Juan Pablo Montoya	Williams FW24 - BMW V10

10) 7 Jul - BRITAIN (Silverstone)
1)	Michael Schumacher	Ferrari F2002 - V10
2/ FL)	Rubens Barrichello	Ferrari F2002 - V10
3/ PP)	Juan Pablo Montoya	Williams FW24 - BMW V10

11) 21 Jul - FRANCE (Magny-Cours)
1)	Michael Schumacher	Ferrari F2002 - V10
2)	Kimi Räikkönen	McLaren MP4-17 - Mercedes V10
3/ FL)	David Coulthard	McLaren MP4-17 - Mercedes V10
PP)	Juan Pablo Montoya	Williams FW24 - BMW V10

12) 28 Jul - GERMANY (Hockenheim)
1/ PP/ FL)	Michael Schumacher	Ferrari F2002 - V10
2)	Juan Pablo Montoya	Williams FW24 - BMW V10
3)	Ralf Schumacher	Williams FW24 - BMW V10

13) 18 Aug - HUNGARY (Hungaroring)
1/ PP)	Rubens Barrichello	Ferrari F2002 - V10
2/ FL)	Michael Schumacher	Ferrari F2002 - V10
3)	Ralf Schumacher	Williams FW24 - BMW V10

14) 1 Sep - BELGIUM (Spa-Francorchamps)
1/ PP/ FL)	Michael Schumacher	Ferrari F2002 - V10
2)	Rubens Barrichello	Ferrari F2002 - V10
3)	Juan Pablo Montoya	Williams FW24 - BMW V10

15) 15 Sep - ITALY (Monza)
1/ FL)	Rubens Barrichello	Ferrari F2002 - V10
2)	Michael Schumacher	Ferrari F2002 - V10
3)	Eddie Irvine	Jaguar R3 - Ford Cosworth V10
PP)	Juan Pablo Montoya	Williams FW24 - BMW V10

16) 29 Sep - UNITED STATES (Indianapolis)
1/ FL)	Rubens Barrichello	Ferrari F2002 - V10
2/ PP)	Michael Schumacher	Ferrari F2002 - V10
3)	David Coulthard	McLaren MP4-17 - Mercedes V10

17) 13 Oct - JAPAN (Suzuka)
1/ PP/ FL)	Michael Schumacher	Ferrari F2002 - V10
2)	Rubens Barrichello	Ferrari F2002 - V10
3)	Kimi Räikkönen	McLaren MP4-17 - Mercedes V10

Drivers' championship		Constructors' championship	
1) Michael Schumacher	144	1) Ferrari	221
2) Rubens Barrichello	77	2) Williams - BMW	92
3) Juan Pablo Montoya	50	3) McLaren - Mercedes	65

2003

1) 9 Mar - AUSTRALIA (Melbourne)
1)	David Coulthard	McLaren MP4-17D - Mercedes V10
2)	Juan Pablo Montoya	Williams FW25 - BMW V10
3/ FL)	Kimi Räikkönen	McLaren MP4-17D - Mercedes V10
PP)	Michael Schumacher	Ferrari F2002 - V10

2) 23 Mar - MALAYSIA (Sepang)
1)	Kimi Räikkönen	McLaren MP4-17D - Mercedes V10
2)	Rubens Barrichello	Ferrari F2002 - V10
3/ PP)	Fernando Alonso	Renault R23 - V10
FL)	Michael Schumacher	Ferrari F2002 - V10

3) 6 Apr - BRAZIL (Interlagos)
1)	Giancarlo Fisichella	Jordan EJ13 - Ford Cosworth V10
2)	Kimi Räikkönen	McLaren MP4-17D - Mercedes V10
3)	Fernando Alonso	Renault R23 - V10
PP/ FL)	Rubens Barrichello	Ferrari F2002 - V10

4) 20 Apr - SAN MARINO (Imola)
1/ PP/ FL)	Michael Schumacher	Ferrari F2002 - V10
2)	Kimi Räikkönen	McLaren MP4-17D - Mercedes V10
3)	Rubens Barrichello	Ferrari F2002 - V10

5) 4 May - SPAIN (Catalunya)
1/ PP)	Michael Schumacher	Ferrari F2003-GA - V10
2)	Fernando Alonso	Renault R23 - V10
3/ FL)	Rubens Barrichello	Ferrari F2003-GA - V10

6) 18 May - AUSTRIA (A1-Ring)
1/ PP/ FL)	Michael Schumacher	Ferrari F2003-GA - V10
2)	Kimi Räikkönen	McLaren MP4-17D - Mercedes V10
3)	Rubens Barrichello	Ferrari F2003-GA - V10

7) 1 Jun - MONACO (Monte-Carlo)
1)	Juan Pablo Montoya	Williams FW25 - BMW V10
2/ FL)	Kimi Räikkönen	McLaren MP4-17D - Mercedes V10
3)	Michael Schumacher	Ferrari F2003-GA - V10
PP)	Ralf Schumacher	Williams FW25 - BMW V10

8) 15 Jun - CANADA (Montréal)
1)	Michael Schumacher	Ferrari F2003-GA - V10
2/ PP)	Ralf Schumacher	Williams FW25 - BMW V10
3)	Juan Pablo Montoya	Williams FW25 - BMW V10
FL)	Fernando Alonso	Renault R23 - V10

9) 29 Jun - EUROPE (Nürburgring)

1)	Ralf Schumacher	Williams FW25 - BMW V10
2)	Juan Pablo Montoya	Williams FW25 - BMW V10
3)	Rubens Barrichello	Ferrari F2003-GA - V10
PP/ FL)	Kimi Räikkönen	McLaren MP4-17D - Mercedes V10

10) 6 Jul - FRANCE (Magny-Cours)

1/ PP)	Ralf Schumacher	Williams FW25 - BMW V10
2/ FL)	Juan Pablo Montoya	Williams FW25 - BMW V10
3)	Michael Schumacher	Ferrari F2003-GA - V10

11) 20 Jul - BRITAIN (Silverstone)

1/ PP/ FL)	Rubens Barrichello	Ferrari F2003-GA - V10
2)	Juan Pablo Montoya	Williams FW25 - BMW V10
3)	Kimi Räikkönen	McLaren MP4-17D - Mercedes V10

12) 3 Aug - GERMANY (Hockenheim)

1/ PP/ FL)	Juan Pablo Montoya	Williams FW25 - BMW V10
2)	David Coulthard	McLaren MP4-17D - Mercedes V10
3)	Jarno Trulli	Renault R23B - V10

13) 24 Aug - HUNGARY (Hungaroring)

1/ PP)	Fernando Alonso	Renault R23B - V10
2)	Kimi Räikkönen	McLaren MP4-17D - Mercedes V10
3/ FL)	Juan Pablo Montoya	Williams FW25 - BMW V10

14) 14 Sep - ITALY (Monza)

1/ PP/ FL)	Michael Schumacher	Ferrari F2003-GA - V10
2)	Juan Pablo Montoya	Williams FW25 - BMW V10
3)	Rubens Barrichello	Ferrari F2003-GA - V10

15) 28 Sep - UNITED STATES (Indianapolis)

1/ FL)	Michael Schumacher	Ferrari F2003-GA - V10
2/ PP)	Kimi Räikkönen	McLaren MP4-17D - Mercedes V10
3)	Heinz-Harald Frentzen	Sauber C22 - Petronas V10

16) 12 Oct - JAPAN (Suzuka)

1/ PP)	Rubens Barrichello	Ferrari F2003-GA - V10
2)	Kimi Räikkönen	McLaren MP4-17D - Mercedes V10
3)	David Coulthard	McLaren MP4-17D - Mercedes V10
FL)	Ralf Schumacher	Williams FW25 - BMW V10

Drivers' championship		Constructors' championship	
1) Michael Schumacher	93	1) Ferrari	158
2) Kimi Räikkönen	91	2) Williams - BMW	144
3) Juan Pablo Montoya	82	3) McLaren - Mercedes	142

2004

1) 7 Mar - AUSTRALIA (Melbourne)

1/ PP/ FL)	Michael Schumacher	Ferrari F2004 - V10
2)	Rubens Barrichello	Ferrari F2004 - V10
3)	Fernando Alonso	Renault R24 - V10

2) 21 Mar - MALAYSIA (Sepang)

1/ PP)	Michael Schumacher	Ferrari F2004 - V10
2/ FL)	Juan Pablo Montoya	Williams FW26 - BMW V10
3)	Jenson Button	BAR 006 - Honda V10

3) 4 Apr - BAHRAIN (Sakhir)

1/ PP/ FL)	Michael Schumacher	Ferrari F2004 - V10
2)	Rubens Barrichello	Ferrari F2004 - V10
3)	Jenson Button	BAR 006 - Honda V10

4) 25 Apr - SAN MARINO (Imola)

1/ FL)	Michael Schumacher	Ferrari F2004 - V10
2/ PP)	Jenson Button	BAR 006 - Honda V10
3)	Juan Pablo Montoya	Williams FW26 - BMW V10

5) 9 May - SPAIN (Catalunya)

1/ PP/ FL)	Michael Schumacher	Ferrari F2004 - V10
2)	Rubens Barrichello	Ferrari F2004 - V10
3)	Jarno Trulli	Renault R24 - V10

6) 23 May - MONACO (Monte-Carlo)

1/ PP)	Jarno Trulli	Renault R24 - V10
2)	Jenson Button	BAR 006 - Honda V10
3)	Rubens Barrichello	Ferrari F2004 - V10
FL)	Michael Schumacher	Ferrari F2004 - V10

7) 30 May - EUROPE (Nürburgring)

1/ PP/ FL)	Michael Schumacher	Ferrari F2004 - V10
2)	Rubens Barrichello	Ferrari F2004 - V10
3)	Jenson Button	BAR 006 - Honda V10

8) 13 Jun - CANADA (Montréal)

1)	Michael Schumacher	Ferrari F2004 - V10
2/ FL)	Rubens Barrichello	Ferrari F2004 - V10
3)	Jenson Button	BAR 006 - Honda V10
PP)	Ralf Schumacher	Williams FW26 - BMW V10

Ralf Schumacher finished 2nd, but was disqualified for having illegal brake ducts.

9) 20 Jun - UNITED STATES (Indianapolis)

1)	Michael Schumacher	Ferrari F2004 - V10
2/ PP/ FL)	Rubens Barrichello	Ferrari F2004 - V10
3)	Takuma Sato	BAR 006 - Honda V10

10) 4 Jul - FRANCE (Magny-Cours)

1/ FL)	Michael Schumacher	Ferrari F2004 - V10
2/ PP)	Fernando Alonso	Renault R24 - V10
3)	Rubens Barrichello	Ferrari F2004 - V10

11) 11 Jul - BRITAIN (Silverstone)

1/ FL)	Michael Schumacher	Ferrari F2004 - V10
2/ PP)	Kimi Räikkönen	McLaren MP4-19B - Mercedes V10
3)	Rubens Barrichello	Ferrari F2004 - V10

12) 25 Jul - GERMANY (Hockenheim)

1/ PP)	Michael Schumacher	Ferrari F2004 - V10
2)	Jenson Button	BAR 006 - Honda V10
3)	Fernando Alonso	Renault R24 - V10
FL)	Kimi Räikkönen	McLaren MP4-19B - Mercedes V10

13) 15 Aug - HUNGARY (Hungaroring)

1/ PP/ FL)	Michael Schumacher	Ferrari F2004 - V10
2)	Rubens Barrichello	Ferrari F2004 - V10
3)	Fernando Alonso	Renault R24 - V10

14) 29 Aug - BELGIUM (Spa-Francorchamps)

1/ FL)	Kimi Räikkönen	McLaren MP4-19B - Mercedes V10
2)	Michael Schumacher	Ferrari F2004 - V10
3)	Rubens Barrichello	Ferrari F2004 - V10
PP)	Jarno Trulli	Renault R24 - V10

15) 12 Sep - ITALY (Monza)

1/ PP/ FL)	Rubens Barrichello	Ferrari F2004 - V10
2)	Michael Schumacher	Ferrari F2004 - V10
3)	Jenson Button	BAR 006 - Honda V10

16) 26 Sep - CHINA (Shanghai)

1/ PP)	Rubens Barrichello	Ferrari F2004 - V10
2)	Jenson Button	BAR 006 - Honda V10
3)	Kimi Räikkönen	McLaren MP4-19B - Mercedes V10
FL)	Michael Schumacher	Ferrari F2004 - V10

17) 10 Oct - JAPAN (Suzuka)

1/ PP)	Michael Schumacher	Ferrari F2004 - V10
2)	Ralf Schumacher	Williams FW26 - BMW V10
3)	Jenson Button	BAR 006 - Honda V10
FL)	Rubens Barrichello	Ferrari F2004 - V10

18) 24 Oct - BRAZIL (Interlagos)

1/ FL)	Juan Pablo Montoya	Williams FW26 - BMW V10
2)	Kimi Räikkönen	McLaren MP4-19B - Mercedes V10
3/ PP)	Rubens Barrichello	Ferrari F2004 - V10

Drivers' championship

1) Michael Schumacher 148
2) Rubens Barrichello 114
3) Jenson Button 85

Constructors' championship

1) Ferrari 262
2) BAR - Honda 119
3) Renault 105

2005

1) 6 Mar - AUSTRALIA (Melbourne)

1/ PP)	Giancarlo Fisichella	Renault R25 - V10
2)	Rubens Barrichello	Ferrari F2004M - V10
3/ FL)	Fernando Alonso	Renault R25 - V10

2) 20 Mar - MALAYSIA (Sepang)

1/ PP)	Fernando Alonso	Renault R25 - V10
2)	Jarno Trulli	Toyota TF105 - V10
3)	Nick Heidfeld	Williams FW27 - BMW V10
FL)	Kimi Räikkönen	McLaren MP4-20 - Mercedes V10

3) 3 Apr - BAHRAIN (Sakhir)

1/ PP)	Fernando Alonso	Renault R25 - V10
2)	Jarno Trulli	Toyota TF105 - V10
3)	Kimi Räikkönen	McLaren MP4-20 - Mercedes V10
FL)	Pedro de la Rosa	McLaren MP4-20 - Mercedes V10

4) 24 Apr - SAN MARINO (Imola)

1)	Fernando Alonso	Renault R25 - V10
2/ FL)	Michael Schumacher	Ferrari F2005 - V10
3)	Alexander Wurz	McLaren MP4-20 - Mercedes V10
PP)	Kimi Räikkönen	McLaren MP4-20 - Mercedes V10

Jenson Button (BAR 007 - Honda V10) finished 3rd, but was disqualified for car being under the minimum weight limit.

5) 8 May - SPAIN (Catalunya)

1/ PP)	Kimi Räikkönen	McLaren MP4-20 - Mercedes V10
2)	Fernando Alonso	Renault R25 - V10
3)	Jarno Trulli	Toyota TF105 - V10
FL)	Giancarlo Fisichella	Renault R25 - V10

6) 22 May - MONACO (Monte-Carlo)

1/ PP)	Kimi Räikkönen	McLaren MP4-20 - Mercedes V10
2)	Nick Heidfeld	Williams FW27 - BMW V10
3)	Mark Webber	Williams FW27 - BMW V10
FL)	Michael Schumacher	Ferrari F2005 - V10

7) 29 May - EUROPE (Nürburgring)

1/ FL)	Fernando Alonso	Renault R25 - V10
2/ PP)	Nick Heidfeld	Williams FW27 - BMW V10
3)	Rubens Barrichello	Ferrari F2005 - V10

8) 12 Jun - CANADA (Montréal)

1/ FL)	Kimi Räikkönen	McLaren MP4-20 - Mercedes V10
2)	Michael Schumacher	Ferrari F2005 - V10
3)	Rubens Barrichello	Ferrari F2005 - V10
PP)	Jenson Button	BAR 007 - Honda V10

9) 19 Jun - UNITED STATES (Indianapolis)

1/ FL)	Michael Schumacher	Ferrari F2005 - V10
2)	Rubens Barrichello	Ferrari F2005 - V10
3)	Tiago Monteiro	Jordan EJ15 - Toyota V10
PP)	Jarno Trulli	Toyota TF105 - V10

Jarno Trulli did not start (withdrawn on the parade lap along with all other Michelin runners, due to tyre safety concerns).

10) 3 Jul - FRANCE (Magny-Cours)

1/ PP)	Fernando Alonso	Renault R25 - V10
2/ FL)	Kimi Räikkönen	McLaren MP4-20 - Mercedes V10
3)	Michael Schumacher	Ferrari F2005 - V10

11) 10 Jul - BRITAIN (Silverstone)

1)	Juan Pablo Montoya	McLaren MP4-20 - Mercedes V10
2/ PP)	Fernando Alonso	Renault R25 - V10
3/ FL)	Kimi Räikkönen	McLaren MP4-20 - Mercedes V10

12) 24 Jul - GERMANY (Hockenheim)

1)	Fernando Alonso	Renault R25 - V10
2)	Juan Pablo Montoya	McLaren MP4-20 - Mercedes V10
3)	Jenson Button	BAR 007 - Honda V10
PP/ FL)	Kimi Räikkönen	McLaren MP4-20 - Mercedes V10

13) 31 Jul - HUNGARY (Hungaroring)

1/ FL)	Kimi Räikkönen	McLaren MP4-20 - Mercedes V10
2/ PP)	Michael Schumacher	Ferrari F2005 - V10
3)	Ralf Schumacher	Toyota TF105 - V10

14) 21 Aug - TURKEY (Istanbul)

1/ PP)	Kimi Räikkönen	McLaren MP4-20 - Mercedes V10
2)	Fernando Alonso	Renault R25 - V10
3/ FL)	Juan Pablo Montoya	McLaren MP4-20 - Mercedes V10

15) 4 Sep - ITALY (Monza)

1/ PP)	Juan Pablo Montoya	McLaren MP4-20 - Mercedes V10
2)	Fernando Alonso	Renault R25 - V10
3)	Giancarlo Fisichella	Renault R25 - V10
FL)	Kimi Räikkönen	McLaren MP4-20 - Mercedes V10

Kimi Räikkönen won pole position, but was given a 10-place penalty, due to an engine change.

16) 11 Sep - BELGIUM (Spa-Francorchamps)

1)	Kimi Räikkönen	McLaren MP4-20 - Mercedes V10
2)	Fernando Alonso	Renault R25 - V10
3)	Jenson Button	BAR 007 - Honda V10
PP)	Juan Pablo Montoya	McLaren MP4-20 - Mercedes V10
FL)	Ralf Schumacher	Toyota TF105 - V10

17) 25 Sep - BRAZIL (Interlagos)

1)	Juan Pablo Montoya	McLaren MP4-20 - Mercedes V10
2/ FL)	Kimi Räikkönen	McLaren MP4-20 - Mercedes V10
3/ PP)	Fernando Alonso	Renault R25 - V10

18) 9 Oct - JAPAN (Suzuka)

1/ FL)	Kimi Räikkönen	McLaren MP4-20 - Mercedes V10
2)	Giancarlo Fisichella	Renault R25 - V10
3)	Fernando Alonso	Renault R25 - V10
PP)	Ralf Schumacher	Toyota TF105B - V10

19) 16 Oct - CHINA (Shanghai)

1/ PP)	Fernando Alonso	Renault R25 - V10
2/ FL)	Kimi Räikkönen	McLaren MP4-20 - Mercedes V10
3)	Ralf Schumacher	Toyota TF105B - V10

Drivers' championship		Constructors' championship	
1) Fernando Alonso	133	1) Renault	191
2) Kimi Räikkönen	112	2) McLaren - Mercedes	182
3) Michael Schumacher	62	3) Ferrari	100

2006

1) 12 Mar - BAHRAIN (Sakhir)

1)	Fernando Alonso	Renault R26 - V8
2/ PP)	Michael Schumacher	Ferrari 248 F1 - V8
3)	Kimi Räikkönen	McLaren MP4-21 - Mercedes V8
FL)	Nico Rosberg	Williams FW28 - Cosworth V8

2) 19 Mar - MALAYSIA (Sepang)

1/ PP)	Giancarlo Fisichella	Renault R26 - V8
2/ FL)	Fernando Alonso	Renault R26 - V8
3)	Jenson Button	Honda RA106 - V8

3) 2 Apr - AUSTRALIA (Melbourne)

1)	Fernando Alonso	Renault R26 - V8
2/ FL)	Kimi Räikkönen	McLaren MP4-21 - Mercedes V8
3)	Ralf Schumacher	Toyota TF106 - V8
PP)	Jenson Button	Honda RA106 - V8

4) 23 Apr - SAN MARINO (Imola)

1/ PP)	Michael Schumacher	Ferrari 248 F1 - V8
2/ FL)	Fernando Alonso	Renault R26 - V8
3)	Juan Pablo Montoya	McLaren MP4-21 - Mercedes V8

5) 7 May - EUROPE (Nürburgring)

1/ FL)	Michael Schumacher	Ferrari 248 F1 - V8
2/ PP)	Fernando Alonso	Renault R26 - V8
3)	Felipe Massa	Ferrari 248 F1 - V8

6) 14 May - SPAIN (Catalunya)

1/ PP)	Fernando Alonso	Renault R26 - V8
2)	Michael Schumacher	Ferrari 248 F1 - V8
3)	Giancarlo Fisichella	Renault R26 - V8
FL)	Felipe Massa	Ferrari 248 F1 - V8

7) 28 May - MONACO (Monte-Carlo)

1/ PP)	Fernando Alonso	Renault R26 - V8
2)	Juan Pablo Montoya	McLaren MP4-21 - Mercedes V8
3)	David Coulthard	Red Bull RB2 - Ferrari V8
FL)	Michael Schumacher	Ferrari 248 F1 - V8

Michael Schumacher set the pole position time, but had all times removed, demoting him to the back of the grid. He was accused of deliberately coming to a halt during the final lap of qualifying and preventing others from setting a faster time.

8) 11 Jun - BRITAIN (Silverstone)

1/ PP/ FL)	Fernando Alonso	Renault R26 - V8
2)	Michael Schumacher	Ferrari 248 F1 - V8
3)	Kimi Räikkönen	McLaren MP4-21 - Mercedes V8

9) 25 Jun - CANADA (Montréal)

1/ PP)	Fernando Alonso	Renault R26 - V8
2)	Michael Schumacher	Ferrari 248 F1 - V8
3/ FL)	Kimi Räikkönen	McLaren MP4-21 - Mercedes V8

10) 2 Jul - UNITED STATES (Indianapolis)

1/ PP/ FL)	Michael Schumacher	Ferrari 248 F1 - V8
2)	Felipe Massa	Ferrari 248 F1 - V8
3)	Giancarlo Fisichella	Renault R26 - V8

11) 16 Jul - FRANCE (Magny-Cours)

1/ PP/ FL)	Michael Schumacher	Ferrari 248 F1 - V8
2)	Fernando Alonso	Renault R26 - V8
3)	Felipe Massa	Ferrari 248 F1 - V8

12) 30 Jul - GERMANY (Hockenheim)

1/ FL)	Michael Schumacher	Ferrari 248 F1 - V8
2)	Felipe Massa	Ferrari 248 F1 - V8
3/ PP)	Kimi Räikkönen	McLaren MP4-21 - Mercedes V8

13) 6 Aug - HUNGARY (Hungaroring)

1)	Jenson Button	Honda RA106 - V8
2)	Pedro de la Rosa	McLaren MP4-21 - Mercedes V8
3)	Nick Heidfeld	BMW Sauber F1.06 - BMW V8
PP)	Kimi Räikkönen	McLaren MP4-21 - Mercedes V8
FL)	Felipe Massa	Ferrari 248 F1 - V8

14) 27 Aug - TURKEY (Istanbul)

1/ PP)	Felipe Massa	Ferrari 248 F1 - V8
2)	Fernando Alonso	Renault R26 - V8
3/ FL)	Michael Schumacher	Ferrari 248 F1 - V8

15) 10 Sep - ITALY (Monza)

1)	Michael Schumacher	Ferrari 248 F1 - V8
2/ PP/ FL)	Kimi Räikkönen	McLaren MP4-21 - Mercedes V8
3)	Robert Kubica	BMW Sauber F1.06 - BMW V8

16) 1 Oct - CHINA (Shanghai)

1)	Michael Schumacher	Ferrari 248 F1 - V8
2/ PP/ FL)	Fernando Alonso	Renault R26 - V8
3)	Giancarlo Fisichella	Renault R26 - V8

17) 8 Oct - JAPAN (Suzuka)

1/ FL)	Fernando Alonso	Renault R26 - V8
2/ PP)	Felipe Massa	Ferrari 248 F1 - V8
3)	Giancarlo Fisichella	Renault R26 - V8

18) 22 Oct - BRAZIL (Interlagos)

1/ PP)	Felipe Massa	Ferrari 248 F1 - V8
2)	Fernando Alonso	Renault R26 - V8
3)	Jenson Button	Honda RA106 - V8
FL)	Michael Schumacher	Ferrari 248 F1 - V8

Drivers' championship		Constructors' championship	
1) Fernando Alonso	134	1) Renault	206
2) Michael Schumacher	121	2) Ferrari	201
3) Felipe Massa	80	3) McLaren - Mercedes	110

2007

1) 18 Mar - AUSTRALIA (Melbourne)
1/ PP/ FL)	Kimi Räikkönen	Ferrari F2007 - V8
2)	Fernando Alonso	McLaren MP4-22 - Mercedes V8
3)	Lewis Hamilton	McLaren MP4-22 - Mercedes V8

2) 8 Apr - MALAYSIA (Sepang)
1)	Fernando Alonso	McLaren MP4-22 - Mercedes V8
2/ FL)	Lewis Hamilton	McLaren MP4-22 - Mercedes V8
3)	Kimi Räikkönen	Ferrari F2007 - V8
PP)	Felipe Massa	Ferrari F2007 - V8

3) 15 Apr - BAHRAIN (Sakhir)
1/ PP/ FL)	Felipe Massa	Ferrari F2007 - V8
2)	Lewis Hamilton	McLaren MP4-22 - Mercedes V8
3)	Kimi Räikkönen	Ferrari F2007 - V8

4) 13 May - SPAIN (Catalunya)
1/ PP/ FL)	Felipe Massa	Ferrari F2007 - V8
2)	Lewis Hamilton	McLaren MP4-22 - Mercedes V8
3)	Fernando Alonso	McLaren MP4-22 - Mercedes V8

5) 27 May - MONACO (Monte-Carlo)
1/ PP/ FL)	Fernando Alonso	McLaren MP4-22 - Mercedes V8
2)	Lewis Hamilton	McLaren MP4-22 - Mercedes V8
3)	Felipe Massa	Ferrari F2007 - V8

6) 10 Jun - CANADA (Montréal)
1/ PP)	Lewis Hamilton	McLaren MP4-22 - Mercedes V8
2)	Nick Heidfeld	BMW Sauber F1.07 - BMW V8
3)	Alexander Wurz	Williams FW29 - Toyota V8
FL)	Fernando Alonso	McLaren MP4-22 - Mercedes V8

7) 17 Jun - UNITED STATES (Indianapolis)
1/ PP)	Lewis Hamilton	McLaren MP4-22 - Mercedes V8
2)	Fernando Alonso	McLaren MP4-22 - Mercedes V8
3)	Felipe Massa	Ferrari F2007 - V8
FL)	Kimi Räikkönen	Ferrari F2007 - V8

8) 1 Jul - FRANCE (Magny-Cours)
1)	Kimi Räikkönen	Ferrari F2007 - V8
2/ PP/ FL)	Felipe Massa	Ferrari F2007 - V8
3)	Lewis Hamilton	McLaren MP4-22 - Mercedes V8

9) 8 Jul - BRITAIN (Silverstone)
1/ FL)	Kimi Räikkönen	Ferrari F2007 - V8
2)	Fernando Alonso	McLaren MP4-22 - Mercedes V8
3/ PP)	Lewis Hamilton	McLaren MP4-22 - Mercedes V8

10) 22 Jul - EUROPE (Nürburgring)
1)	Fernando Alonso	McLaren MP4-22 - Mercedes V8
2/ FL)	Felipe Massa	Ferrari F2007 - V8
3)	Mark Webber	Red Bull RB3 - Renault V8
PP)	Kimi Räikkönen	Ferrari F2007 - V8

11) 5 Aug - HUNGARY (Hungaroring)
1/ PP)	Lewis Hamilton	McLaren MP4-22 - Mercedes V8
2/ FL)	Kimi Räikkönen	Ferrari F2007 - V8
3)	Nick Heidfeld	BMW Sauber F1.07 - BMW V8

Fernando Alonso (McLaren MP4-22 - Mercedes V8) set the pole position time, but received a five-place grid penalty for preventing Hamilton from recording a further lap time, by delaying him in the pit lane.

12) 26 Aug - TURKEY (Istanbul)
1/ PP)	Felipe Massa	Ferrari F2007 - V8
2/ FL)	Kimi Räikkönen	Ferrari F2007 - V8
3)	Fernando Alonso	McLaren MP4-22 - Mercedes V8

13) 9 Sep - ITALY (Monza)
1/ PP/ FL)	Fernando Alonso	McLaren MP4-22 - Mercedes V8
2)	Lewis Hamilton	McLaren MP4-22 - Mercedes V8
3)	Kimi Räikkönen	Ferrari F2007 - V8

14) 16 Sep - BELGIUM (Spa-Francorchamps)
1/ PP)	Kimi Räikkönen	Ferrari F2007 - V8
2/ FL)	Felipe Massa	Ferrari F2007 - V8
3)	Fernando Alonso	McLaren MP4-22 - Mercedes V8

15) 30 Sep - JAPAN (Fuji)
1/ PP/ FL)	Lewis Hamilton	McLaren MP4-22 - Mercedes V8
2)	Heikki Kovalainen	Renault R27 - V8
3)	Kimi Räikkönen	Ferrari F2007 - V8

16) 7 Oct - CHINA (Shanghai)
1)	Kimi Räikkönen	Ferrari F2007 - V8
2)	Fernando Alonso	McLaren MP4-22 - Mercedes V8
3/ FL)	Felipe Massa	Ferrari F2007 - V8
PP)	Lewis Hamilton	McLaren MP4-22 - Mercedes V8

17) 21 Oct - BRAZIL (Interlagos)
1/ FL)	Kimi Räikkönen	Ferrari F2007 - V8
2/ PP)	Felipe Massa	Ferrari F2007 - V8
3)	Fernando Alonso	McLaren MP4-22 - Mercedes V8

Drivers' championship		Constructors' championship	
1) Kimi Räikkönen	110	1) Ferrari	204
2) Lewis Hamilton	109	2) BMW Sauber - BMW	101
3) Fernando Alonso	109	3) Renault	51

McLaren had all their points removed due to the spying scandal. The points were not redistributed to other constructors. McLaren's drivers retained their points.

2008

1) 16 Mar - AUSTRALIA (Melbourne)
1/ PP)	Lewis Hamilton	McLaren MP4-23 - Mercedes V8
2)	Nick Heidfeld	BMW Sauber F1.08 - BMW V8
3)	Nico Rosberg	Williams FW30 - Toyota V8
FL)	Heikki Kovalainen	McLaren MP4-23 - Mercedes V8

2) 23 Mar - MALAYSIA (Sepang)
1)	Kimi Räikkönen	Ferrari F2008 - V8
2)	Robert Kubica	BMW Sauber F1.08 - BMW V8
3)	Heikki Kovalainen	McLaren MP4-23 - Mercedes V8
PP)	Felipe Massa	Ferrari F2008 - V8
FL)	Nick Heidfeld	BMW Sauber F1.08 - BMW V8

3) 6 Apr - BAHRAIN (Sakhir)
1)	Felipe Massa	Ferrari F2008 - V8
2)	Kimi Räikkönen	Ferrari F2008 - V8
3/ PP)	Robert Kubica	BMW Sauber F1.08 - BMW V8
FL)	Heikki Kovalainen	McLaren MP4-23 - Mercedes V8

4) 27 Apr - SPAIN (Catalunya)
1/ PP/ FL)	Kimi Räikkönen	Ferrari F2008 - V8
2)	Felipe Massa	Ferrari F2008 - V8
3)	Lewis Hamilton	McLaren MP4-23 - Mercedes V8

5) 11 May - TURKEY (Istanbul)
1/ PP)	Felipe Massa	Ferrari F2008 - V8
2)	Lewis Hamilton	McLaren MP4-23 - Mercedes V8
3/ FL)	Kimi Räikkönen	Ferrari F2008 - V8

6) 25 May - MONACO (Monte-Carlo)
1)	Lewis Hamilton	McLaren MP4-23 - Mercedes V8
2)	Robert Kubica	BMW Sauber F1.08 - BMW V8
3/ PP)	Felipe Massa	Ferrari F2008 - V8
FL)	Kimi Räikkönen	Ferrari F2008 - V8

7) 8 Jun - CANADA (Montréal)
1)	Robert Kubica	BMW Sauber F1.08 - BMW V8
2)	Nick Heidfeld	BMW Sauber F1.08 - BMW V8
3)	David Coulthard	Red Bull RB4 - Renault V8
PP)	Lewis Hamilton	McLaren MP4-23 - Mercedes V8
FL)	Kimi Räikkönen	Ferrari F2008 - V8

8) 22 Jun - FRANCE (Magny-Cours)
1)	Felipe Massa	Ferrari F2008 - V8
2/ PP/ FL)	Kimi Räikkönen	Ferrari F2008 - V8
3)	Jarno Trulli	Toyota TF108 - V8

9) 6 Jul - BRITAIN (Silverstone)
1)	Lewis Hamilton	McLaren MP4-23 - Mercedes V8
2)	Nick Heidfeld	BMW Sauber F1.08 - BMW V8
3)	Rubens Barrichello	Honda RA108 - V8
PP)	Heikki Kovalainen	McLaren MP4-23 - Mercedes V8
FL)	Kimi Räikkönen	Ferrari F2008 - V8

10) 20 Jul - GERMANY (Hockenheim)
1/ PP)	Lewis Hamilton	McLaren MP4-23 - Mercedes V8
2)	Nelsinho Piquet	Renault R28 - V8
3)	Felipe Massa	Ferrari F2008 - V8
FL)	Nick Heidfeld	BMW Sauber F1.08 - BMW V8

11) 3 Aug - HUNGARY (Hungaroring)
1)	Heikki Kovalainen	McLaren MP4-23 - Mercedes V8
2)	Timo Glock	Toyota TF108 - V8
3/ FL)	Kimi Räikkönen	Ferrari F2008 - V8
PP)	Lewis Hamilton	McLaren MP4-23 - Mercedes V8

12) 24 Aug - EUROPE (Valencia)
1/ PP/ FL)	Felipe Massa	Ferrari F2008 - V8
2)	Lewis Hamilton	McLaren MP4-23 - Mercedes V8
3)	Robert Kubica	BMW Sauber F1.08 - BMW V8

13) 7 Sep - BELGIUM (Spa-Francorchamps)
1)	Felipe Massa	Ferrari F2008 - V8
2)	Nick Heidfeld	BMW Sauber F1.08 - BMW V8
3/ PP)	Lewis Hamilton	McLaren MP4-23 - Mercedes V8
FL)	Kimi Räikkönen	Ferrari F2008 - V8

Lewis Hamilton finished 1st, but was given a 25-second penalty for gaining an advantage by cutting the chicane.

14) 14 Sep - ITALY (Monza)
1/ PP)	Sebastian Vettel	Toro Rosso STR3 - Ferrari V8
2)	Heikki Kovalainen	McLaren MP4-23 - Mercedes V8
3)	Robert Kubica	BMW Sauber F1.08 - BMW V8
FL)	Kimi Räikkönen	Ferrari F2008 - V8

15) 28 Sep - SINGAPORE (Marina Bay)
1)	Fernando Alonso	Renault R28 - V8
2)	Nico Rosberg	Williams FW30 - Toyota V8
3)	Lewis Hamilton	McLaren MP4-23 - Mercedes V8
PP)	Felipe Massa	Ferrari F2008 - V8
FL)	Kimi Räikkönen	Ferrari F2008 - V8

16) 12 Oct - JAPAN (Fuji)
1)	Fernando Alonso	Renault R28 - V8
2)	Robert Kubica	BMW Sauber F1.08 - BMW V8
3)	Kimi Räikkönen	Ferrari F2008 - V8
PP)	Lewis Hamilton	McLaren MP4-23 - Mercedes V8
FL)	Felipe Massa	Ferrari F2008 - V8

17) 19 Oct - CHINA (Shanghai)
1/ PP/ FL)	Lewis Hamilton	McLaren MP4-23 - Mercedes V8
2)	Felipe Massa	Ferrari F2008 - V8
3)	Kimi Räikkönen	Ferrari F2008 - V8

18) 2 Nov - BRAZIL (Interlagos)
1/ PP/ FL)	Felipe Massa	Ferrari F2008 - V8
2)	Fernando Alonso	Renault R28 - V8
3)	Kimi Räikkönen	Ferrari F2008 - V8

Drivers' championship		Constructors' championship	
1) Lewis Hamilton	98	1) Ferrari	172
2) Felipe Massa	97	2) McLaren - Mercedes	151
3) Kimi Raikkonen	75	3) BMW Sauber - BMW	135

2009

1) 29 Mar - AUSTRALIA (Melbourne)
1/ PP)	Jenson Button	Brawn BGP 001 - Mercedes V8
2)	Rubens Barrichello	Brawn BGP 001 - Mercedes V8
3)	Jarno Trulli	Toyota TF109 - V8
FL)	Nico Rosberg	Williams FW31 - Toyota V8

2) 5 Apr - MALAYSIA (Sepang)
1/ PP/ FL)	Jenson Button	Brawn BGP 001 - Mercedes V8
2)	Nick Heidfeld	BMW Sauber F1.09 - BMW V8
3)	Timo Glock	Toyota TF109 - V8

Race was stopped early, due to heavy rain. Half points awarded.

3) 19 Apr - CHINA (Shanghai)

1/ PP)	Sebastian Vettel	Red Bull RB5 - Renault V8
2)	Mark Webber	Red Bull RB5 - Renault V8
3)	Jenson Button	Brawn BGP 001 - Mercedes V8
FL)	Rubens Barrichello	Brawn BGP 001 - Mercedes V8

4) 26 Apr - BAHRAIN (Sakhir)

1)	Jenson Button	Brawn BGP 001 - Mercedes V8
2)	Sebastian Vettel	Red Bull RB5 - Renault V8
3/ PP/ FL)	Jarno Trulli	Toyota TF109 - V8

5) 10 May - SPAIN (Catalunya)

1/ PP)	Jenson Button	Brawn BGP 001 - Mercedes V8
2/ FL)	Rubens Barrichello	Brawn BGP 001 - Mercedes V8
3)	Mark Webber	Red Bull RB5 - Renault V8

6) 24 May - MONACO (Monte-Carlo)

1/ PP)	Jenson Button	Brawn BGP 001 - Mercedes V8
2)	Rubens Barrichello	Brawn BGP 001 - Mercedes V8
3)	Kimi Räikkönen	Ferrari F60 - V8
FL)	Felipe Massa	Ferrari F60 - V8

7) 7 Jun - TURKEY (Istanbul)

1/ FL)	Jenson Button	Brawn BGP 001 - Mercedes V8
2)	Mark Webber	Red Bull RB5 - Renault V8
3/ PP)	Sebastian Vettel	Red Bull RB5 - Renault V8

8) 21 Jun - BRITAIN (Silverstone)

1/ PP/ FL)	Sebastian Vettel	Red Bull RB5 - Renault V8
2)	Mark Webber	Red Bull RB5 - Renault V8
3)	Rubens Barrichello	Brawn BGP 001 - Mercedes V8

9) 12 Jul - GERMANY (Nürburgring)

1/ PP)	Mark Webber	Red Bull RB5 - Renault V8
2)	Sebastian Vettel	Red Bull RB5 - Renault V8
3)	Felipe Massa	Ferrari F60 - V8
FL)	Fernando Alonso	Renault R29 - V8

10) 26 Jul - HUNGARY (Hungaroring)

1)	Lewis Hamilton	McLaren MP4-24 - Mercedes V8
2)	Kimi Räikkönen	Ferrari F60 - V8
3/ FL)	Mark Webber	Red Bull RB5 - Renault V8
PP)	Fernando Alonso	Renault R29 - V8

11) 23 Aug - EUROPE (Valencia)

1)	Rubens Barrichello	Brawn BGP 001 - Mercedes V8
2/ PP)	Lewis Hamilton	McLaren MP4-24 - Mercedes V8
3)	Kimi Räikkönen	Ferrari F60 - V8
FL)	Timo Glock	Toyota TF109 - V8

12) 30 Aug - BELGIUM (Spa-Francorchamps)

1)	Kimi Räikkönen	Ferrari F60 - V8
2/ PP)	Giancarlo Fisichella	Force India VJM02 - Mercedes V8
3/ FL)	Sebastian Vettel	Red Bull RB5 - Renault V8

13) 13 Sep - ITALY (Monza)

1)	Rubens Barrichello	Brawn BGP 001 - Mercedes V8
2)	Jenson Button	Brawn BGP 001 - Mercedes V8
3)	Kimi Räikkönen	Ferrari F60 - V8
PP)	Lewis Hamilton	McLaren MP4-24 - Mercedes V8
FL)	Adrian Sutil	Force India VJM02 - Mercedes V8

14) 27 Sep - SINGAPORE (Marina Bay)

1/ PP)	Lewis Hamilton	McLaren MP4-24 - Mercedes V8
2)	Timo Glock	Toyota TF109 - V8
3/ FL)	Fernando Alonso	Renault R29 - V8

15) 4 Oct - JAPAN (Suzuka)

1/ PP)	Sebastian Vettel	Red Bull RB5 - Renault V8
2)	Jarno Trulli	Toyota TF109 - V8
3)	Lewis Hamilton	McLaren MP4-24 - Mercedes V8
FL)	Mark Webber	Red Bull RB5 - Renault V8

16) 18 Oct - BRAZIL (Interlagos)

1/ FL)	Mark Webber	Red Bull RB5 - Renault V8
2)	Robert Kubica	BMW Sauber F1.09 - BMW V8
3)	Lewis Hamilton	McLaren MP4-24 - Mercedes V8
PP)	Rubens Barrichello	Brawn BGP 001 - Mercedes V8

17) 1 Nov - ABU DHABI (Yas Marina)

1/ FL)	Sebastian Vettel	Red Bull RB5 - Renault V8
2)	Mark Webber	Red Bull RB5 - Renault V8
3)	Jenson Button	Brawn BGP 001 - Mercedes V8
PP)	Lewis Hamilton	McLaren MP4-24 - Mercedes V8

Drivers' championship		Constructors' championship	
1) Jenson Button	95	1) Red Bull - Renault	422
2) Sebastian Vettel	84	2) Ferrari	340
3) Rubens Barrichello	77	3)McLaren - Mercedes	318

2010

1) 14 Mar - BAHRAIN (Sakhir)

1/ FL)	Fernando Alonso	Ferrari F10 - V8
2)	Felipe Massa	Ferrari F10 - V8
3)	Lewis Hamilton	McLaren MP4-25 - Mercedes V8
PP)	Sebastian Vettel	Red Bull RB6 - Renault V8

2) 28 Mar - AUSTRALIA (Melbourne)

1)	Jenson Button	McLaren MP4-25 - Mercedes V8
2)	Robert Kubica	Renault R30 - V8
3)	Felipe Massa	Ferrari F10 - V8
PP)	Sebastian Vettel	Red Bull RB6 - Renault V8
FL)	Mark Webber	Red Bull RB6 - Renault V8

3) 4 Apr - MALAYSIA (Sepang)

1)	Sebastian Vettel	Red Bull RB6 - Renault V8
2/ PP/ FL)	Mark Webber	Red Bull RB6 - Renault V8
3)	Nico Rosberg	Mercedes-Benz MGP W01 - V8

4) 18 Apr - CHINA (Shanghai)

1)	Jenson Button	McLaren MP4-25 - Mercedes V8
2/ FL)	Lewis Hamilton	McLaren MP4-25 - Mercedes V8
3)	Nico Rosberg	Mercedes-Benz MGP W01 - V8
PP)	Sebastian Vettel	Red Bull RB6 - Renault V8

5) 9 May - SPAIN (Catalunya)

1/ PP)	Mark Webber	Red Bull RB6 - Renault V8
2)	Fernando Alonso	Ferrari F10 - V8
3)	Sebastian Vettel	Red Bull RB6 - Renault V8
FL)	Lewis Hamilton	McLaren MP4-25 - Mercedes V8

6) 16 May - MONACO (Monte-Carlo)

1/ PP)	Mark Webber	Red Bull RB6 - Renault V8
2/ FL)	Sebastian Vettel	Red Bull RB6 - Renault V8
3)	Robert Kubica	Renault R30 - V8

7) 30 May - TURKEY (Istanbul)

1)	Lewis Hamilton	McLaren MP4-25 - Mercedes V8
2)	Jenson Button	McLaren MP4-25 - Mercedes V8
3/ PP)	Mark Webber	Red Bull RB6 - Renault V8
FL)	Vitaly Petrov	Renault R30 - V8

8) 13 Jun - CANADA (Montréal)

1/ PP)	Lewis Hamilton	McLaren MP4-25 - Mercedes V8
2)	Jenson Button	McLaren MP4-25 - Mercedes V8
3)	Fernando Alonso	Ferrari F10 - V8
FL)	Robert Kubica	Renault R30 - V8

9) 27 Jun - EUROPE (Valencia)

1/ PP)	Sebastian Vettel	Red Bull RB6 - Renault V8
2)	Lewis Hamilton	McLaren MP4-25 - Mercedes V8
3/ FL)	Jenson Button	McLaren MP4-25 - Mercedes V8

10) 11 Jul - BRITAIN (Silverstone)

1)	Mark Webber	Red Bull RB6 - Renault V8
2)	Lewis Hamilton	McLaren MP4-25 - Mercedes V8
3)	Nico Rosberg	Mercedes-Benz MGP W01 - V8
PP)	Sebastian Vettel	Red Bull RB6 - Renault V8
FL)	Fernando Alonso	Ferrari F10 - V8

11) 26 Jul - GERMANY (Hockenheim)

1)	Fernando Alonso	Ferrari F10 - V8
2)	Felipe Massa	Ferrari F10 - V8
3/ PP/ FL)	Sebastian Vettel	Red Bull RB6 - Renault V8

12) 1 Aug - HUNGARY (Hungaroring)

1)	Mark Webber	Red Bull RB6 - Renault V8
2)	Fernando Alonso	Ferrari F10 - V8
3/ PP/ FL)	Sebastian Vettel	Red Bull RB6 - Renault V8

13) 29 Aug - BELGIUM (Spa-Francorchamps)

1/ FL)	Lewis Hamilton	McLaren MP4-25 - Mercedes V8
2/ PP)	Mark Webber	Red Bull RB6 - Renault V8
3)	Robert Kubica	Renault R30 - V8

14) 12 Sep - ITALY (Monza)

1/ PP/ FL)	Fernando Alonso	Ferrari F10 - V8
2)	Jenson Button	McLaren MP4-25 - Mercedes V8
3)	Felipe Massa	Ferrari F10 - V8

15) 26 Sep - SINGAPORE (Marina Bay)

1/ PP/ FL)	Fernando Alonso	Ferrari F10 - V8
2)	Sebastian Vettel	Red Bull RB6 - Renault V8
3)	Mark Webber	Red Bull RB6 - Renault V8

16) 10 Oct - JAPAN (Suzuka)

1/ PP)	Sebastian Vettel	Red Bull RB6 - Renault V8
2/ FL)	Mark Webber	Red Bull RB6 - Renault V8
3)	Fernando Alonso	Ferrari F10 - V8

17) 24 Oct - KOREA (Yeongam)

1/ FL)	Fernando Alonso	Ferrari F10 - V8
2)	Lewis Hamilton	McLaren MP4-25 - Mercedes V8
3)	Felipe Massa	Ferrari F10 - V8
PP)	Sebastian Vettel	Red Bull RB6 - Renault V8

18) 7 Nov - BRAZIL (Interlagos)

1)	Sebastian Vettel	Red Bull RB6 - Renault V8
2)	Mark Webber	Red Bull RB6 - Renault V8
3)	Fernando Alonso	Ferrari F10 - V8
PP)	Nico Hülkenberg	Williams FW32 - Cosworth V8
FL)	Lewis Hamilton	McLaren MP4-25 - Mercedes V8

19) 14 Nov - ABU DHABI (Yas Marina)

1/ PP)	Sebastian Vettel	Red Bull RB6 - Renault V8
2/ FL)	Lewis Hamilton	McLaren MP4-25 - Mercedes V8
3)	Jenson Button	McLaren MP4-25 - Mercedes V8

Drivers' championship

1)	Sebastian Vettel	256
2)	Fernando Alonso	252
3)	Mark Webber	242

Constructors' championship

1)	Red Bull - Renault	498
2)	McLaren - Mercedes	454
3)	Ferrari	396

2011

1) 27 Mar - AUSTRALIA (Melbourne)

1/ PP)	Sebastian Vettel	Red Bull RB7 - Renault V8
2)	Lewis Hamilton	McLaren MP4-26 - Mercedes V8
3)	Vitaly Petrov	Renault R31 - V8
FL)	Felipe Massa	Ferrari F150th Italia - V8

2) 10 Apr - MALAYSIA (Sepang)

1/ PP)	Sebastian Vettel	Red Bull RB7 - Renault V8
2)	Jenson Button	McLaren MP4-26 - Mercedes V8
3)	Nick Heidfeld	Renault R31 - V8
FL)	Mark Webber	Red Bull RB7 - Renault V8

3) 17 Apr - CHINA (Shanghai)

1)	Lewis Hamilton	McLaren MP4-26 - Mercedes V8
2/ PP)	Sebastian Vettel	Red Bull RB7 - Renault V8
3/ FL)	Mark Webber	Red Bull RB7 - Renault V8

4) 8 May - TURKEY (Istanbul)

1/ PP)	Sebastian Vettel	Red Bull RB7 - Renault V8
2/ FL)	Mark Webber	Red Bull RB7 - Renault V8
3)	Fernando Alonso	Ferrari F150th Italia - V8

5) 22 May - SPAIN (Catalunya)

1)	Sebastian Vettel	Red Bull RB7 - Renault V8
2/ FL)	Lewis Hamilton	McLaren MP4-26 - Mercedes V8
3)	Jenson Button	McLaren MP4-26 - Mercedes V8
PP)	Mark Webber	Red Bull RB7 - Renault V8

6) 29 May - MONACO (Monte-Carlo)

1/ PP)	Sebastian Vettel	Red Bull RB7 - Renault V8
2)	Fernando Alonso	Ferrari F150th Italia - V8
3)	Jenson Button	McLaren MP4-26 - Mercedes V8
FL)	Mark Webber	Red Bull RB7 - Renault V8

7) 12 Jun - CANADA (Montréal)

1/ FL)	Jenson Button	McLaren MP4-26 - Mercedes V8
2/ PP)	Sebastian Vettel	Red Bull RB7 - Renault V8
3)	Mark Webber	Red Bull RB7 - Renault V8

8) 26 Jun - EUROPE (Valencia)

1/ PP/ FL)	Sebastian Vettel	Red Bull RB7 - Renault V8
2)	Fernando Alonso	Ferrari F150th Italia - V8
3)	Mark Webber	Red Bull RB7 - Renault V8

9) 10 Jul - BRITAIN (Silverstone)

1/ FL)	Fernando Alonso	Ferrari F150th Italia - V8
2)	Sebastian Vettel	Red Bull RB7 - Renault V8
3/ PP)	Mark Webber	Red Bull RB7 - Renault V8

10) 24 Jul - GERMANY (Nurburgring)

1/ FL)	Lewis Hamilton	McLaren MP4-26 - Mercedes V8
2)	Fernando Alonso	Ferrari F150th Italia - V8
3/ PP)	Mark Webber	Red Bull RB7 - Renault V8

11) 31 Jul - HUNGARY (Hungaroring)

1)	Jenson Button	McLaren MP4-26 - Mercedes V8
2/ PP)	Sebastian Vettel	Red Bull RB7 - Renault V8
3)	Fernando Alonso	Ferrari F150th Italia - V8
FL)	Felipe Massa	Ferrari F150th Italia - V8

12) 28 Aug - BELGIUM (Spa-Francorchamps)

1/ PP)	Sebastian Vettel	Red Bull RB7 - Renault V8
2/ FL)	Mark Webber	Red Bull RB7 - Renault V8
3)	Jenson Button	McLaren MP4-26 - Mercedes V8

13) 11 Sep - ITALY (Monza)

1/ PP)	Sebastian Vettel	Red Bull RB7 - Renault V8
2)	Jenson Button	McLaren MP4-26 - Mercedes V8
3)	Fernando Alonso	Ferrari F150th Italia - V8
FL)	Lewis Hamilton	McLaren MP4-26 - Mercedes V8

14) 25 Sep - SINGAPORE (Marina Bay)

1/ PP)	Sebastian Vettel	Red Bull RB7 - Renault V8
2/ FL)	Jenson Button	McLaren MP4-26 - Mercedes V8
3)	Mark Webber	Red Bull RB7 - Renault V8

15) 9 Oct - JAPAN (Suzuka)

1/ FL)	Jenson Button	McLaren MP4-26 - Mercedes V8
2)	Fernando Alonso	Ferrari F150th Italia - V8
3/ PP)	Sebastian Vettel	Red Bull RB7 - Renault V8

16) 16 Oct - KOREA (Yeongam)

1/ FL)	Sebastian Vettel	Red Bull RB7 - Renault V8
2/ PP)	Lewis Hamilton	McLaren MP4-26 - Mercedes V8
3)	Mark Webber	Red Bull RB7 - Renault V8

17) 30 Oct - INDIA (Buddh)

1/ PP/ FL)	Sebastian Vettel	Red Bull RB7 - Renault V8
2)	Jenson Button	McLaren MP4-26 - Mercedes V8
3)	Fernando Alonso	Ferrari F150th Italia - V8

18) 13 Nov - ABU DHABI (Yas Marina)

1)	Lewis Hamilton	McLaren MP4-26 - Mercedes V8
2)	Fernando Alonso	Ferrari 150th Italia - V8
3)	Jenson Button	McLaren MP4-26 - Mercedes V8
PP)	Sebastian Vettel	Red Bull RB7 - Renault V8
FL)	Mark Webber	Red Bull RB7 - Renault V8

19) 27 Nov - BRAZIL (Interlagos)

1/ FL)	Mark Webber	Red Bull RB7 - Renault V8
2/ PP)	Sebastian Vettel	Red Bull RB7 - Renault V8
3)	Jenson Button	McLaren MP4-26 - Mercedes V8

Drivers' championship		Constructors' championship	
1) Sebastian Vettel	392	1) Red Bull - Renault	650
2) Jenson Button	270	2) McLaren - Mercedes	497
3) Mark Webber	258	3) Ferrari	375

2012

1) 18 Mar - AUSTRALIA (Melbourne)

1/ FL)	Jenson Button	McLaren MP4-27 - Mercedes V8
2)	Sebastian Vettel	Red Bull RB8 - Renault V8
3/ PP)	Lewis Hamilton	McLaren MP4-27 - Mercedes V8

2) 25 Mar - MALAYSIA (Sepang)

1)	Fernando Alonso	Ferrari F2012 - V8
2)	Sergio Pérez	Sauber C31 - Ferrari V8
3/ PP)	Lewis Hamilton	McLaren MP4-27 - Mercedes V8
FL)	Kimi Räikkönen	Lotus E20 - Renault V8

3) 15 Apr - CHINA (Shanghai)

1/ PP)	Nico Rosberg	Mercedes-Benz F1 W03 - V8
2)	Jenson Button	McLaren MP4-27 - Mercedes V8
3)	Lewis Hamilton	McLaren MP4-27 - Mercedes V8
FL)	Kamui Kobayashi	Sauber C31 - Ferrari V8

4) 22 Apr - BAHRAIN (Sakhir)

1/ PP/ FL)	Sebastian Vettel	Red Bull RB8 - Renault V8
2)	Kimi Räikkönen	Lotus E20 - Renault V8
3)	Romain Grosjean	Lotus E20 - Renault V8

5) 13 May - SPAIN (Catalunya)

1/ PP)	Pastor Maldonado	Williams FW34 - Renault V8
2)	Fernando Alonso	Ferrari F2012 - V8
3)	Kimi Räikkönen	Lotus E20 - Renault V8
FL)	Romain Grosjean	Lotus E20 - Renault V8

Lewis Hamilton (McLaren MP4-27 - Mercedes V8) set the pole position time, but had all times removed, demoting him to the back of the grid for having insufficient fuel to provide a sample.

6) 27 May - MONACO (Monte-Carlo)

1/ PP)	Mark Webber	Red Bull RB8 - Renault V8
2)	Nico Rosberg	Mercedes-Benz F1 W03 - V8
3)	Fernando Alonso	Ferrari F2012 - V8
FL)	Sergio Pérez	Sauber C31 - Ferrari V8

Michael Schumacher (Mercedes-Benz F1 W03 - V8) set the pole position time, but received a five-place grid penalty for causing an accident with Bruno Senna in Spain.

7) 10 Jun - CANADA (Montréal)

1)	Lewis Hamilton	McLaren MP4-27 - Mercedes V8
2)	Romain Grosjean	Lotus E20 - Renault V8
3)	Sergio Pérez	Sauber C31 - Ferrari V8
PP/ FL)	Sebastian Vettel	Red Bull RB8 - Renault V8

8) 24 Jun - EUROPE (Valencia)

1)	Fernando Alonso	Ferrari F2012 - V8
2)	Kimi Räikkönen	Lotus E20 - Renault V8
3)	Michael Schumacher	Mercedes-Benz F1 W03 - V8
PP)	Sebastian Vettel	Red Bull RB8 - Renault V8
FL)	Nico Rosberg	Mercedes-Benz F1 W03 - V8

9) 8 Jul - BRITAIN (Silverstone)

1)	Mark Webber	Red Bull RB8 - Renault V8
2/ PP)	Fernando Alonso	Ferrari F2012 - V8
3)	Sebastian Vettel	Red Bull RB8 - Renault V8
FL)	Kimi Räikkönen	Lotus E20 - Renault V8

10) 22 Jul - GERMANY (Hockenheim)

1/ PP)	Fernando Alonso	Ferrari F2012 - V8
2)	Jenson Button	McLaren MP4-27 - Mercedes V8
3)	Kimi Räikkönen	Lotus E20 - Renault V8
FL)	Michael Schumacher	Mercedes-Benz F1 W03 - V8

Sebastian Vettel (Red Bull RB8 - Renault V8), finished 2nd, but was given a 20-second penalty for gaining an advantage by leaving the track. Classified 5th.

11) 29 Jul - HUNGARY (Hungaroring)

1/ PP)	Lewis Hamilton	McLaren MP4-27 - Mercedes V8
2)	Kimi Räikkönen	Lotus E20 - Renault V8
3)	Romain Grosjean	Lotus E20 - Renault V8
FL)	Sebastian Vettel	Red Bull RB8 - Renault V8

12) 2 Sep - BELGIUM (Spa-Francorchamps)

1/ PP)	Jenson Button	McLaren MP4-27 - Mercedes V8
2)	Sebastian Vettel	Red Bull RB8 - Renault V8
3)	Kimi Räikkönen	Lotus E20 - Renault V8
FL)	Bruno Senna	Williams FW34 - Renault V8

13) 9 Sep - ITALY (Monza)

1/ PP)	Lewis Hamilton	McLaren MP4-27 - Mercedes V8
2)	Sergio Pérez	Sauber C31 - Ferrari V8
3)	Fernando Alonso	Ferrari F2012 - V8
FL)	Nico Rosberg	Mercedes-Benz F1 W03 - V8

14) 23 Sep - SINGAPORE (Marina Bay)

1)	Sebastian Vettel	Red Bull RB8 - Renault V8
2)	Jenson Button	McLaren MP4-27 - Mercedes V8
3)	Fernando Alonso	Ferrari F2012 - V8
PP)	Lewis Hamilton	McLaren MP4-27 - Mercedes V8
FL)	Nico Hülkenberg	Force India VJM05 - Mercedes V8

15) 7 Oct - JAPAN (Suzuka)

1/ PP/ FL)	Sebastian Vettel	Red Bull RB8 - Renault V8
2)	Felipe Massa	Ferrari F2012 - V8
3)	Kamui Kobayashi	Sauber C31 - Ferrari V8

16) 14 Oct - KOREA (Yeongam)

1)	Sebastian Vettel	Red Bull RB8 - Renault V8
2/ PP/ FL)	Mark Webber	Red Bull RB8 - Renault V8
3)	Fernando Alonso	Ferrari F2012 - V8

17) 28 Oct - INDIA (Buddh)

1/ PP)	Sebastian Vettel	Red Bull RB8 - Renault V8
2)	Fernando Alonso	Ferrari F2012 - V8
3)	Mark Webber	Red Bull RB8 - Renault V8
FL)	Jenson Button	McLaren MP4-27 - Mercedes V8

18) 4 Nov - ABU DHABI (Yas Marina)

1)	Kimi Räikkönen	Lotus E20 - Renault V8
2)	Fernando Alonso	Ferrari F2012 - V8
3/ FL)	Sebastian Vettel	Red Bull RB8 - Renault V8
PP)	Lewis Hamilton	McLaren MP4-27 - Mercedes V8

19) 18 Nov - UNITED STATES (Austin)

1)	Lewis Hamilton	McLaren MP4-27 - Mercedes V8
2/ PP/ FL)	Sebastian Vettel	Red Bull RB8 - Renault V8
3)	Fernando Alonso	Ferrari F2012 - V8

20) 25 Nov - BRAZIL (Interlagos)

1)	Jenson Button	McLaren MP4-27 - Mercedes V8
2)	Fernando Alonso	Ferrari F2012 - V8
3)	Felipe Massa	Ferrari F2012 - V8
PP/ FL)	Lewis Hamilton	McLaren MP4-27 - Mercedes V8

Drivers' championship		Constructors' championship	
1) Sebastian Vettel	281	1) Red Bull - Renault	460
2) Fernando Alonso	278	2) Ferrari	400
3) Kimi Räikkönen	207	3) McLaren - Mercedes	378

2013

1) 17 Mar - AUSTRALIA (Melbourne)

1/ FL)	Kimi Räikkönen	Lotus E21 - Renault V8
2)	Fernando Alonso	Ferrari F138 - V8
3/ PP)	Sebastian Vettel	Red Bull RB9 - Renault V8

2) 24 Mar - MALAYSIA (Sepang)

1/ PP)	Sebastian Vettel	Red Bull RB9 - Renault V8
2)	Mark Webber	Red Bull RB9 - Renault V8
3)	Lewis Hamilton	Mercedes-Benz F1 W04 - V8
FL)	Sergio Pérez	McLaren MP4-28 - Mercedes V8

3) 14 Apr - CHINA (Shanghai)

1)	Fernando Alonso	Ferrari F138 - V8
2)	Kimi Räikkönen	Lotus E21 - Renault V8
3/ PP)	Lewis Hamilton	Mercedes-Benz F1 W04 - V8
FL)	Sebastian Vettel	Red Bull RB9 - Renault V8

4) 21 Apr - BAHRAIN (Sakhir)

1/ FL)	Sebastian Vettel	Red Bull RB9 - Renault V8
2)	Kimi Räikkönen	Lotus E21 - Renault V8
3)	Romain Grosjean	Lotus E21 - Renault V8
PP)	Nico Rosberg	Mercedes-Benz F1 W04 - V8

5) 12 May - SPAIN (Catalunya)

1)	Fernando Alonso	Ferrari F138 - V8
2)	Kimi Räikkönen	Lotus E21 - Renault V8
3)	Felipe Massa	Ferrari F138 - V8
PP)	Nico Rosberg	Mercedes-Benz F1 W04 - V8
FL)	Esteban Gutiérrez	Sauber C32 - Ferrari

6) 26 May - MONACO (Monte-Carlo)

1/ PP)	Nico Rosberg	Mercedes-Benz F1 W04 - V8
2/ FL)	Sebastian Vettel	Red Bull RB9 - Renault V8
3)	Mark Webber	Red Bull RB9 - Renault V8

7) 9 Jun - CANADA (Montréal)

1/ PP)	Sebastian Vettel	Red Bull RB9 - Renault V8
2)	Fernando Alonso	Ferrari F138 - V8
3)	Lewis Hamilton	Mercedes-Benz F1 W04 - V8
FL)	Mark Webber	Red Bull RB9 - Renault V8

8) 30 Jun - BRITAIN (Silverstone)

1)	Nico Rosberg	Mercedes-Benz F1 W04 - V8
2/ FL)	Mark Webber	Red Bull RB9 - Renault V8
3)	Fernando Alonso	Ferrari F138 - V8
PP)	Lewis Hamilton	Mercedes-Benz F1 W04 - V8

9) 7 Jul - GERMANY (Nürburgring)

1)	Sebastian Vettel	Red Bull RB9 - Renault V8
2)	Kimi Räikkönen	Lotus E21 - Renault V8
3)	Romain Grosjean	Lotus E21 - Renault V8
PP)	Lewis Hamilton	Mercedes-Benz F1 W04 - V8
FL)	Fernando Alonso	Ferrari F138 - V8

10) 28 Jul - HUNGARY (Hungaroring)

1/ PP)	Lewis Hamilton	Mercedes-Benz F1 W04 - V8
2)	Kimi Räikkönen	Lotus E21 - Renault V8
3)	Sebastian Vettel	Red Bull RB9 - Renault V8
FL)	Mark Webber	Red Bull RB9 - Renault V8

11) 25 Aug - BELGIUM (Spa-Francorchamps)

1/ FL)	Sebastian Vettel	Red Bull RB9 - Renault V8
2)	Fernando Alonso	Ferrari F138 - V8
3/ PP)	Lewis Hamilton	Mercedes-Benz F1 W04 - V8

12) 8 Sep - ITALY (Monza)

1/ PP)	Sebastian Vettel	Red Bull RB9 - Renault V8
2)	Fernando Alonso	Ferrari F138 - V8
3)	Mark Webber	Red Bull RB9 - Renault V8
FL)	Lewis Hamilton	Mercedes-Benz F1 W04 - V8

13) 22 Sep - SINGAPORE (Marina Bay)

1/ PP/ FL)	Sebastian Vettel	Red Bull RB9 - Renault V8
2)	Fernando Alonso	Ferrari F138 - V8
3)	Kimi Räikkönen	Lotus E21 - Renault V8

14) 6 Oct - KOREA (Yeongam)

1/ PP/ FL)	Sebastian Vettel	Red Bull RB9 - Renault V8
2)	Kimi Räikkönen	Lotus E21 - Renault V8
3)	Romain Grosjean	Lotus E21 - Renault V8

15) 13 Oct - JAPAN (Suzuka)

1)	Sebastian Vettel	Red Bull RB9 - Renault V8
2/ PP/ FL)	Mark Webber	Red Bull RB9 - Renault V8
3)	Romain Grosjean	Lotus E21 - Renault V8

16) 27 Oct - INDIA (Buddh)

1/ PP)	Sebastian Vettel	Red Bull RB9 - Renault V8
2)	Nico Rosberg	Mercedes-Benz F1 W04 - V8
3)	Romain Grosjean	Lotus E21 - Renault V8
FL)	Kimi Räikkönen	Lotus E21 - Renault V8

17) 3 Nov - ABU DHABI (Yas Marina)

1)	Sebastian Vettel	Red Bull RB9 - Renault V8
2/ PP)	Mark Webber	Red Bull RB9 - Renault V8
3)	Nico Rosberg	Mercedes-Benz F1 W04 - V8
FL)	Fernando Alonso	Ferrari F138 - V8

18) 17 Nov - UNITED STATES (Austin)

1/ PP/FL)	Sebastian Vettel	Red Bull RB9 - Renault V8
2)	Romain Grosjean	Lotus E21 - Renault V8
3)	Mark Webber	Red Bull RB9 - Renault V8

19) 24 Nov - BRAZIL (Interlagos)

1/ PP)	Sebastian Vettel	Red Bull RB9 - Renault V8
2 /FL)	Mark Webber	Red Bull RB9 - Renault V8
3)	Fernando Alonso	Ferrari F138 - V8

Drivers' championship		Constructors' championship	
1) Sebastian Vettel	397	1) Red Bull - Renault	596
2) Fernando Alonso	242	2) Mercedes-Benz	360
3) Mark Webber	199	3) Ferrari	354

2014

1) 16 Mar - AUSTRALIA (Melbourne)

1/ FL)	Nico Rosberg	Mercedes-Benz F1 W05 - V6t
2)	Kevin Magnussen	McLaren MP4-29 - Mercedes V6t
3)	Jenson Button	McLaren MP4-29 - Mercedes V6t
PP)	Lewis Hamilton	Mercedes-Benz F1 W05 - V6t

Daniel Ricciardo (Red Bull RB10 - Renault V6t) finished 2nd, but was disqualified for exceeding the fuel flow limitation.

2) 30 Mar - MALAYSIA (Sepang)

1/ PP/ FL)	Lewis Hamilton	Mercedes-Benz F1 W05 - V6t
2)	Nico Rosberg	Mercedes-Benz F1 W05 - V6t
3)	Sebastian Vettel	Red Bull RB10 - Renault V6t

3) 6 Apr - BAHRAIN (Sakhir)

1)	Lewis Hamilton	Mercedes-Benz F1 W05 - V6t
2/ PP/ FL)	Nico Rosberg	Mercedes-Benz F1 W05 - V6t
3)	Sergio Pérez	Force India VJM07 - Mercedes V6t

4) 20 Apr - CHINA (Shanghai)

1/ PP)	Lewis Hamilton	Mercedes-Benz F1 W05 - V6t
2/ FL)	Nico Rosberg	Mercedes-Benz F1 W05 - V6t
3)	Fernando Alonso	Ferrari F14 T - V6t

5) 11 May - SPAIN (Catalunya)

1/ PP)	Lewis Hamilton	Mercedes-Benz F1 W05 - V6t
2)	Nico Rosberg	Mercedes-Benz F1 W05 - V6t
3)	Daniel Ricciardo	Red Bull RB10 - Renault V6t
FL)	Sebastian Vettel	Red Bull RB10 - Renault V6t

6) 25 May - MONACO (Monte-Carlo)

1/ PP)	Nico Rosberg	Mercedes-Benz F1 W05 - V6t
2)	Lewis Hamilton	Mercedes-Benz F1 W05 - V6t
3)	Daniel Ricciardo	Red Bull RB10 - Renault V6t
FL)	Kimi Räikkönen	Ferrari F14 T - V6t

7) 8 Jun - CANADA (Montréal)

1)	Daniel Ricciardo	Red Bull RB10 - Renault V6t
2/ PP)	Nico Rosberg	Mercedes-Benz F1 W05 - V6t
3)	Sebastian Vettel	Red Bull RB10 - Renault V6t
FL)	Felipe Massa	Williams FW36 - Mercedes V6t

8) 22 Jun - AUSTRIA (Spielberg)

1)	Nico Rosberg	Mercedes-Benz F1 W05 - V6t
2)	Lewis Hamilton	Mercedes-Benz F1 W05 - V6t
3)	Valtteri Bottas	Williams FW36 - Mercedes V6t
PP)	Felipe Massa	Williams FW36 - Mercedes V6t
FL)	Sergio Pérez	Force India VJM07 - Mercedes V6t

9) 6 Jul - BRITAIN (Silverstone)

1/ FL)	Lewis Hamilton	Mercedes-Benz F1 W05 - V6t
2)	Valtteri Bottas	Williams FW36 - Mercedes V6t
3)	Daniel Ricciardo	Red Bull RB10 - Renault V6t
PP)	Nico Rosberg	Mercedes-Benz F1 W05 - V6t

10) 20 Jul - GERMANY (Hockenheim)

1/ PP)	Nico Rosberg	Mercedes-Benz F1 W05 - V6t
2)	Valtteri Bottas	Williams FW36 - Mercedes V6t
3/ FL)	Lewis Hamilton	Mercedes-Benz F1 W05 - V6t

11) 27 Jul - HUNGARY (Hungaroring)

1)	Daniel Ricciardo	Red Bull RB10 - Renault V6t
2)	Fernando Alonso	Ferrari F14 T - V6t
3)	Lewis Hamilton	Mercedes-Benz F1 W05 - V6t
PP/ FL)	Nico Rosberg	Mercedes-Benz F1 W05 - V6t

12) 24 Aug - BELGIUM (Spa-Francorchamps)

1)	Daniel Ricciardo	Red Bull RB10 - Renault V6t
2/ PP/ FL)	Nico Rosberg	Mercedes-Benz F1 W05 - V6t
3)	Valtteri Bottas	Williams FW36 - Mercedes V6t

13) 7 Sep - ITALY (Monza)

1/ PP/ FL)	Lewis Hamilton	Mercedes-Benz F1 W05 - V6t
2)	Nico Rosberg	Mercedes-Benz F1 W05 - V6t
3)	Felipe Massa	Williams FW36 - Mercedes V6t

14) 21 Sep - SINGAPORE (Marina Bay)

1/ PP/ FL)	Lewis Hamilton	Mercedes-Benz F1 W05 - V6t
2)	Sebastian Vettel	Red Bull RB10 - Renault V6t
3)	Daniel Ricciardo	Red Bull RB10 - Renault V6t

15) 5 Oct - JAPAN (Suzuka)

1/ FL)	Lewis Hamilton	Mercedes-Benz F1 W05 - V6t
2/ PP)	Nico Rosberg	Mercedes-Benz F1 W05 - V6t
3)	Sebastian Vettel	Red Bull RB10 - Renault V6t

16) 12 Oct - RUSSIA (Sochi)

1/ PP)	Lewis Hamilton	Mercedes-Benz F1 W05 - V6t
2)	Nico Rosberg	Mercedes-Benz F1 W05 - V6t
3/ FL)	Valtteri Bottas	Williams FW36 - Mercedes V6t

17) 2 Nov - UNITED STATES (Austin)

1)	Lewis Hamilton	Mercedes-Benz F1 W05 - V6t
2/ PP)	Nico Rosberg	Mercedes-Benz F1 W05 - V6t
3)	Daniel Ricciardo	Red Bull RB10 - Renault V6t
FL)	Sebastian Vettel	Red Bull RB10 - Renault V6t

18) 9 Nov - BRAZIL (Interlagos)

1/ PP)	Nico Rosberg	Mercedes-Benz F1 W05 - V6t
2/ FL)	Lewis Hamilton	Mercedes-Benz F1 W05 - V6t
3)	Felipe Massa	Williams FW36 - Mercedes V6t

19) 23 Nov - ABU DHABI (Yas Marina)

1)	Lewis Hamilton	Mercedes-Benz F1 W05 - V6t
2)	Felipe Massa	Williams FW36 - Mercedes V6t
3)	Valtteri Bottas	Williams FW36 - Mercedes V6t
PP)	Nico Rosberg	Mercedes-Benz F1 W05 - V6t
FL)	Daniel Ricciardo	Red Bull RB10 - Renault V6t

Drivers' championship		Constructors' championship	
1) Lewis Hamilton	384	1) Mercedes-Benz	701
2) Nico Rosberg	317	2) Red Bull - Renault	405
3) Daniel Ricciardo	238	3) Williams - Mercedes	320

2015

1) 15 Mar - AUSTRALIA (Melbourne)

1/PP/FL)	Lewis Hamilton	Mercedes-Benz F1 W06 - V6t
2)	Nico Rosberg	Mercedes-Benz F1 W06 - V6t
3)	Sebastian Vettel	Ferrari SF15-T - V6t

2) 29 Mar - MALAYSIA (Sepang)

1)	Sebastian Vettel	Ferrari SF15-T - V6t
2/PP)	Lewis Hamilton	Mercedes-Benz F1 W06 - V6t
3/FL)	Nico Rosberg	Mercedes-Benz F1 W06 - V6t

3) 12 Apr - CHINA (Shanghai)

1/PP/FL)	Lewis Hamilton	Mercedes-Benz F1 W06 - V6t
2)	Nico Rosberg	Mercedes-Benz F1 W06 - V6t
3)	Sebastian Vettel	Ferrari SF15-T - V6t

4) 19 Apr - BAHRAIN (Sakhir)

1/PP)	Lewis Hamilton	Mercedes-Benz F1 W06 - V6t
2/FL)	Kimi Räikkönen	Ferrari SF15-T - V6t
3)	Nico Rosberg	Mercedes-Benz F1 W06 - V6t

5) 10 May - SPAIN (Catalunya)

1/PP)	Nico Rosberg	Mercedes-Benz F1 W06 - V6t
2/FL)	Lewis Hamilton	Mercedes-Benz F1 W06 - V6t
3)	Sebastian Vettel	Ferrari SF15-T - V6t

6) 24 May - MONACO (Monte-Carlo)

1)	Nico Rosberg	Mercedes-Benz F1 W06 - V6t
2)	Sebastian Vettel	Ferrari SF15-T - V6t
3/PP)	Lewis Hamilton	Mercedes-Benz F1 W06 - V6t
FL)	Daniel Ricciardo	Red Bull RB11 - Renault V6t

7) 7 Jun - CANADA (Montréal)

1/PP)	Lewis Hamilton	Mercedes-Benz F1 W06 - V6t
2)	Nico Rosberg	Mercedes-Benz F1 W06 - V6t
3)	Valtteri Bottas	Williams FW37 - Mercedes V6t
FL)	Kimi Räikkönen	Ferrari SF15-T - V6t

8) 21 Jun - AUSTRIA (Spielberg)

1/FL)	Nico Rosberg	Mercedes-Benz F1 W06 - V6t
2/PP)	Lewis Hamilton	Mercedes-Benz F1 W06 - V6t
3)	Felipe Massa	Williams FW37 - Mercedes V6t

9) 5 Jul - BRITAIN (Silverstone)

1/PP/FL)	Lewis Hamilton	Mercedes-Benz F1 W06 - V6t
2)	Nico Rosberg	Mercedes-Benz F1 W06 - V6t
3)	Sebastian Vettel	Ferrari SF15-T - V6t

10) 26 Jul - HUNGARY (Hungaroring)

1)	Sebastian Vettel	Ferrari SF15-T - V6t
2)	Daniil Kvyat	Red Bull RB11 - Renault V6t
3/FL)	Daniel Ricciardo	Red Bull RB11 - Renault V6t
PP)	Lewis Hamilton	Mercedes-Benz F1 W06 - V6t

11) 23 Aug - BELGIUM (Spa-Francorchamps)

1/ PP)	Lewis Hamilton	Mercedes-Benz F1 W06 - V6t
2/ FL)	Nico Rosberg	Mercedes-Benz F1 W06 - V6t
3)	Romain Grosjean	Lotus E23 - Mercedes V6t

12) 6 Sep - ITALY (Monza)

1/ PP/ FL)	Lewis Hamilton	Mercedes-Benz F1 W06 - V6t
2)	Sebastian Vettel	Ferrari SF15-T - V6t
3)	Felipe Massa	Williams FW37 - Mercedes V6t

13) 20 Sep - SINGAPORE (Marina Bay)

1/ PP)	Sebastian Vettel	Ferrari SF15-T - V6t
2/ FL)	Daniel Ricciardo	Red Bull RB11 - Renault V6t
3)	Kimi Räikkönen	Ferrari SF15-T - V6t

14) 27 Sep - JAPAN (Suzuka)

1/ FL)	Lewis Hamilton	Mercedes-Benz F1 W06 - V6t
2/ PP)	Nico Rosberg	Mercedes-Benz F1 W06 - V6t
3)	Sebastian Vettel	Ferrari SF15-T - V6t

15) 11 Oct - RUSSIA (Sochi)

1)	Lewis Hamilton	Mercedes-Benz F1 W06 - V6t
2/ FL)	Sebastian Vettel	Ferrari SF15-T - V6t
3)	Sergio Pérez	Force India VJM08 - Mercedes V6t
PP)	Nico Rosberg	Mercedes-Benz F1 W06 - V6t

16) 25 Oct - UNITED STATES (Austin)

1)	Lewis Hamilton	Mercedes-Benz F1 W06 - V6t
2/ PP/ FL)	Nico Rosberg	Mercedes-Benz F1 W06 - V6t
3)	Sebastian Vettel	Ferrari SF15-T - V6t

17) 1 Nov - MEXICO (Mexico City)

1/ PP/ FL)	Nico Rosberg	Mercedes-Benz F1 W06 - V6t
2)	Lewis Hamilton	Mercedes-Benz F1 W06 - V6t
3)	Valtteri Bottas	Williams FW37 - Mercedes V6t

18) 15 Nov - BRAZIL (Interlagos)

1/PP)	Nico Rosberg	Mercedes-Benz F1 W06 - V6t
2/FL)	Lewis Hamilton	Mercedes-Benz F1 W06 - V6t
3)	Sebastian Vettel	Ferrari SF15-T - V6t

19) 29 Nov - ABU DHABI (Yas Marina)

1/ PP)	Nico Rosberg	Mercedes-Benz F1 W06 - V6t
2/ FL)	Lewis Hamilton	Mercedes-Benz F1 W06 - V6t
3)	Kimi Räikkönen	Ferrari SF15-T - V6t

Drivers' championship		Constructors' championship	
1) Lewis Hamilton	381	1) Mercedes-Benz	703
2) Nico Rosberg	322	2) Ferrari	428
3) Sebastian Vettel	278	3) Williams - Mercedes	257

Bibliography

During compilation of this book, there were numerous sources for research, the most useful being:

Magazines
Autosport
F1 News
Grand Prix International
Motoring News
Motorsport

Web sites
http://forix.com
http://oldracingcars.com
http://GPfactsandnumbers.com

Books
1950 The Races • *Jean-Paul Delsaux (France)*
33 Anni Di Gran Premio Iridati F.1 (1950-82) • *Autosprint, Italy*
50 Ans de Formule 1 • *L'Equipe (France)*
A Record of Grand Prix and Voiturette Racing • *Paul Sheldon, Richard Page, Duncan Rabagliati*
Autocourse
Automobile Year
A-Z of Formula Racing Cars • *David Hodges*
A-Z of Grand Prix Cars • *David Hodges*
Benetton-Ford - A Racing Partnership • *Phil Drackett*
Brabham - The Grand Prix Cars • *Alan Henry*
BRM - The Saga of British Racing Motors Vol.1 (1945-60) • *Doug Nye*
Champion Book of World Championship Motor Racing Facts & Figures • *Mike Kettlewell*
The Complete Book of Formula One • *Simon Arron & Mark Hughes*
The Concise Dictionary of Motorsport • *George Bishop*
Cooper Cars • *Doug Nye*
Directory of Formula One Cars (1966-86) • *Pritchard*
The Encyclopedia of Auto Racing Greats • *Robert Cutter & Bob Fendell, USA*
The Encyclopedia of Motorsport • *G N Georgano*
Ferrari - 1947-1997 • *Ferrari spa, Italy*
Ferrari - The Grand Prix Cars • *Alan Henry*
Ferrari - Monoposto: Catalogue Raisonné 1948-1997 • *Automobilia, Italy*
FIA Yearbook of Automobile Sport • *FIA, France*
Formula 3000 Yearbook (1987-1992) • *Stéphane Barbé etc, France*
Formula Ferrari - 1948-2002 • *Paolo D'Alessio, Italy*
Formula One Championship Computerised Results & Timing Service (1982-1993) • *Longines, Olivetti & TAG/Heuer*
The Formula One Record Book (1961-1965) • *John Thomson*
Grand Prix! (1950-84) • *Mike Lang*
Grand Prix Cars (1945-65) • *Mike Lawrence*
Grand Prix Who's Who • *Steve Small*
The Great Encyclopedia of Formula 1 (1950-2000) • *Pierre Ménard*
Guinness Guide to International Motor Racing • *Peter Higham*
Handbook of Grand Prix Cars - Post-War to Present • *Hans Tanner, USA*
History of the Grand Prix Car (1945-91) • *Doug Nye*
The Illustrated History of the Indianapolis 500 (1911-1994) • *Jack C. Fox, USA*
Kimberley's Team and Driver Guides • *various*
McLaren The Grand Prix, CanAm & Indy Cars • *Doug Nye*
Motor Racing and Motor Rally Directory (1957) • *Motor Racing staff*
The Motor Racing Directory • *Mike Kettlewell*
The Motor Racing Register (1961/62-1966) • *Geoffrey Dempsey*
Palmarès Pilote par Pilote des Grand Prix de Formule 1 • *Christian Naviaux with Jimmy Piget, France*
The Racing Car Pocket Book • *Denis Jenkinson*
Theme Lotus - From Chapman To Ducarouge (1956-1986) • *Doug Nye*
Williams - The Story Of A Racing Team • *Bruce Grant-Braham*